BUS

OVERSIZE

Household
Spending

Household Spending

Who Spends How Much on What

BY THE EDITORS OF NEW STRATEGIST PUBLICATIONS

New Strategist Publications, Inc.
P.O. Box 242, Ithaca, New York 14851
800/848-0842; 607/273-0913
www.newstrategist.com

ISBN 978-1-933588-05-6

Printed in the United States of America

Contents

Chapter 11. Spending on Transportation, 2004

List of Tables

Chapter 3. Spending on Entertainment, 2004

Chapter 4. Spending on Financial Products and Services, 2004

Chapter 5. Spending on Food and Alcoholic Beverages, 2004

Chapter 6. Spending on Gifts for Nonhousehold Members, 2004

Chapter 7. Spending on Health Care, 2004

Chapter 10. Spending on Personal Care, Reading, Education, and Tobacco, 2004

Chapter 11. Spending on Transportation, 2004

Introduction

Welcome to the eleventh edition of *Household Spending*: *Who Spends How Much on What*. This edition provides a comprehensive analysis of the spending of American households in the year 2004.

Since we published the first edition of *Household Spending* in 1991, the economy has cycled through good times and bad. Despite the ups and downs, the average household has held a surprisingly steady course. While spending has grown strongly at the national level over the years, it has increased more moderately at the household level. This caution has served Americans well, helping to insulate their day-to-day lives from the economy's gyrations. Rising energy prices and interest rates are now testing household budgets. These factors begin to surface in the 2004 spending data.

To understand spending trends, it is important to distinguish between aggregate consumer spending and average household spending. Aggregate spending is the big picture, the total expenditures of American consumers, businesses, and government. Aggregate consumer spending in the U.S. has been growing strongly for years because of population growth and the aging of the enormous baby-boom generation into the peak spending age groups. Average household spending, in contrast, is the more intimate world of bills and budgets. It shows how individual households allocate their dollars. Average household spending is growing much more slowly than aggregate spending. Between 1990 and 2004, for example, aggregate spending increased by an enormous 48 percent, after adjusting for inflation. Average household spending grew only 6 percent.

In 2004, the average American household spent $43,395. This was just 4 percent more than it spent in 2000, after adjusting for inflation (see table 1.1). Much of the growth in household spending since 2000 has been involuntary, brought about by the ever-larger claim of necessities on the household budget. After adjusting for inflation, the average household spent 11 percent more on property taxes in 2004 than in 2000. Spending on gasoline rose 13 percent during those years. Spending on vehicle insurance also rose 13 percent. Out-of-pocket spending on health insurance increased by an enormous 24 percent. Spending on education grew an even greater 31 percent.

Declines in discretionary spending are evident in the 2000 to 2004 trends. Spending on "other lodging," a category that includes hotel and motel expenses, fell 10 percent, after adjusting for inflation. Spending on furniture declined 3 percent, women's apparel fell 5 percent, and shoes were down an even larger 13 percent. Spending on public transportation (a category dominated by airline fares) declined 6 percent. Households cut their spending on fees and admissions to entertainment events by 7 percent and reading material by 19 percent.

Analyzing spending trends at the individual household level, as *Household Spending* does, provides deeper insight into the nation's economic ups and downs than any examination of aggregate figures. Unfortunately, the complexity of household spending statistics discourages many from tackling the job of analyzing the data. It is much easier to analyze spending at the national level because it requires an examination of only two figures—today's and yesterday's. But analyzing trends in spending at the household level requires delving into the who, what, and why of spending—the mindset and motivations of individual consumers. The eleventh edition of *Household Spending* is for those who want to know the who, what, and why.

Consumer spending is the result of a complex mix of wants and needs, hopes and fears. This mix determines the success of individual businesses and the health of our economy. Knowing how consumers spend their dollars is key to understanding where our economy is headed, an insight of immense value as the nation copes with uncertainty.

How to use this book

Household Spending is based on unpublished data collected by the Bureau of Labor Statistics' Consumer Expenditure Survey, an ongoing, nationwide survey of household spending. The editors of New Strategist start with the average spending figures collected by the Bureau of Labor Statistics and analyze them in a variety of ways, calculating household spending indexes, total household spending, and household market shares. We do this for hundreds of spending categories by age of householder, household income, household type, race and Hispanic origin of householder, region of residence, and educational attainment of householder.

The Bureau of Labor Statistics' Consumer Expenditure Survey is a complete accounting of household expenditures, and it includes everything from big-ticket items such as homes and cars, to small purchases like laundry detergent and videogames. The survey does not include expenditures by government, business, or institutions. The lag time between data collection and publication is about two years. The data in this book are from the 2004 Consumer Expenditure Survey, unless otherwise noted.

The Consumer Expenditure Survey uses consumer unit as its sampling unit. The Bureau of Labor Statistics defines "consumer unit" as "a single person or group of persons in a sample household related by blood, marriage, adoption or other legal arrangement or who share responsibility for at least two out of three major types of expenses—food, housing, and other expenses." For convenience, consumer units are referred to as households in the text of this book. For more information about the Consumer Expenditure Survey and consumer units, see Appendix A.

Chapter 1 of *Household Spending* is devoted to summary household spending statistics. These are shown for the following consumer segments: age, income, household type, region of residence, race and Hispanic origin, and education.

Chapters 2 through 11 present detailed spending statistics organized by major product and service category (food, housing, transportation, and so on) and include all typical household expenditures. Within each chapter, spending statistics are shown by age of householder, household income, household type, race and Hispanic origin of householder, region of residence, and educational attainment of householder. For each of the demographic variables, tables show average household spending, indexed household spending, total household (or aggregate) spending, and household share of spending.

How to use the tables in this book

The data in *Household Spending* reveal how American households allocate their spending dollars. The starting point for all calculations in *Household Spending* are the unpublished detailed average household spending data collected by the Consumer Expenditure Survey.

These are shown in the average spending tables in chapters 2 through 11. The remaining tables in each chapter were produced by New Strategist's statisticians and are based on the average figures. The indexed household spending tables reveal whether households in a given segment spend more or less than the average for all households (or for all households in that segment), and by how much. The total household spending tables show the overall size of a particular market. The household market share tables reveal how much spending each household segment accounts for. These four types of tables are described in detail below.

• **Average Household Spending Tables.** The average spending tables report the average annual spending of households on each item or category of items in 2004. The Consumer Expenditure Survey produces average spending data for all households in a segment; e.g., all households with a householder aged 25 to 34, not just for those who purchased an item. When reviewing the spending data, it is important to remember that by including both purchasers and nonpurchasers in the calculation, the average is diluted—especially for infrequently purchased items. For example, the average household spent $194 on day care centers in 2004. Since only a small percentage of households spend money on day care, this figure greatly underestimates the amount spent on day care centers by those who make use of them. To get a more realistic idea of how much buyers spend on an item, Appendix C shows the percentage of households purchasing individual products and services during an average quarter of 2004, and the amount spent by purchasers per quarter. According to Appendix C, only 5 percent of households spent on day care centers during an average quarter of 2004. The purchasers spent an average of $884 per quarter, for an estimated annual cost of $3,536—a much more realistic figure than the average of $194 for all households.

For frequently purchased items—such as bread—the average spending figures give a fairly accurate account of actual spending. But for most of the products and services examined in *Household Spending*, the average spending figures are less revealing than the indexes and market shares.

Average spending figures are useful in determining the market potential of a product or service in a local area. By multiplying the average amount married couples spend on children's clothing by the number of married couples in the Dallas metropolitan area, for example, marketers can estimate the size of the market for children's clothing in Dallas. The Dallas media could show those figures to potential advertisers as evidence of the local demand for children's clothing.

Note that because of sampling errors, average values can vary—especially for infrequently purchased items. To examine the standard errors associated with summary average spending figures (Chapter 1), go to http://www.bls.gov/cex/csxstnderror.htm. To examine the standard errors associated with detailed average spending data, contact the Bureau of Labor Statistics Consumer Expenditure Survey statisticians by phone at 202-691-6900 or by email at cexinfo@bls.gov.

• **Indexed Household Spending Tables**. The indexed spending tables compare the spending of each household segment with that of the average household. To compute the indexes, New Strategist's statisticians divide the average amount each household segment spends on a particular item by how much the average household spends on the item and multiplying the resulting figure by 100.

An index of 100 is the average for all households. An index of 125 means the spending of that household segment is 25 percent above average (100 plus 25). An index of 75 indicates spending that is 25 percent below the average for all households (100 minus 25). Indexed spending figures identify the best customers for a product or service. Households with an index of 177 for outdoor furniture, for example, are a strong market for that product. Those with an index below 100 are either a weak or an underserved market.

Spending indexes can reveal hidden markets—household segments with a high propensity to buy a particular product or service but which are overshadowed by larger household segments that account for a bigger share of the total market. Householders aged 65 to 74, for example, spend 39 percent more than the average household on magazine subscriptions (with an index of 139). This is a higher index than that of any other age group, making householders aged 65 to 74 the best customers of this item. Householders aged 35 to 44 spend 15 percent less than average on magazine subscriptions (with an index of 85), meaning they are a weaker or underserved market for this product. But the market share of 35-to-44-year-olds is larger than that of 65-to-74-year-olds (18 versus 13 percent) because there are more households in the younger age group. Using the indexed spending tables, marketers can see that older householders are in fact their better customers and adjust their business strategy accordingly.

Note that because of sampling errors, small differences in index values usually are not significant. But the broader patterns revealed by indexes can guide marketers to the best customers.

• **Total Household Spending Tables**. To produce the total spending tables, New Strategist's statistician's multiplied average spending figures by the number of households in a segment. The result is the dollar size of the total household market and of each market segment. All totals are shown in thousands of dollars. To convert the numbers in the total spending tables to dollars, you must append "000" to the number. For example, households headed by people aged 45 to 54 spent nearly $12 billion ($11,892,042,000) on alcoholic beverages in 2004.

When comparing the total spending figures in *Household Spending* with aggregate spending figures from the Bureau of Economic Analysis, other government agencies, or trade associations, keep in mind that the Consumer Expenditure Survey includes only household spending, not spending by businesses or institutions. Sales data also will differ from household spending totals because sales figures for consumer products include the value of goods sold to industries, government, and foreign markets, which can be a significant proportion of sales.

• **Household Market Share Tables**. New Strategist's statisticians produced the market share tables by converting total spending data to percentages. To calculate the percentage of total household spending on an item that is controlled by each demographic segment—i.e., its market share—each segment's total spending on an item was divided by aggregate household spending on the item.

Market shares reveal the biggest customers—the demographic segments that account for the largest share of household spending on a particular product or service. Businesses can reach a large portion of their customers by targeting the demographic segments in control of the largest market shares. Of course, by single-mindedly targeting the biggest customers, businesses cannot nurture potential growth markets. An additional danger of focusing only on the biggest customers is that businesses may end up ignoring their best customers. This is especially problematic because market shares are unstable, thanks to baby booms and busts over the past half-century. Right now, for example, householders aged 45 to 54 are the biggest customers of gardening and lawn care services, controlling 23 percent of the market—but only because the age group is filled with the large baby-boom generation. In fact, the best customers of lawn and garden services are older householders. Those aged 65 to 74, for example, spend 54 percent more than the average household on gardening and lawn care services. The 45-to-54 age group spends only 14 percent more than the average household on this item. Although the older age group controls only 15 percent of the gardening and lawn care market today, the share will expand as boomers age into their sixties and seventies. The best customers of gardening and lawn care services will become the biggest customers as well. Marketers who ignore their best customers in favor of the biggest customers may end up with no customers.

For more information

The eleventh edition of *Household Spending* offers researchers a detailed analysis of the voluminous and unpublished spending data collected by the Bureau of Labor Statistics. It provides a convenient way to compare and contrast spending on goods and services by demographic characteristic such as age of householder or household type. For more about the Consumer Expenditure Survey, visit the Bureau of Labor Statistics web site (http://www .bls.gov/cex/), where summary average spending figures (as shown in chapter 1 of this book) are available online. The detailed average spending numbers (as shown in chapters 2 through 11) are available only by special request.

For a product-by-product analysis of the best and biggest customers, see the fourth edition of New Strategist's *Best Customers: Demographics of Consumer Demand*. For household spending trends by single product category, see New Strategist's *Who's Buying* reports. To find out more about these books and to view tables of contents and sample pages, visit New Strategist's web site at http://www.newstrategist.com. All New Strategist books and reports are available as downloads or hardcopies.

Chapter 1. Spending Overview

Household Spending Trends: 2000 to 2004

Between 2000 and 2004, spending by the average household rose 4 percent, to $43,395, after adjusting for inflation. At the same time, average household income grew by a larger 11 percent. The considerable gap between income growth and spending growth reveals consumer caution, despite the improving economy. The pundits may accuse Americans of spending beyond their means, but in fact the steady rise in consumer spending at the national level primarily is the result of demographic change—population growth and the aging of the baby-boom generation into the peak earning and spending years.

Much of the growth in household spending between 2000 and 2004 was involuntary, brought about by the ever-larger claim of necessities on the household budget. After adjusting for inflation, the average household spent 11 percent more on property taxes in 2004 than in 2000. Spending on gasoline rose 13 percent during those years. Spending on vehicle insurance also rose 13 percent. Out-of-pocket spending on health insurance increased by an enormous 24 percent. Spending on education grew an even greater 31 percent.

Declines in discretionary spending are evident in the 2000 to 2004 trends. Spending on "other lodging," a category that includes hotel and motel expenses, fell 10 percent, after adjusting for inflation. Spending on furniture declined 3 percent, women's apparel fell 5 percent, and shoes were down an even larger 13 percent. Spending on public transportation (a category dominated by airline fares) declined 6 percent. Households cut their spending on fees and admissions to entertainment events by 7 percent and on reading material by 19 percent.

Contrary to popular perception, Americans are cautious spenders at the individual household level. The recession of 2001 followed by the lackluster recovery forced households to spend less on many discretionary items to make ends meet. Rapidly rising energy costs are now reducing discretionary spending even further. With the aging baby-boom generation entering its sixties and leaving the peak spending years behind, average household spending is not likely to grow much in the years ahead. American businesses will have to adapt to a new economic landscape, one in which affluence is becoming less common and the middle class is struggling to stay afloat. The globalization of the workforce coupled with rising energy prices and an increasingly troubled health insurance system will make our future very different from our past.

Table 1.1 Spending trends, 2000 to 2004

(average annual spending of consumer units by product and service category, 2000 to 2004; percent change 2000–04; in 2004 dollars)

	2004	2000	percent change 2000–04
Number of consumer units (in 000s)	116,282	109,367	6.3%
Average before-tax income	$54,453	$48,975	11.2
Average annual spending	43,395	41,731	4.0
FOOD	5,781	5,658	2.2
Food at home	3,347	3,314	1.0
Cereals and bakery products	461	497	−7.2
Cereals and cereal products	154	171	−10.0
Bakery products	307	326	−5.8
Meats, poultry, fish, and eggs	880	872	0.9
Beef	265	261	1.5
Pork	181	183	−1.2
Other meats	108	111	−2.5
Poultry	156	159	−1.9
Fish and seafood	128	121	6.1
Eggs	42	37	12.6
Dairy products	371	356	4.1
Fresh milk and cream	144	144	0.2
Other dairy products	226	212	6.8
Fruits and vegetables	561	571	−1.8
Fresh fruits	187	179	4.6
Fresh vegetables	183	174	4.9
Processed fruits	110	126	−12.8
Processed vegetables	82	92	−11.0
Other food at home	1,075	1,017	5.7
Sugar and other sweets	128	128	−0.3
Fats and oils	89	91	−2.2
Miscellaneous foods	527	479	9.9
Nonalcoholic beverages	290	274	5.8
Food prepared by consumer unit on trips	41	44	−6.6
Food away from home	2,434	2,344	3.8
ALCOHOLIC BEVERAGES	459	408	12.5
HOUSING	13,918	13,513	3.0
Shelter	7,998	7,803	2.5
Owned dwellings	5,324	5,048	5.5
Mortgage interest and charges	2,936	2,895	1.4
Property taxes	1,391	1,249	11.3
Maintenance, repair, insurance, other expenses	997	905	10.2
Rented dwellings	2,201	2,231	−1.3
Other lodging	473	524	−9.8
Utilities, fuels, and public services	2,927	2,730	7.2
Natural gas	424	337	25.9
Electricity	1,064	999	6.5
Fuel oil and other fuels	121	106	13.7
Telephone	990	962	2.9
Water and other public services	327	325	0.7
Household services	753	750	0.4
Personal services	300	358	−16.1
Other household services	453	393	15.4
Housekeeping supplies	594	529	12.4
Laundry and cleaning supplies	149	144	3.7
Other household products	290	248	17.0
Postage and stationery	155	138	12.1

	2004	2000	percent change 2000–04
Household furnishings and equipment	**$1,646**	**$1,699**	**–3.1%**
Household textiles	158	116	35.9
Furniture	417	429	–2.8
Floor coverings	52	48	7.7
Major appliances	204	207	–1.6
Small appliances, miscellaneous housewares	105	95	10.0
Miscellaneous household equipment	711	802	–11.3
APPAREL AND RELATED SERVICES	**1,816**	**2,036**	**–10.8**
Men and boys	**406**	**483**	**–15.9**
Men, aged 16 or older	317	377	–16.0
Boys, aged 2 to 15	89	105	–15.5
Women and girls	**739**	**795**	**–7.1**
Women, aged 16 or older	631	666	–5.2
Girls, aged 2 to 15	108	129	–16.6
Children under age 2	**79**	**90**	**–12.2**
Footwear	**329**	**376**	**–12.6**
Other apparel products and services	**264**	**292**	**–9.5**
TRANSPORTATION	**7,801**	**8,136**	**–4.1**
Vehicle purchases	**3,397**	**3,749**	**–9.4**
Cars and trucks, new	1,748	1,761	–0.7
Cars and trucks, used	1,582	1,941	–18.5
Gasoline and motor oil	**1,598**	**1,416**	**12.8**
Other vehicle expenses	**2,365**	**2,502**	**–5.5**
Vehicle finance charges	323	360	–10.2
Maintenance and repairs	652	684	–4.7
Vehicle insurance	964	853	13.0
Vehicle rentals, leases, licenses, other charges	426	604	–29.5
Public transportation	**441**	**468**	**–5.8**
HEALTH CARE	**2,574**	**2,266**	**13.6**
Health insurance	1,332	1,078	23.5
Medical services	648	623	4.0
Drugs	480	456	5.2
Medical supplies	114	109	5.0
ENTERTAINMENT	**2,218**	**2,044**	**8.5**
Fees and admissions	528	565	–6.5
Television, radio, and sound equipment	788	682	15.5
Pets, toys, and playground equipment	381	366	4.0
Other entertainment products and services	522	431	21.1
PERSONAL CARE PRODUCTS AND SERVICES	**581**	**619**	**–6.1**
READING	**130**	**160**	**–18.8**
EDUCATION	**905**	**693**	**30.5**
TOBACCO PRODUCTS AND SMOKING SUPPLIES	**288**	**350**	**–17.7**
MISCELLANEOUS	**690**	**851**	**–18.9**
CASH CONTRIBUTIONS	**1,408**	**1,307**	**7.7**
PERSONAL INSURANCE AND PENSIONS	**4,823**	**3,691**	**30.7**
Life and other personal insurance	390	438	–10.9
Pensions and Social Security	4,433	3,253	36.3
PERSONAL TAXES	**2,166**	**3,419**	**–36.6**
Federal income taxes	1,519	2,642	–42.5
State and local income taxes	472	616	–23.4
Other taxes	175	160	9.3
GIFTS FOR NONHOUSEHOLD MEMBERS	**1,215**	**1,188**	**2.3**

Note: The Bureau of Labor Statistics uses consumer unit rather than household as the sampling unit in the Consumer Expenditure Survey. For the definition of consumer unit, see the glossary. Spending on gifts is also included in the preceding product and service categories.
Source: Bureau of Labor Statistics, 2000 and 2004 Consumer Expenditure Surveys, Internet site http://www.bls.gov/cex/; calculations by New Strategist

Spending by Age, 2004

The average household spent $43,395 in 2004, but some spent more while others spent less. Because spending rises with income, affluent householders spend the most. Householders aged 45 to 54 are in their peak earning years, which explains why they spent 22 percent more than the average household in 2004, the highest level of spending among all age groups. Householders aged 35 to 44 were in second place, with spending 17 percent above average.

Households headed by people under age 25 or aged 75 or older spend the least because their incomes are lowest. Householders under age 25 spend just 57 percent as much as the average household, while householders aged 75 or older spend 59 percent as much as the average.

Householders aged 45 to 54 spend the most overall, but other age groups spend more in some categories. Householders under age 25 spend slightly more on alcoholic beverages, for example. Householders aged 25 to 34 spend the most on rented dwellings, used cars and trucks, and infants' apparel. Householders aged 35 to 44 spend the most on children's clothes. Spending on new cars and trucks, public transportation, and entertainment is highest in the 55-to-64 age group. Households headed by people aged 65 or older spend the most on health care, including the individual categories of health insurance and drugs.

With the early retirement trend coming to an end, look for the two-earner couples of the baby-boom generation to boost spending by householders aged 55 to 64 in the years ahead.

Table 1.2 Average spending by age of householder, 2004

(average annual spending of consumer units by product and service category and age of consumer unit reference person, 2004)

	total consumer units	under 25	25 to 34	35 to 44	45 to 54	55 to 64	aged 65 or older total	65 to 74	75 or older
Number of consumer units (in 000s)	116,282	8,817	19,439	24,070	23,712	17,479	22,765	11,230	11,536
Average number of persons per consumer unit	2.5	1.9	2.9	3.2	2.7	2.1	1.7	1.9	1.5
Average income before taxes	$54,453	$22,840	$52,484	$65,515	$70,434	$61,031	$34,988	$42,137	$28,028
Average annual spending	43,395	24,535	42,701	50,402	52,764	47,299	31,104	36,512	25,763
FOOD	**5,781**	**3,715**	**5,705**	**6,752**	**7,038**	**5,898**	**4,206**	**4,871**	**3,518**
Food at home	**3,347**	**1,853**	**3,155**	**3,897**	**4,083**	**3,374**	**2,722**	**3,049**	**2,380**
Cereals and bakery products	461	265	432	552	547	437	394	422	364
Cereals and cereal products	154	99	152	194	181	137	118	126	110
Bakery products	307	166	280	357	366	300	276	296	255
Meats, poultry, fish, and eggs	880	480	812	1,019	1,111	894	694	799	584
Beef	265	148	250	313	338	257	205	236	172
Pork	181	95	161	204	222	203	148	173	122
Other meats	108	53	97	125	140	102	91	113	68
Poultry	156	101	154	182	196	156	108	123	93
Fish and seafood	128	57	112	151	167	130	103	111	95
Eggs	42	26	38	45	48	46	38	44	33
Dairy products	371	205	346	440	436	371	313	353	271
Fresh milk and cream	144	86	147	177	161	137	118	125	110
Other dairy products	226	119	199	263	276	235	195	227	161
Fruits and vegetables	561	285	521	615	673	588	510	548	470
Fresh fruits	187	92	168	199	229	199	174	183	166
Fresh vegetables	183	86	166	200	219	200	167	191	142
Processed fruits	110	64	110	122	126	108	99	97	100
Processed vegetables	82	44	77	94	99	80	70	77	62
Other food at home	1,075	618	1,043	1,271	1,316	1,083	812	927	692
Sugar and other sweets	128	54	113	146	162	137	109	127	91
Fats and oils	89	45	78	97	112	97	77	84	69
Miscellaneous foods	527	334	545	643	623	485	394	446	340
Nonalcoholic beverages	290	171	281	340	370	295	201	226	175
Food prepared by consumer unit on trips	41	15	26	44	49	69	31	45	18
Food away from home	**2,434**	**1,862**	**2,550**	**2,855**	**2,955**	**2,524**	**1,484**	**1,822**	**1,138**
ALCOHOLIC BEVERAGES	**459**	**503**	**522**	**535**	**502**	**457**	**261**	**329**	**190**
HOUSING	**13,918**	**7,649**	**14,379**	**16,794**	**16,164**	**14,339**	**10,259**	**11,152**	**9,381**
Shelter	**7,998**	**4,901**	**8,729**	**9,856**	**9,313**	**7,883**	**5,329**	**5,784**	**4,886**
Owned dwellings	5,324	1,009	4,700	7,025	6,968	5,970	3,523	4,134	2,928
Mortgage interest and charges	2,936	615	3,190	4,575	4,010	2,813	863	1,317	421
Property taxes	1,391	236	909	1,562	1,747	1,760	1,416	1,534	1,302
Maintenance, repair, insurance, other expenses	997	159	601	888	1,211	1,398	1,244	1,283	1,205
Rented dwellings	2,201	3,647	3,802	2,450	1,636	1,169	1,393	1,123	1,655
Other lodging	473	244	227	381	710	743	414	527	303
Utilities, fuels, and public services	**2,927**	**1,413**	**2,687**	**3,309**	**3,413**	**3,222**	**2,580**	**2,881**	**2,287**
Natural gas	424	135	366	474	473	477	442	478	406
Electricity	1,064	507	957	1,211	1,231	1,177	957	1,072	845
Fuel oil and other fuels	121	28	61	104	149	161	163	163	164
Telephone	990	642	1,028	1,145	1,178	1,040	695	815	579
Water and other public services	327	101	275	375	381	367	323	353	294
Household services	**753**	**270**	**915**	**992**	**693**	**645**	**694**	**522**	**861**
Personal services	300	159	584	568	131	43	201	27	370
Other household services	453	110	331	424	562	602	493	495	491
Housekeeping supplies	**594**	**253**	**499**	**677**	**756**	**657**	**509**	**569**	**445**
Laundry and cleaning supplies	149	75	142	170	188	158	111	122	100
Other household products	290	114	223	339	385	318	248	285	210
Postage and stationery	155	64	134	169	183	181	149	162	136
Household furnishings and equipment	**1,646**	**812**	**1,548**	**1,960**	**1,989**	**1,932**	**1,147**	**1,395**	**901**
Household textiles	158	55	104	187	182	203	154	122	188
Furniture	417	261	464	546	415	504	236	322	153
Floor coverings	52	7	36	51	65	87	44	61	26

	total consumer units	under 25	25 to 34	35 to 44	45 to 54	55 to 64	aged 65 or older total	65 to 74	75 or older
Major appliances	$204	$72	$184	$237	$237	$240	$175	$208	$143
Small appliances, miscellaneous housewares	105	62	104	97	125	130	90	109	71
Miscellaneous household equipment	711	355	657	841	966	768	448	573	321
APPAREL AND RELATED SERVICES	**1,816**	**1,371**	**2,134**	**2,142**	**2,217**	**1,863**	**907**	**1,200**	**604**
Men and boys	**406**	**235**	**456**	**532**	**542**	**338**	**204**	**312**	**93**
Men, aged 16 or older	317	214	336	356	455	285	180	273	84
Boys, aged 2 to 15	89	22	120	176	87	53	24	39	9
Women and girls	**739**	**587**	**755**	**801**	**972**	**793**	**431**	**543**	**315**
Women, aged 16 or older	631	558	638	580	841	743	404	504	300
Girls, aged 2 to 15	108	29	118	222	131	50	27	39	15
Children under age 2	**79**	**102**	**182**	**86**	**53**	**47**	**20**	**28**	**13**
Footwear	**329**	**258**	**398**	**416**	**385**	**351**	**123**	**153**	**91**
Other apparel products and services	**264**	**188**	**342**	**306**	**264**	**333**	**129**	**165**	**93**
TRANSPORTATION	**7,801**	**4,704**	**8,485**	**9,183**	**9,343**	**8,421**	**4,875**	**6,506**	**3,286**
Vehicle purchases	**3,397**	**2,035**	**4,033**	**4,190**	**3,790**	**3,616**	**1,966**	**2,822**	**1,132**
Cars and trucks, new	1,748	542	1,901	2,204	1,827	2,311	1,089	1,561	630
Cars and trucks, used	1,582	1,430	2,086	1,907	1,826	1,247	872	1,251	502
Other vehicles	66	63	46	79	138	58	5	9	–
Gasoline and motor oil	**1,598**	**1,130**	**1,679**	**1,877**	**1,980**	**1,666**	**963**	**1,259**	**675**
Other vehicle expenses	**2,365**	**1,326**	**2,407**	**2,681**	**3,061**	**2,532**	**1,546**	**1,902**	**1,200**
Vehicle finance charges	323	147	408	434	398	336	115	182	48
Maintenance and repairs	652	400	602	687	838	742	490	585	398
Vehicle insurance	964	535	944	1,068	1,273	973	711	825	600
Vehicle rentals, leases, licenses, other charges	426	243	453	491	553	481	230	309	153
Public transportation	**441**	**214**	**366**	**435**	**512**	**606**	**400**	**524**	**280**
HEALTH CARE	**2,574**	**654**	**1,519**	**2,263**	**2,695**	**3,262**	**3,899**	**3,799**	**3,995**
Health insurance	1,332	321	842	1,199	1,291	1,567	2,142	2,171	2,115
Medical services	648	184	403	654	809	892	678	631	723
Drugs	480	118	212	318	461	642	920	854	985
Medical supplies	114	31	62	92	133	161	158	144	172
ENTERTAINMENT	**2,218**	**1,166**	**2,122**	**2,504**	**2,711**	**2,823**	**1,429**	**1,879**	**990**
Fees and admissions	528	277	415	666	667	618	361	463	262
Television, radio, and sound equipment	788	500	843	921	926	810	550	628	474
Pets, toys, and playground equipment	381	218	404	460	477	428	204	261	147
Other entertainment products and services	522	172	460	457	641	967	314	527	107
PERSONAL CARE PRODUCTS AND SERVICES	**581**	**334**	**552**	**660**	**690**	**628**	**468**	**514**	**421**
READING	**130**	**51**	**94**	**123**	**149**	**177**	**146**	**158**	**135**
EDUCATION	**905**	**1,821**	**726**	**786**	**1,567**	**730**	**274**	**352**	**198**
TOBACCO PRODUCTS AND SMOKING SUPPLIES	**288**	**236**	**283**	**350**	**375**	**301**	**147**	**197**	**98**
MISCELLANEOUS	**690**	**297**	**600**	**773**	**774**	**825**	**641**	**735**	**547**
CASH CONTRIBUTIONS	**1,408**	**310**	**815**	**1,265**	**1,625**	**1,752**	**2,000**	**2,471**	**1,542**
PERSONAL INSURANCE AND PENSIONS	**4,823**	**1,726**	**4,765**	**6,273**	**6,915**	**5,825**	**1,592**	**2,348**	**856**
Life and other personal insurance	390	31	235	391	505	612	372	472	275
Pensions and Social Security	4,433	1,695	4,529	5,881	6,410	5,214	1,220	1,875	582
PERSONAL TAXES	**2,166**	**333**	**1,665**	**2,313**	**3,673**	**2,987**	**948**	**1,010**	**887**
Federal income taxes	1,519	200	1,098	1,557	2,674	2,168	648	679	618
State and local income taxes	472	123	473	598	756	584	93	119	67
Other taxes	175	10	94	158	244	236	207	213	201
GIFTS FOR NONHOUSEHOLD MEMBERS	**1,215**	**438**	**711**	**1,096**	**1,935**	**1,636**	**1,000**	**1,068**	**926**

Note: Spending by category will not add to total spending because gift spending is also included in the preceding product and service categories and personal taxes are not included in the total. "–" means sample is too small to make a reliable estimate.
Source: Bureau of Labor Statistics, 2004 Consumer Expenditure Survey, Internet site http://www.bls.gov/cex/

Table 1.3 Indexed spending by age of householder, 2004

(indexed average annual spending of consumer units by product and service category and age of consumer unit reference person, 2004; index definition: an index of 100 is the average for all consumer units; an index of 132 means that spending by consumer units in that group is 32 percent above the average for all consumer units; an index of 68 indicates spending that is 32 percent below the average for all consumer units)

	total consumer units	under 25	25 to 34	35 to 44	45 to 54	55 to 64	aged 65 or older total	65 to 74	75 or older
Average spending of consumer units, total	$43,395	$24,535	$42,701	$50,402	$52,764	$47,299	$31,104	$36,512	$25,763
Average spending of consumer units, index	100	57	98	116	122	109	72	84	59
FOOD	100	64	99	117	122	102	73	84	61
Food at home	100	55	94	116	122	101	81	91	71
Cereals and bakery products	100	57	94	120	119	95	85	92	79
Cereals and cereal products	100	64	99	126	118	89	77	82	71
Bakery products	100	54	91	116	119	98	90	96	83
Meats, poultry, fish, and eggs	100	55	92	116	126	102	79	91	66
Beef	100	56	94	118	128	97	77	89	65
Pork	100	52	89	113	123	112	82	96	67
Other meats	100	49	90	116	130	94	84	105	63
Poultry	100	65	99	117	126	100	69	79	60
Fish and seafood	100	45	88	118	130	102	80	87	74
Eggs	100	62	90	107	114	110	90	105	79
Dairy products	100	55	93	119	118	100	84	95	73
Fresh milk and cream	100	60	102	123	112	95	82	87	76
Other dairy products	100	53	88	116	122	104	86	100	71
Fruits and vegetables	100	51	93	110	120	105	91	98	84
Fresh fruits	100	49	90	106	122	106	93	98	89
Fresh vegetables	100	47	91	109	120	109	91	104	78
Processed fruits	100	58	100	111	115	98	90	88	91
Processed vegetables	100	54	94	115	121	98	85	94	76
Other food at home	100	57	97	118	122	101	76	86	64
Sugar and other sweets	100	42	88	114	127	107	85	99	71
Fats and oils	100	51	88	109	126	109	87	94	78
Miscellaneous foods	100	63	103	122	118	92	75	85	65
Nonalcoholic beverages	100	59	97	117	128	102	69	78	60
Food prepared by consumer unit on trips	100	37	63	107	120	168	76	110	44
Food away from home	100	76	105	117	121	104	61	75	47
ALCOHOLIC BEVERAGES	100	110	114	117	109	100	57	72	41
HOUSING	100	55	103	121	116	103	74	80	67
Shelter	100	61	109	123	116	99	67	72	61
Owned dwellings	100	19	88	132	131	112	66	78	55
Mortgage interest and charges	100	21	109	156	137	96	29	45	14
Property taxes	100	17	65	112	126	127	102	110	94
Maintenance, repair, insurance, other expenses	100	16	60	89	121	140	125	129	121
Rented dwellings	100	166	173	111	74	53	63	51	75
Other lodging	100	52	48	81	150	157	88	111	64
Utilities, fuels, and public services	100	48	92	113	117	110	88	98	78
Natural gas	100	32	86	112	112	113	104	113	96
Electricity	100	48	90	114	116	111	90	101	79
Fuel oil and other fuels	100	23	50	86	123	133	135	135	136
Telephone	100	65	104	116	119	105	70	82	58
Water and other public services	100	31	84	115	117	112	99	108	90
Household services	100	36	122	132	92	86	92	69	114
Personal services	100	53	195	189	44	14	67	9	123
Other household services	100	24	73	94	124	133	109	109	108
Housekeeping supplies	100	43	84	114	127	111	86	96	75
Laundry and cleaning supplies	100	50	95	114	126	106	74	82	67
Other household products	100	39	77	117	133	110	86	98	72
Postage and stationery	100	41	86	109	118	117	96	105	88
Household furnishings and equipment	100	49	94	119	121	117	70	85	55
Household textiles	100	35	66	118	115	128	97	77	119
Furniture	100	63	111	131	100	121	57	77	37
Floor coverings	100	13	69	98	125	167	85	117	50

	total consumer units	under 25	25 to 34	35 to 44	45 to 54	55 to 64	aged 65 or older total	65 to 74	75 or older
Major appliances	100	35	90	116	116	118	86	102	70
Small appliances, miscellaneous housewares	100	59	99	92	119	124	86	104	68
Miscellaneous household equipment	100	50	92	118	136	108	63	81	45
APPAREL AND RELATED SERVICES	**100**	**75**	**118**	**118**	**122**	**103**	**50**	**66**	**33**
Men and boys	**100**	**58**	**112**	**131**	**133**	**83**	**50**	**77**	**23**
Men, aged 16 or older	100	68	106	112	144	90	57	86	26
Boys, aged 2 to 15	100	25	135	198	98	60	27	44	10
Women and girls	**100**	**79**	**102**	**108**	**132**	**107**	**58**	**73**	**43**
Women, aged 16 or older	100	88	101	92	133	118	64	80	48
Girls, aged 2 to 15	100	27	109	206	121	46	25	36	14
Children under age 2	**100**	**129**	**230**	**109**	**67**	**59**	**25**	**35**	**16**
Footwear	**100**	**78**	**121**	**126**	**117**	**107**	**37**	**47**	**28**
Other apparel products and services	**100**	**71**	**130**	**116**	**100**	**126**	**49**	**63**	**35**
TRANSPORTATION	**100**	**60**	**109**	**118**	**120**	**108**	**62**	**83**	**42**
Vehicle purchases	**100**	**60**	**119**	**123**	**112**	**106**	**58**	**83**	**33**
Cars and trucks, new	100	31	109	126	105	132	62	89	36
Cars and trucks, used	100	90	132	121	115	79	55	79	32
Other vehicles	100	95	70	120	209	88	8	14	–
Gasoline and motor oil	**100**	**71**	**105**	**117**	**124**	**104**	**60**	**79**	**42**
Other vehicle expenses	**100**	**56**	**102**	**113**	**129**	**107**	**65**	**80**	**51**
Vehicle finance charges	100	46	126	134	123	104	36	56	15
Maintenance and repairs	100	61	92	105	129	114	75	90	61
Vehicle insurance	100	55	98	111	132	101	74	86	62
Vehicle rentals, leases, licenses, other charges	100	57	106	115	130	113	54	73	36
Public transportation	**100**	**49**	**83**	**99**	**116**	**137**	**91**	**119**	**63**
HEALTH CARE	**100**	**25**	**59**	**88**	**105**	**127**	**151**	**148**	**155**
Health insurance	100	24	63	90	97	118	161	163	159
Medical services	100	28	62	101	125	138	105	97	112
Drugs	100	25	44	66	96	134	192	178	205
Medical supplies	100	27	54	81	117	141	139	126	151
ENTERTAINMENT	**100**	**53**	**96**	**113**	**122**	**127**	**64**	**85**	**45**
Fees and admissions	100	52	79	126	126	117	68	88	50
Television, radio, and sound equipment	100	63	107	117	118	103	70	80	60
Pets, toys, and playground equipment	100	57	106	121	125	112	54	69	39
Other entertainment products and services	100	33	88	88	123	185	60	101	20
PERSONAL CARE PRODUCTS AND SERVICES	**100**	**57**	**95**	**114**	**119**	**108**	**81**	**88**	**72**
READING	**100**	**39**	**72**	**95**	**115**	**136**	**112**	**122**	**104**
EDUCATION	**100**	**201**	**80**	**87**	**173**	**81**	**30**	**39**	**22**
TOBACCO PRODUCTS AND SMOKING SUPPLIES	**100**	**82**	**98**	**122**	**130**	**105**	**51**	**68**	**34**
MISCELLANEOUS	**100**	**43**	**87**	**112**	**112**	**120**	**93**	**107**	**79**
CASH CONTRIBUTIONS	**100**	**22**	**58**	**90**	**115**	**124**	**142**	**175**	**110**
PERSONAL INSURANCE AND PENSIONS	**100**	**36**	**99**	**130**	**143**	**121**	**33**	**49**	**18**
Life and other personal insurance	100	8	60	100	129	157	95	121	71
Pensions and Social Security	100	38	102	133	145	118	28	42	13
PERSONAL TAXES	**100**	**15**	**77**	**107**	**170**	**138**	**44**	**47**	**41**
Federal income taxes	100	13	72	103	176	143	43	45	41
State and local income taxes	100	26	100	127	160	124	20	25	14
Other taxes	100	6	54	90	139	135	118	122	115
GIFTS FOR NONHOUSEHOLD MEMBERS	**100**	**36**	**59**	**90**	**159**	**135**	**82**	**88**	**76**

Note: "–" means sample is too small to make a reliable estimate.
Source: Calculations by New Strategist based on the Bureau of Labor Statistics' 2004 Consumer Expenditure Survey

Spending by Income, 2004

The average household spent $43,395 in 2004. Not surprisingly, households with incomes of $70,000 or more spend the most—77 percent more than the average household. The highest income group spends the most on almost every product and service category, with a few exceptions such as rented dwellings and tobacco.

Households with incomes below $40,000 spend less than the average household on most categories. One of the few exceptions is rent. Many households with incomes below $40,000 spend more money than they make. The income they report to government interviewers is less than their reported expenditures. These households make up the difference through borrowing, the use of savings, and unreported income.

Income makes a bigger difference in the purchasing of some products than others. Everyone has to buy food, but only those who can afford to do so will buy a new car. Households with incomes of $70,000 or more spend close to the average on such items as eggs, drugs, and tobacco. They spend well over twice what the average household spends on other lodging (a category that includes hotel and motel expenses as well as housing for children in college), mortgage interest, and fees and admissions to entertainment events.

Table 1.4 Average spending by household income, 2004

(average annual spending of consumer units by product and service category and before-tax income of consumer unit, 2004)

	total consumer units	under $10,000	$10,000– $19,999	$20,000– $29,999	$30,000– $39,999	$40,000– $49,999	$50,000– $69,999	$70,000 or more
Number of consumer units (in 000s)	116,282	11,771	17,127	14,172	13,125	11,374	18,069	30,644
Average number of persons per consumer unit	2.5	1.6	1.9	2.2	2.4	2.6	2.8	3.1
Average income before taxes	$54,453	$5,215	$14,847	$24,767	$34,739	$44,645	$59,259	$118,482
Average annual spending	43,395	15,537	21,153	27,741	33,273	38,204	47,750	76,954
FOOD	**5,781**	**2,705**	**3,261**	**4,076**	**4,986**	**5,452**	**6,312**	**9,042**
Food at home	**3,347**	**1,825**	**2,263**	**2,591**	**3,056**	**3,263**	**3,640**	**4,734**
Cereals and bakery products	461	275	321	359	430	456	506	628
Cereals and cereal products	154	104	118	117	145	152	166	203
Bakery products	307	171	204	242	285	305	340	426
Meats, poultry, fish, and eggs	880	508	599	698	827	900	936	1,209
Beef	265	150	174	205	266	265	278	369
Pork	181	113	133	161	172	195	194	229
Other meats	108	59	72	81	92	111	117	155
Poultry	156	90	109	117	146	149	170	217
Fish and seafood	128	64	77	95	106	141	135	189
Eggs	42	30	35	39	45	41	43	49
Dairy products	371	197	248	289	349	361	403	521
Fresh milk and cream	144	90	111	121	145	143	154	185
Other dairy products	226	106	137	169	204	218	250	336
Fruits and vegetables	561	301	401	425	519	549	592	794
Fresh fruits	187	96	128	147	168	193	184	271
Fresh vegetables	183	99	134	132	165	168	202	262
Processed fruits	110	57	77	84	108	106	117	153
Processed vegetables	82	49	62	62	78	82	88	109
Other food at home	1,075	545	692	819	930	997	1,202	1,582
Sugar and other sweets	128	72	85	97	107	118	136	191
Fats and oils	89	58	66	74	84	96	94	114
Miscellaneous foods	527	241	333	387	452	475	589	801
Nonalcoholic beverages	290	161	195	240	259	278	333	395
Food prepared by consumer unit on trips	41	12	14	21	29	30	50	80
Food away from home	**2,434**	**880**	**998**	**1,485**	**1,930**	**2,189**	**2,672**	**4,308**
ALCOHOLIC BEVERAGES	**459**	**180**	**200**	**262**	**323**	**449**	**484**	**824**
HOUSING	**13,918**	**5,898**	**7,922**	**9,639**	**11,143**	**12,383**	**14,699**	**23,547**
Shelter	**7,998**	**3,601**	**4,502**	**5,538**	**6,371**	**7,074**	**8,421**	**13,571**
Owned dwellings	5,324	1,119	1,804	2,479	3,406	4,363	5,917	11,053
Mortgage interest and charges	2,936	445	610	1,038	1,758	2,431	3,459	6,455
Property taxes	1,391	391	635	772	891	1,098	1,466	2,763
Maintenance, repair, insurance, other expenses	997	283	558	670	757	833	991	1,836
Rented dwellings	2,201	2,325	2,573	2,893	2,753	2,457	2,085	1,362
Other lodging	473	157	125	166	212	255	419	1,156
Utilities, fuels, and public services	**2,927**	**1,442**	**2,064**	**2,425**	**2,645**	**2,935**	**3,270**	**4,125**
Natural gas	424	190	291	357	384	434	450	617
Electricity	1,064	565	815	916	968	1,070	1,156	1,450
Fuel oil and other fuels	121	55	104	93	121	106	130	167
Telephone	990	500	649	804	881	984	1,148	1,411
Water and other public services	327	131	206	255	291	341	386	480
Household services	**753**	**162**	**371**	**452**	**453**	**487**	**690**	**1,597**
Personal services	300	53	159	182	161	163	281	649
Other household services	453	109	212	270	292	323	409	948
Housekeeping supplies	**594**	**262**	**355**	**381**	**513**	**542**	**645**	**948**
Laundry and cleaning supplies	149	79	92	120	141	160	166	202
Other household products	290	123	171	172	253	232	311	486
Postage and stationery	155	61	91	90	119	150	168	260
Household furnishings and equipment	**1,646**	**432**	**630**	**843**	**1,161**	**1,345**	**1,672**	**3,306**
Household textiles	158	49	62	108	127	123	141	302
Furniture	417	92	167	185	205	327	440	899
Floor coverings	52	8	12	18	16	54	68	112

	total consumer units	under $10,000	$10,000– $19,999	$20,000– $29,999	$30,000– $39,999	$40,000– $49,999	$50,000– $69,999	$70,000 or more
Major appliances	$204	$43	$101	$101	$159	$235	$219	$367
Small appliances, miscellaneous housewares	105	33	49	75	106	90	79	190
Miscellaneous household equipment	711	208	240	356	548	517	725	1,436
APPAREL AND RELATED SERVICES	**1,816**	**797**	**860**	**1,047**	**1,384**	**1,490**	**1,774**	**3,349**
Men and boys	**406**	**135**	**167**	**216**	**298**	**344**	**389**	**789**
Men, aged 16 or older	317	100	119	144	223	271	300	639
Boys, aged 2 to 15	89	35	48	72	75	73	89	151
Women and girls	**739**	**344**	**325**	**425**	**539**	**571**	**765**	**1,363**
Women, aged 16 or older	631	312	274	361	455	491	646	1,164
Girls, aged 2 to 15	108	32	51	63	84	80	119	199
Children under age 2	**79**	**44**	**49**	**65**	**60**	**63**	**78**	**127**
Footwear	**329**	**180**	**200**	**209**	**323**	**300**	**325**	**513**
Other apparel products and services	**264**	**94**	**119**	**132**	**164**	**213**	**218**	**558**
TRANSPORTATION	**7,801**	**2,136**	**3,362**	**5,114**	**6,288**	**7,031**	**9,700**	**13,513**
Vehicle purchases	**3,397**	**705**	**1,266**	**2,186**	**2,671**	**2,867**	**4,539**	**6,017**
Cars and trucks, new	1,748	288	482	913	1,237	1,337	2,254	3,477
Cars and trucks, used	1,582	409	779	1,258	1,427	1,449	2,123	2,429
Other vehicles	66	20	4	15	6	81	161	112
Gasoline and motor oil	**1,598**	**647**	**869**	**1,190**	**1,432**	**1,621**	**1,953**	**2,411**
Other vehicle expenses	**2,365**	**664**	**1,077**	**1,525**	**1,942**	**2,259**	**2,795**	**4,092**
Vehicle finance charges	323	49	86	171	253	358	445	577
Maintenance and repairs	652	232	370	423	548	571	755	1,088
Vehicle insurance	964	281	499	718	866	1,032	1,146	1,511
Vehicle rentals, leases, licenses, other charges	426	102	122	213	275	298	450	916
Public transportation	**441**	**122**	**150**	**212**	**243**	**283**	**413**	**992**
HEALTH CARE	**2,574**	**1,061**	**1,903**	**2,157**	**2,383**	**2,552**	**2,874**	**3,630**
Health insurance	1,332	547	1,014	1,147	1,223	1,440	1,521	1,791
Medical services	648	209	352	466	558	519	728	1,107
Drugs	480	258	468	476	495	484	488	557
Medical supplies	114	47	69	68	107	110	138	175
ENTERTAINMENT	**2,218**	**687**	**875**	**1,512**	**1,525**	**1,756**	**2,587**	**4,119**
Fees and admissions	528	142	128	206	286	379	548	1,196
Television, radio, and sound equipment	788	336	456	578	672	734	925	1,231
Pets, toys, and playground equipment	381	121	169	217	356	316	403	686
Other entertainment products and services	522	89	123	511	211	328	711	1,006
PERSONAL CARE PRODUCTS AND SERVICES	**581**	**235**	**306**	**410**	**451**	**550**	**600**	**985**
READING	**130**	**50**	**67**	**83**	**95**	**118**	**137**	**234**
EDUCATION	**905**	**786**	**441**	**316**	**316**	**417**	**706**	**2,031**
TOBACCO PRODUCTS AND SMOKING SUPPLIES	**288**	**185**	**256**	**291**	**320**	**329**	**339**	**285**
MISCELLANEOUS	**690**	**305**	**354**	**502**	**522**	**735**	**748**	**1,128**
CASH CONTRIBUTIONS	**1,408**	**237**	**612**	**738**	**844**	**1,284**	**1,360**	**2,929**
PERSONAL INSURANCE AND PENSIONS	**4,823**	**274**	**733**	**1,594**	**2,692**	**3,656**	**5,430**	**11,338**
Life and other personal insurance	390	82	148	183	270	316	417	804
Pensions and Social Security	4,433	192	584	1,411	2,422	3,340	5,013	10,535
PERSONAL TAXES	**2,166**	**–24**	**–93**	**469**	**541**	**955**	**2,137**	**6,217**
Federal income taxes	1,519	–48	–168	253	234	523	1,484	4,589
State and local income taxes	472	–5	19	89	183	275	447	1,298
Other taxes	175	29	56	127	124	157	206	329
GIFTS FOR NONHOUSEHOLD MEMBERS	**1,215**	**367**	**576**	**516**	**748**	**779**	**1,151**	**2,591**

Note: Spending by category will not add to total spending because gift spending is also included in the preceding product and service categories and personal taxes are not included in the total.
Source: Bureau of Labor Statistics, 2004 Consumer Expenditure Survey, Internet site http://www.bls.gov/cex/; calculations by New Strategist

Table 1.5 Indexed spending by household income, 2004

(indexed average annual spending of consumer units by product and service category and before-tax income of consumer unit reference person, 2004; index definition: an index of 100 is the average for all consumer units; an index of 132 means that spending by consumer units in that group is 32 percent above the average for all consumer units; an index of 68 indicates spending that is 32 percent below the average for all consumer units)

	total consumer units	under $10,000	$10,000– $19,999	$20,000– $29,999	$30,000– $39,999	$40,000– $49,999	$50,000– $69,999	$70,000 or more
Average spending of consumer units, total	$43,395	$15,537	$21,153	$27,741	$33,273	$38,204	$47,750	$76,954
Average spending of consumer units, index	100	36	49	64	77	88	110	177
FOOD	**100**	**47**	**56**	**71**	**86**	**94**	**109**	**156**
Food at home	**100**	**55**	**68**	**77**	**91**	**97**	**109**	**141**
Cereals and bakery products	100	60	70	78	93	99	110	136
Cereals and cereal products	100	67	76	76	94	99	108	132
Bakery products	100	56	66	79	93	99	111	139
Meats, poultry, fish, and eggs	100	58	68	79	94	102	106	137
Beef	100	57	66	77	100	100	105	139
Pork	100	62	73	89	95	108	107	127
Other meats	100	55	67	75	85	103	108	144
Poultry	100	58	70	75	94	96	109	139
Fish and seafood	100	50	60	74	83	110	105	148
Eggs	100	72	82	93	107	98	102	117
Dairy products	100	53	67	78	94	97	109	140
Fresh milk and cream	100	63	77	84	101	99	107	128
Other dairy products	100	47	61	75	90	96	111	149
Fruits and vegetables	100	54	72	76	93	98	106	142
Fresh fruits	100	51	69	79	90	103	98	145
Fresh vegetables	100	54	73	72	90	92	110	143
Processed fruits	100	52	70	76	98	96	106	139
Processed vegetables	100	60	75	76	95	100	107	133
Other food at home	100	51	64	76	87	93	112	147
Sugar and other sweets	100	56	66	76	84	92	106	149
Fats and oils	100	65	74	83	94	108	106	128
Miscellaneous foods	100	46	63	73	86	90	112	152
Nonalcoholic beverages	100	55	67	83	89	96	115	136
Food prepared by consumer unit on trips	100	30	35	51	71	73	122	195
Food away from home	**100**	**36**	**41**	**61**	**79**	**90**	**110**	**177**
ALCOHOLIC BEVERAGES	**100**	**39**	**44**	**57**	**70**	**98**	**105**	**180**
HOUSING	**100**	**42**	**57**	**69**	**80**	**89**	**106**	**169**
Shelter	**100**	**45**	**56**	**69**	**80**	**88**	**105**	**170**
Owned dwellings	100	21	34	47	64	82	111	208
Mortgage interest and charges	100	15	21	35	60	83	118	220
Property taxes	100	28	46	55	64	79	105	199
Maintenance, repair, insurance, other expenses	100	28	56	67	76	84	99	184
Rented dwellings	100	106	117	131	125	112	95	62
Other lodging	100	33	26	35	45	54	89	244
Utilities, fuels, and public services	**100**	**49**	**71**	**83**	**90**	**100**	**112**	**141**
Natural gas	100	45	69	84	91	102	106	146
Electricity	100	53	77	86	91	101	109	136
Fuel oil and other fuels	100	46	86	77	100	88	107	138
Telephone	100	51	66	81	89	99	116	143
Water and other public services	100	40	63	78	89	104	118	147
Household services	**100**	**22**	**49**	**60**	**60**	**65**	**92**	**212**
Personal services	100	18	53	61	54	54	94	216
Other household services	100	24	47	60	64	71	90	209
Housekeeping supplies	**100**	**44**	**60**	**64**	**86**	**91**	**109**	**160**
Laundry and cleaning supplies	100	53	62	81	95	107	111	136
Other household products	100	42	59	59	87	80	107	168
Postage and stationery	100	40	59	58	77	97	108	168
Household furnishings and equipment	**100**	**26**	**38**	**51**	**71**	**82**	**102**	**201**
Household textiles	100	31	39	68	80	78	89	191
Furniture	100	22	40	44	49	78	106	216
Floor coverings	100	15	22	35	31	104	131	215

	total consumer units	under $10,000	$10,000– $19,999	$20,000– $29,999	$30,000– $39,999	$40,000– $49,999	$50,000– $69,999	$70,000 or more
Major appliances	100	21	49	50	78	115	107	180
Small appliances, miscellaneous housewares	100	32	47	71	101	86	75	181
Miscellaneous household equipment	100	29	34	50	77	73	102	202
APPAREL AND RELATED SERVICES	**100**	**44**	**47**	**58**	**76**	**82**	**98**	**184**
Men and boys	**100**	**33**	**41**	**53**	**73**	**85**	**96**	**194**
Men, aged 16 or older	100	32	37	45	70	85	95	202
Boys, aged 2 to 15	100	39	54	81	84	82	100	170
Women and girls	**100**	**47**	**44**	**58**	**73**	**77**	**104**	**184**
Women, aged 16 or older	100	49	43	57	72	78	102	184
Girls, aged 2 to 15	100	30	47	58	78	74	110	184
Children under age 2	**100**	**55**	**62**	**82**	**76**	**80**	**99**	**161**
Footwear	**100**	**55**	**61**	**64**	**98**	**91**	**99**	**156**
Other apparel products and services	**100**	**35**	**45**	**50**	**62**	**81**	**83**	**211**
TRANSPORTATION	**100**	**27**	**43**	**66**	**81**	**90**	**124**	**173**
Vehicle purchases	**100**	**21**	**37**	**64**	**79**	**84**	**134**	**177**
Cars and trucks, new	100	16	28	52	71	76	129	199
Cars and trucks, used	100	26	49	80	90	92	134	154
Other vehicles	100	30	7	23	9	123	244	170
Gasoline and motor oil	**100**	**40**	**54**	**74**	**90**	**101**	**122**	**151**
Other vehicle expenses	**100**	**28**	**46**	**64**	**82**	**96**	**118**	**173**
Vehicle finance charges	100	15	27	53	78	111	138	179
Maintenance and repairs	100	36	57	65	84	88	116	167
Vehicle insurance	100	29	52	74	90	107	119	157
Vehicle rentals, leases, licenses, other charges	100	24	29	50	65	70	106	215
Public transportation	**100**	**28**	**34**	**48**	**55**	**64**	**94**	**225**
HEALTH CARE	**100**	**41**	**74**	**84**	**93**	**99**	**112**	**141**
Health insurance	100	41	76	86	92	108	114	134
Medical services	100	32	54	72	86	80	112	171
Drugs	100	54	98	99	103	101	102	116
Medical supplies	100	41	60	60	94	96	121	154
ENTERTAINMENT	**100**	**31**	**39**	**68**	**69**	**79**	**117**	**186**
Fees and admissions	100	27	24	39	54	72	104	227
Television, radio, and sound equipment	100	43	58	73	85	93	117	156
Pets, toys, and playground equipment	100	32	44	57	93	83	106	180
Other entertainment products and services	100	17	24	98	40	63	136	193
PERSONAL CARE PRODUCTS AND SERVICES	**100**	**40**	**53**	**71**	**78**	**95**	**103**	**170**
READING	**100**	**39**	**52**	**64**	**73**	**91**	**105**	**180**
EDUCATION	**100**	**87**	**49**	**35**	**35**	**46**	**78**	**224**
TOBACCO PRODUCTS AND SMOKING SUPPLIES	**100**	**64**	**89**	**101**	**111**	**114**	**118**	**99**
MISCELLANEOUS	**100**	**44**	**51**	**73**	**76**	**107**	**108**	**163**
CASH CONTRIBUTIONS	**100**	**17**	**43**	**52**	**60**	**91**	**97**	**208**
PERSONAL INSURANCE AND PENSIONS	**100**	**6**	**15**	**33**	**56**	**76**	**113**	**235**
Life and other personal insurance	100	21	38	47	69	81	107	206
Pensions and Social Security	100	4	13	32	55	75	113	238
PERSONAL TAXES	**100**	**−1**	**−4**	**22**	**25**	**44**	**99**	**287**
Federal income taxes	100	−3	−11	17	15	34	98	302
State and local income taxes	100	−1	4	19	39	58	95	275
Other taxes	100	17	32	73	71	90	118	188
GIFTS FOR NONHOUSEHOLD MEMBERS	**100**	**30**	**47**	**42**	**62**	**64**	**95**	**213**

Source: Calculations by New Strategist based on the Bureau of Labor Statistics' 2004 Consumer Expenditure Survey

Spending by High-Income Consumer Units, 2004

The higher the income, the greater the spending. Households with incomes of $100,000 or more spent more than $93,000 in 2004, more than double the $43,395 spending of the average household. The Consumer Expenditure Survey examines the spending of households with incomes up to $150,000 or more. These highest-income households spent more than $119,000 in 2004. Spending surges as income rises, in part because affluent households have more earners—and consequently more expenses—than the average household.

On many products and services, the most affluent households spend four or even five times as much as the average household. On "other lodging" (motels, hotels, vacation homes, college dorms), households with incomes of $150,000 or more spend more than five times as much as the average household. They spend more than four times the average on fees and admissions to entertainment events, public transportation, and education. The most affluent households spend less than average on only two items: rent and tobacco.

Table 1.6 Average spending by high-income consumer units, 2004

(average annual spending of consumer units by product and service category and before-tax income of consumer unit, 2004)

	total consumer units	less than $70,000	$70,000–$79,999	$80,000–$99,999	$100,000 or more total	$100,000–$119,999	$120,000–$149,999	$150,000 or more
Number of consumer units (in 000s)	116,282	85,638	6,461	9,246	14,937	5,625	4,245	5,067
Average number of persons per consumer unit	2.5	2.3	3.0	3.1	3.2	3.1	3.3	3.2
Average income before taxes	$54,453	$31,541	$74,437	$88,811	$155,901	$108,751	$132,292	$228,021
Average annual spending	43,395	31,280	55,012	65,446	93,526	75,213	87,299	119,449
FOOD	**5,781**	**4,562**	**7,337**	**7,467**	**10,733**	**9,444**	**10,419**	**12,555**
Food at home	**3,347**	**2,825**	**4,079**	**4,043**	**5,435**	**5,014**	**5,542**	**5,840**
Cereals and bakery products	461	398	522	545	724	672	741	772
Cereals and cereal products	154	135	176	180	228	217	232	238
Bakery products	307	262	346	366	496	455	509	534
Meats, poultry, fish, and eggs	880	756	1,097	1,033	1,363	1,271	1,396	1,442
Beef	265	226	354	324	403	384	412	419
Pork	181	163	189	209	258	264	267	241
Other meats	108	90	130	137	177	159	165	212
Poultry	156	133	191	185	247	233	254	258
Fish and seafood	128	105	194	136	220	177	241	252
Eggs	42	39	39	43	57	54	57	60
Dairy products	371	314	426	451	604	560	620	641
Fresh milk and cream	144	129	157	169	206	200	209	210
Other dairy products	226	185	269	282	398	360	411	431
Fruits and vegetables	561	473	645	659	941	860	932	1,049
Fresh fruits	187	155	210	221	327	285	329	378
Fresh vegetables	183	153	213	214	312	288	311	342
Processed fruits	110	93	126	134	175	159	172	199
Processed vegetables	82	71	96	89	126	128	120	131
Other food at home	1,075	884	1,389	1,355	1,803	1,651	1,853	1,935
Sugar and other sweets	128	104	141	162	231	184	273	246
Fats and oils	89	79	103	98	129	131	128	128
Miscellaneous foods	527	424	717	693	902	860	896	960
Nonalcoholic beverages	290	250	374	332	443	405	461	472
Food prepared by consumer unit on trips	41	27	55	69	98	72	95	129
Food away from home	**2,434**	**1,737**	**3,259**	**3,424**	**5,299**	**4,429**	**4,877**	**6,715**
ALCOHOLIC BEVERAGES	**459**	**323**	**617**	**702**	**987**	**724**	**887**	**1,405**
HOUSING	**13,918**	**10,456**	**17,422**	**20,397**	**28,140**	**22,273**	**26,339**	**36,246**
Shelter	**7,998**	**6,004**	**10,213**	**11,761**	**16,143**	**12,871**	**14,869**	**20,843**
Owned dwellings	5,324	3,275	8,051	9,604	13,249	10,421	12,527	16,992
Mortgage interest and charges	2,936	1,677	4,871	5,681	7,619	6,139	7,306	9,523
Property taxes	1,391	900	1,884	2,253	3,458	2,570	3,173	4,683
Maintenance, repair, insurance, other expenses	997	697	1,296	1,670	2,172	1,712	2,048	2,786
Rented dwellings	2,201	2,501	1,638	1,325	1,266	1,496	1,019	1,219
Other lodging	473	229	524	833	1,628	954	1,323	2,633
Utilities, fuels, and public services	**2,927**	**2,498**	**3,552**	**3,903**	**4,511**	**3,977**	**4,446**	**5,159**
Natural gas	424	355	540	535	701	587	729	805
Electricity	1,064	926	1,232	1,393	1,580	1,343	1,541	1,875
Fuel oil and other fuels	121	104	129	156	190	167	153	246
Telephone	990	840	1,252	1,370	1,506	1,404	1,494	1,629
Water and other public services	327	273	399	450	534	475	530	604
Household services	**753**	**451**	**895**	**1,332**	**2,064**	**1,407**	**1,799**	**3,016**
Personal services	300	175	381	613	786	558	739	1,080
Other household services	453	276	514	718	1,278	849	1,061	1,936
Housekeeping supplies	**594**	**461**	**677**	**862**	**1,118**	**893**	**1,051**	**1,461**
Laundry and cleaning supplies	149	128	173	181	227	204	246	237
Other household products	290	217	323	423	595	437	493	892
Postage and stationery	155	116	181	257	295	252	312	332
Household furnishings and equipment	**1,646**	**1,042**	**2,085**	**2,539**	**4,304**	**3,125**	**4,174**	**5,767**
Household textiles	158	104	166	266	383	317	380	459
Furniture	417	244	587	576	1,235	791	1,318	1,659
Floor coverings	52	30	45	80	162	88	93	303

	total consumer units	less than $70,000	$70,000–$79,999	$80,000–$99,999	$100,000 or more			
					total	$100,000–$119,999	$120,000–$149,999	$150,000 or more
Major appliances	$204	$145	$321	$323	$413	$316	$390	$539
Small appliances, miscellaneous housewares	105	73	130	150	240	219	235	269
Miscellaneous household equipment	711	445	837	1,144	1,871	1,394	1,759	2,538
APPAREL AND RELATED SERVICES	**1,816**	**1,248**	**2,219**	**2,666**	**4,253**	**3,644**	**3,675**	**5,502**
Men and boys	**406**	**264**	**544**	**613**	**1,003**	**849**	**842**	**1,341**
Men, aged 16 or older	317	197	419	480	831	674	687	1,156
Boys, aged 2 to 15	89	66	126	133	172	175	154	185
Women and girls	**739**	**505**	**854**	**1,159**	**1,706**	**1,490**	**1,597**	**2,074**
Women, aged 16 or older	631	431	695	996	1,468	1,252	1,370	1,824
Girls, aged 2 to 15	108	74	159	162	239	238	226	250
Children under age 2	**79**	**61**	**118**	**92**	**151**	**145**	**148**	**161**
Footwear	**329**	**260**	**380**	**382**	**649**	**634**	**566**	**750**
Other apparel products and services	**264**	**159**	**323**	**420**	**744**	**526**	**523**	**1,175**
TRANSPORTATION	**7,801**	**5,756**	**9,965**	**12,446**	**15,707**	**13,520**	**15,515**	**18,308**
Vehicle purchases	**3,397**	**2,459**	**4,218**	**5,516**	**7,106**	**6,013**	**7,028**	**8,384**
Cars and trucks, new	1,748	1,130	2,139	3,166	4,247	3,210	4,584	5,117
Cars and trucks, used	1,582	1,279	1,974	2,231	2,748	2,723	2,292	3,157
Other vehicles	66	50	104	119	111	79	153	111
Gasoline and motor oil	**1,598**	**1,307**	**2,131**	**2,366**	**2,559**	**2,452**	**2,686**	**2,573**
Other vehicle expenses	**2,365**	**1,747**	**3,184**	**3,812**	**4,659**	**4,162**	**4,582**	**5,278**
Vehicle finance charges	323	233	559	564	593	575	655	562
Maintenance and repairs	652	495	830	1,048	1,225	1,083	1,227	1,383
Vehicle insurance	964	769	1,245	1,431	1,675	1,584	1,744	1,720
Vehicle rentals, leases, licenses, other charges	426	250	550	768	1,165	920	956	1,613
Public transportation	**441**	**244**	**432**	**752**	**1,383**	**894**	**1,219**	**2,073**
HEALTH CARE	**2,574**	**2,195**	**3,029**	**3,384**	**4,042**	**3,732**	**3,812**	**4,581**
Health insurance	1,332	1,167	1,532	1,766	1,918	1,778	1,799	2,173
Medical services	648	484	867	945	1,311	1,163	1,221	1,551
Drugs	480	452	511	528	596	569	594	629
Medical supplies	114	92	119	145	217	222	197	228
ENTERTAINMENT	**2,218**	**1,534**	**2,870**	**3,677**	**4,932**	**3,613**	**4,716**	**6,570**
Fees and admissions	528	289	673	924	1,590	1,055	1,476	2,280
Television, radio, and sound equipment	788	629	1,016	1,142	1,379	1,202	1,321	1,628
Pets, toys, and playground equipment	381	269	560	604	790	615	811	966
Other entertainment products and services	522	347	621	1,007	1,172	742	1,108	1,696
PERSONAL CARE PRODUCTS AND SERVICES	**581**	**433**	**658**	**852**	**1,207**	**1,030**	**1,191**	**1,427**
READING	**130**	**93**	**159**	**197**	**290**	**227**	**298**	**353**
EDUCATION	**905**	**502**	**940**	**1,540**	**2,806**	**1,865**	**2,166**	**4,382**
TOBACCO PRODUCTS AND SMOKING SUPPLIES	**288**	**289**	**337**	**303**	**252**	**279**	**290**	**189**
MISCELLANEOUS	**690**	**532**	**809**	**894**	**1,411**	**1,132**	**1,140**	**1,968**
CASH CONTRIBUTIONS	**1,408**	**864**	**1,551**	**2,052**	**4,067**	**2,445**	**2,672**	**7,037**
PERSONAL INSURANCE AND PENSIONS	**4,823**	**2,492**	**7,099**	**8,871**	**14,699**	**11,284**	**14,178**	**18,927**
Life and other personal insurance	390	242	430	645	1,063	785	904	1,505
Pensions and Social Security	4,433	2,249	6,670	8,225	13,636	10,498	13,274	17,422
PERSONAL TAXES	**2,166**	**716**	**2,201**	**3,927**	**9,371**	**4,950**	**8,019**	**15,411**
Federal income taxes	1,519	420	1,464	2,719	7,100	3,559	6,022	11,933
State and local income taxes	472	177	552	902	1,865	1,072	1,650	2,926
Other taxes	175	119	185	307	406	319	347	552
GIFTS FOR NONHOUSEHOLD MEMBERS	**1,215**	**715**	**1,289**	**1,927**	**3,563**	**2,178**	**3,174**	**5,473**

Note: Spending by category will not add to total spending because gift spending is also included in the preceding product and service categories and personal taxes are not included in the total.
Source: Bureau of Labor Statistics, 2004 Consumer Expenditure Survey, Internet site http://www.bls.gov/cex/

Table 1.7 Indexed spending by high-income consumer units, 2004

(indexed average annual spending of consumer units by product and service category and before-tax income of consumer unit reference person, 2004; index definition: an index of 100 is the average for all consumer units; an index of 132 means that spending by consumer units in that group is 32 percent above the average for all consumer units; an index of 68 indicates spending that is 32 percent below the average for all consumer units)

	total consumer units	less than $70,000	$70,000–$79,999	$80,000–$99,999	$100,000 or more total	$100,000–$119,999	$120,000–$149,999	$150,000 or more
Average spending of consumer units, total	$43,395	$31,280	$55,012	$65,446	$93,526	$75,213	$87,299	$119,449
Average spending of consumer units, index	100	72	127	151	216	173	201	275
FOOD	100	79	127	129	186	163	180	217
Food at home	100	84	122	121	162	150	166	174
Cereals and bakery products	100	86	113	118	157	146	161	167
Cereals and cereal products	100	88	114	117	148	141	151	155
Bakery products	100	85	113	119	162	148	166	174
Meats, poultry, fish, and eggs	100	86	125	117	155	144	159	164
Beef	100	85	134	122	152	145	155	158
Pork	100	90	104	115	143	146	148	133
Other meats	100	83	120	127	164	147	153	196
Poultry	100	85	122	119	158	149	163	165
Fish and seafood	100	82	152	106	172	138	188	197
Eggs	100	93	93	102	136	129	136	143
Dairy products	100	85	115	122	163	151	167	173
Fresh milk and cream	100	90	109	117	143	139	145	146
Other dairy products	100	82	119	125	176	159	182	191
Fruits and vegetables	100	84	115	117	168	153	166	187
Fresh fruits	100	83	112	118	175	152	176	202
Fresh vegetables	100	84	116	117	170	157	170	187
Processed fruits	100	85	115	122	159	145	156	181
Processed vegetables	100	87	117	109	154	156	146	160
Other food at home	100	82	129	126	168	154	172	180
Sugar and other sweets	100	81	110	127	180	144	213	192
Fats and oils	100	89	116	110	145	147	144	144
Miscellaneous foods	100	80	136	131	171	163	170	182
Nonalcoholic beverages	100	86	129	114	153	140	159	163
Food prepared by consumer unit on trips	100	66	134	168	239	176	232	315
Food away from home	100	71	134	141	218	182	200	276
ALCOHOLIC BEVERAGES	100	70	134	153	215	158	193	306
HOUSING	100	75	125	147	202	160	189	260
Shelter	100	75	128	147	202	161	186	261
Owned dwellings	100	62	151	180	249	196	235	319
Mortgage interest and charges	100	57	166	193	260	209	249	324
Property taxes	100	65	135	162	249	185	228	337
Maintenance, repair, insurance, other expenses	100	70	130	168	218	172	205	279
Rented dwellings	100	114	74	60	58	68	46	55
Other lodging	100	48	111	176	344	202	280	557
Utilities, fuels, and public services	100	85	121	133	154	136	152	176
Natural gas	100	84	127	126	165	138	172	190
Electricity	100	87	116	131	148	126	145	176
Fuel oil and other fuels	100	86	107	129	157	138	126	203
Telephone	100	85	126	138	152	142	151	165
Water and other public services	100	83	122	138	163	145	162	185
Household services	100	60	119	177	274	187	239	401
Personal services	100	58	127	204	262	186	246	360
Other household services	100	61	113	158	282	187	234	427
Housekeeping supplies	100	78	114	145	188	150	177	246
Laundry and cleaning supplies	100	86	116	121	152	137	165	159
Other household products	100	75	111	146	205	151	170	308
Postage and stationery	100	75	117	166	190	163	201	214
Household furnishings and equipment	100	63	127	154	261	190	254	350
Household textiles	100	66	105	168	242	201	241	291
Furniture	100	59	141	138	296	190	316	398
Floor coverings	100	58	87	154	312	169	179	583

	total consumer units	less than $70,000	$70,000– $79,999	$80,000– $99,999	$100,000 or more total	$100,000– $119,999	$120,000– $149,999	$150,000 or more
Major appliances	100	71	157	158	202	155	191	264
Small appliances, miscellaneous housewares	100	70	124	143	229	209	224	256
Miscellaneous household equipment	100	63	118	161	263	196	247	357
APPAREL AND RELATED SERVICES	**100**	**69**	**122**	**147**	**234**	**201**	**202**	**303**
Men and boys	**100**	**65**	**134**	**151**	**247**	**209**	**207**	**330**
Men, aged 16 or older	100	62	132	151	262	213	217	365
Boys, aged 2 to 15	100	74	142	149	193	197	173	208
Women and girls	**100**	**68**	**116**	**157**	**231**	**202**	**216**	**281**
Women, aged 16 or older	100	68	110	158	233	198	217	289
Girls, aged 2 to 15	100	69	147	150	221	220	209	231
Children under age 2	**100**	**77**	**149**	**116**	**191**	**184**	**187**	**204**
Footwear	**100**	**79**	**116**	**116**	**197**	**193**	**172**	**228**
Other apparel products and services	**100**	**60**	**122**	**159**	**282**	**199**	**198**	**445**
TRANSPORTATION	**100**	**74**	**128**	**160**	**201**	**173**	**199**	**235**
Vehicle purchases	**100**	**72**	**124**	**162**	**209**	**177**	**207**	**247**
Cars and trucks, new	100	65	122	181	243	184	262	293
Cars and trucks, used	100	81	125	141	174	172	145	200
Other vehicles	100	76	158	180	168	120	232	168
Gasoline and motor oil	**100**	**82**	**133**	**148**	**160**	**153**	**168**	**161**
Other vehicle expenses	**100**	**74**	**135**	**161**	**197**	**176**	**194**	**223**
Vehicle finance charges	100	72	173	175	184	178	203	174
Maintenance and repairs	100	76	127	161	188	166	188	212
Vehicle insurance	100	80	129	148	174	164	181	178
Vehicle rentals, leases, licenses, other charges	100	59	129	180	273	216	224	379
Public transportation	**100**	**55**	**98**	**171**	**314**	**203**	**276**	**470**
HEALTH CARE	**100**	**85**	**118**	**131**	**157**	**145**	**148**	**178**
Health insurance	100	88	115	133	144	133	135	163
Medical services	100	75	134	146	202	179	188	239
Drugs	100	94	106	110	124	119	124	131
Medical supplies	100	81	104	127	190	195	173	200
ENTERTAINMENT	**100**	**69**	**129**	**166**	**222**	**163**	**213**	**296**
Fees and admissions	100	55	127	175	301	200	280	432
Television, radio, and sound equipment	100	80	129	145	175	153	168	207
Pets, toys, and playground equipment	100	71	147	159	207	161	213	254
Other entertainment products and services	100	66	119	193	225	142	212	325
PERSONAL CARE PRODUCTS AND SERVICES	**100**	**75**	**113**	**147**	**208**	**177**	**205**	**246**
READING	**100**	**72**	**122**	**152**	**223**	**175**	**229**	**272**
EDUCATION	**100**	**55**	**104**	**170**	**310**	**206**	**239**	**484**
TOBACCO PRODUCTS AND SMOKING SUPPLIES	**100**	**100**	**117**	**105**	**88**	**97**	**101**	**66**
MISCELLANEOUS	**100**	**77**	**117**	**130**	**204**	**164**	**165**	**285**
CASH CONTRIBUTIONS	**100**	**61**	**110**	**146**	**289**	**174**	**190**	**500**
PERSONAL INSURANCE AND PENSIONS	**100**	**52**	**147**	**184**	**305**	**234**	**294**	**392**
Life and other personal insurance	100	62	110	165	273	201	232	386
Pensions and Social Security	100	51	150	186	308	237	299	393
PERSONAL TAXES	**100**	**33**	**102**	**181**	**433**	**229**	**370**	**711**
Federal income taxes	100	28	96	179	467	234	396	786
State and local income taxes	100	38	117	191	395	227	350	620
Other taxes	100	68	106	175	232	182	198	315
GIFTS FOR NONHOUSEHOLD MEMBERS	**100**	**59**	**106**	**159**	**293**	**179**	**261**	**450**

Source: Calculations by New Strategist based on the Bureau of Labor Statistics' 2004 Consumer Expenditure Survey

Spending by Household Type, 2004

Married couples spent 28 percent more than the average household in 2004. Among married couples, those with adult children at home spend the most—$64,162 in 2004. Behind the higher spending levels of married couples are their higher incomes, due primarily to the greater number of earners in the household. Married couples with children at home average 2.0 earners per household. Those with adult children at home average 2.5 earners. The more earners, the greater the spending—particularly on products and services needed by workers such as food away from home, men's and women's clothes, and transportation.

Married couples with children under age 18 at home have distinct spending patterns. Couples with school-aged children spend 40 percent more than the average household overall. They spend 62 percent more than the average household on milk and 60 percent more on cereal. They spend 88 percent more than average on fees and admissions to entertainment events and three times the average on children's clothes. The biggest spenders on household personal services (mostly day care) are married couples with preschoolers, while couples without children at home (mostly empty-nesters) spend the most on alcoholic beverages and health care.

Single parents spend less than the average household on most items. Some of the exceptions are rent, children's clothes, and household personal services (mostly day care).

Table 1.8 Average spending by household type, 2004

(average annual spending of consumer units by product and service category and type of consumer unit, 2004)

	total married couples	married couples, no children	married couples with children				single parent, at least one child <18	single person
			total	oldest child under 6	oldest child 6 to 17	oldest child 18 or older		
Number of consumer units (in 000s)	59,797	25,585	29,279	5,604	15,376	8,300	6,892	33,686
Average number of persons per consumer unit	3.2	2.0	3.9	3.5	4.1	3.9	2.9	1.0
Average income before taxes	$73,001	$64,434	$79,764	$75,293	$78,508	$85,109	$31,055	$28,143
Average annual spending	55,607	49,690	60,661	55,981	60,578	64,162	32,824	25,423
FOOD	7,379	6,268	8,089	6,300	8,484	8,682	4,873	3,095
Food at home	4,303	3,574	4,711	3,765	4,887	5,104	3,015	1,681
Cereals and bakery products	593	472	668	492	718	705	443	229
Cereals and cereal products	198	148	227	160	246	242	162	73
Bakery products	395	324	441	333	472	463	281	156
Meats, poultry, fish, and eggs	1,121	923	1,210	875	1,216	1,465	835	411
Beef	342	270	377	244	380	480	258	117
Pork	227	190	240	175	236	300	188	83
Other meats	140	115	155	100	162	184	106	49
Poultry	197	154	217	165	225	243	135	75
Fish and seafood	164	151	165	147	159	191	112	63
Eggs	52	43	55	45	54	66	37	24
Dairy products	480	390	542	437	580	549	317	183
Fresh milk and cream	187	137	220	190	233	219	140	69
Other dairy products	293	254	322	246	347	330	176	114
Fruits and vegetables	726	644	756	634	771	823	456	298
Fresh fruits	244	225	248	211	255	263	149	101
Fresh vegetables	241	222	242	205	239	278	130	93
Processed fruits	138	112	154	136	160	155	102	62
Processed vegetables	103	85	112	82	116	128	75	42
Other food at home	1,383	1,145	1,535	1,327	1,602	1,561	964	560
Sugar and other sweets	168	148	176	140	187	183	123	63
Fats and oils	113	98	121	88	125	137	78	47
Miscellaneous foods	683	538	788	772	813	750	474	274
Nonalcoholic beverages	361	298	399	292	421	439	269	155
Food prepared by consumer unit on trips	58	64	50	35	55	51	19	20
Food away from home	3,076	2,694	3,378	2,535	3,597	3,578	1,858	1,414
ALCOHOLIC BEVERAGES	493	567	443	330	455	506	219	359
HOUSING	17,005	14,706	18,912	21,045	18,900	17,503	12,030	9,244
Shelter	9,427	8,031	10,658	11,944	10,838	9,455	7,043	5,841
Owned dwellings	7,291	5,947	8,473	9,254	8,644	7,628	3,314	2,916
Mortgage interest and charges	4,152	2,793	5,315	6,243	5,433	4,470	2,037	1,360
Property taxes	1,885	1,814	1,958	1,907	1,961	1,987	729	832
Maintenance, repair, insurance, other expenses	1,255	1,340	1,200	1,104	1,250	1,171	548	725
Rented dwellings	1,463	1,308	1,558	2,334	1,545	1,058	3,510	2,659
Other lodging	673	776	628	357	650	769	219	265
Utilities, fuels, and public services	3,572	3,176	3,839	3,325	3,809	4,240	2,755	1,830
Natural gas	512	448	561	546	549	594	380	274
Electricity	1,302	1,173	1,381	1,114	1,419	1,489	1,065	649
Fuel oil and other fuels	156	163	149	110	149	177	67	84
Telephone	1,179	1,013	1,300	1,166	1,249	1,487	979	634
Water and other public services	422	378	447	389	444	492	263	188
Household services	996	638	1,299	2,699	1,167	599	759	443
Personal services	416	19	749	2,146	608	69	483	125
Other household services	580	619	550	554	558	531	276	318
Housekeeping supplies	771	729	815	820	824	794	453	315
Laundry and cleaning supplies	183	145	206	174	217	208	158	73
Other household products	387	368	413	450	415	379	193	147
Postage and stationery	202	215	196	196	192	207	102	95
Household furnishings and equipment	2,238	2,133	2,301	2,257	2,262	2,415	1,020	816
Household textiles	204	211	199	168	164	299	85	87
Furniture	575	541	587	626	590	556	357	174
Floor coverings	72	78	61	47	64	66	42	24

	total married couples	married couples, no children	married couples with children				single parent, at least one child <18	single person
			total	oldest child under 6	oldest child 6 to 17	oldest child 18 or older		
Major appliances	$286	$278	$297	$333	$276	$311	$101	$88
Small appliances, miscellaneous housewares	139	136	141	180	130	133	70	59
Miscellaneous household equipment	963	889	1,015	903	1,038	1,049	365	385
APPAREL AND RELATED SERVICES	**2,263**	**1,745**	**2,680**	**2,583**	**2,757**	**2,617**	**1,859**	**949**
Men and boys	**547**	**399**	**673**	**575**	**739**	**618**	**304**	**169**
Men, aged 16 or older	423	369	469	443	456	516	111	153
Boys, aged 2 to 15	124	30	204	132	283	103	193	16
Women and girls	**897**	**741**	**1,033**	**873**	**1,023**	**1,189**	**880**	**416**
Women, aged 16 or older	743	706	782	719	671	1,061	608	401
Girls, aged 2 to 15	153	35	251	154	352	128	272	14
Children under age 2	**116**	**42**	**168**	**518**	**100**	**35**	**89**	**12**
Footwear	**389**	**255**	**485**	**323**	**545**	**490**	**424**	**186**
Other apparel products and services	**314**	**307**	**321**	**294**	**351**	**285**	**164**	**166**
TRANSPORTATION	**10,486**	**8,975**	**11,884**	**10,599**	**11,377**	**13,694**	**5,446**	**3,941**
Vehicle purchases	**4,724**	**3,806**	**5,579**	**5,142**	**5,370**	**6,263**	**2,304**	**1,600**
Cars and trucks, new	2,609	2,295	2,969	2,944	2,769	3,354	798	796
Cars and trucks, used	2,021	1,369	2,546	2,169	2,526	2,837	1,463	776
Other vehicles	94	142	65	29	75	72	44	28
Gasoline and motor oil	**2,087**	**1,752**	**2,362**	**1,991**	**2,277**	**2,770**	**1,216**	**806**
Other vehicle expenses	**3,080**	**2,753**	**3,381**	**3,015**	**3,188**	**3,986**	**1,716**	**1,281**
Vehicle finance charges	451	372	519	484	516	548	211	127
Maintenance and repairs	830	771	881	722	881	987	477	404
Vehicle insurance	1,226	1,075	1,356	1,105	1,199	1,818	725	537
Vehicle rentals, leases, licenses, other charges	573	534	625	703	593	634	302	213
Public transportation	**595**	**664**	**561**	**451**	**542**	**674**	**209**	**254**
HEALTH CARE	**3,345**	**3,761**	**3,009**	**2,369**	**2,948**	**3,554**	**1,384**	**1,697**
Health insurance	1,750	1,945	1,589	1,275	1,579	1,820	705	850
Medical services	863	880	859	690	872	947	415	391
Drugs	581	762	427	305	372	611	213	383
Medical supplies	151	175	134	99	125	176	51	73
ENTERTAINMENT	**2,945**	**2,919**	**3,051**	**2,442**	**3,320**	**2,975**	**1,573**	**1,162**
Fees and admissions	722	656	819	479	991	729	391	283
Television, radio, and sound equipment	946	814	1,060	1,001	1,070	1,081	695	516
Pets, toys, and playground equipment	496	456	537	520	570	495	285	196
Other entertainment products and services	782	993	636	442	690	670	203	167
PERSONAL CARE PRODUCTS AND SERVICES	**711**	**656**	**748**	**604**	**732**	**891**	**517**	**355**
READING	**166**	**186**	**153**	**139**	**158**	**154**	**68**	**97**
EDUCATION	**1,154**	**828**	**1,485**	**414**	**1,439**	**2,294**	**700**	**629**
TOBACCO PRODUCTS AND SMOKING SUPPLIES	**301**	**249**	**324**	**211**	**318**	**413**	**277**	**167**
MISCELLANEOUS	**800**	**790**	**757**	**687**	**650**	**1,011**	**643**	**517**
CASH CONTRIBUTIONS	**1,836**	**2,316**	**1,481**	**1,189**	**1,517**	**1,610**	**587**	**1,027**
PERSONAL INSURANCE AND PENSIONS	**6,722**	**5,723**	**7,645**	**7,069**	**7,524**	**8,257**	**2,648**	**2,184**
Life and other personal insurance	594	604	570	389	543	742	204	146
Pensions and Social Security	6,128	5,119	7,075	6,680	6,981	7,516	2,444	2,039
PERSONAL TAXES	**2,953**	**3,326**	**2,881**	**2,891**	**2,738**	**3,142**	**103**	**1,383**
Federal income taxes	2,069	2,416	1,970	1,947	1,836	2,233	-195	990
State and local income taxes	650	630	712	788	697	690	217	280
Other taxes	234	281	199	156	205	219	82	113
GIFTS FOR NONHOUSEHOLD MEMBERS	**1,575**	**1,855**	**1,425**	**1,078**	**1,393**	**1,722**	**649**	**860**

Note: Spending by category will not add to total spending because gift spending is also included in the preceding product and service categories and personal taxes are not included in the total.

Source: Bureau of Labor Statistics, 2004 Consumer Expenditure Survey, Internet site http://www.bls.gov/cex/; calculations by New Strategist

Table 1.9 Indexed spending by household type, 2004

(indexed average annual spending of consumer units by product and service category and type of consumer unit, 2004; index definition: an index of 100 is the average for all consumer units; an index of 132 means that spending by consumer units in that group is 32 percent above the average for all consumer units; an index of 68 indicates spending that is 32 percent below the average for all consumer units)

	total married couples	married couples, no children	married couples with children total	oldest child under 6	oldest child 6 to 17	oldest child 18 or older	single parent, at least one child <18	single person
Average spending of consumer units, total	$55,607	$49,690	$60,661	$55,981	$60,578	$64,162	$32,824	$25,423
Average spending of consumer units, index	128	115	140	129	140	148	76	59
FOOD	128	108	140	109	147	150	84	54
Food at home	129	107	141	112	146	152	90	50
Cereals and bakery products	129	102	145	107	156	153	96	50
Cereals and cereal products	129	96	147	104	160	157	105	47
Bakery products	129	106	144	108	154	151	92	51
Meats, poultry, fish, and eggs	127	105	138	99	138	166	95	47
Beef	129	102	142	92	143	181	97	44
Pork	125	105	133	97	130	166	104	46
Other meats	130	106	144	93	150	170	98	45
Poultry	126	99	139	106	144	156	87	48
Fish and seafood	128	118	129	115	124	149	88	49
Eggs	124	102	131	107	129	157	88	57
Dairy products	129	105	146	118	156	148	85	49
Fresh milk and cream	130	95	153	132	162	152	97	48
Other dairy products	130	112	142	109	154	146	78	50
Fruits and vegetables	129	115	135	113	137	147	81	53
Fresh fruits	130	120	133	113	136	141	80	54
Fresh vegetables	132	121	132	112	131	152	71	51
Processed fruits	125	102	140	124	145	141	93	56
Processed vegetables	126	104	137	100	141	156	91	51
Other food at home	129	107	143	123	149	145	90	52
Sugar and other sweets	131	116	138	109	146	143	96	49
Fats and oils	127	110	136	99	140	154	88	53
Miscellaneous foods	130	102	150	146	154	142	90	52
Nonalcoholic beverages	124	103	138	101	145	151	93	53
Food prepared by consumer unit on trips	141	156	122	85	134	124	46	49
Food away from home	126	111	139	104	148	147	76	58
ALCOHOLIC BEVERAGES	107	124	97	72	99	110	48	78
HOUSING	122	106	136	151	136	126	86	66
Shelter	118	100	133	149	136	118	88	73
Owned dwellings	137	112	159	174	162	143	62	55
Mortgage interest and charges	141	95	181	213	185	152	69	46
Property taxes	136	130	141	137	141	143	52	60
Maintenance, repair, insurance, other expenses	126	134	120	111	125	117	55	73
Rented dwellings	66	59	71	106	70	48	159	121
Other lodging	142	164	133	75	137	163	46	56
Utilities, fuels, and public services	122	109	131	114	130	145	94	63
Natural gas	121	106	132	129	129	140	90	65
Electricity	122	110	130	105	133	140	100	61
Fuel oil and other fuels	129	135	123	91	123	146	55	69
Telephone	119	102	131	118	126	150	99	64
Water and other public services	129	116	137	119	136	150	80	57
Household services	132	85	173	358	155	80	101	59
Personal services	139	6	250	715	203	23	161	42
Other household services	128	137	121	122	123	117	61	70
Housekeeping supplies	130	123	137	138	139	134	76	53
Laundry and cleaning supplies	123	97	138	117	146	140	106	49
Other household products	133	127	142	155	143	131	67	51
Postage and stationery	130	139	126	126	124	134	66	61
Household furnishings and equipment	136	130	140	137	137	147	62	50
Household textiles	129	134	126	106	104	189	54	55
Furniture	138	130	141	150	141	133	86	42
Floor coverings	138	150	117	90	123	127	81	46

	total married couples	married couples, no children	married couples with children				single parent, at least one child <18	single person
			total	oldest child under 6	oldest child 6 to 17	oldest child 18 or older		
Major appliances	140	136	146	163	135	152	50	43
Small appliances, miscellaneous housewares	132	130	134	171	124	127	67	56
Miscellaneous household equipment	135	125	143	127	146	148	51	54
APPAREL AND RELATED SERVICES	**125**	**96**	**148**	**142**	**152**	**144**	**102**	**52**
Men and boys	**135**	**98**	**166**	**142**	**182**	**152**	**75**	**42**
Men, aged 16 or older	133	116	148	140	144	163	35	48
Boys, aged 2 to 15	139	34	229	148	318	116	217	18
Women and girls	**121**	**100**	**140**	**118**	**138**	**161**	**119**	**56**
Women, aged 16 or older	118	112	124	114	106	168	96	64
Girls, aged 2 to 15	142	32	232	143	326	119	252	13
Children under age 2	**147**	**53**	**213**	**656**	**127**	**44**	**113**	**15**
Footwear	**118**	**78**	**147**	**98**	**166**	**149**	**129**	**57**
Other apparel products and services	**119**	**116**	**122**	**111**	**133**	**108**	**62**	**63**
TRANSPORTATION	**134**	**115**	**152**	**136**	**146**	**176**	**70**	**51**
Vehicle purchases	**139**	**112**	**164**	**151**	**158**	**184**	**68**	**47**
Cars and trucks, new	149	131	170	168	158	192	46	46
Cars and trucks, used	128	87	161	137	160	179	92	49
Other vehicles	142	215	98	44	114	109	67	42
Gasoline and motor oil	**131**	**110**	**148**	**125**	**142**	**173**	**76**	**50**
Other vehicle expenses	**130**	**116**	**143**	**127**	**135**	**169**	**73**	**54**
Vehicle finance charges	140	115	161	150	160	170	65	39
Maintenance and repairs	127	118	135	111	135	151	73	62
Vehicle insurance	127	112	141	115	124	189	75	56
Vehicle rentals, leases, licenses, other charges	135	125	147	165	139	149	71	50
Public transportation	**135**	**151**	**127**	**102**	**123**	**153**	**47**	**58**
HEALTH CARE	**130**	**146**	**117**	**92**	**115**	**138**	**54**	**66**
Health insurance	131	146	119	96	119	137	53	64
Medical services	133	136	133	106	135	146	64	60
Drugs	121	159	89	64	78	127	44	80
Medical supplies	132	154	118	87	110	154	45	64
ENTERTAINMENT	**133**	**132**	**138**	**110**	**150**	**134**	**71**	**52**
Fees and admissions	137	124	155	91	188	138	74	54
Television, radio, and sound equipment	120	103	135	127	136	137	88	65
Pets, toys, and playground equipment	130	120	141	136	150	130	75	51
Other entertainment products and services	150	190	122	85	132	128	39	32
PERSONAL CARE PRODUCTS AND SERVICES	**122**	**113**	**129**	**104**	**126**	**153**	**89**	**61**
READING	**128**	**143**	**118**	**107**	**122**	**118**	**52**	**75**
EDUCATION	**128**	**91**	**164**	**46**	**159**	**253**	**77**	**70**
TOBACCO PRODUCTS AND SMOKING SUPPLIES	**105**	**86**	**113**	**73**	**110**	**143**	**96**	**58**
MISCELLANEOUS	**116**	**114**	**110**	**100**	**94**	**147**	**93**	**75**
CASH CONTRIBUTIONS	**130**	**164**	**105**	**84**	**108**	**114**	**42**	**73**
PERSONAL INSURANCE AND PENSIONS	**139**	**119**	**159**	**147**	**156**	**171**	**55**	**45**
Life and other personal insurance	152	155	146	100	139	190	52	37
Pensions and Social Security	138	115	160	151	157	170	55	46
PERSONAL TAXES	**136**	**154**	**133**	**133**	**126**	**145**	**5**	**64**
Federal income taxes	136	159	130	128	121	147	-13	65
State and local income taxes	138	133	151	167	148	146	46	59
Other taxes	134	161	114	89	117	125	47	65
GIFTS FOR NONHOUSEHOLD MEMBERS	**130**	**153**	**117**	**89**	**115**	**142**	**53**	**71**

Note: Spending index for total consumer units is 100.
Source: Calculations by New Strategist based on the Bureau of Labor Statistics' 2004 Consumer Expenditure Survey

Spending by Race and Hispanic Origin, 2004

Asians spend more than the average household, while Hispanics and blacks spend less. The $49,459 spent by the average Asian household in 2004 was 14 percent above the national average and surpassed the spending of every other racial or ethnic group. Black households spent $30,481 in 2004, or 30 percent less than average. Hispanic spending, at $37,578, was 13 percent below average.

Asian spending reflects their above-average incomes, a consequence of their high educational attainment. Asian households spend more than twice the average on education.

Hispanic and black spending exceeds that of the average household in many categories. Because of their larger families, Hispanic households spend 16 percent more than the average household on food at home. They spend 34 percent more than the average household on laundry and cleaning supplies and 82 percent more on infants' apparel.

Blacks spend 41 percent more than the average household on rented dwellings, 15 percent more on pork, and 23 percent more on fish and seafood. They spend 11 to 35 percent more on clothes for boys and girls, and 54 percent more on shoes.

(average annual spending of consumer units by product and service category and by race and Hispanic origin of consumer unit reference person, 2004)

	total consumer units	Asian	black	Hispanic	non-Hispanic white and other
Number of consumer units (in 000s)	116,282	3,957	13,773	12,298	90,424
Average number of persons per consumer unit	2.5	2.8	2.6	3.3	2.3
Average income before taxes	$54,453	$67,705	$38,503	$43,693	$58,314
Average annual spending	43,395	49,459	30,481	37,578	46,163
FOOD	**5,781**	**6,742**	**4,265**	**5,911**	**5,999**
Food at home	**3,347**	**3,689**	**2,749**	**3,883**	**3,367**
Cereals and bakery products	461	527	388	517	464
Cereals and cereal products	154	243	152	202	147
Bakery products	307	284	236	315	317
Meats, poultry, fish, and eggs	880	1,021	898	1,175	836
Beef	265	231	216	367	259
Pork	181	183	208	236	169
Other meats	108	64	87	113	111
Poultry	156	192	186	231	140
Fish and seafood	128	305	157	159	119
Eggs	42	46	44	68	38
Dairy products	371	286	249	425	382
Fresh milk and cream	144	135	100	201	143
Other dairy products	226	151	149	224	239
Fruits and vegetables	561	870	442	712	559
Fresh fruits	187	329	130	249	187
Fresh vegetables	183	359	120	250	183
Processed fruits	110	118	107	127	108
Processed vegetables	82	63	86	86	80
Other food at home	1,075	985	772	1,054	1,125
Sugar and other sweets	128	137	94	116	135
Fats and oils	89	76	85	107	87
Miscellaneous foods	527	479	353	471	562
Nonalcoholic beverages	290	245	227	328	294
Food prepared by consumer unit on trips	41	47	13	31	46
Food away from home	**2,434**	**3,053**	**1,516**	**2,027**	**2,633**
ALCOHOLIC BEVERAGES	**459**	**325**	**171**	**320**	**523**
HOUSING	**13,918**	**17,418**	**11,043**	**12,884**	**14,503**
Shelter	**7,998**	**11,728**	**6,411**	**7,833**	**8,266**
Owned dwellings	5,324	7,734	3,165	4,107	5,817
Mortgage interest and charges	2,936	4,810	1,936	2,589	3,134
Property taxes	1,391	1,900	743	866	1,560
Maintenance, repair, insurance, other expenses	997	1,024	486	652	1,123
Rented dwellings	2,201	3,537	3,097	3,501	1,894
Other lodging	473	458	149	226	555
Utilities, fuels, and public services	**2,927**	**2,781**	**2,884**	**2,671**	**2,966**
Natural gas	424	442	452	337	432
Electricity	1,064	876	1,088	909	1,081
Fuel oil and other fuels	121	40	52	73	138
Telephone	990	1,078	1,025	1,031	979
Water and other public services	327	345	267	320	337
Household services	**753**	**885**	**466**	**574**	**820**
Personal services	300	450	241	331	304
Other household services	453	435	225	243	516
Housekeeping supplies	**594**	**472**	**374**	**503**	**641**
Laundry and cleaning supplies	149	115	124	199	145
Other household products	290	217	152	210	323
Postage and stationery	155	140	98	94	173
Household furnishings and equipment	**1,646**	**1,552**	**907**	**1,303**	**1,809**
Household textiles	158	96	107	110	172
Furniture	417	513	326	351	442
Floor coverings	52	64	25	22	60

	total consumer units	Asian	black	Hispanic	non-Hispanic white and other
Major appliances	$204	$139	$109	$205	$218
Small appliances, miscellaneous housewares	105	167	46	78	117
Miscellaneous household equipment	711	573	294	536	800
APPAREL AND RELATED SERVICES	**1,816**	**1,885**	**1,765**	**1,817**	**1,830**
Men and boys	**406**	**548**	**334**	**413**	**416**
Men, aged 16 or older	317	446	214	290	337
Boys, aged 2 to 15	89	101	120	123	79
Women and girls	**739**	**718**	**665**	**586**	**776**
Women, aged 16 or older	631	614	544	473	671
Girls, aged 2 to 15	108	104	120	113	105
Children under age 2	**79**	**82**	**50**	**144**	**74**
Footwear	**329**	**313**	**508**	**424**	**289**
Other apparel products and services	**264**	**224**	**208**	**250**	**274**
TRANSPORTATION	**7,801**	**8,556**	**4,976**	**7,497**	**8,273**
Vehicle purchases	**3,397**	**3,676**	**1,759**	**3,445**	**3,639**
Cars and trucks, new	1,748	2,307	786	1,604	1,917
Cars and trucks, used	1,582	1,354	960	1,833	1,639
Other vehicles	66	15	13	8	82
Gasoline and motor oil	**1,598**	**1,637**	**1,231**	**1,650**	**1,646**
Other vehicle expenses	**2,365**	**2,330**	**1,696**	**2,048**	**2,511**
Vehicle finance charges	323	260	240	285	341
Maintenance and repairs	652	701	427	574	697
Vehicle insurance	964	954	745	865	1,012
Vehicle rentals, leases, licenses, other charges	426	414	283	325	461
Public transportation	**441**	**913**	**290**	**355**	**477**
HEALTH CARE	**2,574**	**2,101**	**1,368**	**1,588**	**2,891**
Health insurance	1,332	1,177	846	850	1,471
Medical services	648	502	220	402	746
Drugs	480	294	263	252	544
Medical supplies	114	127	39	85	129
ENTERTAINMENT	**2,218**	**1,789**	**1,040**	**1,443**	**2,503**
Fees and admissions	528	614	185	308	610
Television, radio, and sound equipment	788	792	657	656	826
Pets, toys, and playground equipment	381	156	122	239	439
Other entertainment products and services	522	227	75	240	628
PERSONAL CARE PRODUCTS AND SERVICES	**581**	**506**	**503**	**519**	**602**
READING	**130**	**112**	**53**	**53**	**152**
EDUCATION	**905**	**2,087**	**573**	**438**	**1,019**
TOBACCO PRODUCTS AND SMOKING SUPPLIES	**288**	**103**	**200**	**155**	**319**
MISCELLANEOUS	**690**	**569**	**457**	**477**	**754**
CASH CONTRIBUTIONS	**1,408**	**1,089**	**835**	**710**	**1,589**
PERSONAL INSURANCE AND PENSIONS	**4,823**	**6,176**	**3,230**	**3,765**	**5,207**
Life and other personal insurance	390	306	292	155	437
Pensions and Social Security	4,433	5,871	2,938	3,610	4,770
PERSONAL TAXES	**2,166**	**2,131**	**507**	**895**	**2,587**
Federal income taxes	1,519	1,492	243	630	1,831
State and local income taxes	472	504	206	185	551
Other taxes	175	134	59	80	205
GIFTS FOR NONHOUSEHOLD MEMBERS	**1,215**	**1,274**	**684**	**723**	**1,363**

Note: "Asian" and "black" include Hispanics and non-Hispanics who identify themselves as being of the respective race alone. "Hispanic" includes people of any race who identify themselves as Hispanic. "Other" includes people who identify themselves as non-Hispanic and as Alaska Native, American Indian, Asian (who are also included in the "Asian" column), Native Hawaiian or other Pacific Islander, as well as non-Hispanics reporting more than one race. Spending by category will not add to total spending because gift spending is also included in the preceding product and service categories and personal taxes are not included in the total.
Source: Bureau of Labor Statistics, 2004 Consumer Expenditure Survey, Internet site http://www.bls.gov/cex/

Table 1.11 Indexed spending by race and Hispanic origin of householder, 2004

(indexed average annual spending of consumer units by product and service category and by race and Hispanic origin of consumer unit reference person, 2004; index definition: an index of 100 is the average for all consumer units; an index of 132 means that spending by consumer units in that group is 32 percent above the average for all consumer units; an index of 68 indicates spending that is 32 percent below the average for all consumer units)

	total consumer units	Asian	black	Hispanic	non-Hispanic white and other
Average spending of consumer units, total	$43,395	$49,459	$30,481	$37,578	$46,163
Average spending of consumer units, index	100	114	70	87	106
FOOD	**100**	**117**	**74**	**102**	**104**
Food at home	**100**	**110**	**82**	**116**	**101**
Cereals and bakery products	100	114	84	112	101
Cereals and cereal products	100	158	99	131	95
Bakery products	100	93	77	103	103
Meats, poultry, fish, and eggs	100	116	102	134	95
Beef	100	87	82	138	98
Pork	100	101	115	130	93
Other meats	100	59	81	105	103
Poultry	100	123	119	148	90
Fish and seafood	100	238	123	124	93
Eggs	100	110	105	162	90
Dairy products	100	77	67	115	103
Fresh milk and cream	100	94	69	140	99
Other dairy products	100	67	66	99	106
Fruits and vegetables	100	155	79	127	100
Fresh fruits	100	176	70	133	100
Fresh vegetables	100	196	66	137	100
Processed fruits	100	107	97	115	98
Processed vegetables	100	77	105	105	98
Other food at home	100	92	72	98	105
Sugar and other sweets	100	107	73	91	105
Fats and oils	100	85	96	120	98
Miscellaneous foods	100	91	67	89	107
Nonalcoholic beverages	100	84	78	113	101
Food prepared by consumer unit on trips	100	115	32	76	112
Food away from home	**100**	**125**	**62**	**83**	**108**
ALCOHOLIC BEVERAGES	**100**	**71**	**37**	**70**	**114**
HOUSING	**100**	**125**	**79**	**93**	**104**
Shelter	**100**	**147**	**80**	**98**	**103**
Owned dwellings	100	145	59	77	109
Mortgage interest and charges	100	164	66	88	107
Property taxes	100	137	53	62	112
Maintenance, repair, insurance, other expenses	100	103	49	65	113
Rented dwellings	100	161	141	159	86
Other lodging	100	97	32	48	117
Utilities, fuels, and public services	**100**	**95**	**99**	**91**	**101**
Natural gas	100	104	107	79	102
Electricity	100	82	102	85	102
Fuel oil and other fuels	100	33	43	60	114
Telephone	100	109	104	104	99
Water and other public services	100	106	82	98	103
Household services	**100**	**118**	**62**	**76**	**109**
Personal services	100	150	80	110	101
Other household services	100	96	50	54	114
Housekeeping supplies	**100**	**79**	**63**	**85**	**108**
Laundry and cleaning supplies	100	77	83	134	97
Other household products	100	75	52	72	111
Postage and stationery	100	90	63	61	112
Household furnishings and equipment	**100**	**94**	**55**	**79**	**110**
Household textiles	100	61	68	70	109
Furniture	100	123	78	84	106
Floor coverings	100	123	48	42	115

	total consumer units	Asian	black	Hispanic	non-Hispanic white and other
Major appliances	100	68	53	100	107
Small appliances, miscellaneous housewares	100	159	44	74	111
Miscellaneous household equipment	100	81	41	75	113
APPAREL AND RELATED SERVICES	**100**	**104**	**97**	**100**	**101**
Men and boys	**100**	**135**	**82**	**102**	**102**
Men, aged 16 or older	100	141	68	91	106
Boys, aged 2 to 15	100	113	135	138	89
Women and girls	**100**	**97**	**90**	**79**	**105**
Women, aged 16 or older	100	97	86	75	106
Girls, aged 2 to 15	100	96	111	105	97
Children under age 2	**100**	**104**	**63**	**182**	**94**
Footwear	**100**	**95**	**154**	**129**	**88**
Other apparel products and services	**100**	**85**	**79**	**95**	**104**
TRANSPORTATION	**100**	**110**	**64**	**96**	**106**
Vehicle purchases	**100**	**108**	**52**	**101**	**107**
Cars and trucks, new	100	132	45	92	110
Cars and trucks, used	100	86	61	116	104
Other vehicles	100	23	20	12	124
Gasoline and motor oil	**100**	**102**	**77**	**103**	**103**
Other vehicle expenses	**100**	**99**	**72**	**87**	**106**
Vehicle finance charges	100	80	74	88	106
Maintenance and repairs	100	108	65	88	107
Vehicle insurance	100	99	77	90	105
Vehicle rentals, leases, licenses, other charges	100	97	66	76	108
Public transportation	**100**	**207**	**66**	**80**	**108**
HEALTH CARE	**100**	**82**	**53**	**62**	**112**
Health insurance	100	88	64	64	110
Medical services	100	77	34	62	115
Drugs	100	61	55	53	113
Medical supplies	100	111	34	75	113
ENTERTAINMENT	**100**	**81**	**47**	**65**	**113**
Fees and admissions	100	116	35	58	116
Television, radio, and sound equipment	100	101	83	83	105
Pets, toys, and playground equipment	100	41	32	63	115
Other entertainment products and services	100	43	14	46	120
PERSONAL CARE PRODUCTS AND SERVICES	**100**	**87**	**87**	**89**	**104**
READING	**100**	**86**	**41**	**41**	**117**
EDUCATION	**100**	**231**	**63**	**48**	**113**
TOBACCO PRODUCTS AND SMOKING SUPPLIES	**100**	**36**	**69**	**54**	**111**
MISCELLANEOUS	**100**	**82**	**66**	**69**	**109**
CASH CONTRIBUTIONS	**100**	**77**	**59**	**50**	**113**
PERSONAL INSURANCE AND PENSIONS	**100**	**128**	**67**	**78**	**108**
Life and other personal insurance	100	78	75	40	112
Pensions and Social Security	100	132	66	81	108
PERSONAL TAXES	**100**	**98**	**23**	**41**	**119**
Federal income taxes	100	98	16	41	121
State and local income taxes	100	107	44	39	117
Other taxes	100	77	34	46	117
GIFTS FOR NONHOUSEHOLD MEMBERS	**100**	**105**	**56**	**60**	**112**

Note: "Asian" and "black" include Hispanics and non-Hispanics who identify themselves as being of the respective race alone. "Hispanic" includes people of any race who identify themselves as Hispanic. "Other" includes people who identify themselves as non-Hispanic and as Alaska Native, American Indian, Asian (who are also included in the "Asian" column), Native Hawaiian or other Pacific Islander, as well as non-Hispanics reporting more than one race.
Source: Calculations by New Strategist based on the Bureau of Labor Statistics' 2004 Consumer Expenditure Survey

Spending by Region, 2004

Households in the West spent $47,922 in 2004, 10 percent more than the average household and more than households in any other region. Spending by households in the Northeast is 6 percent above average, at $46,115 in 2004. Households in the Midwest spent $43,371, or just about the average amount. In the South, average household spending was 10 percent below the national average, at $39,174 in 2004.

Households in the Northeast and West spend more than the average household on most products and services. Those in the Midwest spend close to the average, while households in the South spend less than average on most items. Households in the Northeast spend the most on property taxes. Those in the West spend the most on mortgage interest and rent. Households in the Midwest spend the most on tobacco. Households in the South spend 24 percent less than average on alcoholic beverages.

The biggest consumers of natural gas are households in the Midwest, spending 49 percent more than the average household on this item. Households in the South spend the most on electricity, while those in the Northeast spend the most on fuel oil. Western households spend 24 percent more than the average household on water and other public services.

Households in the West spend the most on entertainment. Public transportation spending is highest in the Northeast. Spending on housekeeping supplies is 11 percent above average in the Midwest. Households in the South spend 11 percent more than average on drugs.

Table 1.12 Average spending by region, 2004

(average annual spending of consumer units by product and service category and region of residence, 2004)

	total	Northeast	Midwest	South	West
Number of consumer units (in 000s)	116,282	22,051	26,539	41,801	25,891
Average number of persons per consumer unit	2.5	2.4	2.4	2.5	2.6
Average income before taxes	$54,453	$61,050	$53,567	$50,775	$55,682
Average annual spending	43,395	46,115	43,371	39,174	47,922
FOOD	**5,781**	**6,368**	**5,592**	**5,318**	**6,224**
Food at home	**3,347**	**3,634**	**3,189**	**3,119**	**3,634**
Cereals and bakery products	461	521	446	427	480
Cereals and cereal products	154	176	141	143	165
Bakery products	307	346	305	284	314
Meats, poultry, fish, and eggs	880	1,008	781	849	922
Beef	265	279	242	263	283
Pork	181	189	170	189	172
Other meats	108	135	119	92	100
Poultry	156	194	127	149	163
Fish and seafood	128	164	91	117	154
Eggs	42	47	32	40	51
Dairy products	371	417	358	329	411
Fresh milk and cream	144	156	137	133	161
Other dairy products	226	261	221	197	249
Fruits and vegetables	561	638	510	501	645
Fresh fruits	187	213	171	161	222
Fresh vegetables	183	208	148	166	225
Processed fruits	110	127	112	93	120
Processed vegetables	82	89	78	82	78
Other food at home	1,075	1,050	1,094	1,013	1,177
Sugar and other sweets	128	137	129	118	135
Fats and oils	89	93	83	84	100
Miscellaneous foods	527	505	560	491	572
Nonalcoholic beverages	290	279	278	286	316
Food prepared by consumer unit on trips	41	36	44	33	54
Food away from home	**2,434**	**2,733**	**2,403**	**2,199**	**2,590**
ALCOHOLIC BEVERAGES	**459**	**625**	**427**	**348**	**532**
HOUSING	**13,918**	**15,734**	**13,438**	**12,250**	**15,557**
Shelter	**7,998**	**9,626**	**7,339**	**6,621**	**9,513**
Owned dwellings	5,324	6,387	5,260	4,456	5,887
Mortgage interest and charges	2,936	3,057	2,750	2,531	3,678
Property taxes	1,391	2,131	1,530	1,046	1,176
Maintenance, repair, insurance, other expenses	997	1,200	980	879	1,034
Rented dwellings	2,201	2,674	1,556	1,826	3,066
Other lodging	473	565	523	339	560
Utilities, fuels, and public services	**2,927**	**3,098**	**2,957**	**2,975**	**2,672**
Natural gas	424	564	631	255	365
Electricity	1,064	985	958	1,288	880
Fuel oil and other fuels	121	322	105	69	48
Telephone	990	988	946	1,031	971
Water and other public services	327	240	317	331	407
Household services	**753**	**793**	**707**	**673**	**894**
Personal services	300	352	301	257	323
Other household services	453	442	406	417	571
Housekeeping supplies	**594**	**586**	**661**	**549**	**606**
Laundry and cleaning supplies	149	146	153	147	149
Other household products	290	294	340	268	271
Postage and stationery	155	146	169	134	186
Household furnishings and equipment	**1,646**	**1,630**	**1,775**	**1,432**	**1,871**
Household textiles	158	209	126	151	158
Furniture	417	381	438	356	523
Floor coverings	52	44	57	35	81

	total	Northeast	Midwest	South	West
Major appliances	$204	$216	$234	$161	$232
Small appliances, miscellaneous housewares	105	94	98	99	130
Miscellaneous household equipment	711	685	822	630	748
APPAREL AND RELATED SERVICES	**1,816**	**2,176**	**1,672**	**1,643**	**1,936**
Men and boys	**406**	**460**	**407**	**377**	**406**
Men, aged 16 or older	317	366	317	288	324
Boys, aged 2 to 15	89	94	90	90	82
Women and girls	**739**	**933**	**661**	**662**	**777**
Women, aged 16 or older	631	809	547	565	673
Girls, aged 2 to 15	108	124	114	97	104
Children under age 2	**79**	**69**	**79**	**73**	**95**
Footwear	**329**	**427**	**271**	**312**	**332**
Other apparel products and services	**264**	**287**	**254**	**220**	**325**
TRANSPORTATION	**7,801**	**7,622**	**7,710**	**7,233**	**8,966**
Vehicle purchases	**3,397**	**3,196**	**3,315**	**3,195**	**3,979**
Cars and trucks, new	1,748	1,590	1,610	1,627	2,221
Cars and trucks, used	1,582	1,512	1,621	1,520	1,703
Other vehicles	66	94	83	48	55
Gasoline and motor oil	**1,598**	**1,386**	**1,620**	**1,598**	**1,755**
Other vehicle expenses	**2,365**	**2,396**	**2,413**	**2,160**	**2,622**
Vehicle finance charges	323	256	331	357	318
Maintenance and repairs	652	590	654	578	821
Vehicle insurance	964	991	924	944	1,017
Vehicle rentals, leases, licenses, other charges	426	559	504	281	466
Public transportation	**441**	**644**	**363**	**280**	**609**
HEALTH CARE	**2,574**	**2,371**	**2,861**	**2,508**	**2,560**
Health insurance	1,332	1,307	1,492	1,287	1,261
Medical services	648	597	714	583	731
Drugs	480	375	526	533	438
Medical supplies	114	92	128	106	131
ENTERTAINMENT	**2,218**	**2,017**	**2,208**	**2,134**	**2,538**
Fees and admissions	528	545	586	398	664
Television, radio, and sound equipment	788	840	768	753	818
Pets, toys, and playground equipment	381	360	373	364	434
Other entertainment products and services	522	272	481	619	622
PERSONAL CARE PRODUCTS AND SERVICES	**581**	**631**	**563**	**542**	**620**
READING	**130**	**145**	**150**	**98**	**150**
EDUCATION	**905**	**1,152**	**928**	**631**	**1,115**
TOBACCO PRODUCTS AND SMOKING SUPPLIES	**288**	**296**	**340**	**291**	**223**
MISCELLANEOUS	**690**	**760**	**797**	**512**	**809**
CASH CONTRIBUTIONS	**1,408**	**1,108**	**1,790**	**1,252**	**1,525**
PERSONAL INSURANCE AND PENSIONS	**4,823**	**5,110**	**4,895**	**4,414**	**5,167**
Life and other personal insurance	390	364	439	394	357
Pensions and Social Security	4,433	4,746	4,456	4,020	4,809
PERSONAL TAXES	**2,166**	**2,377**	**2,445**	**1,695**	**2,460**
Federal income taxes	1,519	1,581	1,613	1,217	1,857
State and local income taxes	472	561	586	330	510
Other taxes	175	235	246	149	93
GIFTS FOR NONHOUSEHOLD MEMBERS	**1,215**	**1,511**	**1,234**	**986**	**1,316**

Note: Spending by category will not add to total spending because gift spending is also included in the preceding product and service categories and personal taxes are not included in the total.
Source: Bureau of Labor Statistics, 2004 Consumer Expenditure Survey, Internet site http://www.bls.gov/cex/

Table 1.13 Indexed spending by region, 2004

(indexed average annual spending of consumer units by product and service category and region of residence, 2004; index definition: an index of 100 is the average for all consumer units; an index of 132 means that spending by consumer units in that group is 32 percent above the average for all consumer units; an index of 68 indicates spending that is 32 percent below the average for all consumer units)

	total	Northeast	Midwest	South	West
Average spending of consumer units, total	$43,395	$46,115	$43,371	$39,174	$47,922
Average spending of consumer units, index	100	106	100	90	110
FOOD	100	110	97	92	108
Food at home	100	109	95	93	109
Cereals and bakery products	100	113	97	93	104
Cereals and cereal products	100	114	92	93	107
Bakery products	100	113	99	93	102
Meats, poultry, fish, and eggs	100	115	89	96	105
Beef	100	105	91	99	107
Pork	100	104	94	104	95
Other meats	100	125	110	85	93
Poultry	100	124	81	96	104
Fish and seafood	100	128	71	91	120
Eggs	100	112	76	95	121
Dairy products	100	112	96	89	111
Fresh milk and cream	100	108	95	92	112
Other dairy products	100	115	98	87	110
Fruits and vegetables	100	114	91	89	115
Fresh fruits	100	114	91	86	119
Fresh vegetables	100	114	81	91	123
Processed fruits	100	115	102	85	109
Processed vegetables	100	109	95	100	95
Other food at home	100	98	102	94	109
Sugar and other sweets	100	107	101	92	105
Fats and oils	100	104	93	94	112
Miscellaneous foods	100	96	106	93	109
Nonalcoholic beverages	100	96	96	99	109
Food prepared by consumer unit on trips	100	88	107	80	132
Food away from home	100	112	99	90	106
ALCOHOLIC BEVERAGES	100	136	93	76	116
HOUSING	100	113	97	88	112
Shelter	100	120	92	83	119
Owned dwellings	100	120	99	84	111
Mortgage interest and charges	100	104	94	86	125
Property taxes	100	153	110	75	85
Maintenance, repair, insurance, other expenses	100	120	98	88	104
Rented dwellings	100	121	71	83	139
Other lodging	100	119	111	72	118
Utilities, fuels, and public services	100	106	101	102	91
Natural gas	100	133	149	60	86
Electricity	100	93	90	121	83
Fuel oil and other fuels	100	266	87	57	40
Telephone	100	100	96	104	98
Water and other public services	100	73	97	101	124
Household services	100	105	94	89	119
Personal services	100	117	100	86	108
Other household services	100	98	90	92	126
Housekeeping supplies	100	99	111	92	102
Laundry and cleaning supplies	100	98	103	99	100
Other household products	100	101	117	92	93
Postage and stationery	100	94	109	86	120
Household furnishings and equipment	100	99	108	87	114
Household textiles	100	132	80	96	100
Furniture	100	91	105	85	125
Floor coverings	100	85	110	67	156

	total	Northeast	Midwest	South	West
Major appliances	100	106	115	79	114
Small appliances, miscellaneous housewares	100	90	93	94	124
Miscellaneous household equipment	100	96	116	89	105
APPAREL AND RELATED SERVICES	**100**	**120**	**92**	**90**	**107**
Men and boys	**100**	**113**	**100**	**93**	**100**
Men, aged 16 or older	100	115	100	91	102
Boys, aged 2 to 15	100	106	101	101	92
Women and girls	**100**	**126**	**89**	**90**	**105**
Women, aged 16 or older	100	128	87	90	107
Girls, aged 2 to 15	100	115	106	90	96
Children under age 2	**100**	**87**	**100**	**92**	**120**
Footwear	**100**	**130**	**82**	**95**	**101**
Other apparel products and services	**100**	**109**	**96**	**83**	**123**
TRANSPORTATION	**100**	**98**	**99**	**93**	**115**
Vehicle purchases	**100**	**94**	**98**	**94**	**117**
Cars and trucks, new	100	91	92	93	127
Cars and trucks, used	100	96	102	96	108
Other vehicles	100	142	126	73	83
Gasoline and motor oil	**100**	**87**	**101**	**100**	**110**
Other vehicle expenses	**100**	**101**	**102**	**91**	**111**
Vehicle finance charges	100	79	102	111	98
Maintenance and repairs	100	90	100	89	126
Vehicle insurance	100	103	96	98	105
Vehicle rentals, leases, licenses, other charges	100	131	118	66	109
Public transportation	**100**	**146**	**82**	**63**	**138**
HEALTH CARE	**100**	**92**	**111**	**97**	**99**
Health insurance	100	98	112	97	95
Medical services	100	92	110	90	113
Drugs	100	78	110	111	91
Medical supplies	100	81	112	93	115
ENTERTAINMENT	**100**	**91**	**100**	**96**	**114**
Fees and admissions	100	103	111	75	126
Television, radio, and sound equipment	100	107	97	96	104
Pets, toys, and playground equipment	100	94	98	96	114
Other entertainment products and services	100	52	92	119	119
PERSONAL CARE PRODUCTS AND SERVICES	**100**	**109**	**97**	**93**	**107**
READING	**100**	**112**	**115**	**75**	**115**
EDUCATION	**100**	**127**	**103**	**70**	**123**
TOBACCO PRODUCTS AND SMOKING SUPPLIES	**100**	**103**	**118**	**101**	**77**
MISCELLANEOUS	**100**	**110**	**116**	**74**	**117**
CASH CONTRIBUTIONS	**100**	**79**	**127**	**89**	**108**
PERSONAL INSURANCE AND PENSIONS	**100**	**106**	**101**	**92**	**107**
Life and other personal insurance	100	93	113	101	92
Pensions and Social Security	100	107	101	91	108
PERSONAL TAXES	**100**	**110**	**113**	**78**	**114**
Federal income taxes	100	104	106	80	122
State and local income taxes	100	119	124	70	108
Other taxes	100	134	141	85	53
GIFTS FOR NONHOUSEHOLD MEMBERS	**100**	**124**	**102**	**81**	**108**

Source: Calculations by New Strategist based on the Bureau of Labor Statistics' 2004 Consumer Expenditure Survey

Spending by Education, 2004

Because college graduates have the highest incomes, their spending is well above average. The average household headed by a college graduate spent $60,712 in 2004, or 40 percent more than the average household. In contrast, households headed by people who did not graduate from high school spent only $25,421 in 2004, fully 41 percent less than the average household.

Households headed by the least educated—those without a high school diploma—spend more than average on only a few items. These include meat, eggs, rent, and tobacco.

High school graduates who did not go on to college spent $35,439 in 2004, or 18 percent less than the average household. Their spending is below average in most categories, with some exceptions such as tobacco.

Householders with some college experience or an associate's degree make up the largest share of households (31 percent). Their spending is close to the average on most items.

College graduates, who account for 28 percent of householders, far outspend the average household on most items—particularly those favored by the affluent. These include food away from home (41 percent above average) and alcoholic beverages (55 percent more). They spend nearly twice the average on other lodging (which includes college dorms, vacation homes, and hotel and motel expenses) and public transportation (which includes airfares). They are also big spenders on education, and on fees and admissions to entertainment events.

Table 1.14 Average spending by education of householder, 2004

(average annual spending of consumer units by product and service category and educational attainment of consumer unit reference person, 2004)

	total consumer units	not a high school graduate	high school graduate	some college or associate's degree	college degree or more
Number of consumer units (in 000s)	116,282	16,829	31,005	35,995	32,452
Average number of persons per consumer unit	2.5	2.7	2.5	2.4	2.5
Average income before taxes	$54,453	$29,094	$42,334	$50,267	$83,825
Average annual spending	43,395	25,421	35,439	43,043	60,712
FOOD	**5,781**	**4,260**	**5,182**	**5,717**	**7,206**
Food at home	**3,347**	**2,991**	**3,229**	**3,212**	**3,779**
Cereals and bakery products	461	413	466	437	504
Cereals and cereal products	154	151	157	142	164
Bakery products	307	262	309	295	340
Meats, poultry, fish, and eggs	880	889	890	835	911
Beef	265	269	277	258	259
Pork	181	206	195	171	165
Other meats	108	100	110	100	118
Poultry	156	153	149	147	171
Fish and seafood	128	108	116	119	158
Eggs	42	51	42	37	41
Dairy products	371	325	346	353	436
Fresh milk and cream	144	153	140	137	152
Other dairy products	226	173	206	216	283
Fruits and vegetables	561	507	510	517	682
Fresh fruits	187	168	163	171	234
Fresh vegetables	183	173	161	167	227
Processed fruits	110	94	99	102	136
Processed vegetables	82	72	88	78	85
Other food at home	1,075	856	1,017	1,071	1,246
Sugar and other sweets	128	99	125	128	147
Fats and oils	89	91	93	84	89
Miscellaneous foods	527	377	485	524	648
Nonalcoholic beverages	290	270	288	295	295
Food prepared by consumer unit on trips	41	20	27	39	66
Food away from home	**2,434**	**1,269**	**1,952**	**2,505**	**3,428**
ALCOHOLIC BEVERAGES	**459**	**202**	**345**	**451**	**711**
HOUSING	**13,918**	**8,724**	**11,208**	**13,491**	**19,676**
Shelter	**7,998**	**4,913**	**6,177**	**7,668**	**11,706**
Owned dwellings	5,324	2,412	3,869	5,050	8,530
Mortgage interest and charges	2,936	1,245	2,044	2,848	4,764
Property taxes	1,391	689	1,058	1,241	2,240
Maintenance, repair, insurance, other expenses	997	477	767	961	1,527
Rented dwellings	2,201	2,425	2,066	2,172	2,246
Other lodging	473	76	242	446	930
Utilities, fuels, and public services	**2,927**	**2,414**	**2,837**	**2,852**	**3,361**
Natural gas	424	335	415	387	519
Electricity	1,064	937	1,070	1,042	1,150
Fuel oil and other fuels	121	103	134	114	124
Telephone	990	778	921	989	1,168
Water and other public services	327	261	298	320	399
Household services	**753**	**318**	**475**	**713**	**1,288**
Personal services	300	156	201	302	467
Other household services	453	163	274	412	821
Housekeeping supplies	**594**	**394**	**507**	**591**	**786**
Laundry and cleaning supplies	149	148	142	144	160
Other household products	290	163	241	299	395
Postage and stationery	155	83	124	147	231
Household furnishings and equipment	**1,646**	**685**	**1,212**	**1,667**	**2,536**
Household textiles	158	70	138	152	227
Furniture	417	184	289	426	651
Floor coverings	52	20	21	45	106

	total consumer units	not a high school graduate	high school graduate	some college or associate's degree	college degree or more
Major appliances	$204	$114	$166	$229	$260
Small appliances, miscellaneous housewares	105	62	84	109	142
Miscellaneous household equipment	711	235	515	706	1,151
APPAREL AND RELATED SERVICES	**1,816**	**1,150**	**1,405**	**1,848**	**2,526**
Men and boys	**406**	**258**	**296**	**420**	**576**
Men, aged 16 or older	317	190	217	327	471
Boys, aged 2 to 15	89	68	79	93	105
Women and girls	**739**	**438**	**568**	**803**	**994**
Women, aged 16 or older	631	363	475	700	851
Girls, aged 2 to 15	108	74	92	104	143
Children under age 2	**79**	**73**	**68**	**72**	**98**
Footwear	**329**	**248**	**301**	**311**	**415**
Other apparel products and services	**264**	**133**	**172**	**243**	**443**
TRANSPORTATION	**7,801**	**4,472**	**6,819**	**8,435**	**9,766**
Vehicle purchases	**3,397**	**1,922**	**3,046**	**3,942**	**3,893**
Cars and trucks, new	1,748	668	1,445	2,154	2,148
Cars and trucks, used	1,582	1,232	1,541	1,691	1,683
Other vehicles	66	21	60	97	62
Gasoline and motor oil	**1,598**	**1,142**	**1,537**	**1,656**	**1,826**
Other vehicle expenses	**2,365**	**1,259**	**2,027**	**2,480**	**3,140**
Vehicle finance charges	323	168	315	354	378
Maintenance and repairs	652	332	497	723	889
Vehicle insurance	964	604	927	984	1,166
Vehicle rentals, leases, licenses, other charges	426	154	288	419	706
Public transportation	**441**	**149**	**209**	**356**	**908**
HEALTH CARE	**2,574**	**1,874**	**2,450**	**2,437**	**3,208**
Health insurance	1,332	994	1,308	1,249	1,622
Medical services	648	383	542	632	906
Drugs	480	433	507	448	515
Medical supplies	114	64	93	109	165
ENTERTAINMENT	**2,218**	**953**	**1,685**	**2,332**	**3,259**
Fees and admissions	528	103	270	485	1,043
Television, radio, and sound equipment	788	505	703	819	980
Pets, toys, and playground equipment	381	180	323	409	510
Other entertainment products and services	522	167	388	619	726
PERSONAL CARE PRODUCTS AND SERVICES	**581**	**361**	**481**	**593**	**779**
READING	**130**	**45**	**85**	**120**	**229**
EDUCATION	**905**	**133**	**364**	**930**	**1,797**
TOBACCO PRODUCTS AND SMOKING SUPPLIES	**288**	**347**	**380**	**309**	**147**
MISCELLANEOUS	**690**	**382**	**607**	**700**	**918**
CASH CONTRIBUTIONS	**1,408**	**544**	**949**	**1,182**	**2,546**
PERSONAL INSURANCE AND PENSIONS	**4,823**	**1,974**	**3,480**	**4,499**	**7,943**
Life and other personal insurance	390	210	302	339	625
Pensions and Social Security	4,433	1,764	3,178	4,160	7,318
PERSONAL TAXES	**2,166**	**143**	**1,203**	**1,843**	**4,494**
Federal income taxes	1,519	-5	808	1,240	3,298
State and local income taxes	472	79	268	420	929
Other taxes	175	70	127	182	267
GIFTS FOR NONHOUSEHOLD MEMBERS	**1,215**	**523**	**804**	**1,048**	**2,151**

Note: Spending by category will not add to total spending because gift spending is also included in the preceding product and service categories and personal taxes are not included in the total.
Source: Bureau of Labor Statistics, 2004 Consumer Expenditure Survey, Internet site http://www.bls.gov/cex/

Table 1.15 Indexed spending by education of householder, 2004

(indexed average annual spending of consumer units by product and service category and educational attainment of consumer unit reference person, 2004; index definition: an index of 100 is the average for all consumer units; an index of 132 means that spending by consumer units in that group is 32 percent above the average for all consumer units; an index of 68 indicates spending that is 32 percent below the average for all consumer units)

	total consumer units	not a high school graduate	high school graduate	some college or associate's degree	college degree or more
Average spending of consumer units, total	$43,395	$25,421	$35,439	$43,043	$60,712
Average spending of consumer units, index	100	59	82	99	140
FOOD	100	74	90	99	125
Food at home	100	89	96	96	113
Cereals and bakery products	100	90	101	95	109
Cereals and cereal products	100	98	102	92	106
Bakery products	100	85	101	96	111
Meats, poultry, fish, and eggs	100	101	101	95	104
Beef	100	102	105	97	98
Pork	100	114	108	94	91
Other meats	100	93	102	93	109
Poultry	100	98	96	95	110
Fish and seafood	100	84	91	93	123
Eggs	100	121	100	89	98
Dairy products	100	88	93	95	118
Fresh milk and cream	100	106	97	95	106
Other dairy products	100	77	91	96	125
Fruits and vegetables	100	90	91	92	122
Fresh fruits	100	90	87	92	125
Fresh vegetables	100	95	88	91	124
Processed fruits	100	85	90	92	124
Processed vegetables	100	88	107	95	104
Other food at home	100	80	95	100	116
Sugar and other sweets	100	77	98	100	115
Fats and oils	100	102	104	94	100
Miscellaneous foods	100	72	92	99	123
Nonalcoholic beverages	100	93	99	102	102
Food prepared by consumer unit on trips	100	49	66	96	161
Food away from home	100	52	80	103	141
ALCOHOLIC BEVERAGES	100	44	75	98	155
HOUSING	100	63	81	97	141
Shelter	100	61	77	96	146
Owned dwellings	100	45	73	95	160
Mortgage interest and charges	100	42	70	97	162
Property taxes	100	50	76	89	161
Maintenance, repair, insurance, other expenses	100	48	77	96	153
Rented dwellings	100	110	94	99	102
Other lodging	100	16	51	94	197
Utilities, fuels, and public services	100	82	97	97	115
Natural gas	100	79	98	91	122
Electricity	100	88	101	98	108
Fuel oil and other fuels	100	85	111	94	102
Telephone	100	79	93	100	118
Water and other public services	100	80	91	98	122
Household services	100	42	63	95	171
Personal services	100	52	67	101	156
Other household services	100	36	60	91	181
Housekeeping supplies	100	66	85	99	132
Laundry and cleaning supplies	100	99	95	97	107
Other household products	100	56	83	103	136
Postage and stationery	100	54	80	95	149
Household furnishings and equipment	100	42	74	101	154
Household textiles	100	44	87	96	144
Furniture	100	44	69	102	156
Floor coverings	100	38	40	87	204

	total consumer units	not a high school graduate	high school graduate	some college or associate's degree	college degree or more
Major appliances	100	56	81	112	127
Small appliances, miscellaneous housewares	100	59	80	104	135
Miscellaneous household equipment	100	33	72	99	162
APPAREL AND RELATED SERVICES	**100**	**63**	**77**	**102**	**139**
Men and boys	**100**	**64**	**73**	**103**	**142**
Men, aged 16 or older	100	60	68	103	149
Boys, aged 2 to 15	100	76	89	104	118
Women and girls	**100**	**59**	**77**	**109**	**135**
Women, aged 16 or older	100	58	75	111	135
Girls, aged 2 to 15	100	69	85	96	132
Children under age 2	**100**	**92**	**86**	**92**	**124**
Footwear	**100**	**75**	**91**	**94**	**126**
Other apparel products and services	**100**	**50**	**65**	**92**	**168**
TRANSPORTATION	**100**	**57**	**87**	**108**	**125**
Vehicle purchases	**100**	**57**	**90**	**116**	**115**
Cars and trucks, new	100	38	83	123	123
Cars and trucks, used	100	78	97	107	106
Other vehicles	100	32	91	147	94
Gasoline and motor oil	**100**	**71**	**96**	**104**	**114**
Other vehicle expenses	**100**	**53**	**86**	**105**	**133**
Vehicle finance charges	100	52	98	110	117
Maintenance and repairs	100	51	76	111	136
Vehicle insurance	100	63	96	102	121
Vehicle rentals, leases, licenses, other charges	100	36	68	98	166
Public transportation	**100**	**34**	**47**	**81**	**206**
HEALTH CARE	**100**	**73**	**95**	**95**	**125**
Health insurance	100	75	98	94	122
Medical services	100	59	84	98	140
Drugs	100	90	106	93	107
Medical supplies	100	56	82	95	145
ENTERTAINMENT	**100**	**43**	**76**	**105**	**147**
Fees and admissions	100	20	51	92	198
Television, radio, and sound equipment	100	64	89	104	124
Pets, toys, and playground equipment	100	47	85	107	134
Other entertainment products and services	100	32	74	119	139
PERSONAL CARE PRODUCTS AND SERVICES	**100**	**62**	**83**	**102**	**134**
READING	**100**	**35**	**65**	**92**	**176**
EDUCATION	**100**	**15**	**40**	**103**	**199**
TOBACCO PRODUCTS AND SMOKING SUPPLIES	**100**	**120**	**132**	**107**	**51**
MISCELLANEOUS	**100**	**55**	**88**	**101**	**133**
CASH CONTRIBUTIONS	**100**	**39**	**67**	**84**	**181**
PERSONAL INSURANCE AND PENSIONS	**100**	**41**	**72**	**93**	**165**
Life and other personal insurance	100	54	77	87	160
Pensions and Social Security	100	40	72	94	165
PERSONAL TAXES	**100**	**7**	**56**	**85**	**207**
Federal income taxes	100	0	53	82	217
State and local income taxes	100	17	57	89	197
Other taxes	100	40	73	104	153
GIFTS FOR NONHOUSEHOLD MEMBERS	**100**	**43**	**66**	**86**	**177**

Source: Calculations by New Strategist based on the Bureau of Labor Statistics' 2004 Consumer Expenditure Survey

Chapter 2. Spending on Apparel, 2004

Americans are spending less on apparel than they once did. In 2004, the average household spent $1,816 on clothes, shoes, and related items. This figure is 11 percent less than the $2,036 spent by the average household on apparel in 2000, after adjusting for inflation. Overall, Americans devoted 4.2 percent of their spending to clothes, shoes, and related products and services in 2004, down from 4.9 percent in 2000.

Households headed by people aged 45 to 54 spend the most on apparel, more than $2,217 in 2004. Apparel spending patterns differ sharply by age. Householders aged 35 to 44 spend the most on boys' and girls' apparel. Those aged 25 to 34 spend the most on infants' apparel. Householders aged 45 to 54 spend the most on men's clothes (43 percent more than average) and women's clothes (33 percent more).

Spending on apparel rises with income. Households with incomes of $100,000 or more spend more than twice the average on apparel. This income level accounts for just 13 percent of households but for 44 percent of the market for men's suits, 46 percent of the market for men's sports coats, 40 percent of the market for jewelry, and 47 percent of the market for professional dry cleaning. In contrast, households with incomes of $100,000 or more control only 25 percent of footwear spending.

Married couples with school-aged children at home spend more on apparel than any other household type—more than $2,750 in 2004. In part, this is because their households are larger than average. Married couples without children at home (most of them empty-nesters) spend 12 percent more than average on women's clothes and 16 percent more on men's clothes.

Among race and Hispanic origin groups, Asian households are the biggest spenders on apparel, devoting $1,885 to this category in 2004, or 4 percent more than the average household. Blacks are the biggest spenders on footwear, shelling out 55 percent more than the average household to shoes. Blacks and Hispanics together control more than 32 percent of the footwear market (although there is some overlap because Hispanics may be of any race and some are black).

Spending on apparel is greatest in the Northeast, where households devoted $2,176 to clothes in 2004—20 percent more than the average household. The West was second, with spending 7 percent above average. In the Midwest, apparel spending is average, and in the South it is fully 10 percent below average.

The most educated householders spend the most on clothes because they have the highest incomes. Householders with a college degree averaged spending of $2,526 on clothes in 2004—39 percent more than the average household. College graduates accounted for only 35 percent of the market for infants' clothes, but close to half the market for watches and jewelry and more than half the market for professional dry cleaning.

Table 2.1 Apparel: Average spending by age, 2004

(average annual spending of consumer units (CU) on apparel, accessories, and related services, by age of consumer unit reference person, 2004)

	total consumer units	under 25	25 to 34	35 to 44	45 to 54	55 to 64	65 to 74	75+
Number of consumer units (in 000s)	116,282	8,817	19,439	24,070	23,712	17,479	11,230	11,536
Average number of persons per CU	2.5	1.9	2.9	3.2	2.7	2.1	1.9	1.5
Average before-tax income of CU	$54,453.00	$22,840.00	$52,484.00	$65,515.00	$70,434.00	$61,031.00	$42,137.00	$28,028.00
Average spending of CU, total	43,394.87	24,534.56	42,700.54	50,401.62	52,764.36	47,298.58	36,511.98	25,763.32
Apparel, average spending	**1,815.95**	**1,370.56**	**2,133.60**	**2,141.57**	**2,216.76**	**1,863.33**	**1,200.32**	**604.49**
MEN'S APPAREL	**317.28**	**213.68**	**335.86**	**356.07**	**455.07**	**285.22**	**273.38**	**83.92**
Suits	23.99	9.79	26.49	28.62	34.05	27.60	15.40	3.16
Sport coats and tailored jackets	8.38	5.30	7.89	8.83	10.05	10.02	10.02	3.12
Coats and jackets	25.50	3.23	22.75	24.19	59.70	15.31	16.56	3.84
Underwear	16.99	10.69	16.45	15.23	31.11	15.97	10.23	5.54
Hosiery	15.09	6.27	11.77	22.70	17.94	14.92	13.96	6.61
Nightwear	2.10	1.42	1.76	2.44	2.21	2.44	2.86	1.03
Accessories	25.06	15.53	22.02	22.96	46.06	22.67	21.73	5.30
Sweaters and vests	9.84	7.90	7.79	10.55	11.90	13.03	11.30	2.84
Active sportswear	22.80	53.02	17.57	22.36	26.28	21.00	21.28	5.23
Shirts	82.51	48.59	110.12	87.71	102.63	74.75	76.17	24.19
Pants	62.63	38.09	66.09	81.89	83.57	51.12	52.78	16.79
Shorts and shorts sets	14.82	8.16	16.44	18.59	20.93	8.84	14.82	5.19
Uniforms	3.99	2.72	4.26	6.53	3.94	3.89	2.54	0.92
Costumes	3.57	2.97	4.45	3.45	4.71	3.67	3.71	0.15
BOYS' (AGED 2 TO 15) APPAREL	**88.88**	**21.63**	**120.15**	**175.95**	**87.22**	**53.15**	**38.66**	**9.25**
Coats and jackets	5.99	1.61	8.59	11.38	6.57	3.25	1.87	0.65
Sweaters	2.98	0.79	3.33	4.97	3.50	2.35	2.59	0.24
Shirts	19.65	1.89	24.54	38.73	18.59	13.61	11.87	2.48
Underwear	4.77	2.20	6.97	8.20	4.59	2.95	2.70	0.58
Nightwear	3.27	1.61	3.56	7.46	2.16	3.25	0.51	0.00
Hosiery	5.00	0.89	7.14	10.17	4.55	2.35	1.96	1.27
Accessories	3.82	0.18	2.80	10.50	3.88	1.13	1.26	0.45
Suits, sport coats, and vests	2.59	1.03	4.68	4.10	2.68	1.49	0.66	0.48
Pants	22.39	7.08	32.28	43.33	21.79	14.19	7.43	1.92
Shorts and shorts sets	7.77	2.68	12.95	14.89	6.78	3.63	3.75	0.25
Uniforms	3.82	0.56	4.39	8.40	4.25	1.97	0.88	0.56
Active sportswear	4.29	0.74	5.13	8.52	5.05	1.90	2.70	0.32
Costumes	2.55	0.37	3.80	5.31	2.84	1.06	0.46	0.06
WOMEN'S APPAREL	**631.01**	**558.49**	**637.51**	**579.52**	**840.87**	**743.44**	**503.89**	**299.55**
Coats and jackets	48.87	21.86	36.77	41.37	79.07	78.24	29.20	19.47
Dresses	66.25	47.80	134.49	37.44	83.34	68.74	32.65	16.36
Sport coats and tailored jackets	8.76	3.89	6.31	8.09	12.30	12.87	9.05	4.21
Sweaters and vests	46.31	30.62	38.05	44.67	54.45	68.92	50.34	20.65
Shirts, blouses, and tops	120.91	130.81	136.47	107.41	158.29	120.20	88.91	68.97
Skirts	17.07	8.51	16.84	16.52	23.11	17.12	11.11	18.97
Pants	96.25	102.51	97.31	92.00	124.50	109.65	75.65	38.40
Shorts and shorts sets	12.59	7.40	14.80	13.12	17.55	10.78	11.60	4.90
Active sportswear	36.31	40.12	21.86	38.57	44.95	36.27	48.16	23.52
Nightwear	29.94	18.19	19.35	29.67	42.95	42.58	28.45	13.23
Undergarments	43.77	55.05	32.13	45.11	57.51	45.03	42.86	22.03
Hosiery	18.77	13.96	13.00	20.00	25.51	22.50	12.56	16.61
Suits	23.57	12.08	19.25	27.82	25.47	31.75	25.33	12.75
Accessories	50.57	59.22	40.19	46.06	77.59	64.97	27.83	15.52
Uniforms	5.97	4.25	4.94	7.09	7.98	8.15	3.50	1.71
Costumes	5.09	2.21	5.74	4.60	6.31	5.69	6.70	2.24

	total consumer units	under 25	25 to 34	35 to 44	45 to 54	55 to 64	65 to 74	75+
GIRLS' (AGED 2 TO 15) APPAREL	**$107.60**	**$28.81**	**$117.54**	**$221.96**	**$131.29**	**$49.73**	**$38.68**	**$14.99**
Coats and jackets	7.49	2.06	9.50	14.80	8.05	4.21	3.03	1.14
Dresses and suits	9.49	3.07	7.61	16.02	15.07	4.44	8.06	1.01
Shirts, blouses, and sweaters	23.95	5.69	20.07	52.07	35.98	4.79	7.62	4.38
Skirts and pants	24.32	6.59	29.99	49.01	24.69	14.45	10.96	3.98
Shorts and shorts sets	8.40	3.54	13.16	14.73	9.80	4.06	1.86	0.92
Active sportswear	10.05	3.27	8.02	26.18	8.70	6.92	0.37	1.07
Underwear and nightwear	6.28	1.29	8.55	12.53	6.09	4.27	2.13	0.72
Hosiery	3.77	0.84	4.16	7.49	5.02	0.77	2.08	0.94
Accessories	5.93	0.32	4.90	13.25	9.53	2.07	0.42	0.09
Uniforms	3.84	1.09	6.03	7.61	3.41	2.08	1.39	0.29
Costumes	4.10	1.02	5.54	8.28	4.95	1.68	0.76	0.46
CHILDREN'S (UNDER AGE 2) APPAREL	**78.51**	**101.99**	**182.34**	**85.58**	**53.00**	**47.43**	**27.75**	**13.01**
Coats, jackets, and snowsuits	2.48	2.83	4.70	2.17	2.07	2.27	2.29	0.41
Outerwear including dresses	20.72	22.77	34.70	22.98	16.82	21.67	12.69	5.23
Underwear	44.17	60.50	116.20	49.50	27.98	15.69	8.09	4.98
Nightwear and loungewear	3.49	2.93	6.38	3.43	3.08	3.42	2.54	1.02
Accessories	7.66	12.96	20.36	7.50	3.05	4.38	2.14	1.36
FOOTWEAR	**328.74**	**257.66**	**398.40**	**416.32**	**385.17**	**351.45**	**152.74**	**91.01**
Men's	110.67	70.41	147.98	133.32	136.36	112.54	63.83	15.95
Boys'	35.92	6.66	53.40	81.46	27.49	18.54	6.25	2.58
Women's	153.81	169.72	148.96	149.58	191.51	210.38	78.72	67.29
Girls'	28.34	10.87	48.05	51.95	29.80	9.99	3.94	5.20
OTHER APPAREL PRODUCTS AND SERVICES	**263.94**	**188.30**	**341.80**	**306.17**	**264.13**	**332.91**	**165.21**	**92.77**
Material for making clothes	13.05	10.53	25.68	13.19	8.84	15.44	7.29	3.15
Sewing patterns and notions	7.82	4.24	3.65	8.32	7.33	13.24	11.99	5.41
Watches	21.51	10.48	26.84	29.92	18.65	28.78	14.01	5.58
Jewelry	113.72	71.62	155.24	134.85	110.04	154.57	58.33	31.44
Shoe repair and other shoe services	1.12	0.44	0.65	0.71	1.55	2.47	0.89	0.59
Coin-operated apparel laundry and dry cleaning	34.86	66.36	62.72	35.60	25.90	19.96	17.98	19.67
Apparel alteration, repair, and tailoring services	5.12	2.42	5.12	3.46	6.14	7.95	6.45	2.92
Clothing rental	2.28	3.48	3.30	3.10	1.82	2.46	0.52	0.30
Watch and jewelry repair	3.82	0.46	2.57	3.24	4.62	6.02	4.84	3.69
Professional laundry, dry cleaning	60.18	18.17	55.77	73.73	78.63	81.40	41.64	19.38
Clothing storage	0.47	0.09	0.25	0.04	0.62	0.63	1.28	0.65

Note: Subcategories may not add to total because some are not shown.
Source: Bureau of Labor Statistics, unpublished data from the 2004 Consumer Expenditure Survey

Table 2.2 Apparel: Indexed spending by age, 2004

(indexed average annual spending of consumer units (CU) on apparel, accessories, and related services, by age of consumer unit reference person, 2004; index definition: an index of 100 is the average for all consumer units; an index of 132 means that spending by consumer units in that group is 32 percent above the average for all consumer units; an index of 68 indicates spending that is 32 percent below the average for all consumer units)

	total consumer units	under 25	25 to 34	35 to 44	45 to 54	55 to 64	65 to 74	75+
Average spending of CU, total	$43,395	$24,535	$42,701	$50,402	$52,764	$47,299	$36,512	$25,763
Average spending of CU, index	100	57	98	116	122	109	84	59
Apparel, spending index	**100**	**75**	**117**	**118**	**122**	**103**	**66**	**33**
MEN'S APPAREL	**100**	**67**	**106**	**112**	**143**	**90**	**86**	**26**
Suits	100	41	110	119	142	115	64	13
Sport coats and tailored jackets	100	63	94	105	120	120	120	37
Coats and jackets	100	13	89	95	234	60	65	15
Underwear	100	63	97	90	183	94	60	33
Hosiery	100	42	78	150	119	99	93	44
Nightwear	100	68	84	116	105	116	136	49
Accessories	100	62	88	92	184	90	87	21
Sweaters and vests	100	80	79	107	121	132	115	29
Active sportswear	100	233	77	98	115	92	93	23
Shirts	100	59	133	106	124	91	92	29
Pants	100	61	106	131	133	82	84	27
Shorts and shorts sets	100	55	111	125	141	60	100	35
Uniforms	100	68	107	164	99	97	64	23
Costumes	100	83	125	97	132	103	104	4
BOYS' (AGED 2 TO 15) APPAREL	**100**	**24**	**135**	**198**	**98**	**60**	**43**	**10**
Coats and jackets	100	27	143	190	110	54	31	11
Sweaters	100	27	112	167	117	79	87	8
Shirts	100	10	125	197	95	69	60	13
Underwear	100	46	146	172	96	62	57	12
Nightwear	100	49	109	228	66	99	16	0
Hosiery	100	18	143	203	91	47	39	25
Accessories	100	5	73	275	102	30	33	12
Suits, sport coats, and vests	100	40	181	158	103	58	25	19
Pants	100	32	144	194	97	63	33	9
Shorts and shorts sets	100	34	167	192	87	47	48	3
Uniforms	100	15	115	220	111	52	23	15
Active sportswear	100	17	120	199	118	44	63	7
Costumes	100	15	149	208	111	42	18	2
WOMEN'S APPAREL	**100**	**89**	**101**	**92**	**133**	**118**	**80**	**47**
Coats and jackets	100	45	75	85	162	160	60	40
Dresses	100	72	203	57	126	104	49	25
Sport coats and tailored jackets	100	44	72	92	140	147	103	48
Sweaters and vests	100	66	82	96	118	149	109	45
Shirts, blouses, and tops	100	108	113	89	131	99	74	57
Skirts	100	50	99	97	135	100	65	111
Pants	100	107	101	96	129	114	79	40
Shorts and shorts sets	100	59	118	104	139	86	92	39
Active sportswear	100	110	60	106	124	100	133	65
Nightwear	100	61	65	99	143	142	95	44
Undergarments	100	126	73	103	131	103	98	50
Hosiery	100	74	69	107	136	120	67	88
Suits	100	51	82	118	108	135	107	54
Accessories	100	117	79	91	153	128	55	31
Uniforms	100	71	83	119	134	137	59	29
Costumes	100	43	113	90	124	112	132	44

	total consumer units	under 25	25 to 34	35 to 44	45 to 54	55 to 64	65 to 74	75+
GIRLS' (AGED 2 TO 15) APPAREL	**100**	**27**	**109**	**206**	**122**	**46**	**36**	**14**
Coats and jackets	100	28	127	198	107	56	40	15
Dresses and suits	100	32	80	169	159	47	85	11
Shirts, blouses, and sweaters	100	24	84	217	150	20	32	18
Skirts and pants	100	27	123	202	102	59	45	16
Shorts and shorts sets	100	42	157	175	117	48	22	11
Active sportswear	100	33	80	260	87	69	4	11
Underwear and nightwear	100	21	136	200	97	68	34	11
Hosiery	100	22	110	199	133	20	55	25
Accessories	100	5	83	223	161	35	7	2
Uniforms	100	28	157	198	89	54	36	8
Costumes	100	25	135	202	121	41	19	11
CHILDREN'S (UNDER AGE 2) APPAREL	**100**	**130**	**232**	**109**	**68**	**60**	**35**	**17**
Coats, jackets, and snowsuits	100	114	190	88	83	92	92	17
Outerwear including dresses	100	110	167	111	81	105	61	25
Underwear	100	137	263	112	63	36	18	11
Nightwear and loungewear	100	84	183	98	88	98	73	29
Accessories	100	169	266	98	40	57	28	18
FOOTWEAR	**100**	**78**	**121**	**127**	**117**	**107**	**46**	**28**
Men's	100	64	134	120	123	102	58	14
Boys'	100	19	149	227	77	52	17	7
Women's	100	110	97	97	125	137	51	44
Girls'	100	38	170	183	105	35	14	18
OTHER APPAREL PRODUCTS AND SERVICES	**100**	**71**	**129**	**116**	**100**	**126**	**63**	**35**
Material for making clothes	100	81	197	101	68	118	56	24
Sewing patterns and notions	100	54	47	106	94	169	153	69
Watches	100	49	125	139	87	134	65	26
Jewelry	100	63	137	119	97	136	51	28
Shoe repair and other shoe services	100	39	58	63	138	221	79	53
Coin-operated apparel laundry and dry cleaning	100	190	180	102	74	57	52	56
Apparel alteration, repair, and tailoring services	100	47	100	68	120	155	126	57
Clothing rental	100	153	145	136	80	108	23	13
Watch and jewelry repair	100	12	67	85	121	158	127	97
Professional laundry, dry cleaning	100	30	93	123	131	135	69	32
Clothing storage	100	19	53	9	132	134	272	138

Source: Calculations by New Strategist based on the 2004 Consumer Expenditure Survey

Table 2.3 Apparel: Total spending by age, 2004

(total annual spending on apparel, accessories, and related services, by consumer unit (CU) age group, 2004; consumer units and dollars in thousands)

	total consumer units	under 25	25 to 34	35 to 44	45 to 54	55 to 64	65 to 74	75+
Number of consumer units	116,282	8,817	19,439	24,070	23,712	17,479	11,230	11,536
Total spending of all CUs	$5,046,042,273	$216,321,216	$830,055,797	$1,213,166,993	$1,251,148,504	$826,731,880	$410,029,535	$297,205,660
Apparel, total spending	**211,162,298**	**12,084,228**	**41,475,050**	**51,547,590**	**52,563,813**	**32,569,145**	**13,479,594**	**6,973,397**
MEN'S APPAREL	**36,893,953**	**1,884,017**	**6,528,783**	**8,570,605**	**10,790,620**	**4,985,360**	**3,070,057**	**968,101**
Suits	2,789,605	86,318	514,939	688,883	807,394	482,420	172,942	36,454
Sport coats and tailored jackets	974,443	46,730	153,374	212,538	238,306	175,140	112,525	35,992
Coats and jackets	2,965,191	28,479	442,237	582,253	1,415,606	267,603	185,969	44,298
Underwear	1,975,631	94,254	319,772	366,586	737,680	279,140	114,883	63,909
Hosiery	1,754,695	55,283	228,797	546,389	425,393	260,787	156,771	76,253
Nightwear	244,192	12,520	34,213	58,731	52,404	42,649	32,118	11,882
Accessories	2,914,027	136,928	428,047	552,647	1,092,175	396,249	244,028	61,141
Sweaters and vests	1,144,215	69,654	151,430	253,939	282,173	227,751	126,899	32,762
Active sportswear	2,651,230	467,477	341,543	538,205	623,151	367,059	238,974	60,333
Shirts	9,594,428	428,418	2,140,623	2,111,180	2,433,563	1,306,555	855,389	279,056
Pants	7,282,742	335,840	1,284,724	1,971,092	1,981,612	893,526	592,719	193,689
Shorts and shorts sets	1,723,299	71,947	319,577	447,461	496,292	154,514	166,429	59,872
Uniforms	463,965	23,982	82,810	157,177	93,425	67,993	28,524	10,613
Costumes	415,127	26,186	86,504	83,042	111,684	64,148	41,663	1,730
BOYS' (AGED 2 TO 15) APPAREL	**10,335,144**	**190,712**	**2,335,596**	**4,235,117**	**2,068,161**	**929,009**	**434,152**	**106,708**
Coats and jackets	696,529	14,195	166,981	273,917	155,788	56,807	21,000	7,498
Sweaters	346,520	6,965	64,732	119,628	82,992	41,076	29,086	2,769
Shirts	2,284,941	16,664	477,033	932,231	440,806	237,889	133,300	28,609
Underwear	554,665	19,397	135,490	197,374	108,838	51,563	30,321	6,691
Nightwear	380,242	14,195	69,203	179,562	51,218	56,807	5,727	0
Hosiery	581,410	7,847	138,794	244,792	107,890	41,076	22,011	14,651
Accessories	444,197	1,587	54,429	252,735	92,003	19,751	14,150	5,191
Suits, sport coats, and vests	301,170	9,082	90,975	98,687	63,548	26,044	7,412	5,537
Pants	2,603,554	62,424	627,491	1,042,953	516,684	248,027	83,439	22,149
Shorts and shorts sets	903,511	23,630	251,735	358,402	160,767	63,449	42,113	2,884
Uniforms	444,197	4,938	85,337	202,188	100,776	34,434	9,882	6,460
Active sportswear	498,850	6,525	99,722	205,076	119,746	33,210	30,321	3,692
Costumes	296,519	3,262	73,868	127,812	67,342	18,528	5,166	692
WOMEN'S APPAREL	**73,375,105**	**4,924,206**	**12,392,557**	**13,949,046**	**19,938,709**	**12,994,588**	**5,658,685**	**3,455,609**
Coats and jackets	5,682,701	192,740	714,772	995,776	1,874,908	1,367,557	327,916	224,606
Dresses	7,703,683	421,453	2,614,351	901,181	1,976,158	1,201,506	366,660	188,729
Sport coats and tailored jackets	1,018,630	34,298	122,660	194,726	291,658	224,955	101,632	48,567
Sweaters and vests	5,385,019	269,977	739,654	1,075,207	1,291,118	1,204,653	565,318	238,218
Shirts, blouses, and tops	14,059,657	1,153,352	2,652,840	2,585,359	3,753,372	2,100,976	998,459	795,638
Skirts	1,984,934	75,033	327,353	397,636	547,984	299,240	124,765	218,838
Pants	11,192,143	903,831	1,891,609	2,214,440	2,952,144	1,916,572	849,550	442,982
Shorts and shorts sets	1,463,990	65,246	287,697	315,798	416,146	188,424	130,268	56,526
Active sportswear	4,222,199	353,738	424,937	928,380	1,065,854	633,963	540,837	271,327
Nightwear	3,481,483	160,381	376,145	714,157	1,018,430	744,256	319,494	152,621
Undergarments	5,089,663	485,376	624,575	1,085,798	1,363,677	787,079	481,318	254,138
Hosiery	2,182,613	123,085	252,707	481,400	604,893	393,278	141,049	191,613
Suits	2,740,767	106,509	374,201	669,627	603,945	554,958	284,456	147,084
Accessories	5,880,381	522,143	781,253	1,108,664	1,839,814	1,135,611	312,531	179,039
Uniforms	694,204	37,472	96,029	170,656	189,222	142,454	39,305	19,727
Costumes	591,875	19,486	111,580	110,722	149,623	99,456	75,241	25,841

	total consumer units	under 25	25 to 34	35 to 44	45 to 54	55 to 64	65 to 74	75+
GIRLS' (AGED 2 TO 15) APPAREL	**$12,511,943**	**$254,018**	**$2,284,860**	**$5,342,577**	**$3,113,148**	**$869,231**	**$434,376**	**$172,925**
Coats and jackets	870,952	18,163	184,671	356,236	190,882	73,587	34,027	13,151
Dresses and suits	1,103,516	27,068	147,931	385,601	357,340	77,607	90,514	11,651
Shirts, blouses, and sweaters	2,784,954	50,169	390,141	1,253,325	853,158	83,724	85,573	50,528
Skirts and pants	2,827,978	58,104	582,976	1,179,671	585,449	252,572	123,081	45,913
Shorts and shorts sets	976,769	31,212	255,817	354,551	232,378	70,965	20,888	10,613
Active sportswear	1,168,634	28,832	155,901	630,153	206,294	120,955	4,155	12,344
Underwear and nightwear	730,251	11,374	166,203	301,597	144,406	74,635	23,920	8,306
Hosiery	438,383	7,406	80,866	180,284	119,034	13,459	23,358	10,844
Accessories	689,552	2,821	95,251	318,928	225,975	36,182	4,717	1,038
Uniforms	446,523	9,611	117,217	183,173	80,858	36,356	15,610	3,345
Costumes	476,756	8,993	107,692	199,300	117,374	29,365	8,535	5,307
CHILDREN'S (UNDER AGE 2) APPAREL	**9,129,300**	**899,246**	**3,544,507**	**2,059,911**	**1,256,736**	**829,029**	**311,633**	**150,083**
Coats, jackets, and snowsuits	288,379	24,952	91,363	52,232	49,084	39,677	25,717	4,730
Outerwear including dresses	2,409,363	200,763	674,533	553,129	398,836	378,770	142,509	60,333
Underwear	5,136,176	533,429	2,258,812	1,191,465	663,462	274,246	90,851	57,449
Nightwear and loungewear	405,824	25,834	124,021	82,560	73,033	59,778	28,524	11,767
Accessories	890,720	114,268	395,778	180,525	72,322	76,558	24,032	15,689
FOOTWEAR	**38,226,545**	**2,271,788**	**7,744,498**	**10,020,822**	**9,133,151**	**6,142,995**	**1,715,270**	**1,049,891**
Men's	12,868,929	620,805	2,876,583	3,209,012	3,233,368	1,967,087	716,811	183,999
Boys'	4,176,849	58,721	1,038,043	1,960,742	651,843	324,061	70,188	29,763
Women's	17,885,334	1,496,421	2,895,633	3,600,391	4,541,085	3,677,232	884,026	776,257
Girls'	3,295,432	95,841	934,044	1,250,437	706,618	174,615	44,246	59,987
OTHER APPAREL PRODUCTS AND SERVICES	**30,691,471**	**1,660,241**	**6,644,250**	**7,369,512**	**6,263,051**	**5,818,934**	**1,855,308**	**1,070,195**
Material for making clothes	1,517,480	92,843	499,194	317,483	209,614	269,876	81,867	36,338
Sewing patterns and notions	909,325	37,384	70,952	200,262	173,809	231,422	134,648	62,410
Watches	2,501,226	92,402	521,743	720,174	442,229	503,046	157,332	64,371
Jewelry	13,223,589	631,474	3,017,710	3,245,840	2,609,268	2,701,729	655,046	362,692
Shoe repair and other shoe services	130,236	3,879	12,635	17,090	36,754	43,173	9,995	6,806
Coin-operated apparel laundry and dry cleaning	4,053,591	585,096	1,219,214	856,892	614,141	348,881	201,915	226,913
Apparel alteration, repair, and tailoring services	595,364	21,337	99,528	83,282	145,592	138,958	72,434	33,685
Clothing rental	265,123	30,683	64,149	74,617	43,156	42,998	5,840	3,461
Watch and jewelry repair	444,197	4,056	49,958	77,987	109,549	105,224	54,353	42,568
Professional laundry, dry cleaning	6,997,851	160,205	1,084,113	1,774,681	1,864,475	1,422,791	467,617	223,568
Clothing storage	54,653	794	4,860	963	14,701	11,012	14,374	7,498

Note: Numbers may not add to total because of rounding and missing subcategories.
Source: Calculations by New Strategist based on the 2004 Consumer Expenditure Survey

Table 2.4 Apparel: Market shares by age, 2004

(percentage of total annual spending on apparel, accessories, and related services accounted for by consumer unit age groups, 2004)

	total consumer units	under 25	25 to 34	35 to 44	45 to 54	55 to 64	65 to 74	75+
Share of total consumer units	100.0%	7.6%	16.7%	20.7%	20.4%	15.0%	9.7%	9.9%
Share of total before-tax income	100.0	3.2	16.1	24.9	26.4	16.8	7.5	5.1
Share of total spending	100.0	4.3	16.4	24.0	24.8	16.4	8.1	5.9
Share of apparel spending	100.0	5.7	19.6	24.4	24.9	15.4	6.4	3.3
MEN'S APPAREL	100.0	5.1	17.7	23.2	29.2	13.5	8.3	2.6
Suits	100.0	3.1	18.5	24.7	28.9	17.3	6.2	1.3
Sport coats and tailored jackets	100.0	4.8	15.7	21.8	24.5	18.0	11.5	3.7
Coats and jackets	100.0	1.0	14.9	19.6	47.7	9.0	6.3	1.5
Underwear	100.0	4.8	16.2	18.6	37.3	14.1	5.8	3.2
Hosiery	100.0	3.2	13.0	31.1	24.2	14.9	8.9	4.3
Nightwear	100.0	5.1	14.0	24.1	21.5	17.5	13.2	4.9
Accessories	100.0	4.7	14.7	19.0	37.5	13.6	8.4	2.1
Sweaters and vests	100.0	6.1	13.2	22.2	24.7	19.9	11.1	2.9
Active sportswear	100.0	17.6	12.9	20.3	23.5	13.8	9.0	2.3
Shirts	100.0	4.5	22.3	22.0	25.4	13.6	8.9	2.9
Pants	100.0	4.6	17.6	27.1	27.2	12.3	8.1	2.7
Shorts and shorts sets	100.0	4.2	18.5	26.0	28.8	9.0	9.7	3.5
Uniforms	100.0	5.2	17.8	33.9	20.1	14.7	6.1	2.3
Costumes	100.0	6.3	20.8	20.0	26.9	15.5	10.0	0.4
BOYS' (AGED 2 TO 15) APPAREL	100.0	1.8	22.6	41.0	20.0	9.0	4.2	1.0
Coats and jackets	100.0	2.0	24.0	39.3	22.4	8.2	3.0	1.1
Sweaters	100.0	2.0	18.7	34.5	24.0	11.9	8.4	0.8
Shirts	100.0	0.7	20.9	40.8	19.3	10.4	5.8	1.3
Underwear	100.0	3.5	24.4	35.6	19.6	9.3	5.5	1.2
Nightwear	100.0	3.7	18.2	47.2	13.5	14.9	1.5	0.0
Hosiery	100.0	1.3	23.9	42.1	18.6	7.1	3.8	2.5
Accessories	100.0	0.4	12.3	56.9	20.7	4.4	3.2	1.2
Suits, sport coats, and vests	100.0	3.0	30.2	32.8	21.1	8.6	2.5	1.8
Pants	100.0	2.4	24.1	40.1	19.8	9.5	3.2	0.9
Shorts and shorts sets	100.0	2.6	27.9	39.7	17.8	7.0	4.7	0.3
Uniforms	100.0	1.1	19.2	45.5	22.7	7.8	2.2	1.5
Active sportswear	100.0	1.3	20.0	41.1	24.0	6.7	6.1	0.7
Costumes	100.0	1.1	24.9	43.1	22.7	6.2	1.7	0.2
WOMEN'S APPAREL	100.0	6.7	16.9	19.0	27.2	17.7	7.7	4.7
Coats and jackets	100.0	3.4	12.6	17.5	33.0	24.1	5.8	4.0
Dresses	100.0	5.5	33.9	11.7	25.7	15.6	4.8	2.4
Sport coats and tailored jackets	100.0	3.4	12.0	19.1	28.6	22.1	10.0	4.8
Sweaters and vests	100.0	5.0	13.7	20.0	24.0	22.4	10.5	4.4
Shirts, blouses, and tops	100.0	8.2	18.9	18.4	26.7	14.9	7.1	5.7
Skirts	100.0	3.8	16.5	20.0	27.6	15.1	6.3	11.0
Pants	100.0	8.1	16.9	19.8	26.4	17.1	7.6	4.0
Shorts and shorts sets	100.0	4.5	19.7	21.6	28.4	12.9	8.9	3.9
Active sportswear	100.0	8.4	10.1	22.0	25.2	15.0	12.8	6.4
Nightwear	100.0	4.6	10.8	20.5	29.3	21.4	9.2	4.4
Undergarments	100.0	9.5	12.3	21.3	26.8	15.5	9.5	5.0
Hosiery	100.0	5.6	11.6	22.1	27.7	18.0	6.5	8.8
Suits	100.0	3.9	13.7	24.4	22.0	20.2	10.4	5.4
Accessories	100.0	8.9	13.3	18.9	31.3	19.3	5.3	3.0
Uniforms	100.0	5.4	13.8	24.6	27.3	20.5	5.7	2.8
Costumes	100.0	3.3	18.9	18.7	25.3	16.8	12.7	4.4

	total consumer units	under 25	25 to 34	35 to 44	45 to 54	55 to 64	65 to 74	75+
GIRLS' (AGED 2 TO 15) APPAREL	**100.0%**	**2.0%**	**18.3%**	**42.7%**	**24.9%**	**6.9%**	**3.5%**	**1.4%**
Coats and jackets	100.0	2.1	21.2	40.9	21.9	8.4	3.9	1.5
Dresses and suits	100.0	2.5	13.4	34.9	32.4	7.0	8.2	1.1
Shirts, blouses, and sweaters	100.0	1.8	14.0	45.0	30.6	3.0	3.1	1.8
Skirts and pants	100.0	2.1	20.6	41.7	20.7	8.9	4.4	1.6
Shorts and shorts sets	100.0	3.2	26.2	36.3	23.8	7.3	2.1	1.1
Active sportswear	100.0	2.5	13.3	53.9	17.7	10.4	0.4	1.1
Underwear and nightwear	100.0	1.6	22.8	41.3	19.8	10.2	3.3	1.1
Hosiery	100.0	1.7	18.4	41.1	27.2	3.1	5.3	2.5
Accessories	100.0	0.4	13.8	46.3	32.8	5.2	0.7	0.2
Uniforms	100.0	2.2	26.3	41.0	18.1	8.1	3.5	0.7
Costumes	100.0	1.9	22.6	41.8	24.6	6.2	1.8	1.1
CHILDREN'S (UNDER AGE 2) APPAREL	**100.0**	**9.9**	**38.8**	**22.6**	**13.8**	**9.1**	**3.4**	**1.6**
Coats, jackets, and snowsuits	100.0	8.7	31.7	18.1	17.0	13.8	8.9	1.6
Outerwear including dresses	100.0	8.3	28.0	23.0	16.6	15.7	5.9	2.5
Underwear	100.0	10.4	44.0	23.2	12.9	5.3	1.8	1.1
Nightwear and loungewear	100.0	6.4	30.6	20.3	18.0	14.7	7.0	2.9
Accessories	100.0	12.8	44.4	20.3	8.1	8.6	2.7	1.8
FOOTWEAR	**100.0**	**5.9**	**20.3**	**26.2**	**23.9**	**16.1**	**4.5**	**2.7**
Men's	100.0	4.8	22.4	24.9	25.1	15.3	5.6	1.4
Boys'	100.0	1.4	24.9	46.9	15.6	7.8	1.7	0.7
Women's	100.0	8.4	16.2	20.1	25.4	20.6	4.9	4.3
Girls'	100.0	2.9	28.3	37.9	21.4	5.3	1.3	1.8
OTHER APPAREL PRODUCTS AND SERVICES	**100.0**	**5.4**	**21.6**	**24.0**	**20.4**	**19.0**	**6.0**	**3.5**
Material for making clothes	100.0	6.1	32.9	20.9	13.8	17.8	5.4	2.4
Sewing patterns and notions	100.0	4.1	7.8	22.0	19.1	25.4	14.8	6.9
Watches	100.0	3.7	20.9	28.8	17.7	20.1	6.3	2.6
Jewelry	100.0	4.8	22.8	24.5	19.7	20.4	5.0	2.7
Shoe repair and other shoe services	100.0	3.0	9.7	13.1	28.2	33.1	7.7	5.2
Coin-operated apparel laundry and dry cleaning	100.0	14.4	30.1	21.1	15.2	8.6	5.0	5.6
Apparel alteration, repair, and tailoring services	100.0	3.6	16.7	14.0	24.5	23.3	12.2	5.7
Clothing rental	100.0	11.6	24.2	28.1	16.3	16.2	2.2	1.3
Watch and jewelry repair	100.0	0.9	11.2	17.6	24.7	23.7	12.2	9.6
Professional laundry, dry cleaning	100.0	2.3	15.5	25.4	26.6	20.3	6.7	3.2
Clothing storage	100.0	1.5	8.9	1.8	26.9	20.1	26.3	13.7

Note: Numbers may not add to total because of rounding.
Source: Calculations by New Strategist based on the 2004 Consumer Expenditure Survey

Table 2.5 Apparel: Average spending by income, 2004

(average annual spending on apparel, accessories, and related services, by before-tax income of consumer units (CU), 2004)

	total consumer units	under $20,000	$20,000– $39,999	$40,000– $49,999	$50,000– $69,999	$70,000– $79,999	$80,000– $99,999	$100,000 or more
Number of consumer units (in 000s)	116,282	28,898	27,297	11,374	18,069	6,461	9,246	14,937
Average number of persons per CU	2.5	1.8	2.3	2.6	2.8	3.0	3.1	3.2
Average before-tax income of CU	$54,453.00	$10,923.47	$29,561.76	$44,645.00	$59,259.00	$74,437.00	$88,811.00	$155,901.00
Average spending of CU, total	43,394.87	18,865.37	30,400.94	38,204.07	47,750.13	55,012.03	65,446.39	93,525.67
Apparel, average spending	**1,815.95**	**834.02**	**1,209.16**	**1,490.50**	**1,774.17**	**2,218.80**	**2,666.02**	**4,253.37**
MEN'S APPAREL	**317.28**	**111.41**	**182.23**	**270.80**	**300.21**	**418.93**	**479.80**	**830.68**
Suits	23.99	5.66	7.98	12.96	29.26	35.14	29.06	82.74
Sport coats and tailored jackets	8.38	2.41	4.19	2.93	8.12	10.97	10.09	29.89
Coats and jackets	25.50	6.22	8.20	20.05	26.24	71.34	39.32	64.72
Underwear	16.99	7.56	9.85	23.89	16.04	17.32	26.04	35.98
Hosiery	15.09	5.37	9.87	13.58	24.65	16.80	18.84	28.56
Nightwear	2.10	1.07	1.41	1.98	2.22	2.25	2.66	4.92
Accessories	25.06	7.57	10.04	15.19	23.48	34.37	37.67	79.58
Sweaters and vests	9.84	2.60	5.72	6.70	10.72	12.53	15.05	28.32
Active sportswear	22.80	8.42	10.18	11.08	23.34	30.49	69.19	47.33
Shirts	82.51	27.54	52.40	80.87	59.78	87.68	118.58	232.35
Pants	62.63	26.01	48.86	50.35	53.25	67.99	85.89	152.33
Shorts and shorts sets	14.82	7.94	8.79	22.17	13.99	23.17	13.64	29.84
Uniforms	3.99	1.34	2.25	4.03	6.23	7.10	7.16	6.28
Costumes	3.57	1.70	2.49	5.01	2.87	1.78	6.62	7.84
BOYS' (AGED 2 TO 15) APPAREL	**88.88**	**42.45**	**73.32**	**72.80**	**88.78**	**125.51**	**132.70**	**172.30**
Coats and jackets	5.99	2.63	5.70	5.74	6.02	6.62	7.49	11.96
Sweaters	2.98	1.73	2.67	2.19	2.26	4.01	3.29	6.83
Shirts	19.65	9.83	19.16	11.63	16.01	22.59	35.16	36.62
Underwear	4.77	2.53	5.37	3.59	5.05	7.80	4.69	6.73
Nightwear	3.27	2.25	1.99	0.96	3.40	2.16	–	11.54
Hosiery	5.00	3.57	4.72	3.22	3.79	8.28	3.21	10.41
Accessories	3.82	2.05	1.98	1.63	2.12	12.67	5.74	8.75
Suits, sport coats, and vests	2.59	0.76	0.73	2.69	5.32	2.93	4.13	5.06
Pants	22.39	9.50	18.06	24.36	26.35	30.46	35.08	37.59
Shorts and shorts sets	7.77	3.70	6.80	5.91	7.88	11.66	13.98	13.16
Uniforms	3.82	2.11	1.94	4.24	3.70	6.54	5.43	8.22
Active sportswear	4.29	1.15	2.80	4.38	4.08	7.49	8.40	9.31
Costumes	2.55	0.64	1.42	2.27	2.79	2.31	6.13	6.13
WOMEN'S APPAREL	**631.01**	**289.15**	**406.23**	**491.40**	**646.27**	**694.94**	**996.41**	**1,467.69**
Coats and jackets	48.87	18.84	29.02	34.68	56.60	29.29	92.62	119.81
Dresses	66.25	13.87	40.38	59.32	65.41	63.78	211.79	120.40
Sport coats and tailored jackets	8.76	2.74	3.79	7.15	11.06	9.26	11.90	25.77
Sweaters and vests	46.31	19.42	28.91	31.37	54.57	67.56	78.79	97.51
Shirts, blouses, and tops	120.91	62.64	79.23	114.59	109.33	144.38	161.56	278.88
Skirts	17.07	7.35	8.19	19.90	20.88	19.06	20.22	40.38
Pants	96.25	55.85	73.59	63.10	95.32	93.35	134.16	211.43
Shorts and shorts sets	12.59	5.63	9.04	11.38	9.64	14.10	10.79	35.41
Active sportswear	36.31	16.63	24.79	14.86	34.26	32.72	62.27	95.24
Nightwear	29.94	10.56	13.71	20.10	42.55	36.75	41.53	76.07
Undergarments	43.77	22.85	32.38	40.76	42.64	63.01	50.25	91.54
Hosiery	18.77	13.14	13.77	16.20	21.16	14.17	23.83	35.55
Suits	23.57	8.15	9.57	16.12	20.37	37.10	31.71	77.66
Accessories	50.57	27.53	32.34	29.81	51.85	62.07	43.25	136.50
Uniforms	5.97	1.70	4.76	5.24	8.02	5.89	9.16	12.60
Costumes	5.09	2.24	2.78	6.84	2.64	2.47	12.58	12.94

	total consumer units	under $20,000	$20,000– $39,999	$40,000– $49,999	$50,000– $69,999	$70,000– $79,999	$80,000– $99,999	$100,000 or more
GIRLS' (AGED 2 TO 15) APPAREL	**$107.60**	**$43.45**	**$73.23**	**$79.66**	**$118.75**	**$158.83**	**$162.41**	**$238.57**
Coats and jackets	7.49	3.82	5.74	7.50	8.03	7.74	9.41	15.81
Dresses and suits	9.49	6.55	6.16	0.37	2.81	16.17	11.31	31.02
Shirts, blouses, and sweaters	23.95	6.46	15.92	13.49	30.38	37.14	32.95	57.74
Skirts and pants	24.32	11.16	18.98	23.61	25.48	32.54	40.15	45.29
Shorts and shorts sets	8.40	3.41	6.33	8.35	9.83	9.92	13.35	16.41
Active sportswear	10.05	4.58	3.12	9.79	10.19	17.41	22.05	22.80
Underwear and nightwear	6.28	2.90	4.68	5.80	8.41	8.63	9.03	10.83
Hosiery	3.77	1.46	3.93	3.03	4.48	4.15	4.68	6.45
Accessories	5.93	0.81	4.02	1.65	8.04	12.43	7.95	15.17
Uniforms	3.84	2.24	1.56	3.50	6.71	5.59	3.92	7.07
Costumes	4.10	1.08	2.79	2.56	4.39	7.11	7.59	9.98
CHILDREN'S (UNDER AGE 2) APPAREL	**78.51**	**46.91**	**62.49**	**63.21**	**77.88**	**117.87**	**92.14**	**151.44**
Coats, jackets, and snowsuits	2.48	1.54	2.13	1.24	2.32	1.95	4.04	5.30
Outerwear including dresses	20.72	9.99	16.92	19.12	22.41	28.08	29.35	39.04
Underwear	44.17	28.89	32.93	34.80	44.77	69.73	44.13	86.31
Nightwear and loungewear	3.49	1.65	2.65	3.61	3.65	4.95	4.17	7.21
Accessories	7.66	4.84	7.85	4.43	4.73	13.17	10.44	13.57
FOOTWEAR	**328.74**	**191.87**	**263.93**	**299.87**	**324.59**	**380.05**	**382.19**	**648.66**
Men's	110.67	50.19	74.59	130.34	113.61	114.70	151.19	232.79
Boys'	35.92	22.62	34.47	15.85	18.30	82.75	35.89	75.94
Women's	153.81	103.96	123.81	133.15	161.76	149.18	163.10	295.71
Girls'	28.34	15.09	31.06	20.53	30.93	33.41	32.00	44.22
OTHER APPAREL PRODUCTS AND SERVICES	**263.94**	**108.79**	**147.74**	**212.76**	**217.69**	**322.66**	**420.37**	**744.03**
Material for making clothes	13.05	3.14	6.04	40.00	6.70	11.18	23.63	23.05
Sewing patterns and notions	7.82	2.94	8.69	9.25	4.96	5.85	7.45	17.47
Watches	21.51	6.97	10.29	11.69	18.31	20.54	16.60	84.95
Jewelry	113.72	29.66	43.68	67.85	99.06	171.32	241.41	353.07
Shoe repair and other shoe services	1.12	0.19	0.79	0.62	0.88	0.95	1.96	3.78
Coin-operated apparel laundry and dry cleaning	34.86	50.43	47.55	39.60	24.63	19.68	11.78	11.14
Apparel alteration, repair, and tailoring services	5.12	2.04	3.08	3.38	4.43	6.02	8.27	14.57
Clothing rental	2.28	0.80	1.11	1.61	3.58	5.31	3.37	4.60
Watch and jewelry repair	3.82	1.32	1.87	2.46	4.62	4.67	7.68	9.49
Professional laundry, dry cleaning	60.18	11.33	24.17	34.89	50.26	77.06	97.32	221.46
Clothing storage	0.47	0.17	0.47	1.43	0.24	0.08	0.90	0.46

Note: Subcategories may not add to total because some are not shown. "–" means sample is too small to make a reliable estimate.
Source: Bureau of Labor Statistics, unpublished data from the 2004 Consumer Expenditure Survey; calculations by New Strategist

Table 2.6 Apparel: Indexed spending by income, 2004

(indexed average annual spending of consumer units (CU) on apparel, accessories, and related services, by before-tax income of consumer unit, 2004; index definition: an index of 100 is the average for all consumer units; an index of 132 means that spending by consumer units in that group is 32 percent above the average for all consumer units; an index of 68 indicates spending that is 32 percent below the average for all consumer units)

	total consumer units	under $20,000	$20,000– $39,999	$40,000– $49,999	$50,000– $69,999	$70,000– $79,999	$80,000– $99,999	$100,000 or more
Average spending of CU, total	$43,395	$18,865	$30,401	$38,204	$47,750	$55,012	$65,446	$93,526
Average spending of CU, index	100	43	70	88	110	127	151	216
Apparel, spending index	**100**	**46**	**67**	**82**	**98**	**122**	**147**	**234**
MEN'S APPAREL	**100**	**35**	**57**	**85**	**95**	**132**	**151**	**262**
Suits	100	24	33	54	122	146	121	345
Sport coats and tailored jackets	100	29	50	35	97	131	120	357
Coats and jackets	100	24	32	79	103	280	154	254
Underwear	100	45	58	141	94	102	153	212
Hosiery	100	36	65	90	163	111	125	189
Nightwear	100	51	67	94	106	107	127	234
Accessories	100	30	40	61	94	137	150	318
Sweaters and vests	100	26	58	68	109	127	153	288
Active sportswear	100	37	45	49	102	134	303	208
Shirts	100	33	64	98	72	106	144	282
Pants	100	42	78	80	85	109	137	243
Shorts and shorts sets	100	54	59	150	94	156	92	201
Uniforms	100	34	56	101	156	178	179	157
Costumes	100	48	70	140	80	50	185	220
BOYS' (AGED 2 TO 15) APPAREL	**100**	**48**	**82**	**82**	**100**	**141**	**149**	**194**
Coats and jackets	100	44	95	96	101	111	125	200
Sweaters	100	58	90	73	76	135	110	229
Shirts	100	50	98	59	81	115	179	186
Underwear	100	53	112	75	106	164	98	141
Nightwear	100	69	61	29	104	66	–	353
Hosiery	100	71	94	64	76	166	64	208
Accessories	100	54	52	43	55	332	150	229
Suits, sport coats, and vests	100	29	28	104	205	113	159	195
Pants	100	42	81	109	118	136	157	168
Shorts and shorts sets	100	48	88	76	101	150	180	169
Uniforms	100	55	51	111	97	171	142	215
Active sportswear	100	27	65	102	95	175	196	217
Costumes	100	25	56	89	109	91	240	240
WOMEN'S APPAREL	**100**	**46**	**64**	**78**	**102**	**110**	**158**	**233**
Coats and jackets	100	39	59	71	116	60	190	245
Dresses	100	21	61	90	99	96	320	182
Sport coats and tailored jackets	100	31	43	82	126	106	136	294
Sweaters and vests	100	42	62	68	118	146	170	211
Shirts, blouses, and tops	100	52	66	95	90	119	134	231
Skirts	100	43	48	117	122	112	118	237
Pants	100	58	76	66	99	97	139	220
Shorts and shorts sets	100	45	72	90	77	112	86	281
Active sportswear	100	46	68	41	94	90	171	262
Nightwear	100	35	46	67	142	123	139	254
Undergarments	100	52	74	93	97	144	115	209
Hosiery	100	70	73	86	113	75	127	189
Suits	100	35	41	68	86	157	135	329
Accessories	100	54	64	59	103	123	86	270
Uniforms	100	28	80	88	134	99	153	211
Costumes	100	44	55	134	52	49	247	254

	total consumer units	under $20,000	$20,000– $39,999	$40,000– $49,999	$50,000– $69,999	$70,000– $79,999	$80,000– $99,999	$100,000 or more
GIRLS' (AGED 2 TO 15) APPAREL	**100**	**40**	**68**	**74**	**110**	**148**	**151**	**222**
Coats and jackets	100	51	77	100	107	103	126	211
Dresses and suits	100	69	65	4	30	170	119	327
Shirts, blouses, and sweaters	100	27	66	56	127	155	138	241
Skirts and pants	100	46	78	97	105	134	165	186
Shorts and shorts sets	100	41	75	99	117	118	159	195
Active sportswear	100	46	31	97	101	173	219	227
Underwear and nightwear	100	46	74	92	134	137	144	172
Hosiery	100	39	104	80	119	110	124	171
Accessories	100	14	68	28	136	210	134	256
Uniforms	100	58	41	91	175	146	102	184
Costumes	100	26	68	62	107	173	185	243
CHILDREN'S (UNDER AGE 2) APPAREL	**100**	**60**	**80**	**81**	**99**	**150**	**117**	**193**
Coats, jackets, and snowsuits	100	62	86	50	94	79	163	214
Outerwear including dresses	100	48	82	92	108	136	142	188
Underwear	100	65	75	79	101	158	100	195
Nightwear and loungewear	100	47	76	103	105	142	119	207
Accessories	100	63	102	58	62	172	136	177
FOOTWEAR	**100**	**58**	**80**	**91**	**99**	**116**	**116**	**197**
Men's	100	45	67	118	103	104	137	210
Boys'	100	63	96	44	51	230	100	211
Women's	100	68	80	87	105	97	106	192
Girls'	100	53	110	72	109	118	113	156
OTHER APPAREL PRODUCTS AND SERVICES	**100**	**41**	**56**	**81**	**82**	**122**	**159**	**282**
Material for making clothes	100	24	46	307	51	86	181	177
Sewing patterns and notions	100	38	111	118	63	75	95	223
Watches	100	32	48	54	85	95	77	395
Jewelry	100	26	38	60	87	151	212	310
Shoe repair and other shoe services	100	17	70	55	79	85	175	338
Coin-operated apparel laundry and dry cleaning	100	145	136	114	71	56	34	32
Apparel alteration, repair, and tailoring services	100	40	60	66	87	118	162	285
Clothing rental	100	35	49	71	157	233	148	202
Watch and jewelry repair	100	35	49	64	121	122	201	248
Professional laundry, dry cleaning	100	19	40	58	84	128	162	368
Clothing storage	100	37	100	304	51	17	191	98

Note: "–" means sample is too small to make a reliable estimate.
Source: Calculations by New Strategist based on the 2004 Consumer Expenditure Survey

Table 2.7 Apparel: Total spending by income, 2004

(total annual spending on apparel, accessories, and related services, by before-tax income group of consumer units (CU), 2004; consumer units and dollars in thousands)

	total consumer units	under $20,000	$20,000–$39,999	$40,000–$49,999	$50,000–$69,999	$70,000–$79,999	$80,000–$99,999	$100,000 or more
Number of consumer units	116,282	28,898	27,297	11,374	18,069	6,461	9,246	14,937
Total spending of all CUs	$5,046,042,273	$545,171,431	$829,854,379	$434,533,092	$862,797,099	$355,432,726	$605,117,322	$1,396,992,933
Apparel, total spending	**211,162,298**	**24,101,653**	**33,006,575**	**16,952,947**	**32,057,478**	**14,335,667**	**24,650,021**	**63,532,588**
MEN'S APPAREL	**36,893,953**	**3,219,408**	**4,974,379**	**3,080,079**	**5,424,494**	**2,706,707**	**4,436,231**	**12,407,867**
Suits	2,789,605	163,632	217,956	147,407	528,699	227,040	268,689	1,235,887
Sport coats and tailored jackets	974,443	69,623	114,357	33,326	146,720	70,877	93,292	446,467
Coats and jackets	2,965,191	179,719	223,860	228,049	474,131	460,928	363,553	966,723
Underwear	1,975,631	218,560	268,836	271,725	289,827	111,905	240,766	537,433
Hosiery	1,754,695	155,105	269,498	154,459	445,401	108,545	174,195	426,601
Nightwear	244,192	30,790	38,353	22,521	40,113	14,537	24,594	73,490
Accessories	2,914,027	218,634	273,962	172,771	424,260	222,065	348,297	1,188,686
Sweaters and vests	1,144,215	75,214	156,211	76,206	193,700	80,956	139,152	423,016
Active sportswear	2,651,230	243,453	277,787	126,024	421,730	196,996	639,731	706,968
Shirts	9,594,428	795,881	1,430,312	919,815	1,080,165	566,500	1,096,391	3,470,612
Pants	7,282,742	751,623	1,333,674	572,681	962,174	439,283	794,139	2,275,353
Shorts and shorts sets	1,723,299	229,477	240,058	252,162	252,785	149,701	126,115	445,720
Uniforms	463,965	38,643	61,483	45,837	112,570	45,873	66,201	93,804
Costumes	415,127	49,015	67,901	56,984	51,858	11,501	61,209	117,106
BOYS' (AGED 2 TO 15) APPAREL	**10,335,144**	**1,226,640**	**2,001,430**	**828,027**	**1,604,166**	**810,920**	**1,226,944**	**2,573,645**
Coats and jackets	696,529	75,926	155,526	65,287	108,775	42,772	69,253	178,647
Sweaters	346,520	50,025	72,835	24,909	40,836	25,909	30,419	102,020
Shirts	2,284,941	284,194	523,076	132,280	289,285	145,954	325,089	546,993
Underwear	554,665	73,034	146,460	40,833	91,248	50,396	43,364	100,526
Nightwear	380,242	65,106	54,252	10,919	61,435	13,956	–	172,373
Hosiery	581,410	103,134	128,904	36,624	68,482	53,497	29,680	155,494
Accessories	444,197	59,273	54,001	18,540	38,306	81,861	53,072	130,699
Suits, sport coats, and vests	301,170	21,858	19,896	30,596	96,127	18,931	38,186	75,581
Pants	2,603,554	274,392	492,982	277,071	476,118	196,802	324,350	561,482
Shorts and shorts sets	903,511	106,886	185,647	67,220	142,384	75,335	129,259	196,571
Uniforms	444,197	60,972	52,836	48,226	66,855	42,255	50,206	122,782
Active sportswear	498,850	33,246	76,457	49,818	73,722	48,393	77,666	139,063
Costumes	296,519	18,575	38,841	25,819	50,413	14,925	56,678	91,564
WOMEN'S APPAREL	**73,375,105**	**8,355,946**	**11,088,932**	**5,589,184**	**11,677,453**	**4,490,007**	**9,212,807**	**21,922,886**
Coats and jackets	5,682,701	544,513	792,294	394,450	1,022,705	189,243	856,365	1,789,602
Dresses	7,703,683	400,860	1,102,281	674,706	1,181,893	412,083	1,958,210	1,798,415
Sport coats and tailored jackets	1,018,630	79,267	103,349	81,324	199,843	59,829	110,027	384,926
Sweaters and vests	5,385,019	561,161	789,111	356,802	986,025	436,505	728,492	1,456,507
Shirts, blouses, and tops	14,059,657	1,810,217	2,162,662	1,303,347	1,975,484	932,839	1,493,784	4,165,631
Skirts	1,984,934	212,520	223,587	226,343	377,281	123,147	186,954	603,156
Pants	11,192,143	1,613,975	2,008,747	717,699	1,722,337	603,134	1,240,443	3,158,130
Shorts and shorts sets	1,463,990	162,644	246,884	129,436	174,185	91,100	99,764	528,919
Active sportswear	4,222,199	480,542	676,693	169,018	619,044	211,404	575,748	1,422,600
Nightwear	3,481,483	305,302	374,212	228,617	768,836	237,442	383,986	1,136,258
Undergarments	5,089,663	660,280	883,837	463,604	770,462	407,108	464,612	1,367,333
Hosiery	2,182,613	379,771	375,958	184,259	382,340	91,552	220,332	531,010
Suits	2,740,767	235,449	261,127	183,349	368,066	239,703	293,191	1,160,007
Accessories	5,880,381	795,663	882,867	339,059	936,878	401,034	399,890	2,038,901
Uniforms	694,204	49,136	130,052	59,600	144,913	38,055	84,693	188,206
Costumes	591,875	64,874	75,957	77,798	47,702	15,959	116,315	193,285

	total consumer units	under $20,000	$20,000–$39,999	$40,000–$49,999	$50,000–$69,999	$70,000–$79,999	$80,000–$99,999	$100,000 or more
GIRLS' (AGED 2 TO 15) APPAREL	**$12,511,943**	**$1,255,751**	**$1,998,842**	**$906,053**	**$2,145,694**	**$1,026,201**	**$1,501,643**	**$3,563,520**
Coats and jackets	870,952	110,464	156,700	85,305	145,094	50,008	87,005	236,154
Dresses and suits	1,103,516	189,197	168,070	4,208	50,774	104,474	104,572	463,346
Shirts, blouses, and sweaters	2,784,954	186,618	434,480	153,435	548,936	239,962	304,656	862,462
Skirts and pants	2,827,978	322,588	518,059	268,540	460,398	210,241	371,227	676,497
Shorts and shorts sets	976,769	98,600	172,655	94,973	177,618	64,093	123,434	245,116
Active sportswear	1,168,634	132,359	85,264	111,351	184,123	112,486	203,874	340,564
Underwear and nightwear	730,251	83,735	127,689	65,969	151,960	55,758	83,491	161,768
Hosiery	438,383	42,254	107,262	34,463	80,949	26,813	43,271	96,344
Accessories	689,552	23,354	109,798	18,767	145,275	80,310	73,506	226,594
Uniforms	446,523	64,729	42,462	39,809	121,243	36,117	36,244	105,605
Costumes	476,756	31,214	76,273	29,117	79,323	45,938	70,177	149,071
CHILDREN'S (UNDER AGE 2) APPAREL	**9,129,300**	**1,355,545**	**1,705,725**	**718,951**	**1,407,214**	**761,558**	**851,926**	**2,262,059**
Coats, jackets, and snowsuits	288,379	44,543	58,141	14,104	41,920	12,599	37,354	79,166
Outerwear including dresses	2,409,363	288,643	461,895	217,471	404,926	181,425	271,370	583,140
Underwear	5,136,176	834,955	898,917	395,815	808,949	450,526	408,026	1,289,212
Nightwear and loungewear	405,824	47,785	72,447	41,060	65,952	31,982	38,556	107,696
Accessories	890,720	139,790	214,182	50,387	85,466	85,091	96,528	202,695
FOOTWEAR	**38,226,545**	**5,544,560**	**7,204,614**	**3,410,721**	**5,865,017**	**2,455,503**	**3,533,729**	**9,689,034**
Men's	12,868,929	1,450,283	2,036,179	1,482,487	2,052,819	741,077	1,397,903	3,477,184
Boys'	4,176,849	653,553	940,986	180,278	330,663	534,648	331,839	1,134,316
Women's	17,885,334	3,004,299	3,379,716	1,514,448	2,922,841	963,852	1,508,023	4,417,020
Girls'	3,295,432	436,209	847,733	233,508	558,874	215,862	295,872	660,514
OTHER APPAREL PRODUCTS AND SERVICES	**30,691,471**	**3,143,885**	**4,032,785**	**2,419,932**	**3,933,441**	**2,084,706**	**3,886,741**	**11,113,576**
Material for making clothes	1,517,480	90,723	164,943	454,960	121,062	72,234	218,483	344,298
Sewing patterns and notions	909,325	85,092	237,303	105,210	89,622	37,797	68,883	260,949
Watches	2,501,226	201,448	280,823	132,962	330,843	132,709	153,484	1,268,898
Jewelry	13,223,589	856,977	1,192,306	771,726	1,789,915	1,106,899	2,232,077	5,273,807
Shoe repair and other shoe services	130,236	5,346	21,444	7,052	15,901	6,138	18,122	56,462
Coin-operated apparel laundry and dry cleaning	4,053,591	1,457,248	1,297,955	450,410	445,039	127,152	108,918	166,398
Apparel alteration, repair, and tailoring services	595,364	59,045	84,191	38,444	80,046	38,895	76,464	217,632
Clothing rental	265,123	23,103	30,242	18,312	64,687	34,308	31,159	68,710
Watch and jewelry repair	444,197	38,197	51,167	27,980	83,479	30,173	71,009	141,752
Professional laundry, dry cleaning	6,997,851	327,357	659,765	396,839	908,148	497,885	899,821	3,307,948
Clothing storage	54,653	5,022	12,767	16,265	4,337	517	8,321	6,871

Note: Numbers may not add to total because of rounding and missing subcategories. "–" means sample is too small to make a reliable estimate.
Source: Calculations by New Strategist based on the 2004 Consumer Expenditure Survey

Table 2.8 Apparel: Market shares by income, 2004

(percentage of total annual spending on apparel, accessories, and related services accounted for by before-tax income group of consumer units, 2004)

	total consumer units	under $20,000	$20,000–$39,999	$40,000–$49,999	$50,000–$69,999	$70,000–$79,999	$80,000–$99,999	$100,000 or more
Share of total consumer units	100.0%	24.9%	23.5%	9.8%	15.5%	5.6%	8.0%	12.8%
Share of total before-tax income	100.0	5.0	12.7	8.0	16.9	7.6	13.0	36.8
Share of total spending	100.0	10.8	16.4	8.6	17.1	7.0	12.0	27.7
Share of apparel spending	100.0	11.4	15.6	8.0	15.2	6.8	11.7	30.1
MEN'S APPAREL	100.0	8.7	13.5	8.3	14.7	7.3	12.0	33.6
Suits	100.0	5.9	7.8	5.3	19.0	8.1	9.6	44.3
Sport coats and tailored jackets	100.0	7.1	11.7	3.4	15.1	7.3	9.6	45.8
Coats and jackets	100.0	6.1	7.5	7.7	16.0	15.5	12.3	32.6
Underwear	100.0	11.1	13.6	13.8	14.7	5.7	12.2	27.2
Hosiery	100.0	8.8	15.4	8.8	25.4	6.2	9.9	24.3
Nightwear	100.0	12.6	15.7	9.2	16.4	6.0	10.1	30.1
Accessories	100.0	7.5	9.4	5.9	14.6	7.6	12.0	40.8
Sweaters and vests	100.0	6.6	13.7	6.7	16.9	7.1	12.2	37.0
Active sportswear	100.0	9.2	10.5	4.8	15.9	7.4	24.1	26.7
Shirts	100.0	8.3	14.9	9.6	11.3	5.9	11.4	36.2
Pants	100.0	10.3	18.3	7.9	13.2	6.0	10.9	31.2
Shorts and shorts sets	100.0	13.3	13.9	14.6	14.7	8.7	7.3	25.9
Uniforms	100.0	8.3	13.3	9.9	24.3	9.9	14.3	20.2
Costumes	100.0	11.8	16.4	13.7	12.5	2.8	14.7	28.2
BOYS' (AGED 2 TO 15) APPAREL	100.0	11.9	19.4	8.0	15.5	7.8	11.9	24.9
Coats and jackets	100.0	10.9	22.3	9.4	15.6	6.1	9.9	25.6
Sweaters	100.0	14.4	21.0	7.2	11.8	7.5	8.8	29.4
Shirts	100.0	12.4	22.9	5.8	12.7	6.4	14.2	23.9
Underwear	100.0	13.2	26.4	7.4	16.5	9.1	7.8	18.1
Nightwear	100.0	17.1	14.3	2.9	16.2	3.7	–	45.3
Hosiery	100.0	17.7	22.2	6.3	11.8	9.2	5.1	26.7
Accessories	100.0	13.3	12.2	4.2	8.6	18.4	11.9	29.4
Suits, sport coats, and vests	100.0	7.3	6.6	10.2	31.9	6.3	12.7	25.1
Pants	100.0	10.5	18.9	10.6	18.3	7.6	12.5	21.6
Shorts and shorts sets	100.0	11.8	20.5	7.4	15.8	8.3	14.3	21.8
Uniforms	100.0	13.7	11.9	10.9	15.1	9.5	11.3	27.6
Active sportswear	100.0	6.7	15.3	10.0	14.8	9.7	15.6	27.9
Costumes	100.0	6.3	13.1	8.7	17.0	5.0	19.1	30.9
WOMEN'S APPAREL	100.0	11.4	15.1	7.6	15.9	6.1	12.6	29.9
Coats and jackets	100.0	9.6	13.9	6.9	18.0	3.3	15.1	31.5
Dresses	100.0	5.2	14.3	8.8	15.3	5.3	25.4	23.3
Sport coats and tailored jackets	100.0	7.8	10.1	8.0	19.6	5.9	10.8	37.8
Sweaters and vests	100.0	10.4	14.7	6.6	18.3	8.1	13.5	27.0
Shirts, blouses, and tops	100.0	12.9	15.4	9.3	14.1	6.6	10.6	29.6
Skirts	100.0	10.7	11.3	11.4	19.0	6.2	9.4	30.4
Pants	100.0	14.4	17.9	6.4	15.4	5.4	11.1	28.2
Shorts and shorts sets	100.0	11.1	16.9	8.8	11.9	6.2	6.8	36.1
Active sportswear	100.0	11.4	16.0	4.0	14.7	5.0	13.6	33.7
Nightwear	100.0	8.8	10.7	6.6	22.1	6.8	11.0	32.6
Undergarments	100.0	13.0	17.4	9.1	15.1	8.0	9.1	26.9
Hosiery	100.0	17.4	17.2	8.4	17.5	4.2	10.1	24.3
Suits	100.0	8.6	9.5	6.7	13.4	8.7	10.7	42.3
Accessories	100.0	13.5	15.0	5.8	15.9	6.8	6.8	34.7
Uniforms	100.0	7.1	18.7	8.6	20.9	5.5	12.2	27.1
Costumes	100.0	11.0	12.8	13.1	8.1	2.7	19.7	32.7

	total consumer units	under $20,000	$20,000– $39,999	$40,000– $49,999	$50,000– $69,999	$70,000– $79,999	$80,000– $99,999	$100,000 or more
GIRLS' (AGED 2 TO 15) APPAREL	**100.0%**	**10.0%**	**16.0%**	**7.2%**	**17.1%**	**8.2%**	**12.0%**	**28.5%**
Coats and jackets	100.0	12.7	18.0	9.8	16.7	5.7	10.0	27.1
Dresses and suits	100.0	17.1	15.2	0.4	4.6	9.5	9.5	42.0
Shirts, blouses, and sweaters	100.0	6.7	15.6	5.5	19.7	8.6	10.9	31.0
Skirts and pants	100.0	11.4	18.3	9.5	16.3	7.4	13.1	23.9
Shorts and shorts sets	100.0	10.1	17.7	9.7	18.2	6.6	12.6	25.1
Active sportswear	100.0	11.3	7.3	9.5	15.8	9.6	17.4	29.1
Underwear and nightwear	100.0	11.5	17.5	9.0	20.8	7.6	11.4	22.2
Hosiery	100.0	9.6	24.5	7.9	18.5	6.1	9.9	22.0
Accessories	100.0	3.4	15.9	2.7	21.1	11.6	10.7	32.9
Uniforms	100.0	14.5	9.5	8.9	27.2	8.1	8.1	23.7
Costumes	100.0	6.5	16.0	6.1	16.6	9.6	14.7	31.3
CHILDREN'S (UNDER AGE 2) APPAREL	**100.0**	**14.8**	**18.7**	**7.9**	**15.4**	**8.3**	**9.3**	**24.8**
Coats, jackets, and snowsuits	100.0	15.4	20.2	4.9	14.5	4.4	13.0	27.5
Outerwear including dresses	100.0	12.0	19.2	9.0	16.8	7.5	11.3	24.2
Underwear	100.0	16.3	17.5	7.7	15.8	8.8	7.9	25.1
Nightwear and loungewear	100.0	11.8	17.9	10.1	16.3	7.9	9.5	26.5
Accessories	100.0	15.7	24.0	5.7	9.6	9.6	10.8	22.8
FOOTWEAR	**100.0**	**14.5**	**18.8**	**8.9**	**15.3**	**6.4**	**9.2**	**25.3**
Men's	100.0	11.3	15.8	11.5	16.0	5.8	10.9	27.0
Boys'	100.0	15.6	22.5	4.3	7.9	12.8	7.9	27.2
Women's	100.0	16.8	18.9	8.5	16.3	5.4	8.4	24.7
Girls'	100.0	13.2	25.7	7.1	17.0	6.6	9.0	20.0
OTHER APPAREL PRODUCTS AND SERVICES	**100.0**	**10.2**	**13.1**	**7.9**	**12.8**	**6.8**	**12.7**	**36.2**
Material for making clothes	100.0	6.0	10.9	30.0	8.0	4.8	14.4	22.7
Sewing patterns and notions	100.0	9.4	26.1	11.6	9.9	4.2	7.6	28.7
Watches	100.0	8.1	11.2	5.3	13.2	5.3	6.1	50.7
Jewelry	100.0	6.5	9.0	5.8	13.5	8.4	16.9	39.9
Shoe repair and other shoe services	100.0	4.1	16.5	5.4	12.2	4.7	13.9	43.4
Coin-operated apparel laundry and dry cleaning	100.0	35.9	32.0	11.1	11.0	3.1	2.7	4.1
Apparel alteration, repair, and tailoring services	100.0	9.9	14.1	6.5	13.4	6.5	12.8	36.6
Clothing rental	100.0	8.7	11.4	6.9	24.4	12.9	11.8	25.9
Watch and jewelry repair	100.0	8.6	11.5	6.3	18.8	6.8	16.0	31.9
Professional laundry, dry cleaning	100.0	4.7	9.4	5.7	13.0	7.1	12.9	47.3
Clothing storage	100.0	9.2	23.4	29.8	7.9	0.9	15.2	12.6

Note: Numbers may not add to total because of rounding. "–" means sample is too small to make a reliable estimate.
Source: Calculations by New Strategist based on the 2004 Consumer Expenditure Survey

Table 2.9 Apparel: Average spending by high-income consumer units, 2004

(average annual spending on apparel, accessories, and related services, by before-tax income of high-income consumer units (CU), 2004)

	total consumer units	$100,000 or more	$100,000– $119,999	$120,000– $149,999	$150,000 or more
Number of consumer units (in 000s)	116,282	14,937	5,625	4,245	5,067
Average number of persons per CU	2.5	3.2	3.1	3.3	3.2
Average before-tax income of CU	$54,453.00	$155,901.00	$108,751.00	$132,292.00	$228,021.00
Average spending of CU, total	43,394.87	93,525.67	75,213.14	87,298.57	119,448.79
Apparel, average spending	1,815.95	4,253.37	3,643.90	3,675.00	5,501.81
MEN'S APPAREL	**317.28**	**830.68**	**674.38**	**687.43**	**1,156.36**
Suits	23.99	82.74	54.42	63.96	129.90
Sport coats and tailored jackets	8.38	29.89	24.40	23.12	41.67
Coats and jackets	25.50	64.72	65.41	37.07	91.82
Underwear	16.99	35.98	35.18	26.13	46.93
Hosiery	15.09	28.56	24.33	32.80	29.48
Nightwear	2.10	4.92	4.16	3.81	6.70
Accessories	25.06	79.58	72.57	65.71	102.22
Sweaters and vests	9.84	28.32	19.75	24.10	41.37
Active sportswear	22.80	47.33	36.65	51.51	56.25
Shirts	82.51	232.35	160.80	193.98	359.07
Pants	62.63	152.33	146.66	134.07	177.76
Shorts and shorts sets	14.82	29.84	21.30	17.77	52.53
Uniforms	3.99	6.28	5.33	3.58	9.59
Costumes	3.57	7.84	3.43	9.83	11.08
BOYS' (AGED 2 TO 15) APPAREL	**88.88**	**172.30**	**174.65**	**154.17**	**184.78**
Coats and jackets	5.99	11.96	10.01	13.10	13.16
Sweaters	2.98	6.83	5.49	4.54	10.22
Shirts	19.65	36.62	41.86	29.76	37.11
Underwear	4.77	6.73	5.32	9.18	5.98
Nightwear	3.27	11.54	11.52	12.48	10.62
Hosiery	5.00	10.41	9.75	11.02	10.60
Accessories	3.82	8.75	10.44	8.90	6.53
Suits, sport coats, and vests	2.59	5.06	2.65	3.62	8.95
Pants	22.39	37.59	39.95	31.12	40.41
Shorts and shorts sets	7.77	13.16	16.06	10.66	12.02
Uniforms	3.82	8.22	9.11	7.23	8.07
Active sportswear	4.29	9.31	7.90	7.64	12.28
Costumes	2.55	6.13	4.59	4.91	8.85
WOMEN'S APPAREL	**631.01**	**1,467.69**	**1,251.62**	**1,370.14**	**1,824.24**
Coats and jackets	48.87	119.81	74.51	138.21	156.92
Dresses	66.25	120.40	146.02	118.91	90.41
Sport coats and tailored jackets	8.76	25.77	13.06	33.50	33.41
Sweaters and vests	46.31	97.51	99.21	95.52	97.44
Shirts, blouses, and tops	120.91	278.88	236.84	265.58	343.99
Skirts	17.07	40.38	40.64	33.94	46.57
Pants	96.25	211.43	144.67	241.45	263.16
Shorts and shorts sets	12.59	35.41	33.41	31.63	41.67
Active sportswear	36.31	95.24	72.52	63.40	155.34
Nightwear	29.94	76.07	91.69	51.92	81.27
Undergarments	43.77	91.54	77.47	67.69	132.95
Hosiery	18.77	35.55	31.14	37.14	39.38
Suits	23.57	77.66	55.62	56.71	119.67
Accessories	50.57	136.50	122.96	106.61	183.35
Uniforms	5.97	12.60	4.42	13.06	21.30
Costumes	5.09	12.94	7.44	14.87	17.41

	total consumer units	$100,000 or more	$100,000– $119,999	$120,000– $149,999	$150,000 or more
GIRLS' (AGED 2 TO 15) APPAREL	**$107.60**	**$238.57**	**$238.01**	**$226.41**	**$249.94**
Coats and jackets	7.49	15.81	9.80	19.25	19.60
Dresses and suits	9.49	31.02	51.60	21.32	15.53
Shirts, blouses, and sweaters	23.95	57.74	40.40	66.81	69.90
Skirts and pants	24.32	45.29	42.02	44.29	49.77
Shorts and shorts sets	8.40	16.41	9.54	22.06	19.29
Active sportswear	10.05	22.80	31.87	9.30	25.28
Underwear and nightwear	6.28	10.83	9.38	9.10	13.87
Hosiery	3.77	6.45	6.08	8.40	4.92
Accessories	5.93	15.17	21.19	11.70	11.27
Uniforms	3.84	7.07	6.27	7.12	7.93
Costumes	4.10	9.98	9.86	7.05	12.57
CHILDREN'S (UNDER AGE 2) APPAREL	**78.51**	**151.44**	**145.28**	**147.78**	**161.02**
Coats, jackets, and snowsuits	2.48	5.30	3.71	3.54	8.55
Outerwear including dresses	20.72	39.04	36.23	36.68	44.13
Underwear	44.17	86.31	86.77	90.46	81.56
Nightwear and loungewear	3.49	7.21	5.94	5.53	10.04
Accessories	7.66	13.57	12.63	11.57	16.75
FOOTWEAR	**328.74**	**648.66**	**633.85**	**566.07**	**750.33**
Men's	110.67	232.79	245.61	204.04	246.08
Boys'	35.92	75.94	98.26	58.91	65.70
Women's	153.81	295.71	252.37	251.63	393.54
Girls'	28.34	44.22	37.61	51.49	45.01
OTHER APPAREL PRODUCTS AND SERVICES	**263.94**	**744.03**	**526.11**	**523.01**	**1,175.14**
Material for making clothes	13.05	23.05	8.44	17.34	46.79
Sewing patterns and notions	7.82	17.47	13.41	12.77	27.22
Watches	21.51	84.95	66.40	43.82	139.99
Jewelry	113.72	353.07	257.16	213.23	576.69
Shoe repair and other shoe services	1.12	3.78	2.26	2.72	6.35
Coin-operated apparel laundry and dry cleaning	34.86	11.14	13.79	8.90	10.06
Apparel alteration, repair, and tailoring services	5.12	14.57	11.45	14.16	18.39
Clothing rental	2.28	4.60	5.39	5.81	2.71
Watch and jewelry repair	3.82	9.49	5.43	9.46	14.04
Professional laundry, dry cleaning	60.18	221.46	142.22	194.51	331.99
Clothing storage	0.47	0.46	0.16	0.31	0.92

Note: Subcategories may not add to total because some are not shown.
Source: Bureau of Labor Statistics, unpublished data from the 2004 Consumer Expenditure Survey; calculations by New Strategist

Table 2.10 Apparel: Indexed spending by high-income consumer units, 2004

(indexed average annual spending of high-income consumer units (CU) on apparel, accessories, and related services, by before-tax income of consumer unit, 2004; index definition: an index of 100 is the average for all consumer units; an index of 132 means that spending by consumer units in that group is 32 percent above the average for all consumer units; an index of 68 indicates spending that is 32 percent below the average for all consumer units)

	total consumer units	$100,000 or more	$100,000–$119,999	$120,000–$149,999	$150,000 or more
Average spending of CU, total	$43,395	$93,526	$75,213	$87,299	$119,449
Average spending of CU, index	100	216	173	201	275
Apparel, spending index	100	234	201	202	303
MEN'S APPAREL	100	262	213	217	364
Suits	100	345	227	267	541
Sport coats and tailored jackets	100	357	291	276	497
Coats and jackets	100	254	257	145	360
Underwear	100	212	207	154	276
Hosiery	100	189	161	217	195
Nightwear	100	234	198	181	319
Accessories	100	318	290	262	408
Sweaters and vests	100	288	201	245	420
Active sportswear	100	208	161	226	247
Shirts	100	282	195	235	435
Pants	100	243	234	214	284
Shorts and shorts sets	100	201	144	120	354
Uniforms	100	157	134	90	240
Costumes	100	220	96	275	310
BOYS' (AGED 2 TO 15) APPAREL	100	194	197	173	208
Coats and jackets	100	200	167	219	220
Sweaters	100	229	184	152	343
Shirts	100	186	213	151	189
Underwear	100	141	112	192	125
Nightwear	100	353	352	382	325
Hosiery	100	208	195	220	212
Accessories	100	229	273	233	171
Suits, sport coats, and vests	100	195	102	140	346
Pants	100	168	178	139	180
Shorts and shorts sets	100	169	207	137	155
Uniforms	100	215	238	189	211
Active sportswear	100	217	184	178	286
Costumes	100	240	180	193	347
WOMEN'S APPAREL	100	233	198	217	289
Coats and jackets	100	245	152	283	321
Dresses	100	182	220	179	136
Sport coats and tailored jackets	100	294	149	382	381
Sweaters and vests	100	211	214	206	210
Shirts, blouses, and tops	100	231	196	220	285
Skirts	100	237	238	199	273
Pants	100	220	150	251	273
Shorts and shorts sets	100	281	265	251	331
Active sportswear	100	262	200	175	428
Nightwear	100	254	306	173	271
Undergarments	100	209	177	155	304
Hosiery	100	189	166	198	210
Suits	100	329	236	241	508
Accessories	100	270	243	211	363
Uniforms	100	211	74	219	357
Costumes	100	254	146	292	342

	total consumer units	$100,000 or more	$100,000–$119,999	$120,000–$149,999	$150,000 or more
GIRLS' (AGED 2 TO 15) APPAREL	**100**	**222**	**221**	**210**	**232**
Coats and jackets	100	211	131	257	262
Dresses and suits	100	327	544	225	164
Shirts, blouses, and sweaters	100	241	169	279	292
Skirts and pants	100	186	173	182	205
Shorts and shorts sets	100	195	114	263	230
Active sportswear	100	227	317	93	252
Underwear and nightwear	100	172	149	145	221
Hosiery	100	171	161	223	131
Accessories	100	256	357	197	190
Uniforms	100	184	163	185	207
Costumes	100	243	240	172	307
CHILDREN'S (UNDER AGE 2) APPAREL	**100**	**193**	**185**	**188**	**205**
Coats, jackets, and snowsuits	100	214	150	143	345
Outerwear including dresses	100	188	175	177	213
Underwear	100	195	196	205	185
Nightwear and loungewear	100	207	170	158	288
Accessories	100	177	165	151	219
FOOTWEAR	**100**	**197**	**193**	**172**	**228**
Men's	100	210	222	184	222
Boys'	100	211	274	164	183
Women's	100	192	164	164	256
Girls'	100	156	133	182	159
OTHER APPAREL PRODUCTS AND SERVICES	**100**	**282**	**199**	**198**	**445**
Material for making clothes	100	177	65	133	359
Sewing patterns and notions	100	223	171	163	348
Watches	100	395	309	204	651
Jewelry	100	310	226	188	507
Shoe repair and other shoe services	100	338	202	243	567
Coin-operated apparel laundry and dry cleaning	100	32	40	26	29
Apparel alteration, repair, and tailoring services	100	285	224	277	359
Clothing rental	100	202	236	255	119
Watch and jewelry repair	100	248	142	248	368
Professional laundry, dry cleaning	100	368	236	323	552
Clothing storage	100	98	34	66	196

Source: Calculations by New Strategist based on the 2004 Consumer Expenditure Survey

Table 2.11 Apparel: Total spending by high-income consumer units, 2004

(total annual spending on apparel, accessories, and related services, by before-tax income group of high-income consumer units (CU), 2004; consumer units and dollars in thousands)

	total consumer units	$100,000 or more	$100,000– $119,999	$120,000– $149,999	$150,000 or more
Number of consumer units	116,282	14,937	5,625	4,245	5,067
Total spending of all CUs	$5,046,042,273	$1,396,992,933	$423,073,913	$370,582,430	$605,247,019
Apparel, total spending	**211,162,298**	**63,532,588**	**20,496,938**	**15,600,375**	**27,877,671**
MEN'S APPAREL	**36,893,953**	**12,407,867**	**3,793,388**	**2,918,140**	**5,859,276**
Suits	2,789,605	1,235,887	306,113	271,510	658,203
Sport coats and tailored jackets	974,443	446,467	137,250	98,144	211,142
Coats and jackets	2,965,191	966,723	367,931	157,362	465,252
Underwear	1,975,631	537,433	197,888	110,922	237,794
Hosiery	1,754,695	426,601	136,856	139,236	149,375
Nightwear	244,192	73,490	23,400	16,173	33,949
Accessories	2,914,027	1,188,686	408,206	278,939	517,949
Sweaters and vests	1,144,215	423,016	111,094	102,305	209,622
Active sportswear	2,651,230	706,968	206,156	218,660	285,019
Shirts	9,594,428	3,470,612	904,500	823,445	1,819,408
Pants	7,282,742	2,275,353	824,963	569,127	900,710
Shorts and shorts sets	1,723,299	445,720	119,813	75,434	266,170
Uniforms	463,965	93,804	29,981	15,197	48,593
Costumes	415,127	117,106	19,294	41,728	56,142
BOYS' (AGED 2 TO 15) APPAREL	**10,335,144**	**2,573,645**	**982,406**	**654,452**	**936,280**
Coats and jackets	696,529	178,647	56,306	55,610	66,682
Sweaters	346,520	102,020	30,881	19,272	51,785
Shirts	2,284,941	546,993	235,463	126,331	188,036
Underwear	554,665	100,526	29,925	38,969	30,301
Nightwear	380,242	172,373	64,800	52,978	53,812
Hosiery	581,410	155,494	54,844	46,780	53,710
Accessories	444,197	130,699	58,725	37,781	33,088
Suits, sport coats, and vests	301,170	75,581	14,906	15,367	45,350
Pants	2,603,554	561,482	224,719	132,104	204,757
Shorts and shorts sets	903,511	196,571	90,338	45,252	60,905
Uniforms	444,197	122,782	51,244	30,691	40,891
Active sportswear	498,850	139,063	44,438	32,432	62,223
Costumes	296,519	91,564	25,819	20,843	44,843
WOMEN'S APPAREL	**73,375,105**	**21,922,886**	**7,040,363**	**5,816,244**	**9,243,424**
Coats and jackets	5,682,701	1,789,602	419,119	586,701	795,114
Dresses	7,703,683	1,798,415	821,363	504,773	458,107
Sport coats and tailored jackets	1,018,630	384,926	73,463	142,208	169,288
Sweaters and vests	5,385,019	1,456,507	558,056	405,482	493,728
Shirts, blouses, and tops	14,059,657	4,165,631	1,332,225	1,127,387	1,742,997
Skirts	1,984,934	603,156	228,600	144,075	235,970
Pants	11,192,143	3,158,130	813,769	1,024,955	1,333,432
Shorts and shorts sets	1,463,990	528,919	187,931	134,269	211,142
Active sportswear	4,222,199	1,422,600	407,925	269,133	787,108
Nightwear	3,481,483	1,136,258	515,756	220,400	411,795
Undergarments	5,089,663	1,367,333	435,769	287,344	673,658
Hosiery	2,182,613	531,010	175,163	157,659	199,538
Suits	2,740,767	1,160,007	312,863	240,734	606,368
Accessories	5,880,381	2,038,901	691,650	452,559	929,034
Uniforms	694,204	188,206	24,863	55,440	107,927
Costumes	591,875	193,285	41,850	63,123	88,216

	total consumer units	$100,000 or more	$100,000– $119,999	$120,000– $149,999	$150,000 or more
GIRLS' (AGED 2 TO 15) APPAREL	**$12,511,943**	**$3,563,520**	**$1,338,806**	**$961,110**	**$1,266,446**
Coats and jackets	870,952	236,154	55,125	81,716	99,313
Dresses and suits	1,103,516	463,346	290,250	90,503	78,691
Shirts, blouses, and sweaters	2,784,954	862,462	227,250	283,608	354,183
Skirts and pants	2,827,978	676,497	236,363	188,011	252,185
Shorts and shorts sets	976,769	245,116	53,663	93,645	97,742
Active sportswear	1,168,634	340,564	179,269	39,479	128,094
Underwear and nightwear	730,251	161,768	52,763	38,630	70,279
Hosiery	438,383	96,344	34,200	35,658	24,930
Accessories	689,552	226,594	119,194	49,667	57,105
Uniforms	446,523	105,605	35,269	30,224	40,181
Costumes	476,756	149,071	55,463	29,927	63,692
CHILDREN'S (UNDER AGE 2) APPAREL	**9,129,300**	**2,262,059**	**817,200**	**627,326**	**815,888**
Coats, jackets, and snowsuits	288,379	79,166	20,869	15,027	43,323
Outerwear including dresses	2,409,363	583,140	203,794	155,707	223,607
Underwear	5,136,176	1,289,212	488,081	384,003	413,265
Nightwear and loungewear	405,824	107,696	33,413	23,475	50,873
Accessories	890,720	202,695	71,044	49,115	84,872
FOOTWEAR	**38,226,545**	**9,689,034**	**3,565,406**	**2,402,967**	**3,801,922**
Men's	12,868,929	3,477,184	1,381,556	866,150	1,246,887
Boys'	4,176,849	1,134,316	552,713	250,073	332,902
Women's	17,885,334	4,417,020	1,419,581	1,068,169	1,994,067
Girls'	3,295,432	660,514	211,556	218,575	228,066
OTHER APPAREL PRODUCTS AND SERVICES	**30,691,471**	**11,113,576**	**2,959,369**	**2,220,177**	**5,954,434**
Material for making clothes	1,517,480	344,298	47,475	73,608	237,085
Sewing patterns and notions	909,325	260,949	75,431	54,209	137,924
Watches	2,501,226	1,268,898	373,500	186,016	709,329
Jewelry	13,223,589	5,273,807	1,446,525	905,161	2,922,088
Shoe repair and other shoe services	130,236	56,462	12,713	11,546	32,175
Coin-operated apparel laundry and dry cleaning	4,053,591	166,398	77,569	37,781	50,974
Apparel alteration, repair, and tailoring services	595,364	217,632	64,406	60,109	93,182
Clothing rental	265,123	68,710	30,319	24,663	13,732
Watch and jewelry repair	444,197	141,752	30,544	40,158	71,141
Professional laundry, dry cleaning	6,997,851	3,307,948	799,988	825,695	1,682,193
Clothing storage	54,653	6,871	900	1,316	4,662

Note: Numbers may not add to total because of rounding and missing subcategories.
Source: Calculations by New Strategist based on the 2004 Consumer Expenditure Survey

Table 2.12 Apparel: Market shares by high-income consumer units, 2004

(percentage of total annual spending on apparel, accessories, and related services accounted for by before-tax income group of high-income consumer units, 2004)

	total consumer units	$100,000 or more	$100,000– $119,999	$120,000– $149,999	$150,000 or more
Share of total consumer units	100.0%	12.8%	4.8%	3.7%	4.4%
Share of total before-tax income	100.0	36.8	9.7	8.9	18.2
Share of total spending	100.0	27.7	8.4	7.3	12.0
Share of apparel spending	100.0	30.1	9.7	7.4	13.2
MEN'S APPAREL	100.0	33.6	10.3	7.9	15.9
Suits	100.0	44.3	11.0	9.7	23.6
Sport coats and tailored jackets	100.0	45.8	14.1	10.1	21.7
Coats and jackets	100.0	32.6	12.4	5.3	15.7
Underwear	100.0	27.2	10.0	5.6	12.0
Hosiery	100.0	24.3	7.8	7.9	8.5
Nightwear	100.0	30.1	9.6	6.6	13.9
Accessories	100.0	40.8	14.0	9.6	17.8
Sweaters and vests	100.0	37.0	9.7	8.9	18.3
Active sportswear	100.0	26.7	7.8	8.2	10.8
Shirts	100.0	36.2	9.4	8.6	19.0
Pants	100.0	31.2	11.3	7.8	12.4
Shorts and shorts sets	100.0	25.9	7.0	4.4	15.4
Uniforms	100.0	20.2	6.5	3.3	10.5
Costumes	100.0	28.2	4.6	10.1	13.5
BOYS' (AGED 2 TO 15) APPAREL	100.0	24.9	9.5	6.3	9.1
Coats and jackets	100.0	25.6	8.1	8.0	9.6
Sweaters	100.0	29.4	8.9	5.6	14.9
Shirts	100.0	23.9	10.3	5.5	8.2
Underwear	100.0	18.1	5.4	7.0	5.5
Nightwear	100.0	45.3	17.0	13.9	14.2
Hosiery	100.0	26.7	9.4	8.0	9.2
Accessories	100.0	29.4	13.2	8.5	7.4
Suits, sport coats, and vests	100.0	25.1	4.9	5.1	15.1
Pants	100.0	21.6	8.6	5.1	7.9
Shorts and shorts sets	100.0	21.8	10.0	5.0	6.7
Uniforms	100.0	27.6	11.5	6.9	9.2
Active sportswear	100.0	27.9	8.9	6.5	12.5
Costumes	100.0	30.9	8.7	7.0	15.1
WOMEN'S APPAREL	100.0	29.9	9.6	7.9	12.6
Coats and jackets	100.0	31.5	7.4	10.3	14.0
Dresses	100.0	23.3	10.7	6.6	5.9
Sport coats and tailored jackets	100.0	37.8	7.2	14.0	16.6
Sweaters and vests	100.0	27.0	10.4	7.5	9.2
Shirts, blouses, and tops	100.0	29.6	9.5	8.0	12.4
Skirts	100.0	30.4	11.5	7.3	11.9
Pants	100.0	28.2	7.3	9.2	11.9
Shorts and shorts sets	100.0	36.1	12.8	9.2	14.4
Active sportswear	100.0	33.7	9.7	6.4	18.6
Nightwear	100.0	32.6	14.8	6.3	11.8
Undergarments	100.0	26.9	8.6	5.6	13.2
Hosiery	100.0	24.3	8.0	7.2	9.1
Suits	100.0	42.3	11.4	8.8	22.1
Accessories	100.0	34.7	11.8	7.7	15.8
Uniforms	100.0	27.1	3.6	8.0	15.5
Costumes	100.0	32.7	7.1	10.7	14.9

	total consumer units	$100,000 or more	$100,000– $119,999	$120,000– $149,999	$150,000 or more
GIRLS' (AGED 2 TO 15) APPAREL	**100.0%**	**28.5%**	**10.7%**	**7.7%**	**10.1%**
Coats and jackets	100.0	27.1	6.3	9.4	11.4
Dresses and suits	100.0	42.0	26.3	8.2	7.1
Shirts, blouses, and sweaters	100.0	31.0	8.2	10.2	12.7
Skirts and pants	100.0	23.9	8.4	6.6	8.9
Shorts and shorts sets	100.0	25.1	5.5	9.6	10.0
Active sportswear	100.0	29.1	15.3	3.4	11.0
Underwear and nightwear	100.0	22.2	7.2	5.3	9.6
Hosiery	100.0	22.0	7.8	8.1	5.7
Accessories	100.0	32.9	17.3	7.2	8.3
Uniforms	100.0	23.7	7.9	6.8	9.0
Costumes	100.0	31.3	11.6	6.3	13.4
CHILDREN'S (UNDER AGE 2) APPAREL	**100.0**	**24.8**	**9.0**	**6.9**	**8.9**
Coats, jackets, and snowsuits	100.0	27.5	7.2	5.2	15.0
Outerwear including dresses	100.0	24.2	8.5	6.5	9.3
Underwear	100.0	25.1	9.5	7.5	8.0
Nightwear and loungewear	100.0	26.5	8.2	5.8	12.5
Accessories	100.0	22.8	8.0	5.5	9.5
FOOTWEAR	**100.0**	**25.3**	**9.3**	**6.3**	**9.9**
Men's	100.0	27.0	10.7	6.7	9.7
Boys'	100.0	27.2	13.2	6.0	8.0
Women's	100.0	24.7	7.9	6.0	11.1
Girls'	100.0	20.0	6.4	6.6	6.9
OTHER APPAREL PRODUCTS AND SERVICES	**100.0**	**36.2**	**9.6**	**7.2**	**19.4**
Material for making clothes	100.0	22.7	3.1	4.9	15.6
Sewing patterns and notions	100.0	28.7	8.3	6.0	15.2
Watches	100.0	50.7	14.9	7.4	28.4
Jewelry	100.0	39.9	10.9	6.8	22.1
Shoe repair and other shoe services	100.0	43.4	9.8	8.9	24.7
Coin-operated apparel laundry and dry cleaning	100.0	4.1	1.9	0.9	1.3
Apparel alteration, repair, and tailoring services	100.0	36.6	10.8	10.1	15.7
Clothing rental	100.0	25.9	11.4	9.3	5.2
Watch and jewelry repair	100.0	31.9	6.9	9.0	16.0
Professional laundry, dry cleaning	100.0	47.3	11.4	11.8	24.0
Clothing storage	100.0	12.6	1.6	2.4	8.5

Note: Numbers may not add to total because of rounding.
Source: Calculations by New Strategist based on the 2004 Consumer Expenditure Survey

Table 2.13 Apparel: Average spending by household type, 2004

(average annual spending of consumer units (CU) on apparel, accessories, and related services, by type of consumer unit, 2004)

	total married couples	married couples, no children	married couples with children				single parent, at least one child <18	single person
			total	oldest child under 6	oldest child 6 to 17	oldest child 18 or older		
Number of consumer units (in 000s)	59,797	25,585	29,279	5,604	15,376	8,300	6,892	33,686
Average number of persons per CU	3.2	2.0	3.9	3.5	4.1	3.9	2.9	1.0
Average before-tax income of CU	$73,001.00	$64,434.00	$79,764.00	$75,293.00	$78,508.00	$85,109.00	$31,055.00	$28,143.00
Average spending of CU, total	55,606.57	49,690.43	60,660.88	55,981.04	60,577.88	64,161.69	32,824.46	25,423.35
Apparel, average spending	**2,262.95**	**1,744.83**	**2,680.43**	**2,583.48**	**2,756.89**	**2,617.18**	**1,859.38**	**949.30**
MEN'S APPAREL	**423.04**	**369.16**	**469.30**	**443.11**	**455.87**	**515.74**	**110.75**	**153.20**
Suits	33.37	25.80	41.60	25.04	45.68	45.21	8.82	14.38
Sport coats and tailored jackets	11.48	11.90	12.01	8.98	11.84	14.37	4.58	4.91
Coats and jackets	35.93	23.73	42.61	30.72	47.71	41.51	24.96	5.75
Underwear	22.00	17.94	24.96	27.75	21.82	29.26	0.68	6.49
Hosiery	20.50	17.34	24.04	45.82	17.06	21.10	3.34	5.81
Nightwear	2.72	2.65	2.90	1.34	3.02	3.72	0.99	1.26
Accessories	35.03	32.78	36.36	31.93	33.36	46.18	3.51	10.26
Sweaters and vests	13.20	13.13	13.66	8.35	13.72	17.13	2.74	6.30
Active sportswear	28.76	24.09	31.32	16.08	30.03	46.25	12.33	9.94
Shirts	109.64	113.69	110.67	164.59	87.45	115.82	15.65	46.03
Pants	84.05	64.96	99.70	59.11	114.11	102.22	21.29	26.33
Shorts and shorts sets	16.60	13.45	17.39	10.79	19.01	19.30	4.23	10.44
Uniforms	5.06	3.56	6.50	6.42	7.12	5.41	4.84	2.29
Costumes	4.69	4.12	5.59	6.18	3.93	8.26	2.79	3.03
BOYS' (AGED 2 TO 15) APPAREL	**124.05**	**30.26**	**203.79**	**132.25**	**282.65**	**102.54**	**192.81**	**16.28**
Coats and jackets	7.56	1.91	12.27	6.08	18.61	4.69	19.33	0.78
Sweaters	3.25	1.07	5.03	2.95	7.45	1.97	8.98	1.53
Shirts	29.23	6.17	48.79	27.48	65.48	31.09	27.51	3.77
Underwear	5.86	1.17	9.35	7.56	12.37	4.50	11.59	1.39
Nightwear	4.61	1.57	7.63	7.25	10.44	2.06	7.60	1.02
Hosiery	6.81	1.65	10.88	6.09	16.25	3.51	10.58	1.23
Accessories	6.37	1.00	10.40	12.51	11.56	6.29	3.43	0.72
Suits, sport coats, and vests	4.12	1.23	6.71	3.14	6.04	10.37	3.03	0.20
Pants	30.96	7.47	51.39	32.35	73.27	23.70	54.66	3.58
Shorts and shorts sets	10.37	3.09	16.74	11.81	25.31	4.20	20.85	0.83
Uniforms	5.20	1.56	8.30	3.88	13.00	2.57	9.84	0.18
Active sportswear	5.95	1.78	9.64	5.43	14.23	3.98	9.74	0.63
Costumes	3.75	0.61	6.66	5.71	8.66	3.60	5.67	0.42
WOMEN'S APPAREL	**743.46**	**706.46**	**781.95**	**719.41**	**671.30**	**1,061.01**	**608.14**	**401.20**
Coats and jackets	53.49	52.99	59.04	33.14	51.59	95.35	39.42	45.17
Dresses	62.80	68.61	56.35	45.17	48.92	80.82	57.30	37.22
Sport coats and tailored jackets	10.50	11.94	9.96	6.62	8.82	14.35	7.94	5.89
Sweaters and vests	57.81	57.96	60.18	65.59	48.33	80.56	33.13	32.46
Shirts, blouses, and tops	148.99	120.89	172.91	172.79	134.64	252.89	112.74	75.49
Skirts	20.71	21.47	19.36	26.72	12.56	27.63	17.44	12.08
Pants	114.60	93.55	126.64	123.71	103.02	178.27	107.76	52.87
Shorts and shorts sets	18.43	17.08	20.65	15.20	21.71	22.84	9.05	5.74
Active sportswear	44.33	44.18	42.54	50.49	34.60	52.71	39.28	22.88
Nightwear	36.59	34.33	40.09	29.45	37.16	54.74	25.09	16.39
Undergarments	49.89	54.07	47.29	55.39	36.79	62.71	43.33	28.37
Hosiery	21.32	20.84	21.98	17.77	17.99	33.70	20.81	11.51
Suits	31.21	36.66	28.14	24.30	28.87	29.40	17.78	13.19
Accessories	58.35	58.41	60.81	38.52	73.91	51.37	63.93	36.60
Uniforms	7.30	6.89	7.75	5.17	6.62	11.57	7.94	2.94
Costumes	7.11	6.58	8.27	9.39	5.80	12.10	5.22	2.39

	total married couples	married couples, no children	married couples with children				single parent, at least one child <18	single person
			total	oldest child under 6	oldest child 6 to 17	oldest child 18 or older		
GIRLS' (AGED 2 TO 15) APPAREL	**$153.49**	**$34.68**	**$251.44**	**$153.74**	**$351.50**	**$127.87**	**$271.69**	**$14.42**
Coats and jackets	9.72	2.43	15.74	11.87	22.58	5.70	22.78	1.63
Dresses and suits	14.28	6.12	20.41	23.07	27.84	2.77	19.80	2.04
Shirts, blouses, and sweaters	36.03	4.98	60.39	26.31	83.27	39.99	41.56	2.34
Skirts and pants	32.98	8.97	52.21	26.09	76.78	24.33	66.84	4.39
Shorts and shorts sets	11.53	2.00	18.98	14.27	27.17	7.00	26.16	0.94
Active sportswear	15.89	2.16	29.39	22.81	36.75	19.32	23.96	0.18
Underwear and nightwear	8.51	2.15	13.43	11.88	18.23	5.58	18.51	1.02
Hosiery	5.03	0.52	8.32	2.62	12.14	4.92	11.27	0.54
Accessories	8.44	2.95	13.67	3.74	19.18	10.12	16.52	0.53
Uniforms	4.84	1.18	7.96	2.51	12.48	3.28	15.21	0.56
Costumes	6.24	1.23	10.94	8.57	15.08	4.88	9.08	0.26
CHILDREN'S (UNDER AGE 2) APPAREL	**115.90**	**42.22**	**167.70**	**518.11**	**99.68**	**35.27**	**88.50**	**11.97**
Coats, jackets, and snowsuits	3.52	1.31	5.03	16.11	2.61	2.03	1.67	0.98
Outerwear including dresses	29.18	18.99	35.47	101.54	21.56	16.63	12.93	6.86
Underwear	67.42	14.74	104.60	338.80	59.51	10.64	61.09	2.07
Nightwear and loungewear	4.91	3.39	6.07	19.21	2.90	3.05	1.90	1.07
Accessories	10.87	3.78	16.54	42.45	13.09	2.92	10.92	1.00
FOOTWEAR	**389.30**	**255.28**	**485.03**	**323.31**	**544.89**	**489.95**	**423.85**	**185.90**
Men's	139.08	93.48	166.78	103.24	171.76	207.41	29.88	67.60
Boys'	46.73	8.97	78.78	32.81	123.52	22.32	94.53	8.59
Women's	162.51	148.26	164.78	128.50	138.82	248.09	218.08	106.27
Girls'	40.97	4.57	74.68	58.77	110.79	12.13	81.38	3.44
OTHER APPAREL PRODUCTS AND SERVICES	**313.71**	**306.77**	**321.23**	**293.54**	**350.99**	**284.81**	**163.63**	**166.33**
Material for making clothes	11.35	10.76	11.66	5.87	15.59	8.12	0.41	5.72
Sewing patterns and notions	9.76	11.41	7.52	4.86	8.12	8.42	2.14	5.22
Watches	30.79	18.69	42.45	44.08	47.10	32.73	8.61	8.81
Jewelry	142.14	155.45	133.09	101.51	150.41	122.34	40.29	63.19
Shoe repair and other shoe services	1.51	2.15	1.04	0.89	0.97	1.28	0.16	0.92
Coin-operated apparel laundry and dry cleaning	22.96	15.74	25.88	37.86	27.36	15.05	75.27	36.10
Apparel alteration, repair, and tailoring services	6.34	8.49	5.13	5.08	4.49	6.36	2.74	3.96
Clothing rental	3.14	2.47	3.85	3.42	3.53	4.75	1.58	0.72
Watch and jewelry repair	5.75	6.64	4.84	5.12	5.41	3.60	2.76	1.58
Professional laundry, dry cleaning	79.73	74.68	85.57	84.85	87.73	82.04	29.65	39.47
Clothing storage	0.25	0.29	0.19	–	0.29	0.12	–	0.65

Note: Average spending figures for total consumer units can be found on Average Spending by Age and Average Spending by Region tables. Subcategories may not add to total because some are not shown. "–" means sample is too small to make a reliable estimate.
Source: Bureau of Labor Statistics, unpublished data from the 2004 Consumer Expenditure Survey

Table 2.14 Apparel: Indexed spending by household type, 2004

(indexed average annual spending of consumer units (CU) on apparel, accessories, and related services, by type of consumer unit, 2004; index definition: an index of 100 is the average for all consumer units; an index of 132 means that spending by consumer units in that group is 32 percent above the average for all consumer units; an index of 68 indicates spending that is 32 percent below the average for all consumer units)

	total married couples	married couples, no children	married couples with children				single parent, at least one child <18	single person
			total	oldest child under 6	oldest child 6 to 17	oldest child 18 or older		
Average spending of CU, total	$55,607	$49,690	$60,661	$55,981	$60,578	$64,162	$32,824	$25,423
Average spending of CU, index	128	115	140	129	140	148	76	59
Apparel, spending index	**125**	**96**	**148**	**142**	**152**	**144**	**102**	**52**
MEN'S APPAREL	**133**	**116**	**148**	**140**	**144**	**163**	**35**	**48**
Suits	139	108	173	104	190	188	37	60
Sport coats and tailored jackets	137	142	143	107	141	171	55	59
Coats and jackets	141	93	167	120	187	163	98	23
Underwear	129	106	147	163	128	172	4	38
Hosiery	136	115	159	304	113	140	22	39
Nightwear	130	126	138	64	144	177	47	60
Accessories	140	131	145	127	133	184	14	41
Sweaters and vests	134	133	139	85	139	174	28	64
Active sportswear	126	106	137	71	132	203	54	44
Shirts	133	138	134	199	106	140	19	56
Pants	134	104	159	94	182	163	34	42
Shorts and shorts sets	112	91	117	73	128	130	29	70
Uniforms	127	89	163	161	178	136	121	57
Costumes	131	115	157	173	110	231	78	85
BOYS' (AGED 2 TO 15) APPAREL	**140**	**34**	**229**	**149**	**318**	**115**	**217**	**18**
Coats and jackets	126	32	205	102	311	78	323	13
Sweaters	109	36	169	99	250	66	301	51
Shirts	149	31	248	140	333	158	140	19
Underwear	123	25	196	158	259	94	243	29
Nightwear	141	48	233	222	319	63	232	31
Hosiery	136	33	218	122	325	70	212	25
Accessories	167	26	272	327	303	165	90	19
Suits, sport coats, and vests	159	47	259	121	233	400	117	8
Pants	138	33	230	144	327	106	244	16
Shorts and shorts sets	133	40	215	152	326	54	268	11
Uniforms	136	41	217	102	340	67	258	5
Active sportswear	139	41	225	127	332	93	227	15
Costumes	147	24	261	224	340	141	222	16
WOMEN'S APPAREL	**118**	**112**	**124**	**114**	**106**	**168**	**96**	**64**
Coats and jackets	109	108	121	68	106	195	81	92
Dresses	95	104	85	68	74	122	86	56
Sport coats and tailored jackets	120	136	114	76	101	164	91	67
Sweaters and vests	125	125	130	142	104	174	72	70
Shirts, blouses, and tops	123	100	143	143	111	209	93	62
Skirts	121	126	113	157	74	162	102	71
Pants	119	97	132	129	107	185	112	55
Shorts and shorts sets	146	136	164	121	172	181	72	46
Active sportswear	122	122	117	139	95	145	108	63
Nightwear	122	115	134	98	124	183	84	55
Undergarments	114	124	108	127	84	143	99	65
Hosiery	114	111	117	95	96	180	111	61
Suits	132	156	119	103	122	125	75	56
Accessories	115	116	120	76	146	102	126	72
Uniforms	122	115	130	87	111	194	133	49
Costumes	140	129	162	184	114	238	103	47

	total married couples	married couples, no children	married couples with children				single parent, at least one child <18	single person
			total	oldest child under 6	oldest child 6 to 17	oldest child 18 or older		
GIRLS' (AGED 2 TO 15) APPAREL	**143**	**32**	**234**	**143**	**327**	**119**	**253**	**13**
Coats and jackets	130	32	210	158	301	76	304	22
Dresses and suits	150	64	215	243	293	29	209	21
Shirts, blouses, and sweaters	150	21	252	110	348	167	174	10
Skirts and pants	136	37	215	107	316	100	275	18
Shorts and shorts sets	137	24	226	170	323	83	311	11
Active sportswear	158	21	292	227	366	192	238	2
Underwear and nightwear	136	34	214	189	290	89	295	16
Hosiery	133	14	221	69	322	131	299	14
Accessories	142	50	231	63	323	171	279	9
Uniforms	126	31	207	65	325	85	396	15
Costumes	152	30	267	209	368	119	221	6
CHILDREN'S (UNDER AGE 2) APPAREL	**148**	**54**	**214**	**660**	**127**	**45**	**113**	**15**
Coats, jackets, and snowsuits	142	53	203	650	105	82	67	40
Outerwear including dresses	141	92	171	490	104	80	62	33
Underwear	153	33	237	767	135	24	138	5
Nightwear and loungewear	141	97	174	550	83	87	54	31
Accessories	142	49	216	554	171	38	143	13
FOOTWEAR	**118**	**78**	**148**	**98**	**166**	**149**	**129**	**57**
Men's	126	84	151	93	155	187	27	61
Boys'	130	25	219	91	344	62	263	24
Women's	106	96	107	84	90	161	142	69
Girls'	145	16	264	207	391	43	287	12
OTHER APPAREL PRODUCTS AND SERVICES	**119**	**116**	**122**	**111**	**133**	**108**	**62**	**63**
Material for making clothes	87	82	89	45	119	62	3	44
Sewing patterns and notions	125	146	96	62	104	108	27	67
Watches	143	87	197	205	219	152	40	41
Jewelry	125	137	117	89	132	108	35	56
Shoe repair and other shoe services	135	192	93	79	87	114	14	82
Coin-operated apparel laundry and dry cleaning	66	45	74	109	78	43	216	104
Apparel alteration, repair, and tailoring services	124	166	100	99	88	124	54	77
Clothing rental	138	108	169	150	155	208	69	32
Watch and jewelry repair	151	174	127	134	142	94	72	41
Professional laundry, dry cleaning	132	124	142	141	146	136	49	66
Clothing storage	53	62	40	–	62	26	–	138

Note: Spending index for total consumer units is 100. "–" means sample is too small to make a reliable estimate.
Source: Calculations by New Strategist based on the 2004 Consumer Expenditure Survey

Table 2.15 Apparel: Total spending by household type, 2004

(total annual spending on apparel, accessories, and related services, by consumer unit (CU) type, 2004; consumer units and dollars in thousands)

	total married couples	married couples, no children	married couples with children				single parent, at least one child <18	single person
			total	oldest child under 6	oldest child 6 to 17	oldest child 18 or older		
Number of consumer units	59,797	25,585	29,279	5,604	15,376	8,300	6,892	33,686
Total spending of all CUs	$3,325,106,066	$1,271,329,652	$1,776,089,906	$313,717,748	$931,445,483	$532,542,027	$226,226,178	$856,410,968
Apparel, total spending	**135,317,621**	**44,641,476**	**78,480,310**	**14,477,822**	**42,389,941**	**21,722,594**	**12,814,847**	**31,978,120**
MEN'S APPAREL	**25,296,523**	**9,444,959**	**13,740,635**	**2,483,188**	**7,009,457**	**4,280,642**	**763,289**	**5,160,695**
Suits	1,995,426	660,093	1,218,006	140,324	702,376	375,243	60,787	484,405
Sport coats and tailored jackets	686,470	304,462	351,641	50,324	182,052	119,271	31,565	165,398
Coats and jackets	2,148,506	607,132	1,247,578	172,155	733,589	344,533	172,024	193,695
Underwear	1,315,534	458,995	730,804	155,511	335,504	242,858	4,687	218,622
Hosiery	1,225,839	443,644	703,867	256,775	262,315	175,130	23,019	195,716
Nightwear	162,648	67,800	84,909	7,509	46,436	30,876	6,823	42,444
Accessories	2,094,689	838,676	1,064,584	178,936	512,943	383,294	24,191	345,618
Sweaters and vests	789,320	335,931	399,951	46,793	210,959	142,179	18,884	212,222
Active sportswear	1,719,762	616,343	917,018	90,112	461,741	383,875	84,978	334,839
Shirts	6,556,143	2,908,759	3,240,307	922,362	1,344,631	961,306	107,860	1,550,567
Pants	5,025,938	1,662,002	2,919,116	331,252	1,754,555	848,426	146,731	886,952
Shorts and shorts sets	992,630	344,118	509,162	60,467	292,298	160,190	29,153	351,682
Uniforms	302,573	91,083	190,314	35,978	109,477	44,903	33,357	77,141
Costumes	280,448	105,410	163,670	34,633	60,428	68,558	19,229	102,069
BOYS' (AGED 2 TO 15) APPAREL	**7,417,818**	**774,202**	**5,966,767**	**741,129**	**4,346,026**	**851,082**	**1,328,847**	**548,408**
Coats and jackets	452,065	48,867	359,253	34,072	286,147	38,927	133,222	26,275
Sweaters	194,340	27,376	147,273	16,532	114,551	16,351	61,890	51,540
Shirts	1,747,866	157,859	1,428,522	153,998	1,006,820	258,047	189,599	126,996
Underwear	350,410	29,934	273,759	42,366	190,201	37,350	79,878	46,824
Nightwear	275,664	40,168	223,399	40,629	160,525	17,098	52,379	34,360
Hosiery	407,218	42,215	318,556	34,128	249,860	29,133	72,917	41,434
Accessories	380,907	25,585	304,502	70,106	177,747	52,207	23,640	24,254
Suits, sport coats, and vests	246,364	31,470	196,462	17,597	92,871	86,071	20,883	6,737
Pants	1,851,315	191,120	1,504,648	181,289	1,126,600	196,710	376,717	120,596
Shorts and shorts sets	620,095	79,058	490,130	66,183	389,167	34,860	143,698	27,959
Uniforms	310,944	39,913	243,016	21,744	199,888	21,331	67,817	6,063
Active sportswear	355,792	45,541	282,250	30,430	218,800	33,034	67,128	21,222
Costumes	224,239	15,607	194,998	31,999	133,156	29,880	39,078	14,148
WOMEN'S APPAREL	**44,456,678**	**18,074,779**	**22,894,714**	**4,031,574**	**10,321,909**	**8,806,383**	**4,191,301**	**13,514,823**
Coats and jackets	3,198,542	1,355,749	1,728,632	185,717	793,248	791,405	271,683	1,521,597
Dresses	3,755,252	1,755,387	1,649,872	253,133	752,194	670,806	394,912	1,253,793
Sport coats and tailored jackets	627,869	305,485	291,619	37,098	135,616	119,105	54,722	198,411
Sweaters and vests	3,456,865	1,482,907	1,762,010	367,566	743,122	668,648	228,332	1,093,448
Shirts, blouses, and tops	8,909,155	3,092,971	5,062,632	968,315	2,070,225	2,098,987	777,004	2,542,956
Skirts	1,238,396	549,310	566,841	149,739	193,123	229,329	120,196	406,927
Pants	6,852,736	2,393,477	3,707,893	693,271	1,584,036	1,479,641	742,682	1,780,979
Shorts and shorts sets	1,102,059	436,992	604,611	85,181	333,813	189,572	62,373	193,358
Active sportswear	2,650,801	1,130,345	1,245,529	282,946	532,010	437,493	270,718	770,736
Nightwear	2,187,972	878,333	1,173,795	165,038	571,372	454,342	172,920	552,114
Undergarments	2,983,272	1,383,381	1,384,604	310,406	565,683	520,493	298,630	955,672
Hosiery	1,274,872	533,191	643,552	99,583	276,614	279,710	143,423	387,726
Suits	1,866,264	937,946	823,911	136,177	443,905	244,020	122,540	444,318
Accessories	3,489,155	1,494,420	1,780,456	215,866	1,136,440	426,371	440,606	1,232,908
Uniforms	436,518	176,281	226,912	28,973	101,789	96,031	54,722	99,037
Costumes	425,157	168,349	242,137	52,622	89,181	100,430	35,976	80,510

	total married couples	married couples, no children	married couples with children				single parent, at least one child <18	single person
			total	oldest child under 6	oldest child 6 to 17	oldest child 18 or older		
GIRLS' (AGED 2 TO 15) APPAREL	**$9,178,242**	**$887,288**	**$7,361,912**	**$861,559**	**$5,404,664**	**$1,061,321**	**$1,872,487**	**$485,752**
Coats and jackets	581,227	62,172	460,851	66,519	347,190	47,310	157,000	54,908
Dresses and suits	853,901	156,580	597,584	129,284	428,068	22,991	136,462	68,719
Shirts, blouses, and sweaters	2,154,486	127,413	1,768,159	147,441	1,280,360	331,917	286,432	78,825
Skirts and pants	1,972,105	229,497	1,528,657	146,208	1,180,569	201,939	460,661	147,882
Shorts and shorts sets	689,459	51,170	555,715	79,969	417,766	58,100	180,295	31,665
Active sportswear	950,174	55,264	860,510	127,827	565,068	160,356	165,132	6,063
Underwear and nightwear	508,872	55,008	393,217	66,576	280,304	46,314	127,571	34,360
Hosiery	300,779	13,304	243,601	14,682	186,665	40,836	77,673	18,190
Accessories	504,687	75,476	400,244	20,959	294,912	83,996	113,856	17,854
Uniforms	289,417	30,190	233,061	14,066	191,892	27,224	104,827	18,864
Costumes	373,133	31,470	320,312	48,026	231,870	40,504	62,579	8,758
CHILDREN'S (UNDER AGE 2) APPAREL	**6,930,472**	**1,080,199**	**4,910,088**	**2,903,488**	**1,532,680**	**292,741**	**609,942**	**403,221**
Coats, jackets, and snowsuits	210,485	33,516	147,273	90,280	40,131	16,849	11,510	33,012
Outerwear including dresses	1,744,876	485,859	1,038,526	569,030	331,507	138,029	89,114	231,086
Underwear	4,031,514	377,123	3,062,583	1,898,635	915,026	88,312	421,032	69,730
Nightwear and loungewear	293,603	86,733	177,724	107,653	44,590	25,315	13,095	36,044
Accessories	649,993	96,711	484,275	237,890	201,272	24,236	75,261	33,686
FOOTWEAR	**23,278,972**	**6,531,339**	**14,201,193**	**1,811,829**	**8,378,229**	**4,066,585**	**2,921,174**	**6,262,227**
Men's	8,316,567	2,391,686	4,883,152	578,557	2,640,982	1,721,503	205,933	2,277,174
Boys'	2,794,314	229,497	2,306,600	183,867	1,899,244	185,256	651,501	289,363
Women's	9,717,610	3,793,232	4,824,594	720,114	2,134,496	2,059,147	1,503,007	3,579,811
Girls'	2,449,883	116,923	2,186,556	329,347	1,703,507	100,679	560,871	115,880
OTHER APPAREL PRODUCTS, SERVICES	**18,758,917**	**7,848,710**	**9,405,293**	**1,644,998**	**5,396,822**	**2,363,923**	**1,127,738**	**5,602,992**
Material for making clothes	678,696	275,295	341,393	32,895	239,712	67,396	2,826	192,684
Sewing patterns and notions	583,619	291,925	220,178	27,235	124,853	69,886	14,749	175,841
Watches	1,841,150	478,184	1,242,894	247,024	724,210	271,659	59,340	296,774
Jewelry	8,499,546	3,977,188	3,896,742	568,862	2,312,704	1,015,422	277,679	2,128,618
Shoe repair and other shoe services	90,293	55,008	30,450	4,988	14,915	10,624	1,103	30,991
Coin-operated apparel laundry and dry cleaning	1,372,939	402,708	757,741	212,167	420,687	124,915	518,761	1,216,065
Apparel alteration, repair, and tailoring services	379,113	217,217	150,201	28,468	69,038	52,788	18,884	133,397
Clothing rental	187,763	63,195	112,724	19,166	54,277	39,425	10,889	24,254
Watch and jewelry repair	343,833	169,884	141,710	28,692	83,184	29,880	19,022	53,224
Professional laundry, dry cleaning	4,767,615	1,910,688	2,505,404	475,499	1,348,936	680,932	204,348	1,329,586
Clothing storage	14,949	7,420	5,563	–	4,459	996	–	21,896

Note: Total spending figures for total consumer units can be found on Total Spending by Age and Total Spending by Region tables. Spending by type of consumer unit will not add to total because not all types of consumer units are shown. Numbers may not add to category total because of rounding and missing subcategories. "–" means sample is too small to make a reliable estimate.
Source: Calculations by New Strategist based on the 2004 Consumer Expenditure Survey

Table 2.16 Apparel: Market shares by household type, 2004

(percentage of total annual spending on apparel, accessories, and related services accounted for by types of consumer units, 2004)

	total married couples	married couples, no children	married couples with children				single parent, at least one child <18	single person
			total	oldest child under 6	oldest child 6 to 17	oldest child 18 or older		
Share of total consumer units	51.4%	22.0%	25.2%	4.8%	13.2%	7.1%	5.9%	29.0%
Share of total before-tax income	68.9	26.0	36.9	6.7	19.1	11.2	3.4	15.0
Share of total spending	65.9	25.2	35.2	6.2	18.5	10.6	4.5	17.0
Share of apparel spending	64.1	21.1	37.2	6.9	20.1	10.3	6.1	15.1
MEN'S APPAREL	**68.6**	**25.6**	**37.2**	**6.7**	**19.0**	**11.6**	**2.1**	**14.0**
Suits	71.5	23.7	43.7	5.0	25.2	13.5	2.2	17.4
Sport coats and tailored jackets	70.4	31.2	36.1	5.2	18.7	12.2	3.2	17.0
Coats and jackets	72.5	20.5	42.1	5.8	24.7	11.6	5.8	6.5
Underwear	66.6	23.2	37.0	7.9	17.0	12.3	0.2	11.1
Hosiery	69.9	25.3	40.1	14.6	14.9	10.0	1.3	11.2
Nightwear	66.6	27.8	34.8	3.1	19.0	12.6	2.8	17.4
Accessories	71.9	28.8	36.5	6.1	17.6	13.2	0.8	11.9
Sweaters and vests	69.0	29.4	35.0	4.1	18.4	12.4	1.7	18.5
Active sportswear	64.9	23.2	34.6	3.4	17.4	14.5	3.2	12.6
Shirts	68.3	30.3	33.8	9.6	14.0	10.0	1.1	16.2
Pants	69.0	22.8	40.1	4.5	24.1	11.6	2.0	12.2
Shorts and shorts sets	57.6	20.0	29.5	3.5	17.0	9.3	1.7	20.4
Uniforms	65.2	19.6	41.0	7.8	23.6	9.7	7.2	16.6
Costumes	67.6	25.4	39.4	8.3	14.6	16.5	4.6	24.6
BOYS' (AGED 2 TO 15) APPAREL	**71.8**	**7.5**	**57.7**	**7.2**	**42.1**	**8.2**	**12.9**	**5.3**
Coats and jackets	64.9	7.0	51.6	4.9	41.1	5.6	19.1	3.8
Sweaters	56.1	7.9	42.5	4.8	33.1	4.7	17.9	14.9
Shirts	76.5	6.9	62.5	6.7	44.1	11.3	8.3	5.6
Underwear	63.2	5.4	49.4	7.6	34.3	6.7	14.4	8.4
Nightwear	72.5	10.6	58.8	10.7	42.2	4.5	13.8	9.0
Hosiery	70.0	7.3	54.8	5.9	43.0	5.0	12.5	7.1
Accessories	85.8	5.8	68.6	15.8	40.0	11.8	5.3	5.5
Suits, sport coats, and vests	81.8	10.4	65.2	5.8	30.8	28.6	6.9	2.2
Pants	71.1	7.3	57.8	7.0	43.3	7.6	14.5	4.6
Shorts and shorts sets	68.6	8.8	54.2	7.3	43.1	3.9	15.9	3.1
Uniforms	70.0	9.0	54.7	4.9	45.0	4.8	15.3	1.4
Active sportswear	71.3	9.1	56.6	6.1	43.9	6.6	13.5	4.3
Costumes	75.6	5.3	65.8	10.8	44.9	10.1	13.2	4.8
WOMEN'S APPAREL	**60.6**	**24.6**	**31.2**	**5.5**	**14.1**	**12.0**	**5.7**	**18.4**
Coats and jackets	56.3	23.9	30.4	3.3	14.0	13.9	4.8	26.8
Dresses	48.7	22.8	21.4	3.3	9.8	8.7	5.1	16.3
Sport coats and tailored jackets	61.6	30.0	28.6	3.6	13.3	11.7	5.4	19.5
Sweaters and vests	64.2	27.5	32.7	6.8	13.8	12.4	4.2	20.3
Shirts, blouses, and tops	63.4	22.0	36.0	6.9	14.7	14.9	5.5	18.1
Skirts	62.4	27.7	28.6	7.5	9.7	11.6	6.1	20.5
Pants	61.2	21.4	33.1	6.2	14.2	13.2	6.6	15.9
Shorts and shorts sets	75.3	29.8	41.3	5.8	22.8	12.9	4.3	13.2
Active sportswear	62.8	26.8	29.5	6.7	12.6	10.4	6.4	18.3
Nightwear	62.8	25.2	33.7	4.7	16.4	13.1	5.0	15.9
Undergarments	58.6	27.2	27.2	6.1	11.1	10.2	5.9	18.8
Hosiery	58.4	24.4	29.5	4.6	12.7	12.8	6.6	17.8
Suits	68.1	34.2	30.1	5.0	16.2	8.9	4.5	16.2
Accessories	59.3	25.4	30.3	3.7	19.3	7.3	7.5	21.0
Uniforms	62.9	25.4	32.7	4.2	14.7	13.8	7.9	14.3
Costumes	71.8	28.4	40.9	8.9	15.1	17.0	6.1	13.6

	total married couples	married couples, no children	married couples with children				single parent, at least one child <18	single person
			total	oldest child under 6	oldest child 6 to 17	oldest child 18 or older		
GIRLS' (AGED 2 TO 15) APPAREL	**73.4%**	**7.1%**	**58.8%**	**6.9%**	**43.2%**	**8.5%**	**15.0%**	**3.9%**
Coats and jackets	66.7	7.1	52.9	7.6	39.9	5.4	18.0	6.3
Dresses and suits	77.4	14.2	54.2	11.7	38.8	2.1	12.4	6.2
Shirts, blouses, and sweaters	77.4	4.6	63.5	5.3	46.0	11.9	10.3	2.8
Skirts and pants	69.7	8.1	54.1	5.2	41.7	7.1	16.3	5.2
Shorts and shorts sets	70.6	5.2	56.9	8.2	42.8	5.9	18.5	3.2
Active sportswear	81.3	4.7	73.6	10.9	48.4	13.7	14.1	0.5
Underwear and nightwear	69.7	7.5	53.8	9.1	38.4	6.3	17.5	4.7
Hosiery	68.6	3.0	55.6	3.3	42.6	9.3	17.7	4.1
Accessories	73.2	10.9	58.0	3.0	42.8	12.2	16.5	2.6
Uniforms	64.8	6.8	52.2	3.2	43.0	6.1	23.5	4.2
Costumes	78.3	6.6	67.2	10.1	48.6	8.5	13.1	1.8
CHILDREN'S (UNDER AGE 2) APPAREL	**75.9**	**11.8**	**53.8**	**31.8**	**16.8**	**3.2**	**6.7**	**4.4**
Coats, jackets, and snowsuits	73.0	11.6	51.1	31.3	13.9	5.8	4.0	11.4
Outerwear including dresses	72.4	20.2	43.1	23.6	13.8	5.7	3.7	9.6
Underwear	78.5	7.3	59.6	37.0	17.8	1.7	8.2	1.4
Nightwear and loungewear	72.3	21.4	43.8	26.5	11.0	6.2	3.2	8.9
Accessories	73.0	10.9	54.4	26.7	22.6	2.7	8.4	3.8
FOOTWEAR	**60.9**	**17.1**	**37.2**	**4.7**	**21.9**	**10.6**	**7.6**	**16.4**
Men's	64.6	18.6	37.9	4.5	20.5	13.4	1.6	17.7
Boys'	66.9	5.5	55.2	4.4	45.5	4.4	15.6	6.9
Women's	54.3	21.2	27.0	4.0	11.9	11.5	8.4	20.0
Girls'	74.3	3.5	66.4	10.0	51.7	3.1	17.0	3.5
OTHER APPAREL PRODUCTS AND SERVICES	**61.1**	**25.6**	**30.6**	**5.4**	**17.6**	**7.7**	**3.7**	**18.3**
Material for making clothes	44.7	18.1	22.5	2.2	15.8	4.4	0.2	12.7
Sewing patterns and notions	64.2	32.1	24.2	3.0	13.7	7.7	1.6	19.3
Watches	73.6	19.1	49.7	9.9	29.0	10.9	2.4	11.9
Jewelry	64.3	30.1	29.5	4.3	17.5	7.7	2.1	16.1
Shoe repair and other shoe services	69.3	42.2	23.4	3.8	11.5	8.2	0.8	23.8
Coin-operated apparel laundry and dry cleaning	33.9	9.9	18.7	5.2	10.4	3.1	12.8	30.0
Apparel alteration, repair, and tailoring services	63.7	36.5	25.2	4.8	11.6	8.9	3.2	22.4
Clothing rental	70.8	23.8	42.5	7.2	20.5	14.9	4.1	9.1
Watch and jewelry repair	77.4	38.2	31.9	6.5	18.7	6.7	4.3	12.0
Professional laundry, dry cleaning	68.1	27.3	35.8	6.8	19.3	9.7	2.9	19.0
Clothing storage	27.4	13.6	10.2	–	8.2	1.8	–	40.1

Note: Market share for total consumer units is 100.0%. Market shares by type of consumer unit will not add to total because not all types of consumer units are shown. "–" means sample is too small to make a reliable estimate.
Source: Calculations by New Strategist based on the 2004 Consumer Expenditure Survey

Table 2.17 Apparel: Average spending by race and Hispanic origin, 2004

(average annual spending of consumer units (CU) on apparel, accessories, and related services, by race and Hispanic origin of consumer unit reference person, 2004)

	total consumer units	Asian	black	Hispanic	non-Hispanic white and other
Number of consumer units (in 000s)	116,282	3,957	13,773	12,298	90,424
Average number of persons per CU	2.5	2.8	2.6	3.3	2.3
Average before-tax income of CU	$54,453.00	$67,705.00	$38,503.00	$43,693.00	$58,314.00
Average spending of CU, total	43,394.87	49,458.68	30,481.49	37,578.03	46,163.26
Apparel, average spending	**1,815.95**	**1,884.52**	**1,764.69**	**1,816.62**	**1,830.08**
MEN'S APPAREL	**317.28**	**446.41**	**213.87**	**289.78**	**336.66**
Suits	23.99	18.67	30.16	19.30	23.64
Sport coats and tailored jackets	8.38	5.85	3.76	7.44	9.21
Coats and jackets	25.50	123.65	15.71	23.62	27.24
Underwear	16.99	14.03	12.89	16.11	17.73
Hosiery	15.09	10.09	7.63	13.81	16.40
Nightwear	2.10	1.45	1.57	2.28	2.16
Accessories	25.06	20.69	16.27	22.06	26.80
Sweaters and vests	9.84	11.03	6.79	9.34	10.41
Active sportswear	22.80	13.88	5.60	16.43	26.32
Shirts	82.51	117.65	50.48	64.23	89.92
Pants	62.63	94.78	43.73	77.40	63.37
Shorts and shorts sets	14.82	11.21	13.12	11.38	15.54
Uniforms	3.99	2.34	5.16	5.22	3.64
Costumes	3.57	1.10	1.01	1.17	4.28
BOYS' (AGED 2 TO 15) APPAREL	**88.88**	**101.20**	**119.92**	**122.82**	**79.46**
Coats and jackets	5.99	7.00	9.07	8.87	5.13
Sweaters	2.98	3.51	3.54	3.71	2.80
Shirts	19.65	18.25	20.93	26.47	18.45
Underwear	4.77	11.04	6.11	7.28	4.19
Nightwear	3.27	3.52	8.37	5.40	2.17
Hosiery	5.00	6.21	11.31	5.50	3.95
Accessories	3.82	1.56	2.13	1.91	4.34
Suits, sport coats, and vests	2.59	4.34	7.07	3.14	1.83
Pants	22.39	22.04	29.06	32.58	20.02
Shorts and shorts sets	7.77	6.19	9.83	12.53	6.84
Uniforms	3.82	9.10	7.21	5.68	3.08
Active sportswear	4.29	5.21	3.15	6.78	4.11
Costumes	2.55	3.23	2.14	2.96	2.55
WOMEN'S APPAREL	**631.01**	**613.61**	**544.45**	**472.94**	**670.99**
Coats and jackets	48.87	42.77	50.31	19.63	52.68
Dresses	66.25	66.72	45.20	54.17	72.07
Sport coats and tailored jackets	8.76	4.96	6.24	6.12	9.48
Sweaters and vests	46.31	43.48	25.83	31.19	51.82
Shirts, blouses, and tops	120.91	138.23	103.22	92.36	128.12
Skirts	17.07	22.62	11.71	6.33	19.38
Pants	96.25	85.29	104.69	84.48	97.83
Shorts and shorts sets	12.59	16.07	11.08	10.15	13.34
Active sportswear	36.31	26.59	25.24	20.77	40.16
Nightwear	29.94	12.39	25.89	34.69	30.47
Undergarments	43.77	38.17	33.12	42.36	46.62
Hosiery	18.77	9.73	22.96	14.75	18.77
Suits	23.57	8.88	27.75	16.55	23.91
Accessories	50.57	87.72	41.36	30.86	54.70
Uniforms	5.97	6.23	6.26	5.53	6.04
Costumes	5.09	3.76	3.60	2.99	5.60

	total consumer units	Asian	black	Hispanic	non-Hispanic white and other
GIRLS' (AGED 2 TO 15) APPAREL	**$107.60**	**$104.06**	**$120.46**	**$113.24**	**$105.11**
Coats and jackets	7.49	7.52	10.48	9.03	6.84
Dresses and suits	9.49	11.66	11.43	13.10	8.70
Shirts, blouses, and sweaters	23.95	21.45	19.99	22.69	24.72
Skirts and pants	24.32	20.43	28.77	30.08	22.94
Shorts and shorts sets	8.40	8.95	10.76	10.24	7.78
Active sportswear	10.05	8.68	4.93	3.57	11.74
Underwear and nightwear	6.28	3.35	7.93	8.68	5.71
Hosiery	3.77	5.62	6.90	3.38	3.36
Accessories	5.93	10.80	7.97	2.95	6.05
Uniforms	3.84	1.13	7.55	4.96	3.16
Costumes	4.10	4.47	3.74	4.56	4.10
CHILDREN'S (UNDER AGE 2) APPAREL	**78.51**	**81.79**	**49.65**	**143.82**	**74.18**
Coats, jackets, and snowsuits	2.48	1.32	2.75	3.82	2.25
Outerwear including dresses	20.72	22.93	14.24	33.52	20.02
Underwear	44.17	51.69	25.39	87.68	41.26
Nightwear and loungewear	3.49	3.86	2.37	5.31	3.40
Accessories	7.66	1.98	4.91	13.49	7.25
FOOTWEAR	**328.74**	**313.03**	**508.10**	**423.94**	**289.25**
Men's	110.67	85.82	131.72	139.11	103.52
Boys'	35.92	54.51	104.55	44.57	23.98
Women's	153.81	140.02	222.40	203.39	137.94
Girls'	28.34	32.69	49.43	36.86	23.81
OTHER APPAREL PRODUCTS AND SERVICES	**263.94**	**224.42**	**208.24**	**250.08**	**274.43**
Material for making clothes	13.05	6.20	2.85	0.73	16.35
Sewing patterns and notions	7.82	7.70	2.25	2.93	9.36
Watches	21.51	52.57	13.76	20.83	22.84
Jewelry	113.72	48.39	53.47	75.21	127.92
Shoe repair and other shoe services	1.12	0.28	0.65	0.22	1.31
Coin-operated apparel laundry and dry cleaning	34.86	48.86	63.85	96.57	22.10
Apparel alteration, repair, and tailoring services	5.12	3.10	3.90	3.82	5.53
Clothing rental	2.28	0.42	2.15	3.11	2.18
Watch and jewelry repair	3.82	2.94	1.59	1.89	4.41
Professional laundry, dry cleaning	60.18	53.96	63.16	44.39	61.94
Clothing storage	0.47	–	0.61	0.39	0.49

Note: "Asian" and "black" include Hispanics and non-Hispanics who identify themselves as being of the respective race alone. "Hispanic" includes people of any race who identify themselves as Hispanic. "Other" includes people who identify themselves as non-Hispanic and as Alaska Native, American Indian, Asian (who are also included in the "Asian" column), Native Hawaiian or other Pacific Islander, as well as non-Hispanics reporting more than one race. Subcategories may not add to total because some are not shown. "–" means sample is too small to make a reliable estimate.
Source: Bureau of Labor Statistics, unpublished data from the 2004 Consumer Expenditure Survey

Table 2.18 Apparel: Indexed spending by race and Hispanic origin, 2004

(indexed average annual spending of consumer units (CU) on apparel, accessories, and related services, by race and Hispanic origin of consumer unit reference person, 2004; index definition: an index of 100 is the average for all consumer units; an index of 132 means that spending by consumer units in that group is 32 percent above the average for all consumer units; an index of 68 indicates spending that is 32 percent below the average for all consumer units)

	total consumer units	Asian	black	Hispanic	non-Hispanic white and other
Average spending of CU, total	$43,395	$49,459	$30,481	$37,578	$46,163
Average spending of CU, index	100	114	70	87	106
Apparel, spending index	**100**	**104**	**97**	**100**	**101**
MEN'S APPAREL	**100**	**141**	**67**	**91**	**106**
Suits	100	78	126	80	99
Sport coats and tailored jackets	100	70	45	89	110
Coats and jackets	100	485	62	93	107
Underwear	100	83	76	95	104
Hosiery	100	67	51	92	109
Nightwear	100	69	75	109	103
Accessories	100	83	65	88	107
Sweaters and vests	100	112	69	95	106
Active sportswear	100	61	25	72	115
Shirts	100	143	61	78	109
Pants	100	151	70	124	101
Shorts and shorts sets	100	76	89	77	105
Uniforms	100	59	129	131	91
Costumes	100	31	28	33	120
BOYS' (AGED 2 TO 15) APPAREL	**100**	**114**	**135**	**138**	**89**
Coats and jackets	100	117	151	148	86
Sweaters	100	118	119	124	94
Shirts	100	93	107	135	94
Underwear	100	231	128	153	88
Nightwear	100	108	256	165	66
Hosiery	100	124	226	110	79
Accessories	100	41	56	50	114
Suits, sport coats, and vests	100	168	273	121	71
Pants	100	98	130	146	89
Shorts and shorts sets	100	80	127	161	88
Uniforms	100	238	189	149	81
Active sportswear	100	121	73	158	96
Costumes	100	127	84	116	100
WOMEN'S APPAREL	**100**	**97**	**86**	**75**	**106**
Coats and jackets	100	88	103	40	108
Dresses	100	101	68	82	109
Sport coats and tailored jackets	100	57	71	70	108
Sweaters and vests	100	94	56	67	112
Shirts, blouses, and tops	100	114	85	76	106
Skirts	100	133	69	37	114
Pants	100	89	109	88	102
Shorts and shorts sets	100	128	88	81	106
Active sportswear	100	73	70	57	111
Nightwear	100	41	86	116	102
Undergarments	100	87	76	97	107
Hosiery	100	52	122	79	100
Suits	100	38	118	70	101
Accessories	100	173	82	61	108
Uniforms	100	104	105	93	101
Costumes	100	74	71	59	110

	total consumer units	Asian	black	Hispanic	non-Hispanic white and other
GIRLS' (AGED 2 TO 15) APPAREL	**100**	**97**	**112**	**105**	**98**
Coats and jackets	100	100	140	121	91
Dresses and suits	100	123	120	138	92
Shirts, blouses, and sweaters	100	90	83	95	103
Skirts and pants	100	84	118	124	94
Shorts and shorts sets	100	107	128	122	93
Active sportswear	100	86	49	36	117
Underwear and nightwear	100	53	126	138	91
Hosiery	100	149	183	90	89
Accessories	100	182	134	50	102
Uniforms	100	29	197	129	82
Costumes	100	109	91	111	100
CHILDREN'S (UNDER AGE 2) APPAREL	**100**	**104**	**63**	**183**	**94**
Coats, jackets, and snowsuits	100	53	111	154	91
Outerwear including dresses	100	111	69	162	97
Underwear	100	117	57	199	93
Nightwear and loungewear	100	111	68	152	97
Accessories	100	26	64	176	95
FOOTWEAR	**100**	**95**	**155**	**129**	**88**
Men's	100	78	119	126	94
Boys'	100	152	291	124	67
Women's	100	91	145	132	90
Girls'	100	115	174	130	84
OTHER APPAREL PRODUCTS AND SERVICES	**100**	**85**	**79**	**95**	**104**
Material for making clothes	100	48	22	6	125
Sewing patterns and notions	100	98	29	37	120
Watches	100	244	64	97	106
Jewelry	100	43	47	66	112
Shoe repair and other shoe services	100	25	58	20	117
Coin-operated apparel laundry and dry cleaning	100	140	183	277	63
Apparel alteration, repair, and tailoring services	100	61	76	75	108
Clothing rental	100	18	94	136	96
Watch and jewelry repair	100	77	42	49	115
Professional laundry, dry cleaning	100	90	105	74	103
Clothing storage	100	–	130	83	104

Note: "Asian" and "black" include Hispanics and non-Hispanics who identify themselves as being of the respective race alone. "Hispanic" includes people of any race who identify themselves as Hispanic. "Other" includes people who identify themselves as non-Hispanic and as Alaska Native, American Indian, Asian (who are also included in the "Asian" column), Native Hawaiian or other Pacific Islander, as well as non-Hispanics reporting more than one race. "–" means sample is too small to make a reliable estimate.
Source: Calculations by New Strategist based on the 2004 Consumer Expenditure Survey

Table 2.19 Apparel: Total spending by race and Hispanic origin, 2004

(total annual spending on apparel, accessories, and related services, by race and Hispanic origin groups, 2004; consumer units and dollars in thousands)

	total consumer units	Asian	black	Hispanic	non-Hispanic white and other
Number of consumer units	116,282	3,957	13,773	12,298	90,424
Total spending of all consumer units	$5,046,042,273	$195,707,997	$419,821,562	$462,134,613	$4,174,266,622
Apparel, total spending	**211,162,298**	**7,457,046**	**24,305,075**	**22,340,793**	**165,483,154**
MEN'S APPAREL	**36,893,953**	**1,766,444**	**2,945,632**	**3,563,714**	**30,442,144**
Suits	2,789,605	73,877	415,394	237,351	2,137,623
Sport coats and tailored jackets	974,443	23,148	51,786	91,497	832,805
Coats and jackets	2,965,191	489,283	216,374	290,479	2,463,150
Underwear	1,975,631	55,517	177,534	198,121	1,603,218
Hosiery	1,754,695	39,926	105,088	169,835	1,482,954
Nightwear	244,192	5,738	21,624	28,039	195,316
Accessories	2,914,027	81,870	224,087	271,294	2,423,363
Sweaters and vests	1,144,215	43,646	93,519	114,863	941,314
Active sportswear	2,651,230	54,923	77,129	202,056	2,379,960
Shirts	9,594,428	465,541	695,261	789,901	8,130,926
Pants	7,282,742	375,044	602,293	951,865	5,730,169
Shorts and shorts sets	1,723,299	44,358	180,702	139,951	1,405,189
Uniforms	463,965	9,259	71,069	64,196	329,143
Costumes	415,127	4,353	13,911	14,389	387,015
BOYS' (AGED 2 TO 15) APPAREL	**10,335,144**	**400,448**	**1,651,658**	**1,510,440**	**7,185,091**
Coats and jackets	696,529	27,699	124,921	109,083	463,875
Sweaters	346,520	13,889	48,756	45,626	253,187
Shirts	2,284,941	72,215	288,269	325,528	1,668,323
Underwear	554,665	43,685	84,153	89,529	378,877
Nightwear	380,242	13,929	115,280	66,409	196,220
Hosiery	581,410	24,573	155,773	67,639	357,175
Accessories	444,197	6,173	29,336	23,489	392,440
Suits, sport coats, and vests	301,170	17,173	97,375	38,616	165,476
Pants	2,603,554	87,212	400,243	400,669	1,810,288
Shorts and shorts sets	903,511	24,494	135,389	154,094	618,500
Uniforms	444,197	36,009	99,303	69,853	278,506
Active sportswear	498,850	20,616	43,385	83,380	371,643
Costumes	296,519	12,781	29,474	36,402	230,581
WOMEN'S APPAREL	**73,375,105**	**2,428,055**	**7,498,710**	**5,816,216**	**60,673,600**
Coats and jackets	5,682,701	169,241	692,920	241,410	4,763,536
Dresses	7,703,683	264,011	622,540	666,183	6,516,858
Sport coats and tailored jackets	1,018,630	19,627	85,944	75,264	857,220
Sweaters and vests	5,385,019	172,050	355,757	383,575	4,685,772
Shirts, blouses, and tops	14,059,657	546,976	1,421,649	1,135,843	11,585,123
Skirts	1,984,934	89,507	161,282	77,846	1,752,417
Pants	11,192,143	337,493	1,441,895	1,038,935	8,846,180
Shorts and shorts sets	1,463,990	63,589	152,605	124,825	1,206,256
Active sportswear	4,222,199	105,217	347,631	255,429	3,631,428
Nightwear	3,481,483	49,027	356,583	426,618	2,755,219
Undergarments	5,089,663	151,039	456,162	520,943	4,215,567
Hosiery	2,182,613	38,502	316,228	181,396	1,697,258
Suits	2,740,767	35,138	382,201	203,532	2,162,038
Accessories	5,880,381	347,108	569,651	379,516	4,946,193
Uniforms	694,204	24,652	86,219	68,008	546,161
Costumes	591,875	14,878	49,583	36,771	506,374

	total consumer units	Asian	black	Hispanic	non-Hispanic white and other
GIRLS' (AGED 2 TO 15) APPAREL	**$12,511,943**	**$411,765**	**$1,659,096**	**$1,392,626**	**$9,504,467**
Coats and jackets	870,952	29,757	144,341	111,051	618,500
Dresses and suits	1,103,516	46,139	157,425	161,104	786,689
Shirts, blouses, and sweaters	2,784,954	84,878	275,322	279,042	2,235,281
Skirts and pants	2,827,978	80,842	396,249	369,924	2,074,327
Shorts and shorts sets	976,769	35,415	148,197	125,932	703,499
Active sportswear	1,168,634	34,347	67,901	43,904	1,061,578
Underwear and nightwear	730,251	13,256	109,220	106,747	516,321
Hosiery	438,383	22,238	95,034	41,567	303,825
Accessories	689,552	42,736	109,771	36,279	547,065
Uniforms	446,523	4,471	103,986	60,998	285,740
Costumes	476,756	17,688	51,511	56,079	370,738
CHILDREN'S (UNDER AGE 2) APPAREL	**9,129,300**	**323,643**	**683,829**	**1,768,698**	**6,707,652**
Coats, jackets, and snowsuits	288,379	5,223	37,876	46,978	203,454
Outerwear including dresses	2,409,363	90,734	196,128	412,229	1,810,288
Underwear	5,136,176	204,537	349,696	1,078,289	3,730,894
Nightwear and loungewear	405,824	15,274	32,642	65,302	307,442
Accessories	890,720	7,835	67,625	165,900	655,574
FOOTWEAR	**38,226,545**	**1,238,660**	**6,998,061**	**5,213,614**	**26,155,142**
Men's	12,868,929	339,590	1,814,180	1,710,775	9,360,692
Boys'	4,176,849	215,696	1,439,967	548,122	2,168,368
Women's	17,885,334	554,059	3,063,115	2,501,290	12,473,087
Girls'	3,295,432	129,354	680,799	453,304	2,152,995
OTHER APPAREL PRODUCTS AND SERVICES	**30,691,471**	**888,030**	**2,868,090**	**3,075,484**	**24,815,058**
Material for making clothes	1,517,480	24,533	39,253	8,978	1,478,432
Sewing patterns and notions	909,325	30,469	30,989	36,033	846,369
Watches	2,501,226	208,019	189,516	256,167	2,065,284
Jewelry	13,223,589	191,479	736,442	924,933	11,567,038
Shoe repair and other shoe services	130,236	1,108	8,952	2,706	118,455
Coin-operated apparel laundry and dry cleaning	4,053,591	193,339	879,406	1,187,618	1,998,370
Apparel alteration, repair, and tailoring services	595,364	12,267	53,715	46,978	500,045
Clothing rental	265,123	1,662	29,612	38,247	197,124
Watch and jewelry repair	444,197	11,634	21,899	23,243	398,770
Professional laundry, dry cleaning	6,997,851	213,520	869,903	545,908	5,600,863
Clothing storage	54,653	–	8,402	4,796	44,308

Note: "Asian" and "black" include Hispanics and non-Hispanics who identify themselves as being of the respective race alone. "Hispanic" includes people of any race who identify themselves as Hispanic. "Other" includes people who identify themselves as non-Hispanic and as Alaska Native, American Indian, Asian (who are also included in the "Asian" column), Native Hawaiian or other Pacific Islander, as well as non-Hispanics reporting more than one race. Numbers may not add to total because of rounding and missing subcategories. "–" means sample is too small to make a reliable estimate.
Source: Calculations by New Strategist based on the 2004 Consumer Expenditure Survey

Table 2.20 Apparel: Market shares by race and Hispanic origin, 2004

(percentage of total annual spending on apparel, accessories, and related services accounted for by race and Hispanic origin groups, 2004)

	total consumer units	Asian	black	Hispanic	non-Hispanic white and other
Share of total consumer units	100.0%	3.4%	11.8%	10.6%	77.8%
Share of total before-tax income	100.0	4.2	8.4	8.5	83.3
Share of total spending	100.0	3.9	8.3	9.2	82.7
Share of apparel spending	100.0	3.5	11.5	10.6	78.4
MEN'S APPAREL	100.0	4.8	8.0	9.7	82.5
Suits	100.0	2.6	14.9	8.5	76.6
Sport coats and tailored jackets	100.0	2.4	5.3	9.4	85.5
Coats and jackets	100.0	16.5	7.3	9.8	83.1
Underwear	100.0	2.8	9.0	10.0	81.1
Hosiery	100.0	2.3	6.0	9.7	84.5
Nightwear	100.0	2.3	8.9	11.5	80.0
Accessories	100.0	2.8	7.7	9.3	83.2
Sweaters and vests	100.0	3.8	8.2	10.0	82.3
Active sportswear	100.0	2.1	2.9	7.6	89.8
Shirts	100.0	4.9	7.2	8.2	84.7
Pants	100.0	5.1	8.3	13.1	78.7
Shorts and shorts sets	100.0	2.6	10.5	8.1	81.5
Uniforms	100.0	2.0	15.3	13.8	70.9
Costumes	100.0	1.0	3.4	3.5	93.2
BOYS' (AGED 2 TO 15) APPAREL	100.0	3.9	16.0	14.6	69.5
Coats and jackets	100.0	4.0	17.9	15.7	66.6
Sweaters	100.0	4.0	14.1	13.2	73.1
Shirts	100.0	3.2	12.6	14.2	73.0
Underwear	100.0	7.9	15.2	16.1	68.3
Nightwear	100.0	3.7	30.3	17.5	51.6
Hosiery	100.0	4.2	26.8	11.6	61.4
Accessories	100.0	1.4	6.6	5.3	88.3
Suits, sport coats, and vests	100.0	5.7	32.3	12.8	54.9
Pants	100.0	3.3	15.4	15.4	69.5
Shorts and shorts sets	100.0	2.7	15.0	17.1	68.5
Uniforms	100.0	8.1	22.4	15.7	62.7
Active sportswear	100.0	4.1	8.7	16.7	74.5
Costumes	100.0	4.3	9.9	12.3	77.8
WOMEN'S APPAREL	100.0	3.3	10.2	7.9	82.7
Coats and jackets	100.0	3.0	12.2	4.2	83.8
Dresses	100.0	3.4	8.1	8.6	84.6
Sport coats and tailored jackets	100.0	1.9	8.4	7.4	84.2
Sweaters and vests	100.0	3.2	6.6	7.1	87.0
Shirts, blouses, and tops	100.0	3.9	10.1	8.1	82.4
Skirts	100.0	4.5	8.1	3.9	88.3
Pants	100.0	3.0	12.9	9.3	79.0
Shorts and shorts sets	100.0	4.3	10.4	8.5	82.4
Active sportswear	100.0	2.5	8.2	6.0	86.0
Nightwear	100.0	1.4	10.2	12.3	79.1
Undergarments	100.0	3.0	9.0	10.2	82.8
Hosiery	100.0	1.8	14.5	8.3	77.8
Suits	100.0	1.3	13.9	7.4	78.9
Accessories	100.0	5.9	9.7	6.5	84.1
Uniforms	100.0	3.6	12.4	9.8	78.7
Costumes	100.0	2.5	8.4	6.2	85.6

	total consumer units	Asian	black	Hispanic	non-Hispanic white and other
GIRLS' (AGED 2 TO 15) APPAREL	**100.0%**	**3.3%**	**13.3%**	**11.1%**	**76.0%**
Coats and jackets	100.0	3.4	16.6	12.8	71.0
Dresses and suits	100.0	4.2	14.3	14.6	71.3
Shirts, blouses, and sweaters	100.0	3.0	9.9	10.0	80.3
Skirts and pants	100.0	2.9	14.0	13.1	73.4
Shorts and shorts sets	100.0	3.6	15.2	12.9	72.0
Active sportswear	100.0	2.9	5.8	3.8	90.8
Underwear and nightwear	100.0	1.8	15.0	14.6	70.7
Hosiery	100.0	5.1	21.7	9.5	69.3
Accessories	100.0	6.2	15.9	5.3	79.3
Uniforms	100.0	1.0	23.3	13.7	64.0
Costumes	100.0	3.7	10.8	11.8	77.8
CHILDREN'S (UNDER AGE 2) APPAREL	**100.0**	**3.5**	**7.5**	**19.4**	**73.5**
Coats, jackets, and snowsuits	100.0	1.8	13.1	16.3	70.6
Outerwear including dresses	100.0	3.8	8.1	17.1	75.1
Underwear	100.0	4.0	6.8	21.0	72.6
Nightwear and loungewear	100.0	3.8	8.0	16.1	75.8
Accessories	100.0	0.9	7.6	18.6	73.6
FOOTWEAR	**100.0**	**3.2**	**18.3**	**13.6**	**68.4**
Men's	100.0	2.6	14.1	13.3	72.7
Boys'	100.0	5.2	34.5	13.1	51.9
Women's	100.0	3.1	17.1	14.0	69.7
Girls'	100.0	3.9	20.7	13.8	65.3
OTHER APPAREL PRODUCTS AND SERVICES	**100.0**	**2.9**	**9.3**	**10.0**	**80.9**
Material for making clothes	100.0	1.6	2.6	0.6	97.4
Sewing patterns and notions	100.0	3.4	3.4	4.0	93.1
Watches	100.0	8.3	7.6	10.2	82.6
Jewelry	100.0	1.4	5.6	7.0	87.5
Shoe repair and other shoe services	100.0	0.9	6.9	2.1	91.0
Coin-operated apparel laundry and dry cleaning	100.0	4.8	21.7	29.3	49.3
Apparel alteration, repair, and tailoring services	100.0	2.1	9.0	7.9	84.0
Clothing rental	100.0	0.6	11.2	14.4	74.4
Watch and jewelry repair	100.0	2.6	4.9	5.2	89.8
Professional laundry, dry cleaning	100.0	3.1	12.4	7.8	80.0
Clothing storage	100.0	–	15.4	8.8	81.1

Note: "Asian" and "black" include Hispanics and non-Hispanics who identify themselves as being of the respective race alone. "Hispanic" includes people of any race who identify themselves as Hispanic. "Other" includes people who identify themselves as non-Hispanic and as Alaska Native, American Indian, Asian (who are also included in the "Asian" column), Native Hawaiian or other Pacific Islander, as well as non-Hispanics reporting more than one race. "–" means sample is too small to make a reliable estimate.
Source: Calculations by New Strategist based on the 2004 Consumer Expenditure Survey

Table 2.21 Apparel: Average spending by region, 2004

(average annual spending of consumer units (CU) on apparel, accessories, and related services, by region in which consumer unit lives, 2004)

	total consumer units	Northeast	Midwest	South	West
Number of consumer units (in 000s)	116,282	22,051	26,539	41,801	25,891
Average number of persons per CU	2.5	2.4	2.4	2.5	2.6
Average before-tax income of CU	$54,453.00	$61,050.00	$53,567.00	$50,775.00	$55,682.00
Average spending of CU, total	43,394.87	46,114.89	43,370.77	39,173.65	47,921.74
Apparel, average spending	**1,815.95**	**2,176.24**	**1,672.35**	**1,643.03**	**1,936.07**
MEN'S APPAREL	**317.28**	**365.63**	**317.46**	**287.61**	**323.78**
Suits	23.99	27.86	24.91	21.66	23.49
Sport coats and tailored jackets	8.38	10.27	10.36	7.03	6.94
Coats and jackets	25.50	32.32	29.30	18.69	26.74
Underwear	16.99	25.86	15.07	14.49	15.42
Hosiery	15.09	16.97	20.68	11.15	14.03
Nightwear	2.10	1.71	2.35	1.85	2.59
Accessories	25.06	31.97	24.74	21.96	24.47
Sweaters and vests	9.84	14.68	10.15	6.87	10.21
Active sportswear	22.80	28.07	21.48	17.68	27.96
Shirts	82.51	96.80	64.10	84.27	86.54
Pants	62.63	64.74	67.03	60.00	60.49
Shorts and shorts sets	14.82	11.21	12.75	16.91	16.70
Uniforms	3.99	1.92	2.03	4.86	6.38
Costumes	3.57	1.26	12.53	0.19	1.82
BOYS' (AGED 2 TO 15) APPAREL	**88.88**	**94.21**	**89.65**	**89.69**	**82.20**
Coats and jackets	5.99	6.30	6.75	6.19	4.60
Sweaters	2.98	5.31	2.71	2.81	1.56
Shirts	19.65	23.51	19.94	17.51	19.48
Underwear	4.77	4.63	4.67	4.27	5.79
Nightwear	3.27	2.16	3.03	4.16	3.02
Hosiery	5.00	3.07	5.58	6.18	4.15
Accessories	3.82	2.91	4.66	4.18	3.14
Suits, sport coats, and vests	2.59	6.81	1.84	1.78	1.06
Pants	22.39	20.33	21.14	25.24	20.81
Shorts and shorts sets	7.77	7.59	7.70	8.05	7.53
Uniforms	3.82	4.23	2.11	4.36	4.34
Active sportswear	4.29	5.47	3.99	3.57	4.73
Costumes	2.55	1.87	5.50	1.40	1.96
WOMEN'S APPAREL	**631.01**	**809.01**	**547.18**	**564.59**	**673.12**
Coats and jackets	48.87	71.66	43.89	40.57	47.89
Dresses	66.25	121.39	50.85	50.29	60.62
Sport coats and tailored jackets	8.76	11.11	10.37	6.74	8.37
Sweaters and vests	46.31	63.58	41.13	38.41	49.69
Shirts, blouses, and tops	120.91	130.60	111.15	118.28	127.01
Skirts	17.07	25.57	16.06	13.36	16.81
Pants	96.25	119.02	82.56	89.22	102.33
Shorts and shorts sets	12.59	13.03	7.65	16.46	11.06
Active sportswear	36.31	37.94	29.46	30.40	51.72
Nightwear	29.94	38.99	21.65	23.62	41.10
Undergarments	43.77	52.15	35.98	43.18	45.61
Hosiery	18.77	19.76	15.48	19.73	19.77
Suits	23.57	33.61	22.82	22.92	16.83
Accessories	50.57	62.07	37.91	44.48	63.80
Uniforms	5.97	5.90	5.87	5.91	6.25
Costumes	5.09	2.65	14.32	1.02	4.26

	total consumer units	Northeast	Midwest	South	West
GIRLS' (AGED 2 TO 15) APPAREL	**$107.60**	**$124.42**	**$113.56**	**$97.11**	**$103.97**
Coats and jackets	7.49	12.01	8.46	5.08	6.52
Dresses and suits	9.49	13.25	8.81	9.09	7.60
Shirts, blouses, and sweaters	23.95	26.10	25.02	22.69	23.02
Skirts and pants	24.32	26.92	24.67	22.80	24.18
Shorts and shorts sets	8.40	10.29	7.77	8.98	6.48
Active sportswear	10.05	17.30	10.50	5.88	10.11
Underwear and nightwear	6.28	5.76	6.78	5.39	7.65
Hosiery	3.77	3.04	4.06	3.50	4.55
Accessories	5.93	5.14	6.41	5.92	6.10
Uniforms	3.84	1.65	3.50	4.96	4.24
Costumes	4.10	2.97	7.59	2.83	3.53
CHILDREN'S (UNDER AGE 2) APPAREL	**78.51**	**68.85**	**79.35**	**72.70**	**95.46**
Coats, jackets, and snowsuits	2.48	4.52	2.24	1.45	2.63
Outerwear including dresses	20.72	21.56	20.02	18.03	25.05
Underwear	44.17	33.14	46.09	43.19	53.33
Nightwear and loungewear	3.49	4.66	3.69	2.42	4.01
Accessories	7.66	4.97	7.31	7.61	10.44
FOOTWEAR	**328.74**	**426.95**	**271.06**	**311.53**	**332.08**
Men's	110.67	155.42	101.88	99.00	100.14
Boys'	35.92	36.90	33.85	37.33	34.95
Women's	153.81	198.12	108.54	146.88	174.07
Girls'	28.34	36.51	26.79	28.32	22.93
OTHER APPAREL PRODUCTS AND SERVICES	**263.94**	**287.18**	**254.09**	**219.79**	**325.46**
Material for making clothes	13.05	3.27	29.79	7.10	13.74
Sewing patterns and notions	7.82	5.81	5.72	8.62	10.46
Watches	21.51	16.61	19.96	15.34	37.22
Jewelry	113.72	118.44	112.42	90.86	147.94
Shoe repair and other shoe services	1.12	1.27	1.03	1.00	1.28
Coin-operated apparel laundry and dry cleaning	34.86	52.59	24.90	25.57	44.95
Apparel alteration, repair, and tailoring services	5.12	5.90	4.43	4.66	5.88
Clothing rental	2.28	2.67	2.86	1.57	2.48
Watch and jewelry repair	3.82	4.40	3.90	2.96	4.62
Professional laundry, dry cleaning	60.18	75.58	48.77	61.54	56.55
Clothing storage	0.47	0.63	0.31	0.56	0.33

Note: Subcategories may not add to total because some are not shown.
Source: Bureau of Labor Statistics, unpublished data from the 2004 Consumer Expenditure Survey

Table 2.22 Apparel: Indexed spending by region, 2004

(indexed average annual spending of consumer units (CU) on apparel, accessories, and related services, by region in which consumer unit lives, 2004; index definition: an index of 100 is the average for all consumer units; an index of 132 means that spending by consumer units in that group is 32 percent above the average for all consumer units; an index of 68 indicates spending that is 32 percent below the average for all consumer units)

	total consumer units	Northeast	Midwest	South	West
Average spending of CU, total	$43,395	$46,115	$43,371	$39,174	$47,922
Average spending of CU, index	100	106	100	90	110
Apparel, spending index	**100**	**120**	**92**	**90**	**107**
MEN'S APPAREL	**100**	**115**	**100**	**91**	**102**
Suits	100	116	104	90	98
Sport coats and tailored jackets	100	123	124	84	83
Coats and jackets	100	127	115	73	105
Underwear	100	152	89	85	91
Hosiery	100	112	137	74	93
Nightwear	100	81	112	88	123
Accessories	100	128	99	88	98
Sweaters and vests	100	149	103	70	104
Active sportswear	100	123	94	78	123
Shirts	100	117	78	102	105
Pants	100	103	107	96	97
Shorts and shorts sets	100	76	86	114	113
Uniforms	100	48	51	122	160
Costumes	100	35	351	5	51
BOYS' (AGED 2 TO 15) APPAREL	**100**	**106**	**101**	**101**	**92**
Coats and jackets	100	105	113	103	77
Sweaters	100	178	91	94	52
Shirts	100	120	101	89	99
Underwear	100	97	98	90	121
Nightwear	100	66	93	127	92
Hosiery	100	61	112	124	83
Accessories	100	76	122	109	82
Suits, sport coats, and vests	100	263	71	69	41
Pants	100	91	94	113	93
Shorts and shorts sets	100	98	99	104	97
Uniforms	100	111	55	114	114
Active sportswear	100	128	93	83	110
Costumes	100	73	216	55	77
WOMEN'S APPAREL	**100**	**128**	**87**	**89**	**107**
Coats and jackets	100	147	90	83	98
Dresses	100	183	77	76	92
Sport coats and tailored jackets	100	127	118	77	96
Sweaters and vests	100	137	89	83	107
Shirts, blouses, and tops	100	108	92	98	105
Skirts	100	150	94	78	98
Pants	100	124	86	93	106
Shorts and shorts sets	100	103	61	131	88
Active sportswear	100	104	81	84	142
Nightwear	100	130	72	79	137
Undergarments	100	119	82	99	104
Hosiery	100	105	82	105	105
Suits	100	143	97	97	71
Accessories	100	123	75	88	126
Uniforms	100	99	98	99	105
Costumes	100	52	281	20	84

	total consumer units	Northeast	Midwest	South	West
GIRLS' (AGED 2 TO 15) APPAREL	**100**	**116**	**106**	**90**	**97**
Coats and jackets	100	160	113	68	87
Dresses and suits	100	140	93	96	80
Shirts, blouses, and sweaters	100	109	104	95	96
Skirts and pants	100	111	101	94	99
Shorts and shorts sets	100	123	93	107	77
Active sportswear	100	172	104	59	101
Underwear and nightwear	100	92	108	86	122
Hosiery	100	81	108	93	121
Accessories	100	87	108	100	103
Uniforms	100	43	91	129	110
Costumes	100	72	185	69	86
CHILDREN'S (UNDER AGE 2) APPAREL	**100**	**88**	**101**	**93**	**122**
Coats, jackets, and snowsuits	100	182	90	58	106
Outerwear including dresses	100	104	97	87	121
Underwear	100	75	104	98	121
Nightwear and loungewear	100	134	106	69	115
Accessories	100	65	95	99	136
FOOTWEAR	**100**	**130**	**82**	**95**	**101**
Men's	100	140	92	89	90
Boys'	100	103	94	104	97
Women's	100	129	71	95	113
Girls'	100	129	95	100	81
OTHER APPAREL PRODUCTS AND SERVICES	**100**	**109**	**96**	**83**	**123**
Material for making clothes	100	25	228	54	105
Sewing patterns and notions	100	74	73	110	134
Watches	100	77	93	71	173
Jewelry	100	104	99	80	130
Shoe repair and other shoe services	100	113	92	89	114
Coin-operated apparel laundry and dry cleaning	100	151	71	73	129
Apparel alteration, repair, and tailoring services	100	115	87	91	115
Clothing rental	100	117	125	69	109
Watch and jewelry repair	100	115	102	77	121
Professional laundry, dry cleaning	100	126	81	102	94
Clothing storage	100	134	66	119	70

Source: Calculations by New Strategist based on the 2004 Consumer Expenditure Survey

Table 2.23 Apparel: Total spending by region, 2004

(total annual spending on apparel, accessories, and related services, by region in which consumer units live, 2004; consumer units and dollars in thousands)

	total consumer units	Northeast	Midwest	South	West
Number of consumer units	116,282	22,051	26,539	41,801	25,891
Total spending of all consumer units	$5,046,042,273	$1,016,879,439	$1,151,016,865	$1,637,497,744	$1,240,741,770
Apparel, total spending	**211,162,298**	**47,988,268**	**44,382,497**	**68,680,297**	**50,126,788**
MEN'S APPAREL	**36,893,953**	**8,062,507**	**8,425,071**	**12,022,386**	**8,382,988**
Suits	2,789,605	614,341	661,086	905,410	608,180
Sport coats and tailored jackets	974,443	226,464	274,944	293,861	179,684
Coats and jackets	2,965,191	712,688	777,593	781,261	692,325
Underwear	1,975,631	570,239	399,943	605,696	399,239
Hosiery	1,754,695	374,205	548,827	466,081	363,251
Nightwear	244,192	37,707	62,367	77,332	67,058
Accessories	2,914,027	704,970	656,575	917,950	633,553
Sweaters and vests	1,144,215	323,709	269,371	287,173	264,347
Active sportswear	2,651,230	618,972	570,058	739,042	723,912
Shirts	9,594,428	2,134,537	1,701,150	3,522,570	2,240,607
Pants	7,282,742	1,427,582	1,778,909	2,508,060	1,566,147
Shorts and shorts sets	1,723,299	247,192	338,372	706,855	432,380
Uniforms	463,965	42,338	53,874	203,153	165,185
Costumes	415,127	27,784	332,534	7,942	47,122
BOYS' (AGED 2 TO 15) APPAREL	**10,335,144**	**2,077,425**	**2,379,221**	**3,749,132**	**2,128,240**
Coats and jackets	696,529	138,921	179,138	258,748	119,099
Sweaters	346,520	117,091	71,921	117,461	40,390
Shirts	2,284,941	518,419	529,188	731,936	504,357
Underwear	554,665	102,096	123,937	178,490	149,909
Nightwear	380,242	47,630	80,413	173,892	78,191
Hosiery	581,410	67,697	148,088	258,330	107,448
Accessories	444,197	64,168	123,672	174,728	81,298
Suits, sport coats, and vests	301,170	150,167	48,832	74,406	27,444
Pants	2,603,554	448,297	561,034	1,055,057	538,792
Shorts and shorts sets	903,511	167,367	204,350	336,498	194,959
Uniforms	444,197	93,276	55,997	182,252	112,367
Active sportswear	498,850	120,619	105,891	149,230	122,464
Costumes	296,519	41,235	145,965	58,521	50,746
WOMEN'S APPAREL	**73,375,105**	**17,839,480**	**14,521,610**	**23,600,427**	**17,427,750**
Coats and jackets	5,682,701	1,580,175	1,164,797	1,695,867	1,239,920
Dresses	7,703,683	2,676,771	1,349,508	2,102,172	1,569,512
Sport coats and tailored jackets	1,018,630	244,987	275,209	281,739	216,708
Sweaters and vests	5,385,019	1,402,003	1,091,549	1,605,576	1,286,524
Shirts, blouses, and tops	14,059,657	2,879,861	2,949,810	4,944,222	3,288,416
Skirts	1,984,934	563,844	426,216	558,461	435,228
Pants	11,192,143	2,624,510	2,191,060	3,729,485	2,649,426
Shorts and shorts sets	1,463,990	287,325	203,023	688,044	286,354
Active sportswear	4,222,199	836,615	781,839	1,270,750	1,339,083
Nightwear	3,481,483	859,768	574,569	987,340	1,064,120
Undergarments	5,089,663	1,149,960	954,873	1,804,967	1,180,889
Hosiery	2,182,613	435,728	410,824	824,734	511,865
Suits	2,740,767	741,134	605,620	958,079	435,746
Accessories	5,880,381	1,368,706	1,006,093	1,859,308	1,651,846
Uniforms	694,204	130,101	155,784	247,044	161,819
Costumes	591,875	58,435	380,038	42,637	110,296

	total consumer units	Northeast	Midwest	South	West
GIRLS' (AGED 2 TO 15) APPAREL	**$12,511,943**	**$2,743,585**	**$3,013,769**	**$4,059,295**	**$2,691,887**
Coats and jackets	870,952	264,833	224,520	212,349	168,809
Dresses and suits	1,103,516	292,176	233,809	379,971	196,772
Shirts, blouses, and sweaters	2,784,954	575,531	664,006	948,465	596,011
Skirts and pants	2,827,978	593,613	654,717	953,063	626,044
Shorts and shorts sets	976,769	226,905	206,208	375,373	167,774
Active sportswear	1,168,634	381,482	278,660	245,790	261,758
Underwear and nightwear	730,251	127,014	179,934	225,307	198,066
Hosiery	438,383	67,035	107,748	146,304	117,804
Accessories	689,552	113,342	170,115	247,462	157,935
Uniforms	446,523	36,384	92,887	207,333	109,778
Costumes	476,756	65,491	201,431	118,297	91,395
CHILDREN'S (UNDER AGE 2) APPAREL	**9,129,300**	**1,518,211**	**2,105,870**	**3,038,933**	**2,471,555**
Coats, jackets, and snowsuits	288,379	99,671	59,447	60,611	68,093
Outerwear including dresses	2,409,363	475,420	531,311	753,672	648,570
Underwear	5,136,176	730,770	1,223,183	1,805,385	1,380,767
Nightwear and loungewear	405,824	102,758	97,929	101,158	103,823
Accessories	890,720	109,593	194,000	318,106	270,302
FOOTWEAR	**38,226,545**	**9,414,674**	**7,193,661**	**13,022,266**	**8,597,883**
Men's	12,868,929	3,427,166	2,703,793	4,138,299	2,592,725
Boys'	4,176,849	813,682	898,345	1,560,431	904,890
Women's	17,885,334	4,368,744	2,880,543	6,139,731	4,506,846
Girls'	3,295,432	805,082	710,980	1,183,804	593,681
OTHER APPAREL PRODUCTS AND SERVICES	**30,691,471**	**6,332,606**	**6,743,295**	**9,187,442**	**8,426,485**
Material for making clothes	1,517,480	72,107	790,597	296,787	355,742
Sewing patterns and notions	909,325	128,116	151,803	360,325	270,820
Watches	2,501,226	366,267	529,718	641,227	963,663
Jewelry	13,223,589	2,611,720	2,983,514	3,798,039	3,830,315
Shoe repair and other shoe services	130,236	28,005	27,335	41,801	33,140
Coin-operated apparel laundry and dry cleaning	4,053,591	1,159,662	660,821	1,068,852	1,163,800
Apparel alteration, repair, and tailoring services	595,364	130,101	117,568	194,793	152,239
Clothing rental	265,123	58,876	75,902	65,628	64,210
Watch and jewelry repair	444,197	97,024	103,502	123,731	119,616
Professional laundry, dry cleaning	6,997,851	1,666,615	1,294,307	2,572,434	1,464,136
Clothing storage	54,653	13,892	8,227	23,409	8,544

Note: Numbers may not add to total because of rounding and missing subcategories.
Source: Calculations by New Strategist based on the 2004 Consumer Expenditure Survey

Table 2.24 Apparel: Market shares by region, 2004

(percentage of total annual spending on apparel, accessories, and related services accounted for by consumer units by region, 2004)

	total consumer units	Northeast	Midwest	South	West
Share of total consumer units	100.0%	19.0%	22.8%	35.9%	22.3%
Share of total before-tax income	100.0	21.3	22.5	33.5	22.8
Share of total spending	100.0	20.2	22.8	32.5	24.6
Share of apparel spending	100.0	22.7	21.0	32.5	23.7
MEN'S APPAREL	**100.0**	**21.9**	**22.8**	**32.6**	**22.7**
Suits	100.0	22.0	23.7	32.5	21.8
Sport coats and tailored jackets	100.0	23.2	28.2	30.2	18.4
Coats and jackets	100.0	24.0	26.2	26.3	23.3
Underwear	100.0	28.9	20.2	30.7	20.2
Hosiery	100.0	21.3	31.3	26.6	20.7
Nightwear	100.0	15.4	25.5	31.7	27.5
Accessories	100.0	24.2	22.5	31.5	21.7
Sweaters and vests	100.0	28.3	23.5	25.1	23.1
Active sportswear	100.0	23.3	21.5	27.9	27.3
Shirts	100.0	22.2	17.7	36.7	23.4
Pants	100.0	19.6	24.4	34.4	21.5
Shorts and shorts sets	100.0	14.3	19.6	41.0	25.1
Uniforms	100.0	9.1	11.6	43.8	35.6
Costumes	100.0	6.7	80.1	1.9	11.4
BOYS' (AGED 2 TO 15) APPAREL	**100.0**	**20.1**	**23.0**	**36.3**	**20.6**
Coats and jackets	100.0	19.9	25.7	37.1	17.1
Sweaters	100.0	33.8	20.8	33.9	11.7
Shirts	100.0	22.7	23.2	32.0	22.1
Underwear	100.0	18.4	22.3	32.2	27.0
Nightwear	100.0	12.5	21.1	45.7	20.6
Hosiery	100.0	11.6	25.5	44.4	18.5
Accessories	100.0	14.4	27.8	39.3	18.3
Suits, sport coats, and vests	100.0	49.9	16.2	24.7	9.1
Pants	100.0	17.2	21.5	40.5	20.7
Shorts and shorts sets	100.0	18.5	22.6	37.2	21.6
Uniforms	100.0	21.0	12.6	41.0	25.3
Active sportswear	100.0	24.2	21.2	29.9	24.5
Costumes	100.0	13.9	49.2	19.7	17.1
WOMEN'S APPAREL	**100.0**	**24.3**	**19.8**	**32.2**	**23.8**
Coats and jackets	100.0	27.8	20.5	29.8	21.8
Dresses	100.0	34.7	17.5	27.3	20.4
Sport coats and tailored jackets	100.0	24.1	27.0	27.7	21.3
Sweaters and vests	100.0	26.0	20.3	29.8	23.9
Shirts, blouses, and tops	100.0	20.5	21.0	35.2	23.4
Skirts	100.0	28.4	21.5	28.1	21.9
Pants	100.0	23.4	19.6	33.3	23.7
Shorts and shorts sets	100.0	19.6	13.9	47.0	19.6
Active sportswear	100.0	19.8	18.5	30.1	31.7
Nightwear	100.0	24.7	16.5	28.4	30.6
Undergarments	100.0	22.6	18.8	35.5	23.2
Hosiery	100.0	20.0	18.8	37.8	23.5
Suits	100.0	27.0	22.1	35.0	15.9
Accessories	100.0	23.3	17.1	31.6	28.1
Uniforms	100.0	18.7	22.4	35.6	23.3
Costumes	100.0	9.9	64.2	7.2	18.6

	total consumer units	Northeast	Midwest	South	West
GIRLS' (AGED 2 TO 15) APPAREL	**100.0%**	**21.9%**	**24.1%**	**32.4%**	**21.5%**
Coats and jackets	100.0	30.4	25.8	24.4	19.4
Dresses and suits	100.0	26.5	21.2	34.4	17.8
Shirts, blouses, and sweaters	100.0	20.7	23.8	34.1	21.4
Skirts and pants	100.0	21.0	23.2	33.7	22.1
Shorts and shorts sets	100.0	23.2	21.1	38.4	17.2
Active sportswear	100.0	32.6	23.8	21.0	22.4
Underwear and nightwear	100.0	17.4	24.6	30.9	27.1
Hosiery	100.0	15.3	24.6	33.4	26.9
Accessories	100.0	16.4	24.7	35.9	22.9
Uniforms	100.0	8.1	20.8	46.4	24.6
Costumes	100.0	13.7	42.3	24.8	19.2
CHILDREN'S (UNDER AGE 2) APPAREL	**100.0**	**16.6**	**23.1**	**33.3**	**27.1**
Coats, jackets, and snowsuits	100.0	34.6	20.6	21.0	23.6
Outerwear including dresses	100.0	19.7	22.1	31.3	26.9
Underwear	100.0	14.2	23.8	35.2	26.9
Nightwear and loungewear	100.0	25.3	24.1	24.9	25.6
Accessories	100.0	12.3	21.8	35.7	30.3
FOOTWEAR	**100.0**	**24.6**	**18.8**	**34.1**	**22.5**
Men's	100.0	26.6	21.0	32.2	20.1
Boys'	100.0	19.5	21.5	37.4	21.7
Women's	100.0	24.4	16.1	34.3	25.2
Girls'	100.0	24.4	21.6	35.9	18.0
OTHER APPAREL PRODUCTS AND SERVICES	**100.0**	**20.6**	**22.0**	**29.9**	**27.5**
Material for making clothes	100.0	4.8	52.1	19.6	23.4
Sewing patterns and notions	100.0	14.1	16.7	39.6	29.8
Watches	100.0	14.6	21.2	25.6	38.5
Jewelry	100.0	19.8	22.6	28.7	29.0
Shoe repair and other shoe services	100.0	21.5	21.0	32.1	25.4
Coin-operated apparel laundry and dry cleaning	100.0	28.6	16.3	26.4	28.7
Apparel alteration, repair, and tailoring services	100.0	21.9	19.7	32.7	25.6
Clothing rental	100.0	22.2	28.6	24.8	24.2
Watch and jewelry repair	100.0	21.8	23.3	27.9	26.9
Professional laundry, dry cleaning	100.0	23.8	18.5	36.8	20.9
Clothing storage	100.0	25.4	15.1	42.8	15.6

Note: Numbers may not add to total because of rounding.
Source: Calculations by New Strategist based on the 2004 Consumer Expenditure Survey

Table 2.25 Apparel: Average spending by education, 2004

(average annual spending of consumer units (CU) on apparel, accessories, and related services, by education of consumer unit reference person, 2004)

	total consumer units	less than high school graduate	high school graduate	some college	associate's degree	college graduate total	bachelor's degree	master's, professional, doctorate
Number of consumer units (in 000s)	116,282	16,829	31,005	25,317	10,678	32,452	20,684	11,768
Average number of persons per CU	2.5	2.7	2.5	2.3	2.6	2.5	2.4	2.5
Average before-tax income of CU	$54,453.00	$29,094.00	$42,334.00	$46,756.00	$58,593.00	$83,825.00	$75,647.00	$98,201.00
Average spending of CU, total	43,394.87	25,421.18	35,438.55	40,877.68	48,177.36	60,712.28	56,728.41	67,801.38
Apparel, average spending	**1,815.95**	**1,149.61**	**1,404.86**	**1,805.84**	**1,947.73**	**2,526.12**	**2,435.97**	**2,690.37**
MEN'S APPAREL	**317.28**	**189.54**	**217.14**	**345.94**	**280.76**	**471.14**	**444.51**	**520.77**
Suits	23.99	6.57	13.24	19.40	19.53	48.33	44.94	54.30
Sport coats and tailored jackets	8.38	2.72	4.60	8.12	6.40	15.80	13.02	20.67
Coats and jackets	25.50	7.57	22.50	32.87	19.91	34.03	32.20	37.54
Underwear	16.99	17.80	12.74	16.74	15.23	21.43	21.77	20.78
Hosiery	15.09	9.14	13.41	12.94	9.97	22.81	19.23	29.63
Nightwear	2.10	1.13	1.55	2.31	1.74	3.10	3.04	3.19
Accessories	25.06	12.72	13.40	24.65	29.05	41.80	39.99	45.24
Sweaters and vests	9.84	4.01	6.83	8.37	7.49	17.68	16.28	20.13
Active sportswear	22.80	13.45	15.45	32.24	20.13	28.82	34.88	17.26
Shirts	82.51	46.86	50.45	84.90	71.30	133.57	126.93	146.25
Pants	62.63	53.56	40.60	79.35	63.96	76.44	64.70	98.85
Shorts and shorts sets	14.82	9.88	16.59	16.20	7.98	16.69	17.16	15.79
Uniforms	3.99	3.04	3.42	3.87	4.76	4.89	4.58	5.45
Costumes	3.57	1.10	2.38	3.98	3.32	5.75	5.79	5.69
BOYS' (AGED 2 TO 15) APPAREL	**88.88**	**68.27**	**78.59**	**86.81**	**107.48**	**105.07**	**106.29**	**102.58**
Coats and jackets	5.99	5.23	5.45	5.10	6.63	7.38	6.16	9.51
Sweaters	2.98	2.16	2.57	3.35	2.70	3.61	3.53	3.76
Shirts	19.65	14.30	16.78	21.26	25.78	22.19	24.84	17.12
Underwear	4.77	5.52	4.26	4.95	3.41	5.14	5.92	3.66
Nightwear	3.27	1.70	2.56	3.57	2.22	4.85	4.18	6.13
Hosiery	5.00	3.79	4.93	4.47	8.18	5.12	5.78	3.86
Accessories	3.82	1.17	4.14	2.01	4.68	5.88	4.80	7.95
Suits, sport coats, and vests	2.59	2.11	1.65	3.29	2.26	3.30	2.26	5.12
Pants	22.39	18.95	20.49	21.36	29.89	24.31	25.17	22.80
Shorts and shorts sets	7.77	6.12	6.80	7.77	9.06	9.12	9.87	7.80
Uniforms	3.82	3.45	3.14	3.25	4.41	4.91	4.31	5.96
Active sportswear	4.29	2.02	4.00	4.20	4.94	5.58	5.58	5.59
Costumes	2.55	1.74	1.80	2.25	3.32	3.68	3.87	3.34
WOMEN'S APPAREL	**631.01**	**363.09**	**475.37**	**690.58**	**719.96**	**850.84**	**824.86**	**899.53**
Coats and jackets	48.87	31.19	29.19	56.46	68.52	65.80	57.85	80.99
Dresses	66.25	33.29	45.09	114.63	46.02	75.43	84.08	58.92
Sport coats and tailored jackets	8.76	2.30	4.97	8.71	9.64	15.47	13.87	18.29
Sweaters and vests	46.31	23.95	29.43	47.22	48.88	72.75	73.75	70.85
Shirts, blouses, and tops	120.91	86.05	101.02	123.39	128.43	154.05	139.41	182.00
Skirts	17.07	15.16	14.49	11.35	19.03	24.01	22.41	27.07
Pants	96.25	64.20	77.95	111.59	100.42	118.31	113.54	127.40
Shorts and shorts sets	12.59	7.68	11.08	10.28	13.06	18.07	20.24	13.92
Active sportswear	36.31	19.66	29.20	28.76	50.69	52.78	57.04	44.65
Nightwear	29.94	11.73	30.73	28.32	44.89	35.16	38.72	28.35
Undergarments	43.77	30.88	29.31	51.47	64.32	52.80	48.91	60.23
Hosiery	18.77	11.28	16.90	17.86	22.75	23.86	23.08	25.35
Suits	23.57	7.75	15.03	18.73	15.53	46.35	40.39	56.83
Accessories	50.57	14.69	32.71	50.62	74.44	79.10	73.27	90.22
Uniforms	5.97	2.54	4.75	6.66	8.21	7.65	8.26	6.57
Costumes	5.09	0.77	3.52	4.52	5.13	9.26	10.04	7.89

	total consumer units	less than high school graduate	high school graduate	some college	associate's degree	college graduate		
						total	bachelor's degree	master's, professional, doctorate
GIRLS' (AGED 2 TO 15) APPAREL	**$107.60**	**$74.47**	**$92.33**	**$92.54**	**$129.19**	**$143.46**	**$141.25**	**$147.22**
Coats and jackets	7.49	5.87	7.82	6.27	8.93	8.49	7.17	10.81
Dresses and suits	9.49	6.31	6.00	7.64	17.67	13.36	12.31	15.38
Shirts, blouses, and sweaters	23.95	17.68	18.33	20.85	26.82	33.94	36.83	28.43
Skirts and pants	24.32	18.47	23.10	24.22	27.86	27.42	26.49	29.07
Shorts and shorts sets	8.40	6.83	6.83	8.21	11.57	9.81	9.21	10.86
Active sportswear	10.05	5.23	7.86	5.63	10.81	17.53	17.31	17.97
Underwear and nightwear	6.28	4.71	5.13	6.64	7.98	7.36	7.39	7.30
Hosiery	3.77	2.37	4.31	2.87	4.65	4.34	3.15	6.60
Accessories	5.93	2.32	4.99	3.55	4.07	10.92	11.32	10.14
Uniforms	3.84	2.40	4.23	3.52	4.30	4.30	4.39	4.13
Costumes	4.10	2.27	3.73	3.16	4.53	5.98	5.68	6.52
CHILDREN'S (UNDER AGE 2) APPAREL	**78.51**	**72.86**	**68.17**	**67.00**	**85.14**	**97.67**	**101.34**	**90.64**
Coats, jackets, and snowsuits	2.48	1.96	1.77	2.72	2.45	3.23	2.63	4.28
Outerwear including dresses	20.72	15.24	18.65	19.22	22.06	26.25	26.80	25.30
Underwear	44.17	45.19	38.10	34.88	52.24	53.73	55.95	49.50
Nightwear and loungewear	3.49	1.87	3.08	3.13	4.94	4.52	4.41	4.73
Accessories	7.66	8.60	6.57	7.05	3.45	9.93	11.55	6.83
FOOTWEAR	**328.74**	**248.31**	**301.29**	**282.92**	**376.58**	**414.66**	**418.65**	**407.04**
Men's	110.67	75.18	103.61	105.88	108.17	139.80	135.18	148.63
Boys'	35.92	26.99	37.14	30.08	45.63	40.54	46.57	29.03
Women's	153.81	122.54	131.49	127.08	180.74	202.36	211.68	184.55
Girls'	28.34	23.61	29.06	19.89	42.04	31.96	25.21	44.84
OTHER APPAREL PRODUCTS AND SERVICES	**263.94**	**133.07**	**171.95**	**240.05**	**248.62**	**443.27**	**399.07**	**522.58**
Material for making clothes	13.05	6.30	4.22	9.75	6.11	29.51	19.29	49.02
Sewing patterns and notions	7.82	3.41	4.51	10.60	9.11	10.94	10.51	11.77
Watches	21.51	6.19	15.57	20.11	18.70	37.14	39.60	32.82
Jewelry	113.72	29.71	75.00	108.74	120.87	195.81	177.55	227.90
Shoe repair and other shoe services	1.12	0.27	0.57	0.86	0.79	2.40	2.02	3.07
Coin-operated apparel laundry and dry cleaning	34.86	67.14	35.25	32.73	27.18	21.93	22.62	20.70
Apparel alteration, repair, and tailoring services	5.12	2.49	2.47	4.47	5.64	9.34	8.44	10.91
Clothing rental	2.28	0.95	2.53	2.08	2.22	2.89	3.35	2.09
Watch and jewelry repair	3.82	0.42	3.57	3.88	4.11	5.67	4.18	8.29
Professional laundry, dry cleaning	60.18	16.13	28.00	46.51	53.84	126.51	110.34	154.94
Clothing storage	0.47	0.06	0.25	0.32	0.05	1.14	1.17	1.08

Note: Subcategories may not add to total because some are not shown.
Source: Bureau of Labor Statistics, unpublished data from the 2004 Consumer Expenditure Survey

Table 2.26 Apparel: Indexed spending by education, 2004

(indexed average annual spending of consumer units (CU) on apparel, accessories, and related services, by education of consumer unit reference person, 2004; index definition: an index of 100 is the average for all consumer units; an index of 132 means that spending by consumer units in that group is 32 percent above the average for all consumer units; an index of 68 indicates spending that is 32 percent below the average for all consumer units)

	total consumer units	less than high school graduate	high school graduate	some college	associate's degree	college graduate total	college graduate bachelor's degree	college graduate master's, professional, doctorate
Average spending of CU, total	$43,395	$25,421	$35,439	$40,878	$48,177	$60,712	$56,728	$67,801
Average spending of CU, index	100	59	82	94	111	140	131	156
Apparel, spending index	100	63	77	99	107	139	134	148
MEN'S APPAREL	**100**	**60**	**68**	**109**	**88**	**148**	**140**	**164**
Suits	100	27	55	81	81	201	187	226
Sport coats and tailored jackets	100	32	55	97	76	189	155	247
Coats and jackets	100	30	88	129	78	133	126	147
Underwear	100	105	75	99	90	126	128	122
Hosiery	100	61	89	86	66	151	127	196
Nightwear	100	54	74	110	83	148	145	152
Accessories	100	51	53	98	116	167	160	181
Sweaters and vests	100	41	69	85	76	180	165	205
Active sportswear	100	59	68	141	88	126	153	76
Shirts	100	57	61	103	86	162	154	177
Pants	100	86	65	127	102	122	103	158
Shorts and shorts sets	100	67	112	109	54	113	116	107
Uniforms	100	76	86	97	119	123	115	137
Costumes	100	31	67	111	93	161	162	159
BOYS' (AGED 2 TO 15) APPAREL	**100**	**77**	**88**	**98**	**121**	**118**	**120**	**115**
Coats and jackets	100	87	91	85	111	123	103	159
Sweaters	100	72	86	112	91	121	118	126
Shirts	100	73	85	108	131	113	126	87
Underwear	100	116	89	104	71	108	124	77
Nightwear	100	52	78	109	68	148	128	187
Hosiery	100	76	99	89	164	102	116	77
Accessories	100	31	108	53	123	154	126	208
Suits, sport coats, and vests	100	81	64	127	87	127	87	198
Pants	100	85	92	95	133	109	112	102
Shorts and shorts sets	100	79	88	100	117	117	127	100
Uniforms	100	90	82	85	115	129	113	156
Active sportswear	100	47	93	98	115	130	130	130
Costumes	100	68	71	88	130	144	152	131
WOMEN'S APPAREL	**100**	**58**	**75**	**109**	**114**	**135**	**131**	**143**
Coats and jackets	100	64	60	116	140	135	118	166
Dresses	100	50	68	173	69	114	127	89
Sport coats and tailored jackets	100	26	57	99	110	177	158	209
Sweaters and vests	100	52	64	102	106	157	159	153
Shirts, blouses, and tops	100	71	84	102	106	127	115	151
Skirts	100	89	85	66	111	141	131	159
Pants	100	67	81	116	104	123	118	132
Shorts and shorts sets	100	61	88	82	104	144	161	111
Active sportswear	100	54	80	79	140	145	157	123
Nightwear	100	39	103	95	150	117	129	95
Undergarments	100	71	67	118	147	121	112	138
Hosiery	100	60	90	95	121	127	123	135
Suits	100	33	64	79	66	197	171	241
Accessories	100	29	65	100	147	156	145	178
Uniforms	100	43	80	112	138	128	138	110
Costumes	100	15	69	89	101	182	197	155

	total consumer units	less than high school graduate	high school graduate	some college	associate's degree	college graduate		
						total	bachelor's degree	master's, professional, doctorate
GIRLS' (AGED 2 TO 15) APPAREL	**100**	**69**	**86**	**86**	**120**	**133**	**131**	**137**
Coats and jackets	100	78	104	84	119	113	96	144
Dresses and suits	100	66	63	81	186	141	130	162
Shirts, blouses, and sweaters	100	74	77	87	112	142	154	119
Skirts and pants	100	76	95	100	115	113	109	120
Shorts and shorts sets	100	81	81	98	138	117	110	129
Active sportswear	100	52	78	56	108	174	172	179
Underwear and nightwear	100	75	82	106	127	117	118	116
Hosiery	100	63	114	76	123	115	84	175
Accessories	100	39	84	60	69	184	191	171
Uniforms	100	63	110	92	112	112	114	108
Costumes	100	55	91	77	110	146	139	159
CHILDREN'S (UNDER AGE 2) APPAREL	**100**	**93**	**87**	**85**	**108**	**124**	**129**	**115**
Coats, jackets, and snowsuits	100	79	71	110	99	130	106	173
Outerwear including dresses	100	74	90	93	106	127	129	122
Underwear	100	102	86	79	118	122	127	112
Nightwear and loungewear	100	54	88	90	142	130	126	136
Accessories	100	112	86	92	45	130	151	89
FOOTWEAR	**100**	**76**	**92**	**86**	**115**	**126**	**127**	**124**
Men's	100	68	94	96	98	126	122	134
Boys'	100	75	103	84	127	113	130	81
Women's	100	80	85	83	118	132	138	120
Girls'	100	83	103	70	148	113	89	158
OTHER APPAREL PRODUCTS AND SERVICES	**100**	**50**	**65**	**91**	**94**	**168**	**151**	**198**
Material for making clothes	100	48	32	75	47	226	148	376
Sewing patterns and notions	100	44	58	136	116	140	134	151
Watches	100	29	72	93	87	173	184	153
Jewelry	100	26	66	96	106	172	156	200
Shoe repair and other shoe services	100	24	51	77	71	214	180	274
Coin-operated apparel laundry and dry cleaning	100	193	101	94	78	63	65	59
Apparel alteration, repair, and tailoring services	100	49	48	87	110	182	165	213
Clothing rental	100	42	111	91	97	127	147	92
Watch and jewelry repair	100	11	93	102	108	148	109	217
Professional laundry, dry cleaning	100	27	47	77	89	210	183	257
Clothing storage	100	13	53	68	11	243	249	230

Source: Calculations by New Strategist based on the 2004 Consumer Expenditure Survey

Table 2.27 Apparel: Total spending by education, 2004

(total annual spending on apparel, accessories, and related services, by consumer unit (CU) educational attainment group, 2004; consumer units and dollars in thousands)

	total consumer units	less than high school graduate	high school graduate	some college	associate's degree	college graduate total	bachelor's degree	master's, professional, doctorate
Number of consumer units	116,282	16,829	31,005	25,317	10,678	32,452	20,684	11,768
Total spending of all CUs	$5,046,042,273	$427,813,038	$1,098,772,243	$1,034,900,225	$514,437,850	$1,970,234,911	$1,173,370,432	$797,886,640
Apparel, total spending	211,162,298	19,346,787	43,557,684	45,718,451	20,797,861	81,977,646	50,385,603	31,660,274
MEN'S APPAREL	**36,893,953**	**3,189,769**	**6,732,426**	**8,758,163**	**2,997,955**	**15,289,435**	**9,194,245**	**6,128,421**
Suits	2,789,605	110,567	410,506	491,150	208,541	1,568,405	929,539	639,002
Sport coats and tailored jackets	974,443	45,775	142,623	205,574	68,339	512,742	269,306	243,245
Coats and jackets	2,965,191	127,396	697,613	832,170	212,599	1,104,342	666,025	441,771
Underwear	1,975,631	299,556	395,004	423,807	162,626	695,446	450,291	244,539
Hosiery	1,754,695	153,817	415,777	327,602	106,460	740,230	397,753	348,686
Nightwear	244,192	19,017	48,058	58,482	18,580	100,601	62,879	37,540
Accessories	2,914,027	214,065	415,467	624,064	310,196	1,356,494	827,153	532,384
Sweaters and vests	1,144,215	67,484	211,764	211,903	79,978	573,751	336,736	236,890
Active sportswear	2,651,230	226,350	479,027	816,220	214,948	935,267	721,458	203,116
Shirts	9,594,428	788,607	1,564,202	2,149,413	761,341	4,334,614	2,625,420	1,721,070
Pants	7,282,742	901,361	1,258,803	2,008,904	682,965	2,480,631	1,338,255	1,163,267
Shorts and shorts sets	1,723,299	166,271	514,373	410,135	85,210	541,624	354,937	185,817
Uniforms	463,965	51,160	106,037	97,977	50,827	158,690	94,733	64,136
Costumes	415,127	18,512	73,792	100,762	35,451	186,599	119,760	66,960
BOYS' (AGED 2 TO 15) APPAREL	**10,335,144**	**1,148,916**	**2,436,683**	**2,197,769**	**1,147,671**	**3,409,732**	**2,198,502**	**1,207,161**
Coats and jackets	696,529	88,016	168,977	129,117	70,795	239,496	127,413	111,914
Sweaters	346,520	36,351	79,683	84,812	28,831	117,152	73,015	44,248
Shirts	2,284,941	240,655	520,264	538,239	275,279	720,110	513,791	201,468
Underwear	554,665	92,896	132,081	125,319	36,412	166,803	122,449	43,071
Nightwear	380,242	28,609	79,373	90,382	23,705	157,392	86,459	72,138
Hosiery	581,410	63,782	152,855	113,167	87,346	166,154	119,554	45,424
Accessories	444,197	19,690	128,361	50,887	49,973	190,818	99,283	93,556
Suits, sport coats, and vests	301,170	35,509	51,158	83,293	24,132	107,092	46,746	60,252
Pants	2,603,554	318,910	635,292	540,771	319,165	788,908	520,616	268,310
Shorts and shorts sets	903,511	102,993	210,834	196,713	96,743	295,962	204,151	91,790
Uniforms	444,197	58,060	97,356	82,280	47,090	159,339	89,148	70,137
Active sportswear	498,850	33,995	124,020	106,331	52,749	181,082	115,417	65,783
Costumes	296,519	29,282	55,809	56,963	35,451	119,423	80,047	39,305
WOMEN'S APPAREL	**73,375,105**	**6,110,442**	**14,738,847**	**17,483,414**	**7,687,733**	**27,611,460**	**17,061,404**	**10,585,669**
Coats and jackets	5,682,701	524,897	905,036	1,429,398	731,657	2,135,342	1,196,569	953,090
Dresses	7,703,683	560,237	1,398,015	2,902,088	491,402	2,447,854	1,739,111	693,371
Sport coats and tailored jackets	1,018,630	38,707	154,095	220,511	102,936	502,032	286,887	215,237
Sweaters and vests	5,385,019	403,055	912,477	1,195,469	521,941	2,360,883	1,525,445	833,763
Shirts, blouses, and tops	14,059,657	1,448,135	3,132,125	3,123,865	1,371,376	4,999,231	2,883,556	2,141,776
Skirts	1,984,934	255,128	449,262	287,348	203,202	779,173	463,528	318,560
Pants	11,192,143	1,080,422	2,416,840	2,825,124	1,072,285	3,839,396	2,348,461	1,499,243
Shorts and shorts sets	1,463,990	129,247	343,535	260,259	139,455	586,408	418,644	163,811
Active sportswear	4,222,199	330,858	905,346	728,117	541,268	1,712,817	1,179,815	525,441
Nightwear	3,481,483	197,404	952,784	716,977	479,335	1,141,012	800,884	333,623
Undergarments	5,089,663	519,680	908,757	1,303,066	686,809	1,713,466	1,011,654	708,787
Hosiery	2,182,613	189,831	523,985	452,162	242,925	774,305	477,387	298,319
Suits	2,740,767	130,425	466,005	474,187	165,829	1,504,150	835,427	668,775
Accessories	5,880,381	247,218	1,014,174	1,281,547	794,870	2,566,953	1,515,517	1,061,709
Uniforms	694,204	42,746	147,274	168,611	87,666	248,258	170,850	77,316
Costumes	591,875	12,958	109,138	114,433	54,778	300,506	207,667	92,850

	total consumer units	less than high school graduate	high school graduate	some college	associate's degree	college graduate		
						total	bachelor's degree	master's, professional, doctorate
GIRLS' (AGED 2 TO 15) APPAREL	**$12,511,943**	**$1,253,256**	**$2,862,692**	**$2,342,835**	**$1,379,491**	**$4,655,564**	**$2,921,615**	**$1,732,485**
Coats and jackets	870,952	98,786	242,459	158,738	95,355	275,517	148,304	127,212
Dresses and suits	1,103,516	106,191	186,030	193,422	188,680	433,559	254,620	180,992
Shirts, blouses, and sweaters	2,784,954	297,537	568,322	527,859	286,384	1,101,421	761,792	334,564
Skirts and pants	2,827,978	310,832	716,216	613,178	297,489	889,834	547,919	342,096
Shorts and shorts sets	976,769	114,942	211,764	207,853	123,544	318,354	190,500	127,800
Active sportswear	1,168,634	88,016	243,699	142,535	115,429	568,884	358,040	211,471
Underwear and nightwear	730,251	79,265	159,056	168,105	85,210	238,847	152,855	85,906
Hosiery	438,383	39,885	133,632	72,660	49,653	140,842	65,155	77,669
Accessories	689,552	39,043	154,715	89,875	43,459	354,376	234,143	119,328
Uniforms	446,523	40,390	131,151	89,116	45,915	139,544	90,803	48,602
Costumes	476,756	38,202	115,649	80,002	48,371	194,063	117,485	76,727
CHILDREN'S (UNDER AGE 2) APPAREL	**9,129,300**	**1,226,161**	**2,113,611**	**1,696,239**	**909,125**	**3,169,587**	**2,096,117**	**1,066,652**
Coats, jackets, and snowsuits	288,379	32,985	54,879	68,862	26,161	104,820	54,399	50,367
Outerwear including dresses	2,409,363	256,474	578,243	486,593	235,557	851,865	554,331	297,730
Underwear	5,136,176	760,503	1,181,291	883,057	557,819	1,743,646	1,157,270	582,516
Nightwear and loungewear	405,824	31,470	95,495	79,242	52,749	146,683	91,216	55,663
Accessories	890,720	144,729	203,703	178,485	36,839	322,248	238,900	80,375
FOOTWEAR	**38,226,545**	**4,178,809**	**9,341,496**	**7,162,686**	**4,021,121**	**13,456,546**	**8,659,357**	**4,790,047**
Men's	12,868,929	1,265,204	3,212,428	2,680,564	1,155,039	4,536,790	2,796,063	1,749,078
Boys'	4,176,849	454,215	1,151,526	761,535	487,237	1,315,604	963,254	341,625
Women's	17,885,334	2,062,226	4,076,847	3,217,284	1,929,942	6,566,987	4,378,389	2,171,784
Girls'	3,295,432	397,333	901,005	503,555	448,903	1,037,166	521,444	527,677
OTHER APPAREL PRODUCTS, SERVICES	**30,691,471**	**2,239,435**	**5,331,310**	**6,077,346**	**2,654,764**	**14,384,998**	**8,254,364**	**6,149,721**
Material for making clothes	1,517,480	106,023	130,841	246,841	65,243	957,659	398,994	576,867
Sewing patterns and notions	909,325	57,387	139,833	268,360	97,277	355,025	217,389	138,509
Watches	2,501,226	104,172	482,748	509,125	199,679	1,205,267	819,086	386,226
Jewelry	13,223,589	499,990	2,325,375	2,752,971	1,290,650	6,354,426	3,672,444	2,681,927
Shoe repair and other shoe services	130,236	4,544	17,673	21,773	8,436	77,885	41,782	36,128
Coin-operated apparel laundry and dry cleaning	4,053,591	1,129,899	1,092,926	828,625	290,228	711,672	467,872	243,598
Apparel alteration, repair, and tailoring services	595,364	41,904	76,582	113,167	60,224	303,102	174,573	128,389
Clothing rental	265,123	15,988	78,443	52,659	23,705	93,786	69,291	24,595
Watch and jewelry repair	444,197	7,068	110,688	98,230	43,887	184,003	86,459	97,557
Professional laundry, dry cleaning	6,997,851	271,452	868,140	1,177,494	574,904	4,105,503	2,282,273	1,823,334
Clothing storage	54,653	1,010	7,751	8,101	534	36,995	24,200	12,709

Note: Numbers may not add to total because of rounding and missing subcategories.
Source: Calculations by New Strategist based on the 2004 Consumer Expenditure Survey

Table 2.28 Apparel: Market shares by education, 2004

(percentage of total annual spending on apparel, accessories, and related services accounted for by consumer unit educational attainment groups, 2004)

	total consumer units	less than high school graduate	high school graduate	some college	associate's degree	college graduate total	bachelor's degree	master's, professional, doctorate
Share of total consumer units	100.0%	14.5%	26.7%	21.8%	9.2%	27.9%	17.8%	10.1%
Share of total before-tax income	100.0	7.7	20.7	18.7	9.9	43.0	24.7	18.3
Share of total spending	100.0	8.5	21.8	20.5	10.2	39.0	23.3	15.8
Share of apparel spending	100.0	9.2	20.6	21.7	9.8	38.8	23.9	15.0
MEN'S APPAREL	100.0	8.6	18.2	23.7	8.1	41.4	24.9	16.6
Suits	100.0	4.0	14.7	17.6	7.5	56.2	33.3	22.9
Sport coats and tailored jackets	100.0	4.7	14.6	21.1	7.0	52.6	27.6	25.0
Coats and jackets	100.0	4.3	23.5	28.1	7.2	37.2	22.5	14.9
Underwear	100.0	15.2	20.0	21.5	8.2	35.2	22.8	12.4
Hosiery	100.0	8.8	23.7	18.7	6.1	42.2	22.7	19.9
Nightwear	100.0	7.8	19.7	23.9	7.6	41.2	25.7	15.4
Accessories	100.0	7.3	14.3	21.4	10.6	46.6	28.4	18.3
Sweaters and vests	100.0	5.9	18.5	18.5	7.0	50.1	29.4	20.7
Active sportswear	100.0	8.5	18.1	30.8	8.1	35.3	27.2	7.7
Shirts	100.0	8.2	16.3	22.4	7.9	45.2	27.4	17.9
Pants	100.0	12.4	17.3	27.6	9.4	34.1	18.4	16.0
Shorts and shorts sets	100.0	9.6	29.8	23.8	4.9	31.4	20.6	10.8
Uniforms	100.0	11.0	22.9	21.1	11.0	34.2	20.4	13.8
Costumes	100.0	4.5	17.8	24.3	8.5	44.9	28.8	16.1
BOYS' (AGED 2 TO 15) APPAREL	100.0	11.1	23.6	21.3	11.1	33.0	21.3	11.7
Coats and jackets	100.0	12.6	24.3	18.5	10.2	34.4	18.3	16.1
Sweaters	100.0	10.5	23.0	24.5	8.3	33.8	21.1	12.8
Shirts	100.0	10.5	22.8	23.6	12.0	31.5	22.5	8.8
Underwear	100.0	16.7	23.8	22.6	6.6	30.1	22.1	7.8
Nightwear	100.0	7.5	20.9	23.8	6.2	41.4	22.7	19.0
Hosiery	100.0	11.0	26.3	19.5	15.0	28.6	20.6	7.8
Accessories	100.0	4.4	28.9	11.5	11.3	43.0	22.4	21.1
Suits, sport coats, and vests	100.0	11.8	17.0	27.7	8.0	35.6	15.5	20.0
Pants	100.0	12.2	24.4	20.8	12.3	30.3	20.0	10.3
Shorts and shorts sets	100.0	11.4	23.3	21.8	10.7	32.8	22.6	10.2
Uniforms	100.0	13.1	21.9	18.5	10.6	35.9	20.1	15.8
Active sportswear	100.0	6.8	24.9	21.3	10.6	36.3	23.1	13.2
Costumes	100.0	9.9	18.8	19.2	12.0	40.3	27.0	13.3
WOMEN'S APPAREL	100.0	8.3	20.1	23.8	10.5	37.6	23.3	14.4
Coats and jackets	100.0	9.2	15.9	25.2	12.9	37.6	21.1	16.8
Dresses	100.0	7.3	18.1	37.7	6.4	31.8	22.6	9.0
Sport coats and tailored jackets	100.0	3.8	15.1	21.6	10.1	49.3	28.2	21.1
Sweaters and vests	100.0	7.5	16.9	22.2	9.7	43.8	28.3	15.5
Shirts, blouses, and tops	100.0	10.3	22.3	22.2	9.8	35.6	20.5	15.2
Skirts	100.0	12.9	22.6	14.5	10.2	39.3	23.4	16.0
Pants	100.0	9.7	21.6	25.2	9.6	34.3	21.0	13.4
Shorts and shorts sets	100.0	8.8	23.5	17.8	9.5	40.1	28.6	11.2
Active sportswear	100.0	7.8	21.4	17.2	12.8	40.6	27.9	12.4
Nightwear	100.0	5.7	27.4	20.6	13.8	32.8	23.0	9.6
Undergarments	100.0	10.2	17.9	25.6	13.5	33.7	19.9	13.9
Hosiery	100.0	8.7	24.0	20.7	11.1	35.5	21.9	13.7
Suits	100.0	4.8	17.0	17.3	6.1	54.9	30.5	24.4
Accessories	100.0	4.2	17.2	21.8	13.5	43.7	25.8	18.1
Uniforms	100.0	6.2	21.2	24.3	12.6	35.8	24.6	11.1
Costumes	100.0	2.2	18.4	19.3	9.3	50.8	35.1	15.7

	total consumer units	less than high school graduate	high school graduate	some college	associate's degree	college graduate		
						total	bachelor's degree	master's, professional, doctorate
GIRLS' (AGED 2 TO 15) APPAREL	**100.0%**	**10.0%**	**22.9%**	**18.7%**	**11.0%**	**37.2%**	**23.4%**	**13.8%**
Coats and jackets	100.0	11.3	27.8	18.2	10.9	31.6	17.0	14.6
Dresses and suits	100.0	9.6	16.9	17.5	17.1	39.3	23.1	16.4
Shirts, blouses, and sweaters	100.0	10.7	20.4	19.0	10.3	39.5	27.4	12.0
Skirts and pants	100.0	11.0	25.3	21.7	10.5	31.5	19.4	12.1
Shorts and shorts sets	100.0	11.8	21.7	21.3	12.6	32.6	19.5	13.1
Active sportswear	100.0	7.5	20.9	12.2	9.9	48.7	30.6	18.1
Underwear and nightwear	100.0	10.9	21.8	23.0	11.7	32.7	20.9	11.8
Hosiery	100.0	9.1	30.5	16.6	11.3	32.1	14.9	17.7
Accessories	100.0	5.7	22.4	13.0	6.3	51.4	34.0	17.3
Uniforms	100.0	9.0	29.4	20.0	10.3	31.3	20.3	10.9
Costumes	100.0	8.0	24.3	16.8	10.1	40.7	24.6	16.1
CHILDREN'S (UNDER AGE 2) APPAREL	**100.0**	**13.4**	**23.2**	**18.6**	**10.0**	**34.7**	**23.0**	**11.7**
Coats, jackets, and snowsuits	100.0	11.4	19.0	23.9	9.1	36.3	18.9	17.5
Outerwear including dresses	100.0	10.6	24.0	20.2	9.8	35.4	23.0	12.4
Underwear	100.0	14.8	23.0	17.2	10.9	33.9	22.5	11.3
Nightwear and loungewear	100.0	7.8	23.5	19.5	13.0	36.1	22.5	13.7
Accessories	100.0	16.2	22.9	20.0	4.1	36.2	26.8	9.0
FOOTWEAR	**100.0**	**10.9**	**24.4**	**18.7**	**10.5**	**35.2**	**22.7**	**12.5**
Men's	100.0	9.8	25.0	20.8	9.0	35.3	21.7	13.6
Boys'	100.0	10.9	27.6	18.2	11.7	31.5	23.1	8.2
Women's	100.0	11.5	22.8	18.0	10.8	36.7	24.5	12.1
Girls'	100.0	12.1	27.3	15.3	13.6	31.5	15.8	16.0
OTHER APPAREL PRODUCTS AND SERVICES	**100.0**	**7.3**	**17.4**	**19.8**	**8.6**	**46.9**	**26.9**	**20.0**
Material for making clothes	100.0	7.0	8.6	16.3	4.3	63.1	26.3	38.0
Sewing patterns and notions	100.0	6.3	15.4	29.5	10.7	39.0	23.9	15.2
Watches	100.0	4.2	19.3	20.4	8.0	48.2	32.7	15.4
Jewelry	100.0	3.8	17.6	20.8	9.8	48.1	27.8	20.3
Shoe repair and other shoe services	100.0	3.5	13.6	16.7	6.5	59.8	32.1	27.7
Coin-operated apparel laundry and dry cleaning	100.0	27.9	27.0	20.4	7.2	17.6	11.5	6.0
Apparel alteration, repair, and tailoring services	100.0	7.0	12.9	19.0	10.1	50.9	29.3	21.6
Clothing rental	100.0	6.0	29.6	19.9	8.9	35.4	26.1	9.3
Watch and jewelry repair	100.0	1.6	24.9	22.1	9.9	41.4	19.5	22.0
Professional laundry, dry cleaning	100.0	3.9	12.4	16.8	8.2	58.7	32.6	26.1
Clothing storage	100.0	1.8	14.2	14.8	1.0	67.7	44.3	23.3

Note: Numbers may not add to total because of rounding.
Source: Calculations by New Strategist based on the 2004 Consumer Expenditure Survey

Chapter 3. Spending on Entertainment, 2004

Entertainment spending has grown since 2000, despite the volatility in the economy. The average household spent $2,218 on entertainment in 2004, up from $2,044 in 2000, a nearly 9 percent rise after adjusting for inflation. Overall, Americans devoted 5.1 percent of their spending to entertainment in 2004, up slightly from 4.9 percent in 2000. The average American household now spends substantially more on entertainment than it does on clothes.

Households headed by people aged 55 to 64 spend the most on entertainment, $2,823 on average in 2004—27 percent more than the average household. Interestingly, older householders spend more on entertainment than younger ones. Households headed by 45-to-54-year-olds spent $2,711 on entertainment in 2004, more than households headed by people under age 45. Even householders aged 65 to 74 are big spenders on many entertainment categories including admission to sports events, rental of recreational vehicles, docking and landing fees.

Households with incomes of $100,000 or more spent $4,932 on entertainment in 2004, more than twice what the average household spends. High-income households spend far more than average on nearly every entertainment category. Households with incomes of $100,000 or more account for 13 percent of households, but they control a larger 29 percent of entertainment spending. They account for 44 percent of spending on playground equipment, 45 percent of spending on fees for recreational lessons, and 46 percent of spending on club memberships.

Married couples with children aged 6 to 17 at home spend much more on entertainment than other household types—50 percent more than the average household. They are especially big spenders on fees for recreational lessons, devoting nearly four times as much as the average household to this item. They spend two-and-one-half times the average on videogame hardware and software. Married couples without children at home, many of them empty-nesters, spend nearly triple the average on motorized recreational vehicles.

Asians, blacks, and Hispanics spend less than the average household on entertainment. In some categories, however, they spend more. Asians spend more than double the average on fees for recreational lessons. Blacks spend much more than average on television and VCR rentals. Hispanics spend more than average on table-top televisions. Non-Hispanic whites spend 19 percent more than average on pets, while Asians, blacks, and Hispanics spend less than average on this item.

Households in the West spend more on entertainment than households in other regions–$2,538 in 2004, or 14 percent more than average. Western households spend 65 percent more than average on musical instruments and nearly twice the average on motorized campers. Households in the Northeast spend 9 percent less than average on entertainment, but they spend 25 percent more than average on fees for recreational lessons.

College graduates spend 47 percent more than the average household on entertainment. They account for 80 percent of the market for musical instrument rental and repair. They also control 64 percent of household spending on fees for recreational lessons. Householders without a college degree account for 70 percent of spending on pet food.

Table 3.1 Entertainment: Average spending by age, 2004

(average annual spending of consumer units (CU) on entertainment, by age of consumer unit reference person, 2004)

	total consumer units	under 25	25 to 34	35 to 44	45 to 54	55 to 64	65 to 74	75+
Number of consumer units (in 000s)	116,282	8,817	19,439	24,070	23,712	17,479	11,230	11,536
Average number of persons per CU	2.5	1.9	2.9	3.2	2.7	2.1	1.9	1.5
Average before-tax income of CU	$54,453.00	$22,840.00	$52,484.00	$65,515.00	$70,434.00	$61,031.00	$42,137.00	$28,028.00
Average spending of CU, total	43,394.87	24,534.56	42,700.54	50,401.62	52,764.36	47,298.58	36,511.98	25,763.32
Entertainment, average spending	2,218.47	1,165.85	2,121.68	2,504.33	2,711.13	2,822.81	1,878.87	990.38
FEES AND ADMISSIONS	527.94	276.97	415.15	666.40	666.68	618.44	462.60	262.21
Recreation expenses on trips	27.04	17.24	22.53	28.65	36.03	34.91	24.93	10.43
Social, recreation, civic club membership	98.19	43.82	66.35	99.06	108.02	162.57	113.45	58.96
Fees for participant sports	73.98	27.96	53.50	82.08	80.31	89.32	70.21	94.20
Participant sports on trips	26.72	13.59	18.41	30.14	37.43	36.87	21.95	10.89
Movie, theater, opera, ballet	92.46	85.42	94.15	108.12	113.75	93.17	74.58	34.86
Movie, other admissions on trips	48.03	24.58	39.64	59.59	59.82	61.01	40.01	19.82
Admission to sports events	36.05	19.33	27.78	43.24	50.26	32.01	55.72	5.57
Admission to sports events on trips	16.01	8.19	13.21	19.86	19.94	20.33	13.33	6.61
Fees for recreational lessons	82.42	19.59	57.05	167.02	125.07	53.32	23.49	10.45
Other entertainment services on trips	27.04	17.24	22.53	28.65	36.03	34.91	24.93	10.43
TELEVISION, RADIO, SOUND EQUIPMENT	787.64	499.75	842.81	920.68	926.18	809.73	628.17	473.96
Television	652.61	372.01	672.64	741.32	749.94	712.70	566.90	440.55
Cable service and community antenna	471.01	215.60	443.50	513.74	543.40	537.61	473.76	371.08
Color TV sets, consoles	52.46	44.51	71.26	61.40	52.00	58.79	28.93	22.46
Color TV sets, portable and table models	39.80	29.64	41.21	43.56	45.73	49.60	24.61	25.05
VCRs and video disc players	24.05	12.08	27.91	34.38	29.96	22.22	11.87	7.60
Video cassettes, tapes, and discs	42.63	44.18	60.90	54.18	53.80	31.06	16.63	6.41
Video game hardware and software	18.34	19.75	24.02	28.82	20.22	9.66	7.84	5.33
Repair of TV, radio, and sound equipment	3.02	2.04	3.02	3.96	2.78	3.18	2.45	2.62
Rental of television sets	0.81	3.64	0.80	0.91	0.93	0.16	–	–
Radio and sound equipment	135.03	127.74	170.17	179.36	176.24	97.03	61.27	33.41
Radios	3.67	6.29	1.81	2.90	6.84	3.41	1.62	2.38
Tape recorders and players	9.71	4.67	9.31	11.60	18.60	6.64	5.11	0.90
Sound components and component systems	14.08	16.76	21.70	13.18	17.80	12.42	7.27	2.60
Miscellaneous sound equipment	1.37	–	2.25	1.33	1.49	1.87	0.38	0.97
Sound equipment accessories	7.94	3.53	3.40	12.56	12.87	6.22	5.26	4.40
Satellite dishes	0.77	0.94	0.59	0.72	1.22	0.50	0.84	0.50
Compact disc, tape, record, video mail order clubs	4.15	2.44	7.30	4.63	4.11	2.86	4.16	1.23
Records, CDs, audio tapes, needles	35.26	41.83	41.24	43.74	46.04	30.18	16.12	6.68
Rental of VCR, radio, sound equipment	0.11	0.33	0.19	0.07	0.20	–	0.01	0.01
Musical instruments and accessories	20.06	8.80	30.68	35.57	23.37	7.31	8.45	2.25
Rental and repair of musical instruments	2.28	0.59	1.11	3.54	1.65	0.78	0.26	8.47
Rental of video cassettes, tapes, discs, films	35.61	41.55	50.60	49.52	42.05	24.84	11.80	3.03
PETS, TOYS, HOBBIES, AND PLAYGROUND EQUIPMENT	380.64	217.50	403.74	460.19	476.95	427.92	261.39	146.95
Pets	271.61	165.28	232.14	306.02	387.61	307.98	195.57	128.18
Pet food	110.31	48.83	70.63	125.07	181.69	120.12	86.58	56.22
Pet purchase, supplies, and medicines	57.85	70.40	62.34	66.74	68.27	62.75	19.82	29.04
Pet services	25.07	8.76	20.38	26.36	36.18	30.61	21.81	14.70
Veterinarian services	78.38	37.29	78.79	87.85	101.47	94.50	67.37	28.21
Toys, games, hobbies, and tricycles	99.21	50.90	162.45	147.57	85.70	85.37	58.80	16.72
Playground equipment	3.33	0.88	7.31	5.06	1.58	4.31	0.15	0.15

	total consumer units	under 25	25 to 34	35 to 44	45 to 54	55 to 64	65 to 74	75+
OTHER ENTERTAINMENT SUPPLIES, EQUIPMENT, SERVICES	**$522.26**	**$171.62**	**$459.98**	**$457.06**	**$641.31**	**$966.73**	**$526.71**	**$107.27**
Unmotored recreational vehicles	**55.39**	**–**	**46.77**	**53.87**	**57.21**	**114.76**	**35.27**	**41.29**
Boat without motor and boat trailers	17.57	–	2.45	42.27	22.99	24.76	–	–
Trailer and other attachable campers	37.82	–	44.33	11.60	34.22	90.00	35.27	41.29
Motorized recreational vehicles	**229.60**	**29.99**	**180.80**	**111.26**	**215.71**	**638.95**	**352.52**	**–**
Motorized camper	73.72	–	19.92	15.06	73.47	146.95	312.71	–
Other vehicle	35.62	29.99	29.50	39.53	60.94	44.24	11.90	–
Motorboats	120.27	–	131.38	56.66	81.29	447.76	27.91	–
Rental of recreational vehicles	**6.21**	**0.72**	**6.38**	**5.82**	**7.65**	**5.48**	**11.56**	**3.88**
Docking and landing fees	**5.62**	**1.13**	**1.02**	**4.76**	**4.61**	**11.76**	**13.64**	**3.53**
Sports, recreation, exercise equipment	**132.93**	**81.22**	**122.57**	**160.15**	**236.96**	**98.91**	**61.73**	**38.83**
Athletic gear, game tables, exercise equipment	53.07	33.88	51.22	83.03	72.66	33.94	28.11	19.26
Bicycles	11.34	5.95	12.59	14.97	17.10	11.51	3.56	1.29
Camping equipment	13.48	5.27	16.46	15.14	20.66	9.16	7.92	8.34
Hunting and fishing equipment	31.82	19.11	19.28	22.33	85.90	24.08	10.72	4.64
Winter sports equipment	4.17	6.19	4.27	5.03	5.67	4.32	1.39	0.04
Water sports equipment	4.65	3.75	7.05	4.37	7.57	4.00	0.26	1.14
Other sports equipment	11.89	5.27	8.87	13.12	24.60	8.36	6.99	3.49
Rental and repair of miscellaneous sports equipment	2.49	1.80	2.83	2.17	2.81	3.53	2.78	0.63
Photographic equipment and supplies	**82.86**	**54.67**	**86.88**	**106.27**	**106.25**	**92.90**	**50.48**	**17.21**
Film	12.18	9.92	12.66	15.05	14.45	13.13	9.07	4.03
Other photographic supplies	4.24	0.44	2.22	2.71	8.50	8.40	3.06	–
Film processing	20.31	14.24	22.71	25.42	23.47	22.38	14.16	6.62
Repair and rental of photographic equipment	0.99	0.58	0.14	2.66	1.12	0.49	0.67	0.04
Photographic equipment	28.92	20.74	23.75	40.48	35.38	36.45	19.09	4.62
Photographer fees	16.23	8.77	25.40	19.96	23.33	12.04	4.43	1.89
Fireworks	**3.75**	**1.63**	**8.44**	**3.76**	**4.72**	**2.61**	**–**	**0.53**
Pinball, electronic video games	**1.51**	**1.25**	**3.99**	**1.58**	**1.88**	**0.13**	**–**	**–**

Note: Subcategories may not add to total because some are not shown. "–" means sample is too small to make a reliable estimate.
Source: Bureau of Labor Statistics, unpublished data from the 2004 Consumer Expenditure Survey

Table 3.2 Entertainment: Indexed spending by age, 2004

(indexed average annual spending of consumer units (CU) on entertainment by age of consumer unit reference person, 2004; index definition: an index of 100 is the average for all consumer units; an index of 132 means that spending by consumer units in that group is 32 percent above the average for all consumer units; an index of 68 indicates spending that is 32 percent below the average for all consumer units)

	total consumer units	under 25	25 to 34	35 to 44	45 to 54	55 to 64	65 to 74	75+
Average spending of CU, total	$43,395	$24,535	$42,701	$50,402	$52,764	$47,299	$36,512	$25,763
Average spending of CU, index	100	57	98	116	122	109	84	59
Entertainment, spending index	100	53	96	113	122	127	85	45
FEES AND ADMISSIONS	100	52	79	126	126	117	88	50
Recreation expenses on trips	100	64	83	106	133	129	92	39
Social, recreation, civic club membership	100	45	68	101	110	166	116	60
Fees for participant sports	100	38	72	111	109	121	95	127
Participant sports on trips	100	51	69	113	140	138	82	41
Movie, theater, opera, ballet	100	92	102	117	123	101	81	38
Movie, other admissions on trips	100	51	83	124	125	127	83	41
Admission to sports events	100	54	77	120	139	89	155	15
Admission to sports events on trips	100	51	83	124	125	127	83	41
Fees for recreational lessons	100	24	69	203	152	65	29	13
Other entertainment services on trips	100	64	83	106	133	129	92	39
TELEVISION, RADIO, AND SOUND EQUIPMENT	100	63	107	117	118	103	80	60
Television	100	57	103	114	115	109	87	68
Cable service and community antenna	100	46	94	109	115	114	101	79
Color TV sets, consoles	100	85	136	117	99	112	55	43
Color TV sets, portable and table models	100	74	104	109	115	125	62	63
VCRs and video disc players	100	50	116	143	125	92	49	32
Video cassettes, tapes, and discs	100	104	143	127	126	73	39	15
Video game hardware and software	100	108	131	157	110	53	43	29
Repair of TV, radio, and sound equipment	100	68	100	131	92	105	81	87
Rental of television sets	100	449	99	112	115	20	–	–
Radio and sound equipment	100	95	126	133	131	72	45	25
Radios	100	171	49	79	186	93	44	65
Tape recorders and players	100	48	96	119	192	68	53	9
Sound components and component systems	100	119	154	94	126	88	52	18
Miscellaneous sound equipment	100	–	164	97	109	136	28	71
Sound equipment accessories	100	44	43	158	162	78	66	55
Satellite dishes	100	122	77	94	158	65	109	65
Compact disc, tape, record, video mail order clubs	100	59	176	112	99	69	100	30
Records, CDs, audio tapes, needles	100	119	117	124	131	86	46	19
Rental of VCR, radio, sound equipment	100	300	173	64	182	–	9	9
Musical instruments and accessories	100	44	153	177	117	36	42	11
Rental and repair of musical instruments	100	26	49	155	72	34	11	371
Rental of video cassettes, tapes, discs, films	100	117	142	139	118	70	33	9
PETS, TOYS, HOBBIES, AND PLAYGROUND EQUIPMENT	100	57	106	121	125	112	69	39
Pets	100	61	85	113	143	113	72	47
Pet food	100	44	64	113	165	109	78	51
Pet purchase, supplies, and medicines	100	122	108	115	118	108	34	50
Pet services	100	35	81	105	144	122	87	59
Veterinarian services	100	48	101	112	129	121	86	36
Toys, games, hobbies, and tricycles	100	51	164	149	86	86	59	17
Playground equipment	100	26	220	152	47	129	5	5

	total consumer units	under 25	25 to 34	35 to 44	45 to 54	55 to 64	65 to 74	75+
OTHER ENTERTAINMENT SUPPLIES, EQUIPMENT, SERVICES	100	33	88	88	123	185	101	21
Unmotored recreational vehicles	100	–	84	97	103	207	64	75
Boat without motor and boat trailers	100	–	14	241	131	141	–	–
Trailer and other attachable campers	100	–	117	31	90	238	93	109
Motorized recreational vehicles	100	13	79	48	94	278	154	–
Motorized camper	100	–	27	20	100	199	424	–
Other vehicle	100	84	83	111	171	124	33	–
Motorboats	100	–	109	47	68	372	23	–
Rental of recreational vehicles	100	12	103	94	123	88	186	62
Docking and landing fees	100	20	18	85	82	209	243	63
Sports, recreation, exercise equipment	100	61	92	120	178	74	46	29
Athletic gear, game tables, exercise equipment	100	64	97	156	137	64	53	36
Bicycles	100	52	111	132	151	101	31	11
Camping equipment	100	39	122	112	153	68	59	62
Hunting and fishing equipment	100	60	61	70	270	76	34	15
Winter sports equipment	100	148	102	121	136	104	33	1
Water sports equipment	100	81	152	94	163	86	6	25
Other sports equipment	100	44	75	110	207	70	59	29
Rental and repair of miscellaneous sports equipment	100	72	114	87	113	142	112	25
Photographic equipment and supplies	100	66	105	128	128	112	61	21
Film	100	81	104	124	119	108	74	33
Other photographic supplies	100	10	52	64	200	198	72	–
Film processing	100	70	112	125	116	110	70	33
Repair and rental of photographic equipment	100	59	14	269	113	49	68	4
Photographic equipment	100	72	82	140	122	126	66	16
Photographer fees	100	54	157	123	144	74	27	12
Fireworks	100	43	225	100	126	70	–	14
Pinball, electronic video games	100	83	264	105	125	9	–	–

Note: "–" means sample is too small to make a reliable estimate.
Source: Calculations by New Strategist based on the 2004 Consumer Expenditure Survey

Table 3.3 Entertainment: Total spending by age, 2004

(total annual spending on entertainment, by consumer unit (CU) age groups, 2004; consumer units and dollars in thousands)

	total consumer units	under 25	25 to 34	35 to 44	45 to 54	55 to 64	65 to 74	75+
Number of consumer units	116,282	8,817	19,439	24,070	23,712	17,479	11,230	11,536
Total spending of all CUs	$5,046,042,273	$216,321,216	$830,055,797	$1,213,166,993	$1,251,148,504	$826,731,880	$410,029,535	$297,205,660
Entertainment, total spending	257,968,129	10,279,299	41,243,338	60,279,223	64,286,315	49,339,896	21,099,710	11,425,024
FEES AND ADMISSIONS	61,389,919	2,442,044	8,070,101	16,040,248	15,808,316	10,809,713	5,194,998	3,024,855
Recreation expenses on trips	3,144,265	152,005	437,961	689,606	854,343	610,192	279,964	120,320
Social, recreation, civic club membership	11,417,730	386,361	1,289,778	2,384,374	2,561,370	2,841,561	1,274,044	680,163
Fees for participant sports	8,602,542	246,523	1,039,987	1,975,666	1,904,311	1,561,224	788,458	1,086,691
Participant sports on trips	3,107,055	119,823	357,872	725,470	887,540	644,451	246,499	125,627
Movie, theater, opera, ballet	10,751,434	753,148	1,830,182	2,602,448	2,697,240	1,628,518	837,533	402,145
Movie, other admissions on trips	5,585,024	216,722	770,562	1,434,331	1,418,452	1,066,394	449,312	228,644
Admission to sports events	4,191,966	170,433	540,015	1,040,787	1,191,765	559,503	625,736	64,256
Admission to sports events on trips	1,861,675	72,211	256,789	478,030	472,817	355,348	149,696	76,253
Fees for recreational lessons	9,583,962	172,725	1,108,995	4,020,171	2,965,660	931,980	263,793	120,551
Other entertainment services on trips	3,144,265	152,005	437,961	689,606	854,343	610,192	279,964	120,320
TELEVISION, RADIO, SOUND EQUIPMENT	91,588,354	4,406,296	16,383,384	22,160,768	21,961,580	14,153,271	7,054,349	5,467,603
Television	75,886,796	3,280,012	13,075,449	17,843,572	17,782,577	12,457,283	6,366,287	5,082,185
Cable service and community antenna	54,769,985	1,900,945	8,621,197	12,365,722	12,885,101	9,396,885	5,320,325	4,280,779
Color TV sets, consoles	6,100,154	392,445	1,385,223	1,477,898	1,233,024	1,027,590	324,884	259,099
Color TV sets, portable and table models	4,628,024	261,336	801,081	1,048,489	1,084,350	866,958	276,370	288,977
VCRs and video disc players	2,796,582	106,509	542,542	827,527	710,412	388,383	133,300	87,674
Video cassettes, tapes, and discs	4,957,102	389,535	1,183,835	1,304,113	1,275,706	542,898	186,755	73,946
Video game hardware and software	2,132,612	174,136	466,925	693,697	479,457	168,847	88,043	61,487
Repair of TV, radio, and sound equipment	351,172	17,987	58,706	95,317	65,919	55,583	27,514	30,224
Rental of television sets	94,188	32,094	15,551	21,904	22,052	2,797	–	–
Radio and sound equipment	15,701,558	1,126,284	3,307,935	4,317,195	4,179,003	1,695,987	688,062	385,418
Radios	426,755	55,459	35,185	69,803	162,190	59,603	18,193	27,456
Tape recorders and players	1,129,098	41,175	180,977	279,212	441,043	116,061	57,385	10,382
Sound components and component systems	1,637,251	147,773	421,826	317,243	422,074	217,089	81,642	29,994
Miscellaneous sound equipment	159,306	–	43,738	32,013	35,331	32,686	4,267	11,190
Sound equipment accessories	923,279	31,124	66,093	302,319	305,173	108,719	59,070	50,758
Satellite dishes	89,537	8,288	11,469	17,330	28,929	8,740	9,433	5,768
Compact disc, tape, record, video mail order clubs	482,570	21,513	141,905	111,444	97,456	49,990	46,717	14,189
Records, CDs, audio tapes, needles	4,100,103	368,815	801,664	1,052,822	1,091,700	527,516	181,028	77,060
Rental of VCR, radio, sound equipment	12,791	2,910	3,693	1,685	4,742	–	112	115
Musical instruments and accessories	2,332,617	77,590	596,389	856,170	554,149	127,771	94,894	25,956
Rental and repair of musical instruments	265,123	5,202	21,577	85,208	39,125	13,634	2,920	97,710
Rental of video cassettes, tapes, discs, films	4,140,802	366,346	983,613	1,191,946	997,090	434,178	132,514	34,954
PETS, TOYS, HOBBIES, AND PLAYGROUND EQUIPMENT	44,261,580	1,917,698	7,848,302	11,076,773	11,309,438	7,479,614	2,935,410	1,695,215
Pets	31,583,354	1,457,274	4,512,569	7,365,901	9,191,008	5,383,182	2,196,251	1,478,684
Pet food	12,827,067	430,534	1,372,977	3,010,435	4,308,233	2,099,577	972,293	648,554
Pet purchase, supplies, and medicines	6,726,914	620,717	1,211,827	1,606,432	1,618,818	1,096,807	222,579	335,005
Pet services	2,915,190	77,237	396,167	634,485	857,900	535,032	244,926	169,579
Veterinarian services	9,114,183	328,786	1,531,599	2,114,550	2,406,057	1,651,766	756,565	325,431
Toys, games, hobbies, and tricycles	11,536,337	448,785	3,157,866	3,552,010	2,032,118	1,492,182	660,324	192,882
Playground equipment	387,219	7,759	142,099	121,794	37,465	75,334	1,685	1,730

	total consumer units	under 25	25 to 34	35 to 44	45 to 54	55 to 64	65 to 74	75+
OTHER ENTERTAINMENT SUPPLIES, EQUIPMENT, SERVICES	$60,729,437	$1,513,174	$8,941,551	$11,001,434	$15,206,743	$16,897,474	$5,914,953	$1,237,467
Unmotored recreational vehicles	6,440,860	–	909,162	1,296,651	1,356,564	2,005,890	396,082	476,321
Boat without motor and boat trailers	2,043,075	–	47,626	1,017,439	545,139	432,780	–	–
Trailer and other attachable campers	4,397,785	–	861,731	279,212	811,425	1,573,110	396,082	476,321
Motorized recreational vehicles	26,698,347	264,422	3,514,571	2,678,028	5,114,916	11,168,207	3,958,800	–
Motorized camper	8,572,309	–	387,225	362,494	1,742,121	2,568,539	3,511,733	–
Other vehicle	4,141,965	264,422	573,451	951,487	1,445,009	773,271	133,637	–
Motorboats	13,985,236	–	2,553,896	1,363,806	1,927,548	7,826,397	313,429	–
Rental of recreational vehicles	722,111	6,348	124,021	140,087	181,397	95,785	129,819	44,760
Docking and landing fees	653,505	9,963	19,828	114,573	109,312	205,553	153,177	40,722
Sports, recreation, exercise equipment	15,457,366	716,117	2,382,638	3,854,811	5,618,796	1,728,848	693,228	447,943
Athletic gear, game tables, exercise equipment	6,171,086	298,720	995,666	1,998,532	1,722,914	593,237	315,675	222,183
Bicycles	1,318,638	52,461	244,737	360,328	405,475	201,183	39,979	14,881
Camping equipment	1,567,481	46,466	319,966	364,420	489,890	160,108	88,942	96,210
Hunting and fishing equipment	3,700,093	168,493	374,784	537,483	2,036,861	420,894	120,386	53,527
Winter sports equipment	484,896	54,577	83,005	121,072	134,447	75,509	15,610	461
Water sports equipment	540,711	33,064	137,045	105,186	179,500	69,916	2,920	13,151
Other sports equipment	1,382,593	46,466	172,424	315,798	583,315	146,124	78,498	40,261
Rental and repair of miscellaneous sports equipment	289,542	15,871	55,012	52,232	66,631	61,701	31,219	7,268
Photographic equipment and supplies	9,635,127	482,025	1,688,860	2,557,919	2,519,400	1,623,799	566,890	198,535
Film	1,416,315	87,465	246,098	362,254	342,638	229,499	101,856	46,490
Other photographic supplies	493,036	3,879	43,155	65,230	201,552	146,824	34,364	–
Film processing	2,361,687	125,554	441,460	611,859	556,521	391,180	159,017	76,368
Repair and rental of photographic equipment	115,119	5,114	2,721	64,026	26,557	8,565	7,524	461
Photographic equipment	3,362,875	182,865	461,676	974,354	838,931	637,110	214,381	53,296
Photographer fees	1,887,257	77,325	493,751	480,437	553,201	210,447	49,749	21,803
Fireworks	436,058	14,372	164,065	90,503	111,921	45,620	–	6,114
Pinball, electronic video games	175,586	11,021	77,562	38,031	44,579	2,272	–	–

Note: Numbers may not add to total because of rounding and missing subcategories. "–" means sample is too small to make a reliable estimate.

Source: Calculations by New Strategist based on the 2004 Consumer Expenditure Survey

Table 3.4 Entertainment: Market shares by age, 2004

(percentage of total annual spending on entertainment accounted for by consumer unit age groups, 2004)

	total consumer units	under 25	25 to 34	35 to 44	45 to 54	55 to 64	65 to 74	75+
Share of total consumer units	100.0%	7.6%	16.7%	20.7%	20.4%	15.0%	9.7%	9.9%
Share of total before-tax income	100.0	3.2	16.1	24.9	26.4	16.8	7.5	5.1
Share of total spending	100.0	4.3	16.4	24.0	24.8	16.4	8.1	5.9
Share of entertainment spending	100.0	4.0	16.0	23.4	24.9	19.1	8.2	4.4
FEES AND ADMISSIONS	100.0	4.0	13.1	26.1	25.8	17.6	8.5	4.9
Recreation expenses on trips	100.0	4.8	13.9	21.9	27.2	19.4	8.9	3.8
Social, recreation, civic club membership	100.0	3.4	11.3	20.9	22.4	24.9	11.2	6.0
Fees for participant sports	100.0	2.9	12.1	23.0	22.1	18.1	9.2	12.6
Participant sports on trips	100.0	3.9	11.5	23.3	28.6	20.7	7.9	4.0
Movie, theater, opera, ballet	100.0	7.0	17.0	24.2	25.1	15.1	7.8	3.7
Movie, other admissions on trips	100.0	3.9	13.8	25.7	25.4	19.1	8.0	4.1
Admission to sports events	100.0	4.1	12.9	24.8	28.4	13.3	14.9	1.5
Admission to sports events on trips	100.0	3.9	13.8	25.7	25.4	19.1	8.0	4.1
Fees for recreational lessons	100.0	1.8	11.6	41.9	30.9	9.7	2.8	1.3
Other entertainment services on trips	100.0	4.8	13.9	21.9	27.2	19.4	8.9	3.8
TELEVISION, RADIO, AND SOUND EQUIPMENT	100.0	4.8	17.9	24.2	24.0	15.5	7.7	6.0
Television	100.0	4.3	17.2	23.5	23.4	16.4	8.4	6.7
Cable service and community antenna	100.0	3.5	15.7	22.6	23.5	17.2	9.7	7.8
Color TV sets, consoles	100.0	6.4	22.7	24.2	20.2	16.8	5.3	4.2
Color TV sets, portable and table models	100.0	5.6	17.3	22.7	23.4	18.7	6.0	6.2
VCRs and video disc players	100.0	3.8	19.4	29.6	25.4	13.9	4.8	3.1
Video cassettes, tapes, and discs	100.0	7.9	23.9	26.3	25.7	11.0	3.8	1.5
Video game hardware and software	100.0	8.2	21.9	32.5	22.5	7.9	4.1	2.9
Repair of TV, radio, and sound equipment	100.0	5.1	16.7	27.1	18.8	15.8	7.8	8.6
Rental of television sets	100.0	34.1	16.5	23.3	23.4	3.0	–	–
Radio and sound equipment	100.0	7.2	21.1	27.5	26.6	10.8	4.4	2.5
Radios	100.0	13.0	8.2	16.4	38.0	14.0	4.3	6.4
Tape recorders and players	100.0	3.6	16.0	24.7	39.1	10.3	5.1	0.9
Sound components and component systems	100.0	9.0	25.8	19.4	25.8	13.3	5.0	1.8
Miscellaneous sound equipment	100.0	–	27.5	20.1	22.2	20.5	2.7	7.0
Sound equipment accessories	100.0	3.4	7.2	32.7	33.1	11.8	6.4	5.5
Satellite dishes	100.0	9.3	12.8	19.4	32.3	9.8	10.5	6.4
Compact disc, tape, record, video mail order clubs	100.0	4.5	29.4	23.1	20.2	10.4	9.7	2.9
Records, CDs, audio tapes, needles	100.0	9.0	19.6	25.7	26.6	12.9	4.4	1.9
Rental of VCR, radio, sound equipment	100.0	22.7	28.9	13.2	37.1	–	0.9	0.9
Musical instruments and accessories	100.0	3.3	25.6	36.7	23.8	5.5	4.1	1.1
Rental and repair of musical instruments	100.0	2.0	8.1	32.1	14.8	5.1	1.1	36.9
Rental of video cassettes, tapes, discs, films	100.0	8.8	23.8	28.8	24.1	10.5	3.2	0.8
PETS, TOYS, HOBBIES, AND PLAYGROUND EQUIPMENT	100.0	4.3	17.7	25.0	25.6	16.9	6.6	3.8
Pets	100.0	4.6	14.3	23.3	29.1	17.0	7.0	4.7
Pet food	100.0	3.4	10.7	23.5	33.6	16.4	7.6	5.1
Pet purchase, supplies, and medicines	100.0	9.2	18.0	23.9	24.1	16.3	3.3	5.0
Pet services	100.0	2.6	13.6	21.8	29.4	18.4	8.4	5.8
Veterinarian services	100.0	3.6	16.8	23.2	26.4	18.1	8.3	3.6
Toys, games, hobbies, and tricycles	100.0	3.9	27.4	30.8	17.6	12.9	5.7	1.7
Playground equipment	100.0	2.0	36.7	31.5	9.7	19.5	0.4	0.4

	total consumer units	under 25	25 to 34	35 to 44	45 to 54	55 to 64	65 to 74	75+
OTHER ENTERTAINMENT SUPPLIES, EQUIPMENT, SERVICES	**100.0%**	**2.5%**	**14.7%**	**18.1%**	**25.0%**	**27.8%**	**9.7%**	**2.0%**
Unmotored recreational vehicles	**100.0**	–	**14.1**	**20.1**	**21.1**	**31.1**	**6.1**	**7.4**
Boat without motor and boat trailers	100.0	–	2.3	49.8	26.7	21.2	–	–
Trailer and other attachable campers	100.0	–	19.6	6.3	18.5	35.8	9.0	10.8
Motorized recreational vehicles	**100.0**	**1.0**	**13.2**	**10.0**	**19.2**	**41.8**	**14.8**	–
Motorized camper	100.0	–	4.5	4.2	20.3	30.0	41.0	–
Other vehicle	100.0	6.4	13.8	23.0	34.9	18.7	3.2	–
Motorboats	100.0	–	18.3	9.8	13.8	56.0	2.2	–
Rental of recreational vehicles	**100.0**	**0.9**	**17.2**	**19.4**	**25.1**	**13.3**	**18.0**	**6.2**
Docking and landing fees	**100.0**	**1.5**	**3.0**	**17.5**	**16.7**	**31.5**	**23.4**	**6.2**
Sports, recreation, exercise equipment	**100.0**	**4.6**	**15.4**	**24.9**	**36.4**	**11.2**	**4.5**	**2.9**
Athletic gear, game tables, exercise equipment	100.0	4.8	16.1	32.4	27.9	9.6	5.1	3.6
Bicycles	100.0	4.0	18.6	27.3	30.7	15.3	3.0	1.1
Camping equipment	100.0	3.0	20.4	23.2	31.3	10.2	5.7	6.1
Hunting and fishing equipment	100.0	4.6	10.1	14.5	55.0	11.4	3.3	1.4
Winter sports equipment	100.0	11.3	17.1	25.0	27.7	15.6	3.2	0.1
Water sports equipment	100.0	6.1	25.3	19.5	33.2	12.9	0.5	2.4
Other sports equipment	100.0	3.4	12.5	22.8	42.2	10.6	5.7	2.9
Rental and repair of miscellaneous sports equipment	100.0	5.5	19.0	18.0	23.0	21.3	10.8	2.5
Photographic equipment and supplies	**100.0**	**5.0**	**17.5**	**26.5**	**26.1**	**16.9**	**5.9**	**2.1**
Film	100.0	6.2	17.4	25.6	24.2	16.2	7.2	3.3
Other photographic supplies	100.0	0.8	8.8	13.2	40.9	29.8	7.0	–
Film processing	100.0	5.3	18.7	25.9	23.6	16.6	6.7	3.2
Repair and rental of photographic equipment	100.0	4.4	2.4	55.6	23.1	7.4	6.5	0.4
Photographic equipment	100.0	5.4	13.7	29.0	24.9	18.9	6.4	1.6
Photographer fees	100.0	4.1	26.2	25.5	29.3	11.2	2.6	1.2
Fireworks	**100.0**	**3.3**	**37.6**	**20.8**	**25.7**	**10.5**	–	**1.4**
Pinball, electronic video games	**100.0**	**6.3**	**44.2**	**21.7**	**25.4**	**1.3**	–	–

Note: Numbers may not add to total because of rounding. "–" means sample is too small to make a reliable estimate.
Source: Calculations by New Strategist based on the 2004 Consumer Expenditure Survey

Table 3.5 Entertainment: Average spending by income, 2004

(average annual spending on entertainment, by before-tax income of consumer units (CU), 2004)

	total consumer units	under $20,000	$20,000–$39,999	$40,000–$49,999	$50,000–$69,999	$70,000–$79,999	$80,000–$99,999	$100,000 or more
Number of consumer units (in 000s)	116,282	28,898	27,297	11,374	18,069	6,461	9,246	14,937
Average number of persons per CU	2.5	1.8	2.3	2.6	2.8	3.0	3.1	3.2
Average before-tax income of CU	$54,453.00	$10,923.47	$29,561.76	$44,645.00	$59,259.00	$74,437.00	$88,811.00	$155,901.00
Average spending of CU, total	43,394.87	18,865.37	30,400.94	38,204.07	47,750.13	55,012.03	65,446.39	93,525.67
Entertainment, average spending	**2,218.47**	**798.76**	**1,518.17**	**1,755.81**	**2,586.50**	**2,870.01**	**3,676.55**	**4,931.74**
FEES AND ADMISSIONS	**527.94**	**133.42**	**244.72**	**379.04**	**547.65**	**673.37**	**924.17**	**1,590.15**
Recreation expenses on trips	27.04	7.23	12.17	20.17	31.72	39.33	44.82	75.78
Social, recreation, civic club membership	98.19	25.13	35.37	46.11	86.06	113.03	181.39	350.73
Fees for participant sports	73.98	19.77	44.18	76.43	76.96	97.99	115.43	191.82
Participant sports on trips	26.72	3.40	6.63	15.71	34.36	23.80	48.87	95.26
Movie, theater, opera, ballet	92.46	34.17	56.34	73.97	96.95	125.82	147.55	231.36
Movie, other admissions on trips	48.03	11.37	26.97	31.09	59.26	59.16	96.08	122.19
Admission to sports events	36.05	7.81	19.13	16.91	39.12	51.83	53.36	114.95
Admission to sports events on trips	16.01	3.79	8.99	10.36	19.75	19.72	32.01	40.72
Fees for recreational lessons	82.42	13.51	22.78	68.12	71.75	103.36	159.84	291.55
Other entertainment services on trips	27.04	7.23	12.17	20.17	31.72	39.33	44.82	75.78
TELEVISION, RADIO, AND SOUND EQUIPMENT	**787.64**	**407.03**	**623.01**	**733.52**	**924.63**	**1,016.09**	**1,141.80**	**1,379.39**
Television	**652.61**	**354.94**	**527.52**	**623.76**	**763.43**	**818.15**	**956.84**	**1,085.08**
Cable service and community antenna	471.01	283.26	409.03	475.56	543.18	593.79	634.57	702.44
Color TV sets, consoles	52.46	15.77	30.60	36.10	70.53	55.00	108.58	118.16
Color TV sets, portable and table models	39.80	18.21	25.03	27.65	47.68	58.07	60.31	87.65
VCRs and video disc players	24.05	8.37	16.64	22.23	24.39	27.71	46.25	53.55
Video cassettes, tapes, and discs	42.63	19.28	29.85	40.36	54.14	53.62	63.05	81.53
Video game hardware and software	18.34	7.49	12.96	18.49	19.89	27.32	34.35	33.38
Repair of TV, radio, and sound equipment	3.02	1.40	1.95	2.14	3.15	2.51	7.55	6.04
Rental of television sets	0.81	0.90	1.17	1.23	0.10	0.05	1.99	0.12
Radio and sound equipment	**135.03**	**52.09**	**95.49**	**109.75**	**161.20**	**197.94**	**184.95**	**294.31**
Radios	3.67	0.85	2.22	0.78	8.73	11.85	2.26	5.47
Tape recorders and players	9.71	–	6.04	9.71	8.80	12.49	5.52	27.43
Sound components and component systems	14.08	5.30	8.81	9.40	11.46	17.41	22.40	40.87
Miscellaneous sound equipment	1.37	0.02	0.55	1.77	0.87	0.50	4.27	4.02
Sound equipment accessories	7.94	2.50	3.07	8.21	10.00	7.30	11.51	22.92
Satellite dishes	0.77	0.12	0.73	0.65	0.88	0.27	1.05	2.12
Compact disc, tape, record, video mail order clubs	4.15	2.10	3.49	4.53	5.87	8.25	5.93	4.11
Records, CDs, audio tapes, needles	35.26	16.24	27.27	31.27	39.01	50.11	51.81	68.51
Rental of VCR, radio, sound equipment	0.11	0.24	0.19	0.08	0.11	–	0.06	0.05
Musical instruments and accessories	20.06	4.07	10.73	6.20	30.22	38.64	23.55	56.14
Rental and repair of musical instruments	2.28	0.21	4.20	1.51	2.26	1.99	1.33	4.28
Rental of video cassettes, tapes, discs, films	35.61	16.90	28.18	35.65	42.99	49.13	55.25	58.42
PETS, TOYS, HOBBIES, AND PLAYGROUND EQUIPMENT	**380.64**	**149.14**	**283.73**	**315.59**	**402.94**	**559.75**	**603.52**	**790.31**
Pets	**271.61**	**106.77**	**205.03**	**219.08**	**289.04**	**407.30**	**425.27**	**554.93**
Pet food	110.31	52.63	87.02	101.04	110.07	154.25	154.47	211.44
Pet purchase, supplies, and medicines	57.85	22.81	54.37	35.54	64.05	95.48	82.05	101.82
Pet services	25.07	8.07	13.50	16.99	28.48	33.82	41.68	67.09
Veterinarian services	78.38	23.26	50.14	65.51	86.44	123.74	147.07	174.57
Toys, games, hobbies, and tricycles	**99.21**	**41.13**	**75.38**	**88.94**	**109.79**	**148.67**	**164.20**	**188.53**
Playground equipment	**3.33**	**0.27**	**1.34**	**1.58**	**2.74**	**2.00**	**10.26**	**11.35**

	total consumer units	under $20,000	$20,000–$39,999	$40,000–$49,999	$50,000–$69,999	$70,000–$79,999	$80,000–$99,999	$100,000 or more
OTHER ENTERTAINMENT SUPPLIES, EQUIPMENT, SERVICES	**$522.26**	**$109.17**	**$366.71**	**$327.66**	**$711.27**	**$620.80**	**$1,007.07**	**$1,171.89**
Unmotored recreational vehicles	**55.39**	–	**8.03**	**19.43**	**120.97**	**33.91**	**90.33**	**164.25**
Boat without motor and boat trailers	17.57	4.49	–	1.33	5.77	16.32	8.03	114.27
Trailer and other attachable campers	37.82	–	8.03	18.10	115.19	17.59	82.30	49.98
Motorized recreational vehicles	**229.60**	**48.49**	**225.57**	**153.32**	**327.12**	**249.03**	**453.92**	**430.21**
Motorized camper	73.72	–	29.13	123.54	205.96	72.01	39.21	85.69
Other vehicle	35.62	–	27.40	25.20	53.74	61.03	124.18	32.24
Motorboats	120.27	0.11	169.04	4.57	67.42	115.99	290.53	312.28
Rental of recreational vehicles	**6.21**	**0.14**	**2.29**	**1.14**	**6.80**	**5.07**	**14.37**	**23.79**
Docking and landing fees	**5.62**	**0.89**	**3.24**	**4.33**	**5.23**	**10.42**	**11.42**	**15.69**
Sports, recreation, exercise equipment	**132.93**	**46.07**	**77.78**	**85.34**	**131.31**	**204.52**	**272.65**	**311.64**
Athletic gear, game tables, exercise equipment	53.07	13.00	18.82	27.13	69.93	113.43	106.91	126.17
Bicycles	11.34	3.85	7.27	6.76	10.53	14.21	13.42	35.23
Camping equipment	13.48	11.06	7.46	11.96	9.65	9.59	32.00	24.84
Hunting and fishing equipment	31.82	12.99	33.75	18.47	20.53	48.74	73.74	51.78
Winter sports equipment	4.17	2.23	0.96	1.72	3.96	1.64	10.45	13.10
Water sports equipment	4.65	0.67	1.88	1.85	5.03	3.51	6.60	18.40
Other sports equipment	11.89	1.46	7.30	15.09	8.59	9.62	26.89	33.71
Rental and repair of miscellaneous sports equipment	2.49	0.82	0.35	2.36	3.07	3.79	2.64	8.40
Photographic equipment and supplies	**82.86**	**23.95**	**45.60**	**60.96**	**99.20**	**113.28**	**153.86**	**204.73**
Film	12.18	5.11	8.27	10.98	15.13	14.13	18.95	25.31
Other photographic supplies	4.24	1.26	1.25	0.31	12.36	1.89	0.85	12.32
Film processing	20.31	7.54	12.22	16.66	24.59	26.28	33.91	46.42
Repair and rental of photographic equipment	0.99	0.13	0.80	0.46	0.63	0.62	5.93	0.98
Photographic equipment	28.92	6.06	14.52	22.66	28.84	43.27	62.41	77.37
Photographer fees	16.23	4.19	8.53	9.89	17.65	27.10	31.82	42.35
Fireworks	**3.75**	–	**2.16**	**0.28**	**8.03**	**2.58**	**8.44**	**1.30**
Pinball, electronic video games	**1.51**	–	**0.46**	**1.73**	**2.64**	**0.58**	**0.72**	**4.13**

Note: Subcategories may not add to total because some are not shown. "–" means sample is too small to make a reliable estimate.
Source: Bureau of Labor Statistics, unpublished data from the 2004 Consumer Expenditure Survey; calculations by New Strategist

Table 3.6 Entertainment: Indexed spending by income, 2004

(indexed average annual spending of consumer units (CU) on entertainment by before-tax income of consumer unit, 2004; index definition: an index of 100 is the average for all consumer units; an index of 132 means that spending by consumer units in that group is 32 percent above the average for all consumer units; an index of 68 indicates spending that is 32 percent below the average for all consumer units)

	total consumer units	under $20,000	$20,000–$39,999	$40,000–$49,999	$50,000–$69,999	$70,000–$79,999	$80,000–$99,999	$100,000 or more
Average spending of CU, total	$43,395	$18,865	$30,401	$38,204	$47,750	$55,012	$65,446	$93,526
Average spending of CU, index	100	43	70	88	110	127	151	216
Entertainment, spending index	**100**	**36**	**68**	**79**	**117**	**129**	**166**	**222**
FEES AND ADMISSIONS	**100**	**25**	**46**	**72**	**104**	**128**	**175**	**301**
Recreation expenses on trips	100	27	45	75	117	145	166	280
Social, recreation, civic club membership	100	26	36	47	88	115	185	357
Fees for participant sports	100	27	60	103	104	132	156	259
Participant sports on trips	100	13	25	59	129	89	183	357
Movie, theater, opera, ballet	100	37	61	80	105	136	160	250
Movie, other admissions on trips	100	24	56	65	123	123	200	254
Admission to sports events	100	22	53	47	109	144	148	319
Admission to sports events on trips	100	24	56	65	123	123	200	254
Fees for recreational lessons	100	16	28	83	87	125	194	354
Other entertainment services on trips	100	27	45	75	117	145	166	280
TELEVISION, RADIO, AND SOUND EQUIPMENT	**100**	**52**	**79**	**93**	**117**	**129**	**145**	**175**
Television	**100**	**54**	**81**	**96**	**117**	**125**	**147**	**166**
Cable service and community antenna	100	60	87	101	115	126	135	149
Color TV sets, consoles	100	30	58	69	134	105	207	225
Color TV sets, portable and table models	100	46	63	69	120	146	152	220
VCRs and video disc players	100	35	69	92	101	115	192	223
Video cassettes, tapes, and discs	100	45	70	95	127	126	148	191
Video game hardware and software	100	41	71	101	108	149	187	182
Repair of TV, radio, and sound equipment	100	46	64	71	104	83	250	200
Rental of television sets	100	112	145	152	12	6	246	15
Radio and sound equipment	**100**	**39**	**71**	**81**	**119**	**147**	**137**	**218**
Radios	100	23	61	21	238	323	62	149
Tape recorders and players	100	–	62	100	91	129	57	282
Sound components and component systems	100	38	63	67	81	124	159	290
Miscellaneous sound equipment	100	1	40	129	64	36	312	293
Sound equipment accessories	100	32	39	103	126	92	145	289
Satellite dishes	100	16	95	84	114	35	136	275
Compact disc, tape, record, video mail order clubs	100	51	84	109	141	199	143	99
Records, CDs, audio tapes, needles	100	46	77	89	111	142	147	194
Rental of VCR, radio, sound equipment	100	221	172	73	100	–	55	45
Musical instruments and accessories	100	20	53	31	151	193	117	280
Rental and repair of musical instruments	100	9	184	66	99	87	58	188
Rental of video cassettes, tapes, discs, films	100	47	79	100	121	138	155	164
PETS, TOYS, HOBBIES, AND PLAYGROUND EQUIPMENT	**100**	**39**	**75**	**83**	**106**	**147**	**159**	**208**
Pets	**100**	**39**	**75**	**81**	**106**	**150**	**157**	**204**
Pet food	100	48	79	92	100	140	140	192
Pet purchase, supplies, and medicines	100	39	94	61	111	165	142	176
Pet services	100	32	54	68	114	135	166	268
Veterinarian services	100	30	64	84	110	158	188	223
Toys, games, hobbies, and tricycles	**100**	**41**	**76**	**90**	**111**	**150**	**166**	**190**
Playground equipment	**100**	**8**	**40**	**47**	**82**	**60**	**308**	**341**

	total consumer units	under $20,000	$20,000– $39,999	$40,000– $49,999	$50,000– $69,999	$70,000– $79,999	$80,000– $99,999	$100,000 or more
OTHER ENTERTAINMENT SUPPLIES, EQUIPMENT, SERVICES	**100**	**21**	**70**	**63**	**136**	**119**	**193**	**224**
Unmotored recreational vehicles	**100**	**–**	**14**	**35**	**218**	**61**	**163**	**297**
Boat without motor and boat trailers	100	26	–	8	33	93	46	650
Trailer and other attachable campers	100	–	21	48	305	47	218	132
Motorized recreational vehicles	**100**	**21**	**98**	**67**	**142**	**108**	**198**	**187**
Motorized camper	100	–	40	168	279	98	53	116
Other vehicle	100	–	77	71	151	171	349	91
Motorboats	100	0	141	4	56	96	242	260
Rental of recreational vehicles	**100**	**2**	**37**	**18**	**110**	**82**	**231**	**383**
Docking and landing fees	**100**	**16**	**58**	**77**	**93**	**185**	**203**	**279**
Sports, recreation, exercise equipment	**100**	**35**	**59**	**64**	**99**	**154**	**205**	**234**
Athletic gear, game tables, exercise equipment	100	24	35	51	132	214	201	238
Bicycles	100	34	64	60	93	125	118	311
Camping equipment	100	82	55	89	72	71	237	184
Hunting and fishing equipment	100	41	106	58	65	153	232	163
Winter sports equipment	100	54	23	41	95	39	251	314
Water sports equipment	100	14	40	40	108	75	142	396
Other sports equipment	100	12	61	127	72	81	226	284
Rental and repair of miscellaneous sports equipment	100	33	14	95	123	152	106	337
Photographic equipment and supplies	**100**	**29**	**55**	**74**	**120**	**137**	**186**	**247**
Film	100	42	68	90	124	116	156	208
Other photographic supplies	100	30	30	7	292	45	20	291
Film processing	100	37	60	82	121	129	167	229
Repair and rental of photographic equipment	100	13	81	46	64	63	599	99
Photographic equipment	100	21	50	78	100	150	216	268
Photographer fees	100	26	53	61	109	167	196	261
Fireworks	**100**	**–**	**57**	**7**	**214**	**69**	**225**	**35**
Pinball, electronic video games	**100**	**–**	**30**	**115**	**175**	**38**	**48**	**274**

Note: "–" means sample is too small to make a reliable estimate.
Source: Calculations by New Strategist based on the 2004 Consumer Expenditure Survey

Table 3.7 Entertainment: Total spending by income, 2004

(total annual spending on entertainment, by before-tax income group of consumer units (CU), 2004; consumer units and dollars in thousands)

	total consumer units	under $20,000	$20,000– $39,999	$40,000– $49,999	$50,000– $69,999	$70,000– $79,999	$80,000– $99,999	$100,000 or more
Number of consumer units	116,282	28,898	27,297	11,374	18,069	6,461	9,246	14,937
Total spending of all CUs	$5,046,042,273	$545,171,431	$829,854,379	$434,533,092	$862,797,099	$355,432,726	$605,117,322	$1,396,992,933
Entertainment, total spending	**257,968,129**	**23,082,558**	**41,441,505**	**19,970,583**	**46,735,469**	**18,543,135**	**33,993,381**	**73,665,400**
FEES AND ADMISSIONS	**61,389,919**	**3,855,578**	**6,680,175**	**4,311,201**	**9,895,488**	**4,350,644**	**8,544,876**	**23,752,071**
Recreation expenses on trips	3,144,265	208,968	332,227	229,414	573,149	254,111	414,406	1,131,926
Social, recreation, civic club membership	11,417,730	726,177	965,537	524,455	1,555,018	730,287	1,677,132	5,238,854
Fees for participant sports	8,602,542	571,418	1,205,898	869,315	1,390,590	633,113	1,067,266	2,865,215
Participant sports on trips	3,107,055	98,139	181,081	178,686	620,851	153,772	451,852	1,422,899
Movie, theater, opera, ballet	10,751,434	987,444	1,537,790	841,335	1,751,790	812,923	1,364,247	3,455,824
Movie, other admissions on trips	5,585,024	328,527	736,164	353,618	1,070,769	382,233	888,356	1,825,152
Admission to sports events	4,191,966	225,768	522,220	192,334	706,859	334,874	493,367	1,717,008
Admission to sports events on trips	1,861,675	109,494	245,301	117,835	356,863	127,411	295,964	608,235
Fees for recreational lessons	9,583,962	390,504	621,730	774,797	1,296,451	667,809	1,477,881	4,354,882
Other entertainment services on trips	3,144,265	208,968	332,227	229,414	573,149	254,111	414,406	1,131,926
TELEVISION, RADIO, SOUND EQUIPMENT	**91,588,354**	**11,762,404**	**17,006,292**	**8,343,056**	**16,707,139**	**6,564,957**	**10,557,083**	**20,603,948**
Television	**75,886,796**	**10,257,006**	**14,399,694**	**7,094,646**	**13,794,417**	**5,286,067**	**8,846,943**	**16,207,840**
Cable service and community antenna	54,769,985	8,185,583	11,165,195	5,409,019	9,814,719	3,836,477	5,867,234	10,492,346
Color TV sets, consoles	6,100,154	455,608	835,411	410,601	1,274,407	355,355	1,003,931	1,764,956
Color TV sets, portable and table models	4,628,024	526,356	683,305	314,491	861,530	375,190	557,626	1,309,228
VCRs and video disc players	2,796,582	241,932	454,344	252,844	440,703	179,034	427,628	799,876
Video cassettes, tapes, and discs	4,957,102	557,294	814,907	459,055	978,256	346,439	582,960	1,217,814
Video game hardware and software	2,132,612	216,360	353,752	210,305	359,392	176,515	317,600	498,597
Repair of TV, radio, and sound equipment	351,172	40,488	53,157	24,340	56,917	16,217	69,807	90,219
Rental of television sets	94,188	26,110	32,069	13,990	1,807	323	18,400	1,792
Radio and sound equipment	**15,701,558**	**1,505,425**	**2,606,457**	**1,248,297**	**2,912,723**	**1,278,890**	**1,710,048**	**4,396,108**
Radios	426,755	24,559	60,720	8,872	157,742	76,563	20,896	81,705
Tape recorders and players	1,129,098	–	164,947	110,442	159,007	80,698	51,038	409,722
Sound components and component systems	1,637,251	153,273	240,431	106,916	207,071	112,486	207,110	610,475
Miscellaneous sound equipment	159,306	578	14,899	20,132	15,720	3,231	39,480	60,047
Sound equipment accessories	923,279	72,369	83,850	93,381	180,690	47,165	106,421	342,356
Satellite dishes	89,537	3,454	19,984	7,393	15,901	1,744	9,708	31,666
Compact disc, tape, record, video mail order clubs	482,570	60,622	95,372	51,524	106,065	53,303	54,829	61,391
Records, CDs, audio tapes, needles	4,100,103	469,384	744,503	355,665	704,872	323,761	479,035	1,023,334
Rental of VCR, radio, sound equipment	12,791	7,019	5,150	910	1,988	–	555	747
Musical instruments and accessories	2,332,617	117,636	292,810	70,519	546,045	249,653	217,743	838,563
Rental and repair of musical instruments	265,123	5,985	114,669	17,175	40,836	12,857	12,297	63,930
Rental of video cassettes, tapes, discs, films	4,140,802	488,368	769,253	405,483	776,786	317,429	510,842	872,620
PETS, TOYS, HOBBIES, AND PLAYGROUND EQUIPMENT	**44,261,580**	**4,309,783**	**7,744,848**	**3,589,521**	**7,280,723**	**3,616,545**	**5,580,146**	**11,804,860**
Pets	**31,583,354**	**3,085,310**	**5,596,696**	**2,491,816**	**5,222,664**	**2,631,565**	**3,932,046**	**8,288,989**
Pet food	12,827,067	1,520,818	2,375,449	1,149,229	1,988,855	996,609	1,428,230	3,158,279
Pet purchase, supplies, and medicines	6,726,914	659,285	1,484,085	404,232	1,157,319	616,896	758,634	1,520,885
Pet services	2,915,190	233,087	368,376	193,244	514,605	218,511	385,373	1,002,123
Veterinarian services	9,114,183	672,075	1,368,654	745,111	1,561,884	799,484	1,359,809	2,607,552
Toys, games, hobbies, and tricycles	**11,536,337**	**1,188,652**	**2,057,540**	**1,011,604**	**1,983,796**	**960,557**	**1,518,193**	**2,816,073**
Playground equipment	**387,219**	**7,772**	**36,486**	**17,971**	**49,509**	**12,922**	**94,864**	**169,535**

	total consumer units	under $20,000	$20,000–$39,999	$40,000–$49,999	$50,000–$69,999	$70,000–$79,999	$80,000–$99,999	$100,000 or more
OTHER ENTERTAINMENT SUPPLIES, EQUIPMENT, SERVICES	$60,729,437	$3,154,793	$10,010,059	$3,726,805	$12,851,938	$4,010,989	$9,311,369	$17,504,521
Unmotored recreational vehicles	**6,440,860**	–	**219,146**	**220,997**	**2,185,807**	**219,093**	**835,191**	**2,453,402**
Boat without motor and boat trailers	2,043,075	129,752	–	15,127	104,258	105,444	74,245	1,706,851
Trailer and other attachable campers	4,397,785	–	219,146	205,869	2,081,368	113,649	760,946	746,551
Motorized recreational vehicles	**26,698,347**	**1,401,233**	**6,157,415**	**1,743,862**	**5,910,731**	**1,608,983**	**4,196,944**	**6,426,047**
Motorized camper	8,572,309	–	795,246	1,405,144	3,721,491	465,257	362,536	1,279,952
Other vehicle	4,141,965		–	747,850	286,625	971,028	394,315	1,148,168	481,569
Motorboats	13,985,236	3,179	4,614,188	51,979	1,218,212	749,411	2,686,240	4,664,526
Rental of recreational vehicles	**722,111**	**4,028**	**62,393**	**12,966**	**122,869**	**32,757**	**132,865**	**355,351**
Docking and landing fees	**653,505**	**25,733**	**88,456**	**49,249**	**94,501**	**67,324**	**105,589**	**234,362**
Sports, recreation, exercise equipment	**15,457,366**	**1,331,320**	**2,123,167**	**970,657**	**2,372,640**	**1,321,404**	**2,520,922**	**4,654,967**
Athletic gear, game tables, exercise equipment	6,171,086	375,570	513,658	308,577	1,263,565	732,871	988,490	1,884,601
Bicycles	1,318,638	111,115	198,381	76,888	190,267	91,811	124,081	526,231
Camping equipment	1,567,481	319,476	203,685	136,033	174,366	61,961	295,872	371,035
Hunting and fishing equipment	3,700,093	375,329	921,156	210,078	370,957	314,909	681,800	773,438
Winter sports equipment	484,896	64,550	26,079	19,563	71,553	10,596	96,621	195,675
Water sports equipment	540,711	19,263	51,193	21,042	90,887	22,678	61,024	274,841
Other sports equipment	1,382,593	42,233	199,267	171,634	155,213	62,155	248,625	503,526
Rental and repair of miscellaneous sports equipment	289,542	23,695	9,476	26,843	55,472	24,487	24,409	125,471
Photographic equipment and supplies	**9,635,127**	**691,991**	**1,244,642**	**693,359**	**1,792,445**	**731,902**	**1,422,590**	**3,058,052**
Film	1,416,315	147,596	225,802	124,887	273,384	91,294	175,212	378,055
Other photographic supplies	493,036	36,472	34,229	3,526	223,333	12,211	7,859	184,024
Film processing	2,361,687	217,759	333,564	189,491	444,317	169,795	313,532	693,376
Repair and rental of photographic equipment	115,119	3,756	21,796	5,232	11,383	4,006	54,829	14,638
Photographic equipment	3,362,875	175,107	396,348	257,735	521,110	279,567	577,043	1,155,676
Photographer fees	1,887,257	121,002	232,760	112,489	318,918	175,093	294,208	632,582
Fireworks	**436,058**	–	**58,841**	**3,185**	**145,094**	**16,669**	**78,036**	**19,418**
Pinball, electronic video games	**175,586**	–	**12,562**	**19,677**	**47,702**	**3,747**	**6,657**	**61,690**

Note: Numbers may not add to total because of rounding and missing subcategories. "–" means sample is too small to make a reliable estimate.
Source: Calculations by New Strategist based on the 2004 Consumer Expenditure Survey

Table 3.08 Entertainment: Market shares by income, 2004

(percentage of total annual spending on entertainment accounted for by before-tax income group of consumer units, 2004)

	total consumer units	under $20,000	$20,000– $39,999	$40,000– $49,999	$50,000– $69,999	$70,000– $79,999	$80,000– $99,999	$100,000 or more
Share of total consumer units	100.0%	24.9%	23.5%	9.8%	15.5%	5.6%	8.0%	12.8%
Share of total before-tax income	100.0	5.0	12.7	8.0	16.9	7.6	13.0	36.8
Share of total spending	100.0	10.8	16.4	8.6	17.1	7.0	12.0	27.7
Share of entertainment spending	100.0	8.9	16.1	7.7	18.1	7.2	13.2	28.6
FEES AND ADMISSIONS	100.0	6.3	10.9	7.0	16.1	7.1	13.9	38.7
Recreation expenses on trips	100.0	6.6	10.6	7.3	18.2	8.1	13.2	36.0
Social, recreation, civic club membership	100.0	6.4	8.5	4.6	13.6	6.4	14.7	45.9
Fees for participant sports	100.0	6.6	14.0	10.1	16.2	7.4	12.4	33.3
Participant sports on trips	100.0	3.2	5.8	5.8	20.0	4.9	14.5	45.8
Movie, theater, opera, ballet	100.0	9.2	14.3	7.8	16.3	7.6	12.7	32.1
Movie, other admissions on trips	100.0	5.9	13.2	6.3	19.2	6.8	15.9	32.7
Admission to sports events	100.0	5.4	12.5	4.6	16.9	8.0	11.8	41.0
Admission to sports events on trips	100.0	5.9	13.2	6.3	19.2	6.8	15.9	32.7
Fees for recreational lessons	100.0	4.1	6.5	8.1	13.5	7.0	15.4	45.4
Other entertainment services on trips	100.0	6.6	10.6	7.3	18.2	8.1	13.2	36.0
TELEVISION, RADIO, AND SOUND EQUIPMENT	100.0	12.8	18.6	9.1	18.2	7.2	11.5	22.5
Television	100.0	13.5	19.0	9.3	18.2	7.0	11.7	21.4
Cable service and community antenna	100.0	14.9	20.4	9.9	17.9	7.0	10.7	19.2
Color TV sets, consoles	100.0	7.5	13.7	6.7	20.9	5.8	16.5	28.9
Color TV sets, portable and table models	100.0	11.4	14.8	6.8	18.6	8.1	12.0	28.3
VCRs and video disc players	100.0	8.7	16.2	9.0	15.8	6.4	15.3	28.6
Video cassettes, tapes, and discs	100.0	11.2	16.4	9.3	19.7	7.0	11.8	24.6
Video game hardware and software	100.0	10.1	16.6	9.9	16.9	8.3	14.9	23.4
Repair of TV, radio, and sound equipment	100.0	11.5	15.1	6.9	16.2	4.6	19.9	25.7
Rental of television sets	100.0	27.7	34.0	14.9	1.9	0.3	19.5	1.9
Radio and sound equipment	100.0	9.6	16.6	8.0	18.6	8.1	10.9	28.0
Radios	100.0	5.8	14.2	2.1	37.0	17.9	4.9	19.1
Tape recorders and players	100.0	–	14.6	9.8	14.1	7.1	4.5	36.3
Sound components and component systems	100.0	9.4	14.7	6.5	12.6	6.9	12.6	37.3
Miscellaneous sound equipment	100.0	0.4	9.4	12.6	9.9	2.0	24.8	37.7
Sound equipment accessories	100.0	7.8	9.1	10.1	19.6	5.1	11.5	37.1
Satellite dishes	100.0	3.9	22.3	8.3	17.8	1.9	10.8	35.4
Compact disc, tape, record, video mail order clubs	100.0	12.6	19.8	10.7	22.0	11.0	11.4	12.7
Records, CDs, audio tapes, needles	100.0	11.4	18.2	8.7	17.2	7.9	11.7	25.0
Rental of VCR, radio, sound equipment	100.0	54.9	40.3	7.1	15.5	–	4.3	5.8
Musical instruments and accessories	100.0	5.0	12.6	3.0	23.4	10.7	9.3	35.9
Rental and repair of musical instruments	100.0	2.3	43.3	6.5	15.4	4.8	4.6	24.1
Rental of video cassettes, tapes, discs, films	100.0	11.8	18.6	9.8	18.8	7.7	12.3	21.1
PETS, TOYS, HOBBIES, AND PLAYGROUND EQUIPMENT	100.0	9.7	17.5	8.1	16.4	8.2	12.6	26.7
Pets	100.0	9.8	17.7	7.9	16.5	8.3	12.4	26.2
Pet food	100.0	11.9	18.5	9.0	15.5	7.8	11.1	24.6
Pet purchase, supplies, and medicines	100.0	9.8	22.1	6.0	17.2	9.2	11.3	22.6
Pet services	100.0	8.0	12.6	6.6	17.7	7.5	13.2	34.4
Veterinarian services	100.0	7.4	15.0	8.2	17.1	8.8	14.9	28.6
Toys, games, hobbies, and tricycles	100.0	10.3	17.8	8.8	17.2	8.3	13.2	24.4
Playground equipment	100.0	2.0	9.4	4.6	12.8	3.3	24.5	43.8

	total consumer units	under $20,000	$20,000–$39,999	$40,000–$49,999	$50,000–$69,999	$70,000–$79,999	$80,000–$99,999	$100,000 or more
OTHER ENTERTAINMENT SUPPLIES, EQUIPMENT, SERVICES	100.0%	5.2%	16.5%	6.1%	21.2%	6.6%	15.3%	28.8%
Unmotored recreational vehicles	100.0	–	3.4	3.4	33.9	3.4	13.0	38.1
Boat without motor and boat trailers	100.0	6.4	–	0.7	5.1	5.2	3.6	83.5
Trailer and other attachable campers	100.0	–	5.0	4.7	47.3	2.6	17.3	17.0
Motorized recreational vehicles	100.0	5.2	23.1	6.5	22.1	6.0	15.7	24.1
Motorized camper	100.0	–	9.3	16.4	43.4	5.4	4.2	14.9
Other vehicle	100.0	–	18.1	6.9	23.4	9.5	27.7	11.6
Motorboats	100.0	0.0	33.0	0.4	8.7	5.4	19.2	33.4
Rental of recreational vehicles	100.0	0.6	8.6	1.8	17.0	4.5	18.4	49.2
Docking and landing fees	100.0	3.9	13.5	7.5	14.5	10.3	16.2	35.9
Sports, recreation, exercise equipment	100.0	8.6	13.7	6.3	15.3	8.5	16.3	30.1
Athletic gear, game tables, exercise equipment	100.0	6.1	8.3	5.0	20.5	11.9	16.0	30.5
Bicycles	100.0	8.4	15.0	5.8	14.4	7.0	9.4	39.9
Camping equipment	100.0	20.4	13.0	8.7	11.1	4.0	18.9	23.7
Hunting and fishing equipment	100.0	10.1	24.9	5.7	10.0	8.5	18.4	20.9
Winter sports equipment	100.0	13.3	5.4	4.0	14.8	2.2	19.9	40.4
Water sports equipment	100.0	3.6	9.5	3.9	16.8	4.2	11.3	50.8
Other sports equipment	100.0	3.1	14.4	12.4	11.2	4.5	18.0	36.4
Rental and repair of miscellaneous sports equipment	100.0	8.2	3.3	9.3	19.2	8.5	8.4	43.3
Photographic equipment and supplies	100.0	7.2	12.9	7.2	18.6	7.6	14.8	31.7
Film	100.0	10.4	15.9	8.8	19.3	6.4	12.4	26.7
Other photographic supplies	100.0	7.4	6.9	0.7	45.3	2.5	1.6	37.3
Film processing	100.0	9.2	14.1	8.0	18.8	7.2	13.3	29.4
Repair and rental of photographic equipment	100.0	3.3	18.9	4.5	9.9	3.5	47.6	12.7
Photographic equipment	100.0	5.2	11.8	7.7	15.5	8.3	17.2	34.4
Photographer fees	100.0	6.4	12.3	6.0	16.9	9.3	15.6	33.5
Fireworks	100.0	–	13.5	0.7	33.3	3.8	17.9	4.5
Pinball, electronic video games	100.0	–	7.2	11.2	27.2	2.1	3.8	35.1

Note: Numbers may not add to total because of rounding. "–" means sample is too small to make a reliable estimate.
Source: Calculations by New Strategist based on the 2004 Consumer Expenditure Survey

Table 3.9 Entertainment: Average spending by high-income consumer units, 2004

(average annual spending on entertainment, by before-tax income of high-income consumer units (CU), 2004)

	total consumer units	$100,000 or more	$100,000– $119,999	$120,000– $149,999	$150,000 or more
Number of consumer units (in 000s)	116,282	14,937	5,625	4,245	5,067
Average number of persons per CU	2.5	3.2	3.1	3.3	3.2
Average before-tax income of CU	$54,453.00	$155,901.00	$108,751.00	$132,292.00	$228,021.00
Average spending of CU, total	43,394.87	93,525.67	75,213.14	87,298.57	119,448.79
Entertainment, average spending	**2,218.47**	**4,931.74**	**3,613.43**	**4,715.50**	**6,569.63**
FEES AND ADMISSIONS	**527.94**	**1,590.15**	**1,055.17**	**1,475.55**	**2,280.02**
Recreation expenses on trips	27.04	75.78	44.53	70.77	114.68
Social, recreation, civic club membership	98.19	350.73	234.38	308.41	515.35
Fees for participant sports	73.98	191.82	149.36	163.17	262.97
Participant sports on trips	26.72	95.26	66.76	94.15	127.83
Movie, theater, opera, ballet	92.46	231.36	174.33	225.22	299.81
Movie, other admissions on trips	48.03	122.19	88.84	146.99	138.42
Admission to sports events	36.05	114.95	59.67	90.41	196.87
Admission to sports events on trips	16.01	40.72	29.61	49.00	46.13
Fees for recreational lessons	82.42	291.55	163.17	256.67	463.28
Other entertainment services on trips	27.04	75.78	44.53	70.77	114.68
TELEVISION, RADIO, AND SOUND EQUIPMENT	**787.64**	**1,379.39**	**1,201.61**	**1,321.39**	**1,627.93**
Television	**652.61**	**1,085.08**	**955.84**	**1,068.44**	**1,242.49**
Cable service and community antenna	471.01	702.44	645.16	707.30	761.94
Color TV sets, consoles	52.46	118.16	66.04	117.44	176.61
Color TV sets, portable and table models	39.80	87.65	84.57	58.28	115.67
VCRs and video disc players	24.05	53.55	46.28	59.95	56.27
Video cassettes, tapes, and discs	42.63	81.53	75.23	77.12	92.21
Video game hardware and software	18.34	33.38	32.14	39.57	29.58
Repair of TV, radio, and sound equipment	3.02	6.04	4.35	6.24	7.75
Rental of television sets	0.81	0.12	–	0.41	–
Radio and sound equipment	**135.03**	**294.31**	**245.76**	**252.96**	**385.44**
Radios	3.67	5.47	1.36	14.01	1.88
Tape recorders and players	9.71	27.43	41.29	5.95	32.10
Sound components and component systems	14.08	40.87	16.89	24.81	80.95
Miscellaneous sound equipment	1.37	4.02	6.53	4.06	0.87
Sound equipment accessories	7.94	22.92	26.13	10.08	31.94
Satellite dishes	0.77	2.12	0.76	3.40	2.56
Compact disc, tape, record, video mail order clubs	4.15	4.11	4.58	2.29	5.11
Records, CDs, audio tapes, needles	35.26	68.51	57.62	66.39	82.35
Rental of VCR, radio, sound equipment	0.11	0.05	–	0.12	0.04
Musical instruments and accessories	20.06	56.14	34.43	55.32	80.93
Rental and repair of musical instruments	2.28	4.28	2.67	4.24	6.10
Rental of video cassettes, tapes, discs, films	35.61	58.42	53.51	62.29	60.61
PETS, TOYS, HOBBIES, PLAYGROUND EQUIPMENT	**380.64**	**790.31**	**614.67**	**810.83**	**966.02**
Pets	**271.61**	**554.93**	**424.42**	**626.01**	**638.18**
Pet food	110.31	211.44	143.42	284.99	220.73
Pet purchase, supplies, and medicines	57.85	101.82	95.63	91.47	119.91
Pet services	25.07	67.09	44.45	65.64	93.44
Veterinarian services	78.38	174.57	140.92	183.92	204.10
Toys, games, hobbies, and tricycles	**99.21**	**188.53**	**161.97**	**177.29**	**227.44**
Playground equipment	**3.33**	**11.35**	**25.88**	**4.46**	**0.99**

	total consumer units	$100,000 or more	$100,000– $119,999	$120,000– $149,999	$150,000 or more
OTHER ENTERTAINMENT SUPPLIES, EQUIPMENT, SERVICES	**$522.26**	**$1,171.89**	**$741.97**	**$1,107.73**	**$1,695.65**
Unmotored recreational vehicles	**55.39**	**164.25**	**51.83**	**52.55**	**382.63**
Boat without motor and boat trailers	17.57	114.27	29.71	8.13	297.06
Trailer and other attachable campers	37.82	49.98	22.12	44.42	85.56
Motorized recreational vehicles	**229.60**	**430.21**	**233.23**	**382.41**	**688.92**
Motorized camper	73.72	85.69	–	301.53	–
Other vehicle	35.62	32.24	40.16	52.62	6.37
Motorboats	120.27	312.28	193.07	28.27	682.55
Rental of recreational vehicles	**6.21**	**23.79**	**8.93**	**28.58**	**36.27**
Docking and landing fees	**5.62**	**15.69**	**14.73**	**23.87**	**9.89**
Sports, recreation, exercise equipment	**132.93**	**311.64**	**236.06**	**411.38**	**302.42**
Athletic gear, game tables, exercise equipment	53.07	126.17	76.66	174.02	138.68
Bicycles	11.34	35.23	28.85	40.06	38.26
Camping equipment	13.48	24.84	34.86	25.98	11.37
Hunting and fishing equipment	31.82	51.78	34.99	97.03	26.70
Winter sports equipment	4.17	13.10	6.04	18.02	16.81
Water sports equipment	4.65	18.40	18.52	12.11	23.54
Other sports equipment	11.89	33.71	32.30	35.86	33.48
Rental and repair of miscellaneous sports equipment	2.49	8.40	3.83	8.29	13.57
Photographic equipment and supplies	**82.86**	**204.73**	**181.54**	**182.08**	**251.51**
Film	12.18	25.31	24.90	22.26	28.32
Other photographic supplies	4.24	12.32	5.42	5.23	27.96
Film processing	20.31	46.42	40.88	47.08	52.02
Repair and rental of photographic equipment	0.99	0.98	0.65	0.65	1.61
Photographic equipment	28.92	77.37	67.96	78.69	86.69
Photographer fees	16.23	42.35	41.73	28.17	54.90
Fireworks	**3.75**	**1.30**	**0.09**	**4.05**	**–**
Pinball, electronic video games	**1.51**	**4.13**	**3.32**	**6.78**	**2.44**

Note: Subcategories may not add to total because some are not shown. "–" means sample is too small to make a reliable estimate.
Source: Bureau of Labor Statistics, unpublished data from the 2004 Consumer Expenditure Survey; calculations by New Strategist

Table 3.10 Entertainment: Indexed spending by high-income consumer units, 2004

(indexed average annual spending of high-income consumer units (CU) on entertainment by before-tax income of consumer unit, 2004; index definition: an index of 100 is the average for all consumer units; an index of 132 means that spending by consumer units in that group is 32 percent above the average for all consumer units; an index of 68 indicates spending that is 32 percent below the average for all consumer units)

	total consumer units	$100,000 or more	$100,000–$119,999	$120,000–$149,999	$150,000 or more
Average spending of CU, total	$43,395	$93,526	$75,213	$87,299	$119,449
Average spending of CU, index	100	216	173	201	275
Entertainment, spending index	100	222	163	213	296
FEES AND ADMISSIONS	100	301	200	279	432
Recreation expenses on trips	100	280	165	262	424
Social, recreation, civic club membership	100	357	239	314	525
Fees for participant sports	100	259	202	221	355
Participant sports on trips	100	357	250	352	478
Movie, theater, opera, ballet	100	250	189	244	324
Movie, other admissions on trips	100	254	185	306	288
Admission to sports events	100	319	166	251	546
Admission to sports events on trips	100	254	185	306	288
Fees for recreational lessons	100	354	198	311	562
Other entertainment services on trips	100	280	165	262	424
TELEVISION, RADIO, AND SOUND EQUIPMENT	100	175	153	168	207
Television	100	166	146	164	190
Cable service and community antenna	100	149	137	150	162
Color TV sets, consoles	100	225	126	224	337
Color TV sets, portable and table models	100	220	212	146	291
VCRs and video disc players	100	223	192	249	234
Video cassettes, tapes, and discs	100	191	176	181	216
Video game hardware and software	100	182	175	216	161
Repair of TV, radio, and sound equipment	100	200	144	207	257
Rental of television sets	100	15	–	51	–
Radio and sound equipment	100	218	182	187	285
Radios	100	149	37	382	51
Tape recorders and players	100	282	425	61	331
Sound components and component systems	100	290	120	176	575
Miscellaneous sound equipment	100	293	477	296	64
Sound equipment accessories	100	289	329	127	402
Satellite dishes	100	275	99	442	332
Compact disc, tape, record, video mail order clubs	100	99	110	55	123
Records, CDs, audio tapes, needles	100	194	163	188	234
Rental of VCR, radio, sound equipment	100	45	–	109	36
Musical instruments and accessories	100	280	172	276	403
Rental and repair of musical instruments	100	188	117	186	268
Rental of video cassettes, tapes, discs, films	100	164	150	175	170
PETS, TOYS, HOBBIES, PLAYGROUND EQUIPMENT	100	208	161	213	254
Pets	100	204	156	230	235
Pet food	100	192	130	258	200
Pet purchase, supplies, and medicines	100	176	165	158	207
Pet services	100	268	177	262	373
Veterinarian services	100	223	180	235	260
Toys, games, hobbies, and tricycles	100	190	163	179	229
Playground equipment	100	341	777	134	30

	total consumer units	$100,000 or more	$100,000– $119,999	$120,000– $149,999	$150,000 or more
OTHER ENTERTAINMENT SUPPLIES, EQUIPMENT, SERVICES	**100**	**224**	**142**	**212**	**325**
Unmotored recreational vehicles	**100**	**297**	**94**	**95**	**691**
Boat without motor and boat trailers	100	650	169	46	1,691
Trailer and other attachable campers	100	132	58	117	226
Motorized recreational vehicles	**100**	**187**	**102**	**167**	**300**
Motorized camper	100	116	–	409	–
Other vehicle	100	91	113	148	18
Motorboats	100	260	161	24	568
Rental of recreational vehicles	**100**	**383**	**144**	**460**	**584**
Docking and landing fees	**100**	**279**	**262**	**425**	**176**
Sports, recreation, exercise equipment	**100**	**234**	**178**	**309**	**228**
Athletic gear, game tables, exercise equipment	100	238	144	328	261
Bicycles	100	311	254	353	337
Camping equipment	100	184	259	193	84
Hunting and fishing equipment	100	163	110	305	84
Winter sports equipment	100	314	145	432	403
Water sports equipment	100	396	398	260	506
Other sports equipment	100	284	272	302	282
Rental and repair of miscellaneous sports equipment	100	337	154	333	545
Photographic equipment and supplies	**100**	**247**	**219**	**220**	**304**
Film	100	208	204	183	233
Other photographic supplies	100	291	128	123	659
Film processing	100	229	201	232	256
Repair and rental of photographic equipment	100	99	66	66	163
Photographic equipment	100	268	235	272	300
Photographer fees	100	261	257	174	338
Fireworks	**100**	**35**	**2**	**108**	**–**
Pinball, electronic video games	**100**	**274**	**220**	**449**	**162**

Note: "–" means sample is too small to make a reliable estimate.
Source: Calculations by New Strategist based on the 2004 Consumer Expenditure Survey

Table 3.11 Entertainment: Total spending by high-income consumer units, 2004

(total annual spending on entertainment, by before-tax income group of high-income consumer units (CU), 2004; consumer units and dollars in thousands)

	total consumer units	$100,000 or more	$100,000–$119,999	$120,000–$149,999	$150,000 or more
Number of consumer units	116,282	14,937	5,625	4,245	5,067
Total spending of all CUs	$5,046,042,273	$1,396,992,933	$423,073,913	$370,582,430	$605,247,019
Entertainment, total spending	**257,968,129**	**73,665,400**	**20,325,544**	**20,017,298**	**33,288,315**
FEES AND ADMISSIONS	**61,389,919**	**23,752,071**	**5,935,331**	**6,263,710**	**11,552,861**
Recreation expenses on trips	3,144,265	1,131,926	250,481	300,419	581,084
Social, recreation, civic club membership	11,417,730	5,238,854	1,318,388	1,309,200	2,611,278
Fees for participant sports	8,602,542	2,865,215	840,150	692,657	1,332,469
Participant sports on trips	3,107,055	1,422,899	375,525	399,667	647,715
Movie, theater, opera, ballet	10,751,434	3,455,824	980,606	956,059	1,519,137
Movie, other admissions on trips	5,585,024	1,825,152	499,725	623,973	701,374
Admission to sports events	4,191,966	1,717,008	335,644	383,790	997,540
Admission to sports events on trips	1,861,675	608,235	166,556	208,005	233,741
Fees for recreational lessons	9,583,962	4,354,882	917,831	1,089,564	2,347,440
Other entertainment services on trips	3,144,265	1,131,926	250,481	300,419	581,084
TELEVISION, RADIO, AND SOUND EQUIPMENT	**91,588,354**	**20,603,948**	**6,759,056**	**5,609,301**	**8,248,721**
Television	**75,886,796**	**16,207,840**	**5,376,600**	**4,535,528**	**6,295,697**
Cable service and community antenna	54,769,985	10,492,346	3,629,025	3,002,489	3,860,750
Color TV sets, consoles	6,100,154	1,764,956	371,475	498,533	894,883
Color TV sets, portable and table models	4,628,024	1,309,228	475,706	247,399	586,100
VCRs and video disc players	2,796,582	799,876	260,325	254,488	285,120
Video cassettes, tapes, and discs	4,957,102	1,217,814	423,169	327,374	467,228
Video game hardware and software	2,132,612	498,597	180,788	167,975	149,882
Repair of TV, radio, and sound equipment	351,172	90,219	24,469	26,489	39,269
Rental of television sets	94,188	1,792	–	1,740	–
Radio and sound equipment	**15,701,558**	**4,396,108**	**1,382,400**	**1,073,815**	**1,953,024**
Radios	426,755	81,705	7,650	59,472	9,526
Tape recorders and players	1,129,098	409,722	232,256	25,258	162,651
Sound components and component systems	1,637,251	610,475	95,006	105,318	410,174
Miscellaneous sound equipment	159,306	60,047	36,731	17,235	4,408
Sound equipment accessories	923,279	342,356	146,981	42,790	161,840
Satellite dishes	89,537	31,666	4,275	14,433	12,972
Compact disc, tape, record, video mail order clubs	482,570	61,391	25,763	9,721	25,892
Records, CDs, audio tapes, needles	4,100,103	1,023,334	324,113	281,826	417,267
Rental of VCR, radio, sound equipment	12,791	747	–	509	203
Musical instruments and accessories	2,332,617	838,563	193,669	234,833	410,072
Rental and repair of musical instruments	265,123	63,930	15,019	17,999	30,909
Rental of video cassettes, tapes, discs, films	4,140,802	872,620	300,994	264,421	307,111
PETS, TOYS, HOBBIES, PLAYGROUND EQUIPMENT	**44,261,580**	**11,804,860**	**3,457,519**	**3,441,973**	**4,894,823**
Pets	**31,583,354**	**8,288,989**	**2,387,363**	**2,657,412**	**3,233,658**
Pet food	12,827,067	3,158,279	806,738	1,209,783	1,118,439
Pet purchase, supplies, and medicines	6,726,914	1,520,885	537,919	388,290	607,584
Pet services	2,915,190	1,002,123	250,031	278,642	473,460
Veterinarian services	9,114,183	2,607,552	792,675	780,740	1,034,175
Toys, games, hobbies, and tricycles	**11,536,337**	**2,816,073**	**911,081**	**752,596**	**1,152,438**
Playground equipment	**387,219**	**169,535**	**145,575**	**18,933**	**5,016**

	total consumer units	$100,000 or more	$100,000– $119,999	$120,000– $149,999	$150,000 or more
OTHER ENTERTAINMENT SUPPLIES, EQUIPMENT, SERVICES	**$60,729,437**	**$17,504,521**	**$4,173,581**	**$4,702,314**	**$8,591,859**
Unmotored recreational vehicles	**6,440,860**	**2,453,402**	**291,544**	**223,075**	**1,938,786**
Boat without motor and boat trailers	2,043,075	1,706,851	167,119	34,512	1,505,203
Trailer and other attachable campers	4,397,785	746,551	124,425	188,563	433,533
Motorized recreational vehicles	**26,698,347**	**6,426,047**	**1,311,919**	**1,623,330**	**3,490,758**
Motorized camper	8,572,309	1,279,952	–	1,279,995	–
Other vehicle	4,141,965	481,569	225,900	223,372	32,277
Motorboats	13,985,236	4,664,526	1,086,019	120,006	3,458,481
Rental of recreational vehicles	**722,111**	**355,351**	**50,231**	**121,322**	**183,780**
Docking and landing fees	**653,505**	**234,362**	**82,856**	**101,328**	**50,113**
Sports, recreation, exercise equipment	**15,457,366**	**4,654,967**	**1,327,838**	**1,746,308**	**1,532,362**
Athletic gear, game tables, exercise equipment	6,171,086	1,884,601	431,213	738,715	702,692
Bicycles	1,318,638	526,231	162,281	170,055	193,863
Camping equipment	1,567,481	371,035	196,088	110,285	57,612
Hunting and fishing equipment	3,700,093	773,438	196,819	411,892	135,289
Winter sports equipment	484,896	195,675	33,975	76,495	85,176
Water sports equipment	540,711	274,841	104,175	51,407	119,277
Other sports equipment	1,382,593	503,526	181,688	152,226	169,643
Rental and repair of miscellaneous sports equipment	289,542	125,471	21,544	35,191	68,759
Photographic equipment and supplies	**9,635,127**	**3,058,052**	**1,021,163**	**772,930**	**1,274,401**
Film	1,416,315	378,055	140,063	94,494	143,497
Other photographic supplies	493,036	184,024	30,488	22,201	141,673
Film processing	2,361,687	693,376	229,950	199,855	263,585
Repair and rental of photographic equipment	115,119	14,638	3,656	2,759	8,158
Photographic equipment	3,362,875	1,155,676	382,275	334,039	439,258
Photographer fees	1,887,257	632,582	234,731	119,582	278,178
Fireworks	**436,058**	**19,418**	**506**	**17,192**	**–**
Pinball, electronic video games	**175,586**	**61,690**	**18,675**	**28,781**	**12,363**

Note: Numbers may not add to total because of rounding and missing subcategories. "–" means sample is too small to make a reliable estimate.
Source: Calculations by New Strategist based on the 2004 Consumer Expenditure Survey

Table 3.12 Entertainment: Market shares by high-income consumer units, 2004

(percentage of total annual spending on entertainment accounted for by before-tax income group of high-income consumer units, 2004)

	total consumer units	$100,000 or more	$100,000– $119,999	$120,000– $149,999	$150,000 or more
Share of total consumer units	100.0%	12.8%	4.8%	3.7%	4.4%
Share of total before-tax income	100.0	36.8	9.7	8.9	18.2
Share of total spending	100.0	27.7	8.4	7.3	12.0
Share of entertainment spending	100.0	28.6	7.9	7.8	12.9
FEES AND ADMISSIONS	100.0	38.7	9.7	10.2	18.8
Recreation expenses on trips	100.0	36.0	8.0	9.6	18.5
Social, recreation, civic club membership	100.0	45.9	11.5	11.5	22.9
Fees for participant sports	100.0	33.3	9.8	8.1	15.5
Participant sports on trips	100.0	45.8	12.1	12.9	20.8
Movie, theater, opera, ballet	100.0	32.1	9.1	8.9	14.1
Movie, other admissions on trips	100.0	32.7	8.9	11.2	12.6
Admission to sports events	100.0	41.0	8.0	9.2	23.8
Admission to sports events on trips	100.0	32.7	8.9	11.2	12.6
Fees for recreational lessons	100.0	45.4	9.6	11.4	24.5
Other entertainment services on trips	100.0	36.0	8.0	9.6	18.5
TELEVISION, RADIO, AND SOUND EQUIPMENT	100.0	22.5	7.4	6.1	9.0
Television	100.0	21.4	7.1	6.0	8.3
Cable service and community antenna	100.0	19.2	6.6	5.5	7.0
Color TV sets, consoles	100.0	28.9	6.1	8.2	14.7
Color TV sets, portable and table models	100.0	28.3	10.3	5.3	12.7
VCRs and video disc players	100.0	28.6	9.3	9.1	10.2
Video cassettes, tapes, and discs	100.0	24.6	8.5	6.6	9.4
Video game hardware and software	100.0	23.4	8.5	7.9	7.0
Repair of TV, radio, and sound equipment	100.0	25.7	7.0	7.5	11.2
Rental of television sets	100.0	1.9	–	1.8	–
Radio and sound equipment	100.0	28.0	8.8	6.8	12.4
Radios	100.0	19.1	1.8	13.9	2.2
Tape recorders and players	100.0	36.3	20.6	2.2	14.4
Sound components and component systems	100.0	37.3	5.8	6.4	25.1
Miscellaneous sound equipment	100.0	37.7	23.1	10.8	2.8
Sound equipment accessories	100.0	37.1	15.9	4.6	17.5
Satellite dishes	100.0	35.4	4.8	16.1	14.5
Compact disc, tape, record, video mail order clubs	100.0	12.7	5.3	2.0	5.4
Records, CDs, audio tapes, needles	100.0	25.0	7.9	6.9	10.2
Rental of VCR, radio, sound equipment	100.0	5.8	–	4.0	1.6
Musical instruments and accessories	100.0	35.9	8.3	10.1	17.6
Rental and repair of musical instruments	100.0	24.1	5.7	6.8	11.7
Rental of video cassettes, tapes, discs, films	100.0	21.1	7.3	6.4	7.4
PETS, TOYS, HOBBIES, PLAYGROUND EQUIPMENT	100.0	26.7	7.8	7.8	11.1
Pets	100.0	26.2	7.6	8.4	10.2
Pet food	100.0	24.6	6.3	9.4	8.7
Pet purchase, supplies, and medicines	100.0	22.6	8.0	5.8	9.0
Pet services	100.0	34.4	8.6	9.6	16.2
Veterinarian services	100.0	28.6	8.7	8.6	11.3
Toys, games, hobbies, and tricycles	100.0	24.4	7.9	6.5	10.0
Playground equipment	100.0	43.8	37.6	4.9	1.3

	total consumer units	$100,000 or more	$100,000– $119,999	$120,000– $149,999	$150,000 or more
OTHER ENTERTAINMENT SUPPLIES, EQUIPMENT, SERVICES	100.0%	28.8%	6.9%	7.7%	14.1%
Unmotored recreational vehicles	100.0	38.1	4.5	3.5	30.1
Boat without motor and boat trailers	100.0	83.5	8.2	1.7	73.7
Trailer and other attachable campers	100.0	17.0	2.8	4.3	9.9
Motorized recreational vehicles	100.0	24.1	4.9	6.1	13.1
Motorized camper	100.0	14.9	–	14.9	–
Other vehicle	100.0	11.6	5.5	5.4	0.8
Motorboats	100.0	33.4	7.8	0.9	24.7
Rental of recreational vehicles	100.0	49.2	7.0	16.8	25.5
Docking and landing fees	100.0	35.9	12.7	15.5	7.7
Sports, recreation, exercise equipment	100.0	30.1	8.6	11.3	9.9
Athletic gear, game tables, exercise equipment	100.0	30.5	7.0	12.0	11.4
Bicycles	100.0	39.9	12.3	12.9	14.7
Camping equipment	100.0	23.7	12.5	7.0	3.7
Hunting and fishing equipment	100.0	20.9	5.3	11.1	3.7
Winter sports equipment	100.0	40.4	7.0	15.8	17.6
Water sports equipment	100.0	50.8	19.3	9.5	22.1
Other sports equipment	100.0	36.4	13.1	11.0	12.3
Rental and repair of miscellaneous sports equipment	100.0	43.3	7.4	12.2	23.7
Photographic equipment and supplies	100.0	31.7	10.6	8.0	13.2
Film	100.0	26.7	9.9	6.7	10.1
Other photographic supplies	100.0	37.3	6.2	4.5	28.7
Film processing	100.0	29.4	9.7	8.5	11.2
Repair and rental of photographic equipment	100.0	12.7	3.2	2.4	7.1
Photographic equipment	100.0	34.4	11.4	9.9	13.1
Photographer fees	100.0	33.5	12.4	6.3	14.7
Fireworks	100.0	4.5	0.1	3.9	–
Pinball, electronic video games	100.0	35.1	10.6	16.4	7.0

Note: Numbers may not add to total because of rounding. "–" means sample is too small to make a reliable estimate.
Source: Calculations by New Strategist based on the 2004 Consumer Expenditure Survey

Table 3.13 Entertainment: Average spending by household type, 2004

(average annual spending of consumer units (CU) on entertainment, by type of consumer unit, 2004)

	total married couples	married couples, no children	married couples with children				single parent, at least one child <18	single person
			total	oldest child under 6	oldest child 6 to 17	oldest child 18 or older		
Number of consumer units (in 000s)	59,797	25,585	29,279	5,604	15,376	8,300	6,892	33,686
Average number of persons per CU	3.2	2.0	3.9	3.5	4.1	3.9	2.9	1.0
Average before-tax income of CU	$73,001.00	$64,434.00	$79,764.00	$75,293.00	$78,508.00	$85,109.00	$31,055.00	$28,143.00
Average spending of CU, total	55,606.57	49,690.43	60,660.88	55,981.04	60,577.88	64,161.69	32,824.46	25,423.35
Entertainment, average spending	2,945.47	2,919.15	3,051.45	2,442.34	3,320.20	2,974.96	1,573.25	1,161.83
FEES AND ADMISSIONS	**722.45**	**656.35**	**818.69**	**479.21**	**990.64**	**729.37**	**391.03**	**282.94**
Recreation expenses on trips	37.01	41.24	34.21	19.47	35.92	40.97	17.31	13.02
Social, recreation, civic club membership	142.58	170.99	127.70	103.43	153.96	95.46	56.42	50.52
Fees for participant sports	99.90	105.01	101.75	73.68	114.51	97.07	43.27	46.13
Participant sports on trips	37.37	41.17	35.51	15.29	36.87	46.64	13.05	11.01
Movie, theater, opera, ballet	111.15	97.11	125.80	78.89	145.26	121.42	84.07	63.85
Movie, other admissions on trips	65.09	63.93	69.39	37.68	79.28	72.49	27.36	24.76
Admission to sports events	47.12	45.93	49.52	25.16	51.05	63.13	19.88	22.66
Admission to sports events on trips	21.69	21.31	23.13	12.56	26.42	24.15	9.11	8.25
Fees for recreational lessons	123.53	28.42	217.48	93.57	311.44	127.08	103.25	29.71
Other entertainment services on trips	37.01	41.24	34.21	19.47	35.92	40.97	17.31	13.02
TELEVISION, RADIO, SOUND EQUIPMENT	**945.84**	**814.01**	**1,059.95**	**1,001.31**	**1,069.84**	**1,081.34**	**694.66**	**516.15**
Television	**779.92**	**707.78**	**848.19**	**823.29**	**837.76**	**884.32**	**569.35**	**436.38**
Cable service and community antenna	551.35	529.13	569.84	508.57	561.52	626.61	430.53	334.69
Color TV sets, consoles	66.57	66.57	74.50	121.58	53.60	81.44	24.17	30.09
Color TV sets, portable and table models	49.41	44.28	52.87	51.47	54.44	50.91	23.51	25.10
VCRs and video disc players	33.06	20.58	43.98	49.99	45.75	36.64	18.53	11.14
Video cassettes, tapes, and discs	50.39	32.20	64.94	63.49	70.21	56.15	42.50	25.30
Video game hardware and software	24.03	10.71	35.93	22.78	47.13	24.08	24.30	8.21
Repair of TV, radio, and sound equipment	3.62	3.57	3.78	4.01	3.65	3.88	2.73	1.68
Rental of television sets	0.77	0.45	1.18	0.64	1.14	1.62	3.07	0.01
Radio and sound equipment	**165.91**	**106.23**	**211.76**	**178.01**	**232.08**	**197.03**	**125.31**	**79.77**
Radios	4.75	3.85	6.29	8.35	4.63	8.08	–	3.21
Tape recorders and players	11.89	5.07	16.51	6.32	23.79	9.51	5.52	4.60
Sound components and component systems	17.44	11.80	23.16	51.03	14.90	19.65	6.72	7.44
Miscellaneous sound equipment	1.92	1.98	2.01	0.14	3.42	0.55	–	1.16
Sound equipment accessories	9.03	8.72	7.53	4.47	7.08	10.91	6.59	4.92
Satellite dishes	1.21	1.00	1.30	1.70	0.97	1.64	0.71	0.07
Compact disc, tape, record, video mail order clubs	4.26	4.16	4.16	5.60	4.21	3.12	4.63	3.51
Records, CDs, audio tapes, needles	39.92	27.57	51.02	38.61	53.88	54.10	36.26	25.29
Rental of VCR, radio, sound equipment	0.15	0.19	0.11	0.27	0.11	0.01	0.31	–
Musical instruments and accessories	30.17	15.78	38.72	14.71	47.81	38.09	18.01	7.08
Rental and repair of musical instruments	1.83	0.23	3.31	0.17	5.49	1.39	3.38	3.60
Rental of video cassettes, tapes, discs, films	43.37	25.87	57.65	46.64	65.80	49.97	43.19	18.89
PETS, TOYS, HOBBIES, AND								
PLAYGROUND EQUIPMENT	**495.65**	**455.86**	**536.62**	**520.22**	**570.20**	**494.57**	**285.02**	**195.63**
Pets	**343.11**	**371.70**	**328.04**	**216.09**	**346.08**	**379.27**	**150.46**	**155.42**
Pet food	145.11	150.30	143.04	59.89	153.08	188.83	69.34	57.71
Pet purchase, supplies, and medicines	65.31	66.06	65.25	43.68	73.59	65.17	22.48	33.30
Pet services	32.01	37.53	28.57	25.06	32.78	23.13	14.23	18.91
Veterinarian services	100.68	117.81	91.18	87.46	86.62	102.14	44.41	45.50
Toys, games, hobbies, and tricycles	**136.18**	**60.12**	**198.88**	**276.19**	**217.20**	**112.74**	**132.31**	**37.32**
Playground equipment	**6.04**	**1.54**	**8.62**	**27.04**	**5.78**	**1.44**	**0.58**	**0.07**

	total married couples	married couples, no children	married couples with children				single parent, at least one child <18	single person
			total	oldest child under 6	oldest child 6 to 17	oldest child 18 or older		
OTHER ENTERTAINMENT SUPPLIES, EQUIPMENT, SERVICES	**$781.53**	**$992.93**	**$636.19**	**$441.61**	**$689.52**	**$669.68**	**$202.54**	**$167.12**
Unmotored recreational vehicles	**87.21**	**94.94**	**94.89**	**31.19**	**97.71**	**132.68**	**1.00**	**2.39**
Boat without motor and boat trailers	31.07	6.96	57.10	1.17	57.77	93.64	–	1.72
Trailer and other attachable campers	56.15	87.98	37.79	30.02	39.95	39.03	1.00	0.67
Motorized recreational vehicles	**384.47**	**658.89**	**154.99**	**98.14**	**170.32**	**164.99**	**40.77**	**38.51**
Motorized camper	106.81	166.42	29.86	–	25.19	58.69	–	16.10
Other vehicle	55.00	102.66	22.54	–	20.85	40.87	40.77	9.01
Motorboats	222.66	389.81	102.59	98.14	124.28	65.43	–	13.40
Rental of recreational vehicles	**9.21**	**12.80**	**6.17**	**4.37**	**8.06**	**3.88**	**4.02**	**1.89**
Docking and landing fees	**8.31**	**15.03**	**3.71**	**0.88**	**3.96**	**5.17**	**3.86**	**2.72**
Sports, recreation, exercise equipment	**160.79**	**104.76**	**215.41**	**118.82**	**255.51**	**207.26**	**82.67**	**86.31**
Athletic gear, game tables, exercise equipment	71.88	34.05	109.55	39.14	150.26	81.12	18.95	26.69
Bicycles	15.20	10.55	19.91	18.11	20.83	19.42	12.89	6.82
Camping equipment	18.91	12.66	22.82	29.32	21.56	20.22	9.62	7.39
Hunting and fishing equipment	23.72	21.56	25.11	9.77	24.93	37.80	15.86	34.34
Winter sports equipment	5.27	3.19	7.27	1.93	8.94	7.78	4.53	2.62
Water sports equipment	6.05	4.72	8.11	6.56	11.29	3.25	0.97	2.41
Other sports equipment	16.47	14.75	19.04	11.13	14.33	33.09	18.02	4.55
Rental and repair of miscellaneous sports equipment	3.29	3.27	3.61	2.85	3.36	4.58	1.82	1.48
Photographic equipment and supplies	**118.26**	**96.75**	**144.10**	**182.66**	**135.13**	**134.45**	**62.01**	**31.38**
Film	16.17	13.37	18.94	22.64	18.63	17.03	11.00	6.09
Other photographic supplies	4.89	7.28	3.60	4.57	4.06	1.84	1.14	0.26
Film processing	28.02	23.75	32.91	43.85	31.83	27.51	14.39	9.86
Repair and rental of photographic equipment	1.41	0.59	2.27	9.77	0.59	0.33	1.31	0.31
Photographic equipment	42.23	35.19	51.44	67.28	48.59	46.02	15.98	12.67
Photographer fees	25.53	16.56	34.94	34.54	31.43	41.72	18.18	2.20
Fireworks	**4.54**	**4.98**	**4.89**	**–**	**4.11**	**10.44**	**3.56**	**1.09**
Pinball, electronic video games	**1.78**	**0.51**	**2.80**	**3.70**	**2.73**	**2.21**	**4.30**	**0.68**

Note: Average spending figures for total consumer units can be found on Average Spending by Age and Average Spending by Region tables. Subcategories may not add to total because some are not shown. "–" means sample is too small to make a reliable estimate.
Source: Bureau of Labor Statistics, unpublished data from the 2004 Consumer Expenditure Survey

Table 3.14 Entertainment: Indexed spending by household type, 2004

(indexed average annual spending of consumer units (CU) on entertainment by type of consumer unit, 2004; index definition: an index of 100 is the average for all consumer units; an index of 132 means that spending by consumer units in that group is 32 percent above the average for all consumer units; an index of 68 indicates spending that is 32 percent below the average for all consumer units)

	total married couples	married couples, no children	married couples with children				single parent, at least one child <18	single person
			total	oldest child under 6	oldest child 6 to 17	oldest child 18 or older		
Average spending of CU, total	$55,607	$49,690	$60,661	$55,981	$60,578	$64,162	$32,824	$25,423
Average spending of CU, index	128	115	140	129	140	148	76	59
Entertainment, spending index	**133**	**132**	**138**	**110**	**150**	**134**	**71**	**52**
FEES AND ADMISSIONS	**137**	**124**	**155**	**91**	**188**	**138**	**74**	**54**
Recreation expenses on trips	137	153	127	72	133	152	64	48
Social, recreation, civic club membership	145	174	130	105	157	97	57	51
Fees for participant sports	135	142	138	100	155	131	58	62
Participant sports on trips	140	154	133	57	138	175	49	41
Movie, theater, opera, ballet	120	105	136	85	157	131	91	69
Movie, other admissions on trips	136	133	144	78	165	151	57	52
Admission to sports events	131	127	137	70	142	175	55	63
Admission to sports events on trips	135	133	144	78	165	151	57	52
Fees for recreational lessons	150	34	264	114	378	154	125	36
Other entertainment services on trips	137	153	127	72	133	152	64	48
TELEVISION, RADIO, AND SOUND EQUIPMENT	**120**	**103**	**135**	**127**	**136**	**137**	**88**	**66**
Television	**120**	**108**	**130**	**126**	**128**	**136**	**87**	**67**
Cable service and community antenna	117	112	121	108	119	133	91	71
Color TV sets, consoles	127	127	142	232	102	155	46	57
Color TV sets, portable and table models	124	111	133	129	137	128	59	63
VCRs and video disc players	137	86	183	208	190	152	77	46
Video cassettes, tapes, and discs	118	76	152	149	165	132	100	59
Video game hardware and software	131	58	196	124	257	131	132	45
Repair of TV, radio, and sound equipment	120	118	125	133	121	128	90	56
Rental of television sets	95	56	146	79	141	200	379	1
Radio and sound equipment	**123**	**79**	**157**	**132**	**172**	**146**	**93**	**59**
Radios	129	105	171	228	126	220	–	87
Tape recorders and players	122	52	170	65	245	98	57	47
Sound components and component systems	124	84	164	362	106	140	48	53
Miscellaneous sound equipment	140	145	147	10	250	40	–	85
Sound equipment accessories	114	110	95	56	89	137	83	62
Satellite dishes	157	130	169	221	126	213	92	9
Compact disc, tape, record, video mail order clubs	103	100	100	135	101	75	112	85
Records, CDs, audio tapes, needles	113	78	145	110	153	153	103	72
Rental of VCR, radio, sound equipment	136	173	100	245	100	9	282	–
Musical instruments and accessories	150	79	193	73	238	190	90	35
Rental and repair of musical instruments	80	10	145	7	241	61	148	158
Rental of video cassettes, tapes, discs, films	122	73	162	131	185	140	121	53
PETS, TOYS, HOBBIES, AND PLAYGROUND EQUIPMENT	**130**	**120**	**141**	**137**	**150**	**130**	**75**	**51**
Pets	**126**	**137**	**121**	**80**	**127**	**140**	**55**	**57**
Pet food	132	136	130	54	139	171	63	52
Pet purchase, supplies, and medicines	113	114	113	76	127	113	39	58
Pet services	128	150	114	100	131	92	57	75
Veterinarian services	128	150	116	112	111	130	57	58
Toys, games, hobbies, and tricycles	**137**	**61**	**200**	**278**	**219**	**114**	**133**	**38**
Playground equipment	**181**	**46**	**259**	**812**	**174**	**43**	**17**	**2**

	total married couples	married couples, no children	married couples with children				single parent, at least one child <18	single person
			total	oldest child under 6	oldest child 6 to 17	oldest child 18 or older		
OTHER ENTERTAINMENT SUPPLIES, EQUIPMENT, SERVICES	**150**	**190**	**122**	**85**	**132**	**128**	**39**	**32**
Unmotored recreational vehicles	**157**	**171**	**171**	**56**	**176**	**240**	**2**	**4**
Boat without motor and boat trailers	177	40	325	7	329	533	–	10
Trailer and other attachable campers	148	233	100	79	106	103	3	2
Motorized recreational vehicles	**167**	**287**	**68**	**43**	**74**	**72**	**18**	**17**
Motorized camper	145	226	41	–	34	80	–	22
Other vehicle	154	288	63	–	59	115	114	25
Motorboats	185	324	85	82	103	54	–	11
Rental of recreational vehicles	**148**	**206**	**99**	**70**	**130**	**62**	**65**	**30**
Docking and landing fees	**148**	**267**	**66**	**16**	**70**	**92**	**69**	**48**
Sports, recreation, exercise equipment	**121**	**79**	**162**	**89**	**192**	**156**	**62**	**65**
Athletic gear, game tables, exercise equipment	135	64	206	74	283	153	36	50
Bicycles	134	93	176	160	184	171	114	60
Camping equipment	140	94	169	218	160	150	71	55
Hunting and fishing equipment	75	68	79	31	78	119	50	108
Winter sports equipment	126	76	174	46	214	187	109	63
Water sports equipment	130	102	174	141	243	70	21	52
Other sports equipment	139	124	160	94	121	278	152	38
Rental and repair of miscellaneous sports equipment	132	131	145	114	135	184	73	59
Photographic equipment and supplies	**143**	**117**	**174**	**220**	**163**	**162**	**75**	**38**
Film	133	110	156	186	153	140	90	50
Other photographic supplies	115	172	85	108	96	43	27	6
Film processing	138	117	162	216	157	135	71	49
Repair and rental of photographic equipment	142	60	229	987	60	33	132	31
Photographic equipment	146	122	178	233	168	159	55	44
Photographer fees	157	102	215	213	194	257	112	14
Fireworks	**121**	**133**	**130**	**–**	**110**	**278**	**95**	**29**
Pinball, electronic video games	**118**	**34**	**185**	**245**	**181**	**146**	**285**	**45**

Note: Spending index for total consumer units is 100. "–" means sample is too small to make a reliable estimate.
Source: Calculations by New Strategist based on the 2004 Consumer Expenditure Survey

Table 3.15 Entertainment: Total spending by household type, 2004

(total annual spending on entertainment, by consumer unit (CU) type, 2004; consumer units and dollars in thousands)

	total married couples	married couples, no children	married couples with children total	oldest child under 6	oldest child 6 to 17	oldest child 18 or older	single parent, at least one child <18	single person
Number of consumer units	59,797	25,585	29,279	5,604	15,376	8,300	6,892	33,686
Total spending of all CUs	$3,325,106,066	$1,271,329,652	$1,776,089,906	$313,717,748	$931,445,483	$532,542,027	$226,226,178	$856,410,968
Entertainment, total spending	**176,130,270**	**74,686,453**	**89,343,405**	**13,686,873**	**51,051,395**	**24,692,168**	**10,842,839**	**39,137,405**
FEES AND ADMISSIONS	**43,200,343**	**16,792,715**	**23,970,425**	**2,685,493**	**15,232,081**	**6,053,771**	**2,694,979**	**9,531,117**
Recreation expenses on trips	2,213,087	1,055,125	1,001,635	109,110	552,306	340,051	119,301	438,592
Social, recreation, civic club membership	8,525,856	4,374,779	3,738,928	579,622	2,367,289	792,318	388,847	1,701,817
Fees for participant sports	5,973,720	2,686,681	2,979,138	412,903	1,760,706	805,681	298,217	1,553,935
Participant sports on trips	2,234,614	1,053,334	1,039,697	85,685	566,913	387,112	89,941	370,883
Movie, theater, opera, ballet	6,646,437	2,484,559	3,683,298	442,100	2,233,518	1,007,786	579,410	2,150,851
Movie, other admissions on trips	3,892,187	1,635,649	2,031,670	211,159	1,219,009	601,667	188,565	834,065
Admission to sports events	2,817,635	1,175,119	1,449,896	140,997	784,945	523,979	137,013	763,325
Admission to sports events on trips	1,296,997	545,216	677,223	70,386	406,234	200,445	62,786	277,910
Fees for recreational lessons	7,386,723	727,126	6,367,597	524,366	4,788,701	1,054,764	711,599	1,000,811
Other entertainment services on trips	2,213,087	1,055,125	1,001,635	109,110	552,306	340,051	119,301	438,592
TELEVISION, RADIO, SOUND EQUIPMENT	**56,558,394**	**20,826,446**	**31,034,276**	**5,611,341**	**16,449,860**	**8,975,122**	**4,787,597**	**17,387,029**
Television	**46,636,876**	**18,108,551**	**24,834,155**	**4,613,717**	**12,881,398**	**7,339,856**	**3,923,960**	**14,699,897**
Cable service and community antenna	32,969,076	13,537,791	16,684,345	2,850,026	8,633,932	5,200,863	2,967,213	11,274,367
Color TV sets, consoles	3,980,686	1,703,193	2,181,286	681,334	824,154	675,952	166,580	1,013,612
Color TV sets, portable and table models	2,954,570	1,132,904	1,547,981	288,438	837,069	422,553	162,031	845,519
VCRs and video disc players	1,976,889	526,539	1,287,690	280,144	703,452	304,112	127,709	375,262
Video cassettes, tapes, and discs	3,013,171	823,837	1,901,378	355,798	1,079,549	466,045	292,910	852,256
Video game hardware and software	1,436,922	274,015	1,051,994	127,659	724,671	199,864	167,476	276,562
Repair of TV, radio, and sound equipment	216,465	91,338	110,675	22,472	56,122	32,204	18,815	56,592
Rental of television sets	46,044	11,513	34,549	3,587	17,529	13,446	21,158	337
Radio and sound equipment	**9,920,920**	**2,717,895**	**6,200,121**	**997,568**	**3,568,462**	**1,635,349**	**863,637**	**2,687,132**
Radios	284,036	98,502	184,165	46,793	71,191	67,064	–	108,132
Tape recorders and players	710,986	129,716	483,396	35,417	365,795	78,933	38,044	154,956
Sound components and component systems	1,042,860	301,903	678,102	285,972	229,102	163,095	46,314	250,624
Miscellaneous sound equipment	114,810	50,658	58,851	785	52,586	4,565	–	39,076
Sound equipment accessories	539,967	223,101	220,471	25,050	108,862	90,553	45,418	165,735
Satellite dishes	72,354	25,585	38,063	9,527	14,915	13,612	4,893	2,358
Compact disc, tape, record, video mail order clubs	254,735	106,434	121,801	31,382	64,733	25,896	31,910	118,238
Records, CDs, audio tapes, needles	2,387,096	705,378	1,493,815	216,370	828,459	449,030	249,904	851,919
Rental of VCR, radio, sound equipment	8,970	4,861	3,221	1,513	1,691	83	2,137	–
Musical instruments and accessories	1,804,075	403,731	1,133,683	82,435	735,127	316,147	124,125	238,497
Rental and repair of musical instruments	109,429	5,885	96,913	953	84,414	11,537	23,295	121,270
Rental of video cassettes, tapes, discs, films	2,593,396	661,884	1,687,934	261,371	1,011,741	414,751	297,665	636,329
PETS, TOYS, HOBBIES, AND PLAYGROUND EQUIPMENT	**29,638,383**	**11,663,178**	**15,711,697**	**2,915,313**	**8,767,395**	**4,104,931**	**1,964,358**	**6,589,992**
Pets	**20,516,949**	**9,509,945**	**9,604,683**	**1,210,968**	**5,321,326**	**3,147,941**	**1,036,970**	**5,235,478**
Pet food	8,677,143	3,845,426	4,188,068	335,624	2,353,758	1,567,289	477,891	1,944,019
Pet purchase, supplies, and medicines	3,905,342	1,690,145	1,910,455	244,783	1,131,520	540,911	154,932	1,121,744
Pet services	1,914,102	960,205	836,501	140,436	504,025	191,979	98,073	637,002
Veterinarian services	6,020,362	3,014,169	2,669,659	490,126	1,331,869	847,762	306,074	1,532,713
Toys, games, hobbies, and tricycles	**8,143,155**	**1,538,170**	**5,823,008**	**1,547,769**	**3,339,667**	**935,742**	**911,881**	**1,257,162**
Playground equipment	**361,174**	**39,401**	**252,385**	**151,532**	**88,873**	**11,952**	**3,997**	**2,358**

	total married couples	married couples, no children	married couples with children				single parent, at least one child <18	single person
			total	oldest child under 6	oldest child 6 to 17	oldest child 18 or older		
OTHER ENTERTAINMENT SUPPLIES, EQUIPMENT, SERVICES	$46,733,149	$25,404,114	$18,627,007	$2,474,782	$10,602,060	$5,558,344	$1,395,906	$5,629,604
Unmotored recreational vehicles	5,214,896	2,429,040	2,778,284	174,789	1,502,389	1,101,244	6,892	80,510
Boat without motor and boat trailers	1,857,893	178,072	1,671,831	6,557	888,272	777,212	–	57,940
Trailer and other attachable campers	3,357,602	2,250,968	1,106,453	168,232	614,271	323,949	6,892	22,570
Motorized recreational vehicles	22,990,153	16,857,701	4,537,952	549,977	2,618,840	1,369,417	280,987	1,297,248
Motorized camper	6,386,918	4,257,856	874,271	–	387,321	487,127	–	542,345
Other vehicle	3,288,835	2,626,556	659,949	–	320,590	339,221	280,987	303,511
Motorboats	13,314,400	9,973,289	3,003,733	549,977	1,910,929	543,069	–	451,392
Rental of recreational vehicles	550,730	327,488	180,651	24,489	123,931	32,204	27,706	63,667
Docking and landing fees	496,913	384,543	108,625	4,932	60,889	42,911	26,603	91,626
Sports, recreation, exercise equipment	9,614,760	2,680,285	6,306,989	665,867	3,928,722	1,720,258	569,762	2,907,439
Athletic gear, game tables, exercise equipment	4,298,208	871,169	3,207,514	219,341	2,310,398	673,296	130,603	899,079
Bicycles	908,914	269,922	582,945	101,488	320,282	161,186	88,838	229,739
Camping equipment	1,130,761	323,906	668,147	164,309	331,507	167,826	66,301	248,940
Hunting and fishing equipment	1,418,385	551,613	735,196	54,751	383,324	313,740	109,307	1,156,777
Winter sports equipment	315,130	81,616	212,858	10,816	137,461	64,574	31,221	88,257
Water sports equipment	361,772	120,761	237,453	36,762	173,595	26,975	6,685	81,183
Other sports equipment	984,857	377,379	557,472	62,373	220,338	274,647	124,194	153,271
Rental and repair of miscellaneous sports equipment	196,732	83,663	105,697	15,971	51,663	38,014	12,543	49,855
Photographic equipment and supplies	7,071,593	2,475,349	4,219,104	1,023,627	2,077,759	1,115,935	427,373	1,057,067
Film	966,917	342,071	554,544	126,875	286,455	141,349	75,812	205,148
Other photographic supplies	292,407	186,259	105,404	25,610	62,427	15,272	7,857	8,758
Film processing	1,675,512	607,644	963,572	245,735	489,418	228,333	99,176	332,144
Repair and rental of photographic equipment	84,314	15,095	66,463	54,751	9,072	2,739	9,029	10,443
Photographic equipment	2,525,227	900,336	1,506,112	377,037	747,120	381,966	110,134	426,802
Photographer fees	1,526,617	423,688	1,023,008	193,562	483,268	346,276	125,297	74,109
Fireworks	271,478	127,413	143,174	–	63,195	86,652	24,536	36,718
Pinball, electronic video games	106,439	13,048	81,981	20,735	41,976	18,343	29,636	22,906

Note: Total spending figures for total consumer units can be found on Total Spending by Age and Total Spending by Region tables. Spending by type of consumer unit will not add to total because not all types of consumer units are shown. Numbers may not add to category total because of rounding and missing subcategories. "–" means sample is too small to make a reliable estimate.
Source: Calculations by New Strategist based on the 2004 Consumer Expenditure Survey

Table 3.16 Entertainment: Market shares by household type, 2004

(percentage of total annual spending on entertainment accounted for by types of consumer units, 2004)

	total married couples	married couples, no children	married couples with children				single parent, at least one child <18	single person
			total	oldest child under 6	oldest child 6 to 17	oldest child 18 or older		
Share of total consumer units	51.4%	22.0%	25.2%	4.8%	13.2%	7.1%	5.9%	29.0%
Share of total before-tax income	68.9	26.0	36.9	6.7	19.1	11.2	3.4	15.0
Share of total spending	65.9	25.2	35.2	6.2	18.5	10.6	4.5	17.0
Share of entertainment spending	68.3	29.0	34.6	5.3	19.8	9.6	4.2	15.2
FEES AND ADMISSIONS	**70.4**	**27.4**	**39.0**	**4.4**	**24.8**	**9.9**	**4.4**	**15.5**
Recreation expenses on trips	70.4	33.6	31.9	3.5	17.6	10.8	3.8	13.9
Social, recreation, civic club membership	74.7	38.3	32.7	5.1	20.7	6.9	3.4	14.9
Fees for participant sports	69.4	31.2	34.6	4.8	20.5	9.4	3.5	18.1
Participant sports on trips	71.9	33.9	33.5	2.8	18.2	12.5	2.9	11.9
Movie, theater, opera, ballet	61.8	23.1	34.3	4.1	20.8	9.4	5.4	20.0
Movie, other admissions on trips	69.7	29.3	36.4	3.8	21.8	10.8	3.4	14.9
Admission to sports events	67.2	28.0	34.6	3.4	18.7	12.5	3.3	18.2
Admission to sports events on trips	69.7	29.3	36.4	3.8	21.8	10.8	3.4	14.9
Fees for recreational lessons	77.1	7.6	66.4	5.5	50.0	11.0	7.4	10.4
Other entertainment services on trips	70.4	33.6	31.9	3.5	17.6	10.8	3.8	13.9
TELEVISION, RADIO, AND SOUND EQUIPMENT	**61.8**	**22.7**	**33.9**	**6.1**	**18.0**	**9.8**	**5.2**	**19.0**
Television	**61.5**	**23.9**	**32.7**	**6.1**	**17.0**	**9.7**	**5.2**	**19.4**
Cable service and community antenna	60.2	24.7	30.5	5.2	15.8	9.5	5.4	20.6
Color TV sets, consoles	65.3	27.9	35.8	11.2	13.5	11.1	2.7	16.6
Color TV sets, portable and table models	63.8	24.5	33.4	6.2	18.1	9.1	3.5	18.3
VCRs and video disc players	70.7	18.8	46.0	10.0	25.2	10.9	4.6	13.4
Video cassettes, tapes, and discs	60.8	16.6	38.4	7.2	21.8	9.4	5.9	17.2
Video game hardware and software	67.4	12.8	49.3	6.0	34.0	9.4	7.9	13.0
Repair of TV, radio, and sound equipment	61.6	26.0	31.5	6.4	16.0	9.2	5.4	16.1
Rental of television sets	48.9	12.2	36.7	3.8	18.6	14.3	22.5	0.4
Radio and sound equipment	**63.2**	**17.3**	**39.5**	**6.4**	**22.7**	**10.4**	**5.5**	**17.1**
Radios	66.6	23.1	43.2	11.0	16.7	15.7	–	25.3
Tape recorders and players	63.0	11.5	42.8	3.1	32.4	7.0	3.4	13.7
Sound components and component systems	63.7	18.4	41.4	17.5	14.0	10.0	2.8	15.3
Miscellaneous sound equipment	72.1	31.8	36.9	0.5	33.0	2.9	–	24.5
Sound equipment accessories	58.5	24.2	23.9	2.7	11.8	9.8	4.9	18.0
Satellite dishes	80.8	28.6	42.5	10.6	16.7	15.2	5.5	2.6
Compact disc, tape, record, video mail order clubs	52.8	22.1	25.2	6.5	13.4	5.4	6.6	24.5
Records, CDs, audio tapes, needles	58.2	17.2	36.4	5.3	20.2	11.0	6.1	20.8
Rental of VCR, radio, sound equipment	70.1	38.0	25.2	11.8	13.2	0.6	16.7	–
Musical instruments and accessories	77.3	17.3	48.6	3.5	31.5	13.6	5.3	10.2
Rental and repair of musical instruments	41.3	2.2	36.6	0.4	31.8	4.4	8.8	45.7
Rental of video cassettes, tapes, discs, films	62.6	16.0	40.8	6.3	24.4	10.0	7.2	15.4
PETS, TOYS, HOBBIES, AND PLAYGROUND EQUIPMENT	**67.0**	**26.4**	**35.5**	**6.6**	**19.8**	**9.3**	**4.4**	**14.9**
Pets	**65.0**	**30.1**	**30.4**	**3.8**	**16.8**	**10.0**	**3.3**	**16.6**
Pet food	67.6	30.0	32.7	2.6	18.3	12.2	3.7	15.2
Pet purchase, supplies, and medicines	58.1	25.1	28.4	3.6	16.8	8.0	2.3	16.7
Pet services	65.7	32.9	28.7	4.8	17.3	6.6	3.4	21.9
Veterinarian services	66.1	33.1	29.3	5.4	14.6	9.3	3.4	16.8
Toys, games, hobbies, and tricycles	**70.6**	**13.3**	**50.5**	**13.4**	**28.9**	**8.1**	**7.9**	**10.9**
Playground equipment	**93.3**	**10.2**	**65.2**	**39.1**	**23.0**	**3.1**	**1.0**	**0.6**

	total married couples	married couples, no children	married couples with children				single parent, at least one child <18	single person
			total	oldest child under 6	oldest child 6 to 17	oldest child 18 or older		
OTHER ENTERTAINMENT SUPPLIES, EQUIPMENT, SERVICES	**77.0%**	**41.8%**	**30.7%**	**4.1%**	**17.5%**	**9.2%**	**2.3%**	**9.3%**
Unmotored recreational vehicles	**81.0**	**37.7**	**43.1**	**2.7**	**23.3**	**17.1**	**0.1**	**1.2**
Boat without motor and boat trailers	90.9	8.7	81.8	0.3	43.5	38.0	–	2.8
Trailer and other attachable campers	76.3	51.2	25.2	3.8	14.0	7.4	0.2	0.5
Motorized recreational vehicles	**86.1**	**63.1**	**17.0**	**2.1**	**9.8**	**5.1**	**1.1**	**4.9**
Motorized camper	74.5	49.7	10.2	–	4.5	5.7	–	6.3
Other vehicle	79.4	63.4	15.9	–	7.7	8.2	6.8	7.3
Motorboats	95.2	71.3	21.5	3.9	13.7	3.9	–	3.2
Rental of recreational vehicles	**76.3**	**45.4**	**25.0**	**3.4**	**17.2**	**4.5**	**3.8**	**8.8**
Docking and landing fees	**76.0**	**58.8**	**16.6**	**0.8**	**9.3**	**6.6**	**4.1**	**14.0**
Sports, recreation, exercise equipment	**62.2**	**17.3**	**40.8**	**4.3**	**25.4**	**11.1**	**3.7**	**18.8**
Athletic gear, game tables, exercise equipment	69.7	14.1	52.0	3.6	37.4	10.9	2.1	14.6
Bicycles	68.9	20.5	44.2	7.7	24.3	12.2	6.7	17.4
Camping equipment	72.1	20.7	42.6	10.5	21.1	10.7	4.2	15.9
Hunting and fishing equipment	38.3	14.9	19.9	1.5	10.4	8.5	3.0	31.3
Winter sports equipment	65.0	16.8	43.9	2.2	28.3	13.3	6.4	18.2
Water sports equipment	66.9	22.3	43.9	6.8	32.1	5.0	1.2	15.0
Other sports equipment	71.2	27.3	40.3	4.5	15.9	19.9	9.0	11.1
Rental and repair of miscellaneous sports equipment	67.9	28.9	36.5	5.5	17.8	13.1	4.3	17.2
Photographic equipment and supplies	**73.4**	**25.7**	**43.8**	**10.6**	**21.6**	**11.6**	**4.4**	**11.0**
Film	68.3	24.2	39.2	9.0	20.2	10.0	5.4	14.5
Other photographic supplies	59.3	37.8	21.4	5.2	12.7	3.1	1.6	1.8
Film processing	70.9	25.7	40.8	10.4	20.7	9.7	4.2	14.1
Repair and rental of photographic equipment	73.2	13.1	57.7	47.6	7.9	2.4	7.8	9.1
Photographic equipment	75.1	26.8	44.8	11.2	22.2	11.4	3.3	12.7
Photographer fees	80.9	22.4	54.2	10.3	25.6	18.3	6.6	3.9
Fireworks	**62.3**	**29.2**	**32.8**	**–**	**14.5**	**19.9**	**5.6**	**8.4**
Pinball, electronic video games	**60.6**	**7.4**	**46.7**	**11.8**	**23.9**	**10.4**	**16.9**	**13.0**

Note: Market share for total consumer units is 100.0%. Market shares by type of consumer unit will not add to total because not all types of consumer units are shown. "–" means sample is too small to make a reliable estimate.
Source: Calculations by New Strategist based on the 2004 Consumer Expenditure Survey

Table 3.17 Entertainment: Average spending by race and Hispanic origin, 2004

(average annual spending of consumer units (CU) on entertainment, by race and Hispanic origin of consumer unit reference person, 2004)

	total consumer units	Asian	black	Hispanic	non-Hispanic white and other
Number of consumer units (in 000s)	116,282	3,957	13,773	12,298	90,424
Average number of persons per CU	2.5	2.8	2.6	3.3	2.3
Average before-tax income of CU	$54,453.00	$67,705.00	$38,503.00	$43,693.00	$58,314.00
Average spending of CU, total	43,394.87	49,458.68	30,481.49	37,578.03	46,163.26
Entertainment, average spending	2,218.47	1,788.87	1,039.54	1,443.08	2,502.73
FEES AND ADMISSIONS	527.94	613.69	185.36	307.69	609.65
Recreation expenses on trips	27.04	43.88	10.80	25.44	29.71
Social, recreation, civic club membership	98.19	40.63	21.82	33.13	118.53
Fees for participant sports	73.98	85.70	17.67	36.08	87.55
Participant sports on trips	26.72	22.16	6.23	12.03	31.78
Movie, theater, opera, ballet	92.46	96.85	50.43	70.73	101.79
Movie, other admissions on trips	48.03	61.36	20.61	27.35	54.93
Admission to sports events	36.05	15.60	11.82	17.78	42.15
Admission to sports events on trips	16.01	20.45	6.87	9.12	18.31
Fees for recreational lessons	82.42	183.16	28.31	50.58	95.19
Other entertainment services on trips	27.04	43.88	10.80	25.44	29.71
TELEVISION, RADIO, AND SOUND EQUIPMENT	787.64	792.10	657.20	656.02	825.55
Television	652.61	579.72	585.33	525.18	679.88
Cable service and community antenna	471.01	361.28	469.02	349.92	487.55
Color TV sets, consoles	52.46	66.26	33.45	36.45	57.46
Color TV sets, portable and table models	39.80	40.60	24.85	57.92	39.51
VCRs and video disc players	24.05	40.56	11.40	21.15	26.35
Video cassettes, tapes, and discs	42.63	47.38	29.77	38.88	45.20
Video game hardware and software	18.34	21.68	11.52	16.25	19.66
Repair of TV, radio, and sound equipment	3.02	1.94	2.43	2.55	3.17
Rental of television sets	0.81	0.03	2.85	0.81	0.52
Radio and sound equipment	135.03	212.38	71.87	130.83	145.67
Radios	3.67	0.23	0.63	3.49	4.16
Tape recorders and players	9.71	11.25	2.95	9.01	10.84
Sound components and component systems	14.08	14.92	10.32	14.81	14.81
Miscellaneous sound equipment	1.37	1.10	–	1.16	1.61
Sound equipment accessories	7.94	16.34	1.43	6.81	9.09
Satellite dishes	0.77	0.08	0.11	1.47	0.78
Compact disc, tape, record, video mail order clubs	4.15	2.17	2.96	3.07	4.49
Records, CDs, audio tapes, needles	35.26	29.62	28.48	34.67	36.50
Rental of VCR, radio, sound equipment	0.11	–	0.26	0.18	0.08
Musical instruments and accessories	20.06	97.29	2.67	16.93	23.09
Rental and repair of musical instruments	2.28	0.49	0.38	0.97	2.80
Rental of video cassettes, tapes, discs, films	35.61	38.89	21.70	38.25	37.42
PETS, TOYS, HOBBIES, AND PLAYGROUND EQUIPMENT	380.64	155.97	121.94	239.22	439.36
Pets	271.61	90.67	51.27	139.13	323.38
Pet food	110.31	39.60	26.60	68.53	129.01
Pet purchase, supplies, and medicines	57.85	16.76	12.46	36.41	67.82
Pet services	25.07	5.60	3.67	6.33	30.84
Veterinarian services	78.38	28.72	8.53	27.86	95.71
Toys, games, hobbies, and tricycles	99.21	64.11	70.02	96.59	103.94
Playground equipment	3.33	0.79	0.09	2.56	3.93

	total consumer units	Asian	black	Hispanic	non-Hispanic white and other
OTHER ENTERTAINMENT SUPPLIES, EQUIPMENT, SERVICES	**$522.26**	**$227.11**	**$75.03**	**$240.17**	**$628.17**
Unmotored recreational vehicles	**55.39**	**1.26**	**–**	**5.08**	**70.54**
Boat without motor and boat trailers	17.57	1.26	–	5.08	21.90
Trailer and other attachable campers	37.82	–	–	–	48.64
Motorized recreational vehicles	**229.60**	**43.40**	**3.23**	**84.99**	**283.21**
Motorized camper	73.72	–	2.28	69.85	84.95
Other vehicle	35.62	13.18	0.96	–	45.65
Motorboats	120.27	30.22	–	15.14	152.60
Rental of recreational vehicles	**6.21**	**2.31**	**0.63**	**3.73**	**7.38**
Docking and landing fees	**5.62**	**0.03**	**0.01**	**1.74**	**6.99**
Sports, recreation, exercise equipment	**132.93**	**69.26**	**37.84**	**85.00**	**154.07**
Athletic gear, game tables, exercise equipment	53.07	37.90	23.53	29.35	60.91
Bicycles	11.34	5.26	5.48	11.26	12.22
Camping equipment	13.48	6.32	1.07	12.20	15.57
Hunting and fishing equipment	31.82	0.36	3.24	19.54	37.94
Winter sports equipment	4.17	5.32	0.07	1.53	5.14
Water sports equipment	4.65	0.29	0.30	1.09	5.79
Other sports equipment	11.89	13.49	2.29	8.77	13.75
Rental and repair of miscellaneous sports equipment	2.49	0.33	1.86	1.25	2.75
Photographic equipment and supplies	**82.86**	**95.90**	**31.04**	**56.34**	**94.32**
Film	12.18	8.96	5.28	10.25	13.52
Other photographic supplies	4.24	–	–	2.78	5.10
Film processing	20.31	16.10	6.53	14.49	23.23
Repair and rental of photographic equipment	0.99	–	0.06	0.63	1.18
Photographic equipment	28.92	57.90	8.27	20.92	33.08
Photographer fees	16.23	12.94	10.90	7.28	18.22
Fireworks	**3.75**	**–**	**2.00**	**1.79**	**4.28**
Pinball, electronic video games	**1.51**	**4.51**	**0.28**	**1.17**	**1.74**

Note: "Asian" and "black" include Hispanics and non-Hispanics who identify themselves as being of the respective race alone. "Hispanic" includes people of any race who identify themselves as Hispanic. "Other" includes people who identify themselves as non-Hispanic and as Alaska Native, American Indian, Asian (who are also included in the "Asian" column), Native Hawaiian or other Pacific Islander, as well as non-Hispanics reporting more than one race. Subcategories may not add to total because some are not shown. "–" means sample is too small to make a reliable estimate.
Source: Bureau of Labor Statistics, unpublished data from the 2004 Consumer Expenditure Survey

Table 3.18 Entertainment: Indexed spending by race and Hispanic origin, 2004

(indexed average annual spending of consumer units (CU) on entertainment by race and Hispanic origin of consumer unit reference person, 2004; index definition: an index of 100 is the average for all consumer units; an index of 132 means that spending by consumer units in that group is 32 percent above the average for all consumer units; an index of 68 indicates spending that is 32 percent below the average for all consumer units)

	total consumer units	Asian	black	Hispanic	non-Hispanic white and other
Average spending of CU, total	$43,395	$49,459	$30,481	$37,578	$46,163
Average spending of CU, index	100	114	70	87	106
Entertainment, spending index	**100**	**81**	**47**	**65**	**113**
FEES AND ADMISSIONS	**100**	**116**	**35**	**58**	**115**
Recreation expenses on trips	100	162	40	94	110
Social, recreation, civic club membership	100	41	22	34	121
Fees for participant sports	100	116	24	49	118
Participant sports on trips	100	83	23	45	119
Movie, theater, opera, ballet	100	105	55	76	110
Movie, other admissions on trips	100	128	43	57	114
Admission to sports events	100	43	33	49	117
Admission to sports events on trips	100	128	43	57	114
Fees for recreational lessons	100	222	34	61	115
Other entertainment services on trips	100	162	40	94	110
TELEVISION, RADIO, AND SOUND EQUIPMENT	**100**	**101**	**83**	**83**	**105**
Television	**100**	**89**	**90**	**80**	**104**
Cable service and community antenna	100	77	100	74	104
Color TV sets, consoles	100	126	64	69	110
Color TV sets, portable and table models	100	102	62	146	99
VCRs and video disc players	100	169	47	88	110
Video cassettes, tapes, and discs	100	111	70	91	106
Video game hardware and software	100	118	63	89	107
Repair of TV, radio, and sound equipment	100	64	80	84	105
Rental of television sets	100	4	352	100	64
Radio and sound equipment	**100**	**157**	**53**	**97**	**108**
Radios	100	6	17	95	113
Tape recorders and players	100	116	30	93	112
Sound components and component systems	100	106	73	105	105
Miscellaneous sound equipment	100	80	–	85	118
Sound equipment accessories	100	206	18	86	114
Satellite dishes	100	10	14	191	101
Compact disc, tape, record, video mail order clubs	100	52	71	74	108
Records, CDs, audio tapes, needles	100	84	81	98	104
Rental of VCR, radio, sound equipment	100	–	236	164	73
Musical instruments and accessories	100	485	13	84	115
Rental and repair of musical instruments	100	21	17	43	123
Rental of video cassettes, tapes, discs, films	100	109	61	107	105
PETS, TOYS, HOBBIES, AND PLAYGROUND EQUIPMENT	**100**	**41**	**32**	**63**	**115**
Pets	**100**	**33**	**19**	**51**	**119**
Pet food	100	36	24	62	117
Pet purchase, supplies, and medicines	100	29	22	63	117
Pet services	100	22	15	25	123
Veterinarian services	100	37	11	36	122
Toys, games, hobbies, and tricycles	**100**	**65**	**71**	**97**	**105**
Playground equipment	**100**	**24**	**3**	**77**	**118**

	total consumer units	Asian	black	Hispanic	non-Hispanic white and other
OTHER ENTERTAINMENT SUPPLIES, EQUIPMENT, SERVICES	**100**	**43**	**14**	**46**	**120**
Unmotored recreational vehicles	**100**	**2**	**–**	**9**	**127**
Boat without motor and boat trailers	100	7	–	29	125
Trailer and other attachable campers	100	–	–	–	129
Motorized recreational vehicles	**100**	**19**	**1**	**37**	**123**
Motorized camper	100	–	3	95	115
Other vehicle	100	37	3	–	128
Motorboats	100	25	–	13	127
Rental of recreational vehicles	**100**	**37**	**10**	**60**	**119**
Docking and landing fees	**100**	**1**	**0**	**31**	**124**
Sports, recreation, exercise equipment	**100**	**52**	**28**	**64**	**116**
Athletic gear, game tables, exercise equipment	100	71	44	55	115
Bicycles	100	46	48	99	108
Camping equipment	100	47	8	91	116
Hunting and fishing equipment	100	1	10	61	119
Winter sports equipment	100	128	2	37	123
Water sports equipment	100	6	6	23	125
Other sports equipment	100	113	19	74	116
Rental and repair of miscellaneous sports equipment	100	13	75	50	110
Photographic equipment and supplies	**100**	**116**	**37**	**68**	**114**
Film	100	74	43	84	111
Other photographic supplies	100	–	–	66	120
Film processing	100	79	32	71	114
Repair and rental of photographic equipment	100	–	6	64	119
Photographic equipment	100	200	29	72	114
Photographer fees	100	80	67	45	112
Fireworks	**100**	**–**	**53**	**48**	**114**
Pinball, electronic video games	**100**	**299**	**19**	**77**	**115**

Note: "Asian" and "black" include Hispanics and non-Hispanics who identify themselves as being of the respective race alone. "Hispanic" includes people of any race who identify themselves as Hispanic. "Other" includes people who identify themselves as non-Hispanic and as Alaska Native, American Indian, Asian (who are also included in the "Asian" column), Native Hawaiian or other Pacific Islander, as well as non-Hispanics reporting more than one race. "–" means sample is too small to make a reliable estimate.
Source: Calculations by New Strategist based on the 2004 Consumer Expenditure Survey

Table 3.19 Entertainment: Total spending by race and Hispanic origin, 2004

(total annual spending on entertainment, by consumer unit race and Hispanic origin groups, 2004; consumer units and dollars in thousands)

	total consumer units	Asian	black	Hispanic	non-Hispanic white and other
Number of consumer units	116,282	3,957	13,773	12,298	90,424
Total spending of all consumer units	$5,046,042,273	$195,707,997	$419,821,562	$462,134,613	$4,174,266,622
Entertainment, total spending	**257,968,129**	**7,078,559**	**14,317,584**	**17,746,998**	**226,306,858**
FEES AND ADMISSIONS	**61,389,919**	**2,428,371**	**2,552,963**	**3,783,972**	**55,126,992**
Recreation expenses on trips	3,144,265	173,633	148,748	312,861	2,686,497
Social, recreation, civic club membership	11,417,730	160,773	300,527	407,433	10,717,957
Fees for participant sports	8,602,542	339,115	243,369	443,712	7,916,621
Participant sports on trips	3,107,055	87,687	85,806	147,945	2,873,675
Movie, theater, opera, ballet	10,751,434	383,235	694,572	869,838	9,204,259
Movie, other admissions on trips	5,585,024	242,802	283,862	336,350	4,966,990
Admission to sports events	4,191,966	61,729	162,797	218,658	3,811,372
Admission to sports events on trips	1,861,675	80,921	94,621	112,158	1,655,663
Fees for recreational lessons	9,583,962	724,764	389,914	622,033	8,607,461
Other entertainment services on trips	3,144,265	173,633	148,748	312,861	2,686,497
TELEVISION, RADIO, AND SOUND EQUIPMENT	**91,588,354**	**3,134,340**	**9,051,616**	**8,067,734**	**74,649,533**
Television	**75,886,796**	**2,293,952**	**8,061,750**	**6,458,664**	**61,477,469**
Cable service and community antenna	54,769,985	1,429,585	6,459,812	4,303,316	44,086,221
Color TV sets, consoles	6,100,154	262,191	460,707	448,262	5,195,763
Color TV sets, portable and table models	4,628,024	160,654	342,259	712,300	3,572,652
VCRs and video disc players	2,796,582	160,496	157,012	260,103	2,382,672
Video cassettes, tapes, and discs	4,957,102	187,483	410,022	478,146	4,087,165
Video game hardware and software	2,132,612	85,788	158,665	199,843	1,777,736
Repair of TV, radio, and sound equipment	351,172	7,677	33,468	31,360	286,644
Rental of television sets	94,188	119	39,253	9,961	47,020
Radio and sound equipment	**15,701,558**	**840,388**	**989,866**	**1,608,947**	**13,172,064**
Radios	426,755	910	8,677	42,920	376,164
Tape recorders and players	1,129,098	44,516	40,630	110,805	980,196
Sound components and component systems	1,637,251	59,038	142,137	182,133	1,339,179
Miscellaneous sound equipment	159,306	4,353	–	14,266	145,583
Sound equipment accessories	923,279	64,657	19,695	83,749	821,954
Satellite dishes	89,537	317	1,515	18,078	70,531
Compact disc, tape, record, video mail order clubs	482,570	8,587	40,768	37,755	406,004
Records, CDs, audio tapes, needles	4,100,103	117,206	392,255	426,372	3,300,476
Rental of VCR, radio, sound equipment	12,791	–	3,581	2,214	7,234
Musical instruments and accessories	2,332,617	384,977	36,774	208,205	2,087,890
Rental and repair of musical instruments	265,123	1,939	5,234	11,929	253,187
Rental of video cassettes, tapes, discs, films	4,140,802	153,888	298,874	470,399	3,383,666
PETS, TOYS, HOBBIES, AND PLAYGROUND EQUIPMENT	**44,261,580**	**617,173**	**1,679,480**	**2,941,928**	**39,728,689**
Pets	**31,583,354**	**358,781**	**706,142**	**1,711,021**	**29,241,313**
Pet food	12,827,067	156,697	366,362	842,782	11,665,600
Pet purchase, supplies, and medicines	6,726,914	66,319	171,612	447,770	6,132,556
Pet services	2,915,190	22,159	50,547	77,846	2,788,676
Veterinarian services	9,114,183	113,645	117,484	342,622	8,654,481
Toys, games, hobbies, and tricycles	**11,536,337**	**253,683**	**964,385**	**1,187,864**	**9,398,671**
Playground equipment	**387,219**	**3,126**	**1,240**	**31,483**	**355,366**

	total consumer units	Asian	black	Hispanic	non-Hispanic white and other
OTHER ENTERTAINMENT SUPPLIES, EQUIPMENT, SERVICES	**$60,729,437**	**$898,674**	**$1,033,388**	**$2,953,611**	**$56,801,644**
Unmotored recreational vehicles	**6,440,860**	**4,986**	**–**	**62,474**	**6,378,509**
Boat without motor and boat trailers	2,043,075	4,986	–	62,474	1,980,286
Trailer and other attachable campers	4,397,785	–	–	–	4,398,223
Motorized recreational vehicles	**26,698,347**	**171,734**	**44,487**	**1,045,207**	**25,608,981**
Motorized camper	8,572,309	–	31,402	859,015	7,681,519
Other vehicle	4,141,965	52,153	13,222	–	4,127,856
Motorboats	13,985,236	119,581	–	186,192	13,798,702
Rental of recreational vehicles	**722,111**	**9,141**	**8,677**	**45,872**	**667,329**
Docking and landing fees	**653,505**	**119**	**138**	**21,399**	**632,064**
Sports, recreation, exercise equipment	**15,457,366**	**274,062**	**521,170**	**1,045,330**	**13,931,626**
Athletic gear, game tables, exercise equipment	6,171,086	149,970	324,079	360,946	5,507,726
Bicycles	1,318,638	20,814	75,476	138,475	1,104,981
Camping equipment	1,567,481	25,008	14,737	150,036	1,407,902
Hunting and fishing equipment	3,700,093	1,425	44,625	240,303	3,430,687
Winter sports equipment	484,896	21,051	964	18,816	464,779
Water sports equipment	540,711	1,148	4,132	13,405	523,555
Other sports equipment	1,382,593	53,380	31,540	107,853	1,243,330
Rental and repair of miscellaneous sports equipment	289,542	1,306	25,618	15,373	248,666
Photographic equipment and supplies	**9,635,127**	**379,476**	**427,514**	**692,869**	**8,528,792**
Film	1,416,315	35,455	72,721	126,055	1,222,532
Other photographic supplies	493,036	–	–	34,188	461,162
Film processing	2,361,687	63,708	89,938	178,198	2,100,550
Repair and rental of photographic equipment	115,119	–	826	7,748	106,700
Photographic equipment	3,362,875	229,110	113,903	257,274	2,991,226
Photographer fees	1,887,257	51,204	150,126	89,529	1,647,525
Fireworks	436,058	–	27,546	22,013	387,015
Pinball, electronic video games	**175,586**	**17,846**	**3,856**	**14,389**	**157,338**

Note: "Asian" and "black" include Hispanics and non-Hispanics who identify themselves as being of the respective race alone. "Hispanic" includes people of any race who identify themselves as Hispanic. "Other" includes people who identify themselves as non-Hispanic and as Alaska Native, American Indian, Asian (who are also included in the "Asian" column), Native Hawaiian or other Pacific Islander, as well as non-Hispanics reporting more than one race. Numbers may not add to total because of rounding and missing subcategories. "–" means sample is too small to make a reliable estimate.
Source: Calculations by New Strategist based on the 2004 Consumer Expenditure Survey

Table 3.20 Entertainment: Market shares by race and Hispanic origin, 2004

(percentage of total annual spending on entertainment accounted for by consumer unit race and Hispanic origin groups, 2004)

	total consumer units	Asian	black	Hispanic	non-Hispanic white and other
Share of total consumer units	100.0%	3.4%	11.8%	10.6%	77.8%
Share of total before-tax income	100.0	4.2	8.4	8.5	83.3
Share of total spending	100.0	3.9	8.3	9.2	82.7
Share of entertainment spending	100.0	2.7	5.6	6.9	87.7
FEES AND ADMISSIONS	100.0	4.0	4.2	6.2	89.8
Recreation expenses on trips	100.0	5.5	4.7	10.0	85.4
Social, recreation, civic club membership	100.0	1.4	2.6	3.6	93.9
Fees for participant sports	100.0	3.9	2.8	5.2	92.0
Participant sports on trips	100.0	2.8	2.8	4.8	92.5
Movie, theater, opera, ballet	100.0	3.6	6.5	8.1	85.6
Movie, other admissions on trips	100.0	4.3	5.1	6.0	88.9
Admission to sports events	100.0	1.5	3.9	5.2	90.9
Admission to sports events on trips	100.0	4.3	5.1	6.0	88.9
Fees for recreational lessons	100.0	7.6	4.1	6.5	89.8
Other entertainment services on trips	100.0	5.5	4.7	10.0	85.4
TELEVISION, RADIO, AND SOUND EQUIPMENT	100.0	3.4	9.9	8.8	81.5
Television	100.0	3.0	10.6	8.5	81.0
Cable service and community antenna	100.0	2.6	11.8	7.9	80.5
Color TV sets, consoles	100.0	4.3	7.6	7.3	85.2
Color TV sets, portable and table models	100.0	3.5	7.4	15.4	77.2
VCRs and video disc players	100.0	5.7	5.6	9.3	85.2
Video cassettes, tapes, and discs	100.0	3.8	8.3	9.6	82.5
Video game hardware and software	100.0	4.0	7.4	9.4	83.4
Repair of TV, radio, and sound equipment	100.0	2.2	9.5	8.9	81.6
Rental of television sets	100.0	0.1	41.7	10.6	49.9
Radio and sound equipment	100.0	5.4	6.3	10.2	83.9
Radios	100.0	0.2	2.0	10.1	88.1
Tape recorders and players	100.0	3.9	3.6	9.8	86.8
Sound components and component systems	100.0	3.6	8.7	11.1	81.8
Miscellaneous sound equipment	100.0	2.7	–	9.0	91.4
Sound equipment accessories	100.0	7.0	2.1	9.1	89.0
Satellite dishes	100.0	0.4	1.7	20.2	78.8
Compact disc, tape, record, video mail order clubs	100.0	1.8	8.4	7.8	84.1
Records, CDs, audio tapes, needles	100.0	2.9	9.6	10.4	80.5
Rental of VCR, radio, sound equipment	100.0	–	28.0	17.3	56.6
Musical instruments and accessories	100.0	16.5	1.6	8.9	89.5
Rental and repair of musical instruments	100.0	0.7	2.0	4.5	95.5
Rental of video cassettes, tapes, discs, films	100.0	3.7	7.2	11.4	81.7
PETS, TOYS, HOBBIES, AND PLAYGROUND EQUIPMENT	100.0	1.4	3.8	6.6	89.8
Pets	100.0	1.1	2.2	5.4	92.6
Pet food	100.0	1.2	2.9	6.6	90.9
Pet purchase, supplies, and medicines	100.0	1.0	2.6	6.7	91.2
Pet services	100.0	0.8	1.7	2.7	95.7
Veterinarian services	100.0	1.2	1.3	3.8	95.0
Toys, games, hobbies, and tricycles	100.0	2.2	8.4	10.3	81.5
Playground equipment	100.0	0.8	0.3	8.1	91.8

	total consumer units	Asian	black	Hispanic	non-Hispanic white and other
OTHER ENTERTAINMENT SUPPLIES, EQUIPMENT, SERVICES	**100.0%**	**1.5%**	**1.7%**	**4.9%**	**93.5%**
Unmotored recreational vehicles	**100.0**	**0.1**	**–**	**1.0**	**99.0**
Boat without motor and boat trailers	100.0	0.2	–	3.1	96.9
Trailer and other attachable campers	100.0	–	–	–	100.0
Motorized recreational vehicles	**100.0**	**0.6**	**0.2**	**3.9**	**95.9**
Motorized camper	100.0	–	0.4	10.0	89.6
Other vehicle	100.0	1.3	0.3	–	99.7
Motorboats	100.0	0.9	–	1.3	98.7
Rental of recreational vehicles	**100.0**	**1.3**	**1.2**	**6.4**	**92.4**
Docking and landing fees	**100.0**	**0.0**	**0.0**	**3.3**	**96.7**
Sports, recreation, exercise equipment	**100.0**	**1.8**	**3.4**	**6.8**	**90.1**
Athletic gear, game tables, exercise equipment	100.0	2.4	5.3	5.8	89.3
Bicycles	100.0	1.6	5.7	10.5	83.8
Camping equipment	100.0	1.6	0.9	9.6	89.8
Hunting and fishing equipment	100.0	0.0	1.2	6.5	92.7
Winter sports equipment	100.0	4.3	0.2	3.9	95.9
Water sports equipment	100.0	0.2	0.8	2.5	96.8
Other sports equipment	100.0	3.9	2.3	7.8	89.9
Rental and repair of miscellaneous sports equipment	100.0	0.5	8.8	5.3	85.9
Photographic equipment and supplies	**100.0**	**3.9**	**4.4**	**7.2**	**88.5**
Film	100.0	2.5	5.1	8.9	86.3
Other photographic supplies	100.0	–	–	6.9	93.5
Film processing	100.0	2.7	3.8	7.5	88.9
Repair and rental of photographic equipment	100.0	–	0.7	6.7	92.7
Photographic equipment	100.0	6.8	3.4	7.7	88.9
Photographer fees	100.0	2.7	8.0	4.7	87.3
Fireworks	**100.0**	**–**	**6.3**	**5.0**	**88.8**
Pinball, electronic video games	**100.0**	**10.2**	**2.2**	**8.2**	**89.6**

Note: "Asian" and "black" include Hispanics and non-Hispanics who identify themselves as being of the respective race alone. "Hispanic" includes people of any race who identify themselves as Hispanic. "Other" includes people who identify themselves as non-Hispanic and as Alaska Native, American Indian, Asian (who are also included in the "Asian" column), Native Hawaiian or other Pacific Islander, as well as non-Hispanics reporting more than one race. "–" means sample is too small to make a reliable estimate.
Source: Calculations by New Strategist based on the 2004 Consumer Expenditure Survey

Table 3.21 Entertainment: Average spending by region, 2004

(average annual spending of consumer units (CU) on entertainment, by region in which consumer unit lives, 2004)

	total consumer units	Northeast	Midwest	South	West
Number of consumer units (in 000s)	116,282	22,051	26,539	41,801	25,891
Average number of persons per CU	2.5	2.4	2.4	2.5	2.6
Average before-tax income of CU	$54,453.00	$61,050.00	$53,567.00	$50,775.00	$55,682.00
Average spending of CU, total	43,394.87	46,114.89	43,370.77	39,173.65	47,921.74
Entertainment, average spending	**$2,218.47**	**$2,016.89**	**$2,208.13**	**$2,133.86**	**$2,538.26**
FEES AND ADMISSIONS	**527.94**	**544.76**	**586.21**	**397.65**	**664.24**
Recreation expenses on trips	27.04	24.82	31.36	20.21	35.54
Social, recreation, civic club membership	98.19	94.49	112.32	80.05	116.13
Fees for participant sports	73.98	70.39	85.26	58.42	90.61
Participant sports on trips	26.72	30.22	32.04	14.97	37.26
Movie, theater, opera, ballet	92.46	104.18	88.19	68.31	125.85
Movie, other admissions on trips	48.03	47.17	46.30	38.31	66.21
Admission to sports events	36.05	30.16	49.82	28.40	39.32
Admission to sports events on trips	16.01	15.72	15.43	12.77	22.07
Fees for recreational lessons	82.42	102.79	94.13	56.01	95.71
Other entertainment services on trips	27.04	24.82	31.36	20.21	35.54
TELEVISION, RADIO, AND SOUND EQUIPMENT	**787.64**	**839.88**	**768.47**	**753.27**	**818.39**
Television	**652.61**	**718.49**	**626.52**	**642.23**	**640.00**
Cable service and community antenna	471.01	534.03	446.17	484.69	420.73
Color TV sets, consoles	52.46	64.86	44.66	40.94	68.51
Color TV sets, portable and table models	39.80	33.98	37.49	41.82	43.85
VCRs and video disc players	24.05	20.24	28.70	21.33	26.90
Video cassettes, tapes, and discs	42.63	41.93	44.94	33.58	55.46
Video game hardware and software	18.34	17.96	20.53	16.06	20.10
Repair of TV, radio, and sound equipment	3.02	2.95	2.70	3.32	2.92
Rental of television sets	0.81	1.89	0.84	0.42	0.50
Radio and sound equipment	**135.03**	**121.39**	**141.95**	**111.03**	**178.39**
Radios	3.67	1.50	2.79	2.47	8.44
Tape recorders and players	9.71	6.37	10.78	12.13	7.53
Sound components and component systems	14.08	17.07	12.29	9.51	20.76
Miscellaneous sound equipment	1.37	1.61	0.96	0.76	2.59
Sound equipment accessories	7.94	6.05	6.24	9.92	8.12
Satellite dishes	0.77	0.65	0.86	0.31	1.54
Compact disc, tape, record, video mail order clubs	4.15	5.36	4.23	2.95	4.99
Records, CDs, audio tapes, needles	35.26	35.03	36.14	29.45	43.94
Rental of VCR, radio, sound equipment	0.11	0.25	0.12	0.07	0.07
Musical instruments and accessories	20.06	18.61	24.06	10.22	33.08
Rental and repair of musical instruments	2.28	1.02	5.71	1.35	1.35
Rental of video cassettes, tapes, discs, films	35.61	27.88	37.77	31.89	46.00
PETS, TOYS, HOBBIES, PLAYGROUND EQUIPMENT	**380.64**	**360.05**	**372.64**	**363.89**	**433.89**
Pets	**271.61**	**259.12**	**258.48**	**259.60**	**315.61**
Pet food	110.31	98.18	103.90	106.54	133.67
Pet purchase, supplies, and medicines	57.85	43.51	59.42	62.70	60.72
Pet services	25.07	23.03	24.43	21.09	33.90
Veterinarian services	78.38	94.40	70.73	69.26	87.32
Toys, games, hobbies, and tricycles	**99.21**	**94.78**	**106.30**	**100.01**	**94.42**
Playground equipment	**3.33**	**4.18**	**4.25**	**2.55**	**2.94**

	total consumer units	Northeast	Midwest	South	West
OTHER ENTERTAINMENT SUPPLIES, EQUIPMENT, SERVICES	**$522.26**	**$272.21**	**$480.82**	**$619.06**	**$621.73**
Unmotored recreational vehicles	**55.39**	**18.37**	**94.01**	**20.09**	**104.32**
Boat without motor and boat trailers	17.57	18.37	49.66	4.40	5.24
Trailer and other attachable campers	37.82	–	44.35	15.69	99.07
Motorized recreational vehicles	**229.60**	**40.11**	**117.07**	**415.13**	**206.81**
Motorized camper	73.72	–	0.58	117.63	140.57
Other vehicle	35.62	11.53	58.12	42.57	21.82
Motorboats	120.27	28.58	58.37	254.92	44.41
Rental of recreational vehicles	**6.21**	**2.73**	**5.23**	**4.14**	**13.53**
Docking and landing fees	**5.62**	**7.39**	**6.44**	**5.58**	**3.32**
Sports, recreation, exercise equipment	**132.93**	**116.89**	**147.75**	**99.76**	**185.26**
Athletic gear, game tables, exercise equipment	53.07	47.36	69.51	45.51	53.17
Bicycles	11.34	9.09	14.32	6.53	17.98
Camping equipment	13.48	8.43	13.88	11.81	20.18
Hunting and fishing equipment	31.82	23.17	30.12	21.19	58.48
Winter sports equipment	4.17	5.48	4.79	1.03	7.48
Water sports equipment	4.65	4.88	3.02	4.11	7.01
Other sports equipment	11.89	16.09	9.35	7.39	18.18
Rental and repair of miscellaneous sports equipment	2.49	2.38	2.77	2.20	2.78
Photographic equipment and supplies	**82.86**	**80.20**	**96.64**	**67.77**	**95.32**
Film	12.18	11.20	13.36	10.92	13.84
Other photographic supplies	4.24	14.02	1.82	1.21	3.24
Film processing	20.31	19.11	23.39	16.63	24.11
Repair and rental of photographic equipment	0.99	0.82	2.47	0.50	0.41
Photographic equipment	28.92	18.98	31.78	26.65	38.11
Photographer fees	16.23	16.07	23.82	11.87	15.62
Fireworks	**3.75**	**1.14**	**6.02**	**4.39**	**2.57**
Pinball, electronic video games	**1.51**	**1.75**	**1.16**	**0.90**	**2.64**

Note: Subcategories may not add to total because some are not shown. "–" means sample is too small to make a reliable estimate.
Source: Bureau of Labor Statistics, unpublished data from the 2004 Consumer Expenditure Survey

Table 3.22 Entertainment: Indexed spending by region, 2004

(indexed average annual spending of consumer units (CU) on entertainment by region in which consumer unit lives, 2004; index definition: an index of 100 is the average for all consumer units; an index of 132 means that spending by consumer units in that group is 32 percent above the average for all consumer units; an index of 68 indicates spending that is 32 percent below the average for all consumer units)

	total consumer units	Northeast	Midwest	South	West
Average spending of CU, total	$43,395	$46,115	$43,371	$39,174	$47,922
Average spending of CU, index	100	106	100	90	110
Entertainment, spending index	**100**	**91**	**100**	**96**	**114**
FEES AND ADMISSIONS	**100**	**103**	**111**	**75**	**126**
Recreation expenses on trips	100	92	116	75	131
Social, recreation, civic club membership	100	96	114	82	118
Fees for participant sports	100	95	115	79	122
Participant sports on trips	100	113	120	56	139
Movie, theater, opera, ballet	100	113	95	74	136
Movie, other admissions on trips	100	98	96	80	138
Admission to sports events	100	84	138	79	109
Admission to sports events on trips	100	98	96	80	138
Fees for recreational lessons	100	125	114	68	116
Other entertainment services on trips	100	92	116	75	131
TELEVISION, RADIO, AND SOUND EQUIPMENT	**100**	**107**	**98**	**96**	**104**
Television	**100**	**110**	**96**	**98**	**98**
Cable service and community antenna	100	113	95	103	89
Color TV sets, consoles	100	124	85	78	131
Color TV sets, portable and table models	100	85	94	105	110
VCRs and video disc players	100	84	119	89	112
Video cassettes, tapes, and discs	100	98	105	79	130
Video game hardware and software	100	98	112	88	110
Repair of TV, radio, and sound equipment	100	98	89	110	97
Rental of television sets	100	233	104	52	62
Radio and sound equipment	**100**	**90**	**105**	**82**	**132**
Radios	100	41	76	67	230
Tape recorders and players	100	66	111	125	78
Sound components and component systems	100	121	87	68	147
Miscellaneous sound equipment	100	118	70	55	189
Sound equipment accessories	100	76	79	125	102
Satellite dishes	100	84	112	40	200
Compact disc, tape, record, video mail order clubs	100	129	102	71	120
Records, CDs, audio tapes, needles	100	99	102	84	125
Rental of VCR, radio, sound equipment	100	227	109	64	64
Musical instruments and accessories	100	93	120	51	165
Rental and repair of musical instruments	100	45	250	59	59
Rental of video cassettes, tapes, discs, films	100	78	106	90	129
PETS, TOYS, HOBBIES, AND PLAYGROUND EQUIPMENT	**100**	**95**	**98**	**96**	**114**
Pets	**100**	**95**	**95**	**96**	**116**
Pet food	100	89	94	97	121
Pet purchase, supplies, and medicines	100	75	103	108	105
Pet services	100	92	97	84	135
Veterinarian services	100	120	90	88	111
Toys, games, hobbies, and tricycles	**100**	**96**	**107**	**101**	**95**
Playground equipment	**100**	**126**	**128**	**77**	**88**

	total consumer units	Northeast	Midwest	South	West
OTHER ENTERTAINMENT SUPPLIES, EQUIPMENT, SERVICES	**100**	**52**	**92**	**119**	**119**
Unmotored recreational vehicles	**100**	**33**	**170**	**36**	**188**
Boat without motor and boat trailers	100	105	283	25	30
Trailer and other attachable campers	100	–	117	41	262
Motorized recreational vehicles	**100**	**17**	**51**	**181**	**90**
Motorized camper	100	–	1	160	191
Other vehicle	100	32	163	120	61
Motorboats	100	24	49	212	37
Rental of recreational vehicles	**100**	**44**	**84**	**67**	**218**
Docking and landing fees	**100**	**131**	**115**	**99**	**59**
Sports, recreation, exercise equipment	**100**	**88**	**111**	**75**	**139**
Athletic gear, game tables, exercise equipment	100	89	131	86	100
Bicycles	100	80	126	58	159
Camping equipment	100	63	103	88	150
Hunting and fishing equipment	100	73	95	67	184
Winter sports equipment	100	131	115	25	179
Water sports equipment	100	105	65	88	151
Other sports equipment	100	135	79	62	153
Rental and repair of miscellaneous sports equipment	100	96	111	88	112
Photographic equipment and supplies	**100**	**97**	**117**	**82**	**115**
Film	100	92	110	90	114
Other photographic supplies	100	331	43	29	76
Film processing	100	94	115	82	119
Repair and rental of photographic equipment	100	83	249	51	41
Photographic equipment	100	66	110	92	132
Photographer fees	100	99	147	73	96
Fireworks	**100**	**30**	**161**	**117**	**69**
Pinball, electronic video games	**100**	**116**	**77**	**60**	**175**

Note: "–" means sample is too small to make a reliable estimate.
Source: Calculations by New Strategist based on the 2004 Consumer Expenditure Survey

Table 3.23 Entertainment: Total spending by region, 2004

(total annual spending on entertainment, by region in which consumer units live, 2004; consumer units and dollars in thousands)

	total consumer units	Northeast	Midwest	South	West
Number of consumer units	116,282	22,051	26,539	41,801	25,891
Total spending of all consumer units	$5,046,042,273	$1,016,879,439	$1,151,016,865	$1,637,497,744	$1,240,741,770
Entertainment, total spending	257,968,129	44,474,441	58,601,562	89,197,482	65,718,090
FEES AND ADMISSIONS	61,389,919	12,012,503	15,557,427	16,622,168	17,197,838
Recreation expenses on trips	3,144,265	547,306	832,263	844,798	920,166
Social, recreation, civic club membership	11,417,730	2,083,599	2,980,860	3,346,170	3,006,722
Fees for participant sports	8,602,542	1,552,170	2,262,715	2,442,014	2,345,984
Participant sports on trips	3,107,055	666,381	850,310	625,761	964,699
Movie, theater, opera, ballet	10,751,434	2,297,273	2,340,474	2,855,426	3,258,382
Movie, other admissions on trips	5,585,024	1,040,146	1,228,756	1,601,396	1,714,243
Admission to sports events	4,191,966	665,058	1,322,173	1,187,148	1,018,034
Admission to sports events on trips	1,861,675	346,642	409,497	533,799	571,414
Fees for recreational lessons	9,583,962	2,266,622	2,498,116	2,341,274	2,478,028
Other entertainment services on trips	3,144,265	547,306	832,263	844,798	920,166
TELEVISION, RADIO, AND SOUND EQUIPMENT	91,588,354	18,520,194	20,394,425	31,487,439	21,188,935
Television	75,886,796	15,843,423	16,627,214	26,845,856	16,570,240
Cable service and community antenna	54,769,985	11,775,896	11,840,906	20,260,527	10,893,120
Color TV sets, consoles	6,100,154	1,430,228	1,185,232	1,711,333	1,773,792
Color TV sets, portable and table models	4,628,024	749,293	994,947	1,748,118	1,135,320
VCRs and video disc players	2,796,582	446,312	761,669	891,615	696,468
Video cassettes, tapes, and discs	4,957,102	924,598	1,192,663	1,403,678	1,435,915
Video game hardware and software	2,132,612	396,036	544,846	671,324	520,409
Repair of TV, radio, and sound equipment	351,172	65,050	71,655	138,779	75,602
Rental of television sets	94,188	41,676	22,293	17,556	12,946
Radio and sound equipment	15,701,558	2,676,771	3,767,211	4,641,165	4,618,695
Radios	426,755	33,077	74,044	103,248	218,520
Tape recorders and players	1,129,098	140,465	286,090	507,046	194,959
Sound components and component systems	1,637,251	376,411	326,164	397,528	537,497
Miscellaneous sound equipment	159,306	35,502	25,477	31,769	67,058
Sound equipment accessories	923,279	133,409	165,603	414,666	210,235
Satellite dishes	89,537	14,333	22,824	12,958	39,872
Compact disc, tape, record, video mail order clubs	482,570	118,193	112,260	123,313	129,196
Records, CDs, audio tapes, needles	4,100,103	772,447	959,119	1,231,039	1,137,651
Rental of VCR, radio, sound equipment	12,791	5,513	3,185	2,926	1,812
Musical instruments and accessories	2,332,617	410,369	638,528	427,206	856,474
Rental and repair of musical instruments	265,123	22,492	151,538	56,431	34,953
Rental of video cassettes, tapes, discs, films	4,140,802	614,782	1,002,378	1,333,034	1,190,986
PETS, TOYS, HOBBIES, PLAYGROUND EQUIPMENT	44,261,580	7,939,463	9,889,493	15,210,966	11,233,846
Pets	31,583,354	5,713,855	6,859,801	10,851,540	8,171,459
Pet food	12,827,067	2,164,967	2,757,402	4,453,479	3,460,850
Pet purchase, supplies, and medicines	6,726,914	959,439	1,576,947	2,620,923	1,572,102
Pet services	2,915,190	507,835	648,348	881,583	877,705
Veterinarian services	9,114,183	2,081,614	1,877,103	2,895,137	2,260,802
Toys, games, hobbies, and tricycles	11,536,337	2,089,994	2,821,096	4,180,518	2,444,628
Playground equipment	387,219	92,173	112,791	106,593	76,120

	total consumer units	Northeast	Midwest	South	West
OTHER ENTERTAINMENT SUPPLIES, EQUIPMENT, SERVICES	**$60,729,437**	**$6,002,503**	**$12,760,482**	**$25,877,327**	**$16,097,211**
Unmotored recreational vehicles	**6,440,860**	**405,077**	**2,494,931**	**839,782**	**2,700,949**
Boat without motor and boat trailers	2,043,075	405,077	1,317,927	183,924	135,669
Trailer and other attachable campers	4,397,785	–	1,177,005	655,858	2,565,021
Motorized recreational vehicles	**26,698,347**	**884,466**	**3,106,921**	**17,352,849**	**5,354,518**
Motorized camper	8,572,309	–	15,393	4,917,052	3,639,498
Other vehicle	4,141,965	254,248	1,542,447	1,779,469	564,942
Motorboats	13,985,236	630,218	1,549,081	10,655,911	1,149,819
Rental of recreational vehicles	**722,111**	**60,199**	**138,799**	**173,056**	**350,305**
Docking and landing fees	**653,505**	**162,957**	**170,911**	**233,250**	**85,958**
Sports, recreation, exercise equipment	**15,457,366**	**2,577,541**	**3,921,137**	**4,170,068**	**4,796,567**
Athletic gear, game tables, exercise equipment	6,171,086	1,044,335	1,844,726	1,902,364	1,376,624
Bicycles	1,318,638	200,444	380,038	272,961	465,520
Camping equipment	1,567,481	185,890	368,361	493,670	522,480
Hunting and fishing equipment	3,700,093	510,922	799,355	885,763	1,514,106
Winter sports equipment	484,896	120,839	127,122	43,055	193,665
Water sports equipment	540,711	107,609	80,148	171,802	181,496
Other sports equipment	1,382,593	354,801	248,140	308,909	470,698
Rental and repair of miscellaneous sports equipment	289,542	52,481	73,513	91,962	71,977
Photographic equipment and supplies	**9,635,127**	**1,768,490**	**2,564,729**	**2,832,854**	**2,467,930**
Film	1,416,315	246,971	354,561	456,467	358,331
Other photographic supplies	493,036	309,155	48,301	50,579	83,887
Film processing	2,361,687	421,395	620,747	695,151	624,232
Repair and rental of photographic equipment	115,119	18,082	65,551	20,901	10,615
Photographic equipment	3,362,875	418,528	843,409	1,113,997	986,706
Photographer fees	1,887,257	354,360	632,159	496,178	404,417
Fireworks	**436,058**	**25,138**	**159,765**	**183,506**	**66,540**
Pinball, electronic video games	**175,586**	**38,589**	**30,785**	**37,621**	**68,352**

Note: Numbers may not add to total because of rounding and missing subcategories. "–" means sample is too small to make a reliable estimate.
Source: Calculations by New Strategist based on the 2004 Consumer Expenditure Survey

Table 3.24 Entertainment: Market shares by region, 2004

(percentage of total annual spending on entertainment accounted for by consumer units by region, 2004)

	total consumer units	Northeast	Midwest	South	West
Share of total consumer units	100.0%	19.0%	22.8%	35.9%	22.3%
Share of total before-tax income	100.0	21.3	22.5	33.5	22.8
Share of total spending	100.0	20.2	22.8	32.5	24.6
Share of entertainment spending	100.0	17.2	22.7	34.6	25.5
FEES AND ADMISSIONS	**100.0**	**19.6**	**25.3**	**27.1**	**28.0**
Recreation expenses on trips	100.0	17.4	26.5	26.9	29.3
Social, recreation, civic club membership	100.0	18.2	26.1	29.3	26.3
Fees for participant sports	100.0	18.0	26.3	28.4	27.3
Participant sports on trips	100.0	21.4	27.4	20.1	31.0
Movie, theater, opera, ballet	100.0	21.4	21.8	26.6	30.3
Movie, other admissions on trips	100.0	18.6	22.0	28.7	30.7
Admission to sports events	100.0	15.9	31.5	28.3	24.3
Admission to sports events on trips	100.0	18.6	22.0	28.7	30.7
Fees for recreational lessons	100.0	23.7	26.1	24.4	25.9
Other entertainment services on trips	100.0	17.4	26.5	26.9	29.3
TELEVISION, RADIO, AND SOUND EQUIPMENT	**100.0**	**20.2**	**22.3**	**34.4**	**23.1**
Television	**100.0**	**20.9**	**21.9**	**35.4**	**21.8**
Cable service and community antenna	100.0	21.5	21.6	37.0	19.9
Color TV sets, consoles	100.0	23.4	19.4	28.1	29.1
Color TV sets, portable and table models	100.0	16.2	21.5	37.8	24.5
VCRs and video disc players	100.0	16.0	27.2	31.9	24.9
Video cassettes, tapes, and discs	100.0	18.7	24.1	28.3	29.0
Video game hardware and software	100.0	18.6	25.5	31.5	24.4
Repair of TV, radio, and sound equipment	100.0	18.5	20.4	39.5	21.5
Rental of television sets	100.0	44.2	23.7	18.6	13.7
Radio and sound equipment	**100.0**	**17.0**	**24.0**	**29.6**	**29.4**
Radios	100.0	7.8	17.4	24.2	51.2
Tape recorders and players	100.0	12.4	25.3	44.9	17.3
Sound components and component systems	100.0	23.0	19.9	24.3	32.8
Miscellaneous sound equipment	100.0	22.3	16.0	19.9	42.1
Sound equipment accessories	100.0	14.4	17.9	44.9	22.8
Satellite dishes	100.0	16.0	25.5	14.5	44.5
Compact disc, tape, record, video mail order clubs	100.0	24.5	23.3	25.6	26.8
Records, CDs, audio tapes, needles	100.0	18.8	23.4	30.0	27.7
Rental of VCR, radio, sound equipment	100.0	43.1	24.9	22.9	14.2
Musical instruments and accessories	100.0	17.6	27.4	18.3	36.7
Rental and repair of musical instruments	100.0	8.5	57.2	21.3	13.2
Rental of video cassettes, tapes, discs, films	100.0	14.8	24.2	32.2	28.8
PETS, TOYS, HOBBIES, AND PLAYGROUND EQUIPMENT	**100.0**	**17.9**	**22.3**	**34.4**	**25.4**
Pets	**100.0**	**18.1**	**21.7**	**34.4**	**25.9**
Pet food	100.0	16.9	21.5	34.7	27.0
Pet purchase, supplies, and medicines	100.0	14.3	23.4	39.0	23.4
Pet services	100.0	17.4	22.2	30.2	30.1
Veterinarian services	100.0	22.8	20.6	31.8	24.8
Toys, games, hobbies, and tricycles	**100.0**	**18.1**	**24.5**	**36.2**	**21.2**
Playground equipment	**100.0**	**23.8**	**29.1**	**27.5**	**19.7**

	total consumer units	Northeast	Midwest	South	West
OTHER ENTERTAINMENT SUPPLIES, EQUIPMENT, SERVICES	**100.0%**	**9.9%**	**21.0%**	**42.6%**	**26.5%**
Unmotored recreational vehicles	**100.0**	**6.3**	**38.7**	**13.0**	**41.9**
Boat without motor and boat trailers	100.0	19.8	64.5	9.0	6.6
Trailer and other attachable campers	100.0	–	26.8	14.9	58.3
Motorized recreational vehicles	**100.0**	**3.3**	**11.6**	**65.0**	**20.1**
Motorized camper	100.0	–	0.2	57.4	42.5
Other vehicle	100.0	6.1	37.2	43.0	13.6
Motorboats	100.0	4.5	11.1	76.2	8.2
Rental of recreational vehicles	**100.0**	**8.3**	**19.2**	**24.0**	**48.5**
Docking and landing fees	**100.0**	**24.9**	**26.2**	**35.7**	**13.2**
Sports, recreation, exercise equipment	**100.0**	**16.7**	**25.4**	**27.0**	**31.0**
Athletic gear, game tables, exercise equipment	100.0	16.9	29.9	30.8	22.3
Bicycles	100.0	15.2	28.8	20.7	35.3
Camping equipment	100.0	11.9	23.5	31.5	33.3
Hunting and fishing equipment	100.0	13.8	21.6	23.9	40.9
Winter sports equipment	100.0	24.9	26.2	8.9	39.9
Water sports equipment	100.0	19.9	14.8	31.8	33.6
Other sports equipment	100.0	25.7	17.9	22.3	34.0
Rental and repair of miscellaneous sports equipment	100.0	18.1	25.4	31.8	24.9
Photographic equipment and supplies	**100.0**	**18.4**	**26.6**	**29.4**	**25.6**
Film	100.0	17.4	25.0	32.2	25.3
Other photographic supplies	100.0	62.7	9.8	10.3	17.0
Film processing	100.0	17.8	26.3	29.4	26.4
Repair and rental of photographic equipment	100.0	15.7	56.9	18.2	9.2
Photographic equipment	100.0	12.4	25.1	33.1	29.3
Photographer fees	100.0	18.8	33.5	26.3	21.4
Fireworks	**100.0**	**5.8**	**36.6**	**42.1**	**15.3**
Pinball, electronic video games	**100.0**	**22.0**	**17.5**	**21.4**	**38.9**

Note: Numbers may not add to total because of rounding. "–" means sample is too small to make a reliable estimate.
Source: Calculations by New Strategist based on the 2004 Consumer Expenditure Survey

Table 3.25 Entertainment: Average spending by education, 2004

(average annual spending of consumer units (CU) on entertainment, by education of consumer unit reference person, 2004)

	total consumer units	less than high school graduate	high school graduate	some college	associate's degree	college graduate total	college graduate bachelor's degree	college graduate master's, professional, doctorate
Number of consumer units (in 000s)	116,282	16,829	31,005	25,317	10,678	32,452	20,684	11,768
Average number of persons per CU	2.5	2.7	2.5	2.3	2.6	2.5	2.4	2.5
Average before-tax income of CU	$54,453.00	$29,094.00	$42,334.00	$46,756.00	$58,593.00	$83,825.00	$75,647.00	$98,201.00
Average spending of CU, total	43,394.87	25,421.18	35,438.55	40,877.68	48,177.36	60,712.28	56,728.41	67,801.38
Entertainment, average spending	**2,218.47**	**953.45**	**1,684.52**	**2,275.87**	**2,464.75**	**3,259.40**	**3,044.96**	**3,639.26**
FEES AND ADMISSIONS	**527.94**	**102.60**	**269.52**	**463.85**	**534.54**	**1,043.24**	**909.90**	**1,277.61**
Recreation expenses on trips	27.04	6.62	13.33	21.88	29.09	54.08	47.73	65.23
Social, recreation, civic club membership	98.19	11.96	39.19	78.12	105.15	212.63	181.51	267.33
Fees for participant sports	73.98	18.36	48.19	72.45	68.14	130.59	123.86	142.41
Participant sports on trips	26.72	4.34	12.56	26.05	34.09	49.96	44.62	59.35
Movie, theater, opera, ballet	92.46	25.11	53.11	86.98	94.66	168.53	151.54	198.40
Movie, other admissions on trips	48.03	10.64	26.59	50.09	53.51	84.48	72.89	104.84
Admission to sports events	36.05	6.10	20.65	30.95	27.31	73.17	63.92	89.43
Admission to sports events on trips	16.01	3.55	8.86	16.69	17.84	28.15	24.29	34.94
Fees for recreational lessons	82.42	9.30	33.71	58.75	75.65	187.57	151.81	250.44
Other entertainment services on trips	27.04	6.62	13.33	21.88	29.09	54.08	47.73	65.23
TELEVISION, RADIO, AND SOUND EQUIPMENT	**787.64**	**504.54**	**703.20**	**786.65**	**895.30**	**980.33**	**965.77**	**1,006.31**
Television	**652.61**	**448.92**	**604.74**	**645.79**	**746.02**	**778.56**	**786.01**	**765.47**
Cable service and community antenna	471.01	344.36	467.55	463.87	511.20	532.35	541.82	515.72
Color TV sets, consoles	52.46	36.72	37.33	44.00	75.62	74.06	77.19	68.56
Color TV sets, portable and table models	39.80	20.45	35.51	48.85	37.39	47.66	42.46	56.80
VCRs and video disc players	24.05	16.79	16.85	21.10	27.12	35.99	32.65	41.86
Video cassettes, tapes, and discs	42.63	16.24	32.28	43.93	63.27	58.39	61.27	53.32
Video game hardware and software	18.34	11.39	12.30	19.61	26.03	24.20	25.18	22.46
Repair of TV, radio, and sound equipment	3.02	1.51	1.48	3.59	4.49	4.34	3.99	4.97
Rental of television sets	0.81	0.76	1.29	0.57	0.76	0.58	0.83	0.15
Radio and sound equipment	**135.03**	**55.62**	**98.47**	**140.87**	**149.27**	**201.77**	**179.76**	**240.84**
Radios	3.67	1.87	5.65	4.52	2.56	2.40	1.60	3.92
Tape recorders and players	9.71	4.23	9.14	7.78	8.55	14.77	14.85	14.64
Sound components and component systems	14.08	6.27	7.49	22.18	12.81	18.54	17.40	20.53
Miscellaneous sound equipment	1.37	0.14	0.68	3.05	1.81	1.34	0.82	2.33
Sound equipment accessories	7.94	2.17	7.58	7.22	9.64	11.23	9.92	13.72
Satellite dishes	0.77	0.44	0.59	0.37	0.76	1.44	1.24	1.79
Compact disc, tape, record, video mail order clubs	4.15	2.87	3.15	3.46	5.31	5.94	5.72	6.33
Records, CDs, audio tapes, needles	35.26	17.71	26.38	37.69	40.70	49.17	45.82	55.06
Rental of VCR, radio, sound equipment	0.11	0.22	0.14	0.09	0.23	0.02	0.02	0.01
Musical instruments and accessories	20.06	2.58	8.81	17.05	21.16	41.87	25.91	69.92
Rental and repair of musical instruments	2.28	0.20	0.57	1.02	0.70	6.50	8.09	3.69
Rental of video cassettes, tapes, discs, films	35.61	16.91	28.30	36.42	45.05	48.55	48.36	48.90
PETS, TOYS, HOBBIES, AND PLAYGROUND EQUIPMENT	**380.64**	**179.73**	**323.50**	**351.17**	**544.77**	**510.02**	**488.39**	**549.33**
Pets	**271.61**	**120.45**	**234.14**	**243.97**	**403.54**	**365.59**	**361.46**	**374.12**
Pet food	110.31	65.39	110.05	96.63	196.96	117.26	109.02	132.99
Pet purchase, supplies, and medicines	57.85	19.76	60.16	54.48	89.28	68.04	67.86	68.38
Pet services	25.07	7.24	14.53	25.25	25.28	44.19	42.55	47.07
Veterinarian services	78.38	28.05	49.40	67.61	92.02	136.10	142.03	125.67
Toys, games, hobbies, and tricycles	**99.21**	**57.36**	**86.65**	**101.88**	**130.14**	**120.64**	**115.35**	**129.94**
Playground equipment	**3.33**	**0.98**	**0.66**	**1.74**	**6.61**	**7.27**	**9.29**	**3.71**

	total consumer units	less than high school graduate	high school graduate	some college	associate's degree	college graduate		
						total	bachelor's degree	master's, professional, doctorate
OTHER ENTERTAINMENT SUPPLIES, EQUIPMENT, SERVICES	**$522.26**	**$166.59**	**$388.30**	**$674.20**	**$490.14**	**$725.81**	**$680.90**	**$806.02**
Unmotored recreational vehicles	**55.39**	**52.09**	**55.12**	**57.56**	**18.27**	**67.88**	**54.74**	**90.97**
Boat without motor and boat trailers	17.57	–	30.63	5.22	1.59	29.09	18.54	47.63
Trailer and other attachable campers	37.82	52.09	24.49	52.34	16.68	38.79	36.20	43.34
Motorized recreational vehicles	**229.60**	**52.33**	**159.71**	**386.32**	**227.51**	**266.74**	**256.96**	**283.93**
Motorized camper	73.72	32.23	26.86	143.66	1.44	109.22	67.93	181.78
Other vehicle	35.62	19.46	50.87	32.39	79.43	17.52	5.94	37.87
Motorboats	120.27	0.65	81.97	210.27	146.63	140.00	183.09	64.28
Rental of recreational vehicles	**6.21**	**0.59**	**2.24**	**6.75**	**3.89**	**13.26**	**8.30**	**21.97**
Docking and landing fees	**5.62**	**0.06**	**3.56**	**7.89**	**2.68**	**9.65**	**11.30**	**6.76**
Sports, recreation, exercise equipment	**132.93**	**38.44**	**103.47**	**122.63**	**140.07**	**214.79**	**203.50**	**235.73**
Athletic gear, game tables, exercise equipment	53.07	8.39	45.52	46.11	54.79	87.66	88.32	86.40
Bicycles	11.34	3.57	5.96	8.15	13.30	22.37	22.10	22.84
Camping equipment	13.48	13.03	14.07	6.24	28.74	13.70	12.65	15.70
Hunting and fishing equipment	31.82	9.84	22.74	34.59	18.93	53.78	46.97	66.78
Winter sports equipment	4.17	0.42	1.11	4.02	6.11	8.50	9.54	6.67
Water sports equipment	4.65	0.88	0.66	4.29	6.51	10.09	8.10	13.58
Other sports equipment	11.89	1.89	11.29	17.53	9.45	14.06	11.27	18.96
Rental and repair of miscellaneous sports equipment	2.49	0.43	2.12	1.69	2.24	4.64	4.54	4.81
Photographic equipment and supplies	**82.86**	**21.17**	**55.24**	**80.60**	**86.80**	**141.40**	**133.26**	**156.23**
Film	12.18	4.26	9.78	12.62	13.48	17.80	17.18	18.88
Other photographic supplies	4.24	0.79	1.97	1.52	0.26	11.32	7.92	17.81
Film processing	20.31	5.69	14.59	20.33	20.98	33.13	30.47	37.81
Repair and rental of photographic equipment	0.99	0.01	0.25	0.40	0.59	2.79	1.56	4.95
Photographic equipment	28.92	5.84	17.17	28.70	33.34	50.82	49.58	53.01
Photographer fees	16.23	4.57	11.50	17.03	18.14	25.54	26.55	23.78
Fireworks	**3.75**	**0.69**	**1.02**	**7.87**	**8.62**	**3.58**	**5.29**	**0.30**
Pinball, electronic video games	**1.51**	**0.74**	**2.07**	**1.62**	**0.61**	**1.55**	**1.44**	**1.76**

Note: Subcategories may not add to total because some are not shown. "–" means sample is too small to make a reliable estimate.
Source: Bureau of Labor Statistics, unpublished data from the 2004 Consumer Expenditure Survey

Table 3.26 Entertainment: Indexed spending by education, 2004

(indexed average annual spending of consumer units (CU) on entertainment by education of consumer unit reference person, 2004; index definition: an index of 100 is the average for all consumer units; an index of 132 means that spending by consumer units in that group is 32 percent above the average for all consumer units; an index of 68 indicates spending that is 32 percent below the average for all consumer units)

	total consumer units	less than high school graduate	high school graduate	some college	associate's degree	college graduate total	bachelor's degree	master's, professional, doctorate
Average spending of CU, total	$43,395	$25,421	$35,439	$40,878	$48,177	$60,712	$56,728	$67,801
Average spending of CU, index	100	59	82	94	111	140	131	156
Entertainment, spending index	100	43	76	103	111	147	137	164
FEES AND ADMISSIONS	100	19	51	88	101	198	172	242
Recreation expenses on trips	100	24	49	81	108	200	177	241
Social, recreation, civic club membership	100	12	40	80	107	217	185	272
Fees for participant sports	100	25	65	98	92	177	167	192
Participant sports on trips	100	16	47	97	128	187	167	222
Movie, theater, opera, ballet	100	27	57	94	102	182	164	215
Movie, other admissions on trips	100	22	55	104	111	176	152	218
Admission to sports events	100	17	57	86	76	203	177	248
Admission to sports events on trips	100	22	55	104	111	176	152	218
Fees for recreational lessons	100	11	41	71	92	228	184	304
Other entertainment services on trips	100	24	49	81	108	200	177	241
TELEVISION, RADIO, AND SOUND EQUIPMENT	100	64	89	100	114	124	123	128
Television	100	69	93	99	114	119	120	117
Cable service and community antenna	100	73	99	98	109	113	115	109
Color TV sets, consoles	100	70	71	84	144	141	147	131
Color TV sets, portable and table models	100	51	89	123	94	120	107	143
VCRs and video disc players	100	70	70	88	113	150	136	174
Video cassettes, tapes, and discs	100	38	76	103	148	137	144	125
Video game hardware and software	100	62	67	107	142	132	137	122
Repair of TV, radio, and sound equipment	100	50	49	119	149	144	132	165
Rental of television sets	100	94	159	70	94	72	102	19
Radio and sound equipment	100	41	73	104	111	149	133	178
Radios	100	51	154	123	70	65	44	107
Tape recorders and players	100	44	94	80	88	152	153	151
Sound components and component systems	100	45	53	158	91	132	124	146
Miscellaneous sound equipment	100	10	50	223	132	98	60	170
Sound equipment accessories	100	27	95	91	121	141	125	173
Satellite dishes	100	57	77	48	99	187	161	232
Compact disc, tape, record, video mail order clubs	100	69	76	83	128	143	138	153
Records, CDs, audio tapes, needles	100	50	75	107	115	139	130	156
Rental of VCR, radio, sound equipment	100	200	127	82	209	18	18	9
Musical instruments and accessories	100	13	44	85	105	209	129	349
Rental and repair of musical instruments	100	9	25	45	31	285	355	162
Rental of video cassettes, tapes, discs, films	100	47	79	102	127	136	136	137
PETS, TOYS, HOBBIES, AND PLAYGROUND EQUIPMENT	100	47	85	92	143	134	128	144
Pets	100	44	86	90	149	135	133	138
Pet food	100	59	100	88	179	106	99	121
Pet purchase, supplies, and medicines	100	34	104	94	154	118	117	118
Pet services	100	29	58	101	101	176	170	188
Veterinarian services	100	36	63	86	117	174	181	160
Toys, games, hobbies, and tricycles	100	58	87	103	131	122	116	131
Playground equipment	100	29	20	52	198	218	279	111

	total consumer units	less than high school graduate	high school graduate	some college	associate's degree	college graduate		
						total	bachelor's degree	master's, professional, doctorate
OTHER ENTERTAINMENT SUPPLIES, EQUIPMENT, SERVICES	**100**	**32**	**74**	**129**	**94**	**139**	**130**	**154**
Unmotored recreational vehicles	**100**	**94**	**100**	**104**	**33**	**123**	**99**	**164**
Boat without motor and boat trailers	100	–	174	30	9	166	106	271
Trailer and other attachable campers	100	138	65	138	44	103	96	115
Motorized recreational vehicles	**100**	**23**	**70**	**168**	**99**	**116**	**112**	**124**
Motorized camper	100	44	36	195	2	148	92	247
Other vehicle	100	55	143	91	223	49	17	106
Motorboats	100	1	68	175	122	116	152	53
Rental of recreational vehicles	**100**	**10**	**36**	**109**	**63**	**214**	**134**	**354**
Docking and landing fees	**100**	**1**	**63**	**140**	**48**	**172**	**201**	**120**
Sports, recreation, exercise equipment	**100**	**29**	**78**	**92**	**105**	**162**	**153**	**177**
Athletic gear, game tables, exercise equipment	100	16	86	87	103	165	166	163
Bicycles	100	31	53	72	117	197	195	201
Camping equipment	100	97	104	46	213	102	94	116
Hunting and fishing equipment	100	31	71	109	59	169	148	210
Winter sports equipment	100	10	27	96	147	204	229	160
Water sports equipment	100	19	14	92	140	217	174	292
Other sports equipment	100	16	95	147	79	118	95	159
Rental and repair of miscellaneous sports equipment	100	17	85	68	90	186	182	193
Photographic equipment and supplies	**100**	**26**	**67**	**97**	**105**	**171**	**161**	**189**
Film	100	35	80	104	111	146	141	155
Other photographic supplies	100	19	46	36	6	267	187	420
Film processing	100	28	72	100	103	163	150	186
Repair and rental of photographic equipment	100	1	25	40	60	282	158	500
Photographic equipment	100	20	59	99	115	176	171	183
Photographer fees	100	28	71	105	112	157	164	147
Fireworks	**100**	**18**	**27**	**210**	**230**	**95**	**141**	**8**
Pinball, electronic video games	**100**	**49**	**137**	**107**	**40**	**103**	**95**	**117**

Note: "–" means sample is too small to make a reliable estimate.
Source: Calculations by New Strategist based on the 2004 Consumer Expenditure Survey

Table 3.27 Entertainment: Total spending by education, 2004

(total annual spending on entertainment, by consumer unit (CU) educational attainment group, 2004; consumer units and dollars in thousands)

	total consumer units	less than high school graduate	high school graduate	some college	associate's degree	college graduate total	bachelor's degree	master's, professional, doctorate
Number of consumer units	116,282	16,829	31,005	25,317	10,678	32,452	20,684	11,768
Total spending of all CUs	$5,046,042,273	$427,813,038	$1,098,772,243	$1,034,900,225	$514,437,850	$1,970,234,911	$1,173,370,432	$797,886,640
Entertainment, total spending	257,968,129	16,045,610	52,228,543	57,618,201	26,318,601	105,774,049	62,981,953	42,826,812
FEES AND ADMISSIONS	61,389,919	1,726,655	8,356,468	11,743,290	5,707,818	33,855,224	18,820,372	15,034,914
Recreation expenses on trips	3,144,265	111,408	413,297	553,936	310,623	1,755,004	987,247	767,627
Social, recreation, civic club membership	11,417,730	201,275	1,215,086	1,977,764	1,122,792	6,900,269	3,754,353	3,145,939
Fees for participant sports	8,602,542	308,980	1,494,131	1,834,217	727,599	4,237,907	2,561,920	1,675,881
Participant sports on trips	3,107,055	73,038	389,423	659,508	364,013	1,621,302	922,920	698,431
Movie, theater, opera, ballet	10,751,434	422,576	1,646,676	2,202,073	1,010,779	5,469,136	3,134,453	2,334,771
Movie, other admissions on trips	5,585,024	179,061	824,423	1,268,129	571,380	2,741,545	1,507,657	1,233,757
Admission to sports events	4,191,966	102,657	640,253	783,561	291,616	2,374,513	1,322,121	1,052,412
Admission to sports events on trips	1,861,675	59,743	274,704	422,541	190,496	913,524	502,414	411,174
Fees for recreational lessons	9,583,962	156,510	1,045,179	1,487,374	807,791	6,087,022	3,140,038	2,947,178
Other entertainment services on trips	3,144,265	111,408	413,297	553,936	310,623	1,755,004	987,247	767,627
TELEVISION, RADIO, SOUND EQUIPMENT	91,588,354	8,490,904	21,802,716	19,915,618	9,560,013	31,813,669	19,975,987	11,842,256
Television	75,886,796	7,554,875	18,749,964	16,349,465	7,966,002	25,265,829	16,257,831	9,008,051
Cable service and community antenna	54,769,985	5,795,234	14,496,388	11,743,797	5,458,594	17,275,822	11,207,005	6,068,993
Color TV sets, consoles	6,100,154	617,961	1,157,417	1,113,948	807,470	2,403,395	1,596,598	806,814
Color TV sets, portable and table models	4,628,024	344,153	1,100,988	1,236,735	399,250	1,546,662	878,243	668,422
VCRs and video disc players	2,796,582	282,559	522,434	534,189	289,587	1,167,947	675,333	492,608
Video cassettes, tapes, and discs	4,957,102	273,303	1,000,841	1,112,176	675,597	1,894,872	1,267,309	627,470
Video game hardware and software	2,132,612	191,682	381,362	496,466	277,948	785,338	520,823	264,309
Repair of TV, radio, and sound equipment	351,172	25,412	45,887	90,888	47,944	140,842	82,529	58,487
Rental of television sets	94,188	12,790	39,996	14,431	8,115	18,822	17,168	1,765
Radio and sound equipment	15,701,558	936,029	3,053,062	3,566,406	1,593,905	6,547,840	3,718,156	2,834,205
Radios	426,755	31,470	175,178	114,433	27,336	77,885	33,094	46,131
Tape recorders and players	1,129,098	71,187	283,386	196,966	91,297	479,316	307,157	172,284
Sound components and component systems	1,637,251	105,518	232,227	561,531	136,785	601,660	359,902	241,597
Miscellaneous sound equipment	159,306	2,356	21,083	77,217	19,327	43,486	16,961	27,419
Sound equipment accessories	923,279	36,519	235,018	182,789	102,936	364,436	205,185	161,457
Satellite dishes	89,537	7,405	18,293	9,367	8,115	46,731	25,648	21,065
Compact disc, tape, record, video mail order clubs	482,570	48,299	97,666	87,597	56,700	192,765	118,312	74,491
Records, CDs, audio tapes, needles	4,100,103	298,042	817,912	954,198	434,595	1,595,665	947,741	647,946
Rental of VCR, radio, sound equipment	12,791	3,702	4,341	2,279	2,456	649	414	118
Musical instruments and accessories	2,332,617	43,419	273,154	431,655	225,946	1,358,765	535,922	822,819
Rental and repair of musical instruments	265,123	3,366	17,673	25,823	7,475	210,938	167,334	43,424
Rental of video cassettes, tapes, discs, films	4,140,802	284,578	877,442	922,045	481,044	1,575,545	1,000,278	575,455
PETS, TOYS, HOBBIES, AND PLAYGROUND EQUIPMENT	44,261,580	3,024,676	10,030,118	8,890,571	5,817,054	16,551,169	10,101,859	6,464,515
Pets	31,583,354	2,027,053	7,259,511	6,176,588	4,309,000	11,864,127	7,476,439	4,402,644
Pet food	12,827,067	1,100,448	3,412,100	2,446,382	2,103,139	3,805,322	2,254,970	1,565,026
Pet purchase, supplies, and medicines	6,726,914	332,541	1,865,261	1,379,270	953,332	2,208,034	1,403,616	804,696
Pet services	2,915,190	121,842	450,503	639,254	269,940	1,434,054	880,104	553,920
Veterinarian services	9,114,183	472,053	1,531,647	1,711,682	982,590	4,416,717	2,937,749	1,478,885
Toys, games, hobbies, and tricycles	11,536,337	965,311	2,686,583	2,579,296	1,389,635	3,915,009	2,385,899	1,529,134
Playground equipment	387,219	16,492	20,463	44,052	70,582	235,926	192,154	43,659

	total consumer units	less than high school graduate	high school graduate	some college	associate's degree	college graduate total	bachelor's degree	master's, professional, doctorate
OTHER ENTERTAINMENT SUPPLIES, EQUIPMENT, SERVICES	**$60,729,437**	**$2,803,543**	**$12,039,242**	**$17,068,721**	**$5,233,715**	**$23,553,986**	**$14,083,736**	**$9,485,243**
Unmotored recreational vehicles	**6,440,860**	**876,623**	**1,708,996**	**1,457,247**	**195,087**	**2,202,842**	**1,132,242**	**1,070,535**
Boat without motor and boat trailers	2,043,075	–	949,683	132,155	16,978	944,029	383,481	560,510
Trailer and other attachable campers	4,397,785	876,623	759,312	1,325,092	178,109	1,258,813	748,761	510,025
Motorized recreational vehicles	**26,698,347**	**880,662**	**4,951,809**	**9,780,463**	**2,429,352**	**8,656,246**	**5,314,961**	**3,341,288**
Motorized camper	8,572,309	542,399	832,794	3,637,040	15,376	3,544,407	1,405,064	2,139,187
Other vehicle	4,141,965	327,492	1,577,224	820,018	848,154	568,559	122,863	445,654
Motorboats	13,985,236	10,939	2,541,480	5,323,406	1,565,715	4,543,280	3,787,034	756,447
Rental of recreational vehicles	**722,111**	**9,929**	**69,451**	**170,890**	**41,537**	**430,314**	**171,677**	**258,543**
Docking and landing fees	**653,505**	**1,010**	**110,378**	**199,751**	**28,617**	**313,162**	**233,729**	**79,552**
Sports, recreation, exercise equipment	**15,457,366**	**646,907**	**3,208,087**	**3,104,624**	**1,495,667**	**6,970,365**	**4,209,194**	**2,774,071**
Athletic gear, game tables, exercise equipment	6,171,086	141,195	1,411,348	1,167,367	585,048	2,844,742	1,826,811	1,016,755
Bicycles	1,318,638	60,080	184,790	206,334	142,017	725,951	457,116	268,781
Camping equipment	1,567,481	219,282	436,240	157,978	306,886	444,592	261,653	184,758
Hunting and fishing equipment	3,700,093	165,597	705,054	875,715	202,135	1,745,269	971,527	785,867
Winter sports equipment	484,896	7,068	34,416	101,774	65,243	275,842	197,325	78,493
Water sports equipment	540,711	14,810	20,463	108,610	69,514	327,441	167,540	159,809
Other sports equipment	1,382,593	31,807	350,046	443,807	100,907	456,275	233,109	223,121
Rental and repair of miscellaneous sports equipment	289,542	7,236	65,731	42,786	23,919	150,577	93,905	56,604
Photographic equipment and supplies	**9,635,127**	**356,270**	**1,712,716**	**2,040,550**	**926,850**	**4,588,713**	**2,756,350**	**1,838,515**
Film	1,416,315	71,692	303,229	319,501	143,939	577,646	355,351	222,180
Other photographic supplies	493,036	13,295	61,080	38,482	2,776	367,357	163,817	209,588
Film processing	2,361,687	95,757	452,363	514,695	224,024	1,075,135	630,241	444,948
Repair and rental of photographic equipment	115,119	168	7,751	10,127	6,300	90,541	32,267	58,252
Photographic equipment	3,362,875	98,281	532,356	726,598	356,005	1,649,211	1,025,513	623,822
Photographer fees	1,887,257	76,909	356,558	431,149	193,699	828,824	549,160	279,843
Fireworks	**436,058**	**11,612**	**31,625**	**199,245**	**92,044**	**116,178**	**109,418**	**3,530**
Pinball, electronic video games	**175,586**	**12,453**	**64,180**	**41,014**	**6,514**	**50,301**	**29,785**	**20,712**

Note: Numbers may not add to total because of rounding and missing subcategories. "–" means sample is too small to make a reliable estimate.
Source: Calculations by New Strategist based on the 2004 Consumer Expenditure Survey

Table 3.28 Entertainment: Market shares by education, 2004

(percentage of total annual spending on entertainment accounted for by consumer unit educational attainment groups, 2004)

	total consumer units	less than high school graduate	high school graduate	some college	associate's degree	college graduate total	bachelor's degree	master's, professional, doctorate
Share of total consumer units	100.0%	14.5%	26.7%	21.8%	9.2%	27.9%	17.8%	10.1%
Share of total before-tax income	100.0	7.7	20.7	18.7	9.9	43.0	24.7	18.3
Share of total spending	100.0	8.5	21.8	20.5	10.2	39.0	23.3	15.8
Share of entertainment spending	100.0	6.2	20.2	22.3	10.2	41.0	24.4	16.6
FEES AND ADMISSIONS	100.0	2.8	13.6	19.1	9.3	55.1	30.7	24.5
Recreation expenses on trips	100.0	3.5	13.1	17.6	9.9	55.8	31.4	24.4
Social, recreation, civic club membership	100.0	1.8	10.6	17.3	9.8	60.4	32.9	27.6
Fees for participant sports	100.0	3.6	17.4	21.3	8.5	49.3	29.8	19.5
Participant sports on trips	100.0	2.4	12.5	21.2	11.7	52.2	29.7	22.5
Movie, theater, opera, ballet	100.0	3.9	15.3	20.5	9.4	50.9	29.2	21.7
Movie, other admissions on trips	100.0	3.2	14.8	22.7	10.2	49.1	27.0	22.1
Admission to sports events	100.0	2.4	15.3	18.7	7.0	56.6	31.5	25.1
Admission to sports events on trips	100.0	3.2	14.8	22.7	10.2	49.1	27.0	22.1
Fees for recreational lessons	100.0	1.6	10.9	15.5	8.4	63.5	32.8	30.8
Other entertainment services on trips	100.0	3.5	13.1	17.6	9.9	55.8	31.4	24.4
TELEVISION, RADIO, AND SOUND EQUIPMENT	100.0	9.3	23.8	21.7	10.4	34.7	21.8	12.9
Television	100.0	10.0	24.7	21.5	10.5	33.3	21.4	11.9
Cable service and community antenna	100.0	10.6	26.5	21.4	10.0	31.5	20.5	11.1
Color TV sets, consoles	100.0	10.1	19.0	18.3	13.2	39.4	26.2	13.2
Color TV sets, portable and table models	100.0	7.4	23.8	26.7	8.6	33.4	19.0	14.4
VCRs and video disc players	100.0	10.1	18.7	19.1	10.4	41.8	24.1	17.6
Video cassettes, tapes, and discs	100.0	5.5	20.2	22.4	13.6	38.2	25.6	12.7
Video game hardware and software	100.0	9.0	17.9	23.3	13.0	36.8	24.4	12.4
Repair of TV, radio, and sound equipment	100.0	7.2	13.1	25.9	13.7	40.1	23.5	16.7
Rental of television sets	100.0	13.6	42.5	15.3	8.6	20.0	18.2	1.9
Radio and sound equipment	100.0	6.0	19.4	22.7	10.2	41.7	23.7	18.1
Radios	100.0	7.4	41.0	26.8	6.4	18.3	7.8	10.8
Tape recorders and players	100.0	6.3	25.1	17.4	8.1	42.5	27.2	15.3
Sound components and component systems	100.0	6.4	14.2	34.3	8.4	36.7	22.0	14.8
Miscellaneous sound equipment	100.0	1.5	13.2	48.5	12.1	27.3	10.6	17.2
Sound equipment accessories	100.0	4.0	25.5	19.8	11.1	39.5	22.2	17.5
Satellite dishes	100.0	8.3	20.4	10.5	9.1	52.2	28.6	23.5
Compact disc, tape, record, video mail order clubs	100.0	10.0	20.2	18.2	11.7	39.9	24.5	15.4
Records, CDs, audio tapes, needles	100.0	7.3	19.9	23.3	10.6	38.9	23.1	15.8
Rental of VCR, radio, sound equipment	100.0	28.9	33.9	17.8	19.2	5.1	3.2	0.9
Musical instruments and accessories	100.0	1.9	11.7	18.5	9.7	58.3	23.0	35.3
Rental and repair of musical instruments	100.0	1.3	6.7	9.7	2.8	79.6	63.1	16.4
Rental of video cassettes, tapes, discs, films	100.0	6.9	21.2	22.3	11.6	38.0	24.2	13.9
PETS, TOYS, HOBBIES, AND PLAYGROUND EQUIPMENT	100.0	6.8	22.7	20.1	13.1	37.4	22.8	14.6
Pets	100.0	6.4	23.0	19.6	13.6	37.6	23.7	13.9
Pet food	100.0	8.6	26.6	19.1	16.4	29.7	17.6	12.2
Pet purchase, supplies, and medicines	100.0	4.9	27.7	20.5	14.2	32.8	20.9	12.0
Pet services	100.0	4.2	15.5	21.9	9.3	49.2	30.2	19.0
Veterinarian services	100.0	5.2	16.8	18.8	10.8	48.5	32.2	16.2
Toys, games, hobbies, and tricycles	100.0	8.4	23.3	22.4	12.0	33.9	20.7	13.3
Playground equipment	100.0	4.3	5.3	11.4	18.2	60.9	49.6	11.3

	total consumer units	less than high school graduate	high school graduate	some college	associate's degree	college graduate total	bachelor's degree	master's, professional, doctorate
OTHER ENTERTAINMENT SUPPLIES, EQUIPMENT, SERVICES	**100.0%**	**4.6%**	**19.8%**	**28.1%**	**8.6%**	**38.8%**	**23.2%**	**15.6%**
Unmotored recreational vehicles	**100.0**	**13.6**	**26.5**	**22.6**	**3.0**	**34.2**	**17.6**	**16.6**
Boat without motor and boat trailers	100.0	–	46.5	6.5	0.8	46.2	18.8	27.4
Trailer and other attachable campers	100.0	19.9	17.3	30.1	4.0	28.6	17.0	11.6
Motorized recreational vehicles	**100.0**	**3.3**	**18.5**	**36.6**	**9.1**	**32.4**	**19.9**	**12.5**
Motorized camper	100.0	6.3	9.7	42.4	0.2	41.3	16.4	25.0
Other vehicle	100.0	7.9	38.1	19.8	20.5	13.7	3.0	10.8
Motorboats	100.0	0.1	18.2	38.1	11.2	32.5	27.1	5.4
Rental of recreational vehicles	**100.0**	**1.4**	**9.6**	**23.7**	**5.8**	**59.6**	**23.8**	**35.8**
Docking and landing fees	**100.0**	**0.2**	**16.9**	**30.6**	**4.4**	**47.9**	**35.8**	**12.2**
Sports, recreation, exercise equipment	**100.0**	**4.2**	**20.8**	**20.1**	**9.7**	**45.1**	**27.2**	**17.9**
Athletic gear, game tables, exercise equipment	100.0	2.3	22.9	18.9	9.5	46.1	29.6	16.5
Bicycles	100.0	4.6	14.0	15.6	10.8	55.1	34.7	20.4
Camping equipment	100.0	14.0	27.8	10.1	19.6	28.4	16.7	11.8
Hunting and fishing equipment	100.0	4.5	19.1	23.7	5.5	47.2	26.3	21.2
Winter sports equipment	100.0	1.5	7.1	21.0	13.5	56.9	40.7	16.2
Water sports equipment	100.0	2.7	3.8	20.1	12.9	60.6	31.0	29.6
Other sports equipment	100.0	2.3	25.3	32.1	7.3	33.0	16.9	16.1
Rental and repair of miscellaneous sports equipment	100.0	2.5	22.7	14.8	8.3	52.0	32.4	19.5
Photographic equipment and supplies	**100.0**	**3.7**	**17.8**	**21.2**	**9.6**	**47.6**	**28.6**	**19.1**
Film	100.0	5.1	21.4	22.6	10.2	40.8	25.1	15.7
Other photographic supplies	100.0	2.7	12.4	7.8	0.6	74.5	33.2	42.5
Film processing	100.0	4.1	19.2	21.8	9.5	45.5	26.7	18.8
Repair and rental of photographic equipment	100.0	0.1	6.7	8.8	5.5	78.6	28.0	50.6
Photographic equipment	100.0	2.9	15.8	21.6	10.6	49.0	30.5	18.6
Photographer fees	100.0	4.1	18.9	22.8	10.3	43.9	29.1	14.8
Fireworks	**100.0**	**2.7**	**7.3**	**45.7**	**21.1**	**26.6**	**25.1**	**0.8**
Pinball, electronic video games	**100.0**	**7.1**	**36.6**	**23.4**	**3.7**	**28.6**	**17.0**	**11.8**

Note: Numbers may not add to total because of rounding. "–" means sample is too small to make a reliable estimate.
Source: Calculations by New Strategist based on the 2004 Consumer Expenditure Survey

Chapter 4. Spending on Financial Products and Services, 2004

Trends in spending on financial products and services have been mixed since 2000. Spending on financial services (such as bank fees, accounting fees, credit card fees, and legal fees) fell between 2000 and 2004—by 19 percent after adjusting for inflation. Spending on cash contributions (a category that includes child support as well as gifts to charities) rose 8 percent between 2000 and 2004. Spending on pensions and Social Security climbed 36 percent, while spending on life and other personal insurance fell 11 percent. Households spent less on federal and state taxes, but other taxes rose 9 percent.

Households headed by 55-to-64-year-olds spend more than other age groups on financial services, $825 in 2004. The biggest spenders on personal insurance and pensions, however, are householders aged 45 to 54. Householders aged 65 to 74 spend the most on cash contributions—75 percent more than the average household. Not surprisingly, support for college students peaks in the 45-to-54 age group, while child support spending is greatest among householders aged 35 to 44.

Households with incomes of $100,000 or more represent just 13 percent of consumer units but account for 31 percent of consumer spending on legal fees and 56 percent of spending on support for college students. These affluent households account for 59 percent of contributions to charities and for an even larger 77 percent of contributions to educational institutions.

Married couples with adult children at home spend more than other household types on most financial categories because their households are larger and more likely to include two or more wage earners. Married couples without children at home spend the most on cash gifts to nonhousehold members and on gifts to charities. Single parents spend more than twice the average on legal fees.

Blacks and Hispanics spend less than average on nearly every financial product and service, while non-Hispanic whites spend more. Asian households spend 77 percent more than the average on support for college students.

Households in the West spend more than the average household on many financial products and services including accounting fees and shopping club and credit card memberships. Households in the Northeast spend (or lose) the most on lotteries and gambling. Households in the Midwest spend the most on life and other personal insurance.

Households headed by college graduates account for 28 percent of households, but they control fully 71 percent of cash gifts to charities and 91 percent of cash contributions to educational institutions. Households headed by college graduates spend nearly three times the average on contributions to political organizations and devote more than twice the average to support for college students.

Table 4.1 Financial: Average spending by age, 2004

(average annual spending of consumer units (CU) on financial products and services, cash contributions, and miscellaneous items, by age of consumer unit reference person, 2004)

	total consumer units	under 25	25 to 34	35 to 44	45 to 54	55 to 64	65 to 74	75+
Number of consumer units (in 000s)	116,282	8,817	19,439	24,070	23,712	17,479	11,230	11,536
Average number of persons per CU	2.5	1.9	2.9	3.2	2.7	2.1	1.9	1.5
Average before-tax income of CU	$54,453.00	$22,840.00	$52,484.00	$65,515.00	$70,434.00	$61,031.00	$42,137.00	$28,028.00
Average spending of CU, total	43,394.87	24,534.56	42,700.54	50,401.62	52,764.36	47,298.58	36,511.98	25,763.32
FINANCIAL PRODUCTS AND SERVICES	690.02	296.63	599.67	773.31	774.05	824.59	735.43	547.09
Miscellaneous fees	4.57	2.96	8.34	3.27	3.89	6.19	3.49	2.03
Lottery and gambling losses	66.54	20.34	65.75	43.71	79.45	89.95	118.21	38.62
Legal fees	127.50	53.61	101.28	186.65	153.09	146.19	68.65	81.13
Funeral expenses	65.78	26.03	25.05	37.05	44.78	63.50	169.06	170.86
Safe deposit box rental	3.22	0.08	0.86	2.30	3.74	4.62	6.17	5.51
Checking accounts, other bank service charges	18.70	16.66	22.54	22.05	23.72	18.05	9.42	6.47
Cemetery lots, vaults, and maintenance fees	13.48	0.91	2.17	5.58	7.81	27.75	43.16	19.80
Accounting fees	51.22	7.73	32.21	45.77	57.78	72.85	62.14	70.99
Miscellaneous personal services	36.79	73.98	37.01	54.72	20.24	31.65	6.80	40.51
Finance charges, except mortgage and vehicles	158.18	70.36	181.02	215.27	197.87	166.31	89.67	40.53
Occupational expenses	43.10	15.36	51.53	56.89	58.62	51.64	15.12	3.70
Expenses for other properties	91.63	6.31	64.44	88.96	111.76	134.62	131.65	62.76
Credit card memberships	2.41	0.74	2.36	2.98	2.74	2.91	2.10	1.42
Shopping club membership fees	5.72	1.56	3.76	6.97	6.44	8.30	7.15	2.76
CASH CONTRIBUTIONS	1,408.04	309.70	815.48	1,265.35	1,624.83	1,751.83	2,471.07	1,542.38
Support for college students	82.49	0.24	3.09	34.33	214.43	96.11	163.98	8.45
Alimony expenditures	47.29	–	17.16	29.78	79.66	102.89	49.79	17.51
Child support expenditures	165.10	63.38	197.15	343.32	218.45	65.62	16.95	2.25
Gifts to non–CU members of stocks, bonds, and mutual funds	24.97	–	12.80	23.78	11.94	50.08	26.71	54.12
Cash contributions to charities and other organizations	157.51	11.84	52.22	95.71	142.09	216.48	505.49	178.80
Cash contributions to church, religious organizations	565.11	168.68	392.32	500.27	661.78	728.31	773.73	645.52
Cash contributions to educational institutions	46.06	1.27	12.80	43.26	32.76	35.99	184.19	50.30
Cash contributions to political organizations	16.58	1.41	12.21	9.97	18.29	24.99	34.55	15.57
Other cash gifts	302.93	62.88	115.73	184.92	245.44	431.36	715.67	569.86
PERSONAL INSURANCE AND PENSIONS	4,823.20	1,726.06	4,764.63	6,272.69	6,915.21	5,825.32	2,347.56	856.09
Life and other personal insurance	390.34	30.59	235.22	391.38	504.72	611.59	472.21	274.53
Life, endowment, annuity, other personal insurance	378.18	26.47	228.84	384.57	492.02	595.41	450.61	251.62
Other nonhealth insurance	12.16	4.12	6.37	6.80	12.69	16.18	21.61	22.90
Pensions and Social Security	4,432.85	1,695.47	4,529.41	5,881.31	6,410.49	5,213.73	1,875.34	581.56
Deductions for government retirement	78.45	20.56	57.30	94.75	99.77	152.34	42.34	3.66
Deductions for railroad retirement	2.67	–	0.83	5.21	5.88	1.36	0.51	–
Deductions for private pensions	518.59	55.12	433.41	799.85	828.24	605.15	155.03	15.75
Nonpayroll deposit to retirement plans	400.54	19.75	219.52	350.55	654.71	846.75	210.35	87.51
Deductions for Social Security	3,432.61	1,600.05	3,818.36	4,630.95	4,821.89	3,608.12	1,467.12	474.64
PERSONAL TAXES	2,165.85	333.10	1,664.61	2,312.72	3,673.16	2,987.40	1,010.38	886.54
Federal income taxes	1,518.95	200.11	1,097.98	1,557.26	2,673.77	2,167.53	678.72	617.92
State and local income taxes	472.12	122.85	472.75	597.69	755.64	584.20	118.95	67.19
Other taxes	174.78	10.14	93.88	157.77	243.75	235.68	212.71	201.42

Note: Subcategories may not add to total because some are not shown. "–" means sample is too small to make a reliable estimate.
Source: Bureau of Labor Statistics, unpublished tables from the 2004 Consumer Expenditure Survey

Table 4.2 Financial: Indexed spending by age, 2004

(indexed average annual spending of consumer units (CU) on financial products and services, cash contributions, and miscellaneous items, by age of consumer unit reference person, 2004; index definition: an index of 100 is the average for all consumer units; an index of 132 means that spending by consumer units in that group is 32 percent above the average for all consumer units; an index of 68 indicates spending that is 32 percent below the average for all consumer units)

	total consumer units	under 25	25 to 34	35 to 44	45 to 54	55 to 64	65 to 74	75+
Average spending of CU, total	$43,395	$24,535	$42,701	$50,402	$52,764	$47,299	$36,512	$25,763
Average spending of CU, index	100	57	98	116	122	109	84	59
FINANCIAL PRODUCTS AND SERVICES	100	43	87	112	112	120	107	79
Miscellaneous fees	100	65	182	72	85	135	76	44
Lottery and gambling losses	100	31	99	66	119	135	178	58
Legal fees	100	42	79	146	120	115	54	64
Funeral expenses	100	40	38	56	68	97	257	260
Safe deposit box rental	100	2	27	71	116	143	192	171
Checking accounts, other bank service charges	100	89	121	118	127	97	50	35
Cemetery lots, vaults, and maintenance fees	100	7	16	41	58	206	320	147
Accounting fees	100	15	63	89	113	142	121	139
Miscellaneous personal services	100	201	101	149	55	86	18	110
Finance charges, except mortgage and vehicles	100	44	114	136	125	105	57	26
Occupational expenses	100	36	120	132	136	120	35	9
Expenses for other properties	100	7	70	97	122	147	144	68
Credit card memberships	100	31	98	124	114	121	87	59
Shopping club membership fees	100	27	66	122	113	145	125	48
CASH CONTRIBUTIONS	100	22	58	90	115	124	175	110
Support for college students	100	0	4	42	260	117	199	10
Alimony expenditures	100	–	36	63	168	218	105	37
Child support expenditures	100	38	119	208	132	40	10	1
Gifts to non–CU members of stocks, bonds, and mutual funds	100	–	51	95	48	201	107	217
Cash contributions to charities and other organizations	100	8	33	61	90	137	321	114
Cash contributions to church, religious organizations	100	30	69	89	117	129	137	114
Cash contributions to educational institutions	100	3	28	94	71	78	400	109
Cash contributions to political organizations	100	9	74	60	110	151	208	94
Other cash gifts	100	21	38	61	81	142	236	188
PERSONAL INSURANCE AND PENSIONS	100	36	99	130	143	121	49	18
Life and other personal insurance	100	8	60	100	129	157	121	70
Life, endowment, annuity, other personal insurance	100	7	61	102	130	157	119	67
Other nonhealth insurance	100	34	52	56	104	133	178	188
Pensions and Social Security	100	38	102	133	145	118	42	13
Deductions for government retirement	100	26	73	121	127	194	54	5
Deductions for railroad retirement	100	–	31	195	220	51	19	–
Deductions for private pensions	100	11	84	154	160	117	30	3
Nonpayroll deposit to retirement plans	100	5	55	88	163	211	53	22
Deductions for Social Security	100	47	111	135	140	105	43	14
PERSONAL TAXES	100	15	77	107	170	138	47	41
Federal income taxes	100	13	72	103	176	143	45	41
State and local income taxes	100	26	100	127	160	124	25	14
Other taxes	100	6	54	90	139	135	122	115

Note: "–" means sample is too small to make a reliable estimate.
Source: Calculations by New Strategist based on the 2004 Consumer Expenditure Survey

Table 4.3 Financial: Total spending by age, 2004

(total annual spending on financial products and services, cash contributions, and miscellaneous items, by consumer unit (CU) age groups, 2004; consumer units and dollars in thousands)

	total consumer units	under 25	25 to 34	35 to 44	45 to 54	55 to 64	65 to 74	75+
Number of consumer units	116,282	8,817	19,439	24,070	23,712	17,479	11,230	11,536
Total spending of all CUs	$5,046,042,273	$216,321,216	$830,055,797	$1,213,166,993	$1,251,148,504	$826,731,880	$410,029,535	$297,205,660
FINANCIAL PRODUCTS AND SERVICES	80,236,906	2,615,387	11,656,985	18,613,572	18,354,274	14,413,009	8,258,879	6,311,230
Miscellaneous fees	531,409	26,098	162,121	78,709	92,240	108,195	39,193	23,418
Lottery and gambling losses	7,737,404	179,338	1,278,114	1,052,100	1,883,918	1,572,236	1,327,498	445,520
Legal fees	14,825,955	472,679	1,968,782	4,492,666	3,630,070	2,555,255	770,940	935,916
Funeral expenses	7,649,030	229,507	486,947	891,794	1,061,823	1,109,917	1,898,544	1,971,041
Safe deposit box rental	374,428	705	16,718	55,361	88,683	80,753	69,289	63,563
Checking accounts, other bank service charges	2,174,473	146,891	438,155	530,744	562,449	315,496	105,787	74,638
Cemetery lots, vaults, and maintenance fees	1,567,481	8,023	42,183	134,311	185,191	485,042	484,687	228,413
Accounting fees	5,955,964	68,155	626,130	1,101,684	1,370,079	1,273,345	697,832	818,941
Miscellaneous personal services	4,278,015	652,282	719,437	1,317,110	479,931	553,210	76,364	467,323
Finance charges, except mortgage and vehicles	18,393,487	620,364	3,518,848	5,181,549	4,691,893	2,906,932	1,006,994	467,554
Occupational expenses	5,011,754	135,429	1,001,692	1,369,342	1,389,997	902,616	169,798	42,683
Expenses for other properties	10,654,920	55,635	1,252,649	2,141,267	2,650,053	2,353,023	1,478,430	723,999
Credit card memberships	280,240	6,525	45,876	71,729	64,971	50,864	23,583	16,381
Shopping club membership fees	665,133	13,755	73,091	167,768	152,705	145,076	80,295	31,839
CASH CONTRIBUTIONS	163,729,707	2,730,625	15,852,116	30,456,975	38,527,969	30,620,237	27,750,116	17,792,896
Support for college students	9,592,102	2,116	60,067	826,323	5,084,564	1,679,907	1,841,495	97,479
Alimony expenditures	5,498,976	–	333,573	716,805	1,888,898	1,798,414	559,142	201,995
Child support expenditures	19,198,158	558,821	3,832,399	8,263,712	5,179,886	1,146,972	190,349	25,956
Gifts to non–CU members of stocks, bonds, and mutual funds	2,903,562	–	248,819	572,385	283,121	875,348	299,953	624,328
Cash contributions to charities and other organizations	18,315,578	104,393	1,015,105	2,303,740	3,369,238	3,783,854	5,676,653	2,062,637
Cash contributions to church, religious organizations	65,712,121	1,487,252	7,626,308	12,041,499	15,692,127	12,730,130	8,688,988	7,446,719
Cash contributions to educational institutions	5,355,949	11,198	248,819	1,041,268	776,805	629,069	2,068,454	580,261
Cash contributions to political organizations	1,927,956	12,432	237,350	239,978	433,692	436,800	387,997	179,616
Other cash gifts	35,225,306	554,413	2,249,675	4,451,024	5,819,873	7,539,741	8,036,974	6,573,905
PERSONAL INSURANCE AND PENSIONS	560,851,342	15,218,671	92,619,643	150,983,648	163,973,460	101,820,768	26,363,099	9,875,854
Life and other personal insurance	45,389,516	269,712	4,572,442	9,420,517	11,967,921	10,689,982	5,302,918	3,166,978
Life, endowment, annuity, other personal insurance	43,975,527	233,386	4,448,421	9,256,600	11,666,778	10,407,171	5,060,350	2,902,688
Other nonhealth insurance	1,413,989	36,326	123,826	163,676	300,905	282,810	242,680	264,174
Pensions and Social Security	515,460,664	14,948,959	88,047,201	141,563,132	152,005,539	91,130,787	21,060,068	6,708,876
Deductions for government retirement	9,122,323	181,278	1,113,855	2,280,633	2,365,746	2,662,751	475,478	42,222
Deductions for railroad retirement	310,473	–	16,134	125,405	139,427	23,771	5,727	–
Deductions for private pensions	60,302,682	485,993	8,425,057	19,252,390	19,639,227	10,577,417	1,740,987	181,692
Nonpayroll deposit to retirement plans	46,575,592	174,136	4,267,249	8,437,739	15,524,484	14,800,343	2,362,231	1,009,515
Deductions for Social Security	399,150,756	14,107,641	74,225,100	111,466,967	114,336,656	63,066,329	16,475,758	5,475,447
PERSONAL TAXES	251,849,370	2,936,943	32,358,354	55,667,170	87,097,970	52,216,765	11,346,567	10,227,125
Federal income taxes	176,626,544	1,764,370	21,343,633	37,483,248	63,400,434	37,886,257	7,622,026	7,128,325
State and local income taxes	54,899,058	1,083,168	9,189,787	14,386,398	17,917,736	10,211,232	1,335,809	775,104
Other taxes	20,323,768	89,404	1,824,933	3,797,524	5,779,800	4,119,451	2,388,733	2,323,581

Note: Numbers may not add to total because of rounding and missing subcategories. "–" means sample is too small to make a reliable estimate.
Source: Calculations by New Strategist based on the 2004 Consumer Expenditure Survey

Table 4.4 Financial: Market shares by age, 2004

(percentage of total annual spending on financial products and services, cash contributions, and miscellaneous items accounted for by consumer unit age groups, 2004)

	total consumer units	under 25	25 to 34	35 to 44	45 to 54	55 to 64	65 to 74	75+
Share of total consumer units	**100.0%**	**7.6%**	**16.7%**	**20.7%**	**20.4%**	**15.0%**	**9.7%**	**9.9%**
Share of total before-tax income	**100.0**	**3.2**	**16.1**	**24.9**	**26.4**	**16.8**	**7.5**	**5.1**
Share of total spending	**100.0**	**4.3**	**16.4**	**24.0**	**24.8**	**16.4**	**8.1**	**5.9**
FINANCIAL PRODUCTS AND SERVICES	**100.0**	**3.3**	**14.5**	**23.2**	**22.9**	**18.0**	**10.3**	**7.9**
Miscellaneous fees	100.0	4.9	30.5	14.8	17.4	20.4	7.4	4.4
Lottery and gambling losses	100.0	2.3	16.5	13.6	24.3	20.3	17.2	5.8
Legal fees	100.0	3.2	13.3	30.3	24.5	17.2	5.2	6.3
Funeral expenses	100.0	3.0	6.4	11.7	13.9	14.5	24.8	25.8
Safe deposit box rental	100.0	0.2	4.5	14.8	23.7	21.6	18.5	17.0
Checking accounts, other bank service charges	100.0	6.8	20.1	24.4	25.9	14.5	4.9	3.4
Cemetery lots, vaults, and maintenance fees	100.0	0.5	2.7	8.6	11.8	30.9	30.9	14.6
Accounting fees	100.0	1.1	10.5	18.5	23.0	21.4	11.7	13.7
Miscellaneous personal services	100.0	15.2	16.8	30.8	11.2	12.9	1.8	10.9
Finance charges, except mortgage and vehicles	100.0	3.4	19.1	28.2	25.5	15.8	5.5	2.5
Occupational expenses	100.0	2.7	20.0	27.3	27.7	18.0	3.4	0.9
Expenses for other properties	100.0	0.5	11.8	20.1	24.9	22.1	13.9	6.8
Credit card memberships	100.0	2.3	16.4	25.6	23.2	18.2	8.4	5.8
Shopping club membership fees	100.0	2.1	11.0	25.2	23.0	21.8	12.1	4.8
CASH CONTRIBUTIONS	**100.0**	**1.7**	**9.7**	**18.6**	**23.5**	**18.7**	**16.9**	**10.9**
Support for college students	100.0	0.0	0.6	8.6	53.0	17.5	19.2	1.0
Alimony expenditures	100.0	–	6.1	13.0	34.3	32.7	10.2	3.7
Child support expenditures	100.0	2.9	20.0	43.0	27.0	6.0	1.0	0.1
Gifts to non–CU members of stocks, bonds, and mutual funds	100.0	–	8.6	19.7	9.8	30.1	10.3	21.5
Cash contributions to charities and other organizations	100.0	0.6	5.5	12.6	18.4	20.7	31.0	11.3
Cash contributions to church, religious organizations	100.0	2.3	11.6	18.3	23.9	19.4	13.2	11.3
Cash contributions to educational institutions	100.0	0.2	4.6	19.4	14.5	11.7	38.6	10.8
Cash contributions to political organizations	100.0	0.6	12.3	12.4	22.5	22.7	20.1	9.3
Other cash gifts	100.0	1.6	6.4	12.6	16.5	21.4	22.8	18.7
PERSONAL INSURANCE AND PENSIONS	**100.0**	**2.7**	**16.5**	**26.9**	**29.2**	**18.2**	**4.7**	**1.8**
Life and other personal insurance	**100.0**	**0.6**	**10.1**	**20.8**	**26.4**	**23.6**	**11.7**	**7.0**
Life, endowment, annuity, other personal insurance	100.0	0.5	10.1	21.0	26.5	23.7	11.5	6.6
Other nonhealth insurance	100.0	2.6	8.8	11.6	21.3	20.0	17.2	18.7
Pensions and Social Security	**100.0**	**2.9**	**17.1**	**27.5**	**29.5**	**17.7**	**4.1**	**1.3**
Deductions for government retirement	100.0	2.0	12.2	25.0	25.9	29.2	5.2	0.5
Deductions for railroad retirement	100.0	–	5.2	40.4	44.9	7.7	1.8	–
Deductions for private pensions	100.0	0.8	14.0	31.9	32.6	17.5	2.9	0.3
Nonpayroll deposit to retirement plans	100.0	0.4	9.2	18.1	33.3	31.8	5.1	2.2
Deductions for Social Security	100.0	3.5	18.6	27.9	28.6	15.8	4.1	1.4
PERSONAL TAXES	**100.0**	**1.2**	**12.8**	**22.1**	**34.6**	**20.7**	**4.5**	**4.1**
Federal income taxes	100.0	1.0	12.1	21.2	35.9	21.4	4.3	4.0
State and local income taxes	100.0	2.0	16.7	26.2	32.6	18.6	2.4	1.4
Other taxes	100.0	0.4	9.0	18.7	28.4	20.3	11.8	11.4

Note: Numbers may not add to total because of rounding. "–" means sample is too small to make a reliable estimate.
Source: Calculations by New Strategist based on the 2004 Consumer Expenditure Survey

Table 4.5 Financial: Average spending by income, 2004

(average annual spending on financial products and services, cash contributions, and miscellaneous items, by before-tax income of consumer units (CU), 2004)

	total consumer units	under $20,000	$20,000–$39,999	$40,000–$49,999	$50,000–$69,999	$70,000–$79,999	$80,000–$99,999	$100,000 or more
Number of consumer units (in 000s)	116,282	28,898	27,297	11,374	18,069	6,461	9,246	14,937
Average number of persons per CU	2.5	1.8	2.3	2.6	2.8	3.0	3.1	3.2
Average before-tax income of CU	$54,453.00	$10,923.47	$29,561.76	$44,645.00	$59,259.00	$74,437.00	$88,811.00	$155,901.00
Average spending of CU, total	43,394.87	18,865.37	30,400.94	38,204.07	47,750.13	55,012.03	65,446.39	93,525.67
FINANCIAL PRODUCTS AND SERVICES	**690.02**	**333.88**	**511.90**	**735.35**	**748.19**	**808.51**	**893.86**	**1,410.70**
Miscellaneous fees	4.57	3.12	–	6.69	6.63	2.60	6.61	3.72
Lottery and gambling losses	66.54	27.65	40.03	119.60	60.96	129.76	38.36	134.62
Legal fees	127.50	57.47	119.69	72.78	136.70	83.06	154.09	310.57
Funeral expenses	65.78	67.28	73.01	111.13	39.10	77.17	43.09	56.55
Safe deposit box rental	3.22	1.40	2.65	2.85	2.84	3.14	5.32	7.30
Checking accounts, other bank service charges	18.70	11.04	13.52	16.38	23.47	23.45	28.45	30.89
Cemetery lots, vaults, and maintenance fees	13.48	6.96	15.66	20.73	12.42	10.69	12.74	19.56
Accounting fees	51.22	21.04	30.51	40.97	62.58	49.90	71.02	129.83
Miscellaneous personal services	36.79	28.93	20.32	21.02	52.72	20.85	34.02	84.35
Finance charges, except mortgage and vehicles	158.18	70.57	112.97	184.05	199.34	215.18	261.72	252.08
Occupational expenses	43.10	7.96	16.53	44.96	60.79	62.01	76.27	108.11
Expenses for other properties	91.63	29.53	55.22	85.77	80.79	119.11	145.03	250.96
Credit card memberships	2.41	0.63	1.79	1.95	1.96	2.66	3.76	6.90
Shopping club membership fees	5.72	1.28	3.58	6.03	7.50	6.90	10.99	12.04
CASH CONTRIBUTIONS	**1,408.04**	**459.28**	**788.97**	**1,283.72**	**1,359.84**	**1,550.72**	**2,052.40**	**4,067.30**
Support for college students	82.49	9.12	23.00	42.19	64.26	96.14	115.68	359.45
Alimony expenditures	47.29	2.09	5.39	34.22	32.54	24.66	107.47	213.53
Child support expenditures	165.10	31.94	102.98	215.20	190.77	266.57	217.41	390.74
Gifts to non–CU members of stocks, bonds, and mutual funds	24.97	14.90	8.09	70.78	31.24	15.60	19.40	44.92
Cash contributions to charities and other organizations	157.51	26.93	61.09	63.00	105.38	156.40	163.40	718.20
Cash contributions to church, religious organizations	565.11	196.49	353.51	466.91	641.64	695.64	919.20	1,371.55
Cash contributions to educational institutions	46.06	4.52	8.75	11.41	9.10	29.73	42.43	274.98
Cash contributions to political organizations	16.58	1.56	5.53	5.63	10.07	18.15	24.21	76.62
Other cash gifts	302.93	175.06	220.64	374.38	274.84	247.82	443.21	617.30
PERSONAL INSURANCE AND PENSIONS	**4,823.20**	**545.99**	**2,122.24**	**3,655.87**	**5,430.10**	**7,099.50**	**8,870.51**	**14,699.01**
Life and other personal insurance	**390.34**	**121.28**	**224.77**	**315.97**	**416.85**	**429.93**	**645.04**	**1,063.25**
Life, endowment, annuity, other personal insurance	378.18	117.61	216.69	310.05	401.73	418.40	625.13	1,030.55
Other nonhealth insurance	12.16	3.67	8.09	5.92	15.13	11.53	19.91	32.71
Pensions and Social Security	**4,432.85**	**424.71**	**1,897.48**	**3,339.90**	**5,013.24**	**6,669.57**	**8,225.47**	**13,635.76**
Deductions for government retirement	78.45	1.62	19.29	66.57	87.94	125.34	152.71	266.50
Deductions for railroad retirement	2.67	–	0.89	–	3.84	5.46	8.24	7.90
Deductions for private pensions	518.59	8.38	88.70	218.83	511.97	810.70	1,049.12	2,072.77
Nonpayroll deposit to retirement plans	400.54	35.87	105.97	172.41	318.52	387.05	661.56	1,761.58
Deductions for Social Security	3,432.61	378.85	1,683.08	2,882.09	4,090.98	5,341.03	6,353.84	9,527.00
PERSONAL TAXES	**2,165.85**	**–64.74**	**503.54**	**955.32**	**2,136.80**	**2,200.83**	**3,927.08**	**9,370.73**
Federal income taxes	1,518.95	–118.73	243.77	523.26	1,483.97	1,463.70	2,718.65	7,099.51
State and local income taxes	472.12	9.16	134.41	275.34	446.57	551.85	901.78	1,865.26
Other taxes	174.78	44.84	125.37	156.72	206.27	185.28	306.64	405.95

Note: Subcategories may not add to total because some are not shown. "–" means sample is too small to make a reliable estimate.
Source: Bureau of Labor Statistics, unpublished tables from the 2004 Consumer Expenditure Survey; calculations by New Strategist

Table 4.6 Financial: Indexed spending by income, 2004

(indexed average annual spending of consumer units (CU) on financial products and services, cash contributions, and miscellaneous items, by before-tax income of consumer unit, 2004; index definition: an index of 100 is the average for all consumer units; an index of 132 means that spending by consumer units in that group is 32 percent above the average for all consumer units; an index of 68 indicates spending that is 32 percent below the average for all consumer units)

	total consumer units	under $20,000	$20,000– $39,999	$40,000– $49,999	$50,000– $69,999	$70,000– $79,999	$80,000– $99,999	$100,000 or more
Average spending of CU, total	$43,395	$18,865	$30,401	$38,204	$47,750	$55,012	$65,446	$93,526
Average spending of CU, index	**100**	**43**	**70**	**88**	**110**	**127**	**151**	**216**
FINANCIAL PRODUCTS AND SERVICES	**100**	**48**	**74**	**107**	**108**	**117**	**130**	**204**
Miscellaneous fees	100	68	–	146	145	57	145	81
Lottery and gambling losses	100	42	60	180	92	195	58	202
Legal fees	100	45	94	57	107	65	121	244
Funeral expenses	100	102	111	169	59	117	66	86
Safe deposit box rental	100	44	82	89	88	98	165	227
Checking accounts, other bank service charges	100	59	72	88	126	125	152	165
Cemetery lots, vaults, and maintenance fees	100	52	116	154	92	79	95	145
Accounting fees	100	41	60	80	122	97	139	253
Miscellaneous personal services	100	79	55	57	143	57	92	229
Finance charges, except mortgage and vehicles	100	45	71	116	126	136	165	159
Occupational expenses	100	18	38	104	141	144	177	251
Expenses for other properties	100	32	60	94	88	130	158	274
Credit card memberships	100	26	74	81	81	110	156	286
Shopping club membership fees	100	22	63	105	131	121	192	210
CASH CONTRIBUTIONS	**100**	**33**	**56**	**91**	**97**	**110**	**146**	**289**
Support for college students	100	11	28	51	78	117	140	436
Alimony expenditures	100	4	11	72	69	52	227	452
Child support expenditures	100	19	62	130	116	161	132	237
Gifts to non–CU members of stocks, bonds, and mutual funds	100	60	32	283	125	62	78	180
Cash contributions to charities and other organizations	100	17	39	40	67	99	104	456
Cash contributions to church, religious organizations	100	35	63	83	114	123	163	243
Cash contributions to educational institutions	100	10	19	25	20	65	92	597
Cash contributions to political organizations	100	9	33	34	61	109	146	462
Other cash gifts	100	58	73	124	91	82	146	204
PERSONAL INSURANCE AND PENSIONS	**100**	**11**	**44**	**76**	**113**	**147**	**184**	**305**
Life and other personal insurance	**100**	**31**	**58**	**81**	**107**	**110**	**165**	**272**
Life, endowment, annuity, other personal insurance	100	31	57	82	106	111	165	273
Other nonhealth insurance	100	30	66	49	124	95	164	269
Pensions and Social Security	**100**	**10**	**43**	**75**	**113**	**150**	**186**	**308**
Deductions for government retirement	100	2	25	85	112	160	195	340
Deductions for railroad retirement	100	–	33	–	144	204	309	296
Deductions for private pensions	100	2	17	42	99	156	202	400
Nonpayroll deposit to retirement plans	100	9	26	43	80	97	165	440
Deductions for Social Security	100	11	49	84	119	156	185	278
PERSONAL TAXES	**100**	**–**	**23**	**44**	**99**	**102**	**181**	**433**
Federal income taxes	100	–	16	34	98	96	179	467
State and local income taxes	100	2	28	58	95	117	191	395
Other taxes	100	26	72	90	118	106	175	232

Note: "–" means sample is too small to make a reliable estimate.
Source: Calculations by New Strategist based on the 2004 Consumer Expenditure Survey

Table 4.7 Financial: Total spending by income, 2004

(total annual spending on financial products and services, cash contributions, and miscellaneous items, by before-tax income group of consumer units (CU), 2004; consumer units and dollars in thousands)

	total consumer units	under $20,000	$20,000– $39,999	$40,000– $49,999	$50,000– $69,999	$70,000– $79,999	$80,000– $99,999	$100,000 or more
Number of consumer units	116,282	28,898	27,297	11,374	18,069	6,461	9,246	14,937
Total spending of all CUs	$5,046,042,273	$545,171,431	$829,854,379	$434,533,092	$862,797,099	$355,432,726	$605,117,322	$1,396,992,933
FINANCIAL PRODUCTS AND SERVICES	80,236,906	9,648,517	13,973,416	8,363,871	13,519,045	5,223,783	8,264,630	21,071,626
Miscellaneous fees	531,409	90,278	–	76,092	119,797	16,799	61,116	55,566
Lottery and gambling losses	7,737,404	798,996	1,092,700	1,360,330	1,101,486	838,379	354,677	2,010,819
Legal fees	14,825,955	1,660,746	3,267,273	827,800	2,470,032	536,651	1,424,716	4,638,984
Funeral expenses	7,649,030	1,944,377	1,992,986	1,263,993	706,498	498,595	398,410	844,687
Safe deposit box rental	374,428	40,534	72,206	32,416	51,316	20,288	49,189	109,040
Checking accounts, other bank service charges	2,174,473	318,925	368,991	186,306	424,079	151,510	263,049	461,404
Cemetery lots, vaults, and maintenance fees	1,567,481	201,028	427,495	235,783	224,417	69,068	117,794	292,168
Accounting fees	5,955,964	607,943	832,959	465,993	1,130,758	322,404	656,651	1,939,271
Miscellaneous personal services	4,278,015	836,044	554,553	239,081	952,598	134,712	314,549	1,259,936
Finance charges, except mortgage and vehicles	18,393,487	2,039,251	3,083,827	2,093,385	3,601,874	1,390,278	2,419,863	3,765,319
Occupational expenses	5,011,754	229,953	451,129	511,375	1,098,415	400,647	705,192	1,614,839
Expenses for other properties	10,654,920	853,389	1,507,281	975,548	1,459,795	769,570	1,340,947	3,748,590
Credit card memberships	280,240	18,174	48,926	22,179	35,415	17,186	34,765	103,065
Shopping club membership fees	665,133	36,884	97,645	68,585	135,518	44,581	101,614	179,841
CASH CONTRIBUTIONS	163,729,707	13,272,299	21,536,446	14,601,031	24,570,949	10,019,202	18,976,490	60,753,260
Support for college students	9,592,102	263,659	627,701	479,869	1,161,114	621,161	1,069,577	5,369,105
Alimony expenditures	5,498,976	60,264	147,026	389,218	587,965	159,328	993,668	3,189,498
Child support expenditures	19,198,158	923,110	2,811,014	2,447,685	3,447,023	1,722,309	2,010,173	5,836,483
Gifts to non–CU members of stocks, bonds, and mutual funds	2,903,562	430,531	220,726	805,052	564,476	100,792	179,372	670,970
Cash contributions to charities and other organizations	18,315,578	778,245	1,667,542	716,562	1,904,111	1,010,500	1,510,796	10,727,753
Cash contributions to church, religious organizations	65,712,121	5,678,120	9,649,870	5,310,634	11,593,793	4,494,530	8,498,923	20,486,842
Cash contributions to educational institutions	5,355,949	130,759	238,968	129,777	164,428	192,086	392,308	4,107,376
Cash contributions to political organizations	1,927,956	45,013	150,921	64,036	181,955	117,267	223,846	1,144,473
Other cash gifts	35,225,306	5,058,849	6,022,678	4,258,198	4,966,084	1,601,165	4,097,920	9,220,610
PERSONAL INSURANCE AND PENSIONS	560,851,342	15,777,998	57,930,852	41,581,865	98,116,477	45,869,870	82,016,735	219,559,112
Life and other personal insurance	45,389,516	3,504,745	6,135,594	3,593,843	7,532,063	2,777,778	5,964,040	15,881,765
Life, endowment, annuity, other personal insurance	43,975,527	3,398,671	5,914,880	3,526,509	7,258,859	2,703,282	5,779,952	15,393,325
Other nonhealth insurance	1,413,989	106,082	220,714	67,334	273,384	74,495	184,088	488,589
Pensions and Social Security	515,460,664	12,273,280	51,795,390	37,988,023	90,584,234	43,092,092	76,052,696	203,677,347
Deductions for government retirement	9,122,323	46,778	526,591	757,167	1,588,988	809,822	1,411,957	3,980,711
Deductions for railroad retirement	310,473	–	24,294	–	69,385	35,277	76,187	118,002
Deductions for private pensions	60,302,682	242,299	2,421,362	2,488,972	9,250,786	5,237,933	9,700,164	30,960,965
Nonpayroll deposit to retirement plans	46,575,592	1,036,509	2,892,584	1,960,991	5,755,338	2,500,730	6,116,784	26,312,720
Deductions for Social Security	399,150,756	10,947,909	45,943,030	32,780,892	73,919,918	34,508,395	58,747,605	142,304,799
PERSONAL TAXES	251,849,370	–1,870,789	13,745,198	10,865,810	38,609,839	14,219,563	36,309,782	139,970,594
Federal income taxes	176,626,544	–3,431,142	6,654,309	5,951,559	26,813,854	9,456,966	25,136,638	106,045,381
State and local income taxes	54,899,058	264,646	3,668,915	3,131,717	8,069,073	3,565,503	8,337,858	27,861,389
Other taxes	20,323,768	1,295,707	3,422,116	1,782,533	3,727,093	1,197,094	2,835,193	6,063,675

Note: Numbers may not add to total because of rounding and missing subcategories. "–" means sample is too small to make a reliable estimate.
Source: Calculations by New Strategist based on the 2004 Consumer Expenditure Survey

Table 4.8 Financial: Market shares by income, 2004

(percentage of total annual spending on financial products and services, cash contributions, and miscellaneous items accounted for by before-tax income group of consumer units, 2004)

	total consumer units	under $20,000	$20,000–$39,999	$40,000–$49,999	$50,000–$69,999	$70,000–$79,999	$80,000–$99,999	$100,000 or more
Share of total consumer units	100.0%	24.9%	23.5%	9.8%	15.5%	5.6%	8.0%	12.8%
Share of total before-tax income	100.0	5.0	12.7	8.0	16.9	7.6	13.0	36.8
Share of total spending	100.0	10.8	16.4	8.6	17.1	7.0	12.0	27.7
FINANCIAL PRODUCTS AND SERVICES	100.0	12.0	17.4	10.4	16.8	6.5	10.3	26.3
Miscellaneous fees	100.0	17.0	–	14.3	22.5	3.2	11.5	10.5
Lottery and gambling losses	100.0	10.3	14.1	17.6	14.2	10.8	4.6	26.0
Legal fees	100.0	11.2	22.0	5.6	16.7	3.6	9.6	31.3
Funeral expenses	100.0	25.4	26.1	16.5	9.2	6.5	5.2	11.0
Safe deposit box rental	100.0	10.8	19.3	8.7	13.7	5.4	13.1	29.1
Checking accounts, other bank service charges	100.0	14.7	17.0	8.6	19.5	7.0	12.1	21.2
Cemetery lots, vaults, and maintenance fees	100.0	12.8	27.3	15.0	14.3	4.4	7.5	18.6
Accounting fees	100.0	10.2	14.0	7.8	19.0	5.4	11.0	32.6
Miscellaneous personal services	100.0	19.5	13.0	5.6	22.3	3.1	7.4	29.5
Finance charges, except mortgage and vehicles	100.0	11.1	16.8	11.4	19.6	7.6	13.2	20.5
Occupational expenses	100.0	4.6	9.0	10.2	21.9	8.0	14.1	32.2
Expenses for other properties	100.0	8.0	14.1	9.2	13.7	7.2	12.6	35.2
Credit card memberships	100.0	6.5	17.5	7.9	12.6	6.1	12.4	36.8
Shopping club membership fees	100.0	5.5	14.7	10.3	20.4	6.7	15.3	27.0
CASH CONTRIBUTIONS	100.0	8.1	13.2	8.9	15.0	6.1	11.6	37.1
Support for college students	100.0	2.7	6.5	5.0	12.1	6.5	11.2	56.0
Alimony expenditures	100.0	1.1	2.7	7.1	10.7	2.9	18.1	58.0
Child support expenditures	100.0	4.8	14.6	12.7	18.0	9.0	10.5	30.4
Gifts to non–CU members of stocks, bonds, and mutual funds	100.0	14.8	7.6	27.7	19.4	3.5	6.2	23.1
Cash contributions to charities and other organizations	100.0	4.2	9.1	3.9	10.4	5.5	8.2	58.6
Cash contributions to church, religious organizations	100.0	8.6	14.7	8.1	17.6	6.8	12.9	31.2
Cash contributions to educational institutions	100.0	2.4	4.5	2.4	3.1	3.6	7.3	76.7
Cash contributions to political organizations	100.0	2.3	7.8	3.3	9.4	6.1	11.6	59.4
Other cash gifts	100.0	14.4	17.1	12.1	14.1	4.5	11.6	26.2
PERSONAL INSURANCE AND PENSIONS	100.0	2.8	10.3	7.4	17.5	8.2	14.6	39.1
Life and other personal insurance	100.0	7.7	13.5	7.9	16.6	6.1	13.1	35.0
Life, endowment, annuity, other personal insurance	100.0	7.7	13.5	8.0	16.5	6.1	13.1	35.0
Other nonhealth insurance	100.0	7.5	15.6	4.8	19.3	5.3	13.0	34.6
Pensions and Social Security	100.0	2.4	10.0	7.4	17.6	8.4	14.8	39.5
Deductions for government retirement	100.0	0.5	5.8	8.3	17.4	8.9	15.5	43.6
Deductions for railroad retirement	100.0	–	7.8	–	22.3	11.4	24.5	38.0
Deductions for private pensions	100.0	0.4	4.0	4.1	15.3	8.7	16.1	51.3
Nonpayroll deposit to retirement plans	100.0	2.2	6.2	4.2	12.4	5.4	13.1	56.5
Deductions for Social Security	100.0	2.7	11.5	8.2	18.5	8.6	14.7	35.7
PERSONAL TAXES	100.0	–	5.5	4.3	15.3	5.6	14.4	55.6
Federal income taxes	100.0	–	3.8	3.4	15.2	5.4	14.2	60.0
State and local income taxes	100.0	0.5	6.7	5.7	14.7	6.5	15.2	50.8
Other taxes	100.0	6.4	16.8	8.8	18.3	5.9	14.0	29.8

Note: Numbers may not add to total because of rounding. "–" means sample is too small to make a reliable estimate.
Source: Calculations by New Strategist based on the 2004 Consumer Expenditure Survey

Table 4.9 Financial: Average spending by high-income consumer units, 2004

(average annual spending on financial products and services, cash contributions, and miscellaneous items, by before-tax income of high-income consumer units (CU), 2004)

	total consumer units	$100,000 or more	$100,000–$119,999	$120,000–$149,999	$150,000 or more
Number of consumer units (in 000s)	116,282	14,937	5,625	4,245	5,067
Average number of persons per CU	2.5	3.2	3.1	3.3	3.2
Average before-tax income of CU	$54,453.00	$155,901.00	$108,751.00	$132,292.00	$228,021.00
Average spending of CU, total	43,394.87	93,525.67	75,213.14	87,298.57	119,448.79
FINANCIAL PRODUCTS AND SERVICES	**690.02**	**1,410.70**	**1,131.62**	**1,140.05**	**1,968.11**
Miscellaneous fees	4.57	3.72	7.30	1.94	1.12
Lottery and gambling losses	66.54	134.62	139.32	38.58	225.91
Legal fees	127.50	310.57	93.98	194.96	647.86
Funeral expenses	65.78	56.55	82.84	69.96	16.12
Safe deposit box rental	3.22	7.30	6.46	7.37	8.16
Checking accounts, other bank service charges	18.70	30.89	27.47	30.70	34.85
Cemetery lots, vaults, and maintenance fees	13.48	19.56	7.78	46.70	9.89
Accounting fees	51.22	129.83	59.84	116.67	218.55
Miscellaneous personal services	36.79	84.35	125.57	27.16	91.47
Finance charges, except mortgage and vehicles	158.18	252.08	296.76	258.42	197.18
Occupational expenses	43.10	108.11	105.74	91.19	124.91
Expenses for other properties	91.63	250.96	157.62	238.01	365.42
Credit card memberships	2.41	6.90	6.23	5.76	8.60
Shopping club membership fees	5.72	12.04	11.38	12.60	12.30
CASH CONTRIBUTIONS	**1,408.04**	**4,067.30**	**2,445.21**	**2,672.44**	**7,036.51**
Support for college students	82.49	359.45	160.86	120.42	780.15
Alimony expenditures	47.29	213.53	20.76	81.15	538.43
Child support expenditures	165.10	390.74	294.29	314.19	561.94
Gifts to non–CU members of stocks, bonds, and mutual funds	24.97	44.92	54.01	22.95	53.25
Cash contributions to charities and other organizations	157.51	718.20	258.90	330.10	1,553.19
Cash contributions to church, religious organizations	565.11	1,371.55	1,130.03	1,090.94	1,874.75
Cash contributions to educational institutions	46.06	274.98	62.05	103.97	654.62
Cash contributions to political organizations	16.58	76.62	49.87	43.87	133.76
Other cash gifts	302.93	617.30	414.44	564.85	886.44
PERSONAL INSURANCE AND PENSIONS	**4,823.20**	**14,699.01**	**11,283.53**	**14,177.86**	**18,927.05**
Life and other personal insurance	**390.34**	**1,063.25**	**785.38**	**904.07**	**1,505.07**
Life, endowment, annuity, other personal insurance	378.18	1,030.55	768.89	871.50	1,454.25
Other nonhealth insurance	12.16	32.71	16.49	32.57	50.82
Pensions and Social Security	**4,432.85**	**13,635.76**	**10,498.15**	**13,273.79**	**17,421.99**
Deductions for government retirement	78.45	266.50	258.04	324.35	227.43
Deductions for railroad retirement	2.67	7.90	9.27	1.34	11.88
Deductions for private pensions	518.59	2,072.77	1,431.69	2,090.86	2,769.27
Nonpayroll deposit to retirement plans	400.54	1,761.58	1,045.92	1,842.60	2,488.14
Deductions for Social Security	3,432.61	9,527.00	7,753.23	9,014.65	11,925.26
PERSONAL TAXES	**2,165.85**	**9,370.73**	**4,949.80**	**8,018.50**	**15,411.13**
Federal income taxes	1,518.95	7,099.51	3,559.01	6,021.64	11,932.73
State and local income taxes	472.12	1,865.26	1,071.85	1,649.86	2,926.47
Other taxes	174.78	405.95	318.94	347.00	551.93

Note: Subcategories may not add to total because some are not shown.
Source: Bureau of Labor Statistics, unpublished tables from the 2004 Consumer Expenditure Survey; calculations by New Strategist

Table 4.10 Financial: Indexed spending by high-income consumer units, 2004

(indexed average annual spending of high-income consumer units (CU) on financial products and services, cash contributions, and miscellaneous items, by before-tax income of consumer unit, 2004; index definition: an index of 100 is the average for all consumer units; an index of 132 means that spending by consumer units in that group is 32 percent above the average for all consumer units; an index of 68 indicates spending that is 32 percent below the average for all consumer units)

	total consumer units	$100,000 or more	$100,000– $119,999	$120,000– $149,999	$150,000 or more
Average spending of CU, total	$43,395	$93,526	$75,213	$87,299	$119,449
Average spending of CU, index	100	216	173	201	275
FINANCIAL PRODUCTS AND SERVICES	100	204	164	165	285
Miscellaneous fees	100	81	160	42	25
Lottery and gambling losses	100	202	209	58	340
Legal fees	100	244	74	153	508
Funeral expenses	100	86	126	106	25
Safe deposit box rental	100	227	201	229	253
Checking accounts, other bank service charges	100	165	147	164	186
Cemetery lots, vaults, and maintenance fees	100	145	58	346	73
Accounting fees	100	253	117	228	427
Miscellaneous personal services	100	229	341	74	249
Finance charges, except mortgage and vehicles	100	159	188	163	125
Occupational expenses	100	251	245	212	290
Expenses for other properties	100	274	172	260	399
Credit card memberships	100	286	259	239	357
Shopping club membership fees	100	210	199	220	215
CASH CONTRIBUTIONS	100	289	174	190	500
Support for college students	100	436	195	146	946
Alimony expenditures	100	452	44	172	1139
Child support expenditures	100	237	178	190	340
Gifts to non–CU members of stocks, bonds, and mutual funds	100	180	216	92	213
Cash contributions to charities and other organizations	100	456	164	210	986
Cash contributions to church, religious organizations	100	243	200	193	332
Cash contributions to educational institutions	100	597	135	226	1421
Cash contributions to political organizations	100	462	301	265	807
Other cash gifts	100	204	137	186	293
PERSONAL INSURANCE AND PENSIONS	100	305	234	294	392
Life and other personal insurance	100	272	201	232	386
Life, endowment, annuity, other personal insurance	100	273	203	230	385
Other nonhealth insurance	100	269	136	268	418
Pensions and Social Security	100	308	237	299	393
Deductions for government retirement	100	340	329	413	290
Deductions for railroad retirement	100	296	347	50	445
Deductions for private pensions	100	400	276	403	534
Nonpayroll deposit to retirement plans	100	440	261	460	621
Deductions for Social Security	100	278	226	263	347
PERSONAL TAXES	100	433	229	370	712
Federal income taxes	100	467	234	396	786
State and local income taxes	100	395	227	349	620
Other taxes	100	232	182	199	316

Source: Calculations by New Strategist based on the 2004 Consumer Expenditure Survey

Table 4.11 Financial: Total spending by high-income consumer units, 2004

(total annual spending on financial products and services, cash contributions, and miscellaneous items, by before-tax income group of high-income consumer units (CU), 2004; consumer units and dollars in thousands)

	total consumer units	$100,000 or more	$100,000–$119,999	$120,000–$149,999	$150,000 or more
Number of consumer units	116,282	14,937	5,625	4,245	5,067
Total spending of all CUs	$5,046,042,273	$1,396,992,933	$423,073,913	$370,582,430	$605,247,019
FINANCIAL PRODUCTS AND SERVICES	**80,236,906**	**21,071,626**	**6,365,363**	**4,839,512**	**9,972,413**
Miscellaneous fees	531,409	55,566	41,063	8,235	5,675
Lottery and gambling losses	7,737,404	2,010,819	783,675	163,772	1,144,686
Legal fees	14,825,955	4,638,984	528,638	827,605	3,282,707
Funeral expenses	7,649,030	844,687	465,975	296,980	81,680
Safe deposit box rental	374,428	109,040	36,338	31,286	41,347
Checking accounts, other bank service charges	2,174,473	461,404	154,519	130,322	176,585
Cemetery lots, vaults, and maintenance fees	1,567,481	292,168	43,763	198,242	50,113
Accounting fees	5,955,964	1,939,271	336,600	495,264	1,107,393
Miscellaneous personal services	4,278,015	1,259,936	706,331	115,294	463,478
Finance charges, except mortgage and vehicles	18,393,487	3,765,319	1,669,275	1,096,993	999,111
Occupational expenses	5,011,754	1,614,839	594,788	387,102	632,919
Expenses for other properties	10,654,920	3,748,590	886,613	1,010,352	1,851,583
Credit card memberships	280,240	103,065	35,044	24,451	43,576
Shopping club membership fees	665,133	179,841	64,013	53,487	62,324
CASH CONTRIBUTIONS	**163,729,707**	**60,753,260**	**13,754,306**	**11,344,508**	**35,653,996**
Support for college students	9,592,102	5,369,105	904,838	511,183	3,953,020
Alimony expenditures	5,498,976	3,189,498	116,775	344,482	2,728,225
Child support expenditures	19,198,158	5,836,483	1,655,381	1,333,737	2,847,350
Gifts to non–CU members of stocks, bonds, and mutual funds	2,903,562	670,970	303,806	97,423	269,818
Cash contributions to charities and other organizations	18,315,578	10,727,753	1,456,313	1,401,275	7,870,014
Cash contributions to church, religious organizations	65,712,121	20,486,842	6,356,419	4,631,040	9,499,358
Cash contributions to educational institutions	5,355,949	4,107,376	349,031	441,353	3,316,960
Cash contributions to political organizations	1,927,956	1,144,473	280,519	186,228	677,762
Other cash gifts	35,225,306	9,220,610	2,331,225	2,397,788	4,491,591
PERSONAL INSURANCE AND PENSIONS	**560,851,342**	**219,559,112**	**63,469,856**	**60,185,016**	**95,903,362**
Life and other personal insurance	**45,389,516**	**15,881,765**	**4,417,763**	**3,837,777**	**7,626,190**
Life, endowment, annuity, other personal insurance	43,975,527	15,393,325	4,325,006	3,699,518	7,368,685
Other nonhealth insurance	1,413,989	488,589	92,756	138,260	257,505
Pensions and Social Security	**515,460,664**	**203,677,347**	**59,052,094**	**56,347,239**	**88,277,223**
Deductions for government retirement	9,122,323	3,980,711	1,451,475	1,376,866	1,152,388
Deductions for railroad retirement	310,473	118,002	52,144	5,688	60,196
Deductions for private pensions	60,302,682	30,960,965	8,053,256	8,875,701	14,031,891
Nonpayroll deposit to retirement plans	46,575,592	26,312,720	5,883,300	7,821,837	12,607,405
Deductions for Social Security	399,150,756	142,304,799	43,611,919	38,267,189	60,425,292
PERSONAL TAXES	**251,849,370**	**139,970,594**	**27,842,625**	**34,038,533**	**78,088,196**
Federal income taxes	176,626,544	106,045,381	20,019,431	25,561,862	60,463,143
State and local income taxes	54,899,058	27,861,389	6,029,156	7,003,656	14,828,423
Other taxes	20,323,768	6,063,675	1,794,038	1,473,015	2,796,629

Note: Numbers may not add to total because of rounding and missing subcategories.
Source: Calculations by New Strategist based on the 2004 Consumer Expenditure Survey

Table 4.12 Financial: Market shares by high-income consumer units, 2004

(percentage of total annual spending on financial products and services, cash contributions, and miscellaneous items accounted for by before-tax income group of high-income consumer units, 2004)

	total consumer units	$100,000 or more	$100,000– $119,999	$120,000– $149,999	$150,000 or more
Share of total consumer units	100.0%	12.8%	4.8%	3.7%	4.4%
Share of total before-tax income	100.0	36.8	9.7	8.9	18.2
Share of total spending	100.0	27.7	8.4	7.3	12.0
FINANCIAL PRODUCTS AND SERVICES	100.0	26.3	7.9	6.0	12.4
Miscellaneous fees	100.0	10.5	7.7	1.5	1.1
Lottery and gambling losses	100.0	26.0	10.1	2.1	14.8
Legal fees	100.0	31.3	3.6	5.6	22.1
Funeral expenses	100.0	11.0	6.1	3.9	1.1
Safe deposit box rental	100.0	29.1	9.7	8.4	11.0
Checking accounts, other bank service charges	100.0	21.2	7.1	6.0	8.1
Cemetery lots, vaults, and maintenance fees	100.0	18.6	2.8	12.6	3.2
Accounting fees	100.0	32.6	5.7	8.3	18.6
Miscellaneous personal services	100.0	29.5	16.5	2.7	10.8
Finance charges, except mortgage and vehicles	100.0	20.5	9.1	6.0	5.4
Occupational expenses	100.0	32.2	11.9	7.7	12.6
Expenses for other properties	100.0	35.2	8.3	9.5	17.4
Credit card memberships	100.0	36.8	12.5	8.7	15.5
Shopping club membership fees	100.0	27.0	9.6	8.0	9.4
CASH CONTRIBUTIONS	100.0	37.1	8.4	6.9	21.8
Support for college students	100.0	56.0	9.4	5.3	41.2
Alimony expenditures	100.0	58.0	2.1	6.3	49.6
Child support expenditures	100.0	30.4	8.6	6.9	14.8
Gifts to non–CU members of stocks, bonds, and mutual funds	100.0	23.1	10.5	3.4	9.3
Cash contributions to charities and other organizations	100.0	58.6	8.0	7.7	43.0
Cash contributions to church, religious organizations	100.0	31.2	9.7	7.0	14.5
Cash contributions to educational institutions	100.0	76.7	6.5	8.2	61.9
Cash contributions to political organizations	100.0	59.4	14.6	9.7	35.2
Other cash gifts	100.0	26.2	6.6	6.8	12.8
PERSONAL INSURANCE AND PENSIONS	100.0	39.1	11.3	10.7	17.1
Life and other personal insurance	100.0	35.0	9.7	8.5	16.8
Life, endowment, annuity, other personal insurance	100.0	35.0	9.8	8.4	16.8
Other nonhealth insurance	100.0	34.6	6.6	9.8	18.2
Pensions and Social Security	100.0	39.5	11.5	10.9	17.1
Deductions for government retirement	100.0	43.6	15.9	15.1	12.6
Deductions for railroad retirement	100.0	38.0	16.8	1.8	19.4
Deductions for private pensions	100.0	51.3	13.4	14.7	23.3
Nonpayroll deposit to retirement plans	100.0	56.5	12.6	16.8	27.1
Deductions for Social Security	100.0	35.7	10.9	9.6	15.1
PERSONAL TAXES	100.0	55.6	11.1	13.5	31.0
Federal income taxes	100.0	60.0	11.3	14.5	34.2
State and local income taxes	100.0	50.8	11.0	12.8	27.0
Other taxes	100.0	29.8	8.8	7.2	13.8

Note: Numbers may not add to total because of rounding.
Source: Calculations by New Strategist based on the 2004 Consumer Expenditure Survey

Table 4.13 Financial: Average spending by household type, 2004

(average annual spending of consumer units (CU) on financial products and services, cash contributions, and miscellaneous items, by type of consumer unit, 2004)

	total married couples	married couples, no children	married couples with children				single parent, at least one child <18	single person
			total	oldest child under 6	oldest child 6 to 17	oldest child 18 or older		
Number of consumer units (in 000s)	59,797	25,585	29,279	5,604	15,376	8,300	6,892	33,686
Average number of persons per CU	3.2	2.0	3.9	3.5	4.1	3.9	2.9	1.0
Average before-tax income of CU	$73,001.00	$64,434.00	$79,764.00	$75,293.00	$78,508.00	$85,109.00	$31,055.00	$28,143.00
Average spending of CU, total	55,606.57	49,690.43	60,660.88	55,981.04	60,577.88	64,161.69	32,824.46	25,423.35
FINANCIAL PRODUCTS AND SERVICES	**799.62**	**790.47**	**756.66**	**687.21**	**649.83**	**1,011.06**	**642.59**	**516.92**
Miscellaneous fees	5.27	5.31	5.82	5.75	1.44	15.01	4.63	1.44
Lottery and gambling losses	67.89	81.72	58.84	13.94	51.42	110.35	13.43	77.61
Legal fees	128.36	103.02	123.12	64.15	133.41	143.89	337.21	96.00
Funeral expenses	73.99	111.08	31.28	26.27	12.48	69.48	11.47	51.10
Safe deposit box rental	4.21	5.11	3.52	1.91	3.51	4.64	1.42	2.53
Checking accounts, other bank service charges	21.20	16.02	25.02	28.94	24.65	23.05	19.30	12.60
Cemetery lots, vaults, and maintenance fees	16.79	18.84	6.18	1.27	0.89	19.28	5.52	10.51
Accounting fees	62.18	74.13	53.56	58.43	41.94	71.80	32.47	40.43
Miscellaneous personal services	35.78	14.21	51.67	99.39	20.90	77.57	65.92	26.78
Finance charges, except mortgage and vehicles	185.48	159.35	200.10	158.43	214.03	202.43	100.20	118.41
Occupational expenses	60.33	49.74	70.86	73.11	62.24	85.33	26.08	21.49
Expenses for other properties	125.78	139.14	114.78	146.11	72.05	172.80	21.04	53.64
Credit card memberships	2.95	3.30	2.72	2.46	3.12	2.14	0.82	1.52
Shopping club membership fees	8.17	8.36	7.98	7.05	7.75	9.03	3.08	2.29
CASH CONTRIBUTIONS	**1,836.35**	**2,315.97**	**1,480.73**	**1,188.67**	**1,517.25**	**1,610.27**	**586.92**	**1,027.17**
Support for college students	128.25	162.61	104.30	10.66	116.32	145.27	47.62	37.60
Alimony expenditures	23.23	39.66	12.79	33.66	12.08	–	18.34	93.19
Child support expenditures	141.20	114.50	155.87	191.08	177.91	91.27	65.80	183.29
Gifts to non–CU members of stocks, bonds, and mutual funds	27.73	42.37	17.52	43.28	12.57	9.31	56.11	20.56
Cash contributions to charities and other organizations	235.27	376.22	135.31	96.77	147.84	138.10	50.48	78.11
Cash contributions to church, religious organizations	849.78	910.39	808.46	618.00	798.39	955.71	205.88	288.67
Cash contributions to educational institutions	73.26	121.97	38.86	22.74	58.25	13.82	8.70	23.18
Cash contributions to political organizations	24.29	30.83	18.37	10.31	24.32	12.79	4.82	10.26
Other cash gifts	333.34	517.41	189.25	162.17	169.57	244.01	129.17	292.31
PERSONAL INSURANCE AND PENSIONS	**6,722.40**	**5,722.64**	**7,644.67**	**7,068.96**	**7,523.89**	**8,257.13**	**2,647.88**	**2,184.44**
Life and other personal insurance	**594.12**	**603.67**	**569.93**	**389.31**	**543.12**	**741.56**	**204.31**	**145.53**
Life, endowment, annuity, other personal insurance	578.78	586.47	557.33	380.18	531.28	725.20	200.06	135.94
Other nonhealth insurance	15.34	17.20	12.60	9.13	11.83	16.36	4.24	9.59
Pensions and Social Security	**6,128.28**	**5,118.97**	**7,074.74**	**6,679.65**	**6,980.78**	**7,515.57**	**2,443.58**	**2,038.91**
Deductions for government retirement	103.94	119.58	97.02	89.46	105.16	87.04	56.38	40.44
Deductions for railroad retirement	3.62	0.84	6.17	3.75	5.59	8.87	1.26	0.91
Deductions for private pensions	748.90	689.77	853.11	842.78	920.18	735.83	232.37	258.03
Nonpayroll deposit to retirement plans	594.55	705.23	553.47	447.30	479.49	762.22	198.12	186.02
Deductions for Social Security	4,677.27	3,603.56	5,564.98	5,296.36	5,470.36	5,921.62	1,955.44	1,553.51
PERSONAL TAXES	**2,953.49**	**3,325.80**	**2,881.44**	**2,890.71**	**2,737.66**	**3,141.55**	**103.48**	**1,382.64**
Federal income taxes	2,069.35	2,415.57	1,970.04	1,946.78	1,836.47	2,233.19	−194.80	989.79
State and local income taxes	650.45	629.52	712.09	788.09	696.57	689.51	216.51	280.33
Other taxes	233.69	280.72	199.31	155.84	204.62	218.84	81.76	112.53

Note: Average spending figures for total consumer units can be found on Average Spending by Age and Average Spending by Region tables. Subcategories may not add to total because some are not shown. "–" means sample is too small to make a reliable estimate.
Source: Bureau of Labor Statistics, unpublished tables from the 2004 Consumer Expenditure Survey

Table 4.14 Financial: Indexed spending by household type, 2004

(indexed average annual spending of consumer units (CU) on financial products and services, cash contributions, and miscellaneous items, by type of consumer unit, 2004; index definition: an index of 100 is the average for all consumer units; an index of 132 means that spending by consumer units in that group is 32 percent above the average for all consumer units; an index of 68 indicates spending that is 32 percent below the average for all consumer units)

| | total married couples | married couples, no children | married couples with children | | | | single parent, at least one child <18 | single person |
			total	oldest child under 6	oldest child 6 to 17	oldest child 18 or older		
Average spending of CU, total	$55,607	$49,690	$60,661	$55,981	$60,578	$64,162	$32,824	$25,423
Average spending of CU, index	128	115	140	129	140	148	76	59
FINANCIAL PRODUCTS AND SERVICES	**116**	**115**	**110**	**100**	**94**	**147**	**93**	**75**
Miscellaneous fees	115	116	127	126	32	328	101	32
Lottery and gambling losses	102	123	88	21	77	166	20	117
Legal fees	101	81	97	50	105	113	264	75
Funeral expenses	112	169	48	40	19	106	17	78
Safe deposit box rental	131	159	109	59	109	144	44	79
Checking accounts, other bank service charges	113	86	134	155	132	123	103	67
Cemetery lots, vaults, and maintenance fees	125	140	46	9	7	143	41	78
Accounting fees	121	145	105	114	82	140	63	79
Miscellaneous personal services	97	39	140	270	57	211	179	73
Finance charges, except mortgage and vehicles	117	101	127	100	135	128	63	75
Occupational expenses	140	115	164	170	144	198	61	50
Expenses for other properties	137	152	125	159	79	189	23	59
Credit card memberships	122	137	113	102	129	89	34	63
Shopping club membership fees	143	146	140	123	135	158	54	40
CASH CONTRIBUTIONS	**130**	**164**	**105**	**84**	**108**	**114**	**42**	**73**
Support for college students	155	197	126	13	141	176	58	46
Alimony expenditures	49	84	27	71	26	–	39	197
Child support expenditures	86	69	94	116	108	55	40	111
Gifts to non–CU members of stocks, bonds, and mutual funds	111	170	70	173	50	37	225	82
Cash contributions to charities and other organizations	149	239	86	61	94	88	32	50
Cash contributions to church, religious organizations	150	161	143	109	141	169	36	51
Cash contributions to educational institutions	159	265	84	49	126	30	19	50
Cash contributions to political organizations	147	186	111	62	147	77	29	62
Other cash gifts	110	171	62	54	56	81	43	96
PERSONAL INSURANCE AND PENSIONS	**139**	**119**	**158**	**147**	**156**	**171**	**55**	**45**
Life and other personal insurance	**152**	**155**	**146**	**100**	**139**	**190**	**52**	**37**
Life, endowment, annuity, other personal insurance	153	155	147	101	140	192	53	36
Other nonhealth insurance	126	141	104	75	97	135	35	79
Pensions and Social Security	**138**	**115**	**160**	**151**	**157**	**170**	**55**	**46**
Deductions for government retirement	132	152	124	114	134	111	72	52
Deductions for railroad retirement	136	31	231	140	209	332	47	34
Deductions for private pensions	144	133	165	163	177	142	45	50
Nonpayroll deposit to retirement plans	148	176	138	112	120	190	49	46
Deductions for Social Security	136	105	162	154	159	173	57	45
PERSONAL TAXES	**136**	**154**	**133**	**133**	**126**	**145**	**5**	**64**
Federal income taxes	136	159	130	128	121	147	–	65
State and local income taxes	138	133	151	167	148	146	46	59
Other taxes	134	161	114	89	117	125	47	64

Note: Spending index for total consumer units is 100. "–" means sample is too small to make a reliable estimate.
Source: Calculations by New Strategist based on the 2004 Consumer Expenditure Survey

Table 4.15 Financial: Total spending by household type, 2004

(total annual spending on financial products and services, cash contributions, and miscellaneous items, by consumer unit (CU) type, 2004; consumer units and dollars in thousands)

	total married couples	married couples, no children	married couples with children				single parent, at least one child <18	single person
			total	oldest child under 6	oldest child 6 to 17	oldest child 18 or older		
Number of consumer units	59,797	25,585	29,279	5,604	15,376	8,300	6,892	33,686
Total spending of all CUs	$3,325,106,066	$1,271,329,652	$1,776,089,906	$313,717,748	$931,445,483	$532,542,027	$226,226,178	$856,410,968
FINANCIAL PRODUCTS AND SERVICES	**47,814,877**	**20,224,175**	**22,154,248**	**3,851,125**	**9,991,786**	**8,391,798**	**4,428,730**	**17,412,967**
Miscellaneous fees	315,130	135,856	170,404	32,223	22,141	124,583	31,910	48,508
Lottery and gambling losses	4,059,618	2,090,806	1,722,776	78,120	790,634	915,905	92,560	2,614,370
Legal fees	7,675,543	2,635,767	3,604,830	359,497	2,051,312	1,194.287	2,324,051	3,233,856
Funeral expenses	4,424,380	2,841,982	915,847	147,217	191,892	576,684	79,051	1,721,355
Safe deposit box rental	251,745	130,739	103,062	10,704	53,970	38,512	9,787	85,226
Checking accounts, other bank service charges	1,267,696	409,872	732,561	162,180	379,018	191,315	133,016	424,444
Cemetery lots, vaults, and maintenance fees	1,003,992	482,021	180,944	7,117	13,685	160,024	38,044	354,040
Accounting fees	3,718,177	1,896,616	1,568,183	327,442	644,869	595,940	223,783	1,361,925
Miscellaneous personal services	2,139,537	363,563	1,512,846	556,982	321,358	643,831	454,321	902,111
Finance charges, except mortgage and vehicles	11,091,148	4,076,970	5,858,728	887,842	3,290,925	1,680,169	690,578	3,988,759
Occupational expenses	3,607,553	1,272,598	2,074,710	409,708	957,002	708,239	179,743	723,912
Expenses for other properties	7,521,267	3,559,897	3,360,644	818,800	1,107,841	1,434,240	145,008	1,806,917
Credit card memberships	176,401	84,431	79,639	13,786	47,973	17,762	5,651	51,203
Shopping club membership fees	488,541	213,891	233,646	39,508	119,164	74,949	21,227	77,141
CASH CONTRIBUTIONS	**109,808,221**	**59,254,092**	**43,354,294**	**6,661,307**	**23,329,236**	**13,365,241**	**4,045,053**	**34,601,249**
Support for college students	7,668,965	4,160,377	3,053,800	59,739	1,788,536	1,205,741	328,197	1,266,594
Alimony expenditures	1,389,084	1,014,701	374,478	188,631	185,742	–	126,399	3,139,198
Child support expenditures	8,443,336	2,929,483	4,563,718	1,070,812	2,735,544	757,541	453,494	6,174,307
Gifts to non–CU members of stocks, bonds, and mutual funds	1,658,171	1,084,036	512,968	242,541	193,276	77,273	386,710	692,584
Cash contributions to charities and other organizations	14,068,440	9,625,589	3,961,741	542,299	2,273,188	1,146,230	347,908	2,631,213
Cash contributions to church, religious organizations	50,814,295	23,292,328	23,670,900	3,463,272	12,276,045	7,932,393	1,418,925	9,724,138
Cash contributions to educational institutions	4,380,728	3,120,602	1,137,782	127,435	895,652	114,706	59,960	780,841
Cash contributions to political organizations	1,452,469	788,786	537,855	57,777	373,944	106,157	33,219	345,618
Other cash gifts	19,932,732	13,237,935	5,541,051	908,801	2,607,308	2,025,283	890,240	9,846,755
PERSONAL INSURANCE AND PENSIONS	**401,979,353**	**146,413,744**	**223,828,293**	**39,614,452**	**115,687,333**	**68,534,179**	**18,249,189**	**73,585,046**
Life and other personal insurance	**35,526,594**	**15,444,897**	**16,686,980**	**2,181,693**	**8,351,013**	**6,154,948**	**1,408,105**	**4,902,324**
Life, endowment, annuity, other personal insurance	34,609,308	15,004,835	16,318,065	2,130,529	8,168,961	6,019,160	1,378,814	4,579,275
Other nonhealth insurance	917,286	440,062	368,915	51,165	181,898	135,788	29,222	323,049
Pensions and Social Security	**366,452,759**	**130,968,847**	**207,141,312**	**37,432,759**	**107,336,473**	**62,379,231**	**16,841,153**	**68,682,722**
Deductions for government retirement	6,215,300	3,059,454	2,840,649	501,334	1,616,940	722,432	388,571	1,362,262
Deductions for railroad retirement	216,465	21,491	180,651	21,015	85,952	73,621	8,684	30,654
Deductions for private pensions	44,781,973	17,647,765	24,978,208	4,722,939	14,148,688	6,107,389	1,601,494	8,691,999
Nonpayroll deposit to retirement plans	35,552,306	18,043,310	16,205,048	2,506,669	7,372,638	6,326,426	1,365,443	6,266,270
Deductions for Social Security	279,686,714	92,197,083	162,937,049	29,680,801	84,112,255	49,149,446	13,476,892	52,331,538
PERSONAL TAXES	**176,609,842**	**85,090,593**	**84,365,682**	**16,199,539**	**42,094,260**	**26,074,865**	**713,184**	**46,575,611**
Federal income taxes	123,740,922	61,802,358	57,680,801	10,909,755	28,237,563	18,535,477	-1,342,562	33,342,066
State and local income taxes	38,894,959	16,106,269	20,849,283	4,416,456	10,710,460	5,722,933	1,492,187	9,443,196
Other taxes	13,973,961	7,182,221	5,835,597	873,327	3,146,237	1,816,372	563,490	3,790,686

Note: Total spending figures for total consumer units can be found on Total Spending by Age and Total Spending by Region tables. Spending by type of consumer unit will not add to total because not all types of consumer units are shown. Numbers may not add to category total because of rounding and missing subcategories. "–" means sample is too small to make a reliable estimate.
Source: Calculations by New Strategist based on the 2004 Consumer Expenditure Survey

Table 4.16 Financial: Market shares by household type, 2004

(percentage of total annual spending on financial products and services, cash contributions, and miscellaneous items accounted for by types of consumer units, 2004)

	total married couples	married couples, no children	married couples with children total	oldest child under 6	oldest child 6 to 17	oldest child 18 or older	single parent, at least one child <18	single person
Share of total consumer units	51.4%	22.0%	25.2%	4.8%	13.2%	7.1%	5.9%	29.0%
Share of total before-tax income	68.9	26.0	36.9	6.7	19.1	11.2	3.4	15.0
Share of total spending	65.9	25.2	35.2	6.2	18.5	10.6	4.5	17.0
FINANCIAL PRODUCTS AND SERVICES	**59.6**	**25.2**	**27.6**	**4.8**	**12.5**	**10.5**	**5.5**	**21.7**
Miscellaneous fees	59.3	25.6	32.1	6.1	4.2	23.4	6.0	9.1
Lottery and gambling losses	52.5	27.0	22.3	1.0	10.2	11.8	1.2	33.8
Legal fees	51.8	17.8	24.3	2.4	13.8	8.1	15.7	21.8
Funeral expenses	57.8	37.2	12.0	1.9	2.5	7.5	1.0	22.5
Safe deposit box rental	67.2	34.9	27.5	2.9	14.4	10.3	2.6	22.8
Checking accounts, other bank service charges	58.3	18.8	33.7	7.5	17.4	8.8	6.1	19.5
Cemetery lots, vaults, and maintenance fees	64.1	30.8	11.5	0.5	0.9	10.2	2.4	22.6
Accounting fees	62.4	31.8	26.3	5.5	10.8	10.0	3.8	22.9
Miscellaneous personal services	50.0	8.5	35.4	13.0	7.5	15.0	10.6	21.1
Finance charges, except mortgage and vehicles	60.3	22.2	31.9	4.8	17.9	9.1	3.8	21.7
Occupational expenses	72.0	25.4	41.4	8.2	19.1	14.1	3.6	14.4
Expenses for other properties	70.6	33.4	31.5	7.7	10.4	13.5	1.4	17.0
Credit card memberships	62.9	30.1	28.4	4.9	17.1	6.3	2.0	18.3
Shopping club membership fees	73.5	32.2	35.1	5.9	17.9	11.3	3.2	11.6
CASH CONTRIBUTIONS	**67.1**	**36.2**	**26.5**	**4.1**	**14.2**	**8.2**	**2.5**	**21.1**
Support for college students	80.0	43.4	31.8	0.6	18.6	12.6	3.4	13.2
Alimony expenditures	25.3	18.5	6.8	3.4	3.4	–	2.3	57.1
Child support expenditures	44.0	15.3	23.8	5.6	14.2	3.9	2.4	32.2
Gifts to non–CU members of stocks, bonds, and mutual funds	57.1	37.3	17.7	8.4	6.7	2.7	13.3	23.9
Cash contributions to charities and other organizations	76.8	52.6	21.6	3.0	12.4	6.3	1.9	14.4
Cash contributions to church, religious organizations	77.3	35.4	36.0	5.3	18.7	12.1	2.2	14.8
Cash contributions to educational institutions	81.8	58.3	21.2	2.4	16.7	2.1	1.1	14.6
Cash contributions to political organizations	75.3	40.9	27.9	3.0	19.4	5.5	1.7	17.9
Other cash gifts	56.6	37.6	15.7	2.6	7.4	5.7	2.5	28.0
PERSONAL INSURANCE AND PENSIONS	**71.7**	**26.1**	**39.9**	**7.1**	**20.6**	**12.2**	**3.3**	**13.1**
Life and other personal insurance	**78.3**	**34.0**	**36.8**	**4.8**	**18.4**	**13.6**	**3.1**	**10.8**
Life, endowment, annuity, other personal insurance	78.7	34.1	37.1	4.8	18.6	13.7	3.1	10.4
Other nonhealth insurance	64.9	31.1	26.1	3.6	12.9	9.6	2.1	22.8
Pensions and Social Security	**71.1**	**25.4**	**40.2**	**7.3**	**20.8**	**12.1**	**3.3**	**13.3**
Deductions for government retirement	68.1	33.5	31.1	5.5	17.7	7.9	4.3	14.9
Deductions for railroad retirement	69.7	6.9	58.2	6.8	27.7	23.7	2.8	9.9
Deductions for private pensions	74.3	29.3	41.4	7.8	23.5	10.1	2.7	14.4
Nonpayroll deposit to retirement plans	76.3	38.7	34.8	5.4	15.8	13.6	2.9	13.5
Deductions for Social Security	70.1	23.1	40.8	7.4	21.1	12.3	3.4	13.1
PERSONAL TAXES	**70.1**	**33.8**	**33.5**	**6.4**	**16.7**	**10.4**	**0.3**	**18.5**
Federal income taxes	70.1	35.0	32.7	6.2	16.0	10.5	–	18.9
State and local income taxes	70.8	29.3	38.0	8.0	19.5	10.4	2.7	17.2
Other taxes	68.8	35.3	28.7	4.3	15.5	8.9	2.8	18.7

Note: Market share for total consumer units is 100.0%. Market shares by type of consumer unit will not add to total because not all types of consumer units are shown. "–" means sample is too small to make a reliable estimate.
Source: Calculations by New Strategist based on the 2004 Consumer Expenditure Survey

Table 4.17 Financial: Average spending by race and Hispanic origin, 2004

(average annual spending of consumer units (CU) on financial products and services, cash contributions, and miscellaneous items, by race and Hispanic origin of consumer unit reference person, 2004)

	total consumer units	Asian	black	Hispanic	non-Hispanic white and other
Number of consumer units (in 000s)	116,282	3,957	13,773	12,298	90,424
Average number of persons per CU	2.5	2.8	2.6	3.3	2.3
Average before-tax income of CU	$54,453.00	$67,705.00	$38,503.00	$43,693.00	$58,314.00
Average spending of CU, total	43,394.87	49,458.68	30,481.49	37,578.03	46,163.26
FINANCIAL PRODUCTS AND SERVICES	**690.02**	**569.39**	**457.14**	**476.76**	**754.06**
Miscellaneous fees	4.57	1.79	–	2.16	5.62
Lottery and gambling losses	66.54	105.38	16.12	45.50	77.22
Legal fees	127.50	35.85	91.97	77.98	139.64
Funeral expenses	65.78	49.23	86.75	38.95	66.09
Safe deposit box rental	3.22	6.03	0.70	1.45	3.84
Checking accounts, other bank service charges	18.70	11.73	16.96	17.54	19.18
Cemetery lots, vaults, and maintenance fees	13.48	1.76	7.61	6.81	15.25
Accounting fees	51.22	26.64	16.46	28.18	59.61
Miscellaneous personal services	36.79	60.23	31.65	22.58	39.52
Finance charges, except mortgage and vehicles	158.18	49.08	119.35	136.19	166.95
Occupational expenses	43.10	65.09	26.26	35.51	46.65
Expenses for other properties	91.63	144.10	38.08	54.68	104.60
Credit card memberships	2.41	4.52	1.80	1.90	2.56
Shopping club membership fees	5.72	7.94	3.44	5.11	6.13
CASH CONTRIBUTIONS	**1,408.04**	**1,088.84**	**835.34**	**710.32**	**1,588.74**
Support for college students	82.49	145.80	41.02	27.19	96.13
Alimony expenditures	47.29	21.99	5.97	16.30	57.69
Child support expenditures	165.10	106.97	145.73	162.66	168.39
Gifts to non–CU members of stocks, bonds, and mutual funds	24.97	15.45	1.50	30.39	27.75
Cash contributions to charities and other organizations	157.51	76.25	29.17	41.39	192.54
Cash contributions to church, religious organizations	565.11	344.41	492.84	188.16	627.44
Cash contributions to educational institutions	46.06	30.61	3.77	8.30	57.54
Cash contributions to political organizations	16.58	6.41	2.53	7.01	19.99
Other cash gifts	302.93	340.96	112.80	228.92	341.27
PERSONAL INSURANCE AND PENSIONS	**4,823.20**	**6,176.40**	**3,230.32**	**3,765.15**	**5,206.62**
Life and other personal insurance	**390.34**	**305.56**	**291.82**	**155.48**	**436.87**
Life, endowment, annuity, other personal insurance	378.18	300.60	289.38	152.90	421.94
Other nonhealth insurance	12.16	4.96	2.44	2.58	14.92
Pensions and Social Security	**4,432.85**	**5,870.83**	**2,938.50**	**3,609.68**	**4,769.76**
Deductions for government retirement	78.45	58.99	58.43	55.94	84.37
Deductions for railroad retirement	2.67	–	5.45	0.54	2.53
Deductions for private pensions	518.59	822.60	215.08	250.17	600.66
Nonpayroll deposit to retirement plans	400.54	410.38	139.83	233.69	462.02
Deductions for Social Security	3,432.61	4,578.86	2,519.71	3,069.34	3,620.18
PERSONAL TAXES	**2,165.85**	**2,130.93**	**507.40**	**894.78**	**2,586.53**
Federal income taxes	1,518.95	1,492.42	242.87	630.29	1,830.62
State and local income taxes	472.12	504.43	205.69	184.73	550.97
Other taxes	174.78	134.08	58.84	79.76	204.94

Note: "Asian" and "black" include Hispanics and non-Hispanics who identify themselves as being of the respective race alone. "Hispanic" includes people of any race who identify themselves as Hispanic. "Other" includes people who identify themselves as non-Hispanic and as Alaska Native, American Indian, Asian (who are also included in the "Asian" column), Native Hawaiian or other Pacific Islander, as well as non-Hispanics reporting more than one race. Subcategories may not add to total because some are not shown. "–" means sample is too small to make a reliable estimate.
Source: Bureau of Labor Statistics, unpublished tables from the 2004 Consumer Expenditure Survey

Table 4.18 Financial: Indexed spending by race and Hispanic origin, 2004

(indexed average annual spending of consumer units (CU) on financial products and services, cash contributions, and miscellaneous items, by race and Hispanic origin of consumer unit reference person, 2004; index definition: an index of 100 is the average for all consumer units; an index of 132 means that spending by consumer units in that group is 32 percent above the average for all consumer units; an index of 68 indicates spending that is 32 percent below the average for all consumer units)

	total consumer units	Asian	black	Hispanic	non-Hispanic white and other
Average spending of CU, total	$43,395	$49,459	$30,481	$37,578	$46,163
Average spending of CU, index	100	114	70	87	106
FINANCIAL PRODUCTS AND SERVICES	**100**	**83**	**66**	**69**	**109**
Miscellaneous fees	100	39	–	47	123
Lottery and gambling losses	100	158	24	68	116
Legal fees	100	28	72	61	110
Funeral expenses	100	75	132	59	100
Safe deposit box rental	100	187	22	45	119
Checking accounts, other bank service charges	100	63	91	94	103
Cemetery lots, vaults, and maintenance fees	100	13	56	51	113
Accounting fees	100	52	32	55	116
Miscellaneous personal services	100	164	86	61	107
Finance charges, except mortgage and vehicles	100	31	75	86	106
Occupational expenses	100	151	61	82	108
Expenses for other properties	100	157	42	60	114
Credit card memberships	100	188	75	79	106
Shopping club membership fees	100	139	60	89	107
CASH CONTRIBUTIONS	**100**	**77**	**59**	**50**	**113**
Support for college students	100	177	50	33	117
Alimony expenditures	100	47	13	34	122
Child support expenditures	100	65	88	99	102
Gifts to non–CU members of stocks, bonds, and mutual funds	100	62	6	122	111
Cash contributions to charities and other organizations	100	48	19	26	122
Cash contributions to church, religious organizations	100	61	87	33	111
Cash contributions to educational institutions	100	66	8	18	125
Cash contributions to political organizations	100	39	15	42	121
Other cash gifts	100	113	37	76	113
PERSONAL INSURANCE AND PENSIONS	**100**	**128**	**67**	**78**	**108**
Life and other personal insurance	**100**	**78**	**75**	**40**	**112**
Life, endowment, annuity, other personal insurance	100	79	77	40	112
Other nonhealth insurance	100	41	20	21	123
Pensions and Social Security	**100**	**132**	**66**	**81**	**108**
Deductions for government retirement	100	75	74	71	108
Deductions for railroad retirement	100	–	204	20	95
Deductions for private pensions	100	159	41	48	116
Nonpayroll deposit to retirement plans	100	102	35	58	115
Deductions for Social Security	100	133	73	89	105
PERSONAL TAXES	**100**	**98**	**23**	**41**	**119**
Federal income taxes	100	98	16	41	121
State and local income taxes	100	107	44	39	117
Other taxes	100	77	34	46	117

Note: "Asian" and "black" include Hispanics and non-Hispanics who identify themselves as being of the respective race alone. "Hispanic" includes people of any race who identify themselves as Hispanic. "Other" includes people who identify themselves as non-Hispanic and as Alaska Native, American Indian, Asian (who are also included in the "Asian" column), Native Hawaiian or other Pacific Islander, as well as non-Hispanics reporting more than one race. "–" means sample is too small to make a reliable estimate.
Source: Calculations by New Strategist based on the 2004 Consumer Expenditure Survey

Table 4.19 Financial: Total spending by race and Hispanic origin, 2004

(total annual spending on financial products and services, cash contributions, and miscellaneous items, by consumer unit race and Hispanic origin groups, 2004; consumer units and dollars in thousands)

	total consumer units	Asian	black	Hispanic	non-Hispanic white and other
Number of consumer units	116,282	3,957	13,773	12,298	90,424
Total spending of all consumer units	$5,046,042,273	$195,707,997	$419,821,562	$462,134,613	$4,174,266,622
FINANCIAL PRODUCTS AND SERVICES	**80,236,906**	**2,253,076**	**6,296,189**	**5,863,194**	**68,185,121**
Miscellaneous fees	531,409	7,083	–	26,564	508,183
Lottery and gambling losses	7,737,404	416,989	222,021	559,559	6,982,541
Legal fees	14,825,955	141,858	1,266,703	958,998	12,626,807
Funeral expenses	7,649,030	194,803	1,194,808	479,007	5,976,122
Safe deposit box rental	374,428	23,861	9,641	17,832	347,228
Checking accounts, other bank service charges	2,174,473	46,416	233,590	215,707	1,734,332
Cemetery lots, vaults, and maintenance fees	1,567,481	6,964	104,813	83,749	1,378,966
Accounting fees	5,955,964	105,414	226,704	346,558	5,390,175
Miscellaneous personal services	4,278,015	238,330	435,915	277,689	3,573,556
Finance charges, except mortgage and vehicles	18,393,487	194,210	1,643,808	1,674,865	15,096,287
Occupational expenses	5,011,754	257,561	361,679	436,702	4,218,280
Expenses for other properties	10,654,920	570,204	524,476	672,455	9,458,350
Credit card memberships	280,240	17,886	24,791	23,366	231,485
Shopping club membership fees	665,133	31,419	47,379	62,843	554,299
CASH CONTRIBUTIONS	**163,729,707**	**4,308,540**	**11,505,138**	**8,735,515**	**143,660,226**
Support for college students	9,592,102	576,931	564,968	334,383	8,692,459
Alimony expenditures	5,498,976	87,014	82,225	200,457	5,216,561
Child support expenditures	19,198,158	423,280	2,007,139	2,000,393	15,226,497
Gifts to non–CU members of stocks, bonds, and mutual funds	2,903,562	61,136	20,660	373,736	2,509,266
Cash contributions to charities and other organizations	18,315,578	301,721	401,758	509,014	17,410,237
Cash contributions to church, religious organizations	65,712,121	1,362,830	6,787,885	2,313,992	56,735,635
Cash contributions to educational institutions	5,355,949	121,124	51,924	102,073	5,202,997
Cash contributions to political organizations	1,927,956	25,364	34,846	86,209	1,807,576
Other cash gifts	35,225,306	1,349,179	1,553,594	2,815,258	30,858,998
PERSONAL INSURANCE AND PENSIONS	**560,851,342**	**24,440,015**	**44,491,197**	**46,303,815**	**470,803,407**
Life and other personal insurance	**45,389,516**	**1,209,101**	**4,019,237**	**1,912,093**	**39,503,533**
Life, endowment, annuity, other personal insurance	43,975,527	1,189,474	3,985,631	1,880,364	38,153,503
Other nonhealth insurance	1,413,989	19,627	33,606	31,729	1,349,126
Pensions and Social Security	**515,460,664**	**23,230,874**	**40,471,961**	**44,391,845**	**431,300,778**
Deductions for government retirement	9,122,323	233,423	804,756	687,950	7,629,073
Deductions for railroad retirement	310,473	–	75,063	6,641	228,773
Deductions for private pensions	60,302,682	3,255,028	2,962,297	3,076,591	54,314,080
Nonpayroll deposit to retirement plans	46,575,592	1,623,874	1,925,879	2,873,920	41,777,696
Deductions for Social Security	399,150,756	18,118,549	34,703,966	37,746,743	327,351,156
PERSONAL TAXES	**251,849,370**	**8,432,090**	**6,988,420**	**11,004,004**	**233,884,389**
Federal income taxes	176,626,544	5,905,506	3,345,049	7,751,306	165,531,983
State and local income taxes	54,899,058	1,996,030	2,832,968	2,271,810	49,820,911
Other taxes	20,323,768	530,555	810,403	980,888	18,531,495

Note: "Asian" and "black" include Hispanics and non-Hispanics who identify themselves as being of the respective race alone. "Hispanic" includes people of any race who identify themselves as Hispanic. "Other" includes people who identify themselves as non-Hispanic and as Alaska Native, American Indian, Asian (who are also included in the "Asian" column), Native Hawaiian or other Pacific Islander, as well as non-Hispanics reporting more than one race. Numbers may not add to total because of rounding and missing subcategories. "–" means sample is too small to make a reliable estimate.
Source: Calculations by New Strategist based on the 2004 Consumer Expenditure Survey

Table 4.20 Financial: Market shares by race and Hispanic origin, 2004

(percentage of total annual spending on financial products and services, cash contributions, and miscellaneous items accounted for by consumer unit race and Hispanic origin groups, 2004)

	total consumer units	Asian	black	Hispanic	non-Hispanic white and other
Share of total consumer units	100.0%	3.4%	11.8%	10.6%	77.8%
Share of total before-tax income	100.0	4.2	8.4	8.5	83.3
Share of total spending	100.0	3.9	8.3	9.2	82.7
FINANCIAL PRODUCTS AND SERVICES	100.0	2.8	7.8	7.3	85.0
Miscellaneous fees	100.0	1.3	–	5.0	95.6
Lottery and gambling losses	100.0	5.4	2.9	7.2	90.2
Legal fees	100.0	1.0	8.5	6.5	85.2
Funeral expenses	100.0	2.5	15.6	6.3	78.1
Safe deposit box rental	100.0	6.4	2.6	4.8	92.7
Checking accounts, other bank service charges	100.0	2.1	10.7	9.9	79.8
Cemetery lots, vaults, and maintenance fees	100.0	0.4	6.7	5.3	88.0
Accounting fees	100.0	1.8	3.8	5.8	90.5
Miscellaneous personal services	100.0	5.6	10.2	6.5	83.5
Finance charges, except mortgage and vehicles	100.0	1.1	8.9	9.1	82.1
Occupational expenses	100.0	5.1	7.2	8.7	84.2
Expenses for other properties	100.0	5.4	4.9	6.3	88.8
Credit card memberships	100.0	6.4	8.8	8.3	82.6
Shopping club membership fees	100.0	4.7	7.1	9.4	83.3
CASH CONTRIBUTIONS	100.0	2.6	7.0	5.3	87.7
Support for college students	100.0	6.0	5.9	3.5	90.6
Alimony expenditures	100.0	1.6	1.5	3.6	94.9
Child support expenditures	100.0	2.2	10.5	10.4	79.3
Gifts to non–CU members of stocks, bonds, and mutual funds	100.0	2.1	0.7	12.9	86.4
Cash contributions to charities and other organizations	100.0	1.6	2.2	2.8	95.1
Cash contributions to church, religious organizations	100.0	2.1	10.3	3.5	86.3
Cash contributions to educational institutions	100.0	2.3	1.0	1.9	97.1
Cash contributions to political organizations	100.0	1.3	1.8	4.5	93.8
Other cash gifts	100.0	3.8	4.4	8.0	87.6
PERSONAL INSURANCE AND PENSIONS	100.0	4.4	7.9	8.3	83.9
Life and other personal insurance	100.0	2.7	8.9	4.2	87.0
Life, endowment, annuity, other personal insurance	100.0	2.7	9.1	4.3	86.8
Other nonhealth insurance	100.0	1.4	2.4	2.2	95.4
Pensions and Social Security	100.0	4.5	7.9	8.6	83.7
Deductions for government retirement	100.0	2.6	8.8	7.5	83.6
Deductions for railroad retirement	100.0	–	24.2	2.1	73.7
Deductions for private pensions	100.0	5.4	4.9	5.1	90.1
Nonpayroll deposit to retirement plans	100.0	3.5	4.1	6.2	89.7
Deductions for Social Security	100.0	4.5	8.7	9.5	82.0
PERSONAL TAXES	100.0	3.3	2.8	4.4	92.9
Federal income taxes	100.0	3.3	1.9	4.4	93.7
State and local income taxes	100.0	3.6	5.2	4.1	90.8
Other taxes	100.0	2.6	4.0	4.8	91.2

Note: "Asian" and "black" include Hispanics and non-Hispanics who identify themselves as being of the respective race alone. "Hispanic" includes people of any race who identify themselves as Hispanic. "Other" includes people who identify themselves as non-Hispanic and as Alaska Native, American Indian, Asian (who are also included in the "Asian" column), Native Hawaiian or other Pacific Islander, as well as non-Hispanics reporting more than one race. "–" means sample is too small to make a reliable estimate.
Source: Calculations by New Strategist based on the 2004 Consumer Expenditure Survey

Table 4.21 Financial: Average spending by region, 2004

(average annual spending of consumer units (CU) on financial products and services, cash contributions, and miscellaneous items, by region in which consumer unit lives, 2004)

	total consumer units	Northeast	Midwest	South	West
Number of consumer units (in 000s)	116,282	22,051	26,539	41,801	25,891
Average number of persons per CU	2.5	2.4	2.4	2.5	2.6
Average before-tax income of CU	$54,453.00	$61,050.00	$53,567.00	$50,775.00	$55,682.00
Average spending of CU, total	43,394.87	46,114.89	43,370.77	39,173.65	47,921.74
FINANCIAL PRODUCTS AND SERVICES	**$690.02**	**$759.51**	**$796.63**	**$512.00**	**$808.54**
Miscellaneous fees	4.57	2.07	9.19	3.01	4.46
Lottery and gambling losses	66.54	137.13	66.30	26.81	70.48
Legal fees	127.50	103.13	155.67	89.84	180.19
Funeral expenses	65.78	77.35	96.50	54.91	42.01
Safe deposit box rental	3.22	2.88	4.48	3.12	2.40
Checking accounts, other bank service charges	18.70	17.55	18.97	15.73	24.18
Cemetery lots, vaults, and maintenance fees	13.48	28.19	10.21	9.70	10.41
Accounting fees	51.22	58.67	47.93	40.36	65.78
Miscellaneous personal services	36.79	34.18	58.29	16.73	49.33
Finance charges, except mortgage and vehicles	158.18	156.50	165.92	152.64	160.64
Occupational expenses	43.10	38.75	60.88	22.03	62.59
Expenses for other properties	91.63	96.17	93.37	69.58	121.59
Credit card memberships	2.41	2.76	2.21	1.78	3.31
Shopping club membership fees	5.72	4.17	4.47	4.63	10.06
CASH CONTRIBUTIONS	**1,408.04**	**1,108.47**	**1,789.55**	**1,251.64**	**1,524.60**
Support for college students	82.49	66.75	112.10	68.81	87.62
Alimony expenditures	47.29	44.70	30.82	34.45	87.10
Child support expenditures	165.10	177.59	203.41	135.16	163.53
Gifts to non–CU members of stocks, bonds, and mutual funds	24.97	14.24	27.47	17.84	43.09
Cash contributions to charities and other organizations	157.51	156.75	279.00	90.64	141.58
Cash contributions to church, religious organizations	565.11	293.21	618.65	634.10	630.43
Cash contributions to educational institutions	46.06	45.46	87.71	26.74	35.06
Cash contributions to political organizations	16.58	11.75	17.79	14.39	22.98
Other cash gifts	302.93	298.03	412.61	229.51	313.21
PERSONAL INSURANCE AND PENSIONS	**4,823.20**	**5,110.28**	**4,894.70**	**4,413.71**	**5,166.51**
Life and other personal insurance	**390.34**	**364.01**	**438.80**	**393.95**	**357.28**
Life, endowment, annuity, other personal insurance	378.18	354.75	425.91	385.20	337.85
Other nonhealth insurance	12.16	9.27	12.88	8.74	19.42
Pensions and Social Security	**4,432.85**	**4,746.26**	**4,455.90**	**4,019.77**	**4,809.23**
Deductions for government retirement	78.45	52.67	89.84	77.73	89.87
Deductions for railroad retirement	2.67	1.54	1.03	3.45	4.05
Deductions for private pensions	518.59	499.61	575.12	433.33	614.45
Nonpayroll deposit to retirement plans	400.54	405.33	379.16	316.39	554.22
Deductions for Social Security	3,432.61	3,787.11	3,410.75	3,188.87	3,546.64
PERSONAL TAXES	**2,165.85**	**2,376.75**	**2,445.13**	**1,695.14**	**2,459.90**
Federal income taxes	1,518.95	1,581.17	1,613.34	1,216.74	1,857.12
State and local income taxes	472.12	560.59	586.20	329.56	510.00
Other taxes	174.78	234.99	245.59	148.84	92.78

Note: Subcategories may not add to total because some are not shown.
Source: Bureau of Labor Statistics, unpublished tables from the 2004 Consumer Expenditure Survey

Table 4.22 Financial: Indexed spending by region, 2004

(indexed average annual spending of consumer units (CU) on financial products and services, cash contributions, and miscellaneous items, by region in which consumer unit lives, 2004; index definition: an index of 100 is the average for all consumer units; an index of 132 means that spending by consumer units in that group is 32 percent above the average for all consumer units; an index of 68 indicates spending that is 32 percent below the average for all consumer units)

	total consumer units	Northeast	Midwest	South	West
Average spending of CU, total	$43,395	$46,115	$43,371	$39,174	$47,922
Average spending of CU, index	**100**	**106**	**100**	**90**	**110**
FINANCIAL PRODUCTS AND SERVICES	**100**	**110**	**115**	**74**	**117**
Miscellaneous fees	100	45	201	66	98
Lottery and gambling losses	100	206	100	40	106
Legal fees	100	81	122	70	141
Funeral expenses	100	118	147	83	64
Safe deposit box rental	100	89	139	97	75
Checking accounts, other bank service charges	100	94	101	84	129
Cemetery lots, vaults, and maintenance fees	100	209	76	72	77
Accounting fees	100	115	94	79	128
Miscellaneous personal services	100	93	158	45	134
Finance charges, except mortgage and vehicles	100	99	105	96	102
Occupational expenses	100	90	141	51	145
Expenses for other properties	100	105	102	76	133
Credit card memberships	100	115	92	74	137
Shopping club membership fees	100	73	78	81	176
CASH CONTRIBUTIONS	**100**	**79**	**127**	**89**	**108**
Support for college students	100	81	136	83	106
Alimony expenditures	100	95	65	73	184
Child support expenditures	100	108	123	82	99
Gifts to non–CU members of stocks, bonds, and mutual funds	100	57	110	71	173
Cash contributions to charities and other organizations	100	100	177	58	90
Cash contributions to church, religious organizations	100	52	109	112	112
Cash contributions to educational institutions	100	99	190	58	76
Cash contributions to political organizations	100	71	107	87	139
Other cash gifts	100	98	136	76	103
PERSONAL INSURANCE AND PENSIONS	**100**	**106**	**101**	**92**	**107**
Life and other personal insurance	**100**	**93**	**112**	**101**	**92**
Life, endowment, annuity, other personal insurance	100	94	113	102	89
Other nonhealth insurance	100	76	106	72	160
Pensions and Social Security	**100**	**107**	**101**	**91**	**108**
Deductions for government retirement	100	67	115	99	115
Deductions for railroad retirement	100	58	39	129	152
Deductions for private pensions	100	96	111	84	118
Nonpayroll deposit to retirement plans	100	101	95	79	138
Deductions for Social Security	100	110	99	93	103
PERSONAL TAXES	**100**	**110**	**113**	**78**	**114**
Federal income taxes	100	104	106	80	122
State and local income taxes	100	119	124	70	108
Other taxes	100	134	141	85	53

Source: Calculations by New Strategist based on the 2004 Consumer Expenditure Survey

Table 4.23 Financial: Total spending by region, 2004

(total annual spending on financial products and services, cash contributions, and miscellaneous items, by region in which consumer units live, 2004; consumer units and dollars in thousands)

	total consumer units	Northeast	Midwest	South	West
Number of consumer units	116,282	22,051	26,539	41,801	25,891
Total spending of all consumer units	$5,046,042,273	$1,016,879,439	$1,151,016,865	$1,637,497,744	$1,240,741,770
FINANCIAL PRODUCTS AND SERVICES	**80,236,906**	**16,747,955**	**21,141,764**	**21,402,112**	**20,933,909**
Miscellaneous fees	531,409	45,646	243,893	125,821	115,474
Lottery and gambling losses	7,737,404	3,023,854	1,759,536	1,120,685	1,824,798
Legal fees	14,825,955	2,274,120	4,131,326	3,755,402	4,665,299
Funeral expenses	7,649,030	1,705,645	2,561,014	2,295,293	1,087,681
Safe deposit box rental	374,428	63,507	118,895	130,419	62,138
Checking accounts, other bank service charges	2,174,473	386,995	503,445	657,530	626,044
Cemetery lots, vaults, and maintenance fees	1,567,481	621,618	270,963	405,470	269,525
Accounting fees	5,955,964	1,293,732	1,272,014	1,687,088	1,703,110
Miscellaneous personal services	4,278,015	753,703	1,546,958	699,331	1,277,203
Finance charges, except mortgage and vehicles	18,393,487	3,450,982	4,403,351	6,380,505	4,159,130
Occupational expenses	5,011,754	854,476	1,615,694	920,876	1,620,518
Expenses for other properties	10,654,920	2,120,645	2,477,946	2,908,514	3,148,087
Credit card memberships	280,240	60,861	58,651	74,406	85,699
Shopping club membership fees	665,133	91,953	118,629	193,539	260,463
CASH CONTRIBUTIONS	**163,729,707**	**24,442,872**	**47,492,867**	**52,319,804**	**39,473,419**
Support for college students	9,592,102	1,471,904	2,975,022	2,876,327	2,268,569
Alimony expenditures	5,498,976	985,680	817,932	1,440,044	2,255,106
Child support expenditures	19,198,158	3,916,037	5,398,298	5,649,823	4,233,955
Gifts to non–CU members of stocks, bonds, and mutual funds	2,903,562	314,006	729,026	745,730	1,115,643
Cash contributions to charities and other organizations	18,315,578	3,456,494	7,404,381	3,788,843	3,665,648
Cash contributions to church, religious organizations	65,712,121	6,465,574	16,418,352	26,506,014	16,322,463
Cash contributions to educational institutions	5,355,949	1,002,438	2,327,736	1,117,759	907,738
Cash contributions to political organizations	1,927,956	259,099	472,129	601,516	594,975
Other cash gifts	35,225,306	6,571,860	10,950,257	9,593,748	8,109,320
PERSONAL INSURANCE AND PENSIONS	**560,851,342**	**112,686,784**	**129,900,443**	**184,497,492**	**133,766,110**
Life and other personal insurance	**45,389,516**	**8,026,785**	**11,645,313**	**16,467,504**	**9,250,336**
Life, endowment, annuity, other personal insurance	43,975,527	7,822,592	11,303,225	16,101,745	8,747,274
Other nonhealth insurance	1,413,989	204,413	341,822	365,341	502,803
Pensions and Social Security	**515,460,664**	**104,659,779**	**118,255,130**	**168,030,406**	**124,515,774**
Deductions for government retirement	9,122,323	1,161,426	2,384,264	3,249,192	2,326,824
Deductions for railroad retirement	310,473	33,959	27,335	144,213	104,859
Deductions for private pensions	60,302,682	11,016,900	15,263,110	18,113,627	15,908,725
Nonpayroll deposit to retirement plans	46,575,592	8,937,932	10,062,527	13,225,418	14,349,310
Deductions for Social Security	399,150,756	83,509,563	90,517,894	133,297,955	91,826,056
PERSONAL TAXES	**251,849,370**	**52,409,714**	**64,891,305**	**70,858,547**	**63,689,271**
Federal income taxes	176,626,544	34,866,380	42,816,430	50,860,949	48,082,694
State and local income taxes	54,899,058	12,361,570	15,557,162	13,775,938	13,204,410
Other taxes	20,323,768	5,181,764	6,517,713	6,221,661	2,402,167

Note: Numbers may not add to total because of rounding and missing subcategories.
Source: Calculations by New Strategist based on the 2004 Consumer Expenditure Survey

Table 4.24 Financial: Market shares by region, 2004

(percentage of total annual spending on financial products and services, cash contributions, and miscellaneous items accounted for by consumer units (CU) by region, 2004)

	total consumer units	Northeast	Midwest	South	West
Share of total consumer units	**100.0%**	**19.0%**	**22.8%**	**35.9%**	**22.3%**
Share of total before-tax income	**100.0**	**21.3**	**22.5**	**33.5**	**22.8**
Share of total spending	**100.0**	**20.2**	**22.8**	**32.5**	**24.6**
FINANCIAL PRODUCTS AND SERVICES	**100.0**	**20.9**	**26.3**	**26.7**	**26.1**
Miscellaneous fees	100.0	8.6	45.9	23.7	21.7
Lottery and gambling losses	100.0	39.1	22.7	14.5	23.6
Legal fees	100.0	15.3	27.9	25.3	31.5
Funeral expenses	100.0	22.3	33.5	30.0	14.2
Safe deposit box rental	100.0	17.0	31.8	34.8	16.6
Checking accounts, other bank service charges	100.0	17.8	23.2	30.2	28.8
Cemetery lots, vaults, and maintenance fees	100.0	39.7	17.3	25.9	17.2
Accounting fees	100.0	21.7	21.4	28.3	28.6
Miscellaneous personal services	100.0	17.6	36.2	16.3	29.9
Finance charges, except mortgage and vehicles	100.0	18.8	23.9	34.7	22.6
Occupational expenses	100.0	17.0	32.2	18.4	32.3
Expenses for other properties	100.0	19.9	23.3	27.3	29.5
Credit card memberships	100.0	21.7	20.9	26.6	30.6
Shopping club membership fees	100.0	13.8	17.8	29.1	39.2
CASH CONTRIBUTIONS	**100.0**	**14.9**	**29.0**	**32.0**	**24.1**
Support for college students	100.0	15.3	31.0	30.0	23.7
Alimony expenditures	100.0	17.9	14.9	26.2	41.0
Child support expenditures	100.0	20.4	28.1	29.4	22.1
Gifts to non–CU members of stocks, bonds, and mutual funds	100.0	10.8	25.1	25.7	38.4
Cash contributions to charities and other organizations	100.0	18.9	40.4	20.7	20.0
Cash contributions to church, religious organizations	100.0	9.8	25.0	40.3	24.8
Cash contributions to educational institutions	100.0	18.7	43.5	20.9	16.9
Cash contributions to political organizations	100.0	13.4	24.5	31.2	30.9
Other cash gifts	100.0	18.7	31.1	27.2	23.0
PERSONAL INSURANCE AND PENSIONS	**100.0**	**20.1**	**23.2**	**32.9**	**23.9**
Life and other personal insurance	**100.0**	**17.7**	**25.7**	**36.3**	**20.4**
Life, endowment, annuity, other personal insurance	100.0	17.8	25.7	36.6	19.9
Other nonhealth insurance	100.0	14.5	24.2	25.8	35.6
Pensions and Social Security	**100.0**	**20.3**	**22.9**	**32.6**	**24.2**
Deductions for government retirement	100.0	12.7	26.1	35.6	25.5
Deductions for railroad retirement	100.0	10.9	8.8	46.4	33.8
Deductions for private pensions	100.0	18.3	25.3	30.0	26.4
Nonpayroll deposit to retirement plans	100.0	19.2	21.6	28.4	30.8
Deductions for Social Security	100.0	20.9	22.7	33.4	23.0
PERSONAL TAXES	**100.0**	**20.8**	**25.8**	**28.1**	**25.3**
Federal income taxes	100.0	19.7	24.2	28.8	27.2
State and local income taxes	100.0	22.5	28.3	25.1	24.1
Other taxes	100.0	25.5	32.1	30.6	11.8

Note: Numbers may not add to total because of rounding.
Source: Calculations by New Strategist based on the 2004 Consumer Expenditure Survey

Table 4.25 Financial: Average spending by education, 2004

(average annual spending of consumer units (CU) on financial products and services, cash contributions, and miscellaneous items, by education of consumer unit reference person, 2004)

	total consumer units	less than high school graduate	high school graduate	some college	associate's degree	college graduate total	bachelor's degree	master's, professional, doctorate
Number of consumer units (in 000s)	116,282	16,829	31,005	25,317	10,678	32,452	20,684	11,768
Average number of persons per CU	2.5	2.7	2.5	2.3	2.6	2.5	2.4	2.5
Average before-tax income of CU	$54,453.00	$29,094.00	$42,334.00	$46,756.00	$58,593.00	$83,825.00	$75,647.00	$98,201.00
Average spending of CU, total	43,394.87	25,421.18	35,438.55	40,877.68	48,177.36	60,712.28	56,728.41	67,801.38
FINANCIAL PRODUCTS AND SERVICES	**690.02**	**382.26**	**607.34**	**673.81**	**759.81**	**917.83**	**827.22**	**1,083.82**
Miscellaneous fees	4.57	5.66	6.81	4.18	3.20	2.54	3.33	1.03
Lottery and gambling losses	66.54	32.26	66.30	78.55	43.19	82.76	58.43	129.21
Legal fees	127.50	30.01	105.23	143.15	177.78	170.59	158.32	192.17
Funeral expenses	65.78	106.28	83.61	38.71	82.28	43.44	43.18	43.91
Safe deposit box rental	3.22	1.31	2.34	3.00	3.40	5.17	3.97	7.29
Checking accounts, other bank service charges	18.70	8.38	15.57	21.86	22.78	23.23	22.48	24.55
Cemetery lots, vaults, and maintenance fees	13.48	13.25	16.12	2.83	7.26	21.44	17.18	28.93
Accounting fees	51.22	18.83	37.16	48.50	41.63	86.72	83.10	93.08
Miscellaneous personal services	36.79	20.36	40.38	38.39	31.08	42.27	21.45	82.04
Finance charges, except mortgage and vehicles	158.18	78.22	130.57	159.26	180.98	217.68	224.48	205.73
Occupational expenses	43.10	11.06	32.41	38.70	52.97	70.10	55.98	94.91
Expenses for other properties	91.63	54.53	63.83	87.93	102.45	136.76	122.76	161.37
Credit card memberships	2.41	0.56	1.46	2.57	2.32	4.17	3.36	5.59
Shopping club membership fees	5.72	1.55	4.24	5.83	7.95	8.47	7.96	9.36
CASH CONTRIBUTIONS	**1,408.04**	**543.71**	**948.64**	**1,094.22**	**1,390.30**	**2,545.84**	**2,045.85**	**3,424.66**
Support for college students	82.49	11.13	36.70	38.52	64.97	203.31	129.52	333.02
Alimony expenditures	47.29	7.10	36.86	65.49	30.23	69.51	68.69	70.95
Child support expenditures	165.10	76.60	169.16	161.13	268.42	176.21	176.39	175.89
Gifts to non–CU members of stocks, bonds, and mutual funds	24.97	0.67	18.15	30.17	3.88	46.99	64.52	16.17
Cash contributions to charities and other organizations	157.51	21.72	55.44	87.80	90.14	402.00	215.05	730.60
Cash contributions to church, religious organizations	565.11	206.40	380.51	487.12	526.26	1,001.15	901.79	1,175.79
Cash contributions to educational institutions	46.06	0.82	2.19	9.70	14.34	150.23	64.87	300.26
Cash contributions to political organizations	16.58	1.33	3.39	9.23	5.56	46.44	34.79	66.92
Other cash gifts	302.93	217.94	246.24	205.07	386.52	450.00	390.24	555.05
PERSONAL INSURANCE AND PENSIONS	**4,823.20**	**1,974.03**	**3,480.23**	**4,041.53**	**5,583.57**	**7,943.47**	**7,168.75**	**9,305.20**
Life and other personal insurance	**390.34**	**209.59**	**302.29**	**310.73**	**406.22**	**625.09**	**550.58**	**756.05**
Life, endowment, annuity, other personal insurance	378.18	202.12	295.48	298.43	396.02	604.83	532.05	732.76
Other nonhealth insurance	12.16	7.47	6.81	12.30	10.19	20.26	18.53	23.29
Pensions and Social Security	**4,432.85**	**1,764.44**	**3,177.94**	**3,730.80**	**5,177.35**	**7,318.38**	**6,618.17**	**8,549.15**
Deductions for government retirement	78.45	7.48	29.78	57.84	88.23	174.61	125.80	260.40
Deductions for railroad retirement	2.67	–	2.50	2.56	5.04	3.52	5.53	–
Deductions for private pensions	518.59	70.38	261.23	344.28	612.78	1,101.89	966.89	1,339.18
Nonpayroll deposit to retirement plans	400.54	41.02	230.17	277.83	464.55	824.42	659.03	1,115.14
Deductions for Social Security	3,432.61	1,645.56	2,654.26	3,048.30	4,006.75	5,213.93	4,860.92	5,834.42
PERSONAL TAXES	**2,165.85**	**143.44**	**1,202.59**	**1,638.61**	**2,325.33**	**4,493.81**	**3,790.12**	**5,730.68**
Federal income taxes	1,518.95	−5.11	808.36	1,127.22	1,506.99	3,297.78	2,729.44	4,296.74
State and local income taxes	472.12	78.87	267.61	361.40	560.48	928.75	822.17	1,116.08
Other taxes	174.78	69.68	126.62	149.99	257.85	267.29	238.51	317.87

Note: Subcategories may not add to total because some are not shown. "–" means sample is too small to make a reliable estimate.
Source: Bureau of Labor Statistics, unpublished tables from the 2004 Consumer Expenditure Survey

Table 4.26 Financial: Indexed spending by education, 2004

(indexed average annual spending of consumer units (CU) on financial products and services, cash contributions, and miscellaneous items, by education of consumer unit reference person, 2004; index definition: an index of 100 is the average for all consumer units; an index of 132 means that spending by consumer units in that group is 32 percent above the average for all consumer units; an index of 68 indicates spending that is 32 percent below the average for all consumer units)

	total consumer units	less than high school graduate	high school graduate	some college	associate's degree	college graduate total	bachelor's degree	master's, professional, doctorate
Average spending of CU, total	$43,395	$25,421	$35,439	$40,878	$48,177	$60,712	$56,728	$67,801
Average spending of CU, index	100	59	82	94	111	140	131	156
FINANCIAL PRODUCTS AND SERVICES	**100**	**55**	**88**	**98**	**110**	**133**	**120**	**157**
Miscellaneous fees	100	124	149	91	70	56	73	23
Lottery and gambling losses	100	48	100	118	65	124	88	194
Legal fees	100	24	83	112	139	134	124	151
Funeral expenses	100	162	127	59	125	66	66	67
Safe deposit box rental	100	41	73	93	106	161	123	226
Checking accounts, other bank service charges	100	45	83	117	122	124	120	131
Cemetery lots, vaults, and maintenance fees	100	98	120	21	54	159	127	215
Accounting fees	100	37	73	95	81	169	162	182
Miscellaneous personal services	100	55	110	104	84	115	58	223
Finance charges, except mortgage and vehicles	100	49	83	101	114	138	142	130
Occupational expenses	100	26	75	90	123	163	130	220
Expenses for other properties	100	60	70	96	112	149	134	176
Credit card memberships	100	23	61	107	96	173	139	232
Shopping club membership fees	100	27	74	102	139	148	139	164
CASH CONTRIBUTIONS	**100**	**39**	**67**	**78**	**99**	**181**	**145**	**243**
Support for college students	100	13	44	47	79	246	157	404
Alimony expenditures	100	15	78	138	64	147	145	150
Child support expenditures	100	46	102	98	163	107	107	107
Gifts to non–CU members of stocks, bonds, and mutual funds	100	3	73	121	16	188	258	65
Cash contributions to charities and other organizations	100	14	35	56	57	255	137	464
Cash contributions to church, religious organizations	100	37	67	86	93	177	160	208
Cash contributions to educational institutions	100	2	5	21	31	326	141	652
Cash contributions to political organizations	100	8	20	56	34	280	210	404
Other cash gifts	100	72	81	68	128	149	129	183
PERSONAL INSURANCE AND PENSIONS	**100**	**41**	**72**	**84**	**116**	**165**	**149**	**193**
Life and other personal insurance	**100**	**54**	**77**	**80**	**104**	**160**	**141**	**194**
Life, endowment, annuity, other personal insurance	100	53	78	79	105	160	141	194
Other nonhealth insurance	100	61	56	101	84	167	152	192
Pensions and Social Security	**100**	**40**	**72**	**84**	**117**	**165**	**149**	**193**
Deductions for government retirement	100	10	38	74	112	223	160	332
Deductions for railroad retirement	100	–	94	96	189	132	207	–
Deductions for private pensions	100	14	50	66	118	212	186	258
Nonpayroll deposit to retirement plans	100	10	57	69	116	206	165	278
Deductions for Social Security	100	48	77	89	117	152	142	170
PERSONAL TAXES	**100**	**7**	**56**	**76**	**107**	**207**	**175**	**265**
Federal income taxes	100	–	53	74	99	217	180	283
State and local income taxes	100	17	57	77	119	197	174	236
Other taxes	100	40	72	86	148	153	136	182

Note: "–" means sample is too small to make a reliable estimate.
Source: Calculations by New Strategist based on the 2004 Consumer Expenditure Survey

Table 4.27 Financial: Total spending by education, 2004

(total annual spending on financial products and services, cash contributions, and miscellaneous items, by consumer unit (CU) educational attainment group, 2004; consumer units and dollars in thousands)

	total consumer units	less than high school graduate	high school graduate	some college	associate's degree	college graduate total	bachelor's degree	master's, professional, doctorate
Number of consumer units	116,282	16,829	31,005	25,317	10,678	32,452	20,684	11,768
Total spending of all CUs	$5,046,042,273	$427,813,038	$1,098,772,243	$1,034,900,225	$514,437,850	$1,970,234,911	$1,173,370,432	$797,886,640
FINANCIAL PRODUCTS AND SERVICES	80,236,906	6,433,054	18,830,577	17,058,848	8,113,251	29,785,419	17,110,218	12,754,394
Miscellaneous fees	531,409	95,252	211,144	105,825	34,170	82,428	68,878	12,121
Lottery and gambling losses	7,737,404	542,904	2,055,632	1,988,650	461,183	2,685,728	1,208,566	1,520,543
Legal fees	14,825,955	505,038	3,262,656	3,624,129	1,898,335	5,535,987	3,274,691	2,261,457
Funeral expenses	7,649,030	1,788,586	2,592,328	980,021	878,586	1,409,715	893,135	516,733
Safe deposit box rental	374,428	22,046	72,552	75,951	36,305	167,777	82,115	85,789
Checking accounts, other bank service charges	2,174,473	141,027	482,748	553,430	243,245	753,860	464,976	288,904
Cemetery lots, vaults, and maintenance fees	1,567,481	222,984	499,801	71,647	77,522	695,771	355,351	340,448
Accounting fees	5,955,964	316,890	1,152,146	1,227,875	444,525	2,814,237	1,718,840	1,095,365
Miscellaneous personal services	4,278,015	342,638	1,251,982	971,920	331,872	1,371,746	443,672	965,447
Finance charges, except mortgage and vehicles	18,393,487	1,316,364	4,048,323	4,031,985	1,932,504	7,064,151	4,643,144	2,421,031
Occupational expenses	5,011,754	186,129	1,004,872	979,768	565,614	2,274,885	1,157,890	1,116,901
Expenses for other properties	10,654,920	917,685	1,979,049	2,226,124	1,093,961	4,438,136	2,539,168	1,899,002
Credit card memberships	280,240	9,424	45,267	65,065	24,773	135,325	69,498	65,783
Shopping club membership fees	665,133	26,085	131,461	147,598	84,890	274,868	164,645	110,148
CASH CONTRIBUTIONS	163,729,707	9,150,096	29,412,583	27,702,368	14,845,623	82,617,600	42,316,361	40,301,399
Support for college students	9,592,102	187,307	1,137,884	975,211	693,750	6,597,816	2,678,992	3,918,979
Alimony expenditures	5,498,976	119,486	1,142,844	1,658,010	322,796	2,255,739	1,420,784	834,940
Child support expenditures	19,198,158	1,289,101	5,244,806	4,079,328	2,866,189	5,718,367	3,648,451	2,069,874
Gifts to non–CU members of stocks, bonds, and mutual funds	2,903,562	11,275	562,741	763,814	41,431	1,524,919	1,334,532	190,289
Cash contributions to charities and other organizations	18,315,578	365,526	1,718,917	2,222,833	962,515	13,045,704	4,448,094	8,597,701
Cash contributions to church, religious organizations	65,712,121	3,473,506	11,797,713	12,332,417	5,619,404	32,489,320	18,652,624	13,836,697
Cash contributions to educational institutions	5,355,949	13,800	67,901	245,575	153,123	4,875,264	1,341,771	3,533,460
Cash contributions to political organizations	1,927,956	22,383	105,107	233,676	59,370	1,507,071	719,596	787,515
Other cash gifts	35,225,306	3,667,712	7,634,671	5,191,757	4,127,261	14,603,400	8,071,724	6,531,828
PERSONAL INSURANCE AND PENSIONS	560,851,342	33,220,951	107,904,531	102,319,415	59,621,360	257,781,488	148,278,425	109,503,594
Life and other personal insurance	45,389,516	3,527,190	9,372,501	7,866,751	4,337,617	20,285,421	11,388,197	8,897,196
Life, endowment, annuity, other personal insurance	43,975,527	3,401,477	9,161,357	7,555,352	4,228,702	19,627,943	11,004,922	8,623,120
Other nonhealth insurance	1,413,989	125,713	211,144	311,399	108,809	657,478	383,275	274,077
Pensions and Social Security	515,460,664	29,693,761	98,532,030	94,452,664	55,283,743	237,496,068	136,890,228	100,606,397
Deductions for government retirement	9,122,323	125,881	923,329	1,464,335	942,120	5,666,444	2,602,047	3,064,387
Deductions for railroad retirement	310,473	–	77,513	64,812	53,817	114,231	114,383	–
Deductions for private pensions	60,302,682	1,184,425	8,099,436	8,716,137	6,543,265	35,758,534	19,999,153	15,759,470
Nonpayroll deposit to retirement plans	46,575,592	690,326	7,136,421	7,033,822	4,960,465	26,754,078	13,631,377	13,122,968
Deductions for Social Security	399,150,756	27,693,129	82,295,331	77,173,811	42,784,077	169,202,456	100,543,269	68,659,455
PERSONAL TAXES	251,849,370	2,413,952	37,286,303	41,484,689	24,829,874	145,833,122	78,394,842	67,438,642
Federal income taxes	176,626,544	-85,996	25,063,202	28,537,829	16,091,639	107,019,557	56,455,737	50,564,036
State and local income taxes	54,899,058	1,327,303	8,297,248	9,149,564	5,984,805	30,139,795	17,005,764	13,134,029
Other taxes	20,323,768	1,172,645	3,925,853	3,797,297	2,753,322	8,674,095	4,933,341	3,740,694

Note: Numbers may not add to total because of rounding and missing subcategories. "–" means sample is too small to make a reliable estimate.
Source: Calculations by New Strategist based on the 2004 Consumer Expenditure Survey

Table 4.28 Financial: Market shares by education, 2004

(percentage of total annual spending on financial products and services, cash contributions, and miscellaneous items accounted for by consumer unit educational attainment groups, 2004)

	total consumer units	less than high school graduate	high school graduate	some college	associate's degree	college graduate total	bachelor's degree	master's, professional, doctorate
Share of total consumer units	100.0%	14.5%	26.7%	21.8%	9.2%	27.9%	17.8%	10.1%
Share of total before-tax income	100.0	7.7	20.7	18.7	9.9	43.0	24.7	18.3
Share of total spending	100.0	8.5	21.8	20.5	10.2	39.0	23.3	15.8
FINANCIAL PRODUCTS AND SERVICES	**100.0**	**8.0**	**23.5**	**21.3**	**10.1**	**37.1**	**21.3**	**15.9**
Miscellaneous fees	100.0	17.9	39.7	19.9	6.4	15.5	13.0	2.3
Lottery and gambling losses	100.0	7.0	26.6	25.7	6.0	34.7	15.6	19.7
Legal fees	100.0	3.4	22.0	24.4	12.8	37.3	22.1	15.3
Funeral expenses	100.0	23.4	33.9	12.8	11.5	18.4	11.7	6.8
Safe deposit box rental	100.0	5.9	19.4	20.3	9.7	44.8	21.9	22.9
Checking accounts, other bank service charges	100.0	6.5	22.2	25.5	11.2	34.7	21.4	13.3
Cemetery lots, vaults, and maintenance fees	100.0	14.2	31.9	4.6	4.9	44.4	22.7	21.7
Accounting fees	100.0	5.3	19.3	20.6	7.5	47.3	28.9	18.4
Miscellaneous personal services	100.0	8.0	29.3	22.7	7.8	32.1	10.4	22.6
Finance charges, except mortgage and vehicles	100.0	7.2	22.0	21.9	10.5	38.4	25.2	13.2
Occupational expenses	100.0	3.7	20.1	19.5	11.3	45.4	23.1	22.3
Expenses for other properties	100.0	8.6	18.6	20.9	10.3	41.7	23.8	17.8
Credit card memberships	100.0	3.4	16.2	23.2	8.8	48.3	24.8	23.5
Shopping club membership fees	100.0	3.9	19.8	22.2	12.8	41.3	24.8	16.6
CASH CONTRIBUTIONS	**100.0**	**5.6**	**18.0**	**16.9**	**9.1**	**50.5**	**25.8**	**24.6**
Support for college students	100.0	2.0	11.9	10.2	7.2	68.8	27.9	40.9
Alimony expenditures	100.0	2.2	20.8	30.2	5.9	41.0	25.8	15.2
Child support expenditures	100.0	6.7	27.3	21.2	14.9	29.8	19.0	10.8
Gifts to non–CU members of stocks, bonds, and mutual funds	100.0	0.4	19.4	26.3	1.4	52.5	46.0	6.6
Cash contributions to charities and other organizations	100.0	2.0	9.4	12.1	5.3	71.2	24.3	46.9
Cash contributions to church, religious organizations	100.0	5.3	18.0	18.8	8.6	49.4	28.4	21.1
Cash contributions to educational institutions	100.0	0.3	1.3	4.6	2.9	91.0	25.1	66.0
Cash contributions to political organizations	100.0	1.2	5.5	12.1	3.1	78.2	37.3	40.8
Other cash gifts	100.0	10.4	21.7	14.7	11.7	41.5	22.9	18.5
PERSONAL INSURANCE AND PENSIONS	**100.0**	**5.9**	**19.2**	**18.2**	**10.6**	**46.0**	**26.4**	**19.5**
Life and other personal insurance	**100.0**	**7.8**	**20.6**	**17.3**	**9.6**	**44.7**	**25.1**	**19.6**
Life, endowment, annuity, other personal insurance	100.0	7.7	20.8	17.2	9.6	44.6	25.0	19.6
Other nonhealth insurance	100.0	8.9	14.9	22.0	7.7	46.5	27.1	19.4
Pensions and Social Security	**100.0**	**5.8**	**19.1**	**18.3**	**10.7**	**46.1**	**26.6**	**19.5**
Deductions for government retirement	100.0	1.4	10.1	16.1	10.3	62.1	28.5	33.6
Deductions for railroad retirement	100.0	–	25.0	20.9	17.3	36.8	36.8	–
Deductions for private pensions	100.0	2.0	13.4	14.5	10.9	59.3	33.2	26.1
Nonpayroll deposit to retirement plans	100.0	1.5	15.3	15.1	10.7	57.4	29.3	28.2
Deductions for Social Security	100.0	6.9	20.6	19.3	10.7	42.4	25.2	17.2
PERSONAL TAXES	**100.0**	**1.0**	**14.8**	**16.5**	**9.9**	**57.9**	**31.1**	**26.8**
Federal income taxes	100.0	–	14.2	16.2	9.1	60.6	32.0	28.6
State and local income taxes	100.0	2.4	15.1	16.7	10.9	54.9	31.0	23.9
Other taxes	100.0	5.8	19.3	18.7	13.5	42.7	24.3	18.4

Note: Numbers may not add to total because of rounding. "–" means sample is too small to make a reliable estimate.
Source: Calculations by New Strategist based on the 2004 Consumer Expenditure Survey

Chapter 5. Spending on Food and Alcoholic Beverages, 2004

The average household spent 6 percent more on food away from home (primarily sit-down meals and take-outs from restaurants) in 2004 than in 2000, after adjusting for inflation. Spending on food at home (groceries) rose 1 percent during those years. Overall, Americans devoted 13.3 percent of their expenditures to food in 2004, down from 13.6 percent in 2000. Spending on alcoholic beverages rose 13 percent between 2000 and 2004, after adjusting for inflation.

Householders aged 45 to 54 spend the most on food, both at home and away from home. In 2004, householders aged 45 to 54 spent an average of $7,038 on food, 22 percent more than the average household. When eating out, householders aged 25 to 34 spend the most on breakfast and lunch at fast-food restaurants. Householders aged 55 to 64 are the biggest spenders on breakfast, lunch, and dinner at full-service restaurants. Householders aged 25 to 44 spend the most on alcoholic beverages.

Households with incomes of $100,000 or more spend more than twice as much as the average household on restaurant meals and alcoholic beverages. Only 13 percent of households have incomes of $100,000 or more, but they control 31 percent of consumer spending on dinners in full-service restaurants and 35 percent of spending on wine consumed at home.

Married couples with adult children at home spend more on food than any other household type—$8,682 in 2004. These households are not only larger than average, but also have the highest incomes. Married couples without children at home (most of them empty-nesters) and couples with adult children at home are the best customers of full-service restaurants. Married couples with school-aged children spend 54 percent more than the average household on fast-food lunches and 59 percent more on fast-food dinners. Spending on alcoholic beverages is highest among couples without children at home—23 percent above average.

Hispanic households spend more on food at home than any other racial or ethnic group—16 percent more than the average household in 2004. Behind the higher spending of Hispanics is their larger household size, with 3.3 people per household versus 2.5 in the average household. Asians spend more on food away from home than any other racial or ethnic group—25 percent more than the average household. They spend 63 percent more than average on lunch at full-service restaurants. Non-Hispanic whites spend the most on alcoholic beverages—14 percent more than average.

Spending on food at home is above average in the Northeast and West and below average in the Midwest and South. Households in the Northeast spend 12 percent more than average on food away from home, while households in the West spend 6 percent more. Spending on wine consumed at home is 83 percent above average in the Northeast and 30 percent above average in the West. Spending on alcoholic beverages is 7 percent below average in the Midwest and fully 24 percent below average in the South.

Because college graduates dominate the affluent, they account for a large share of the food-away-from-home market. College graduates control 44 percent of consumer spending on dinners at full-service restaurants, for example, a much greater percentage than their 28 percent share of all households. They account for 57 percent of household spending on wine consumed at home, but for only 26 percent of spending on beer consumed at home.

Table 5.1 Food and Alcohol: Average spending by age, 2004

(average annual spending of consumer units (CU) on food and alcoholic beverages, by age of consumer unit reference person, 2004)

	total consumer units	under 25	25 to 34	35 to 44	45 to 54	55 to 64	65 to 74	75+
Number of consumer units (in 000s)	116,282	8,817	19,439	24,070	23,712	17,479	11,230	11,536
Average number of persons per CU	2.5	1.9	2.9	3.2	2.7	2.1	1.9	1.5
Average before-tax income of CU	$54,453.00	$22,840.00	$52,484.00	$65,515.00	$70,434.00	$61,031.00	$42,137.00	$28,028.00
Average spending of CU, total	43,394.87	24,534.56	42,700.54	50,401.62	52,764.36	47,298.58	36,511.98	25,763.32
Food, average spending	**5,780.82**	**3,715.00**	**5,705.10**	**6,752.11**	**7,038.05**	**5,897.57**	**4,870.76**	**3,518.05**
Alcoholic beverages, average spending	**459.27**	**502.53**	**521.87**	**534.72**	**501.52**	**456.55**	**329.36**	**190.13**
FOOD AT HOME	**3,346.82**	**1,853.47**	**3,155.17**	**3,897.29**	**4,083.42**	**3,373.53**	**3,048.98**	**2,380.20**
Cereals and bakery products	**460.90**	**265.16**	**432.17**	**551.69**	**547.13**	**436.89**	**422.02**	**364.41**
Cereals and cereal products	153.80	98.69	152.41	194.23	180.66	136.78	125.73	109.61
Flour	8.32	4.82	8.31	8.26	9.11	7.17	8.27	11.54
Prepared flour mixes	13.78	8.12	12.42	16.61	17.21	11.85	12.06	12.02
Ready-to-eat and cooked cereals	86.69	54.50	85.06	109.73	99.55	77.12	74.21	65.07
Rice	18.46	13.42	19.19	26.29	22.25	15.93	11.85	6.51
Pasta, cornmeal, and other cereal products	26.55	17.83	27.43	33.34	32.54	24.72	19.34	14.48
Bakery products	307.10	166.48	279.77	357.46	366.47	300.11	296.29	254.80
Bread	87.63	49.96	76.52	93.97	104.28	90.81	86.77	84.86
White bread	35.04	22.74	34.47	39.44	39.39	34.84	32.06	30.45
Bread, other than white	52.59	27.23	42.04	54.53	64.89	55.98	54.72	54.41
Crackers and cookies	71.16	41.98	65.40	82.60	84.98	65.32	69.04	61.87
Cookies	46.57	28.70	43.50	54.69	56.38	40.76	44.18	39.25
Crackers	24.60	13.28	21.90	27.91	28.60	24.56	24.86	22.61
Frozen and refrigerated bakery products	26.32	15.87	24.72	35.56	27.78	24.08	26.34	17.48
Other bakery products	121.99	58.66	113.13	145.33	149.43	119.91	114.13	90.59
Biscuits and rolls	42.11	19.44	34.11	49.35	55.80	41.86	40.91	31.43
Cakes and cupcakes	39.04	15.13	45.82	49.85	42.41	36.66	35.53	22.34
Bread and cracker products	3.25	1.52	2.36	3.85	4.76	2.96	2.76	2.70
Sweetrolls, coffee cakes, doughnuts	23.59	14.07	19.97	26.75	28.31	22.78	25.14	20.49
Pies, tarts, turnovers	13.99	8.51	10.86	15.53	18.15	15.64	9.79	13.63
Meats, poultry, fish, and eggs	**879.71**	**480.11**	**812.03**	**1,019.37**	**1,111.05**	**894.38**	**799.10**	**583.69**
Beef	265.34	148.28	249.58	312.69	337.98	257.22	235.69	172.24
Ground beef	96.92	60.06	93.58	113.28	124.17	94.73	83.34	55.88
Roast	45.58	19.43	41.80	48.64	57.24	43.04	51.87	39.52
Chuck roast	11.72	4.19	11.10	12.56	15.24	10.98	12.76	9.69
Round roast	10.27	3.46	10.24	11.71	11.24	9.55	12.19	9.78
Other roast	23.58	11.77	20.46	24.36	30.76	22.51	26.92	20.04
Steak	103.45	59.38	94.19	127.72	132.70	102.69	81.57	63.47
Round steak	16.37	8.28	15.11	21.85	20.45	16.17	11.49	9.65
Sirloin steak	32.38	18.73	30.54	40.32	42.72	28.12	24.87	21.49
Other steak	54.71	32.36	48.53	65.56	69.53	58.39	45.20	32.33
Other beef	19.39	9.41	20.01	23.05	23.87	16.76	18.91	13.37
Pork	181.14	95.46	161.12	204.38	222.34	203.17	172.54	121.93
Bacon	31.08	14.07	27.89	34.04	37.47	33.18	34.14	24.05
Pork chops	37.92	25.23	34.17	42.29	53.71	38.93	27.15	21.16
Ham	39.65	17.25	33.94	44.57	43.76	50.94	37.68	32.91
Ham, not canned	38.67	16.42	33.31	43.90	42.54	50.14	36.36	31.12
Canned ham	0.98	0.83	0.62	0.67	1.22	0.80	1.33	1.79
Sausage	27.91	11.17	23.93	34.95	34.00	32.64	25.69	14.92
Other pork	44.59	27.74	41.19	48.54	53.40	47.49	47.87	28.90
Other meats	107.98	52.78	97.18	125.20	140.41	102.17	113.46	68.39
Frankfurters	22.52	11.98	22.85	27.06	27.02	22.38	19.78	13.81
Lunch meats (cold cuts)	72.99	35.18	64.58	87.10	99.86	67.04	65.14	47.70
Bologna, liverwurst, salami	21.07	10.30	19.48	25.36	27.54	19.90	18.51	13.90
Other lunch meats	51.91	24.87	45.09	61.74	72.32	47.14	46.62	33.80
Lamb, organ meats, and others	12.48	5.63	9.75	11.03	13.53	12.76	28.54	6.88
Poultry	155.61	100.63	154.42	181.61	195.57	155.92	122.55	93.03
Fresh and frozen chicken	122.64	88.37	120.44	144.20	154.88	121.36	96.66	66.45
Fresh and frozen whole chicken	36.59	26.26	36.73	38.90	45.10	39.66	32.33	21.00
Fresh and frozen chicken parts	86.04	62.11	83.71	105.29	109.77	81.70	64.33	45.45
Other poultry	32.97	12.26	33.98	37.41	40.70	34.56	25.89	26.58

	total consumer units	under 25	25 to 34	35 to 44	45 to 54	55 to 64	65 to 74	75+
Fish and seafood	$127.80	$56.68	$111.56	$150.57	$166.66	$130.10	$111.12	$95.35
Canned fish and seafood	15.38	9.46	9.73	16.56	18.81	18.15	15.90	15.67
Fresh fish and shellfish	74.88	30.45	66.06	88.32	100.00	77.73	67.31	46.89
Frozen fish and shellfish	37.54	16.78	35.77	45.69	47.84	34.21	27.91	32.79
Eggs	41.84	26.27	38.19	44.93	48.09	45.80	43.74	32.75
Dairy products	**370.57**	**204.92**	**346.41**	**440.32**	**436.43**	**371.39**	**352.64**	**270.79**
Fresh milk and cream	144.33	86.19	147.50	177.02	160.79	136.61	125.33	109.90
Fresh milk, all types	128.94	79.18	132.79	159.16	143.87	120.21	109.30	97.47
Cream	15.39	7.01	14.71	17.86	16.92	16.40	16.04	12.43
Other dairy products	226.24	118.73	198.91	263.30	275.64	234.78	227.31	160.90
Butter	21.81	9.81	16.59	23.34	28.19	24.93	23.42	17.51
Cheese	113.67	58.66	98.17	135.27	143.21	117.80	110.28	72.36
Ice cream and related products	60.22	31.18	52.90	67.98	70.78	62.32	59.58	54.84
Miscellaneous dairy products	30.54	19.08	31.25	36.71	33.47	29.72	34.03	16.18
Fruits and vegetables	**560.95**	**285.31**	**521.29**	**615.40**	**672.73**	**587.72**	**548.27**	**469.54**
Fresh fruits	186.74	91.79	167.88	198.79	229.14	199.32	182.61	165.87
Apples	32.42	16.56	30.07	40.07	39.30	33.73	26.75	21.74
Bananas	30.17	16.71	29.84	30.32	35.77	30.29	29.24	30.35
Oranges	19.48	9.40	20.15	21.53	23.72	17.62	21.40	13.82
Citrus fruits, excluding oranges	15.41	7.65	13.48	15.88	19.32	16.94	14.51	14.34
Other fresh fruits	89.25	41.46	74.35	90.98	111.03	100.73	90.70	85.62
Fresh vegetables	182.94	85.61	166.11	200.19	219.31	199.71	191.32	141.90
Potatoes	28.07	12.69	26.28	32.63	32.09	28.21	30.20	22.73
Lettuce	22.87	12.01	20.30	25.23	28.43	25.38	22.43	15.78
Tomatoes	35.74	19.73	35.19	38.87	39.99	37.44	38.91	27.84
Other fresh vegetables	96.25	41.18	84.33	103.45	118.80	108.68	99.78	75.55
Processed fruits	109.63	63.89	109.92	121.97	125.60	108.33	97.19	99.98
Frozen fruits and fruit juices	9.97	5.34	8.03	10.82	11.03	10.46	9.94	12.36
Frozen orange juice	4.17	2.48	3.79	4.57	4.13	3.58	3.65	6.91
Frozen fruits	3.53	0.70	2.25	3.41	4.55	4.80	4.29	3.46
Frozen fruit juices, excluding orange	2.27	2.16	1.99	2.85	2.36	2.08	2.00	1.99
Canned fruits	16.19	7.24	13.88	18.37	18.42	16.17	14.52	19.93
Dried fruits	6.35	1.76	5.08	7.49	5.95	7.70	6.54	8.40
Fresh fruit juice	22.07	9.88	23.45	24.17	25.68	25.09	19.44	15.14
Canned and bottled fruit juice	55.05	39.67	59.48	61.11	64.52	48.92	46.75	44.15
Processed vegetables	81.64	44.02	77.38	94.45	98.68	80.37	77.16	61.79
Frozen vegetables	28.50	11.67	24.77	34.98	37.48	27.43	26.08	19.58
Canned and dried vegetables and juices	53.14	32.35	52.61	59.47	61.21	52.94	51.08	42.21
Canned beans	11.39	7.46	11.12	13.31	12.74	11.23	11.36	8.24
Canned corn	6.33	5.10	7.50	7.71	7.08	5.63	4.26	3.78
Canned miscellaneous vegetables	16.77	6.89	15.37	17.35	20.09	18.95	16.42	15.95
Dried peas	0.60	0.35	0.55	0.81	0.67	0.55	0.56	0.42
Dried beans	2.47	1.74	3.11	2.77	2.56	2.57	1.43	2.01
Dried miscellaneous vegetables	6.21	5.74	6.39	6.59	7.20	5.64	6.41	4.00
Dried processed vegetables	0.30	0.09	0.53	0.54	0.18	0.25	–	0.18
Fresh and canned vegetable juices	8.91	4.83	7.93	10.31	10.49	7.92	10.48	7.42
Sugar and other sweets	**128.12**	**53.61**	**112.93**	**145.95**	**162.42**	**137.32**	**126.68**	**90.62**
Candy and chewing gum	83.13	33.77	74.48	97.01	107.67	88.20	77.96	53.19
Sugar	16.10	8.64	16.36	18.84	18.51	15.14	15.90	12.13
Artificial sweeteners	6.85	1.48	3.59	5.03	9.78	8.79	9.69	9.03
Jams, preserves, other sweets	22.04	9.73	18.50	25.07	26.47	25.18	23.13	16.26
Fats and oils	**88.89**	**44.52**	**78.32**	**97.12**	**111.98**	**96.97**	**84.08**	**69.01**
Margarine	9.57	3.32	6.69	8.83	12.21	11.09	11.61	11.39
Fats and oils	28.56	16.78	26.12	32.36	35.26	31.00	24.17	20.58
Salad dressings	27.44	16.49	25.86	29.58	34.55	28.65	26.73	18.12
Nondairy cream and imitation milk	10.80	3.18	8.17	11.64	14.38	13.23	11.27	8.02
Peanut butter	12.52	4.77	11.48	14.72	15.58	13.00	10.29	10.90

	total consumer units	under 25	25 to 34	35 to 44	45 to 54	55 to 64	65 to 74	75+
Miscellaneous foods	**$527.29**	**$333.86**	**$544.98**	**$643.48**	**$623.38**	**$485.00**	**$445.72**	**$339.61**
Frozen prepared foods	109.90	79.44	112.60	133.64	134.85	88.88	93.60	73.45
Frozen meals	31.79	22.59	29.55	33.48	38.28	28.75	27.96	34.58
Other frozen prepared foods	78.11	56.86	83.06	100.16	96.57	60.13	65.64	38.87
Canned and packaged soups	36.50	18.25	31.65	36.91	44.95	41.62	34.11	35.78
Potato chips, nuts, and other snacks	117.08	58.55	108.78	147.71	144.60	115.03	107.67	65.69
Potato chips and other snacks	86.06	47.76	89.50	116.86	105.48	75.86	64.31	39.43
Nuts	31.01	10.80	19.28	30.85	39.12	39.16	43.36	26.26
Condiments and seasonings	93.65	49.48	86.62	115.67	115.09	94.15	85.98	54.71
Salt, spices, and other seasonings	22.22	12.50	22.63	25.31	27.13	21.09	23.38	12.59
Olives, pickles, relishes	10.52	3.82	7.93	11.42	14.03	11.87	10.45	9.17
Sauces and gravies	40.94	24.67	39.98	55.27	49.04	39.24	32.50	18.04
Baking needs and miscellaneous products	19.97	8.48	16.09	23.66	24.89	21.96	19.64	14.90
Other canned/packaged prepared foods	170.16	128.15	205.32	209.56	183.89	145.32	124.37	109.98
Prepared salads	25.43	10.83	18.63	26.11	32.75	29.88	28.83	22.08
Prepared desserts	10.91	4.88	10.05	11.86	12.18	10.93	11.97	11.45
Baby food	30.08	39.71	69.51	44.96	15.05	7.76	9.69	5.69
Miscellaneous prepared foods	102.74	72.73	106.85	125.36	123.28	93.53	73.87	69.88
Nonalcoholic beverages	**289.52**	**170.72**	**281.19**	**340.13**	**369.72**	**295.02**	**225.91**	**174.75**
Cola	93.81	55.21	90.96	107.59	118.84	104.63	73.88	49.98
Other carbonated drinks	48.08	34.14	44.15	57.97	61.06	50.43	35.20	26.47
Coffee	39.12	11.69	27.91	37.44	56.15	46.18	42.33	34.91
Roasted coffee	24.48	6.71	17.86	23.18	34.60	29.99	27.78	20.22
Instant and freeze-dried coffee	14.64	4.98	10.04	14.26	21.55	16.19	14.55	14.68
Noncarbonated fruit-flavored drinks	19.79	16.46	23.24	28.62	21.58	15.78	12.15	6.93
Tea	17.63	13.24	14.75	18.96	23.28	19.36	14.91	11.54
Other nonalcoholic beverages and ice	70.10	39.99	79.32	89.43	86.61	57.78	46.49	43.42
Food prepared by CU on trips	**40.86**	**15.25**	**25.85**	**43.82**	**48.57**	**68.84**	**44.56**	**17.77**
FOOD AWAY FROM HOME	**2,434.00**	**1,861.52**	**2,549.94**	**2,854.82**	**2,954.62**	**2,524.04**	**1,821.78**	**1,137.85**
Meals at restaurants, carry-outs, other	**2,028.17**	**1,628.27**	**2,202.53**	**2,369.68**	**2,386.25**	**2,090.22**	**1,465.06**	**995.83**
Lunch	725.07	597.73	822.77	898.18	831.01	669.03	477.58	383.38
At fast-food restaurants*	409.17	413.09	523.53	499.46	470.47	338.47	232.35	159.63
At full-service restaurants	236.65	133.81	226.22	246.54	256.33	277.97	232.66	215.14
At vending machines, mobile vendors	6.02	5.79	5.25	6.36	7.65	9.56	1.91	2.06
At employer and school cafeterias	73.24	45.04	67.76	145.82	96.57	43.03	10.66	6.55
Dinner	795.59	573.99	809.14	888.51	954.26	903.41	653.92	382.41
At fast-food restaurants*	253.07	253.02	294.77	324.09	312.17	196.95	158.60	78.02
At full-service restaurants	538.22	312.64	512.58	557.91	639.31	699.21	493.74	302.39
At vending machines, mobile vendors	1.50	0.53	0.35	0.69	1.23	5.68	0.98	0.76
At employer and school cafeterias	2.79	7.79	1.44	5.82	1.54	1.58	0.60	1.24
Snacks and nonalcoholic beverages	297.45	286.39	347.35	364.81	358.67	284.76	159.11	97.60
At fast-food restaurants*	217.16	188.43	261.20	270.62	258.17	206.05	119.63	72.04
At full-service restaurants	28.87	31.53	26.81	26.61	35.85	34.35	21.77	19.31
At vending machines, mobile vendors	41.07	53.63	47.00	52.18	52.16	36.57	15.62	4.89
At employer and school cafeterias	10.34	12.81	12.34	15.40	12.49	7.79	2.09	1.37
Breakfast and brunch	210.06	170.17	223.28	218.18	242.31	233.01	174.46	132.44
At fast-food restaurants*	103.28	105.40	126.58	115.47	121.41	100.99	59.63	42.04
At full-service restaurants	100.36	57.01	90.56	94.07	111.62	125.94	113.57	89.74
At vending machines, mobile vendors	1.42	2.38	1.55	1.35	1.87	1.70	0.41	0.24
At employer and school cafeterias	5.00	5.38	4.60	7.30	7.41	4.38	0.86	0.42
Board (including at school)	**27.89**	**58.21**	**1.99**	**11.84**	**69.77**	**35.72**	**1.69**	**9.37**
Catered affairs	**58.56**	**28.78**	**90.68**	**32.44**	**91.76**	**49.89**	**76.01**	**9.55**
Food on trips	**231.55**	**102.65**	**175.77**	**247.78**	**290.73**	**313.38**	**260.97**	**115.93**
School lunches	**63.39**	**6.16**	**43.66**	**157.11**	**94.50**	**17.99**	**7.64**	**3.99**
Meals as pay	**24.45**	**37.46**	**35.30**	**35.97**	**21.62**	**16.84**	**10.41**	**3.17**

	total consumer units	under 25	25 to 34	35 to 44	45 to 54	55 to 64	65 to 74	75+
ALCOHOLIC BEVERAGES	$459.27	$502.53	$521.87	$534.72	$501.52	$456.55	$329.36	$190.13
At home	277.59	277.79	281.72	363.54	294.30	279.03	199.75	120.08
Beer and ale	131.31	182.80	182.57	172.98	132.46	93.87	55.45	37.72
Whiskey	21.66	24.54	11.95	26.93	21.55	26.69	23.09	15.94
Wine	94.55	38.62	59.49	135.56	111.59	115.32	92.66	45.09
Other alcoholic beverages	30.07	31.83	27.71	28.06	28.69	43.15	28.56	21.32
Away from home	181.68	224.73	240.15	171.18	207.22	177.53	129.61	70.05
Beer and ale	76.32	102.53	106.75	68.69	88.64	69.58	49.59	28.45
At fast-food restaurants*	16.44	30.84	26.16	15.53	14.61	13.75	10.67	3.08
At full-service restaurants	56.01	71.49	78.31	52.21	61.27	54.24	34.28	25.32
Wine	22.29	32.57	29.61	19.29	25.68	20.67	15.80	9.28
At fast-food restaurants*	3.06	5.84	5.55	2.63	2.83	1.76	2.32	0.50
At full-service restaurants	18.76	26.73	23.99	16.66	21.55	18.86	11.51	8.77
Other alcoholic beverages	44.71	62.90	63.87	44.28	48.82	38.24	26.82	15.83
At fast-food restaurants*	3.82	7.91	8.24	4.06	2.59	1.62	1.48	0.43
At full-service restaurants	39.44	54.99	55.30	40.00	40.79	36.26	23.36	15.37
Alcoholic beverages purchased on trips	38.37	26.73	39.93	38.92	44.08	49.04	37.40	16.49

The category fast-food restaurants also includes take-out, delivery, concession stands, buffets, and cafeterias other than employer and school.
Note: Subcategories may not add to total because some are not shown. "–" means sample is too small to make a reliable estimate.
Source: Bureau of Labor Statistics, unpublished tables from the 2004 Consumer Expenditure Survey

Table 5.2 Food and Alcohol: Indexed spending by age, 2004

(indexed average annual spending of consumer units (CU) on food and alcoholic beverages, by age of consumer unit reference person, 2004; index definition: an index of 100 is the average for all consumer units; an index of 132 means that spending by consumer units in that group is 32 percent above the average for all consumer units; an index of 68 indicates spending that is 32 percent below the average for all consumer units)

	total consumer units	under 25	25 to 34	35 to 44	45 to 54	55 to 64	65 to 74	75+
Average spending of CU, total	$43,395	$24,535	$42,701	$50,402	$52,764	$47,299	$36,512	$25,763
Average spending of CU, index	100	57	98	116	122	109	84	59
Food, spending index	100	64	99	117	122	102	84	61
Alcoholic beverages, spending index	100	109	114	116	109	99	72	41
FOOD AT HOME	100	55	94	116	122	101	91	71
Cereals and bakery products	100	58	94	120	119	95	92	79
Cereals and cereal products	100	64	99	126	117	89	82	71
Flour	100	58	100	99	109	86	99	139
Prepared flour mixes	100	59	90	121	125	86	88	87
Ready-to-eat and cooked cereals	100	63	98	127	115	89	86	75
Rice	100	73	104	142	121	86	64	35
Pasta, cornmeal, and other cereal products	100	67	103	126	123	93	73	55
Bakery products	100	54	91	116	119	98	96	83
Bread	100	57	87	107	119	104	99	97
White bread	100	65	98	113	112	99	91	87
Bread, other than white	100	52	80	104	123	106	104	103
Crackers and cookies	100	59	92	116	119	92	97	87
Cookies	100	62	93	117	121	88	95	84
Crackers	100	54	89	113	116	100	101	92
Frozen and refrigerated bakery products	100	60	94	135	106	91	100	66
Other bakery products	100	48	93	119	122	98	94	74
Biscuits and rolls	100	46	81	117	133	99	97	75
Cakes and cupcakes	100	39	117	128	109	94	91	57
Bread and cracker products	100	47	73	118	146	91	85	83
Sweetrolls, coffee cakes, doughnuts	100	60	85	113	120	97	107	87
Pies, tarts, turnovers	100	61	78	111	130	112	70	97
Meats, poultry, fish, and eggs	100	55	92	116	126	102	91	66
Beef	100	56	94	118	127	97	89	65
Ground beef	100	62	97	117	128	98	86	58
Roast	100	43	92	107	126	94	114	87
Chuck roast	100	36	95	107	130	94	109	83
Round roast	100	34	100	114	109	93	119	95
Other roast	100	50	87	103	130	95	114	85
Steak	100	57	91	123	128	99	79	61
Round steak	100	51	92	133	125	99	70	59
Sirloin steak	100	58	94	125	132	87	77	66
Other steak	100	59	89	120	127	107	83	59
Other beef	100	49	103	119	123	86	98	69
Pork	100	53	89	113	123	112	95	67
Bacon	100	45	90	110	121	107	110	77
Pork chops	100	67	90	112	142	103	72	56
Ham	100	44	86	112	110	128	95	83
Ham, not canned	100	42	86	114	110	130	94	80
Canned ham	100	85	63	68	124	82	136	183
Sausage	100	40	86	125	122	117	92	53
Other pork	100	62	92	109	120	107	107	65
Other meats	100	49	90	116	130	95	105	63
Frankfurters	100	53	101	120	120	99	88	61
Lunch meats (cold cuts)	100	48	88	119	137	92	89	65
Bologna, liverwurst, salami	100	49	92	120	131	94	88	66
Other lunch meats	100	48	87	119	139	91	90	65
Lamb, organ meats, and others	100	45	78	88	108	102	229	55
Poultry	100	65	99	117	126	100	79	60
Fresh and frozen chicken	100	72	98	118	126	99	79	54
Fresh and frozen whole chicken	100	72	100	106	123	108	88	57
Fresh and frozen chicken parts	100	72	97	122	128	95	75	53
Other poultry	100	37	103	113	123	105	79	81

	total consumer units	under 25	25 to 34	35 to 44	45 to 54	55 to 64	65 to 74	75+
Fish and seafood	100	44	87	118	130	102	87	75
Canned fish and seafood	100	62	63	108	122	118	103	102
Fresh fish and shellfish	100	41	88	118	134	104	90	63
Frozen fish and shellfish	100	45	95	122	127	91	74	87
Eggs	100	63	91	107	115	109	105	78
Dairy products	**100**	**55**	**93**	**119**	**118**	**100**	**95**	**73**
Fresh milk and cream	100	60	102	123	111	95	87	76
Fresh milk, all types	100	61	103	123	112	93	85	76
Cream	100	46	96	116	110	107	104	81
Other dairy products	100	52	88	116	122	104	100	71
Butter	100	45	76	107	129	114	107	80
Cheese	100	52	86	119	126	104	97	64
Ice cream and related products	100	52	88	113	118	103	99	91
Miscellaneous dairy products	100	62	102	120	110	97	111	53
Fruits and vegetables	**100**	**51**	**93**	**110**	**120**	**105**	**98**	**84**
Fresh fruits	100	49	90	106	123	107	98	89
Apples	100	51	93	124	121	104	83	67
Bananas	100	55	99	100	119	100	97	101
Oranges	100	48	103	111	122	90	110	71
Citrus fruits, excluding oranges	100	50	87	103	125	110	94	93
Other fresh fruits	100	46	83	102	124	113	102	96
Fresh vegetables	100	47	91	109	120	109	105	78
Potatoes	100	45	94	116	114	100	108	81
Lettuce	100	53	89	110	124	111	98	69
Tomatoes	100	55	98	109	112	105	109	78
Other fresh vegetables	100	43	88	107	123	113	104	78
Processed fruits	100	58	100	111	115	99	89	91
Frozen fruits and fruit juices	100	54	81	109	111	105	100	124
Frozen orange juice	100	59	91	110	99	86	88	166
Frozen fruits	100	20	64	97	129	136	122	98
Frozen fruit juices, excluding orange	100	95	88	126	104	92	88	88
Canned fruits	100	45	86	113	114	100	90	123
Dried fruits	100	28	80	118	94	121	103	132
Fresh fruit juice	100	45	106	110	116	114	88	69
Canned and bottled fruit juice	100	72	108	111	117	89	85	80
Processed vegetables	100	54	95	116	121	98	95	76
Frozen vegetables	100	41	87	123	132	96	92	69
Canned and dried vegetables and juices	100	61	99	112	115	100	96	79
Canned beans	100	65	98	117	112	99	100	72
Canned corn	100	81	118	122	112	89	67	60
Canned miscellaneous vegetables	100	41	92	103	120	113	98	95
Dried peas	100	58	92	135	112	92	93	70
Dried beans	100	70	126	112	104	104	58	81
Dried miscellaneous vegetables	100	92	103	106	116	91	103	64
Dried processed vegetables	100	30	177	180	60	83	–	60
Fresh and canned vegetable juices	100	54	89	116	118	89	118	83
Sugar and other sweets	**100**	**42**	**88**	**114**	**127**	**107**	**99**	**71**
Candy and chewing gum	100	41	90	117	130	106	94	64
Sugar	100	54	102	117	115	94	99	75
Artificial sweeteners	100	22	52	73	143	128	141	132
Jams, preserves, other sweets	100	44	84	114	120	114	105	74
Fats and oils	**100**	**50**	**88**	**109**	**126**	**109**	**95**	**78**
Margarine	100	35	70	92	128	116	121	119
Fats and oils	100	59	91	113	123	109	85	72
Salad dressings	100	60	94	108	126	104	97	66
Nondairy cream and imitation milk	100	29	76	108	133	123	104	74
Peanut butter	100	38	92	118	124	104	82	87

	total consumer units	under 25	25 to 34	35 to 44	45 to 54	55 to 64	65 to 74	75+
Miscellaneous foods	**100**	**63**	**103**	**122**	**118**	**92**	**85**	**64**
Frozen prepared foods	100	72	102	122	123	81	85	67
Frozen meals	100	71	93	105	120	90	88	109
Other frozen prepared foods	100	73	106	128	124	77	84	50
Canned and packaged soups	100	50	87	101	123	114	93	98
Potato chips, nuts, and other snacks	100	50	93	126	124	98	92	56
Potato chips and other snacks	100	55	104	136	123	88	75	46
Nuts	100	35	62	99	126	126	140	85
Condiments and seasonings	100	53	92	124	123	101	92	58
Salt, spices, and other seasonings	100	56	102	114	122	95	105	57
Olives, pickles, relishes	100	36	75	109	133	113	99	87
Sauces and gravies	100	60	98	135	120	96	79	44
Baking needs and miscellaneous products	100	42	81	118	125	110	98	75
Other canned/packaged prepared foods	100	75	121	123	108	85	73	65
Prepared salads	100	43	73	103	129	117	113	87
Prepared desserts	100	45	92	109	112	100	110	105
Baby food	100	132	231	149	50	26	32	19
Miscellaneous prepared foods	100	71	104	122	120	91	72	68
Nonalcoholic beverages	**100**	**59**	**97**	**117**	**128**	**102**	**78**	**60**
Cola	100	59	97	115	127	112	79	53
Other carbonated drinks	100	71	92	121	127	105	73	55
Coffee	100	30	71	96	144	118	108	89
Roasted coffee	100	27	73	95	141	123	113	83
Instant and freeze-dried coffee	100	34	69	97	147	111	99	100
Noncarbonated fruit-flavored drinks	100	83	117	145	109	80	61	35
Tea	100	75	84	108	132	110	85	65
Other nonalcoholic beverages and ice	100	57	113	128	124	82	66	62
Food prepared by CU on trips	**100**	**37**	**63**	**107**	**119**	**168**	**109**	**43**
FOOD AWAY FROM HOME	**100**	**76**	**105**	**117**	**121**	**104**	**75**	**47**
Meals at restaurants, carry-outs, other	**100**	**80**	**109**	**117**	**118**	**103**	**72**	**49**
Lunch	100	82	113	124	115	92	66	53
At fast-food restaurants*	100	101	128	122	115	83	57	39
At full-service restaurants	100	57	96	104	108	117	98	91
At vending machines, mobile vendors	100	96	87	106	127	159	32	34
At employer and school cafeterias	100	61	93	199	132	59	15	9
Dinner	100	72	102	112	120	114	82	48
At fast-food restaurants*	100	100	116	128	123	78	63	31
At full-service restaurants	100	58	95	104	119	130	92	56
At vending machines, mobile vendors	100	35	23	46	82	379	65	51
At employer and school cafeterias	100	279	52	209	55	57	22	44
Snacks and nonalcoholic beverages	100	96	117	123	121	96	53	33
At fast-food restaurants*	100	87	120	125	119	95	55	33
At full-service restaurants	100	109	93	92	124	119	75	67
At vending machines, mobile vendors	100	131	114	127	127	89	38	12
At employer and school cafeterias	100	124	119	149	121	75	20	13
Breakfast and brunch	100	81	106	104	115	111	83	63
At fast-food restaurants*	100	102	123	112	118	98	58	41
At full-service restaurants	100	57	90	94	111	125	113	89
At vending machines, mobile vendors	100	168	109	95	132	120	29	17
At employer and school cafeterias	100	108	92	146	148	88	17	8
Board (including at school)	**100**	**209**	**7**	**42**	**250**	**128**	**6**	**34**
Catered affairs	**100**	**49**	**155**	**55**	**157**	**85**	**130**	**16**
Food on trips	**100**	**44**	**76**	**107**	**126**	**135**	**113**	**50**
School lunches	**100**	**10**	**69**	**248**	**149**	**28**	**12**	**6**
Meals as pay	**100**	**153**	**144**	**147**	**88**	**69**	**43**	**13**

	total consumer units	under 25	25 to 34	35 to 44	45 to 54	55 to 64	65 to 74	75+
ALCOHOLIC BEVERAGES	**100**	**109**	**114**	**116**	**109**	**99**	**72**	**41**
At home	**100**	**100**	**101**	**131**	**106**	**101**	**72**	**43**
Beer and ale	100	139	139	132	101	71	42	29
Whiskey	100	113	55	124	99	123	107	74
Wine	100	41	63	143	118	122	98	48
Other alcoholic beverages	100	106	92	93	95	143	95	71
Away from home	**100**	**124**	**132**	**94**	**114**	**98**	**71**	**39**
Beer and ale	100	134	140	90	116	91	65	37
At fast-food restaurants*	100	188	159	94	89	84	65	19
At full-service restaurants	100	128	140	93	109	97	61	45
Wine	100	146	133	87	115	93	71	42
At fast-food restaurants*	100	191	181	86	92	58	76	16
At full-service restaurants	100	142	128	89	115	101	61	47
Other alcoholic beverages	100	141	143	99	109	86	60	35
At fast-food restaurants*	100	207	216	106	68	42	39	11
At full-service restaurants	100	139	140	101	103	92	59	39
Alcoholic beverages purchased on trips	100	70	104	101	115	128	97	43

The category fast-food restaurants also includes take-out, delivery, concession stands, buffets, and cafeterias other than employer and school.

Note: "–" means sample is too small to make a reliable estimate.

Source: Calculations by New Strategist based on the 2004 Consumer Expenditure Survey

Table 5.3 Food and Alcohol: Total spending by age, 2004

(total annual spending on food and alcoholic beverages, by consumer unit (CU) age groups, 2004; consumer units and dollars in thousands)

	total consumer units	under 25	25 to 34	35 to 44	45 to 54	55 to 64	65 to 74	75+
Number of consumer units	116,282	8,817	19,439	24,070	23,712	17,479	11,230	11,536
Total spending of all CUs	$5,046,042,273	$216,321,216	$830,055,797	$1,213,166,993	$1,251,148,504	$826,731,880	$410,029,535	$297,205,660
Food, total spending	672,205,311	32,755,155	110,901,439	162,523,288	166,886,242	103,083,626	54,698,635	40,584,225
Alcoholic beverages, total spending	53,404,834	4,430,807	10,144,631	12,870,710	11,892,042	7,980,037	3,698,713	2,193,340
FOOD AT HOME	389,174,923	16,342,045	61,333,350	93,807,770	96,826,055	58,965,931	34,240,045	27,457,987
Cereals and bakery products	53,594,374	2,337,916	8,400,953	13,279,178	12,973,547	7,636,400	4,739,285	4,203,834
Cereals and cereal products	17,884,172	870,150	2,962,698	4,675,116	4,283,810	2,390,778	1,411,948	1,264,461
Flour	967,466	42,498	161,538	198,818	216,016	125,324	92,872	133,125
Prepared flour mixes	1,602,366	71,594	241,432	399,803	408,084	207,126	135,434	138,663
Ready-to-eat and cooked cereals	10,080,487	480,527	1,653,481	2,641,201	2,360,530	1,347,980	833,378	750,648
Rice	2,146,566	118,324	373,034	632,800	527,592	278,440	133,076	75,099
Pasta, cornmeal, and other cereal products	3,087,287	157,207	533,212	802,494	771,588	432,081	217,188	167,041
Bakery products	35,710,202	1,467,854	5,438,449	8,604,062	8,689,737	5,245,623	3,327,337	2,939,373
Bread	10,189,792	440,497	1,487,472	2,261,858	2,472,687	1,587,268	974,427	978,945
White bread	4,074,521	200,499	670,062	949,321	934,016	608,968	360,034	351,271
Bread, other than white	6,115,270	240,087	817,216	1,312,537	1,538,672	978,474	614,506	627,674
Crackers and cookies	8,274,627	370,138	1,271,311	1,988,182	2,015,046	1,141,728	775,319	713,732
Cookies	5,415,253	253,048	845,597	1,316,388	1,336,883	712,444	496,141	452,788
Crackers	2,860,537	117,090	425,714	671,794	678,163	429,284	279,178	260,829
Frozen and refrigerated bakery products	3,060,542	139,926	480,532	855,929	658,719	420,894	295,798	201,649
Other bakery products	14,185,241	517,205	2,199,134	3,498,093	3,543,284	2,095,907	1,281,680	1,045,046
Biscuits and rolls	4,896,635	171,402	663,064	1,187,855	1,323,130	731,671	459,419	362,576
Cakes and cupcakes	4,539,649	133,401	890,695	1,199,890	1,005,626	640,780	399,002	257,714
Bread and cracker products	377,917	13,402	45,876	92,670	112,869	51,738	30,995	31,147
Sweetrolls, coffee cakes, doughnuts	2,743,092	124,055	388,197	643,873	671,287	398,172	282,322	236,373
Pies, tarts, turnovers	1,626,785	75,033	211,108	373,807	430,373	273,372	109,942	157,236
Meats, poultry, fish, and eggs	102,294,438	4,233,130	15,785,051	24,536,236	26,345,218	15,632,868	8,973,893	6,733,448
Beef	30,854,266	1,307,385	4,851,586	7,526,448	8,014,182	4,495,948	2,646,799	1,986,961
Ground beef	11,270,051	529,549	1,819,102	2,726,650	2,944,319	1,655,786	935,908	644,632
Roast	5,300,134	171,314	812,550	1,170,765	1,357,275	752,296	582,500	455,903
Chuck roast	1,362,825	36,943	215,773	302,319	361,371	191,919	143,295	111,784
Round roast	1,194,216	30,507	199,055	281,860	266,523	166,924	136,894	112,822
Other roast	2,741,930	103,776	397,722	586,345	729,381	393,452	302,312	231,181
Steak	12,029,373	523,553	1,830,959	3,074,220	3,146,582	1,794,919	916,031	732,190
Round steak	1,903,536	73,005	293,723	525,930	484,910	282,635	129,033	111,322
Sirloin steak	3,765,211	165,142	593,667	970,502	1,012,977	491,509	279,290	247,909
Other steak	6,361,788	285,318	943,375	1,578,029	1,648,695	1,020,599	507,596	372,959
Other beef	2,254,708	82,968	388,974	554,814	566,005	292,948	212,359	154,236
Pork	21,063,321	841,671	3,132,012	4,919,427	5,272,126	3,551,208	1,937,624	1,406,584
Bacon	3,614,045	124,055	542,154	819,343	888,489	579,953	383,392	277,441
Pork chops	4,409,413	222,453	664,231	1,017,920	1,273,572	680,457	304,895	244,102
Ham	4,610,581	152,093	659,760	1,072,800	1,037,637	890,380	423,146	379,650
Ham, not canned	4,496,625	144,775	647,513	1,056,673	1,008,708	876,397	408,323	359,000
Canned ham	113,956	7,318	12,052	16,127	28,929	13,983	14,936	20,649
Sausage	3,245,431	98,486	465,175	841,247	806,208	570,515	288,499	172,117
Other pork	5,185,014	244,584	800,692	1,168,358	1,266,221	830,078	537,580	333,390
Other meats	12,556,130	465,361	1,889,082	3,013,564	3,329,402	1,785,829	1,274,156	788,947
Frankfurters	2,618,671	105,628	444,181	651,334	640,698	391,180	222,129	159,312
Lunch meats (cold cuts)	8,487,423	310,182	1,255,371	2,096,497	2,367,880	1,171,792	731,522	550,267
Bologna, liverwurst, salami	2,450,062	90,815	378,672	610,415	653,028	347,832	207,867	160,350
Other lunch meats	6,036,199	219,279	876,505	1,486,082	1,714,852	823,960	523,543	389,917
Lamb, organ meats, and others	1,451,199	49,640	189,530	265,492	320,823	223,032	320,504	79,368
Poultry	18,094,642	887,255	3,001,770	4,371,353	4,637,356	2,725,326	1,376,237	1,073,194
Fresh and frozen chicken	14,260,824	779,158	2,341,233	3,470,894	3,672,515	2,121,251	1,085,492	766,567
Fresh and frozen whole chicken	4,254,758	231,534	713,994	936,323	1,069,411	693,217	363,066	242,256
Fresh and frozen chicken parts	10,004,903	547,624	1,627,239	2,534,330	2,602,866	1,428,034	722,426	524,311
Other poultry	3,833,818	108,096	660,537	900,459	965,078	604,074	290,745	306,627

	total consumer units	under 25	25 to 34	35 to 44	45 to 54	55 to 64	65 to 74	75+
Fish and seafood	$14,860,840	$499,748	$2,168,615	$3,624,220	$3,951,842	$2,274,018	$1,247,878	$1,099,958
Canned fish and seafood	1,788,417	83,409	189,141	398,599	446,023	317,244	178,557	180,769
Fresh fish and shellfish	8,707,196	268,478	1,284,140	2,125,862	2,371,200	1,358,643	755,891	540,923
Frozen fish and shellfish	4,365,226	147,949	695,333	1,099,758	1,134,382	597,957	313,429	378,265
Eggs	4,865,239	231,623	742,375	1,081,465	1,140,310	800,538	491,200	377,804
Dairy products	**43,090,621**	**1,806,780**	**6,733,864**	**10,598,502**	**10,348,628**	**6,491,526**	**3,960,147**	**3,123,833**
Fresh milk and cream	16,782,981	759,937	2,867,253	4,260,871	3,812,652	2,387,806	1,407,456	1,267,806
Fresh milk, all types	14,993,401	698,130	2,581,305	3,830,981	3,411,445	2,101,151	1,227,439	1,124,414
Cream	1,789,580	61,807	285,948	429,890	401,207	286,656	180,129	143,392
Other dairy products	26,307,640	1,046,842	3,866,611	6,337,631	6,535,976	4,103,720	2,552,691	1,856,142
Butter	2,536,110	86,495	322,493	561,794	668,441	435,751	263,007	201,995
Cheese	13,217,775	517,205	1,908,327	3,255,949	3,395,796	2,059,026	1,238,444	834,745
Ice cream and related products	7,002,502	274,914	1,028,323	1,636,279	1,678,335	1,089,291	669,083	632,634
Miscellaneous dairy products	3,551,252	168,228	607,469	883,610	793,641	519,476	382,157	186,652
Fruits and vegetables	**65,228,388**	**2,515,578**	**10,133,356**	**14,812,678**	**15,951,774**	**10,272,758**	**6,157,072**	**5,416,613**
Fresh fruits	21,714,501	809,312	3,263,419	4,784,875	5,433,368	3,483,914	2,050,710	1,913,476
Apples	3,769,862	146,010	584,531	964,485	931,882	589,567	300,403	250,793
Bananas	3,508,228	147,332	580,060	729,802	848,178	529,439	328,365	350,118
Oranges	2,265,173	82,880	391,696	518,227	562,449	307,980	240,322	159,428
Citrus fruits, excluding oranges	1,791,906	67,450	262,038	382,232	458,116	296,094	162,947	165,426
Other fresh fruits	10,378,169	365,553	1,445,290	2,189,889	2,632,743	1,760,660	1,018,561	987,712
Fresh vegetables	21,272,629	754,823	3,229,012	4,818,573	5,200,279	3,490,731	2,148,524	1,636,958
Potatoes	3,264,036	111,888	510,857	785,404	760,918	493,083	339,146	262,213
Lettuce	2,659,369	105,892	394,612	607,286	674,132	443,617	251,889	182,038
Tomatoes	4,155,919	173,959	684,058	935,601	948,243	654,414	436,959	321,162
Other fresh vegetables	11,192,143	363,084	1,639,291	2,490,042	2,816,986	1,899,618	1,120,529	871,545
Processed fruits	12,747,996	563,318	2,136,735	2,935,818	2,978,227	1,893,500	1,091,444	1,153,369
Frozen fruits and fruit juices	1,159,332	47,083	156,095	260,437	261,543	182,830	111,626	142,585
Frozen orange juice	484,896	21,866	73,674	110,000	97,931	62,575	40,990	79,714
Frozen fruits	410,475	6,172	43,738	82,079	107,890	83,899	48,177	39,915
Frozen fruit juices, excluding orange	263,960	19,045	38,684	68,600	55,960	36,356	22,460	22,957
Canned fruits	1,882,606	63,835	269,813	442,166	436,775	282,635	163,060	229,912
Dried fruits	738,391	15,518	98,750	180,284	141,086	134,588	73,444	96,902
Fresh fruit juice	2,566,344	87,112	455,845	581,772	608,924	438,548	218,311	174,655
Canned and bottled fruit juice	6,401,324	349,770	1,156,232	1,470,918	1,529,898	855,073	525,003	509,314
Processed vegetables	9,493,262	388,124	1,504,190	2,273,412	2,339,900	1,404,787	866,507	712,809
Frozen vegetables	3,314,037	102,894	481,504	841,969	888,726	479,449	292,878	225,875
Canned and dried vegetables and juices	6,179,225	285,230	1,022,686	1,431,443	1,451,412	925,338	573,628	486,935
Canned beans	1,324,452	65,775	216,162	320,372	302,091	196,289	127,573	95,057
Canned corn	736,065	44,967	145,793	185,580	167,881	98,407	47,840	43,606
Canned miscellaneous vegetables	1,950,049	60,749	298,777	417,615	476,374	331,227	184,397	183,999
Dried peas	69,769	3,086	10,691	19,497	15,887	9,613	6,289	4,845
Dried beans	287,217	15,342	60,455	66,674	60,703	44,921	16,059	23,187
Dried miscellaneous vegetables	722,111	50,610	124,215	158,621	170,726	98,582	71,984	46,144
Dried processed vegetables	34,885	794	10,303	12,998	4,268	4,370	–	2,076
Fresh and canned vegetable juices	1,036,073	42,586	154,151	248,162	248,739	138,434	117,690	85,597
Sugar and other sweets	**14,898,050**	**472,679**	**2,195,246**	**3,513,017**	**3,851,303**	**2,400,216**	**1,422,616**	**1,045,392**
Candy and chewing gum	9,666,523	297,750	1,447,817	2,335,031	2,553,071	1,541,648	875,491	613,600
Sugar	1,872,140	76,179	318,022	453,479	438,909	264,632	178,557	139,932
Artificial sweeteners	796,532	13,049	69,786	121,072	231,903	153,640	108,819	104,170
Jams, preserves, other sweets	2,562,855	85,789	359,622	603,435	627,657	440,121	259,750	187,575
Fats and oils	**10,336,307**	**392,533**	**1,522,462**	**2,337,678**	**2,655,270**	**1,694,939**	**944,218**	**796,099**
Margarine	1,112,819	29,272	130,047	212,538	289,524	193,842	130,380	131,395
Fats and oils	3,321,014	147,949	507,747	778,905	836,085	541,849	271,429	237,411
Salad dressings	3,190,778	145,392	502,693	711,991	819,250	500,773	300,178	209,032
Nondairy cream and imitation milk	1,255,846	28,038	158,817	280,175	340,979	231,247	126,562	92,519
Peanut butter	1,455,851	42,057	223,160	354,310	369,433	227,227	115,557	125,742

	total consumer units	under 25	25 to 34	35 to 44	45 to 54	55 to 64	65 to 74	75+
Miscellaneous foods	**$61,314,336**	**$2,943,644**	**$10,593,866**	**$15,488,564**	**$14,781,587**	**$8,477,315**	**$5,005,436**	**$3,917,741**
Frozen prepared foods	12,779,392	700,422	2,188,831	3,216,715	3,197,563	1,553,534	1,051,128	847,319
Frozen meals	3,696,605	199,176	574,422	805,864	907,695	502,521	313,991	398,915
Other frozen prepared foods	9,082,787	501,335	1,614,603	2,410,851	2,289,868	1,051,012	737,137	448,404
Canned and packaged soups	4,244,293	160,910	615,244	888,424	1,065,854	727,476	383,055	412,758
Potato chips, nuts, and other snacks	13,614,297	516,235	2,114,574	3,555,380	3,428,755	2,010,609	1,209,134	757,800
Potato chips and other snacks	10,007,229	421,100	1,739,791	2,812,820	2,501,142	1,325,957	722,201	454,864
Nuts	3,605,905	95,224	374,784	742,560	927,613	684,478	486,933	302,935
Condiments and seasonings	10,889,809	436,265	1,683,806	2,784,177	2,729,014	1,645,648	965,555	631,135
Salt, spices, and other seasonings	2,583,786	110,213	439,905	609,212	643,307	368,632	262,557	145,238
Olives, pickles, relishes	1,223,287	33,681	154,151	274,879	332,679	207,476	117,354	105,785
Sauces and gravies	4,760,585	217,515	777,171	1,330,349	1,162,836	685,876	364,975	208,109
Baking needs and miscellaneous products	2,322,152	74,768	312,774	569,496	590,192	383,839	220,557	171,886
Other canned/packaged prepared foods	19,786,545	1,129,899	3,991,215	5,044,109	4,360,400	2,540,048	1,396,675	1,268,729
Prepared salads	2,957,051	95,488	362,149	628,468	776,568	522,273	323,761	254,715
Prepared desserts	1,268,637	43,027	195,362	285,470	288,812	191,045	134,423	132,087
Baby food	3,497,763	350,123	1,351,205	1,082,187	356,866	135,637	108,819	65,640
Miscellaneous prepared foods	11,946,813	641,260	2,077,057	3,017,415	2,923,215	1,634,811	829,560	806,136
Nonalcoholic beverages	**33,665,965**	**1,505,238**	**5,466,052**	**8,186,929**	**8,766,801**	**5,156,655**	**2,536,969**	**2,015,916**
Cola	10,908,414	486,787	1,768,171	2,589,691	2,817,934	1,828,828	829,672	576,569
Other carbonated drinks	5,590,839	301,012	858,232	1,395,338	1,447,855	881,466	395,296	305,358
Coffee	4,548,952	103,071	542,542	901,181	1,331,429	807,180	475,366	402,722
Roasted coffee	2,846,583	59,162	347,181	557,943	820,435	524,195	311,969	233,258
Instant and freeze-dried coffee	1,702,368	43,909	195,168	343,238	510,994	282,985	163,397	169,348
Noncarbonated fruit-flavored drinks	2,301,221	145,128	451,762	688,883	511,705	275,819	136,445	79,944
Tea	2,050,052	116,737	286,725	456,367	552,015	338,393	167,439	133,125
Other nonalcoholic beverages and ice	8,151,368	352,592	1,541,901	2,152,580	2,053,696	1,009,937	522,083	500,893
Food prepared by CU on trips	**4,751,283**	**134,459**	**502,498**	**1,054,747**	**1,151,692**	**1,203,254**	**500,409**	**204,995**
FOOD AWAY FROM HOME	**283,030,388**	**16,413,022**	**49,568,284**	**68,715,517**	**70,059,949**	**44,117,695**	**20,458,589**	**13,126,238**
Meals at restaurants, carry-outs, other	**235,839,664**	**14,356,457**	**42,814,981**	**57,038,198**	**56,582,760**	**36,534,955**	**16,452,624**	**11,487,895**
Lunch	84,312,590	5,270,185	15,993,826	21,619,193	19,704,909	11,693,975	5,363,223	4,422,672
At fast-food restaurants*	47,579,106	3,642,215	10,176,900	12,022,002	11,155,785	5,916,117	2,609,291	1,841,492
At full-service restaurants	27,518,135	1,179,803	4,397,491	5,934,218	6,078,097	4,858,638	2,612,772	2,481,855
At vending machines, mobile vendors	700,018	51,050	102,055	153,085	181,397	167,099	21,449	23,764
At employer and school cafeterias	8,516,494	397,118	1,317,187	3,509,887	2,289,868	752,121	119,712	75,561
Dinner	92,512,796	5,060,870	15,728,872	21,386,436	22,627,413	15,790,703	7,343,522	4,411,482
At fast-food restaurants*	29,427,486	2,230,877	5,730,034	7,800,846	7,402,175	3,442,489	1,781,078	900,039
At full-service restaurants	62,585,298	2,756,547	9,964,043	13,428,894	15,159,319	12,221,492	5,544,700	3,488,371
At vending machines, mobile vendors	174,423	4,673	6,804	16,608	29,166	99,281	11,005	8,767
At employer and school cafeterias	324,427	68,684	27,992	140,087	36,516	27,617	6,738	14,305
Snacks and nonalcoholic beverages	34,588,081	2,525,101	6,752,137	8,780,977	8,504,783	4,977,320	1,786,805	1,125,914
At fast-food restaurants*	25,251,799	1,661,387	5,077,467	6,513,823	6,121,727	3,601,548	1,343,445	831,053
At full-service restaurants	3,357,061	278,000	521,160	640,503	850,075	600,404	244,477	222,760
At vending machines, mobile vendors	4,775,702	472,856	913,633	1,255,973	1,236,818	639,207	175,413	56,411
At employer and school cafeterias	1,202,356	112,946	239,877	370,678	296,163	136,161	23,471	15,804
Breakfast and brunch	24,426,197	1,500,389	4,340,340	5,251,593	5,745,655	4,072,782	1,959,186	1,527,828
At fast-food restaurants*	12,009,605	929,312	2,460,589	2,779,363	2,878,874	1,765,204	669,645	484,973
At full-service restaurants	11,670,062	502,657	1,760,396	2,264,265	2,646,733	2,201,305	1,275,391	1,035,241
At vending machines, mobile vendors	165,120	20,984	30,130	32,495	44,341	29,714	4,604	2,769
At employer and school cafeterias	581,410	47,435	89,419	175,711	175,706	76,558	9,658	4,845
Board (including at school)	**3,243,105**	**513,238**	**38,684**	**284,989**	**1,654,386**	**624,350**	**18,979**	**108,092**
Catered affairs	**6,809,474**	**253,753**	**1,762,729**	**780,831**	**2,175,813**	**872,027**	**853,592**	**110,169**
Food on trips	**26,925,097**	**905,065**	**3,416,793**	**5,964,065**	**6,893,790**	**5,477,569**	**2,930,693**	**1,337,368**
School lunches	**7,371,116**	**54,313**	**848,707**	**3,781,638**	**2,240,784**	**314,447**	**85,797**	**46,029**
Meals as pay	**2,843,095**	**330,285**	**686,197**	**865,798**	**512,653**	**294,346**	**116,904**	**36,569**

	total consumer units	under 25	25 to 34	35 to 44	45 to 54	55 to 64	65 to 74	75+
ALCOHOLIC BEVERAGES	**$53,404,834**	**$4,430,807**	**$10,144,631**	**$12,870,710**	**$11,892,042**	**$7,980,037**	**$3,698,713**	**$2,193,340**
At home	**32,278,720**	**2,449,274**	**5,476,355**	**8,750,408**	**6,978,442**	**4,877,165**	**2,243,193**	**1,385,243**
Beer and ale	15,268,989	1,611,748	3,548,978	4,163,629	3,140,892	1,640,754	622,704	435,138
Whiskey	2,518,668	216,369	232,296	648,205	510,994	466,515	259,301	183,884
Wine	10,994,463	340,513	1,156,426	3,262,929	2,646,022	2,015,678	1,040,572	520,158
Other alcoholic beverages	3,496,600	280,645	538,655	675,404	680,297	754,219	320,729	245,948
Away from home	**21,126,114**	**1,981,444**	**4,668,276**	**4,120,303**	**4,913,601**	**3,103,047**	**1,455,520**	**808,097**
Beer and ale	8,874,642	904,007	2,075,113	1,653,368	2,101,832	1,216,189	556,896	328,199
At fast-food restaurants*	1,911,676	271,916	508,524	373,807	346,432	240,336	119,824	35,531
At full-service restaurants	6,512,955	630,327	1,522,268	1,256,695	1,452,834	948,061	384,964	292,092
Wine	2,591,926	287,170	575,589	464,310	608,924	361,291	177,434	107,054
At fast-food restaurants*	355,823	51,491	107,886	63,304	67,105	30,763	26,054	5,768
At full-service restaurants	2,181,450	235,678	466,342	401,006	510,994	329,654	129,257	101,171
Other alcoholic beverages	5,198,968	554,589	1,241,569	1,065,820	1,157,620	668,397	301,189	182,615
At fast-food restaurants*	444,197	69,742	160,177	97,724	61,414	28,316	16,620	4,960
At full-service restaurants	4,586,162	484,847	1,074,977	962,800	967,212	633,789	262,333	177,308
Alcoholic beverages purchased on trips	4,461,740	235,678	776,199	936,804	1,045,225	857,170	420,002	190,229

* The category fast-food restaurants also includes take-out, delivery, concession stands, buffets, and cafeterias other than employer and school.
Note: Numbers may not add to total because of rounding and missing subcategories. "–" means sample is too small to make a reliable estimate.
Source: Calculations by New Strategist based on the 2004 Consumer Expenditure Survey

Table 5.4 Food and Alcohol: Market shares by age, 2004

(percentage of total annual spending on food and alcoholic beverages accounted for by consumer unit age groups, 2004)

	total consumer units	under 25	25 to 34	35 to 44	45 to 54	55 to 64	65 to 74	75+
Share of total consumer units	100.0%	7.6%	16.7%	20.7%	20.4%	15.0%	9.7%	9.9%
Share of total before-tax income	100.0	3.2	16.1	24.9	26.4	16.8	7.5	5.1
Share of total spending	100.0	4.3	16.4	24.0	24.8	16.4	8.1	5.9
Share of food spending	100.0	4.9	16.5	24.2	24.8	15.3	8.1	6.0
Share of alcoholic beverages spending	100.0	8.3	19.0	24.1	22.3	14.9	6.9	4.1
FOOD AT HOME	100.0	4.2	15.8	24.1	24.9	15.2	8.8	7.1
Cereals and bakery products	100.0	4.4	15.7	24.8	24.2	14.2	8.8	7.8
Cereals and cereal products	100.0	4.9	16.6	26.1	24.0	13.4	7.9	7.1
Flour	100.0	4.4	16.7	20.6	22.3	13.0	9.6	13.8
Prepared flour mixes	100.0	4.5	15.1	25.0	25.5	12.9	8.5	8.7
Ready-to-eat and cooked cereals	100.0	4.8	16.4	26.2	23.4	13.4	8.3	7.4
Rice	100.0	5.5	17.4	29.5	24.6	13.0	6.2	3.5
Pasta, cornmeal, and other cereal products	100.0	5.1	17.3	26.0	25.0	14.0	7.0	5.4
Bakery products	100.0	4.1	15.2	24.1	24.3	14.7	9.3	8.2
Bread	100.0	4.3	14.6	22.2	24.3	15.6	9.6	9.6
White bread	100.0	4.9	16.4	23.3	22.9	14.9	8.8	8.6
Bread, other than white	100.0	3.9	13.4	21.5	25.2	16.0	10.0	10.3
Crackers and cookies	100.0	4.5	15.4	24.0	24.4	13.8	9.4	8.6
Cookies	100.0	4.7	15.6	24.3	24.7	13.2	9.2	8.4
Crackers	100.0	4.1	14.9	23.5	23.7	15.0	9.8	9.1
Frozen and refrigerated bakery products	100.0	4.6	15.7	28.0	21.5	13.8	9.7	6.6
Other bakery products	100.0	3.6	15.5	24.7	25.0	14.8	9.0	7.4
Biscuits and rolls	100.0	3.5	13.5	24.3	27.0	14.9	9.4	7.4
Cakes and cupcakes	100.0	2.9	19.6	26.4	22.2	14.1	8.8	5.7
Bread and cracker products	100.0	3.5	12.1	24.5	29.9	13.7	8.2	8.2
Sweetrolls, coffee cakes, doughnuts	100.0	4.5	14.2	23.5	24.5	14.5	10.3	8.6
Pies, tarts, turnovers	100.0	4.6	13.0	23.0	26.5	16.8	6.8	9.7
Meats, poultry, fish, and eggs	100.0	4.1	15.4	24.0	25.8	15.3	8.8	6.6
Beef	100.0	4.2	15.7	24.4	26.0	14.6	8.6	6.4
Ground beef	100.0	4.7	16.1	24.2	26.1	14.7	8.3	5.7
Roast	100.0	3.2	15.3	22.1	25.6	14.2	11.0	8.6
Chuck roast	100.0	2.7	15.8	22.2	26.5	14.1	10.5	8.2
Round roast	100.0	2.6	16.7	23.6	22.3	14.0	11.5	9.4
Other roast	100.0	3.8	14.5	21.4	26.6	14.3	11.0	8.4
Steak	100.0	4.4	15.2	25.6	26.2	14.9	7.6	6.1
Round steak	100.0	3.8	15.4	27.6	25.5	14.8	6.8	5.8
Sirloin steak	100.0	4.4	15.8	25.8	26.9	13.1	7.4	6.6
Other steak	100.0	4.5	14.8	24.8	25.9	16.0	8.0	5.9
Other beef	100.0	3.7	17.3	24.6	25.1	13.0	9.4	6.8
Pork	100.0	4.0	14.9	23.4	25.0	16.9	9.2	6.7
Bacon	100.0	3.4	15.0	22.7	24.6	16.0	10.6	7.7
Pork chops	100.0	5.0	15.1	23.1	28.9	15.4	6.9	5.5
Ham	100.0	3.3	14.3	23.3	22.5	19.3	9.2	8.2
Ham, not canned	100.0	3.2	14.4	23.5	22.4	19.5	9.1	8.0
Canned ham	100.0	6.4	10.6	14.2	25.4	12.3	13.1	18.1
Sausage	100.0	3.0	14.3	25.9	24.8	17.6	8.9	5.3
Other pork	100.0	4.7	15.4	22.5	24.4	16.0	10.4	6.4
Other meats	100.0	3.7	15.0	24.0	26.5	14.2	10.1	6.3
Frankfurters	100.0	4.0	17.0	24.9	24.5	14.9	8.5	6.1
Lunch meats (cold cuts)	100.0	3.7	14.8	24.7	27.9	13.8	8.6	6.5
Bologna, liverwurst, salami	100.0	3.7	15.5	24.9	26.7	14.2	8.5	6.5
Other lunch meats	100.0	3.6	14.5	24.6	28.4	13.7	8.7	6.5
Lamb, organ meats, and others	100.0	3.4	13.1	18.3	22.1	15.4	22.1	5.5
Poultry	100.0	4.9	16.6	24.2	25.6	15.1	7.6	5.9
Fresh and frozen chicken	100.0	5.5	16.4	24.3	25.8	14.9	7.6	5.4
Fresh and frozen whole chicken	100.0	5.4	16.8	22.0	25.1	16.3	8.5	5.7
Fresh and frozen chicken parts	100.0	5.5	16.3	25.3	26.0	14.3	7.2	5.2
Other poultry	100.0	2.8	17.2	23.5	25.2	15.8	7.6	8.0

	total consumer units	under 25	25 to 34	35 to 44	45 to 54	55 to 64	65 to 74	75+
Fish and seafood	100.0%	3.4%	14.6%	24.4%	26.6%	15.3%	8.4%	7.4%
Canned fish and seafood	100.0	4.7	10.6	22.3	24.9	17.7	10.0	10.1
Fresh fish and shellfish	100.0	3.1	14.7	24.4	27.2	15.6	8.7	6.2
Frozen fish and shellfish	100.0	3.4	15.9	25.2	26.0	13.7	7.2	8.7
Eggs	100.0	4.8	15.3	22.2	23.4	16.5	10.1	7.8
Dairy products	**100.0**	**4.2**	**15.6**	**24.6**	**24.0**	**15.1**	**9.2**	**7.2**
Fresh milk and cream	100.0	4.5	17.1	25.4	22.7	14.2	8.4	7.6
Fresh milk, all types	100.0	4.7	17.2	25.6	22.8	14.0	8.2	7.5
Cream	100.0	3.5	16.0	24.0	22.4	16.0	10.1	8.0
Other dairy products	100.0	4.0	14.7	24.1	24.8	15.6	9.7	7.1
Butter	100.0	3.4	12.7	22.2	26.4	17.2	10.4	8.0
Cheese	100.0	3.9	14.4	24.6	25.7	15.6	9.4	6.3
Ice cream and related products	100.0	3.9	14.7	23.4	24.0	15.6	9.6	9.0
Miscellaneous dairy products	100.0	4.7	17.1	24.9	22.3	14.6	10.8	5.3
Fruits and vegetables	**100.0**	**3.9**	**15.5**	**22.7**	**24.5**	**15.7**	**9.4**	**8.3**
Fresh fruits	100.0	3.7	15.0	22.0	25.0	16.0	9.4	8.8
Apples	100.0	3.9	15.5	25.6	24.7	15.6	8.0	6.7
Bananas	100.0	4.2	16.5	20.8	24.2	15.1	9.4	10.0
Oranges	100.0	3.7	17.3	22.9	24.8	13.6	10.6	7.0
Citrus fruits, excluding oranges	100.0	3.8	14.6	21.3	25.6	16.5	9.1	9.2
Other fresh fruits	100.0	3.5	13.9	21.1	25.4	17.0	9.8	9.5
Fresh vegetables	100.0	3.5	15.2	22.7	24.4	16.4	10.1	7.7
Potatoes	100.0	3.4	15.7	24.1	23.3	15.1	10.4	8.0
Lettuce	100.0	4.0	14.8	22.8	25.3	16.7	9.5	6.8
Tomatoes	100.0	4.2	16.5	22.5	22.8	15.7	10.5	7.7
Other fresh vegetables	100.0	3.2	14.6	22.2	25.2	17.0	10.0	7.8
Processed fruits	100.0	4.4	16.8	23.0	23.4	14.9	8.6	9.0
Frozen fruits and fruit juices	100.0	4.1	13.5	22.5	22.6	15.8	9.6	12.3
Frozen orange juice	100.0	4.5	15.2	22.7	20.2	12.9	8.5	16.4
Frozen fruits	100.0	1.5	10.7	20.0	26.3	20.4	11.7	9.7
Frozen fruit juices, excluding orange	100.0	7.2	14.7	26.0	21.2	13.8	8.5	8.7
Canned fruits	100.0	3.4	14.3	23.5	23.2	15.0	8.7	12.2
Dried fruits	100.0	2.1	13.4	24.4	19.1	18.2	9.9	13.1
Fresh fruit juice	100.0	3.4	17.8	22.7	23.7	17.1	8.5	6.8
Canned and bottled fruit juice	100.0	5.5	18.1	23.0	23.9	13.4	8.2	8.0
Processed vegetables	100.0	4.1	15.8	23.9	24.6	14.8	9.1	7.5
Frozen vegetables	100.0	3.1	14.5	25.4	26.8	14.5	8.8	6.8
Canned and dried vegetables and juices	100.0	4.6	16.6	23.2	23.5	15.0	9.3	7.9
Canned beans	100.0	5.0	16.3	24.2	22.8	14.8	9.6	7.2
Canned corn	100.0	6.1	19.8	25.2	22.8	13.4	6.5	5.9
Canned miscellaneous vegetables	100.0	3.1	15.3	21.4	24.4	17.0	9.5	9.4
Dried peas	100.0	4.4	15.3	27.9	22.8	13.8	9.0	6.9
Dried beans	100.0	5.3	21.0	23.2	21.1	15.6	5.6	8.1
Dried miscellaneous vegetables	100.0	7.0	17.2	22.0	23.6	13.7	10.0	6.4
Dried processed vegetables	100.0	2.3	29.5	37.3	12.2	12.5	–	6.0
Fresh and canned vegetable juices	100.0	4.1	14.9	24.0	24.0	13.4	11.4	8.3
Sugar and other sweets	**100.0**	**3.2**	**14.7**	**23.6**	**25.9**	**16.1**	**9.5**	**7.0**
Candy and chewing gum	100.0	3.1	15.0	24.2	26.4	15.9	9.1	6.3
Sugar	100.0	4.1	17.0	24.2	23.4	14.1	9.5	7.5
Artificial sweeteners	100.0	1.6	8.8	15.2	29.1	19.3	13.7	13.1
Jams, preserves, other sweets	100.0	3.3	14.0	23.5	24.5	17.2	10.1	7.3
Fats and oils	**100.0**	**3.8**	**14.7**	**22.6**	**25.7**	**16.4**	**9.1**	**7.7**
Margarine	100.0	2.6	11.7	19.1	26.0	17.4	11.7	11.8
Fats and oils	100.0	4.5	15.3	23.5	25.2	16.3	8.2	7.1
Salad dressings	100.0	4.6	15.8	22.3	25.7	15.7	9.4	6.6
Nondairy cream and imitation milk	100.0	2.2	12.6	22.3	27.2	18.4	10.1	7.4
Peanut butter	100.0	2.9	15.3	24.3	25.4	15.6	7.9	8.6

	total consumer units	under 25	25 to 34	35 to 44	45 to 54	55 to 64	65 to 74	75+
Miscellaneous foods	100.0%	4.8%	17.3%	25.3%	24.1%	13.8%	8.2%	6.4%
Frozen prepared foods	100.0	5.5	17.1	25.2	25.0	12.2	8.2	6.6
Frozen meals	100.0	5.4	15.5	21.8	24.6	13.6	8.5	10.8
Other frozen prepared foods	100.0	5.5	17.8	26.5	25.2	11.6	8.1	4.9
Canned and packaged soups	100.0	3.8	14.5	20.9	25.1	17.1	9.0	9.7
Potato chips, nuts, and other snacks	100.0	3.8	15.5	26.1	25.2	14.8	8.9	5.6
Potato chips and other snacks	100.0	4.2	17.4	28.1	25.0	13.2	7.2	4.5
Nuts	100.0	2.6	10.4	20.6	25.7	19.0	13.5	8.4
Condiments and seasonings	100.0	4.0	15.5	25.6	25.1	15.1	8.9	5.8
Salt, spices, and other seasonings	100.0	4.3	17.0	23.6	24.9	14.3	10.2	5.6
Olives, pickles, relishes	100.0	2.8	12.6	22.5	27.2	17.0	9.6	8.6
Sauces and gravies	100.0	4.6	16.3	27.9	24.4	14.4	7.7	4.4
Baking needs and miscellaneous products	100.0	3.2	13.5	24.5	25.4	16.5	9.5	7.4
Other canned/packaged prepared foods	100.0	5.7	20.2	25.5	22.0	12.8	7.1	6.4
Prepared salads	100.0	3.2	12.2	21.3	26.3	17.7	10.9	8.6
Prepared desserts	100.0	3.4	15.4	22.5	22.8	15.1	10.6	10.4
Baby food	100.0	10.0	38.6	30.9	10.2	3.9	3.1	1.9
Miscellaneous prepared foods	100.0	5.4	17.4	25.3	24.5	13.7	6.9	6.7
Nonalcoholic beverages	100.0	4.5	16.2	24.3	26.0	15.3	7.5	6.0
Cola	100.0	4.5	16.2	23.7	25.8	16.8	7.6	5.3
Other carbonated drinks	100.0	5.4	15.4	25.0	25.9	15.8	7.1	5.5
Coffee	100.0	2.3	11.9	19.8	29.3	17.7	10.5	8.9
Roasted coffee	100.0	2.1	12.2	19.6	28.8	18.4	11.0	8.2
Instant and freeze-dried coffee	100.0	2.6	11.5	20.2	30.0	16.6	9.6	9.9
Noncarbonated fruit-flavored drinks	100.0	6.3	19.6	29.9	22.2	12.0	5.9	3.5
Tea	100.0	5.7	14.0	22.3	26.9	16.5	8.2	6.5
Other nonalcoholic beverages and ice	100.0	4.3	18.9	26.4	25.2	12.4	6.4	6.1
Food prepared by CU on trips	100.0	2.8	10.6	22.2	24.2	25.3	10.5	4.3
FOOD AWAY FROM HOME	100.0	5.8	17.5	24.3	24.8	15.6	7.2	4.6
Meals at restaurants, carry-outs, other	100.0	6.1	18.2	24.2	24.0	15.5	7.0	4.9
Lunch	100.0	6.3	19.0	25.6	23.4	13.9	6.4	5.2
At fast-food restaurants*	100.0	7.7	21.4	25.3	23.4	12.4	5.5	3.9
At full-service restaurants	100.0	4.3	16.0	21.6	22.1	17.7	9.5	9.0
At vending machines, mobile vendors	100.0	7.3	14.6	21.9	25.9	23.9	3.1	3.4
At employer and school cafeterias	100.0	4.7	15.5	41.2	26.9	8.8	1.4	0.9
Dinner	100.0	5.5	17.0	23.1	24.5	17.1	7.9	4.8
At fast-food restaurants*	100.0	7.6	19.5	26.5	25.2	11.7	6.1	3.1
At full-service restaurants	100.0	4.4	15.9	21.5	24.2	19.5	8.9	5.6
At vending machines, mobile vendors	100.0	2.7	3.9	9.5	16.7	56.9	6.3	5.0
At employer and school cafeterias	100.0	21.2	8.6	43.2	11.3	8.5	2.1	4.4
Snacks and nonalcoholic beverages	100.0	7.3	19.5	25.4	24.6	14.4	5.2	3.3
At fast-food restaurants*	100.0	6.6	20.1	25.8	24.2	14.3	5.3	3.3
At full-service restaurants	100.0	8.3	15.5	19.1	25.3	17.9	7.3	6.6
At vending machines, mobile vendors	100.0	9.9	19.1	26.3	25.9	13.4	3.7	1.2
At employer and school cafeterias	100.0	9.4	20.0	30.8	24.6	11.3	2.0	1.3
Breakfast and brunch	100.0	6.1	17.8	21.5	23.5	16.7	8.0	6.3
At fast-food restaurants*	100.0	7.7	20.5	23.1	24.0	14.7	5.6	4.0
At full-service restaurants	100.0	4.3	15.1	19.4	22.7	18.9	10.9	8.9
At vending machines, mobile vendors	100.0	12.7	18.2	19.7	26.9	18.0	2.8	1.7
At employer and school cafeterias	100.0	8.2	15.4	30.2	30.2	13.2	1.7	0.8
Board (including at school)	100.0	15.8	1.2	8.8	51.0	19.3	0.6	3.3
Catered affairs	100.0	3.7	25.9	11.5	32.0	12.8	12.5	1.6
Food on trips	100.0	3.4	12.7	22.2	25.6	20.3	10.9	5.0
School lunches	100.0	0.7	11.5	51.3	30.4	4.3	1.2	0.6
Meals as pay	100.0	11.6	24.1	30.5	18.0	10.4	4.1	1.3

	total consumer units	under 25	25 to 34	35 to 44	45 to 54	55 to 64	65 to 74	75+
ALCOHOLIC BEVERAGES	**100.0%**	**8.3%**	**19.0%**	**24.1%**	**22.3%**	**14.9%**	**6.9%**	**4.1%**
At home	**100.0**	**7.6**	**17.0**	**27.1**	**21.6**	**15.1**	**6.9**	**4.3**
Beer and ale	100.0	10.6	23.2	27.3	20.6	10.7	4.1	2.8
Whiskey	100.0	8.6	9.2	25.7	20.3	18.5	10.3	7.3
Wine	100.0	3.1	10.5	29.7	24.1	18.3	9.5	4.7
Other alcoholic beverages	100.0	8.0	15.4	19.3	19.5	21.6	9.2	7.0
Away from home	**100.0**	**9.4**	**22.1**	**19.5**	**23.3**	**14.7**	**6.9**	**3.8**
Beer and ale	100.0	10.2	23.4	18.6	23.7	13.7	6.3	3.7
At fast-food restaurants*	100.0	14.2	26.6	19.6	18.1	12.6	6.3	1.9
At full-service restaurants	100.0	9.7	23.4	19.3	22.3	14.6	5.9	4.5
Wine	100.0	11.1	22.2	17.9	23.5	13.9	6.8	4.1
At fast-food restaurants*	100.0	14.5	30.3	17.8	18.9	8.6	7.3	1.6
At full-service restaurants	100.0	10.8	21.4	18.4	23.4	15.1	5.9	4.6
Other alcoholic beverages	100.0	10.7	23.9	20.5	22.3	12.9	5.8	3.5
At fast-food restaurants*	100.0	15.7	36.1	22.0	13.8	6.4	3.7	1.1
At full-service restaurants	100.0	10.6	23.4	21.0	21.1	13.8	5.7	3.9
Alcoholic beverages purchased on trips	100.0	5.3	17.4	21.0	23.4	19.2	9.4	4.3

The category fast-food restaurants also includes take-out, delivery, concession stands, buffets, and cafeterias other than employer and school.
Note: Numbers may not add to total because of rounding. "–" means sample is too small to make a reliable estimate.
Source: Calculations by New Strategist based on the 2004 Consumer Expenditure Survey

Table 5.5 Food and Alcohol: Average spending by income, 2004

(average annual spending on food and alcoholic beverages, by before-tax income of consumer units (CU), 2004)

	total consumer units	under $20,000	$20,000– $39,999	$40,000– $49,999	$50,000– $69,999	$70,000– $79,999	$80,000– $99,999	$100,000 or more
Number of consumer units (in 000s)	116,282	28,898	27,297	11,374	18,069	6,461	9,246	14,937
Average number of persons per CU	2.5	1.8	2.3	2.6	2.8	3.0	3.1	3.2
Average before-tax income of CU	$54,453.00	$10,923.47	$29,561.76	$44,645.00	$59,259.00	$74,437.00	$88,811.00	$155,901.00
Average spending of CU, total	43,394.87	18,865.37	30,400.94	38,204.07	47,750.13	55,012.03	65,446.39	93,525.67
Food, average spending	5,780.82	3,034.27	4,513.30	5,452.06	6,311.87	7,337.45	7,466.54	10,733.39
Alcoholic beverages, average spending	459.27	192.20	291.59	449.21	483.62	617.46	701.51	986.82
FOOD AT HOME	3,346.82	2,084.40	2,814.17	3,263.47	3,640.26	4,078.94	4,042.53	5,434.75
Cereals and bakery products	460.90	302.48	393.02	456.43	506.47	522.29	545.18	724.36
Cereals and cereal products	153.80	112.13	130.67	151.67	166.20	176.32	179.61	228.01
Flour	8.32	9.93	8.79	7.56	7.30	8.18	4.64	8.78
Prepared flour mixes	13.78	9.04	9.67	17.09	14.77	14.65	17.73	22.82
Ready-to-eat and cooked cereals	86.69	60.20	75.83	84.90	95.07	99.02	104.42	126.79
Rice	18.46	14.80	16.48	15.92	20.60	21.83	14.74	28.32
Pasta, cornmeal, and other cereal products	26.55	18.17	19.91	26.21	28.47	32.65	38.09	41.29
Bakery products	307.10	190.35	262.35	304.76	340.27	345.97	365.57	496.35
Bread	87.63	59.29	79.45	85.79	100.46	97.04	97.65	126.93
White bread	35.04	26.23	33.98	33.30	39.99	39.04	37.04	44.67
Bread, other than white	52.59	33.07	45.48	52.49	60.47	58.00	60.61	82.27
Crackers and cookies	71.16	44.24	60.22	67.95	78.23	82.03	83.63	118.46
Cookies	46.57	30.08	40.07	45.49	51.02	52.67	50.51	76.82
Crackers	24.60	14.17	20.15	22.45	27.20	29.36	33.11	41.64
Frozen and refrigerated bakery products	26.32	13.33	22.84	25.46	27.73	27.47	33.39	48.67
Other bakery products	121.99	73.48	99.83	125.57	133.85	139.43	150.90	202.29
Biscuits and rolls	42.11	22.43	31.17	39.14	49.30	52.54	53.99	77.61
Cakes and cupcakes	39.04	23.34	34.77	42.21	40.38	41.00	43.83	65.29
Bread and cracker products	3.25	2.07	2.18	3.15	4.14	3.76	4.30	5.39
Sweetrolls, coffee cakes, doughnuts	23.59	15.90	20.65	25.29	25.31	25.25	29.47	34.32
Pies, tarts, turnovers	13.99	9.74	11.04	15.77	14.72	16.88	19.31	19.68
Meats, poultry, fish, and eggs	879.71	562.00	760.12	900.47	936.44	1,096.66	1,033.40	1,362.83
Beef	265.34	164.41	234.21	264.53	277.56	353.59	323.90	403.49
Ground beef	96.92	67.47	89.98	99.44	106.63	121.97	113.47	125.05
Roast	45.58	31.21	42.09	45.73	42.70	61.24	50.07	69.55
Chuck roast	11.72	10.32	11.66	9.05	11.44	13.21	15.24	13.65
Round roast	10.27	7.92	10.16	9.65	8.71	9.70	12.82	15.42
Other roast	23.58	12.96	20.26	27.03	22.55	38.33	22.00	40.47
Steak	103.45	52.36	84.76	106.16	106.86	149.21	135.98	177.15
Round steak	16.37	8.80	14.12	16.43	19.65	18.96	24.03	23.48
Sirloin steak	32.38	16.63	25.93	33.09	30.09	53.95	40.58	58.00
Other steak	54.71	26.94	44.71	56.65	57.12	76.30	71.37	95.67
Other beef	19.39	13.38	17.39	13.20	21.38	21.16	24.38	31.74
Pork	181.14	124.79	166.27	195.15	194.01	188.66	208.62	257.83
Bacon	31.08	22.06	30.62	30.48	35.76	29.89	35.10	40.39
Pork chops	37.92	28.19	35.76	46.18	39.00	38.90	35.64	51.46
Ham	39.65	27.67	34.39	40.19	46.77	35.22	44.95	59.69
Ham, not canned	38.67	26.93	33.19	39.58	46.25	34.06	44.41	57.76
Canned ham	0.98	0.74	1.20	0.61	0.53	1.16	0.55	1.93
Sausage	27.91	17.86	25.32	31.21	30.60	35.52	32.74	37.77
Other pork	44.59	29.01	40.17	47.08	41.87	49.13	60.19	68.51
Other meats	107.98	66.68	86.32	110.61	116.72	130.14	137.36	177.38
Frankfurters	22.52	16.22	19.26	21.76	23.33	27.33	28.81	32.78
Lunch meats (cold cuts)	72.99	41.58	60.31	69.32	82.92	92.91	98.13	116.76
Bologna, liverwurst, salami	21.07	15.19	19.23	23.36	22.60	22.74	23.21	28.83
Other lunch meats	51.91	26.39	41.08	45.96	60.32	70.17	74.92	87.93
Lamb, organ meats, and others	12.48	8.88	6.75	19.54	10.47	9.90	10.42	27.84
Poultry	155.61	101.60	131.02	148.98	169.64	191.30	184.83	247.22
Fresh and frozen chicken	122.64	80.26	108.06	114.29	135.11	152.96	139.26	189.56
Fresh and frozen whole chicken	36.59	25.27	36.67	37.33	36.27	48.13	37.26	49.80
Fresh and frozen chicken parts	86.04	54.99	71.39	76.96	98.84	104.83	102.00	139.76
Other poultry	32.97	21.34	22.97	34.69	34.53	38.34	45.57	57.66

	total consumer units	under $20,000	$20,000– $39,999	$40,000– $49,999	$50,000– $69,999	$70,000– $79,999	$80,000– $99,999	$100,000 or more
Fish and seafood	$127.80	$71.87	$100.44	$140.59	$135.12	$193.77	$135.56	$220.16
Canned fish and seafood	15.38	10.47	12.22	16.98	17.43	15.77	16.46	24.98
Fresh fish and shellfish	74.88	40.24	60.09	77.21	76.39	122.56	77.50	134.59
Frozen fish and shellfish	37.54	21.16	28.13	46.40	41.30	55.44	41.60	60.59
Eggs	41.84	32.65	41.85	40.61	43.38	39.21	43.13	56.76
Dairy products	**370.57**	**227.37**	**318.08**	**361.01**	**403.47**	**426.39**	**450.50**	**603.81**
Fresh milk and cream	144.33	102.63	132.51	142.52	153.65	157.18	168.95	205.79
Fresh milk, all types	128.94	93.50	120.79	128.65	136.51	138.50	147.07	179.41
Cream	15.39	9.14	11.72	13.87	17.13	18.68	21.88	26.39
Other dairy products	226.24	124.73	185.57	218.49	249.82	269.21	281.55	398.02
Butter	21.81	13.58	17.31	19.27	30.84	26.54	26.88	30.75
Cheese	113.67	60.58	88.75	107.62	120.21	132.39	148.80	216.02
Ice cream and related products	60.22	33.71	53.84	61.00	66.05	75.35	67.40	98.30
Miscellaneous dairy products	30.54	16.86	25.68	30.61	32.73	34.93	38.47	52.95
Fruits and vegetables	**560.95**	**360.41**	**470.31**	**548.56**	**591.61**	**644.84**	**658.52**	**940.95**
Fresh fruits	186.74	114.89	157.27	192.97	184.36	210.13	221.47	327.37
Apples	32.42	19.51	28.08	32.47	33.24	32.37	41.98	55.38
Bananas	30.17	21.52	28.85	33.92	30.55	32.62	32.40	41.13
Oranges	19.48	13.49	17.53	25.72	17.60	20.13	22.32	28.30
Citrus fruits, excluding oranges	15.41	9.06	12.22	14.44	14.75	19.45	19.35	29.18
Other fresh fruits	89.25	51.31	70.58	86.42	88.23	105.55	105.42	173.38
Fresh vegetables	182.94	119.79	147.54	167.92	201.76	212.99	214.00	311.86
Potatoes	28.07	20.94	25.01	27.18	30.91	33.11	33.77	37.41
Lettuce	22.87	14.15	16.94	21.56	25.53	29.19	28.43	40.35
Tomatoes	35.74	25.55	29.74	33.58	40.63	37.78	40.12	56.33
Other fresh vegetables	96.25	59.14	75.84	85.60	104.69	112.91	111.69	177.77
Processed fruits	109.63	69.23	95.45	105.76	117.33	125.98	134.16	175.33
Frozen fruits and fruit juices	9.97	7.07	7.86	9.02	11.86	9.85	12.94	15.43
Frozen orange juice	4.17	3.15	3.49	5.01	5.01	4.97	5.65	4.20
Frozen fruits	3.53	2.21	2.15	2.82	4.17	2.83	4.54	7.77
Frozen fruit juices, excluding orange	2.27	1.71	2.21	1.19	2.69	2.05	2.75	3.45
Canned fruits	16.19	10.59	13.57	16.68	15.98	16.98	26.20	23.82
Dried fruits	6.35	3.63	5.15	5.41	7.92	6.90	8.20	10.64
Fresh fruit juice	22.07	11.62	19.03	23.28	22.09	22.86	26.91	40.82
Canned and bottled fruit juice	55.05	36.32	49.84	51.37	59.48	69.38	59.92	84.62
Processed vegetables	81.64	56.50	70.06	81.92	88.16	95.74	88.89	126.39
Frozen vegetables	28.50	16.67	23.19	29.13	31.59	34.19	33.89	48.27
Canned and dried vegetables and juices	53.14	39.83	46.88	52.79	56.57	61.55	55.01	78.12
Canned beans	11.39	8.61	10.59	10.59	12.03	13.90	12.94	15.35
Canned corn	6.33	5.43	5.87	8.71	6.02	6.10	5.17	7.94
Canned miscellaneous vegetables	16.77	12.01	13.06	17.65	18.92	19.17	18.43	26.22
Dried peas	0.60	0.53	0.46	0.50	0.61	0.91	0.57	0.94
Dried beans	2.47	2.58	2.67	3.27	2.30	1.72	1.42	2.39
Dried miscellaneous vegetables	6.21	4.50	5.57	5.33	7.16	8.02	6.14	9.15
Dried processed vegetables	0.30	0.70	0.32	0.33	0.02	0.13	–	0.59
Fresh and canned vegetable juices	8.91	5.67	8.16	6.41	9.23	11.52	10.13	15.46
Sugar and other sweets	**128.12**	**79.45**	**101.85**	**117.58**	**136.48**	**140.60**	**162.26**	**230.63**
Candy and chewing gum	83.13	44.63	60.23	72.53	91.64	95.23	110.36	166.75
Sugar	16.10	14.76	16.75	15.99	16.36	17.38	14.34	17.33
Artificial sweeteners	6.85	5.99	5.31	4.88	5.15	9.11	10.13	11.56
Jams, preserves, other sweets	22.04	14.06	19.56	24.19	23.34	18.89	27.44	34.99
Fats and oils	**88.89**	**62.59**	**78.57**	**95.79**	**93.59**	**103.11**	**98.44**	**129.12**
Margarine	9.57	7.26	9.21	10.84	8.88	12.03	10.27	12.36
Fats and oils	28.56	21.99	25.89	34.97	28.01	26.36	28.39	41.14
Salad dressings	27.44	17.18	22.54	28.64	30.59	36.50	32.23	42.32
Nondairy cream and imitation milk	10.80	6.50	9.41	11.58	12.81	13.10	13.44	15.08
Peanut butter	12.52	9.65	11.52	9.77	13.30	15.11	14.10	18.22

	total consumer units	under $20,000	$20,000– $39,999	$40,000– $49,999	$50,000– $69,999	$70,000– $79,999	$80,000– $99,999	$100,000 or more
Miscellaneous foods	$527.29	$295.79	$418.45	$475.20	$589.49	$716.69	$692.87	$902.30
Frozen prepared foods	109.90	65.92	93.14	104.02	121.55	152.22	135.07	171.66
Frozen meals	31.79	23.93	32.24	25.67	27.79	40.51	40.20	44.24
Other frozen prepared foods	78.11	41.99	60.90	78.35	93.76	111.71	94.87	127.42
Canned and packaged soups	36.50	24.35	31.59	34.03	37.69	44.85	46.55	56.58
Potato chips, nuts, and other snacks	117.08	61.26	87.53	104.19	129.15	166.65	161.84	212.70
Potato chips and other snacks	86.06	44.52	67.88	75.49	97.39	116.85	116.82	152.46
Nuts	31.01	16.73	19.64	28.70	31.76	49.80	45.02	60.24
Condiments and seasonings	93.65	51.33	71.91	85.09	114.45	123.76	118.97	159.39
Salt, spices, and other seasonings	22.22	12.60	17.12	22.50	25.10	30.40	24.91	39.07
Olives, pickles, relishes	10.52	5.95	7.98	9.48	13.50	13.89	13.65	16.90
Sauces and gravies	40.94	21.20	31.68	34.18	52.76	54.25	55.93	68.23
Baking needs and miscellaneous products	19.97	11.58	15.15	18.93	23.09	25.22	24.48	35.19
Other canned/packaged prepared foods	170.16	92.94	134.29	147.86	186.65	229.20	230.44	301.97
Prepared salads	25.43	13.20	17.55	22.39	29.46	30.19	35.14	50.41
Prepared desserts	10.91	6.49	8.24	12.15	10.74	11.45	13.66	20.46
Baby food	30.08	13.65	29.82	22.67	28.02	43.97	44.63	50.98
Miscellaneous prepared foods	102.74	59.61	78.51	90.16	117.03	143.59	136.42	175.28
Nonalcoholic beverages	**289.52**	**180.82**	**249.19**	**278.07**	**333.21**	**373.53**	**332.48**	**443.01**
Cola	93.81	64.06	88.13	94.73	106.66	105.78	110.48	123.03
Other carbonated drinks	48.08	29.13	45.66	46.10	54.83	71.38	50.29	67.03
Coffee	39.12	24.14	32.60	33.45	44.36	59.01	41.76	64.70
Roasted coffee	24.48	14.54	20.26	20.24	29.19	35.05	27.07	40.88
Instant and freeze-dried coffee	14.64	9.61	12.33	13.21	15.17	23.96	14.69	23.82
Noncarbonated fruit-flavored drinks	19.79	13.38	20.20	20.00	22.37	26.57	21.81	22.65
Tea	17.63	10.84	12.58	16.75	22.61	18.73	18.79	32.26
Other nonalcoholic beverages and ice	70.10	39.26	49.36	65.76	81.96	89.88	89.17	129.74
Food prepared by CU on trips	**40.86**	**13.49**	**24.60**	**30.35**	**49.50**	**54.83**	**68.88**	**97.74**
FOOD AWAY FROM HOME	2,434.00	949.88	1,699.12	2,188.59	2,671.61	3,258.51	3,424.00	5,298.64
Meals at restaurants, carry-outs, other	**2,028.17**	**826.24**	**1,494.42**	**1,929.01**	**2,204.30**	**2,788.78**	**2,702.02**	**4,165.65**
Lunch	725.07	302.08	542.14	707.72	797.54	1,003.95	955.31	1,442.80
At fast-food restaurants*	409.17	189.12	326.59	404.85	444.45	573.40	524.46	752.08
At full-service restaurants	236.65	82.75	166.26	228.81	245.31	331.69	337.21	519.21
At vending machines, mobile vendors	6.02	3.79	5.81	6.20	8.68	6.32	3.64	8.30
At employer and school cafeterias	73.24	26.43	43.48	67.86	99.10	92.54	89.99	163.21
Dinner	795.59	290.19	519.05	721.60	859.75	1,146.88	1,102.97	1,798.01
At fast-food restaurants*	253.07	111.62	199.83	233.01	293.40	336.14	317.95	482.54
At full-service restaurants	538.22	175.72	314.97	484.87	562.61	809.18	783.12	1,304.96
At vending machines, mobile vendors	1.50	0.79	2.30	2.25	1.25	0.84	0.13	2.57
At employer and school cafeterias	2.79	2.41	1.95	1.47	2.49	0.72	1.77	7.94
Snacks and nonalcoholic beverages	297.45	146.04	247.59	288.96	317.58	370.33	390.80	539.19
At fast-food restaurants*	217.16	103.91	173.58	203.49	234.13	272.97	291.14	410.03
At full-service restaurants	28.87	16.44	26.62	27.62	29.23	35.60	32.80	49.14
At vending machines, mobile vendors	41.07	20.41	40.42	49.47	41.31	46.99	50.94	61.59
At employer and school cafeterias	10.34	5.28	6.98	8.38	12.92	14.76	15.93	18.43
Breakfast and brunch	210.06	87.92	185.64	210.72	229.42	267.62	252.94	385.65
At fast-food restaurants*	103.28	48.12	101.31	114.99	111.86	122.74	130.19	155.34
At full-service restaurants	100.36	35.46	79.07	90.76	109.19	137.01	116.71	219.81
At vending machines, mobile vendors	1.42	1.36	1.62	0.64	1.60	1.62	1.96	1.13
At employer and school cafeterias	5.00	2.99	3.63	4.32	6.77	6.26	4.09	9.37
Board (including at school)	**27.89**	**17.80**	**6.22**	**5.88**	**14.22**	**16.39**	**33.41**	**121.85**
Catered affairs	**58.56**	**11.07**	**14.50**	**4.94**	**71.87**	**54.92**	**132.35**	**211.57**
Food on trips	**231.55**	**64.73**	**120.74**	**164.49**	**260.04**	**282.37**	**406.75**	**642.94**
School lunches	**63.39**	**8.58**	**37.38**	**62.73**	**85.80**	**91.64**	**127.67**	**138.35**
Meals as pay	**24.45**	**21.46**	**25.87**	**21.55**	**35.37**	**24.40**	**21.81**	**18.28**

	total consumer units	under $20,000	$20,000–$39,999	$40,000–$49,999	$50,000–$69,999	$70,000–$79,999	$80,000–$99,999	$100,000 or more
ALCOHOLIC BEVERAGES	$459.27	$192.20	$291.59	$449.21	$483.62	$617.46	$701.51	$986.82
At home	**277.59**	**128.73**	**188.27**	**285.91**	**285.72**	**368.74**	**414.54**	**554.27**
Beer and ale	131.31	73.32	116.75	131.99	159.24	180.98	168.44	179.85
Whiskey	21.66	14.31	11.37	29.49	18.58	30.14	21.21	46.93
Wine	94.55	27.81	39.46	103.08	76.79	129.05	170.77	260.23
Other alcoholic beverages	30.07	13.29	20.68	21.35	31.11	28.57	54.12	67.26
Away from home	**181.68**	**63.47**	**103.33**	**163.30**	**197.90**	**248.71**	**286.98**	**432.54**
Beer and ale	76.32	30.63	47.94	78.57	80.44	104.52	112.18	164.72
At fast-food restaurants*	16.44	11.41	11.36	15.11	18.74	28.55	16.81	27.12
At full-service restaurants	56.01	19.13	36.32	62.24	60.45	71.47	89.13	117.47
Wine	22.29	7.05	14.35	22.92	24.98	30.91	36.99	46.39
At fast-food restaurants*	3.06	1.90	2.51	2.83	2.89	6.51	3.00	4.91
At full-service restaurants	18.76	5.15	11.83	20.06	22.10	23.94	33.41	38.54
Other alcoholic beverages	44.71	12.37	24.48	38.17	47.66	68.26	76.21	108.79
At fast-food restaurants*	3.82	2.08	2.94	2.91	3.13	13.39	3.44	6.76
At full-service restaurants	39.44	10.79	21.47	35.03	44.47	52.94	70.29	93.98
Alcoholic beverages purchased on trips	38.37	13.43	16.55	23.64	44.82	45.02	61.60	112.64

The category fast-food restaurants also includes take-out, delivery, concession stands, buffets, and cafeterias other than employer and school.
Note: Subcategories may not add to total because some are not shown. "–" means sample is too small to make a reliable estimate.
Source: Bureau of Labor Statistics, unpublished tables from the 2004 Consumer Expenditure Survey; calculations by New Strategist

Table 5.6 Food and Alcohol: Indexed spending by income, 2004

(indexed average annual spending of consumer units (CU) on food and beverages, by before-tax income of consumer unit, 2004; index definition: an index of 100 is the average for all consumer units; an index of 132 means that spending by consumer units in that group is 32 percent above the average for all consumer units; an index of 68 indicates spending that is 32 percent below the average for all consumer units)

	total consumer units	under $20,000	$20,000–$39,999	$40,000–$49,999	$50,000–$69,999	$70,000–$79,999	$80,000–$99,999	$100,000 or more
Average spending of CU, total	$43,395	$18,865	$30,401	$38,204	$47,750	$55,012	$65,446	$93,526
Average spending of CU, index	100	43	70	88	110	127	151	216
Food, spending index	**100**	**52**	**78**	**94**	**109**	**127**	**129**	**186**
Alcoholic beverages, spending index	**100**	**42**	**63**	**98**	**105**	**134**	**153**	**215**
FOOD AT HOME	**100**	**62**	**84**	**98**	**109**	**122**	**121**	**162**
Cereals and bakery products	**100**	**66**	**85**	**99**	**110**	**113**	**118**	**157**
Cereals and cereal products	100	73	85	99	108	115	117	148
Flour	100	119	106	91	88	98	56	106
Prepared flour mixes	100	66	70	124	107	106	129	166
Ready-to-eat and cooked cereals	100	69	87	98	110	114	120	146
Rice	100	80	89	86	112	118	80	153
Pasta, cornmeal, and other cereal products	100	68	75	99	107	123	143	156
Bakery products	100	62	85	99	111	113	119	162
Bread	100	68	91	98	115	111	111	145
White bread	100	75	97	95	114	111	106	127
Bread, other than white	100	63	86	100	115	110	115	156
Crackers and cookies	100	62	85	95	110	115	118	166
Cookies	100	65	86	98	110	113	108	165
Crackers	100	58	82	91	111	119	135	169
Frozen and refrigerated bakery products	100	51	87	97	105	104	127	185
Other bakery products	100	60	82	103	110	114	124	166
Biscuits and rolls	100	53	74	93	117	125	128	184
Cakes and cupcakes	100	60	89	108	103	105	112	167
Bread and cracker products	100	64	67	97	127	116	132	166
Sweetrolls, coffee cakes, doughnuts	100	67	88	107	107	107	125	145
Pies, tarts, turnovers	100	70	79	113	105	121	138	141
Meats, poultry, fish, and eggs	**100**	**64**	**86**	**102**	**106**	**125**	**117**	**155**
Beef	100	62	88	100	105	133	122	152
Ground beef	100	70	93	103	110	126	117	129
Roast	100	68	92	100	94	134	110	153
Chuck roast	100	88	100	77	98	113	130	116
Round roast	100	77	99	94	85	94	125	150
Other roast	100	55	86	115	96	163	93	172
Steak	100	51	82	103	103	144	131	171
Round steak	100	54	86	100	120	116	147	143
Sirloin steak	100	51	80	102	93	167	125	179
Other steak	100	49	82	104	104	139	130	175
Other beef	100	69	90	68	110	109	126	164
Pork	100	69	92	108	107	104	115	142
Bacon	100	71	99	98	115	96	113	130
Pork chops	100	74	94	122	103	103	94	136
Ham	100	70	87	101	118	89	113	151
Ham, not canned	100	70	86	102	120	88	115	149
Canned ham	100	75	122	62	54	118	56	197
Sausage	100	64	91	112	110	127	117	135
Other pork	100	65	90	106	94	110	135	154
Other meats	100	62	80	102	108	121	127	164
Frankfurters	100	72	86	97	104	121	128	146
Lunch meats (cold cuts)	100	57	83	95	114	127	134	160
Bologna, liverwurst, salami	100	72	91	111	107	108	110	137
Other lunch meats	100	51	79	89	116	135	144	169
Lamb, organ meats, and others	100	71	54	157	84	79	83	223
Poultry	100	65	84	96	109	123	119	159
Fresh and frozen chicken	100	65	88	93	110	125	114	155
Fresh and frozen whole chicken	100	69	100	102	99	132	102	136
Fresh and frozen chicken parts	100	64	83	89	115	122	119	162
Other poultry	100	65	70	105	105	116	138	175

	total consumer units	under $20,000	$20,000– $39,999	$40,000– $49,999	$50,000– $69,999	$70,000– $79,999	$80,000– $99,999	$100,000 or more
Fish and seafood	100	56	79	110	106	152	106	172
Canned fish and seafood	100	68	79	110	113	103	107	162
Fresh fish and shellfish	100	54	80	103	102	164	103	180
Frozen fish and shellfish	100	56	75	124	110	148	111	161
Eggs	100	78	100	97	104	94	103	136
Dairy products	**100**	**61**	**86**	**97**	**109**	**115**	**122**	**163**
Fresh milk and cream	100	71	92	99	106	109	117	143
Fresh milk, all types	100	73	94	100	106	107	114	139
Cream	100	59	76	90	111	121	142	171
Other dairy products	100	55	82	97	110	119	124	176
Butter	100	62	79	88	141	122	123	141
Cheese	100	53	78	95	106	116	131	190
Ice cream and related products	100	56	89	101	110	125	112	163
Miscellaneous dairy products	100	55	84	100	107	114	126	173
Fruits and vegetables	**100**	**64**	**84**	**98**	**105**	**115**	**117**	**168**
Fresh fruits	100	62	84	103	99	113	119	175
Apples	100	60	87	100	103	100	129	171
Bananas	100	71	96	112	101	108	107	136
Oranges	100	69	90	132	90	103	115	145
Citrus fruits, excluding oranges	100	59	79	94	96	126	126	189
Other fresh fruits	100	57	79	97	99	118	118	194
Fresh vegetables	100	65	81	92	110	116	117	170
Potatoes	100	75	89	97	110	118	120	133
Lettuce	100	62	74	94	112	128	124	176
Tomatoes	100	72	83	94	114	106	112	158
Other fresh vegetables	100	61	79	89	109	117	116	185
Processed fruits	100	63	87	96	107	115	122	160
Frozen fruits and fruit juices	100	71	79	90	119	99	130	155
Frozen orange juice	100	76	84	120	120	119	135	101
Frozen fruits	100	63	61	80	118	80	129	220
Frozen fruit juices, excluding orange	100	75	97	52	119	90	121	152
Canned fruits	100	65	84	103	99	105	162	147
Dried fruits	100	57	81	85	125	109	129	168
Fresh fruit juice	100	53	86	105	100	104	122	185
Canned and bottled fruit juice	100	66	91	93	108	126	109	154
Processed vegetables	100	69	86	100	108	117	109	155
Frozen vegetables	100	58	81	102	111	120	119	169
Canned and dried vegetables and juices	100	75	88	99	106	116	104	147
Canned beans	100	76	93	93	106	122	114	135
Canned corn	100	86	93	138	95	96	82	125
Canned miscellaneous vegetables	100	72	78	105	113	114	110	156
Dried peas	100	88	76	83	102	152	95	157
Dried beans	100	104	108	132	93	70	57	97
Dried miscellaneous vegetables	100	72	90	86	115	129	99	147
Dried processed vegetables	100	233	105	110	7	43	–	197
Fresh and canned vegetable juices	100	64	92	72	104	129	114	174
Sugar and other sweets	**100**	**62**	**79**	**92**	**107**	**110**	**127**	**180**
Candy and chewing gum	100	54	72	87	110	115	133	201
Sugar	100	92	104	99	102	108	89	108
Artificial sweeteners	100	87	77	71	75	133	148	169
Jams, preserves, other sweets	100	64	89	110	106	86	125	159
Fats and oils	**100**	**70**	**88**	**108**	**105**	**116**	**111**	**145**
Margarine	100	76	96	113	93	126	107	129
Fats and oils	100	77	91	122	98	92	99	144
Salad dressings	100	63	82	104	111	133	117	154
Nondairy cream and imitation milk	100	60	87	107	119	121	124	140
Peanut butter	100	77	92	78	106	121	113	146

	total consumer units	under $20,000	$20,000– $39,999	$40,000– $49,999	$50,000– $69,999	$70,000– $79,999	$80,000– $99,999	$100,000 or more
Miscellaneous foods	**100**	**56**	**79**	**90**	**112**	**136**	**131**	**171**
Frozen prepared foods	100	60	85	95	111	139	123	156
Frozen meals	100	75	101	81	87	127	126	139
Other frozen prepared foods	100	54	78	100	120	143	121	163
Canned and packaged soups	100	67	87	93	103	123	128	155
Potato chips, nuts, and other snacks	100	52	75	89	110	142	138	182
Potato chips and other snacks	100	52	79	88	113	136	136	177
Nuts	100	54	63	93	102	161	145	194
Condiments and seasonings	100	55	77	91	122	132	127	170
Salt, spices, and other seasonings	100	57	77	101	113	137	112	176
Olives, pickles, relishes	100	57	76	90	128	132	130	161
Sauces and gravies	100	52	77	83	129	133	137	167
Baking needs and miscellaneous products	100	58	76	95	116	126	123	176
Other canned/packaged prepared foods	100	55	79	87	110	135	135	177
Prepared salads	100	52	69	88	116	119	138	198
Prepared desserts	100	59	76	111	98	105	125	188
Baby food	100	45	99	75	93	146	148	169
Miscellaneous prepared foods	100	58	76	88	114	140	133	171
Nonalcoholic beverages	**100**	**62**	**86**	**96**	**115**	**129**	**115**	**153**
Cola	100	68	94	101	114	113	118	131
Other carbonated drinks	100	61	95	96	114	148	105	139
Coffee	100	62	83	86	113	151	107	165
Roasted coffee	100	59	83	83	119	143	111	167
Instant and freeze-dried coffee	100	66	84	90	104	164	100	163
Noncarbonated fruit-flavored drinks	100	68	102	101	113	134	110	114
Tea	100	61	71	95	128	106	107	183
Other nonalcoholic beverages and ice	100	56	70	94	117	128	127	185
Food prepared by CU on trips	**100**	**33**	**60**	**74**	**121**	**134**	**169**	**239**
FOOD AWAY FROM HOME	**100**	**39**	**70**	**90**	**110**	**134**	**141**	**218**
Meals at restaurants, carry-outs, other	**100**	**41**	**74**	**95**	**109**	**138**	**133**	**205**
Lunch	100	42	75	98	110	138	132	199
At fast-food restaurants*	100	46	80	99	109	140	128	184
At full-service restaurants	100	35	70	97	104	140	142	219
At vending machines, mobile vendors	100	63	97	103	144	105	60	138
At employer and school cafeterias	100	36	59	93	135	126	123	223
Dinner	100	36	65	91	108	144	139	226
At fast-food restaurants*	100	44	79	92	116	133	126	191
At full-service restaurants	100	33	59	90	105	150	146	242
At vending machines, mobile vendors	100	53	154	150	83	56	9	171
At employer and school cafeterias	100	86	70	53	89	26	63	285
Snacks and nonalcoholic beverages	100	49	83	97	107	125	131	181
At fast-food restaurants*	100	48	80	94	108	126	134	189
At full-service restaurants	100	57	92	96	101	123	114	170
At vending machines, mobile vendors	100	50	98	120	101	114	124	150
At employer and school cafeterias	100	51	67	81	125	143	154	178
Breakfast and brunch	100	42	88	100	109	127	120	184
At fast-food restaurants*	100	47	98	111	108	119	126	150
At full-service restaurants	100	35	79	90	109	137	116	219
At vending machines, mobile vendors	100	96	114	45	113	114	138	80
At employer and school cafeterias	100	60	73	86	135	125	82	187
Board (including at school)	**100**	**64**	**22**	**21**	**51**	**59**	**120**	**437**
Catered affairs	**100**	**19**	**25**	**8**	**123**	**94**	**226**	**361**
Food on trips	**100**	**28**	**52**	**71**	**112**	**122**	**176**	**278**
School lunches	**100**	**14**	**59**	**99**	**135**	**145**	**201**	**218**
Meals as pay	**100**	**88**	**106**	**88**	**145**	**100**	**89**	**75**

	total consumer units	under $20,000	$20,000– $39,999	$40,000– $49,999	$50,000– $69,999	$70,000– $79,999	$80,000– $99,999	$100,000 or more
ALCOHOLIC BEVERAGES	**100**	**42**	**63**	**98**	**105**	**134**	**153**	**215**
At home	**100**	**46**	**68**	**103**	**103**	**133**	**149**	**200**
Beer and ale	100	56	89	101	121	138	128	137
Whiskey	100	66	53	136	86	139	98	217
Wine	100	29	42	109	81	136	181	275
Other alcoholic beverages	100	44	69	71	103	95	180	224
Away from home	**100**	**35**	**57**	**90**	**109**	**137**	**158**	**238**
Beer and ale	100	40	63	103	105	137	147	216
At fast-food restaurants*	100	69	69	92	114	174	102	165
At full-service restaurants	100	34	65	111	108	128	159	210
Wine	100	32	64	103	112	139	166	208
At fast-food restaurants*	100	62	82	92	94	213	98	160
At full-service restaurants	100	27	63	107	118	128	178	205
Other alcoholic beverages	100	28	55	85	107	153	170	243
At fast-food restaurants*	100	55	77	76	82	351	90	177
At full-service restaurants	100	27	54	89	113	134	178	238
Alcoholic beverages purchased on trips	100	35	43	62	117	117	161	294

*The category fast-food restaurants also includes take-out, delivery, concession stands, buffets, and cafeterias other than employer and school.
Note: "–" means sample is too small to make a reliable estimate.
Source: Calculations by New Strategist based on the 2004 Consumer Expenditure Survey

Table 5.7 Food and Alcohol: Total spending by income, 2004

(total annual spending on food and alcoholic beverages, by before-tax income group of consumer units (CU), 2004; consumer units and dollars in thousands)

	total consumer units	under $20,000	$20,000– $39,999	$40,000– $49,999	$50,000– $69,999	$70,000– $79,999	$80,000– $99,999	$100,000 or more
Number of consumer units	116,282	28,898	27,297	11,374	18,069	6,461	9,246	14,937
Total spending of all CUs	$5,046,042,273	$545,171,431	$829,854,379	$434,533,092	$862,797,099	$355,432,726	$605,117,322	$1,396,992,933
Food, total spending	672,205,311	87,684,456	123,199,555	62,011,730	114,049,179	47,407,264	69,035,629	160,324,646
Alcoholic beverages, total spending	53,404,834	5,554,122	7,959,557	5,109,315	8,738,530	3,989,409	6,486,161	14,740,130
FOOD AT HOME	389,174,923	60,234,885	76,818,439	37,118,708	65,775,858	26,354,031	37,377,232	81,178,861
Cereals and bakery products	53,594,374	8,741,070	10,728,196	5,191,435	9,151,406	3,374,516	5,040,734	10,819,765
Cereals and cereal products	17,884,172	3,240,339	3,566,897	1,725,095	3,003,068	1,139,204	1,660,674	3,405,785
Flour	967,466	286,880	239,876	85,987	131,904	52,851	42,901	131,147
Prepared flour mixes	1,602,366	261,094	263,978	194,382	266,879	94,654	163,932	340,862
Ready-to-eat and cooked cereals	10,080,487	1,739,579	2,069,875	965,653	1,717,820	639,768	965,467	1,893,862
Rice	2,146,566	427,777	449,862	181,074	372,221	141,044	136,286	423,016
Pasta, cornmeal, and other cereal products	3,087,287	525,216	543,447	298,113	514,424	210,952	352,180	616,749
Bakery products	35,710,202	5,500,741	7,161,299	3,466,340	6,148,339	2,235,312	3,380,060	7,413,980
Bread	10,189,792	1,713,467	2,168,838	975,775	1,815,212	626,975	902,872	1,895,953
White bread	4,074,521	757,858	927,421	378,754	722,579	252,237	342,472	667,236
Bread, other than white	6,115,270	955,537	1,241,416	597,021	1,092,632	374,738	560,400	1,228,867
Crackers and cookies	8,274,627	1,278,514	1,643,873	772,863	1,413,538	529,996	773,243	1,769,437
Cookies	5,415,253	869,140	1,093,848	517,403	921,880	340,301	467,015	1,147,460
Crackers	2,860,537	409,375	550,166	255,346	491,477	189,695	306,135	621,977
Frozen and refrigerated bakery products	3,060,542	385,290	623,526	289,582	501,053	177,484	308,724	726,984
Other bakery products	14,185,241	2,123,541	2,725,063	1,428,233	2,418,536	900,857	1,395,221	3,021,606
Biscuits and rolls	4,896,635	648,242	850,897	445,178	890,802	339,461	499,192	1,159,261
Cakes and cupcakes	4,539,649	674,592	949,227	480,097	729,626	264,901	405,252	975,237
Bread and cracker products	377,917	59,782	59,598	35,828	74,806	24,293	39,758	80,510
Sweetrolls, coffee cakes, doughnuts	2,743,092	459,516	563,757	287,648	457,326	163,140	272,480	512,638
Pies, tarts, turnovers	1,626,785	281,481	301,453	179,368	265,976	109,062	178,540	293,960
Meats, poultry, fish, and eggs	102,294,438	16,240,706	20,748,868	10,241,946	16,920,534	7,085,520	9,554,816	20,356,592
Beef	30,854,266	4,751,066	6,393,140	3,008,764	5,015,232	2,284,545	2,994,779	6,026,930
Ground beef	11,270,051	1,949,655	2,456,119	1,131,031	1,926,697	788,048	1,049,144	1,867,872
Roast	5,300,134	901,828	1,148,948	520,133	771,546	395,672	462,947	1,038,868
Chuck roast	1,362,825	298,242	318,342	102,935	206,709	85,350	140,909	203,890
Round roast	1,194,216	228,950	277,410	109,759	157,381	62,672	118,534	230,329
Other roast	2,741,930	374,636	553,064	307,439	407,456	247,650	203,412	604,500
Steak	12,029,373	1,512,959	2,313,598	1,207,464	1,930,853	964,046	1,257,271	2,646,090
Round steak	1,903,536	254,178	385,302	186,875	355,056	122,501	222,181	350,721
Sirloin steak	3,765,211	480,525	707,808	376,366	543,696	348,571	375,203	866,346
Other steak	6,361,788	778,392	1,220,489	644,337	1,032,101	492,974	659,887	1,429,023
Other beef	2,254,708	386,623	474,607	150,137	386,315	136,715	225,417	474,100
Pork	21,063,321	3,606,078	4,538,768	2,219,636	3,505,567	1,218,932	1,928,901	3,851,207
Bacon	3,614,045	637,548	835,944	346,680	646,147	193,119	324,535	603,305
Pork chops	4,409,413	814,568	976,138	525,251	704,691	251,333	329,527	768,658
Ham	4,610,581	799,481	938,860	457,121	845,087	227,556	415,608	891,590
Ham, not canned	4,496,625	778,224	906,077	450,183	835,691	220,062	410,615	862,761
Canned ham	113,956	21,257	32,652	6,938	9,577	7,495	5,085	28,828
Sausage	3,245,431	516,026	691,291	354,983	552,911	229,495	302,714	564,170
Other pork	5,185,014	838,246	1,096,404	535,488	756,549	317,429	556,517	1,023,334
Other meats	12,556,130	1,927,026	2,356,323	1,258,078	2,109,014	840,835	1,270,031	2,649,525
Frankfurters	2,618,671	468,700	525,759	247,498	421,550	176,579	266,377	489,635
Lunch meats (cold cuts)	8,487,423	1,201,717	1,646,398	788,446	1,498,281	600,292	907,310	1,744,044
Bologna, liverwurst, salami	2,450,062	438,884	524,906	265,697	408,359	146,923	214,600	430,634
Other lunch meats	6,036,199	762,743	1,121,492	522,749	1,089,922	453,368	692,710	1,313,410
Lamb, organ meats, and others	1,451,199	256,563	184,166	222,248	189,182	63,964	96,343	415,846
Poultry	18,094,642	2,936,094	3,576,563	1,694,499	3,065,225	1,235,989	1,708,938	3,692,725
Fresh and frozen chicken	14,260,824	2,319,386	2,949,605	1,299,934	2,441,303	988,275	1,287,598	2,831,458
Fresh and frozen whole chicken	4,254,758	730,255	1,000,861	424,591	655,363	310,968	344,506	743,863
Fresh and frozen chicken parts	10,004,903	1,589,041	1,948,745	875,343	1,785,940	677,307	943,092	2,087,595
Other poultry	3,833,818	616,708	626,958	394,564	623,923	247,715	421,340	861,267

	total consumer units	under $20,000	$20,000–$39,999	$40,000–$49,999	$50,000–$69,999	$70,000–$79,999	$80,000–$99,999	$100,000 or more
Fish and seafood	$14,860,840	$2,077,023	$2,741,658	$1,599,071	$2,441,483	$1,251,948	$1,253,388	$3,288,530
Canned fish and seafood	1,788,417	302,528	333,564	193,131	314,943	101,890	152,189	373,126
Fresh fish and shellfish	8,707,196	1,162,797	1,640,232	878,187	1,380,291	791,860	716,565	2,010,371
Frozen fish and shellfish	4,365,226	611,626	767,730	527,754	746,250	358,198	384,634	905,033
Eggs	4,865,239	943,383	1,142,415	461,898	783,833	253,336	398,780	847,824
Dairy products	**43,090,621**	**6,570,428**	**8,682,621**	**4,106,128**	**7,290,299**	**2,754,906**	**4,165,323**	**9,019,110**
Fresh milk and cream	16,782,981	2,965,931	3,617,004	1,621,022	2,776,302	1,015,540	1,562,112	3,073,885
Fresh milk, all types	14,993,401	2,701,844	3,297,070	1,463,265	2,466,599	894,849	1,359,809	2,679,847
Cream	1,789,580	264,221	319,934	157,757	309,522	120,691	202,302	394,187
Other dairy products	26,307,640	3,604,362	5,065,617	2,485,105	4,513,998	1,739,366	2,603,211	5,945,225
Butter	2,536,110	392,444	472,483	219,177	557,248	171,475	248,532	459,313
Cheese	13,217,775	1,750,655	2,422,579	1,224,070	2,172,074	855,372	1,375,805	3,226,691
Ice cream and related products	7,002,502	974,114	1,469,688	693,814	1,193,457	486,836	623,180	1,468,307
Miscellaneous dairy products	3,551,252	487,212	700,856	348,158	591,398	225,683	355,694	790,914
Fruits and vegetables	**65,228,388**	**10,415,097**	**12,838,172**	**6,239,321**	**10,689,801**	**4,166,311**	**6,088,676**	**14,054,970**
Fresh fruits	21,714,501	3,320,057	4,292,940	2,194,841	3,331,201	1,357,650	2,047,712	4,889,926
Apples	3,769,862	563,780	766,548	369,314	600,614	209,143	388,147	827,211
Bananas	3,508,228	621,975	787,623	385,806	552,008	210,758	299,570	614,359
Oranges	2,265,173	389,830	478,485	292,539	318,014	130,060	206,371	422,717
Citrus fruits, excluding oranges	1,791,906	261,798	333,576	164,241	266,518	125,666	178,910	435,862
Other fresh fruits	10,378,169	1,482,712	1,926,577	982,941	1,594,228	681,959	974,713	2,589,777
Fresh vegetables	21,272,629	3,461,744	4,027,285	1,909,922	3,645,601	1,376,128	1,978,644	4,658,253
Potatoes	3,264,036	605,082	682,661	309,145	558,513	213,924	312,237	558,793
Lettuce	2,659,369	409,025	462,299	245,223	461,302	188,597	262,864	602,708
Tomatoes	4,155,919	738,478	811,823	381,939	734,143	244,097	370,950	841,401
Other fresh vegetables	11,192,143	1,709,160	2,070,229	973,614	1,891,644	729,512	1,032,686	2,655,350
Processed fruits	12,747,996	2,000,533	2,605,387	1,202,914	2,120,036	813,957	1,240,443	2,618,904
Frozen fruits and fruit juices	1,159,332	204,448	214,494	102,593	214,298	63,641	119,643	230,478
Frozen orange juice	484,896	91,045	95,296	56,984	90,526	32,111	52,240	62,735
Frozen fruits	410,475	63,898	58,785	32,075	75,348	18,285	41,977	116,060
Frozen fruit juices, excluding orange	263,960	49,423	60,282	13,535	48,606	13,245	25,427	51,533
Canned fruits	1,882,606	305,958	370,396	189,718	288,743	109,708	242,245	355,799
Dried fruits	738,391	104,779	140,709	61,533	143,106	44,581	75,817	158,930
Fresh fruit juice	2,566,344	335,687	519,424	264,787	399,144	147,698	248,810	609,728
Canned and bottled fruit juice	6,401,324	1,049,555	1,360,374	584,282	1,074,744	448,264	554,020	1,263,969
Processed vegetables	9,493,262	1,632,636	1,912,561	931,758	1,592,963	618,576	821,877	1,887,887
Frozen vegetables	3,314,037	481,699	632,922	331,325	570,800	220,902	313,347	721,009
Canned and dried vegetables and juices	6,179,225	1,151,009	1,279,629	600,433	1,022,163	397,675	508,622	1,166,878
Canned beans	1,324,452	248,938	288,983	120,451	217,370	89,808	119,643	229,283
Canned corn	736,065	156,791	160,111	99,068	108,775	39,412	47,802	118,600
Canned miscellaneous vegetables	1,950,049	347,056	356,470	200,751	341,865	123,857	170,404	391,648
Dried peas	69,769	15,182	12,441	5,687	11,022	5,880	5,270	14,041
Dried beans	287,217	74,561	72,810	37,193	41,559	11,113	13,129	35,699
Dried miscellaneous vegetables	722,111	129,944	152,027	60,623	129,374	51,817	56,770	136,674
Dried processed vegetables	34,885	20,194	8,599	3,753	361	840	–	8,813
Fresh and canned vegetable juices	1,036,073	163,880	222,612	72,907	166,777	74,431	93,662	230,926
Sugar and other sweets	**14,898,050**	**2,296,001**	**2,780,076**	**1,337,355**	**2,466,057**	**908,417**	**1,500,256**	**3,444,920**
Candy and chewing gum	9,666,523	1,289,832	1,644,043	824,956	1,655,843	615,281	1,020,389	2,490,745
Sugar	1,872,140	426,548	457,341	181,870	295,609	112,292	132,588	258,858
Artificial sweeteners	796,532	173,121	144,835	55,505	93,055	58,860	93,662	172,672
Jams, preserves, other sweets	2,562,855	406,374	533,858	275,137	421,730	122,048	253,710	522,646
Fats and oils	**10,336,307**	**1,808,704**	**2,144,645**	**1,089,515**	**1,691,078**	**666,194**	**910,176**	**1,928,665**
Margarine	1,112,819	209,849	251,475	123,294	160,453	77,726	94,956	184,621
Fats and oils	3,321,014	635,541	706,583	397,749	506,113	170,312	262,494	614,508
Salad dressings	3,190,778	496,565	615,281	325,751	552,731	235,827	297,999	632,134
Nondairy cream and imitation milk	1,255,846	187,773	256,828	131,711	231,464	84,639	124,266	225,250
Peanut butter	1,455,851	278,904	314,337	111,124	240,318	97,626	130,369	272,152

	total consumer units	under $20,000	$20,000– $39,999	$40,000– $49,999	$50,000– $69,999	$70,000– $79,999	$80,000– $99,999	$100,000 or more
Miscellaneous foods	$61,314,336	$8,547,854	$11,422,339	$5,404,925	$10,651,495	$4,630,534	$6,406,276	$13,477,655
Frozen prepared foods	12,779,392	1,904,966	2,542,448	1,183,123	2,196,287	983,493	1,248,857	2,564,085
Frozen meals	3,696,605	691,436	879,984	291,971	502,138	261,735	371,689	660,813
Other frozen prepared foods	9,082,787	1,213,441	1,662,322	891,153	1,694,149	721,758	877,168	1,903,273
Canned and packaged soups	4,244,293	703,681	862,226	387,057	681,021	289,776	430,401	845,135
Potato chips, nuts, and other snacks	13,614,297	1,770,203	2,389,210	1,185,057	2,333,611	1,076,726	1,496,373	3,177,100
Potato chips and other snacks	10,007,229	1,286,679	1,852,996	858,623	1,759,740	754,968	1,080,118	2,277,295
Nuts	3,605,905	483,570	536,072	326,434	573,871	321,758	416,255	899,805
Condiments and seasonings	10,889,809	1,483,245	1,963,062	967,814	2,067,997	799,613	1,099,997	2,380,808
Salt, spices, and other seasonings	2,583,786	364,044	467,298	255,915	453,532	196,414	230,318	583,589
Olives, pickles, relishes	1,223,287	171,910	217,720	107,826	243,932	89,743	126,208	252,435
Sauces and gravies	4,760,585	612,655	864,759	388,763	953,320	350,509	517,129	1,019,152
Baking needs and miscellaneous products	2,322,152	334,554	413,417	215,310	417,213	162,946	226,342	525,633
Other canned/packaged prepared foods	19,786,545	2,685,714	3,665,678	1,681,760	3,372,579	1,480,861	2,130,648	4,510,526
Prepared salads	2,957,051	381,338	478,973	254,664	532,313	195,058	324,904	752,974
Prepared desserts	1,268,637	187,537	224,988	138,194	194,061	73,978	126,300	305,611
Baby food	3,497,763	394,408	813,970	257,849	506,293	284,090	412,649	761,488
Miscellaneous prepared foods	11,946,813	1,722,474	2,143,142	1,025,480	2,114,615	927,735	1,261,339	2,618,157
Nonalcoholic beverages	**33,665,965**	**5,225,450**	**6,802,120**	**3,162,768**	**6,020,771**	**2,413,377**	**3,074,110**	**6,617,240**
Cola	10,908,414	1,851,210	2,405,758	1,077,459	1,927,240	683,445	1,021,498	1,837,699
Other carbonated drinks	5,590,839	841,924	1,246,383	524,341	990,723	461,186	464,981	1,001,227
Coffee	4,548,952	697,606	889,782	380,460	801,541	381,264	386,113	966,424
Roasted coffee	2,846,583	420,039	553,114	230,210	527,434	226,458	250,289	610,625
Instant and freeze-dried coffee	1,702,368	277,577	336,669	150,251	274,107	154,806	135,824	355,799
Noncarbonated fruit-flavored drinks	2,301,221	386,709	551,522	227,480	404,204	171,669	201,655	338,323
Tea	2,050,052	313,224	343,486	190,515	408,540	121,015	173,732	481,868
Other nonalcoholic beverages and ice	8,151,368	1,134,643	1,347,356	747,954	1,480,935	580,715	824,466	1,937,926
Food prepared by CU on trips	**4,751,283**	**389,765**	**671,402**	**345,201**	**894,416**	**354,257**	**636,864**	**1,459,942**
FOOD AWAY FROM HOME	283,030,388	27,449,570	46,380,974	24,893,023	48,273,321	21,053,233	31,658,304	79,145,786
Meals at restaurants, carry-outs, other	235,839,664	23,876,570	40,793,210	21,940,560	39,829,497	18,018,308	24,982,877	62,222,314
Lunch	84,312,590	8,729,459	14,798,788	8,049,607	14,410,750	6,486,521	8,832,796	21,551,104
At fast-food restaurants*	47,579,106	5,465,059	8,914,866	4,604,764	8,030,767	3,704,737	4,849,157	11,233,819
At full-service restaurants	27,518,135	2,391,339	4,538,340	2,602,485	4,432,506	2,143,049	3,117,844	7,755,440
At vending machines, mobile vendors	700,018	109,433	158,724	70,519	156,839	40,834	33,655	123,977
At employer and school cafeterias	8,516,494	763,646	1,186,989	771,840	1,790,638	597,901	832,048	2,437,868
Dinner	92,512,796	8,386,038	14,168,567	8,207,478	15,534,823	7,409,992	10,198,061	26,856,875
At fast-food restaurants*	29,427,486	3,225,665	5,454,802	2,650,256	5,301,445	2,171,801	2,939,766	7,207,700
At full-service restaurants	62,585,298	5,077,829	8,597,603	5,514,911	10,165,800	5,228,112	7,240,728	19,492,188
At vending machines, mobile vendors	174,423	22,881	62,873	25,592	22,586	5,427	1,202	38,388
At employer and school cafeterias	324,427	69,670	53,289	16,720	44,992	4,652	16,365	118,600
Snacks and nonalcoholic beverages	34,588,081	4,220,234	6,758,339	3,286,631	5,738,353	2,392,702	3,613,337	8,053,881
At fast-food restaurants*	25,251,799	3,002,806	4,738,107	2,314,495	4,230,495	1,763,659	2,691,880	6,124,618
At full-service restaurants	3,357,061	475,227	726,585	314,150	528,157	230,012	303,269	734,004
At vending machines, mobile vendors	4,775,702	589,705	1,103,231	562,672	746,430	303,602	470,991	919,970
At employer and school cafeterias	1,202,356	152,585	190,415	95,314	233,451	95,364	147,289	275,289
Breakfast and brunch	24,426,197	2,540,830	5,067,516	2,396,729	4,145,390	1,729,093	2,338,683	5,760,454
At fast-food restaurants*	12,009,605	1,390,580	2,765,447	1,307,896	2,021,198	793,023	1,203,737	2,320,314
At full-service restaurants	11,670,062	1,024,832	2,158,406	1,032,304	1,972,954	885,222	1,079,101	3,283,302
At vending machines, mobile vendors	165,120	39,191	44,323	7,279	28,910	10,467	18,122	16,879
At employer and school cafeterias	581,410	86,272	99,068	49,136	122,327	40,446	37,816	139,960
Board (including at school)	**3,243,105**	**514,394**	**169,695**	**66,879**	**256,941**	**105,896**	**308,909**	**1,820,073**
Catered affairs	**6,809,474**	**319,821**	**395,691**	**56,188**	**1,298,619**	**354,838**	**1,223,708**	**3,160,221**
Food on trips	**26,925,097**	**1,870,602**	**3,295,782**	**1,870,909**	**4,698,663**	**1,824,393**	**3,760,811**	**9,603,595**
School lunches	**7,371,116**	**248,009**	**1,020,479**	**713,491**	**1,550,320**	**592,086**	**1,180,437**	**2,066,534**
Meals as pay	**2,843,095**	**620,193**	**706,116**	**245,110**	**639,101**	**157,648**	**201,655**	**273,048**

	total consumer units	under $20,000	$20,000– $39,999	$40,000– $49,999	$50,000– $69,999	$70,000– $79,999	$80,000– $99,999	$100,000 or more
ALCOHOLIC BEVERAGES	**$53,404,834**	**$5,554,122**	**$7,959,557**	**$5,109,315**	**$8,738,530**	**$3,989,409**	**$6,486,161**	**$14,740,130**
At home	**32,278,720**	**3,719,987**	**5,139,229**	**3,251,940**	**5,162,675**	**2,382,429**	**3,832,837**	**8,279,131**
Beer and ale	15,268,989	2,118,841	3,187,012	1,501,254	2,877,308	1,169,312	1,557,396	2,686,419
Whiskey	2,518,668	413,420	310,456	335,419	335,722	194,735	196,108	700,993
Wine	10,994,463	803,752	1,077,019	1,172,432	1,387,519	833,792	1,578,939	3,887,056
Other alcoholic beverages	3,496,600	384,008	564,470	242,835	562,127	184,591	500,394	1,004,663
Away from home	**21,126,114**	**1,834,063**	**2,820,470**	**1,857,374**	**3,575,855**	**1,606,915**	**2,653,417**	**6,460,850**
Beer and ale	8,874,642	885,088	1,308,585	893,655	1,453,470	675,304	1,037,216	2,460,423
At fast-food restaurants*	1,911,676	329,643	310,009	171,861	338,613	184,462	155,425	405,091
At full-service restaurants	6,512,955	552,681	991,430	707,918	1,092,271	461,768	824,096	1,754,649
Wine	2,591,926	203,714	391,638	260,692	451,364	199,710	342,010	692,927
At fast-food restaurants*	355,823	54,852	68,512	32,188	52,219	42,061	27,738	73,341
At full-service restaurants	2,181,450	148,862	322,984	228,162	399,325	154,676	308,909	575,672
Other alcoholic beverages	5,198,968	357,416	668,361	434,146	861,169	441,028	704,638	1,624,996
At fast-food restaurnts*	444,197	60,205	80,346	33,098	56,556	86,513	31,806	100,974
At full-service restaurants	4,586,162	311,941	586,005	398,431	803,528	342,045	649,901	1,403,779
Alcoholic beverages purchased on trips	4,461,740	387,980	451,886	268,881	809,853	290,874	569,554	1,682,504

The category fast-food restaurants also includes take-out, delivery, concession stands, buffets, and cafeterias other than employer and school.
Note: Numbers may not add to total because of rounding and missing subcategories. "–" means sample is too small to make a reliable estimate.
Source: Calculations by New Strategist based on the 2004 Consumer Expenditure Survey

Table 5.8 Food and Alcohol: Market shares by income, 2004

(percentage of total annual spending on food and alcoholic beverages accounted for by before-tax income group of consumer units, 2004)

	total consumer units	under $20,000	$20,000– $39,999	$40,000– $49,999	$50,000– $69,999	$70,000– $79,999	$80,000– $99,999	$100,000 or more
Share of total consumer units	100.0%	24.9%	23.5%	9.8%	15.5%	5.6%	8.0%	12.8%
Share of total before-tax income	100.0	5.0	12.7	8.0	16.9	7.6	13.0	36.8
Share of total spending	100.0	10.8	16.4	8.6	17.1	7.0	12.0	27.7
Share of food spending	100.0	13.0	18.3	9.2	17.0	7.1	10.3	23.9
Share of alcoholic beverages spending	100.0	10.4	14.9	9.6	16.4	7.5	12.1	27.6
FOOD AT HOME	100.0	15.5	19.7	9.5	16.9	6.8	9.6	20.9
Cereals and bakery products	100.0	16.3	20.0	9.7	17.1	6.3	9.4	20.2
Cereals and cereal products	100.0	18.1	19.9	9.6	16.8	6.4	9.3	19.0
Flour	100.0	29.7	24.8	8.9	13.6	5.5	4.4	13.6
Prepared flour mixes	100.0	16.3	16.5	12.1	16.7	5.9	10.2	21.3
Ready-to-eat and cooked cereals	100.0	17.3	20.5	9.6	17.0	6.3	9.6	18.8
Rice	100.0	19.9	21.0	8.4	17.3	6.6	6.3	19.7
Pasta, cornmeal, and other cereal products	100.0	17.0	17.6	9.7	16.7	6.8	11.4	20.0
Bakery products	100.0	15.4	20.1	9.7	17.2	6.3	9.5	20.8
Bread	100.0	16.8	21.3	9.6	17.8	6.2	8.9	18.6
White bread	100.0	18.6	22.8	9.3	17.7	6.2	8.4	16.4
Bread, other than white	100.0	15.6	20.3	9.8	17.9	6.1	9.2	20.1
Crackers and cookies	100.0	15.5	19.9	9.3	17.1	6.4	9.3	21.4
Cookies	100.0	16.0	20.2	9.6	17.0	6.3	8.6	21.2
Crackers	100.0	14.3	19.2	8.9	17.2	6.6	10.7	21.7
Frozen and refrigerated bakery products	100.0	12.6	20.4	9.5	16.4	5.8	10.1	23.8
Other bakery products	100.0	15.0	19.2	10.1	17.0	6.4	9.8	21.3
Biscuits and rolls	100.0	13.2	17.4	9.1	18.2	6.9	10.2	23.7
Cakes and cupcakes	100.0	14.9	20.9	10.6	16.1	5.8	8.9	21.5
Bread and cracker products	100.0	15.8	15.8	9.5	19.8	6.4	10.5	21.3
Sweetrolls, coffee cakes, doughnuts	100.0	16.8	20.6	10.5	16.7	5.9	9.9	18.7
Pies, tarts, turnovers	100.0	17.3	18.5	11.0	16.3	6.7	11.0	18.1
Meats, poultry, fish, and eggs	100.0	15.9	20.3	10.0	16.5	6.9	9.3	19.9
Beef	100.0	15.4	20.7	9.8	16.3	7.4	9.7	19.5
Ground beef	100.0	17.3	21.8	10.0	17.1	7.0	9.3	16.6
Roast	100.0	17.0	21.7	9.8	14.6	7.5	8.7	19.6
Chuck roast	100.0	21.9	23.4	7.6	15.2	6.3	10.3	15.0
Round roast	100.0	19.2	23.2	9.2	13.2	5.2	9.9	19.3
Other roast	100.0	13.7	20.2	11.2	14.9	9.0	7.4	22.0
Steak	100.0	12.6	19.2	10.0	16.1	8.0	10.5	22.0
Round steak	100.0	13.4	20.2	9.8	18.7	6.4	11.7	18.4
Sirloin steak	100.0	12.8	18.8	10.0	14.4	9.3	10.0	23.0
Other steak	100.0	12.2	19.2	10.1	16.2	7.7	10.4	22.5
Other beef	100.0	17.1	21.0	6.7	17.1	6.1	10.0	21.0
Pork	100.0	17.1	21.5	10.5	16.6	5.8	9.2	18.3
Bacon	100.0	17.6	23.1	9.6	17.9	5.3	9.0	16.7
Pork chops	100.0	18.5	22.1	11.9	16.0	5.7	7.5	17.4
Ham	100.0	17.3	20.4	9.9	18.3	4.9	9.0	19.3
Ham, not canned	100.0	17.3	20.2	10.0	18.6	4.9	9.1	19.2
Canned ham	100.0	18.7	28.7	6.1	8.4	6.6	4.5	25.3
Sausage	100.0	15.9	21.3	10.9	17.0	7.1	9.3	17.4
Other pork	100.0	16.2	21.1	10.3	14.6	6.1	10.7	19.7
Other meats	100.0	15.3	18.8	10.0	16.8	6.7	10.1	21.1
Frankfurters	100.0	17.9	20.1	9.5	16.1	6.7	10.2	18.7
Lunch meats (cold cuts)	100.0	14.2	19.4	9.3	17.7	7.1	10.7	20.5
Bologna, liverwurst, salami	100.0	17.9	21.4	10.8	16.7	6.0	8.8	17.6
Other lunch meats	100.0	12.6	18.6	8.7	18.1	7.5	11.5	21.8
Lamb, organ meats, and others	100.0	17.7	12.7	15.3	13.0	4.4	6.6	28.7
Poultry	100.0	16.2	19.8	9.4	16.9	6.8	9.4	20.4
Fresh and frozen chicken	100.0	16.3	20.7	9.1	17.1	6.9	9.0	19.9
Fresh and frozen whole chicken	100.0	17.2	23.5	10.0	15.4	7.3	8.1	17.5
Fresh and frozen chicken parts	100.0	15.9	19.5	8.7	17.9	6.8	9.4	20.9
Other poultry	100.0	16.1	16.4	10.3	16.3	6.5	11.0	22.5

	total consumer units	under $20,000	$20,000– $39,999	$40,000– $49,999	$50,000– $69,999	$70,000– $79,999	$80,000– $99,999	$100,000 or more
Fish and seafood	100.0%	14.0%	18.4%	10.8%	16.4%	8.4%	8.4%	22.1%
Canned fish and seafood	100.0	16.9	18.7	10.8	17.6	5.7	8.5	20.9
Fresh fish and shellfish	100.0	13.4	18.8	10.1	15.9	9.1	8.2	23.1
Frozen fish and shellfish	100.0	14.0	17.6	12.1	17.1	8.2	8.8	20.7
Eggs	100.0	19.4	23.5	9.5	16.1	5.2	8.2	17.4
Dairy products	**100.0**	**15.2**	**20.1**	**9.5**	**16.9**	**6.4**	**9.7**	**20.9**
Fresh milk and cream	100.0	17.7	21.6	9.7	16.5	6.1	9.3	18.3
Fresh milk, all types	100.0	18.0	22.0	9.8	16.5	6.0	9.1	17.9
Cream	100.0	14.8	17.9	8.8	17.3	6.7	11.3	22.0
Other dairy products	100.0	13.7	19.3	9.4	17.2	6.6	9.9	22.6
Butter	100.0	15.5	18.6	8.6	22.0	6.8	9.8	18.1
Cheese	100.0	13.2	18.3	9.3	16.4	6.5	10.4	24.4
Ice cream and related products	100.0	13.9	21.0	9.9	17.0	7.0	8.9	21.0
Miscellaneous dairy products	100.0	13.7	19.7	9.8	16.7	6.4	10.0	22.3
Fruits and vegetables	**100.0**	**16.0**	**19.7**	**9.6**	**16.4**	**6.4**	**9.3**	**21.5**
Fresh fruits	100.0	15.3	19.8	10.1	15.3	6.3	9.4	22.5
Apples	100.0	15.0	20.3	9.8	15.9	5.5	10.3	21.9
Bananas	100.0	17.7	22.5	11.0	15.7	6.0	8.5	17.5
Oranges	100.0	17.2	21.1	12.9	14.0	5.7	9.1	18.7
Citrus fruits, excluding oranges	100.0	14.6	18.6	9.2	14.9	7.0	10.0	24.3
Other fresh fruits	100.0	14.3	18.6	9.5	15.4	6.6	9.4	25.0
Fresh vegetables	100.0	16.3	18.9	9.0	17.1	6.5	9.3	21.9
Potatoes	100.0	18.5	20.9	9.5	17.1	6.6	9.6	17.1
Lettuce	100.0	15.4	17.4	9.2	17.3	7.1	9.9	22.7
Tomatoes	100.0	17.8	19.5	9.2	17.7	5.9	8.9	20.2
Other fresh vegetables	100.0	15.3	18.5	8.7	16.9	6.5	9.2	23.7
Processed fruits	100.0	15.7	20.4	9.4	16.6	6.4	9.7	20.5
Frozen fruits and fruit juices	100.0	17.6	18.5	8.8	18.5	5.5	10.3	19.9
Frozen orange juice	100.0	18.8	19.7	11.8	18.7	6.6	10.8	12.9
Frozen fruits	100.0	15.6	14.3	7.8	18.4	4.5	10.2	28.3
Frozen fruit juices, excluding orange	100.0	18.7	22.8	5.1	18.4	5.0	9.6	19.5
Canned fruits	100.0	16.3	19.7	10.1	15.3	5.8	12.9	18.9
Dried fruits	100.0	14.2	19.1	8.3	19.4	6.0	10.3	21.5
Fresh fruit juice	100.0	13.1	20.2	10.3	15.6	5.8	9.7	23.8
Canned and bottled fruit juice	100.0	16.4	21.3	9.1	16.8	7.0	8.7	19.7
Processed vegetables	100.0	17.2	20.1	9.8	16.8	6.5	8.7	19.9
Frozen vegetables	100.0	14.5	19.1	10.0	17.2	6.7	9.5	21.8
Canned and dried vegetables and juices	100.0	18.6	20.7	9.7	16.5	6.4	8.2	18.9
Canned beans	100.0	18.8	21.8	9.1	16.4	6.8	9.0	17.3
Canned corn	100.0	21.3	21.8	13.5	14.8	5.4	6.5	16.1
Canned miscellaneous vegetables	100.0	17.8	18.3	10.3	17.5	6.4	8.7	20.1
Dried peas	100.0	21.8	17.8	8.2	15.8	8.4	7.6	20.1
Dried beans	100.0	26.0	25.4	12.9	14.5	3.9	4.6	12.4
Dried miscellaneous vegetables	100.0	18.0	21.1	8.4	17.9	7.2	7.9	18.9
Dried processed vegetables	100.0	57.9	24.6	10.8	1.0	2.4	–	25.3
Fresh and canned vegetable juices	100.0	15.8	21.5	7.0	16.1	7.2	9.0	22.3
Sugar and other sweets	**100.0**	**15.4**	**18.7**	**9.0**	**16.6**	**6.1**	**10.1**	**23.1**
Candy and chewing gum	100.0	13.3	17.0	8.5	17.1	6.4	10.6	25.8
Sugar	100.0	22.8	24.4	9.7	15.8	6.0	7.1	13.8
Artificial sweeteners	100.0	21.7	18.2	7.0	11.7	7.4	11.8	21.7
Jams, preserves, other sweets	100.0	15.9	20.8	10.7	16.5	4.8	9.9	20.4
Fats and oils	**100.0**	**17.5**	**20.7**	**10.5**	**16.4**	**6.4**	**8.8**	**18.7**
Margarine	100.0	18.9	22.6	11.1	14.4	7.0	8.5	16.6
Fats and oils	100.0	19.1	21.3	12.0	15.2	5.1	7.9	18.5
Salad dressings	100.0	15.6	19.3	10.2	17.3	7.4	9.3	19.8
Nondairy cream and imitation milk	100.0	15.0	20.5	10.5	18.4	6.7	9.9	17.9
Peanut butter	100.0	19.2	21.6	7.6	16.5	6.7	9.0	18.7

	total consumer units	under $20,000	$20,000–$39,999	$40,000–$49,999	$50,000–$69,999	$70,000–$79,999	$80,000–$99,999	$100,000 or more
Miscellaneous foods	100.0%	13.9%	18.6%	8.8%	17.4%	7.6%	10.4%	22.0%
Frozen prepared foods	100.0	14.9	19.9	9.3	17.2	7.7	9.8	20.1
Frozen meals	100.0	18.7	23.8	7.9	13.6	7.1	10.1	17.9
Other frozen prepared foods	100.0	13.4	18.3	9.8	18.7	7.9	9.7	21.0
Canned and packaged soups	100.0	16.6	20.3	9.1	16.0	6.8	10.1	19.9
Potato chips, nuts, and other snacks	100.0	13.0	17.5	8.7	17.1	7.9	11.0	23.3
Potato chips and other snacks	100.0	12.9	18.5	8.6	17.6	7.5	10.8	22.8
Nuts	100.0	13.4	14.9	9.1	15.9	8.9	11.5	25.0
Condiments and seasonings	100.0	13.6	18.0	8.9	19.0	7.3	10.1	21.9
Salt, spices, and other seasonings	100.0	14.1	18.1	9.9	17.6	7.6	8.9	22.6
Olives, pickles, relishes	100.0	14.1	17.8	8.8	19.9	7.3	10.3	20.6
Sauces and gravies	100.0	12.9	18.2	8.2	20.0	7.4	10.9	21.4
Baking needs and miscellaneous products	100.0	14.4	17.8	9.3	18.0	7.0	9.7	22.6
Other canned/packaged prepared foods	100.0	13.6	18.5	8.5	17.0	7.5	10.8	22.8
Prepared salads	100.0	12.9	16.2	8.6	18.0	6.6	11.0	25.5
Prepared desserts	100.0	14.8	17.7	10.9	15.3	5.8	10.0	24.1
Baby food	100.0	11.3	23.3	7.4	14.5	8.1	11.8	21.8
Miscellaneous prepared foods	100.0	14.4	17.9	8.6	17.7	7.8	10.6	21.9
Nonalcoholic beverages	100.0	15.5	20.2	9.4	17.9	7.2	9.1	19.7
Cola	100.0	17.0	22.1	9.9	17.7	6.3	9.4	16.8
Other carbonated drinks	100.0	15.1	22.3	9.4	17.7	8.2	8.3	17.9
Coffee	100.0	15.3	19.6	8.4	17.6	8.4	8.5	21.2
Roasted coffee	100.0	14.8	19.4	8.1	18.5	8.0	8.8	21.5
Instant and freeze-dried coffee	100.0	16.3	19.8	8.8	16.1	9.1	8.0	20.9
Noncarbonated fruit-flavored drinks	100.0	16.8	24.0	9.9	17.6	7.5	8.8	14.7
Tea	100.0	15.3	16.8	9.3	19.9	5.9	8.5	23.5
Other nonalcoholic beverages and ice	100.0	13.9	16.5	9.2	18.2	7.1	10.1	23.8
Food prepared by CU on trips	100.0	8.2	14.1	7.3	18.8	7.5	13.4	30.7
FOOD AWAY FROM HOME	100.0	9.7	16.4	8.8	17.1	7.4	11.2	28.0
Meals at restaurants, carry-outs, other	100.0	10.1	17.3	9.3	16.9	7.6	10.6	26.4
Lunch	100.0	10.4	17.6	9.5	17.1	7.7	10.5	25.6
At fast-food restaurants*	100.0	11.5	18.7	9.7	16.9	7.8	10.2	23.6
At full-service restaurants	100.0	8.7	16.5	9.5	16.1	7.8	11.3	28.2
At vending machines, mobile vendors	100.0	15.6	22.7	10.1	22.4	5.8	4.8	17.7
At employer and school cafeterias	100.0	9.0	13.9	9.1	21.0	7.0	9.8	28.6
Dinner	100.0	9.1	15.3	8.9	16.8	8.0	11.0	29.0
At fast-food restaurants*	100.0	11.0	18.5	9.0	18.0	7.4	10.0	24.5
At full-service restaurants	100.0	8.1	13.7	8.8	16.2	8.4	11.6	31.1
At vending machines, mobile vendors	100.0	13.1	36.0	14.7	12.9	3.1	0.7	22.0
At employer and school cafeterias	100.0	21.5	16.4	5.2	13.9	1.4	5.0	36.6
Snacks and nonalcoholic beverages	100.0	12.2	19.5	9.5	16.6	6.9	10.4	23.3
At fast-food restaurants*	100.0	11.9	18.8	9.2	16.8	7.0	10.7	24.3
At full-service restaurants	100.0	14.2	21.6	9.4	15.7	6.9	9.0	21.9
At vending machines, mobile vendors	100.0	12.3	23.1	11.8	15.6	6.4	9.9	19.3
At employer and school cafeterias	100.0	12.7	15.8	7.9	19.4	7.9	12.3	22.9
Breakfast and brunch	100.0	10.4	20.7	9.8	17.0	7.1	9.6	23.6
At fast-food restaurants*	100.0	11.6	23.0	10.9	16.8	6.6	10.0	19.3
At full-service restaurants	100.0	8.8	18.5	8.8	16.9	7.6	9.2	28.1
At vending machines, mobile vendors	100.0	23.7	26.8	4.4	17.5	6.3	11.0	10.2
At employer and school cafeterias	100.0	14.8	17.0	8.5	21.0	7.0	6.5	24.1
Board (including at school)	100.0	15.9	5.2	2.1	7.9	3.3	9.5	56.1
Catered affairs	100.0	4.7	5.8	0.8	19.1	5.2	18.0	46.4
Food on trips	100.0	6.9	12.2	6.9	17.5	6.8	14.0	35.7
School lunches	100.0	3.4	13.8	9.7	21.0	8.0	16.0	28.0
Meals as pay	100.0	21.8	24.8	8.6	22.5	5.5	7.1	9.6

	total consumer units	under $20,000	$20,000– $39,999	$40,000– $49,999	$50,000– $69,999	$70,000– $79,999	$80,000– $99,999	$100,000 or more
ALCOHOLIC BEVERAGES	**100.0%**	**10.4%**	**14.9%**	**9.6%**	**16.4%**	**7.5%**	**12.1%**	**27.6%**
At home	**100.0**	**11.5**	**15.9**	**10.1**	**16.0**	**7.4**	**11.9**	**25.6**
Beer and ale	100.0	13.9	20.9	9.8	18.8	7.7	10.2	17.6
Whiskey	100.0	16.4	12.3	13.3	13.3	7.7	7.8	27.8
Wine	100.0	7.3	9.8	10.7	12.6	7.6	14.4	35.4
Other alcoholic beverages	100.0	11.0	16.1	6.9	16.1	5.3	14.3	28.7
Away from home	**100.0**	**8.7**	**13.4**	**8.8**	**16.9**	**7.6**	**12.6**	**30.6**
Beer and ale	100.0	10.0	14.7	10.1	16.4	7.6	11.7	27.7
At fast-food restaurants*	100.0	17.2	16.2	9.0	17.7	9.6	8.1	21.2
At full-service restaurants	100.0	8.5	15.2	10.9	16.8	7.1	12.7	26.9
Wine	100.0	7.9	15.1	10.1	17.4	7.7	13.2	26.7
At fast-food restaurants*	100.0	15.4	19.3	9.0	14.7	11.8	7.8	20.6
At full-service restaurants	100.0	6.8	14.8	10.5	18.3	7.1	14.2	26.4
Other alcoholic beverages	100.0	6.9	12.9	8.4	16.6	8.5	13.6	31.3
At fast-food restaurants*	100.0	13.6	18.1	7.5	12.7	19.5	7.2	22.7
At full-service restaurants	100.0	6.8	12.8	8.7	17.5	7.5	14.2	30.6
Alcoholic beverages purchased on trips	100.0	8.7	10.1	6.0	18.2	6.5	12.8	37.7

The category fast-food restaurants also includes take-out, delivery, concession stands, buffets, and cafeterias other than employer and school.

Note: Numbers may not add to total because of rounding. "–" means sample is too small to make a reliable estimate.

Source: Calculations by New Strategist based on the 2004 Consumer Expenditure Survey

Table 5.9 Food and Alcohol: Average spending by high-income consumer units, 2004

(average annual spending on food and alcoholic beverages, by before-tax income of high-income consumer units (CU), 2004)

	total consumer units	$100,000 or more	$100,000–$119,999	$120,000–$149,999	$150,000 or more
Number of consumer units (in 000s)	116,282	14,937	5,625	4,245	5,067
Average number of persons per CU	2.5	3.2	3.1	3.3	3.2
Average before-tax income of CU	$54,453.00	$155,901.00	$108,751.00	$132,292.00	$228,021.00
Average spending of CU, total	43,394.87	93,525.67	75,213.14	87,298.57	119,448.79
Food, average spending	**5,780.82**	**10,733.39**	**9,443.59**	**10,419.38**	**12,554.55**
Alcoholic beverages, average spending	**459.27**	**986.82**	**723.80**	**887.24**	**1,405.43**
FOOD AT HOME	**3,346.82**	**5,434.75**	**5,014.31**	**5,542.15**	**5,839.53**
Cereals and bakery products	**460.90**	**724.36**	**671.87**	**740.95**	**772.13**
Cereals and cereal products	153.80	228.01	216.58	232.20	237.84
Flour	8.32	8.78	11.12	6.74	7.98
Prepared flour mixes	13.78	22.82	19.08	28.82	21.37
Ready-to-eat and cooked cereals	86.69	126.79	118.19	122.48	141.72
Rice	18.46	28.32	30.98	29.28	24.10
Pasta, cornmeal, and other cereal products	26.55	41.29	37.21	44.88	42.67
Bakery products	307.10	496.35	455.29	508.75	534.29
Bread	87.63	126.93	114.37	130.97	138.29
White bread	35.04	44.67	40.84	49.41	44.57
Bread, other than white	52.59	82.27	73.53	81.56	93.72
Crackers and cookies	71.16	118.46	114.82	120.89	120.47
Cookies	46.57	76.82	75.42	76.76	78.61
Crackers	24.60	41.64	39.40	44.13	41.86
Frozen and refrigerated bakery products	26.32	48.67	40.15	55.17	52.58
Other bakery products	121.99	202.29	185.94	201.71	222.96
Biscuits and rolls	42.11	77.61	69.08	68.26	97.54
Cakes and cupcakes	39.04	65.29	57.30	71.88	68.45
Bread and cracker products	3.25	5.39	5.02	4.49	6.75
Sweetrolls, coffee cakes, doughnuts	23.59	34.32	33.16	37.07	32.97
Pies, tarts, turnovers	13.99	19.68	21.39	20.01	17.24
Meats, poultry, fish, and eggs	**879.71**	**1,362.83**	**1,270.90**	**1,396.46**	**1,441.87**
Beef	265.34	403.49	383.95	411.51	419.40
Ground beef	96.92	125.05	126.92	131.49	116.25
Roast	45.58	69.55	57.58	66.07	87.77
Chuck roast	11.72	13.65	13.45	11.33	16.25
Round roast	10.27	15.42	9.12	16.30	22.28
Other roast	23.58	40.47	35.02	38.44	49.24
Steak	103.45	177.15	161.82	184.84	188.22
Round steak	16.37	23.48	21.83	29.31	19.61
Sirloin steak	32.38	58.00	52.26	53.01	70.09
Other steak	54.71	95.67	87.72	102.51	98.52
Other beef	19.39	31.74	37.62	29.11	27.17
Pork	181.14	257.83	263.82	266.83	241.37
Bacon	31.08	40.39	42.10	40.13	38.56
Pork chops	37.92	51.46	52.68	55.32	46.07
Ham	39.65	59.69	53.57	64.21	62.65
Ham, not canned	38.67	57.76	52.13	62.14	60.27
Canned ham	0.98	1.93	1.44	2.07	2.38
Sausage	27.91	37.77	41.09	37.62	33.84
Other pork	44.59	68.51	74.38	69.56	60.25
Other meats	107.98	177.38	159.20	165.36	211.89
Frankfurters	22.52	32.78	35.24	29.56	33.00
Lunch meats (cold cuts)	72.99	116.76	108.05	114.00	130.26
Bologna, liverwurst, salami	21.07	28.83	27.01	26.85	33.08
Other lunch meats	51.91	87.93	81.05	87.15	97.18
Lamb, organ meats, and others	12.48	27.84	15.90	21.79	48.64
Poultry	155.61	247.22	233.16	254.07	257.56
Fresh and frozen chicken	122.64	189.56	178.02	201.08	192.10
Fresh and frozen whole chicken	36.59	49.80	52.17	50.52	46.16
Fresh and frozen chicken parts	86.04	139.76	125.85	150.57	145.94
Other poultry	32.97	57.66	55.14	52.99	65.46

	total consumer units	$100,000 or more	$100,000– $119,999	$120,000– $149,999	$150,000 or more
Fish and seafood	$127.80	$220.16	$176.71	$241.43	$252.09
Canned fish and seafood	15.38	24.98	22.09	26.31	27.19
Fresh fish and shellfish	74.88	134.59	102.94	156.92	150.94
Frozen fish and shellfish	37.54	60.59	51.68	58.20	73.96
Eggs	41.84	56.76	54.07	57.26	59.55
Dairy products	**370.57**	**603.81**	**559.71**	**620.32**	**641.33**
Fresh milk and cream	144.33	205.79	199.83	209.05	209.83
Fresh milk, all types	128.94	179.41	175.51	178.65	184.95
Cream	15.39	26.39	24.32	30.39	24.88
Other dairy products	226.24	398.02	359.88	411.28	431.50
Butter	21.81	30.75	23.30	38.46	32.10
Cheese	113.67	216.02	192.37	219.23	241.86
Ice cream and related products	60.22	98.30	93.61	98.91	103.45
Miscellaneous dairy products	30.54	52.95	50.60	54.68	54.09
Fruits and vegetables	**560.95**	**940.95**	**860.49**	**931.65**	**1,049.28**
Fresh fruits	186.74	327.37	285.25	328.85	377.66
Apples	32.42	55.38	47.29	56.23	64.45
Bananas	30.17	41.13	38.32	40.60	45.14
Oranges	19.48	28.30	26.37	28.56	30.41
Citrus fruits, excluding oranges	15.41	29.18	25.17	33.45	29.81
Other fresh fruits	89.25	173.38	148.10	170.01	207.86
Fresh vegetables	182.94	311.86	288.27	310.68	342.05
Potatoes	28.07	37.41	37.83	37.74	36.54
Lettuce	22.87	40.35	37.86	41.44	42.32
Tomatoes	35.74	56.33	45.77	54.72	70.93
Other fresh vegetables	96.25	177.77	166.81	176.77	192.26
Processed fruits	109.63	175.33	159.43	171.65	198.58
Frozen fruits and fruit juices	9.97	15.43	14.88	16.99	14.52
Frozen orange juice	4.17	4.20	4.01	4.36	4.27
Frozen fruits	3.53	7.77	7.18	9.09	7.17
Frozen fruit juices, excluding orange	2.27	3.45	3.69	3.54	3.08
Canned fruits	16.19	23.82	20.69	25.72	25.75
Dried fruits	6.35	10.64	9.96	8.83	13.31
Fresh fruit juice	22.07	40.82	40.57	33.92	48.09
Canned and bottled fruit juice	55.05	84.62	73.33	86.18	96.91
Processed vegetables	81.64	126.39	127.54	120.47	130.98
Frozen vegetables	28.50	48.27	50.32	46.96	47.09
Canned and dried vegetables and juices	53.14	78.12	77.22	73.50	83.89
Canned beans	11.39	15.35	16.07	13.33	16.51
Canned corn	6.33	7.94	7.09	7.33	9.60
Canned miscellaneous vegetables	16.77	26.22	24.91	25.37	28.70
Dried peas	0.60	0.94	0.71	1.18	0.98
Dried beans	2.47	2.39	2.51	1.80	2.85
Dried miscellaneous vegetables	6.21	9.15	7.85	9.79	10.10
Dried processed vegetables	0.30	0.59	1.30	0.33	–
Fresh and canned vegetable juices	8.91	15.46	16.67	14.38	15.06
Sugar and other sweets	**128.12**	**230.63**	**183.74**	**272.81**	**245.65**
Candy and chewing gum	83.13	166.75	125.25	200.41	183.76
Sugar	16.10	17.33	17.63	20.54	13.71
Artificial sweeteners	6.85	11.56	12.33	9.58	12.60
Jams, preserves, other sweets	22.04	34.99	28.53	42.28	35.58
Fats and oils	**88.89**	**129.12**	**130.92**	**127.98**	**128.05**
Margarine	9.57	12.36	12.06	12.00	13.09
Fats and oils	28.56	41.14	44.37	41.02	37.29
Salad dressings	27.44	42.32	44.10	38.30	44.19
Nondairy cream and imitation milk	10.80	15.08	14.64	16.57	14.11
Peanut butter	12.52	18.22	15.76	20.09	19.36

	total consumer units	$100,000 or more	$100,000–$119,999	$120,000–$149,999	$150,000 or more
Miscellaneous foods	**$527.29**	**$902.30**	**$860.22**	**$896.24**	**$960.16**
Frozen prepared foods	109.90	171.66	174.48	168.58	171.30
Frozen meals	31.79	44.24	44.51	44.55	43.59
Other frozen prepared foods	78.11	127.42	129.97	124.03	127.71
Canned and packaged soups	36.50	56.58	53.86	55.40	61.12
Potato chips, nuts, and other snacks	117.08	212.70	186.81	212.02	245.24
Potato chips and other snacks	86.06	152.46	142.61	146.80	170.28
Nuts	31.01	60.24	44.19	65.22	74.95
Condiments and seasonings	93.65	159.39	143.32	176.78	161.57
Salt, spices, and other seasonings	22.22	39.07	38.06	46.45	32.85
Olives, pickles, relishes	10.52	16.90	13.74	22.42	15.22
Sauces and gravies	40.94	68.23	60.90	72.03	73.40
Baking needs and miscellaneous products	19.97	35.19	30.62	35.88	40.09
Other canned/packaged prepared foods	170.16	301.97	301.76	283.47	320.93
Prepared salads	25.43	50.41	48.78	42.09	60.82
Prepared desserts	10.91	20.46	21.06	23.63	16.53
Baby food	30.08	50.98	60.45	47.90	42.44
Miscellaneous prepared foods	102.74	175.28	167.58	169.84	190.24
Nonalcoholic beverages	**289.52**	**443.01**	**404.69**	**460.68**	**472.25**
Cola	93.81	123.03	118.70	133.67	117.62
Other carbonated drinks	48.08	67.03	62.01	68.90	71.31
Coffee	39.12	64.70	59.12	60.13	76.18
Roasted coffee	24.48	40.88	36.98	40.08	46.47
Instant and freeze-dried coffee	14.64	23.82	22.14	20.05	29.71
Noncarbonated fruit-flavored drinks	19.79	22.65	21.48	28.62	18.06
Tea	17.63	32.26	26.77	31.93	39.34
Other nonalcoholic beverages and ice	70.10	129.74	114.53	136.42	141.69
Food prepared by CU on trips	**40.86**	**97.74**	**71.77**	**95.06**	**128.82**
FOOD AWAY FROM HOME	**2,434.00**	**5,298.64**	**4,429.28**	**4,877.23**	**6,715.01**
Meals at restaurants, carry-outs, other	**2,028.17**	**4,165.65**	**3,688.50**	**3,926.25**	**4,994.16**
Lunch	725.07	1,442.80	1,286.58	1,377.18	1,701.17
At fast-food restaurants*	409.17	752.08	680.70	723.89	868.33
At full-service restaurants	236.65	519.21	409.68	520.95	652.09
At vending machines, mobile vendors	6.02	8.30	13.57	7.19	2.97
At employer and school cafeterias	73.24	163.21	182.64	125.16	177.78
Dinner	795.59	1,798.01	1,514.19	1,620.59	2,326.21
At fast-food restaurants*	253.07	482.54	436.47	434.28	587.96
At full-service restaurants	538.22	1,304.96	1,059.12	1,182.26	1,731.20
At vending machines, mobile vendors	1.50	2.57	1.69	0.63	5.60
At employer and school cafeterias	2.79	7.94	16.92	3.42	1.46
Snacks and nonalcoholic beverages	297.45	539.19	551.61	537.22	525.91
At fast-food restaurants*	217.16	410.03	408.29	408.16	414.06
At full-service restaurants	28.87	49.14	56.11	41.49	48.28
At vending machines, mobile vendors	41.07	61.59	65.17	70.68	48.01
At employer and school cafeterias	10.34	18.43	22.03	16.89	15.55
Breakfast and brunch	210.06	385.65	336.10	391.26	440.88
At fast-food restaurants*	103.28	155.34	156.61	140.18	169.08
At full-service restaurants	100.36	219.81	169.51	239.84	261.39
At vending machines, mobile vendors	1.42	1.13	2.05	0.65	0.49
At employer and school cafeterias	5.00	9.37	7.93	10.59	9.92
Board (including at school)	**27.89**	**121.85**	**45.67**	**91.46**	**231.87**
Catered affairs	**58.56**	**211.57**	**112.35**	**97.40**	**417.37**
Food on trips	**231.55**	**642.94**	**427.43**	**603.84**	**914.91**
School lunches	**63.39**	**138.35**	**138.75**	**142.43**	**134.48**
Meals as pay	**24.45**	**18.28**	**16.58**	**15.85**	**22.22**

	total consumer units	$100,000 or more	$100,000–$119,999	$120,000–$149,999	$150,000 or more
ALCOHOLIC BEVERAGES	**$459.27**	**$986.82**	**$723.80**	**$887.24**	**$1,405.43**
At home	**277.59**	**554.27**	**411.20**	**488.41**	**796.72**
Beer and ale	131.31	179.85	169.04	210.25	162.41
Whiskey	21.66	46.93	38.86	56.15	47.53
Wine	94.55	260.23	164.16	156.29	483.38
Other alcoholic beverages	30.07	67.26	39.14	65.73	103.39
Away from home	**181.68**	**432.54**	**312.60**	**398.82**	**608.72**
Beer and ale	76.32	164.72	131.91	135.68	234.40
At fast-food restaurants*	16.44	27.12	29.98	22.58	28.20
At full-service restaurants	56.01	117.47	100.48	107.40	148.52
Wine	22.29	46.39	31.80	38.65	72.16
At fast-food restaurants*	3.06	4.91	2.25	5.40	7.68
At full-service restaurants	18.76	38.54	29.55	33.06	55.14
Other alcoholic beverages	44.71	108.79	86.39	108.23	136.90
At fast-food restaurants*	3.82	6.76	6.23	7.13	7.03
At full-service restaurants	39.44	93.98	79.74	100.09	105.31
Alcoholic beverages purchased on trips	38.37	112.64	62.50	116.27	165.26

The category fast-food restaurants also includes take-out, delivery, concession stands, buffets, and cafeterias other than employer and school.
Note: Subcategories may not add to total because some are not shown. "–" means sample is too small to make a reliable estimate.
Source: Bureau of Labor Statistics, unpublished tables from the 2004 Consumer Expenditure Survey; calculations by New Strategist

Table 5.10 Food and Alcohol: Indexed spending by high-income consumer units, 2004

(indexed average annual spending of high-income consumer units (CU) on food and beverages, by before-tax income of consumer unit, 2004; index definition: an index of 100 is the average for all consumer units; an index of 132 means that spending by consumer units in that group is 32 percent above the average for all consumer units; an index of 68 indicates spending that is 32 percent below the average for all consumer units)

	total consumer units	$100,000 or more	$100,000–$119,999	$120,000–$149,999	$150,000 or more
Average spending of CU, total	$43,395	$93,526	$75,213	$87,299	$119,449
Average spending of CU, index	100	216	173	201	275
Food, spending index	100	186	163	180	217
Alcoholic beverages, spending index	100	215	158	193	306
FOOD AT HOME	100	162	150	166	174
Cereals and bakery products	100	157	146	161	168
Cereals and cereal products	100	148	141	151	155
Flour	100	106	134	81	96
Prepared flour mixes	100	166	138	209	155
Ready-to-eat and cooked cereals	100	146	136	141	163
Rice	100	153	168	159	131
Pasta, cornmeal, and other cereal products	100	156	140	169	161
Bakery products	100	162	148	166	174
Bread	100	145	131	149	158
White bread	100	127	117	141	127
Bread, other than white	100	156	140	155	178
Crackers and cookies	100	166	161	170	169
Cookies	100	165	162	165	169
Crackers	100	169	160	179	170
Frozen and refrigerated bakery products	100	185	153	210	200
Other bakery products	100	166	152	165	183
Biscuits and rolls	100	184	164	162	232
Cakes and cupcakes	100	167	147	184	175
Bread and cracker products	100	166	154	138	208
Sweetrolls, coffee cakes, doughnuts	100	145	141	157	140
Pies, tarts, turnovers	100	141	153	143	123
Meats, poultry, fish, and eggs	100	155	144	159	164
Beef	100	152	145	155	158
Ground beef	100	129	131	136	120
Roast	100	153	126	145	193
Chuck roast	100	116	115	97	139
Round roast	100	150	89	159	217
Other roast	100	172	149	163	209
Steak	100	171	156	179	182
Round steak	100	143	133	179	120
Sirloin steak	100	179	161	164	216
Other steak	100	175	160	187	180
Other beef	100	164	194	150	140
Pork	100	142	146	147	133
Bacon	100	130	135	129	124
Pork chops	100	136	139	146	121
Ham	100	151	135	162	158
Ham, not canned	100	149	135	161	156
Canned ham	100	197	147	211	243
Sausage	100	135	147	135	121
Other pork	100	154	167	156	135
Other meats	100	164	147	153	196
Frankfurters	100	146	156	131	147
Lunch meats (cold cuts)	100	160	148	156	178
Bologna, liverwurst, salami	100	137	128	127	157
Other lunch meats	100	169	156	168	187
Lamb, organ meats, and others	100	223	127	175	390
Poultry	100	159	150	163	166
Fresh and frozen chicken	100	155	145	164	157
Fresh and frozen whole chicken	100	136	143	138	126
Fresh and frozen chicken parts	100	162	146	175	170
Other poultry	100	175	167	161	199

	total consumer units	$100,000 or more	$100,000– $119,999	$120,000– $149,999	$150,000 or more
Fish and seafood	100	172	138	189	197
Canned fish and seafood	100	162	144	171	177
Fresh fish and shellfish	100	180	137	210	202
Frozen fish and shellfish	100	161	138	155	197
Eggs	100	136	129	137	142
Dairy products	**100**	**163**	**151**	**167**	**173**
Fresh milk and cream	100	143	138	145	145
Fresh milk, all types	100	139	136	139	143
Cream	100	171	158	197	162
Other dairy products	100	176	159	182	191
Butter	100	141	107	176	147
Cheese	100	190	169	193	213
Ice cream and related products	100	163	155	164	172
Miscellaneous dairy products	100	173	166	179	177
Fruits and vegetables	**100**	**168**	**153**	**166**	**187**
Fresh fruits	100	175	153	176	202
Apples	100	171	146	173	199
Bananas	100	136	127	135	150
Oranges	100	145	135	147	156
Citrus fruits, excluding oranges	100	189	163	217	193
Other fresh fruits	100	194	166	190	233
Fresh vegetables	100	170	158	170	187
Potatoes	100	133	135	134	130
Lettuce	100	176	166	181	185
Tomatoes	100	158	128	153	198
Other fresh vegetables	100	185	173	184	200
Processed fruits	100	160	145	157	181
Frozen fruits and fruit juices	100	155	149	170	146
Frozen orange juice	100	101	96	105	102
Frozen fruits	100	220	203	258	203
Frozen fruit juices, excluding orange	100	152	163	156	136
Canned fruits	100	147	128	159	159
Dried fruits	100	168	157	139	210
Fresh fruit juice	100	185	184	154	218
Canned and bottled fruit juice	100	154	133	157	176
Processed vegetables	100	155	156	148	160
Frozen vegetables	100	169	177	165	165
Canned and dried vegetables and juices	100	147	145	138	158
Canned beans	100	135	141	117	145
Canned corn	100	125	112	116	152
Canned miscellaneous vegetables	100	156	149	151	171
Dried peas	100	157	118	197	163
Dried beans	100	97	102	73	115
Dried miscellaneous vegetables	100	147	126	158	163
Dried processed vegetables	100	197	433	110	–
Fresh and canned vegetable juices	100	174	187	161	169
Sugar and other sweets	**100**	**180**	**143**	**213**	**192**
Candy and chewing gum	100	201	151	241	221
Sugar	100	108	110	128	85
Artificial sweeteners	100	169	180	140	184
Jams, preserves, other sweets	100	159	129	192	161
Fats and oils	**100**	**145**	**147**	**144**	**144**
Margarine	100	129	126	125	137
Fats and oils	100	144	155	144	131
Salad dressings	100	154	161	140	161
Nondairy cream and imitation milk	100	140	136	153	131
Peanut butter	100	146	126	160	155

	total consumer units	$100,000 or more	$100,000– $119,999	$120,000– $149,999	$150,000 or more
Miscellaneous foods	100	171	163	170	182
Frozen prepared foods	100	156	159	153	156
Frozen meals	100	139	140	140	137
Other frozen prepared foods	100	163	166	159	164
Canned and packaged soups	100	155	148	152	167
Potato chips, nuts, and other snacks	100	182	160	181	209
Potato chips and other snacks	100	177	166	171	198
Nuts	100	194	143	210	242
Condiments and seasonings	100	170	153	189	173
Salt, spices, and other seasonings	100	176	171	209	148
Olives, pickles, relishes	100	161	131	213	145
Sauces and gravies	100	167	149	176	179
Baking needs and miscellaneous products	100	176	153	180	201
Other canned/packaged prepared foods	100	177	177	167	189
Prepared salads	100	198	192	166	239
Prepared desserts	100	188	193	217	152
Baby food	100	169	201	159	141
Miscellaneous prepared foods	100	171	163	165	185
Nonalcoholic beverages	100	153	140	159	163
Cola	100	131	127	142	125
Other carbonated drinks	100	139	129	143	148
Coffee	100	165	151	154	195
Roasted coffee	100	167	151	164	190
Instant and freeze-dried coffee	100	163	151	137	203
Noncarbonated fruit-flavored drinks	100	114	109	145	91
Tea	100	183	152	181	223
Other nonalcoholic beverages and ice	100	185	163	195	202
Food prepared by CU on trips	100	239	176	233	315
FOOD AWAY FROM HOME	100	218	182	200	276
Meals at restaurants, carry-outs, other	100	205	182	194	246
Lunch	100	199	177	190	235
At fast-food restaurants*	100	184	166	177	212
At full-service restaurants	100	219	173	220	276
At vending machines, mobile vendors	100	138	225	119	49
At employer and school cafeterias	100	223	249	171	243
Dinner	100	226	190	204	292
At fast-food restaurants*	100	191	172	172	232
At full-service restaurants	100	242	197	220	322
At vending machines, mobile vendors	100	171	113	42	373
At employer and school cafeterias	100	285	606	123	52
Snacks and nonalcoholic beverages	100	181	185	181	177
At fast-food restaurants*	100	189	188	188	191
At full-service restaurants	100	170	194	144	167
At vending machines, mobile vendors	100	150	159	172	117
At employer and school cafeterias	100	178	213	163	150
Breakfast and brunch	100	184	160	186	210
At fast-food restaurants*	100	150	152	136	164
At full-service restaurants	100	219	169	239	260
At vending machines, mobile vendors	100	80	144	46	35
At employer and school cafeterias	100	187	159	212	198
Board (including at school)	100	437	164	328	831
Catered affairs	100	361	192	166	713
Food on trips	100	278	185	261	395
School lunches	100	218	219	225	212
Meals as pay	100	75	68	65	91

	total consumer units	$100,000 or more	$100,000– $119,999	$120,000– $149,999	$150,000 or more
ALCOHOLIC BEVERAGES	**100**	**215**	**158**	**193**	**306**
At home	**100**	**200**	**148**	**176**	**287**
Beer and ale	100	137	129	160	124
Whiskey	100	217	179	259	219
Wine	100	275	174	165	511
Other alcoholic beverages	100	224	130	219	344
Away from home	**100**	**238**	**172**	**220**	**335**
Beer and ale	100	216	173	178	307
At fast-food restaurants*	100	165	182	137	172
At full-service restaurants	100	210	179	192	265
Wine	100	208	143	173	324
At fast-food restaurants*	100	160	74	176	251
At full-service restaurants	100	205	158	176	294
Other alcoholic beverages	100	243	193	242	306
At fast-food restaurants*	100	177	163	187	184
At full-service restaurants	100	238	202	254	267
Alcoholic beverages purchased on trips	100	294	163	303	431

* The category fast-food restaurants also includes take-out, delivery, concession stands, buffets, and cafeterias other than employer and school.
Note: "–" means sample is too small to make a reliable estimate.
Source: Calculations by New Strategist based on the 2004 Consumer Expenditure Survey

Table 5.11 Food and Alcohol: Total spending by high-income consumer units, 2004

(total annual spending on food and alcoholic beverages, by before-tax income group of high-income consumer units (CU), 2004; consumer units and dollars in thousands)

	total consumer units	$100,000 or more	$100,000–$119,999	$120,000–$149,999	$150,000 or more
Number of consumer units	116,282	14,937	5,625	4,245	5,067
Total spending of all CUs	$5,046,042,273	$1,396,992,933	$423,073,913	$370,582,430	$605,247,019
Food, total spending	672,205,311	160,324,646	53,120,194	44,230,268	63,613,905
Alcoholic beverages, total spending	53,404,834	14,740,130	4,071,375	3,766,334	7,121,314
FOOD AT HOME	389,174,923	81,178,861	28,205,494	23,526,427	29,588,899
Cereals and bakery products	53,594,374	10,819,765	3,779,269	3,145,333	3,912,383
Cereals and cereal products	17,884,172	3,405,785	1,218,263	985,689	1,205,135
Flour	967,466	131,147	62,550	28,611	40,435
Prepared flour mixes	1,602,366	340,862	107,325	122,341	108,282
Ready-to-eat and cooked cereals	10,080,487	1,893,862	664,819	519,928	718,095
Rice	2,146,566	423,016	174,263	124,294	122,115
Pasta, cornmeal, and other cereal products	3,087,287	616,749	209,306	190,516	216,209
Bakery products	35,710,202	7,413,980	2,561,006	2,159,644	2,707,247
Bread	10,189,792	1,895,953	643,331	555,968	700,715
White bread	4,074,521	667,236	229,725	209,745	225,836
Bread, other than white	6,115,270	1,228,867	413,606	346,222	474,879
Crackers and cookies	8,274,627	1,769,437	645,863	513,178	610,421
Cookies	5,415,253	1,147,460	424,238	325,846	398,317
Crackers	2,860,537	621,977	221,625	187,332	212,105
Frozen and refrigerated bakery products	3,060,542	726,984	225,844	234,197	266,423
Other bakery products	14,185,241	3,021,606	1,045,913	856,259	1,129,738
Biscuits and rolls	4,896,635	1,159,261	388,575	289,764	494,235
Cakes and cupcakes	4,539,649	975,237	322,313	305,131	346,836
Bread and cracker products	377,917	80,510	28,238	19,060	34,202
Sweetrolls, coffee cakes, doughnuts	2,743,092	512,638	186,525	157,362	167,059
Pies, tarts, turnovers	1,626,785	293,960	120,319	84,942	87,355
Meats, poultry, fish, and eggs	102,294,438	20,356,592	7,148,813	5,927,973	7,305,955
Beef	30,854,266	6,026,930	2,159,719	1,746,860	2,125,100
Ground beef	11,270,051	1,867,872	713,925	558,175	589,039
Roast	5,300,134	1,038,868	323,888	280,467	444,731
Chuck roast	1,362,825	203,890	75,656	48,096	82,339
Round roast	1,194,216	230,329	51,300	69,194	112,893
Other roast	2,741,930	604,500	196,988	163,178	249,499
Steak	12,029,373	2,646,090	910,238	784,646	953,711
Round steak	1,903,536	350,721	122,794	124,421	99,364
Sirloin steak	3,765,211	866,346	293,963	225,027	355,146
Other steak	6,361,788	1,429,023	493,425	435,155	499,201
Other beef	2,254,708	474,100	211,613	123,572	137,670
Pork	21,063,321	3,851,207	1,483,988	1,132,693	1,223,022
Bacon	3,614,045	603,305	236,813	170,352	195,384
Pork chops	4,409,413	768,658	296,325	234,833	233,437
Ham	4,610,581	891,590	301,331	272,571	317,448
Ham, not canned	4,496,625	862,761	293,231	263,784	305,388
Canned ham	113,956	28,828	8,100	8,787	12,059
Sausage	3,245,431	564,170	231,131	159,697	171,467
Other pork	5,185,014	1,023,334	418,388	295,282	305,287
Other meats	12,556,130	2,649,525	895,500	701,953	1,073,647
Frankfurters	2,618,671	489,635	198,225	125,482	167,211
Lunch meats (cold cuts)	8,487,423	1,744,044	607,781	483,930	660,027
Bologna, liverwurst, salami	2,450,062	430,634	151,931	113,978	167,616
Other lunch meats	6,036,199	1,313,410	455,906	369,952	492,411
Lamb, organ meats, and others	1,451,199	415,846	89,438	92,499	246,459
Poultry	18,094,642	3,692,725	1,311,525	1,078,527	1,305,057
Fresh and frozen chicken	14,260,824	2,831,458	1,001,363	853,585	973,371
Fresh and frozen whole chicken	4,254,758	743,863	293,456	214,457	233,893
Fresh and frozen chicken parts	10,004,903	2,087,595	707,906	639,170	739,478
Other poultry	3,833,818	861,267	310,163	224,943	331,686

	total consumer units	$100,000 or more	$100,000– $119,999	$120,000– $149,999	$150,000 or more
Fish and seafood	$14,860,840	$3,288,530	$993,994	$1,024,870	$1,277,340
Canned fish and seafood	1,788,417	373,126	124,256	111,686	137,772
Fresh fish and shellfish	8,707,196	2,010,371	579,038	666,125	764,813
Frozen fish and shellfish	4,365,226	905,033	290,700	247,059	374,755
Eggs	4,865,239	847,824	304,144	243,069	301,740
Dairy products	**43,090,621**	**9,019,110**	**3,148,369**	**2,633,258**	**3,249,619**
Fresh milk and cream	16,782,981	3,073,885	1,124,044	887,417	1,063,209
Fresh milk, all types	14,993,401	2,679,847	987,244	758,369	937,142
Cream	1,789,580	394,187	136,800	129,006	126,067
Other dairy products	26,307,640	5,945,225	2,024,325	1,745,884	2,186,411
Butter	2,536,110	459,313	131,063	163,263	162,651
Cheese	13,217,775	3,226,691	1,082,081	930,631	1,225,505
Ice cream and related products	7,002,502	1,468,307	526,556	419,873	524,181
Miscellaneous dairy products	3,551,252	790,914	284,625	232,117	274,074
Fruits and vegetables	**65,228,388**	**14,054,970**	**4,840,256**	**3,954,854**	**5,316,702**
Fresh fruits	21,714,501	4,889,926	1,604,531	1,395,968	1,913,603
Apples	3,769,862	827,211	266,006	238,696	326,568
Bananas	3,508,228	614,359	215,550	172,347	228,724
Oranges	2,265,173	422,717	148,331	121,237	154,087
Citrus fruits, excluding oranges	1,791,906	435,862	141,581	141,995	151,047
Other fresh fruits	10,378,169	2,589,777	833,063	721,692	1,053,227
Fresh vegetables	21,272,629	4,658,253	1,621,519	1,318,837	1,733,167
Potatoes	3,264,036	558,793	212,794	160,206	185,148
Lettuce	2,659,369	602,708	212,963	175,913	214,435
Tomatoes	4,155,919	841,401	257,456	232,286	359,402
Other fresh vegetables	11,192,143	2,655,350	938,306	750,389	974,181
Processed fruits	12,747,996	2,618,904	896,794	728,654	1,006,205
Frozen fruits and fruit juices	1,159,332	230,478	83,700	72,123	73,573
Frozen orange juice	484,896	62,735	22,556	18,508	21,636
Frozen fruits	410,475	116,060	40,388	38,587	36,330
Frozen fruit juices, excluding orange	263,960	51,533	20,756	15,027	15,606
Canned fruits	1,882,606	355,799	116,381	109,181	130,475
Dried fruits	738,391	158,930	56,025	37,483	67,442
Fresh fruit juice	2,566,344	609,728	228,206	143,990	243,672
Canned and bottled fruit juice	6,401,324	1,263,969	412,481	365,834	491,043
Processed vegetables	9,493,262	1,887,887	717,413	511,395	663,676
Frozen vegetables	3,314,037	721,009	283,050	199,345	238,605
Canned and dried vegetables and juices	6,179,225	1,166,878	434,363	312,008	425,071
Canned beans	1,324,452	229,283	90,394	56,586	83,656
Canned corn	736,065	118,600	39,881	31,116	48,643
Canned miscellaneous vegetables	1,950,049	391,648	140,119	107,696	145,423
Dried peas	69,769	14,041	3,994	5,009	4,966
Dried beans	287,217	35,699	14,119	7,641	14,441
Dried miscellaneous vegetables	722,111	136,674	44,156	41,559	51,177
Dried processed vegetables	34,885	8,813	7,313	1,401	–
Fresh and canned vegetable juices	1,036,073	230,926	93,769	61,043	76,309
Sugar and other sweets	**14,898,050**	**3,444,920**	**1,033,538**	**1,158,078**	**1,244,709**
Candy and chewing gum	9,666,523	2,490,745	704,531	850,740	931,112
Sugar	1,872,140	258,858	99,169	87,192	69,469
Artificial sweeteners	796,532	172,672	69,356	40,667	63,844
Jams, preserves, other sweets	2,562,855	522,646	160,481	179,479	180,284
Fats and oils	**10,336,307**	**1,928,665**	**736,425**	**543,275**	**648,829**
Margarine	1,112,819	184,621	67,838	50,940	66,327
Fats and oils	3,321,014	614,508	249,581	174,130	188,948
Salad dressings	3,190,778	632,134	248,063	162,584	223,911
Nondairy cream and imitation milk	1,255,846	225,250	82,350	70,340	71,495
Peanut butter	1,455,851	272,152	88,650	85,282	98,097

	total consumer units	$100,000 or more	$100,000– $119,999	$120,000– $149,999	$150,000 or more
Miscellaneous foods	**$61,314,336**	**$13,477,655**	**$4,838,738**	**$3,804,539**	**$4,865,131**
Frozen prepared foods	12,779,392	2,564,085	981,450	715,622	867,977
Frozen meals	3,696,605	660,813	250,369	189,115	220,871
Other frozen prepared foods	9,082,787	1,903,273	731,081	526,507	647,107
Canned and packaged soups	4,244,293	845,135	302,963	235,173	309,695
Potato chips, nuts, and other snacks	13,614,297	3,177,100	1,050,806	900,025	1,242,631
Potato chips and other snacks	10,007,229	2,277,295	802,181	623,166	862,809
Nuts	3,605,905	899,805	248,569	276,859	379,772
Condiments and seasonings	10,889,809	2,380,808	806,175	750,431	818,675
Salt, spices, and other seasonings	2,583,786	583,589	214,088	197,180	166,451
Olives, pickles, relishes	1,223,287	252,435	77,288	95,173	77,120
Sauces and gravies	4,760,585	1,019,152	342,563	305,767	371,918
Baking needs and miscellaneous products	2,322,152	525,633	172,238	152,311	203,136
Other canned/packaged prepared foods	19,786,545	4,510,526	1,697,400	1,203,330	1,626,152
Prepared salads	2,957,051	752,974	274,388	178,672	308,175
Prepared desserts	1,268,637	305,611	118,463	100,309	83,758
Baby food	3,497,763	761,488	340,031	203,336	215,043
Miscellaneous prepared foods	11,946,813	2,618,157	942,638	720,971	963,946
Nonalcoholic beverages	**33,665,965**	**6,617,240**	**2,276,381**	**1,955,587**	**2,392,891**
Cola	10,908,414	1,837,699	667,688	567,429	595,981
Other carbonated drinks	5,590,839	1,001,227	348,806	292,481	361,328
Coffee	4,548,952	966,424	332,550	255,252	386,004
Roasted coffee	2,846,583	610,625	208,013	170,140	235,463
Instant and freeze-dried coffee	1,702,368	355,799	124,538	85,112	150,541
Noncarbonated fruit-flavored drinks	2,301,221	338,323	120,825	121,492	91,510
Tea	2,050,052	481,868	150,581	135,543	199,336
Other nonalcoholic beverages and ice	8,151,368	1,937,926	644,231	579,103	717,943
Food prepared by CU on trips	**4,751,283**	**1,459,942**	**403,706**	**403,530**	**652,731**
FOOD AWAY FROM HOME	283,030,388	79,145,786	24,914,700	20,703,841	34,024,956
Meals at restaurants, carry-outs, other	**235,839,664**	**62,222,314**	**20,747,813**	**16,666,931**	**25,305,409**
Lunch	84,312,590	21,551,104	7,237,013	5,846,129	8,619,828
At fast-food restaurants*	47,579,106	11,233,819	3,828,938	3,072,913	4,399,828
At full-service restaurants	27,518,135	7,755,440	2,304,450	2,211,433	3,304,140
At vending machines, mobile vendors	700,018	123,977	76,331	30,522	15,049
At employer and school cafeterias	8,516,494	2,437,868	1,027,350	531,304	900,811
Dinner	92,512,796	26,856,875	8,517,319	6,879,405	11,786,906
At fast-food restaurants*	29,427,486	7,207,700	2,455,144	1,843,519	2,979,193
At full-service restaurants	62,585,298	19,492,188	5,957,550	5,018,694	8,771,990
At vending machines, mobile vendors	174,423	38,388	9,506	2,674	28,375
At employer and school cafeterias	324,427	118,600	95,175	14,518	7,398
Snacks and nonalcoholic beverages	34,588,081	8,053,881	3,102,806	2,280,499	2,664,786
At fast-food restaurants*	25,251,799	6,124,618	2,296,631	1,732,639	2,098,042
At full-service restaurants	3,357,061	734,004	315,619	176,125	244,635
At vending machines, mobile vendors	4,775,702	919,970	366,581	300,037	243,267
At employer and school cafeterias	1,202,356	275,289	123,919	71,698	78,792
Breakfast and brunch	24,426,197	5,760,454	1,890,563	1,660,899	2,233,939
At fast-food restaurants*	12,009,605	2,320,314	880,931	595,064	856,728
At full-service restaurants	11,670,062	3,283,302	953,494	1,018,121	1,324,463
At vending machines, mobile vendors	165,120	16,879	11,531	2,759	2,483
At employer and school cafeterias	581,410	139,960	44,606	44,955	50,265
Board (including at school)	**3,243,105**	**1,820,073**	**256,894**	**388,248**	**1,174,885**
Catered affairs	**6,809,474**	**3,160,221**	**631,969**	**413,463**	**2,114,814**
Food on trips	**26,925,097**	**9,603,595**	**2,404,294**	**2,563,301**	**4,635,849**
School lunches	**7,371,116**	**2,066,534**	**780,469**	**604,615**	**681,410**
Meals as pay	**2,843,095**	**273,048**	**93,263**	**67,283**	**112,589**

	total consumer units	$100,000 or more	$100,000– $119,999	$120,000– $149,999	$150,000 or more
ALCOHOLIC BEVERAGES	**$53,404,834**	**$14,740,130**	**$4,071,375**	**$3,766,334**	**$7,121,314**
At home	**32,278,720**	**8,279,131**	**2,313,000**	**2,073,300**	**4,036,980**
Beer and ale	15,268,989	2,686,419	950,850	892,511	822,931
Whiskey	2,518,668	700,993	218,588	238,357	240,835
Wine	10,994,463	3,887,056	923,400	663,451	2,449,286
Other alcoholic beverages	3,496,600	1,004,663	220,163	279,024	523,877
Away from home	**21,126,114**	**6,460,850**	**1,758,375**	**1,692,991**	**3,084,384**
Beer and ale	8,874,642	2,460,423	741,994	575,962	1,187,705
At fast-food restaurants*	1,911,676	405,091	168,638	95,852	142,889
At full-service restaurants	6,512,955	1,754,649	565,200	455,913	752,551
Wine	2,591,926	692,927	178,875	164,069	365,635
At fast-food restaurants*	355,823	73,341	12,656	22,923	38,915
At full-service restaurants	2,181,450	575,672	166,219	140,340	279,394
Other alcoholic beverages	5,198,968	1,624,996	485,944	459,436	693,672
At fast-food restaurants*	444,197	100,974	35,044	30,267	35,621
At full-service restaurants	4,586,162	1,403,779	448,538	424,882	533,606
Alcoholic beverages purchased on trips	4,461,740	1,682,504	351,563	493,566	837,372

* The category fast-food restaurants also includes take-out, delivery, concession stands, buffets, and cafeterias other than employer and school.
Note: Numbers may not add to total because of rounding and missing subcategories. "–" means sample is too small to make a reliable estimate.
Source: Calculations by New Strategist based on the 2004 Consumer Expenditure Survey

Table 5.12 Food and Alcohol: Market shares by high-income consumer units, 2004

(percentage of total annual spending on food and alcoholic beverages accounted for by before-tax income group of high-income consumer units, 2004)

	total consumer units	$100,000 or more	$100,000–$119,999	$120,000–$149,999	$150,000 or more
Share of total consumer units	100.0%	12.8%	4.8%	3.7%	4.4%
Share of total before-tax income	100.0	36.8	9.7	8.9	18.2
Share of total spending	100.0	27.7	8.4	7.3	12.0
Share of food spending	100.0	23.9	7.9	6.6	9.5
Share of alcoholic beverages spending	100.0	27.6	7.6	7.1	13.3
FOOD AT HOME	**100.0**	**20.9**	**7.2**	**6.0**	**7.6**
Cereals and bakery products	**100.0**	**20.2**	**7.1**	**5.9**	**7.3**
Cereals and cereal products	100.0	19.0	6.8	5.5	6.7
Flour	100.0	13.6	6.5	3.0	4.2
Prepared flour mixes	100.0	21.3	6.7	7.6	6.8
Ready-to-eat and cooked cereals	100.0	18.8	6.6	5.2	7.1
Rice	100.0	19.7	8.1	5.8	5.7
Pasta, cornmeal, and other cereal products	100.0	20.0	6.8	6.2	7.0
Bakery products	100.0	20.8	7.2	6.0	7.6
Bread	100.0	18.6	6.3	5.5	6.9
White bread	100.0	16.4	5.6	5.1	5.5
Bread, other than white	100.0	20.1	6.8	5.7	7.8
Crackers and cookies	100.0	21.4	7.8	6.2	7.4
Cookies	100.0	21.2	7.8	6.0	7.4
Crackers	100.0	21.7	7.7	6.5	7.4
Frozen and refrigerated bakery products	100.0	23.8	7.4	7.7	8.7
Other bakery products	100.0	21.3	7.4	6.0	8.0
Biscuits and rolls	100.0	23.7	7.9	5.9	10.1
Cakes and cupcakes	100.0	21.5	7.1	6.7	7.6
Bread and cracker products	100.0	21.3	7.5	5.0	9.1
Sweetrolls, coffee cakes, doughnuts	100.0	18.7	6.8	5.7	6.1
Pies, tarts, turnovers	100.0	18.1	7.4	5.2	5.4
Meats, poultry, fish, and eggs	**100.0**	**19.9**	**7.0**	**5.8**	**7.1**
Beef	100.0	19.5	7.0	5.7	6.9
Ground beef	100.0	16.6	6.3	5.0	5.2
Roast	100.0	19.6	6.1	5.3	8.4
Chuck roast	100.0	15.0	5.6	3.5	6.0
Round roast	100.0	19.3	4.3	5.8	9.5
Other roast	100.0	22.0	7.2	6.0	9.1
Steak	100.0	22.0	7.6	6.5	7.9
Round steak	100.0	18.4	6.5	6.5	5.2
Sirloin steak	100.0	23.0	7.8	6.0	9.4
Other steak	100.0	22.5	7.8	6.8	7.8
Other beef	100.0	21.0	9.4	5.5	6.1
Pork	100.0	18.3	7.0	5.4	5.8
Bacon	100.0	16.7	6.6	4.7	5.4
Pork chops	100.0	17.4	6.7	5.3	5.3
Ham	100.0	19.3	6.5	5.9	6.9
Ham, not canned	100.0	19.2	6.5	5.9	6.8
Canned ham	100.0	25.3	7.1	7.7	10.6
Sausage	100.0	17.4	7.1	4.9	5.3
Other pork	100.0	19.7	8.1	5.7	5.9
Other meats	100.0	21.1	7.1	5.6	8.6
Frankfurters	100.0	18.7	7.6	4.8	6.4
Lunch meats (cold cuts)	100.0	20.5	7.2	5.7	7.8
Bologna, liverwurst, salami	100.0	17.6	6.2	4.7	6.8
Other lunch meats	100.0	21.8	7.6	6.1	8.2
Lamb, organ meats, and others	100.0	28.7	6.2	6.4	17.0
Poultry	100.0	20.4	7.2	6.0	7.2
Fresh and frozen chicken	100.0	19.9	7.0	6.0	6.8
Fresh and frozen whole chicken	100.0	17.5	6.9	5.0	5.5
Fresh and frozen chicken parts	100.0	20.9	7.1	6.4	7.4
Other poultry	100.0	22.5	8.1	5.9	8.7

	total consumer units	$100,000 or more	$100,000–$119,999	$120,000–$149,999	$150,000 or more
Fish and seafood	100.0%	22.1%	6.7%	6.9%	8.6%
Canned fish and seafood	100.0	20.9	6.9	6.2	7.7
Fresh fish and shellfish	100.0	23.1	6.7	7.7	8.8
Frozen fish and shellfish	100.0	20.7	6.7	5.7	8.6
Eggs	100.0	17.4	6.3	5.0	6.2
Dairy products	**100.0**	**20.9**	**7.3**	**6.1**	**7.5**
Fresh milk and cream	100.0	18.3	6.7	5.3	6.3
Fresh milk, all types	100.0	17.9	6.6	5.1	6.3
Cream	100.0	22.0	7.6	7.2	7.0
Other dairy products	100.0	22.6	7.7	6.6	8.3
Butter	100.0	18.1	5.2	6.4	6.4
Cheese	100.0	24.4	8.2	7.0	9.3
Ice cream and related products	100.0	21.0	7.5	6.0	7.5
Miscellaneous dairy products	100.0	22.3	8.0	6.5	7.7
Fruits and vegetables	**100.0**	**21.5**	**7.4**	**6.1**	**8.2**
Fresh fruits	100.0	22.5	7.4	6.4	8.8
Apples	100.0	21.9	7.1	6.3	8.7
Bananas	100.0	17.5	6.1	4.9	6.5
Oranges	100.0	18.7	6.5	5.4	6.8
Citrus fruits, excluding oranges	100.0	24.3	7.9	7.9	8.4
Other fresh fruits	100.0	25.0	8.0	7.0	10.1
Fresh vegetables	100.0	21.9	7.6	6.2	8.1
Potatoes	100.0	17.1	6.5	4.9	5.7
Lettuce	100.0	22.7	8.0	6.6	8.1
Tomatoes	100.0	20.2	6.2	5.6	8.6
Other fresh vegetables	100.0	23.7	8.4	6.7	8.7
Processed fruits	100.0	20.5	7.0	5.7	7.9
Frozen fruits and fruit juices	100.0	19.9	7.2	6.2	6.3
Frozen orange juice	100.0	12.9	4.7	3.8	4.5
Frozen fruits	100.0	28.3	9.8	9.4	8.9
Frozen fruit juices, excluding orange	100.0	19.5	7.9	5.7	5.9
Canned fruits	100.0	18.9	6.2	5.8	6.9
Dried fruits	100.0	21.5	7.6	5.1	9.1
Fresh fruit juice	100.0	23.8	8.9	5.6	9.5
Canned and bottled fruit juice	100.0	19.7	6.4	5.7	7.7
Processed vegetables	100.0	19.9	7.6	5.4	7.0
Frozen vegetables	100.0	21.8	8.5	6.0	7.2
Canned and dried vegetables and juices	100.0	18.9	7.0	5.0	6.9
Canned beans	100.0	17.3	6.8	4.3	6.3
Canned corn	100.0	16.1	5.4	4.2	6.6
Canned miscellaneous vegetables	100.0	20.1	7.2	5.5	7.5
Dried peas	100.0	20.1	5.7	7.2	7.1
Dried beans	100.0	12.4	4.9	2.7	5.0
Dried miscellaneous vegetables	100.0	18.9	6.1	5.8	7.1
Dried processed vegetables	100.0	25.3	21.0	4.0	–
Fresh and canned vegetable juices	100.0	22.3	9.1	5.9	7.4
Sugar and other sweets	**100.0**	**23.1**	**6.9**	**7.8**	**8.4**
Candy and chewing gum	100.0	25.8	7.3	8.8	9.6
Sugar	100.0	13.8	5.3	4.7	3.7
Artificial sweeteners	100.0	21.7	8.7	5.1	8.0
Jams, preserves, other sweets	100.0	20.4	6.3	7.0	7.0
Fats and oils	**100.0**	**18.7**	**7.1**	**5.3**	**6.3**
Margarine	100.0	16.6	6.1	4.6	6.0
Fats and oils	100.0	18.5	7.5	5.2	5.7
Salad dressings	100.0	19.8	7.8	5.1	7.0
Nondairy cream and imitation milk	100.0	17.9	6.6	5.6	5.7
Peanut butter	100.0	18.7	6.1	5.9	6.7

	total consumer units	$100,000 or more	$100,000– $119,999	$120,000– $149,999	$150,000 or more
Miscellaneous foods	100.0%	22.0%	7.9%	6.2%	7.9%
Frozen prepared foods	100.0	20.1	7.7	5.6	6.8
Frozen meals	100.0	17.9	6.8	5.1	6.0
Other frozen prepared foods	100.0	21.0	8.0	5.8	7.1
Canned and packaged soups	100.0	19.9	7.1	5.5	7.3
Potato chips, nuts, and other snacks	100.0	23.3	7.7	6.6	9.1
Potato chips and other snacks	100.0	22.8	8.0	6.2	8.6
Nuts	100.0	25.0	6.9	7.7	10.5
Condiments and seasonings	100.0	21.9	7.4	6.9	7.5
Salt, spices, and other seasonings	100.0	22.6	8.3	7.6	6.4
Olives, pickles, relishes	100.0	20.6	6.3	7.8	6.3
Sauces and gravies	100.0	21.4	7.2	6.4	7.8
Baking needs and miscellaneous products	100.0	22.6	7.4	6.6	8.7
Other canned/packaged prepared foods	100.0	22.8	8.6	6.1	8.2
Prepared salads	100.0	25.5	9.3	6.0	10.4
Prepared desserts	100.0	24.1	9.3	7.9	6.6
Baby food	100.0	21.8	9.7	5.8	6.1
Miscellaneous prepared foods	100.0	21.9	7.9	6.0	8.1
Nonalcoholic beverages	100.0	19.7	6.8	5.8	7.1
Cola	100.0	16.8	6.1	5.2	5.5
Other carbonated drinks	100.0	17.9	6.2	5.2	6.5
Coffee	100.0	21.2	7.3	5.6	8.5
Roasted coffee	100.0	21.5	7.3	6.0	8.3
Instant and freeze-dried coffee	100.0	20.9	7.3	5.0	8.8
Noncarbonated fruit-flavored drinks	100.0	14.7	5.3	5.3	4.0
Tea	100.0	23.5	7.3	6.6	9.7
Other nonalcoholic beverages and ice	100.0	23.8	7.9	7.1	8.8
Food prepared by CU on trips	100.0	30.7	8.5	8.5	13.7
FOOD AWAY FROM HOME	100.0	28.0	8.8	7.3	12.0
Meals at restaurants, carry-outs, other	100.0	26.4	8.8	7.1	10.7
Lunch	100.0	25.6	8.6	6.9	10.2
At fast-food restaurants*	100.0	23.6	8.0	6.5	9.2
At full-service restaurants	100.0	28.2	8.4	8.0	12.0
At vending machines, mobile vendors	100.0	17.7	10.9	4.4	2.1
At employer and school cafeterias	100.0	28.6	12.1	6.2	10.6
Dinner	100.0	29.0	9.2	7.4	12.7
At fast-food restaurants*	100.0	24.5	8.3	6.3	10.1
At full-service restaurants	100.0	31.1	9.5	8.0	14.0
At vending machines, mobile vendors	100.0	22.0	5.5	1.5	16.3
At employer and school cafeterias	100.0	36.6	29.3	4.5	2.3
Snacks and nonalcoholic beverages	100.0	23.3	9.0	6.6	7.7
At fast-food restaurants*	100.0	24.3	9.1	6.9	8.3
At full-service restaurants	100.0	21.9	9.4	5.2	7.3
At vending machines, mobile vendors	100.0	19.3	7.7	6.3	5.1
At employer and school cafeterias	100.0	22.9	10.3	6.0	6.6
Breakfast and brunch	100.0	23.6	7.7	6.8	9.1
At fast-food restaurants*	100.0	19.3	7.3	5.0	7.1
At full-service restaurants	100.0	28.1	8.2	8.7	11.3
At vending machines, mobile vendors	100.0	10.2	7.0	1.7	1.5
At employer and school cafeterias	100.0	24.1	7.7	7.7	8.6
Board (including at school)	100.0	56.1	7.9	12.0	36.2
Catered affairs	100.0	46.4	9.3	6.1	31.1
Food on trips	100.0	35.7	8.9	9.5	17.2
School lunches	100.0	28.0	10.6	8.2	9.2
Meals as pay	100.0	9.6	3.3	2.4	4.0

	total consumer units	$100,000 or more	$100,000– $119,999	$120,000– $149,999	$150,000 or more
ALCOHOLIC BEVERAGES	**100.0%**	**27.6%**	**7.6%**	**7.1%**	**13.3%**
At home	**100.0**	**25.6**	**7.2**	**6.4**	**12.5**
Beer and ale	100.0	17.6	6.2	5.8	5.4
Whiskey	100.0	27.8	8.7	9.5	9.6
Wine	100.0	35.4	8.4	6.0	22.3
Other alcoholic beverages	100.0	28.7	6.3	8.0	15.0
Away from home	**100.0**	**30.6**	**8.3**	**8.0**	**14.6**
Beer and ale	100.0	27.7	8.4	6.5	13.4
At fast-food restaurants*	100.0	21.2	8.8	5.0	7.5
At full-service restaurants	100.0	26.9	8.7	7.0	11.6
Wine	100.0	26.7	6.9	6.3	14.1
At fast-food restaurants*	100.0	20.6	3.6	6.4	10.9
At full-service restaurants	100.0	26.4	7.6	6.4	12.8
Other alcoholic beverages	100.0	31.3	9.3	8.8	13.3
At fast-food restaurants*	100.0	22.7	7.9	6.8	8.0
At full-service restaurants	100.0	30.6	9.8	9.3	11.6
Alcoholic beverages purchased on trips	100.0	37.7	7.9	11.1	18.8

The category fast-food restaurants also includes take-out, delivery, concession stands, buffets, and cafeterias other than employer and school.
Note: Numbers may not add to total because of rounding. "–" means sample is too small to make a reliable estimate.
Source: Calculations by New Strategist based on the 2004 Consumer Expenditure Survey

Table 5.13 Food and Alcohol: Average spending by household type, 2004

(average annual spending of consumer units (CU) on food and alcoholic beverages, by type of consumer unit, 2004)

	total married couples	married couples, no children	married couples with children total	oldest child under 6	oldest child 6 to 17	oldest child 18 or older	single parent, at least one child <18	single person
Number of consumer units (in 000s)	59,797	25,585	29,279	5,604	15,376	8,300	6,892	33,686
Average number of persons per CU	3.2	2.0	3.9	3.5	4.1	3.9	2.9	1.0
Average before-tax income of CU	$73,001.00	$64,434.00	$79,764.00	$75,293.00	$78,508.00	$85,109.00	$31,055.00	$28,143.00
Average spending of CU, total	55,606.57	49,690.43	60,660.88	55,981.04	60,577.88	64,161.69	32,824.46	25,423.35
Food, average spending	**7,379.30**	**6,268.38**	**8,089.22**	**6,300.10**	**8,483.62**	**8,681.56**	**4,873.15**	**3,094.64**
Alcoholic beverages, average spending	**493.23**	**567.05**	**442.56**	**329.70**	**455.05**	**505.98**	**219.37**	**358.66**
FOOD AT HOME	**4,303.09**	**3,573.95**	**4,711.21**	**3,764.87**	**4,886.67**	**5,104.05**	**3,014.69**	**1,681.07**
Cereals and bakery products	**593.14**	**472.11**	**668.19**	**492.24**	**718.28**	**704.95**	**443.00**	**228.72**
Cereals and cereal products	197.78	148.31	227.40	159.52	246.47	242.09	162.45	72.89
Flour	9.51	7.41	8.86	7.86	9.08	9.23	5.86	5.67
Prepared flour mixes	19.03	15.73	21.11	15.34	21.89	24.13	13.72	5.27
Ready-to-eat and cooked cereals	110.87	84.34	128.74	90.13	144.76	126.33	100.94	41.20
Rice	24.40	16.83	28.80	18.80	31.53	31.15	18.92	7.38
Pasta, cornmeal, and other cereal products	33.97	24.00	39.87	27.40	39.22	51.25	23.02	13.38
Bakery products	395.36	323.79	440.79	332.72	471.81	462.86	280.55	155.83
Bread	109.62	95.40	117.91	80.31	124.18	135.02	77.12	47.59
White bread	42.39	32.18	47.53	31.01	49.56	56.56	39.60	17.45
Bread, other than white	67.23	63.22	70.38	49.30	74.62	78.46	37.52	30.13
Crackers and cookies	92.54	77.83	105.47	86.88	113.21	104.24	67.95	36.24
Cookies	59.23	46.56	69.53	54.02	75.71	69.08	49.45	24.58
Crackers	33.31	31.27	35.94	32.86	37.50	35.16	18.50	11.66
Frozen and refrigerated bakery products	34.23	24.38	41.29	34.09	46.72	35.75	30.14	12.33
Other bakery products	158.97	126.19	176.12	131.44	187.69	187.85	105.33	59.67
Biscuits and rolls	57.49	48.79	62.90	40.29	68.10	70.20	34.99	19.17
Cakes and cupcakes	50.24	34.27	58.88	53.53	60.79	59.20	35.66	18.61
Bread and cracker products	4.27	3.60	4.89	2.54	5.28	5.95	2.63	1.60
Sweetrolls, coffee cakes, doughnuts	30.31	24.59	32.65	26.91	35.07	32.24	19.05	11.93
Pies, tarts, turnovers	16.66	14.94	16.79	8.17	18.45	20.26	13.00	8.37
Meats, poultry, fish, and eggs	**1,121.18**	**922.69**	**1,209.69**	**875.35**	**1,215.97**	**1,465.01**	**835.45**	**411.32**
Beef	341.63	269.95	377.42	243.62	379.91	479.64	257.77	116.53
Ground beef	121.24	92.45	135.45	78.06	142.80	166.20	113.22	42.52
Roast	62.15	52.57	67.08	40.41	66.29	90.14	34.87	16.49
Chuck roast	14.92	11.23	16.66	8.54	19.32	17.64	9.32	5.12
Round roast	13.79	12.05	14.56	7.29	15.31	18.82	10.87	3.76
Other roast	33.44	29.29	35.85	24.57	31.65	53.68	14.69	7.62
Steak	133.49	105.21	148.38	109.04	140.37	196.69	93.16	49.99
Round steak	21.52	15.94	24.00	15.69	23.86	30.95	15.23	7.40
Sirloin steak	41.15	34.39	44.36	43.44	39.47	55.29	32.32	15.92
Other steak	70.82	54.88	80.03	49.91	77.03	110.44	45.61	26.67
Other beef	24.75	19.72	26.50	16.12	30.45	26.60	16.52	7.53
Pork	226.76	189.58	240.19	174.76	236.49	300.45	187.73	83.49
Bacon	38.54	35.10	39.65	28.72	40.02	47.65	33.12	14.83
Pork chops	46.25	34.63	52.05	38.73	46.34	74.66	50.16	17.24
Ham	51.87	43.90	54.95	41.31	56.28	63.15	31.72	19.65
Ham, not canned	50.61	42.07	54.19	40.60	55.59	62.17	31.24	18.92
Canned ham	1.26	1.83	0.76	0.71	0.68	0.97	0.48	0.73
Sausage	34.25	27.11	36.76	24.83	38.05	43.66	30.24	11.89
Other pork	55.84	48.85	56.78	41.18	55.81	71.34	42.49	19.89
Other meats	140.38	115.27	154.93	100.23	161.94	184.23	105.61	48.63
Frankfurters	27.95	20.16	31.06	22.42	32.30	35.40	29.48	9.70
Lunch meats (cold cuts)	95.51	72.44	112.03	67.46	117.55	136.29	65.12	33.58
Bologna, liverwurst, salami	25.99	20.83	28.71	16.73	29.74	36.17	25.69	9.69
Other lunch meats	69.52	51.61	83.32	50.73	87.81	100.12	39.43	23.89
Lamb, organ meats, and others	16.92	22.66	11.85	10.35	12.09	12.55	11.02	5.34
Poultry	196.84	154.18	216.96	164.62	224.69	242.85	134.83	75.37
Fresh and frozen chicken	152.92	116.54	170.79	134.31	174.08	193.24	111.42	61.09
Fresh and frozen whole chicken	44.77	31.77	50.21	38.60	50.22	59.52	31.00	18.64
Fresh and frozen chicken parts	108.15	84.76	120.58	95.72	123.86	133.71	80.42	42.45
Other poultry	43.92	37.65	46.16	30.30	50.61	49.61	23.41	14.28

	total married couples	married couples, no children	married couples with children				single parent, at least one child <18	single person
			total	oldest child under 6	oldest child 6 to 17	oldest child 18 or older		
Fish and seafood	$163.78	$150.82	$164.99	$147.00	$159.27	$191.36	$112.03	$63.20
Canned fish and seafood	17.49	15.97	17.26	12.46	17.03	21.59	10.30	9.12
Fresh fish and shellfish	98.29	90.39	98.26	93.38	90.05	119.28	58.29	34.45
Frozen fish and shellfish	48.00	44.46	49.48	41.16	52.19	50.49	43.44	19.63
Eggs	51.78	42.88	55.20	45.12	53.67	66.48	37.48	24.09
Dairy products	**480.37**	**390.30**	**542.48**	**436.53**	**579.95**	**549.37**	**316.54**	**183.23**
Fresh milk and cream	186.96	136.66	220.49	190.29	232.77	219.12	140.11	68.93
Fresh milk, all types	166.56	118.67	198.70	171.98	210.08	196.41	128.33	61.43
Cream	20.40	18.00	21.79	18.32	22.69	22.71	11.78	7.51
Other dairy products	293.40	253.63	321.99	246.24	347.18	330.25	176.43	114.29
Butter	26.03	23.16	27.88	20.19	30.68	28.22	16.36	10.78
Cheese	150.36	128.53	166.63	129.59	176.78	175.17	85.72	57.00
Ice cream and related products	77.63	69.06	82.50	53.95	90.56	88.63	51.89	29.74
Miscellaneous dairy products	39.39	32.88	44.97	42.50	49.16	38.23	22.47	16.77
Fruits and vegetables	**725.73**	**643.62**	**756.01**	**634.23**	**770.56**	**823.41**	**455.68**	**297.89**
Fresh fruits	243.80	225.06	247.97	211.01	255.12	262.71	148.76	101.15
Apples	43.15	36.80	47.11	37.44	49.84	49.18	21.46	16.45
Bananas	37.50	33.45	37.63	33.54	37.81	40.53	26.64	17.97
Oranges	25.52	23.60	24.58	19.68	25.11	27.41	19.16	9.89
Citrus fruits, excluding oranges	19.98	18.64	19.71	17.73	21.01	18.58	14.01	8.27
Other fresh fruits	117.65	112.58	118.94	102.62	121.35	127.02	67.49	48.56
Fresh vegetables	240.55	222.27	241.84	204.76	238.80	277.95	129.90	93.17
Potatoes	36.12	31.92	36.64	32.73	36.11	40.90	27.87	13.65
Lettuce	29.54	27.26	30.98	22.29	30.87	38.19	16.38	12.75
Tomatoes	46.71	41.04	47.94	43.41	46.53	54.53	24.99	18.93
Other fresh vegetables	128.18	122.05	126.27	106.33	125.29	144.33	60.66	47.84
Processed fruits	137.89	111.64	153.89	136.01	160.25	154.97	101.79	61.94
Frozen fruits and fruit juices	13.17	11.41	14.81	10.01	16.81	14.51	6.98	5.37
Frozen orange juice	5.37	3.96	6.69	4.89	6.94	7.61	2.31	2.31
Frozen fruits	4.76	5.14	4.98	2.92	6.34	3.78	3.39	1.99
Frozen fruit juices, excluding orange	3.03	2.31	3.15	2.20	3.52	3.12	1.28	1.07
Canned fruits	21.23	18.66	22.74	22.65	24.98	18.13	13.15	9.37
Dried fruits	8.55	8.99	8.59	7.79	8.33	9.77	2.75	3.54
Fresh fruit juice	27.64	21.31	31.09	23.11	31.06	37.55	18.04	12.03
Canned and bottled fruit juice	67.29	51.27	76.66	72.45	79.06	75.02	60.87	31.63
Processed vegetables	103.49	84.66	112.31	82.45	116.39	127.78	75.23	41.63
Frozen vegetables	36.03	27.75	40.03	26.83	41.45	47.65	27.96	15.54
Canned and dried vegetables and juices	67.47	56.91	72.29	55.62	74.94	80.13	47.27	26.09
Canned beans	14.38	12.06	15.49	11.67	16.04	17.43	11.54	6.26
Canned corn	7.49	5.22	8.52	5.48	9.21	9.50	6.56	3.16
Canned miscellaneous vegetables	22.61	21.38	22.88	15.85	22.42	29.47	12.79	7.58
Dried peas	0.68	0.70	0.69	0.66	0.67	0.78	0.62	0.36
Dried beans	2.62	2.11	2.62	1.94	3.07	2.25	2.46	1.22
Dried miscellaneous vegetables	8.05	6.14	9.10	7.19	10.03	8.69	4.81	2.40
Dried processed vegetables	0.48	0.30	0.71	–	1.14	0.38	–	0.16
Fresh and canned vegetable juices	10.99	8.90	12.08	12.42	12.20	11.55	8.47	4.82
Sugar and other sweets	**167.55**	**148.15**	**176.48**	**140.35**	**187.16**	**183.21**	**122.89**	**62.85**
Candy and chewing gum	109.65	95.09	116.90	99.73	124.39	115.05	83.94	40.15
Sugar	19.20	14.98	21.10	13.24	22.85	23.77	17.80	7.41
Artificial sweeteners	8.60	10.71	6.52	3.53	6.05	9.89	2.21	4.87
Jams, preserves, other sweets	30.09	27.37	31.97	23.86	33.87	34.50	18.94	10.42
Fats and oils	**112.88**	**97.74**	**120.62**	**87.76**	**125.25**	**137.35**	**78.41**	**47.14**
Margarine	11.98	11.80	11.71	6.44	12.07	15.20	8.58	5.70
Fats and oils	36.31	30.22	38.96	33.74	39.72	41.55	26.59	13.71
Salad dressings	34.14	29.56	37.04	27.99	39.31	39.56	24.41	15.04
Nondairy cream and imitation milk	14.49	13.24	14.94	10.35	14.92	18.68	6.53	5.49
Peanut butter	15.96	12.92	17.98	9.25	19.23	22.36	12.30	7.19

	total married couples	married couples, no children	married couples with children				single parent, at least one child <18	single person
			total	oldest child under 6	oldest child 6 to 17	oldest child 18 or older		
Miscellaneous foods	**$683.29**	**$537.50**	**$788.40**	**$772.12**	**$813.07**	**$749.99**	**$474.03**	**$274.44**
Frozen prepared foods	130.13	100.29	149.24	120.30	152.34	165.98	117.20	67.62
Frozen meals	33.01	29.30	36.53	30.74	33.06	48.40	35.82	28.40
Other frozen prepared foods	97.13	70.98	112.71	89.57	119.28	117.58	81.37	39.22
Canned and packaged soups	44.28	42.93	42.47	36.84	41.66	48.68	34.13	22.78
Potato chips, nuts, and other snacks	158.03	127.36	184.66	126.27	205.21	188.65	107.34	53.09
Potato chips and other snacks	115.97	80.17	145.71	102.92	166.39	136.94	91.77	34.78
Nuts	42.06	47.19	38.94	23.35	38.83	51.71	15.57	18.31
Condiments and seasonings	122.97	107.24	134.35	105.86	140.51	144.37	76.56	47.48
Salt, spices, and other seasonings	29.33	26.83	30.21	29.11	30.09	31.33	20.08	10.20
Olives, pickles, relishes	13.67	13.63	13.45	6.36	13.11	19.87	9.41	5.19
Sauces and gravies	53.55	43.69	60.78	51.91	64.20	60.75	32.13	21.27
Baking needs and miscellaneous products	26.43	23.10	29.91	18.49	33.11	32.40	14.94	10.82
Other canned/packaged prepared foods	227.87	159.68	277.69	382.85	273.35	202.32	138.80	83.48
Prepared salads	31.82	31.66	32.17	23.48	32.28	38.92	21.93	17.27
Prepared desserts	14.94	15.31	14.56	9.56	16.64	14.24	8.26	4.87
Baby food	46.31	7.18	78.66	223.48	53.01	15.92	22.99	3.15
Miscellaneous prepared foods	133.23	103.96	152.07	126.32	171.00	133.25	85.63	57.54
Nonalcoholic beverages	**360.54**	**298.33**	**399.31**	**291.78**	**421.49**	**439.34**	**269.26**	**155.27**
Cola	115.84	95.17	129.04	96.16	129.91	153.62	88.94	48.80
Other carbonated drinks	60.32	44.64	69.39	43.06	72.62	83.78	51.01	24.10
Coffee	48.40	56.00	42.33	29.91	44.57	47.64	24.04	24.94
Roasted coffee	30.47	35.70	26.43	19.50	27.70	29.34	14.34	15.34
Instant and freeze-dried coffee	17.93	20.30	15.90	10.41	16.87	18.30	9.70	9.60
Noncarbonated fruit-flavored drinks	24.48	13.57	32.54	18.43	40.81	26.61	30.11	8.38
Tea	23.10	22.37	23.25	13.01	22.72	32.60	13.43	9.16
Other nonalcoholic beverages and ice	87.66	65.31	102.37	90.84	110.62	94.41	61.74	39.53
Food prepared by CU on trips	**58.42**	**63.51**	**50.03**	**34.50**	**54.94**	**51.42**	**19.41**	**20.20**
FOOD AWAY FROM HOME	3,076.21	2,694.43	3,378.00	2,535.22	3,596.96	3,577.51	1,858.46	1,413.57
Meals at restaurants, carry-outs, other	**2,514.05**	**2,184.89**	**2,769.05**	**2,248.41**	**2,898.87**	**2,916.17**	**1,540.70**	**1,229.76**
Lunch	903.05	718.16	1,049.47	884.52	1,135.86	1,001.65	612.83	418.27
At fast-food restaurants*	491.92	349.91	603.74	572.10	631.33	571.56	368.03	228.46
At full-service restaurants	305.13	336.83	275.77	265.95	275.61	284.00	113.78	160.00
At vending machines, mobile vendors	6.56	4.98	7.82	2.60	6.17	15.46	5.91	5.92
At employer and school cafeterias	99.44	26.44	162.14	43.86	222.75	130.64	125.12	23.89
Dinner	1,011.23	960.26	1,052.33	839.28	1,050.39	1,227.42	477.13	488.30
At fast-food restaurants*	311.98	227.77	382.87	341.29	402.01	376.30	237.03	133.14
At full-service restaurants	693.36	727.77	662.50	494.83	638.38	847.45	238.12	352.61
At vending machines, mobile vendors	2.34	3.83	0.83	–	1.16	0.78	0.13	0.38
At employer and school cafeterias	3.56	0.89	6.13	3.16	8.83	2.89	1.86	2.18
Snacks and nonalcoholic beverages	343.67	264.92	403.24	322.36	446.03	378.90	278.98	193.14
At fast-food restaurants*	253.72	197.12	300.24	250.55	331.57	274.75	198.05	141.31
At full-service restaurants	33.05	34.22	30.83	22.36	30.69	37.92	21.05	19.60
At vending machines, mobile vendors	44.20	27.25	54.38	42.61	59.24	53.66	44.16	26.62
At employer and school cafeterias	12.69	6.33	17.79	6.83	24.52	12.56	15.72	5.62
Breakfast and brunch	256.09	241.56	264.01	202.25	266.59	308.20	171.75	130.04
At fast-food restaurants*	116.77	88.18	134.97	108.61	139.56	146.56	108.24	66.21
At full-service restaurants	132.34	149.31	119.99	90.40	114.76	154.68	54.12	58.50
At vending machines, mobile vendors	1.46	1.53	1.49	0.67	1.53	2.09	1.93	1.54
At employer and school cafeterias	5.53	2.54	7.55	2.57	10.74	4.87	7.46	3.78
Board (including at school)	**39.51**	**37.21**	**42.61**	**0.04**	**46.02**	**65.04**	**10.91**	**18.84**
Catered affairs	**80.48**	**100.09**	**58.58**	**36.90**	**39.65**	**108.28**	**13.26**	**14.52**
Food on trips	**326.21**	**357.68**	**306.93**	**203.40**	**325.94**	**341.61**	**103.03**	**122.16**
School lunches	**96.43**	**0.35**	**181.93**	**9.00**	**271.64**	**132.51**	**156.63**	**–**
Meals as pay	**19.54**	**14.21**	**18.90**	**37.48**	**14.83**	**13.89**	**33.94**	**28.29**

	total married couples	married couples, no children	married couples with children				single parent, at least one child <18	single person
			total	oldest child under 6	oldest child 6 to 17	oldest child 18 or older		
ALCOHOLIC BEVERAGES	**$493.23**	**$567.05**	**$442.56**	**$329.70**	**$455.05**	**$505.98**	**$219.37**	**$358.66**
At home	**295.09**	**316.14**	**283.71**	**206.44**	**307.27**	**296.58**	**149.26**	**200.10**
Beer and ale	135.23	109.10	151.42	119.52	165.69	147.28	82.16	101.71
Whiskey	21.15	30.96	15.19	12.44	16.11	15.49	6.18	15.84
Wine	104.86	126.10	93.91	60.35	98.57	111.14	42.52	61.93
Other alcoholic beverages	33.85	49.98	23.17	14.13	26.89	22.67	18.40	20.63
Away from home	**198.14**	**250.91**	**158.86**	**123.27**	**147.78**	**209.40**	**70.11**	**158.56**
Beer and ale	77.55	95.95	65.83	51.44	59.01	91.62	30.41	76.77
At fast-food restaurants*	15.29	17.50	13.86	12.48	15.52	11.50	5.50	18.96
At full-service restaurants	55.55	73.82	42.66	38.81	42.78	45.51	24.64	57.05
Wine	23.69	32.38	16.96	14.11	16.10	21.02	7.79	18.12
At fast-food restaurants*	2.85	3.25	2.31	1.81	2.29	2.75	1.30	2.96
At full-service restaurants	19.94	28.14	13.70	12.29	13.79	14.66	6.49	15.14
Other alcoholic beverages	47.32	62.90	36.56	26.20	33.65	50.95	15.94	37.25
At fast-food restaurants*	2.96	3.46	2.71	1.98	2.92	2.86	1.75	3.99
At full-service restaurants	41.70	57.96	29.84	24.23	30.49	33.01	14.02	33.18
Alcoholic beverages purchased on trips	49.59	59.67	39.51	31.52	39.02	45.81	15.96	26.42

The category fast-food restaurants also includes take-out, delivery, concession stands, buffets, and cafeterias other than employer and school.

Note: Average spending figures for total consumer units can be found on Average Spending by Age and Average Spending by Region tables. Subcategories may not add to total because some are not shown. "–" means sample is too small to make a reliable estimate.

Source: Bureau of Labor Statistics, unpublished tables from the 2004 Consumer Expenditure Survey

Table 5.14 Food and Alcohol: Indexed spending by household type, 2004

(indexed average annual spending of consumer units (CU) on food and alcoholic beverages, by type of consumer unit, 2004; index definition: an index of 100 is the average for all consumer units; an index of 132 means that spending by consumer units in that group is 32 percent above the average for all consumer units; an index of 68 indicates spending that is 32 percent below the average for all consumer units)

| | total married couples | married couples, no children | married couples with children | | | | single parent, at least one child <18 | single person |
			total	oldest child under 6	oldest child 6 to 17	oldest child 18 or older		
Average spending of CU, total	$55,607	$49,690	$60,661	$55,981	$60,578	$64,162	$32,824	$25,423
Average spending of CU, index	128	115	140	129	140	148	76	59
Food, spending index	**128**	**108**	**140**	**109**	**147**	**150**	**84**	**54**
Alcoholic beverages, spending index	**107**	**123**	**96**	**72**	**99**	**110**	**48**	**78**
FOOD AT HOME	**129**	**107**	**141**	**112**	**146**	**153**	**90**	**50**
Cereals and bakery products	**129**	**102**	**145**	**107**	**156**	**153**	**96**	**50**
Cereals and cereal products	129	96	148	104	160	157	106	47
Flour	114	89	106	94	109	111	70	68
Prepared flour mixes	138	114	153	111	159	175	100	38
Ready-to-eat and cooked cereals	128	97	149	104	167	146	116	48
Rice	132	91	156	102	171	169	102	40
Pasta, cornmeal, and other cereal products	128	90	150	103	148	193	87	50
Bakery products	129	105	144	108	154	151	91	51
Bread	125	109	135	92	142	154	88	54
White bread	121	92	136	88	141	161	113	50
Bread, other than white	128	120	134	94	142	149	71	57
Crackers and cookies	130	109	148	122	159	146	95	51
Cookies	127	100	149	116	163	148	106	53
Crackers	135	127	146	134	152	143	75	47
Frozen and refrigerated bakery products	130	93	157	130	178	136	115	47
Other bakery products	130	103	144	108	154	154	86	49
Biscuits and rolls	137	116	149	96	162	167	83	46
Cakes and cupcakes	129	88	151	137	156	152	91	48
Bread and cracker products	131	111	150	78	162	183	81	49
Sweetrolls, coffee cakes, doughnuts	128	104	138	114	149	137	81	51
Pies, tarts, turnovers	119	107	120	58	132	145	93	60
Meats, poultry, fish, and eggs	**127**	**105**	**138**	**100**	**138**	**167**	**95**	**47**
Beef	129	102	142	92	143	181	97	44
Ground beef	125	95	140	81	147	171	117	44
Roast	136	115	147	89	145	198	77	36
Chuck roast	127	96	142	73	165	151	80	44
Round roast	134	117	142	71	149	183	106	37
Other roast	142	124	152	104	134	228	62	32
Steak	129	102	143	105	136	190	90	48
Round steak	131	97	147	96	146	189	93	45
Sirloin steak	127	106	137	134	122	171	100	49
Other steak	129	100	146	91	141	202	83	49
Other beef	128	102	137	83	157	137	85	39
Pork	125	105	133	96	131	166	104	46
Bacon	124	113	128	92	129	153	107	48
Pork chops	122	91	137	102	122	197	132	45
Ham	131	111	139	104	142	159	80	50
Ham, not canned	131	109	140	105	144	161	81	49
Canned ham	129	187	78	72	69	99	49	74
Sausage	123	97	132	89	136	156	108	43
Other pork	125	110	127	92	125	160	95	45
Other meats	130	107	143	93	150	171	98	45
Frankfurters	124	90	138	100	143	157	131	43
Lunch meats (cold cuts)	131	99	153	92	161	187	89	46
Bologna, liverwurst, salami	123	99	136	79	141	172	122	46
Other lunch meats	134	99	161	98	169	193	76	46
Lamb, organ meats, and others	136	182	95	83	97	101	88	43
Poultry	126	99	139	106	144	156	87	48
Fresh and frozen chicken	125	95	139	110	142	158	91	50
Fresh and frozen whole chicken	122	87	137	105	137	163	85	51
Fresh and frozen chicken parts	126	99	140	111	144	155	93	49
Other poultry	133	114	140	92	154	150	71	43

	total married couples	married couples, no children	married couples with children				single parent, at least one child <18	single person
			total	oldest child under 6	oldest child 6 to 17	oldest child 18 or older		
Fish and seafood	128	118	129	115	125	150	88	49
Canned fish and seafood	114	104	112	81	111	140	67	59
Fresh fish and shellfish	131	121	131	125	120	159	78	46
Frozen fish and shellfish	128	118	132	110	139	134	116	52
Eggs	124	102	132	108	128	159	90	58
Dairy products	**130**	**105**	**146**	**118**	**157**	**148**	**85**	**49**
Fresh milk and cream	130	95	153	132	161	152	97	48
Fresh milk, all types	129	92	154	133	163	152	100	48
Cream	133	117	142	119	147	148	77	49
Other dairy products	130	112	142	109	153	146	78	51
Butter	119	106	128	93	141	129	75	49
Cheese	132	113	147	114	156	154	75	50
Ice cream and related products	129	115	137	90	150	147	86	49
Miscellaneous dairy products	129	108	147	139	161	125	74	55
Fruits and vegetables	**129**	**115**	**135**	**113**	**137**	**147**	**81**	**53**
Fresh fruits	131	121	133	113	137	141	80	54
Apples	133	114	145	115	154	152	66	51
Bananas	124	111	125	111	125	134	88	60
Oranges	131	121	126	101	129	141	98	51
Citrus fruits, excluding oranges	130	121	128	115	136	121	91	54
Other fresh fruits	132	126	133	115	136	142	76	54
Fresh vegetables	131	121	132	112	131	152	71	51
Potatoes	129	114	131	117	129	146	99	49
Lettuce	129	119	135	97	135	167	72	56
Tomatoes	131	115	134	121	130	153	70	53
Other fresh vegetables	133	127	131	110	130	150	63	50
Processed fruits	126	102	140	124	146	141	93	56
Frozen fruits and fruit juices	132	114	149	100	169	146	70	54
Frozen orange juice	129	95	160	117	166	182	55	55
Frozen fruits	135	146	141	83	180	107	96	56
Frozen fruit juices, excluding orange	133	102	139	97	155	137	56	47
Canned fruits	131	115	140	140	154	112	81	58
Dried fruits	135	142	135	123	131	154	43	56
Fresh fruit juice	125	97	141	105	141	170	82	55
Canned and bottled fruit juice	122	93	139	132	144	136	111	57
Processed vegetables	127	104	138	101	143	157	92	51
Frozen vegetables	126	97	140	94	145	167	98	55
Canned and dried vegetables and juices	127	107	136	105	141	151	89	49
Canned beans	126	106	136	102	141	153	101	55
Canned corn	118	82	135	87	145	150	104	50
Canned miscellaneous vegetables	135	127	136	95	134	176	76	45
Dried peas	113	117	115	110	112	130	103	60
Dried beans	106	85	106	79	124	91	100	49
Dried miscellaneous vegetables	130	99	147	116	162	140	77	39
Dried processed vegetables	160	100	237	–	380	127	–	53
Fresh and canned vegetable juices	123	100	136	139	137	130	95	54
Sugar and other sweets	**131**	**116**	**138**	**110**	**146**	**143**	**96**	**49**
Candy and chewing gum	132	114	141	120	150	138	101	48
Sugar	119	93	131	82	142	148	111	46
Artificial sweeteners	126	156	95	52	88	144	32	71
Jams, preserves, other sweets	137	124	145	108	154	157	86	47
Fats and oils	**127**	**110**	**136**	**99**	**141**	**155**	**88**	**53**
Margarine	125	123	122	67	126	159	90	60
Fats and oils	127	106	136	118	139	145	93	48
Salad dressings	124	108	135	102	143	144	89	55
Nondairy cream and imitation milk	134	123	138	96	138	173	60	51
Peanut butter	127	103	144	74	154	179	98	57

	total married couples	married couples, no children	married couples with children				single parent, at least one child <18	single person
			total	oldest child under 6	oldest child 6 to 17	oldest child 18 or older		
Miscellaneous foods	**130**	**102**	**150**	**146**	**154**	**142**	**90**	**52**
Frozen prepared foods	118	91	136	109	139	151	107	62
Frozen meals	104	92	115	97	104	152	113	89
Other frozen prepared foods	124	91	144	115	153	151	104	50
Canned and packaged soups	121	118	116	101	114	133	94	62
Potato chips, nuts, and other snacks	135	109	158	108	175	161	92	45
Potato chips and other snacks	135	93	169	120	193	159	107	40
Nuts	136	152	126	75	125	167	50	59
Condiments and seasonings	131	115	143	113	150	154	82	51
Salt, spices, and other seasonings	132	121	136	131	135	141	90	46
Olives, pickles, relishes	130	130	128	60	125	189	89	49
Sauces and gravies	131	107	148	127	157	148	78	52
Baking needs and miscellaneous products	132	116	150	93	166	162	75	54
Other canned/packaged prepared foods	134	94	163	225	161	119	82	49
Prepared salads	125	124	127	92	127	153	86	68
Prepared desserts	137	140	133	88	153	131	76	45
Baby food	154	24	262	743	176	53	76	10
Miscellaneous prepared foods	130	101	148	123	166	130	83	56
Nonalcoholic beverages	**125**	**103**	**138**	**101**	**146**	**152**	**93**	**54**
Cola	123	101	138	103	138	164	95	52
Other carbonated drinks	125	93	144	90	151	174	106	50
Coffee	124	143	108	76	114	122	61	64
Roasted coffee	124	146	108	80	113	120	59	63
Instant and freeze-dried coffee	122	139	109	71	115	125	66	66
Noncarbonated fruit-flavored drinks	124	69	164	93	206	134	152	42
Tea	131	127	132	74	129	185	76	52
Other nonalcoholic beverages and ice	125	93	146	130	158	135	88	56
Food prepared by CU on trips	**143**	**155**	**122**	**84**	**134**	**126**	**48**	**49**
FOOD AWAY FROM HOME	**126**	**111**	**139**	**104**	**148**	**147**	**76**	**58**
Meals at restaurants, carry-outs, other	**124**	**108**	**137**	**111**	**143**	**144**	**76**	**61**
Lunch	125	99	145	122	157	138	85	58
At fast-food restaurants*	120	86	148	140	154	140	90	56
At full-service restaurants	129	142	117	112	116	120	48	68
At vending machines, mobile vendors	109	83	130	43	102	257	98	98
At employer and school cafeterias	136	36	221	60	304	178	171	33
Dinner	127	121	132	105	132	154	60	61
At fast-food restaurants*	123	90	151	135	159	149	94	53
At full-service restaurants	129	135	123	92	119	157	44	66
At vending machines, mobile vendors	156	255	55	–	77	52	9	25
At employer and school cafeterias	128	32	220	113	316	104	67	78
Snacks and nonalcoholic beverages	116	89	136	108	150	127	94	65
At fast-food restaurants*	117	91	138	115	153	127	91	65
At full-service restaurants	114	119	107	77	106	131	73	68
At vending machines, mobile vendors	108	66	132	104	144	131	108	65
At employer and school cafeterias	123	61	172	66	237	121	152	54
Breakfast and brunch	122	115	126	96	127	147	82	62
At fast-food restaurants*	113	85	131	105	135	142	105	64
At full-service restaurants	132	149	120	90	114	154	54	58
At vending machines, mobile vendors	103	108	105	47	108	147	136	108
At employer and school cafeterias	111	51	151	51	215	97	149	76
Board (including at school)	**142**	**133**	**153**	**0**	**165**	**233**	**39**	**68**
Catered affairs	**137**	**171**	**100**	**63**	**68**	**185**	**23**	**25**
Food on trips	**141**	**154**	**133**	**88**	**141**	**148**	**44**	**53**
School lunches	**152**	**1**	**287**	**14**	**429**	**209**	**247**	**–**
Meals as pay	**80**	**58**	**77**	**153**	**61**	**57**	**139**	**116**

	total married couples	married couples, no children	married couples with children				single parent, at least one child <18	single person
			total	oldest child under 6	oldest child 6 to 17	oldest child 18 or older		
ALCOHOLIC BEVERAGES	**107**	**123**	**96**	**72**	**99**	**110**	**48**	**78**
At home	**106**	**114**	**102**	**74**	**111**	**107**	**54**	**72**
Beer and ale	103	83	115	91	126	112	63	77
Whiskey	98	143	70	57	74	72	29	73
Wine	111	133	99	64	104	118	45	65
Other alcoholic beverages	113	166	77	47	89	75	61	69
Away from home	**109**	**138**	**87**	**68**	**81**	**115**	**39**	**87**
Beer and ale	102	126	86	67	77	120	40	101
At fast-food restaurants*	93	106	84	76	94	70	33	115
At full-service restaurants	99	132	76	69	76	81	44	102
Wine	106	145	76	63	72	94	35	81
At fast-food restaurants*	93	106	75	59	75	90	42	97
At full-service restaurants	106	150	73	66	74	78	35	81
Other alcoholic beverages	106	141	82	59	75	114	36	83
At fast-food restaurants*	77	91	71	52	76	75	46	104
At full-service restaurants	106	147	76	61	77	84	36	84
Alcoholic beverages purchased on trips	129	156	103	82	102	119	42	69

The category fast-food restaurants also includes take-out, delivery, concession stands, buffets, and cafeterias other than employer and school.
Note: Spending index for total consumer units is 100. "–" means sample is too small to make a reliable estimate.
Source: Calculations by New Strategist based on the 2004 Consumer Expenditure Survey

Table 5.15 Food and Alcohol: Total spending by household type, 2004

(total annual spending on food and alcoholic beverages, by consumer unit (CU) type, 2004; consumer units and dollars in thousands)

	total married couples	married couples, no children	married couples with children				single parent, at least one child <18	single person
			total	oldest child under 6	oldest child 6 to 17	oldest child 18 or older		
Number of consumer units	59,797	25,585	29,279	5,604	15,376	8,300	6,892	33,686
Total spending of all CUs	$3,325,106,066	$1,271,329,652	$1,776,089,906	$313,717,748	$931,445,483	$532,542,027	$226,226,178	$856,410,968
Food, total spending	441,260,002	160,376,502	236,844,272	35,305,760	130,444,141	72,056,948	33,585,750	104,246,043
Alcoholic beverages, total spending	29,493,674	14,507,974	12,957,714	1,847,639	6,996,849	4,199,634	1,511,898	12,081,821
FOOD AT HOME	257,311,873	91,439,511	137,939,518	21,098,331	75,137,438	42,363,615	20,777,243	56,628,524
Cereals and bakery products	35,467,993	12,078,934	19,563,935	2,758,513	11,044,273	5,851,085	3,053,156	7,704,662
Cereals and cereal products	11,826,651	3,794,511	6,658,045	893,950	3,789,723	2,009,347	1,119,605	2,455,373
Flour	568,669	189,585	259,412	44,047	139,614	76,609	40,387	191,000
Prepared flour mixes	1,137,937	402,452	618,080	85,965	336,581	200,279	94,558	177,525
Ready-to-eat and cooked cereals	6,629,693	2,157,839	3,769,378	505,089	2,225,830	1,048,539	695,678	1,387,863
Rice	1,459,047	430,596	843,235	105,355	484,805	258,545	130,397	248,603
Pasta, cornmeal, and other cereal products	2,031,304	614,040	1,167,354	153,550	603,047	425,375	158,654	450,719
Bakery products	23,641,342	8,284,167	12,905,890	1,864,563	7,254,551	3,841,738	1,933,551	5,249,289
Bread	6,554,947	2,440,809	3,452,287	450,057	1,909,392	1,120,666	531,511	1,603,117
White bread	2,534,795	823,325	1,391,631	173,780	762,035	469,448	272,923	587,821
Bread, other than white	4,020,152	1,617,484	2,060,656	276,277	1,147,357	651,218	258,588	1,014,959
Crackers and cookies	5,533,614	1,991,281	3,088,056	486,876	1,740,717	865,192	468,311	1,220,781
Cookies	3,541,776	1,191,238	2,035,769	302,728	1,164,117	573,364	340,809	828,002
Crackers	1,991,838	800,043	1,052,287	184,147	576,600	291,828	127,502	392,779
Frozen and refrigerated bakery products	2,046,851	623,762	1,208,930	191,040	718,367	296,725	207,725	415,348
Other bakery products	9,505,929	3,228,571	5,156,617	736,590	2,885,921	1,559,155	725,934	2,010,044
Biscuits and rolls	3,437,730	1,248,292	1,841,649	225,785	1,047,106	582,660	241,151	645,761
Cakes and cupcakes	3,004,201	876,798	1,723,948	299,982	934,707	491,360	245,769	626,896
Bread and cracker products	255,333	92,106	143,174	14,234	81,185	49,385	18,126	53,898
Sweetrolls, coffee cakes, doughnuts	1,812,447	629,135	955,959	150,804	539,236	267,592	131,293	401,874
Pies, tarts, turnovers	996,218	382,240	491,594	45,785	283,687	168,158	89,596	281,952
Meats, poultry, fish, and eggs	67,043,200	23,607,024	35,418,514	4,905,461	18,696,755	12,159,583	5,757,921	13,855,726
Beef	20,428,449	6,906,671	11,050,480	1,365,246	5,841,496	3,981,012	1,776,551	3,925,430
Ground beef	7,249,788	2,365,333	3,965,841	437,448	2,195,693	1,379,460	780,312	1,432,329
Roast	3,716,384	1,345,003	1,964,035	226,458	1,019,275	748,162	240,324	555,482
Chuck roast	892,171	287,320	487,788	47,858	297,064	146,412	64,233	172,472
Round roast	824,601	308,299	426,302	40,853	235,407	156,206	74,916	126,659
Other roast	1,999,612	749,385	1,049,652	137,690	486,650	445,544	101,243	256,687
Steak	7,982,302	2,691,798	4,344,418	611,060	2,158,329	1,632,527	642,059	1,683,963
Round steak	1,286,831	407,825	702,696	87,927	366,871	256,885	104,965	249,276
Sirloin steak	2,460,647	879,868	1,298,816	243,438	606,891	458,907	222,749	536,281
Other steak	4,234,824	1,404,105	2,343,198	279,696	1,184,413	916,652	314,344	898,406
Other beef	1,479,976	504,536	775,894	90,336	468,199	220,780	113,856	253,656
Pork	13,559,568	4,850,404	7,032,523	979,355	3,636,270	2,493,735	1,293,835	2,812,444
Bacon	2,304,576	898,034	1,160,912	160,947	615,348	395,495	228,263	499,563
Pork chops	2,765,611	886,009	1,523,972	217,043	712,524	619,678	345,703	580,747
Ham	3,101,670	1,123,182	1,608,881	231,501	865,361	524,145	218,614	661,930
Ham, not canned	3,026,326	1,076,361	1,586,629	227,522	854,752	516,011	215,306	637,339
Canned ham	75,344	46,821	22,252	3,979	10,456	8,051	3,308	24,591
Sausage	2,048,047	693,609	1,076,296	139,147	585,057	362,378	208,414	400,527
Other pork	3,339,064	1,249,827	1,662,462	230,773	858,135	592,122	292,841	670,015
Other meats	8,394,303	2,949,183	4,536,195	561,689	2,489,989	1,529,109	727,864	1,638,150
Frankfurters	1,671,326	515,794	909,406	125,642	496,645	293,820	203,176	326,754
Lunch meats (cold cuts)	5,711,211	1,853,377	3,280,126	378,046	1,807,449	1,131,207	448,807	1,131,176
Bologna, liverwurst, salami	1,554,124	532,936	840,600	93,755	457,282	300,211	177,055	326,417
Other lunch meats	4,157,087	1,320,442	2,439,526	284,291	1,350,167	830,996	271,752	804,759
Lamb, organ meats, and others	1,011,765	579,756	346,956	58,001	185,896	104,165	75,950	179,883
Poultry	11,770,441	3,944,695	6,352,372	922,530	3,454,833	2,015,655	929,248	2,538,914
Fresh and frozen chicken	9,144,157	2,981,676	5,000,560	752,673	2,676,654	1,603,892	767,907	2,057,878
Fresh and frozen whole chicken	2,677,112	812,835	1,470,099	216,314	772,183	494,016	213,652	627,907
Fresh and frozen chicken parts	6,467,046	2,168,585	3,530,462	536,415	1,904,471	1,109,793	554,255	1,429,971
Other poultry	2,626,284	963,275	1,351,519	169,801	778,179	411,763	161,342	481,036

	total married couples	married couples, no children	married couples with children				single parent, at least one child <18	single person
			total	oldest child under 6	oldest child 6 to 17	oldest child 18 or older		
Fish and seafood	$9,793,553	$3,858,730	$4,830,742	$823,788	$2,448,936	$1,588,288	$772,111	$2,128,955
Canned fish and seafood	1,045,850	408,592	505,356	69,826	261,853	179,197	70,988	307,216
Fresh fish and shellfish	5,877,447	2,312,628	2,876,955	523,302	1,384,609	990,024	401,735	1,160,483
Frozen fish and shellfish	2,870,256	1,137,509	1,448,725	230,661	802,473	419,067	299,388	661,256
Eggs	3,096,289	1,097,085	1,616,201	252,852	825,230	551,784	258,312	811,496
Dairy products	**28,724,685**	**9,985,826**	**15,883,272**	**2,446,314**	**8,917,311**	**4,559,771**	**2,181,594**	**6,172,286**
Fresh milk and cream	11,179,647	3,496,446	6,455,727	1,066,385	3,579,072	1,818,696	965,638	2,321,976
Fresh milk, all types	9,959,788	3,036,172	5,817,737	963,776	3,230,190	1,630,203	884,450	2,069,331
Cream	1,219,859	460,530	637,989	102,665	348,881	188,493	81,188	252,982
Other dairy products	17,544,440	6,489,124	9,427,545	1,379,929	5,338,240	2,741,075	1,215,956	3,849,973
Butter	1,556,516	592,549	816,299	113,145	471,736	234,226	112,753	363,135
Cheese	8,991,077	3,288,440	4,878,760	726,222	2,718,169	1,453,911	590,782	1,920,102
Ice cream and related products	4,642,041	1,766,900	2,415,518	302,336	1,392,451	735,629	357,626	1,001,822
Miscellaneous dairy products	2,355,404	841,235	1,316,677	238,170	755,884	317,309	154,863	564,914
Fruits and vegetables	**43,396,477**	**16,467,018**	**22,135,217**	**3,554,225**	**11,848,131**	**6,834,303**	**3,140,547**	**10,034,723**
Fresh fruits	14,578,509	5,758,160	7,260,314	1,182,500	3,922,725	2,180,493	1,025,254	3,407,339
Apples	2,580,241	941,528	1,379,334	209,814	766,340	408,194	147,902	554,135
Bananas	2,242,388	855,818	1,101,769	187,958	581,367	336,399	183,603	605,337
Oranges	1,526,019	603,806	719,678	110,287	386,091	227,503	132,051	333,155
Citrus fruits, excluding oranges	1,194,744	476,904	577,089	99,359	323,050	154,214	96,557	278,583
Other fresh fruits	7,035,117	2,880,359	3,482,444	575,082	1,865,878	1,054,266	465,141	1,635,792
Fresh vegetables	14,384,168	5,686,778	7,080,833	1,147,475	3,671,789	2,306,985	895,271	3,138,525
Potatoes	2,159,868	816,673	1,072,783	183,419	555,227	339,470	192,080	459,814
Lettuce	1,766,403	697,447	907,063	124,913	474,657	316,977	112,891	429,497
Tomatoes	2,793,118	1,050,008	1,403,635	243,270	715,445	452,599	172,231	637,676
Other fresh vegetables	7,664,779	3,122,649	3,697,059	595,873	1,926,459	1,197,939	418,069	1,611,538
Processed fruits	8,245,408	2,856,309	4,505,745	762,200	2,464,004	1,286,251	701,537	2,086,511
Frozen fruits and fruit juices	787,526	291,925	433,622	56,096	258,471	120,433	48,106	180,894
Frozen orange juice	321,110	101,317	195,877	27,404	106,709	63,163	15,921	77,815
Frozen fruits	284,634	131,507	145,809	16,364	97,484	31,374	23,364	67,035
Frozen fruit juices, excluding orange	181,185	59,101	92,229	12,329	54,124	25,896	8,822	36,044
Canned fruits	1,269,490	477,416	665,804	126,931	384,092	150,479	90,630	315,638
Dried fruits	511,264	230,009	251,507	43,655	128,082	81,091	18,953	119,248
Fresh fruit juice	1,652,789	545,216	910,284	129,508	477,579	311,665	124,332	405,243
Canned and bottled fruit juice	4,023,740	1,311,743	2,244,528	406,010	1,215,627	622,666	419,516	1,065,488
Processed vegetables	6,188,392	2,166,026	3,288,324	462,050	1,789,613	1,060,574	518,485	1,402,348
Frozen vegetables	2,154,486	709,984	1,172,038	150,355	637,335	395,495	192,700	523,480
Canned and dried vegetables and juices	4,034,504	1,456,042	2,116,579	311,694	1,152,277	665,079	325,785	878,868
Canned beans	859,881	308,555	453,532	65,399	246,631	144,669	79,534	210,874
Canned corn	447,880	133,554	249,457	30,710	141,613	78,850	45,212	106,448
Canned miscellaneous vegetables	1,352,010	547,007	669,904	88,823	344,730	244,601	88,149	255,340
Dried peas	40,662	17,910	20,203	3,699	10,302	6,474	4,273	12,127
Dried beans	156,668	53,984	76,711	10,872	47,204	18,675	16,954	41,097
Dried miscellaneous vegetables	481,366	157,092	266,439	40,293	154,221	72,127	33,151	80,846
Dried processed vegetables	28,703	7,676	20,788	–	17,529	3,154	–	5,390
Fresh and canned vegetable juices	657,169	227,707	353,690	69,602	187,587	95,865	58,375	162,367
Sugar and other sweets	**10,018,987**	**3,790,418**	**5,167,158**	**786,521**	**2,877,772**	**1,520,643**	**846,958**	**2,117,165**
Candy and chewing gum	6,556,741	2,432,878	3,422,715	558,887	1,912,621	954,915	578,514	1,352,493
Sugar	1,148,102	383,263	617,787	74,197	351,342	197,291	122,678	249,613
Artificial sweeteners	514,254	274,015	190,899	19,782	93,025	82,087	15,231	164,051
Jams, preserves, other sweets	1,799,292	700,261	936,050	133,711	520,785	286,350	130,534	351,008
Fats and oils	**6,749,885**	**2,500,678**	**3,531,633**	**491,807**	**1,925,844**	**1,140,005**	**540,402**	**1,587,958**
Margarine	716,368	301,903	342,857	36,090	185,588	126,160	59,133	192,010
Fats and oils	2,171,229	773,179	1,140,710	189,079	610,735	344,865	183,258	461,835
Salad dressings	2,041,470	756,293	1,084,494	156,856	604,431	328,348	168,234	506,637
Nondairy cream and imitation milk	866,459	338,745	437,428	58,001	229,410	155,044	45,005	184,936
Peanut butter	954,360	330,558	526,436	51,837	295,680	185,588	84,772	242,202

	total married couples	married couples, no children	married couples with children				single parent, at least one child <18	single person
			total	oldest child under 6	oldest child 6 to 17	oldest child 18 or older		
Miscellaneous foods	$40,858,692	$13,751,938	$23,083,564	$4,326,960	$12,501,764	$6,224,917	$3,267,015	$9,244,786
Frozen prepared foods	7,781,384	2,565,920	4,369,598	674,161	2,342,380	1,377,634	807,742	2,277,847
Frozen meals	1,973,899	749,641	1,069,562	172,267	508,331	401,720	246,871	956,682
Other frozen prepared foods	5,808,083	1,816,023	3,300,036	501,950	1,834,049	975,914	560,802	1,321,165
Canned and packaged soups	2,647,811	1,098,364	1,243,479	206,451	640,564	404,044	235,224	767,367
Potato chips, nuts, and other snacks	9,449,720	3,258,506	5,406,660	707,617	3,155,309	1,565,795	739,787	1,788,390
Potato chips and other snacks	6,934,658	2,051,149	4,266,243	576,764	2,558,413	1,136,602	632,479	1,171,599
Nuts	2,515,062	1,207,356	1,140,124	130,853	597,050	429,193	107,308	616,791
Condiments and seasonings	7,353,237	2,743,735	3,933,634	593,239	2,160,482	1,198,271	527,652	1,599,411
Salt, spices, and other seasonings	1,753,846	686,446	884,519	163,132	462,664	260,039	138,391	343,597
Olives, pickles, relishes	817,425	348,724	393,803	35,641	201,579	164,921	64,854	174,830
Sauces and gravies	3,202,129	1,117,809	1,779,578	290,904	987,139	504,225	221,440	716,501
Baking needs and miscellaneous products	1,580,435	591,014	875,735	103,618	509,099	268,920	102,966	364,483
Other canned/packaged prepared foods	13,625,942	4,085,413	8,130,486	2,145,491	4,203,030	1,679,256	956,610	2,812,107
Prepared salads	1,902,741	810,021	941,905	131,582	496,337	323,036	151,142	581,757
Prepared desserts	893,367	391,706	426,302	53,574	255,857	118,192	56,928	164,051
Baby food	2,769,199	183,700	2,303,086	1,252,382	815,082	132,136	158,447	106,111
Miscellaneous prepared foods	7,966,754	2,659,817	4,452,458	707,897	2,629,296	1,105,975	590,162	1,938,292
Nonalcoholic beverages	21,559,210	7,632,773	11,691,397	1,635,135	6,480,830	3,646,522	1,855,740	5,230,425
Cola	6,926,884	2,434,924	3,778,162	538,881	1,997,496	1,275,046	612,974	1,643,877
Other carbonated drinks	3,606,955	1,142,114	2,031,670	241,308	1,116,605	695,374	351,561	811,833
Coffee	2,894,175	1,432,760	1,239,380	167,616	685,308	395,412	165,684	840,129
Roasted coffee	1,822,015	913,385	773,844	109,278	425,915	243,522	98,831	516,743
Instant and freeze-dried coffee	1,072,160	519,376	465,536	58,338	259,393	151,890	66,852	323,386
Noncarbonated fruit-flavored drinks	1,463,831	347,188	952,739	103,282	627,495	220,863	207,518	282,289
Tea	1,381,311	572,336	680,737	72,908	349,343	270,580	92,560	308,564
Other nonalcoholic beverages and ice	5,241,805	1,670,956	2,997,291	509,067	1,700,893	783,603	425,512	1,331,608
Food prepared by CU on trips	3,493,341	1,624,903	1,464,828	193,338	844,757	426,786	133,774	680,457
FOOD AWAY FROM HOME	183,948,129	68,936,992	98,904,462	14,207,373	55,306,857	29,693,333	12,808,506	47,617,519
Meals at restaurants, carry-outs, other	150,332,648	55,900,411	81,075,015	12,600,090	44,573,025	24,204,211	10,618,504	41,425,695
Lunch	53,999,681	18,374,124	30,727,432	4,956,850	17,464,983	8,313,695	4,223,624	14,089,843
At fast-food restaurants*	29,415,340	8,952,447	17,676,903	3,206,048	9,707,330	4,743,948	2,536,463	7,695,904
At full-service restaurants	18,245,859	8,617,796	8,074,270	1,490,384	4,237,779	2,357,200	784,172	5,389,760
At vending machines, mobile vendors	392,268	127,413	228,962	14,570	94,870	128,318	40,732	199,421
At employer and school cafeterias	5,946,214	676,467	4,747,297	245,791	3,425,004	1,084,312	862,327	804,759
Dinner	60,468,520	24,568,252	30,811,170	4,703,325	16,150,797	10,187,586	3,288,380	16,448,874
At fast-food restaurants*	18,655,468	5,827,495	11,210,051	1,912,589	6,181,306	3,123,290	1,633,611	4,484,954
At full-service restaurants	41,460,848	18,619,995	19,397,338	2,773,027	9,815,731	7,033,835	1,641,123	11,878,020
At vending machines, mobile vendors	139,925	97,991	24,302	–	17,836	6,474	896	12,801
At employer and school cafeterias	212,877	22,771	179,480	17,709	135,770	23,987	12,819	73,435
Snacks and nonalcoholic beverages	20,550,435	6,777,978	11,806,464	1,806,505	6,858,157	3,144,870	1,922,730	6,506,114
At fast-food restaurants*	15,171,695	5,043,315	8,790,727	1,404,082	5,098,220	2,280,425	1,364,961	4,760,169
At full-service restaurants	1,976,291	875,519	902,672	125,305	471,889	314,736	145,077	660,246
At vending machines, mobile vendors	2,643,027	697,191	1,592,192	238,786	910,874	445,378	304,351	896,721
At employer and school cafeterias	758,824	161,953	520,873	38,275	377,020	104,248	108,342	189,315
Breakfast and brunch	15,313,414	6,180,313	7,729,949	1,133,409	4,099,088	2,558,060	1,183,701	4,380,527
At fast-food restaurants*	6,982,496	2,256,085	3,951,787	608,650	2,145,875	1,216,448	745,990	2,230,350
At full-service restaurants	7,913,535	3,820,096	3,513,187	506,602	1,764,550	1,283,844	372,995	1,970,631
At vending machines, mobile vendors	87,304	39,145	43,626	3,755	23,525	17,347	13,302	51,876
At employer and school cafeterias	330,677	64,986	221,056	14,402	165,138	40,421	51,414	127,333
Board (including at school)	2,362,579	952,018	1,247,578	224	707,604	539,832	75,192	634,644
Catered affairs	4,812,463	2,560,803	1,715,164	206,788	609,658	898,724	91,388	489,121
Food on trips	19,506,379	9,151,243	8,986,603	1,139,854	5,011,653	2,835,363	710,083	4,115,082
School lunches	5,766,225	8,955	5,326,728	50,436	4,176,737	1,099,833	1,079,494	–
Meals as pay	1,168,433	363,563	553,373	210,038	228,026	115,287	233,914	952,977

	total married couples	married couples, no children	married couples with children				single parent, at least one child <18	single person
			total	oldest child under 6	oldest child 6 to 17	oldest child 18 or older		
ALCOHOLIC BEVERAGES	**$29,493,674**	**$14,507,974**	**$12,957,714**	**$1,847,639**	**$6,996,849**	**$4,199,634**	**$1,511,898**	**$12,081,821**
At home	**17,645,497**	**8,088,442**	**8,306,745**	**1,156,890**	**4,724,584**	**2,461,614**	**1,028,700**	**6,740,569**
Beer and ale	8,086,348	2,791,324	4,433,426	669,790	2,547,649	1,222,424	566,247	3,426,203
Whiskey	1,264,707	792,112	444,748	69,714	247,707	128,567	42,593	533,586
Wine	6,270,313	3,226,269	2,749,591	338,201	1,515,612	922,462	293,048	2,086,174
Other alcoholic beverages	2,024,128	1,278,738	678,394	79,185	413,461	188,161	126,813	694,942
Away from home	**11,848,178**	**6,419,532**	**4,651,262**	**690,805**	**2,272,265**	**1,738,020**	**483,198**	**5,341,252**
Beer and ale	4,637,257	2,454,881	1,927,437	288,270	907,338	760,446	209,586	2,586,074
At fast-food restaurants*	914,296	447,738	405,807	69,938	238,636	95,450	37,906	638,687
At full-service restaurants	3,321,723	1,888,685	1,249,042	217,491	657,785	377,733	169,819	1,921,786
Wine	1,416,591	828,442	496,572	79,072	247,554	174,466	53,689	610,390
At fast-food restaurants*	170,421	83,151	67,634	10,143	35,211	22,825	8,960	99,711
At full-service restaurants	1,192,352	719,962	401,122	68,873	212,035	121,678	44,729	510,006
Other alcoholic beverages	2,829,594	1,609,297	1,070,440	146,825	517,402	422,885	109,858	1,254,804
At fast-food restaurants*	176,999	88,524	79,346	11,096	44,898	23,738	12,061	134,407
At full-service restaurants	2,493,535	1,482,907	873,685	135,785	468,814	273,983	96,626	1,117,701
Alcoholic beverages purchased on trips	2,965,333	1,526,657	1,156,813	176,638	599,972	380,223	109,996	889,984

The category fast-food restaurants also includes take-out, delivery, concession stands, buffets, and cafeterias other than employer and school.
Note: Total spending figures for total consumer units can be found on Total Spending by Age and Total Spending by Region tables. Spending by type of consumer unit will not add to total because not all types of consumer units are shown. Numbers may not add to category total because of rounding and missing subcategories. "–" means sample is too small to make a reliable estimate.
Source: Calculations by New Strategist based on the 2004 Consumer Expenditure Survey

Table 5.16 Food and Alcohol: Market shares by household type, 2004

(percentage of total annual spending on food and alcoholic beverages accounted for by types of consumer units, 2004)

	total married couples	married couples, no children	married couples with children				single parent, at least one child <18	single person
			total	oldest child under 6	oldest child 6 to 17	oldest child 18 or older		
Share of total consumer units	51.4%	22.0%	25.2%	4.8%	13.2%	7.1%	5.9%	29.0%
Share of total before-tax income	68.9	26.0	36.9	6.7	19.1	11.2	3.4	15.0
Share of total spending	65.9	25.2	35.2	6.2	18.5	10.6	4.5	17.0
Share of food spending	65.6	23.9	35.2	5.3	19.4	10.7	5.0	15.5
Share of alcoholic beverages spending	55.2	27.2	24.3	3.5	13.1	7.9	2.8	22.6
FOOD AT HOME	66.1	23.5	35.4	5.4	19.3	10.9	5.3	14.6
Cereals and bakery products	66.2	22.5	36.5	5.1	20.6	10.9	5.7	14.4
Cereals and cereal products	66.1	21.2	37.2	5.0	21.2	11.2	6.3	13.7
Flour	58.8	19.6	26.8	4.6	14.4	7.9	4.2	19.7
Prepared flour mixes	71.0	25.1	38.6	5.4	21.0	12.5	5.9	11.1
Ready-to-eat and cooked cereals	65.8	21.4	37.4	5.0	22.1	10.4	6.9	13.8
Rice	68.0	20.1	39.3	4.9	22.6	12.0	6.1	11.6
Pasta, cornmeal, and other cereal products	65.8	19.9	37.8	5.0	19.5	13.8	5.1	14.6
Bakery products	66.2	23.2	36.1	5.2	20.3	10.8	5.4	14.7
Bread	64.3	24.0	33.9	4.4	18.7	11.0	5.2	15.7
White bread	62.2	20.2	34.2	4.3	18.7	11.5	6.7	14.4
Bread, other than white	65.7	26.4	33.7	4.5	18.8	10.6	4.2	16.6
Crackers and cookies	66.9	24.1	37.3	5.9	21.0	10.5	5.7	14.8
Cookies	65.4	22.0	37.6	5.6	21.5	10.6	6.3	15.3
Crackers	69.6	28.0	36.8	6.4	20.2	10.2	4.5	13.7
Frozen and refrigerated bakery products	66.9	20.4	39.5	6.2	23.5	9.7	6.8	13.6
Other bakery products	67.0	22.8	36.4	5.2	20.3	11.0	5.1	14.2
Biscuits and rolls	70.2	25.5	37.6	4.6	21.4	11.9	4.9	13.2
Cakes and cupcakes	66.2	19.3	38.0	6.6	20.6	10.8	5.4	13.8
Bread and cracker products	67.6	24.4	37.9	3.8	21.5	13.1	4.8	14.3
Sweetrolls, coffee cakes, doughnuts	66.1	22.9	34.8	5.5	19.7	9.8	4.8	14.7
Pies, tarts, turnovers	61.2	23.5	30.2	2.8	17.4	10.3	5.5	17.3
Meats, poultry, fish, and eggs	65.5	23.1	34.6	4.8	18.3	11.9	5.6	13.5
Beef	66.2	22.4	35.8	4.4	18.9	12.9	5.8	12.7
Ground beef	64.3	21.0	35.2	3.9	19.5	12.2	6.9	12.7
Roast	70.1	25.4	37.1	4.3	19.2	14.1	4.5	10.5
Chuck roast	65.5	21.1	35.8	3.5	21.8	10.7	4.7	12.7
Round roast	69.0	25.8	35.7	3.4	19.7	13.1	6.3	10.6
Other roast	72.9	27.3	38.3	5.0	17.7	16.2	3.7	9.4
Steak	66.4	22.4	36.1	5.1	17.9	13.6	5.3	14.0
Round steak	67.6	21.4	36.9	4.6	19.3	13.5	5.5	13.1
Sirloin steak	65.4	23.4	34.5	6.5	16.1	12.2	5.9	14.2
Other steak	66.6	22.1	36.8	4.4	18.6	14.4	4.9	14.1
Other beef	65.6	22.4	34.4	4.0	20.8	9.8	5.0	11.3
Pork	64.4	23.0	33.4	4.6	17.3	11.8	6.1	13.4
Bacon	63.8	24.8	32.1	4.5	17.0	10.9	6.3	13.8
Pork chops	62.7	20.1	34.6	4.9	16.2	14.1	7.8	13.2
Ham	67.3	24.4	34.9	5.0	18.8	11.4	4.7	14.4
Ham, not canned	67.3	23.9	35.3	5.1	19.0	11.5	4.8	14.2
Canned ham	66.1	41.1	19.5	3.5	9.2	7.1	2.9	21.6
Sausage	63.1	21.4	33.2	4.3	18.0	11.2	6.4	12.3
Other pork	64.4	24.1	32.1	4.5	16.6	11.4	5.6	12.9
Other meats	66.9	23.5	36.1	4.5	19.8	12.2	5.8	13.0
Frankfurters	63.8	19.7	34.7	4.8	19.0	11.2	7.8	12.5
Lunch meats (cold cuts)	67.3	21.8	38.6	4.5	21.3	13.3	5.3	13.3
Bologna, liverwurst, salami	63.4	21.8	34.3	3.8	18.7	12.3	7.2	13.3
Other lunch meats	68.9	21.9	40.4	4.7	22.4	13.8	4.5	13.3
Lamb, organ meats, and others	69.7	40.0	23.9	4.0	12.8	7.2	5.2	12.4
Poultry	65.0	21.8	35.1	5.1	19.1	11.1	5.1	14.0
Fresh and frozen chicken	64.1	20.9	35.1	5.3	18.8	11.2	5.4	14.4
Fresh and frozen whole chicken	62.9	19.1	34.6	5.1	18.1	11.6	5.0	14.8
Fresh and frozen chicken parts	64.6	21.7	35.3	5.4	19.0	11.1	5.5	14.3
Other poultry	68.5	25.1	35.3	4.4	20.3	10.7	4.2	12.5

	total married couples	married couples, no children	married couples with children				single parent, at least one child <18	single person
			total	oldest child under 6	oldest child 6 to 17	oldest child 18 or older		
Fish and seafood	65.9%	26.0%	32.5%	5.5%	16.5%	10.7%	5.2%	14.3%
Canned fish and seafood	58.5	22.8	28.3	3.9	14.6	10.0	4.0	17.2
Fresh fish and shellfish	67.5	26.6	33.0	6.0	15.9	11.4	4.6	13.3
Frozen fish and shellfish	65.8	26.1	33.2	5.3	18.4	9.6	6.9	15.1
Eggs	63.6	22.5	33.2	5.2	17.0	11.3	5.3	16.7
Dairy products	**66.7**	**23.2**	**36.9**	**5.7**	**20.7**	**10.6**	**5.1**	**14.3**
Fresh milk and cream	66.6	20.8	38.5	6.4	21.3	10.8	5.8	13.8
Fresh milk, all types	66.4	20.3	38.8	6.4	21.5	10.9	5.9	13.8
Cream	68.2	25.7	35.7	5.7	19.5	10.5	4.5	14.1
Other dairy products	66.7	24.7	35.8	5.2	20.3	10.4	4.6	14.6
Butter	61.4	23.4	32.2	4.5	18.6	9.2	4.4	14.3
Cheese	68.0	24.9	36.9	5.5	20.6	11.0	4.5	14.5
Ice cream and related products	66.3	25.2	34.5	4.3	19.9	10.5	5.1	14.3
Miscellaneous dairy products	66.3	23.7	37.1	6.7	21.3	8.9	4.4	15.9
Fruits and vegetables	**66.5**	**25.2**	**33.9**	**5.4**	**18.2**	**10.5**	**4.8**	**15.4**
Fresh fruits	67.1	26.5	33.4	5.4	18.1	10.0	4.7	15.7
Apples	68.4	25.0	36.6	5.6	20.3	10.8	3.9	14.7
Bananas	63.9	24.4	31.4	5.4	16.6	9.6	5.2	17.3
Oranges	67.4	26.7	31.8	4.9	17.0	10.0	5.8	14.7
Citrus fruits, excluding oranges	66.7	26.6	32.2	5.5	18.0	8.6	5.4	15.5
Other fresh fruits	67.8	27.8	33.6	5.5	18.0	10.2	4.5	15.8
Fresh vegetables	67.6	26.7	33.3	5.4	17.3	10.8	4.2	14.8
Potatoes	66.2	25.0	32.9	5.6	17.0	10.4	5.9	14.1
Lettuce	66.4	26.2	34.1	4.7	17.8	11.9	4.2	16.2
Tomatoes	67.2	25.3	33.8	5.9	17.2	10.9	4.1	15.3
Other fresh vegetables	68.5	27.9	33.0	5.3	17.2	10.7	3.7	14.4
Processed fruits	64.7	22.4	35.3	6.0	19.3	10.1	5.5	16.4
Frozen fruits and fruit juices	67.9	25.2	37.4	4.8	22.3	10.4	4.1	15.6
Frozen orange juice	66.2	20.9	40.4	5.7	22.0	13.0	3.3	16.0
Frozen fruits	69.3	32.0	35.5	4.0	23.7	7.6	5.7	16.3
Frozen fruit juices, excluding orange	68.6	22.4	34.9	4.7	20.5	9.8	3.3	13.7
Canned fruits	67.4	25.4	35.4	6.7	20.4	8.0	4.8	16.8
Dried fruits	69.2	31.2	34.1	5.9	17.3	11.0	2.6	16.1
Fresh fruit juice	64.4	21.2	35.5	5.0	18.6	12.1	4.8	15.8
Canned and bottled fruit juice	62.9	20.5	35.1	6.3	19.0	9.7	6.6	16.6
Processed vegetables	65.2	22.8	34.6	4.9	18.9	11.2	5.5	14.8
Frozen vegetables	65.0	21.4	35.4	4.5	19.2	11.9	5.8	15.8
Canned and dried vegetables and juices	65.3	23.6	34.3	5.0	18.6	10.8	5.3	14.2
Canned beans	64.9	23.3	34.2	4.9	18.6	10.9	6.0	15.9
Canned corn	60.8	18.1	33.9	4.2	19.2	10.7	6.1	14.5
Canned miscellaneous vegetables	69.3	28.1	34.4	4.6	17.7	12.5	4.5	13.1
Dried peas	58.3	25.7	29.0	5.3	14.8	9.3	6.1	17.4
Dried beans	54.5	18.8	26.7	3.8	16.4	6.5	5.9	14.3
Dried miscellaneous vegetables	66.7	21.8	36.9	5.6	21.4	10.0	4.6	11.2
Dried processed vegetables	82.3	22.0	59.6	–	50.2	9.0	–	15.5
Fresh and canned vegetable juices	63.4	22.0	34.1	6.7	18.1	9.3	5.6	15.7
Sugar and other sweets	**67.3**	**25.4**	**34.7**	**5.3**	**19.3**	**10.2**	**5.7**	**14.2**
Candy and chewing gum	67.8	25.2	35.4	5.8	19.8	9.9	6.0	14.0
Sugar	61.3	20.5	33.0	4.0	18.8	10.5	6.6	13.3
Artificial sweeteners	64.6	34.4	24.0	2.5	11.7	10.3	1.9	20.6
Jams, preserves, other sweets	70.2	27.3	36.5	5.2	20.3	11.2	5.1	13.7
Fats and oils	**65.3**	**24.2**	**34.2**	**4.8**	**18.6**	**11.0**	**5.2**	**15.4**
Margarine	64.4	27.1	30.8	3.2	16.7	11.3	5.3	17.3
Fats and oils	65.4	23.3	34.3	5.7	18.4	10.4	5.5	13.9
Salad dressings	64.0	23.7	34.0	4.9	18.9	10.3	5.3	15.9
Nondairy cream and imitation milk	69.0	27.0	34.8	4.6	18.3	12.3	3.6	14.7
Peanut butter	65.6	22.7	36.2	3.6	20.3	12.7	5.8	16.6

	total married couples	married couples, no children	married couples with children				single parent, at least one child <18	single person
			total	oldest child under 6	oldest child 6 to 17	oldest child 18 or older		
Miscellaneous foods	**66.6%**	**22.4%**	**37.6%**	**7.1%**	**20.4%**	**10.2%**	**5.3%**	**15.1%**
Frozen prepared foods	60.9	20.1	34.2	5.3	18.3	10.8	6.3	17.8
Frozen meals	53.4	20.3	28.9	4.7	13.8	10.9	6.7	25.9
Other frozen prepared foods	63.9	20.0	36.3	5.5	20.2	10.7	6.2	14.5
Canned and packaged soups	62.4	25.9	29.3	4.9	15.1	9.5	5.5	18.1
Potato chips, nuts, and other snacks	69.4	23.9	39.7	5.2	23.2	11.5	5.4	13.1
Potato chips and other snacks	69.3	20.5	42.6	5.8	25.6	11.4	6.3	11.7
Nuts	69.7	33.5	31.6	3.6	16.6	11.9	3.0	17.1
Condiments and seasonings	67.5	25.2	36.1	5.4	19.8	11.0	4.8	14.7
Salt, spices, and other seasonings	67.9	26.6	34.2	6.3	17.9	10.1	5.4	13.3
Olives, pickles, relishes	66.8	28.5	32.2	2.9	16.5	13.5	5.3	14.3
Sauces and gravies	67.3	23.5	37.4	6.1	20.7	10.6	4.7	15.1
Baking needs and miscellaneous products	68.1	25.5	37.7	4.5	21.9	11.6	4.4	15.7
Other canned/packaged prepared foods	68.9	20.6	41.1	10.8	21.2	8.5	4.8	14.2
Prepared salads	64.3	27.4	31.9	4.4	16.8	10.9	5.1	19.7
Prepared desserts	70.4	30.9	33.6	4.2	20.2	9.3	4.5	12.9
Baby food	79.2	5.3	65.8	35.8	23.3	3.8	4.5	3.0
Miscellaneous prepared foods	66.7	22.3	37.3	5.9	22.0	9.3	4.9	16.2
Nonalcoholic beverages	**64.0**	**22.7**	**34.7**	**4.9**	**19.3**	**10.8**	**5.5**	**15.5**
Cola	63.5	22.3	34.6	4.9	18.3	11.7	5.6	15.1
Other carbonated drinks	64.5	20.4	36.3	4.3	20.0	12.4	6.3	14.5
Coffee	63.6	31.5	27.2	3.7	15.1	8.7	3.6	18.5
Roasted coffee	64.0	32.1	27.2	3.8	15.0	8.6	3.5	18.2
Instant and freeze-dried coffee	63.0	30.5	27.3	3.4	15.2	8.9	3.9	19.0
Noncarbonated fruit-flavored drinks	63.6	15.1	41.4	4.5	27.3	9.6	9.0	12.3
Tea	67.4	27.9	33.2	3.6	17.0	13.2	4.5	15.1
Other nonalcoholic beverages and ice	64.3	20.5	36.8	6.2	20.9	9.6	5.2	16.3
Food prepared by CU on trips	**73.5**	**34.2**	**30.8**	**4.1**	**17.8**	**9.0**	**2.8**	**14.3**
FOOD AWAY FROM HOME	**65.0**	**24.4**	**34.9**	**5.0**	**19.5**	**10.5**	**4.5**	**16.8**
Meals at restaurants, carry-outs, other	63.7	23.7	34.4	5.3	18.9	10.3	4.5	17.6
Lunch	64.0	21.8	36.4	5.9	20.7	9.9	5.0	16.7
At fast-food restaurants*	61.8	18.8	37.2	6.7	20.4	10.0	5.3	16.2
At full-service restaurants	66.3	31.3	29.3	5.4	15.4	8.6	2.8	19.6
At vending machines, mobile vendors	56.0	18.2	32.7	2.1	13.6	18.3	5.8	28.5
At employer and school cafeterias	69.8	7.9	55.7	2.9	40.2	12.7	10.1	9.4
Dinner	65.4	26.6	33.3	5.1	17.5	11.0	3.6	17.8
At fast-food restaurants*	63.4	19.8	38.1	6.5	21.0	10.6	5.6	15.2
At full-service restaurants	66.2	29.8	31.0	4.4	15.7	11.2	2.6	19.0
At vending machines, mobile vendors	80.2	56.2	13.9	–	10.2	3.7	0.5	7.3
At employer and school cafeterias	65.6	7.0	55.3	5.5	41.8	7.4	4.0	22.6
Snacks and nonalcoholic beverages	59.4	19.6	34.1	5.2	19.8	9.1	5.6	18.8
At fast-food restaurants*	60.1	20.0	34.8	5.6	20.2	9.0	5.4	18.9
At full-service restaurants	58.9	26.1	26.9	3.7	14.1	9.4	4.3	19.7
At vending machines, mobile vendors	55.3	14.6	33.3	5.0	19.1	9.3	6.4	18.8
At employer and school cafeterias	63.1	13.5	43.3	3.2	31.4	8.7	9.0	15.7
Breakfast and brunch	62.7	25.3	31.6	4.6	16.8	10.5	4.8	17.9
At fast-food restaurants*	58.1	18.8	32.9	5.1	17.9	10.1	6.2	18.6
At full-service restaurants	67.8	32.7	30.1	4.3	15.1	11.0	3.2	16.9
At vending machines, mobile vendors	52.9	23.7	26.4	2.3	14.2	10.5	8.1	31.4
At employer and school cafeterias	56.9	11.2	38.0	2.5	28.4	7.0	8.8	21.9
Board (including at school)	**72.8**	**29.4**	**38.5**	**0.0**	**21.8**	**16.6**	**2.3**	**19.6**
Catered affairs	**70.7**	**37.6**	**25.2**	**3.0**	**9.0**	**13.2**	**1.3**	**7.2**
Food on trips	**72.4**	**34.0**	**33.4**	**4.2**	**18.6**	**10.5**	**2.6**	**15.3**
School lunches	**78.2**	**0.1**	**72.3**	**0.7**	**56.7**	**14.9**	**14.6**	**–**
Meals as pay	**41.1**	**12.8**	**19.5**	**7.4**	**8.0**	**4.1**	**8.2**	**33.5**

	total married couples	married couples, no children	married couples with children			single parent, at least one child <18	single person
			total	oldest child under 6	oldest child 6 to 17	oldest child 18 or older	
ALCOHOLIC BEVERAGES	**55.2%**	**27.2%**	**24.3%**	**3.5%**	**13.1%**	**7.9%**	**2.8%**	**22.6%**
At home	**54.7**	**25.1**	**25.7**	**3.6**	**14.6**	**7.6**	**3.2**	**20.9**
Beer and ale	53.0	18.3	29.0	4.4	16.7	8.0	3.7	22.4
Whiskey	50.2	31.4	17.7	2.8	9.8	5.1	1.7	21.2
Wine	57.0	29.3	25.0	3.1	13.8	8.4	2.7	19.0
Other alcoholic beverages	57.9	36.6	19.4	2.3	11.8	5.4	3.6	19.9
Away from home	**56.1**	**30.4**	**22.0**	**3.3**	**10.8**	**8.2**	**2.3**	**25.3**
Beer and ale	52.3	27.7	21.7	3.2	10.2	8.6	2.4	29.1
At fast-food restaurants*	47.8	23.4	21.2	3.7	12.5	5.0	2.0	33.4
At full-service restaurants	51.0	29.0	19.2	3.3	10.1	5.8	2.6	29.5
Wine	54.7	32.0	19.2	3.1	9.6	6.7	2.1	23.5
At fast-food restaurants*	47.9	23.4	19.0	2.9	9.9	6.4	2.5	28.0
At full-service restaurants	54.7	33.0	18.4	3.2	9.7	5.6	2.1	23.4
Other alcoholic beverages	54.4	31.0	20.6	2.8	10.0	8.1	2.1	24.1
At fast-food restaurants*	39.8	19.9	17.9	2.5	10.1	5.3	2.7	30.3
At full-service restaurants	54.4	32.3	19.1	3.0	10.2	6.0	2.1	24.4
Alcoholic beverages purchased on trips	66.5	34.2	25.9	4.0	13.4	8.5	2.5	19.9

The category fast-food restaurants also includes take-out, delivery, concession stands, buffets, and cafeterias other than employer and school.
Note: Market share for total consumer units is 100.0%. Market shares by type of consumer unit will not add to total because not all types of consumer units are shown. "–" means sample is too small to make a reliable estimate.
Source: Calculations by New Strategist based on the 2004 Consumer Expenditure Survey

Table 5.17 Food and Alcohol: Average spending by race and Hispanic origin, 2004

(average annual spending of consumer units (CU) on food and alcoholic beverages, by race and Hispanic origin of consumer unit reference person, 2004)

	total consumer units	Asian	black	Hispanic	non-Hispanic white and other
Number of consumer units (in 000s)	116,282	3,957	13,773	12,298	90,424
Average number of persons per CU	2.5	2.8	2.6	3.3	2.3
Average before-tax income of CU	$54,453.00	$67,705.00	$38,503.00	$43,693.00	$58,314.00
Average spending of CU, total	43,394.87	49,458.68	30,481.49	37,578.03	46,163.26
Food, average spending	**5,780.82**	**6,741.86**	**4,265.37**	**5,910.71**	**5,999.27**
Alcoholic beverages, average spending	**459.27**	**325.05**	**171.14**	**320.35**	**522.81**
FOOD AT HOME	**3,346.82**	**3,688.75**	**2,749.11**	**3,883.27**	**3,366.58**
Cereals and bakery products	**460.90**	**527.28**	**387.98**	**517.00**	**464.41**
Cereals and cereal products	153.80	242.86	152.10	201.86	147.44
Flour	8.32	8.34	12.05	22.83	5.68
Prepared flour mixes	13.78	4.99	10.95	12.65	14.35
Ready-to-eat and cooked cereals	86.69	54.86	84.48	102.67	85.02
Rice	18.46	138.59	21.65	31.38	16.13
Pasta, cornmeal, and other cereal products	26.55	36.09	22.97	32.33	26.26
Bakery products	307.10	284.41	235.87	315.13	316.97
Bread	87.63	91.14	72.05	98.52	88.48
White bread	35.04	40.13	33.99	47.03	33.52
Bread, other than white	52.59	51.01	38.07	51.49	54.96
Crackers and cookies	71.16	55.79	50.54	67.58	74.93
Cookies	46.57	34.96	38.01	47.40	47.83
Crackers	24.60	20.83	12.53	20.18	27.10
Frozen and refrigerated bakery products	26.32	17.59	23.20	18.27	27.89
Other bakery products	121.99	119.88	90.08	130.77	125.67
Biscuits and rolls	42.11	35.88	24.52	30.75	46.46
Cakes and cupcakes	39.04	44.28	32.62	55.86	37.61
Bread and cracker products	3.25	0.86	1.65	1.58	3.73
Sweetrolls, coffee cakes, doughnuts	23.59	22.59	18.67	29.04	23.63
Pies, tarts, turnovers	13.99	16.27	12.61	13.53	14.24
Meats, poultry, fish, and eggs	**879.71**	**1,020.56**	**897.94**	**1,175.16**	**836.10**
Beef	265.34	231.29	215.76	367.20	258.89
Ground beef	96.92	62.73	94.18	124.51	93.49
Roast	45.58	43.66	44.93	61.78	43.50
Chuck roast	11.72	8.72	12.49	19.40	10.50
Round roast	10.27	6.92	9.07	13.23	10.08
Other roast	23.58	28.02	23.36	29.15	22.92
Steak	103.45	96.87	59.11	143.91	104.71
Round steak	16.37	15.20	10.17	28.93	15.54
Sirloin steak	32.38	35.67	18.03	51.12	32.06
Other steak	54.71	46.01	30.91	63.87	57.11
Other beef	19.39	28.02	17.55	37.01	17.20
Pork	181.14	182.77	208.27	236.40	169.40
Bacon	31.08	12.78	39.23	35.42	29.16
Pork chops	37.92	35.24	53.85	57.96	32.77
Ham	39.65	28.19	32.07	56.43	38.44
Ham, not canned	38.67	27.33	31.36	54.60	37.55
Canned ham	0.98	0.86	0.72	1.83	0.89
Sausage	27.91	22.67	42.83	26.65	25.86
Other pork	44.59	83.88	40.28	59.93	43.17
Other meats	107.98	63.93	86.92	112.58	110.67
Frankfurters	22.52	10.44	24.72	25.14	21.85
Lunch meats (cold cuts)	72.99	28.93	51.10	70.29	76.81
Bologna, liverwurst, salami	21.07	7.42	21.89	26.49	20.16
Other lunch meats	51.91	21.51	29.21	43.80	56.65
Lamb, organ meats, and others	12.48	24.55	11.10	17.15	12.02
Poultry	155.61	192.10	185.67	231.21	140.36
Fresh and frozen chicken	122.64	158.46	141.72	196.03	109.39
Fresh and frozen whole chicken	36.59	70.44	43.58	76.57	29.91
Fresh and frozen chicken parts	86.04	88.02	98.13	119.46	79.48
Other poultry	32.97	33.65	43.95	35.18	30.98

	total consumer units	Asian	black	Hispanic	non-Hispanic white and other
Fish and seafood	$127.80	$304.55	$157.45	$159.40	$118.95
Canned fish and seafood	15.38	12.14	11.64	17.61	15.66
Fresh fish and shellfish	74.88	199.26	104.49	103.46	66.47
Frozen fish and shellfish	37.54	93.15	41.32	38.34	36.81
Eggs	41.84	45.93	43.85	68.37	37.82
Dairy products	**370.57**	**286.19**	**248.71**	**425.16**	**382.21**
Fresh milk and cream	144.33	134.95	99.56	201.36	143.47
Fresh milk, all types	128.94	128.57	94.96	184.77	126.59
Cream	15.39	6.38	4.60	16.59	16.89
Other dairy products	226.24	151.24	149.15	223.80	238.74
Butter	21.81	15.55	23.14	15.13	22.54
Cheese	113.67	44.87	59.12	116.18	121.91
Ice cream and related products	60.22	58.45	47.17	59.63	62.38
Miscellaneous dairy products	30.54	32.37	19.72	32.86	31.92
Fruits and vegetables	**560.95**	**869.97**	**441.98**	**712.21**	**558.92**
Fresh fruits	186.74	329.28	129.63	249.12	186.93
Apples	32.42	47.12	21.80	41.33	32.83
Bananas	30.17	51.20	26.83	46.81	28.38
Oranges	19.48	49.37	17.48	30.22	18.26
Citrus fruits, excluding oranges	15.41	24.44	7.13	26.67	15.09
Other fresh fruits	89.25	157.15	56.38	104.08	92.37
Fresh vegetables	182.94	358.72	120.19	250.30	183.43
Potatoes	28.07	42.39	28.31	36.65	26.86
Lettuce	22.87	34.86	11.59	30.02	23.65
Tomatoes	35.74	66.28	23.23	64.88	33.62
Other fresh vegetables	96.25	215.20	57.06	118.74	99.30
Processed fruits	109.63	118.47	106.58	126.63	108.08
Frozen fruits and fruit juices	9.97	6.80	7.52	8.91	10.48
Frozen orange juice	4.17	2.49	3.52	3.78	4.32
Frozen fruits	3.53	3.18	1.42	1.92	4.07
Frozen fruit juices, excluding orange	2.27	1.13	2.58	3.21	2.09
Canned fruits	16.19	14.97	11.86	11.00	17.60
Dried fruits	6.35	9.22	2.81	4.57	7.13
Fresh fruit juice	22.07	28.16	22.52	26.10	21.42
Canned and bottled fruit juice	55.05	59.32	61.88	76.05	51.45
Processed vegetables	81.64	63.50	85.59	86.17	80.48
Frozen vegetables	28.50	21.11	32.46	15.86	29.68
Canned and dried vegetables and juices	53.14	42.38	53.12	70.31	50.81
Canned beans	11.39	6.88	14.23	16.44	10.26
Canned corn	6.33	5.30	8.74	10.46	5.38
Canned miscellaneous vegetables	16.77	9.53	15.15	14.37	17.34
Dried peas	0.60	0.94	0.66	0.49	0.61
Dried beans	2.47	2.43	2.04	8.73	1.68
Dried miscellaneous vegetables	6.21	6.13	5.70	8.53	5.98
Dried processed vegetables	0.30	0.12	0.17	0.87	0.24
Fresh and canned vegetable juices	8.91	10.89	6.42	10.26	9.14
Sugar and other sweets	**128.12**	**137.05**	**93.82**	**116.41**	**135.11**
Candy and chewing gum	83.13	107.64	47.76	65.61	91.01
Sugar	16.10	11.97	22.44	24.19	14.05
Artificial sweeteners	6.85	5.45	7.62	5.76	6.88
Jams, preserves, other sweets	22.04	11.99	16.00	20.85	23.17
Fats and oils	**88.89**	**76.21**	**85.36**	**107.34**	**86.94**
Margarine	9.57	4.38	9.75	7.26	9.86
Fats and oils	28.56	40.13	36.34	54.22	23.87
Salad dressings	27.44	17.71	22.92	26.04	28.34
Nondairy cream and imitation milk	10.80	7.11	7.39	7.79	11.74
Peanut butter	12.52	6.88	8.96	12.03	13.14

	total consumer units	Asian	black	Hispanic	non-Hispanic white and other
Miscellaneous foods	**$527.29**	**$479.20**	**$353.23**	**$471.33**	**$562.44**
Frozen prepared foods	109.90	70.70	78.49	66.34	120.71
Frozen meals	31.79	21.72	24.34	16.25	35.08
Other frozen prepared foods	78.11	48.98	54.15	50.09	85.63
Canned and packaged soups	36.50	40.62	25.77	28.93	39.31
Potato chips, nuts, and other snacks	117.08	97.71	73.18	87.11	127.96
Potato chips and other snacks	86.06	53.70	58.78	67.70	92.78
Nuts	31.01	44.01	14.41	19.41	35.17
Condiments and seasonings	93.65	98.25	63.44	80.11	100.32
Salt, spices, and other seasonings	22.22	40.64	19.01	26.19	22.21
Olives, pickles, relishes	10.52	4.56	4.26	7.63	11.90
Sauces and gravies	40.94	38.22	29.61	31.77	44.03
Baking needs and miscellaneous products	19.97	14.84	10.56	14.52	22.18
Other canned/packaged prepared foods	170.16	171.91	112.35	208.84	174.14
Prepared salads	25.43	16.74	14.02	13.11	28.91
Prepared desserts	10.91	4.38	4.61	9.95	12.00
Baby food	30.08	58.63	30.89	58.86	26.38
Miscellaneous prepared foods	102.74	90.70	62.82	126.91	105.56
Nonalcoholic beverages	**289.52**	**245.21**	**226.76**	**328.03**	**294.05**
Cola	93.81	54.39	70.54	118.92	93.84
Other carbonated drinks	48.08	28.59	39.52	42.72	50.15
Coffee	39.12	38.97	22.81	33.95	42.45
Roasted coffee	24.48	23.89	13.75	18.07	27.02
Instant and freeze-dried coffee	14.64	15.08	9.06	15.88	15.43
Noncarbonated fruit-flavored drinks	19.79	11.36	28.27	32.14	16.89
Tea	17.63	20.72	12.62	16.49	18.68
Other nonalcoholic beverages and ice	70.10	91.19	50.04	83.54	71.28
Food prepared by CU on trips	**40.86**	**47.09**	**13.32**	**30.63**	**46.40**
FOOD AWAY FROM HOME	2,434.00	3,053.11	1,516.26	2,027.44	2,632.69
Meals at restaurants, carry-outs, other	2,028.17	2,506.17	1,331.82	1,731.29	2,178.68
Lunch	725.07	1,044.21	526.70	691.92	760.89
At fast-food restaurants*	409.17	575.18	333.59	470.06	412.91
At full-service restaurants	236.65	385.21	106.66	145.55	269.56
At vending machines, mobile vendors	6.02	4.73	5.90	14.85	4.78
At employer and school cafeterias	73.24	79.09	80.54	61.45	73.63
Dinner	795.59	959.86	413.03	578.02	885.28
At fast-food restaurants*	253.07	274.71	205.13	273.20	257.81
At full-service restaurants	538.22	684.62	197.57	301.00	624.06
At vending machines, mobile vendors	1.50	–	3.57	2.12	1.09
At employer and school cafeterias	2.79	0.52	6.77	1.70	2.32
Snacks and nonalcoholic beverages	297.45	328.62	225.22	280.55	311.05
At fast-food restaurants*	217.16	242.19	155.95	189.66	230.54
At full-service restaurants	28.87	40.36	15.34	27.31	31.16
At vending machines, mobile vendors	41.07	35.21	43.61	53.80	38.95
At employer and school cafeterias	10.34	10.85	10.31	9.79	10.41
Breakfast and brunch	210.06	173.48	166.88	180.80	221.45
At fast-food restaurants*	103.28	101.28	109.60	123.60	100.19
At full-service restaurants	100.36	64.45	48.14	48.90	115.54
At vending machines, mobile vendors	1.42	0.68	2.49	3.28	1.00
At employer and school cafeterias	5.00	7.07	6.65	5.02	4.73
Board (including at school)	**27.89**	**76.53**	**12.74**	**13.47**	**32.10**
Catered affairs	**58.56**	**35.25**	**39.67**	**32.19**	**64.91**
Food on trips	**231.55**	**248.65**	**75.17**	**158.92**	**264.88**
School lunches	**63.39**	**93.85**	**46.31**	**59.94**	**66.44**
Meals as pay	**24.45**	**92.65**	**10.54**	**31.63**	**25.68**

	total consumer units	Asian	black	Hispanic	non-Hispanic white and other
ALCOHOLIC BEVERAGES	$459.27	$325.05	$171.14	$320.35	$522.81
At home	277.59	148.83	112.28	220.15	311.00
Beer and ale	131.31	61.83	61.14	163.56	137.46
Whiskey	21.66	18.00	16.34	8.27	24.33
Wine	94.55	64.51	22.72	29.06	114.87
Other alcoholic beverages	30.07	4.49	12.08	19.26	34.35
Away from home	181.68	176.22	58.87	100.20	211.80
Beer and ale	76.32	74.04	24.16	42.16	89.16
At fast-food restaurants*	16.44	9.28	8.25	9.52	18.72
At full-service restaurants	56.01	64.36	15.10	31.46	65.72
Wine	22.29	25.66	6.79	12.50	26.04
At fast-food restaurants*	3.06	2.00	2.82	1.30	3.34
At full-service restaurants	18.76	23.65	3.91	11.17	22.10
Other alcoholic beverages	44.71	50.13	17.54	24.17	51.74
At fast-food restaurants*	3.82	3.29	2.18	1.02	4.47
At full-service restaurants	39.44	46.84	15.09	22.88	45.49
Alcoholic beverages purchased on trips	38.37	26.39	10.38	21.37	44.86

* The category fast-food restaurants also includes take-out, delivery, concession stands, buffets, and cafeterias other than employer and school.

Note: "Asian" and "black" include Hispanics and non-Hispanics who identify themselves as being of the respective race alone. "Hispanic" includes people of any race who identify themselves as Hispanic. "Other" includes people who identify themselves as non-Hispanic and as Alaska Native, American Indian, Asian (who are also included in the "Asian" column), Native Hawaiian or other Pacific Islander, as well as non-Hispanics reporting more than one race. Subcategories may not add to total because some are not shown. "–" means sample is too small to make a reliable estimate.

Source: Bureau of Labor Statistics, unpublished tables from the 2004 Consumer Expenditure Survey

Table 5.18 Food and Alcohol: Indexed spending by race and Hispanic origin, 2004

(indexed average annual spending of consumer units (CU) on food and alcoholic beverages, by race and Hispanic origin of consumer unit reference person, 2004; index definition: an index of 100 is the average for all consumer units; an index of 132 means that spending by consumer units in that group is 32 percent above the average for all consumer units; an index of 68 indicates spending that is 32 percent below the average for all consumer units)

	total consumer units	Asian	black	Hispanic	non-Hispanic white and other
Average spending of CU, total	$43,395	$49,459	$30,481	$37,578	$46,163
Average spending of CU, index	100	114	70	87	106
Food, spending index	100	117	74	102	104
Alcoholic beverages, spending index	100	71	37	70	114
FOOD AT HOME	100	110	82	116	101
Cereals and bakery products	100	114	84	112	101
Cereals and cereal products	100	158	99	131	96
Flour	100	100	145	274	68
Prepared flour mixes	100	36	79	92	104
Ready-to-eat and cooked cereals	100	63	97	118	98
Rice	100	751	117	170	87
Pasta, cornmeal, and other cereal products	100	136	87	122	99
Bakery products	100	93	77	103	103
Bread	100	104	82	112	101
White bread	100	115	97	134	96
Bread, other than white	100	97	72	98	105
Crackers and cookies	100	78	71	95	105
Cookies	100	75	82	102	103
Crackers	100	85	51	82	110
Frozen and refrigerated bakery products	100	67	88	69	106
Other bakery products	100	98	74	107	103
Biscuits and rolls	100	85	58	73	110
Cakes and cupcakes	100	113	84	143	96
Bread and cracker products	100	26	51	49	115
Sweetrolls, coffee cakes, doughnuts	100	96	79	123	100
Pies, tarts, turnovers	100	116	90	97	102
Meats, poultry, fish, and eggs	100	116	102	134	95
Beef	100	87	81	138	98
Ground beef	100	65	97	128	96
Roast	100	96	99	136	95
Chuck roast	100	74	107	166	90
Round roast	100	67	88	129	98
Other roast	100	119	99	124	97
Steak	100	94	57	139	101
Round steak	100	93	62	177	95
Sirloin steak	100	110	56	158	99
Other steak	100	84	56	117	104
Other beef	100	145	91	191	89
Pork	100	101	115	131	94
Bacon	100	41	126	114	94
Pork chops	100	93	142	153	86
Ham	100	71	81	142	97
Ham, not canned	100	71	81	141	97
Canned ham	100	88	73	187	91
Sausage	100	81	153	95	93
Other pork	100	188	90	134	97
Other meats	100	59	80	104	102
Frankfurters	100	46	110	112	97
Lunch meats (cold cuts)	100	40	70	96	105
Bologna, liverwurst, salami	100	35	104	126	96
Other lunch meats	100	41	56	84	109
Lamb, organ meats, and others	100	197	89	137	96
Poultry	100	123	119	149	90
Fresh and frozen chicken	100	129	116	160	89
Fresh and frozen whole chicken	100	193	119	209	82
Fresh and frozen chicken parts	100	102	114	139	92
Other poultry	100	102	133	107	94

	total consumer units	Asian	black	Hispanic	non-Hispanic white and other
Fish and seafood	100	238	123	125	93
Canned fish and seafood	100	79	76	114	102
Fresh fish and shellfish	100	266	140	138	89
Frozen fish and shellfish	100	248	110	102	98
Eggs	100	110	105	163	90
Dairy products	**100**	**77**	**67**	**115**	**103**
Fresh milk and cream	100	94	69	140	99
Fresh milk, all types	100	100	74	143	98
Cream	100	41	30	108	110
Other dairy products	100	67	66	99	106
Butter	100	71	106	69	103
Cheese	100	39	52	102	107
Ice cream and related products	100	97	78	99	104
Miscellaneous dairy products	100	106	65	108	105
Fruits and vegetables	**100**	**155**	**79**	**127**	**100**
Fresh fruits	100	176	69	133	100
Apples	100	145	67	127	101
Bananas	100	170	89	155	94
Oranges	100	253	90	155	94
Citrus fruits, excluding oranges	100	159	46	173	98
Other fresh fruits	100	176	63	117	103
Fresh vegetables	100	196	66	137	100
Potatoes	100	151	101	131	96
Lettuce	100	152	51	131	103
Tomatoes	100	185	65	182	94
Other fresh vegetables	100	224	59	123	103
Processed fruits	100	108	97	116	99
Frozen fruits and fruit juices	100	68	75	89	105
Frozen orange juice	100	60	84	91	104
Frozen fruits	100	90	40	54	115
Frozen fruit juices, excluding orange	100	50	114	141	92
Canned fruits	100	92	73	68	109
Dried fruits	100	145	44	72	112
Fresh fruit juice	100	128	102	118	97
Canned and bottled fruit juice	100	108	112	138	93
Processed vegetables	100	78	105	106	99
Frozen vegetables	100	74	114	56	104
Canned and dried vegetables and juices	100	80	100	132	96
Canned beans	100	60	125	144	90
Canned corn	100	84	138	165	85
Canned miscellaneous vegetables	100	57	90	86	103
Dried peas	100	157	110	82	102
Dried beans	100	98	83	353	68
Dried miscellaneous vegetables	100	99	92	137	96
Dried processed vegetables	100	40	57	290	80
Fresh and canned vegetable juices	100	122	72	115	103
Sugar and other sweets	**100**	**107**	**73**	**91**	**105**
Candy and chewing gum	100	129	57	79	109
Sugar	100	74	139	150	87
Artificial sweeteners	100	80	111	84	100
Jams, preserves, other sweets	100	54	73	95	105
Fats and oils	**100**	**86**	**96**	**121**	**98**
Margarine	100	46	102	76	103
Fats and oils	100	141	127	190	84
Salad dressings	100	65	84	95	103
Nondairy cream and imitation milk	100	66	68	72	109
Peanut butter	100	55	72	96	105

	total consumer units	Asian	black	Hispanic	non-Hispanic white and other
Miscellaneous foods	**100**	**91**	**67**	**89**	**107**
Frozen prepared foods	100	64	71	60	110
Frozen meals	100	68	77	51	110
Other frozen prepared foods	100	63	69	64	110
Canned and packaged soups	100	111	71	79	108
Potato chips, nuts, and other snacks	100	83	63	74	109
Potato chips and other snacks	100	62	68	79	108
Nuts	100	142	46	63	113
Condiments and seasonings	100	105	68	86	107
Salt, spices, and other seasonings	100	183	86	118	100
Olives, pickles, relishes	100	43	40	73	113
Sauces and gravies	100	93	72	78	108
Baking needs and miscellaneous products	100	74	53	73	111
Other canned/packaged prepared foods	100	101	66	123	102
Prepared salads	100	66	55	52	114
Prepared desserts	100	40	42	91	110
Baby food	100	195	103	196	88
Miscellaneous prepared foods	100	88	61	124	103
Nonalcoholic beverages	**100**	**85**	**78**	**113**	**102**
Cola	100	58	75	127	100
Other carbonated drinks	100	59	82	89	104
Coffee	100	100	58	87	109
Roasted coffee	100	98	56	74	110
Instant and freeze-dried coffee	100	103	62	108	105
Noncarbonated fruit-flavored drinks	100	57	143	162	85
Tea	100	118	72	94	106
Other nonalcoholic beverages and ice	100	130	71	119	102
Food prepared by CU on trips	**100**	**115**	**33**	**75**	**114**
FOOD AWAY FROM HOME	**100**	**125**	**62**	**83**	**108**
Meals at restaurants, carry-outs, other	**100**	**124**	**66**	**85**	**107**
Lunch	100	144	73	95	105
At fast-food restaurants*	100	141	82	115	101
At full-service restaurants	100	163	45	62	114
At vending machines, mobile vendors	100	79	98	247	79
At employer and school cafeterias	100	108	110	84	101
Dinner	100	121	52	73	111
At fast-food restaurants*	100	109	81	108	102
At full-service restaurants	100	127	37	56	116
At vending machines, mobile vendors	100	–	238	141	73
At employer and school cafeterias	100	19	243	61	83
Snacks and nonalcoholic beverages	100	110	76	94	105
At fast-food restaurants*	100	112	72	87	106
At full-service restaurants	100	140	53	95	108
At vending machines, mobile vendors	100	86	106	131	95
At employer and school cafeterias	100	105	100	95	101
Breakfast and brunch	100	83	79	86	105
At fast-food restaurants*	100	98	106	120	97
At full-service restaurants	100	64	48	49	115
At vending machines, mobile vendors	100	48	175	231	70
At employer and school cafeterias	100	141	133	100	95
Board (including at school)	**100**	**274**	**46**	**48**	**115**
Catered affairs	**100**	**60**	**68**	**55**	**111**
Food on trips	**100**	**107**	**32**	**69**	**114**
School lunches	**100**	**148**	**73**	**95**	**105**
Meals as pay	**100**	**379**	**43**	**129**	**105**

	total consumer units	Asian	black	Hispanic	non-Hispanic white and other
ALCOHOLIC BEVERAGES	**100**	**71**	**37**	**70**	**114**
At home	**100**	**54**	**40**	**79**	**112**
Beer and ale	100	47	47	125	105
Whiskey	100	83	75	38	112
Wine	100	68	24	31	121
Other alcoholic beverages	100	15	40	64	114
Away from home	**100**	**97**	**32**	**55**	**117**
Beer and ale	100	97	32	55	117
At fast-food restaurants*	100	56	50	58	114
At full-service restaurants	100	115	27	56	117
Wine	100	115	30	56	117
At fast-food restaurants*	100	65	92	42	109
At full-service restaurants	100	126	21	60	118
Other alcoholic beverages	100	112	39	54	116
At fast-food restaurants*	100	86	57	27	117
At full-service restaurants	100	119	38	58	115
Alcoholic beverages purchased on trips	100	69	27	56	117

* The category fast-food restaurants also includes take-out, delivery, concession stands, buffets, and cafeterias other than employer and school.
Note: "Asian" and "black" include Hispanics and non-Hispanics who identify themselves as being of the respective race alone. "Hispanic" includes people of any race who identify themselves as Hispanic. "Other" includes people who identify themselves as non-Hispanic and as Alaska Native, American Indian, Asian (who are also included in the "Asian" column), Native Hawaiian or other Pacific Islander, as well as non-Hispanics reporting more than one race. "–" means sample is too small to make a reliable estimate.
Source: Calculations by New Strategist based on the 2004 Consumer Expenditure Survey

Table 5.19 Food and Alcohol: Total spending by race and Hispanic origin, 2004

(total annual spending on food and alcoholic beverages, by consumer unit race and Hispanic origin groups, 2004; consumer units and dollars in thousands)

	total consumer units	Asian	black	Hispanic	non-Hispanic white and other
Number of consumer units	116,282	3,957	13,773	12,298	90,424
Total spending of all consumer units	$5,046,042,273	$195,707,997	$419,821,562	$462,134,613	$4,174,266,622
Food, total spending	672,205,311	26,677,540	58,746,941	72,689,912	542,477,990
Alcoholic beverages, total spending	53,404,834	1,286,223	2,357,111	3,939,664	47,274,571
FOOD AT HOME	389,174,923	14,596,384	37,863,492	47,756,454	304,419,630
Cereals and bakery products	53,594,374	2,086,447	5,343,649	6,358,066	41,993,810
Cereals and cereal products	17,884,172	960,997	2,094,873	2,482,474	13,332,115
Flour	967,466	33,001	165,965	280,763	513,608
Prepared flour mixes	1,602,366	19,745	150,814	155,570	1,297,584
Ready-to-eat and cooked cereals	10,080,487	217,081	1,163,543	1,262,636	7,687,848
Rice	2,146,566	548,401	298,185	385,911	1,458,539
Pasta, cornmeal, and other cereal products	3,087,287	142,808	316,366	397,594	2,374,534
Bakery products	35,710,202	1,125,410	3,248,638	3,875,469	28,661,695
Bread	10,189,792	360,641	992,345	1,211,599	8,000,716
White bread	4,074,521	158,794	468,144	578,375	3,031,012
Bread, other than white	6,115,270	201,847	524,338	633,224	4,969,703
Crackers and cookies	8,274,627	220,761	696,087	831,099	6,775,470
Cookies	5,415,253	138,337	523,512	582,925	4,324,980
Crackers	2,860,537	82,424	172,576	248,174	2,450,490
Frozen and refrigerated bakery products	3,060,542	69,604	319,534	224,684	2,521,925
Other bakery products	14,185,241	474,365	1,240,672	1,608,209	11,363,584
Biscuits and rolls	4,896,635	141,977	337,714	378,164	4,201,099
Cakes and cupcakes	4,539,649	175,216	449,275	686,966	3,400,847
Bread and cracker products	377,917	3,403	22,725	19,431	337,282
Sweetrolls, coffee cakes, doughnuts	2,743,092	89,389	257,142	357,134	2,136,719
Pies, tarts, turnovers	1,626,785	64,380	173,678	166,392	1,287,638
Meats, poultry, fish, and eggs	102,294,438	4,038,356	12,367,328	14,452,118	75,603,506
Beef	30,854,266	915,215	2,971,662	4,515,826	23,409,869
Ground beef	11,270,051	248,223	1,297,141	1,531,224	8,453,740
Roast	5,300,134	172,763	618,821	759,770	3,933,444
Chuck roast	1,362,825	34,505	172,025	238,581	949,452
Round roast	1,194,216	27,382	124,921	162,703	911,474
Other roast	2,741,930	110,875	321,737	358,487	2,072,518
Steak	12,029,373	383,315	814,122	1,769,805	9,468,297
Round steak	1,903,536	60,146	140,071	355,781	1,405,189
Sirloin steak	3,765,211	141,146	248,327	628,674	2,898,993
Other steak	6,361,788	182,062	425,723	785,473	5,164,115
Other beef	2,254,708	110,875	241,716	455,149	1,555,293
Pork	21,063,321	723,221	2,868,503	2,907,247	15,317,826
Bacon	3,614,045	50,570	540,315	435,595	2,636,764
Pork chops	4,409,413	139,445	741,676	712,792	2,963,194
Ham	4,610,581	111,548	441,700	693,976	3,475,899
Ham, not canned	4,496,625	108,145	431,921	671,471	3,395,421
Canned ham	113,956	3,403	9,917	22,505	80,477
Sausage	3,245,431	89,705	589,898	327,742	2,338,365
Other pork	5,185,014	331,913	554,776	737,019	3,903,604
Other meats	12,556,130	252,971	1,197,149	1,384,509	10,007,224
Frankfurters	2,618,671	41,311	340,469	309,172	1,975,764
Lunch meats (cold cuts)	8,487,423	114,476	703,800	864,426	6,945,467
Bologna, liverwurst, salami	2,450,062	29,361	301,491	325,774	1,822,948
Other lunch meats	6,036,199	85,115	402,309	538,652	5,122,520
Lamb, organ meats, and others	1,451,199	97,144	152,880	210,911	1,086,896
Poultry	18,094,642	760,140	2,557,233	2,843,421	12,691,913
Fresh and frozen chicken	14,260,824	627,026	1,951,910	2,410,777	9,891,481
Fresh and frozen whole chicken	4,254,758	278,731	600,227	941,658	2,704,582
Fresh and frozen chicken parts	10,004,903	348,295	1,351,544	1,469,119	7,186,900
Other poultry	3,833,818	133,153	605,323	432,644	2,801,336

	total consumer units	Asian	black	Hispanic	non-Hispanic white and other
Fish and seafood	$14,860,840	$1,205,104	$2,168,559	$1,960,301	$10,755,935
Canned fish and seafood	1,788,417	48,038	160,318	216,568	1,416,040
Fresh fish and shellfish	8,707,196	788,472	1,439,141	1,272,351	6,010,483
Frozen fish and shellfish	4,365,226	368,595	569,100	471,505	3,328,507
Eggs	4,865,239	181,745	603,946	840,814	3,419,836
Dairy products	**43,090,621**	**1,132,454**	**3,425,483**	**5,228,618**	**34,560,957**
Fresh milk and cream	16,782,981	533,997	1,371,240	2,476,325	12,973,131
Fresh milk, all types	14,993,401	508,751	1,307,884	2,272,301	11,446,774
Cream	1,789,580	25,246	63,356	204,024	1,527,261
Other dairy products	26,307,640	598,457	2,054,243	2,752,292	21,587,826
Butter	2,536,110	61,531	318,707	186,069	2,038,157
Cheese	13,217,775	177,551	814,260	1,428,782	11,023,590
Ice cream and related products	7,002,502	231,287	649,672	733,330	5,640,649
Miscellaneous dairy products	3,551,252	128,088	271,604	404,112	2,886,334
Fruits and vegetables	**65,228,388**	**3,442,471**	**6,087,391**	**8,758,759**	**50,539,782**
Fresh fruits	21,714,501	1,302,961	1,785,394	3,063,678	16,902,958
Apples	3,769,862	186,454	300,251	508,276	2,968,620
Bananas	3,508,228	202,598	369,530	575,669	2,566,233
Oranges	2,265,173	195,357	240,752	371,646	1,651,142
Citrus fruits, excluding oranges	1,791,906	96,709	98,201	327,988	1,364,498
Other fresh fruits	10,378,169	621,843	776,522	1,279,976	8,352,465
Fresh vegetables	21,272,629	1,419,455	1,655,377	3,078,189	16,586,474
Potatoes	3,264,036	167,737	389,914	450,722	2,428,789
Lettuce	2,659,369	137,941	159,629	369,186	2,138,528
Tomatoes	4,155,919	262,270	319,947	797,894	3,040,055
Other fresh vegetables	11,192,143	851,546	785,887	1,460,265	8,979,103
Processed fruits	12,747,996	468,786	1,467,926	1,557,296	9,773,026
Frozen fruits and fruit juices	1,159,332	26,908	103,573	109,575	947,644
Frozen orange juice	484,896	9,853	48,481	46,486	390,632
Frozen fruits	410,475	12,583	19,558	23,612	368,026
Frozen fruit juices, excluding orange	263,960	4,471	35,534	39,477	188,986
Canned fruits	1,882,606	59,236	163,348	135,278	1,591,462
Dried fruits	738,391	36,484	38,702	56,202	644,723
Fresh fruit juice	2,566,344	111,429	310,168	320,978	1,936,882
Canned and bottled fruit juice	6,401,324	234,729	852,273	935,263	4,652,315
Processed vegetables	9,493,262	251,270	1,178,831	1,059,719	7,277,324
Frozen vegetables	3,314,037	83,532	447,072	195,046	2,683,784
Canned and dried vegetables and juices	6,179,225	167,698	731,622	864,672	4,594,443
Canned beans	1,324,452	27,224	195,990	202,179	927,750
Canned corn	736,065	20,972	120,376	128,637	486,481
Canned miscellaneous vegetables	1,950,049	37,710	208,661	176,722	1,567,952
Dried peas	69,769	3,720	9,090	6,026	55,159
Dried beans	287,217	9,616	28,097	107,362	151,912
Dried miscellaneous vegetables	722,111	24,256	78,506	104,902	540,736
Dried processed vegetables	34,885	475	2,341	10,699	21,702
Fresh and canned vegetable juices	1,036,073	43,092	88,423	126,177	826,475
Sugar and other sweets	**14,898,050**	**542,307**	**1,292,183**	**1,431,610**	**12,217,187**
Candy and chewing gum	9,666,523	425,931	657,798	806,872	8,229,488
Sugar	1,872,140	47,365	309,066	297,489	1,270,457
Artificial sweeteners	796,532	21,566	104,950	70,836	622,117
Jams, preserves, other sweets	2,562,855	47,444	220,368	256,413	2,095,124
Fats and oils	**10,336,307**	**301,563**	**1,175,663**	**1,320,067**	**7,861,463**
Margarine	1,112,819	17,332	134,287	89,283	891,581
Fats and oils	3,321,014	158,794	500,511	666,798	2,158,421
Salad dressings	3,190,778	70,078	315,677	320,240	2,562,616
Nondairy cream and imitation milk	1,255,846	28,134	101,782	95,801	1,061,578
Peanut butter	1,455,851	27,224	123,406	147,945	1,188,171

	total consumer units	Asian	black	Hispanic	non-Hispanic white and other
Miscellaneous foods	$61,314,336	$1,896,194	$4,865,037	$5,796,416	$50,858,075
Frozen prepared foods	12,779,392	279,760	1,081,043	815,849	10,915,081
Frozen meals	3,696,605	85,946	335,235	199,843	3,172,074
Other frozen prepared foods	9,082,787	193,814	745,808	616,007	7,743,007
Canned and packaged soups	4,244,293	160,733	354,930	355,781	3,554,567
Potato chips, nuts, and other snacks	13,614,297	386,638	1,007,908	1,071,279	11,570,655
Potato chips and other snacks	10,007,229	212,491	809,577	832,575	8,389,539
Nuts	3,605,905	174,148	198,469	238,704	3,180,212
Condiments and seasonings	10,889,809	388,775	873,759	985,193	9,071,336
Salt, spices, and other seasonings	2,583,786	160,812	261,825	322,085	2,008,317
Olives, pickles, relishes	1,223,287	18,044	58,673	93,834	1,076,046
Sauces and gravies	4,760,585	151,237	407,819	390,707	3,981,369
Baking needs and miscellaneous products	2,322,152	58,722	145,443	178,567	2,005,604
Other canned/packaged prepared foods	19,786,545	680,248	1,547,397	2,568,314	15,746,435
Prepared salads	2,957,051	66,240	193,097	161,227	2,614,158
Prepared desserts	1,268,637	17,332	63,494	122,365	1,085,088
Baby food	3,497,763	231,999	425,448	723,860	2,385,385
Miscellaneous prepared foods	11,946,813	358,900	865,220	1,560,739	9,545,157
Nonalcoholic beverages	33,665,965	970,296	3,123,165	4,034,113	26,589,177
Cola	10,908,414	215,221	971,547	1,462,478	8,485,388
Other carbonated drinks	5,590,839	113,131	544,309	525,371	4,534,764
Coffee	4,548,952	154,204	314,162	417,517	3,838,499
Roasted coffee	2,846,583	94,533	189,379	222,225	2,443,256
Instant and freeze-dried coffee	1,702,368	59,672	124,783	195,292	1,395,242
Noncarbonated fruit-flavored drinks	2,301,221	44,952	389,363	395,258	1,527,261
Tea	2,050,052	81,989	173,815	202,794	1,689,120
Other nonalcoholic beverages and ice	8,151,368	360,839	689,201	1,027,375	6,445,423
Food prepared by CU on trips	4,751,283	186,335	183,456	376,688	4,195,674
FOOD AWAY FROM HOME	283,030,388	12,081,156	20,883,449	24,933,457	238,058,361
Meals at restaurants, carry-outs, other	235,839,664	9,916,915	18,343,157	21,291,404	197,004,960
Lunch	84,312,590	4,131,939	7,254,239	8,509,232	68,802,717
At fast-food restaurants*	47,579,106	2,275,987	4,594,535	5,780,798	37,336,974
At full-service restaurants	27,518,135	1,524,276	1,469,028	1,789,974	24,374,693
At vending machines, mobile vendors	700,018	18,717	81,261	182,625	432,227
At employer and school cafeterias	8,516,494	312,959	1,109,277	755,712	6,657,919
Dinner	92,512,796	3,798,166	5,688,662	7,108,490	80,050,559
At fast-food restaurants*	29,427,486	1,087,027	2,825,255	3,359,814	23,312,211
At full-service restaurants	62,585,298	2,709,041	2,721,132	3,701,698	56,430,001
At vending machines, mobile vendors	174,423	–	49,170	26,072	98,562
At employer and school cafeterias	324,427	2,058	93,243	20,907	209,784
Snacks and nonalcoholic beverages	34,588,081	1,300,349	3,101,955	3,450,204	28,126,385
At fast-food restaurants*	25,251,799	958,346	2,147,899	2,332,439	20,846,349
At full-service restaurants	3,357,061	159,705	211,278	335,858	2,817,612
At vending machines, mobile vendors	4,775,702	139,326	600,641	661,632	3,522,015
At employer and school cafeterias	1,202,356	42,933	142,000	120,397	941,314
Breakfast and brunch	24,426,197	686,460	2,298,438	2,223,478	20,024,395
At fast-food restaurants*	12,009,605	400,765	1,509,521	1,520,033	9,059,581
At full-service restaurants	11,670,062	255,029	663,032	601,372	10,447,589
At vending machines, mobile vendors	165,120	2,691	34,295	40,337	90,424
At employer and school cafeterias	581,410	27,976	91,590	61,736	427,706
Board (including at school)	3,243,105	302,829	175,468	165,654	2,902,610
Catered affairs	6,809,474	139,484	546,375	395,873	5,869,422
Food on trips	26,925,097	983,908	1,035,316	1,954,398	23,951,509
School lunches	7,371,116	371,364	637,828	737,142	6,007,771
Meals as pay	2,843,095	366,616	145,167	388,986	2,322,088

	total consumer units	Asian	black	Hispanic	non-Hispanic white and other
ALCOHOLIC BEVERAGES	**$53,404,834**	**$1,286,223**	**$2,357,111**	**$3,939,664**	**$47,274,571**
At home	**32,278,720**	**588,920**	**1,546,432**	**2,707,405**	**28,121,864**
Beer and ale	15,268,989	244,661	842,081	2,011,461	12,429,683
Whiskey	2,518,668	71,226	225,051	101,704	2,200,016
Wine	10,994,463	255,266	312,923	357,380	10,387,005
Other alcoholic beverages	3,496,600	17,767	166,378	236,859	3,106,064
Away from home	**21,126,114**	**697,303**	**810,817**	**1,232,260**	**19,151,803**
Beer and ale	8,874,642	292,976	332,756	518,484	8,062,204
At fast-food restaurants*	1,911,676	36,721	113,627	117,077	1,692,737
At full-service restaurants	6,512,955	254,673	207,972	386,895	5,942,665
Wine	2,591,926	101,537	93,519	153,725	2,354,641
At fast-food restaurants*	355,823	7,914	38,840	15,987	302,016
At full-service restaurants	2,181,450	93,583	53,852	137,369	1,998,370
Other alcoholic beverages	5,198,968	198,364	241,578	297,243	4,678,538
At fast-food restaurants*	444,197	13,019	30,025	12,544	404,195
At full-service restaurants	4,586,162	185,346	207,835	281,378	4,113,388
Alcoholic beverages purchased on trips	4,461,740	104,425	142,964	262,808	4,056,421

The category fast-food restaurants also includes take-out, delivery, concession stands, buffets, and cafeterias other than employer and school.

Note: "Asian" and "black" include Hispanics and non-Hispanics who identify themselves as being of the respective race alone. "Hispanic" includes people of any race who identify themselves as Hispanic. "Other" includes people who identify themselves as non-Hispanic and as Alaska Native, American Indian, Asian (who are also included in the "Asian" column), Native Hawaiian or other Pacific Islander, as well as non-Hispanics reporting more than one race. Numbers may not add to total because of rounding and missing subcategories. "–" means sample is too small to make a reliable estimate.

Source: Calculations by New Strategist based on the 2004 Consumer Expenditure Survey

Table 5.20 Food and Alcohol: Market shares by race and Hispanic origin, 2004

(percentage of total annual spending on food and alcoholic beverages accounted for by consumer unit race and Hispanic origin groups, 2004)

	total consumer units	Asian	black	Hispanic	non-Hispanic white and other
Share of total consumer units	100.0%	3.4%	11.8%	10.6%	77.8%
Share of total before-tax income	100.0	4.2	8.4	8.5	83.3
Share of total spending	100.0	3.9	8.3	9.2	82.7
Share of food spending	100.0	4.0	8.7	10.8	80.7
Share of alcoholic beverages spending	100.0	2.4	4.4	7.4	88.5
FOOD AT HOME	100.0	3.8	9.7	12.3	78.2
Cereals and bakery products	100.0	3.9	10.0	11.9	78.4
Cereals and cereal products	100.0	5.4	11.7	13.9	74.5
Flour	100.0	3.4	17.2	29.0	53.1
Prepared flour mixes	100.0	1.2	9.4	9.7	81.0
Ready-to-eat and cooked cereals	100.0	2.2	11.5	12.5	76.3
Rice	100.0	25.5	13.9	18.0	67.9
Pasta, cornmeal, and other cereal products	100.0	4.6	10.2	12.9	76.9
Bakery products	100.0	3.2	9.1	10.9	80.3
Bread	100.0	3.5	9.7	11.9	78.5
White bread	100.0	3.9	11.5	14.2	74.4
Bread, other than white	100.0	3.3	8.6	10.4	81.3
Crackers and cookies	100.0	2.7	8.4	10.0	81.9
Cookies	100.0	2.6	9.7	10.8	79.9
Crackers	100.0	2.9	6.0	8.7	85.7
Frozen and refrigerated bakery products	100.0	2.3	10.4	7.3	82.4
Other bakery products	100.0	3.3	8.7	11.3	80.1
Biscuits and rolls	100.0	2.9	6.9	7.7	85.8
Cakes and cupcakes	100.0	3.9	9.9	15.1	74.9
Bread and cracker products	100.0	0.9	6.0	5.1	89.2
Sweetrolls, coffee cakes, doughnuts	100.0	3.3	9.4	13.0	77.9
Pies, tarts, turnovers	100.0	4.0	10.7	10.2	79.2
Meats, poultry, fish, and eggs	100.0	3.9	12.1	14.1	73.9
Beef	100.0	3.0	9.6	14.6	75.9
Ground beef	100.0	2.2	11.5	13.6	75.0
Roast	100.0	3.3	11.7	14.3	74.2
Chuck roast	100.0	2.5	12.6	17.5	69.7
Round roast	100.0	2.3	10.5	13.6	76.3
Other roast	100.0	4.0	11.7	13.1	75.6
Steak	100.0	3.2	6.8	14.7	78.7
Round steak	100.0	3.2	7.4	18.7	73.8
Sirloin steak	100.0	3.7	6.6	16.7	77.0
Other steak	100.0	2.9	6.7	12.3	81.2
Other beef	100.0	4.9	10.7	20.2	69.0
Pork	100.0	3.4	13.6	13.8	72.7
Bacon	100.0	1.4	15.0	12.1	73.0
Pork chops	100.0	3.2	16.8	16.2	67.2
Ham	100.0	2.4	9.6	15.1	75.4
Ham, not canned	100.0	2.4	9.6	14.9	75.5
Canned ham	100.0	3.0	8.7	19.7	70.6
Sausage	100.0	2.8	18.2	10.1	72.1
Other pork	100.0	6.4	10.7	14.2	75.3
Other meats	100.0	2.0	9.5	11.0	79.7
Frankfurters	100.0	1.6	13.0	11.8	75.4
Lunch meats (cold cuts)	100.0	1.3	8.3	10.2	81.8
Bologna, liverwurst, salami	100.0	1.2	12.3	13.3	74.4
Other lunch meats	100.0	1.4	6.7	8.9	84.9
Lamb, organ meats, and others	100.0	6.7	10.5	14.5	74.9
Poultry	100.0	4.2	14.1	15.7	70.1
Fresh and frozen chicken	100.0	4.4	13.7	16.9	69.4
Fresh and frozen whole chicken	100.0	6.6	14.1	22.1	63.6
Fresh and frozen chicken parts	100.0	3.5	13.5	14.7	71.8
Other poultry	100.0	3.5	15.8	11.3	73.1

	total consumer units	Asian	black	Hispanic	non-Hispanic white and other
Fish and seafood	100.0%	8.1%	14.6%	13.2%	72.4%
Canned fish and seafood	100.0	2.7	9.0	12.1	79.2
Fresh fish and shellfish	100.0	9.1	16.5	14.6	69.0
Frozen fish and shellfish	100.0	8.4	13.0	10.8	76.3
Eggs	100.0	3.7	12.4	17.3	70.3
Dairy products	**100.0**	**2.6**	**7.9**	**12.1**	**80.2**
Fresh milk and cream	100.0	3.2	8.2	14.8	77.3
Fresh milk, all types	100.0	3.4	8.7	15.2	76.3
Cream	100.0	1.4	3.5	11.4	85.3
Other dairy products	100.0	2.3	7.8	10.5	82.1
Butter	100.0	2.4	12.6	7.3	80.4
Cheese	100.0	1.3	6.2	10.8	83.4
Ice cream and related products	100.0	3.3	9.3	10.5	80.6
Miscellaneous dairy products	100.0	3.6	7.6	11.4	81.3
Fruits and vegetables	**100.0**	**5.3**	**9.3**	**13.4**	**77.5**
Fresh fruits	100.0	6.0	8.2	14.1	77.8
Apples	100.0	4.9	8.0	13.5	78.7
Bananas	100.0	5.8	10.5	16.4	73.1
Oranges	100.0	8.6	10.6	16.4	72.9
Citrus fruits, excluding oranges	100.0	5.4	5.5	18.3	76.1
Other fresh fruits	100.0	6.0	7.5	12.3	80.5
Fresh vegetables	100.0	6.7	7.8	14.5	78.0
Potatoes	100.0	5.1	11.9	13.8	74.4
Lettuce	100.0	5.2	6.0	13.9	80.4
Tomatoes	100.0	6.3	7.7	19.2	73.2
Other fresh vegetables	100.0	7.6	7.0	13.0	80.2
Processed fruits	100.0	3.7	11.5	12.2	76.7
Frozen fruits and fruit juices	100.0	2.3	8.9	9.5	81.7
Frozen orange juice	100.0	2.0	10.0	9.6	80.6
Frozen fruits	100.0	3.1	4.8	5.8	89.7
Frozen fruit juices, excluding orange	100.0	1.7	13.5	15.0	71.6
Canned fruits	100.0	3.1	8.7	7.2	84.5
Dried fruits	100.0	4.9	5.2	7.6	87.3
Fresh fruit juice	100.0	4.3	12.1	12.5	75.5
Canned and bottled fruit juice	100.0	3.7	13.3	14.6	72.7
Processed vegetables	100.0	2.6	12.4	11.2	76.7
Frozen vegetables	100.0	2.5	13.5	5.9	81.0
Canned and dried vegetables and juices	100.0	2.7	11.8	14.0	74.4
Canned beans	100.0	2.1	14.8	15.3	70.0
Canned corn	100.0	2.8	16.4	17.5	66.1
Canned miscellaneous vegetables	100.0	1.9	10.7	9.1	80.4
Dried peas	100.0	5.3	13.0	8.6	79.1
Dried beans	100.0	3.3	9.8	37.4	52.9
Dried miscellaneous vegetables	100.0	3.4	10.9	14.5	74.9
Dried processed vegetables	100.0	1.4	6.7	30.7	62.2
Fresh and canned vegetable juices	100.0	4.2	8.5	12.2	79.8
Sugar and other sweets	**100.0**	**3.6**	**8.7**	**9.6**	**82.0**
Candy and chewing gum	100.0	4.4	6.8	8.3	85.1
Sugar	100.0	2.5	16.5	15.9	67.9
Artificial sweeteners	100.0	2.7	13.2	8.9	78.1
Jams, preserves, other sweets	100.0	1.9	8.6	10.0	81.7
Fats and oils	**100.0**	**2.9**	**11.4**	**12.8**	**76.1**
Margarine	100.0	1.6	12.1	8.0	80.1
Fats and oils	100.0	4.8	15.1	20.1	65.0
Salad dressings	100.0	2.2	9.9	10.0	80.3
Nondairy cream and imitation milk	100.0	2.2	8.1	7.6	84.5
Peanut butter	100.0	1.9	8.5	10.2	81.6

	total consumer units	Asian	black	Hispanic	non-Hispanic white and other
Miscellaneous foods	100.0%	3.1%	7.9%	9.5%	82.9%
Frozen prepared foods	100.0	2.2	8.5	6.4	85.4
Frozen meals	100.0	2.3	9.1	5.4	85.8
Other frozen prepared foods	100.0	2.1	8.2	6.8	85.2
Canned and packaged soups	100.0	3.8	8.4	8.4	83.7
Potato chips, nuts, and other snacks	100.0	2.8	7.4	7.9	85.0
Potato chips and other snacks	100.0	2.1	8.1	8.3	83.8
Nuts	100.0	4.8	5.5	6.6	88.2
Condiments and seasonings	100.0	3.6	8.0	9.0	83.3
Salt, spices, and other seasonings	100.0	6.2	10.1	12.5	77.7
Olives, pickles, relishes	100.0	1.5	4.8	7.7	88.0
Sauces and gravies	100.0	3.2	8.6	8.2	83.6
Baking needs and miscellaneous products	100.0	2.5	6.3	7.7	86.4
Other canned/packaged prepared foods	100.0	3.4	7.8	13.0	79.6
Prepared salads	100.0	2.2	6.5	5.5	88.4
Prepared desserts	100.0	1.4	5.0	9.6	85.5
Baby food	100.0	6.6	12.2	20.7	68.2
Miscellaneous prepared foods	100.0	3.0	7.2	13.1	79.9
Nonalcoholic beverages	100.0	2.9	9.3	12.0	79.0
Cola	100.0	2.0	8.9	13.4	77.8
Other carbonated drinks	100.0	2.0	9.7	9.4	81.1
Coffee	100.0	3.4	6.9	9.2	84.4
Roasted coffee	100.0	3.3	6.7	7.8	85.8
Instant and freeze-dried coffee	100.0	3.5	7.3	11.5	82.0
Noncarbonated fruit-flavored drinks	100.0	2.0	16.9	17.2	66.4
Tea	100.0	4.0	8.5	9.9	82.4
Other nonalcoholic beverages and ice	100.0	4.4	8.5	12.6	79.1
Food prepared by CU on trips	100.0	3.9	3.9	7.9	88.3
FOOD AWAY FROM HOME	100.0	4.3	7.4	8.8	84.1
Meals at restaurants, carry-outs, other	100.0	4.2	7.8	9.0	83.5
Lunch	100.0	4.9	8.6	10.1	81.6
At fast-food restaurants*	100.0	4.8	9.7	12.1	78.5
At full-service restaurants	100.0	5.5	5.3	6.5	88.6
At vending machines, mobile vendors	100.0	2.7	11.6	26.1	61.7
At employer and school cafeterias	100.0	3.7	13.0	8.9	78.2
Dinner	100.0	4.1	6.1	7.7	86.5
At fast-food restaurants*	100.0	3.7	9.6	11.4	79.2
At full-service restaurants	100.0	4.3	4.3	5.9	90.2
At vending machines, mobile vendors	100.0	–	28.2	14.9	56.5
At employer and school cafeterias	100.0	0.6	28.7	6.4	64.7
Snacks and nonalcoholic beverages	100.0	3.8	9.0	10.0	81.3
At fast-food restaurants*	100.0	3.8	8.5	9.2	82.6
At full-service restaurants	100.0	4.8	6.3	10.0	83.9
At vending machines, mobile vendors	100.0	2.9	12.6	13.9	73.7
At employer and school cafeterias	100.0	3.6	11.8	10.0	78.3
Breakfast and brunch	100.0	2.8	9.4	9.1	82.0
At fast-food restaurants*	100.0	3.3	12.6	12.7	75.4
At full-service restaurants	100.0	2.2	5.7	5.2	89.5
At vending machines, mobile vendors	100.0	1.6	20.8	24.4	54.8
At employer and school cafeterias	100.0	4.8	15.8	10.6	73.6
Board (including at school)	100.0	9.3	5.4	5.1	89.5
Catered affairs	100.0	2.0	8.0	5.8	86.2
Food on trips	100.0	3.7	3.8	7.3	89.0
School lunches	100.0	5.0	8.7	10.0	81.5
Meals as pay	100.0	12.9	5.1	13.7	81.7

	total consumer units	Asian	black	Hispanic	non-Hispanic white and other
ALCOHOLIC BEVERAGES	**100.0%**	**2.4%**	**4.4%**	**7.4%**	**88.5%**
At home	**100.0**	**1.8**	**4.8**	**8.4**	**87.1**
Beer and ale	100.0	1.6	5.5	13.2	81.4
Whiskey	100.0	2.8	8.9	4.0	87.3
Wine	100.0	2.3	2.8	3.3	94.5
Other alcoholic beverages	100.0	0.5	4.8	6.8	88.8
Away from home	**100.0**	**3.3**	**3.8**	**5.8**	**90.7**
Beer and ale	100.0	3.3	3.7	5.8	90.8
At fast-food restaurants*	100.0	1.9	5.9	6.1	88.5
At full-service restaurants	100.0	3.9	3.2	5.9	91.2
Wine	100.0	3.9	3.6	5.9	90.8
At fast-food restaurants*	100.0	2.2	10.9	4.5	84.9
At full-service restaurants	100.0	4.3	2.5	6.3	91.6
Other alcoholic beverages	100.0	3.8	4.6	5.7	90.0
At fast-food restaurants*	100.0	2.9	6.8	2.8	91.0
At full-service restaurants	100.0	4.0	4.5	6.1	89.7
Alcoholic beverages purchased on trips	100.0	2.3	3.2	5.9	90.9

The category fast-food restaurants also includes take-out, delivery, concession stands, buffets, and cafeterias other than employer and school.

Note: "Asian" and "black" include Hispanics and non-Hispanics who identify themselves as being of the respective race alone. "Hispanic" includes people of any race who identify themselves as Hispanic. "Other" includes people who identify themselves as non-Hispanic and as Alaska Native, American Indian, Asian (who are also included in the "Asian" column), Native Hawaiian or other Pacific Islander, as well as non-Hispanics reporting more than one race. "–" means sample is too small to make a reliable estimate.

Source: Calculations by New Strategist based on the 2004 Consumer Expenditure Survey

Table 5.21 Food and Alcohol: Average spending by region, 2004

(average annual spending of consumer units (CU) on food and alcoholic beverages, by region in which consumer unit lives, 2004)

	total consumer units	Northeast	Midwest	South	West
Number of consumer units (in 000s)	116,282	22,051	26,539	41,801	25,891
Average number of persons per CU	2.5	2.4	2.4	2.5	2.6
Average before-tax income of CU	$54,453.00	$61,050.00	$53,567.00	$50,775.00	$55,682.00
Average spending of CU, total	43,394.87	46,114.89	43,370.77	39,173.65	47,921.74
Food, average spending	**5,780.82**	**6,367.80**	**5,592.21**	**5,318.35**	**6,224.12**
Alcoholic beverages, average spending	**459.27**	**624.80**	**426.63**	**347.55**	**532.22**
FOOD AT HOME	**3,346.82**	**3,634.42**	**3,188.76**	**3,119.25**	**3,634.37**
Cereals and bakery products	**460.90**	**521.48**	**445.67**	**427.05**	**479.59**
Cereals and cereal products	153.80	175.76	141.05	143.24	165.35
Flour	8.32	9.05	6.99	7.06	11.12
Prepared flour mixes	13.78	13.33	17.13	11.92	13.68
Ready-to-eat and cooked cereals	86.69	97.25	84.21	79.03	92.66
Rice	18.46	22.65	10.60	20.60	19.57
Pasta, cornmeal, and other cereal products	26.55	33.50	22.12	24.62	28.32
Bakery products	307.10	345.72	304.62	283.82	314.24
Bread	87.63	102.06	84.14	76.61	96.76
White bread	35.04	38.62	34.87	32.76	35.84
Bread, other than white	52.59	63.44	49.26	43.85	60.93
Crackers and cookies	71.16	76.80	70.69	67.23	73.21
Cookies	46.57	52.04	44.80	44.14	47.64
Crackers	24.60	24.76	25.89	23.09	25.57
Frozen and refrigerated bakery products	26.32	25.84	25.03	29.27	23.27
Other bakery products	121.99	141.03	124.76	110.71	121.00
Biscuits and rolls	42.11	51.05	43.66	37.18	40.80
Cakes and cupcakes	39.04	45.38	37.98	35.91	39.76
Bread and cracker products	3.25	3.23	4.10	2.67	3.33
Sweetrolls, coffee cakes, doughnuts	23.59	25.34	24.63	21.00	25.24
Pies, tarts, turnovers	13.99	16.02	14.38	13.96	11.88
Meats, poultry, fish, and eggs	**879.71**	**1,007.85**	**781.25**	**848.70**	**922.31**
Beef	265.34	279.01	241.79	262.57	282.67
Ground beef	96.92	97.67	102.20	99.34	86.81
Roast	45.58	40.40	37.69	53.30	45.70
Chuck roast	11.72	7.89	11.33	15.11	9.92
Round roast	10.27	10.77	7.89	11.23	10.79
Other roast	23.58	21.75	18.47	26.96	24.99
Steak	103.45	116.66	84.96	94.88	125.34
Round steak	16.37	16.15	14.93	15.35	19.71
Sirloin steak	32.38	43.53	23.41	26.17	42.22
Other steak	54.71	56.97	46.62	53.35	63.41
Other beef	19.39	24.28	16.94	15.05	24.82
Pork	181.14	189.23	170.45	189.05	172.40
Bacon	31.08	28.60	30.41	33.38	30.18
Pork chops	37.92	40.75	37.89	39.45	32.97
Ham	39.65	44.64	35.28	41.07	37.57
Ham, not canned	38.67	43.72	34.41	40.13	36.39
Canned ham	0.98	0.92	0.87	0.94	1.18
Sausage	27.91	29.65	26.82	30.25	23.70
Other pork	44.59	45.60	40.05	44.89	47.98
Other meats	107.98	134.65	119.00	91.84	99.70
Frankfurters	22.52	26.07	24.39	20.84	20.21
Lunch meats (cold cuts)	72.99	93.43	78.83	59.76	70.75
Bologna, liverwurst, salami	21.07	26.46	20.72	18.63	20.77
Other lunch meats	51.91	66.98	58.10	41.13	49.98
Lamb, organ meats, and others	12.48	15.14	15.78	11.24	8.75
Poultry	155.61	194.23	126.92	148.82	163.24
Fresh and frozen chicken	122.64	153.55	99.46	118.21	127.32
Fresh and frozen whole chicken	36.59	45.32	23.41	36.10	43.63
Fresh and frozen chicken parts	86.04	108.23	76.06	82.11	83.68
Other poultry	32.97	40.68	27.45	30.61	35.92

	total consumer units	Northeast	Midwest	South	West
Fish and seafood	$127.80	$163.86	$90.84	$116.50	$153.65
Canned fish and seafood	15.38	18.44	13.45	13.48	17.87
Fresh fish and shellfish	74.88	103.88	40.64	70.02	93.50
Frozen fish and shellfish	37.54	41.54	36.75	33.00	42.28
Eggs	41.84	46.87	32.25	39.91	50.65
Dairy products	**370.57**	**416.99**	**358.20**	**329.31**	**410.67**
Fresh milk and cream	144.33	155.85	136.91	132.58	161.30
Fresh milk, all types	128.94	138.31	122.53	119.37	143.16
Cream	15.39	17.54	14.38	13.20	18.14
Other dairy products	226.24	261.14	221.28	196.73	249.37
Butter	21.81	26.91	24.92	18.19	20.06
Cheese	113.67	129.56	113.81	99.63	122.67
Ice cream and related products	60.22	68.44	54.46	55.23	67.28
Miscellaneous dairy products	30.54	36.23	28.09	23.68	39.36
Fruits and vegetables	**560.95**	**638.11**	**509.67**	**501.28**	**645.15**
Fresh fruits	186.74	213.43	171.37	160.74	222.14
Apples	32.42	34.95	31.26	28.40	38.02
Bananas	30.17	35.59	27.40	26.28	34.73
Oranges	19.48	22.42	17.45	16.11	24.57
Citrus fruits, excluding oranges	15.41	16.83	12.98	13.05	20.55
Other fresh fruits	89.25	103.65	82.28	76.89	104.26
Fresh vegetables	182.94	208.50	147.69	166.36	224.73
Potatoes	28.07	29.31	24.44	29.94	27.74
Lettuce	22.87	28.99	19.80	18.29	28.25
Tomatoes	35.74	41.38	24.23	34.27	45.32
Other fresh vegetables	96.25	108.82	79.21	83.86	123.42
Processed fruits	109.63	126.78	112.15	92.55	120.02
Frozen fruits and fruit juices	9.97	9.20	12.02	6.04	14.89
Frozen orange juice	4.17	4.11	5.18	2.41	6.03
Frozen fruits	3.53	3.63	4.36	1.96	5.11
Frozen fruit juices, excluding orange	2.27	1.45	2.48	1.67	3.74
Canned fruits	16.19	13.65	20.13	14.58	16.92
Dried fruits	6.35	6.30	6.68	5.13	8.02
Fresh fruit juice	22.07	29.79	22.76	17.79	21.64
Canned and bottled fruit juice	55.05	67.84	50.56	49.01	58.54
Processed vegetables	81.64	89.41	78.46	81.62	78.26
Frozen vegetables	28.50	35.06	28.99	28.19	22.81
Canned and dried vegetables and juices	53.14	54.35	49.47	53.43	55.45
Canned beans	11.39	10.22	11.56	12.91	9.76
Canned corn	6.33	6.09	5.37	6.60	7.09
Canned miscellaneous vegetables	16.77	16.50	16.10	17.51	16.48
Dried peas	0.60	0.71	0.48	0.52	0.77
Dried beans	2.47	2.29	0.77	2.76	3.95
Dried miscellaneous vegetables	6.21	6.46	5.68	6.16	6.63
Dried processed vegetables	0.30	0.32	0.50	0.29	0.10
Fresh and canned vegetable juices	8.91	11.72	8.81	6.55	10.42
Sugar and other sweets	**128.12**	**137.23**	**129.48**	**118.49**	**134.54**
Candy and chewing gum	83.13	91.68	86.97	73.29	87.77
Sugar	16.10	17.15	16.01	16.85	14.04
Artificial sweeteners	6.85	6.59	4.74	8.87	6.00
Jams, preserves, other sweets	22.04	21.82	21.75	19.47	26.74
Fats and oils	**88.89**	**92.65**	**82.61**	**84.00**	**100.19**
Margarine	9.57	9.20	10.30	9.02	10.00
Fats and oils	28.56	33.87	22.66	27.89	31.22
Salad dressings	27.44	26.23	25.41	26.30	32.48
Nondairy cream and imitation milk	10.80	11.37	11.55	9.73	11.28
Peanut butter	12.52	11.98	12.70	11.06	15.20

	total consumer units	Northeast	Midwest	South	West
Miscellaneous foods	**$527.29**	**$505.28**	**$559.77**	**$490.86**	**$571.89**
Frozen prepared foods	109.90	100.01	129.81	103.35	108.34
Frozen meals	31.79	31.22	34.66	30.45	31.49
Other frozen prepared foods	78.11	68.79	95.15	72.90	76.85
Canned and packaged soups	36.50	41.51	36.00	32.28	39.56
Potato chips, nuts, and other snacks	117.08	104.35	129.72	112.66	122.10
Potato chips and other snacks	86.06	74.92	97.89	85.13	84.87
Nuts	31.01	29.43	31.83	27.53	37.23
Condiments and seasonings	93.65	96.65	90.77	88.38	102.69
Salt, spices, and other seasonings	22.22	21.09	20.72	21.70	25.63
Olives, pickles, relishes	10.52	12.60	10.01	9.19	11.43
Sauces and gravies	40.94	42.78	37.16	39.10	46.29
Baking needs and miscellaneous products	19.97	20.17	22.88	18.39	19.34
Other canned/packaged prepared foods	170.16	162.77	173.46	154.19	199.20
Prepared salads	25.43	28.27	25.00	22.30	28.55
Prepared desserts	10.91	13.01	10.59	8.77	12.91
Baby food	30.08	29.73	36.92	25.69	30.39
Miscellaneous prepared foods	102.74	89.14	100.44	96.73	126.75
Nonalcoholic beverages	**289.52**	**278.86**	**278.03**	**286.47**	**315.73**
Cola	93.81	80.57	99.75	95.00	97.13
Other carbonated drinks	48.08	45.58	53.44	48.35	44.22
Coffee	39.12	41.99	35.14	35.86	46.11
Roasted coffee	24.48	25.80	21.93	22.60	29.06
Instant and freeze-dried coffee	14.64	16.19	13.21	13.26	17.06
Noncarbonated fruit-flavored drinks	19.79	20.17	17.05	19.81	22.30
Tea	17.63	22.81	14.60	16.56	18.07
Other nonalcoholic beverages and ice	70.10	66.86	57.54	69.64	86.79
Food prepared by CU on trips	**40.86**	**35.95**	**44.08**	**33.09**	**54.30**
FOOD AWAY FROM HOME	2,434.00	2,733.39	2,403.45	2,199.11	2,589.75
Meals at restaurants, carry-outs, other	**2,028.17**	**2,262.86**	**1,965.14**	**1,898.71**	**2,102.09**
Lunch	725.07	734.64	686.86	729.09	750.21
At fast-food restaurants*	409.17	394.48	380.01	416.58	440.31
At full-service restaurants	236.65	247.64	219.31	237.94	243.16
At vending machines, mobile vendors	6.02	4.88	4.57	6.86	7.16
At employer and school cafeterias	73.24	87.64	82.97	67.71	59.59
Dinner	795.59	989.56	773.06	694.87	815.48
At fast-food restaurants*	253.07	252.66	264.76	232.08	275.46
At full-service restaurants	538.22	731.97	506.16	457.72	535.28
At vending machines, mobile vendors	1.50	1.00	0.86	2.08	1.67
At employer and school cafeterias	2.79	3.92	1.28	2.99	3.07
Snacks and nonalcoholic beverages	297.45	322.23	296.96	272.41	317.36
At fast-food restaurants*	217.16	241.41	215.49	188.44	244.77
At full-service restaurants	28.87	27.26	25.79	30.78	30.38
At vending machines, mobile vendors	41.07	41.59	45.15	44.46	30.82
At employer and school cafeterias	10.34	11.97	10.52	8.73	11.38
Breakfast and brunch	210.06	216.43	208.26	202.34	219.04
At fast-food restaurants*	103.28	92.78	101.07	106.55	109.35
At full-service restaurants	100.36	114.35	101.73	89.50	104.52
At vending machines, mobile vendors	1.42	2.44	1.15	1.29	1.05
At employer and school cafeterias	5.00	6.86	4.31	4.99	4.12
Board (including at school)	**27.89**	**30.16**	**29.61**	**14.59**	**45.65**
Catered affairs	**58.56**	**99.41**	**71.59**	**36.22**	**46.46**
Food on trips	**231.55**	**238.73**	**235.36**	**182.23**	**301.15**
School lunches	**63.39**	**71.51**	**78.32**	**54.02**	**56.32**
Meals as pay	**24.45**	**30.72**	**23.44**	**13.35**	**38.07**

	total consumer units	Northeast	Midwest	South	West
ALCOHOLIC BEVERAGES	$459.27	$624.80	$426.63	$347.55	$532.22
At home	277.59	373.63	233.69	225.19	325.84
Beer and ale	131.31	138.19	130.43	120.67	143.63
Whiskey	21.66	25.47	17.88	22.15	21.52
Wine	94.55	172.81	60.42	57.79	122.45
Other alcoholic beverages	30.07	37.17	24.96	24.58	38.23
Away from home	181.68	251.17	192.94	122.36	206.38
Beer and ale	76.32	108.98	88.29	47.64	82.30
At fast-food restaurants*	16.44	25.80	19.22	8.63	18.18
At full-service restaurants	56.01	81.12	56.54	37.78	63.44
Wine	22.29	29.96	23.49	15.54	25.41
At fast-food restaurants*	3.06	3.43	3.32	2.36	3.61
At full-service restaurants	18.76	26.42	18.32	13.12	21.78
Other alcoholic beverages	44.71	71.27	43.17	30.86	45.92
At fast-food restaurants*	3.82	5.56	4.14	2.59	4.01
At full-service restaurants	39.44	65.22	33.90	27.88	41.77
Alcoholic beverages purchased on trips	38.37	40.96	37.98	28.33	52.76

The category fast-food restaurants also includes take-out, delivery, concession stands, buffets, and cafeterias other than employer and school.
Note: Subcategories may not add to total because some are not shown.
Source: Bureau of Labor Statistics, unpublished tables from the 2004 Consumer Expenditure Survey

Table 5.22 Food and Alcohol: Indexed spending by region, 2004

(indexed average annual spending of consumer units (CU) on food and alcoholic beverages, by region in which consumer unit lives, 2004; index definition: an index of 100 is the average for all consumer units; an index of 132 means that spending by consumer units in that group is 32 percent above the average for all consumer units; an index of 68 indicates spending that is 32 percent below the average for all consumer units)

	total consumer units	Northeast	Midwest	South	West
Average spending of CU, total	$43,395	$46,115	$43,371	$39,174	$47,922
Average spending of CU, index	100	106	100	90	110
Food, spending index	**100**	**110**	**97**	**92**	**108**
Alcoholic beverages, spending index	**100**	**136**	**93**	**76**	**116**
FOOD AT HOME	**100**	**109**	**95**	**93**	**109**
Cereals and bakery products	**100**	**113**	**97**	**93**	**104**
Cereals and cereal products	100	114	92	93	108
Flour	100	109	84	85	134
Prepared flour mixes	100	97	124	87	99
Ready-to-eat and cooked cereals	100	112	97	91	107
Rice	100	123	57	112	106
Pasta, cornmeal, and other cereal products	100	126	83	93	107
Bakery products	100	113	99	92	102
Bread	100	116	96	87	110
White bread	100	110	100	93	102
Bread, other than white	100	121	94	83	116
Crackers and cookies	100	108	99	94	103
Cookies	100	112	96	95	102
Crackers	100	101	105	94	104
Frozen and refrigerated bakery products	100	98	95	111	88
Other bakery products	100	116	102	91	99
Biscuits and rolls	100	121	104	88	97
Cakes and cupcakes	100	116	97	92	102
Bread and cracker products	100	99	126	82	102
Sweetrolls, coffee cakes, doughnuts	100	107	104	89	107
Pies, tarts, turnovers	100	115	103	100	85
Meats, poultry, fish, and eggs	**100**	**115**	**89**	**96**	**105**
Beef	100	105	91	99	107
Ground beef	100	101	105	102	90
Roast	100	89	83	117	100
Chuck roast	100	67	97	129	85
Round roast	100	105	77	109	105
Other roast	100	92	78	114	106
Steak	100	113	82	92	121
Round steak	100	99	91	94	120
Sirloin steak	100	134	72	81	130
Other steak	100	104	85	98	116
Other beef	100	125	87	78	128
Pork	100	104	94	104	95
Bacon	100	92	98	107	97
Pork chops	100	107	100	104	87
Ham	100	113	89	104	95
Ham, not canned	100	113	89	104	94
Canned ham	100	94	89	96	120
Sausage	100	106	96	108	85
Other pork	100	102	90	101	108
Other meats	100	125	110	85	92
Frankfurters	100	116	108	93	90
Lunch meats (cold cuts)	100	128	108	82	97
Bologna, liverwurst, salami	100	126	98	88	99
Other lunch meats	100	129	112	79	96
Lamb, organ meats, and others	100	121	126	90	70
Poultry	100	125	82	96	105
Fresh and frozen chicken	100	125	81	96	104
Fresh and frozen whole chicken	100	124	64	99	119
Fresh and frozen chicken parts	100	126	88	95	97
Other poultry	100	123	83	93	109

	total consumer units	Northeast	Midwest	South	West
Fish and seafood	100	128	71	91	120
Canned fish and seafood	100	120	87	88	116
Fresh fish and shellfish	100	139	54	94	125
Frozen fish and shellfish	100	111	98	88	113
Eggs	100	112	77	95	121
Dairy products	**100**	**113**	**97**	**89**	**111**
Fresh milk and cream	100	108	95	92	112
Fresh milk, all types	100	107	95	93	111
Cream	100	114	93	86	118
Other dairy products	100	115	98	87	110
Butter	100	123	114	83	92
Cheese	100	114	100	88	108
Ice cream and related products	100	114	90	92	112
Miscellaneous dairy products	100	119	92	78	129
Fruits and vegetables	**100**	**114**	**91**	**89**	**115**
Fresh fruits	100	114	92	86	119
Apples	100	108	96	88	117
Bananas	100	118	91	87	115
Oranges	100	115	90	83	126
Citrus fruits, excluding oranges	100	109	84	85	133
Other fresh fruits	100	116	92	86	117
Fresh vegetables	100	114	81	91	123
Potatoes	100	104	87	107	99
Lettuce	100	127	87	80	124
Tomatoes	100	116	68	96	127
Other fresh vegetables	100	113	82	87	128
Processed fruits	100	116	102	84	109
Frozen fruits and fruit juices	100	92	121	61	149
Frozen orange juice	100	99	124	58	145
Frozen fruits	100	103	124	56	145
Frozen fruit juices, excluding orange	100	64	109	74	165
Canned fruits	100	84	124	90	105
Dried fruits	100	99	105	81	126
Fresh fruit juice	100	135	103	81	98
Canned and bottled fruit juice	100	123	92	89	106
Processed vegetables	100	110	96	100	96
Frozen vegetables	100	123	102	99	80
Canned and dried vegetables and juices	100	102	93	101	104
Canned beans	100	90	101	113	86
Canned corn	100	96	85	104	112
Canned miscellaneous vegetables	100	98	96	104	98
Dried peas	100	118	80	87	128
Dried beans	100	93	31	112	160
Dried miscellaneous vegetables	100	104	91	99	107
Dried processed vegetables	100	107	167	97	33
Fresh and canned vegetable juices	100	132	99	74	117
Sugar and other sweets	**100**	**107**	**101**	**92**	**105**
Candy and chewing gum	100	110	105	88	106
Sugar	100	107	99	105	87
Artificial sweeteners	100	96	69	129	88
Jams, preserves, other sweets	100	99	99	88	121
Fats and oils	**100**	**104**	**93**	**94**	**113**
Margarine	100	96	108	94	104
Fats and oils	100	119	79	98	109
Salad dressings	100	96	93	96	118
Nondairy cream and imitation milk	100	105	107	90	104
Peanut butter	100	96	101	88	121

	total consumer units	Northeast	Midwest	South	West
Miscellaneous foods	**100**	**96**	**106**	**93**	**108**
Frozen prepared foods	100	91	118	94	99
Frozen meals	100	98	109	96	99
Other frozen prepared foods	100	88	122	93	98
Canned and packaged soups	100	114	99	88	108
Potato chips, nuts, and other snacks	100	89	111	96	104
Potato chips and other snacks	100	87	114	99	99
Nuts	100	95	103	89	120
Condiments and seasonings	100	103	97	94	110
Salt, spices, and other seasonings	100	95	93	98	115
Olives, pickles, relishes	100	120	95	87	109
Sauces and gravies	100	104	91	96	113
Baking needs and miscellaneous products	100	101	115	92	97
Other canned/packaged prepared foods	100	96	102	91	117
Prepared salads	100	111	98	88	112
Prepared desserts	100	119	97	80	118
Baby food	100	99	123	85	101
Miscellaneous prepared foods	100	87	98	94	123
Nonalcoholic beverages	**100**	**96**	**96**	**99**	**109**
Cola	100	86	106	101	104
Other carbonated drinks	100	95	111	101	92
Coffee	100	107	90	92	118
Roasted coffee	100	105	90	92	119
Instant and freeze-dried coffee	100	111	90	91	117
Noncarbonated fruit-flavored drinks	100	102	86	100	113
Tea	100	129	83	94	102
Other nonalcoholic beverages and ice	100	95	82	99	124
Food prepared by CU on trips	**100**	**88**	**108**	**81**	**133**
FOOD AWAY FROM HOME	**100**	**112**	**99**	**90**	**106**
Meals at restaurants, carry-outs, other	**100**	**112**	**97**	**94**	**104**
Lunch	100	101	95	101	103
At fast-food restaurants*	100	96	93	102	108
At full-service restaurants	100	105	93	101	103
At vending machines, mobile vendors	100	81	76	114	119
At employer and school cafeterias	100	120	113	92	81
Dinner	100	124	97	87	103
At fast-food restaurants*	100	100	105	92	109
At full-service restaurants	100	136	94	85	99
At vending machines, mobile vendors	100	67	57	139	111
At employer and school cafeterias	100	141	46	107	110
Snacks and nonalcoholic beverages	100	108	100	92	107
At fast-food restaurants*	100	111	99	87	113
At full-service restaurants	100	94	89	107	105
At vending machines, mobile vendors	100	101	110	108	75
At employer and school cafeterias	100	116	102	84	110
Breakfast and brunch	100	103	99	96	104
At fast-food restaurants*	100	90	98	103	106
At full-service restaurants	100	114	101	89	104
At vending machines, mobile vendors	100	172	81	91	74
At employer and school cafeterias	100	137	86	100	82
Board (including at school)	**100**	**108**	**106**	**52**	**164**
Catered affairs	**100**	**170**	**122**	**62**	**79**
Food on trips	**100**	**103**	**102**	**79**	**130**
School lunches	**100**	**113**	**124**	**85**	**89**
Meals as pay	**100**	**126**	**96**	**55**	**156**

	total consumer units	Northeast	Midwest	South	West
ALCOHOLIC BEVERAGES	**100**	**136**	**93**	**76**	**116**
At home	**100**	**135**	**84**	**81**	**117**
Beer and ale	100	105	99	92	109
Whiskey	100	118	83	102	99
Wine	100	183	64	61	130
Other alcoholic beverages	100	124	83	82	127
Away from home	**100**	**138**	**106**	**67**	**114**
Beer and ale	100	143	116	62	108
At fast-food restaurants*	100	157	117	52	111
At full-service restaurants	100	145	101	67	113
Wine	100	134	105	70	114
At fast-food restaurants*	100	112	108	77	118
At full-service restaurants	100	141	98	70	116
Other alcoholic beverages	100	159	97	69	103
At fast-food restaurants*	100	146	108	68	105
At full-service restaurants	100	165	86	71	106
Alcoholic beverages purchased on trips	100	107	99	74	138

The category fast-food restaurants also includes take-out, delivery, concession stands, buffets, and cafeterias other than employer and school.
Source: Calculations by New Strategist based on the 2004 Consumer Expenditure Survey

Table 5.23 Food and Alcohol: Total spending by region, 2004

(total annual spending on food and alcoholic beverages, by region in which consumer units live, 2004; consumer units and dollars in thousands)

	total consumer units	Northeast	Midwest	South	West
Number of consumer units	116,282	22,051	26,539	41,801	25,891
Total spending of all consumer units	$5,046,042,273	$1,016,879,439	$1,151,016,865	$1,637,497,744	$1,240,741,770
Food, total spending	672,205,311	140,416,358	148,411,661	222,312,348	161,148,691
Alcoholic beverages, total spending	53,404,834	13,777,465	11,322,334	14,527,938	13779708.02
FOOD AT HOME	**389,174,923**	**80,142,595**	**84,626,502**	**130,387,769**	**94,097,474**
Cereals and bakery products	**53,594,374**	**11,499,155**	**11,827,636**	**17,851,117**	**12,417,065**
Cereals and cereal products	17,884,172	3,875,684	3,743,326	5,987,575	4,281,077
Flour	967,466	199,562	185,508	295,115	287,908
Prepared flour mixes	1,602,366	293,940	454,613	498,268	354,189
Ready-to-eat and cooked cereals	10,080,487	2,144,460	2,234,849	3,303,533	2,399,060
Rice	2,146,566	499,455	281,313	861,101	506,687
Pasta, cornmeal, and other cereal products	3,087,287	738,709	587,043	1,029,141	733,233
Bakery products	35,710,202	7,623,472	8,084,310	11,863,960	8,135,988
Bread	10,189,792	2,250,525	2,232,991	3,202,375	2,505,213
White bread	4,074,521	851,610	925,415	1,369,401	927,933
Bread, other than white	6,115,270	1,398,915	1,307,311	1,832,974	1,577,539
Crackers and cookies	8,274,627	1,693,517	1,876,042	2,810,281	1,895,480
Cookies	5,415,253	1,147,534	1,188,947	1,845,096	1,233,447
Crackers	2,860,537	545,983	687,095	965,185	662,033
Frozen and refrigerated bakery products	3,060,542	569,798	664,271	1,223,515	602,484
Other bakery products	14,185,241	3,109,853	3,311,006	4,627,789	3,132,811
Biscuits and rolls	4,896,635	1,125,704	1,158,693	1,554,161	1,056,353
Cakes and cupcakes	4,539,649	1,000,674	1,007,951	1,501,074	1,029,426
Bread and cracker products	377,917	71,225	108,810	111,609	86,217
Sweetrolls, coffee cakes, doughnuts	2,743,092	558,772	653,656	877,821	653,489
Pies, tarts, turnovers	1,626,785	353,257	381,631	583,542	307,585
Meats, poultry, fish, and eggs	**102,294,438**	**22,224,100**	**20,733,594**	**35,476,509**	**23,879,528**
Beef	30,854,266	6,152,450	6,416,865	10,975,689	7,318,609
Ground beef	11,270,051	2,153,721	2,712,286	4,152,511	2,247,598
Roast	5,300,134	890,860	1,000,255	2,227,993	1,183,219
Chuck roast	1,362,825	173,982	300,687	631,613	256,839
Round roast	1,194,216	237,489	209,393	469,425	279,364
Other roast	2,741,930	479,609	490,175	1,126,955	647,016
Steak	12,029,373	2,572,470	2,254,753	3,966,079	3,245,178
Round steak	1,903,536	356,124	396,227	641,645	510,312
Sirloin steak	3,765,211	959,880	621,278	1,093,932	1,093,118
Other steak	6,361,788	1,256,245	1,237,248	2,230,083	1,641,748
Other beef	2,254,708	535,398	449,571	629,105	642,615
Pork	21,063,321	4,172,711	4,523,573	7,902,479	4,463,608
Bacon	3,614,045	630,659	807,051	1,395,317	781,390
Pork chops	4,409,413	898,578	1,005,563	1,649,049	853,626
Ham	4,610,581	984,357	936,296	1,716,767	972,725
Ham, not canned	4,496,625	964,070	913,207	1,677,474	942,173
Canned ham	113,956	20,287	23,089	39,293	30,551
Sausage	3,245,431	653,812	711,776	1,264,480	613,617
Other pork	5,185,014	1,005,526	1,062,887	1,876,447	1,242,250
Other meats	12,556,130	2,969,167	3,158,141	3,839,004	2,581,333
Frankfurters	2,618,671	574,870	647,286	871,133	523,257
Lunch meats (cold cuts)	8,487,423	2,060,225	2,092,069	2,498,028	1,831,788
Bologna, liverwurst, salami	2,450,062	583,469	549,888	778,753	537,756
Other lunch meats	6,036,199	1,476,976	1,541,916	1,719,275	1,294,032
Lamb, organ meats, and others	1,451,199	333,852	418,785	469,843	226,546
Poultry	18,094,642	4,282,966	3,368,330	6,220,825	4,226,447
Fresh and frozen chicken	14,260,824	3,385,931	2,639,569	4,941,296	3,296,442
Fresh and frozen whole chicken	4,254,758	999,351	621,278	1,509,016	1,129,624
Fresh and frozen chicken parts	10,004,903	2,386,580	2,018,556	3,432,280	2,166,559
Other poultry	3,833,818	897,035	728,496	1,279,529	930,005

	total consumer units	Northeast	Midwest	South	West
Fish and seafood	$14,860,840	$3,613,277	$2,410,803	$4,869,817	$3,978,152
Canned fish and seafood	1,788,417	406,620	356,950	563,477	462,672
Fresh fish and shellfish	8,707,196	2,290,658	1,078,545	2,926,906	2,420,809
Frozen fish and shellfish	4,365,226	915,999	975,308	1,379,433	1,094,671
Eggs	4,865,239	1,033,530	855,883	1,668,278	1,311,379
Dairy products	**43,090,621**	**9,195,046**	**9,506,270**	**13,765,487**	**10,632,657**
Fresh milk and cream	16,782,981	3,436,648	3,633,454	5,541,977	4,176,218
Fresh milk, all types	14,993,401	3,049,874	3,251,824	4,989,785	3,706,556
Cream	1,789,580	386,775	381,631	551,773	469,663
Other dairy products	26,307,640	5,758,398	5,872,550	8,223,511	6,456,439
Butter	2,536,110	593,392	661,352	760,360	519,373
Cheese	13,217,775	2,856,928	3,020,404	4,164,634	3,176,049
Ice cream and related products	7,002,502	1,509,170	1,445,314	2,308,669	1,741,946
Miscellaneous dairy products	3,551,252	798,908	745,481	989,848	1,019,070
Fruits and vegetables	**65,228,388**	**14,070,964**	**13,526,132**	**20,954,005**	**16,703,579**
Fresh fruits	21,714,501	4,706,345	4,547,988	6,719,093	5,751,427
Apples	3,769,862	770,682	829,609	1,187,148	984,376
Bananas	3,508,228	784,795	727,169	1,098,530	899,194
Oranges	2,265,173	494,383	463,106	673,414	636,142
Citrus fruits, excluding oranges	1,791,906	371,118	344,476	545,503	532,060
Other fresh fruits	10,378,169	2,285,586	2,183,629	3,214,079	2,699,396
Fresh vegetables	21,272,629	4,597,634	3,919,545	6,954,014	5,818,484
Potatoes	3,264,036	646,315	648,613	1,251,522	718,216
Lettuce	2,659,369	639,258	525,472	764,540	731,421
Tomatoes	4,155,919	912,470	643,040	1,432,520	1,173,380
Other fresh vegetables	11,192,143	2,399,590	2,102,154	3,505,432	3,195,467
Processed fruits	12,747,996	2,795,626	2,976,349	3,868,683	3,107,438
Frozen fruits and fruit juices	1,159,332	202,869	318,999	252,478	385,517
Frozen orange juice	484,896	90,630	137,472	100,740	156,123
Frozen fruits	410,475	80,045	115,710	81,930	132,303
Frozen fruit juices, excluding orange	263,960	31,974	65,817	69,808	96,832
Canned fruits	1,882,606	300,996	534,230	609,459	438,076
Dried fruits	738,391	138,921	177,281	214,439	207,646
Fresh fruit juice	2,566,344	656,899	604,028	743,640	560,281
Canned and bottled fruit juice	6,401,324	1,495,940	1,341,812	2,048,667	1,515,659
Processed vegetables	9,493,262	1,971,580	2,082,250	3,411,798	2,026,230
Frozen vegetables	3,314,037	773,108	769,366	1,178,370	590,574
Canned and dried vegetables and juices	6,179,225	1,198,472	1,312,884	2,233,427	1,435,656
Canned beans	1,324,452	225,361	306,791	539,651	252,696
Canned corn	736,065	134,291	142,514	275,887	183,567
Canned miscellaneous vegetables	1,950,049	363,842	427,278	731,936	426,684
Dried peas	69,769	15,656	12,739	21,737	19,936
Dried beans	287,217	50,497	20,435	115,371	102,269
Dried miscellaneous vegetables	722,111	142,449	150,742	257,494	171,657
Dried processed vegetables	34,885	7,056	13,270	12,122	2,589
Fresh and canned vegetable juices	1,036,073	258,438	233,809	273,797	269,784
Sugar and other sweets	**14,898,050**	**3,026,059**	**3,436,270**	**4,953,000**	**3,483,375**
Candy and chewing gum	9,666,523	2,021,636	2,308,097	3,063,595	2,272,453
Sugar	1,872,140	378,175	424,889	704,347	363,510
Artificial sweeteners	796,532	145,316	125,795	370,775	155,346
Jams, preserves, other sweets	2,562,855	481,153	577,223	813,865	692,325
Fats and oils	**10,336,307**	**2,043,025**	**2,192,387**	**3,511,284**	**2,594,019**
Margarine	1,112,819	202,869	273,352	377,045	258,910
Fats and oils	3,321,014	746,867	601,374	1,165,830	808,317
Salad dressings	3,190,778	578,398	674,356	1,099,366	840,940
Nondairy cream and imitation milk	1,255,846	250,720	306,525	406,724	292,050
Peanut butter	1,455,851	264,171	337,045	462,319	393,543

	total consumer units	Northeast	Midwest	South	West
Miscellaneous foods	**$61,314,336**	**$11,141,929**	**$14,855,736**	**$20,518,439**	**$14,806,804**
Frozen prepared foods	12,779,392	2,205,321	3,445,028	4,320,133	2,805,031
Frozen meals	3,696,605	688,432	919,842	1,272,840	815,308
Other frozen prepared foods	9,082,787	1,516,888	2,525,186	3,047,293	1,989,723
Canned and packaged soups	4,244,293	915,337	955,404	1,349,336	1,024,248
Potato chips, nuts, and other snacks	13,614,297	2,301,022	3,442,639	4,709,301	3,161,291
Potato chips and other snacks	10,007,229	1,652,061	2,597,903	3,558,519	2,197,369
Nuts	3,605,905	648,961	844,736	1,150,782	963,922
Condiments and seasonings	10,889,809	2,131,229	2,408,945	3,694,372	2,658,747
Salt, spices, and other seasonings	2,583,786	465,056	549,888	907,082	663,586
Olives, pickles, relishes	1,223,287	277,843	265,655	384,151	295,934
Sauces and gravies	4,760,585	943,342	986,189	1,634,419	1,198,494
Baking needs and miscellaneous products	2,322,152	444,769	607,212	768,720	500,732
Other canned/packaged prepared foods	19,786,545	3,589,241	4,603,455	6,445,296	5,157,487
Prepared salads	2,957,051	623,382	663,475	932,162	739,188
Prepared desserts	1,268,637	286,884	281,048	366,595	334,253
Baby food	3,497,763	655,576	979,820	1,073,868	786,827
Miscellaneous prepared foods	11,946,813	1,965,626	2,665,577	4,043,411	3,281,684
Nonalcoholic beverages	**33,665,965**	**6,149,142**	**7,378,638**	**11,974,732**	**8,174,565**
Cola	10,908,414	1,776,649	2,647,265	3,971,095	2,514,793
Other carbonated drinks	5,590,839	1,005,085	1,418,244	2,021,078	1,144,900
Coffee	4,548,952	925,921	932,580	1,498,984	1,193,834
Roasted coffee	2,846,583	568,916	582,000	944,703	752,392
Instant and freeze-dried coffee	1,702,368	357,006	350,580	554,281	441,700
Noncarbonated fruit-flavored drinks	2,301,221	444,769	452,490	828,078	577,369
Tea	2,050,052	502,983	387,469	692,225	467,850
Other nonalcoholic beverages and ice	8,151,368	1,474,330	1,527,054	2,911,022	2,247,080
Food prepared by CU on trips	**4,751,283**	**792,733**	**1,169,839**	**1,383,195**	**1,405,881**
FOOD AWAY FROM HOME	283,030,388	60,273,983	63,785,160	91,924,997	67,051,217
Meals at restaurants, carry-outs, other	**235,839,664**	**49,898,326**	**52,152,850**	**79,367,977**	**54,425,212**
Lunch	84,312,590	16,199,547	18,228,578	30,476,691	19,423,687
At fast-food restaurants*	47,579,106	8,698,678	10,085,085	17,413,461	11,400,066
At full-service restaurants	27,518,135	5,460,710	5,820,268	9,946,130	6,295,656
At vending machines, mobile vendors	700,018	107,609	121,283	286,755	185,380
At employer and school cafeterias	8,516,494	1,932,550	2,201,941	2,830,346	1,542,845
Dinner	92,512,796	21,820,788	20,516,239	29,046,261	21,113,593
At fast-food restaurants*	29,427,486	5,571,406	7,026,466	9,701,176	7,131,935
At full-service restaurants	62,585,298	16,140,670	13,432,980	19,133,154	13,858,934
At vending machines, mobile vendors	174,423	22,051	22,824	86,946	43,238
At employer and school cafeterias	324,427	86,440	33,970	124,985	79,485
Snacks and nonalcoholic beverages	34,588,081	7,105,494	7,881,021	11,387,010	8,216,768
At fast-food restaurants*	25,251,799	5,323,332	5,718,889	7,876,980	6,337,340
At full-service restaurants	3,357,061	601,110	684,441	1,286,635	786,569
At vending machines, mobile vendors	4,775,702	917,101	1,198,236	1,858,472	797,961
At employer and school cafeterias	1,202,356	263,950	279,190	364,923	294,640
Breakfast and brunch	24,426,197	4,772,498	5,527,012	8,458,014	5,671,165
At fast-food restaurants*	12,009,605	2,045,892	2,682,297	4,453,897	2,831,181
At full-service restaurants	11,670,062	2,521,532	2,699,812	3,741,190	2,706,127
At vending machines, mobile vendors	165,120	53,804	30,520	53,923	27,186
At employer and school cafeterias	581,410	151,270	114,383	208,587	106,671
Board (including at school)	**3,243,105**	**665,058**	**785,820**	**609,877**	**1,181,924**
Catered affairs	**6,809,474**	**2,192,090**	**1,899,927**	**1,514,032**	**1,202,896**
Food on trips	**26,925,097**	**5,264,235**	**6,246,219**	**7,617,396**	**7,797,075**
School lunches	**7,371,116**	**1,576,867**	**2,078,534**	**2,258,090**	**1,458,181**
Meals as pay	**2,843,095**	**677,407**	**622,074**	**558,043**	**985,670**

	total consumer units	Northeast	Midwest	South	West
ALCOHOLIC BEVERAGES	$53,404,834	$13,777,465	$11,322,334	$14,527,938	$13,779,708
At home	32,278,720	8,238,915	6,201,899	9,413,167	8,436,323
Beer and ale	15,268,989	3,047,228	3,461,482	5,044,127	3,718,724
Whiskey	2,518,668	561,639	474,517	925,892	557,174
Wine	10,994,463	3,810,633	1,603,486	2,415,680	3,170,353
Other alcoholic beverages	3,496,600	819,636	662,413	1,027,469	989,813
Away from home	21,126,114	5,538,550	5,120,435	5,114,770	5,343,385
Beer and ale	8,874,642	2,403,118	2,343,128	1,991,400	2,130,829
At fast-food restaurants*	1,911,676	568,916	510,080	360,743	470,698
At full-service restaurants	6,512,955	1,788,777	1,500,515	1,579,242	1,642,525
Wine	2,591,926	660,648	623,401	649,588	657,890
At fast-food restaurants*	355,823	75,635	88,109	98,650	93,467
At full-service restaurants	2,181,450	582,587	486,194	548,429	563,906
Other alcoholic beverages	5,198,968	1,571,575	1,145,689	1,289,979	1,188,915
At fast-food restaurants*	444,197	122,604	109,871	108,265	103,823
At full-service restaurants	4,586,162	1,438,166	899,672	1,165,412	1,081,467
Alcoholic beverages purchased on trips	4,461,740	903,209	1,007,951	1,184,222	1,366,009

The category fast-food restaurants also includes take-out, delivery, concession stands, buffets, and cafeterias other than employer and school.
Note: Numbers may not add to total because of rounding and missing subcategories.
Source: Calculations by New Strategist based on the 2004 Consumer Expenditure Survey

Table 5.24 Food and Alcohol: Market shares by region, 2004

(percentage of total annual spending on food and alcoholic beverages accounted for by consumer units by region, 2004)

	total consumer units	Northeast	Midwest	South	West
Share of total consumer units	100.0%	19.0%	22.8%	35.9%	22.3%
Share of total before-tax income	100.0	21.3	22.5	33.5	22.8
Share of total spending	100.0	20.2	22.8	32.5	24.6
Share of food spending	100.0	20.9	22.1	33.1	24.0
Share of alcoholic beverages spending	100.0	25.8	21.2	27.2	25.8
FOOD AT HOME	100.0	20.6	21.7	33.5	24.2
Cereals and bakery products	100.0	21.5	22.1	33.3	23.2
Cereals and cereal products	100.0	21.7	20.9	33.5	23.9
Flour	100.0	20.6	19.2	30.5	29.8
Prepared flour mixes	100.0	18.3	28.4	31.1	22.1
Ready-to-eat and cooked cereals	100.0	21.3	22.2	32.8	23.8
Rice	100.0	23.3	13.1	40.1	23.6
Pasta, cornmeal, and other cereal products	100.0	23.9	19.0	33.3	23.8
Bakery products	100.0	21.3	22.6	33.2	22.8
Bread	100.0	22.1	21.9	31.4	24.6
White bread	100.0	20.9	22.7	33.6	22.8
Bread, other than white	100.0	22.9	21.4	30.0	25.8
Crackers and cookies	100.0	20.5	22.7	34.0	22.9
Cookies	100.0	21.2	22.0	34.1	22.8
Crackers	100.0	19.1	24.0	33.7	23.1
Frozen and refrigerated bakery products	100.0	18.6	21.7	40.0	19.7
Other bakery products	100.0	21.9	23.3	32.6	22.1
Biscuits and rolls	100.0	23.0	23.7	31.7	21.6
Cakes and cupcakes	100.0	22.0	22.2	33.1	22.7
Bread and cracker products	100.0	18.8	28.8	29.5	22.8
Sweetrolls, coffee cakes, doughnuts	100.0	20.4	23.8	32.0	23.8
Pies, tarts, turnovers	100.0	21.7	23.5	35.9	18.9
Meats, poultry, fish, and eggs	100.0	21.7	20.3	34.7	23.3
Beef	100.0	19.9	20.8	35.6	23.7
Ground beef	100.0	19.1	24.1	36.8	19.9
Roast	100.0	16.8	18.9	42.0	22.3
Chuck roast	100.0	12.8	22.1	46.3	18.8
Round roast	100.0	19.9	17.5	39.3	23.4
Other roast	100.0	17.5	17.9	41.1	23.6
Steak	100.0	21.4	18.7	33.0	27.0
Round steak	100.0	18.7	20.8	33.7	26.8
Sirloin steak	100.0	25.5	16.5	29.1	29.0
Other steak	100.0	19.7	19.4	35.1	25.8
Other beef	100.0	23.7	19.9	27.9	28.5
Pork	100.0	19.8	21.5	37.5	21.2
Bacon	100.0	17.5	22.3	38.6	21.6
Pork chops	100.0	20.4	22.8	37.4	19.4
Ham	100.0	21.3	20.3	37.2	21.1
Ham, not canned	100.0	21.4	20.3	37.3	21.0
Canned ham	100.0	17.8	20.3	34.5	26.8
Sausage	100.0	20.1	21.9	39.0	18.9
Other pork	100.0	19.4	20.5	36.2	24.0
Other meats	100.0	23.6	25.2	30.6	20.6
Frankfurters	100.0	22.0	24.7	33.3	20.0
Lunch meats (cold cuts)	100.0	24.3	24.6	29.4	21.6
Bologna, liverwurst, salami	100.0	23.8	22.4	31.8	21.9
Other lunch meats	100.0	24.5	25.5	28.5	21.4
Lamb, organ meats, and others	100.0	23.0	28.9	32.4	15.6
Poultry	100.0	23.7	18.6	34.4	23.4
Fresh and frozen chicken	100.0	23.7	18.5	34.6	23.1
Fresh and frozen whole chicken	100.0	23.5	14.6	35.5	26.5
Fresh and frozen chicken parts	100.0	23.9	20.2	34.3	21.7
Other poultry	100.0	23.4	19.0	33.4	24.3

	total consumer units	Northeast	Midwest	South	West
Fish and seafood	100.0%	24.3%	16.2%	32.8%	26.8%
Canned fish and seafood	100.0	22.7	20.0	31.5	25.9
Fresh fish and shellfish	100.0	26.3	12.4	33.6	27.8
Frozen fish and shellfish	100.0	21.0	22.3	31.6	25.1
Eggs	100.0	21.2	17.6	34.3	27.0
Dairy products	**100.0**	**21.3**	**22.1**	**31.9**	**24.7**
Fresh milk and cream	100.0	20.5	21.6	33.0	24.9
Fresh milk, all types	100.0	20.3	21.7	33.3	24.7
Cream	100.0	21.6	21.3	30.8	26.2
Other dairy products	100.0	21.9	22.3	31.3	24.5
Butter	100.0	23.4	26.1	30.0	20.5
Cheese	100.0	21.6	22.9	31.5	24.0
Ice cream and related products	100.0	21.6	20.6	33.0	24.9
Miscellaneous dairy products	100.0	22.5	21.0	27.9	28.7
Fruits and vegetables	**100.0**	**21.6**	**20.7**	**32.1**	**25.6**
Fresh fruits	100.0	21.7	20.9	30.9	26.5
Apples	100.0	20.4	22.0	31.5	26.1
Bananas	100.0	22.4	20.7	31.3	25.6
Oranges	100.0	21.8	20.4	29.7	28.1
Citrus fruits, excluding oranges	100.0	20.7	19.2	30.4	29.7
Other fresh fruits	100.0	22.0	21.0	31.0	26.0
Fresh vegetables	100.0	21.6	18.4	32.7	27.4
Potatoes	100.0	19.8	19.9	38.3	22.0
Lettuce	100.0	24.0	19.8	28.7	27.5
Tomatoes	100.0	22.0	15.5	34.5	28.2
Other fresh vegetables	100.0	21.4	18.8	31.3	28.6
Processed fruits	100.0	21.9	23.3	30.3	24.4
Frozen fruits and fruit juices	100.0	17.5	27.5	21.8	33.3
Frozen orange juice	100.0	18.7	28.4	20.8	32.2
Frozen fruits	100.0	19.5	28.2	20.0	32.2
Frozen fruit juices, excluding orange	100.0	12.1	24.9	26.4	36.7
Canned fruits	100.0	16.0	28.4	32.4	23.3
Dried fruits	100.0	18.8	24.0	29.0	28.1
Fresh fruit juice	100.0	25.6	23.5	29.0	21.8
Canned and bottled fruit juice	100.0	23.4	21.0	32.0	23.7
Processed vegetables	100.0	20.8	21.9	35.9	21.3
Frozen vegetables	100.0	23.3	23.2	35.6	17.8
Canned and dried vegetables and juices	100.0	19.4	21.2	36.1	23.2
Canned beans	100.0	17.0	23.2	40.7	19.1
Canned corn	100.0	18.2	19.4	37.5	24.9
Canned miscellaneous vegetables	100.0	18.7	21.9	37.5	21.9
Dried peas	100.0	22.4	18.3	31.2	28.6
Dried beans	100.0	17.6	7.1	40.2	35.6
Dried miscellaneous vegetables	100.0	19.7	20.9	35.7	23.8
Dried processed vegetables	100.0	20.2	38.0	34.7	7.4
Fresh and canned vegetable juices	100.0	24.9	22.6	26.4	26.0
Sugar and other sweets	**100.0**	**20.3**	**23.1**	**33.2**	**23.4**
Candy and chewing gum	100.0	20.9	23.9	31.7	23.5
Sugar	100.0	20.2	22.7	37.6	19.4
Artificial sweeteners	100.0	18.2	15.8	46.5	19.5
Jams, preserves, other sweets	100.0	18.8	22.5	31.8	27.0
Fats and oils	**100.0**	**19.8**	**21.2**	**34.0**	**25.1**
Margarine	100.0	18.2	24.6	33.9	23.3
Fats and oils	100.0	22.5	18.1	35.1	24.3
Salad dressings	100.0	18.1	21.1	34.5	26.4
Nondairy cream and imitation milk	100.0	20.0	24.4	32.4	23.3
Peanut butter	100.0	18.1	23.2	31.8	27.0

	total consumer units	Northeast	Midwest	South	West
Miscellaneous foods	100.0%	18.2%	24.2%	33.5%	24.1%
Frozen prepared foods	100.0	17.3	27.0	33.8	21.9
Frozen meals	100.0	18.6	24.9	34.4	22.1
Other frozen prepared foods	100.0	16.7	27.8	33.6	21.9
Canned and packaged soups	100.0	21.6	22.5	31.8	24.1
Potato chips, nuts, and other snacks	100.0	16.9	25.3	34.6	23.2
Potato chips and other snacks	100.0	16.5	26.0	35.6	22.0
Nuts	100.0	18.0	23.4	31.9	26.7
Condiments and seasonings	100.0	19.6	22.1	33.9	24.4
Salt, spices, and other seasonings	100.0	18.0	21.3	35.1	25.7
Olives, pickles, relishes	100.0	22.7	21.7	31.4	24.2
Sauces and gravies	100.0	19.8	20.7	34.3	25.2
Baking needs and miscellaneous products	100.0	19.2	26.1	33.1	21.6
Other canned/packaged prepared foods	100.0	18.1	23.3	32.6	26.1
Prepared salads	100.0	21.1	22.4	31.5	25.0
Prepared desserts	100.0	22.6	22.2	28.9	26.3
Baby food	100.0	18.7	28.0	30.7	22.5
Miscellaneous prepared foods	100.0	16.5	22.3	33.8	27.5
Nonalcoholic beverages	100.0	18.3	21.9	35.6	24.3
Cola	100.0	16.3	24.3	36.4	23.1
Other carbonated drinks	100.0	18.0	25.4	36.1	20.5
Coffee	100.0	20.4	20.5	33.0	26.2
Roasted coffee	100.0	20.0	20.4	33.2	26.4
Instant and freeze-dried coffee	100.0	21.0	20.6	32.6	25.9
Noncarbonated fruit-flavored drinks	100.0	19.3	19.7	36.0	25.1
Tea	100.0	24.5	18.9	33.8	22.8
Other nonalcoholic beverages and ice	100.0	18.1	18.7	35.7	27.6
Food prepared by CU on trips	100.0	16.7	24.6	29.1	29.6
FOOD AWAY FROM HOME	100.0	21.3	22.5	32.5	23.7
Meals at restaurants, carry-outs, other	100.0	21.2	22.1	33.7	23.1
Lunch	100.0	19.2	21.6	36.1	23.0
At fast-food restaurants*	100.0	18.3	21.2	36.6	24.0
At full-service restaurants	100.0	19.8	21.2	36.1	22.9
At vending machines, mobile vendors	100.0	15.4	17.3	41.0	26.5
At employer and school cafeterias	100.0	22.7	25.9	33.2	18.1
Dinner	100.0	23.6	22.2	31.4	22.8
At fast-food restaurants*	100.0	18.9	23.9	33.0	24.2
At full-service restaurants	100.0	25.8	21.5	30.6	22.1
At vending machines, mobile vendors	100.0	12.6	13.1	49.8	24.8
At employer and school cafeterias	100.0	26.6	10.5	38.5	24.5
Snacks and nonalcoholic beverages	100.0	20.5	22.8	32.9	23.8
At fast-food restaurants*	100.0	21.1	22.6	31.2	25.1
At full-service restaurants	100.0	17.9	20.4	38.3	23.4
At vending machines, mobile vendors	100.0	19.2	25.1	38.9	16.7
At employer and school cafeterias	100.0	22.0	23.2	30.4	24.5
Breakfast and brunch	100.0	19.5	22.6	34.6	23.2
At fast-food restaurants*	100.0	17.0	22.3	37.1	23.6
At full-service restaurants	100.0	21.6	23.1	32.1	23.2
At vending machines, mobile vendors	100.0	32.6	18.5	32.7	16.5
At employer and school cafeterias	100.0	26.0	19.7	35.9	18.3
Board (including at school)	100.0	20.5	24.2	18.8	36.4
Catered affairs	100.0	32.2	27.9	22.2	17.7
Food on trips	100.0	19.6	23.2	28.3	29.0
School lunches	100.0	21.4	28.2	30.6	19.8
Meals as pay	100.0	23.8	21.9	19.6	34.7

	total consumer units	Northeast	Midwest	South	West
ALCOHOLIC BEVERAGES	**100.0%**	**25.8%**	**21.2%**	**27.2%**	**25.8%**
At home	**100.0**	**25.5**	**19.2**	**29.2**	**26.1**
Beer and ale	100.0	20.0	22.7	33.0	24.4
Whiskey	100.0	22.3	18.8	36.8	22.1
Wine	100.0	34.7	14.6	22.0	28.8
Other alcoholic beverages	100.0	23.4	18.9	29.4	28.3
Away from home	**100.0**	**26.2**	**24.2**	**24.2**	**25.3**
Beer and ale	100.0	27.1	26.4	22.4	24.0
At fast-food restaurants*	100.0	29.8	26.7	18.9	24.6
At full-service restaurants	100.0	27.5	23.0	24.2	25.2
Wine	100.0	25.5	24.1	25.1	25.4
At fast-food restaurants*	100.0	21.3	24.8	27.7	26.3
At full-service restaurants	100.0	26.7	22.3	25.1	25.9
Other alcoholic beverages	100.0	30.2	22.0	24.8	22.9
At fast-food restaurants*	100.0	27.6	24.7	24.4	23.4
At full-service restaurants	100.0	31.4	19.6	25.4	23.6
Alcoholic beverages purchased on trips	100.0	20.2	22.6	26.5	30.6

* The category fast-food restaurants also includes take-out, delivery, concession stands, buffets, and cafeterias other than employer and school.
Note: Numbers may not add to total because of rounding.
Source: Calculations by New Strategist based on the 2004 Consumer Expenditure Survey

Table 5.25 Food and Alcohol: Average spending by education, 2004

(average annual spending of consumer units (CU) on food and alcoholic beverages, by education of consumer unit reference person, 2004)

	total consumer units	less than high school graduate	high school graduate	some college	associate's degree	college graduate total	bachelor's degree	master's, professional, doctorate
Number of consumer units (in 000s)	116,282	16,829	31,005	25,317	10,678	32,452	20,684	11,768
Average number of persons per CU	2.5	2.7	2.5	2.3	2.6	2.5	2.4	2.5
Average before-tax income of CU	$54,453.00	$29,094.00	$42,334.00	$46,756.00	$58,593.00	$83,825.00	$75,647.00	$98,201.00
Average spending of CU, total	43,394.87	25,421.18	35,438.55	40,877.68	48,177.36	60,712.28	56,728.41	67,801.38
Food, average spending	**5,780.82**	**4,259.90**	**5,181.74**	**5,504.98**	**6,217.99**	**7,206.40**	**6,847.82**	**7,876.86**
Alcoholic beverages, average spending	**459.27**	**201.70**	**344.92**	**451.72**	**447.93**	**711.05**	**692.80**	**745.51**
FOOD AT HOME	**3346.82**	**2990.87**	**3229.42**	**3097.90**	**3481.64**	**3778.85**	**3625.54**	**4070.65**
Cereals and bakery products	**460.90**	**413.43**	**465.99**	**425.01**	**465.41**	**504.26**	**493.95**	**523.95**
Cereals and cereal products	153.80	151.31	156.92	137.71	151.94	163.99	158.23	174.98
Flour	8.32	12.94	8.73	5.84	5.72	8.09	6.05	11.99
Prepared flour mixes	13.78	12.15	13.46	12.26	19.33	14.33	15.02	13.01
Ready-to-eat and cooked cereals	86.69	77.45	88.72	78.52	87.88	94.88	93.06	98.36
Rice	18.46	25.22	16.78	16.74	15.56	18.74	16.80	22.43
Pasta, cornmeal, and other cereal products	26.55	23.55	29.25	24.35	23.45	27.95	27.30	29.19
Bakery products	307.10	262.12	309.07	287.30	313.47	340.27	335.72	348.97
Bread	87.63	85.25	88.73	79.07	91.27	92.75	91.53	95.07
White bread	35.04	42.84	37.74	30.42	33.19	32.26	31.72	33.29
Bread, other than white	52.59	42.41	50.99	48.64	58.09	60.49	59.82	61.78
Crackers and cookies	71.16	54.28	68.34	69.72	76.59	81.92	80.71	84.25
Cookies	46.57	38.10	45.32	46.74	48.34	51.45	50.75	52.79
Crackers	24.60	16.19	23.02	22.98	28.26	30.47	29.96	31.46
Frozen and refrigerated bakery products	26.32	17.24	25.04	28.11	29.61	29.95	28.25	33.20
Other bakery products	121.99	105.35	126.96	110.40	115.99	135.65	135.23	136.46
Biscuits and rolls	42.11	27.60	42.77	39.08	41.45	51.23	50.65	52.34
Cakes and cupcakes	39.04	39.01	43.15	29.82	35.09	42.77	42.62	43.07
Bread and cracker products	3.25	1.84	3.09	3.64	2.89	3.96	3.98	3.93
Sweetrolls, coffee cakes, doughnuts	23.59	24.82	22.65	23.93	21.78	24.19	25.06	22.52
Pies, tarts, turnovers	13.99	12.08	15.30	13.93	14.79	13.50	12.92	14.60
Meats, poultry, fish, and eggs	**879.71**	**888.84**	**889.53**	**807.89**	**898.03**	**910.88**	**872.04**	**985.05**
Beef	265.34	269.32	277.27	244.73	290.36	258.82	253.41	269.15
Ground beef	96.92	105.50	111.04	91.03	101.95	81.49	83.83	77.02
Roast	45.58	46.60	45.07	39.46	48.27	49.07	48.23	50.66
Chuck roast	11.72	17.81	11.45	9.82	10.57	10.56	8.85	13.84
Round roast	10.27	10.03	10.18	9.58	7.48	11.82	9.41	16.43
Other roast	23.58	18.76	23.44	20.07	30.23	26.68	29.97	20.39
Steak	103.45	93.66	102.26	95.37	123.77	109.24	104.21	118.85
Round steak	16.37	16.85	19.32	13.60	17.47	14.88	15.36	13.96
Sirloin steak	32.38	29.37	28.52	29.87	45.86	35.40	31.86	42.16
Other steak	54.71	47.44	54.42	51.90	60.44	58.96	56.99	62.73
Other beef	19.39	23.55	18.89	18.88	16.37	19.03	17.15	22.63
Pork	181.14	206.18	195.31	164.50	186.63	164.73	155.52	182.33
Bacon	31.08	32.20	34.28	29.30	33.52	27.91	25.98	31.62
Pork chops	37.92	43.80	43.62	32.57	43.22	31.56	30.91	32.82
Ham	39.65	48.68	43.45	32.11	36.23	37.71	34.90	43.07
Ham, not canned	38.67	47.45	42.44	31.49	35.64	36.52	33.87	41.58
Canned ham	0.98	1.23	1.00	0.61	0.59	1.19	1.03	1.49
Sausage	27.91	27.10	28.95	29.59	32.67	24.69	23.43	27.08
Other pork	44.59	54.38	45.00	40.93	40.99	42.86	40.30	47.74
Other meats	107.98	100.48	109.69	99.10	104.16	117.59	116.76	119.16
Frankfurters	22.52	23.49	23.89	20.76	18.82	23.03	22.90	23.26
Lunch meats (cold cuts)	72.99	63.47	77.87	69.20	75.43	75.04	72.30	80.28
Bologna, liverwurst, salami	21.07	25.05	23.66	19.85	18.43	18.18	17.39	19.70
Other lunch meats	51.91	38.42	54.21	49.35	57.00	56.86	54.91	60.58
Lamb, organ meats, and others	12.48	13.52	7.92	9.14	9.91	19.52	21.56	15.62
Poultry	155.61	153.33	149.05	143.45	158.08	171.02	163.01	186.32
Fresh and frozen chicken	122.64	126.78	119.94	112.39	126.58	129.22	127.17	133.14
Fresh and frozen whole chicken	36.59	48.67	36.23	33.85	32.41	33.96	34.72	32.51
Fresh and frozen chicken parts	86.04	78.11	83.70	78.54	94.16	95.27	92.45	100.63
Other poultry	32.97	26.55	29.11	31.06	31.50	41.80	35.84	53.18

	total consumer units	less than high school graduate	high school graduate	some college	associate's degree	college graduate		
						total	bachelor's degree	master's, professional, doctorate
Fish and seafood	$127.80	$108.28	$116.09	$119.64	$117.55	$158.00	$145.17	$182.49
Canned fish and seafood	15.38	13.29	16.46	13.03	12.87	17.83	16.29	20.76
Fresh fish and shellfish	74.88	68.73	66.43	64.12	69.47	95.47	85.92	113.70
Frozen fish and shellfish	37.54	26.27	33.19	42.49	35.22	44.70	42.95	48.04
Eggs	41.84	51.26	42.13	36.48	41.26	40.72	38.17	45.59
Dairy products	**370.57**	**325.32**	**346.32**	**334.79**	**394.31**	**435.52**	**415.39**	**473.95**
Fresh milk and cream	144.33	152.61	140.03	129.87	152.38	152.12	149.05	157.99
Fresh milk, all types	128.94	141.83	125.50	115.44	136.21	133.11	131.40	136.37
Cream	15.39	10.78	14.53	14.44	16.17	19.01	17.65	21.62
Other dairy products	226.24	172.71	206.29	204.92	241.93	283.40	266.34	315.96
Butter	21.81	15.51	20.62	20.42	34.69	23.33	21.01	27.74
Cheese	113.67	82.87	101.10	105.20	114.59	147.34	138.88	163.50
Ice cream and related products	60.22	52.24	57.66	54.74	63.30	69.75	66.85	75.30
Miscellaneous dairy products	30.54	22.09	26.91	24.56	29.35	42.98	39.60	49.43
Fruits and vegetables	**560.95**	**507.27**	**510.43**	**502.16**	**551.26**	**682.03**	**640.43**	**761.44**
Fresh fruits	186.74	168.35	163.10	169.84	175.35	234.49	217.31	267.28
Apples	32.42	29.72	29.50	28.99	33.25	38.84	37.08	42.20
Bananas	30.17	34.08	28.80	26.31	30.28	32.21	30.44	35.60
Oranges	19.48	21.13	17.26	17.93	19.64	21.86	19.80	25.79
Citrus fruits, excluding oranges	15.41	13.58	11.98	15.09	13.90	20.34	18.05	24.73
Other fresh fruits	89.25	69.85	75.56	81.52	78.29	121.24	111.95	138.97
Fresh vegetables	182.94	172.57	160.88	159.61	181.93	226.52	209.86	258.32
Potatoes	28.07	30.61	30.13	23.48	28.99	27.75	25.42	32.21
Lettuce	22.87	18.50	19.35	22.16	22.63	29.10	27.57	32.02
Tomatoes	35.74	40.93	31.96	30.26	32.10	41.76	38.50	47.97
Other fresh vegetables	96.25	82.53	79.44	83.71	98.22	127.91	118.37	146.12
Processed fruits	109.63	94.36	98.84	98.62	107.91	136.24	132.99	142.45
Frozen fruits and fruit juices	9.97	8.57	9.05	8.35	11.15	12.36	11.88	13.29
Frozen orange juice	4.17	3.84	3.96	3.67	5.06	4.63	4.58	4.71
Frozen fruits	3.53	2.42	3.12	3.00	2.53	5.16	4.45	6.51
Frozen fruit juices, excluding orange	2.27	2.31	1.97	1.68	3.56	2.58	2.85	2.07
Canned fruits	16.19	11.95	15.89	14.88	19.04	18.73	18.41	19.35
Dried fruits	6.35	3.47	6.36	5.22	5.23	8.93	8.01	10.68
Fresh fruit juice	22.07	19.94	19.64	18.12	21.22	28.58	27.59	30.45
Canned and bottled fruit juice	55.05	50.43	47.90	52.05	51.27	67.64	67.10	68.67
Processed vegetables	81.64	71.98	87.62	74.09	86.07	84.78	80.27	93.38
Frozen vegetables	28.50	18.76	32.15	25.88	33.55	30.27	28.60	33.46
Canned and dried vegetables and juices	53.14	53.22	55.47	48.21	52.52	54.51	51.67	59.93
Canned beans	11.39	10.51	13.37	9.84	10.87	11.18	9.78	13.86
Canned corn	6.33	8.10	7.25	5.69	6.46	4.95	4.69	5.44
Canned miscellaneous vegetables	16.77	14.69	16.25	15.26	19.96	18.44	17.28	20.67
Dried peas	0.60	0.51	0.54	0.64	0.67	0.65	0.57	0.82
Dried beans	2.47	5.62	2.49	1.59	1.21	1.85	1.86	1.84
Dried miscellaneous vegetables	6.21	5.83	6.57	6.39	5.46	6.16	5.70	7.04
Dried processed vegetables	0.30	0.78	0.29	0.02	–	0.36	0.13	0.80
Fresh and canned vegetable juices	8.91	7.04	8.64	8.72	7.75	10.59	11.28	9.29
Sugar and other sweets	**128.12**	**98.56**	**124.67**	**119.58**	**147.20**	**146.92**	**145.22**	**150.16**
Candy and chewing gum	83.13	53.03	78.04	75.87	100.63	103.36	104.09	101.96
Sugar	16.10	21.54	18.06	15.13	16.78	11.89	10.93	13.72
Artificial sweeteners	6.85	5.22	7.30	7.48	6.86	6.81	6.11	8.15
Jams, preserves, other sweets	22.04	18.76	21.28	21.10	22.93	24.86	24.09	26.33
Fats and oils	**88.89**	**90.64**	**92.83**	**81.22**	**89.51**	**89.42**	**84.77**	**98.29**
Margarine	9.57	9.50	11.58	7.65	9.30	9.08	8.39	10.38
Fats and oils	28.56	37.98	28.29	24.27	22.37	28.89	26.36	33.72
Salad dressings	27.44	22.96	28.69	27.16	31.40	27.53	27.27	28.03
Nondairy cream and imitation milk	10.80	8.38	12.36	11.10	11.60	10.08	10.29	9.67
Peanut butter	12.52	11.81	11.91	11.04	14.83	13.84	12.46	16.48

	total consumer units	less than high school graduate	high school graduate	some college	associate's degree	college graduate total	bachelor's degree	master's, professional, doctorate
Miscellaneous foods	**$527.29**	**$376.51**	**$484.63**	**$508.37**	**$563.35**	**$648.41**	**$625.87**	**$691.44**
Frozen prepared foods	109.90	66.57	109.00	114.09	131.61	123.45	121.20	127.75
Frozen meals	31.79	21.28	30.85	33.50	42.91	33.55	33.89	32.90
Other frozen prepared foods	78.11	45.29	78.14	80.59	88.70	89.90	87.31	94.85
Canned and packaged soups	36.50	27.14	35.64	32.94	37.52	44.33	44.72	43.59
Potato chips, nuts, and other snacks	117.08	81.22	105.86	113.99	127.14	145.48	144.09	148.13
Potato chips and other snacks	86.06	65.34	81.68	82.47	93.07	101.36	105.28	93.89
Nuts	31.01	15.88	24.18	31.52	34.07	44.12	38.82	54.25
Condiments and seasonings	93.65	67.96	87.02	91.91	100.72	112.34	104.90	126.55
Salt, spices, and other seasonings	22.22	18.74	21.42	20.20	23.03	25.98	23.02	31.62
Olives, pickles, relishes	10.52	6.72	9.00	12.49	10.86	12.44	11.31	14.59
Sauces and gravies	40.94	28.35	38.34	40.73	47.29	48.14	46.92	50.47
Baking needs and miscellaneous products	19.97	14.15	18.27	18.48	19.55	25.78	23.64	29.87
Other canned/packaged prepared foods	170.16	133.62	147.12	155.44	166.36	222.81	210.96	245.42
Prepared salads	25.43	13.66	21.98	22.52	27.74	36.18	35.89	36.72
Prepared desserts	10.91	8.94	10.28	11.31	10.48	12.37	12.01	13.04
Baby food	30.08	26.08	27.93	29.83	25.03	35.90	33.22	41.02
Miscellaneous prepared foods	102.74	84.86	85.12	90.44	103.10	137.61	129.32	153.44
Nonalcoholic beverages	**289.52**	**270.03**	**287.65**	**281.36**	**329.11**	**295.22**	**287.65**	**309.69**
Cola	93.81	101.43	101.63	86.48	116.23	80.80	76.99	88.07
Other carbonated drinks	48.08	43.35	50.81	47.11	52.58	47.20	45.39	50.64
Coffee	39.12	33.83	34.40	38.27	47.31	44.57	43.67	46.28
Roasted coffee	24.48	18.84	21.68	23.45	31.30	28.77	27.87	30.48
Instant and freeze-dried coffee	14.64	14.99	12.73	14.82	16.01	15.80	15.80	15.79
Noncarbonated fruit-flavored drinks	19.79	22.38	18.84	22.98	18.54	17.51	18.06	16.46
Tea	17.63	13.40	16.14	17.35	20.21	20.68	20.13	21.73
Other nonalcoholic beverages and ice	70.10	55.59	65.10	68.26	73.88	82.54	80.69	86.07
Food prepared by CU on trips	**40.86**	**20.28**	**27.37**	**37.52**	**43.46**	**66.18**	**60.21**	**76.68**
FOOD AWAY FROM HOME	**2434.00**	**1269.04**	**1952.32**	**2407.08**	**2736.35**	**3427.55**	**3222.28**	**3806.20**
Meals at restaurants, carry-outs, other	**2028.17**	**1135.59**	**1686.51**	**2041.86**	**2293.07**	**2727.32**	**2609.61**	**2952.07**
Lunch	725.07	428.77	608.77	730.07	859.99	945.60	918.12	998.07
At fast-food restaurants*	409.17	281.91	366.35	444.63	454.31	477.17	481.50	468.90
At full-service restaurants	236.65	99.77	168.89	207.18	312.52	370.63	344.10	421.29
At vending machines, mobile vendors	6.02	7.66	8.36	4.90	7.19	3.35	2.44	5.08
At employer and school cafeterias	73.24	39.43	65.18	73.35	85.97	94.45	90.08	102.81
Dinner	795.59	389.85	616.33	781.91	868.26	1165.07	1094.73	1299.37
At fast-food restaurants*	253.07	164.33	218.47	287.21	279.30	300.01	298.13	303.60
At full-service restaurants	538.22	221.36	395.60	491.19	584.53	858.20	788.71	990.87
At vending machines, mobile vendors	1.50	3.47	0.92	1.12	1.32	1.38	0.39	3.26
At employer and school cafeterias	2.79	0.69	1.33	2.39	3.11	5.48	7.50	1.64
Snacks and nonalcoholic beverages	297.45	192.41	264.54	302.21	343.35	365.98	358.44	380.37
At fast-food restaurants*	217.16	132.92	185.17	219.89	244.04	281.30	269.97	302.95
At full-service restaurants	28.87	19.81	24.79	31.48	35.87	33.53	35.29	30.18
At vending machines, mobile vendors	41.07	33.06	45.10	40.87	48.10	39.29	41.26	35.52
At employer and school cafeterias	10.34	6.61	9.49	9.97	15.34	11.85	11.92	11.72
Breakfast and brunch	210.06	124.56	196.86	227.67	221.48	250.67	238.31	274.26
At fast-food restaurants*	103.28	77.59	104.35	116.92	109.27	103.89	102.31	106.92
At full-service restaurants	100.36	42.97	85.95	104.86	106.78	138.56	127.82	159.07
At vending machines, mobile vendors	1.42	1.56	1.90	1.28	0.94	1.14	1.09	1.24
At employer and school cafeterias	5.00	2.44	4.66	4.60	4.49	7.07	7.10	7.01
Board (including at school)	**27.89**	**5.15**	**5.59**	**29.26**	**16.41**	**63.69**	**46.10**	**94.62**
Catered affairs	**58.56**	**9.58**	**37.75**	**52.34**	**80.99**	**101.30**	**83.81**	**132.05**
Food on trips	**231.55**	**58.98**	**138.34**	**197.89**	**237.48**	**434.40**	**384.15**	**522.71**
School lunches	**63.39**	**34.78**	**58.46**	**57.19**	**87.61**	**79.82**	**73.19**	**91.49**
Meals as pay	**24.45**	**24.97**	**25.68**	**28.54**	**20.80**	**21.02**	**25.43**	**13.27**

	total consumer units	less than high school graduate	high school graduate	some college	associate's degree	college graduate		
						total	bachelor's degree	master's, professional, doctorate
ALCOHOLIC BEVERAGES	**$459.27**	**$201.70**	**$344.92**	**$451.72**	**$447.93**	**$711.05**	**$692.80**	**$745.51**
At home	**277.59**	**156.37**	**225.81**	**275.73**	**278.29**	**390.95**	**362.66**	**444.96**
Beer and ale	131.31	113.40	135.95	141.53	149.87	123.14	132.81	104.68
Whiskey	21.66	11.48	14.11	27.49	16.07	31.75	26.70	41.38
Wine	94.55	19.73	55.72	69.44	81.33	192.26	162.56	248.95
Other alcoholic beverages	30.07	11.76	20.03	37.27	31.02	43.80	40.58	49.95
Away from home	**181.68**	**45.33**	**119.11**	**175.99**	**169.64**	**320.11**	**330.13**	**300.55**
Beer and ale	76.32	21.79	51.90	76.23	71.93	129.28	134.44	119.44
At fast-food restaurants*	16.44	7.23	11.25	18.11	18.70	24.33	22.64	27.55
At full-service restaurants	56.01	14.02	39.31	57.52	52.21	93.74	96.49	88.49
Wine	22.29	6.04	16.08	23.40	17.88	37.16	40.98	29.88
At fast-food restaurants*	3.06	1.93	1.84	4.09	1.99	4.41	4.49	4.25
At full-service restaurants	18.76	4.11	14.13	19.27	15.88	31.24	34.26	25.46
Other alcoholic beverages	44.71	9.47	29.27	41.90	43.45	80.09	83.85	72.91
At fast-food restaurants*	3.82	1.05	2.02	5.09	4.61	5.85	6.75	4.15
At full-service restaurants	39.44	8.42	26.72	36.63	38.70	69.87	70.92	67.86
Alcoholic beverages purchased on trips	38.37	8.03	21.86	34.47	36.37	73.57	70.87	78.32

* The category fast-food restaurants also includes take-out, delivery, concession stands, buffets, and cafeterias other than employer and school.
Note: Subcategories may not add to total because some are not shown. "–" means sample is too small to make a reliable estimate.
Source: Bureau of Labor Statistics, unpublished tables from the 2004 Consumer Expenditure Survey

Table 5.26 Food and Alcohol: Indexed spending by education, 2004

(indexed average annual spending of consumer units (CU) on food and alcoholic beverages, by education of consumer unit reference person, 2004; index definition: an index of 100 is the average for all consumer units; an index of 132 means that spending by consumer units in that group is 32 percent above the average for all consumer units; an index of 68 indicates spending that is 32 percent below the average for all consumer units)

| | | | | | | college graduate | | |
	total consumer units	less than high school graduate	high school graduate	some college	associate's degree	total	bachelor's degree	master's, professional, doctorate
Average spending of CU, total	$43,395	$25,421	$35,439	$40,878	$48,177	$60,712	$56,728	$67,801
Average spending of CU, index	100	59	82	94	111	140	131	156
Food, spending index	100	74	90	95	108	125	118	136
Alcoholic beverages, spending index	100	44	75	98	98	155	151	162
FOOD AT HOME	100	89	96	93	104	113	108	122
Cereals and bakery products	100	90	101	92	101	109	107	114
Cereals and cereal products	100	98	102	90	99	107	103	114
Flour	100	156	105	70	69	97	73	144
Prepared flour mixes	100	88	98	89	140	104	109	94
Ready-to-eat and cooked cereals	100	89	102	91	101	109	107	113
Rice	100	137	91	91	84	102	91	122
Pasta, cornmeal, and other cereal products	100	89	110	92	88	105	103	110
Bakery products	100	85	101	94	102	111	109	114
Bread	100	97	101	90	104	106	104	108
White bread	100	122	108	87	95	92	91	95
Bread, other than white	100	81	97	92	110	115	114	117
Crackers and cookies	100	76	96	98	108	115	113	118
Cookies	100	82	97	100	104	110	109	113
Crackers	100	66	94	93	115	124	122	128
Frozen and refrigerated bakery products	100	66	95	107	113	114	107	126
Other bakery products	100	86	104	90	95	111	111	112
Biscuits and rolls	100	66	102	93	98	122	120	124
Cakes and cupcakes	100	100	111	76	90	110	109	110
Bread and cracker products	100	57	95	112	89	122	122	121
Sweetrolls, coffee cakes, doughnuts	100	105	96	101	92	103	106	95
Pies, tarts, turnovers	100	86	109	100	106	96	92	104
Meats, poultry, fish, and eggs	100	101	101	92	102	104	99	112
Beef	100	101	104	92	109	98	96	101
Ground beef	100	109	115	94	105	84	86	79
Roast	100	102	99	87	106	108	106	111
Chuck roast	100	152	98	84	90	90	76	118
Round roast	100	98	99	93	73	115	92	160
Other roast	100	80	99	85	128	113	127	86
Steak	100	91	99	92	120	106	101	115
Round steak	100	103	118	83	107	91	94	85
Sirloin steak	100	91	88	92	142	109	98	130
Other steak	100	87	99	95	110	108	104	115
Other beef	100	121	97	97	84	98	88	117
Pork	100	114	108	91	103	91	86	101
Bacon	100	104	110	94	108	90	84	102
Pork chops	100	116	115	86	114	83	82	87
Ham	100	123	110	81	91	95	88	109
Ham, not canned	100	123	110	81	92	94	88	108
Canned ham	100	126	102	62	60	121	105	152
Sausage	100	97	104	106	117	88	84	97
Other pork	100	122	101	92	92	96	90	107
Other meats	100	93	102	92	96	109	108	110
Frankfurters	100	104	106	92	84	102	102	103
Lunch meats (cold cuts)	100	87	107	95	103	103	99	110
Bologna, liverwurst, salami	100	119	112	94	87	86	83	93
Other lunch meats	100	74	104	95	110	110	106	117
Lamb, organ meats, and others	100	108	63	73	79	156	173	125
Poultry	100	99	96	92	102	110	105	120
Fresh and frozen chicken	100	103	98	92	103	105	104	109
Fresh and frozen whole chicken	100	133	99	93	89	93	95	89
Fresh and frozen chicken parts	100	91	97	91	109	111	107	117
Other poultry	100	81	88	94	96	127	109	161

	total consumer units	less than high school graduate	high school graduate	some college	associate's degree	college graduate		
						total	bachelor's degree	master's, professional, doctorate
Fish and seafood	100	85	91	94	92	124	114	143
Canned fish and seafood	100	86	107	85	84	116	106	135
Fresh fish and shellfish	100	92	89	86	93	127	115	152
Frozen fish and shellfish	100	70	88	113	94	119	114	128
Eggs	100	123	101	87	99	97	91	109
Dairy products	**100**	**88**	**93**	**90**	**106**	**118**	**112**	**128**
Fresh milk and cream	100	106	97	90	106	105	103	109
Fresh milk, all types	100	110	97	90	106	103	102	106
Cream	100	70	94	94	105	124	115	140
Other dairy products	100	76	91	91	107	125	118	140
Butter	100	71	95	94	159	107	96	127
Cheese	100	73	89	93	101	130	122	144
Ice cream and related products	100	87	96	91	105	116	111	125
Miscellaneous dairy products	100	72	88	80	96	141	130	162
Fruits and vegetables	**100**	**90**	**91**	**90**	**98**	**122**	**114**	**136**
Fresh fruits	100	90	87	91	94	126	116	143
Apples	100	92	91	89	103	120	114	130
Bananas	100	113	95	87	100	107	101	118
Oranges	100	108	89	92	101	112	102	132
Citrus fruits, excluding oranges	100	88	78	98	90	132	117	160
Other fresh fruits	100	78	85	91	88	136	125	156
Fresh vegetables	100	94	88	87	99	124	115	141
Potatoes	100	109	107	84	103	99	91	115
Lettuce	100	81	85	97	99	127	121	140
Tomatoes	100	115	89	85	90	117	108	134
Other fresh vegetables	100	86	83	87	102	133	123	152
Processed fruits	100	86	90	90	98	124	121	130
Frozen fruits and fruit juices	100	86	91	84	112	124	119	133
Frozen orange juice	100	92	95	88	121	111	110	113
Frozen fruits	100	69	88	85	72	146	126	184
Frozen fruit juices, excluding orange	100	102	87	74	157	114	126	91
Canned fruits	100	74	98	92	118	116	114	120
Dried fruits	100	55	100	82	82	141	126	168
Fresh fruit juice	100	90	89	82	96	129	125	138
Canned and bottled fruit juice	100	92	87	95	93	123	122	125
Processed vegetables	100	88	107	91	105	104	98	114
Frozen vegetables	100	66	113	91	118	106	100	117
Canned and dried vegetables and juices	100	100	104	91	99	103	97	113
Canned beans	100	92	117	86	95	98	86	122
Canned corn	100	128	115	90	102	78	74	86
Canned miscellaneous vegetables	100	88	97	91	119	110	103	123
Dried peas	100	85	90	107	112	108	95	137
Dried beans	100	228	101	64	49	75	75	74
Dried miscellaneous vegetables	100	94	106	103	88	99	92	113
Dried processed vegetables	100	260	97	7	–	120	43	267
Fresh and canned vegetable juices	100	79	97	98	87	119	127	104
Sugar and other sweets	**100**	**77**	**97**	**93**	**115**	**115**	**113**	**117**
Candy and chewing gum	100	64	94	91	121	124	125	123
Sugar	100	134	112	94	104	74	68	85
Artificial sweeteners	100	76	107	109	100	99	89	119
Jams, preserves, other sweets	100	85	97	96	104	113	109	119
Fats and oils	**100**	**102**	**104**	**91**	**101**	**101**	**95**	**111**
Margarine	100	99	121	80	97	95	88	108
Fats and oils	100	133	99	85	78	101	92	118
Salad dressings	100	84	105	99	114	100	99	102
Nondairy cream and imitation milk	100	78	114	103	107	93	95	90
Peanut butter	100	94	95	88	118	111	100	132

	total consumer units	less than high school graduate	high school graduate	some college	associate's degree	college graduate		
						total	bachelor's degree	master's, professional, doctorate
Miscellaneous foods	**100**	**71**	**92**	**96**	**107**	**123**	**119**	**131**
Frozen prepared foods	100	61	99	104	120	112	110	116
Frozen meals	100	67	97	105	135	106	107	103
Other frozen prepared foods	100	58	100	103	114	115	112	121
Canned and packaged soups	100	74	98	90	103	121	123	119
Potato chips, nuts, and other snacks	100	69	90	97	109	124	123	127
Potato chips and other snacks	100	76	95	96	108	118	122	109
Nuts	100	51	78	102	110	142	125	175
Condiments and seasonings	100	73	93	98	108	120	112	135
Salt, spices, and other seasonings	100	84	96	91	104	117	104	142
Olives, pickles, relishes	100	64	86	119	103	118	108	139
Sauces and gravies	100	69	94	99	116	118	115	123
Baking needs and miscellaneous products	100	71	91	93	98	129	118	150
Other canned/packaged prepared foods	100	79	86	91	98	131	124	144
Prepared salads	100	54	86	89	109	142	141	144
Prepared desserts	100	82	94	104	96	113	110	120
Baby food	100	87	93	99	83	119	110	136
Miscellaneous prepared foods	100	83	83	88	100	134	126	149
Nonalcoholic beverages	**100**	**93**	**99**	**97**	**114**	**102**	**99**	**107**
Cola	100	108	108	92	124	86	82	94
Other carbonated drinks	100	90	106	98	109	98	94	105
Coffee	100	86	88	98	121	114	112	118
Roasted coffee	100	77	89	96	128	118	114	125
Instant and freeze-dried coffee	100	102	87	101	109	108	108	108
Noncarbonated fruit-flavored drinks	100	113	95	116	94	88	91	83
Tea	100	76	92	98	115	117	114	123
Other nonalcoholic beverages and ice	100	79	93	97	105	118	115	123
Food prepared by CU on trips	**100**	**50**	**67**	**92**	**106**	**162**	**147**	**188**
FOOD AWAY FROM HOME	**100**	**52**	**80**	**99**	**112**	**141**	**132**	**156**
Meals at restaurants, carry-outs, other	**100**	**56**	**83**	**101**	**113**	**134**	**129**	**146**
Lunch	100	59	84	101	119	130	127	138
At fast-food restaurants*	100	69	90	109	111	117	118	115
At full-service restaurants	100	42	71	88	132	157	145	178
At vending machines, mobile vendors	100	127	139	81	119	56	41	84
At employer and school cafeterias	100	54	89	100	117	129	123	140
Dinner	100	49	77	98	109	146	138	163
At fast-food restaurants*	100	65	86	113	110	119	118	120
At full-service restaurants	100	41	74	91	109	159	147	184
At vending machines, mobile vendors	100	231	61	75	88	92	26	217
At employer and school cafeterias	100	25	48	86	111	196	269	59
Snacks and nonalcoholic beverages	100	65	89	102	115	123	121	128
At fast-food restaurants*	100	61	85	101	112	130	124	140
At full-service restaurants	100	69	86	109	124	116	122	105
At vending machines, mobile vendors	100	80	110	100	117	96	100	86
At employer and school cafeterias	100	64	92	96	148	115	115	113
Breakfast and brunch	100	59	94	108	105	119	113	131
At fast-food restaurants*	100	75	101	113	106	101	99	104
At full-service restaurants	100	43	86	104	106	138	127	158
At vending machines, mobile vendors	100	110	134	90	66	80	77	87
At employer and school cafeterias	100	49	93	92	90	141	142	140
Board (including at school)	**100**	**18**	**20**	**105**	**59**	**228**	**165**	**339**
Catered affairs	**100**	**16**	**64**	**89**	**138**	**173**	**143**	**225**
Food on trips	**100**	**25**	**60**	**85**	**103**	**188**	**166**	**226**
School lunches	**100**	**55**	**92**	**90**	**138**	**126**	**115**	**144**
Meals as pay	**100**	**102**	**105**	**117**	**85**	**86**	**104**	**54**

	total consumer units	less than high school graduate	high school graduate	some college	associate's degree	college graduate		
						total	bachelor's degree	master's, professional, doctorate
ALCOHOLIC BEVERAGES	**100**	**44**	**75**	**98**	**98**	**155**	**151**	**162**
At home	**100**	**56**	**81**	**99**	**100**	**141**	**131**	**160**
Beer and ale	100	86	104	108	114	94	101	80
Whiskey	100	53	65	127	74	147	123	191
Wine	100	21	59	73	86	203	172	263
Other alcoholic beverages	100	39	67	124	103	146	135	166
Away from home	**100**	**25**	**66**	**97**	**93**	**176**	**182**	**165**
Beer and ale	100	29	68	100	94	169	176	156
At fast-food restaurants*	100	44	68	110	114	148	138	168
At full-service restaurants	100	25	70	103	93	167	172	158
Wine	100	27	72	105	80	167	184	134
At fast-food restaurants*	100	63	60	134	65	144	147	139
At full-service restaurants	100	22	75	103	85	167	183	136
Other alcoholic beverages	100	21	65	94	97	179	188	163
At fast-food restaurants*	100	27	53	133	121	153	177	109
At full-service restaurants	100	21	68	93	98	177	180	172
Alcoholic beverages purchased on trips	100	21	57	90	95	192	185	204

* The category fast-food restaurants also includes take-out, delivery, concession stands, buffets, and cafeterias other than employer and school.
Note: "–" means sample is too small to make a reliable estimate.
Source: Calculations by New Strategist based on the 2004 Consumer Expenditure Survey

Table 5.27 Food and Alcohol: Total spending by education, 2004

(total annual spending on food and alcoholic beverages, by consumer unit (CU) educational attainment group, 2004; consumer units and dollars in thousands)

	total consumer units	less than high school graduate	high school graduate	some college	associate's degree	college graduate total	bachelor's degree	master's, professional, doctorate
Number of consumer units	116,282	16,829	31,005	25,317	10,678	32,452	20,684	11,768
Total spending of all CUs	$5,046,042,273	$427,813,038	$1,098,772,243	$1,034,900,225	$514,437,850	$1,970,234,911	$1,173,370,432	$797,886,640
Food, total spending	672,205,311	71,689,857	160,659,849	139,369,579	66,395,697	233,862,093	141,640,309	92,694,888
Alcoholic beverages, total spending	53,404,834	3,394,409	10,694,245	11,436,195	4,782,997	23,074,995	14,329,875	8,773,162
FOOD AT HOME	389,174,923	50,333,351	100,128,167	78,429,534	37,176,952	122,631,240	74,990,669	47,903,409
Cereals and bakery products	53,594,374	6,957,613	14,448,020	10,759,978	4,969,648	16,364,246	10,216,862	6,165,844
Cereals and cereal products	17,884,172	2,546,396	4,865,305	3,486,404	1,622,415	5,321,803	3,272,829	2,059,165
Flour	967,466	217,767	270,674	147,851	61,078	262,537	125,138	141,098
Prepared flour mixes	1,602,366	204,472	417,327	310,386	206,406	465,037	310,674	153,102
Ready-to-eat and cooked cereals	10,080,487	1,303,406	2,750,764	1,987,891	938,383	3,079,046	1,924,853	1,157,500
Rice	2,146,566	424,427	520,264	423,807	166,150	608,150	347,491	263,956
Pasta, cornmeal, and other cereal products	3,087,287	396,323	906,896	616,469	250,399	907,033	564,673	343,508
Bakery products	35,710,202	4,411,217	9,582,715	7,273,574	3,347,233	11,042,442	6,944,032	4,106,679
Bread	10,189,792	1,434,672	2,751,074	2,001,815	974,581	3,009,923	1,893,207	1,118,784
White bread	4,074,521	720,954	1,170,129	770,143	354,403	1,046,902	656,096	391,757
Bread, other than white	6,115,270	713,718	1,580,945	1,231,419	620,285	1,963,021	1,237,317	727,027
Crackers and cookies	8,274,627	913,478	2,118,882	1,765,101	817,828	2,658,468	1,669,406	991,454
Cookies	5,415,253	641,185	1,405,147	1,183,317	516,175	1,669,655	1,049,713	621,233
Crackers	2,860,537	272,462	713,735	581,785	301,760	988,812	619,693	370,221
Frozen and refrigerated bakery products	3,060,542	290,132	776,365	711,661	316,176	971,937	584,323	390,698
Other bakery products	14,185,241	1,772,935	3,936,395	2,794,997	1,238,541	4,402,114	2,797,097	1,605,861
Biscuits and rolls	4,896,635	464,480	1,326,084	989,388	442,603	1,662,516	1,047,645	615,937
Cakes and cupcakes	4,539,649	656,499	1,337,866	754,953	374,691	1,387,972	881,552	506,848
Bread and cracker products	377,917	30,965	95,805	92,154	30,859	128,510	82,322	46,248
Sweetrolls, coffee cakes, doughnuts	2,743,092	417,696	702,263	605,836	232,567	785,014	518,341	265,015
Pies, tarts, turnovers	1,626,785	203,294	474,377	352,666	157,928	438,102	267,237	171,813
Meats, poultry, fish, and eggs	102,294,438	14,958,288	27,579,878	20,453,351	9,589,164	29,559,878	18,037,275	11,592,068
Beef	30,854,266	4,532,386	8,596,756	6,195,829	3,100,464	8,399,227	5,241,532	3,167,357
Ground beef	11,270,051	1,775,460	3,442,795	2,304,607	1,088,622	2,644,513	1,733,940	906,371
Roast	5,300,134	784,231	1,397,395	999,009	515,427	1,592,420	997,589	596,167
Chuck roast	1,362,825	299,724	355,007	248,613	112,866	342,693	183,053	162,869
Round roast	1,194,216	168,795	315,631	242,537	79,871	383,583	194,636	193,348
Other roast	2,741,930	315,712	726,757	508,112	322,796	865,819	619,899	239,950
Steak	12,029,373	1,576,204	3,170,571	2,414,482	1,321,616	3,545,056	2,155,480	1,398,627
Round steak	1,903,536	283,569	599,017	344,311	186,545	482,886	317,706	164,281
Sirloin steak	3,765,211	494,268	884,263	756,219	489,693	1,148,801	658,992	496,139
Other steak	6,361,788	798,368	1,687,292	1,313,952	645,378	1,913,370	1,178,781	738,207
Other beef	2,254,708	396,323	585,684	477,985	174,799	617,562	354,731	266,310
Pork	21,063,321	3,469,803	6,055,587	4,164,647	1,992,835	5,345,818	3,216,776	2,145,659
Bacon	3,614,045	541,894	1,062,851	741,788	357,927	905,735	537,370	372,104
Pork chops	4,409,413	737,110	1,352,438	824,575	461,503	1,024,185	639,342	386,226
Ham	4,610,581	819,236	1,347,167	812,929	386,864	1,223,765	721,872	506,848
Ham, not canned	4,496,625	798,536	1,315,852	797,232	380,564	1,185,147	700,567	489,313
Canned ham	113,956	20,700	31,005	15,443	6,300	38,618	21,305	17,534
Sausage	3,245,431	456,066	897,595	749,130	348,850	801,240	484,626	318,677
Other pork	5,185,014	915,161	1,395,225	1,036,225	437,691	1,390,893	833,565	561,804
Other meats	12,556,130	1,690,978	3,400,938	2,508,915	1,112,220	3,816,031	2,415,064	1,402,275
Frankfurters	2,618,671	395,313	740,709	525,581	200,960	747,370	473,664	273,724
Lunch meats (cold cuts)	8,487,423	1,068,137	2,414,359	1,751,936	805,442	2,435,198	1,495,453	944,735
Bologna, liverwurst, salami	2,450,062	421,566	733,578	502,542	196,796	589,977	359,695	231,830
Other lunch meats	6,036,199	646,570	1,680,781	1,249,394	608,646	1,845,221	1,135,758	712,905
Lamb, organ meats, and others	1,451,199	227,528	245,560	231,397	105,819	633,463	445,947	183,816
Poultry	18,094,642	2,580,391	4,621,295	3,631,724	1,687,978	5,549,941	3,371,699	2,192,614
Fresh and frozen chicken	14,260,824	2,133,581	3,718,740	2,845,378	1,351,621	4,193,447	2,630,384	1,566,792
Fresh and frozen whole chicken	4,254,758	819,067	1,123,311	856,980	346,074	1,102,070	718,148	382,578
Fresh and frozen chicken parts	10,004,903	1,314,513	2,595,119	1,988,397	1,005,440	3,091,702	1,912,236	1,184,214
Other poultry	3,833,818	446,810	902,556	786,346	336,357	1,356,494	741,315	625,822

	total consumer units	less than high school graduate	high school graduate	some college	associate's degree	college graduate		
						total	bachelor's degree	master's, professional, doctorate
Fish and seafood	$14,860,840	$1,822,244	$3,599,370	$3,028,926	$1,255,199	$5,127,416	$3,002,696	$2,147,542
Canned fish and seafood	1,788,417	223,657	510,342	329,881	137,426	578,619	336,942	244,304
Fresh fish and shellfish	8,707,196	1,156,657	2,059,662	1,623,326	741,801	3,098,192	1,777,169	1,338,022
Frozen fish and shellfish	4,365,226	442,098	1,029,056	1,075,719	376,079	1,450,604	888,378	565,335
Eggs	4,865,239	862,655	1,306,241	923,564	440,574	1,321,445	789,508	536,503
Dairy products	**43,090,621**	**5,474,810**	**10,737,652**	**8,475,878**	**4,210,442**	**14,133,495**	**8,591,927**	**5,577,444**
Fresh milk and cream	16,782,981	2,568,274	4,341,630	3,287,919	1,627,114	4,936,598	3,082,950	1,859,226
Fresh milk, all types	14,993,401	2,386,857	3,891,128	2,922,594	1,454,450	4,319,686	2,717,878	1,604,802
Cream	1,789,580	181,417	450,503	365,577	172,663	616,913	365,073	254,424
Other dairy products	26,307,640	2,906,537	6,396,021	5,187,960	2,583,329	9,196,897	5,508,977	3,718,217
Butter	2,536,110	261,018	639,323	516,973	370,420	757,105	434,571	326,444
Cheese	13,217,775	1,394,619	3,134,606	2,663,348	1,223,592	4,781,478	2,872,594	1,924,068
Ice cream and related products	7,002,502	879,147	1,787,748	1,385,853	675,917	2,263,527	1,382,725	886,130
Miscellaneous dairy products	3,551,252	371,753	834,345	621,786	313,399	1,394,787	819,086	581,692
Fruits and vegetables	**65,228,388**	**8,536,847**	**15,825,882**	**12,713,185**	**5,886,354**	**22,133,238**	**13,246,654**	**8,960,626**
Fresh fruits	21,714,501	2,833,162	5,056,916	4,299,839	1,872,387	7,609,669	4,494,840	3,145,351
Apples	3,769,862	500,158	914,648	733,940	355,044	1,260,436	766,963	496,610
Bananas	3,508,228	573,532	892,944	666,090	323,330	1,045,279	629,621	418,941
Oranges	2,265,173	355,597	535,146	453,934	209,716	709,401	409,543	303,497
Citrus fruits, excluding oranges	1,791,906	228,538	371,440	382,034	148,424	660,074	373,346	291,023
Other fresh fruits	10,378,169	1,175,506	2,342,738	2,063,842	835,981	3,934,480	2,315,574	1,635,399
Fresh vegetables	21,272,629	2,904,181	4,988,084	4,040,846	1,942,649	7,351,027	4,340,744	3,039,910
Potatoes	3,264,036	515,136	934,181	594,443	309,555	900,543	525,787	379,047
Lettuce	2,659,369	311,337	599,947	561,025	241,643	944,353	570,258	376,811
Tomatoes	4,155,919	688,811	990,920	766,092	342,764	1,355,196	796,334	564,511
Other fresh vegetables	11,192,143	1,388,897	2,463,037	2,119,286	1,048,793	4,150,935	2,448,365	1,719,540
Processed fruits	12,747,996	1,587,984	3,064,534	2,496,763	1,152,263	4,421,260	2,750,765	1,676,352
Frozen fruits and fruit juices	1,159,332	144,225	280,595	211,397	119,060	401,107	245,726	156,397
Frozen orange juice	484,896	64,623	122,780	92,913	54,031	150,253	94,733	55,427
Frozen fruits	410,475	40,726	96,736	75,951	27,015	167,452	92,044	76,610
Frozen fruit juices, excluding orange	263,960	38,875	61,080	42,533	38,014	83,726	58,949	24,360
Canned fruits	1,882,606	201,107	492,669	376,717	203,309	607,826	380,792	227,711
Dried fruits	738,391	58,397	197,192	132,155	55,846	289,796	165,679	125,682
Fresh fruit juice	2,566,344	335,570	608,938	458,744	226,587	927,478	570,672	358,336
Canned and bottled fruit juice	6,401,324	848,686	1,485,140	1,317,750	547,461	2,195,053	1,387,896	808,109
Processed vegetables	9,493,262	1,211,351	2,716,658	1,875,737	919,055	2,751,281	1,660,305	1,098,896
Frozen vegetables	3,314,037	315,712	996,811	655,204	358,247	982,322	591,562	393,757
Canned and dried vegetables and juices	6,179,225	895,639	1,719,847	1,220,533	560,809	1,768,959	1,068,742	705,256
Canned beans	1,324,452	176,873	414,537	249,119	116,070	362,813	202,290	163,104
Canned corn	736,065	136,315	224,786	144,054	68,980	160,637	97,008	64,018
Canned miscellaneous vegetables	1,950,049	247,218	503,831	386,337	213,133	598,415	357,420	243,245
Dried peas	69,769	8,583	16,743	16,203	7,154	21,094	11,790	9,650
Dried beans	287,217	94,579	77,202	40,254	12,920	60,036	38,472	21,653
Dried miscellaneous vegetables	722,111	98,113	203,703	161,776	58,302	199,904	117,899	82,847
Dried processed vegetables	34,885	13,127	8,991	506	–	11,683	2,689	9,414
Fresh and canned vegetable juices	1,036,073	118,476	267,883	220,764	82,755	343,667	233,316	109,325
Sugar and other sweets	**14,898,050**	**1,658,666**	**3,865,393**	**3,027,407**	**1,571,802**	**4,767,848**	**3,003,730**	**1,767,083**
Candy and chewing gum	9,666,523	892,442	2,419,630	1,920,801	1,074,527	3,354,239	2,152,998	1,199,865
Sugar	1,872,140	362,497	559,950	383,046	179,177	385,854	226,076	161,457
Artificial sweeteners	796,532	87,847	226,337	189,371	73,251	220,998	126,379	95,909
Jams, preserves, other sweets	2,562,855	315,712	659,786	534,189	244,847	806,757	498,278	309,851
Fats and oils	**10,336,307**	**1,525,381**	**2,878,194**	**2,056,247**	**955,788**	**2,901,858**	**1,753,383**	**1,156,677**
Margarine	1,112,819	159,876	359,038	193,675	99,305	294,664	173,539	122,152
Fats and oils	3,321,014	639,165	877,131	614,444	238,867	937,538	545,230	396,817
Salad dressings	3,190,778	386,394	889,533	687,610	335,289	893,404	564,053	329,857
Nondairy cream and imitation milk	1,255,846	141,027	383,222	281,019	123,865	327,116	212,838	113,797
Peanut butter	1,455,851	198,750	369,270	279,500	158,355	449,136	257,723	193,937

	total consumer units	less than high school graduate	high school graduate	some college	associate's degree	college graduate		master's, professional, doctorate
						total	bachelor's degree	
Miscellaneous foods	$61,314,336	$6,336,287	$15,025,953	$12,870,403	$6,015,451	$21,042,201	$12,945,495	$8,136,866
Frozen prepared foods	12,779,392	1,120,307	3,379,545	2,888,417	1,405,332	4,006,199	2,506,901	1,503,362
Frozen meals	3,696,605	358,121	956,504	848,120	458,193	1,088,765	700,981	387,167
Other frozen prepared foods	9,082,787	762,185	2,422,731	2,040,297	947,139	2,917,435	1,805,920	1,116,195
Canned and packaged soups	4,244,293	456,739	1,105,018	833,942	400,639	1,438,597	924,988	512,967
Potato chips, nuts, and other snacks	13,614,297	1,366,851	3,282,189	2,885,885	1,357,601	4,721,117	2,980,358	1,743,194
Potato chips and other snacks	10,007,229	1,099,607	2,532,488	2,087,893	993,801	3,289,335	2,177,612	1,104,898
Nuts	3,605,905	267,245	749,701	797,992	363,799	1,431,782	802,953	638,414
Condiments and seasonings	10,889,809	1,143,699	2,698,055	2,326,885	1,075,488	3,645,658	2,169,752	1,489,240
Salt, spices, and other seasonings	2,583,786	315,375	664,127	511,403	245,914	843,103	476,146	372,104
Olives, pickles, relishes	1,223,287	113,091	279,045	316,209	115,963	403,703	233,936	171,695
Sauces and gravies	4,760,585	477,102	1,188,732	1,031,161	504,963	1,562,239	970,493	593,931
Baking needs and miscellaneous products	2,322,152	238,130	566,461	467,858	208,755	836,613	488,970	351,510
Other canned/packaged prepared foods	19,786,545	2,248,691	4,561,456	3,935,274	1,776,392	7,230,630	4,363,497	2,888,103
Prepared salads	2,957,051	229,884	681,490	570,139	296,208	1,174,113	742,349	432,121
Prepared desserts	1,268,637	150,451	318,731	286,335	111,905	401,431	248,415	153,455
Baby food	3,497,763	438,900	865,970	755,206	267,270	1,165,027	687,122	482,723
Miscellaneous prepared foods	11,946,813	1,428,109	2,639,146	2,289,669	1,100,902	4,465,720	2,674,855	1,805,682
Nonalcoholic beverages	33,665,965	4,544,335	8,918,588	7,123,191	3,514,237	9,580,479	5,949,753	3,644,432
Cola	10,908,414	1,706,965	3,151,038	2,189,414	1,241,104	2,622,122	1,592,461	1,036,408
Other carbonated drinks	5,590,839	729,537	1,575,364	1,192,684	561,449	1,531,734	938,847	595,932
Coffee	4,548,952	569,325	1,066,572	968,882	505,176	1,446,386	903,270	544,623
Roasted coffee	2,846,583	317,058	672,188	593,684	334,221	933,644	576,463	358,689
Instant and freeze-dried coffee	1,702,368	252,267	394,694	375,198	170,955	512,742	326,807	185,817
Noncarbonated fruit-flavored drinks	2,301,221	376,633	584,134	581,785	197,970	568,235	373,553	193,701
Tea	2,050,052	225,509	500,421	439,250	215,802	671,107	416,369	255,719
Other nonalcoholic beverages and ice	8,151,368	935,524	2,018,426	1,728,138	788,891	2,678,588	1,668,992	1,012,872
Food prepared by CU on trips	4,751,283	341,292	848,607	949,894	464,066	2,147,673	1,245,384	902,370
FOOD AWAY FROM HOME	283,030,388	21,356,674	60,531,682	60,940,044	29,218,745	111,230,853	66,649,640	44,791,362
Meals at restaurants, carry-outs, other	235,839,664	19,110,844	52,290,243	51,693,770	24,485,401	88,506,989	53,977,173	34,739,960
Lunch	84,312,590	7,215,770	18,874,914	18,483,182	9,182,973	30,686,611	18,990,394	11,745,288
At fast-food restaurants*	47,579,106	4,744,263	11,358,682	11,256,698	4,851,122	15,485,121	9,959,346	5,518,015
At full-service restaurants	27,518,135	1,679,029	5,236,434	5,245,176	3,337,089	12,027,685	7,117,364	4,957,741
At vending machines, mobile vendors	700,018	128,910	259,202	124,053	76,775	108,714	50,469	59,781
At employer and school cafeterias	8,516,494	663,567	2,020,906	1,857,002	917,988	3,065,091	1,863,215	1,209,868
Dinner	92,512,796	6,560,786	19,109,312	19,795,615	9,271,280	37,808,852	22,643,395	15,290,986
At fast-food restaurants*	29,427,486	2,765,510	6,773,662	7,271,296	2,982,365	9,735,925	6,166,521	3,572,765
At full-service restaurants	62,585,298	3,725,267	12,265,578	12,435,457	6,241,611	27,850,306	16,313,678	11,660,558
At vending machines, mobile vendors	174,423	58,397	28,525	28,355	14,095	44,784	8,067	38,364
At employer and school cafeterias	324,427	11,612	41,237	60,508	33,209	177,837	155,130	19,300
Snacks and nonalcoholic beverages	34,588,081	3,238,068	8,202,063	7,651,051	3,666,291	11,876,783	7,413,973	4,476,194
At fast-food restaurants*	25,251,799	2,236,911	5,741,196	5,566,955	2,605,859	9,128,748	5,584,059	3,565,116
At full-service restaurants	3,357,061	333,382	768,614	796,979	383,020	1,088,116	729,938	355,158
At vending machines, mobile vendors	4,775,702	556,367	1,398,326	1,034,706	513,612	1,275,039	853,422	417,999
At employer and school cafeterias	1,202,356	111,240	294,237	252,410	163,801	384,556	246,553	137,921
Breakfast and brunch	24,426,197	2,096,220	6,103,644	5,763,921	2,364,963	8,134,743	4,929,204	3,227,492
At fast-food restaurants*	12,009,605	1,305,762	3,235,372	2,960,064	1,166,785	3,371,438	2,116,180	1,258,235
At full-service restaurants	11,670,062	723,142	2,664,880	2,654,741	1,140,197	4,496,549	2,643,829	1,871,936
At vending machines, mobile vendors	165,120	26,253	58,910	32,406	10,037	36,995	22,546	14,592
At employer and school cafeterias	581,410	41,063	144,483	116,458	47,944	229,436	146,856	82,494
Board (including at school)	3,243,105	86,669	173,318	740,775	175,226	2,066,868	953,532	1,113,488
Catered affairs	6,809,474	161,222	1,170,439	1,325,092	864,811	3,287,388	1,733,526	1,553,964
Food on trips	26,925,097	992,574	4,289,232	5,009,981	2,535,811	14,097,149	7,945,759	6,151,251
School lunches	7,371,116	585,313	1,812,552	1,447,879	935,500	2,590,319	1,513,862	1,076,654
Meals as pay	2,843,095	420,220	796,208	722,547	222,102	682,141	525,994	156,161

	total consumer units	less than high school graduate	high school graduate	some college	associate's degree	college graduate total	bachelor's degree	master's, professional, doctorate
ALCOHOLIC BEVERAGES	**$53,404,834**	**$3,394,409**	**$10,694,245**	**$11,436,195**	**$4,782,997**	**$23,074,995**	**$14,329,875**	**$8,773,162**
At home	**32,278,720**	**2,631,551**	**7,001,239**	**6,980,656**	**2,971,581**	**12,687,109**	**7,501,259**	**5,236,289**
Beer and ale	15,268,989	1,908,409	4,215,130	3,583,115	1,600,312	3,996,139	2,747,042	1,231,874
Whiskey	2,518,668	193,197	437,481	695,964	171,595	1,030,351	552,263	486,960
Wine	10,994,463	332,036	1,727,599	1,758,012	868,442	6,239,222	3,362,391	2,929,644
Other alcoholic beverages	3,496,600	197,909	621,030	943,565	331,232	1,421,398	839,357	587,812
Away from home	**21,126,114**	**762,859**	**3,693,006**	**4,455,539**	**1,811,416**	**10,388,210**	**6,828,409**	**3,536,872**
Beer and ale	8,874,642	366,704	1,609,160	1,929,915	768,069	4,195,395	2,780,757	1,405,570
At fast-food restaurants*	1,911,676	121,674	348,806	458,491	199,679	789,557	468,286	324,208
At full-service restaurants	6,512,955	235,943	1,218,807	1,456,234	557,498	3,042,050	1,995,799	1,041,350
Wine	2,591,926	101,647	498,560	592,418	190,923	1,205,916	847,630	351,628
At fast-food restaurants*	355,823	32,480	57,049	103,547	21,249	143,113	92,871	50,014
At full-service restaurants	2,181,450	69,167	438,101	487,859	169,567	1,013,800	708,634	299,613
Other alcoholic beverages	5,198,968	159,371	907,516	1,060,782	463,959	2,599,081	1,734,353	858,005
At fast-food restaurants*	444,197	17,670	62,630	128,864	49,226	189,844	139,617	48,837
At full-service restaurants	4,586,162	141,700	828,454	927,362	413,239	2,267,421	1,466,909	798,576
Alcoholic beverages purchased on trips	4,461,740	135,137	677,769	872,677	388,359	2,387,494	1,465,875	921,670

(The "college graduate" columns — total, bachelor's degree, and master's, professional, doctorate — are grouped under the heading "college graduate".)

* The category fast-food restaurants also includes take-out, delivery, concession stands, buffets, and cafeterias other than employer and school.
Note: Numbers may not add to total because of rounding and missing subcategories. "–" means sample is too small to make a reliable estimate.
Source: Calculations by New Strategist based on the 2004 Consumer Expenditure Survey

Table 5.28 Food and Alcohol: Market shares by education, 2004

(percentage of total annual spending on food and alcoholic beverages accounted for by consumer unit educational attainment groups, 2004)

	total consumer units	less than high school graduate	high school graduate	some college	associate's degree	college graduate total	bachelor's degree	master's, professional, doctorate
Share of total consumer units	100.0%	14.5%	26.7%	21.8%	9.2%	27.9%	17.8%	10.1%
Share of total before-tax income	100.0	7.7	20.7	18.7	9.9	43.0	24.7	18.3
Share of total spending	100.0	8.5	21.8	20.5	10.2	39.0	23.3	15.8
Share of food spending	100.0	10.7	23.9	20.7	9.9	34.8	21.1	13.8
Share of alcoholic beverages spending	100.0	6.4	20.0	21.4	9.0	43.2	26.8	16.4
FOOD AT HOME	100.0	12.9	25.7	20.2	9.6	31.5	19.3	12.3
Cereals and bakery products	100.0	13.0	27.0	20.1	9.3	30.5	19.1	11.5
Cereals and cereal products	100.0	14.2	27.2	19.5	9.1	29.8	18.3	11.5
Flour	100.0	22.5	28.0	15.3	6.3	27.1	12.9	14.6
Prepared flour mixes	100.0	12.8	26.0	19.4	12.9	29.0	19.4	9.6
Ready-to-eat and cooked cereals	100.0	12.9	27.3	19.7	9.3	30.5	19.1	11.5
Rice	100.0	19.8	24.2	19.7	7.7	28.3	16.2	12.3
Pasta, cornmeal, and other cereal products	100.0	12.8	29.4	20.0	8.1	29.4	18.3	11.1
Bakery products	100.0	12.4	26.8	20.4	9.4	30.9	19.4	11.5
Bread	100.0	14.1	27.0	19.6	9.6	29.5	18.6	11.0
White bread	100.0	17.7	28.7	18.9	8.7	25.7	16.1	9.6
Bread, other than white	100.0	11.7	25.9	20.1	10.1	32.1	20.2	11.9
Crackers and cookies	100.0	11.0	25.6	21.3	9.9	32.1	20.2	12.0
Cookies	100.0	11.8	25.9	21.9	9.5	30.8	19.4	11.5
Crackers	100.0	9.5	25.0	20.3	10.5	34.6	21.7	12.9
Frozen and refrigerated bakery products	100.0	9.5	25.4	23.3	10.3	31.8	19.1	12.8
Other bakery products	100.0	12.5	27.7	19.7	8.7	31.0	19.7	11.3
Biscuits and rolls	100.0	9.5	27.1	20.2	9.0	34.0	21.4	12.6
Cakes and cupcakes	100.0	14.5	29.5	16.6	8.3	30.6	19.4	11.2
Bread and cracker products	100.0	8.2	25.4	24.4	8.2	34.0	21.8	12.2
Sweetrolls, coffee cakes, doughnuts	100.0	15.2	25.6	22.1	8.5	28.6	18.9	9.7
Pies, tarts, turnovers	100.0	12.5	29.2	21.7	9.7	26.9	16.4	10.6
Meats, poultry, fish, and eggs	100.0	14.6	27.0	20.0	9.4	28.9	17.6	11.3
Beef	100.0	14.7	27.9	20.1	10.0	27.2	17.0	10.3
Ground beef	100.0	15.8	30.5	20.4	9.7	23.5	15.4	8.0
Roast	100.0	14.8	26.4	18.8	9.7	30.0	18.8	11.2
Chuck roast	100.0	22.0	26.0	18.2	8.3	25.1	13.4	12.0
Round roast	100.0	14.1	26.4	20.3	6.7	32.1	16.3	16.2
Other roast	100.0	11.5	26.5	18.5	11.8	31.6	22.6	8.8
Steak	100.0	13.1	26.4	20.1	11.0	29.5	17.9	11.6
Round steak	100.0	14.9	31.5	18.1	9.8	25.4	16.7	8.6
Sirloin steak	100.0	13.1	23.5	20.1	13.0	30.5	17.5	13.2
Other steak	100.0	12.5	26.5	20.7	10.1	30.1	18.5	11.6
Other beef	100.0	17.6	26.0	21.2	7.8	27.4	15.7	11.8
Pork	100.0	16.5	28.7	19.8	9.5	25.4	15.3	10.2
Bacon	100.0	15.0	29.4	20.5	9.9	25.1	14.9	10.3
Pork chops	100.0	16.7	30.7	18.7	10.5	23.2	14.5	8.8
Ham	100.0	17.8	29.2	17.6	8.4	26.5	15.7	11.0
Ham, not canned	100.0	17.8	29.3	17.7	8.5	26.4	15.6	10.9
Canned ham	100.0	18.2	27.2	13.6	5.5	33.9	18.7	15.4
Sausage	100.0	14.1	27.7	23.1	10.7	24.7	14.9	9.8
Other pork	100.0	17.7	26.9	20.0	8.4	26.8	16.1	10.8
Other meats	100.0	13.5	27.1	20.0	8.9	30.4	19.2	11.2
Frankfurters	100.0	15.1	28.3	20.1	7.7	28.5	18.1	10.5
Lunch meats (cold cuts)	100.0	12.6	28.4	20.6	9.5	28.7	17.6	11.1
Bologna, liverwurst, salami	100.0	17.2	29.9	20.5	8.0	24.1	14.7	9.5
Other lunch meats	100.0	10.7	27.8	20.7	10.1	30.6	18.8	11.8
Lamb, organ meats, and others	100.0	15.7	16.9	15.9	7.3	43.7	30.7	12.7
Poultry	100.0	14.3	25.5	20.1	9.3	30.7	18.6	12.1
Fresh and frozen chicken	100.0	15.0	26.1	20.0	9.5	29.4	18.4	11.0
Fresh and frozen whole chicken	100.0	19.3	26.4	20.1	8.1	25.9	16.9	9.0
Fresh and frozen chicken parts	100.0	13.1	25.9	19.9	10.0	30.9	19.1	11.8
Other poultry	100.0	11.7	23.5	20.5	8.8	35.4	19.3	16.3

	total consumer units	less than high school graduate	high school graduate	some college	associate's degree	college graduate total	bachelor's degree	master's, professional, doctorate
Fish and seafood	100.0%	12.3%	24.2%	20.4%	8.4%	34.5%	20.2%	14.5%
Canned fish and seafood	100.0	12.5	28.5	18.4	7.7	32.4	18.8	13.7
Fresh fish and shellfish	100.0	13.3	23.7	18.6	8.5	35.6	20.4	15.4
Frozen fish and shellfish	100.0	10.1	23.6	24.6	8.6	33.2	20.4	13.0
Eggs	100.0	17.7	26.8	19.0	9.1	27.2	16.2	11.0
Dairy products	**100.0**	**12.7**	**24.9**	**19.7**	**9.8**	**32.8**	**19.9**	**12.9**
Fresh milk and cream	100.0	15.3	25.9	19.6	9.7	29.4	18.4	11.1
Fresh milk, all types	100.0	15.9	26.0	19.5	9.7	28.8	18.1	10.7
Cream	100.0	10.1	25.2	20.4	9.6	34.5	20.4	14.2
Other dairy products	100.0	11.0	24.3	19.7	9.8	35.0	20.9	14.1
Butter	100.0	10.3	25.2	20.4	14.6	29.9	17.1	12.9
Cheese	100.0	10.6	23.7	20.1	9.3	36.2	21.7	14.6
Ice cream and related products	100.0	12.6	25.5	19.8	9.7	32.3	19.7	12.7
Miscellaneous dairy products	100.0	10.5	23.5	17.5	8.8	39.3	23.1	16.4
Fruits and vegetables	**100.0**	**13.1**	**24.3**	**19.5**	**9.0**	**33.9**	**20.3**	**13.7**
Fresh fruits	100.0	13.0	23.3	19.8	8.6	35.0	20.7	14.5
Apples	100.0	13.3	24.3	19.5	9.4	33.4	20.3	13.2
Bananas	100.0	16.3	25.5	19.0	9.2	29.8	17.9	11.9
Oranges	100.0	15.7	23.6	20.0	9.3	31.3	18.1	13.4
Citrus fruits, excluding oranges	100.0	12.8	20.7	21.3	8.3	36.8	20.8	16.2
Other fresh fruits	100.0	11.3	22.6	19.9	8.1	37.9	22.3	15.8
Fresh vegetables	100.0	13.7	23.4	19.0	9.1	34.6	20.4	14.3
Potatoes	100.0	15.8	28.6	18.2	9.5	27.6	16.1	11.6
Lettuce	100.0	11.7	22.6	21.1	9.1	35.5	21.4	14.2
Tomatoes	100.0	16.6	23.8	18.4	8.2	32.6	19.2	13.6
Other fresh vegetables	100.0	12.4	22.0	18.9	9.4	37.1	21.9	15.4
Processed fruits	100.0	12.5	24.0	19.6	9.0	34.7	21.6	13.1
Frozen fruits and fruit juices	100.0	12.4	24.2	18.2	10.3	34.6	21.2	13.5
Frozen orange juice	100.0	13.3	25.3	19.2	11.1	31.0	19.5	11.4
Frozen fruits	100.0	9.9	23.6	18.5	6.6	40.8	22.4	18.7
Frozen fruit juices, excluding orange	100.0	14.7	23.1	16.1	14.4	31.7	22.3	9.2
Canned fruits	100.0	10.7	26.2	20.0	10.8	32.3	20.2	12.1
Dried fruits	100.0	7.9	26.7	17.9	7.6	39.2	22.4	17.0
Fresh fruit juice	100.0	13.1	23.7	17.9	8.8	36.1	22.2	14.0
Canned and bottled fruit juice	100.0	13.3	23.2	20.6	8.6	34.3	21.7	12.6
Processed vegetables	100.0	12.8	28.6	19.8	9.7	29.0	17.5	11.6
Frozen vegetables	100.0	9.5	30.1	19.8	10.8	29.6	17.9	11.9
Canned and dried vegetables and juices	100.0	14.5	27.8	19.8	9.1	28.6	17.3	11.4
Canned beans	100.0	13.4	31.3	18.8	8.8	27.4	15.3	12.3
Canned corn	100.0	18.5	30.5	19.6	9.4	21.8	13.2	8.7
Canned miscellaneous vegetables	100.0	12.7	25.8	19.8	10.9	30.7	18.3	12.5
Dried peas	100.0	12.3	24.0	23.2	10.3	30.2	16.9	13.8
Dried beans	100.0	32.9	26.9	14.0	4.5	20.9	13.4	7.5
Dried miscellaneous vegetables	100.0	13.6	28.2	22.4	8.1	27.7	16.3	11.5
Dried processed vegetables	100.0	37.6	25.8	1.5	–	33.5	7.7	27.0
Fresh and canned vegetable juices	100.0	11.4	25.9	21.3	8.0	33.2	22.5	10.6
Sugar and other sweets	**100.0**	**11.1**	**25.9**	**20.3**	**10.6**	**32.0**	**20.2**	**11.9**
Candy and chewing gum	100.0	9.2	25.0	19.9	11.1	34.7	22.3	12.4
Sugar	100.0	19.4	29.9	20.5	9.6	20.6	12.1	8.6
Artificial sweeteners	100.0	11.0	28.4	23.8	9.2	27.7	15.9	12.0
Jams, preserves, other sweets	100.0	12.3	25.7	20.8	9.6	31.5	19.4	12.1
Fats and oils	**100.0**	**14.8**	**27.8**	**19.9**	**9.2**	**28.1**	**17.0**	**11.2**
Margarine	100.0	14.4	32.3	17.4	8.9	26.5	15.6	11.0
Fats and oils	100.0	19.2	26.4	18.5	7.2	28.2	16.4	11.9
Salad dressings	100.0	12.1	27.9	21.5	10.5	28.0	17.7	10.3
Nondairy cream and imitation milk	100.0	11.2	30.5	22.4	9.9	26.0	16.9	9.1
Peanut butter	100.0	13.7	25.4	19.2	10.9	30.9	17.7	13.3

	total consumer units	less than high school graduate	high school graduate	some college	associate's degree	college graduate total	college graduate bachelor's degree	college graduate master's, professional, doctorate
Miscellaneous foods	100.0%	10.3%	24.5%	21.0%	9.8%	34.3%	21.1%	13.3%
Frozen prepared foods	100.0	8.8	26.4	22.6	11.0	31.3	19.6	11.8
Frozen meals	100.0	9.7	25.9	22.9	12.4	29.5	19.0	10.5
Other frozen prepared foods	100.0	8.4	26.7	22.5	10.4	32.1	19.9	12.3
Canned and packaged soups	100.0	10.8	26.0	19.6	9.4	33.9	21.8	12.1
Potato chips, nuts, and other snacks	100.0	10.0	24.1	21.2	10.0	34.7	21.9	12.8
Potato chips and other snacks	100.0	11.0	25.3	20.9	9.9	32.9	21.8	11.0
Nuts	100.0	7.4	20.8	22.1	10.1	39.7	22.3	17.7
Condiments and seasonings	100.0	10.5	24.8	21.4	9.9	33.5	19.9	13.7
Salt, spices, and other seasonings	100.0	12.2	25.7	19.8	9.5	32.6	18.4	14.4
Olives, pickles, relishes	100.0	9.2	22.8	25.8	9.5	33.0	19.1	14.0
Sauces and gravies	100.0	10.0	25.0	21.7	10.6	32.8	20.4	12.5
Baking needs and miscellaneous products	100.0	10.3	24.4	20.1	9.0	36.0	21.1	15.1
Other canned/packaged prepared foods	100.0	11.4	23.1	19.9	9.0	36.5	22.1	14.6
Prepared salads	100.0	7.8	23.0	19.3	10.0	39.7	25.1	14.6
Prepared desserts	100.0	11.9	25.1	22.6	8.8	31.6	19.6	12.1
Baby food	100.0	12.5	24.8	21.6	7.6	33.3	19.6	13.8
Miscellaneous prepared foods	100.0	12.0	22.1	19.2	9.2	37.4	22.4	15.1
Nonalcoholic beverages	100.0	13.5	26.5	21.2	10.4	28.5	17.7	10.8
Cola	100.0	15.6	28.9	20.1	11.4	24.0	14.6	9.5
Other carbonated drinks	100.0	13.0	28.2	21.3	10.0	27.4	16.8	10.7
Coffee	100.0	12.5	23.4	21.3	11.1	31.8	19.9	12.0
Roasted coffee	100.0	11.1	23.6	20.9	11.7	32.8	20.3	12.6
Instant and freeze-dried coffee	100.0	14.8	23.2	22.0	10.0	30.1	19.2	10.9
Noncarbonated fruit-flavored drinks	100.0	16.4	25.4	25.3	8.6	24.7	16.2	8.4
Tea	100.0	11.0	24.4	21.4	10.5	32.7	20.3	12.5
Other nonalcoholic beverages and ice	100.0	11.5	24.8	21.2	9.7	32.9	20.5	12.4
Food prepared by CU on trips	100.0	7.2	17.9	20.0	9.8	45.2	26.2	19.0
FOOD AWAY FROM HOME	100.0	7.5	21.4	21.5	10.3	39.3	23.5	15.8
Meals at restaurants, carry-outs, other	100.0	8.1	22.2	21.9	10.4	37.5	22.9	14.7
Lunch	100.0	8.6	22.4	21.9	10.9	36.4	22.5	13.9
At fast-food restaurants*	100.0	10.0	23.9	23.7	10.2	32.5	20.9	11.6
At full-service restaurants	100.0	6.1	19.0	19.1	12.1	43.7	25.9	18.0
At vending machines, mobile vendors	100.0	18.4	37.0	17.7	11.0	15.5	7.2	8.5
At employer and school cafeterias	100.0	7.8	23.7	21.8	10.8	36.0	21.9	14.2
Dinner	100.0	7.1	20.7	21.4	10.0	40.9	24.5	16.5
At fast-food restaurants*	100.0	9.4	23.0	24.7	10.1	33.1	21.0	12.1
At full-service restaurants	100.0	6.0	19.6	19.9	10.0	44.5	26.1	18.6
At vending machines, mobile vendors	100.0	33.5	16.4	16.3	8.1	25.7	4.6	22.0
At employer and school cafeterias	100.0	3.6	12.7	18.7	10.2	54.8	47.8	5.9
Snacks and nonalcoholic beverages	100.0	9.4	23.7	22.1	10.6	34.3	21.4	12.9
At fast-food restaurants*	100.0	8.9	22.7	22.0	10.3	36.2	22.1	14.1
At full-service restaurants	100.0	9.9	22.9	23.7	11.4	32.4	21.7	10.6
At vending machines, mobile vendors	100.0	11.6	29.3	21.7	10.8	26.7	17.9	8.8
At employer and school cafeterias	100.0	9.3	24.5	21.0	13.6	32.0	20.5	11.5
Breakfast and brunch	100.0	8.6	25.0	23.6	9.7	33.3	20.2	13.2
At fast-food restaurants*	100.0	10.9	26.9	24.6	9.7	28.1	17.6	10.5
At full-service restaurants	100.0	6.2	22.8	22.7	9.8	38.5	22.7	16.0
At vending machines, mobile vendors	100.0	15.9	35.7	19.6	6.1	22.4	13.7	8.8
At employer and school cafeterias	100.0	7.1	24.9	20.0	8.2	39.5	25.3	14.2
Board (including at school)	100.0	2.7	5.3	22.8	5.4	63.7	29.4	34.3
Catered affairs	100.0	2.4	17.2	19.5	12.7	48.3	25.5	22.8
Food on trips	100.0	3.7	15.9	18.6	9.4	52.4	29.5	22.8
School lunches	100.0	7.9	24.6	19.6	12.7	35.1	20.5	14.6
Meals as pay	100.0	14.8	28.0	25.4	7.8	24.0	18.5	5.5

	total consumer units	less than high school graduate	high school graduate	some college	associate's degree	college graduate		
						total	bachelor's degree	master's, professional, doctorate
ALCOHOLIC BEVERAGES	**100.0%**	**6.4%**	**20.0%**	**21.4%**	**9.0%**	**43.2%**	**26.8%**	**16.4%**
At home	**100.0**	**8.2**	**21.7**	**21.6**	**9.2**	**39.3**	**23.2**	**16.2**
Beer and ale	100.0	12.5	27.6	23.5	10.5	26.2	18.0	8.1
Whiskey	100.0	7.7	17.4	27.6	6.8	40.9	21.9	19.3
Wine	100.0	3.0	15.7	16.0	7.9	56.7	30.6	26.6
Other alcoholic beverages	100.0	5.7	17.8	27.0	9.5	40.7	24.0	16.8
Away from home	**100.0**	**3.6**	**17.5**	**21.1**	**8.6**	**49.2**	**32.3**	**16.7**
Beer and ale	100.0	4.1	18.1	21.7	8.7	47.3	31.3	15.8
At fast-food restaurants*	100.0	6.4	18.2	24.0	10.4	41.3	24.5	17.0
At full-service restaurants	100.0	3.6	18.7	22.4	8.6	46.7	30.6	16.0
Wine	100.0	3.9	19.2	22.9	7.4	46.5	32.7	13.6
At fast-food restaurants*	100.0	9.1	16.0	29.1	6.0	40.2	26.1	14.1
At full-service restaurants	100.0	3.2	20.1	22.4	7.8	46.5	32.5	13.7
Other alcoholic beverages	100.0	3.1	17.5	20.4	8.9	50.0	33.4	16.5
At fast-food restaurants*	100.0	4.0	14.1	29.0	11.1	42.7	31.4	11.0
At full-service restaurants	100.0	3.1	18.1	20.2	9.0	49.4	32.0	17.4
Alcoholic beverages purchased on trips	100.0	3.0	15.2	19.6	8.7	53.5	32.9	20.7

The category fast-food restaurants also includes take-out, delivery, concession stands, buffets, and cafeterias other than employer and school.
Note: Numbers may not add to total because of rounding. "–" means sample is too small to make a reliable estimate.
Source: Calculations by New Strategist based on the 2004 Consumer Expenditure Survey

Chapter 6. Spending on Gifts for Nonhousehold Members, 2004

Spending on gifts for nonhousehold members stood at $1,215 in 2004, 2 percent greater than in 2000 after adjusting for inflation. Households cut their spending on many gift categories. Spending on gifts of transportation fell 34 percent, while spending on gifts of entertainment declined24 percent. Bucking the trend, spending on gifts of education for nonhousehold members climbed 51 percent, and gifts of housekeeping supplies grew 42 percent.

Households headed by 45-to-54-year-olds spend the most on gifts for nonhousehold members, a total of $1,935 in 2004—59 percent more than the average household. This age group, the most affluent, accounts for 32 percent of all spending on gifts for people in other households—a much greater percentage than its 20 percent share of households. Householders aged 55 to 64 spend 35 percent more than the average household on gifts for nonhousehold members, accounting for another 20 percent of the market. Every other age group spends less than average on gifts for nonhousehold members.

Households with incomes of $100,000 or more averaged spending of $3,563 on gifts for nonhousehold members in 2004, three times as much as the average household. While overall spending on gifts is less in lower-income households, gift spending by category varies by household income. Lower-income households spend more than average on practical gifts such as buying appliances for someone living in another household (such as a grown child living elsewhere).

Among household types, married couples without children at home (most of them empty-nesters) spend the most on gifts for nonhousehold members—53 percent more than the average household. Spending on gifts for nonhousehold members is well below average among married couples with preschoolers, single parents, and people living alone.

Non-Hispanic white and Asian households spend far more than other racial or ethnic groups on gifts for nonhousehold members. In 2004, the average non-Hispanic white household devoted $1,363 to this category, 12 percent more than average, while Asians spent 5 percent more. Black households spent 44 percent less than average on gifts for nonhousehold members in 2004, while Hispanic households spent 40 percent less.

Households in the Northeast spend the most on gifts for nonhousehold members, 24 percent more than the average household. In the South, spending on gifts is 19 percent below average.

Because college graduates dominate the nation's affluent households, they spend the most on gifts for nonhousehold members. In 2004, households headed by college graduates spent $2,151 on gifts for nonhousehold members, 77 percent more than the average household. College graduates spend more than twice the average on gifts of education expenses. They account for 70 percent of the market for gifts of major appliances for nonhousehold members.

Table 6.1 Gifts for Nonhousehold Members: Average spending by age, 2004

(average annual spending of consumer units (CU) on selected gifts of products and services for nonhousehold members by age of consumer unit reference person, 2004)

	total consumer units	under 25	25 to 34	35 to 44	45 to 54	55 to 64	65 to 74	75+
Number of consumer units (in 000s)	116,282	8,817	19,439	24,070	23,712	17,479	11,230	11,536
Average number of persons per CU	2.5	1.9	2.9	3.2	2.7	2.1	1.9	1.5
Average before-tax income of CU	$54,453.00	$22,840.00	$52,484.00	$65,515.00	$70,434.00	$61,031.00	$42,137.00	$28,028.00
Average spending of CU, total	43,394.87	24,534.56	42,700.54	50,401.62	52,764.36	47,298.58	36,511.98	25,763.32
Gifts, average spending	1,215.44	438.02	711.40	1,096.49	1,934.85	1,636.17	1,068.24	926.04
FOOD	74.03	10.18	36.55	56.22	157.17	109.22	51.52	21.12
ALCOHOLIC BEVERAGES	19.91	13.74	18.89	25.55	27.73	18.65	16.10	3.40
HOUSING	282.78	104.34	181.90	299.17	398.00	371.74	213.55	248.20
Housekeeping supplies	61.07	19.68	45.77	88.01	80.13	61.27	51.33	31.61
Laundry and cleaning supplies	5.75	2.11	4.83	6.66	11.63	4.17	1.72	2.51
Other household supplies	19.09	5.59	11.75	39.22	21.96	16.11	10.42	6.04
Postage and stationery	36.23	11.98	29.19	42.13	46.55	40.98	39.18	23.06
Household textiles	18.90	8.96	10.90	19.61	21.98	30.56	23.57	10.16
Appliances and miscellaneous housewares	31.93	13.55	28.38	29.59	31.77	50.96	32.57	27.40
Major appliances	11.71	1.03	4.19	11.44	11.40	26.61	7.31	15.83
Small appliances and miscellaneous housewares	20.22	12.52	24.19	18.15	20.36	24.35	25.26	11.57
Miscellaneous household equipment	71.64	28.24	51.95	106.35	94.54	81.37	41.77	31.15
Other housing	99.23	33.90	44.90	55.61	169.59	147.59	64.31	147.88
APPAREL AND SERVICES	286.38	180.81	260.60	338.76	328.72	372.53	255.98	108.50
Men and boys, aged 2 or older	75.54	37.34	51.33	100.31	87.77	96.96	89.40	21.11
Women and girls, aged 2 or older	101.20	61.73	77.01	113.99	128.13	128.65	99.04	50.02
Children under age 2	38.29	22.27	58.45	43.43	38.92	40.85	25.34	11.40
Other apparel products and services	71.35	59.46	73.82	81.02	73.90	106.07	42.20	25.97
Jewelry and watches	24.03	25.85	33.36	19.96	16.18	47.91	14.23	4.88
All other apparel products and services	47.32	33.61	40.45	61.06	57.71	58.16	27.96	21.10
TRANSPORTATION	50.84	12.21	32.25	47.11	84.98	56.40	47.22	44.12
HEALTH CARE	49.10	7.97	30.07	35.35	44.10	34.35	25.72	196.74
ENTERTAINMENT	78.16	32.70	50.70	73.63	108.20	119.70	86.66	35.98
Toys, games, arts and crafts, and tricycles	27.65	9.55	22.72	22.30	31.36	46.93	40.57	11.52
Other entertainment	50.51	23.14	27.98	51.33	76.84	72.76	46.09	24.46
PERSONAL CARE PRODUCTS AND SERVICES	28.83	17.28	29.62	44.44	32.23	23.12	16.25	16.73
EDUCATION	249.81	16.11	25.16	105.30	662.74	346.16	196.37	165.15
ALL OTHER GIFTS	94.36	42.53	45.32	70.42	89.69	182.10	156.09	84.10

Note: Numbers may not add to total because not all categories are shown. Spending on gifts is also included in the product and service categories in other chapters.
Source: Bureau of Labor Statistics, unpublished tables from the 2004 Consumer Expenditure Survey

Table 6.2 Gifts for Nonhousehold Members: Indexed spending by age, 2004

(indexed average annual spending of consumer units (CU) on selected gifts of products and services for nonhousehold members by age of consumer unit reference person, 2004; index definition: an index of 100 is the average for all consumer units; an index of 132 means that spending by consumer units in that group is 32 percent above the average for all consumer units; an index of 68 indicates spending that is 32 percent below the average for all consumer units)

	total consumer units	under 25	25 to 34	35 to 44	45 to 54	55 to 64	65 to 74	75+
Average spending of CU, total	$43,395	$24,535	$42,701	$50,402	$52,764	$47,299	$36,512	$25,763
Average spending of CU, index	100	57	98	116	122	109	84	59
Gifts, spending index	**100**	**36**	**59**	**90**	**159**	**135**	**88**	**76**
FOOD	**100**	**14**	**49**	**76**	**212**	**148**	**70**	**29**
ALCOHOLIC BEVERAGES	**100**	**69**	**95**	**128**	**139**	**94**	**81**	**17**
HOUSING	**100**	**37**	**64**	**106**	**141**	**131**	**76**	**88**
Housekeeping supplies	**100**	**32**	**75**	**144**	**131**	**100**	**84**	**52**
Laundry and cleaning supplies	100	37	84	116	202	73	30	44
Other household supplies	100	29	62	205	115	84	55	32
Postage and stationery	100	33	81	116	128	113	108	64
Household textiles	**100**	**47**	**58**	**104**	**116**	**162**	**125**	**54**
Appliances and miscellaneous housewares	**100**	**42**	**89**	**93**	**99**	**160**	**102**	**86**
Major appliances	100	9	36	98	97	227	62	135
Small appliances and miscellaneous housewares	100	62	120	90	101	120	125	57
Miscellaneous household equipment	**100**	**39**	**73**	**148**	**132**	**114**	**58**	**43**
Other housing	**100**	**34**	**45**	**56**	**171**	**149**	**65**	**149**
APPAREL AND SERVICES	**100**	**63**	**91**	**118**	**115**	**130**	**89**	**38**
Men and boys, aged 2 or older	100	49	68	133	116	128	118	28
Women and girls, aged 2 or older	100	61	76	113	127	127	98	49
Children under age 2	100	58	153	113	102	107	66	30
Other apparel products and services	100	83	103	114	104	149	59	36
Jewelry and watches	100	108	139	83	67	199	59	20
All other apparel products and services	100	71	85	129	122	123	59	45
TRANSPORTATION	**100**	**24**	**63**	**93**	**167**	**111**	**93**	**87**
HEALTH CARE	**100**	**16**	**61**	**72**	**90**	**70**	**52**	**401**
ENTERTAINMENT	**100**	**42**	**65**	**94**	**138**	**153**	**111**	**46**
Toys, games, arts and crafts, and tricycles	100	35	82	81	113	170	147	42
Other entertainment	100	46	55	102	152	144	91	48
PERSONAL CARE PRODUCTS AND SERVICES	**100**	**60**	**103**	**154**	**112**	**80**	**56**	**58**
EDUCATION	**100**	**6**	**10**	**42**	**265**	**139**	**79**	**66**
ALL OTHER GIFTS	**100**	**45**	**48**	**75**	**95**	**193**	**165**	**89**

Note: Spending on gifts is also included in the product and service categories in other chapters.
Source: Calculations by New Strategist based on the 2004 Consumer Expenditure Survey

Table 6.3 Gifts for Nonhousehold Members: Total spending by age, 2004

(total annual spending on selected gifts of products and services for nonhousehold members by consumer unit (CU) age groups, 2004; consumer units and dollars in thousands)

	total consumer units	under 25	25 to 34	35 to 44	45 to 54	55 to 64	65 to 74	75+
Number of consumer units	116,282	8,817	19,439	24,070	23,712	17,479	11,230	11,536
Total spending of all CUs	$5,046,042,273	$216,321,216	$830,055,797	$1,213,166,993	$1,251,148,504	$826,731,880	$410,029,535	$297,205,660
Gifts, total spending	141,333,794	3,862,022	13,828,905	26,392,514	45,879,163	28,598,615	11,996,335	10,682,797
FOOD	8,608,356	89,757	710,495	1,353,215	3,726,815	1,909,056	578,570	243,640
ALCOHOLIC BEVERAGES	2,315,175	121,146	367,203	614,989	657,534	325,983	180,803	39,222
HOUSING	32,882,224	919,966	3,535,954	7,201,022	9,437,376	6,497,643	2,398,167	2,863,235
Housekeeping supplies	7,101,342	173,519	889,723	2,118,401	1,900,043	1,070,938	576,436	364,653
Laundry and cleaning supplies	668,622	18,604	93,890	160,306	275,771	72,887	19,316	28,955
Other household supplies	2,219,823	49,287	228,408	944,025	520,716	281,587	117,017	69,677
Postage and stationery	4,212,897	105,628	567,424	1,014,069	1,103,794	716,289	439,991	266,020
Household textiles	2,197,730	79,000	211,885	472,013	521,190	534,158	264,691	117,206
Appliances and miscellaneous housewares	3,712,884	119,470	551,679	712,231	753,330	890,730	365,761	316,086
Major appliances	1,361,662	9,082	81,449	275,361	270,317	465,116	82,091	182,615
Small appliances and miscellaneous housewares	2,351,222	110,389	470,229	436,871	482,776	425,614	283,670	133,472
Miscellaneous household equipment	8,330,442	248,992	1,009,856	2,559,845	2,241,732	1,422,266	469,077	359,346
Other housing	11,538,663	298,896	872,811	1,338,533	4,021,318	2,579,726	722,201	1,705,944
APPAREL AND SERVICES	33,300,839	1,594,202	5,065,803	8,153,953	7,794,609	6,511,452	2,874,655	1,251,656
Men and boys, aged 2 or older	8,783,942	329,227	997,804	2,414,462	2,081,202	1,694,764	1,003,962	243,525
Women and girls, aged 2 or older	11,767,738	544,273	1,496,997	2,743,739	3,038,219	2,248,673	1,112,219	577,031
Children under age 2	4,452,438	196,355	1,136,210	1,045,360	922,871	714,017	284,568	131,510
Other apparel products and services	8,296,721	524,259	1,434,987	1,950,151	1,752,317	1,853,998	473,906	299,590
Jewelry and watches	2,794,256	227,919	648,485	480,437	383,660	837,419	159,803	56,296
All other apparel products and services	5,502,464	296,339	786,308	1,469,714	1,368,420	1,016,579	313,991	243,410
TRANSPORTATION	5,911,777	107,656	626,908	1,133,938	2,015,046	985,816	530,281	508,968
HEALTH CARE	5,709,446	70,271	584,531	850,875	1,045,699	600,404	288,836	2,269,593
ENTERTAINMENT	9,088,601	288,316	985,557	1,772,274	2,565,638	2,092,236	973,192	415,065
Toys, games, arts and crafts, and tricycles	3,215,197	84,202	441,654	536,761	743,608	820,289	455,601	132,895
Other entertainment	5,873,404	204,025	543,903	1,235,513	1,822,030	1,271,772	517,591	282,171
PERSONAL CARE PRODUCTS AND SERVICES	3,352,410	152,358	575,783	1,069,671	764,238	404,114	182,488	192,997
EDUCATION	29,048,406	142,042	489,085	2,534,571	15,714,891	6,050,531	2,205,235	1,905,170
ALL OTHER GIFTS	10,972,370	374,987	880,975	1,695,009	2,126,729	3,182,926	1,752,891	970,178

Note: Numbers may not add to total because of rounding and because not all categories are shown. Spending on gifts is also included in the product and service categories in other chapters.
Source: Calculations by New Strategist based on the 2004 Consumer Expenditure Survey

Table 6.4 Gifts for Nonhousehold Members: Market shares by age, 2004

(percentage of total annual spending on selected gifts of products and services for nonhousehold members accounted for by consumer unit age groups, 2004)

	total consumer units	under 25	25 to 34	35 to 44	45 to 54	55 to 64	65 to 74	75+
Share of total consumer units	100.0%	7.6%	16.7%	20.7%	20.4%	15.0%	9.7%	9.9%
Share of total before-tax income	100.0	3.2	16.1	24.9	26.4	16.8	7.5	5.1
Share of total spending	100.0	4.3	16.4	24.0	24.8	16.4	8.1	5.9
Share of gifts spending	100.0	2.7	9.8	18.7	32.5	20.2	8.5	7.6
FOOD	100.0	1.0	8.3	15.7	43.3	22.2	6.7	2.8
ALCOHOLIC BEVERAGES	100.0	5.2	15.9	26.6	28.4	14.1	7.8	1.7
HOUSING	100.0	2.8	10.8	21.9	28.7	19.8	7.3	8.7
Housekeeping supplies	100.0	2.4	12.5	29.8	26.8	15.1	8.1	5.1
Laundry and cleaning supplies	100.0	2.8	14.0	24.0	41.2	10.9	2.9	4.3
Other household supplies	100.0	2.2	10.3	42.5	23.5	12.7	5.3	3.1
Postage and stationery	100.0	2.5	13.5	24.1	26.2	17.0	10.4	6.3
Household textiles	100.0	3.6	9.6	21.5	23.7	24.3	12.0	5.3
Appliances and miscellaneous housewares	100.0	3.2	14.9	19.2	20.3	24.0	9.9	8.5
Major appliances	100.0	0.7	6.0	20.2	19.9	34.2	6.0	13.4
Small appliances and miscellaneous housewares	100.0	4.7	20.0	18.6	20.5	18.1	12.1	5.7
Miscellaneous household equipment	100.0	3.0	12.1	30.7	26.9	17.1	5.6	4.3
Other housing	100.0	2.6	7.6	11.6	34.9	22.4	6.3	14.8
APPAREL AND SERVICES	100.0	4.8	15.2	24.5	23.4	19.6	8.6	3.8
Men and boys, aged 2 or older	100.0	3.7	11.4	27.5	23.7	19.3	11.4	2.8
Women and girls, aged 2 or older	100.0	4.6	12.7	23.3	25.8	19.1	9.5	4.9
Children under age 2	100.0	4.4	25.5	23.5	20.7	16.0	6.4	3.0
Other apparel products and services	100.0	6.3	17.3	23.5	21.1	22.3	5.7	3.6
Jewelry and watches	100.0	8.2	23.2	17.2	13.7	30.0	5.7	2.0
All other apparel products and services	100.0	5.4	14.3	26.7	24.9	18.5	5.7	4.4
TRANSPORTATION	100.0	1.8	10.6	19.2	34.1	16.7	9.0	8.6
HEALTH CARE	100.0	1.2	10.2	14.9	18.3	10.5	5.1	39.8
ENTERTAINMENT	100.0	3.2	10.8	19.5	28.2	23.0	10.7	4.6
Toys, games, arts and crafts, and tricycles	100.0	2.6	13.7	16.7	23.1	25.5	14.2	4.1
Other entertainment	100.0	3.5	9.3	21.0	31.0	21.7	8.8	4.8
PERSONAL CARE PRODUCTS AND SERVICES	100.0	4.5	17.2	31.9	22.8	12.1	5.4	5.8
EDUCATION	100.0	0.5	1.7	8.7	54.1	20.8	7.6	6.6
ALL OTHER GIFTS	100.0	3.4	8.0	15.4	19.4	29.0	16.0	8.8

Note: Numbers may not add to total because of rounding. Spending on gifts is also included in the product and service categories in other chapters.
Source: Calculations by New Strategist based on the 2004 Consumer Expenditure Survey

Table 6.5 Gifts for Nonhousehold Members: Average spending by income, 2004

(average annual spending on selected gifts of products and services for nonhousehold members by before-tax income of consumer units (CU), 2004)

	total consumer units	under $20,000	$20,000–$39,999	$40,000–$49,999	$50,000–$69,999	$70,000–$79,999	$80,000–$99,999	$100,000 or more
Number of consumer units (in 000s)	116,282	28,898	27,297	11,374	18,069	6,461	9,246	14,937
Average number of persons per CU	2.5	1.8	2.3	2.6	2.8	3.0	3.1	3.2
Average before-tax income of CU	$54,453.00	$10,923.47	$29,561.76	$44,645.00	$59,259.00	$74,437.00	$88,811.00	$155,901.00
Average spending of CU, total	43,394.87	18,865.37	30,400.94	38,204.07	47,750.13	55,012.03	65,446.39	93,525.67
Gifts, average spending	**1,215.44**	**490.87**	**627.78**	**778.89**	**1,151.47**	**1,289.10**	**1,927.10**	**3,562.88**
FOOD	**74.03**	**21.04**	**27.82**	**42.97**	**48.54**	**69.18**	**108.18**	**289.59**
ALCOHOLIC BEVERAGES	**19.91**	**4.67**	**8.57**	**23.89**	**22.62**	**19.36**	**31.80**	**53.23**
HOUSING	**282.78**	**145.54**	**146.98**	**177.98**	**251.87**	**359.04**	**499.08**	**724.79**
Housekeeping supplies	**61.07**	**18.38**	**40.54**	**41.97**	**62.94**	**84.68**	**156.33**	**115.53**
Laundry and cleaning supplies	5.75	2.05	5.23	4.18	4.77	9.51	10.46	10.63
Other household supplies	19.09	3.84	11.33	6.19	13.29	29.96	85.21	30.79
Postage and stationery	36.23	12.49	23.98	31.60	44.88	45.22	60.66	74.11
Household textiles	**18.90**	**8.01**	**13.08**	**5.02**	**26.58**	**33.94**	**31.05**	**36.41**
Appliances and miscellaneous housewares	**31.93**	**9.55**	**20.61**	**33.14**	**14.33**	**40.27**	**50.32**	**94.89**
Major appliances	11.71	4.67	4.99	18.69	3.23	16.66	7.21	40.81
Small appliances and miscellaneous housewares	20.22	4.88	15.63	14.45	11.10	23.61	43.11	54.08
Miscellaneous household equipment	**71.64**	**24.08**	**33.19**	**36.91**	**89.87**	**69.20**	**136.57**	**193.86**
Other housing	**99.23**	**85.52**	**39.54**	**60.94**	**58.15**	**130.94**	**124.81**	**284.10**
APPAREL AND SERVICES	**286.38**	**149.38**	**192.20**	**243.96**	**313.97**	**350.79**	**384.20**	**611.10**
Men and boys, aged 2 or older	75.54	37.17	46.90	66.41	81.60	79.57	97.21	179.26
Women and girls, aged 2 or older	101.20	44.33	62.34	93.57	127.63	85.87	128.39	236.96
Children under age 2	38.29	19.76	27.13	28.71	41.37	50.53	46.43	85.35
Other apparel products and services	71.35	48.12	55.82	55.28	63.38	134.81	112.18	109.53
Jewelry and watches	24.03	8.65	13.79	12.21	27.34	65.05	72.32	29.86
All other apparel products and services	47.32	39.48	42.03	43.07	36.04	69.76	39.86	79.67
TRANSPORTATION	**50.84**	**16.61**	**41.52**	**54.43**	**46.92**	**42.21**	**51.35**	**138.92**
HEALTH CARE	**49.10**	**35.74**	**41.31**	**21.89**	**61.95**	**46.00**	**34.26**	**104.03**
ENTERTAINMENT	**78.16**	**34.08**	**56.31**	**63.10**	**77.54**	**115.28**	**110.96**	**174.96**
Toys, games, arts and crafts, and tricycles	27.65	14.96	24.42	23.07	29.05	42.24	34.70	49.22
Other entertainment	50.51	19.12	31.89	40.02	48.49	73.04	76.27	125.74
PERSONAL CARE PRODUCTS AND SERVICES	**28.83**	**9.92**	**21.16**	**25.49**	**27.62**	**22.17**	**38.16**	**75.75**
EDUCATION	**249.81**	**24.39**	**33.34**	**51.51**	**175.39**	**175.78**	**556.04**	**1,165.36**
ALL OTHER GIFTS	**94.36**	**49.10**	**57.57**	**72.99**	**123.00**	**87.02**	**111.43**	**223.02**

Note: Numbers may not add to total because not all categories are shown. Spending on gifts is also included in the product and service categories in other chapters.
Source: Bureau of Labor Statistics, unpublished tables from the 2004 Consumer Expenditure Survey

Table 6.6 Gifts for Nonhousehold Members: Indexed spending by income, 2004

(indexed average annual spending of consumer units (CU) on selected gifts of products and services for nonhousehold members by before-tax income of consumer unit, 2004; index definition: an index of 100 is the average for all consumer units; an index of 132 means that spending by consumer units in that group is 32 percent above the average for all consumer units; an index of 68 indicates spending that is 32 percent below the average for all consumer units)

	total consumer units	under $20,000	$20,000– $39,999	$40,000– $49,999	$50,000– $69,999	$70,000– $79,999	$80,000– $99,999	$100,000 or more
Average spending of CU, total	$43,395	$18,865	$30,401	$38,204	$47,750	$55,012	$65,446	$93,526
Average spending of CU, index	100	43	70	88	110	127	151	216
Gifts, spending index	100	40	52	64	95	106	159	293
FOOD	100	28	38	58	66	93	146	391
ALCOHOLIC BEVERAGES	100	23	43	120	114	97	160	267
HOUSING	100	51	52	63	89	127	176	256
Housekeeping supplies	100	30	66	69	103	139	256	189
Laundry and cleaning supplies	100	36	91	73	83	165	182	185
Other household supplies	100	20	59	32	70	157	446	161
Postage and stationery	100	34	66	87	124	125	167	205
Household textiles	100	42	69	27	141	180	164	193
Appliances and miscellaneous housewares	100	30	65	104	45	126	158	297
Major appliances	100	40	43	160	28	142	62	349
Small appliances and miscellaneous housewares	100	24	77	71	55	117	213	267
Miscellaneous household equipment	100	34	46	52	125	97	191	271
Other housing	100	86	40	61	59	132	126	286
APPAREL AND SERVICES	100	52	67	85	110	122	134	213
Men and boys, aged 2 or older	100	49	62	88	108	105	129	237
Women and girls, aged 2 or older	100	44	62	92	126	85	127	234
Children under age 2	100	52	71	75	108	132	121	223
Other apparel products and services	100	67	78	77	89	189	157	154
Jewelry and watches	100	36	57	51	114	271	301	124
All other apparel products and services	100	83	89	91	76	147	84	168
TRANSPORTATION	100	33	82	107	92	83	101	273
HEALTH CARE	100	73	84	45	126	94	70	212
ENTERTAINMENT	100	44	72	81	99	147	142	224
Toys, games, arts and crafts, and tricycles	100	54	88	83	105	153	125	178
Other entertainment	100	38	63	79	96	145	151	249
PERSONAL CARE PRODUCTS AND SERVICES	100	34	73	88	96	77	132	263
EDUCATION	100	10	13	21	70	70	223	466
ALL OTHER GIFTS	100	52	61	77	130	92	118	236

Note: Spending on gifts is also included in the product and service categories in other chapters.
Source: Calculations by New Strategist based on the 2004 Consumer Expenditure Survey

Table 6.7 Gifts for Nonhousehold Members: Total spending by income, 2004

(total annual spending on selected gifts of products and services for nonhousehold members by before-tax income group of consumer units (CU), 2004; consumer units and dollars in thousands)

	total consumer units	under $20,000	$20,000–$39,999	$40,000–$49,999	$50,000–$69,999	$70,000–$79,999	$80,000–$99,999	$100,000 or more
Number of consumer units	116,282	28,898	27,297	11,374	18,069	6,461	9,246	14,937
Total spending of all CUs	$5,046,042,273	$545,171,431	$829,854,379	$434,533,092	$862,797,099	$355,432,726	$605,117,322	$1,396,992,933
Gifts, total spending	141,333,794.08	14,185,177.27	17,136,410.28	8,859,094.86	20,805,911.43	8,328,875.10	17,817,966.60	53,218,738.56
FOOD	8,608,356	608,067	759,269	488,741	877,069	446,972	1,000,232	4,325,606
ALCOHOLIC BEVERAGES	2,315,175	135,053	233,951	271,725	408,721	125,085	294,023	795,097
HOUSING	32,882,224	4,205,946	4,012,009	2,024,345	4,551,039	2,319,757	4,614,494	10,826,188
Housekeeping supplies	7,101,342	531,166	1,106,723	477,367	1,137,263	547,117	1,445,427	1,725,672
Laundry and cleaning supplies	668,622	59,245	142,787	47,543	86,189	61,444	96,713	158,780
Other household supplies	2,219,823	110,968	309,377	70,405	240,137	193,572	787,852	459,910
Postage and stationery	4,212,897	360,954	654,691	359,418	810,937	292,166	560,862	1,106,981
Household textiles	2,197,730	231,561	357,091	57,097	480,274	219,286	287,088	543,856
Appliances and miscellaneous housewares	3,712,884	275,872	562,701	376,934	258,929	260,184	465,259	1,417,372
Major appliances	1,361,662	134,887	136,132	212,580	58,363	107,640	66,664	609,579
Small appliances and miscellaneous housewares	2,351,222	140,985	426,569	164,354	200,566	152,544	398,595	807,793
Miscellaneous household equipment	8,330,442	695,763	905,931	419,814	1,623,861	447,101	1,262,726	2,895,687
Other housing	11,538,663	2,471,430	1,079,433	693,132	1,050,712	846,003	1,153,993	4,243,602
APPAREL AND SERVICES	33,300,839	4,316,844	5,246,361	2,774,801	5,673,124	2,266,454	3,552,313	9,128,001
Men and boys, aged 2 or older	8,783,942	1,074,248	1,280,279	755,347	1,474,430	514,102	898,804	2,677,607
Women and girls, aged 2 or older	11,767,738	1,281,047	1,701,667	1,064,265	2,306,146	554,806	1,187,094	3,539,472
Children under age 2	4,452,438	570,974	740,671	326,548	747,515	326,474	429,292	1,274,873
Other apparel products and services	8,296,721	1,390,710	1,523,745	628,755	1,145,213	871,007	1,037,216	1,636,050
Jewelry and watches	2,794,256	249,968	376,290	138,877	494,006	420,288	668,671	446,019
All other apparel products and services	5,502,464	1,140,787	1,147,182	489,878	651,207	450,719	368,546	1,190,031
TRANSPORTATION	5,911,777	480,102	1,133,282	619,087	847,797	272,719	474,782	2,075,048
HEALTH CARE	5,709,446	1,032,947	1,127,559	248,977	1,119,375	297,206	316,768	1,553,896
ENTERTAINMENT	9,088,601	984,725	1,537,062	717,699	1,401,070	744,824	1,025,936	2,613,378
Toys, games, arts and crafts, and tricycles	3,215,197	432,285	666,477	262,398	524,904	272,913	320,836	735,199
Other entertainment	5,873,404	552,486	870,443	455,187	876,166	471,911	705,192	1,878,178
PERSONAL CARE PRODUCTS AND SERVICES	3,352,410	286,631	577,600	289,923	499,066	143,240	352,827	1,131,478
EDUCATION	29,048,406	704,795	910,141	585,875	3,169,122	1,135,715	5,141,146	17,406,982
ALL OTHER GIFTS	10,972,370	1,418,856	1,571,559	830,188	2,222,487	562,236	1,030,282	3,331,250

Note: Numbers may not add to total because of rounding and because not all categories are shown. Spending on gifts is also included in the product and service categories in other chapters.
Source: Calculations by New Strategist based on the 2004 Consumer Expenditure Survey

Table 6.8 Gifts for Nonhousehold Members: Market shares by income, 2004

(percentage of total annual spending on selected gifts of products and services for nonhousehold members accounted for by before-tax income group of consumer units, 2004)

	total consumer units	under $20,000	$20,000–$39,999	$40,000–$49,999	$50,000–$69,999	$70,000–$79,999	$80,000–$99,999	$100,000 or more
Share of total consumer units	100.0%	24.9%	23.5%	9.8%	15.5%	5.6%	8.0%	12.8%
Share of total before-tax income	100.0	5.0	12.7	8.0	16.9	7.6	13.0	36.8
Share of total spending	100.0	10.8	16.4	8.6	17.1	7.0	12.0	27.7
Share of gifts spending	100.0	10.0	12.1	6.3	14.7	5.9	12.6	37.7
FOOD	100.0	7.1	8.8	5.7	10.2	5.2	11.6	50.2
ALCOHOLIC BEVERAGES	100.0	5.8	10.1	11.7	17.7	5.4	12.7	34.3
HOUSING	100.0	12.8	12.2	6.2	13.8	7.1	14.0	32.9
Housekeeping supplies	100.0	7.5	15.6	6.7	16.0	7.7	20.4	24.3
Laundry and cleaning supplies	100.0	8.9	21.4	7.1	12.9	9.2	14.5	23.7
Other household supplies	100.0	5.0	13.9	3.2	10.8	8.7	35.5	20.7
Postage and stationery	100.0	8.6	15.5	8.5	19.2	6.9	13.3	26.3
Household textiles	100.0	10.5	16.2	2.6	21.9	10.0	13.1	24.7
Appliances and miscellaneous housewares	100.0	7.4	15.2	10.2	7.0	7.0	12.5	38.2
Major appliances	100.0	9.9	10.0	15.6	4.3	7.9	4.9	44.8
Small appliances and miscellaneous housewares	100.0	6.0	18.1	7.0	8.5	6.5	17.0	34.4
Miscellaneous household equipment	100.0	8.4	10.9	5.0	19.5	5.4	15.2	34.8
Other housing	100.0	21.4	9.4	6.0	9.1	7.3	10.0	36.8
APPAREL AND SERVICES	100.0	13.0	15.8	8.3	17.0	6.8	10.7	27.4
Men and boys, aged 2 or older	100.0	12.2	14.6	8.6	16.8	5.9	10.2	30.5
Women and girls, aged 2 or older	100.0	10.9	14.5	9.0	19.6	4.7	10.1	30.1
Children under age 2	100.0	12.8	16.6	7.3	16.8	7.3	9.6	28.6
Other apparel products and services	100.0	16.8	18.4	7.6	13.8	10.5	12.5	19.7
Jewelry and watches	100.0	8.9	13.5	5.0	17.7	15.0	23.9	16.0
All other apparel products and services	100.0	20.7	20.8	8.9	11.8	8.2	6.7	21.6
TRANSPORTATION	100.0	8.1	19.2	10.5	14.3	4.6	8.0	35.1
HEALTH CARE	100.0	18.1	19.7	4.4	19.6	5.2	5.5	27.2
ENTERTAINMENT	100.0	10.8	16.9	7.9	15.4	8.2	11.3	28.8
Toys, games, arts and crafts, and tricycles	100.0	13.4	20.7	8.2	16.3	8.5	10.0	22.9
Other entertainment	100.0	9.4	14.8	7.7	14.9	8.0	12.0	32.0
PERSONAL CARE PRODUCTS AND SERVICES	100.0	8.6	17.2	8.6	14.9	4.3	10.5	33.8
EDUCATION	100.0	2.4	3.1	2.0	10.9	3.9	17.7	59.9
ALL OTHER GIFTS	100.0	12.9	14.3	7.6	20.3	5.1	9.4	30.4

Note: Numbers may not add to total because of rounding. Spending on gifts is also included in the product and service categories in other chapters.
Source: Calculations by New Strategist based on the 2004 Consumer Expenditure Survey

Table 6.9 Gifts for Nonhousehold Members: Average spending by high-income consumer units, 2004

(average annual spending on selected gifts of products and services for nonhousehold members by before-tax income of high-income consumer units (CU), 2004)

	total consumer units	$100,000 or more	$100,000–$119,999	$120,000–$149,999	$150,000 or more
Number of consumer units (in 000s)	116,282	14,937	5,625	4,245	5,067
Average number of persons per CU	2.5	3.2	3.1	3.3	3.2
Average before-tax income of CU	$54,453.00	$155,901.00	$108,751.00	$132,292.00	$228,021.00
Average spending of CU, total	43,394.87	93,525.67	75,213.14	87,298.57	119,448.79
Gifts, average spending	1,215.44	3,562.88	2,177.63	3,173.81	5,472.50
FOOD	74.03	289.59	175.44	200.50	494.26
ALCOHOLIC BEVERAGES	19.91	53.23	23.71	50.49	92.23
HOUSING	282.78	724.79	445.05	687.99	1,072.90
Housekeeping supplies	61.07	115.53	99.48	122.33	128.40
Laundry and cleaning supplies	5.75	10.63	8.87	12.67	10.75
Other household supplies	19.09	30.79	23.62	26.92	43.53
Postage and stationery	36.23	74.11	67.00	82.74	74.13
Household textiles	18.90	36.41	38.33	40.09	30.05
Appliances and miscellaneous housewares	31.93	94.89	51.67	119.21	122.91
Major appliances	11.71	40.81	11.14	60.39	57.04
Small appliances and miscellaneous housewares	20.22	54.08	40.53	58.82	65.86
Miscellaneous household equipment	71.64	193.86	123.46	182.56	288.33
Other housing	99.23	284.10	132.12	223.81	503.21
APPAREL AND SERVICES	286.38	611.10	475.46	491.76	893.11
Men and boys, aged 2 or older	75.54	179.26	114.54	124.63	309.87
Women and girls, aged 2 or older	101.20	236.96	201.94	195.44	321.53
Children under age 2	38.29	85.35	77.55	78.90	101.58
Other apparel products and services	71.35	109.53	81.44	92.79	160.13
Jewelry and watches	24.03	29.86	29.56	24.10	35.02
All other apparel products and services	47.32	79.67	51.88	68.69	125.10
TRANSPORTATION	50.84	138.92	72.50	171.34	185.72
HEALTH CARE	49.10	104.03	82.46	133.69	101.68
ENTERTAINMENT	78.16	174.96	144.78	190.98	190.59
Toys, games, arts and crafts, and tricycles	27.65	49.22	38.63	46.96	62.86
Other entertainment	50.51	125.74	106.15	144.02	127.73
PERSONAL CARE PRODUCTS AND SERVICES	28.83	75.75	70.71	92.98	64.53
EDUCATION	249.81	1,165.36	566.12	990.64	1,977.47
ALL OTHER GIFTS	94.36	223.02	120.09	160.87	397.34

Note: Numbers may not add to total because not all categories are shown. Spending on gifts is also included in the product and service categories in other chapters.
Source: Bureau of Labor Statistics, unpublished tables from the 2004 Consumer Expenditure Survey

Table 6.10 Gifts for Nonhousehold Members: Indexed spending by high-income consumer units, 2004

(indexed average annual spending of high-income consumer units (CU) on selected gifts of products and services for nonhousehold members by before-tax income of consumer unit, 2004; index definition: an index of 100 is the average for all consumer units; an index of 132 means that spending by consumer units in that group is 32 percent above the average for all consumer units; an index of 68 indicates spending that is 32 percent below the average for all consumer units)

	total consumer units	$100,000 or more	$100,000–$119,999	$120,000–$149,999	$150,000 or more
Average spending of CU, total	$43,395	$93,526	$75,213	$87,299	$119,449
Average spending of CU, index	100	216	173	201	275
Gifts, spending index	100	293	179	261	450
FOOD	100	391	237	271	668
ALCOHOLIC BEVERAGES	100	267	119	254	463
HOUSING	100	256	157	243	379
Housekeeping supplies	100	189	163	200	210
Laundry and cleaning supplies	100	185	154	220	187
Other household supplies	100	161	124	141	228
Postage and stationery	100	205	185	228	205
Household textiles	100	193	203	212	159
Appliances and miscellaneous housewares	100	297	162	373	385
Major appliances	100	349	95	516	487
Small appliances and miscellaneous housewares	100	267	200	291	326
Miscellaneous household equipment	100	271	172	255	402
Other housing	100	286	133	226	507
APPAREL AND SERVICES	100	213	166	172	312
Men and boys, aged 2 or older	100	237	152	165	410
Women and girls, aged 2 or older	100	234	200	193	318
Children under age 2	100	223	203	206	265
Other apparel products and services	100	154	114	130	224
Jewelry and watches	100	124	123	100	146
All other apparel products and services	100	168	110	145	264
TRANSPORTATION	100	273	143	337	365
HEALTH CARE	100	212	168	272	207
ENTERTAINMENT	100	224	185	244	244
Toys, games, arts and crafts, and tricycles	100	178	140	170	227
Other entertainment	100	249	210	285	253
PERSONAL CARE PRODUCTS AND SERVICES	100	263	245	323	224
EDUCATION	100	466	227	397	792
ALL OTHER GIFTS	100	236	127	170	421

Note: Spending on gifts is also included in the product and service categories in other chapters.
Source: Calculations by New Strategist based on the 2004 Consumer Expenditure Survey

Table 6.11 Gifts for Nonhousehold Members: Total spending by high-income consumer units, 2004

(total annual spending on selected gifts of products and services for nonhousehold members by before-tax income group of high-income consumer units (CU), 2004; consumer units and dollars in thousands)

	total consumer units	$100,000 or more	$100,000– $119,999	$120,000– $149,999	$150,000 or more
Number of consumer units	116,282	14,937	5,625	4,245	5,067
Total spending of all CUs	$5,046,042,273	$1,396,992,933	$423,073,913	$370,582,430	$605,247,019
Gifts, total spending	141,333,794	53,218,739	12,249,169	13,472,823	27,729,158
FOOD	8,608,356	4,325,606	986,850	851,123	2,504,415
ALCOHOLIC BEVERAGES	2,315,175	795,097	133,369	214,330	467,329
HOUSING	32,882,224	10,826,188	2,503,406	2,920,518	5,436,384
Housekeeping supplies	7,101,342	1,725,672	559,575	519,291	650,603
Laundry and cleaning supplies	668,622	158,780	49,894	53,784	54,470
Other household supplies	2,219,823	459,910	132,863	114,275	220,567
Postage and stationery	4,212,897	1,106,981	376,875	351,231	375,617
Household textiles	2,197,730	543,856	215,606	170,182	152,263
Appliances and miscellaneous housewares	3,712,884	1,417,372	290,644	506,046	622,785
Major appliances	1,361,662	609,579	62,663	256,356	289,022
Small appliances and miscellaneous housewares	2,351,222	807,793	227,981	249,691	333,713
Miscellaneous household equipment	8,330,442	2,895,687	694,463	774,967	1,460,968
Other housing	11,538,663	4,243,602	743,175	950,073	2,549,765
APPAREL AND SERVICES	33,300,839	9,128,001	2,674,463	2,087,521	4,525,388
Men and boys, aged 2 or older	8,783,942	2,677,607	644,288	529,054	1,570,111
Women and girls, aged 2 or older	11,767,738	3,539,472	1,135,913	829,643	1,629,193
Children under age 2	4,452,438	1,274,873	436,219	334,931	514,706
Other apparel products and services	8,296,721	1,636,050	458,100	393,894	811,379
Jewelry and watches	2,794,256	446,019	166,275	102,305	177,446
All other apparel products and services	5,502,464	1,190,031	291,825	291,589	633,882
TRANSPORTATION	5,911,777	2,075,048	407,813	727,338	941,043
HEALTH CARE	5,709,446	1,553,896	463,838	567,514	515,213
ENTERTAINMENT	9,088,601	2,613,378	814,388	810,710	965,720
Toys, games, arts and crafts, and tricycles	3,215,197	735,199	217,294	199,345	318,512
Other entertainment	5,873,404	1,878,178	597,094	611,365	647,208
PERSONAL CARE PRODUCTS AND SERVICES	3,352,410	1,131,478	397,744	394,700	326,974
EDUCATION	29,048,406	17,406,982	3,184,425	4,205,267	10,019,840
ALL OTHER GIFTS	10,972,370	3,331,250	675,506	682,893	2,013,322

Note: Numbers may not add to total because of rounding and because not all categories are shown. Spending on gifts is also included in the product and service categories in other chapters.
Source: Calculations by New Strategist based on the 2004 Consumer Expenditure Survey

Table 6.12 Gifts for Nonhousehold Members: Market shares by high-income consumer units, 2004

(percentage of total annual spending on selected gifts of products and services for nonhousehold members accounted for by before-tax income group of high-income consumer units, 2004)

	total consumer units	$100,000 or more	$100,000–$119,999	$120,000–$149,999	$150,000 or more
Share of total consumer units	100.0%	12.8%	4.8%	3.7%	4.4%
Share of total before-tax income	100.0	36.8	9.7	8.9	18.2
Share of total spending	100.0	27.7	8.4	7.3	12.0
Share of gifts spending	100.0	37.7	8.7	9.5	19.6
FOOD	100.0	50.2	11.5	9.9	29.1
ALCOHOLIC BEVERAGES	100.0	34.3	5.8	9.3	20.2
HOUSING	100.0	32.9	7.6	8.9	16.5
Housekeeping supplies	100.0	24.3	7.9	7.3	9.2
Laundry and cleaning supplies	100.0	23.7	7.5	8.0	8.1
Other household supplies	100.0	20.7	6.0	5.1	9.9
Postage and stationery	100.0	26.3	8.9	8.3	8.9
Household textiles	100.0	24.7	9.8	7.7	6.9
Appliances and miscellaneous housewares	100.0	38.2	7.8	13.6	16.8
Major appliances	100.0	44.8	4.6	18.8	21.2
Small appliances and miscellaneous housewares	100.0	34.4	9.7	10.6	14.2
Miscellaneous household equipment	100.0	34.8	8.3	9.3	17.5
Other housing	100.0	36.8	6.4	8.2	22.1
APPAREL AND SERVICES	100.0	27.4	8.0	6.3	13.6
Men and boys, aged 2 or older	100.0	30.5	7.3	6.0	17.9
Women and girls, aged 2 or older	100.0	30.1	9.7	7.1	13.8
Children under age 2	100.0	28.6	9.8	7.5	11.6
Other apparel products and services	100.0	19.7	5.5	4.7	9.8
Jewelry and watches	100.0	16.0	6.0	3.7	6.4
All other apparel products and services	100.0	21.6	5.3	5.3	11.5
TRANSPORTATION	100.0	35.1	6.9	12.3	15.9
HEALTH CARE	100.0	27.2	8.1	9.9	9.0
ENTERTAINMENT	100.0	28.8	9.0	8.9	10.6
Toys, games, arts and crafts, and tricycles	100.0	22.9	6.8	6.2	9.9
Other entertainment	100.0	32.0	10.2	10.4	11.0
PERSONAL CARE PRODUCTS AND SERVICES	100.0	33.8	11.9	11.8	9.8
EDUCATION	100.0	59.9	11.0	14.5	34.5
ALL OTHER GIFTS	100.0	30.4	6.2	6.2	18.3

Note: Spending on gifts is also included in the product and service categories in other chapters.
Source: Calculations by New Strategist based on the 2004 Consumer Expenditure Survey

Table 6.13 Gifts for Nonhousehold Members: Average spending by household type, 2004

(average annual spending of consumer units (CU) on selected gifts of products and services for nonhousehold members by type of consumer unit, 2004)

	total married couples	married couples, no children	married couples with children				single parent, at least one child <18	single person
			total	oldest child under 6	oldest child 6 to 17	oldest child 18 or older		
Number of consumer units (in 000s)	59,797	25,585	29,279	5,604	15,376	8,300	6,892	33,686
Average number of persons per CU	3.2	2.0	3.9	3.5	4.1	3.9	2.9	1.0
Average before-tax income of CU	$73,001.00	$64,434.00	$79,764.00	$75,293.00	$78,508.00	$85,109.00	$31,055.00	$28,143.00
Average spending of CU, total	55,606.57	49,690.43	60,660.88	55,981.04	60,577.88	64,161.69	32,824.46	25,423.35
Gifts, average spending	**1,575.50**	**1,855.34**	**1,425.34**	**1,077.78**	**1,393.35**	**1,721.76**	**649.36**	**860.11**
FOOD	**108.67**	**121.27**	**103.99**	**63.26**	**105.58**	**129.45**	**54.93**	**29.41**
ALCOHOLIC BEVERAGES	**21.21**	**26.90**	**17.02**	**23.74**	**15.81**	**14.14**	**14.26**	**16.09**
HOUSING	**364.59**	**421.77**	**338.40**	**310.79**	**333.72**	**363.74**	**157.50**	**192.64**
Housekeeping supplies	**77.71**	**74.43**	**84.16**	**87.33**	**85.15**	**79.55**	**35.39**	**30.44**
Laundry and cleaning supplies	7.93	4.63	10.67	4.43	13.97	8.81	3.99	2.51
Other household supplies	20.68	19.91	21.93	23.48	21.78	20.99	11.31	6.60
Postage and stationery	49.10	49.89	51.56	59.43	49.40	49.75	20.10	21.33
Household textiles	**26.07**	**30.43**	**23.07**	**12.73**	**18.67**	**40.36**	**8.89**	**9.56**
Appliances and miscellaneous housewares	**45.68**	**48.70**	**44.89**	**83.33**	**30.38**	**43.41**	**12.32**	**14.74**
Major appliances	18.27	21.69	16.28	36.67	1.87	29.26	2.25	5.68
Small appliances and miscellaneous housewares	27.41	27.01	28.61	46.66	28.51	14.15	10.08	9.06
Miscellaneous household equipment	**95.06**	**118.22**	**83.46**	**60.87**	**89.79**	**85.88**	**41.04**	**42.27**
Other housing	**120.07**	**150.00**	**102.82**	**66.53**	**109.72**	**114.54**	**59.86**	**95.64**
APPAREL AND SERVICES	**359.96**	**380.42**	**359.13**	**408.35**	**327.28**	**383.68**	**211.85**	**202.12**
Men and boys, aged 2 or older	101.28	116.05	96.76	124.09	77.38	114.71	28.22	48.97
Women and girls, aged 2 or older	135.83	145.02	135.41	108.60	131.78	163.95	67.07	65.13
Children under age 2	54.51	42.14	61.26	136.04	47.37	29.84	38.97	11.88
Other apparel products and services	68.35	77.22	65.70	39.61	70.75	75.18	77.60	76.14
Jewelry and watches	14.29	18.89	11.67	10.64	8.43	18.39	14.82	46.39
All other apparel products and services	54.06	58.32	54.03	28.97	62.33	56.79	62.78	29.75
TRANSPORTATION	**64.06**	**65.99**	**65.69**	**79.81**	**46.93**	**89.83**	**8.54**	**45.36**
HEALTH CARE	**36.51**	**38.58**	**36.08**	**7.31**	**45.14**	**38.59**	**5.58**	**81.25**
ENTERTAINMENT	**97.02**	**109.73**	**88.72**	**52.56**	**94.75**	**103.02**	**39.54**	**63.11**
Toys, games, arts and crafts, and tricycles	33.37	42.18	26.95	21.92	22.81	38.03	12.15	23.86
Other entertainment	63.65	67.55	61.76	30.64	71.94	64.99	27.39	39.26
PERSONAL CARE PRODUCTS AND SERVICES	**35.34**	**22.94**	**47.55**	**34.76**	**32.98**	**88.23**	**15.95**	**20.49**
EDUCATION	**380.00**	**500.64**	**311.93**	**42.38**	**352.68**	**418.04**	**104.15**	**120.06**
ALL OTHER GIFTS	**106.56**	**164.00**	**56.36**	**54.51**	**38.05**	**92.41**	**36.70**	**88.38**

Note: Average spending figures for total consumer units can be found on Average Spending by Age and Average Spending by Region tables. Subcategories may not add to total because some are not shown. Spending on gifts is also included in the product and service categories in other chapters.
Source: Bureau of Labor Statistics, unpublished tables from the 2004 Consumer Expenditure Survey

Table 6.14 Gifts for Nonhousehold Members: Indexed spending by household type, 2004

(indexed average annual spending of consumer units (CU) on selected gifts of products and services for nonhousehold members by type of consumer unit, 2004; index definition: an index of 100 is the average for all consumer units; an index of 132 means that spending by consumer units in that group is 32 percent above the average for all consumer units; an index of 68 indicates spending that is 32 percent below the average for all consumer units)

| | total married couples | married couples, no children | married couples with children | | | | single parent, at least one child <18 | single person |
			total	oldest child under 6	oldest child 6 to 17	oldest child 18 or older		
Average spending of CU, total	$55,607	$49,690	$60,661	$55,981	$60,578	$64,162	$32,824	$25,423
Average spending of CU, index	128	115	140	129	140	148	76	59
Gifts, spending index	**130**	**153**	**117**	**89**	**115**	**142**	**53**	**71**
FOOD	**147**	**164**	**140**	**85**	**143**	**175**	**74**	**40**
ALCOHOLIC BEVERAGES	**107**	**135**	**85**	**119**	**79**	**71**	**72**	**81**
HOUSING	**129**	**149**	**120**	**110**	**118**	**129**	**56**	**68**
Housekeeping supplies	**127**	**122**	**138**	**143**	**139**	**130**	**58**	**50**
Laundry and cleaning supplies	138	81	186	77	243	153	69	44
Other household supplies	108	104	115	123	114	110	59	35
Postage and stationery	136	138	142	164	136	137	55	59
Household textiles	**138**	**161**	**122**	**67**	**99**	**214**	**47**	**51**
Appliances and miscellaneous housewares	**143**	**153**	**141**	**261**	**95**	**136**	**39**	**46**
Major appliances	156	185	139	313	16	250	19	49
Small appliances and miscellaneous housewares	136	134	141	231	141	70	50	45
Miscellaneous household equipment	**133**	**165**	**116**	**85**	**125**	**120**	**57**	**59**
Other housing	**121**	**151**	**104**	**67**	**111**	**115**	**60**	**96**
APPAREL AND SERVICES	**126**	**133**	**125**	**143**	**114**	**134**	**74**	**71**
Men and boys, aged 2 or older	134	154	128	164	102	152	37	65
Women and girls, aged 2 or older	134	143	134	107	130	162	66	64
Children under age 2	142	110	160	355	124	78	102	31
Other apparel products and services	96	108	92	56	99	105	109	107
Jewelry and watches	59	79	49	44	35	77	62	193
All other apparel products and services	114	123	114	61	132	120	133	63
TRANSPORTATION	**126**	**130**	**129**	**157**	**92**	**177**	**17**	**89**
HEALTH CARE	**74**	**79**	**73**	**15**	**92**	**79**	**11**	**165**
ENTERTAINMENT	**124**	**140**	**114**	**67**	**121**	**132**	**51**	**81**
Toys, games, arts and crafts, and tricycles	121	153	97	79	82	138	44	86
Other entertainment	126	134	122	61	142	129	54	78
PERSONAL CARE PRODUCTS AND SERVICES	**123**	**80**	**165**	**121**	**114**	**306**	**55**	**71**
EDUCATION	**152**	**200**	**125**	**17**	**141**	**167**	**42**	**48**
ALL OTHER GIFTS	**113**	**174**	**60**	**58**	**40**	**98**	**39**	**94**

Note: Spending index for total consumer units is 100. Spending on gifts is also included in the product and service categories in other chapters.
Source: Calculations by New Strategist based on the 2004 Consumer Expenditure Survey

Table 6.15 Gifts for Nonhousehold Members: Total spending by household type, 2004

(total annual spending on selected gifts of products and services for nonhousehold members by consumer unit (CU) type, 2004; consumer units and dollars in thousands)

	total married couples	married couples, no children	married couples with children				single parent, at least one child <18	single person
			total	oldest child under 6	oldest child 6 to 17	oldest child 18 or older		
Number of consumer units	59,797	25,585	29,279	5,604	15,376	8,300	6,892	33,686
Total spending of all CUs	$3,325,106,066	$1,271,329,652	$1,776,089,906	$313,717,748	$931,445,483	$532,542,027	$226,226,178	$856,410,968
Gifts, total spending	94,210,174	47,468,874	41,732,530	6,039,879	21,424,150	14,290,608	4,475,389	28,973,665
FOOD	6,498,140	3,102,693	3,044,723	354,509	1,623,398	1,074,435	378,578	990,705
ALCOHOLIC BEVERAGES	1,268,294	688,237	498,329	133,039	243,095	117,362	98,280	542,008
HOUSING	21,801,388	10,790,985	9,908,014	1,741,667	5,131,279	3,019,042	1,085,490	6,489,271
Housekeeping supplies	4,646,825	1,904,292	2,464,121	489,397	1,309,266	660,265	243,908	1,025,402
Laundry and cleaning supplies	474,190	118,459	312,407	24,826	214,803	73,123	27,499	84,552
Other household supplies	1,236,602	509,397	642,088	131,582	334,889	174,217	77,949	222,328
Postage and stationery	2,936,033	1,276,436	1,509,625	333,046	759,574	412,925	138,529	718,522
Household textiles	1,558,908	778,552	675,467	71,339	287,070	334,988	61,270	322,038
Appliances and miscellaneous housewares	2,731,527	1,245,990	1,314,334	466,981	467,123	360,303	84,909	496,532
Major appliances	1,092,491	554,939	476,662	205,499	28,753	242,858	15,507	191,336
Small appliances and miscellaneous housewares	1,639,036	691,051	837,672	261,483	438,370	117,445	69,471	305,195
Miscellaneous household equipment	5,684,303	3,024,659	2,443,625	341,115	1,380,611	712,804	282,848	1,423,907
Other housing	7,179,826	3,837,750	3,010,467	372,834	1,687,055	950,682	412,555	3,221,729
APPAREL AND SERVICES	21,524,528	9,733,046	10,514,967	2,288,393	5,032,257	3,184,544	1,460,070	6,808,614
Men and boys, aged 2 or older	6,056,240	2,969,139	2,833,036	695,400	1,189,795	952,093	194,492	1,649,603
Women and girls, aged 2 or older	8,122,227	3,710,337	3,964,669	608,594	2,026,249	1,360,785	462,246	2,193,969
Children under age 2	3,259,534	1,078,152	1,793,632	762,368	728,361	247,672	268,581	400,190
Other apparel products and services	4,087,125	1,975,674	1,923,630	221,974	1,087,852	623,994	534,819	2,564,852
Jewelry and watches	854,499	483,301	341,686	59,627	129,620	152,637	102,139	1,562,694
All other apparel products and services	3,232,626	1,492,117	1,581,944	162,348	958,386	471,357	432,680	1,002,159
TRANSPORTATION	3,830,596	1,688,354	1,923,338	447,255	721,596	745,589	58,858	1,527,997
HEALTH CARE	2,183,188	987,069	1,056,386	40,965	694,073	320,297	38,457	2,736,988
ENTERTAINMENT	5,801,505	2,807,442	2,597,633	294,546	1,456,876	855,066	272,510	2,125,923
Toys, games, arts and crafts, and tricycles	1,995,426	1,079,175	789,069	122,840	350,727	315,649	83,738	803,748
Other entertainment	3,806,079	1,728,267	1,808,271	171,707	1,106,149	539,417	188,772	1,322,512
PERSONAL CARE PRODUCTS AND SERVICES	2,113,226	586,920	1,392,216	194,795	507,100	732,309	109,927	690,226
EDUCATION	22,722,860	12,808,874	9,132,998	237,498	5,422,808	3,469,732	717,802	4,044,341
ALL OTHER GIFTS	6,371,968	4,195,940	1,650,164	305,474	585,057	767,003	252,936	2,977,169

Note: Total spending figures for total consumer units can be found on Total Spending by Age and Total Spending by Region tables. Spending by type of consumer unit will not add to total because not all types of consumer units are shown. Numbers may not add to category total because of rounding and missing subcategories.
Source: Calculations by New Strategist based on the 2004 Consumer Expenditure Survey

Table 6.16 Gifts for Nonhousehold Members: Market shares by household type, 2004

(percentage of total annual spending on selected gifts of products and services for nonhousehold members accounted for by types of consumer units, 2004)

	total married couples	married couples, no children	married couples with children				single parent, at least one child <18	single person
			total	oldest child under 6	oldest child 6 to 17	oldest child 18 or older		
Share of total consumer units	51.4%	22.0%	25.2%	4.8%	13.2%	7.1%	5.9%	29.0%
Share of total before-tax income	68.9	26.0	36.9	6.7	19.1	11.2	3.4	15.0
Share of total spending	65.9	25.2	35.2	6.2	18.5	10.6	4.5	17.0
Share of gifts spending	66.7	33.6	29.5	4.3	15.2	10.1	3.2	20.5
FOOD	75.5	36.0	35.4	4.1	18.9	12.5	4.4	11.5
ALCOHOLIC BEVERAGES	54.8	29.7	21.5	5.7	10.5	5.1	4.2	23.4
HOUSING	66.3	32.8	30.1	5.3	15.6	9.2	3.3	19.7
Housekeeping supplies	65.4	26.8	34.7	6.9	18.4	9.3	3.4	14.4
Laundry and cleaning supplies	70.9	17.7	46.7	3.7	32.1	10.9	4.1	12.6
Other household supplies	55.7	22.9	28.9	5.9	15.1	7.8	3.5	10.0
Postage and stationery	69.7	30.3	35.8	7.9	18.0	9.8	3.3	17.1
Household textiles	70.9	35.4	30.7	3.2	13.1	15.2	2.8	14.7
Appliances and miscellaneous housewares	73.6	33.6	35.4	12.6	12.6	9.7	2.3	13.4
Major appliances	80.2	40.8	35.0	15.1	2.1	17.8	1.1	14.1
Small appliances and miscellaneous housewares	69.7	29.4	35.6	11.1	18.6	5.0	3.0	13.0
Miscellaneous household equipment	68.2	36.3	29.3	4.1	16.6	8.6	3.4	17.1
Other housing	62.2	33.3	26.1	3.2	14.6	8.2	3.6	27.9
APPAREL AND SERVICES	64.6	29.2	31.6	6.9	15.1	9.6	4.4	20.4
Men and boys, aged 2 or older	68.9	33.8	32.3	7.9	13.5	10.8	2.2	18.8
Women and girls, aged 2 or older	69.0	31.5	33.7	5.2	17.2	11.6	3.9	18.6
Children under age 2	73.2	24.2	40.3	17.1	16.4	5.6	6.0	9.0
Other apparel products and services	49.3	23.8	23.2	2.7	13.1	7.5	6.4	30.9
Jewelry and watches	30.6	17.3	12.2	2.1	4.6	5.5	3.7	55.9
All other apparel products and services	58.7	27.1	28.7	3.0	17.4	8.6	7.9	18.2
TRANSPORTATION	64.8	28.6	32.5	7.6	12.2	12.6	1.0	25.8
HEALTH CARE	38.2	17.3	18.5	0.7	12.2	5.6	0.7	47.9
ENTERTAINMENT	63.8	30.9	28.6	3.2	16.0	9.4	3.0	23.4
Toys, games, arts and crafts, and tricycles	62.1	33.6	24.5	3.8	10.9	9.8	2.6	25.0
Other entertainment	64.8	29.4	30.8	2.9	18.8	9.2	3.2	22.5
PERSONAL CARE PRODUCTS AND SERVICES	63.0	17.5	41.5	5.8	15.1	21.8	3.3	20.6
EDUCATION	78.2	44.1	31.4	0.8	18.7	11.9	2.5	13.9
ALL OTHER GIFTS	58.1	38.2	15.0	2.8	5.3	7.0	2.3	27.1

Note: Market share for total consumer units is 100.0%. Market shares by type of consumer unit will not add to total because not all types of consumer units are shown. Spending on gifts is also included in the product and service categories in other chapters.
Source: Calculations by New Strategist based on the 2004 Consumer Expenditure Survey

Table 6.17 Gifts for Nonhousehold Members: Average spending by race and Hispanic origin, 2004

(average annual spending of consumer units (CU) on selected gifts of products and services for nonhousehold members by race and Hispanic origin of consumer unit reference person, 2004)

	total consumer units	Asian	black	Hispanic	non-Hispanic white and other
Number of consumer units (in 000s)	116,282	3,957	13,773	12,298	90,424
Average number of persons per CU	2.5	2.8	2.6	3.3	2.3
Average before-tax income of CU	$54,453.00	$67,705.00	$38,503.00	$43,693.00	$58,314.00
Average spending of CU, total	43,394.87	49,458.68	30,481.49	37,578.03	46,163.26
Gifts, average spending	**1,215.44**	**1,273.69**	**684.06**	**723.24**	**1,363.33**
FOOD	**74.03**	**158.18**	**34.92**	**37.62**	**85.00**
ALCOHOLIC BEVERAGES	**19.91**	**26.66**	**10.44**	**12.86**	**22.34**
HOUSING	**282.78**	**211.55**	**139.65**	**156.36**	**322.06**
Housekeeping supplies	**61.07**	**41.33**	**41.49**	**35.77**	**67.61**
Laundry and cleaning supplies	5.75	3.73	7.96	5.78	5.44
Other household supplies	19.09	10.25	10.57	8.57	21.87
Postage and stationery	36.23	27.35	22.96	21.42	40.31
Household textiles	**18.90**	**6.51**	**8.69**	**7.14**	**22.10**
Appliances and miscellaneous housewares	**31.93**	**32.60**	**6.95**	**20.60**	**37.31**
Major appliances	11.71	0.47	2.59	7.38	13.70
Small appliances and miscellaneous housewares	20.22	32.13	4.36	13.22	23.61
Miscellaneous household equipment	**71.64**	**28.19**	**18.95**	**33.36**	**85.00**
Other housing	**99.23**	**102.91**	**63.58**	**59.50**	**110.04**
APPAREL AND SERVICES	**286.38**	**190.36**	**233.78**	**272.92**	**296.62**
Men and boys, aged 2 or older	75.54	60.51	49.77	53.17	82.51
Women and girls, aged 2 or older	101.20	50.06	71.50	89.83	107.33
Children under age 2	38.29	26.34	20.61	58.32	38.63
Other apparel products and services	71.35	53.44	91.90	71.60	68.16
Jewelry and watches	24.03	19.23	7.50	21.11	26.89
All other apparel products and services	47.32	34.21	84.40	50.49	41.27
TRANSPORTATION	**50.84**	**38.23**	**16.39**	**50.04**	**56.18**
HEALTH CARE	**49.10**	**56.25**	**17.60**	**22.30**	**57.46**
ENTERTAINMENT	**78.16**	**52.26**	**38.68**	**51.63**	**87.72**
Toys, games, arts and crafts, and tricycles	27.65	12.69	15.57	17.85	30.78
Other entertainment	50.51	39.57	23.11	33.78	56.94
PERSONAL CARE PRODUCTS AND SERVICES	**28.83**	**37.69**	**25.67**	**23.76**	**30.09**
EDUCATION	**249.81**	**428.02**	**98.59**	**57.43**	**298.46**
ALL OTHER GIFTS	**94.36**	**73.30**	**68.23**	**38.11**	**105.85**

Note: "Asian" and "black" include Hispanics and non-Hispanics who identify themselves as being of the respective race alone. "Hispanic" includes people of any race who identify themselves as Hispanic. "Other" includes people who identify themselves as non-Hispanic and as Alaska Native, American Indian, Asian (who are also included in the "Asian" column), Native Hawaiian or other Pacific Islander, as well as non-Hispanics reporting more than one race. Numbers may not add to total because not all categories are shown. Spending on gifts is also included in the product and service categories in other chapters.
Source: Bureau of Labor Statistics, unpublished tables from the 2004 Consumer Expenditure Survey

Table 6.18 Gifts for Nonhousehold Members: Indexed spending by race and Hispanic origin, 2004

(indexed average annual spending of consumer units (CU) on selected gifts of products and services for nonhousehold members by race and Hispanic origin of consumer unit reference person, 2004; index definition: an index of 100 is the average for all consumer units; an index of 132 means that spending by consumer units in that group is 32 percent above the average for all consumer units; an index of 68 indicates spending that is 32 percent below the average for all consumer units)

	total consumer units	Asian	black	Hispanic	non-Hispanic white and other
Average spending of CU, total	$43,395	$49,459	$30,481	$37,578	$46,163
Average spending of CU, index	100	114	70	87	106
Gifts, spending index	100	105	56	60	112
FOOD	100	214	47	51	115
ALCOHOLIC BEVERAGES	100	134	52	65	112
HOUSING	100	75	49	55	114
Housekeeping supplies	100	68	68	59	111
Laundry and cleaning supplies	100	65	138	101	95
Other household supplies	100	54	55	45	115
Postage and stationery	100	75	63	59	111
Household textiles	100	34	46	38	117
Appliances and miscellaneous housewares	100	102	22	65	117
Major appliances	100	4	22	63	117
Small appliances and miscellaneous housewares	100	159	22	65	117
Miscellaneous household equipment	100	39	26	47	119
Other housing	100	104	64	60	111
APPAREL AND SERVICES	100	66	82	95	104
Men and boys, aged 2 or older	100	80	66	70	109
Women and girls, aged 2 or older	100	49	71	89	106
Children under age 2	100	69	54	152	101
Other apparel products and services	100	75	129	100	96
Jewelry and watches	100	80	31	88	112
All other apparel products and services	100	72	178	107	87
TRANSPORTATION	100	75	32	98	111
HEALTH CARE	100	115	36	45	117
ENTERTAINMENT	100	67	49	66	112
Toys, games, arts and crafts, and tricycles	100	46	56	65	111
Other entertainment	100	78	46	67	113
PERSONAL CARE PRODUCTS AND SERVICES	100	131	89	82	104
EDUCATION	100	171	39	23	119
ALL OTHER GIFTS	100	78	72	40	112

Note: "Asian" and "black" include Hispanics and non-Hispanics who identify themselves as being of the respective race alone. "Hispanic" includes people of any race who identify themselves as Hispanic. "Other" includes people who identify themselves as non-Hispanic and as Alaska Native, American Indian, Asian (who are also included in the "Asian" column), Native Hawaiian or other Pacific Islander, as well as non-Hispanics reporting more than one race. Spending on gifts is also included in the product and service categories in other chapters.
Source: Bureau of Labor Statistics, unpublished tables from the 2004 Consumer Expenditure Survey

Table 6.19 Gifts for Nonhousehold Members: Total spending by race and Hispanic origin, 2004

(total annual spending on selected gifts of products and services for nonhousehold members by consumer unit race and Hispanic origin groups, 2004; consumer units and dollars in thousands)

	total consumer units	Asian	black	Hispanic	non-Hispanic white and other
Number of consumer units	116,282	3,957	13,773	12,298	90,424
Total spending of all consumer units	$5,046,042,273	$195,707,997	$419,821,562	$462,134,613	$4,174,266,622
Gifts, total spending	141,333,794	5,039,991	9,421,558	8,894,406	123,277,752
FOOD	8,608,356	625,918	480,953	462,651	7,686,040
ALCOHOLIC BEVERAGES	2,315,175	105,494	143,790	158,152	2,020,072
HOUSING	32,882,224	837,103	1,923,399	1,922,915	29,121,953
Housekeeping supplies	7,101,342	163,543	571,442	439,899	6,113,567
Laundry and cleaning supplies	668,622	14,760	109,633	71,082	491,907
Other household supplies	2,219,823	40,559	145,581	105,394	1,977,573
Postage and stationery	4,212,897	108,224	316,228	263,423	3,644,991
Household textiles	2,197,730	25,760	119,687	87,808	1,998,370
Appliances and miscellaneous housewares	3,712,884	128,998	95,722	253,339	3,373,719
Major appliances	1,361,662	1,860	35,672	90,759	1,238,809
Small appliances and miscellaneous housewares	2,351,222	127,138	60,050	162,580	2,134,911
Miscellaneous household equipment	8,330,442	111,548	260,998	410,261	7,686,040
Other housing	11,538,663	407,215	875,687	731,731	9,950,257
APPAREL AND SERVICES	33,300,839	753,255	3,219,852	3,356,370	26,821,567
Men and boys, aged 2 or older	8,783,942	239,438	685,482	653,885	7,460,884
Women and girls, aged 2 or older	11,767,738	198,087	984,770	1,104,729	9,705,208
Children under age 2	4,452,438	104,227	283,862	717,219	3,493,079
Other apparel products and services	8,296,721	211,462	1,265,739	880,537	6,163,300
Jewelry and watches	2,794,256	76,093	103,298	259,611	2,431,501
All other apparel products and services	5,502,464	135,369	1,162,441	620,926	3,731,798
TRANSPORTATION	5,911,777	151,276	225,739	615,392	5,080,020
HEALTH CARE	5,709,446	222,581	242,405	274,245	5,195,763
ENTERTAINMENT	9,088,601	206,793	532,740	634,946	7,931,993
Toys, games, arts and crafts, and tricycles	3,215,197	50,214	214,446	219,519	2,783,251
Other entertainment	5,873,404	156,578	318,294	415,426	5,148,743
PERSONAL CARE PRODUCTS AND SERVICES	3,352,410	149,139	353,553	292,200	2,720,858
EDUCATION	29,048,406	1,693,675	1,357,880	706,274	26,987,947
ALL OTHER GIFTS	10,972,370	290,048	939,732	468,677	9,571,380

Note: "Asian" and "black" include Hispanics and non-Hispanics who identify themselves as being of the respective race alone. "Hispanic" includes people of any race who identify themselves as Hispanic. "Other" includes people who identify themselves as non-Hispanic and as Alaska Native, American Indian, Asian (who are also included in the "Asian" column), Native Hawaiian or other Pacific Islander, as well as non-Hispanics reporting more than one race. Numbers may not add to total because of rounding and because not all categories are shown. Spending on gifts is also included in the product and service categories in other chapters.
Source: Calculations by New Strategist based on the 2004 Consumer Expenditure Survey

Table 6.20 Gifts for Nonhousehold Members: Market shares by race and Hispanic origin, 2004

(percentage of total annual spending on selected gifts of products and services for nonhousehold members accounted for by consumer unit race and Hispanic origin groups, 2004)

	total consumer units	Asian	black	Hispanic	non-Hispanic white and other
Share of total consumer units	100.0%	3.4%	11.8%	10.6%	77.8%
Share of total before-tax income	100.0	4.2	8.4	8.5	83.3
Share of total spending	100.0	3.9	8.3	9.2	82.7
Share of gifts spending	100.0	3.6	6.7	6.3	87.2
FOOD	100.0	7.3	5.6	5.4	89.3
ALCOHOLIC BEVERAGES	100.0	4.6	6.2	6.8	87.3
HOUSING	100.0	2.5	5.8	5.8	88.6
Housekeeping supplies	100.0	2.3	8.0	6.2	86.1
Laundry and cleaning supplies	100.0	2.2	16.4	10.6	73.6
Other household products	100.0	1.8	6.6	4.7	89.1
Postage and stationery	100.0	2.6	7.5	6.3	86.5
Household textiles	100.0	1.2	5.4	4.0	90.9
Appliances and miscellaneous housewares	100.0	3.5	2.6	6.8	90.9
Major appliances	100.0	0.1	2.6	6.7	91.0
Small appliances and miscellaneous housewares	100.0	5.4	2.6	6.9	90.8
Miscellaneous household equipment	100.0	1.3	3.1	4.9	92.3
Other housing	100.0	3.5	7.6	6.3	86.2
APPAREL AND SERVICES	100.0	2.3	9.7	10.1	80.5
Men and boys, aged 2 or older	100.0	2.7	7.8	7.4	84.9
Women and girls, aged 2 or older	100.0	1.7	8.4	9.4	82.5
Children under age 2	100.0	2.3	6.4	16.1	78.5
Other apparel products and services	100.0	2.5	15.3	10.6	74.3
Jewelry and watches	100.0	2.7	3.7	9.3	87.0
All other apparel products and services	100.0	2.5	21.1	11.3	67.8
TRANSPORTATION	100.0	2.6	3.8	10.4	85.9
HEALTH CARE	100.0	3.9	4.2	4.8	91.0
ENTERTAINMENT	100.0	2.3	5.9	7.0	87.3
Toys, games, hobbies, and tricycles	100.0	1.6	6.7	6.8	86.6
Other entertainment	100.0	2.7	5.4	7.1	87.7
PERSONAL CARE PRODUCTS AND SERVICES	100.0	4.4	10.5	8.7	81.2
EDUCATION	100.0	5.8	4.7	2.4	92.9
ALL OTHER GIFTS	100.0	2.6	8.6	4.3	87.2

Note: "Asian" and "black" include Hispanics and non-Hispanics who identify themselves as being of the respective race alone. "Hispanic" includes people of any race who identify themselves as Hispanic. "Other" includes people who identify themselves as non-Hispanic and as Alaska Native, American Indian, Asian (who are also included in the "Asian" column), Native Hawaiian or other Pacific Islander, as well as non-Hispanics reporting more than one race. Numbers may not add to total because of rounding and because not all categories are shown. Spending on gifts is also included in the product and service categories in other chapters.
Source: Calculations by New Strategist based on the 2004 Consumer Expenditure Survey

Table 6.21 Gifts for Nonhousehold Members: Average spending by region, 2004

(average annual spending of consumer units (CU) on selected gifts of products and services for nonhousehold members by region in which consumer unit lives, 2004)

	total consumer units	Northeast	Midwest	South	West
Number of consumer units (in 000s)	116,282	22,051	26,539	41,801	25,891
Average number of persons per CU	2.5	2.4	2.4	2.5	2.6
Average before-tax income of CU	$54,453.00	$61,050.00	$53,567.00	$50,775.00	$55,682.00
Average spending of CU, total	43,394.87	46,114.89	43,370.77	39,173.65	47,921.74
Gifts, average spending	**1,215.44**	**1,511.05**	**1,233.52**	**985.77**	**1,315.83**
FOOD	**74.03**	**124.98**	**63.33**	**48.67**	**82.53**
ALCOHOLIC BEVERAGES	**19.91**	**29.07**	**15.65**	**15.67**	**23.34**
HOUSING	**282.78**	**317.17**	**284.62**	**241.75**	**317.68**
Housekeeping supplies	**61.07**	**85.68**	**59.27**	**51.30**	**57.60**
Laundry and cleaning supplies	5.75	8.51	5.07	5.42	4.62
Other household supplies	19.09	42.49	16.22	12.81	12.08
Postage and stationery	36.23	34.68	37.98	33.06	40.90
Household textiles	**18.90**	**15.59**	**19.39**	**20.24**	**19.09**
Appliances and miscellaneous housewares	**31.93**	**19.86**	**47.25**	**26.80**	**34.64**
Major appliances	11.71	3.94	26.58	7.75	9.29
Small appliances and miscellaneous housewares	20.22	15.92	20.67	19.05	25.36
Miscellaneous household equipment	**71.64**	**73.70**	**72.53**	**66.23**	**77.85**
Other housing	**99.23**	**122.35**	**86.18**	**77.19**	**128.50**
APPAREL AND SERVICES	**286.38**	**328.55**	**265.93**	**269.11**	**299.15**
Men and boys, aged 2 or older	75.54	95.86	80.61	70.78	60.47
Women and girls, aged 2 or older	101.20	112.17	92.54	103.69	96.72
Children under age 2	38.29	37.44	31.67	34.75	51.69
Other apparel products and services	71.35	83.09	61.12	59.89	90.26
Jewelry and watches	24.03	17.50	21.63	14.63	47.24
All other apparel products and services	47.32	65.60	39.49	45.26	43.02
TRANSPORTATION	**50.84**	**40.57**	**56.65**	**44.13**	**64.37**
HEALTH CARE	**49.10**	**18.32**	**100.62**	**40.64**	**36.22**
ENTERTAINMENT	**78.16**	**75.60**	**95.33**	**67.17**	**80.58**
Toys, games, arts and crafts, and tricycles	27.65	23.77	33.07	28.92	23.34
Other entertainment	50.51	51.83	62.26	38.25	57.24
PERSONAL CARE PRODUCTS AND SERVICES	**28.83**	**29.02**	**19.38**	**32.88**	**31.94**
EDUCATION	**249.81**	**453.96**	**240.35**	**159.75**	**231.12**
ALL OTHER GIFTS	**94.36**	**92.45**	**90.21**	**64.98**	**147.56**

Note: Numbers may not add to total because not all categories are shown. Spending on gifts is also included in the product and service categories in other chapters.
Source: Bureau of Labor Statistics, unpublished tables from the 2004 Consumer Expenditure Survey

Table 6.22 Gifts for Nonhousehold Members: Indexed spending by region, 2004

(indexed average annual spending of consumer units (CU) on selected gifts of products and services for nonhousehold members by region in which consumer unit lives, 2004; index definition: an index of 100 is the average for all consumer units; an index of 132 means that spending by consumer units in that group is 32 percent above the average for all consumer units; an index of 68 indicates spending that is 32 percent below the average for all consumer units)

	total consumer units	Northeast	Midwest	South	West
Average spending of CU, total	$43,395	$46,115	$43,371	$39,174	$47,922
Average spending of CU, index	100	106	100	90	110
Gifts, spending index	100	124	101	81	108
FOOD	100	169	86	66	111
ALCOHOLIC BEVERAGES	100	146	79	79	117
HOUSING	100	112	101	85	112
Housekeeping supplies	100	140	97	84	94
Laundry and cleaning supplies	100	148	88	94	80
Other household supplies	100	223	85	67	63
Postage and stationery	100	96	105	91	113
Household textiles	100	82	103	107	101
Appliances and miscellaneous housewares	100	62	148	84	108
Major appliances	100	34	227	66	79
Small appliances and miscellaneous housewares	100	79	102	94	125
Miscellaneous household equipment	100	103	101	92	109
Other housing	100	123	87	78	129
APPAREL AND SERVICES	100	115	93	94	104
Men and boys, aged 2 or older	100	127	107	94	80
Women and girls, aged 2 or older	100	111	91	102	96
Children under age 2	100	98	83	91	135
Other apparel products and services	100	116	86	84	127
Jewelry and watches	100	73	90	61	197
All other apparel products and services	100	139	83	96	91
TRANSPORTATION	100	80	111	87	127
HEALTH CARE	100	37	205	83	74
ENTERTAINMENT	100	97	122	86	103
Toys, games, arts and crafts, and tricycles	100	86	120	105	84
Other entertainment	100	103	123	76	113
PERSONAL CARE PRODUCTS AND SERVICES	100	101	67	114	111
EDUCATION	100	182	96	64	93
ALL OTHER GIFTS	100	98	96	69	156

Note: Spending on gifts is also included in the product and service categories in other chapters.
Source: Calculations by New Strategist based on the 2004 Consumer Expenditure Survey

Table 6.23 Gifts for Nonhousehold Members: Total spending by region, 2004

(total annual spending on selected gifts of products and services for nonhousehold members by region in which consumer units live, 2004; consumer units and dollars in thousands)

	total consumer units	Northeast	Midwest	South	West
Number of consumer units	116,282	22,051	26,539	41,801	25,891
Total spending of all consumer units	$5,046,042,273	$1,016,879,439	$1,151,016,865	$1,637,497,744	$1,240,741,770
Gifts, total spending	141,333,794	33,320,164	32,736,387	41,206,172	34,068,155
FOOD	8,608,356	2,755,934	1,680,715	2,034,455	2,136,784
ALCOHOLIC BEVERAGES	2,315,175	641,023	415,335	655,022	604,296
HOUSING	32,882,224	6,993,916	7,553,530	10,105,392	8,225,053
Housekeeping supplies	7,101,342	1,889,330	1,572,967	2,144,391	1,491,322
Laundry and cleaning supplies	668,622	187,654	134,553	226,561	119,616
Other household supplies	2,219,823	936,947	430,463	535,471	312,763
Postage and stationery	4,212,897	764,729	1,007,951	1,381,941	1,058,942
Household textiles	2,197,730	343,775	514,591	846,052	494,259
Appliances and miscellaneous housewares	3,712,884	437,933	1,253,968	1,120,267	896,864
Major appliances	1,361,662	86,881	705,407	323,958	240,527
Small appliances and miscellaneous housewares	2,351,222	351,052	548,561	796,309	656,596
Miscellaneous household equipment	8,330,442	1,625,159	1,924,874	2,768,480	2,015,614
Other housing	11,538,663	2,697,940	2,287,131	3,226,619	3,326,994
APPAREL AND SERVICES	33,300,839	7,244,856	7,057,516	11,249,067	7,745,293
Men and boys, aged 2 or older	8,783,942	2,113,809	2,139,309	2,958,675	1,565,629
Women and girls, aged 2 or older	11,767,738	2,473,461	2,455,919	4,334,346	2,504,178
Children under age 2	4,452,438	825,589	840,490	1,452,585	1,338,306
Other apparel products and services	8,296,721	1,832,218	1,622,064	2,503,462	2,336,922
Jewelry and watches	2,794,256	385,893	574,039	611,549	1,223,091
All other apparel products and services	5,502,464	1,446,546	1,048,025	1,891,913	1,113,831
TRANSPORTATION	5,911,777	894,609	1,503,434	1,844,678	1,666,604
HEALTH CARE	5,709,446	403,974	2,670,354	1,698,793	937,772
ENTERTAINMENT	9,088,601	1,667,056	2,529,963	2,807,773	2,086,297
Toys, games, arts and crafts, and tricycles	3,215,197	524,152	877,645	1,208,885	604,296
Other entertainment	5,873,404	1,142,903	1,652,318	1,598,888	1,482,001
PERSONAL CARE PRODUCTS AND SERVICES	3,352,410	639,920	514,326	1,374,417	826,959
EDUCATION	29,048,406	10,010,272	6,378,649	6,677,710	5,983,928
ALL OTHER GIFTS	10,972,370	2,038,615	2,394,083	2,716,229	3,820,476

Note: Numbers may not add to total because of rounding and because not all categories are shown. Spending on gifts is also included in the product and service categories in other chapters.
Source: Calculations by New Strategist based on the 2004 Consumer Expenditure Survey

Table 6.24 Gifts for Nonhousehold Members: Market shares by region, 2004

(percentage of total annual spending on selected gifts of products and services for nonhousehold members accounted for by consumer units by region, 2004)

	total consumer units	Northeast	Midwest	South	West
Share of total consumer units	100.0%	19.0%	22.8%	35.9%	22.3%
Share of total before-tax income	100.0	21.3	22.5	33.5	22.8
Share of total spending	100.0	20.2	22.8	32.5	24.6
Share of gifts spending	100.0	23.6	23.2	29.2	24.1
FOOD	100.0	32.0	19.5	23.6	24.8
ALCOHOLIC BEVERAGES	100.0	27.7	17.9	28.3	26.1
HOUSING	100.0	21.3	23.0	30.7	25.0
Housekeeping supplies	100.0	26.6	22.2	30.2	21.0
Laundry and cleaning supplies	100.0	28.1	20.1	33.9	17.9
Other household products	100.0	42.2	19.4	24.1	14.1
Postage and stationery	100.0	18.2	23.9	32.8	25.1
Household textiles	100.0	15.6	23.4	38.5	22.5
Appliances and miscellaneous housewares	100.0	11.8	33.8	30.2	24.2
Major appliances	100.0	6.4	51.8	23.8	17.7
Small appliances and miscellaneous housewares	100.0	14.9	23.3	33.9	27.9
Miscellaneous household equipment	100.0	19.5	23.1	33.2	24.2
Other housing	100.0	23.4	19.8	28.0	28.8
APPAREL AND SERVICES	100.0	21.8	21.2	33.8	23.3
Men and boys, aged 2 or older	100.0	24.1	24.4	33.7	17.8
Women and girls, aged 2 or older	100.0	21.0	20.9	36.8	21.3
Children under age 2	100.0	18.5	18.9	32.6	30.1
Other apparel products and services	100.0	22.1	19.6	30.2	28.2
Jewelry and watches	100.0	13.8	20.5	21.9	43.8
All other apparel products and services	100.0	26.3	19.0	34.4	20.2
TRANSPORTATION	100.0	15.1	25.4	31.2	28.2
HEALTH CARE	100.0	7.1	46.8	29.8	16.4
ENTERTAINMENT	100.0	18.3	27.8	30.9	23.0
Toys, games, hobbies, and tricycles	100.0	16.3	27.3	37.6	18.8
Other entertainment	100.0	19.5	28.1	27.2	25.2
PERSONAL CARE PRODUCTS AND SERVICES	100.0	19.1	15.3	41.0	24.7
EDUCATION	100.0	34.5	22.0	23.0	20.6
ALL OTHER GIFTS	100.0	18.6	21.8	24.8	34.8

Note: Numbers may not add to total because of rounding. Spending on gifts is also included in the product and service categories in other chapters.
Source: Calculations by New Strategist based on the 2004 Consumer Expenditure Survey

Table 6.25 Gifts for Nonhousehold Members: Average spending by education, 2004

(average annual spending of consumer units (CU) on selected gifts of products and services for nonhousehold members by education of consumer unit reference person, 2004)

	total consumer units	less than high school graduate	high school graduate	some college	associate's degree	college graduate total	college graduate bachelor's degree	college graduate master's, professional, doctorate
Number of consumer units (in 000s)	116,282	16,829	31,005	25,317	10,678	32,452	20,684	11,768
Average number of persons per CU	2.5	2.7	2.5	2.3	2.6	2.5	2.4	2.5
Average before-tax income of CU	$54,453.00	$29,094.00	$42,334.00	$46,756.00	$58,593.00	$83,825.00	$75,647.00	$98,201.00
Average spending of CU, total	43,394.87	25,421.18	35,438.55	40,877.68	48,177.36	60,712.28	56,728.41	67,801.38
Gifts, average spending	1,215.44	522.64	803.58	991.41	1,182.95	2,151.12	1,764.71	2,841.99
FOOD	74.03	12.97	39.83	54.96	75.82	152.52	137.48	178.53
ALCOHOLIC BEVERAGES	19.91	6.72	10.82	14.93	25.20	37.44	36.26	39.68
HOUSING	282.78	112.34	197.88	225.01	291.54	493.85	431.31	608.66
Housekeeping supplies	61.07	25.73	44.17	50.75	65.99	101.41	84.98	132.77
Laundry and cleaning supplies	5.75	3.69	5.32	4.21	6.08	8.22	8.93	6.87
Other household supplies	19.09	5.23	12.49	13.49	13.43	38.26	22.29	68.75
Postage and stationery	36.23	16.81	26.36	33.05	46.48	54.92	53.75	57.15
Household textiles	18.90	3.55	19.79	21.42	19.65	23.85	19.39	32.35
Appliances and miscellaneous housewares	31.93	16.96	17.69	20.04	31.18	62.16	53.70	78.59
Major appliances	11.71	5.86	4.77	4.74	3.00	29.16	18.79	49.21
Small appliances and miscellaneous housewares	20.22	11.10	12.92	15.30	28.18	33.01	34.91	29.38
Miscellaneous household equipment	71.64	19.90	43.44	73.40	87.18	119.51	112.60	131.87
Other housing	99.23	46.20	72.79	59.38	87.53	186.92	160.65	233.08
APPAREL AND SERVICES	286.38	172.26	239.82	262.26	333.13	391.98	378.36	417.80
Men and boys, aged 2 or older	75.54	47.44	57.59	64.07	68.37	117.91	107.50	137.27
Women and girls, aged 2 or older	101.20	54.87	80.99	88.76	143.46	140.76	140.56	140.90
Children under age 2	38.29	25.22	36.43	29.28	45.99	50.87	49.88	52.63
Other apparel products and services	71.35	44.73	64.82	80.16	75.31	82.43	80.42	86.99
Jewelry and watches	24.03	5.80	9.81	36.57	38.12	32.66	37.44	24.25
All other apparel products and services	47.32	38.93	55.01	43.59	37.20	49.78	42.98	62.75
TRANSPORTATION	50.84	16.87	52.81	41.55	68.63	68.14	52.06	96.08
HEALTH CARE	49.10	65.24	40.67	33.98	44.25	61.95	39.69	101.61
ENTERTAINMENT	78.16	42.93	64.44	83.25	82.68	104.37	88.53	133.71
Toys, games, arts and crafts, and tricycles	27.65	16.38	29.24	28.48	33.24	29.48	28.06	31.97
Other entertainment	50.51	26.55	35.19	54.76	49.43	74.90	60.47	101.74
PERSONAL CARE PRODUCTS AND SERVICES	28.83	20.77	25.25	23.36	28.36	40.45	38.33	44.48
EDUCATION	249.81	26.02	63.56	166.04	155.55	640.49	422.58	1,024.74
ALL OTHER GIFTS	94.36	46.22	67.74	84.70	77.03	157.68	138.43	193.43

Note: Numbers may not add to total because not all categories are shown. Spending on gifts is also included in the product and service categories in other chapters.
Source: Bureau of Labor Statistics, unpublished tables from the 2004 Consumer Expenditure Survey

Table 6.26 Gifts for Nonhousehold Members: Indexed spending by education, 2004

(indexed average annual spending of consumer units (CU) on selected gifts of products and services for nonhousehold members by education of consumer unit reference person, 2004; index definition: an index of 100 is the average for all consumer units; an index of 132 means that spending by consumer units in that group is 32 percent above the average for all consumer units; an index of 68 indicates spending that is 32 percent below the average for all consumer units)

	total consumer units	less than high school graduate	high school graduate	some college	associate's degree	college graduate total	bachelor's degree	master's, professional, doctorate
Average spending of CU, total	$43,395	$25,421	$35,439	$40,878	$48,177	$60,712	$56,728	$67,801
Average spending of CU, index	100	59	82	94	111	140	131	156
Gifts, spending index	**100**	**43**	**66**	**82**	**97**	**177**	**145**	**234**
FOOD	**100**	**18**	**54**	**74**	**102**	**206**	**186**	**241**
ALCOHOLIC BEVERAGES	**100**	**34**	**54**	**75**	**127**	**188**	**182**	**199**
HOUSING	**100**	**40**	**70**	**80**	**103**	**175**	**153**	**215**
Housekeeping supplies	**100**	**42**	**72**	**83**	**108**	**166**	**139**	**217**
Laundry and cleaning supplies	100	64	93	73	106	143	155	119
Other household supplies	100	27	65	71	70	200	117	360
Postage and stationery	100	46	73	91	128	152	148	158
Household textiles	**100**	**19**	**105**	**113**	**104**	**126**	**103**	**171**
Appliances and miscellaneous housewares	**100**	**53**	**55**	**63**	**98**	**195**	**168**	**246**
Major appliances	100	50	41	40	26	249	160	420
Small appliances and miscellaneous housewares	100	55	64	76	139	163	173	145
Miscellaneous household equipment	**100**	**28**	**61**	**102**	**122**	**167**	**157**	**184**
Other housing	**100**	**47**	**73**	**60**	**88**	**188**	**162**	**235**
APPAREL AND SERVICES	**100**	**60**	**84**	**92**	**116**	**137**	**132**	**146**
Men and boys, aged 2 or older	100	63	76	85	91	156	142	182
Women and girls, aged 2 or older	100	54	80	88	142	139	139	139
Children under age 2	100	66	95	76	120	133	130	137
Other apparel products and services	100	63	91	112	106	116	113	122
Jewelry and watches	100	24	41	152	159	136	156	101
All other apparel products and services	100	82	116	92	79	105	91	133
TRANSPORTATION	**100**	**33**	**104**	**82**	**135**	**134**	**102**	**189**
HEALTH CARE	**100**	**133**	**83**	**69**	**90**	**126**	**81**	**207**
ENTERTAINMENT	**100**	**55**	**82**	**107**	**106**	**134**	**113**	**171**
Toys, games, arts and crafts, and tricycles	100	59	106	103	120	107	101	116
Other entertainment	100	53	70	108	98	148	120	201
PERSONAL CARE PRODUCTS AND SERVICES	**100**	**72**	**88**	**81**	**98**	**140**	**133**	**154**
EDUCATION	**100**	**10**	**25**	**66**	**62**	**256**	**169**	**410**
ALL OTHER GIFTS	**100**	**49**	**72**	**90**	**82**	**167**	**147**	**205**

Note: Spending on gifts is also included in the product and service categories in other chapters.
Source: Calculations by New Strategist based on the 2004 Consumer Expenditure Survey

Table 6.27 Gifts for Nonhousehold Members: Total spending by education, 2004

(total annual spending on selected gifts of products and services for nonhousehold members by consumer unit (CU) educational attainment group, 2004; consumer units and dollars in thousands)

	total consumer units	less than high school graduate	high school graduate	some college	associate's degree	college graduate total	bachelor's degree	master's, professional, doctorate
Number of consumer units	116,282	16,829	31,005	25,317	10,678	32,452	20,684	11,768
Total spending of all CUs	$5,046,042,273	$427,813,038	$1,098,772,243	$1,034,900,225	$514,437,850	$1,970,234,911	$1,173,370,432	$797,886,640
Gifts, total spending	141,333,794	8,795,509	24,914,998	25,099,527	12,631,540	69,808,146	36,501,262	33,444,538
FOOD	8,608,356	218,272	1,234,929	1,391,422	809,606	4,949,579	2,843,636	2,100,941
ALCOHOLIC BEVERAGES	2,315,175	113,091	335,474	377,983	269,086	1,215,003	750,002	466,954
HOUSING	32,882,224	1,890,570	6,135,269	5,696,578	3,113,064	16,026,420	8,921,216	7,162,711
Housekeeping supplies	7,101,342	433,010	1,369,491	1,284,838	704,641	3,290,957	1,757,726	1,562,437
Laundry and cleaning supplies	668,622	62,099	164,947	106,585	64,922	266,755	184,708	80,846
Other household supplies	2,219,823	88,016	387,252	341,526	143,406	1,241,614	461,046	809,050
Postage and stationery	4,212,897	282,895	817,292	836,727	496,313	1,782,264	1,111,765	672,541
Household textiles	2,197,730	59,743	613,589	542,290	209,823	773,980	401,063	380,695
Appliances and miscellaneous housewares	3,712,884	285,420	548,478	507,353	332,940	2,017,216	1,110,731	924,847
Major appliances	1,361,662	98,618	147,894	120,003	32,034	946,300	388,652	579,103
Small appliances and miscellaneous housewares	2,351,222	186,802	400,585	387,350	300,906	1,071,241	722,078	345,744
Miscellaneous household equipment	8,330,442	334,897	1,346,857	1,858,268	930,908	3,878,339	2,329,018	1,551,846
Other housing	11,538,663	777,500	2,256,854	1,503,323	934,645	6,065,928	3,322,885	2,742,885
APPAREL AND SERVICES	33,300,839	2,898,964	7,435,619	6,639,636	3,557,162	12,720,535	7,825,998	4,916,670
Men and boys, aged 2 or older	8,783,942	798,368	1,785,578	1,622,060	730,055	3,826,415	2,223,530	1,615,393
Women and girls, aged 2 or older	11,767,738	923,407	2,511,095	2,247,137	1,531,866	4,567,944	2,907,343	1,658,111
Children under age 2	4,452,438	424,427	1,129,512	741,282	491,081	1,650,833	1,031,718	619,350
Other apparel products and services	8,296,721	752,761	2,009,744	2,029,411	804,160	2,675,018	1,663,407	1,023,698
Jewelry and watches	2,794,256	97,608	304,159	925,843	407,045	1,059,882	774,409	285,374
All other apparel products and services	5,502,464	655,153	1,705,585	1,103,568	397,222	1,615,461	888,998	738,442
TRANSPORTATION	5,911,777	283,905	1,637,374	1,051,921	732,831	2,211,279	1,076,809	1,130,669
HEALTH CARE	5,709,446	1,097,924	1,260,973	860,272	472,502	2,010,401	820,948	1,195,746
ENTERTAINMENT	9,088,601	722,469	1,997,962	2,107,640	882,857	3,387,015	1,831,155	1,573,499
Toys, games, arts and crafts, and tricycles	3,215,197	275,659	906,586	721,028	354,937	956,685	580,393	376,223
Other entertainment	5,873,404	446,810	1,091,066	1,386,359	527,814	2,430,655	1,250,761	1,197,276
PERSONAL CARE PRODUCTS AND SERVICES	3,352,410	349,538	782,876	591,405	302,828	1,312,683	792,818	523,441
EDUCATION	29,048,406	437,891	1,970,678	4,203,635	1,660,963	20,785,181	8,740,645	12,059,140
ALL OTHER GIFTS	10,972,370	777,836	2,100,279	2,144,350	822,526	5,117,031	2,863,286	2,276,284

Note: Numbers may not add to total because of rounding and because not all categories are shown. Spending on gifts is also included in the product and service categories in other chapters.
Source: Calculations by New Strategist based on the 2004 Consumer Expenditure Survey

Table 6.28 Gifts for Nonhousehold Members: Market shares by education, 2004

(percentage of total annual spending on selected gifts of products and services for nonhousehold members accounted for by consumer unit educational attainment groups, 2004)

	total consumer units	less than high school graduate	high school graduate	some college	associate's degree	college graduate total	bachelor's degree	master's, professional, doctorate
Share of total consumer units	100.0%	14.5%	26.7%	21.8%	9.2%	27.9%	17.8%	10.1%
Share of total before-tax income	100.0	7.7	20.7	18.7	9.9	43.0	24.7	18.3
Share of total spending	100.0	8.5	21.8	20.5	10.2	39.0	23.3	15.8
Share of gifts spending	100.0	6.2	17.6	17.8	8.9	49.4	25.8	23.7
FOOD	100.0	2.5	14.3	16.2	9.4	57.5	33.0	24.4
ALCOHOLIC BEVERAGES	100.0	4.9	14.5	16.3	11.6	52.5	32.4	20.2
HOUSING	100.0	5.7	18.7	17.3	9.5	48.7	27.1	21.8
Housekeeping supplies	100.0	6.1	19.3	18.1	9.9	46.3	24.8	22.0
Laundry and cleaning supplies	100.0	9.3	24.7	15.9	9.7	39.9	27.6	12.1
Other household supplies	100.0	4.0	17.4	15.4	6.5	55.9	20.8	36.4
Postage and stationery	100.0	6.7	19.4	19.9	11.8	42.3	26.4	16.0
Household textiles	100.0	2.7	27.9	24.7	9.5	35.2	18.2	17.3
Appliances and miscellaneous housewares	100.0	7.7	14.8	13.7	9.0	54.3	29.9	24.9
Major appliances	100.0	7.2	10.9	8.8	2.4	69.5	28.5	42.5
Small appliances and miscellaneous housewares	100.0	7.9	17.0	16.5	12.8	45.6	30.7	14.7
Miscellaneous household equipment	100.0	4.0	16.2	22.3	11.2	46.6	28.0	18.6
Other housing	100.0	6.7	19.6	13.0	8.1	52.6	28.8	23.8
APPAREL AND SERVICES	100.0	8.7	22.3	19.9	10.7	38.2	23.5	14.8
Men and boys, aged 2 or older	100.0	9.1	20.3	18.5	8.3	43.6	25.3	18.4
Women and girls, aged 2 or older	100.0	7.8	21.3	19.1	13.0	38.8	24.7	14.1
Children under age 2	100.0	9.5	25.4	16.6	11.0	37.1	23.2	13.9
Other apparel products and services	100.0	9.1	24.2	24.5	9.7	32.2	20.0	12.3
Jewelry and watches	100.0	3.5	10.9	33.1	14.6	37.9	27.7	10.2
All other apparel products and services	100.0	11.9	31.0	20.1	7.2	29.4	16.2	13.4
TRANSPORTATION	100.0	4.8	27.7	17.8	12.4	37.4	18.2	19.1
HEALTH CARE	100.0	19.2	22.1	15.1	8.3	35.2	14.4	20.9
ENTERTAINMENT	100.0	7.9	22.0	23.2	9.7	37.3	20.1	17.3
Toys, games, arts and crafts, and tricycles	100.0	8.6	28.2	22.4	11.0	29.8	18.1	11.7
Other entertainment	100.0	7.6	18.6	23.6	9.0	41.4	21.3	20.4
PERSONAL CARE PRODUCTS AND SERVICES	100.0	10.4	23.4	17.6	9.0	39.2	23.6	15.6
EDUCATION	100.0	1.5	6.8	14.5	5.7	71.6	30.1	41.5
ALL OTHER GIFTS	100.0	7.1	19.1	19.5	7.5	46.6	26.1	20.7

Note: Numbers may not add to total because of rounding. Spending on gifts is also included in the product and service categories in other chapters.
Source: Calculations by New Strategist based on the 2004 Consumer Expenditure Survey

Chapter 7. Spending on Health Care, 2004

American households spent 14 percent more on out-of-pocket health care costs in 2004 than in 2000, after adjusting for inflation. Out-of-pocket spending on health insurance rose a substantial 24 percent during those years, while prescription drug spending increased 4 percent. Out-of-pocket spending on commercial Medicare supplements rose 44 percent over the period. Out-of-pocket health care costs absorbed 5.9 percent of the household budget in 2004, up from 5.4 percent in 2000.

Not surprisingly, out-of-pocket health care spending rises with age, peaking among householders aged 75 or older at more than $3,994 in 2004. Householders aged 65 to 74, however, spend more than any other age group on out-of-pocket health insurance costs ($2,171). Householders aged 75 or older spend the most out-of-pocket on prescription drugs ($813). Householders aged 55 to 64 spend the most on medical services ($892).

Out-of-pocket spending on health care rises with income, largely because household size also grows with income. In 2004, households with incomes of $100,000 or more spent $4,042 out-of-pocket on health care, 57 percent more than the average household. Spending on health care is significantly below average only for households with incomes below $40,000.

Married couples without children at home, most of them older empty-nesters, spend the most out-of-pocket on health care, $3,761 in 2004—46 percent more than the average household. Married couples with children at home spend just 17 percent more than the average household on health care overall, but they spend 44 percent more than average on physician services.

Asians, blacks, and Hispanics spend far less than the average household out-of-pocket on almost every health care category, while non-Hispanic whites spend more. One factor behind these differences is the older age of the non-Hispanic white population. There are some exceptions, however. Asian households spend 41 percent more than average on vitamins, for example.

Households in the Northeast spend 8 percent less than average out-of-pocket on health care, while households in the Midwest spend 11 percent more. Households in the South spend 14 percent more than average out-of-pocket on prescription drugs, while those in the West spend 19 percent less than average on this item. Average household out-of-pocket spending on dental services is 19 percent above average in the Northeast and 18 percent below average in the South.

College graduates spend the most on out-of-pocket health care costs, an average of $3,208 in 2004—25 percent more than the average household. They spend 40 percent more than average out-of-pocket on medical services and 57 percent more than average on eyeglasses and contact lenses. But college graduates spend only an average amount out-of-pocket on prescription drugs, while high school graduates spend 14 percent more than average on that item.

Table 7.1 Health Care: Average spending by age, 2004

(average annual out-of-pocket spending of consumer units (CU) on health care, by age of consumer unit reference person, 2004)

	total consumer units	under 25	25 to 34	35 to 44	45 to 54	55 to 64	65 to 74	75+
Number of consumer units (in 000s)	116,282	8,817	19,439	24,070	23,712	17,479	11,230	11,536
Average number of persons per CU	2.5	1.9	2.9	3.2	2.7	2.1	1.9	1.5
Average before-tax income of CU	$54,453.00	$22,840.00	$52,484.00	$65,515.00	$70,434.00	$61,031.00	$42,137.00	$28,028.00
Average spending of CU, total	43,394.87	24,534.56	42,700.54	50,401.62	52,764.36	47,298.58	36,511.98	25,763.32
Health care, average spending	2,574.21	653.66	1,518.79	2,263.02	2,694.92	3,261.54	3,799.38	3,994.93
HEALTH INSURANCE	1,331.71	321.50	842.41	1,199.37	1,291.12	1,566.89	2,171.04	2,114.57
Commercial health insurance	272.52	107.38	220.00	320.47	344.73	377.61	202.39	147.81
Traditional fee-for-service health plan (not BCBS)	71.95	26.05	29.63	69.18	72.14	119.11	76.97	107.38
Preferred-provider health plan (not BCBS)	200.57	81.33	190.37	251.29	272.58	258.50	125.42	40.43
Blue Cross, Blue Shield	405.89	100.74	281.23	449.19	461.35	544.62	431.36	409.87
Traditional fee-for-service health plan	69.32	15.75	48.39	50.51	68.59	147.90	64.08	72.36
Preferred-provider health plan	169.58	47.81	139.08	212.40	229.16	226.80	109.02	74.46
Health maintenance organization	113.61	30.42	82.89	170.04	137.44	137.65	80.89	57.66
Commercial Medicare supplement	46.84	6.68	10.12	9.15	20.36	18.98	170.57	194.26
Other BCBS health insurance	6.54	0.08	0.76	7.10	5.79	13.29	6.80	11.12
Health maintenance plans (HMOs)	272.11	69.15	268.72	323.38	334.93	376.08	196.04	113.34
Medicare payments	246.20	10.80	20.05	40.97	74.09	165.70	975.09	1,001.63
Commercial Medicare supplements/ other health insurance	134.99	33.43	52.41	65.36	76.03	102.89	366.16	441.92
Commercial Medicare supplement (not BCBS)	92.90	19.03	20.61	33.63	31.96	40.44	296.55	401.32
Other health insurance (not BCBS)	42.10	14.40	31.80	31.73	44.06	62.45	69.60	40.60
MEDICAL SERVICES	648.37	183.59	402.57	653.92	809.45	891.75	631.06	723.18
Physician's services	146.58	54.13	108.47	161.55	195.05	202.41	118.78	93.03
Dental services	240.60	32.20	100.59	248.71	319.28	326.44	322.74	247.16
Eye care services	38.89	16.05	24.14	29.60	55.48	59.51	49.39	25.04
Service by professionals other than physician	39.54	9.85	20.85	47.63	53.19	66.75	25.06	21.68
Lab tests, X-rays	26.75	3.98	16.61	22.91	31.22	57.88	21.47	18.05
Hospital room	40.01	27.65	38.96	41.78	51.79	49.11	21.20	27.85
Hospital services other than room	51.20	37.63	59.00	49.19	62.05	64.96	35.61	24.67
Care in convalescent or nursing home	41.33	–	20.04	20.10	17.33	35.97	10.92	240.15
Other medical services	23.46	2.10	13.91	32.45	24.06	28.72	25.89	25.55
DRUGS	480.29	117.60	211.77	318.00	461.24	642.27	853.69	985.09
Nonprescription drugs	80.31	45.26	56.53	77.89	93.65	90.18	89.20	104.54
Nonprescription vitamins	50.57	26.72	25.46	38.99	56.38	71.26	78.48	67.67
Prescription drugs	349.41	45.63	129.78	201.11	311.21	480.83	686.02	812.88
MEDICAL SUPPLIES	113.83	30.97	62.04	91.72	133.11	160.63	143.58	172.08
Eyeglasses and contact lenses	47.56	12.02	28.42	43.83	70.12	63.09	58.30	34.44
Hearing aids	15.21	0.77	0.35	6.13	9.16	21.53	28.99	59.66
Topicals and dressings	31.53	15.58	23.01	29.29	30.52	45.05	41.77	35.33
Medical equipment for general use	6.75	1.78	3.79	4.56	10.65	9.95	2.89	11.02
Supportive, convalescent medical equipment	7.16	0.60	2.74	3.50	7.84	9.03	6.36	23.81
Rental of medical equipment	1.88	0.19	0.59	1.57	1.33	4.09	1.83	3.80
Rental of supportive, convalescent medical equipment	3.74	0.04	3.14	2.84	3.49	7.89	3.45	4.01

Note: Subcategories may not add to total because some are not shown. "–" means sample is too small to make a reliable estimate.
Source: Bureau of Labor Statistics, unpublished tables from the 2004 Consumer Expenditure Survey

Table 7.2 Health Care: Indexed spending by age, 2004

(indexed average annual out-of-pocket spending of consumer units (CU) on health care, by age of consumer unit reference person, 2004; index definition: an index of 100 is the average for all consumer units; an index of 132 means that spending by consumer units in that group is 32 percent above the average for all consumer units; an index of 68 indicates spending that is 32 percent below the average for all consumer units)

	total consumer units	under 25	25 to 34	35 to 44	45 to 54	55 to 64	65 to 74	75+
Average spending of CU, total	$43,395	$24,535	$42,701	$50,402	$52,764	$47,299	$36,512	$25,763
Average spending of CU, index	100	57	98	116	122	109	84	59
Health care, spending index	**100**	**25**	**59**	**88**	**105**	**127**	**148**	**155**
HEALTH INSURANCE	**100**	**24**	**63**	**90**	**97**	**118**	**163**	**159**
Commercial health insurance	**100**	**39**	**81**	**118**	**126**	**139**	**74**	**54**
Traditional fee-for-service health plan (not BCBS)	100	36	41	96	100	166	107	149
Preferred-provider health plan (not BCBS)	100	41	95	125	136	129	63	20
Blue Cross, Blue Shield	**100**	**25**	**69**	**111**	**114**	**134**	**106**	**101**
Traditional fee-for-service health plan	100	23	70	73	99	213	92	104
Preferred-provider health plan	100	28	82	125	135	134	64	44
Health maintenance organization	100	27	73	150	121	121	71	51
Commercial Medicare supplement	100	14	22	20	43	41	364	415
Other BCBS health insurance	100	1	12	109	89	203	104	170
Health maintenance plans (HMOs)	**100**	**25**	**99**	**119**	**123**	**138**	**72**	**42**
Medicare payments	**100**	**4**	**8**	**17**	**30**	**67**	**396**	**407**
Commercial Medicare supplements/ other health insurance	**100**	**25**	**39**	**48**	**56**	**76**	**271**	**327**
Commercial Medicare supplement (not BCBS)	100	20	22	36	34	44	319	432
Other health insurance (not BCBS)	100	34	76	75	105	148	165	96
MEDICAL SERVICES	**100**	**28**	**62**	**101**	**125**	**138**	**97**	**112**
Physician's services	100	37	74	110	133	138	81	63
Dental services	100	13	42	103	133	136	134	103
Eye care services	100	41	62	76	143	153	127	64
Service by professionals other than physician	100	25	53	120	135	169	63	55
Lab tests, X-rays	100	15	62	86	117	216	80	67
Hospital room	100	69	97	104	129	123	53	70
Hospital services other than room	100	73	115	96	121	127	70	48
Care in convalescent or nursing home	100	–	48	49	42	87	26	581
Other medical services	100	9	59	138	103	122	110	109
DRUGS	**100**	**24**	**44**	**66**	**96**	**134**	**178**	**205**
Nonprescription drugs	100	56	70	97	117	112	111	130
Nonprescription vitamins	100	53	50	77	111	141	155	134
Prescription drugs	100	13	37	58	89	138	196	233
MEDICAL SUPPLIES	**100**	**27**	**55**	**81**	**117**	**141**	**126**	**151**
Eyeglasses and contact lenses	100	25	60	92	147	133	123	72
Hearing aids	100	5	2	40	60	142	191	392
Topicals and dressings	100	49	73	93	97	143	132	112
Medical equipment for general use	100	26	56	68	158	147	43	163
Supportive, convalescent medical equipment	100	8	38	49	109	126	89	333
Rental of medical equipment	100	10	31	84	71	218	97	202
Rental of supportive, convalescent medical equipment	100	1	84	76	93	211	92	107

Note: "–" means sample is too small to make a reliable estimate.
Source: Calculations by New Strategist based on the 2004 Consumer Expenditure Survey

Table 7.3 Health Care: Total spending by age, 2004

(total annual out-of-pocket spending on health care, by consumer unit (CU) age groups, 2004; consumer units and dollars in thousands)

	total consumer units	under 25	25 to 34	35 to 44	45 to 54	55 to 64	65 to 74	75+
Number of consumer units	116,282	8,817	19,439	24,070	23,712	17,479	11,230	11,536
Total spending of all CUs	$5,046,042,273	$216,321,216	$830,055,797	$1,213,166,993	$1,251,148,504	$826,731,880	$410,029,535	$297,205,660
Health care, total spending	299,334,287	5,763,320	29,523,759	54,470,891	63,901,943	57,008,458	42,667,037	46,085,512
HEALTH INSURANCE	154,853,902	2,834,666	16,375,608	28,868,836	30,615,037	27,387,670	24,380,779	24,393,680
Commercial health insurance	31,689,171	946,769	4,276,580	7,713,713	8,174,238	6,600,245	2,272,840	1,705,136
Traditional fee-for-service health plan (not BCBS)	8,366,490	229,683	575,978	1,665,163	1,710,584	2,081,924	864,373	1,238,736
Preferred-provider health plan (not BCBS)	23,322,681	717,087	3,700,602	6,048,550	6,463,417	4,518,322	1,408,467	466,400
Blue Cross, Blue Shield	47,197,701	888,225	5,466,830	10,812,003	10,939,531	9,519,413	4,844,173	4,728,260
Traditional fee-for-service health plan	8,060,668	138,868	940,653	1,215,776	1,626,406	2,585,144	719,618	834,745
Preferred-provider health plan	19,719,102	421,541	2,703,576	5,112,468	5,433,842	3,964,237	1,224,295	858,971
Health maintenance organization	13,210,798	268,213	1,611,299	4,092,863	3,258,977	2,405,984	908,395	665,166
Commercial Medicare supplement	5,446,649	58,898	196,723	220,241	482,776	331,751	1,915,501	2,240,983
Other BCBS health insurance	760,484	705	14,774	170,897	137,292	232,296	76,364	128,280
Health maintenance plans (HMOs)	31,641,495	609,696	5,223,648	7,783,757	7,941,860	6,573,502	2,201,529	1,307,490
Medicare payments	28,628,628	95,224	389,752	986,148	1,756,822	2,896,270	10,950,261	11,554,804
Commercial Medicare supplements/ other health insurance	15,696,907	294,752	1,018,798	1,573,215	1,802,823	1,798,414	4,111,977	5,097,989
Commercial Medicare supplement (not BCBS)	10,802,598	167,788	400,638	809,474	757,836	706,851	3,330,257	4,629,628
Other health insurance (not BCBS)	4,895,472	126,965	618,160	763,741	1,044,751	1,091,564	781,608	468,362
MEDICAL SERVICES	75,393,760	1,618,713	7,825,558	15,739,854	19,193,678	15,586,898	7,086,804	8,342,604
Physician's services	17,044,616	477,264	2,108,548	3,888,509	4,625,026	3,537,924	1,333,899	1,073,194
Dental services	27,977,449	283,907	1,955,369	5,986,450	7,570,767	5,705,845	3,624,370	2,851,238
Eye care services	4,522,207	141,513	469,257	712,472	1,315,542	1,040,175	554,650	288,861
Service by professionals other than physician	4,597,790	86,847	405,303	1,146,454	1,261,241	1,166,723	281,424	250,100
Lab tests, X-rays	3,110,544	35,092	322,882	551,444	740,289	1,011,685	241,108	208,225
Hospital room	4,652,443	243,790	757,343	1,005,645	1,228,044	858,394	238,076	321,278
Hospital services other than room	5,953,638	331,784	1,146,901	1,184,003	1,471,330	1,135,436	399,900	284,593
Care in convalescent or nursing home	4,805,935	–	389,558	483,807	410,929	628,720	122,632	2,770,370
Other medical services	2,727,976	18,516	270,396	781,072	570,511	501,997	290,745	294,745
DRUGS	55,849,082	1,036,879	4,116,597	7,654,260	10,936,923	11,226,237	9,586,939	11,363,998
Nonprescription drugs	9,338,607	399,057	1,098,887	1,874,812	2,220,629	1,576,256	1,001,716	1,205,973
Nonprescription vitamins	5,880,381	235,590	494,917	938,489	1,336,883	1,245,554	881,330	780,641
Prescription drugs	40,630,094	402,320	2,522,793	4,840,718	7,379,412	8,404,428	7,704,005	9,377,384
MEDICAL SUPPLIES	13,236,380	273,062	1,205,996	2,207,700	3,156,304	2,807,652	1,612,403	1,985,115
Eyeglasses and contact lenses	5,530,372	105,980	552,456	1,054,988	1,662,685	1,102,750	654,709	397,300
Hearing aids	1,768,649	6,789	6,804	147,549	217,202	376,323	325,558	688,238
Topicals and dressings	3,666,371	137,369	447,291	705,010	723,690	787,429	469,077	407,567
Medical equipment for general use	784,904	15,694	73,674	109,759	252,533	173,916	32,455	127,127
Supportive, convalescent medical equipment	832,579	5,290	53,263	84,245	185,902	157,835	71,423	274,672
Rental of medical equipment	218,610	1,675	11,469	37,790	31,537	71,489	20,551	43,837
Rental of supportive, convalescent medical equipment	434,895	353	61,038	68,359	82,755	137,909	38,744	46,259

Note: Numbers may not add to total because of rounding and missing subcategories. "–" means sample is too small to make a reliable estimate.
Source: Calculations by New Strategist based on the 2004 Consumer Expenditure Survey

Table 7.4 Health Care: Market shares by age, 2004

(percentage of total annual out-of-pocket spending on health care accounted for by consumer unit age groups, 2004)

	total consumer units	under 25	25 to 34	35 to 44	45 to 54	55 to 64	65 to 74	75+
Share of total consumer units	100.0%	7.6%	16.7%	20.7%	20.4%	15.0%	9.7%	9.9%
Share of total before-tax income	100.0	3.2	16.1	24.9	26.4	16.8	7.5	5.1
Share of total spending	100.0	4.3	16.4	24.0	24.8	16.4	8.1	5.9
Share of health care spending	100.0	1.9	9.9	18.2	21.3	19.0	14.3	15.4
HEALTH INSURANCE	100.0	1.8	10.6	18.6	19.8	17.7	15.7	15.8
Commercial health insurance	100.0	3.0	13.5	24.3	25.8	20.8	7.2	5.4
Traditional fee-for-service health plan (not BCBS)	100.0	2.7	6.9	19.9	20.4	24.9	10.3	14.8
Preferred-provider health plan (not BCBS)	100.0	3.1	15.9	25.9	27.7	19.4	6.0	2.0
Blue Cross, Blue Shield	100.0	1.9	11.6	22.9	23.2	20.2	10.3	10.0
Traditional fee-for-service health plan	100.0	1.7	11.7	15.1	20.2	32.1	8.9	10.4
Preferred-provider health plan	100.0	2.1	13.7	25.9	27.6	20.1	6.2	4.4
Health maintenance organization	100.0	2.0	12.2	31.0	24.7	18.2	6.9	5.0
Commercial Medicare supplement	100.0	1.1	3.6	4.0	8.9	6.1	35.2	41.1
Other BCBS health insurance	100.0	0.1	1.9	22.5	18.1	30.5	10.0	16.9
Health maintenance plans (HMOs)	100.0	1.9	16.5	24.6	25.1	20.8	7.0	4.1
Medicare payments	100.0	0.3	1.4	3.4	6.1	10.1	38.2	40.4
Commercial Medicare supplements/ other health insurance	100.0	1.9	6.5	10.0	11.5	11.5	26.2	32.5
Commercial Medicare supplement (not BCBS)	100.0	1.6	3.7	7.5	7.0	6.5	30.8	42.9
Other health insurance (not BCBS)	100.0	2.6	12.6	15.6	21.3	22.3	16.0	9.6
MEDICAL SERVICES	100.0	2.1	10.4	20.9	25.5	20.7	9.4	11.1
Physician's services	100.0	2.8	12.4	22.8	27.1	20.8	7.8	6.3
Dental services	100.0	1.0	7.0	21.4	27.1	20.4	13.0	10.2
Eye care services	100.0	3.1	10.4	15.8	29.1	23.0	12.3	6.4
Service by professionals other than physician	100.0	1.9	8.8	24.9	27.4	25.4	6.1	5.4
Lab tests, X-rays	100.0	1.1	10.4	17.7	23.8	32.5	7.8	6.7
Hospital room	100.0	5.2	16.3	21.6	26.4	18.5	5.1	6.9
Hospital services other than room	100.0	5.6	19.3	19.9	24.7	19.1	6.7	4.8
Care in convalescent or nursing home	100.0	–	8.1	10.1	8.6	13.1	2.6	57.6
Other medical services	100.0	0.7	9.9	28.6	20.9	18.4	10.7	10.8
DRUGS	100.0	1.9	7.4	13.7	19.6	20.1	17.2	20.3
Nonprescription drugs	100.0	4.3	11.8	20.1	23.8	16.9	10.7	12.9
Nonprescription vitamins	100.0	4.0	8.4	16.0	22.7	21.2	15.0	13.3
Prescription drugs	100.0	1.0	6.2	11.9	18.2	20.7	19.0	23.1
MEDICAL SUPPLIES	100.0	2.1	9.1	16.7	23.8	21.2	12.2	15.0
Eyeglasses and contact lenses	100.0	1.9	10.0	19.1	30.1	19.9	11.8	7.2
Hearing aids	100.0	0.4	0.4	8.3	12.3	21.3	18.4	38.9
Topicals and dressings	100.0	3.7	12.2	19.2	19.7	21.5	12.8	11.1
Medical equipment for general use	100.0	2.0	9.4	14.0	32.2	22.2	4.1	16.2
Supportive, convalescent medical equipment	100.0	0.6	6.4	10.1	22.3	19.0	8.6	33.0
Rental of medical equipment	100.0	0.8	5.2	17.3	14.4	32.7	9.4	20.1
Rental of supportive, convalescent medical equipment	100.0	0.1	14.0	15.7	19.0	31.7	8.9	10.6

Note: Numbers may not add to total because of rounding. "–" means sample is too small to make a reliable estimate.
Source: Calculations by New Strategist based on the 2004 Consumer Expenditure Survey

Table 7.5 Health Care: Average spending by income, 2004

(average annual out-of-pocket spending on health care, by before-tax income of consumer units (CU), 2004)

	total consumer units	under $20,000	$20,000– $39,999	$40,000– $49,999	$50,000– $69,999	$70,000– $79,999	$80,000– $99,999	$100,000 or more
Number of consumer units (in 000s)	116,282	28,898	27,297	11,374	18,069	6,461	9,246	14,937
Average number of persons per CU	2.5	1.8	2.3	2.6	2.8	3.0	3.1	3.2
Average before-tax income of CU	$54,453.00	$10,923.47	$29,561.76	$44,645.00	$59,259.00	$74,437.00	$88,811.00	$155,901.00
Average spending of CU, total	43,394.87	18,865.37	30,400.94	38,204.07	47,750.13	55,012.03	65,446.39	93,525.67
Health care, average spending	2,574.21	1,560.19	2,265.69	2,552.41	2,873.60	3,029.34	3,383.54	4,042.15
HEALTH INSURANCE	**1,331.71**	**824.07**	**1,183.38**	**1,439.97**	**1,520.78**	**1,532.30**	**1,765.67**	**1,918.41**
Commercial health insurance	**272.52**	**84.51**	**188.79**	**328.26**	**328.15**	**347.47**	**419.98**	**555.84**
Traditional fee-for-service health plan (not BCBS)	71.95	36.72	66.44	87.44	84.58	105.58	87.99	98.61
Preferred-provider health plan (not BCBS)	200.57	47.79	122.35	240.82	243.57	241.89	332.00	457.22
Blue Cross, Blue Shield	**405.89**	**154.51**	**322.13**	**442.40**	**552.91**	**513.55**	**644.04**	**645.69**
Traditional fee-for-service health plan	69.32	26.95	51.44	90.87	84.50	90.04	104.21	118.67
Preferred-provider health plan	169.58	38.62	124.91	191.25	227.03	231.72	299.24	311.40
Health maintenance organization	113.61	37.27	79.61	111.75	183.16	157.99	200.69	167.62
Commercial Medicare supplement	46.84	48.60	60.65	38.99	50.91	31.34	29.35	36.77
Other BCBS health insurance	6.54	3.08	5.50	9.53	7.31	2.46	10.55	11.22
Health maintenance plans (HMOs)	**272.11**	**77.48**	**206.31**	**302.22**	**351.93**	**405.08**	**464.98**	**472.51**
Medicare payments	**246.20**	**377.84**	**324.53**	**229.47**	**162.99**	**122.25**	**108.63**	**100.54**
Commercial Medicare supplements/ other health insurance	**134.99**	**129.72**	**141.62**	**137.63**	**124.80**	**143.95**	**128.04**	**143.83**
Commercial Medicare supplement (not BCBS)	92.90	110.21	108.89	86.00	77.49	83.89	62.66	76.68
Other health insurance (not BCBS)	42.10	19.52	32.73	51.63	47.31	60.07	65.38	67.15
MEDICAL SERVICES	**648.37**	**293.92**	**510.44**	**518.55**	**727.65**	**867.10**	**944.87**	**1,310.98**
Physician's services	146.58	67.16	124.09	140.58	166.80	229.41	169.24	271.56
Dental services	240.60	98.29	158.47	173.78	269.58	345.14	379.81	550.47
Eye care services	38.89	13.70	23.14	40.24	44.14	43.11	95.90	71.92
Service by professionals other than physician	39.54	19.18	25.68	26.80	46.43	60.18	59.96	84.08
Lab tests, X-rays	26.75	9.24	23.64	23.88	31.81	30.48	46.51	48.54
Hospital room	40.01	11.80	39.31	31.19	44.19	48.47	62.38	80.03
Hospital services other than room	51.20	16.68	37.88	52.88	54.93	78.05	70.21	113.17
Care in convalescent or nursing home	41.33	44.24	45.36	12.52	47.03	12.82	26.45	64.92
Other medical services	23.46	13.62	32.88	16.66	22.74	19.46	34.40	26.29
DRUGS	**480.29**	**382.59**	**484.94**	**483.72**	**487.52**	**510.58**	**527.62**	**595.75**
Nonprescription drugs	80.31	61.69	64.73	82.92	80.35	88.19	97.67	123.79
Nonprescription vitamins	50.57	27.49	43.91	51.25	46.59	65.71	55.21	95.77
Prescription drugs	349.41	293.40	376.30	349.55	360.58	356.68	374.74	376.20
MEDICAL SUPPLIES	**113.83**	**59.62**	**86.94**	**110.17**	**137.64**	**119.35**	**145.39**	**217.01**
Eyeglasses and contact lenses	47.56	21.10	28.52	41.74	56.11	54.86	76.02	106.89
Hearing aids	15.21	11.88	9.82	21.06	24.15	8.13	9.48	22.81
Topicals and dressings	31.53	16.82	26.39	24.70	40.19	39.16	39.68	52.81
Medical equipment for general use	6.75	4.73	4.29	14.03	4.14	5.81	8.75	11.99
Supportive, convalescent medical equipment	7.16	2.95	9.43	2.91	8.21	7.69	5.67	13.79
Rental of medical equipment	1.88	0.99	2.34	1.02	1.50	1.55	2.44	3.65
Rental of supportive, convalescent medical equipment	3.74	1.15	6.14	4.71	3.34	2.15	3.34	5.06

Note: Subcategories may not add to total because some are not shown.
Source: Bureau of Labor Statistics, unpublished tables from the 2004 Consumer Expenditure Survey; calculations by New Strategist

Table 7.6 Health Care: Indexed spending by income, 2004

(indexed average annual out-of-pocket spending of consumer units (CU) on health care, by before-tax income of consumer unit, 2004; index definition: an index of 100 is the average for all consumer units; an index of 132 means that spending by consumer units in that group is 32 percent above the average for all consumer units; an index of 68 indicates spending that is 32 percent below the average for all consumer units)

	total consumer units	under $20,000	$20,000– $39,999	$40,000– $49,999	$50,000– $69,999	$70,000– $79,999	$80,000– $99,999	$100,000 or more
Average spending of CU, total	$43,395	$18,865	$30,401	$38,204	$47,750	$55,012	$65,446	$93,526
Average spending of CU, index	100	43	70	88	110	127	151	216
Health care, spending index	**100**	**61**	**88**	**99**	**112**	**118**	**131**	**157**
HEALTH INSURANCE	**100**	**62**	**89**	**108**	**114**	**115**	**133**	**144**
Commercial health insurance	**100**	**31**	**69**	**120**	**120**	**128**	**154**	**204**
Traditional fee-for-service health plan (not BCBS)	100	51	92	122	118	147	122	137
Preferred-provider health plan (not BCBS)	100	24	61	120	121	121	166	228
Blue Cross, Blue Shield	**100**	**38**	**79**	**109**	**136**	**127**	**159**	**159**
Traditional fee-for-service health plan	100	39	74	131	122	130	150	171
Preferred-provider health plan	100	23	74	113	134	137	176	184
Health maintenance organization	100	33	70	98	161	139	177	148
Commercial Medicare supplement	100	104	129	83	109	67	63	79
Other BCBS health insurance	100	47	84	146	112	38	161	172
Health maintenance plans (HMOs)	**100**	**28**	**76**	**111**	**129**	**149**	**171**	**174**
Medicare payments	**100**	**153**	**132**	**93**	**66**	**50**	**44**	**41**
Commercial Medicare supplements/ other health insurance	**100**	**96**	**105**	**102**	**92**	**107**	**95**	**107**
Commercial Medicare supplement (not BCBS)	100	119	117	93	83	90	67	83
Other health insurance (not BCBS)	100	46	78	123	112	143	155	160
MEDICAL SERVICES	**100**	**45**	**79**	**80**	**112**	**134**	**146**	**202**
Physician's services	100	46	85	96	114	157	115	185
Dental services	100	41	66	72	112	143	158	229
Eye care services	100	35	59	103	113	111	247	185
Service by professionals other than physician	100	49	65	68	117	152	152	213
Lab tests, X-rays	100	35	88	89	119	114	174	181
Hospital room	100	29	98	78	110	121	156	200
Hospital services other than room	100	33	74	103	107	152	137	221
Care in convalescent or nursing home	100	107	110	30	114	31	64	157
Other medical services	100	58	140	71	97	83	147	112
DRUGS	**100**	**80**	**101**	**101**	**102**	**106**	**110**	**124**
Nonprescription drugs	100	77	81	103	100	110	122	154
Nonprescription vitamins	100	54	87	101	92	130	109	189
Prescription drugs	100	84	108	100	103	102	107	108
MEDICAL SUPPLIES	**100**	**52**	**76**	**97**	**121**	**105**	**128**	**191**
Eyeglasses and contact lenses	100	44	60	88	118	115	160	225
Hearing aids	100	78	65	138	159	53	62	150
Topicals and dressings	100	53	84	78	127	124	126	167
Medical equipment for general use	100	70	64	208	61	86	130	178
Supportive, convalescent medical equipment	100	41	132	41	115	107	79	193
Rental of medical equipment	100	53	125	54	80	82	130	194
Rental of supportive, convalescent medical equipment	100	31	164	126	89	57	89	135

Source: Calculations by New Strategist based on the 2004 Consumer Expenditure Survey

Table 7.7 Health Care: Total spending by income, 2004

(total annual out-of-pocket spending on health care, by before-tax income group of consumer units (CU), 2004; consumer units and dollars in thousands)

	total consumer units	under $20,000	$20,000–$39,999	$40,000–$49,999	$50,000–$69,999	$70,000–$79,999	$80,000–$99,999	$100,000 or more
Number of consumer units	116,282	28,898	27,297	11,374	18,069	6,461	9,246	14,937
Total spending of all CUs	$5,046,042,273	$545,171,431	$829,854,379	$434,533,092	$862,797,099	$355,432,726	$605,117,322	$1,396,992,933
Health care, total spending	299,334,287	45,086,445	61,846,634	29,031,111	51,923,078	19,572,566	31,284,211	60,377,595
HEALTH INSURANCE	154,853,902	23,813,929	32,302,786	16,378,219	27,478,974	9,900,190	16,325,385	28,655,290
Commercial health insurance	31,689,171	2,442,165	5,153,507	3,733,629	5,929,342	2,245,004	3,883,135	8,302,582
Traditional fee-for-service health plan (not BCBS)	8,366,490	1,061,109	1,813,705	994,543	1,528,276	682,152	813,556	1,472,938
Preferred-provider health plan (not BCBS)	23,322,681	1,381,046	3,339,802	2,739,087	4,401,066	1,562,851	3,069,672	6,829,495
Blue Cross, Blue Shield	47,197,701	4,465,088	8,793,133	5,031,858	9,990,531	3,318,047	5,954,794	9,644,672
Traditional fee-for-service health plan	8,060,668	778,807	1,404,203	1,033,555	1,526,831	581,748	963,526	1,772,574
Preferred-provider health plan	19,719,102	1,115,935	3,409,761	2,175,278	4,102,205	1,497,143	2,766,773	4,651,382
Health maintenance organization	13,210,798	1,077,088	2,173,179	1,271,045	3,309,518	1,020,773	1,855,580	2,503,740
Commercial Medicare supplement	5,446,649	1,404,366	1,655,665	443,472	919,893	202,488	271,370	549,233
Other BCBS health insurance	760,484	88,902	150,194	108,394	132,084	15,894	97,545	167,593
Health maintenance plans (HMOs)	31,641,495	2,238,897	5,631,525	3,437,450	6,359,023	2,617,222	4,299,205	7,057,882
Medicare payments	28,628,628	10,918,841	8,858,705	2,609,992	2,945,066	789,857	1,004,393	1,501,766
Commercial Medicare supplements/ other health insurance	15,696,907	3,748,783	3,865,916	1,565,404	2,255,011	930,061	1,183,858	2,148,389
Commercial Medicare supplement (not BCBS)	10,802,598	3,184,869	2,972,498	978,164	1,400,167	542,013	579,354	1,145,369
Other health insurance (not BCBS)	4,895,472	563,977	893,418	587,240	854,844	388,112	604,503	1,003,020
MEDICAL SERVICES	75,393,760	8,493,629	13,933,429	5,897,988	13,147,908	5,602,333	8,736,268	19,582,108
Physician's services	17,044,616	1,940,908	3,387,156	1,598,957	3,013,909	1,482,218	1,564,793	4,056,292
Dental services	27,977,449	2,840,289	4,325,700	1,976,574	4,871,041	2,229,950	3,511,723	8,222,370
Eye care services	4,522,207	395,987	631,632	457,690	797,566	278,534	886,691	1,074,269
Service by professionals other than physician	4,597,790	554,375	700,982	304,823	838,944	388,823	554,390	1,255,903
Lab tests, X-rays	3,110,544	266,988	645,256	271,611	574,775	196,931	430,031	725,042
Hospital room	4,652,443	341,016	1,073,027	354,755	798,469	313,165	576,765	1,195,408
Hospital services other than room	5,953,638	482,095	1,034,145	601,457	992,530	504,281	649,162	1,690,420
Care in convalescent or nursing home	4,805,935	1,278,368	1,238,105	142,402	849,785	82,830	244,557	969,710
Other medical services	2,727,976	393,477	897,569	189,491	410,889	125,731	318,062	392,694
DRUGS	55,849,082	11,055,977	13,237,382	5,501,831	8,808,999	3,298,857	4,878,375	8,898,718
Nonprescription drugs	9,338,607	1,782,741	1,767,057	943,132	1,451,844	569,796	903,057	1,849,051
Nonprescription vitamins	5,880,381	794,426	1,198,533	582,918	841,835	424,552	510,472	1,430,516
Prescription drugs	40,630,094	8,478,811	10,271,802	3,975,782	6,515,320	2,304,509	3,464,846	5,619,299
MEDICAL SUPPLIES	13,236,380	1,722,864	2,373,169	1,253,074	2,487,017	771,120	1,344,276	3,241,478
Eyeglasses and contact lenses	5,530,372	609,817	778,604	474,751	1,013,852	354,450	702,881	1,596,616
Hearing aids	1,768,649	343,209	268,114	239,536	436,366	52,528	87,652	340,713
Topicals and dressings	3,666,371	486,170	720,356	280,938	726,193	253,013	366,881	788,823
Medical equipment for general use	784,904	136,557	117,130	159,577	74,806	37,538	80,903	179,095
Supportive, convalescent medical equipment	832,579	85,291	257,430	33,098	148,346	49,685	52,425	205,981
Rental of medical equipment	218,610	28,559	63,995	11,601	27,104	10,015	22,560	54,520
Rental of supportive, convalescent medical equipment	434,895	33,323	167,539	53,572	60,350	13,891	30,882	75,581

Note: Numbers may not add to total because of rounding and missing subcategories.
Source: Calculations by New Strategist based on the 2004 Consumer Expenditure Survey

Table 7.8 Health Care: Market shares by income, 2004

(percentage of total annual out-of-pocket spending on health care accounted for by before-tax income group of consumer units, 2004)

	total consumer units	under $20,000	$20,000–$39,999	$40,000–$49,999	$50,000–$69,999	$70,000–$79,999	$80,000–$99,999	$100,000 or more
Share of total consumer units	100.0%	24.9%	23.5%	9.8%	15.5%	5.6%	8.0%	12.8%
Share of total before-tax income	100.0	5.0	12.7	8.0	16.9	7.6	13.0	36.8
Share of total spending	100.0	10.8	16.4	8.6	17.1	7.0	12.0	27.7
Share of health care spending	100.0	15.1	20.7	9.7	17.3	6.5	10.5	20.2
HEALTH INSURANCE	**100.0**	**15.4**	**20.9**	**10.6**	**17.7**	**6.4**	**10.5**	**18.5**
Commercial health insurance	**100.0**	**7.7**	**16.3**	**11.8**	**18.7**	**7.1**	**12.3**	**26.2**
Traditional fee-for-service health plan (not BCBS)	100.0	12.7	21.7	11.9	18.3	8.2	9.7	17.6
Preferred-provider health plan (not BCBS)	100.0	5.9	14.3	11.7	18.9	6.7	13.2	29.3
Blue Cross, Blue Shield	**100.0**	**9.5**	**18.6**	**10.7**	**21.2**	**7.0**	**12.6**	**20.4**
Traditional fee-for-service health plan	100.0	9.7	17.4	12.8	18.9	7.2	12.0	22.0
Preferred-provider health plan	100.0	5.7	17.3	11.0	20.8	7.6	14.0	23.6
Health maintenance organization	100.0	8.2	16.5	9.6	25.1	7.7	14.0	19.0
Commercial Medicare supplement	100.0	25.8	30.4	8.1	16.9	3.7	5.0	10.1
Other BCBS health insurance	100.0	11.7	19.7	14.3	17.4	2.1	12.8	22.0
Health maintenance plans (HMOs)	**100.0**	**7.1**	**17.8**	**10.9**	**20.1**	**8.3**	**13.6**	**22.3**
Medicare payments	**100.0**	**38.1**	**30.9**	**9.1**	**10.3**	**2.8**	**3.5**	**5.2**
Commercial Medicare supplements/ other health insurance	**100.0**	**23.9**	**24.6**	**10.0**	**14.4**	**5.9**	**7.5**	**13.7**
Commercial Medicare supplement (not BCBS)	100.0	29.5	27.5	9.1	13.0	5.0	5.4	10.6
Other health insurance (not BCBS)	100.0	11.5	18.2	12.0	17.5	7.9	12.3	20.5
MEDICAL SERVICES	**100.0**	**11.3**	**18.5**	**7.8**	**17.4**	**7.4**	**11.6**	**26.0**
Physician's services	100.0	11.4	19.9	9.4	17.7	8.7	9.2	23.8
Dental services	100.0	10.2	15.5	7.1	17.4	8.0	12.6	29.4
Eye care services	100.0	8.8	14.0	10.1	17.6	6.2	19.6	23.8
Service by professionals other than physician	100.0	12.1	15.2	6.6	18.2	8.5	12.1	27.3
Lab tests, X-rays	100.0	8.6	20.7	8.7	18.5	6.3	13.8	23.3
Hospital room	100.0	7.3	23.1	7.6	17.2	6.7	12.4	25.7
Hospital services other than room	100.0	8.1	17.4	10.1	16.7	8.5	10.9	28.4
Care in convalescent or nursing home	100.0	26.6	25.8	3.0	17.7	1.7	5.1	20.2
Other medical services	100.0	14.4	32.9	6.9	15.1	4.6	11.7	14.4
DRUGS	**100.0**	**19.8**	**23.7**	**9.9**	**15.8**	**5.9**	**8.7**	**15.9**
Nonprescription drugs	100.0	19.1	18.9	10.1	15.5	6.1	9.7	19.8
Nonprescription vitamins	100.0	13.5	20.4	9.9	14.3	7.2	8.7	24.3
Prescription drugs	100.0	20.9	25.3	9.8	16.0	5.7	8.5	13.8
MEDICAL SUPPLIES	**100.0**	**13.0**	**17.9**	**9.5**	**18.8**	**5.8**	**10.2**	**24.5**
Eyeglasses and contact lenses	100.0	11.0	14.1	8.6	18.3	6.4	12.7	28.9
Hearing aids	100.0	19.4	15.2	13.5	24.7	3.0	5.0	19.3
Topicals and dressings	100.0	13.3	19.6	7.7	19.8	6.9	10.0	21.5
Medical equipment for general use	100.0	17.4	14.9	20.3	9.5	4.8	10.3	22.8
Supportive, convalescent medical equipment	100.0	10.2	30.9	4.0	17.8	6.0	6.3	24.7
Rental of medical equipment	100.0	13.1	29.3	5.3	12.4	4.6	10.3	24.9
Rental of supportive, convalescent medical equipment	100.0	7.7	38.5	12.3	13.9	3.2	7.1	17.4

Note: Numbers may not add to total because of rounding.
Source: Calculations by New Strategist based on the 2004 Consumer Expenditure Survey

Table 7.9 Health Care: Average spending by high-income consumer units, 2004

(average annual out-of-pocket spending on health care, by before-tax income of high-income consumer units (CU), 2004)

	total consumer units	$100,000 or more	$100,000–$119,999	$120,000–$149,999	$150,000 or more
Number of consumer units (in 000s)	116,282	14,937	5,625	4,245	5,067
Average number of persons per CU	2.5	3.2	3.1	3.3	3.2
Average before-tax income of CU	$54,453.00	$155,901.00	$108,751.00	$132,292.00	$228,021.00
Average spending of CU, total	43,394.87	93,525.67	75,213.14	87,298.57	119,448.79
Health care, average spending	2,574.21	4,042.15	3,732.38	3,811.54	4,580.92
HEALTH INSURANCE	**1,331.71**	**1,918.41**	**1,778.43**	**1,799.41**	**2,173.48**
Commercial health insurance	**272.52**	**555.84**	**503.52**	**530.21**	**635.39**
Traditional fee-for-service health plan (not BCBS)	71.95	98.61	123.41	83.60	83.66
Preferred-provider health plan (not BCBS)	200.57	457.22	380.10	446.61	551.72
Blue Cross, Blue Shield	**405.89**	**645.69**	**603.84**	**579.48**	**747.60**
Traditional fee-for-service health plan	69.32	118.67	75.91	66.60	209.77
Preferred-provider health plan	169.58	311.40	301.98	305.53	326.79
Health maintenance organization	113.61	167.62	186.39	165.56	148.49
Commercial Medicare supplement	46.84	36.77	38.05	27.65	43.00
Other BCBS health insurance	6.54	11.22	1.51	14.15	19.54
Health maintenance plans (HMOs)	**272.11**	**472.51**	**462.96**	**480.47**	**476.45**
Medicare payments	**246.20**	**100.54**	**109.91**	**88.14**	**100.53**
Commercial Medicare supplements/other health insurance	**134.99**	**143.83**	**98.20**	**121.11**	**213.52**
Commercial Medicare supplement (not BCBS)	92.90	76.68	45.01	55.84	129.30
Other health insurance (not BCBS)	42.10	67.15	53.20	65.27	84.22
MEDICAL SERVICES	**648.37**	**1,310.98**	**1,163.31**	**1,220.65**	**1,550.58**
Physician's services	146.58	271.56	230.81	290.12	301.26
Dental services	240.60	550.47	488.63	486.95	672.33
Eye care services	38.89	71.92	49.62	73.30	95.51
Service by professionals other than physician	39.54	84.08	99.71	51.35	94.16
Lab tests, X-rays	26.75	48.54	56.36	47.28	40.91
Hospital room	40.01	80.03	55.09	95.48	94.77
Hospital services other than room	51.20	113.17	53.29	149.65	149.08
Care in convalescent or nursing home	41.33	64.92	103.47	4.99	72.33
Other medical services	23.46	26.29	26.32	21.53	30.23
DRUGS	**480.29**	**595.75**	**569.12**	**594.23**	**629.30**
Nonprescription drugs	80.31	123.79	99.73	147.45	129.45
Nonprescription vitamins	50.57	95.77	79.76	84.12	127.21
Prescription drugs	349.41	376.20	389.62	362.67	372.64
MEDICAL SUPPLIES	**113.83**	**217.01**	**221.52**	**197.25**	**227.56**
Eyeglasses and contact lenses	47.56	106.89	97.14	101.36	122.37
Hearing aids	15.21	22.81	37.80	10.20	16.74
Topicals and dressings	31.53	52.81	50.25	60.30	48.37
Medical equipment for general use	6.75	11.99	14.49	16.13	5.75
Supportive, convalescent medical equipment	7.16	13.79	13.27	5.82	21.06
Rental of medical equipment	1.88	3.65	4.92	2.06	3.56
Rental of supportive, convalescent medical equipment	3.74	5.06	3.66	1.38	9.70

Note: Subcategories may not add to total because some are not shown.
Source: Bureau of Labor Statistics, unpublished tables from the 2004 Consumer Expenditure Survey; calculations by New Strategist

Table 7.10 Health Care: Indexed spending by high-income consumer units, 2004

(indexed average annual out-of-pocket spending of high-income consumer units (CU) on health care, by before-tax income of consumer unit, 2004; index definition: an index of 100 is the average for all consumer units; an index of 132 means that spending by consumer units in that group is 32 percent above the average for all consumer units; an index of 68 indicates spending that is 32 percent below the average for all consumer units)

	total consumer units	$100,000 or more	$100,000–$119,999	$120,000–$149,999	$150,000 or more
Average spending of CU, total	$43,395	$93,526	$75,213	$87,299	$119,449
Average spending of CU, index	100	216	173	201	275
Health care, spending index	**100**	**157**	**145**	**148**	**178**
HEALTH INSURANCE	**100**	**144**	**134**	**135**	**163**
Commercial health insurance	**100**	**204**	**185**	**195**	**233**
Traditional fee-for-service health plan (not BCBS)	100	137	172	116	116
Preferred-provider health plan (not BCBS)	100	228	190	223	275
Blue Cross, Blue Shield	**100**	**159**	**149**	**143**	**184**
Traditional fee-for-service health plan	100	171	110	96	303
Preferred-provider health plan	100	184	178	180	193
Health maintenance organization	100	148	164	146	131
Commercial Medicare supplement	100	79	81	59	92
Other BCBS health insurance	100	172	23	216	299
Health maintenance plans (HMOs)	**100**	**174**	**170**	**177**	**175**
Medicare payments	**100**	**41**	**45**	**36**	**41**
Commercial Medicare supplements/other health insurance	**100**	**107**	**73**	**90**	**158**
Commercial Medicare supplement (not BCBS)	100	83	48	60	139
Other health insurance (not BCBS)	100	160	126	155	200
MEDICAL SERVICES	**100**	**202**	**179**	**188**	**239**
Physician's services	100	185	157	198	206
Dental services	100	229	203	202	279
Eye care services	100	185	128	188	246
Service by professionals other than physician	100	213	252	130	238
Lab tests, X-rays	100	181	211	177	153
Hospital room	100	200	138	239	237
Hospital services other than room	100	221	104	292	291
Care in convalescent or nursing home	100	157	250	12	175
Other medical services	100	112	112	92	129
DRUGS	**100**	**124**	**118**	**124**	**131**
Nonprescription drugs	100	154	124	184	161
Nonprescription vitamins	100	189	158	166	252
Prescription drugs	100	108	112	104	107
MEDICAL SUPPLIES	**100**	**191**	**195**	**173**	**200**
Eyeglasses and contact lenses	100	225	204	213	257
Hearing aids	100	150	249	67	110
Topicals and dressings	100	167	159	191	153
Medical equipment for general use	100	178	215	239	85
Supportive, convalescent medical equipment	100	193	185	81	294
Rental of medical equipment	100	194	262	110	189
Rental of supportive, convalescent medical equipment	100	135	98	37	259

Source: Calculations by New Strategist based on the 2004 Consumer Expenditure Survey

Table 7.11 Health Care: Total spending by high-income consumer units, 2004

(total annual out-of-pocket spending on health care, by before-tax income group of high-income consumer units (CU), 2004; consumer units and dollars in thousands)

	total consumer units	$100,000 or more	$100,000–$119,999	$120,000–$149,999	$150,000 or more
Number of consumer units	116,282	14,937	5,625	4,245	5,067
Total spending of all CUs	$5,046,042,273	$1,396,992,933	$423,073,913	$370,582,430	$605,247,019
Health care, total spending	299,334,287	60,377,595	20,994,638	16,179,987	23,211,522
HEALTH INSURANCE	154,853,902	28,655,290	10,003,669	7,638,495	11,013,023
Commercial health insurance	31,689,171	8,302,582	2,832,300	2,250,741	3,219,521
Traditional fee-for-service health plan (not BCBS)	8,366,490	1,472,938	694,181	354,882	423,905
Preferred-provider health plan (not BCBS)	23,322,681	6,829,495	2,138,063	1,895,859	2,795,565
Blue Cross, Blue Shield	47,197,701	9,644,672	3,396,600	2,459,893	3,788,089
Traditional fee-for-service health plan	8,060,668	1,772,574	426,994	282,717	1,062,905
Preferred-provider health plan	19,719,102	4,651,382	1,698,638	1,296,975	1,655,845
Health maintenance organization	13,210,798	2,503,740	1,048,444	702,802	752,399
Commercial Medicare supplement	5,446,649	549,233	214,031	117,374	217,881
Other BCBS health insurance	760,484	167,593	8,494	60,067	99,009
Health maintenance plans (HMOs)	31,641,495	7,057,882	2,604,150	2,039,595	2,414,172
Medicare payments	28,628,628	1,501,766	618,244	374,154	509,386
Commercial Medicare supplements/other health insurance	15,696,907	2,148,389	552,375	514,112	1,081,906
Commercial Medicare supplement (not BCBS)	10,802,598	1,145,369	253,181	237,041	655,163
Other health insurance (not BCBS)	4,895,472	1,003,020	299,250	277,071	426,743
MEDICAL SERVICES	75,393,760	19,582,108	6,543,619	5,181,659	7,856,789
Physician's services	17,044,616	4,056,292	1,298,306	1,231,559	1,526,484
Dental services	27,977,449	8,222,370	2,748,544	2,067,103	3,406,696
Eye care services	4,522,207	1,074,269	279,113	311,159	483,949
Service by professionals other than physician	4,597,790	1,255,903	560,869	217,981	477,109
Lab tests, X-rays	3,110,544	725,042	317,025	200,704	207,291
Hospital room	4,652,443	1,195,408	309,881	405,313	480,200
Hospital services other than room	5,953,638	1,690,420	299,756	635,264	755,388
Care in convalescent or nursing home	4,805,935	969,710	582,019	21,183	366,496
Other medical services	2,727,976	392,694	148,050	91,395	153,175
DRUGS	55,849,082	8,898,718	3,201,300	2,522,506	3,188,663
Nonprescription drugs	9,338,607	1,849,051	560,981	625,925	655,923
Nonprescription vitamins	5,880,381	1,430,516	448,650	357,089	644,573
Prescription drugs	40,630,094	5,619,299	2,191,613	1,539,534	1,888,167
MEDICAL SUPPLIES	13,236,380	3,241,478	1,246,050	837,326	1,153,047
Eyeglasses and contact lenses	5,530,372	1,596,616	546,413	430,273	620,049
Hearing aids	1,768,649	340,713	212,625	43,299	84,822
Topicals and dressings	3,666,371	788,823	282,656	255,974	245,091
Medical equipment for general use	784,904	179,095	81,506	68,472	29,135
Supportive, convalescent medical equipment	832,579	205,981	74,644	24,706	106,711
Rental of medical equipment	218,610	54,520	27,675	8,745	18,039
Rental of supportive, convalescent medical equipment	434,895	75,581	20,588	5,858	49,150

Note: Numbers may not add to total because of rounding and missing subcategories.
Source: Calculations by New Strategist based on the 2004 Consumer Expenditure Survey

Table 7.12 Health Care: Market shares by high-income consumer units, 2004

(percentage of total annual out-of-pocket spending on health care accounted for by before-tax income group of high-income consumer units, 2004)

	total consumer units	$100,000 or more	$100,000–$119,999	$120,000–$149,999	$150,000 or more
Share of total consumer units	100.0%	12.8%	4.8%	3.7%	4.4%
Share of total before-tax income	100.0	36.8	9.7	8.9	18.2
Share of total spending	100.0	27.7	8.4	7.3	12.0
Share of health care spending	100.0	20.2	7.0	5.4	7.8
HEALTH INSURANCE	100.0	18.5	6.5	4.9	7.1
Commercial health insurance	100.0	26.2	8.9	7.1	10.2
Traditional fee-for-service health plan (not BCBS)	100.0	17.6	8.3	4.2	5.1
Preferred-provider health plan (not BCBS)	100.0	29.3	9.2	8.1	12.0
Blue Cross, Blue Shield	100.0	20.4	7.2	5.2	8.0
Traditional fee-for-service health plan	100.0	22.0	5.3	3.5	13.2
Preferred-provider health plan	100.0	23.6	8.6	6.6	8.4
Health maintenance organization	100.0	19.0	7.9	5.3	5.7
Commercial Medicare supplement	100.0	10.1	3.9	2.2	4.0
Other BCBS health insurance	100.0	22.0	1.1	7.9	13.0
Health maintenance plans (HMOs)	100.0	22.3	8.2	6.4	7.6
Medicare payments	100.0	5.2	2.2	1.3	1.8
Commercial Medicare supplements/other health insurance	100.0	13.7	3.5	3.3	6.9
Commercial Medicare supplement (not BCBS)	100.0	10.6	2.3	2.2	6.1
Other health insurance (not BCBS)	100.0	20.5	6.1	5.7	8.7
MEDICAL SERVICES	100.0	26.0	8.7	6.9	10.4
Physician's services	100.0	23.8	7.6	7.2	9.0
Dental services	100.0	29.4	9.8	7.4	12.2
Eye care services	100.0	23.8	6.2	6.9	10.7
Service by professionals other than physician	100.0	27.3	12.2	4.7	10.4
Lab tests, X-rays	100.0	23.3	10.2	6.5	6.7
Hospital room	100.0	25.7	6.7	8.7	10.3
Hospital services other than room	100.0	28.4	5.0	10.7	12.7
Care in convalescent or nursing home	100.0	20.2	12.1	0.4	7.6
Other medical services	100.0	14.4	5.4	3.4	5.6
DRUGS	100.0	15.9	5.7	4.5	5.7
Nonprescription drugs	100.0	19.8	6.0	6.7	7.0
Nonprescription vitamins	100.0	24.3	7.6	6.1	11.0
Prescription drugs	100.0	13.8	5.4	3.8	4.6
MEDICAL SUPPLIES	100.0	24.5	9.4	6.3	8.7
Eyeglasses and contact lenses	100.0	28.9	9.9	7.8	11.2
Hearing aids	100.0	19.3	12.0	2.4	4.8
Topicals and dressings	100.0	21.5	7.7	7.0	6.7
Medical equipment for general use	100.0	22.8	10.4	8.7	3.7
Supportive, convalescent medical equipment	100.0	24.7	9.0	3.0	12.8
Rental of medical equipment	100.0	24.9	12.7	4.0	8.3
Rental of supportive, convalescent medical equipment	100.0	17.4	4.7	1.3	11.3

Note: Numbers may not add to total because of rounding.
Source: Calculations by New Strategist based on the 2004 Consumer Expenditure Survey

Table 7.13 Health Care: Average spending by household type, 2004

(average annual out-of-pocket spending of consumer units (CU) on health care, by type of consumer unit, 2004)

	total married couples	married couples, no children	married couples with children				single parent, at least one child <18	single person
			total	oldest child under 6	oldest child 6 to 17	oldest child 18 or older		
Number of consumer units (in 000s)	59,797	25,585	29,279	5,604	15,376	8,300	6,892	33,686
Average number of persons per CU	3.2	2.0	3.9	3.5	4.1	3.9	2.9	1.0
Average before-tax income of CU	$73,001.00	$64,434.00	$79,764.00	$75,293.00	$78,508.00	$85,109.00	$31,055.00	$28,143.00
Average spending of CU, total	55,606.57	49,690.43	60,660.88	55,981.04	60,577.88	64,161.69	32,824.46	25,423.35
Health care, average spending	**3,345.50**	**3,760.92**	**3,008.51**	**2,369.24**	**2,947.83**	**3,554.42**	**1,383.81**	**1,696.50**
HEALTH INSURANCE	**1,750.04**	**1,945.16**	**1,589.20**	**1,275.44**	**1,578.99**	**1,819.97**	**704.97**	**849.99**
Commercial health insurance	**395.29**	**375.58**	**434.63**	**433.95**	**435.79**	**432.93**	**135.67**	**128.96**
Traditional fee-for-service health plan (not BCBS)	90.49	112.23	75.89	70.62	65.92	97.93	42.94	54.46
Preferred-provider health plan (not BCBS)	304.81	263.35	358.73	363.32	369.87	335.00	92.73	74.50
Blue Cross, Blue Shield	**549.86**	**538.31**	**563.02**	**398.50**	**591.18**	**621.92**	**276.73**	**222.18**
Traditional fee-for-service health plan	88.08	99.47	75.25	50.22	81.11	81.28	24.94	45.17
Preferred-provider health plan	245.00	202.62	284.89	216.15	312.65	279.86	161.96	62.74
Health maintenance organization	157.54	137.36	179.36	123.35	174.63	225.93	83.56	53.82
Commercial Medicare supplement	50.87	87.78	18.35	7.20	15.46	31.24	0.67	55.01
Other BCBS health insurance	8.37	11.08	5.17	1.58	7.33	3.62	5.60	5.43
Health maintenance plans (HMOs)	**375.98**	**300.54**	**433.50**	**374.94**	**443.59**	**454.36**	**215.38**	**114.81**
Medicare payments	**266.09**	**488.19**	**60.65**	**17.67**	**23.35**	**158.78**	**47.66**	**264.12**
Commercial Medicare supplements/ other health insurance	**162.81**	**242.53**	**97.40**	**50.38**	**85.08**	**151.98**	**29.53**	**119.92**
Commercial Medicare supplement (not BCBS)	103.03	170.09	47.42	12.65	29.34	104.41	3.70	96.25
Other health insurance (not BCBS)	59.79	72.44	49.98	37.74	55.74	47.57	25.83	23.66
MEDICAL SERVICES	**862.87**	**879.55**	**858.57**	**689.79**	**872.36**	**947.00**	**415.37**	**390.89**
Physician's services	204.34	202.47	210.41	219.07	204.99	214.61	102.34	72.56
Dental services	329.37	349.52	316.12	119.21	344.09	397.26	177.62	128.63
Eye care services	51.62	62.08	45.42	19.17	56.78	42.10	24.22	17.97
Service by professionals other than physician	52.92	48.39	54.45	40.71	65.96	42.39	24.44	24.02
Lab tests, X-rays	34.66	42.95	28.75	25.42	25.06	37.82	17.75	14.06
Hospital room	56.48	41.07	66.05	105.56	54.75	60.33	25.61	20.33
Hospital services other than room	75.87	67.43	82.65	130.17	68.19	77.34	22.09	17.45
Care in convalescent or nursing home	28.79	35.55	24.57	15.03	22.50	34.85	3.87	80.99
Other medical services	28.82	30.08	30.16	15.45	30.04	40.30	17.43	14.87
DRUGS	**581.37**	**761.52**	**426.75**	**305.18**	**371.96**	**611.48**	**212.68**	**382.55**
Nonprescription drugs	96.83	103.98	90.85	77.34	93.12	96.97	55.85	52.26
Nonprescription vitamins	55.92	78.24	41.13	38.31	42.92	39.67	35.11	45.90
Prescription drugs	428.63	579.29	294.76	189.53	235.91	474.84	121.72	284.38
MEDICAL SUPPLIES	**151.22**	**174.70**	**133.98**	**98.83**	**124.52**	**175.97**	**50.79**	**73.07**
Eyeglasses and contact lenses	63.93	61.01	68.08	41.25	69.88	82.87	27.79	25.72
Hearing aids	22.11	34.07	10.70	7.56	7.07	19.56	3.01	10.10
Topicals and dressings	40.88	51.23	33.88	29.45	33.11	39.04	17.22	19.88
Medical equipment for general use	8.84	8.54	9.98	8.57	4.88	20.39	1.06	4.11
Supportive, convalescent medical equipment	7.97	9.79	5.56	5.85	5.55	5.37	1.16	8.83
Rental of medical equipment	2.30	3.36	1.50	1.40	1.54	1.50	0.12	1.82
Rental of supportive, convalescent medical equipment	5.19	6.71	4.27	4.76	2.49	7.24	0.42	2.61

Note: Average spending figures for total consumer units can be found on Average Spending by Age and Average Spending by Region tables. Subcategories may not add to total because some are not shown.
Source: Bureau of Labor Statistics, unpublished tables from the 2004 Consumer Expenditure Survey

Table 7.14 Health Care: Indexed spending by household type, 2004

(indexed average annual out-of-pocket spending of consumer units (CU) on health care, by type of consumer unit, 2004; index definition: an index of 100 is the average for all consumer units; an index of 132 means that spending by consumer units in that group is 32 percent above the average for all consumer units; an index of 68 indicates spending that is 32 percent below the average for all consumer units)

	total married couples	married couples, no children	married couples with children				single parent, at least one child <18	single person
			total	oldest child under 6	oldest child 6 to 17	oldest child 18 or older		
Average spending of CU, total	$55,607	$49,690	$60,661	$55,981	$60,578	$64,162	$32,824	$25,423
Average spending of CU, index	128	115	140	129	140	148	76	59
Health care, spending index	130	146	117	92	115	138	54	66
HEALTH INSURANCE	131	146	119	96	119	137	53	64
Commercial health insurance	145	138	159	159	160	159	50	47
Traditional fee-for-service health plan (not BCBS)	126	156	105	98	92	136	60	76
Preferred-provider health plan (not BCBS)	152	131	179	181	184	167	46	37
Blue Cross, Blue Shield	135	133	139	98	146	153	68	55
Traditional fee-for-service health plan	127	143	109	72	117	117	36	65
Preferred-provider health plan	144	119	168	127	184	165	96	37
Health maintenance organization	139	121	158	109	154	199	74	47
Commercial Medicare supplement	109	187	39	15	33	67	1	117
Other BCBS health insurance	128	169	79	24	112	55	86	83
Health maintenance plans (HMOs)	138	110	159	138	163	167	79	42
Medicare payments	108	198	25	7	9	64	19	107
Commercial Medicare supplements/ other health insurance	121	180	72	37	63	113	22	89
Commercial Medicare supplement (not BCBS)	111	183	51	14	32	112	4	104
Other health insurance (not BCBS)	142	172	119	90	132	113	61	56
MEDICAL SERVICES	133	136	132	106	135	146	64	60
Physician's services	139	138	144	149	140	146	70	50
Dental services	137	145	131	50	143	165	74	53
Eye care services	133	160	117	49	146	108	62	46
Service by professionals other than physician	134	122	138	103	167	107	62	61
Lab tests, X-rays	130	161	107	95	94	141	66	53
Hospital room	141	103	165	264	137	151	64	51
Hospital services other than room	148	132	161	254	133	151	43	34
Care in convalescent or nursing home	70	86	59	36	54	84	9	196
Other medical services	123	128	129	66	128	172	74	63
DRUGS	121	159	89	64	77	127	44	80
Nonprescription drugs	121	129	113	96	116	121	70	65
Nonprescription vitamins	111	155	81	76	85	78	69	91
Prescription drugs	123	166	84	54	68	136	35	81
MEDICAL SUPPLIES	133	153	118	87	109	155	45	64
Eyeglasses and contact lenses	134	128	143	87	147	174	58	54
Hearing aids	145	224	70	50	46	129	20	66
Topicals and dressings	130	162	107	93	105	124	55	63
Medical equipment for general use	131	127	148	127	72	302	16	61
Supportive, convalescent medical equipment	111	137	78	82	78	75	16	123
Rental of medical equipment	122	179	80	74	82	80	6	97
Rental of supportive, convalescent medical equipment	139	179	114	127	67	194	11	70

Note: Spending index for total consumer units is 100.
Source: Calculations by New Strategist based on the 2004 Consumer Expenditure Survey

Table 7.15 Health Care: Total spending by household type, 2004

(total annual out-of-pocket spending on health care, by consumer unit (CU) type, 2004; consumer units and dollars in thousands)

	total married couples	married couples, no children	married couples with children				single parent, at least one child <18	single person
			total	oldest child under 6	oldest child 6 to 17	oldest child 18 or older		
Number of consumer units	59,797	25,585	29,279	5,604	15,376	8,300	6,892	33,686
Total spending of all CUs	$3,325,106,066	$1,271,329,652	$1,776,089,906	$313,717,748	$931,445,483	$532,542,027	$226,226,178	$856,410,968
Health care, total spending	200,050,864	96,223,138	88,086,164	13,277,221	45,325,834	29,501,686	9,537,219	57,148,299
HEALTH INSURANCE	**104,647,142**	**49,766,919**	**46,530,187**	**7,147,566**	**24,278,550**	**15,105,751**	**4,858,653**	**28,632,763**
Commercial health insurance	23,637,156	9,609,214	12,725,532	2,431,856	6,700,707	3,593,319	935,038	4,344,147
Traditional fee-for-service health plan (not BCBS)	5,411,031	2,871,405	2,221,983	395,754	1,013,586	812,819	295,942	1,834,540
Preferred-provider health plan (not BCBS)	18,226,724	6,737,810	10,503,256	2,036,045	5,687,121	2,780,500	639,095	2,509,607
Blue Cross, Blue Shield	**32,879,978**	**13,772,661**	**16,484,663**	**2,233,194**	**9,089,984**	**5,161,936**	**1,907,223**	**7,484,355**
Traditional fee-for-service health plan	5,266,920	2,544,940	2,203,245	281,433	1,247,147	674,624	171,886	1,521,597
Preferred-provider health plan	14,650,265	5,184,033	8,341,294	1,211,305	4,807,306	2,322,838	1,116,228	2,113,460
Health maintenance organization	9,420,419	3,514,356	5,251,481	691,253	2,685,111	1,875,219	575,896	1,812,981
Commercial Medicare supplement	3,041,873	2,245,851	537,270	40,349	237,713	259,292	4,618	1,853,067
Other BCBS health insurance	500,501	283,482	151,372	8,854	112,706	30,046	38,595	182,915
Health maintenance plans (HMOs)	**22,482,476**	**7,689,316**	**12,692,447**	**2,101,164**	**6,820,640**	**3,771,188**	**1,484,399**	**3,867,490**
Medicare payments	**15,911,384**	**12,490,341**	**1,775,771**	**99,023**	**359,030**	**1,317,874**	**328,473**	**8,897,146**
Commercial Medicare supplements/ other health insurance	**9,735,550**	**6,205,130**	**2,851,775**	**282,330**	**1,308,190**	**1,261,434**	**203,521**	**4,039,625**
Commercial Medicare supplement (not BCBS)	6,160,885	4,351,753	1,388,410	70,891	451,132	866,603	25,500	3,242,278
Other health insurance (not BCBS)	3,575,263	1,853,377	1,463,364	211,495	857,058	394,831	178,020	797,011
MEDICAL SERVICES	**51,597,037**	**22,503,287**	**25,138,071**	**3,865,583**	**13,413,407**	**7,860,100**	**2,862,730**	**13,167,521**
Physician's services	12,218,919	5,180,195	6,160,594	1,227,668	3,151,926	1,781,263	705,327	2,444,256
Dental services	19,695,338	8,942,469	9,255,677	668,053	5,290,728	3,297,258	1,224,157	4,333,030
Eye care services	3,086,721	1,588,317	1,329,852	107,429	873,049	349,430	166,924	605,337
Service by professionals other than physician	3,164,457	1,238,058	1,594,242	228,139	1,014,201	351,837	168,440	809,138
Lab tests, X-rays	2,072,564	1,098,876	841,771	142,454	385,323	313,906	122,333	473,625
Hospital room	3,377,335	1,050,776	1,933,878	591,558	841,836	500,739	176,504	684,836
Hospital services other than room	4,536,798	1,725,197	2,419,909	729,473	1,048,489	641,922	152,244	587,821
Care in convalescent or nursing home	1,721,556	909,547	719,385	84,228	345,960	289,255	26,672	2,728,229
Other medical services	1,723,350	769,597	883,055	86,582	461,895	334,490	120,128	500,911
DRUGS	**34,764,182**	**19,483,489**	**12,494,813**	**1,710,229**	**5,719,257**	**5,075,284**	**1,465,791**	**12,886,579**
Nonprescription drugs	5,790,144	2,660,328	2,659,997	433,413	1,431,813	804,851	384,918	1,760,430
Nonprescription vitamins	3,343,848	2,001,770	1,204,245	214,689	659,938	329,261	241,978	1,546,187
Prescription drugs	25,630,788	14,821,135	8,630,278	1,062,126	3,627,352	3,941,172	838,894	9,579,625
MEDICAL SUPPLIES	**9,042,502**	**4,469,700**	**3,922,800**	**553,843**	**1,914,620**	**1,460,551**	**350,045**	**2,461,436**
Eyeglasses and contact lenses	3,822,822	1,560,941	1,993,314	231,165	1,074,475	687,821	191,529	866,404
Hearing aids	1,322,112	871,681	313,285	42,366	108,708	162,348	20,745	340,229
Topicals and dressings	2,444,501	1,310,720	991,973	165,038	509,099	324,032	118,680	669,678
Medical equipment for general use	528,605	218,496	292,204	48,026	75,035	169,237	7,306	138,449
Supportive, convalescent medical equipment	476,582	250,477	162,791	32,783	85,337	44,571	7,995	297,447
Rental of medical equipment	137,533	85,966	43,919	7,846	23,679	12,450	827	61,309
Rental of supportive, convalescent medical equipment	310,346	171,675	125,021	26,675	38,286	60,092	2,895	87,920

Note: Total spending figures for total consumer units can be found on Total Spending by Age and Total Spending by Region tables. Spending by type of consumer unit will not add to total because not all types of consumer units are shown. Numbers may not add to category total because of rounding and missing subcategories.

Table 7.16 Health Care: Market shares by household type, 2004

(percentage of total annual out-of-pocket spending on health care accounted for by types of consumer units, 2004)

	total married couples	married couples, no children	married couples with children				single parent, at least one child <18	single person
			total	oldest child under 6	oldest child 6 to 17	oldest child 18 or older		
Share of total consumer units	51.4%	22.0%	25.2%	4.8%	13.2%	7.1%	5.9%	29.0%
Share of total before-tax income	68.9	26.0	36.9	6.7	19.1	11.2	3.4	15.0
Share of total spending	65.9	25.2	35.2	6.2	18.5	10.6	4.5	17.0
Share of health care spending	66.8	32.1	29.4	4.4	15.1	9.9	3.2	19.1
HEALTH INSURANCE	67.6	32.1	30.0	4.6	15.7	9.8	3.1	18.5
Commercial health insurance	74.6	30.3	40.2	7.7	21.1	11.3	3.0	13.7
Traditional fee-for-service health plan (not BCBS)	64.7	34.3	26.6	4.7	12.1	9.7	3.5	21.9
Preferred-provider health plan (not BCBS)	78.2	28.9	45.0	8.7	24.4	11.9	2.7	10.8
Blue Cross, Blue Shield	69.7	29.2	34.9	4.7	19.3	10.9	4.0	15.9
Traditional fee-for-service health plan	65.3	31.6	27.3	3.5	15.5	8.4	2.1	18.9
Preferred-provider health plan	74.3	26.3	42.3	6.1	24.4	11.8	5.7	10.7
Health maintenance organization	71.3	26.6	39.8	5.2	20.3	14.2	4.4	13.7
Commercial Medicare supplement	55.8	41.2	9.9	0.7	4.4	4.8	0.1	34.0
Other BCBS health insurance	65.8	37.3	19.9	1.2	14.8	4.0	5.1	24.1
Health maintenance plans (HMOs)	71.1	24.3	40.1	6.6	21.6	11.9	4.7	12.2
Medicare payments	55.6	43.6	6.2	0.3	1.3	4.6	1.1	31.1
Commercial Medicare supplements/ other health insurance	62.0	39.5	18.2	1.8	8.3	8.0	1.3	25.7
Commercial Medicare supplement (not BCBS)	57.0	40.3	12.9	0.7	4.2	8.0	0.2	30.0
Other health insurance (not BCBS)	73.0	37.9	29.9	4.3	17.5	8.1	3.6	16.3
MEDICAL SERVICES	68.4	29.8	33.3	5.1	17.8	10.4	3.8	17.5
Physician's services	71.7	30.4	36.1	7.2	18.5	10.5	4.1	14.3
Dental services	70.4	32.0	33.1	2.4	18.9	11.8	4.4	15.5
Eye care services	68.3	35.1	29.4	2.4	19.3	7.7	3.7	13.4
Service by professionals other than physician	68.8	26.9	34.7	5.0	22.1	7.7	3.7	17.6
Lab tests, X-rays	66.6	35.3	27.1	4.6	12.4	10.1	3.9	15.2
Hospital room	72.6	22.6	41.6	12.7	18.1	10.8	3.8	14.7
Hospital services other than room	76.2	29.0	40.6	12.3	17.6	10.8	2.6	9.9
Care in convalescent or nursing home	35.8	18.9	15.0	1.8	7.2	6.0	0.6	56.8
Other medical services	63.2	28.2	32.4	3.2	16.9	12.3	4.4	18.4
DRUGS	62.2	34.9	22.4	3.1	10.2	9.1	2.6	23.1
Nonprescription drugs	62.0	28.5	28.5	4.6	15.3	8.6	4.1	18.9
Nonprescription vitamins	56.9	34.0	20.5	3.7	11.2	5.6	4.1	26.3
Prescription drugs	63.1	36.5	21.2	2.6	8.9	9.7	2.1	23.6
MEDICAL SUPPLIES	68.3	33.8	29.6	4.2	14.5	11.0	2.6	18.6
Eyeglasses and contact lenses	69.1	28.2	36.0	4.2	19.4	12.4	3.5	15.7
Hearing aids	74.8	49.3	17.7	2.4	6.1	9.2	1.2	19.2
Topicals and dressings	66.7	35.7	27.1	4.5	13.9	8.8	3.2	18.3
Medical equipment for general use	67.3	27.8	37.2	6.1	9.6	21.6	0.9	17.6
Supportive, convalescent medical equipment	57.2	30.1	19.6	3.9	10.2	5.4	1.0	35.7
Rental of medical equipment	62.9	39.3	20.1	3.6	10.8	5.7	0.4	28.0
Rental of supportive, convalescent medical equipment	71.4	39.5	28.7	6.1	8.8	13.8	0.7	20.2

Note: Market share for total consumer units is 100.0%. Market shares by type of consumer unit will not add to total because not all types of consumer units are shown.
Source: Calculations by New Strategist based on the 2004 Consumer Expenditure Survey

Table 7.17 Health Care: Average spending by race and Hispanic origin, 2004

(average annual out-of-pocket spending of consumer units (CU) on health care, by race and Hispanic origin of consumer unit reference person, 2004)

	total consumer units	Asian	black	Hispanic	non-Hispanic white and other
Number of consumer units (in 000s)	116,282	3,957	13,773	12,298	90,424
Average number of persons per CU	2.5	2.8	2.6	3.3	2.3
Average before-tax income of CU	$54,453.00	$67,705.00	$38,503.00	$43,693.00	$58,314.00
Average spending of CU, total	43,394.87	49,458.68	30,481.49	37,578.03	46,163.26
Health care, average spending	**2,574.21**	**2,100.56**	**1,368.14**	**1,588.19**	**2,890.52**
HEALTH INSURANCE	**1,331.71**	**1,176.75**	**845.88**	**849.70**	**1,471.25**
Commercial health insurance	**272.52**	**253.86**	**131.32**	**144.94**	**310.77**
Traditional fee-for-service health plan (not BCBS)	71.95	94.42	29.19	26.07	84.53
Preferred-provider health plan (not BCBS)	200.57	159.45	102.13	118.87	226.24
Blue Cross, Blue Shield	**405.89**	**296.75**	**245.03**	**181.10**	**462.21**
Traditional fee-for-service health plan	69.32	50.17	31.76	16.78	82.03
Preferred-provider health plan	169.58	87.25	90.28	73.86	195.52
Health maintenance organization	113.61	131.00	104.28	74.94	120.98
Commercial Medicare supplement	46.84	28.26	14.66	11.18	56.48
Other BCBS health insurance	6.54	0.07	4.05	4.34	7.21
Health maintenance plans (HMOs)	**272.11**	**392.00**	**200.09**	**321.43**	**276.27**
Medicare payments	**246.20**	**114.98**	**201.54**	**150.08**	**265.82**
Commercial Medicare supplements/other health insurance	**134.99**	**119.16**	**67.90**	**52.15**	**156.17**
Commercial Medicare supplement (not BCBS)	92.90	95.10	52.79	26.13	107.87
Other health insurance (not BCBS)	42.10	24.06	15.11	26.03	48.30
MEDICAL SERVICES	**648.37**	**502.24**	**219.97**	**401.95**	**745.94**
Physician's services	146.58	153.25	50.73	94.87	168.02
Dental services	240.60	178.58	93.93	126.02	278.01
Eye care services	38.89	28.23	14.07	19.30	45.25
Service by professionals other than physician	39.54	39.16	9.27	17.94	47.00
Lab tests, X-rays	26.75	15.02	8.67	12.50	31.41
Hospital room	40.01	35.94	13.65	35.79	44.51
Hospital services other than room	51.20	36.04	19.33	57.11	55.23
Care in convalescent or nursing home	41.33	5.52	4.74	19.27	49.80
Other medical services	23.46	10.51	5.57	19.15	26.71
DRUGS	**480.29**	**294.45**	**262.83**	**251.51**	**544.35**
Nonprescription drugs	80.31	56.31	54.77	72.54	85.43
Nonprescription vitamins	50.57	71.35	15.41	28.70	59.02
Prescription drugs	349.41	166.79	192.65	150.27	399.90
MEDICAL SUPPLIES	**113.83**	**127.12**	**39.46**	**85.02**	**128.98**
Eyeglasses and contact lenses	47.56	50.61	20.01	37.50	53.06
Hearing aids	15.21	33.61	2.21	11.29	17.68
Topicals and dressings	31.53	29.52	11.09	20.18	36.24
Medical equipment for general use	6.75	3.34	2.69	2.64	7.92
Supportive, convalescent medical equipment	7.16	2.96	1.69	7.59	7.92
Rental of medical equipment	1.88	0.65	0.23	1.37	2.19
Rental of supportive, convalescent medical equipment	3.74	6.42	1.54	4.45	3.97

Note: "Asian" and "black" include Hispanics and non-Hispanics who identify themselves as being of the respective race alone. "Hispanic" includes people of any race who identify themselves as Hispanic. "Other" includes people who identify themselves as non-Hispanic and as Alaska Native, American Indian, Asian (who are also included in the "Asian" column), Native Hawaiian or other Pacific Islander, as well as non-Hispanics reporting more than one race. Subcategories may not add to total because some are not shown.
Source: Bureau of Labor Statistics, unpublished tables from the 2004 Consumer Expenditure Survey

Table 7.18 Health Care: Indexed spending by race and Hispanic origin, 2004

(indexed average annual out-of-pocket spending of consumer units (CU) on health care, by race and Hispanic origin of consumer unit reference person, 2004; index definition: an index of 100 is the average for all consumer units; an index of 132 means that spending by consumer units in that group is 32 percent above the average for all consumer units; an index of 68 indicates spending that is 32 percent below the average for all consumer units)

	total consumer units	Asian	black	Hispanic	non-Hispanic white and other
Average spending of CU, total	$43,395	$49,459	$30,481	$37,578	$46,163
Average spending of CU, index	100	114	70	87	106
Health care, spending index	100	82	53	62	112
HEALTH INSURANCE	100	88	64	64	110
Commercial health insurance	100	93	48	53	114
Traditional fee-for-service health plan (not BCBS)	100	131	41	36	117
Preferred-provider health plan (not BCBS)	100	79	51	59	113
Blue Cross, Blue Shield	100	73	60	45	114
Traditional fee-for-service health plan	100	72	46	24	118
Preferred-provider health plan	100	51	53	44	115
Health maintenance organization	100	115	92	66	106
Commercial Medicare supplement	100	60	31	24	121
Other BCBS health insurance	100	1	62	66	110
Health maintenance plans (HMOs)	100	144	74	118	102
Medicare payments	100	47	82	61	108
Commercial Medicare supplements/other health insurance	100	88	50	39	116
Commercial Medicare supplement (not BCBS)	100	102	57	28	116
Other health insurance (not BCBS)	100	57	36	62	115
MEDICAL SERVICES	100	77	34	62	115
Physician's services	100	105	35	65	115
Dental services	100	74	39	52	116
Eye care services	100	73	36	50	116
Service by professionals other than physician	100	99	23	45	119
Lab tests, X-rays	100	56	32	47	117
Hospital room	100	90	34	89	111
Hospital services other than room	100	70	38	112	108
Care in convalescent or nursing home	100	13	11	47	120
Other medical services	100	45	24	82	114
DRUGS	100	61	55	52	113
Nonprescription drugs	100	70	68	90	106
Nonprescription vitamins	100	141	30	57	117
Prescription drugs	100	48	55	43	114
MEDICAL SUPPLIES	100	112	35	75	113
Eyeglasses and contact lenses	100	106	42	79	112
Hearing aids	100	221	15	74	116
Topicals and dressings	100	94	35	64	115
Medical equipment for general use	100	49	40	39	117
Supportive, convalescent medical equipment	100	41	24	106	111
Rental of medical equipment	100	35	12	73	116
Rental of supportive, convalescent medical equipment	100	172	41	119	106

Note: "Asian" and "black" include Hispanics and non-Hispanics who identify themselves as being of the respective race alone. "Hispanic" includes people of any race who identify themselves as Hispanic. "Other" includes people who identify themselves as non-Hispanic and as Alaska Native, American Indian, Asian (who are also included in the "Asian" column), Native Hawaiian or other Pacific Islander, as well as non-Hispanics reporting more than one race.
Source: Calculations by New Strategist based on the 2004 Consumer Expenditure Survey

Table 7.19 Health Care: Total spending by race and Hispanic origin, 2004

(total annual out-of-pocket spending on health care, by consumer unit race and Hispanic origin groups, 2004; consumer units and dollars in thousands)

	total consumer units	Asian	black	Hispanic	non-Hispanic white and other
Number of consumer units	116,282	3,957	13,773	12,298	90,424
Total spending of all consumer units	$5,046,042,273	$195,707,997	$419,821,562	$462,134,613	$4,174,266,622
Health care, total spending	299,334,287	8,311,916	18,843,392	19,531,561	261,372,380
HEALTH INSURANCE	154,853,902	4,656,400	11,650,305	10,449,611	133,036,310
Commercial health insurance	31,689,171	1,004,524	1,808,670	1,782,472	28,101,066
Traditional fee-for-service health plan (not BCBS)	8,366,490	373,620	402,034	320,609	7,643,541
Preferred-provider health plan (not BCBS)	23,322,681	630,944	1,406,636	1,461,863	20,457,526
Blue Cross, Blue Shield	47,197,701	1,174,240	3,374,798	2,227,168	41,794,877
Traditional fee-for-service health plan	8,060,668	198,523	437,430	206,360	7,417,481
Preferred-provider health plan	19,719,102	345,248	1,243,426	908,330	17,679,700
Health maintenance organization	13,210,798	518,367	1,436,248	921,612	10,939,496
Commercial Medicare supplement	5,446,649	111,825	201,912	137,492	5,107,148
Other BCBS health insurance	760,484	277	55,781	53,373	651,957
Health maintenance plans (HMOs)	31,641,495	1,551,144	2,755,840	3,952,946	24,981,438
Medicare payments	28,628,628	454,976	2,775,810	1,845,684	24,036,508
Commercial Medicare supplements/other health insurance	15,696,907	471,516	935,187	641,341	14,121,516
Commercial Medicare supplement (not BCBS)	10,802,598	376,311	727,077	321,347	9,754,037
Other health insurance (not BCBS)	4,895,472	95,205	208,110	320,117	4,367,479
MEDICAL SERVICES	75,393,760	1,987,364	3,029,647	4,943,181	67,450,879
Physician's services	17,044,616	606,410	698,704	1,166,711	15,193,040
Dental services	27,977,449	706,641	1,293,698	1,549,794	25,138,776
Eye care services	4,522,207	111,706	193,786	237,351	4,091,686
Service by professionals other than physician	4,597,790	154,956	127,676	220,626	4,249,928
Lab tests, X-rays	3,110,544	59,434	119,412	153,725	2,840,218
Hospital room	4,652,443	142,215	188,001	440,145	4,024,772
Hospital services other than room	5,953,638	142,610	266,232	702,339	4,994,118
Care in convalescent or nursing home	4,805,935	21,843	65,284	236,982	4,503,115
Other medical services	2,727,976	41,588	76,716	235,507	2,415,225
DRUGS	55,849,082	1,165,139	3,619,958	3,093,070	49,222,304
Nonprescription drugs	9,338,607	222,819	754,347	892,097	7,724,922
Nonprescription vitamins	5,880,381	282,332	212,242	352,953	5,336,824
Prescription drugs	40,630,094	659,988	2,653,368	1,848,020	36,160,558
MEDICAL SUPPLIES	13,236,380	503,014	543,483	1,045,576	11,662,888
Eyeglasses and contact lenses	5,530,372	200,264	275,598	461,175	4,797,897
Hearing aids	1,768,649	132,995	30,438	138,844	1,598,696
Topicals and dressings	3,666,371	116,811	152,743	248,174	3,276,966
Medical equipment for general use	784,904	13,216	37,049	32,467	716,158
Supportive, convalescent medical equipment	832,579	11,713	23,276	93,342	716,158
Rental of medical equipment	218,610	2,572	3,168	16,848	198,029
Rental of supportive, convalescent medical equipment	434,895	25,404	21,210	54,726	358,983

Note: "Asian" and "black" include Hispanics and non-Hispanics who identify themselves as being of the respective race alone. "Hispanic" includes people of any race who identify themselves as Hispanic. "Other" includes people who identify themselves as non-Hispanic and as Alaska Native, American Indian, Asian (who are also included in the "Asian" column), Native Hawaiian or other Pacific Islander, as well as non-Hispanics reporting more than one race. Numbers may not add to total because of rounding and missing subcategories.
Source: Calculations by New Strategist based on the 2004 Consumer Expenditure Survey

Table 7.20 Health Care: Market shares by race and Hispanic origin, 2004

(percentage of total annual out-of-pocket spending on health care accounted for by consumer unit race and Hispanic origin groups, 2004)

	total consumer units	Asian	black	Hispanic	non-Hispanic white and other
Share of total consumer units	100.0%	3.4%	11.8%	10.6%	77.8%
Share of total before-tax income	100.0	4.2	8.4	8.5	83.3
Share of total spending	100.0	3.9	8.3	9.2	82.7
Share of health care spending	100.0	2.8	6.3	6.5	87.3
HEALTH INSURANCE	100.0	3.0	7.5	6.7	85.9
Commercial health insurance	100.0	3.2	5.7	5.6	88.7
Traditional fee-for-service health plan (not BCBS)	100.0	4.5	4.8	3.8	91.4
Preferred-provider health plan (not BCBS)	100.0	2.7	6.0	6.3	87.7
Blue Cross, Blue Shield	100.0	2.5	7.2	4.7	88.6
Traditional fee-for-service health plan	100.0	2.5	5.4	2.6	92.0
Preferred-provider health plan	100.0	1.8	6.3	4.6	89.7
Health maintenance organization	100.0	3.9	10.9	7.0	82.8
Commercial Medicare supplement	100.0	2.1	3.7	2.5	93.8
Other BCBS health insurance	100.0	0.0	7.3	7.0	85.7
Health maintenance plans (HMOs)	100.0	4.9	8.7	12.5	79.0
Medicare payments	100.0	1.6	9.7	6.4	84.0
Commercial Medicare supplements/other health insurance	100.0	3.0	6.0	4.1	90.0
Commercial Medicare supplement (not BCBS)	100.0	3.5	6.7	3.0	90.3
Other health insurance (not BCBS)	100.0	1.9	4.3	6.5	89.2
MEDICAL SERVICES	100.0	2.6	4.0	6.6	89.5
Physician's services	100.0	3.6	4.1	6.8	89.1
Dental services	100.0	2.5	4.6	5.5	89.9
Eye care services	100.0	2.5	4.3	5.2	90.5
Service by professionals other than physician	100.0	3.4	2.8	4.8	92.4
Lab tests, X-rays	100.0	1.9	3.8	4.9	91.3
Hospital room	100.0	3.1	4.0	9.5	86.5
Hospital services other than room	100.0	2.4	4.5	11.8	83.9
Care in convalescent or nursing home	100.0	0.5	1.4	4.9	93.7
Other medical services	100.0	1.5	2.8	8.6	88.5
DRUGS	100.0	2.1	6.5	5.5	88.1
Nonprescription drugs	100.0	2.4	8.1	9.6	82.7
Nonprescription vitamins	100.0	4.8	3.6	6.0	90.8
Prescription drugs	100.0	1.6	6.5	4.5	89.0
MEDICAL SUPPLIES	100.0	3.8	4.1	7.9	88.1
Eyeglasses and contact lenses	100.0	3.6	5.0	8.3	86.8
Hearing aids	100.0	7.5	1.7	7.9	90.4
Topicals and dressings	100.0	3.2	4.2	6.8	89.4
Medical equipment for general use	100.0	1.7	4.7	4.1	91.2
Supportive, convalescent medical equipment	100.0	1.4	2.8	11.2	86.0
Rental of medical equipment	100.0	1.2	1.4	7.7	90.6
Rental of supportive, convalescent medical equipment	100.0	5.8	4.9	12.6	82.5

Note: "Asian" and "black" include Hispanics and non-Hispanics who identify themselves as being of the respective race alone. "Hispanic" includes people of any race who identify themselves as Hispanic. "Other" includes people who identify themselves as non-Hispanic and as Alaska Native, American Indian, Asian (who are also included in the "Asian" column), Native Hawaiian or other Pacific Islander, as well as non-Hispanics reporting more than one race.
Source: Calculations by New Strategist based on the 2004 Consumer Expenditure Survey

Table 7.21 Health Care: Average spending by region, 2004

(average annual out-of-pocket spending of consumer units (CU) on health care, by region in which consumer unit lives, 2004)

	total consumer units	Northeast	Midwest	South	West
Number of consumer units (in 000s)	116,282	22,051	26,539	41,801	25,891
Average number of persons per CU	2.5	2.4	2.4	2.5	2.6
Average before-tax income of CU	$54,453.00	$61,050.00	$53,567.00	$50,775.00	$55,682.00
Average spending of CU, total	43,394.87	46,114.89	43,370.77	39,173.65	47,921.74
Health care, average spending	2,574.21	2,370.58	2,860.96	2,508.50	2,560.28
HEALTH INSURANCE	**1,331.71**	**1,307.09**	**1,492.17**	**1,286.86**	**1,260.62**
Commercial health insurance	**272.52**	**179.07**	**335.64**	**285.15**	**267.02**
Traditional fee-for-service health plan (not BCBS)	71.95	85.42	74.99	68.16	63.49
Preferred-provider health plan (not BCBS)	200.57	93.65	260.65	217.00	203.53
Blue Cross, Blue Shield	**405.89**	**433.05**	**456.49**	**419.06**	**309.63**
Traditional fee-for-service health plan	69.32	99.92	82.24	57.92	48.44
Preferred-provider health plan	169.58	102.21	192.09	209.89	138.78
Health maintenance organization	113.61	176.65	105.91	96.25	95.85
Commercial Medicare supplement	46.84	40.64	70.51	50.43	22.05
Other BCBS health insurance	6.54	13.62	5.74	4.58	4.50
Health maintenance plans (HMOs)	**272.11**	**317.51**	**258.53**	**202.17**	**360.26**
Medicare payments	**246.20**	**257.91**	**258.97**	**251.32**	**214.87**
Commercial Medicare supplements/other health insurance	**134.99**	**119.55**	**182.53**	**129.17**	**108.83**
Commercial Medicare supplement (not BCBS)	92.90	81.87	137.04	88.47	64.19
Other health insurance (not BCBS)	42.10	37.68	45.50	40.70	44.63
MEDICAL SERVICES	**648.37**	**596.95**	**714.23**	**582.72**	**730.65**
Physician's services	146.58	129.55	148.12	143.34	164.73
Dental services	240.60	286.83	232.26	196.89	280.34
Eye care services	38.89	42.74	44.81	36.38	33.62
Service by professionals other than physician	39.54	27.73	41.34	32.09	59.79
Lab tests, X-rays	26.75	21.62	28.07	27.58	28.44
Hospital room	40.01	21.78	56.57	43.56	32.83
Hospital services other than room	51.20	31.12	62.78	59.95	42.33
Care in convalescent or nursing home	41.33	22.84	70.51	22.49	57.58
Other medical services	23.46	12.74	29.78	20.44	30.99
DRUGS	**480.29**	**374.92**	**526.22**	**533.20**	**438.01**
Nonprescription drugs	80.31	71.12	77.72	80.77	90.25
Nonprescription vitamins	50.57	45.68	38.60	53.07	63.26
Prescription drugs	349.41	258.13	409.90	399.37	284.50
MEDICAL SUPPLIES	**113.83**	**91.62**	**128.35**	**105.71**	**131.00**
Eyeglasses and contact lenses	47.56	43.11	61.34	39.70	49.93
Hearing aids	15.21	7.79	10.58	19.21	19.80
Topicals and dressings	31.53	30.44	34.62	27.22	36.27
Medical equipment for general use	6.75	4.68	9.84	5.64	7.16
Supportive, convalescent medical equipment	7.16	2.92	6.32	9.92	7.17
Rental of medical equipment	1.88	1.20	1.31	1.16	4.19
Rental of supportive, convalescent medical equipment	3.74	1.49	4.33	2.85	6.50

Note: Subcategories may not add to total because some are not shown.
Source: Bureau of Labor Statistics, unpublished tables from the 2004 Consumer Expenditure Survey

Table 7.22 Health Care: Indexed spending by region, 2004

(indexed average annual out-of-pocket spending of consumer units (CU) on health care, by region in which consumer unit lives, 2004; index definition: an index of 100 is the average for all consumer units; an index of 132 means that spending by consumer units in that group is 32 percent above the average for all consumer units; an index of 68 indicates spending that is 32 percent below the average for all consumer units)

	total consumer units	Northeast	Midwest	South	West
Average spending of CU, total	$43,395	$46,115	$43,371	$39,174	$47,922
Average spending of CU, index	100	106	100	90	110
Health care, spending index	**100**	**92**	**111**	**97**	**99**
HEALTH INSURANCE	**100**	**98**	**112**	**97**	**95**
Commercial health insurance	**100**	**66**	**123**	**105**	**98**
Traditional fee-for-service health plan (not BCBS)	100	119	104	95	88
Preferred-provider health plan (not BCBS)	100	47	130	108	101
Blue Cross, Blue Shield	**100**	**107**	**112**	**103**	**76**
Traditional fee-for-service health plan	100	144	119	84	70
Preferred-provider health plan	100	60	113	124	82
Health maintenance organization	100	155	93	85	84
Commercial Medicare supplement	100	87	151	108	47
Other BCBS health insurance	100	208	88	70	69
Health maintenance plans (HMOs)	**100**	**117**	**95**	**74**	**132**
Medicare payments	**100**	**105**	**105**	**102**	**87**
Commercial Medicare supplements/other health insurance	**100**	**89**	**135**	**96**	**81**
Commercial Medicare supplement (not BCBS)	100	88	148	95	69
Other health insurance (not BCBS)	100	90	108	97	106
MEDICAL SERVICES	**100**	**92**	**110**	**90**	**113**
Physician's services	100	88	101	98	112
Dental services	100	119	97	82	117
Eye care services	100	110	115	94	86
Service by professionals other than physician	100	70	105	81	151
Lab tests, X-rays	100	81	105	103	106
Hospital room	100	54	141	109	82
Hospital services other than room	100	61	123	117	83
Care in convalescent or nursing home	100	55	171	54	139
Other medical services	100	54	127	87	132
DRUGS	**100**	**78**	**110**	**111**	**91**
Nonprescription drugs	100	89	97	101	112
Nonprescription vitamins	100	90	76	105	125
Prescription drugs	100	74	117	114	81
MEDICAL SUPPLIES	**100**	**80**	**113**	**93**	**115**
Eyeglasses and contact lenses	100	91	129	83	105
Hearing aids	100	51	70	126	130
Topicals and dressings	100	97	110	86	115
Medical equipment for general use	100	69	146	84	106
Supportive, convalescent medical equipment	100	41	88	139	100
Rental of medical equipment	100	64	70	62	223
Rental of supportive, convalescent medical equipment	100	40	116	76	174

Source: Calculations by New Strategist based on the 2004 Consumer Expenditure Survey

Table 7.23 Health Care: Total spending by region, 2004

(total annual out-of-pocket spending on health care, by region in which consumer units live, 2004; consumer units and dollars in thousands)

	total consumer units	Northeast	Midwest	South	West
Number of consumer units	116,282	22,051	26,539	41,801	25,891
Total spending of all consumer units	$5,046,042,273	$1,016,879,439	$1,151,016,865	$1,637,497,744	$1,240,741,770
Health care, total spending	299,334,287	52,273,660	75,927,017	104,857,809	66,288,209
HEALTH INSURANCE	154,853,902	28,822,642	39,600,700	53,792,035	32,638,712
Commercial health insurance	31,689,171	3,948,673	8,907,550	11,919,555	6,913,415
Traditional fee-for-service health plan (not BCBS)	8,366,490	1,883,596	1,990,160	2,849,156	1,643,820
Preferred-provider health plan (not BCBS)	23,322,681	2,065,076	6,917,390	9,070,817	5,269,595
Blue Cross, Blue Shield	47,197,701	9,549,186	12,114,788	17,517,127	8,016,630
Traditional fee-for-service health plan	8,060,668	2,203,336	2,182,567	2,421,114	1,254,160
Preferred-provider health plan	19,719,102	2,253,833	5,097,877	8,773,612	3,593,153
Health maintenance organization	13,210,798	3,895,309	2,810,745	4,023,346	2,481,652
Commercial Medicare supplement	5,446,649	896,153	1,871,265	2,108,024	570,897
Other BCBS health insurance	760,484	300,335	152,334	191,449	116,510
Health maintenance plans (HMOs)	31,641,495	7,001,413	6,861,128	8,450,908	9,327,492
Medicare payments	28,628,628	5,687,173	6,872,805	10,505,427	5,563,199
Commercial Medicare supplements/other health insurance	15,696,907	2,636,197	4,844,164	5,399,435	2,817,718
Commercial Medicare supplement (not BCBS)	10,802,598	1,805,315	3,636,905	3,698,134	1,661,943
Other health insurance (not BCBS)	4,895,472	830,882	1,207,525	1,701,301	1,155,515
MEDICAL SERVICES	75,393,760	13,163,344	18,954,950	24,358,279	18,917,259
Physician's services	17,044,616	2,856,707	3,930,957	5,991,755	4,265,024
Dental services	27,977,449	6,324,888	6,163,948	8,230,199	7,258,283
Eye care services	4,522,207	942,460	1,189,213	1,520,720	870,455
Service by professionals other than physician	4,597,790	611,474	1,097,122	1,341,394	1,548,023
Lab tests, X-rays	3,110,544	476,743	744,950	1,152,872	736,340
Hospital room	4,652,443	480,271	1,501,311	1,820,852	850,002
Hospital services other than room	5,953,638	686,227	1,666,118	2,505,970	1,095,966
Care in convalescent or nursing home	4,805,935	503,645	1,871,265	940,104	1,490,804
Other medical services	2,727,976	280,930	790,331	854,412	802,362
DRUGS	55,849,082	8,267,361	13,965,353	22,288,293	11,340,517
Nonprescription drugs	9,338,607	1,568,267	2,062,611	3,376,267	2,336,663
Nonprescription vitamins	5,880,381	1,007,290	1,024,405	2,218,379	1,637,865
Prescription drugs	40,630,094	5,692,025	10,878,336	16,694,065	7,365,990
MEDICAL SUPPLIES	13,236,380	2,020,313	3,406,281	4,418,784	3,391,721
Eyeglasses and contact lenses	5,530,372	950,619	1,627,902	1,659,500	1,292,738
Hearing aids	1,768,649	171,777	280,783	802,997	512,642
Topicals and dressings	3,666,371	671,232	918,780	1,137,823	939,067
Medical equipment for general use	784,904	103,199	261,144	235,758	185,380
Supportive, convalescent medical equipment	832,579	64,389	167,726	414,666	185,638
Rental of medical equipment	218,610	26,461	34,766	48,489	108,483
Rental of supportive, convalescent medical equipment	434,895	32,856	114,914	119,133	168,292

Note: Numbers may not add to total because of rounding and missing subcategories.
Source: Calculations by New Strategist based on the 2004 Consumer Expenditure Survey

Table 7.24 Health Care: Market shares by region, 2004

(percentage of total annual out-of-pocket spending on health care accounted for by consumer units by region, 2004)

	total consumer units	Northeast	Midwest	South	West
Share of total consumer units	100.0%	19.0%	22.8%	35.9%	22.3%
Share of total before-tax income	100.0	21.3	22.5	33.5	22.8
Share of total spending	100.0	20.2	22.8	32.5	24.6
Share of health care spending	100.0	17.5	25.4	35.0	22.1
HEALTH INSURANCE	**100.0**	**18.6**	**25.6**	**34.7**	**21.1**
Commercial health insurance	**100.0**	**12.5**	**28.1**	**37.6**	**21.8**
Traditional fee-for-service health plan (not BCBS)	100.0	22.5	23.8	34.1	19.6
Preferred-provider health plan (not BCBS)	100.0	8.9	29.7	38.9	22.6
Blue Cross, Blue Shield	**100.0**	**20.2**	**25.7**	**37.1**	**17.0**
Traditional fee-for-service health plan	100.0	27.3	27.1	30.0	15.6
Preferred-provider health plan	100.0	11.4	25.9	44.5	18.2
Health maintenance organization	100.0	29.5	21.3	30.5	18.8
Commercial Medicare supplement	100.0	16.5	34.4	38.7	10.5
Other BCBS health insurance	100.0	39.5	20.0	25.2	15.3
Health maintenance plans (HMOs)	**100.0**	**22.1**	**21.7**	**26.7**	**29.5**
Medicare payments	**100.0**	**19.9**	**24.0**	**36.7**	**19.4**
Commercial Medicare supplements/other health insurance	**100.0**	**16.8**	**30.9**	**34.4**	**18.0**
Commercial Medicare supplement (not BCBS)	100.0	16.7	33.7	34.2	15.4
Other health insurance (not BCBS)	100.0	17.0	24.7	34.8	23.6
MEDICAL SERVICES	**100.0**	**17.5**	**25.1**	**32.3**	**25.1**
Physician's services	100.0	16.8	23.1	35.2	25.0
Dental services	100.0	22.6	22.0	29.4	25.9
Eye care services	100.0	20.8	26.3	33.6	19.2
Service by professionals other than physician	100.0	13.3	23.9	29.2	33.7
Lab tests, X-rays	100.0	15.3	23.9	37.1	23.7
Hospital room	100.0	10.3	32.3	39.1	18.3
Hospital services other than room	100.0	11.5	28.0	42.1	18.4
Care in convalescent or nursing home	100.0	10.5	38.9	19.6	31.0
Other medical services	100.0	10.3	29.0	31.3	29.4
DRUGS	**100.0**	**14.8**	**25.0**	**39.9**	**20.3**
Nonprescription drugs	100.0	16.8	22.1	36.2	25.0
Nonprescription vitamins	100.0	17.1	17.4	37.7	27.9
Prescription drugs	100.0	14.0	26.8	41.1	18.1
MEDICAL SUPPLIES	**100.0**	**15.3**	**25.7**	**33.4**	**25.6**
Eyeglasses and contact lenses	100.0	17.2	29.4	30.0	23.4
Hearing aids	100.0	9.7	15.9	45.4	29.0
Topicals and dressings	100.0	18.3	25.1	31.0	25.6
Medical equipment for general use	100.0	13.1	33.3	30.0	23.6
Supportive, convalescent medical equipment	100.0	7.7	20.1	49.8	22.3
Rental of medical equipment	100.0	12.1	15.9	22.2	49.6
Rental of supportive, convalescent medical equipment	100.0	7.6	26.4	27.4	38.7

Note: Numbers may not add to total because of rounding.
Source: Calculations by New Strategist based on the 2004 Consumer Expenditure Survey

Table 7.25 Health Care: Average spending by education, 2004

(average annual out-of-pocket spending of consumer units (CU) on health care, by education of consumer unit reference person, 2004)

	total consumer units	less than high school graduate	high school graduate	some college	associate's degree	college graduate total	college graduate bachelor's degree	college graduate master's, professional, doctorate
Number of consumer units (in 000s)	116,282	16,829	31,005	25,317	10,678	32,452	20,684	11,768
Average number of persons per CU	2.5	2.7	2.5	2.3	2.6	2.5	2.4	2.5
Average before-tax income of CU	$54,453.00	$29,094.00	$42,334.00	$46,756.00	$58,593.00	$83,825.00	$75,647.00	$98,201.00
Average spending of CU, total	43,394.87	25,421.18	35,438.55	40,877.68	48,177.36	60,712.28	56,728.41	67,801.38
Health care, average spending	**2,574.21**	**1,873.76**	**2,449.72**	**2,325.41**	**2,703.11**	**3,207.58**	**3,031.18**	**3,521.87**
HEALTH INSURANCE	**1,331.71**	**994.17**	**1,307.57**	**1,183.01**	**1,405.03**	**1,621.71**	**1,585.09**	**1,686.07**
Commercial health insurance	**272.52**	**97.85**	**221.73**	**253.85**	**327.51**	**408.11**	**420.99**	**385.45**
Traditional fee-for-service health plan (not BCBS)	71.95	39.47	71.84	74.29	92.72	80.23	83.22	74.98
Preferred-provider health plan (not BCBS)	200.57	58.38	149.89	179.55	234.79	327.87	337.77	310.47
Blue Cross, Blue Shield	**405.89**	**207.55**	**410.47**	**342.85**	**447.40**	**539.90**	**525.50**	**565.23**
Traditional fee-for-service health plan	69.32	32.16	71.44	53.71	72.10	97.85	88.49	114.29
Preferred-provider health plan	169.58	79.30	158.30	140.41	190.67	242.97	244.51	240.28
Health maintenance organization	113.61	49.92	112.10	97.48	143.86	150.71	147.28	156.73
Commercial Medicare supplement	46.84	42.23	61.77	46.93	31.21	40.04	37.17	45.09
Other BCBS health insurance	6.54	3.94	6.86	4.31	9.56	8.33	8.05	8.83
Health maintenance plans (HMOs)	**272.11**	**145.68**	**237.53**	**246.16**	**363.06**	**361.02**	**350.44**	**379.60**
Medicare payments	**246.20**	**404.93**	**312.00**	**209.67**	**145.72**	**162.58**	**149.70**	**185.22**
Commercial Medicare supplements/ other health insurance	**134.99**	**138.16**	**125.84**	**130.49**	**121.34**	**150.10**	**138.46**	**170.57**
Commercial Medicare supplement (not BCBS)	92.90	120.14	97.55	87.05	76.88	84.15	81.17	89.40
Other health insurance (not BCBS)	42.10	18.02	28.29	43.44	44.46	65.95	57.29	81.17
MEDICAL SERVICES	**648.37**	**382.58**	**541.98**	**600.48**	**707.83**	**905.64**	**821.26**	**1,053.97**
Physician's services	146.58	76.71	134.58	117.30	157.63	213.47	211.05	217.73
Dental services	240.60	94.58	185.60	235.77	285.22	357.96	308.78	444.41
Eye care services	38.89	13.94	30.30	36.73	41.26	60.95	61.89	59.30
Service by professionals other than physician	39.54	19.26	26.01	38.41	30.26	66.93	60.61	78.04
Lab tests, X-rays	26.75	13.33	18.82	26.41	37.84	37.90	35.36	42.36
Hospital room	40.01	31.94	36.03	26.30	52.64	54.53	55.51	52.82
Hospital services other than room	51.20	46.32	51.17	32.99	67.22	62.72	56.30	73.99
Care in convalescent or nursing home	41.33	68.42	37.23	59.68	21.39	23.44	7.82	50.90
Other medical services	23.46	18.09	22.24	26.87	14.36	27.74	23.94	34.42
DRUGS	**480.29**	**432.81**	**507.03**	**439.64**	**466.71**	**515.15**	**484.84**	**571.47**
Nonprescription drugs	80.31	75.37	73.28	69.74	90.46	94.13	90.40	101.26
Nonprescription vitamins	50.57	24.10	36.97	49.16	52.01	77.87	61.63	108.89
Prescription drugs	349.41	333.34	396.78	320.74	324.23	343.15	332.80	361.32
MEDICAL SUPPLIES	**113.83**	**64.19**	**93.14**	**102.29**	**123.53**	**165.07**	**140.00**	**210.36**
Eyeglasses and contact lenses	47.56	23.73	35.67	38.87	57.60	74.77	64.73	92.42
Hearing aids	15.21	8.05	10.41	14.00	18.26	23.44	18.80	31.60
Topicals and dressings	31.53	21.43	27.83	29.31	34.73	40.89	32.92	56.11
Medical equipment for general use	6.75	4.17	10.41	3.99	3.83	7.72	6.60	9.68
Supportive, convalescent medical equipment	7.16	3.14	4.18	6.79	5.49	12.93	13.75	11.49
Rental of medical equipment	1.88	1.22	2.20	2.03	1.38	1.96	1.26	3.19
Rental of supportive, convalescent medical equipment	3.74	2.44	2.45	7.31	2.24	3.37	1.95	5.87

Note: Subcategories may not add to total because some are not shown.
Source: Bureau of Labor Statistics, unpublished tables from the 2004 Consumer Expenditure Survey

Table 7.26 Health Care: Indexed spending by education, 2004

(indexed average annual out-of-pocket spending of consumer units (CU) on health care, by education of consumer unit reference person, 2004; index definition: an index of 100 is the average for all consumer units; an index of 132 means that spending by consumer units in that group is 32 percent above the average for all consumer units; an index of 68 indicates spending that is 32 percent below the average for all consumer units)

	total consumer units	less than high school graduate	high school graduate	some college	associate's degree	college graduate total	bachelor's degree	master's, professional, doctorate
Average spending of CU, total	$43,395	$25,421	$35,439	$40,878	$48,177	$60,712	$56,728	$67,801
Average spending of CU, index	100	59	82	94	111	140	131	156
Health care, spending index	100	73	95	90	105	125	118	137
HEALTH INSURANCE	**100**	**75**	**98**	**89**	**106**	**122**	**119**	**127**
Commercial health insurance	**100**	**36**	**81**	**93**	**120**	**150**	**154**	**141**
Traditional fee-for-service health plan (not BCBS)	100	55	100	103	129	112	116	104
Preferred-provider health plan (not BCBS)	100	29	75	90	117	163	168	155
Blue Cross, Blue Shield	**100**	**51**	**101**	**84**	**110**	**133**	**129**	**139**
Traditional fee-for-service health plan	100	46	103	77	104	141	128	165
Preferred-provider health plan	100	47	93	83	112	143	144	142
Health maintenance organization	100	44	99	86	127	133	130	138
Commercial Medicare supplement	100	90	132	100	67	85	79	96
Other BCBS health insurance	100	60	105	66	146	127	123	135
Health maintenance plans (HMOs)	**100**	**54**	**87**	**90**	**133**	**133**	**129**	**140**
Medicare payments	**100**	**164**	**127**	**85**	**59**	**66**	**61**	**75**
Commercial Medicare supplements/ other health insurance	**100**	**102**	**93**	**97**	**90**	**111**	**103**	**126**
Commercial Medicare supplement (not BCBS)	100	129	105	94	83	91	87	96
Other health insurance (not BCBS)	100	43	67	103	106	157	136	193
MEDICAL SERVICES	**100**	**59**	**84**	**93**	**109**	**140**	**127**	**163**
Physician's services	100	52	92	80	108	146	144	149
Dental services	100	39	77	98	119	149	128	185
Eye care services	100	36	78	94	106	157	159	152
Service by professionals other than physician	100	49	66	97	77	169	153	197
Lab tests, X-rays	100	50	70	99	141	142	132	158
Hospital room	100	80	90	66	132	136	139	132
Hospital services other than room	100	90	100	64	131	123	110	145
Care in convalescent or nursing home	100	166	90	144	52	57	19	123
Other medical services	100	77	95	115	61	118	102	147
DRUGS	**100**	**90**	**106**	**92**	**97**	**107**	**101**	**119**
Nonprescription drugs	100	94	91	87	113	117	113	126
Nonprescription vitamins	100	48	73	97	103	154	122	215
Prescription drugs	100	95	114	92	93	98	95	103
MEDICAL SUPPLIES	**100**	**56**	**82**	**90**	**109**	**145**	**123**	**185**
Eyeglasses and contact lenses	100	50	75	82	121	157	136	194
Hearing aids	100	53	68	92	120	154	124	208
Topicals and dressings	100	68	88	93	110	130	104	178
Medical equipment for general use	100	62	154	59	57	114	98	143
Supportive, convalescent medical equipment	100	44	58	95	77	181	192	160
Rental of medical equipment	100	65	117	108	73	104	67	170
Rental of supportive, convalescent medical equipment	100	65	66	195	60	90	52	157

Source: Calculations by New Strategist based on the 2004 Consumer Expenditure Survey

Table 7.27 Health Care: Total spending by education, 2004

(total annual out-of-pocket spending on health care, by consumer unit (CU) educational attainment groups, 2004; consumer units and dollars in thousands)

	total consumer units	less than high school graduate	high school graduate	some college	associate's degree	college graduate total	bachelor's degree	master's, professional, doctorate
Number of consumer units	116,282	16,829	31,005	25,317	10,678	32,452	20,684	11,768
Total spending of all CUs	$5,046,042,273	$427,813,038	$1,098,772,243	$1,034,900,225	$514,437,850	$1,970,234,911	$1,173,370,432	$797,886,640
Health care, total spending	**299,334,287**	**31,533,507**	**75,953,569**	**58,872,405**	**28,863,809**	**104,092,386**	**62,696,927**	**41,445,366**
HEALTH INSURANCE	**154,853,902**	**16,730,887**	**40,541,208**	**29,950,264**	**15,002,910**	**52,627,733**	**32,786,002**	**19,841,672**
Commercial health insurance	**31,689,171**	**1,646,718**	**6,874,739**	**6,426,720**	**3,497,152**	**13,243,986**	**8,707,757**	**4,535,976**
Traditional fee-for-service health plan (not BCBS)	8,366,490	664,241	2,227,399	1,880,800	990,064	2,603,624	1,721,322	882,365
Preferred-provider health plan (not BCBS)	23,322,681	982,477	4,647,339	4,545,667	2,507,088	10,640,037	6,986,435	3,653,611
Blue Cross, Blue Shield	**47,197,701**	**3,492,859**	**12,726,622**	**8,679,933**	**4,777,337**	**17,520,835**	**10,869,442**	**6,651,627**
Traditional fee-for-service health plan	8,060,668	541,221	2,214,997	1,359,776	769,884	3,175,428	1,830,327	1,344,965
Preferred-provider health plan	19,719,102	1,334,540	4,908,092	3,554,760	2,035,974	7,884,862	5,057,445	2,827,615
Health maintenance organization	13,210,798	840,104	3,475,661	2,467,901	1,536,137	4,890,841	3,046,340	1,844,399
Commercial Medicare supplement	5,446,649	710,689	1,915,179	1,188,127	333,260	1,299,378	768,824	530,619
Other BCBS health insurance	760,484	66,306	212,694	109,116	102,082	270,325	166,506	103,911
Health maintenance plans (HMOs)	**31,641,495**	**2,451,649**	**7,364,618**	**6,232,033**	**3,876,755**	**11,715,821**	**7,248,501**	**4,467,133**
Medicare payments	**28,628,628**	**6,814,567**	**9,673,560**	**5,308,215**	**1,555,998**	**5,276,046**	**3,096,395**	**2,179,669**
Commercial Medicare supplements/ other health insurance	**15,696,907**	**2,325,095**	**3,901,669**	**3,303,615**	**1,295,669**	**4,871,045**	**2,863,907**	**2,007,268**
Commercial Medicare supplement (not BCBS)	10,802,598	2,021,836	3,024,538	2,203,845	820,925	2,730,836	1,678,920	1,052,059
Other health insurance (not BCBS)	4,895,472	303,259	877,131	1,099,770	474,744	2,140,209	1,184,986	955,209
MEDICAL SERVICES	**75,393,760**	**6,438,439**	**16,804,090**	**15,202,352**	**7,558,209**	**29,389,829**	**16,986,942**	**12,403,119**
Physician's services	17,044,616	1,290,953	4,172,653	2,969,684	1,683,173	6,927,528	4,365,358	2,562,247
Dental services	27,977,449	1,591,687	5,754,528	5,968,989	3,045,579	11,616,518	6,386,806	5,229,817
Eye care services	4,522,207	234,596	939,452	929,893	440,574	1,977,949	1,280,133	697,842
Service by professionals other than physician	4,597,790	324,127	806,440	972,426	323,116	2,172,012	1,253,657	918,375
Lab tests, X-rays	3,110,544	224,331	583,514	668,622	404,056	1,229,931	731,386	498,492
Hospital room	4,652,443	537,518	1,117,110	665,837	562,090	1,769,608	1,148,169	621,586
Hospital services other than room	5,953,638	779,519	1,586,526	835,208	717,775	2,035,389	1,164,509	870,714
Care in convalescent or nursing home	4,805,935	1,151,440	1,154,316	1,510,919	228,402	760,675	161,749	598,991
Other medical services	2,727,976	304,437	689,551	680,268	153,336	900,218	495,175	405,055
DRUGS	**55,849,082**	**7,283,759**	**15,720,465**	**11,130,366**	**4,983,529**	**16,717,648**	**10,028,431**	**6,725,059**
Nonprescription drugs	9,338,607	1,268,402	2,272,046	1,765,608	965,932	3,054,707	1,869,834	1,191,628
Nonprescription vitamins	5,880,381	405,579	1,146,255	1,244,584	555,363	2,527,037	1,274,755	1,281,418
Prescription drugs	40,630,094	5,609,779	12,302,164	8,120,175	3,462,128	11,135,904	6,883,635	4,252,014
MEDICAL SUPPLIES	**13,236,380**	**1,080,254**	**2,887,806**	**2,589,676**	**1,319,053**	**5,356,852**	**2,895,760**	**2,475,516**
Eyeglasses and contact lenses	5,530,372	399,352	1,105,948	984,072	615,053	2,426,436	1,338,875	1,087,599
Hearing aids	1,768,649	135,473	322,762	354,438	194,980	760,675	388,859	371,869
Topicals and dressings	3,666,371	360,645	862,869	742,041	370,847	1,326,962	680,917	660,302
Medical equipment for general use	784,904	70,177	322,762	101,015	40,897	250,529	136,514	113,914
Supportive, convalescent medical equipment	832,579	52,843	129,601	171,902	58,622	419,604	284,405	135,214
Rental of medical equipment	218,610	20,531	68,211	51,394	14,736	63,606	26,062	37,540
Rental of supportive, convalescent medical equipment	434,895	41,063	75,962	185,067	23,919	109,363	40,334	69,078

Note: Numbers may not add to total because of rounding and missing subcategories.
Source: Calculations by New Strategist based on the 2004 Consumer Expenditure Survey

Table 7.28 Health Care: Market shares by education, 2004

(percentage of total annual out-of-pocket spending on health care accounted for by consumer unit educational attainment groups, 2004)

	total consumer units	less than high school graduate	high school graduate	some college	associate's degree	college graduate total	college graduate bachelor's degree	college graduate master's, professional, doctorate
Share of total consumer units	100.0%	14.5%	26.7%	21.8%	9.2%	27.9%	17.8%	10.1%
Share of total before-tax income	100.0	7.7	20.7	18.7	9.9	43.0	24.7	18.3
Share of total spending	100.0	8.5	21.8	20.5	10.2	39.0	23.3	15.8
Share of health care spending	100.0	10.5	25.4	19.7	9.6	34.8	20.9	13.8
HEALTH INSURANCE	100.0	10.8	26.2	19.3	9.7	34.0	21.2	12.8
Commercial health insurance	100.0	5.2	21.7	20.3	11.0	41.8	27.5	14.3
Traditional fee-for-service health plan (not BCBS)	100.0	7.9	26.6	22.5	11.8	31.1	20.6	10.5
Preferred-provider health plan (not BCBS)	100.0	4.2	19.9	19.5	10.7	45.6	30.0	15.7
Blue Cross, Blue Shield	100.0	7.4	27.0	18.4	10.1	37.1	23.0	14.1
Traditional fee-for-service health plan	100.0	6.7	27.5	16.9	9.6	39.4	22.7	16.7
Preferred-provider health plan	100.0	6.8	24.9	18.0	10.3	40.0	25.6	14.3
Health maintenance organization	100.0	6.4	26.3	18.7	11.6	37.0	23.1	14.0
Commercial Medicare supplement	100.0	13.0	35.2	21.8	6.1	23.9	14.1	9.7
Other BCBS health insurance	100.0	8.7	28.0	14.3	13.4	35.5	21.9	13.7
Health maintenance plans (HMOs)	100.0	7.7	23.3	19.7	12.3	37.0	22.9	14.1
Medicare payments	100.0	23.8	33.8	18.5	5.4	18.4	10.8	7.6
Commercial Medicare supplements/ other health insurance	100.0	14.8	24.9	21.0	8.3	31.0	18.2	12.8
Commercial Medicare supplement (not BCBS)	100.0	18.7	28.0	20.4	7.6	25.3	15.5	9.7
Other health insurance (not BCBS)	100.0	6.2	17.9	22.5	9.7	43.7	24.2	19.5
MEDICAL SERVICES	100.0	8.5	22.3	20.2	10.0	39.0	22.5	16.5
Physician's services	100.0	7.6	24.5	17.4	9.9	40.6	25.6	15.0
Dental services	100.0	5.7	20.6	21.3	10.9	41.5	22.8	18.7
Eye care services	100.0	5.2	20.8	20.6	9.7	43.7	28.3	15.4
Service by professionals other than physician	100.0	7.0	17.5	21.1	7.0	47.2	27.3	20.0
Lab tests, X-rays	100.0	7.2	18.8	21.5	13.0	39.5	23.5	16.0
Hospital room	100.0	11.6	24.0	14.3	12.1	38.0	24.7	13.4
Hospital services other than room	100.0	13.1	26.6	14.0	12.1	34.2	19.6	14.6
Care in convalescent or nursing home	100.0	24.0	24.0	31.4	4.8	15.8	3.4	12.5
Other medical services	100.0	11.2	25.3	24.9	5.6	33.0	18.2	14.8
DRUGS	100.0	13.0	28.1	19.9	8.9	29.9	18.0	12.0
Nonprescription drugs	100.0	13.6	24.3	18.9	10.3	32.7	20.0	12.8
Nonprescription vitamins	100.0	6.9	19.5	21.2	9.4	43.0	21.7	21.8
Prescription drugs	100.0	13.8	30.3	20.0	8.5	27.4	16.9	10.5
MEDICAL SUPPLIES	100.0	8.2	21.8	19.6	10.0	40.5	21.9	18.7
Eyeglasses and contact lenses	100.0	7.2	20.0	17.8	11.1	43.9	24.2	19.7
Hearing aids	100.0	7.7	18.2	20.0	11.0	43.0	22.0	21.0
Topicals and dressings	100.0	9.8	23.5	20.2	10.1	36.2	18.6	18.0
Medical equipment for general use	100.0	8.9	41.1	12.9	5.2	31.9	17.4	14.5
Supportive, convalescent medical equipment	100.0	6.3	15.6	20.6	7.0	50.4	34.2	16.2
Rental of medical equipment	100.0	9.4	31.2	23.5	6.7	29.1	11.9	17.2
Rental of supportive, convalescent medical equipment	100.0	9.4	17.5	42.6	5.5	25.1	9.3	15.9

Note: Numbers may not add to total because of rounding.
Source: Calculations by New Strategist based on the 2004 Consumer Expenditure Survey

Chapter 8. Spending on Housing: Household Operations, 2004

Americans are spending big on housing as homeownership rates reach record highs. In 2004, housing costs—including shelter, utilities, and all household operations (household services, housekeeping supplies, furniture, and equipment)—absorbed 32.1 percent of average household expenditures. That figure was slightly below the 32.4 percent of 2000 as lower mortgage interest rates cut some housing costs. Spending on household furnishings and equipment fell 3 percent between 2000 and 2004, after adjusting for inflation. But spending on housekeeping supplies rose 12 percent during those years, and spending on household services remained almost unchanged.

Overall housing costs are highest for householders aged 35 to 44, an average of $16,794 in 2004. The 35-to-44 age group spends the most on household services, $992 in 2004, because of the high cost of day care. Householders spanning the ages from 35 to 64 spend almost the same amount on home furnishings and equipment—more than $1,900 in 2004. Spending on housekeeping supplies peaks among householders aged 45 to 54 at $756.

Households with incomes of $100,000 or more spent an enormous $28,140 on housing in 2004, more than twice the $13,918 spent by the average household. The most affluent households spend far more than average on just about every category of household operations. They account for 53 percent of spending on housekeeping services and half of spending on closet and storage items.

Among household types, married couples with children under age 6 spend the most on housing, more than $21,000 in 2004. Behind this figure is the high cost of housing for recent homebuyers—many married couples with children under age 6 are new homeowners. In addition, these householders spend the most on day care. Married couples with preschoolers spent an average of $1,585 on day care centers in 2004.

Asian households spend 25 percent more than the average household on housing, while the spending of black and Hispanic households is below average. Asian households spend fully double the average on day care centers, and they spend 52 percent more on nonbusiness computer software and accessories. Hispanics spend 34 percent more than average on laundry and cleaning supplies. Blacks spend 65 percent more than average on home security system service fees.

Households in the West spend the most on housing, $15,557 in 2004, because of the high cost of housing in California. Spending on housing is lowest in the South, at $12,250. Southern households spend the most on termite and pest control services, however. Households in the West spend the most on computer hardware and software. Midwesterners are the biggest spenders on water softening services.

Not surprisingly, college graduates (who dominate the nation's affluent households) spend the most on housing, an average of $19,676 in 2004. They spend far more than the average household on almost every category of household operations. They spend more than twice the average on housekeeping services. They spend less than average on rental of appliances and furniture and on sewing machines.

Table 8.1 Housing: Household Operations: Average spending by age, 2004

(average annual spending of consumer units (CU) on household services, supplies, furnishings, and equipment, by age of consumer unit reference person, 2004)

	total consumer units	under 25	25 to 34	35 to 44	45 to 54	55 to 64	65 to 74	75+
Number of consumer units (in 000s)	116,282	8,817	19,439	24,070	23,712	17,479	11,230	11,536
Average number of persons per CU	2.5	1.9	2.9	3.2	2.7	2.1	1.9	1.5
Average before-tax income of CU	$54,453.00	$22,840.00	$52,484.00	$65,515.00	$70,434.00	$61,031.00	$42,137.00	$28,028.00
Average spending of CU, total	43,394.87	24,534.56	42,700.54	50,401.62	52,764.36	47,298.58	36,511.98	25,763.32
Housing, average spending	**13,918.48**	**7,648.84**	**14,378.71**	**16,793.61**	**16,163.91**	**14,339.42**	**11,151.62**	**9,381.21**
HOUSEHOLD SERVICES	**752.83**	**269.81**	**915.14**	**992.04**	**692.84**	**644.90**	**521.99**	**861.08**
Personal services	**299.71**	**159.35**	**584.01**	**567.86**	**131.11**	**42.52**	**26.76**	**370.35**
Babysitting and child care in own home	37.09	6.59	80.90	93.08	18.13	0.12	0.07	0.73
Babysitting and child care in someone else's home	26.12	35.88	64.91	46.41	12.69	0.71	2.12	0.42
Care for elderly, invalids, handicapped, etc.	34.96	–	0.51	4.77	19.43	8.12	6.15	283.33
Day care centers, nurseries, and preschools	193.51	116.88	437.69	423.59	80.78	32.69	18.41	6.39
Other household services	**453.12**	**110.47**	**331.13**	**424.18**	**561.73**	**602.38**	**495.23**	**490.73**
Housekeeping services	88.85	2.79	43.74	74.73	101.76	134.04	107.87	146.60
Gardening, lawn care service	95.08	4.00	43.24	68.25	108.36	127.59	146.68	181.26
Water-softening service	3.06	0.11	2.00	3.16	3.92	3.49	3.39	4.16
Nonclothing laundry and dry cleaning, sent out	0.94	0.85	0.51	0.94	0.92	1.48	1.18	0.76
Nonclothing laundry and dry cleaning, coin-operated	3.71	5.46	6.55	3.77	2.83	3.15	1.82	1.99
Termite and pest control services	12.04	1.83	6.91	9.92	16.41	17.36	18.61	9.51
Home security system service fee	15.57	1.88	13.17	19.06	18.57	17.98	18.81	9.89
Other home services	23.03	1.93	13.64	14.19	29.49	33.97	24.15	42.48
Termite and pest control products	1.53	0.46	0.54	1.19	2.29	2.38	2.25	1.20
Moving, storage, and freight express	33.91	14.50	37.90	27.30	50.26	49.05	23.21	9.67
Appliance repair, including at service center	14.53	1.03	8.21	12.85	20.51	21.61	17.75	12.84
Reupholstering and furniture repair	7.35	0.68	1.58	4.65	6.15	22.71	9.05	5.36
Repairs and rentals of lawn and garden equipment, hand and power tools, etc.	7.29	0.50	3.27	6.02	12.32	8.39	11.06	6.24
Appliance rental	1.75	1.84	1.65	2.12	2.28	1.10	0.19	2.43
Repair of computer systems for nonbusiness use	4.03	2.10	1.82	4.00	6.21	5.78	2.92	3.20
Computer information services	139.46	69.60	145.35	171.48	178.25	152.11	105.73	50.05
HOUSEKEEPING SUPPLIES	**594.47**	**253.11**	**499.34**	**677.31**	**755.81**	**656.82**	**569.07**	**445.46**
Laundry and cleaning supplies	**148.56**	**75.27**	**142.46**	**170.16**	**188.04**	**157.68**	**122.21**	**100.15**
Soaps and detergents	85.44	47.02	86.85	101.58	105.53	89.13	65.10	50.65
Other laundry cleaning products	63.13	28.25	55.61	68.58	82.51	68.55	57.11	49.50
Other household products	**290.41**	**113.64**	**222.65**	**338.61**	**385.10**	**318.39**	**284.97**	**209.77**
Cleansing and toilet tissue, paper towels, and napkins	85.84	49.26	71.11	89.36	99.59	101.66	84.36	82.03
Miscellaneous household products	121.13	51.14	103.47	168.72	154.20	119.29	85.69	73.22
Lawn and garden supplies	83.44	13.25	48.07	80.53	131.30	97.44	114.91	54.52
Postage and stationery	**155.50**	**64.20**	**134.23**	**168.53**	**182.67**	**180.74**	**161.89**	**135.54**
Stationery, stationery supplies, giftwrap	74.86	43.40	69.42	92.12	87.12	72.92	74.90	48.63
Postage	74.12	18.26	49.11	72.01	87.68	104.08	82.45	85.48
Delivery services	6.52	2.53	15.70	4.41	7.86	3.74	4.53	1.43
HOUSEHOLD FURNISHINGS AND EQUIPMENT	**1,646.10**	**812.35**	**1,547.91**	**1,959.80**	**1,988.91**	**1,932.48**	**1,395.02**	**901.19**
Household textiles	**157.66**	**55.47**	**104.09**	**186.93**	**181.57**	**203.01**	**121.93**	**187.51**
Bathroom linens	21.26	10.49	20.67	21.55	21.38	20.06	35.88	16.86
Bedroom linens	85.72	24.18	53.38	109.51	96.99	115.70	41.74	116.65
Kitchen and dining room linens	9.84	4.79	6.44	13.29	12.38	14.05	4.20	6.22
Curtains and draperies	19.22	8.43	12.78	21.37	24.79	23.98	14.29	20.00
Slipcovers and decorative pillows	9.12	3.79	4.95	10.63	11.62	6.83	4.77	20.55
Sewing materials for household items	11.20	3.33	4.88	9.10	12.82	20.56	19.58	6.55
Other linens	1.31	0.46	0.99	1.47	1.59	1.83	1.46	0.68
Furniture	**416.97**	**261.30**	**464.27**	**546.21**	**414.54**	**503.62**	**322.15**	**152.56**
Mattresses and springs	53.56	35.76	47.52	62.23	61.02	73.42	41.51	25.50
Other bedroom furniture	81.32	49.53	108.84	114.18	80.04	80.53	51.03	24.00
Sofas	94.74	87.22	105.89	132.31	90.86	94.96	70.56	34.47
Living room chairs	41.65	21.11	35.99	44.34	47.76	61.85	38.66	21.01
Living room tables	14.77	10.77	18.24	16.08	14.17	21.36	10.63	4.55
Kitchen and dining room furniture	41.26	15.48	51.66	52.04	39.98	49.84	36.01	15.72

	total consumer units	under 25	25 to 34	35 to 44	45 to 54	55 to 64	65 to 74	75+
Infants' furniture	$8.44	$11.16	$14.15	$14.06	$4.14	$4.58	$6.22	$1.83
Outdoor furniture	16.18	2.15	11.80	25.57	13.09	26.10	14.41	7.79
Wall units, cabinets, and other furniture	65.05	28.13	70.18	85.41	63.49	90.99	53.13	17.69
Floor coverings	**51.98**	**7.30**	**35.63**	**51.31**	**64.91**	**87.01**	**61.30**	**26.36**
Wall-to-wall carpeting	27.98	0.78	20.08	30.12	33.12	41.95	41.15	13.01
Floor coverings, nonpermanent	24.00	6.52	15.55	21.19	31.79	45.06	20.15	13.35
Major appliances	**203.94**	**71.93**	**183.82**	**237.08**	**237.37**	**240.00**	**208.27**	**142.93**
Dishwashers (built-in), garbage disposals, range hoods	14.34	2.60	10.98	19.83	13.95	18.05	21.78	5.53
Refrigerators and freezers	51.27	16.50	50.11	53.84	53.69	67.53	65.24	31.18
Washing machines	30.65	8.94	32.08	34.41	33.26	39.42	28.96	19.96
Clothes dryers	22.03	5.79	22.25	24.97	28.16	25.36	17.90	14.34
Cooking stoves, ovens	32.42	6.97	27.67	34.39	44.79	36.49	37.86	18.89
Microwave ovens	8.43	7.22	6.23	7.68	11.65	8.51	11.10	5.31
Portable dishwasher	1.22	0.33	2.41	1.51	1.01	0.13	1.87	0.78
Window air conditioners	4.36	2.85	6.75	3.76	5.84	4.28	3.32	0.81
Electric floor-cleaning equipment	27.71	7.71	22.36	51.57	35.91	9.91	13.58	25.68
Sewing machines	3.59	0.60	1.04	1.70	6.36	6.81	6.66	0.60
Miscellaneous household appliances	7.91	12.44	1.94	3.42	2.74	23.52	–	19.84
Small appliances and miscellaneous housewares	**104.66**	**61.75**	**103.54**	**96.89**	**124.84**	**130.48**	**108.79**	**71.26**
Housewares	82.56	46.54	81.72	73.02	100.89	103.85	90.03	54.51
Plastic dinnerware	1.82	2.56	2.77	1.94	2.12	1.50	0.66	0.40
China and other dinnerware	13.47	3.71	12.47	10.29	15.56	22.37	17.03	8.23
Flatware	4.02	1.54	2.96	4.41	5.84	4.77	4.10	1.96
Glassware	20.88	10.25	16.99	17.14	25.19	29.62	32.20	10.17
Silver serving pieces	0.30	0.06	0.18	0.31	0.44	0.52	0.25	0.07
Other serving pieces	1.76	1.05	1.15	1.91	2.62	2.30	1.63	0.60
Nonelectric cookware	18.10	11.77	23.20	15.41	19.42	18.45	16.73	18.19
Tableware, nonelectric kitchenware	22.20	15.60	22.00	21.61	29.68	24.32	17.42	14.89
Small appliances	22.10	15.21	21.81	23.87	23.96	26.63	18.76	16.76
Small electric kitchen appliances	17.27	13.02	18.24	16.86	18.43	20.83	16.92	12.31
Portable heating and cooling equipment	4.83	2.19	3.57	7.01	5.52	5.80	1.84	4.44
Miscellaneous household equipment	**710.89**	**354.59**	**656.57**	**841.37**	**965.67**	**768.36**	**572.59**	**320.56**
Window coverings	23.47	3.76	23.59	21.21	20.58	40.62	17.05	29.19
Infants' equipment	7.86	9.64	18.78	13.56	1.95	2.44	2.97	–
Laundry and cleaning equipment	15.72	9.79	12.87	16.72	19.16	18.23	16.53	11.32
Outdoor equipment	35.99	–	21.15	34.30	86.34	33.32	19.09	10.31
Clocks	7.64	7.22	4.60	7.10	8.80	13.63	7.28	3.17
Lamps and lighting fixtures	16.40	7.97	12.43	18.14	13.24	35.54	14.64	5.09
Other household decorative items	158.10	58.85	131.87	223.34	205.23	189.38	95.86	55.89
Telephones and accessories	26.83	10.51	10.71	24.98	58.26	31.44	12.68	13.86
Lawn and garden equipment	48.79	8.13	51.24	45.81	53.03	47.99	70.39	53.38
Power tools	33.44	1.21	39.90	38.91	42.07	17.07	54.64	21.13
Office furniture for home use	11.37	5.26	10.94	17.35	14.54	12.29	6.33	1.22
Hand tools	6.11	3.05	7.16	5.26	9.41	8.02	3.14	1.67
Indoor plants and fresh flowers	41.52	13.92	37.04	39.58	55.93	52.19	45.61	24.46
Closet and storage items	17.83	7.85	11.89	33.03	15.95	24.33	9.58	5.21
Rental of furniture	2.22	7.21	4.07	2.34	1.78	0.41	0.39	0.45
Luggage	6.63	5.64	4.02	7.04	7.96	12.03	4.95	1.62
Computers and computer hardware, nonbusiness use	134.57	134.64	134.35	158.03	189.90	130.88	73.63	37.06
Computer software and accessories, nonbusiness use	19.06	12.05	18.84	22.64	30.73	17.95	9.81	4.00
Telephone answering devices	0.62	0.17	0.59	0.68	0.86	0.79	0.52	0.26
Calculators	1.44	1.96	0.96	2.08	2.50	0.72	0.75	0.08
Business equipment for home use	0.94	0.27	0.80	1.12	0.88	1.36	1.41	0.36
Other hardware	39.63	7.43	33.91	42.58	74.52	21.61	55.57	6.79
Smoke alarms	1.03	0.43	1.22	0.90	1.22	1.22	1.28	0.49
Other household appliances	12.53	3.27	10.64	12.81	13.81	16.95	10.49	14.81
Miscellaneous household equipment and parts	41.18	34.34	52.98	51.86	37.02	37.92	37.99	18.74

Note: Subcategories may not add to total because some are not shown. "–" means sample is too small to make a reliable estimate.
Source: Bureau of Labor Statistics, unpublished tables from the 2004 Consumer Expenditure Survey

Table 8.2 Housing: Household Operations: Indexed spending by age, 2004

(indexed average annual spending of consumer units (CU) on household services, supplies, furnishings, and equipment, by age of consumer unit reference person, 2004; index definition: an index of 100 is the average for all consumer units; an index of 132 means that spending by consumer units in that group is 32 percent above the average for all consumer units; an index of 68 indicates spending that is 32 percent below the average for all consumer units)

	total consumer units	under 25	25 to 34	35 to 44	45 to 54	55 to 64	65 to 74	75+
Average spending of CU, total	$43,395	$24,535	$42,701	$50,402	$52,764	$47,299	$36,512	$25,763
Average spending of CU, index	100	57	98	116	122	109	84	59
Housing, spending index	100	55	103	121	116	103	80	67
HOUSEHOLD SERVICES	100	36	122	132	92	86	69	114
Personal services	100	53	195	189	44	14	9	124
Babysitting and child care in own home	100	18	218	251	49	0	0	2
Babysitting and child care in someone else's home	100	137	249	178	49	3	8	2
Care for elderly, invalids, handicapped, etc.	100	–	1	14	56	23	18	810
Day care centers, nurseries, and preschools	100	60	226	219	42	17	10	3
Other household services	100	24	73	94	124	133	109	108
Housekeeping services	100	3	49	84	115	151	121	165
Gardening, lawn care service	100	4	45	72	114	134	154	191
Water-softening service	100	4	65	103	128	114	111	136
Nonclothing laundry and dry cleaning, sent out	100	90	54	100	98	157	126	81
Nonclothing laundry and dry cleaning, coin-operated	100	147	177	102	76	85	49	54
Termite and pest control services	100	15	57	82	136	144	155	79
Home security system service fee	100	12	85	122	119	115	121	64
Other home services	100	8	59	62	128	148	105	184
Termite and pest control products	100	30	35	78	150	156	147	78
Moving, storage, and freight express	100	43	112	81	148	145	68	29
Appliance repair, including at service center	100	7	57	88	141	149	122	88
Reupholstering and furniture repair	100	9	21	63	84	309	123	73
Repairs and rentals of lawn and garden equipment, hand and power tools, etc.	100	7	45	83	169	115	152	86
Appliance rental	100	105	94	121	130	63	11	139
Repair of computer systems for nonbusiness use	100	52	45	99	154	143	72	79
Computer information services	100	50	104	123	128	109	76	36
HOUSEKEEPING SUPPLIES	100	43	84	114	127	110	96	75
Laundry and cleaning supplies	100	51	96	115	127	106	82	67
Soaps and detergents	100	55	102	119	124	104	76	59
Other laundry cleaning products	100	45	88	109	131	109	90	78
Other household products	100	39	77	117	133	110	98	72
Cleansing and toilet tissue, paper towels, and napkins	100	57	83	104	116	118	98	96
Miscellaneous household products	100	42	85	139	127	98	71	60
Lawn and garden supplies	100	16	58	97	157	117	138	65
Postage and stationery	100	41	86	108	117	116	104	87
Stationery, stationery supplies, giftwrap	100	58	93	123	116	97	100	65
Postage	100	25	66	97	118	140	111	115
Delivery services	100	39	241	68	121	57	69	22
HOUSEHOLD FURNISHINGS AND EQUIPMENT	100	49	94	119	121	117	85	55
Household textiles	100	35	66	119	115	129	77	119
Bathroom linens	100	49	97	101	101	94	169	79
Bedroom linens	100	28	62	128	113	135	49	136
Kitchen and dining room linens	100	49	65	135	126	143	43	63
Curtains and draperies	100	44	66	111	129	125	74	104
Slipcovers and decorative pillows	100	42	54	117	127	75	52	225
Sewing materials for household items	100	30	44	81	114	184	175	58
Other linens	100	35	76	112	121	140	111	52
Furniture	100	63	111	131	99	121	77	37
Mattresses and springs	100	67	89	116	114	137	78	48
Other bedroom furniture	100	61	134	140	98	99	63	30
Sofas	100	92	112	140	96	100	74	36
Living room chairs	100	51	86	106	115	148	93	50
Living room tables	100	73	123	109	96	145	72	31
Kitchen and dining room furniture	100	38	125	126	97	121	87	38

	total consumer units	under 25	25 to 34	35 to 44	45 to 54	55 to 64	65 to 74	75+
Infants' furniture	100	132	168	167	49	54	74	22
Outdoor furniture	100	13	73	158	81	161	89	48
Wall units, cabinets, and other furniture	100	43	108	131	98	140	82	27
Floor coverings	**100**	**14**	**69**	**99**	**125**	**167**	**118**	**51**
Wall-to-wall carpeting	100	3	72	108	118	150	147	46
Floor coverings, nonpermanent	100	27	65	88	132	188	84	56
Major appliances	**100**	**35**	**90**	**116**	**116**	**118**	**102**	**70**
Dishwashers (built-in), garbage disposals, range hoods	100	18	77	138	97	126	152	39
Refrigerators and freezers	100	32	98	105	105	132	127	61
Washing machines	100	29	105	112	109	129	94	65
Clothes dryers	100	26	101	113	128	115	81	65
Cooking stoves, ovens	100	21	85	106	138	113	117	58
Microwave ovens	100	86	74	91	138	101	132	63
Portable dishwasher	100	27	198	124	83	11	153	64
Window air conditioners	100	65	155	86	134	98	76	19
Electric floor-cleaning equipment	100	28	81	186	130	36	49	93
Sewing machines	100	17	29	47	177	190	186	17
Miscellaneous household appliances	100	157	25	43	35	297	–	251
Small appliances and miscellaneous housewares	**100**	**59**	**99**	**93**	**119**	**125**	**104**	**68**
Housewares	100	56	99	88	122	126	109	66
Plastic dinnerware	100	141	152	107	116	82	36	22
China and other dinnerware	100	28	93	76	116	166	126	61
Flatware	100	38	74	110	145	119	102	49
Glassware	100	49	81	82	121	142	154	49
Silver serving pieces	100	20	60	103	147	173	83	23
Other serving pieces	100	60	65	109	149	131	93	34
Nonelectric cookware	100	65	128	85	107	102	92	100
Tableware, nonelectric kitchenware	100	70	99	97	134	110	78	67
Small appliances	100	69	99	108	108	120	85	76
Small electric kitchen appliances	100	75	106	98	107	121	98	71
Portable heating and cooling equipment	100	45	74	145	114	120	38	92
Miscellaneous household equipment	**100**	**50**	**92**	**118**	**136**	**108**	**81**	**45**
Window coverings	100	16	101	90	88	173	73	124
Infants' equipment	100	123	239	173	25	31	38	–
Laundry and cleaning equipment	100	62	82	106	122	116	105	72
Outdoor equipment	100	–	59	95	240	93	53	29
Clocks	100	95	60	93	115	178	95	41
Lamps and lighting fixtures	100	49	76	111	81	217	89	31
Other household decorative items	100	37	83	141	130	120	61	35
Telephones and accessories	100	39	40	93	217	117	47	52
Lawn and garden equipment	100	17	105	94	109	98	144	109
Power tools	100	4	119	116	126	51	163	63
Office furniture for home use	100	46	96	153	128	108	56	11
Hand tools	100	50	117	86	154	131	51	27
Indoor plants and fresh flowers	100	34	89	95	135	126	110	59
Closet and storage items	100	44	67	185	89	136	54	29
Rental of furniture	100	325	183	105	80	18	18	20
Luggage	100	85	61	106	120	181	75	24
Computers and computer hardware, nonbusiness use	100	100	100	117	141	97	55	28
Computer software and accessories, nonbusiness use	100	63	99	119	161	94	51	21
Telephone answering devices	100	27	95	110	139	127	84	42
Calculators	100	136	67	144	174	50	52	6
Business equipment for home use	100	29	85	119	94	145	150	38
Other hardware	100	19	86	107	188	55	140	17
Smoke alarms	100	42	118	87	118	118	124	48
Other household appliances	100	26	85	102	110	135	84	118
Miscellaneous household equipment and parts	100	83	129	126	90	92	92	46

Note: "–" means sample is too small to make a reliable estimate.
Source: Calculations by New Strategist based on the 2004 Consumer Expenditure Survey

Table 8.3 Housing: Household Operations: Total spending by age, 2004

(total annual spending on household services, supplies, furnishings, and equipment, by consumer unit (CU) age groups, 2004; consumer units and dollars in thousands)

	total consumer units	under 25	25 to 34	35 to 44	45 to 54	55 to 64	65 to 74	75+
Number of consumer units	116,282	8,817	19,439	24,070	23,712	17,479	11,230	11,536
Total spending of all CUs	$5,046,042,273	$216,321,216	$830,055,797	$1,213,166,993	$1,251,148,504	$826,731,880	$410,029,535	$297,205,660
Housing, total spending	1,618,468,691	67,439,822	279,507,744	404,222,193	383,278,634	250,638,722	125,232,693	108,221,639
HOUSEHOLD SERVICES	87,540,578	2,378,915	17,789,406	23,878,403	16,428,622	11,272,207	5,861,948	9,933,419
Personal services	34,850,878	1,404,989	11,352,570	13,668,390	3,108,880	743,207	300,515	4,272,358
Babysitting and child care in own home	4,312,899	58,104	1,572,615	2,240,436	429,899	2,097	786	8,421
Babysitting and child care in someone else's home	3,037,286	316,354	1,261,785	1,117,089	300,905	12,410	23,808	4,845
Care for elderly, invalids, handicapped, etc.	4,065,219	–	9,914	114,814	460,724	141,929	69,065	3,268,495
Day care centers, nurseries, and preschools	22,501,730	1,030,531	8,508,256	10,195,811	1,915,455	571,389	206,744	73,715
Other household services	52,689,700	974,014	6,436,836	10,210,013	13,319,742	10,529,000	5,561,433	5,661,061
Housekeeping services	10,331,656	24,599	850,262	1,798,751	2,412,933	2,342,885	1,211,380	1,691,178
Gardening, lawn care service	11,056,093	35,268	840,542	1,642,778	2,569,432	2,230,146	1,647,216	2,091,015
Water-softening service	355,823	970	38,878	76,061	92,951	61,002	38,070	47,990
Nonclothing laundry and dry cleaning, sent out	109,305	7,494	9,914	22,626	21,815	25,869	13,251	8,767
Nonclothing laundry and dry cleaning, coin-operated	431,406	48,141	127,325	90,744	67,105	55,059	20,439	22,957
Termite and pest control services	1,400,035	16,135	134,323	238,774	389,114	303,435	208,990	109,707
Home security system service fee	1,810,511	16,576	256,012	458,774	440,332	314,272	211,236	114,091
Other home services	2,677,974	17,017	265,148	341,553	699,267	593,762	271,205	490,049
Termite and pest control products	177,911	4,056	10,497	28,643	54,300	41,600	25,268	13,843
Moving, storage, and freight express	3,943,123	127,847	736,738	657,111	1,191,765	857,345	260,648	111,553
Appliance repair, including at service center	1,689,577	9,082	159,594	309,300	486,333	377,721	199,333	148,122
Reupholstering and furniture repair	854,673	5,996	30,714	111,926	145,829	396,948	101,632	61,833
Repairs and rentals of lawn and garden equipment, hand and power tools, etc.	847,696	4,409	63,566	144,901	292,132	146,649	124,204	71,985
Appliance rental	203,494	16,223	32,074	51,028	54,063	19,227	2,134	28,032
Repair of computer systems for nonbusiness use	468,616	18,516	35,379	96,280	147,252	101,029	32,792	36,915
Computer information services	16,216,688	613,663	2,825,459	4,127,524	4,226,664	2,658,731	1,187,348	577,377
HOUSEKEEPING SUPPLIES	69,126,161	2,231,671	9,706,670	16,302,852	17,921,767	11,480,557	6,390,656	5,138,827
Laundry and cleaning supplies	17,274,854	663,656	2,769,280	4,095,751	4,458,804	2,756,089	1,372,418	1,155,330
Soaps and detergents	9,935,134	414,575	1,688,277	2,445,031	2,502,327	1,557,903	731,073	584,298
Other laundry cleaning products	7,340,883	249,080	1,081,003	1,650,721	1,956,477	1,198,185	641,345	571,032
Other household products	33,769,456	1,001,964	4,328,093	8,150,343	9,131,491	5,565,139	3,200,213	2,419,907
Cleansing and toilet tissue, paper towels, and napkins	9,981,647	434,325	1,382,307	2,150,895	2,361,478	1,776,915	947,363	946,298
Miscellaneous household products	14,085,239	450,901	2,011,353	4,061,090	3,656,390	2,085,070	962,299	844,666
Lawn and garden supplies	9,702,570	116,825	934,433	1,938,357	3,113,386	1,703,154	1,290,439	628,943
Postage and stationery	18,081,851	566,051	2,609,297	4,056,517	4,331,471	3,159,154	1,818,025	1,563,589
Stationery, stationery supplies, giftwrap	8,704,871	382,658	1,349,455	2,217,328	2,065,789	1,274,569	841,127	560,996
Postage	8,618,822	160,998	954,649	1,733,281	2,079,068	1,819,214	925,914	986,097
Delivery services	758,159	22,307	305,192	106,149	186,376	65,371	50,872	16,496
HOUSEHOLD FURNISHINGS, EQUIPMENT	191,411,800	7,162,490	30,089,822	47,172,386	47,161,034	33,777,818	15,666,075	10,396,128
Household textiles	18,333,020	489,079	2,023,406	4,499,405	4,305,388	3,548,412	1,369,274	2,163,115
Bathroom linens	2,472,155	92,490	401,804	518,709	506,963	350,629	402,932	194,497
Bedroom linens	9,967,693	213,195	1,037,654	2,635,906	2,299,827	2,022,320	468,740	1,345,674
Kitchen and dining room linens	1,144,215	42,233	125,187	319,890	293,555	245,580	47,166	71,754
Curtains and draperies	2,234,940	74,327	248,430	514,376	587,820	419,146	160,477	230,720
Slipcovers and decorative pillows	1,060,492	33,416	96,223	255,864	275,533	119,382	53,567	237,065
Sewing materials for household items	1,302,358	29,361	94,862	219,037	303,988	359,368	219,883	75,561
Other linens	152,329	4,056	19,245	35,383	37,702	31,987	16,396	7,844
Furniture	48,486,106	2,303,882	9,024,945	13,147,275	9,829,572	8,802,774	3,617,745	1,759,932
Mattresses and springs	6,228,064	315,296	923,741	1,497,876	1,446,906	1,283,308	466,157	294,168
Other bedroom furniture	9,456,052	436,706	2,115,741	2,748,313	1,897,908	1,407,584	573,067	276,864
Sofas	11,016,557	769,019	2,058,396	3,184,702	2,154,472	1,659,806	792,389	397,646
Living room chairs	4,843,145	186,127	699,610	1,067,264	1,132,485	1,081,076	434,152	242,371
Living room tables	1,717,485	94,959	354,567	387,046	335,999	373,351	119,375	52,489
Kitchen and dining room furniture	4,797,795	136,487	1,004,219	1,252,603	948,006	871,153	404,392	181,346

	total consumer units	under 25	25 to 34	35 to 44	45 to 54	55 to 64	65 to 74	75+
Infants' furniture	$981,420	$98,398	$275,062	$338,424	$98,168	$80,054	$69,851	$21,111
Outdoor furniture	1,881,443	18,957	229,380	615,470	310,390	456,202	161,824	89,865
Wall units, cabinets, and other furniture	7,564,144	248,022	1,364,229	2,055,819	1,505,475	1,590,414	596,650	204,072
Floor coverings	**6,044,338**	**64,364**	**692,612**	**1,235,032**	**1,539,146**	**1,520,848**	**688,399**	**304,089**
Wall-to-wall carpeting	3,253,570	6,877	390,335	724,988	785,341	733,244	462,115	150,083
Floor coverings, nonpermanent	2,790,768	57,487	302,276	510,043	753,804	787,604	226,285	154,006
Major appliances	**23,714,551**	**634,207**	**3,573,277**	**5,706,516**	**5,628,517**	**4,194,960**	**2,338,872**	**1,648,840**
Dishwashers (built-in), garbage disposals, range hoods	1,667,484	22,924	213,440	477,308	330,782	315,496	244,589	63,794
Refrigerators and freezers	5,961,778	145,481	974,088	1,295,929	1,273,097	1,180,357	732,645	359,692
Washing machines	3,564,043	78,824	623,603	828,249	788,661	689,022	325,221	230,259
Clothes dryers	2,561,692	51,050	432,518	601,028	667,730	443,267	201,017	165,426
Cooking stoves, ovens	3,769,862	61,454	537,877	827,767	1,062,060	637,809	425,168	217,915
Microwave ovens	980,257	63,659	121,105	184,858	276,245	148,746	124,653	61,256
Portable dishwasher	141,864	2,910	46,848	36,346	23,949	2,272	21,000	8,998
Window air conditioners	506,990	25,128	131,213	90,503	138,478	74,810	37,284	9,344
Electric floor-cleaning equipment	3,222,174	67,979	434,656	1,241,290	851,498	173,217	152,503	296,244
Sewing machines	417,452	5,290	20,217	40,919	150,808	119,032	74,792	6,922
Miscellaneous household appliances	919,791	109,683	37,712	82,319	64,971	411,106	–	228,874
Small appliances and miscellaneous housewares	**12,170,074**	**544,450**	**2,012,714**	**2,332,142**	**2,960,206**	**2,280,660**	**1,221,712**	**822,055**
Housewares	9,600,242	410,343	1,588,555	1,757,591	2,392,304	1,815,194	1,011,037	628,827
Plastic dinnerware	211,633	22,572	53,846	46,696	50,269	26,219	7,412	4,614
China and other dinnerware	1,566,319	32,711	242,404	247,680	368,959	391,005	191,247	94,941
Flatware	467,454	13,578	57,539	106,149	138,478	83,375	46,043	22,611
Glassware	2,427,968	90,374	330,269	412,560	597,305	517,728	361,606	117,321
Silver serving pieces	34,885	529	3,499	7,462	10,433	9,089	2,808	808
Other serving pieces	204,656	9,258	22,355	45,974	62,125	40,202	18,305	6,922
Nonelectric cookware	2,104,704	103,776	450,985	370,919	460,487	322,488	187,878	209,840
Tableware, nonelectric kitchenware	2,581,460	137,545	427,658	520,153	703,772	425,089	195,627	171,771
Small appliances	2,569,832	134,107	423,965	574,551	568,140	465,466	210,675	193,343
Small electric kitchen appliances	2,008,190	114,797	354,567	405,820	437,012	364,088	190,012	142,008
Portable heating and cooling equipment	561,642	19,309	69,397	168,731	130,890	101,378	20,663	51,220
Miscellaneous household equipment	**82,663,711**	**3,126,420**	**12,763,064**	**20,251,776**	**22,897,967**	**13,430,164**	**6,430,186**	**3,697,980**
Window coverings	2,729,139	33,152	458,566	510,525	487,993	709,997	191,472	336,736
Infants' equipment	913,977	84,996	365,064	326,389	46,238	42,649	33,353	–
Laundry and cleaning equipment	1,827,953	86,318	250,180	402,450	454,322	318,642	185,632	130,588
Outdoor equipment	4,184,989	–	411,135	825,601	2,047,294	582,400	214,381	118,936
Clocks	888,394	63,659	89,419	170,897	208,666	238,239	81,754	36,569
Lamps and lighting fixtures	1,907,025	70,271	241,627	436,630	313,947	621,204	164,407	58,718
Other household decorative items	18,384,184	518,880	2,563,421	5,375,794	4,866,414	3,310,173	1,076,508	644,747
Telephones and accessories	3,119,846	92,667	208,192	601,269	1,381,461	549,540	142,396	159,889
Lawn and garden equipment	5,673,399	71,682	996,054	1,102,647	1,257,447	838,817	790,480	615,792
Power tools	3,888,470	10,669	775,616	936,564	997,564	298,367	613,607	243,756
Office furniture for home use	1,322,126	46,377	212,663	417,615	344,772	214,817	71,086	14,074
Hand tools	710,483	26,892	139,183	126,608	223,130	140,182	35,262	19,265
Indoor plants and fresh flowers	4,828,029	122,733	720,021	952,691	1,326,212	912,229	512,200	282,171
Closet and storage items	2,073,308	69,213	231,130	795,032	378,206	425,264	107,583	60,103
Rental of furniture	258,146	63,571	79,117	56,324	42,207	7,166	4,380	5,191
Luggage	770,950	49,728	78,145	169,453	188,748	210,272	55,589	18,688
Computers and computer hardware, nonbusiness use	15,648,069	1,187,121	2,611,630	3,803,782	4,502,909	2,287,652	826,865	427,524
Computer software and accessories, nonbusiness use	2,216,335	106,245	366,231	544,945	728,670	313,748	110,166	46,144
Telephone answering devices	72,095	1,499	11,469	16,368	20,392	13,808	5,840	2,999
Calculators	167,446	17,281	18,661	50,066	59,280	12,585	8,423	923
Business equipment for home use	109,305	2,381	15,551	26,958	20,867	23,771	15,834	4,153
Other hardware	4,608,256	65,510	659,176	1,024,901	1,767,018	377,721	624,051	78,329
Smoke alarms	119,770	3,791	23,716	21,663	28,929	21,324	14,374	5,653
Other household appliances	1,457,013	28,832	206,831	308,337	327,463	296,269	117,803	170,848
Miscellaneous household equipment and parts	4,788,493	302,776	1,029,878	1,248,270	877,818	662,804	426,628	216,185

Note: Numbers may not add to total because of rounding and missing subcategories. "–" means sample is too small to make a reliable estimate.
Source: Calculations by New Strategist based on the 2004 Consumer Expenditure Survey

Table 8.4 Housing: Household Operations: Market shares by age, 2004

(percentage of total annual spending on household services, supplies, furnishings, and equipment accounted for by consumer unit age groups, 2004)

	total consumer units	under 25	25 to 34	35 to 44	45 to 54	55 to 64	65 to 74	75+
Share of total consumer units	100.0%	7.6%	16.7%	20.7%	20.4%	15.0%	9.7%	9.9%
Share of total before-tax income	100.0	3.2	16.1	24.9	26.4	16.8	7.5	5.1
Share of total spending	100.0	4.3	16.4	24.0	24.8	16.4	8.1	5.9
Share of housing spending	100.0	4.2	17.3	25.0	23.7	15.5	7.7	6.7
HOUSEHOLD SERVICES	100.0	2.7	20.3	27.3	18.8	12.9	6.7	11.3
Personal services	100.0	4.0	32.6	39.2	8.9	2.1	0.9	12.3
Babysitting and child care in own home	100.0	1.3	36.5	51.9	10.0	0.0	0.0	0.2
Babysitting and child care in someone else's home	100.0	10.4	41.5	36.8	9.9	0.4	0.8	0.2
Care for elderly, invalids, handicapped, etc.	100.0	–	0.2	2.8	11.3	3.5	1.7	80.4
Day care centers, nurseries, and preschools	100.0	4.6	37.8	45.3	8.5	2.5	0.9	0.3
Other household services	100.0	1.8	12.2	19.4	25.3	20.0	10.6	10.7
Housekeeping services	100.0	0.2	8.2	17.4	23.4	22.7	11.7	16.4
Gardening, lawn care service	100.0	0.3	7.6	14.9	23.2	20.2	14.9	18.9
Water-softening service	100.0	0.3	10.9	21.4	26.1	17.1	10.7	13.5
Nonclothing laundry and dry cleaning, sent out	100.0	6.9	9.1	20.7	20.0	23.7	12.1	8.0
Nonclothing laundry and dry cleaning, coin-operated	100.0	11.2	29.5	21.0	15.6	12.8	4.7	5.3
Termite and pest control services	100.0	1.2	9.6	17.1	27.8	21.7	14.9	7.8
Home security system service fee	100.0	0.9	14.1	25.3	24.3	17.4	11.7	6.3
Other home services	100.0	0.6	9.9	12.8	26.1	22.2	10.1	18.3
Termite and pest control products	100.0	2.3	5.9	16.1	30.5	23.4	14.2	7.8
Moving, storage, and freight express	100.0	3.2	18.7	16.7	30.2	21.7	6.6	2.8
Appliance repair, including at service center	100.0	0.5	9.4	18.3	28.8	22.4	11.8	8.8
Reupholstering and furniture repair	100.0	0.7	3.6	13.1	17.1	46.4	11.9	7.2
Repairs and rentals of lawn and garden equipment, hand and power tools, etc.	100.0	0.5	7.5	17.1	34.5	17.3	14.7	8.5
Appliance rental	100.0	8.0	15.8	25.1	26.6	9.4	1.0	13.8
Repair of computer systems for nonbusiness use	100.0	4.0	7.5	20.5	31.4	21.6	7.0	7.9
Computer information services	100.0	3.8	17.4	25.5	26.1	16.4	7.3	3.6
HOUSEKEEPING SUPPLIES	100.0	3.2	14.0	23.6	25.9	16.6	9.2	7.4
Laundry and cleaning supplies	100.0	3.8	16.0	23.7	25.8	16.0	7.9	6.7
Soaps and detergents	100.0	4.2	17.0	24.6	25.2	15.7	7.4	5.9
Other laundry cleaning products	100.0	3.4	14.7	22.5	26.7	16.3	8.7	7.8
Other household products	100.0	3.0	12.8	24.1	27.0	16.5	9.5	7.2
Cleansing and toilet tissue, paper towels, and napkins	100.0	4.4	13.8	21.5	23.7	17.8	9.5	9.5
Miscellaneous household products	100.0	3.2	14.3	28.8	26.0	14.8	6.8	6.0
Lawn and garden supplies	100.0	1.2	9.6	20.0	32.1	17.6	13.3	6.5
Postage and stationery	100.0	3.1	14.4	22.4	24.0	17.5	10.1	8.6
Stationery, stationery supplies, giftwrap	100.0	4.4	15.5	25.5	23.7	14.6	9.7	6.4
Postage	100.0	1.9	11.1	20.1	24.1	21.1	10.7	11.4
Delivery services	100.0	2.9	40.3	14.0	24.6	8.6	6.7	2.2
HOUSEHOLD FURNISHINGS AND EQUIPMENT	100.0	3.7	15.7	24.6	24.6	17.6	8.2	5.4
Household textiles	100.0	2.7	11.0	24.5	23.5	19.4	7.5	11.8
Bathroom linens	100.0	3.7	16.3	21.0	20.5	14.2	16.3	7.9
Bedroom linens	100.0	2.1	10.4	26.4	23.1	20.3	4.7	13.5
Kitchen and dining room linens	100.0	3.7	10.9	28.0	25.7	21.5	4.1	6.3
Curtains and draperies	100.0	3.3	11.1	23.0	26.3	18.8	7.2	10.3
Slipcovers and decorative pillows	100.0	3.2	9.1	24.1	26.0	11.3	5.1	22.4
Sewing materials for household items	100.0	2.3	7.3	16.8	23.3	27.6	16.9	5.8
Other linens	100.0	2.7	12.6	23.2	24.8	21.0	10.8	5.1
Furniture	100.0	4.8	18.6	27.1	20.3	18.2	7.5	3.6
Mattresses and springs	100.0	5.1	14.8	24.1	23.2	20.6	7.5	4.7
Other bedroom furniture	100.0	4.6	22.4	29.1	20.1	14.9	6.1	2.9
Sofas	100.0	7.0	18.7	28.9	19.6	15.1	7.2	3.6
Living room chairs	100.0	3.8	14.4	22.0	23.4	22.3	9.0	5.0
Living room tables	100.0	5.5	20.6	22.5	19.6	21.7	7.0	3.1
Kitchen and dining room furniture	100.0	2.8	20.9	26.1	19.8	18.2	8.4	3.8

	total consumer units	under 25	25 to 34	35 to 44	45 to 54	55 to 64	65 to 74	75+
Infants' furniture	100.0%	10.0%	28.0%	34.5%	10.0%	8.2%	7.1%	2.2%
Outdoor furniture	100.0	1.0	12.2	32.7	16.5	24.2	8.6	4.8
Wall units, cabinets, and other furniture	100.0	3.3	18.0	27.2	19.9	21.0	7.9	2.7
Floor coverings	**100.0**	**1.1**	**11.5**	**20.4**	**25.5**	**25.2**	**11.4**	**5.0**
Wall-to-wall carpeting	100.0	0.2	12.0	22.3	24.1	22.5	14.2	4.6
Floor coverings, nonpermanent	100.0	2.1	10.8	18.3	27.0	28.2	8.1	5.5
Major appliances	**100.0**	**2.7**	**15.1**	**24.1**	**23.7**	**17.7**	**9.9**	**7.0**
Dishwashers (built-in), garbage disposals, range hoods	100.0	1.4	12.8	28.6	19.8	18.9	14.7	3.8
Refrigerators and freezers	100.0	2.4	16.3	21.7	21.4	19.8	12.3	6.0
Washing machines	100.0	2.2	17.5	23.2	22.1	19.3	9.1	6.5
Clothes dryers	100.0	2.0	16.9	23.5	26.1	17.3	7.8	6.5
Cooking stoves, ovens	100.0	1.6	14.3	22.0	28.2	16.9	11.3	5.8
Microwave ovens	100.0	6.5	12.4	18.9	28.2	15.2	12.7	6.2
Portable dishwasher	100.0	2.1	33.0	25.6	16.9	1.6	14.8	6.3
Window air conditioners	100.0	5.0	25.9	17.9	27.3	14.8	7.4	1.8
Electric floor-cleaning equipment	100.0	2.1	13.5	38.5	26.4	5.4	4.7	9.2
Sewing machines	100.0	1.3	4.8	9.8	36.1	28.5	17.9	1.7
Miscellaneous household appliances	100.0	11.9	4.1	8.9	7.1	44.7	–	24.9
Small appliances and miscellaneous housewares	**100.0**	**4.5**	**16.5**	**19.2**	**24.3**	**18.7**	**10.0**	**6.8**
Housewares	100.0	4.3	16.5	18.3	24.9	18.9	10.5	6.6
Plastic dinnerware	100.0	10.7	25.4	22.1	23.8	12.4	3.5	2.2
China and other dinnerware	100.0	2.1	15.5	15.8	23.6	25.0	12.2	6.1
Flatware	100.0	2.9	12.3	22.7	29.6	17.8	9.8	4.8
Glassware	100.0	3.7	13.6	17.0	24.6	21.3	14.9	4.8
Silver serving pieces	100.0	1.5	10.0	21.4	29.9	26.1	8.0	2.3
Other serving pieces	100.0	4.5	10.9	22.5	30.4	19.6	8.9	3.4
Nonelectric cookware	100.0	4.9	21.4	17.6	21.9	15.3	8.9	10.0
Tableware, nonelectric kitchenware	100.0	5.3	16.6	20.1	27.3	16.5	7.6	6.7
Small appliances	100.0	5.2	16.5	22.4	22.1	18.1	8.2	7.5
Small electric kitchen appliances	100.0	5.7	17.7	20.2	21.8	18.1	9.5	7.1
Portable heating and cooling equipment	100.0	3.4	12.4	30.0	23.3	18.1	3.7	9.1
Miscellaneous household equipment	**100.0**	**3.8**	**15.4**	**24.5**	**27.7**	**16.2**	**7.8**	**4.5**
Window coverings	100.0	1.2	16.8	18.7	17.9	26.0	7.0	12.3
Infants' equipment	100.0	9.3	39.9	35.7	5.1	4.7	3.6	–
Laundry and cleaning equipment	100.0	4.7	13.7	22.0	24.9	17.4	10.2	7.1
Outdoor equipment	100.0	–	9.8	19.7	48.9	13.9	5.1	2.8
Clocks	100.0	7.2	10.1	19.2	23.5	26.8	9.2	4.1
Lamps and lighting fixtures	100.0	3.7	12.7	22.9	16.5	32.6	8.6	3.1
Other household decorative items	100.0	2.8	13.9	29.2	26.5	18.0	5.9	3.5
Telephones and accessories	100.0	3.0	6.7	19.3	44.3	17.6	4.6	5.1
Lawn and garden equipment	100.0	1.3	17.6	19.4	22.2	14.8	13.9	10.9
Power tools	100.0	0.3	19.9	24.1	25.7	7.7	15.8	6.3
Office furniture for home use	100.0	3.5	16.1	31.6	26.1	16.2	5.4	1.1
Hand tools	100.0	3.8	19.6	17.8	31.4	19.7	5.0	2.7
Indoor plants and fresh flowers	100.0	2.5	14.9	19.7	27.5	18.9	10.6	5.8
Closet and storage items	100.0	3.3	11.1	38.3	18.2	20.5	5.2	2.9
Rental of furniture	100.0	24.6	30.6	21.8	16.4	2.8	1.7	2.0
Luggage	100.0	6.5	10.1	22.0	24.5	27.3	7.2	2.4
Computers and computer hardware, nonbusiness use	100.0	7.6	16.7	24.3	28.8	14.6	5.3	2.7
Computer software and accessories, nonbusiness use	100.0	4.8	16.5	24.6	32.9	14.2	5.0	2.1
Telephone answering devices	100.0	2.1	15.9	22.7	28.3	19.2	8.1	4.2
Calculators	100.0	10.3	11.1	29.9	35.4	7.5	5.0	0.6
Business equipment for home use	100.0	2.2	14.2	24.7	19.1	21.7	14.5	3.8
Other hardware	100.0	1.4	14.3	22.2	38.3	8.2	13.5	1.7
Smoke alarms	100.0	3.2	19.8	18.1	24.2	17.8	12.0	4.7
Other household appliances	100.0	2.0	14.2	21.2	22.5	20.3	8.1	11.7
Miscellaneous household equipment and parts	100.0	6.3	21.5	26.1	18.3	13.8	8.9	4.5

Note: Numbers may not add to total because of rounding. "–" means sample is too small to make a reliable estimate.
Source: Calculations by New Strategist based on the 2004 Consumer Expenditure Survey

Table 8.5 Housing: Household Operations: Average spending by income, 2004

(average annual spending on household services, supplies, furnishings, and equipment, by before-tax income of consumer units (CU), 2004)

	total consumer units	under $20,000	$20,000– $39,999	$40,000– $49,999	$50,000– $69,999	$70,000– $79,999	$80,000– $99,999	$100,000 or more
Number of consumer units (in 000s)	116,282	28,898	27,297	11,374	18,069	6,461	9,246	14,937
Average number of persons per CU	2.5	1.8	2.3	2.6	2.8	3.0	3.1	3.2
Average before-tax income of CU	$54,453.00	$10,923.47	$29,561.76	$44,645.00	$59,259.00	$74,437.00	$88,811.00	$155,901.00
Average spending of CU, total	43,394.87	18,865.37	30,400.94	38,204.07	47,750.13	55,012.03	65,446.39	93,525.67
Housing, average spending	**13,918.48**	**7,098.03**	**10,362.24**	**12,383.34**	**14,698.87**	**17,421.88**	**20,397.04**	**28,139.97**
HOUSEHOLD SERVICES	**752.83**	**285.77**	**452.34**	**486.53**	**690.13**	**895.01**	**1,331.51**	**2,064.29**
Personal services	**299.71**	**115.98**	**171.66**	**163.33**	**280.96**	**380.88**	**613.47**	**786.36**
Babysitting and child care in own home	37.09	3.92	10.05	20.58	22.51	60.79	52.56	161.01
Babysitting and child care in someone else's home	26.12	8.87	21.21	29.10	37.08	38.97	34.32	42.32
Care for elderly, invalids, handicapped, etc.	34.96	46.37	42.38	5.39	24.97	6.45	64.39	28.01
Day care centers, nurseries, and preschools	193.51	35.82	92.42	108.26	187.44	274.67	461.11	554.88
Other household services	**453.12**	**169.78**	**280.68**	**323.21**	**409.17**	**514.13**	**718.04**	**1,277.93**
Housekeeping services	88.85	30.46	37.24	41.89	46.88	74.75	120.87	368.93
Gardening, lawn care service	95.08	41.84	62.68	54.68	74.78	95.18	139.09	285.33
Water-softening service	3.06	1.72	2.14	2.77	3.40	4.17	3.73	6.27
Nonclothing laundry and dry cleaning, sent out	0.94	0.37	0.72	0.52	0.88	0.96	1.36	2.60
Nonclothing laundry and dry cleaning, coin-operated	3.71	4.83	4.47	3.96	2.92	2.35	2.08	2.54
Termite and pest control services	12.04	3.21	7.55	9.06	11.04	13.42	18.13	36.47
Home security system service fee	15.57	4.25	8.29	9.50	17.14	20.34	27.70	43.97
Other home services	23.03	8.65	14.14	17.59	14.28	24.68	47.52	65.95
Termite and pest control products	1.53	0.54	1.13	1.04	1.19	1.33	2.75	4.32
Moving, storage, and freight express	33.91	8.79	21.60	23.83	33.59	23.99	57.23	102.94
Appliance repair, including at service center	14.53	5.11	8.88	9.89	14.21	23.99	29.74	33.47
Reupholstering and furniture repair	7.35	3.29	3.56	5.12	3.54	9.43	12.04	24.62
Repairs and rentals of lawn and garden equipment, hand and power tools, etc.	7.29	2.81	5.34	4.61	6.10	6.56	17.67	16.92
Appliance rental	1.75	2.66	2.19	0.21	1.66	0.83	1.42	1.03
Repair of computer systems for nonbusiness use	4.03	1.34	3.13	4.72	2.66	4.73	7.99	9.24
Computer information services	139.46	49.35	95.69	133.84	174.61	207.42	228.39	271.08
HOUSEKEEPING SUPPLIES	**594.47**	**317.33**	**444.70**	**542.50**	**644.85**	**676.97**	**861.85**	**1,117.54**
Laundry and cleaning supplies	**148.56**	**86.94**	**130.04**	**159.99**	**165.60**	**173.36**	**181.23**	**227.46**
Soaps and detergents	85.44	50.08	74.99	93.87	93.61	102.78	107.08	127.50
Other laundry cleaning products	63.13	36.85	55.05	66.12	72.00	70.58	74.16	99.96
Other household products	**290.41**	**151.39**	**211.04**	**232.36**	**311.47**	**322.55**	**423.43**	**594.72**
Cleansing and toilet tissue, paper towels, and napkins	85.84	62.15	79.19	83.14	82.76	96.93	96.55	131.73
Miscellaneous household products	121.13	53.87	83.64	97.55	136.28	139.92	211.14	240.40
Lawn and garden supplies	83.44	35.37	48.21	51.68	92.43	85.70	115.73	222.59
Postage and stationery	**155.50**	**79.01**	**103.62**	**150.15**	**167.78**	**181.06**	**257.18**	**295.36**
Stationery, stationery supplies, giftwrap	74.86	39.29	47.23	64.43	78.35	91.74	114.98	156.72
Postage	74.12	38.00	54.50	82.09	84.30	84.68	112.34	125.08
Delivery services	6.52	1.71	1.90	3.63	5.13	4.64	29.86	13.57
HOUSEHOLD FURNISHINGS, EQUIPMENT	**1,646.10**	**549.17**	**995.97**	**1,345.00**	**1,672.16**	**2,085.14**	**2,539.18**	**4,303.69**
Household textiles	**157.66**	**56.44**	**116.79**	**122.66**	**141.44**	**165.94**	**265.88**	**382.73**
Bathroom linens	21.26	9.50	19.91	13.66	22.84	19.69	31.52	42.08
Bedroom linens	85.72	30.70	61.36	80.05	66.78	73.13	149.64	214.29
Kitchen and dining room linens	9.84	3.49	4.54	4.33	6.10	15.45	11.77	35.08
Curtains and draperies	19.22	5.25	10.33	7.15	20.62	15.77	42.89	56.87
Slipcovers and decorative pillows	9.12	3.48	11.07	5.09	9.95	24.76	11.86	10.40
Sewing materials for household items	11.20	4.56	8.89	11.67	13.89	13.22	16.76	20.33
Other linens	1.31	0.34	0.69	0.71	1.26	3.91	1.44	3.67
Furniture	**416.97**	**136.14**	**194.73**	**327.38**	**439.95**	**586.86**	**575.70**	**1,235.09**
Mattresses and springs	53.56	17.43	26.51	37.38	54.48	61.68	72.23	169.00
Other bedroom furniture	81.32	30.73	39.92	51.32	103.45	118.63	134.30	202.02
Sofas	94.74	32.82	54.96	86.25	102.29	155.08	99.92	255.25
Living room chairs	41.65	18.85	20.42	33.96	47.09	54.25	55.87	109.56
Living room tables	14.77	5.34	6.66	10.69	15.52	22.57	17.54	44.96
Kitchen and dining room furniture	41.26	9.58	13.24	42.88	37.18	62.82	58.03	137.78

	total consumer units	under $20,000	$20,000– $39,999	$40,000– $49,999	$50,000– $69,999	$70,000– $79,999	$80,000– $99,999	$100,000 or more
Infants' furniture	$8.44	$1.85	$3.78	$5.80	$8.74	$15.27	$11.32	$26.57
Outdoor furniture	16.18	4.71	5.35	10.42	13.95	29.12	19.35	57.72
Wall units, cabinets, and other furniture	65.05	14.82	23.91	48.69	57.26	67.43	107.12	232.25
Floor coverings	**51.98**	**9.87**	**17.09**	**53.64**	**68.47**	**44.79**	**79.64**	**161.99**
Wall-to-wall carpeting	27.98	3.44	7.90	42.72	46.45	30.72	17.85	83.67
Floor coverings, nonpermanent	24.00	6.44	9.19	10.92	22.02	14.07	61.79	78.32
Major appliances	**203.94**	**77.15**	**128.68**	**234.58**	**219.01**	**320.69**	**323.40**	**412.64**
Dishwashers (built-in), garbage disposals, range hoods	14.34	2.95	8.18	6.18	16.95	30.71	26.86	35.91
Refrigerators and freezers	51.27	18.31	37.72	43.55	57.35	105.99	76.79	98.83
Washing machines	30.65	10.21	24.54	24.93	37.40	41.75	52.04	59.48
Clothes dryers	22.03	5.82	13.57	21.20	30.94	28.81	42.75	42.97
Cooking stoves, ovens	32.42	10.26	19.88	24.62	32.69	72.51	69.93	63.27
Microwave ovens	8.43	4.15	6.07	8.66	8.31	10.42	16.09	15.38
Portable dishwasher	1.22	–	0.60	1.84	1.82	2.83	1.53	1.85
Window air conditioners	4.36	2.63	2.70	3.59	4.62	5.80	5.90	9.43
Electric floor-cleaning equipment	27.71	15.20	8.15	95.03	18.21	19.64	23.50	51.96
Sewing machines	3.59	1.30	3.19	2.58	9.06	2.22	3.97	3.29
Miscellaneous household appliances	7.91	9.86	4.07	2.42	1.66	–	4.04	30.26
Small appliances and miscellaneous housewares	**104.66**	**42.65**	**90.27**	**90.19**	**78.53**	**129.96**	**150.45**	**240.32**
Housewares	82.56	32.17	71.08	68.15	56.99	108.55	122.47	193.03
Plastic dinnerware	1.82	0.95	1.14	2.62	1.58	2.63	2.17	3.88
China and other dinnerware	13.47	3.83	10.98	8.39	5.55	24.50	40.13	25.90
Flatware	4.02	1.07	2.33	3.25	3.69	4.59	7.09	11.71
Glassware	20.88	3.14	25.40	13.48	15.07	29.87	15.81	53.68
Silver serving pieces	0.30	0.09	0.22	0.14	0.30	0.25	0.62	0.74
Other serving pieces	1.76	0.29	0.89	0.89	1.33	2.42	2.87	6.45
Nonelectric cookware	18.10	11.09	13.37	19.30	14.40	14.08	23.51	40.10
Tableware, nonelectric kitchenware	22.20	11.73	16.76	20.08	15.09	30.21	30.26	50.57
Small appliances	22.10	10.49	19.19	22.04	21.54	21.40	27.98	47.29
Small electric kitchen appliances	17.27	8.61	15.77	15.97	17.68	16.81	24.54	32.98
Portable heating and cooling equipment	4.83	1.87	3.43	6.07	3.86	4.60	3.44	14.31
Miscellaneous household equipment	**710.89**	**226.91**	**448.43**	**516.54**	**724.76**	**836.89**	**1,144.11**	**1,870.92**
Window coverings	23.47	6.47	8.68	7.22	20.15	27.68	66.65	71.20
Infants' equipment	7.86	4.47	7.32	5.06	7.85	6.46	7.45	17.42
Laundry and cleaning equipment	15.72	8.91	14.28	11.75	17.07	17.67	21.25	27.11
Outdoor equipment	35.99	17.17	16.75	34.23	27.54	22.42	46.71	112.48
Clocks	7.64	3.11	3.59	5.33	4.14	4.89	9.13	28.74
Lamps and lighting fixtures	16.40	3.92	6.40	8.59	14.13	17.39	24.20	62.26
Other household decorative items	158.10	49.78	80.38	93.46	169.03	212.94	179.09	484.20
Telephones and accessories	26.83	5.06	15.74	26.38	20.60	25.48	51.63	76.78
Lawn and garden equipment	48.79	13.38	33.10	47.31	42.56	60.00	150.37	86.88
Power tools	33.44	13.91	28.50	25.61	52.70	37.02	36.62	61.97
Office furniture for home use	11.37	1.96	2.65	7.18	7.21	13.27	10.52	53.42
Hand tools	6.11	2.15	4.45	8.51	7.89	3.70	11.96	10.24
Indoor plants and fresh flowers	41.52	12.20	24.96	27.68	46.15	47.68	73.56	110.97
Closet and storage items	17.83	5.90	5.05	10.33	9.75	35.67	16.28	69.27
Rental of furniture	2.22	1.70	4.24	4.39	0.65	0.14	0.76	1.57
Luggage	6.63	2.78	2.45	4.75	6.34	9.04	9.41	20.71
Computers and computer hardware, nonbusiness use	134.57	54.05	71.46	120.25	144.05	179.95	235.88	322.75
Computer software and accessories, nonbusiness use	19.06	5.09	13.47	12.53	22.50	21.56	35.49	45.87
Telephone answering devices	0.62	0.32	0.34	0.96	0.56	0.36	1.02	1.42
Calculators	1.44	0.79	0.69	0.90	1.64	1.54	1.61	4.10
Business equipment for home use	0.94	0.35	0.73	1.78	1.24	0.39	1.12	1.59
Other hardware	39.63	4.36	60.30	12.17	37.14	30.35	67.18	72.05
Smoke alarms	1.03	0.27	0.82	0.93	1.39	1.27	2.05	1.74
Other household appliances	12.53	3.35	8.88	7.05	14.55	19.96	27.30	26.31
Miscellaneous household equipment and parts	41.18	8.95	33.19	32.19	47.92	40.07	56.86	99.85

Note: Subcategories may not add to total because some are not shown. "–" means sample is too small to make a reliable estimate.
Source: Bureau of Labor Statistics, unpublished tables from the 2004 Consumer Expenditure Survey; calculations by New Strategist

Table 8.6 Housing: Household Operations: Indexed spending by income, 2004

(indexed average annual spending of consumer units (CU) on household services, supplies, furnishings, and equipment, by before-tax income of consumer unit, 2004; index definition: an index of 100 is the average for all consumer units; an index of 132 means that spending by consumer units in that group is 32 percent above the average for all consumer units; an index of 68 indicates spending that is 32 percent below the average for all consumer units)

	total consumer units	under $20,000	$20,000–$39,999	$40,000–$49,999	$50,000–$69,999	$70,000–$79,999	$80,000–$99,999	$100,000 or more
Average spending of CU, total	$43,395	$18,865	$30,401	$38,204	$47,750	$55,012	$65,446	$93,526
Average spending of CU, index	100	43	70	88	110	127	151	216
Housing, spending index	100	51	74	89	106	125	147	202
HOUSEHOLD SERVICES	100	38	60	65	92	119	177	274
Personal services	100	39	57	54	94	127	205	262
Babysitting and child care in own home	100	11	27	55	61	164	142	434
Babysitting and child care in someone else's home	100	34	81	111	142	149	131	162
Care for elderly, invalids, handicapped, etc.	100	133	121	15	71	18	184	80
Day care centers, nurseries, and preschools	100	19	48	56	97	142	238	287
Other household services	100	37	62	71	90	113	158	282
Housekeeping services	100	34	42	47	53	84	136	415
Gardening, lawn care service	100	44	66	58	79	100	146	300
Water-softening service	100	56	70	91	111	136	122	205
Nonclothing laundry and dry cleaning, sent out	100	39	77	55	94	102	145	277
Nonclothing laundry and dry cleaning, coin-operated	100	130	120	107	79	63	56	68
Termite and pest control services	100	27	63	75	92	111	151	303
Home security system service fee	100	27	53	61	110	131	178	282
Other home services	100	38	61	76	62	107	206	286
Termite and pest control products	100	35	74	68	78	87	180	282
Moving, storage, and freight express	100	26	64	70	99	71	169	304
Appliance repair, including at service center	100	35	61	68	98	165	205	230
Reupholstering and furniture repair	100	45	48	70	48	128	164	335
Repairs and rentals of lawn and garden equipment, hand and power tools, etc.	100	38	73	63	84	90	242	232
Appliance rental	100	152	125	12	95	47	81	59
Repair of computer systems for nonbusiness use	100	33	78	117	66	117	198	229
Computer information services	100	35	69	96	125	149	164	194
HOUSEKEEPING SUPPLIES	100	53	75	91	108	114	145	188
Laundry and cleaning supplies	100	59	88	108	111	117	122	153
Soaps and detergents	100	59	88	110	110	120	125	149
Other laundry cleaning products	100	58	87	105	114	112	117	158
Other household products	100	52	73	80	107	111	146	205
Cleansing and toilet tissue, paper towels, and napkins	100	72	92	97	96	113	112	153
Miscellaneous household products	100	44	69	81	113	116	174	198
Lawn and garden supplies	100	42	58	62	111	103	139	267
Postage and stationery	100	51	67	97	108	116	165	190
Stationery, stationery supplies, giftwrap	100	52	63	86	105	123	154	209
Postage	100	51	74	111	114	114	152	169
Delivery services	100	26	29	56	79	71	458	208
HOUSEHOLD FURNISHINGS AND EQUIPMENT	100	33	61	82	102	127	154	261
Household textiles	100	36	74	78	90	105	169	243
Bathroom linens	100	45	94	64	107	93	148	198
Bedroom linens	100	36	72	93	78	85	175	250
Kitchen and dining room linens	100	36	46	44	62	157	120	357
Curtains and draperies	100	27	54	37	107	82	223	296
Slipcovers and decorative pillows	100	38	121	56	109	271	130	114
Sewing materials for household items	100	41	79	104	124	118	150	182
Other linens	100	26	52	54	96	298	110	280
Furniture	100	33	47	79	106	141	138	296
Mattresses and springs	100	33	49	70	102	115	135	316
Other bedroom furniture	100	38	49	63	127	146	165	248
Sofas	100	35	58	91	108	164	105	269
Living room chairs	100	45	49	82	113	130	134	263
Living room tables	100	36	45	72	105	153	119	304
Kitchen and dining room furniture	100	23	32	104	90	152	141	334

	total consumer units	under $20,000	$20,000– $39,999	$40,000– $49,999	$50,000– $69,999	$70,000– $79,999	$80,000– $99,999	$100,000 or more
Infants' furniture	100	22	45	69	104	181	134	315
Outdoor furniture	100	29	33	64	86	180	120	357
Wall units, cabinets, and other furniture	100	23	37	75	88	104	165	357
Floor coverings	**100**	**19**	**33**	**103**	**132**	**86**	**153**	**312**
Wall-to-wall carpeting	100	12	28	153	166	110	64	299
Floor coverings, nonpermanent	100	27	38	46	92	59	257	326
Major appliances	**100**	**38**	**63**	**115**	**107**	**157**	**159**	**202**
Dishwashers (built-in), garbage disposals, range hoods	100	21	57	43	118	214	187	250
Refrigerators and freezers	100	36	74	85	112	207	150	193
Washing machines	100	33	80	81	122	136	170	194
Clothes dryers	100	26	62	96	140	131	194	195
Cooking stoves, ovens	100	32	61	76	101	224	216	195
Microwave ovens	100	49	72	103	99	124	191	182
Portable dishwasher	100	–	49	151	149	232	125	152
Window air conditioners	100	60	62	82	106	133	135	216
Electric floor-cleaning equipment	100	55	29	343	66	71	85	188
Sewing machines	100	36	89	72	252	62	111	92
Miscellaneous household appliances	100	125	51	31	21	–	51	383
Small appliances and miscellaneous housewares	**100**	**41**	**86**	**86**	**75**	**124**	**144**	**230**
Housewares	100	39	86	83	69	131	148	234
Plastic dinnerware	100	52	62	144	87	145	119	213
China and other dinnerware	100	28	82	62	41	182	298	192
Flatware	100	27	58	81	92	114	176	291
Glassware	100	15	122	65	72	143	76	257
Silver serving pieces	100	29	73	47	100	83	207	247
Other serving pieces	100	16	51	51	76	138	163	366
Nonelectric cookware	100	61	74	107	80	78	130	222
Tableware, nonelectric kitchenware	100	53	75	90	68	136	136	228
Small appliances	100	47	87	100	97	97	127	214
Small electric kitchen appliances	100	50	91	92	102	97	142	191
Portable heating and cooling equipment	100	39	71	126	80	95	71	296
Miscellaneous household equipment	**100**	**32**	**63**	**73**	**102**	**118**	**161**	**263**
Window coverings	100	28	37	31	86	118	284	303
Infants' equipment	100	57	93	64	100	82	95	222
Laundry and cleaning equipment	100	57	91	75	109	112	135	172
Outdoor equipment	100	48	47	95	77	62	130	313
Clocks	100	41	47	70	54	64	120	376
Lamps and lighting fixtures	100	24	39	52	86	106	148	380
Other household decorative items	100	31	51	59	107	135	113	306
Telephones and accessories	100	19	59	98	77	95	192	286
Lawn and garden equipment	100	27	68	97	87	123	308	178
Power tools	100	42	85	77	158	111	110	185
Office furniture for home use	100	17	23	63	63	117	93	470
Hand tools	100	35	73	139	129	61	196	168
Indoor plants and fresh flowers	100	29	60	67	111	115	177	267
Closet and storage items	100	33	28	58	55	200	91	389
Rental of furniture	100	77	191	198	29	6	34	71
Luggage	100	42	37	72	96	136	142	312
Computers and computer hardware, nonbusiness use	100	40	53	89	107	134	175	240
Computer software and accessories, nonbusiness use	100	27	71	66	118	113	186	241
Telephone answering devices	100	52	54	155	90	58	165	229
Calculators	100	55	48	63	114	107	112	285
Business equipment for home use	100	37	78	189	132	41	119	169
Other hardware	100	11	152	31	94	77	170	182
Smoke alarms	100	26	80	90	135	123	199	169
Other household appliances	100	27	71	56	116	159	218	210
Miscellaneous household equipment and parts	100	22	81	78	116	97	138	242

Note: "–" means sample is too small to make a reliable estimate.
Source: Calculations by New Strategist based on the 2004 Consumer Expenditure Survey

Table 8.7 Housing: Household Operations: Total spending by income, 2004

(total annual spending on household services, supplies, furnishings, and equipment, by before-tax income group of consumer units (CU), 2004; consumer units and dollars in thousands)

	total consumer units	under $20,000	$20,000–$39,999	$40,000–$49,999	$50,000–$69,999	$70,000–$79,999	$80,000–$99,999	$100,000 or more
Number of consumer units	116,282	28,898	27,297	11,374	18,069	6,461	9,246	14,937
Total spending of all CUs	$5,046,042,273	$545,171,431	$829,854,379	$434,533,092	$862,797,099	$355,432,726	$605,117,322	$1,396,992,933
Housing, total spending	1,618,468,691	205,118,748	282,858,140	140,848,109	265,593,882	112,562,767	188,591,032	420,326,732
HOUSEHOLD SERVICES	87,540,578	8,258,086	12,347,638	5,533,792	12,469,959	5,782,660	12,311,141	30,834,300
Personal services	34,850,878	3,351,716	4,685,878	1,857,715	5,076,666	2,460,866	5,672,144	11,745,859
Babysitting and child care in own home	4,312,899	113,176	274,435	234,077	406,733	392,764	485,970	2,405,006
Babysitting and child care in someone else's home	3,037,286	256,227	579,005	330,983	669,999	251,785	317,323	632,134
Care for elderly, invalids, handicapped, etc.	4,065,219	1,339,915	1,156,943	61,306	451,183	41,673	595,350	418,385
Day care centers, nurseries, and preschools	22,501,730	1,034,996	2,522,721	1,231,349	3,386,853	1,774,643	4,263,423	8,288,243
Other household services	52,689,700	4,906,442	7,661,759	3,676,191	7,393,293	3,321,794	6,638,998	19,088,440
Housekeeping services	10,331,656	880,237	1,016,583	476,457	847,075	482,960	1,117,564	5,510,707
Gardening, lawn care service	11,056,093	1,209,211	1,710,939	621,930	1,351,200	614,958	1,286,026	4,261,974
Water-softening service	355,823	49,596	58,542	31,506	61,435	26,942	34,488	93,655
Nonclothing laundry and dry cleaning, sent out	109,305	10,578	19,639	5,914	15,901	6,203	12,575	38,836
Nonclothing laundry and dry cleaning, coin-operated	431,406	139,546	121,933	45,041	52,761	15,183	19,232	37,940
Termite and pest control services	1,400,035	92,827	206,030	103,048	199,482	86,707	167,630	544,752
Home security system service fee	1,810,511	122,821	226,238	108,053	309,703	131,417	256,114	656,780
Other home services	2,677,974	250,015	385,883	200,069	258,025	159,457	439,370	985,095
Termite and pest control products	177,911	15,586	30,923	11,829	21,502	8,593	25,427	64,528
Moving, storage, and freight express	3,943,123	254,012	589,527	271,042	606,938	154,999	529,149	1,537,615
Appliance repair, including at service center	1,689,577	147,795	242,317	112,489	256,760	154,999	274,976	499,941
Reupholstering and furniture repair	854,673	95,136	97,251	58,235	63,964	60,927	111,322	367,749
Repairs and rentals of lawn and garden equipment, hand and power tools, etc.	847,696	81,075	145,751	52,434	110,221	42,384	163,377	252,734
Appliance rental	203,494	76,836	59,843	2,389	29,995	5,363	13,129	15,385
Repair of computer systems for nonbusiness use	468,616	38,616	85,467	53,685	48,064	30,561	73,876	138,018
Computer information services	16,216,688	1,426,124	2,612,028	1,522,296	3,155,028	1,340,141	2,111,694	4,049,122
HOUSEKEEPING SUPPLIES	69,126,161	9,170,296	12,139,055	6,170,395	11,651,795	4,373,903	7,968,665	16,692,695
Laundry and cleaning supplies	17,274,854	2,512,371	3,549,796	1,819,726	2,992,226	1,120,079	1,675,653	3,397,570
Soaps and detergents	9,935,134	1,447,301	2,047,099	1,067,677	1,691,439	664,062	990,062	1,904,468
Other laundry cleaning products	7,340,883	1,064,998	1,502,697	752,049	1,300,968	456,017	685,683	1,493,103
Other household products	33,769,456	4,374,768	5,760,839	2,642,863	5,627,951	2,083,996	3,915,034	8,883,333
Cleansing and toilet tissue, paper towels, and napkins	9,981,647	1,796,002	2,161,620	945,634	1,495,390	626,265	892,701	1,967,651
Miscellaneous household products	14,085,239	1,556,728	2,283,188	1,109,534	2,462,443	904,023	1,952,200	3,590,855
Lawn and garden supplies	9,702,570	1,022,038	1,315,900	587,808	1,670,118	553,708	1,070,040	3,324,827
Postage and stationery	18,081,851	2,283,203	2,828,552	1,707,806	3,031,617	1,169,829	2,377,886	4,411,792
Stationery, stationery supplies, giftwrap	8,704,871	1,135,448	1,289,145	732,827	1,415,706	592,732	1,063,105	2,340,927
Postage	8,618,822	1,098,112	1,487,621	933,692	1,523,217	547,117	1,038,696	1,868,320
Delivery services	758,159	49,517	51,785	41,288	92,694	29,979	276,086	202,695
HOUSEHOLD FURNISHINGS, EQUIPMENT	191,411,800	15,869,812	27,187,006	15,298,030	30,214,259	13,472,090	23,477,258	64,284,218
Household textiles	18,333,020	1,631,124	3,187,891	1,395,135	2,555,679	1,072,138	2,458,326	5,716,838
Bathroom linens	2,472,155	274,467	543,459	155,369	412,696	127,217	291,434	628,549
Bedroom linens	9,967,693	887,048	1,675,036	910,489	1,206,648	472,493	1,383,571	3,200,850
Kitchen and dining room linens	1,144,215	100,976	123,893	49,249	110,221	99,822	108,825	523,990
Curtains and draperies	2,234,940	151,681	281,848	81,324	372,583	101,890	396,561	849,467
Slipcovers and decorative pillows	1,060,492	100,544	302,275	57,894	179,787	159,974	109,658	155,345
Sewing materials for household items	1,302,358	131,778	242,536	132,735	250,978	85,414	154,963	303,669
Other linens	152,329	9,872	18,704	8,076	22,767	25,263	13,314	54,819
Furniture	48,486,106	3,934,092	5,315,511	3,723,620	7,949,457	3,791,702	5,322,922	18,448,539
Mattresses and springs	6,228,064	503,700	723,522	425,160	984,399	398,514	667,839	2,524,353
Other bedroom furniture	9,456,052	888,100	1,089,662	583,714	1,869,238	766,468	1,241,738	3,017,573
Sofas	11,016,557	948,525	1,500,222	981,008	1,848,278	1,001,972	923,860	3,812,669
Living room chairs	4,843,145	544,847	557,313	386,261	850,869	350,509	516,574	1,636,498
Living room tables	1,717,485	154,458	181,681	121,588	280,431	145,825	162,175	671,568
Kitchen and dining room furniture	4,797,795	276,801	361,492	487,717	671,805	405,880	536,545	2,058,020

	total consumer units	under $20,000	$20,000– $39,999	$40,000– $49,999	$50,000– $69,999	$70,000– $79,999	$80,000– $99,999	$100,000 or more
Infants' furniture	$981,420	$53,569	$103,203	$65,969	$157,923	$98,659	$104,665	$396,876
Outdoor furniture	1,881,443	136,083	145,987	118,517	252,063	188,144	178,910	862,164
Wall units, cabinets, and other furniture	7,564,144	428,145	652,692	553,800	1,034,631	435,665	990,432	3,469,118
Floor coverings	**6,044,338**	**285,323**	**466,529**	**610,101**	**1,237,184**	**289,388**	**736,351**	**2,419,645**
Wall-to-wall carpeting	3,253,570	99,316	215,662	485,897	839,305	198,482	165,041	1,249,779
Floor coverings, nonpermanent	2,790,768	186,007	250,867	124,204	397,879	90,906	571,310	1,169,866
Major appliances	**23,714,551**	**2,229,568**	**3,512,505**	**2,668,113**	**3,957,292**	**2,071,978**	**2,990,156**	**6,163,604**
Dishwashers (built-in), garbage disposals, range hoods	1,667,484	85,152	223,321	70,291	306,270	198,417	248,348	536,388
Refrigerators and freezers	5,961,778	528,999	1,029,567	495,338	1,036,257	684,801	710,000	1,476,224
Washing machines	3,564,043	295,121	669,908	283,554	675,781	269,747	481,162	888,453
Clothes dryers	2,561,692	168,197	370,439	241,129	559,055	186,141	395,267	641,843
Cooking stoves, ovens	3,769,862	296,479	542,652	280,028	590,676	468,487	646,573	945,064
Microwave ovens	980,257	120,004	165,731	98,499	150,153	67,324	148,768	229,731
Portable dishwasher	141,864	–	16,315	20,928	32,886	18,285	14,146	27,633
Window air conditioners	506,990	75,958	73,606	40,833	83,479	37,474	54,551	140,856
Electric floor-cleaning equipment	3,222,174	439,390	222,538	1,080,871	329,036	126,894	217,281	776,127
Sewing machines	417,452	37,648	86,945	29,345	163,705	14,343	36,707	49,143
Miscellaneous household appliances	919,791	284,889	111,069	27,525	29,995	–	37,354	451,994
Small appliances and miscellaneous housewares	**12,170,074**	**1,232,587**	**2,464,108**	**1,025,821**	**1,418,959**	**839,672**	**1,391,061**	**3,589,660**
Housewares	9,600,242	929,625	1,940,196	775,138	1,029,752	701,342	1,132,358	2,883,289
Plastic dinnerware	211,633	27,487	30,992	29,800	28,549	16,992	20,064	57,956
China and other dinnerware	1,566,319	110,751	299,726	95,428	100,283	158,295	371,042	386,868
Flatware	467,454	30,807	63,471	36,966	66,675	29,656	65,554	174,912
Glassware	2,427,968	90,616	693,259	153,322	272,300	192,990	146,179	801,818
Silver serving pieces	34,885	2,553	5,943	1,592	5,421	1,615	5,733	11,053
Other serving pieces	204,656	8,298	24,377	10,123	24,032	15,636	26,536	96,344
Nonelectric cookware	2,104,704	320,463	364,855	219,518	260,194	90,971	217,373	598,974
Tableware, nonelectric kitchenware	2,581,460	338,903	457,442	228,390	272,661	195,187	279,784	755,364
Small appliances	2,569,832	303,043	523,912	250,683	389,206	138,265	258,703	706,371
Small electric kitchen appliances	2,008,190	248,881	430,489	181,643	319,460	108,609	226,897	492,622
Portable heating and cooling equipment	561,642	54,162	93,554	69,040	69,746	29,721	31,806	213,748
Miscellaneous household equipment	**82,663,711**	**6,557,118**	**12,240,744**	**5,875,126**	**13,095,688**	**5,407,146**	**10,578,441**	**27,945,932**
Window coverings	2,729,139	186,868	237,055	82,120	364,090	178,840	616,246	1,063,514
Infants' equipment	913,977	129,126	199,852	57,552	141,842	41,738	68,883	260,203
Laundry and cleaning equipment	1,827,953	257,376	389,779	133,645	308,438	114,166	196,478	404,942
Outdoor equipment	4,184,989	496,301	457,091	389,332	497,620	144,856	431,881	1,680,114
Clocks	888,394	89,958	97,968	60,623	74,806	31,594	84,416	429,289
Lamps and lighting fixtures	1,907,025	113,174	174,798	97,703	255,315	112,357	223,753	929,978
Other household decorative items	18,384,184	1,438,677	2,194,074	1,063,014	3,054,203	1,375,805	1,655,866	7,232,495
Telephones and accessories	3,119,846	146,173	429,779	300,046	372,221	164,626	477,371	1,146,863
Lawn and garden equipment	5,673,399	386,647	903,404	538,104	769,017	387,660	1,390,321	1,297,727
Power tools	3,888,470	401,931	778,029	291,288	952,236	239,186	338,589	925,646
Office furniture for home use	1,322,126	56,547	72,259	81,665	130,277	85,737	97,268	797,935
Hand tools	710,483	62,003	121,573	96,793	142,564	23,906	110,582	152,955
Indoor plants and fresh flowers	4,828,029	352,482	681,225	314,832	833,884	308,060	680,136	1,657,559
Closet and storage items	2,073,308	170,500	137,789	117,493	176,173	230,464	150,525	1,034,686
Rental of furniture	258,146	49,113	115,747	49,932	11,745	905	7,027	23,451
Luggage	770,950	80,339	66,895	54,027	114,557	58,407	87,005	309,345
Computers and computer hardware, nonbusiness use	15,648,069	1,561,857	1,950,618	1,367,724	2,602,839	1,162,657	2,180,946	4,820,917
Computer software and accessories, nonbusiness use	2,216,335	146,975	367,690	142,516	406,553	139,299	328,141	685,160
Telephone answering devices	72,095	9,259	9,208	10,919	10,119	2,326	9,431	21,211
Calculators	167,446	22,742	18,740	10,237	29,633	9,950	14,886	61,242
Business equipment for home use	109,305	10,066	20,027	20,246	22,406	2,520	10,356	23,750
Other hardware	4,608,256	126,037	1,645,933	138,422	671,083	196,091	621,146	1,076,211
Smoke alarms	119,770	7,795	22,363	10,578	25,116	8,205	18,954	25,990
Other household appliances	1,457,013	96,855	242,303	80,187	262,904	128,962	252,416	392,992
Miscellaneous household equipment and parts	4,788,493	258,693	905,989	366,129	865,866	258,892	525,728	1,491,459

Note: Numbers may not add to total because of rounding and missing subcategories. "–" means sample is too small to make a reliable estimate.
Source: Calculations by New Strategist based on the 2004 Consumer Expenditure Survey

Table 8.8 Housing: Household Operations: Market shares by income, 2004

(percentage of total annual spending on household services, supplies, furnishings, and equipment accounted for by before-tax income group of consumer units, 2004)

	total consumer units	under $20,000	$20,000–$39,999	$40,000–$49,999	$50,000–$69,999	$70,000–$79,999	$80,000–$99,999	$100,000 or more
Share of total consumer units	100.0%	24.9%	23.5%	9.8%	15.5%	5.6%	8.0%	12.8%
Share of total before-tax income	100.0	5.0	12.7	8.0	16.9	7.6	13.0	36.8
Share of total spending	100.0	10.8	16.4	8.6	17.1	7.0	12.0	27.7
Share of housing spending	100.0	12.7	17.5	8.7	16.4	7.0	11.7	26.0
HOUSEHOLD SERVICES	100.0	9.4	14.1	6.3	14.2	6.6	14.1	35.2
Personal services	100.0	9.6	13.4	5.3	14.6	7.1	16.3	33.7
Babysitting and child care in own home	100.0	2.6	6.4	5.4	9.4	9.1	11.3	55.8
Babysitting and child care in someone else's home	100.0	8.4	19.1	10.9	22.1	8.3	10.4	20.8
Care for elderly, invalids, handicapped, etc.	100.0	33.0	28.5	1.5	11.1	1.0	14.6	10.3
Day care centers, nurseries, and preschools	100.0	4.6	11.2	5.5	15.1	7.9	18.9	36.8
Other household services	100.0	9.3	14.5	7.0	14.0	6.3	12.6	36.2
Housekeeping services	100.0	8.5	9.8	4.6	8.2	4.7	10.8	53.3
Gardening, lawn care service	100.0	10.9	15.5	5.6	12.2	5.6	11.6	38.5
Water-softening service	100.0	13.9	16.5	8.9	17.3	7.6	9.7	26.3
Nonclothing laundry and dry cleaning, sent out	100.0	9.7	18.0	5.4	14.5	5.7	11.5	35.5
Nonclothing laundry and dry cleaning, coin-operated	100.0	32.3	28.3	10.4	12.2	3.5	4.5	8.8
Termite and pest control services	100.0	6.6	14.7	7.4	14.2	6.2	12.0	38.9
Home security system service fee	100.0	6.8	12.5	6.0	17.1	7.3	14.1	36.3
Other home services	100.0	9.3	14.4	7.5	9.6	6.0	16.4	36.8
Termite and pest control products	100.0	8.8	17.4	6.6	12.1	4.8	14.3	36.3
Moving, storage, and freight express	100.0	6.4	15.0	6.9	15.4	3.9	13.4	39.0
Appliance repair, including at service center	100.0	8.7	14.3	6.7	15.2	9.2	16.3	29.6
Reupholstering and furniture repair	100.0	11.1	11.4	6.8	7.5	7.1	13.0	43.0
Repairs and rentals of lawn and garden equipment, hand and power tools, etc.	100.0	9.6	17.2	6.2	13.0	5.0	19.3	29.8
Appliance rental	100.0	37.8	29.4	1.2	14.7	2.6	6.5	7.6
Repair of computer systems for nonbusiness use	100.0	8.2	18.2	11.5	10.3	6.5	15.8	29.5
Computer information services	100.0	8.8	16.1	9.4	19.5	8.3	13.0	25.0
HOUSEKEEPING SUPPLIES	100.0	13.3	17.6	8.9	16.9	6.3	11.5	24.1
Laundry and cleaning supplies	100.0	14.5	20.5	10.5	17.3	6.5	9.7	19.7
Soaps and detergents	100.0	14.6	20.6	10.7	17.0	6.7	10.0	19.2
Other laundry cleaning products	100.0	14.5	20.5	10.2	17.7	6.2	9.3	20.3
Other household products	100.0	13.0	17.1	7.8	16.7	6.2	11.6	26.3
Cleansing and toilet tissue, paper towels, and napkins	100.0	18.0	21.7	9.5	15.0	6.3	8.9	19.7
Miscellaneous household products	100.0	11.1	16.2	7.9	17.5	6.4	13.9	25.5
Lawn and garden supplies	100.0	10.5	13.6	6.1	17.2	5.7	11.0	34.3
Postage and stationery	100.0	12.6	15.6	9.4	16.8	6.5	13.2	24.4
Stationery, stationery supplies, giftwrap	100.0	13.0	14.8	8.4	16.3	6.8	12.2	26.9
Postage	100.0	12.7	17.3	10.8	17.7	6.3	12.1	21.7
Delivery services	100.0	6.5	6.8	5.4	12.2	4.0	36.4	26.7
HOUSEHOLD FURNISHINGS AND EQUIPMENT	100.0	8.3	14.2	8.0	15.8	7.0	12.3	33.6
Household textiles	100.0	8.9	17.4	7.6	13.9	5.8	13.4	31.2
Bathroom linens	100.0	11.1	22.0	6.3	16.7	5.1	11.8	25.4
Bedroom linens	100.0	8.9	16.8	9.1	12.1	4.7	13.9	32.1
Kitchen and dining room linens	100.0	8.8	10.8	4.3	9.6	8.7	9.5	45.8
Curtains and draperies	100.0	6.8	12.6	3.6	16.7	4.6	17.7	38.0
Slipcovers and decorative pillows	100.0	9.5	28.5	5.5	17.0	15.1	10.3	14.6
Sewing materials for household items	100.0	10.1	18.6	10.2	19.3	6.6	11.9	23.3
Other linens	100.0	6.5	12.3	5.3	14.9	16.6	8.7	36.0
Furniture	100.0	8.1	11.0	7.7	16.4	7.8	11.0	38.0
Mattresses and springs	100.0	8.1	11.6	6.8	15.8	6.4	10.7	40.5
Other bedroom furniture	100.0	9.4	11.5	6.2	19.8	8.1	13.1	31.9
Sofas	100.0	8.6	13.6	8.9	16.8	9.1	8.4	34.6
Living room chairs	100.0	11.2	11.5	8.0	17.6	7.2	10.7	33.8
Living room tables	100.0	9.0	10.6	7.1	16.3	8.5	9.4	39.1
Kitchen and dining room furniture	100.0	5.8	7.5	10.2	14.0	8.5	11.2	42.9

	total consumer units	under $20,000	$20,000– $39,999	$40,000– $49,999	$50,000– $69,999	$70,000– $79,999	$80,000– $99,999	$100,000 or more
Infants' furniture	100.0%	5.5%	10.5%	6.7%	16.1%	10.1%	10.7%	40.4%
Outdoor furniture	100.0	7.2	7.8	6.3	13.4	10.0	9.5	45.8
Wall units, cabinets, and other furniture	100.0	5.7	8.6	7.3	13.7	5.8	13.1	45.9
Floor coverings	**100.0**	**4.7**	**7.7**	**10.1**	**20.5**	**4.8**	**12.2**	**40.0**
Wall-to-wall carpeting	100.0	3.1	6.6	14.9	25.8	6.1	5.1	38.4
Floor coverings, nonpermanent	100.0	6.7	9.0	4.5	14.3	3.3	20.5	41.9
Major appliances	**100.0**	**9.4**	**14.8**	**11.3**	**16.7**	**8.7**	**12.6**	**26.0**
Dishwashers (built-in), garbage disposals, range hoods	100.0	5.1	13.4	4.2	18.4	11.9	14.9	32.2
Refrigerators and freezers	100.0	8.9	17.3	8.3	17.4	11.5	11.9	24.8
Washing machines	100.0	8.3	18.8	8.0	19.0	7.6	13.5	24.9
Clothes dryers	100.0	6.6	14.5	9.4	21.8	7.3	15.4	25.1
Cooking stoves, ovens	100.0	7.9	14.4	7.4	15.7	12.4	17.2	25.1
Microwave ovens	100.0	12.2	16.9	10.0	15.3	6.9	15.2	23.4
Portable dishwasher	100.0	–	11.5	14.8	23.2	12.9	10.0	19.5
Window air conditioners	100.0	15.0	14.5	8.1	16.5	7.4	10.8	27.8
Electric floor-cleaning equipment	100.0	13.6	6.9	33.5	10.2	3.9	6.7	24.1
Sewing machines	100.0	9.0	20.8	7.0	39.2	3.4	8.8	11.8
Miscellaneous household appliances	100.0	31.0	12.1	3.0	3.3	–	4.1	49.1
Small appliances and miscellaneous housewares	**100.0**	**10.1**	**20.2**	**8.4**	**11.7**	**6.9**	**11.4**	**29.5**
Housewares	100.0	9.7	20.2	8.1	10.7	7.3	11.8	30.0
Plastic dinnerware	100.0	13.0	14.6	14.1	13.5	8.0	9.5	27.4
China and other dinnerware	100.0	7.1	19.1	6.1	6.4	10.1	23.7	24.7
Flatware	100.0	6.6	13.6	7.9	14.3	6.3	14.0	37.4
Glassware	100.0	3.7	28.6	6.3	11.2	7.9	6.0	33.0
Silver serving pieces	100.0	7.3	17.0	4.6	15.5	4.6	16.4	31.7
Other serving pieces	100.0	4.1	11.9	4.9	11.7	7.6	13.0	47.1
Nonelectric cookware	100.0	15.2	17.3	10.4	12.4	4.3	10.3	28.5
Tableware, nonelectric kitchenware	100.0	13.1	17.7	8.8	10.6	7.6	10.8	29.3
Small appliances	100.0	11.8	20.4	9.8	15.1	5.4	10.1	27.5
Small electric kitchen appliances	100.0	12.4	21.4	9.0	15.9	5.4	11.3	24.5
Portable heating and cooling equipment	100.0	9.6	16.7	12.3	12.4	5.3	5.7	38.1
Miscellaneous household equipment	**100.0**	**7.9**	**14.8**	**7.1**	**15.8**	**6.5**	**12.8**	**33.8**
Window coverings	100.0	6.8	8.7	3.0	13.3	6.6	22.6	39.0
Infants' equipment	100.0	14.1	21.9	6.3	15.5	4.6	7.5	28.5
Laundry and cleaning equipment	100.0	14.1	21.3	7.3	16.9	6.2	10.7	22.2
Outdoor equipment	100.0	11.9	10.9	9.3	11.9	3.5	10.3	40.1
Clocks	100.0	10.1	11.0	6.8	8.4	3.6	9.5	48.3
Lamps and lighting fixtures	100.0	5.9	9.2	5.1	13.4	5.9	11.7	48.8
Other household decorative items	100.0	7.8	11.9	5.8	16.6	7.5	9.0	39.3
Telephones and accessories	100.0	4.7	13.8	9.6	11.9	5.3	15.3	36.8
Lawn and garden equipment	100.0	6.8	15.9	9.5	13.6	6.8	24.5	22.9
Power tools	100.0	10.3	20.0	7.5	24.5	6.2	8.7	23.8
Office furniture for home use	100.0	4.3	5.5	6.2	9.9	6.5	7.4	60.4
Hand tools	100.0	8.7	17.1	13.6	20.1	3.4	15.6	21.5
Indoor plants and fresh flowers	100.0	7.3	14.1	6.5	17.3	6.4	14.1	34.3
Closet and storage items	100.0	8.2	6.6	5.7	8.5	11.1	7.3	49.9
Rental of furniture	100.0	19.0	44.8	19.3	4.5	0.4	2.7	9.1
Luggage	100.0	10.4	8.7	7.0	14.9	7.6	11.3	40.1
Computers and computer hardware, nonbusiness use	100.0	10.0	12.5	8.7	16.6	7.4	13.9	30.8
Computer software and accessories, nonbusiness use	100.0	6.6	16.6	6.4	18.3	6.3	14.8	30.9
Telephone answering devices	100.0	12.8	12.8	15.1	14.0	3.2	13.1	29.4
Calculators	100.0	13.6	11.2	6.1	17.7	5.9	8.9	36.6
Business equipment for home use	100.0	9.2	18.3	18.5	20.5	2.3	9.5	21.7
Other hardware	100.0	2.7	35.7	3.0	14.6	4.3	13.5	23.4
Smoke alarms	100.0	6.5	18.7	8.8	21.0	6.9	15.8	21.7
Other household appliances	100.0	6.6	16.6	5.5	18.0	8.9	17.3	27.0
Miscellaneous household equipment and parts	100.0	5.4	18.9	7.6	18.1	5.4	11.0	31.1

Note: Numbers may not add to total because of rounding. "–" means sample is too small to make a reliable estimate.
Source: Calculations by New Strategist based on the 2004 Consumer Expenditure Survey

Table 8.9 Housing: Household Operations: Average spending by high-income consumer units, 2004

(average annual spending on household services, supplies, furnishings, and equipment, by before-tax income of high-income consumer units (CU), 2004)

	total consumer units	$100,000 or more	$100,000– $119,999	$120,000– $149,999	$150,000 or more
Number of consumer units (in 000s)	116,282	14,937	5,625	4,245	5,067
Average number of persons per CU	2.5	3.2	3.1	3.3	3.2
Average before-tax income of CU	$54,453.00	$155,901.00	$108,751.00	$132,292.00	$228,021.00
Average spending of CU, total	43,394.87	93,525.67	75,213.14	87,298.57	119,448.79
Housing, average spending	**13,918.48**	**28,139.97**	**22,273.31**	**26,339.36**	**36,246.25**
HOUSEHOLD SERVICES	**752.83**	**2,064.29**	**1,406.78**	**1,799.32**	**3,016.36**
Personal services	**299.71**	**786.36**	**557.67**	**738.68**	**1,080.17**
Babysitting and child care in own home	37.09	161.01	126.41	88.68	260.02
Babysitting and child care in someone else's home	26.12	42.32	29.87	50.30	49.45
Care for elderly, invalids, handicapped, etc.	34.96	28.01	47.12	5.67	25.51
Day care centers, nurseries, and preschools	193.51	554.88	354.27	593.54	745.18
Other household services	**453.12**	**1,277.93**	**849.12**	**1,060.64**	**1,936.19**
Housekeeping services	88.85	368.93	161.68	249.73	698.86
Gardening, lawn care service	95.08	285.33	158.22	235.46	468.22
Water-softening service	3.06	6.27	5.09	6.85	7.08
Nonclothing laundry and dry cleaning, sent out	0.94	2.60	1.23	1.53	5.01
Nonclothing laundry and dry cleaning, coin-operated	3.71	2.54	1.41	3.19	3.25
Termite and pest control services	12.04	36.47	22.52	31.91	55.77
Home security system service fee	15.57	43.97	30.00	45.50	58.21
Other home services	23.03	65.95	39.41	48.33	110.18
Termite and pest control products	1.53	4.32	2.58	3.88	6.61
Moving, storage, and freight express	33.91	102.94	133.01	75.12	92.86
Appliance repair, including at service center	14.53	33.47	22.77	37.76	41.76
Reupholstering and furniture repair	7.35	24.62	10.30	20.71	43.80
Repairs and rentals of lawn and garden equipment, hand and power tools, etc.	7.29	16.92	16.12	15.33	19.14
Appliance rental	1.75	1.03	1.12	1.39	0.64
Repair of computer systems for nonbusiness use	4.03	9.24	5.52	10.98	11.90
Computer information services	139.46	271.08	237.53	270.69	308.64
HOUSEKEEPING SUPPLIES	**594.47**	**1,117.54**	**893.36**	**1,050.61**	**1,460.75**
Laundry and cleaning supplies	**148.56**	**227.46**	**204.43**	**245.97**	**237.06**
Soaps and detergents	85.44	127.50	116.54	130.87	137.55
Other laundry cleaning products	63.13	99.96	87.88	115.10	99.51
Other household products	**290.41**	**594.72**	**436.65**	**493.12**	**891.71**
Cleansing and toilet tissue, paper towels, and napkins	85.84	131.73	119.42	139.58	138.92
Miscellaneous household products	121.13	240.40	188.71	225.07	319.44
Lawn and garden supplies	83.44	222.59	128.52	128.47	433.35
Postage and stationery	**155.50**	**295.36**	**252.28**	**311.52**	**331.98**
Stationery, stationery supplies, giftwrap	74.86	156.72	137.71	173.84	162.78
Postage	74.12	125.08	104.60	135.12	140.10
Delivery services	6.52	13.57	9.98	2.55	29.11
HOUSEHOLD FURNISHINGS AND EQUIPMENT	**1,646.10**	**4,303.69**	**3,125.35**	**4,174.49**	**5,766.84**
Household textiles	**157.66**	**382.73**	**316.81**	**380.17**	**458.53**
Bathroom linens	21.26	42.08	40.36	27.26	59.17
Bedroom linens	85.72	214.29	185.33	236.59	227.36
Kitchen and dining room linens	9.84	35.08	29.50	50.67	26.20
Curtains and draperies	19.22	56.87	30.43	40.25	100.14
Slipcovers and decorative pillows	9.12	10.40	7.78	11.32	12.69
Sewing materials for household items	11.20	20.33	21.36	12.08	26.10
Other linens	1.31	3.67	2.06	1.99	6.86
Furniture	**416.97**	**1,235.09**	**790.81**	**1,317.57**	**1,659.18**
Mattresses and springs	53.56	169.00	70.21	238.32	220.59
Other bedroom furniture	81.32	202.02	181.71	250.03	184.32
Sofas	94.74	255.25	198.93	212.17	353.85
Living room chairs	41.65	109.56	62.05	109.89	162.02
Living room tables	14.77	44.96	31.47	39.74	64.31
Kitchen and dining room furniture	41.26	137.78	79.71	197.31	152.37

	total consumer units	$100,000 or more	$100,000– $119,999	$120,000– $149,999	$150,000 or more
Infants' furniture	$8.44	$26.57	$32.72	$23.36	$22.43
Outdoor furniture	16.18	57.72	34.00	55.40	85.98
Wall units, cabinets, and other furniture	65.05	232.25	100.01	191.37	413.31
Floor coverings	**51.98**	**161.99**	**87.76**	**92.61**	**302.52**
Wall-to-wall carpeting	27.98	83.67	62.59	31.11	151.10
Floor coverings, nonpermanent	24.00	78.32	25.17	61.50	151.42
Major appliances	**203.94**	**412.64**	**316.43**	**389.74**	**539.09**
Dishwashers (built-in), garbage disposals, range hoods	14.34	35.91	24.11	22.05	60.64
Refrigerators and freezers	51.27	98.83	73.21	103.91	123.01
Washing machines	30.65	59.48	46.80	55.16	77.18
Clothes dryers	22.03	42.97	28.31	44.05	58.34
Cooking stoves, ovens	32.42	63.27	45.37	48.47	95.54
Microwave ovens	8.43	15.38	13.49	18.59	14.79
Portable dishwasher	1.22	1.85	2.14	–	3.06
Window air conditioners	4.36	9.43	16.63	4.96	5.16
Electric floor-cleaning equipment	27.71	51.96	60.71	37.96	55.37
Sewing machines	3.59	3.29	2.37	0.53	6.61
Miscellaneous household appliances	7.91	30.26	3.27	54.06	39.40
Small appliances and miscellaneous housewares	**104.66**	**240.32**	**219.39**	**235.07**	**269.28**
Housewares	82.56	193.03	182.87	191.41	206.99
Plastic dinnerware	1.82	3.88	2.69	5.09	4.18
China and other dinnerware	13.47	25.90	18.74	19.74	40.93
Flatware	4.02	11.71	3.92	14.60	17.93
Glassware	20.88	53.68	57.26	56.19	46.74
Silver serving pieces	0.30	0.74	0.42	1.15	0.70
Other serving pieces	1.76	6.45	3.65	9.52	7.00
Nonelectric cookware	18.10	40.10	40.59	39.36	40.24
Tableware, nonelectric kitchenware	22.20	50.57	55.60	45.74	49.27
Small appliances	22.10	47.29	36.52	43.67	62.29
Small electric kitchen appliances	17.27	32.98	31.21	31.89	35.86
Portable heating and cooling equipment	4.83	14.31	5.31	11.78	26.43
Miscellaneous household equipment	**710.89**	**1,870.92**	**1,394.16**	**1,759.32**	**2,538.23**
Window coverings	23.47	71.20	42.85	47.40	122.61
Infants' equipment	7.86	17.42	34.60	5.29	8.56
Laundry and cleaning equipment	15.72	27.11	25.00	32.60	24.15
Outdoor equipment	35.99	112.48	26.97	233.84	94.97
Clocks	7.64	28.74	16.76	16.88	55.46
Lamps and lighting fixtures	16.40	62.26	89.78	37.16	52.74
Other household decorative items	158.10	484.20	297.57	345.40	853.91
Telephones and accessories	26.83	76.78	61.94	44.65	127.50
Lawn and garden equipment	48.79	86.88	81.09	100.26	82.11
Power tools	33.44	61.97	58.73	70.95	56.88
Office furniture for home use	11.37	53.42	16.74	38.63	106.52
Hand tools	6.11	10.24	10.01	11.19	9.71
Indoor plants and fresh flowers	41.52	110.97	84.14	110.00	141.56
Closet and storage items	17.83	69.27	35.40	34.79	145.75
Rental of furniture	2.22	1.57	0.59	0.48	3.57
Luggage	6.63	20.71	11.09	17.88	33.78
Computers and computer hardware, nonbusiness use	134.57	322.75	273.03	295.02	401.18
Computer software and accessories, nonbusiness use	19.06	45.87	35.12	55.11	50.05
Telephone answering devices	0.62	1.42	1.19	0.33	2.58
Calculators	1.44	4.10	2.69	3.36	6.29
Business equipment for home use	0.94	1.59	0.90	1.58	2.37
Other hardware	39.63	72.05	32.87	171.60	19.61
Smoke alarms	1.03	1.74	1.38	2.27	1.73
Other household appliances	12.53	26.31	16.54	23.77	39.28
Miscellaneous household equipment and parts	41.18	99.85	137.17	58.88	95.38

Note: Subcategories may not add to total because some are not shown. "–" means sample is too small to make a reliable estimate.
Source: Bureau of Labor Statistics, unpublished tables from the 2004 Consumer Expenditure Survey; calculations by New Strategist

Table 8.10 Housing: Household Operations: Indexed spending by high-income consumer units, 2004

(indexed average annual spending of high-income consumer units (CU) on household services, supplies, furnishings, and equipment, by before-tax income of consumer unit, 2004; index definition: an index of 100 is the average for all consumer units; an index of 132 means that spending by consumer units in that group is 32 percent above the average for all consumer units; an index of 68 indicates spending that is 32 percent below the average for all consumer units)

	total consumer units	$100,000 or more	$100,000–$119,999	$120,000–$149,999	$150,000 or more
Average spending of CU, total	$43,395	$93,526	$75,213	$87,299	$119,449
Average spending of CU, index	100	216	173	201	275
Housing, spending index	100	202	160	189	260
HOUSEHOLD SERVICES	100	274	187	239	401
Personal services	100	262	186	246	360
Babysitting and child care in own home	100	434	341	239	701
Babysitting and child care in someone else's home	100	162	114	193	189
Care for elderly, invalids, handicapped, etc.	100	80	135	16	73
Day care centers, nurseries, and preschools	100	287	183	307	385
Other household services	100	282	187	234	427
Housekeeping services	100	415	182	281	787
Gardening, lawn care service	100	300	166	248	492
Water-softening service	100	205	166	224	231
Nonclothing laundry and dry cleaning, sent out	100	277	131	163	533
Nonclothing laundry and dry cleaning, coin-operated	100	68	38	86	88
Termite and pest control services	100	303	187	265	463
Home security system service fee	100	282	193	292	374
Other home services	100	286	171	210	478
Termite and pest control products	100	282	169	254	432
Moving, storage, and freight express	100	304	392	222	274
Appliance repair, including at service center	100	230	157	260	287
Reupholstering and furniture repair	100	335	140	282	596
Repairs and rentals of lawn and garden equipment, hand and power tools, etc.	100	232	221	210	263
Appliance rental	100	59	64	79	37
Repair of computer systems for nonbusiness use	100	229	137	272	295
Computer information services	100	194	170	194	221
HOUSEKEEPING SUPPLIES	100	188	150	177	246
Laundry and cleaning supplies	100	153	138	166	160
Soaps and detergents	100	149	136	153	161
Other laundry cleaning products	100	158	139	182	158
Other household products	100	205	150	170	307
Cleansing and toilet tissue, paper towels, and napkins	100	153	139	163	162
Miscellaneous household products	100	198	156	186	264
Lawn and garden supplies	100	267	154	154	519
Postage and stationery	100	190	162	200	213
Stationery, stationery supplies, giftwrap	100	209	184	232	217
Postage	100	169	141	182	189
Delivery services	100	208	153	39	446
HOUSEHOLD FURNISHINGS AND EQUIPMENT	100	261	190	254	350
Household textiles	100	243	201	241	291
Bathroom linens	100	198	190	128	278
Bedroom linens	100	250	216	276	265
Kitchen and dining room linens	100	357	300	515	266
Curtains and draperies	100	296	158	209	521
Slipcovers and decorative pillows	100	114	85	124	139
Sewing materials for household items	100	182	191	108	233
Other linens	100	280	157	152	524
Furniture	100	296	190	316	398
Mattresses and springs	100	316	131	445	412
Other bedroom furniture	100	248	223	307	227
Sofas	100	269	210	224	373
Living room chairs	100	263	149	264	389
Living room tables	100	304	213	269	435
Kitchen and dining room furniture	100	334	193	478	369

	total consumer units	$100,000 or more	$100,000– $119,999	$120,000– $149,999	$150,000 or more
Infants' furniture	100	315	388	277	266
Outdoor furniture	100	357	210	342	531
Wall units, cabinets, and other furniture	100	357	154	294	635
Floor coverings	**100**	**312**	**169**	**178**	**582**
Wall-to-wall carpeting	100	299	224	111	540
Floor coverings, nonpermanent	100	326	105	256	631
Major appliances	**100**	**202**	**155**	**191**	**264**
Dishwashers (built-in), garbage disposals, range hoods	100	250	168	154	423
Refrigerators and freezers	100	193	143	203	240
Washing machines	100	194	153	180	252
Clothes dryers	100	195	129	200	265
Cooking stoves, ovens	100	195	140	150	295
Microwave ovens	100	182	160	221	175
Portable dishwasher	100	152	175	–	251
Window air conditioners	100	216	381	114	118
Electric floor-cleaning equipment	100	188	219	137	200
Sewing machines	100	92	66	15	184
Miscellaneous household appliances	100	383	41	683	498
Small appliances and miscellaneous housewares	**100**	**230**	**210**	**225**	**257**
Housewares	100	234	221	232	251
Plastic dinnerware	100	213	148	280	230
China and other dinnerware	100	192	139	147	304
Flatware	100	291	98	363	446
Glassware	100	257	274	269	224
Silver serving pieces	100	247	140	383	233
Other serving pieces	100	366	207	541	398
Nonelectric cookware	100	222	224	217	222
Tableware, nonelectric kitchenware	100	228	250	206	222
Small appliances	100	214	165	198	282
Small electric kitchen appliances	100	191	181	185	208
Portable heating and cooling equipment	100	296	110	244	547
Miscellaneous household equipment	**100**	**263**	**196**	**247**	**357**
Window coverings	100	303	183	202	522
Infants' equipment	100	222	440	67	109
Laundry and cleaning equipment	100	172	159	207	154
Outdoor equipment	100	313	75	650	264
Clocks	100	376	219	221	726
Lamps and lighting fixtures	100	380	547	227	322
Other household decorative items	100	306	188	218	540
Telephones and accessories	100	286	231	166	475
Lawn and garden equipment	100	178	166	205	168
Power tools	100	185	176	212	170
Office furniture for home use	100	470	147	340	937
Hand tools	100	168	164	183	159
Indoor plants and fresh flowers	100	267	203	265	341
Closet and storage items	100	389	199	195	817
Rental of furniture	100	71	27	22	161
Luggage	100	312	167	270	510
Computers and computer hardware, nonbusiness use	100	240	203	219	298
Computer software and accessories, nonbusiness use	100	241	184	289	263
Telephone answering devices	100	229	192	53	416
Calculators	100	285	187	233	437
Business equipment for home use	100	169	96	168	252
Other hardware	100	182	83	433	49
Smoke alarms	100	169	134	220	168
Other household appliances	100	210	132	190	313
Miscellaneous household equipment and parts	100	242	333	143	232

Note: "–" means sample is too small to make a reliable estimate.
Source: Calculations by New Strategist based on the 2004 Consumer Expenditure Survey

Table 8.11 Housing: Household Operations: Total spending by high-income consumer units, 2004

(total annual spending on household services, supplies, furnishings, and equipment, by before-tax income group of high-income consumer units (CU), 2004; consumer units and dollars in thousands)

	total consumer units	$100,000 or more	$100,000–$119,999	$120,000–$149,999	$150,000 or more
Number of consumer units	116,282	14,937	5,625	4,245	5,067
Total spending of all CUs	$5,046,042,273	$1,396,992,933	$423,073,913	$370,582,430	$605,247,019
Housing, total spending	1,618,468,691	420,326,732	125,287,369	111,810,583	183,659,749
HOUSEHOLD SERVICES	87,540,578	30,834,300	7,913,138	7,638,113	15,283,896
Personal services	34,850,878	11,745,859	3,136,894	3,135,697	5,473,221
Babysitting and child care in own home	4,312,899	2,405,006	711,056	376,447	1,317,521
Babysitting and child care in someone else's home	3,037,286	632,134	168,019	213,524	250,563
Care for elderly, invalids, handicapped, etc.	4,065,219	418,385	265,050	24,069	129,259
Day care centers, nurseries, and preschools	22,501,730	8,288,243	1,992,769	2,519,577	3,775,827
Other household services	52,689,700	19,088,440	4,776,300	4,502,417	9,810,675
Housekeeping services	10,331,656	5,510,707	909,450	1,060,104	3,541,124
Gardening, lawn care service	11,056,093	4,261,974	889,988	999,528	2,372,471
Water-softening service	355,823	93,655	28,631	29,078	35,874
Nonclothing laundry and dry cleaning, sent out	109,305	38,836	6,919	6,495	25,386
Nonclothing laundry and dry cleaning, coin-operated	431,406	37,940	7,931	13,542	16,468
Termite and pest control services	1,400,035	544,752	126,675	135,458	282,587
Home security system service fee	1,810,511	656,780	168,750	193,148	294,950
Other home services	2,677,974	985,095	221,681	205,161	558,282
Termite and pest control products	177,911	64,528	14,513	16,471	33,493
Moving, storage, and freight express	3,943,123	1,537,615	748,181	318,884	470,522
Appliance repair, including at service center	1,689,577	499,941	128,081	160,291	211,598
Reupholstering and furniture repair	854,673	367,749	57,938	87,914	221,935
Repairs and rentals of lawn and garden equipment, hand and power tools, etc.	847,696	252,734	90,675	65,076	96,982
Appliance rental	203,494	15,385	6,300	5,901	3,243
Repair of computer systems for nonbusiness use	468,616	138,018	31,050	46,610	60,297
Computer information services	16,216,688	4,049,122	1,336,106	1,149,079	1,563,879
HOUSEKEEPING SUPPLIES	69,126,161	16,692,695	5,025,150	4,459,839	7,401,620
Laundry and cleaning supplies	17,274,854	3,397,570	1,149,919	1,044,143	1,201,183
Soaps and detergents	9,935,134	1,904,468	655,538	555,543	696,966
Other laundry cleaning products	7,340,883	1,493,103	494,325	488,600	504,217
Other household products	33,769,456	8,883,333	2,456,156	2,093,294	4,518,295
Cleansing and toilet tissue, paper towels, and napkins	9,981,647	1,967,651	671,738	592,517	703,908
Miscellaneous household products	14,085,239	3,590,855	1,061,494	955,422	1,618,602
Lawn and garden supplies	9,702,570	3,324,827	722,925	545,355	2,195,784
Postage and stationery	18,081,851	4,411,792	1,419,075	1,322,402	1,682,143
Stationery, stationery supplies, giftwrap	8,704,871	2,340,927	774,619	737,951	824,806
Postage	8,618,822	1,868,320	588,375	573,584	709,887
Delivery services	758,159	202,695	56,138	10,825	147,500
HOUSEHOLD FURNISHINGS AND EQUIPMENT	191,411,800	64,284,218	17,580,094	17,720,710	29,220,578
Household textiles	18,333,020	5,716,838	1,782,056	1,613,822	2,323,372
Bathroom linens	2,472,155	628,549	227,025	115,719	299,814
Bedroom linens	9,967,693	3,200,850	1,042,481	1,004,325	1,152,033
Kitchen and dining room linens	1,144,215	523,990	165,938	215,094	132,755
Curtains and draperies	2,234,940	849,467	171,169	170,861	507,409
Slipcovers and decorative pillows	1,060,492	155,345	43,763	48,053	64,300
Sewing materials for household items	1,302,358	303,669	120,150	51,280	132,249
Other linens	152,329	54,819	11,588	8,448	34,760
Furniture	48,486,106	18,448,539	4,448,306	5,593,085	8,407,065
Mattresses and springs	6,228,064	2,524,353	394,931	1,011,668	1,117,730
Other bedroom furniture	9,456,052	3,017,573	1,022,119	1,061,377	933,949
Sofas	11,016,557	3,812,669	1,118,981	900,662	1,792,958
Living room chairs	4,843,145	1,636,498	349,031	466,483	820,955
Living room tables	1,717,485	671,568	177,019	168,696	325,859
Kitchen and dining room furniture	4,797,795	2,058,020	448,369	837,581	772,059

	total consumer units	$100,000 or more	$100,000–$119,999	$120,000–$149,999	$150,000 or more
Infants' furniture	$981,420	$396,876	$184,050	$99,163	$113,653
Outdoor furniture	1,881,443	862,164	191,250	235,173	435,661
Wall units, cabinets, and other furniture	7,564,144	3,469,118	562,556	812,366	2,094,242
Floor coverings	**6,044,338**	**2,419,645**	**493,650**	**393,129**	**1,532,869**
Wall-to-wall carpeting	3,253,570	1,249,779	352,069	132,062	765,624
Floor coverings, nonpermanent	2,790,768	1,169,866	141,581	261,068	767,245
Major appliances	**23,714,551**	**6,163,604**	**1,779,919**	**1,654,446**	**2,731,569**
Dishwashers (built-in), garbage disposals, range hoods	1,667,484	536,388	135,619	93,602	307,263
Refrigerators and freezers	5,961,778	1,476,224	411,806	441,098	623,292
Washing machines	3,564,043	888,453	263,250	234,154	391,071
Clothes dryers	2,561,692	641,843	159,244	186,992	295,609
Cooking stoves, ovens	3,769,862	945,064	255,206	205,755	484,101
Microwave ovens	980,257	229,731	75,881	78,915	74,941
Portable dishwasher	141,864	27,633	12,038	–	15,505
Window air conditioners	506,990	140,856	93,544	21,055	26,146
Electric floor-cleaning equipment	3,222,174	776,127	341,494	161,140	280,560
Sewing machines	417,452	49,143	13,331	2,250	33,493
Miscellaneous household appliances	919,791	451,994	18,394	229,485	199,640
Small appliances and miscellaneous housewares	**12,170,074**	**3,589,660**	**1,234,069**	**997,872**	**1,364,442**
Housewares	9,600,242	2,883,289	1,028,644	812,535	1,048,818
Plastic dinnerware	211,633	57,956	15,131	21,607	21,180
China and other dinnerware	1,566,319	386,868	105,413	83,796	207,392
Flatware	467,454	174,912	22,050	61,977	90,851
Glassware	2,427,968	801,818	322,088	238,527	236,832
Silver serving pieces	34,885	11,053	2,363	4,882	3,547
Other serving pieces	204,656	96,344	20,531	40,412	35,469
Nonelectric cookware	2,104,704	598,974	228,319	167,083	203,896
Tableware, nonelectric kitchenware	2,581,460	755,364	312,750	194,166	249,651
Small appliances	2,569,832	706,371	205,425	185,379	315,623
Small electric kitchen appliances	2,008,190	492,622	175,556	135,373	181,703
Portable heating and cooling equipment	561,642	213,748	29,869	50,006	133,921
Miscellaneous household equipment	**82,663,711**	**27,945,932**	**7,842,150**	**7,468,313**	**12,861,211**
Window coverings	2,729,139	1,063,514	241,031	201,213	621,265
Infants' equipment	913,977	260,203	194,625	22,456	43,374
Laundry and cleaning equipment	1,827,953	404,942	140,625	138,387	122,368
Outdoor equipment	4,184,989	1,680,114	151,706	992,651	481,213
Clocks	888,394	429,289	94,275	71,656	281,016
Lamps and lighting fixtures	1,907,025	929,978	505,013	157,744	267,234
Other household decorative items	18,384,184	7,232,495	1,673,831	1,466,223	4,326,762
Telephones and accessories	3,119,846	1,146,863	348,413	189,539	646,043
Lawn and garden equipment	5,673,399	1,297,727	456,131	425,604	416,051
Power tools	3,888,470	925,646	330,356	301,183	288,211
Office furniture for home use	1,322,126	797,935	94,163	163,984	539,737
Hand tools	710,483	152,955	56,306	47,502	49,201
Indoor plants and fresh flowers	4,828,029	1,657,559	473,288	466,950	717,285
Closet and storage items	2,073,308	1,034,686	199,125	147,684	738,515
Rental of furniture	258,146	23,451	3,319	2,038	18,089
Luggage	770,950	309,345	62,381	75,901	171,163
Computers and computer hardware, nonbusiness use	15,648,069	4,820,917	1,535,794	1,252,360	2,032,779
Computer software and accessories, nonbusiness use	2,216,335	685,160	197,550	233,942	253,603
Telephone answering devices	72,095	21,211	6,694	1,401	13,073
Calculators	167,446	61,242	15,131	14,263	31,871
Business equipment for home use	109,305	23,750	5,063	6,707	12,009
Other hardware	4,608,256	1,076,211	184,894	728,442	99,364
Smoke alarms	119,770	25,990	7,763	9,636	8,766
Other household appliances	1,457,013	392,992	93,038	100,904	199,032
Miscellaneous household equipment and parts	4,788,493	1,491,459	771,581	249,946	483,290

Note: Numbers may not add to total because of rounding and missing subcategories. "–" means sample is too small to make a reliable estimate.
Source: Calculations by New Strategist based on the 2004 Consumer Expenditure Survey

Table 8.12 Housing: Household Operations: Market shares by high-income consumer units, 2004

(percentage of total annual spending on household services, supplies, furnishings, and equipment accounted for by before-tax income group of high-income consumer units, 2004)

	total consumer units	$100,000 or more	$100,000– $119,999	$120,000– $149,999	$150,000 or more
Share of total consumer units	100.0%	12.8%	4.8%	3.7%	4.4%
Share of total before-tax income	100.0	36.8	9.7	8.9	18.2
Share of total spending	100.0	27.7	8.4	7.3	12.0
Share of housing spending	100.0	26.0	7.7	6.9	11.3
HOUSEHOLD SERVICES	100.0	35.2	9.0	8.7	17.5
Personal services	100.0	33.7	9.0	9.0	15.7
Babysitting and child care in own home	100.0	55.8	16.5	8.7	30.5
Babysitting and child care in someone else's home	100.0	20.8	5.5	7.0	8.2
Care for elderly, invalids, handicapped, etc.	100.0	10.3	6.5	0.6	3.2
Day care centers, nurseries, and preschools	100.0	36.8	8.9	11.2	16.8
Other household services	100.0	36.2	9.1	8.5	18.6
Housekeeping services	100.0	53.3	8.8	10.3	34.3
Gardening, lawn care service	100.0	38.5	8.0	9.0	21.5
Water-softening service	100.0	26.3	8.0	8.2	10.1
Nonclothing laundry and dry cleaning, sent out	100.0	35.5	6.3	5.9	23.2
Nonclothing laundry and dry cleaning, coin-operated	100.0	8.8	1.8	3.1	3.8
Termite and pest control services	100.0	38.9	9.0	9.7	20.2
Home security system service fee	100.0	36.3	9.3	10.7	16.3
Other home services	100.0	36.8	8.3	7.7	20.8
Termite and pest control products	100.0	36.3	8.2	9.3	18.8
Moving, storage, and freight express	100.0	39.0	19.0	8.1	11.9
Appliance repair, including at service center	100.0	29.6	7.6	9.5	12.5
Reupholstering and furniture repair	100.0	43.0	6.8	10.3	26.0
Repairs and rentals of lawn and garden equipment, hand and power tools, etc.	100.0	29.8	10.7	7.7	11.4
Appliance rental	100.0	7.6	3.1	2.9	1.6
Repair of computer systems for nonbusiness use	100.0	29.5	6.6	9.9	12.9
Computer information services	100.0	25.0	8.2	7.1	9.6
HOUSEKEEPING SUPPLIES	100.0	24.1	7.3	6.5	10.7
Laundry and cleaning supplies	100.0	19.7	6.7	6.0	7.0
Soaps and detergents	100.0	19.2	6.6	5.6	7.0
Other laundry cleaning products	100.0	20.3	6.7	6.7	6.9
Other household products	100.0	26.3	7.3	6.2	13.4
Cleansing and toilet tissue, paper towels, and napkins	100.0	19.7	6.7	5.9	7.1
Miscellaneous household products	100.0	25.5	7.5	6.8	11.5
Lawn and garden supplies	100.0	34.3	7.5	5.6	22.6
Postage and stationery	100.0	24.4	7.8	7.3	9.3
Stationery, stationery supplies, giftwrap	100.0	26.9	8.9	8.5	9.5
Postage	100.0	21.7	6.8	6.7	8.2
Delivery services	100.0	26.7	7.4	1.4	19.5
HOUSEHOLD FURNISHINGS AND EQUIPMENT	100.0	33.6	9.2	9.3	15.3
Household textiles	100.0	31.2	9.7	8.8	12.7
Bathroom linens	100.0	25.4	9.2	4.7	12.1
Bedroom linens	100.0	32.1	10.5	10.1	11.6
Kitchen and dining room linens	100.0	45.8	14.5	18.8	11.6
Curtains and draperies	100.0	38.0	7.7	7.6	22.7
Slipcovers and decorative pillows	100.0	14.6	4.1	4.5	6.1
Sewing materials for household items	100.0	23.3	9.2	3.9	10.2
Other linens	100.0	36.0	7.6	5.5	22.8
Furniture	100.0	38.0	9.2	11.5	17.3
Mattresses and springs	100.0	40.5	6.3	16.2	17.9
Other bedroom furniture	100.0	31.9	10.8	11.2	9.9
Sofas	100.0	34.6	10.2	8.2	16.3
Living room chairs	100.0	33.8	7.2	9.6	17.0
Living room tables	100.0	39.1	10.3	9.8	19.0
Kitchen and dining room furniture	100.0	42.9	9.3	17.5	16.1

	total consumer units	$100,000 or more	$100,000– $119,999	$120,000– $149,999	$150,000 or more
Infants' furniture	100.0%	40.4%	18.8%	10.1%	11.6%
Outdoor furniture	100.0	45.8	10.2	12.5	23.2
Wall units, cabinets, and other furniture	100.0	45.9	7.4	10.7	27.7
Floor coverings	**100.0**	**40.0**	**8.2**	**6.5**	**25.4**
Wall-to-wall carpeting	100.0	38.4	10.8	4.1	23.5
Floor coverings, nonpermanent	100.0	41.9	5.1	9.4	27.5
Major appliances	**100.0**	**26.0**	**7.5**	**7.0**	**11.5**
Dishwashers (built-in), garbage disposals, range hoods	100.0	32.2	8.1	5.6	18.4
Refrigerators and freezers	100.0	24.8	6.9	7.4	10.5
Washing machines	100.0	24.9	7.4	6.6	11.0
Clothes dryers	100.0	25.1	6.2	7.3	11.5
Cooking stoves, ovens	100.0	25.1	6.8	5.5	12.8
Microwave ovens	100.0	23.4	7.7	8.1	7.6
Portable dishwasher	100.0	19.5	8.5	–	10.9
Window air conditioners	100.0	27.8	18.5	4.2	5.2
Electric floor-cleaning equipment	100.0	24.1	10.6	5.0	8.7
Sewing machines	100.0	11.8	3.2	0.5	8.0
Miscellaneous household appliances	100.0	49.1	2.0	24.9	21.7
Small appliances and miscellaneous housewares	**100.0**	**29.5**	**10.1**	**8.2**	**11.2**
Housewares	100.0	30.0	10.7	8.5	10.9
Plastic dinnerware	100.0	27.4	7.1	10.2	10.0
China and other dinnerware	100.0	24.7	6.7	5.3	13.2
Flatware	100.0	37.4	4.7	13.3	19.4
Glassware	100.0	33.0	13.3	9.8	9.8
Silver serving pieces	100.0	31.7	6.8	14.0	10.2
Other serving pieces	100.0	47.1	10.0	19.7	17.3
Nonelectric cookware	100.0	28.5	10.8	7.9	9.7
Tableware, nonelectric kitchenware	100.0	29.3	12.1	7.5	9.7
Small appliances	100.0	27.5	8.0	7.2	12.3
Small electric kitchen appliances	100.0	24.5	8.7	6.7	9.0
Portable heating and cooling equipment	100.0	38.1	5.3	8.9	23.8
Miscellaneous household equipment	**100.0**	**33.8**	**9.5**	**9.0**	**15.6**
Window coverings	100.0	39.0	8.8	7.4	22.8
Infants' equipment	100.0	28.5	21.3	2.5	4.7
Laundry and cleaning equipment	100.0	22.2	7.7	7.6	6.7
Outdoor equipment	100.0	40.1	3.6	23.7	11.5
Clocks	100.0	48.3	10.6	8.1	31.6
Lamps and lighting fixtures	100.0	48.8	26.5	8.3	14.0
Other household decorative items	100.0	39.3	9.1	8.0	23.5
Telephones and accessories	100.0	36.8	11.2	6.1	20.7
Lawn and garden equipment	100.0	22.9	8.0	7.5	7.3
Power tools	100.0	23.8	8.5	7.7	7.4
Office furniture for home use	100.0	60.4	7.1	12.4	40.8
Hand tools	100.0	21.5	7.9	6.7	6.9
Indoor plants and fresh flowers	100.0	34.3	9.8	9.7	14.9
Closet and storage items	100.0	49.9	9.6	7.1	35.6
Rental of furniture	100.0	9.1	1.3	0.8	7.0
Luggage	100.0	40.1	8.1	9.8	22.2
Computers and computer hardware, nonbusiness use	100.0	30.8	9.8	8.0	13.0
Computer software and accessories, nonbusiness use	100.0	30.9	8.9	10.6	11.4
Telephone answering devices	100.0	29.4	9.3	1.9	18.1
Calculators	100.0	36.6	9.0	8.5	19.0
Business equipment for home use	100.0	21.7	4.6	6.1	11.0
Other hardware	100.0	23.4	4.0	15.8	2.2
Smoke alarms	100.0	21.7	6.5	8.0	7.3
Other household appliances	100.0	27.0	6.4	6.9	13.7
Miscellaneous household equipment and parts	100.0	31.1	16.1	5.2	10.1

Note: Numbers may not add to total because of rounding. "–" means sample is too small to make a reliable estimate.
Source: Calculations by New Strategist based on the 2004 Consumer Expenditure Survey

Table 8.13 Housing: Household Operations: Average spending by household type, 2004

(average annual spending of consumer units (CU) on household services, supplies, furnishings, and equipment, by type of consumer unit, 2004)

	total married couples	married couples, no children	married couples with children				single parent, at least one child <18	single person
			total	oldest child under 6	oldest child 6 to 17	oldest child 18 or older		
Number of consumer units (in 000s)	59,797	25,585	29,279	5,604	15,376	8,300	6,892	33,686
Average number of persons per CU	3.2	2.0	3.9	3.5	4.1	3.9	2.9	1.0
Average before-tax income of CU	$73,001.00	$64,434.00	$79,764.00	$75,293.00	$78,508.00	$85,109.00	$31,055.00	$28,143.00
Average spending of CU, total	55,606.57	49,690.43	60,660.88	55,981.04	60,577.88	64,161.69	32,824.46	25,423.35
Housing, average spending	**17,004.54**	**14,706.43**	**18,912.20**	**21,045.02**	**18,900.14**	**17,502.90**	**12,029.78**	**9,244.07**
HOUSEHOLD SERVICES	**996.20**	**637.67**	**1,299.12**	**2,699.16**	**1,166.60**	**599.48**	**759.08**	**442.64**
Personal services	**415.83**	**18.57**	**749.46**	**2,145.56**	**608.11**	**68.70**	**483.06**	**124.96**
Babysitting and child care in own home	62.77	0.03	117.18	356.71	90.73	4.43	51.79	0.07
Babysitting and child care in someone else's home	36.50	0.80	68.37	204.19	54.26	2.82	71.64	0.59
Care for elderly, invalids, handicapped, etc.	14.14	10.24	6.99	–	1.12	22.58	–	89.21
Day care centers, nurseries, and preschools	302.36	7.45	556.85	1,584.66	462.00	38.62	359.63	8.20
Other household services	**580.37**	**619.10**	**549.65**	**553.60**	**558.48**	**530.78**	**276.01**	**317.68**
Housekeeping services	115.82	132.60	103.52	128.93	113.79	67.35	55.46	69.79
Gardening, lawn care service	111.79	140.29	86.66	77.38	91.01	84.87	38.43	91.30
Water-softening service	3.79	2.62	4.73	7.06	4.15	4.23	2.16	2.40
Nonclothing laundry and dry cleaning, sent out	1.20	1.44	0.97	0.50	1.03	1.16	0.32	0.85
Nonclothing laundry and dry cleaning, coin-operated	2.76	1.76	2.91	3.52	3.43	1.52	5.87	3.81
Termite and pest control services	16.96	19.53	14.79	12.31	15.80	14.58	3.68	6.90
Home security system service fee	20.66	20.08	21.19	29.36	21.19	15.67	11.10	10.57
Other home services	33.32	36.66	27.69	28.95	19.82	41.41	4.36	12.63
Termite and pest control products	2.19	2.65	1.76	0.95	2.06	1.76	0.81	0.77
Moving, storage, and freight express	42.71	47.68	36.85	46.90	36.13	31.40	21.08	20.59
Appliance repair, including at service center	20.61	19.49	21.40	19.98	20.64	23.76	7.68	7.73
Reupholstering and furniture repair	11.87	19.85	5.20	11.41	2.79	5.47	0.94	3.84
Repairs and rentals of lawn and garden equipment, hand and power tools, etc.	10.59	9.94	11.93	5.84	15.82	8.83	4.35	3.10
Appliance rental	1.70	2.22	1.40	1.27	1.72	0.91	3.74	0.73
Repair of computer systems for nonbusiness use	5.43	4.22	6.37	1.29	6.81	8.97	3.07	1.67
Computer information services	177.90	156.45	201.48	177.18	201.81	217.28	112.80	80.43
HOUSEKEEPING SUPPLIES	**771.11**	**728.90**	**815.20**	**819.77**	**823.69**	**793.81**	**453.12**	**314.74**
Laundry and cleaning supplies	**182.96**	**145.44**	**205.60**	**173.53**	**216.89**	**207.78**	**158.06**	**72.78**
Soaps and detergents	105.64	76.47	123.01	112.14	127.35	122.67	88.67	38.70
Other laundry cleaning products	77.32	68.97	82.59	61.40	89.53	85.11	69.39	34.08
Other household products	**386.57**	**368.36**	**413.22**	**450.34**	**415.18**	**379.32**	**193.20**	**147.38**
Cleansing and toilet tissue, paper towels, and napkins	104.64	97.28	106.59	88.73	106.69	120.70	72.50	49.55
Miscellaneous household products	160.12	135.11	186.21	269.18	165.70	162.38	85.29	62.82
Lawn and garden supplies	121.81	135.98	120.42	92.43	142.78	96.24	35.41	35.01
Postage and stationery	**201.58**	**215.10**	**196.39**	**195.90**	**191.63**	**206.71**	**101.85**	**94.58**
Stationery, stationery supplies, giftwrap	100.18	91.58	112.48	116.51	112.55	109.11	56.67	38.96
Postage	92.75	110.32	78.16	78.74	72.82	88.83	43.71	49.68
Delivery services	8.64	13.20	5.75	0.65	6.27	8.76	1.47	5.94
HOUSEHOLD FURNISHINGS AND EQUIPMENT	**2,238.14**	**2,132.93**	**2,301.35**	**2,256.65**	**2,262.22**	**2,414.86**	**1,019.94**	**815.95**
Household textiles	**203.77**	**211.00**	**199.48**	**168.43**	**163.65**	**298.91**	**85.04**	**86.55**
Bathroom linens	25.80	25.32	27.44	22.91	22.67	41.02	24.39	11.60
Bedroom linens	112.05	120.67	105.48	87.13	79.87	173.67	40.23	41.64
Kitchen and dining room linens	14.65	13.47	17.02	10.29	14.13	28.46	4.80	4.28
Curtains and draperies	25.97	26.61	23.40	29.91	24.21	17.52	5.24	11.87
Slipcovers and decorative pillows	8.53	6.41	10.73	6.43	10.93	13.79	2.41	9.57
Sewing materials for household items	15.05	16.63	13.85	10.51	10.04	23.17	7.10	6.93
Other linens	1.72	1.88	1.55	1.25	1.81	1.28	0.87	0.65
Furniture	**575.03**	**540.55**	**587.21**	**625.80**	**589.76**	**556.43**	**356.64**	**173.93**
Mattresses and springs	73.37	75.52	75.32	55.45	72.03	94.85	36.96	25.99
Other bedroom furniture	102.87	93.07	104.52	142.93	97.75	91.11	102.62	27.09
Sofas	129.79	113.69	140.37	124.54	156.58	121.02	79.82	44.70
Living room chairs	59.40	64.98	53.30	50.30	56.21	49.95	24.49	18.76
Living room tables	20.87	20.86	21.06	20.37	20.58	22.40	11.98	7.13
Kitchen and dining room furniture	55.89	50.41	54.67	67.83	55.05	45.08	28.67	18.59

	total married couples	married couples, no children	married couples with children				single parent, at least one child <18	single person
			total	oldest child under 6	oldest child 6 to 17	oldest child 18 or older		
Infants' furniture	$13.14	$13.93	$12.88	$39.18	$7.45	$5.20	$3.79	$0.79
Outdoor furniture	24.69	23.97	25.22	23.69	29.29	18.72	10.35	6.01
Wall units, cabinets, and other furniture	95.00	84.11	99.87	101.52	94.83	108.11	57.96	24.88
Floor coverings	**71.98**	**78.44**	**61.46**	**47.18**	**64.15**	**66.12**	**42.44**	**23.60**
Wall-to-wall carpeting	36.74	42.12	28.38	28.14	24.96	34.87	29.34	12.96
Floor coverings, nonpermanent	35.24	36.32	33.08	19.04	39.19	31.25	13.10	10.64
Major appliances	**285.71**	**278.04**	**296.71**	**332.60**	**276.41**	**311.30**	**100.98**	**88.30**
Dishwashers (built-in), garbage disposals, range hoods	21.75	22.57	22.31	27.92	18.21	26.13	8.87	3.72
Refrigerators and freezers	71.63	76.17	69.30	107.19	48.27	82.66	20.97	22.73
Washing machines	41.66	42.75	40.28	44.95	40.58	36.57	24.06	13.39
Clothes dryers	29.27	26.03	31.83	26.65	33.02	33.13	16.34	11.56
Cooking stoves, ovens	44.79	47.58	42.49	54.27	40.95	37.41	8.16	15.14
Microwave ovens	10.42	9.13	11.44	8.55	12.06	12.26	6.01	4.84
Portable dishwasher	1.81	1.39	2.46	4.32	2.54	1.09	0.37	0.34
Window air conditioners	5.08	3.93	5.50	3.07	5.52	7.10	2.78	1.64
Electric floor-cleaning equipment	41.42	23.72	58.65	53.11	60.59	59.03	10.40	13.38
Sewing machines	5.49	5.09	5.11	2.13	7.71	2.31	2.01	1.13
Miscellaneous household appliances	12.39	19.67	7.31	0.44	6.95	13.60	1.04	0.43
Small appliances and miscellaneous housewares	**138.80**	**135.86**	**141.03**	**179.59**	**130.25**	**133.04**	**69.99**	**59.02**
Housewares	111.06	106.60	115.03	142.38	108.05	107.57	54.28	46.16
Plastic dinnerware	2.38	1.48	3.09	5.56	2.30	2.87	1.62	0.88
China and other dinnerware	22.69	24.97	19.44	28.01	19.55	12.31	6.63	2.35
Flatware	5.10	4.95	4.46	4.22	3.77	5.90	2.73	2.49
Glassware	28.29	26.75	31.24	31.34	25.13	43.90	9.09	14.75
Silver serving pieces	0.40	0.39	0.43	0.31	0.51	0.36	0.11	0.19
Other serving pieces	2.47	2.85	2.25	1.40	2.63	2.11	1.30	0.83
Nonelectric cookware	22.56	20.77	25.30	39.92	23.97	16.32	11.77	10.36
Tableware, nonelectric kitchenware	27.18	24.44	28.83	31.62	30.17	23.79	21.04	14.30
Small appliances	27.74	29.26	26.00	37.21	22.20	25.47	15.71	12.86
Small electric kitchen appliances	21.46	23.88	18.52	16.54	18.86	19.22	13.57	10.22
Portable heating and cooling equipment	6.28	5.38	7.48	20.67	3.34	6.25	2.14	2.64
Miscellaneous household equipment	**962.85**	**889.05**	**1,015.46**	**903.04**	**1,038.00**	**1,049.06**	**364.85**	**384.55**
Window coverings	33.21	39.61	25.36	55.20	20.64	13.94	17.70	12.88
Infants' equipment	11.59	15.50	8.81	24.01	6.61	1.20	3.47	0.76
Laundry and cleaning equipment	19.07	16.89	19.58	17.47	19.03	22.43	15.25	10.38
Outdoor equipment	39.74	31.73	49.24	27.58	44.71	76.10	21.43	13.01
Clocks	10.85	14.25	6.98	7.25	6.64	7.49	1.66	3.44
Lamps and lighting fixtures	23.75	31.49	18.21	28.37	17.82	12.05	7.73	7.34
Other household decorative items	216.96	191.58	210.64	215.52	222.19	182.63	60.95	92.71
Telephones and accessories	40.08	23.76	59.50	8.09	60.87	97.89	8.40	11.69
Lawn and garden equipment	69.20	75.27	57.98	58.40	53.62	65.77	21.43	25.28
Power tools	51.31	52.10	53.77	44.88	62.81	42.04	13.98	9.42
Office furniture for home use	16.08	11.49	20.41	12.61	28.45	10.77	7.90	5.20
Hand tools	7.73	8.49	7.40	9.72	5.97	8.48	4.35	3.99
Indoor plants and fresh flowers	57.40	65.05	52.73	46.79	46.98	67.39	17.39	22.47
Closet and storage items	24.88	20.50	29.72	68.75	19.49	19.70	11.93	5.74
Rental of furniture	2.15	0.40	3.30	3.67	3.66	2.38	5.73	0.88
Luggage	8.29	8.16	8.90	7.81	9.29	8.93	3.54	4.77
Computers and computer hardware, nonbusiness use	172.48	134.13	210.54	152.09	206.14	258.15	90.28	81.89
Computer software and accessories, nonbusiness use	24.26	20.92	27.31	15.82	28.61	32.66	10.78	14.43
Telephone answering devices	0.77	0.62	0.95	0.63	1.22	0.67	0.39	0.54
Calculators	1.97	0.51	3.01	0.98	3.87	2.78	0.97	0.93
Business equipment for home use	1.09	1.30	0.78	0.13	1.24	0.38	1.55	0.64
Other hardware	51.08	61.20	43.35	23.34	63.55	17.26	9.99	36.50
Smoke alarms	1.50	1.28	1.51	2.47	1.33	1.20	0.40	0.45
Other household appliances	18.80	17.13	21.24	7.55	21.04	30.87	2.35	6.35
Miscellaneous household equipment and parts	58.60	45.70	74.25	63.91	82.22	65.91	25.27	12.86

Note: Average spending figures for total consumer units can be found on Average Spending by Age and Average Spending by Region tables. Subcategories may not add to total because some are not shown. "–" means sample is too small to make a reliable estimate.
Source: Bureau of Labor Statistics, unpublished tables from the 2004 Consumer Expenditure Survey

Table 8.14 Housing: Household Operations: Indexed spending by household type, 2004

(indexed average annual spending of consumer units (CU) on household services, supplies, furnishings, and equipment, by type of consumer unit, 2004; index definition: an index of 100 is the average for all consumer units; an index of 132 means that spending by consumer units in that group is 32 percent above the average for all consumer units; an index of 68 indicates spending that is 32 percent below the average for all consumer units)

	total married couples	married couples, no children	married couples with children total	oldest child under 6	oldest child 6 to 17	oldest child 18 or older	single parent, at least one child <18	single person
Average spending of CU, total	$55,607	$49,690	$60,661	$55,981	$60,578	$64,162	$32,824	$25,423
Average spending of CU, index	128	115	140	129	140	148	76	59
Housing, spending index	**122**	**106**	**136**	**151**	**136**	**126**	**86**	**66**
HOUSEHOLD SERVICES	132	85	173	359	155	80	101	59
Personal services	139	6	250	716	203	23	161	42
Babysitting and child care in own home	169	0	316	962	245	12	140	0
Babysitting and child care in someone else's home	140	3	262	782	208	11	274	2
Care for elderly, invalids, handicapped, etc.	40	29	20	–	3	65	–	255
Day care centers, nurseries, and preschools	156	4	288	819	239	20	186	4
Other household services	128	137	121	122	123	117	61	70
Housekeeping services	130	149	117	145	128	76	62	79
Gardening, lawn care service	118	148	91	81	96	89	40	96
Water-softening service	124	86	155	231	136	138	71	78
Nonclothing laundry and dry cleaning, sent out	128	153	103	53	110	123	34	90
Nonclothing laundry and dry cleaning, coin-operated	74	47	78	95	92	41	158	103
Termite and pest control services	141	162	123	102	131	121	31	57
Home security system service fee	133	129	136	189	136	101	71	68
Other home services	145	159	120	126	86	180	19	55
Termite and pest control products	143	173	115	62	135	115	53	50
Moving, storage, and freight express	126	141	109	138	107	93	62	61
Appliance repair, including at service center	142	134	147	138	142	164	53	53
Reupholstering and furniture repair	161	270	71	155	38	74	13	52
Repairs and rentals of lawn and garden equipment, hand and power tools, etc.	145	136	164	80	217	121	60	43
Appliance rental	97	127	80	73	98	52	214	42
Repair of computer systems for nonbusiness use	135	105	158	32	169	223	76	41
Computer information services	128	112	144	127	145	156	81	58
HOUSEKEEPING SUPPLIES	130	123	137	138	139	134	76	53
Laundry and cleaning supplies	123	98	138	117	146	140	106	49
Soaps and detergents	124	90	144	131	149	144	104	45
Other laundry cleaning products	122	109	131	97	142	135	110	54
Other household products	133	127	142	155	143	131	67	51
Cleansing and toilet tissue, paper towels, and napkins	122	113	124	103	124	141	84	58
Miscellaneous household products	132	112	154	222	137	134	70	52
Lawn and garden supplies	146	163	144	111	171	115	42	42
Postage and stationery	130	138	126	126	123	133	65	61
Stationery, stationery supplies, giftwrap	134	122	150	156	150	146	76	52
Postage	125	149	105	106	98	120	59	67
Delivery services	133	202	88	10	96	134	23	91
HOUSEHOLD FURNISHINGS AND EQUIPMENT	136	130	140	137	137	147	62	50
Household textiles	129	134	127	107	104	190	54	55
Bathroom linens	121	119	129	108	107	193	115	55
Bedroom linens	131	141	123	102	93	203	47	49
Kitchen and dining room linens	149	137	173	105	144	289	49	43
Curtains and draperies	135	138	122	156	126	91	27	62
Slipcovers and decorative pillows	94	70	118	71	120	151	26	105
Sewing materials for household items	134	148	124	94	90	207	63	62
Other linens	131	144	118	95	138	98	66	50
Furniture	138	130	141	150	141	133	86	42
Mattresses and springs	137	141	141	104	134	177	69	49
Other bedroom furniture	127	114	129	176	120	112	126	33
Sofas	137	120	148	131	165	128	84	47
Living room chairs	143	156	128	121	135	120	59	45
Living room tables	141	141	143	138	139	152	81	48
Kitchen and dining room furniture	135	122	133	164	133	109	69	45

	total married couples	married couples, no children	married couples with children				single parent, at least one child <18	single person
			total	oldest child under 6	oldest child 6 to 17	oldest child 18 or older		
Infants' furniture	156	165	153	464	88	62	45	9
Outdoor furniture	153	148	156	146	181	116	64	37
Wall units, cabinets, and other furniture	146	129	154	156	146	166	89	38
Floor coverings	**138**	**151**	**118**	**91**	**123**	**127**	**82**	**45**
Wall-to-wall carpeting	131	151	101	101	89	125	105	46
Floor coverings, nonpermanent	147	151	138	79	163	130	55	44
Major appliances	**140**	**136**	**145**	**163**	**136**	**153**	**50**	**43**
Dishwashers (built-in), garbage disposals, range hoods	152	157	156	195	127	182	62	26
Refrigerators and freezers	140	149	135	209	94	161	41	44
Washing machines	136	139	131	147	132	119	78	44
Clothes dryers	133	118	144	121	150	150	74	52
Cooking stoves, ovens	138	147	131	167	126	115	25	47
Microwave ovens	124	108	136	101	143	145	71	57
Portable dishwasher	148	114	202	354	208	89	30	28
Window air conditioners	117	90	126	70	127	163	64	38
Electric floor-cleaning equipment	149	86	212	192	219	213	38	48
Sewing machines	153	142	142	59	215	64	56	31
Miscellaneous household appliances	157	249	92	6	88	172	13	5
Small appliances and miscellaneous housewares	**133**	**130**	**135**	**172**	**124**	**127**	**67**	**56**
Housewares	135	129	139	172	131	130	66	56
Plastic dinnerware	131	81	170	305	126	158	89	48
China and other dinnerware	168	185	144	208	145	91	49	17
Flatware	127	123	111	105	94	147	68	62
Glassware	135	128	150	150	120	210	44	71
Silver serving pieces	133	130	143	103	170	120	37	63
Other serving pieces	140	162	128	80	149	120	74	47
Nonelectric cookware	125	115	140	221	132	90	65	57
Tableware, nonelectric kitchenware	122	110	130	142	136	107	95	64
Small appliances	126	132	118	168	100	115	71	58
Small electric kitchen appliances	124	138	107	96	109	111	79	59
Portable heating and cooling equipment	130	111	155	428	69	129	44	55
Miscellaneous household equipment	**135**	**125**	**143**	**127**	**146**	**148**	**51**	**54**
Window coverings	141	169	108	235	88	59	75	55
Infants' equipment	147	197	112	305	84	15	44	10
Laundry and cleaning equipment	121	107	125	111	121	143	97	66
Outdoor equipment	110	88	137	77	124	211	60	36
Clocks	142	187	91	95	87	98	22	45
Lamps and lighting fixtures	145	192	111	173	109	73	47	45
Other household decorative items	137	121	133	136	141	116	39	59
Telephones and accessories	149	89	222	30	227	365	31	44
Lawn and garden equipment	142	154	119	120	110	135	44	52
Power tools	153	156	161	134	188	126	42	28
Office furniture for home use	141	101	180	111	250	95	69	46
Hand tools	127	139	121	159	98	139	71	65
Indoor plants and fresh flowers	138	157	127	113	113	162	42	54
Closet and storage items	140	115	167	386	109	110	67	32
Rental of furniture	97	18	149	165	165	107	258	40
Luggage	125	123	134	118	140	135	53	72
Computers and computer hardware, nonbusiness use	128	100	156	113	153	192	67	61
Computer software and accessories, nonbusiness use	127	110	143	83	150	171	57	76
Telephone answering devices	124	100	153	102	197	108	63	87
Calculators	137	35	209	68	269	193	67	65
Business equipment for home use	116	138	83	14	132	40	165	68
Other hardware	129	154	109	59	160	44	25	92
Smoke alarms	146	124	147	240	129	117	39	44
Other household appliances	150	137	170	60	168	246	19	51
Miscellaneous household equipment and parts	142	111	180	155	200	160	61	31

Note: Spending index for total consumer units is 100. "–" means sample is too small to make a reliable estimate.
Source: Calculations by New Strategist based on the 2004 Consumer Expenditure Survey

Table 8.15 Housing: Household Operations: Total spending by household type, 2004

(total annual spending on household services, supplies, furnishings, and equipment, by consumer unit (CU) type, 2004; consumer units and dollars in thousands)

	total married couples	married couples, no children	married couples with children total	oldest child under 6	oldest child 6 to 17	oldest child 18 or older	single parent, at least one child <18	single person
Number of consumer units	59,797	25,585	29,279	5,604	15,376	8,300	6,892	33,686
Total spending of all CUs	$3,325,106,066	$1,271,329,652	$1,776,089,906	$313,717,748	$931,445,483	$532,542,027	$226,226,178	$856,410,968
Housing, total spending	1,016,820,478	376,264,012	553,730,304	117,936,292	290,608,553	145,274,070	82,909,244	311,395,742
HOUSEHOLD SERVICES	59,569,771	16,314,787	38,036,934	15,126,093	17,937,642	4,975,684	5,231,579	14,910,771
Personal services	24,865,387	475,113	21,943,439	12,023,718	9,350,299	570,210	3,329,250	4,209,403
Babysitting and child care in own home	3,753,458	768	3,430,913	1,999,003	1,395,064	36,769	356,937	2,358
Babysitting and child care in someone else's home	2,182,591	20,468	2,001,805	1,144,281	834,302	23,406	493,743	19,875
Care for elderly, invalids, handicapped, etc.	845,530	261,990	204,660	–	17,221	187,414	–	3,005,128
Day care centers, nurseries, and preschools	18,080,221	190,608	16,304,011	8,880,435	7,103,712	320,546	2,478,570	276,225
Other household services	34,704,385	15,839,674	16,093,202	3,102,374	8,587,188	4,405,474	1,902,261	10,701,368
Housekeeping services	6,925,689	3,392,571	3,030,962	722,524	1,749,635	559,005	382,230	2,350,946
Gardening, lawn care service	6,684,707	3,589,320	2,537,318	433,638	1,399,370	704,421	264,860	3,075,532
Water-softening service	226,631	67,033	138,490	39,564	63,810	35,109	14,887	80,846
Nonclothing laundry and dry cleaning, sent out	71,756	36,842	28,401	2,802	15,837	9,628	2,205	28,633
Nonclothing laundry and dry cleaning, coin-operated	165,040	45,030	85,202	19,726	52,740	12,616	40,456	128,344
Termite and pest control services	1,014,157	499,675	433,036	68,985	242,941	121,014	25,363	232,433
Home security system service fee	1,235,406	513,747	620,422	164,533	325,817	130,061	76,501	356,061
Other home services	1,992,436	937,946	810,736	162,236	304,752	343,703	30,049	425,454
Termite and pest control products	130,955	67,800	51,531	5,324	31,675	14,608	5,583	25,938
Moving, storage, and freight express	2,553,930	1,219,893	1,078,931	262,828	555,535	260,620	145,283	693,595
Appliance repair, including at service center	1,232,416	498,652	626,571	111,968	317,361	197,208	52,931	260,393
Reupholstering and furniture repair	709,790	507,862	152,251	63,942	42,899	45,401	6,478	129,354
Repairs and rentals of lawn and garden equipment, hand and power tools, etc.	633,250	254,315	349,298	32,727	243,248	73,289	29,980	104,427
Appliance rental	101,655	56,799	40,991	7,117	26,447	7,553	25,776	24,591
Repair of computer systems for nonbusiness use	324,698	107,969	186,507	7,229	104,711	74,451	21,158	56,256
Computer information services	10,637,886	4,002,773	5,899,133	992,917	3,103,031	1,803,424	777,418	2,709,365
HOUSEKEEPING SUPPLIES	46,110,065	18,648,907	23,868,241	4,593,991	12,665,057	6,588,623	3,122,903	10,602,332
Laundry and cleaning supplies	10,940,459	3,721,082	6,019,762	972,462	3,334,901	1,724,574	1,089,350	2,451,667
Soaps and detergents	6,316,955	1,956,485	3,601,610	628,433	1,958,134	1,018,161	611,114	1,303,648
Other laundry cleaning products	4,623,504	1,764,597	2,418,153	344,086	1,376,613	706,413	478,236	1,148,019
Other household products	23,115,726	9,424,491	12,098,668	2,523,705	6,383,808	3,148,356	1,331,534	4,964,643
Cleansing and toilet tissue, paper towels, and napkins	6,257,158	2,488,909	3,120,849	497,243	1,640,465	1,001,810	499,670	1,669,141
Miscellaneous household products	9,574,696	3,456,789	5,452,043	1,508,485	2,547,803	1,347,754	587,819	2,116,155
Lawn and garden supplies	7,283,873	3,479,048	3,525,777	517,978	2,195,385	798,792	244,046	1,179,347
Postage and stationery	12,053,879	5,503,334	5,750,103	1,097,824	2,946,503	1,715,693	701,950	3,186,022
Stationery, stationery supplies, giftwrap	5,990,463	2,343,074	3,293,302	652,922	1,730,569	905,613	390,570	1,312,407
Postage	5,546,172	2,822,537	2,288,447	441,259	1,119,680	737,289	301,249	1,673,520
Delivery services	516,646	337,722	168,354	3,643	96,408	72,708	10,131	200,095
HOUSEHOLD FURNISHINGS, EQUIPMENT	133,834,058	54,571,014	67,381,227	12,646,267	34,783,895	20,043,338	7,029,426	27,486,092
Household textiles	12,184,835	5,398,435	5,840,575	943,882	2,516,282	2,480,953	586,096	2,915,523
Bathroom linens	1,542,763	647,812	803,416	128,388	348,574	340,466	168,096	390,758
Bedroom linens	6,700,254	3,087,342	3,088,349	488,277	1,228,081	1,441,461	277,265	1,402,685
Kitchen and dining room linens	876,026	344,630	498,329	57,665	217,263	236,218	33,082	144,176
Curtains and draperies	1,552,928	680,817	685,129	167,616	372,253	145,416	36,114	399,853
Slipcovers and decorative pillows	510,068	164,000	314,164	36,034	168,060	114,457	16,610	322,375
Sewing materials for household items	899,945	425,479	405,514	58,898	154,375	192,311	48,933	233,444
Other linens	102,851	48,100	45,382	7,005	27,831	10,624	5,996	21,896
Furniture	34,385,069	13,829,972	17,192,922	3,506,983	9,068,150	4,618,369	2,457,963	5,859,006
Mattresses and springs	4,387,306	1,932,179	2,205,294	310,742	1,107,533	787,255	254,728	875,499
Other bedroom furniture	6,151,317	2,381,196	3,060,241	800,980	1,503,004	756,213	707,257	912,554
Sofas	7,761,053	2,908,759	4,109,893	697,922	2,407,574	1,004,466	550,119	1,505,764
Living room chairs	3,551,942	1,662,513	1,560,571	281,881	864,285	414,585	168,785	631,949
Living room tables	1,247,963	533,703	616,616	114,153	316,438	185,920	82,566	240,181
Kitchen and dining room furniture	3,342,054	1,289,740	1,600,683	380,119	846,449	374,164	197,594	626,223

	total married couples	married couples, no children	married couples with children				single parent, at least one child <18	single person
			total	oldest child under 6	oldest child 6 to 17	oldest child 18 or older		
Infants' furniture	$785,733	$356,399	$377,114	$219,565	$114,551	$43,160	$26,121	$26,612
Outdoor furniture	1,476,388	613,272	738,416	132,759	450,363	155,376	71,332	202,453
Wall units, cabinets, and other furniture	5,680,715	2,151,954	2,924,094	568,918	1,458,106	897,313	399,460	838,108
Floor coverings	**4,304,188**	**2,006,887**	**1,799,487**	**264,397**	**986,370**	**548,796**	**292,496**	**794,990**
Wall-to-wall carpeting	2,196,942	1,077,640	830,938	157,697	383,785	289,421	202,211	436,571
Floor coverings, nonpermanent	2,107,246	929,247	968,549	106,700	602,585	259,375	90,285	358,419
Major appliances	**17,084,601**	**7,113,653**	**8,687,372**	**1,863,890**	**4,250,080**	**2,583,790**	**695,954**	**2,974,474**
Dishwashers (built-in), garbage disposals, range hoods	1,300,585	577,453	653,214	156,464	279,997	216,879	61,132	125,312
Refrigerators and freezers	4,283,259	1,948,809	2,029,035	600,693	742,200	686,078	144,525	765,683
Washing machines	2,491,143	1,093,759	1,179,358	251,900	623,958	303,531	165,822	451,056
Clothes dryers	1,750,258	665,978	931,951	149,347	507,716	274,979	112,615	389,410
Cooking stoves, ovens	2,678,308	1,217,334	1,244,065	304,129	629,647	310,503	56,239	510,006
Microwave ovens	623,085	233,591	334,952	47,914	185,435	101,758	41,421	163,040
Portable dishwasher	108,233	35,563	72,026	24,209	39,055	9,047	2,550	11,453
Window air conditioners	303,769	100,549	161,035	17,204	84,876	58,930	19,160	55,245
Electric floor-cleaning equipment	2,476,792	606,876	1,717,213	297,628	931,632	489,949	71,677	450,719
Sewing machines	328,286	130,228	149,616	11,937	118,549	19,173	13,853	38,065
Miscellaneous household appliances	740,885	503,257	214,029	2,466	106,863	112,880	7,168	14,485
Small appliances and miscellaneous housewares	**8,299,824**	**3,475,978**	**4,129,217**	**1,006,422**	**2,002,724**	**1,104,232**	**482,371**	**1,988,148**
Housewares	6,641,055	2,727,361	3,367,963	797,898	1,661,377	892,831	374,098	1,554,946
Plastic dinnerware	142,317	37,866	90,472	31,158	35,365	23,821	11,165	29,644
China and other dinnerware	1,356,794	638,857	569,184	156,968	300,601	102,173	45,694	79,162
Flatware	304,965	126,646	130,584	23,649	57,968	48,970	18,815	83,878
Glassware	1,691,657	684,399	914,676	175,629	386,399	364,370	62,648	496,869
Silver serving pieces	23,919	9,978	12,590	1,737	7,842	2,988	758	6,400
Other serving pieces	147,699	72,917	65,878	7,846	40,439	17,513	8,960	27,959
Nonelectric cookware	1,349,020	531,400	740,759	223,712	368,563	135,456	81,119	348,987
Tableware, nonelectric kitchenware	1,625,282	625,297	844,114	177,198	463,894	197,457	145,008	481,710
Small appliances	1,658,769	748,617	761,254	208,525	341,347	211,401	108,273	433,202
Small electric kitchen appliances	1,283,244	610,970	542,247	92,690	289,991	159,526	93,524	344,271
Portable heating and cooling equipment	375,525	137,647	219,007	115,835	51,356	51,875	14,749	88,931
Miscellaneous household equipment	**57,575,541**	**22,746,344**	**29,731,653**	**5,060,636**	**15,960,288**	**8,707,198**	**2,514,546**	**12,953,951**
Window coverings	1,985,858	1,013,422	742,515	309,341	317,361	115,702	121,988	433,876
Infants' equipment	693,047	396,568	257,948	134,552	101,635	9,960	23,915	25,601
Laundry and cleaning equipment	1,140,329	432,131	573,283	97,902	292,605	186,169	105,103	349,661
Outdoor equipment	2,376,333	811,812	1,441,698	154,558	687,461	631,630	147,696	438,255
Clocks	648,797	364,586	204,367	40,629	102,097	62,167	11,441	115,880
Lamps and lighting fixtures	1,420,179	805,672	533,171	158,985	274,000	100,015	53,275	247,255
Other household decorative items	12,973,557	4,901,574	6,167,329	1,207,774	3,416,393	1,515,829	420,067	3,123,029
Telephones and accessories	2,396,664	607,900	1,742,101	45,336	935,937	812,487	57,893	393,789
Lawn and garden equipment	4,137,952	1,925,783	1,697,596	327,274	824,461	545,891	147,696	851,582
Power tools	3,068,184	1,332,979	1,574,332	251,508	965,767	348,932	96,350	317,322
Office furniture for home use	961,536	293,972	597,584	70,666	437,447	89,391	54,447	175,167
Hand tools	462,231	217,217	216,665	54,471	91,795	70,384	29,980	134,407
Indoor plants and fresh flowers	3,432,348	1,664,304	1,543,882	262,211	722,364	559,337	119,852	756,924
Closet and storage items	1,487,749	524,493	870,172	385,275	299,678	163,510	82,222	193,358
Rental of furniture	128,564	10,234	96,621	20,567	56,276	19,754	39,491	29,644
Luggage	495,717	208,774	260,583	43,767	142,843	74,119	24,398	160,682
Computers and computer hardware, nonbusiness use	10,313,787	3,431,716	6,164,401	852,312	3,169,609	2,142,645	622,210	2,758,547
Computer software and accessories, nonbusiness use	1,450,675	535,238	799,609	88,655	439,907	271,078	74,296	486,089
Telephone answering devices	46,044	15,863	27,815	3,531	18,759	5,561	2,688	18,190
Calculators	117,800	13,048	88,130	5,492	59,505	23,074	6,685	31,328
Business equipment for home use	65,179	33,261	22,838	729	19,066	3,154	10,683	21,559
Other hardware	3,054,431	1,565,802	1,269,245	130,797	977,145	143,258	68,851	1,229,539
Smoke alarms	89,696	32,749	44,211	13,842	20,450	9,960	2,757	15,159
Other household appliances	1,124,184	438,271	621,886	42,310	323,511	256,221	16,196	213,906
Miscellaneous household equipment and parts	3,504,104	1,169,235	2,173,966	358,152	1,264,215	547,053	174,161	433,202

Note: Total spending figures for total consumer units can be found on Total Spending by Age and Total Spending by Region tables. Spending by type of consumer unit will not add to total because not all types of consumer units are shown. Numbers may not add to category total because of rounding and missing subcategories. "–" means sample is too small to make a reliable estimate.

Source: Calculations by New Strategist based on the 2004 Consumer Expenditure Survey

Table 8.16 Housing: Household Operations: Market shares by household type, 2004

(percentage of total annual spending on household services, supplies, furnishings, and equipment accounted for by types of consumer units, 2004)

	total married couples	married couples, no children	married couples with children				single parent, at least one child <18	single person
			total	oldest child under 6	oldest child 6 to 17	oldest child 18 or older		
Share of total consumer units	51.4%	22.0%	25.2%	4.8%	13.2%	7.1%	5.9%	29.0%
Share of total before-tax income	68.9	26.0	36.9	6.7	19.1	11.2	3.4	15.0
Share of total spending	65.9	25.2	35.2	6.2	18.5	10.6	4.5	17.0
Share of housing spending	62.8	23.2	34.2	7.3	18.0	9.0	5.1	19.2
HOUSEHOLD SERVICES	68.0	18.6	43.5	17.3	20.5	5.7	6.0	17.0
Personal services	71.3	1.4	63.0	34.5	26.8	1.6	9.6	12.1
Babysitting and child care in own home	87.0	0.0	79.6	46.3	32.3	0.9	8.3	0.1
Babysitting and child care in someone else's home	71.9	0.7	65.9	37.7	27.5	0.8	16.3	0.7
Care for elderly, invalids, handicapped, etc.	20.8	6.4	5.0	–	0.4	4.6	–	73.9
Day care centers, nurseries, and preschools	80.4	0.8	72.5	39.5	31.6	1.4	11.0	1.2
Other household services	65.9	30.1	30.5	5.9	16.3	8.4	3.6	20.3
Housekeeping services	67.0	32.8	29.3	7.0	16.9	5.4	3.7	22.8
Gardening, lawn care service	60.5	32.5	22.9	3.9	12.7	6.4	2.4	27.8
Water-softening service	63.7	18.8	38.9	11.1	17.9	9.9	4.2	22.7
Nonclothing laundry and dry cleaning, sent out	65.6	33.7	26.0	2.6	14.5	8.8	2.0	26.2
Nonclothing laundry and dry cleaning, coin-operated	38.3	10.4	19.7	4.6	12.2	2.9	9.4	29.8
Termite and pest control services	72.4	35.7	30.9	4.9	17.4	8.6	1.8	16.6
Home security system service fee	68.2	28.4	34.3	9.1	18.0	7.2	4.2	19.7
Other home services	74.4	35.0	30.3	6.1	11.4	12.8	1.1	15.9
Termite and pest control products	73.6	38.1	29.0	3.0	17.8	8.2	3.1	14.6
Moving, storage, and freight express	64.8	30.9	27.4	6.7	14.1	6.6	3.7	17.6
Appliance repair, including at service center	72.9	29.5	37.1	6.6	18.8	11.7	3.1	15.4
Reupholstering and furniture repair	83.0	59.4	17.8	7.5	5.0	5.3	0.8	15.1
Repairs and rentals of lawn and garden equipment, hand and power tools, etc.	74.7	30.0	41.2	3.9	28.7	8.6	3.5	12.3
Appliance rental	50.0	27.9	20.1	3.5	13.0	3.7	12.7	12.1
Repair of computer systems for nonbusiness use	69.3	23.0	39.8	1.5	22.3	15.9	4.5	12.0
Computer information services	65.6	24.7	36.4	6.1	19.1	11.1	4.8	16.7
HOUSEKEEPING SUPPLIES	66.7	27.0	34.5	6.6	18.3	9.5	4.5	15.3
Laundry and cleaning supplies	63.3	21.5	34.8	5.6	19.3	10.0	6.3	14.2
Soaps and detergents	63.6	19.7	36.3	6.3	19.7	10.2	6.2	13.1
Other laundry cleaning products	63.0	24.0	32.9	4.7	18.8	9.6	6.5	15.6
Other household products	68.5	27.9	35.8	7.5	18.9	9.3	3.9	14.7
Cleansing and toilet tissue, paper towels, and napkins	62.7	24.9	31.3	5.0	16.4	10.0	5.0	16.7
Miscellaneous household products	68.0	24.5	38.7	10.7	18.1	9.6	4.2	15.0
Lawn and garden supplies	75.1	35.9	36.3	5.3	22.6	8.2	2.5	12.2
Postage and stationery	66.7	30.4	31.8	6.1	16.3	9.5	3.9	17.6
Stationery, stationery supplies, giftwrap	68.8	26.9	37.8	7.5	19.9	10.4	4.5	15.1
Postage	64.3	32.7	26.6	5.1	13.0	8.6	3.5	19.4
Delivery services	68.1	44.5	22.2	0.5	12.7	9.6	1.3	26.4
HOUSEHOLD FURNISHINGS AND EQUIPMENT	69.9	28.5	35.2	6.6	18.2	10.5	3.7	14.4
Household textiles	66.5	29.4	31.9	5.1	13.7	13.5	3.2	15.9
Bathroom linens	62.4	26.2	32.5	5.2	14.1	13.8	6.8	15.8
Bedroom linens	67.2	31.0	31.0	4.9	12.3	14.5	2.8	14.1
Kitchen and dining room linens	76.6	30.1	43.6	5.0	19.0	20.6	2.9	12.6
Curtains and draperies	69.5	30.5	30.7	7.5	16.7	6.5	1.6	17.9
Slipcovers and decorative pillows	48.1	15.5	29.6	3.4	15.8	10.8	1.6	30.4
Sewing materials for household items	69.1	32.7	31.1	4.5	11.9	14.8	3.8	17.9
Other linens	67.5	31.6	29.8	4.6	18.3	7.0	3.9	14.4
Furniture	70.9	28.5	35.5	7.2	18.7	9.5	5.1	12.1
Mattresses and springs	70.4	31.0	35.4	5.0	17.8	12.6	4.1	14.1
Other bedroom furniture	65.1	25.2	32.4	8.5	15.9	8.0	7.5	9.7
Sofas	70.4	26.4	37.3	6.3	21.9	9.1	5.0	13.7
Living room chairs	73.3	34.3	32.2	5.8	17.8	8.6	3.5	13.0
Living room tables	72.7	31.1	35.9	6.6	18.4	10.8	4.8	14.0
Kitchen and dining room furniture	69.7	26.9	33.4	7.9	17.6	7.8	4.1	13.1

	total married couples	married couples, no children	married couples with children				single parent, at least one child <18	single person
			total	oldest child under 6	oldest child 6 to 17	oldest child 18 or older		
Infants' furniture	80.1%	36.3%	38.4%	22.4%	11.7%	4.4%	2.7%	2.7%
Outdoor furniture	78.5	32.6	39.2	7.1	23.9	8.3	3.8	10.8
Wall units, cabinets, and other furniture	75.1	28.4	38.7	7.5	19.3	11.9	5.3	11.1
Floor coverings	**71.2**	**33.2**	**29.8**	**4.4**	**16.3**	**9.1**	**4.8**	**13.2**
Wall-to-wall carpeting	67.5	33.1	25.5	4.8	11.8	8.9	6.2	13.4
Floor coverings, nonpermanent	75.5	33.3	34.7	3.8	21.6	9.3	3.2	12.8
Major appliances	**72.0**	**30.0**	**36.6**	**7.9**	**17.9**	**10.9**	**2.9**	**12.5**
Dishwashers (built-in), garbage disposals, range hoods	78.0	34.6	39.2	9.4	16.8	13.0	3.7	7.5
Refrigerators and freezers	71.8	32.7	34.0	10.1	12.4	11.5	2.4	12.8
Washing machines	69.9	30.7	33.1	7.1	17.5	8.5	4.7	12.7
Clothes dryers	68.3	26.0	36.4	5.8	19.8	10.7	4.4	15.2
Cooking stoves, ovens	71.0	32.3	33.0	8.1	16.7	8.2	1.5	13.5
Microwave ovens	63.6	23.8	34.2	4.9	18.9	10.4	4.2	16.6
Portable dishwasher	76.3	25.1	50.8	17.1	27.5	6.4	1.8	8.1
Window air conditioners	59.9	19.8	31.8	3.4	16.7	11.6	3.8	10.9
Electric floor-cleaning equipment	76.9	18.8	53.3	9.2	28.9	15.2	2.2	14.0
Sewing machines	78.6	31.2	35.8	2.9	28.4	4.6	3.3	9.1
Miscellaneous household appliances	80.5	54.7	23.3	0.3	11.6	12.3	0.8	1.6
Small appliances and miscellaneous housewares	**68.2**	**28.6**	**33.9**	**8.3**	**16.5**	**9.1**	**4.0**	**16.3**
Housewares	69.2	28.4	35.1	8.3	17.3	9.3	3.9	16.2
Plastic dinnerware	67.2	17.9	42.7	14.7	16.7	11.3	5.3	14.0
China and other dinnerware	86.6	40.8	36.3	10.0	19.2	6.5	2.9	5.1
Flatware	65.2	27.1	27.9	5.1	12.4	10.5	4.0	17.9
Glassware	69.7	28.2	37.7	7.2	15.9	15.0	2.6	20.5
Silver serving pieces	68.6	28.6	36.1	5.0	22.5	8.6	2.2	18.3
Other serving pieces	72.2	35.6	32.2	3.8	19.8	8.6	4.4	13.7
Nonelectric cookware	64.1	25.2	35.2	10.6	17.5	6.4	3.9	16.6
Tableware, nonelectric kitchenware	63.0	24.2	32.7	6.9	18.0	7.6	5.6	18.7
Small appliances	64.5	29.1	29.6	8.1	13.3	8.2	4.2	16.9
Small electric kitchen appliances	63.9	30.4	27.0	4.6	14.4	7.9	4.7	17.1
Portable heating and cooling equipment	66.9	24.5	39.0	20.6	9.1	9.2	2.6	15.8
Miscellaneous household equipment	**69.7**	**27.5**	**36.0**	**6.1**	**19.3**	**10.5**	**3.0**	**15.7**
Window coverings	72.8	37.1	27.2	11.3	11.6	4.2	4.5	15.9
Infants' equipment	75.8	43.4	28.2	14.7	11.1	1.1	2.6	2.8
Laundry and cleaning equipment	62.4	23.6	31.4	5.4	16.0	10.2	5.7	19.1
Outdoor equipment	56.8	19.4	34.4	3.7	16.4	15.1	3.5	10.5
Clocks	73.0	41.0	23.0	4.6	11.5	7.0	1.3	13.0
Lamps and lighting fixtures	74.5	42.2	28.0	8.3	14.4	5.2	2.8	13.0
Other household decorative items	70.6	26.7	33.5	6.6	18.6	8.2	2.3	17.0
Telephones and accessories	76.8	19.5	55.8	1.5	30.0	26.0	1.9	12.6
Lawn and garden equipment	72.9	33.9	29.9	5.8	14.5	9.6	2.6	15.0
Power tools	78.9	34.3	40.5	6.5	24.8	9.0	2.5	8.2
Office furniture for home use	72.7	22.2	45.2	5.3	33.1	6.8	4.1	13.2
Hand tools	65.1	30.6	30.5	7.7	12.9	9.9	4.2	18.9
Indoor plants and fresh flowers	71.1	34.5	32.0	5.4	15.0	11.6	2.5	15.7
Closet and storage items	71.8	25.3	42.0	18.6	14.5	7.9	4.0	9.3
Rental of furniture	49.8	4.0	37.4	8.0	21.8	7.7	15.3	11.5
Luggage	64.3	27.1	33.8	5.7	18.5	9.6	3.2	20.8
Computers and computer hardware, nonbusiness use	65.9	21.9	39.4	5.4	20.3	13.7	4.0	17.6
Computer software and accessories, nonbusiness use	65.5	24.1	36.1	4.0	19.8	12.2	3.4	21.9
Telephone answering devices	63.9	22.0	38.6	4.9	26.0	7.7	3.7	25.2
Calculators	70.4	7.8	52.6	3.3	35.5	13.8	4.0	18.7
Business equipment for home use	59.6	30.4	20.9	0.7	17.4	2.9	9.8	19.7
Other hardware	66.3	34.0	27.5	2.8	21.2	3.1	1.5	26.7
Smoke alarms	74.9	27.3	36.9	11.6	17.1	8.3	2.3	12.7
Other household appliances	77.2	30.1	42.7	2.9	22.2	17.6	1.1	14.7
Miscellaneous household equipment and parts	73.2	24.4	45.4	7.5	26.4	11.4	3.6	9.0

Note: Market share for total consumer units is 100.0%. Market shares by type of consumer unit will not add to total because not all types of consumer units are shown. "–" means sample is too small to make a reliable estimate.
Source: Calculations by New Strategist based on the 2004 Consumer Expenditure Survey

Table 8.17 Housing: Household Operations: Average spending by race and Hispanic origin, 2004

(average annual spending of consumer units (CU) on household services, supplies, furnishings, and equipment, by race and Hispanic origin of consumer unit reference person, 2004)

	total consumer units	Asian	black	Hispanic	non-Hispanic white and other
Number of consumer units (in 000s)	116,282	3,957	13,773	12,298	90,424
Average number of persons per CU	2.5	2.8	2.6	3.3	2.3
Average before-tax income of CU	$54,453.00	$67,705.00	$38,503.00	$43,693.00	$58,314.00
Average spending of CU, total	43,394.87	49,458.68	30,481.49	37,578.03	46,163.26
Housing, average spending	13,918.48	17,418.15	11,042.97	12,883.84	14,503.48
HOUSEHOLD SERVICES	752.83	885.50	465.93	573.53	820.04
Personal services	299.71	450.02	240.74	330.53	304.43
Babysitting and child care in own home	37.09	44.24	14.46	48.32	38.91
Babysitting and child care in someone else's home	26.12	12.07	29.23	66.08	20.15
Care for elderly, invalids, handicapped, etc.	34.96	2.92	13.35	16.33	40.70
Day care centers, nurseries, and preschools	193.51	390.79	183.63	199.64	194.37
Other household services	453.12	435.48	225.19	243.00	515.61
Housekeeping services	88.85	49.74	23.72	31.41	106.37
Gardening, lawn care service	95.08	109.66	41.92	41.47	110.24
Water-softening service	3.06	0.44	1.08	2.26	3.46
Nonclothing laundry and dry cleaning, sent out	0.94	2.02	0.30	0.26	1.13
Nonclothing laundry and dry cleaning, coin-operated	3.71	4.30	5.43	10.57	2.54
Termite and pest control services	12.04	8.15	5.00	6.60	13.83
Home security system service fee	15.57	18.41	25.69	8.48	14.96
Other home services	23.03	6.60	6.76	13.39	26.76
Termite and pest control products	1.53	1.39	0.74	0.86	1.74
Moving, storage, and freight express	33.91	19.33	9.07	17.62	39.88
Appliance repair, including at service center	14.53	8.95	7.92	7.24	16.50
Reupholstering and furniture repair	7.35	4.34	3.56	7.89	7.84
Repairs and rentals of lawn and garden equipment, hand and power tools, etc.	7.29	21.00	2.09	2.39	8.73
Appliance rental	1.75	0.65	6.66	1.05	1.09
Repair of computer systems for nonbusiness use	4.03	3.47	2.51	2.04	4.52
Computer information services	139.46	175.39	82.14	89.38	154.85
HOUSEKEEPING SUPPLIES	594.47	471.85	374.50	503.06	641.50
Laundry and cleaning supplies	148.56	115.01	123.90	199.34	145.29
Soaps and detergents	85.44	74.57	78.35	126.05	80.94
Other laundry cleaning products	63.13	40.44	45.54	73.29	64.35
Other household products	290.41	216.63	152.14	209.91	323.12
Cleansing and toilet tissue, paper towels, and napkins	85.84	79.27	75.98	104.96	84.73
Miscellaneous household products	121.13	58.63	54.52	73.84	138.02
Lawn and garden supplies	83.44	78.73	21.65	31.12	100.37
Postage and stationery	155.50	140.21	98.46	93.81	173.09
Stationery, stationery supplies, giftwrap	74.86	83.72	41.42	47.82	83.93
Postage	74.12	46.84	56.21	43.75	81.17
Delivery services	6.52	9.65	0.84	2.24	8.00
HOUSEHOLD FURNISHINGS AND EQUIPMENT	1,646.10	1,551.59	907.45	1,303.06	1,809.48
Household textiles	157.66	95.92	106.99	110.00	172.33
Bathroom linens	21.26	7.10	20.32	15.65	22.45
Bedroom linens	85.72	67.24	63.60	60.03	92.79
Kitchen and dining room linens	9.84	4.88	6.56	5.77	10.93
Curtains and draperies	19.22	6.05	10.23	13.57	21.33
Slipcovers and decorative pillows	9.12	6.72	4.06	8.66	9.95
Sewing materials for household items	11.20	2.59	1.83	5.20	13.41
Other linens	1.31	1.33	0.38	1.11	1.48
Furniture	416.97	513.20	325.67	351.33	441.52
Mattresses and springs	53.56	73.43	30.00	47.99	57.82
Other bedroom furniture	81.32	71.27	104.32	87.91	78.23
Sofas	94.74	180.86	70.85	98.97	97.96
Living room chairs	41.65	21.52	28.41	23.31	46.29
Living room tables	14.77	9.15	10.04	11.29	16.21
Kitchen and dining room furniture	41.26	77.07	33.98	30.35	43.76

	total consumer units	Asian	black	Hispanic	non-Hispanic white and other
Infants' furniture	$8.44	$12.12	$3.06	$9.47	$9.09
Outdoor furniture	16.18	6.41	11.02	7.45	18.16
Wall units, cabinets, and other furniture	65.05	61.37	33.99	34.60	74.00
Floor coverings	**51.98**	**63.72**	**25.11**	**22.45**	**59.97**
Wall-to-wall carpeting	27.98	15.54	13.57	12.89	32.16
Floor coverings, nonpermanent	24.00	48.18	11.54	9.56	27.81
Major appliances	**203.94**	**138.54**	**108.99**	**205.13**	**217.93**
Dishwashers (built-in), garbage disposals, range hoods	14.34	8.01	3.69	8.67	16.71
Refrigerators and freezers	51.27	52.40	33.01	46.38	54.60
Washing machines	30.65	23.34	14.80	32.86	32.70
Clothes dryers	22.03	11.30	7.85	22.73	24.05
Cooking stoves, ovens	32.42	24.22	23.50	40.49	32.62
Microwave ovens	8.43	8.97	6.55	10.66	8.40
Portable dishwasher	1.22	1.30	0.34	1.32	1.34
Window air conditioners	4.36	2.82	3.41	9.93	3.74
Electric floor-cleaning equipment	27.71	5.64	11.67	10.90	32.53
Sewing machines	3.59	0.55	1.34	2.32	4.10
Miscellaneous household appliances	7.91	–	2.86	18.86	7.13
Small appliances and miscellaneous housewares	**104.66**	**167.50**	**46.47**	**77.83**	**117.48**
Housewares	82.56	151.30	35.64	61.76	92.85
Plastic dinnerware	1.82	2.10	0.86	2.80	1.84
China and other dinnerware	13.47	18.29	4.06	7.18	15.81
Flatware	4.02	6.29	1.89	4.87	4.23
Glassware	20.88	46.29	5.29	16.21	23.92
Silver serving pieces	0.30	0.47	0.22	0.16	0.33
Other serving pieces	1.76	2.05	0.45	1.01	2.06
Nonelectric cookware	18.10	58.97	11.28	14.84	19.79
Tableware, nonelectric kitchenware	22.20	16.83	11.58	14.68	24.88
Small appliances	22.10	16.20	10.83	16.07	24.63
Small electric kitchen appliances	17.27	13.80	7.96	13.84	19.15
Portable heating and cooling equipment	4.83	2.40	2.87	2.24	5.48
Miscellaneous household equipment	710.89	572.72	294.20	536.32	800.25
Window coverings	23.47	38.62	10.82	22.59	25.46
Infants' equipment	7.86	13.32	3.00	18.48	7.10
Laundry and cleaning equipment	15.72	12.55	9.32	18.59	16.28
Outdoor equipment	35.99	8.32	18.78	18.74	41.17
Clocks	7.64	4.69	6.06	7.82	7.85
Lamps and lighting fixtures	16.40	13.52	7.62	12.65	18.23
Other household decorative items	158.10	109.50	64.96	83.67	182.96
Telephones and accessories	26.83	8.12	30.17	28.30	27.61
Lawn and garden equipment	48.79	12.38	14.99	14.02	58.55
Power tools	33.44	10.35	14.16	31.91	36.59
Office furniture for home use	11.37	9.50	4.09	3.51	13.52
Hand tools	6.11	4.52	0.70	6.55	6.86
Indoor plants and fresh flowers	41.52	26.82	14.56	29.10	47.42
Closet and storage items	17.83	8.89	3.51	9.99	21.13
Rental of furniture	2.22	3.55	6.16	5.90	1.25
Luggage	6.63	8.03	4.73	5.24	7.09
Computers and computer hardware, nonbusiness use	134.57	182.89	51.50	113.01	149.83
Computer software and accessories, nonbusiness use	19.06	29.00	7.56	13.11	21.58
Telephone answering devices	0.62	0.62	0.15	0.86	0.66
Calculators	1.44	2.49	0.86	1.01	1.58
Business equipment for home use	0.94	1.27	0.89	0.94	0.95
Other hardware	39.63	31.82	4.08	62.90	42.01
Smoke alarms	1.03	0.54	0.48	0.99	1.11
Other household appliances	12.53	3.51	5.73	9.88	13.90
Miscellaneous household equipment and parts	41.18	27.87	9.30	16.57	49.56

Note: "Asian" and "black" include Hispanics and non-Hispanics who identify themselves as being of the respective race alone. "Hispanic" includes people of any race who identify themselves as Hispanic. "Other" includes people who identify themselves as non-Hispanic and as Alaska Native, American Indian, Asian (who are also included in the "Asian" column), Native Hawaiian or other Pacific Islander, as well as non-Hispanics reporting more than one race. Subcategories may not add to total because some are not shown. "–" means sample is too small to make a reliable estimate.
Source: Bureau of Labor Statistics, unpublished tables from the 2004 Consumer Expenditure Survey

Table 8.18 Housing: Household Operations: Indexed spending by race and Hispanic origin, 2004

(indexed average annual spending of consumer units (CU) on household services, supplies, furnishings, and equipment, by race and Hispanic origin of consumer unit reference person, 2004; index definition: an index of 100 is the average for all consumer units; an index of 132 means that spending by consumer units in that group is 32 percent above the average for all consumer units; an index of 68 indicates spending that is 32 percent below the average for all consumer units)

	total consumer units	Asian	black	Hispanic	non-Hispanic white and other
Average spending of CU, total	$43,395	$49,459	$30,481	$37,578	$46,163
Average spending of CU, index	100	114	70	87	106
Housing, spending index	100	125	79	93	104
HOUSEHOLD SERVICES	100	118	62	76	109
Personal services	100	150	80	110	102
Babysitting and child care in own home	100	119	39	130	105
Babysitting and child care in someone else's home	100	46	112	253	77
Care for elderly, invalids, handicapped, etc.	100	8	38	47	116
Day care centers, nurseries, and preschools	100	202	95	103	100
Other household services	100	96	50	54	114
Housekeeping services	100	56	27	35	120
Gardening, lawn care service	100	115	44	44	116
Water-softening service	100	14	35	74	113
Nonclothing laundry and dry cleaning, sent out	100	215	32	28	120
Nonclothing laundry and dry cleaning, coin-operated	100	116	146	285	68
Termite and pest control services	100	68	42	55	115
Home security system service fee	100	118	165	54	96
Other home services	100	29	29	58	116
Termite and pest control products	100	91	48	56	114
Moving, storage, and freight express	100	57	27	52	118
Appliance repair, including at service center	100	62	55	50	114
Reupholstering and furniture repair	100	59	48	107	107
Repairs and rentals of lawn and garden equipment, hand and power tools, etc.	100	288	29	33	120
Appliance rental	100	37	381	60	62
Repair of computer systems for nonbusiness use	100	86	62	51	112
Computer information services	100	126	59	64	111
HOUSEKEEPING SUPPLIES	100	79	63	85	108
Laundry and cleaning supplies	100	77	83	134	98
Soaps and detergents	100	87	92	148	95
Other laundry cleaning products	100	64	72	116	102
Other household products	100	75	52	72	111
Cleansing and toilet tissue, paper towels, and napkins	100	92	89	122	99
Miscellaneous household products	100	48	45	61	114
Lawn and garden supplies	100	94	26	37	120
Postage and stationery	100	90	63	60	111
Stationery, stationery supplies, giftwrap	100	112	55	64	112
Postage	100	63	76	59	110
Delivery services	100	148	13	34	123
HOUSEHOLD FURNISHINGS AND EQUIPMENT	100	94	55	79	110
Household textiles	100	61	68	70	109
Bathroom linens	100	33	96	74	106
Bedroom linens	100	78	74	70	108
Kitchen and dining room linens	100	50	67	59	111
Curtains and draperies	100	31	53	71	111
Slipcovers and decorative pillows	100	74	45	95	109
Sewing materials for household items	100	23	16	46	120
Other linens	100	102	29	85	113
Furniture	100	123	78	84	106
Mattresses and springs	100	137	56	90	108
Other bedroom furniture	100	88	128	108	96
Sofas	100	191	75	104	103
Living room chairs	100	52	68	56	111
Living room tables	100	62	68	76	110
Kitchen and dining room furniture	100	187	82	74	106

	total consumer units	Asian	black	Hispanic	non-Hispanic white and other
Infants' furniture	100	144	36	112	108
Outdoor furniture	100	40	68	46	112
Wall units, cabinets, and other furniture	100	94	52	53	114
Floor coverings	**100**	**123**	**48**	**43**	**115**
Wall-to-wall carpeting	100	56	48	46	115
Floor coverings, nonpermanent	100	201	48	40	116
Major appliances	**100**	**68**	**53**	**101**	**107**
Dishwashers (built-in), garbage disposals, range hoods	100	56	26	60	117
Refrigerators and freezers	100	102	64	90	106
Washing machines	100	76	48	107	107
Clothes dryers	100	51	36	103	109
Cooking stoves, ovens	100	75	72	125	101
Microwave ovens	100	106	78	126	100
Portable dishwasher	100	107	28	108	110
Window air conditioners	100	65	78	228	86
Electric floor-cleaning equipment	100	20	42	39	117
Sewing machines	100	15	37	65	114
Miscellaneous household appliances	100	–	36	238	90
Small appliances and miscellaneous housewares	**100**	**160**	**44**	**74**	**112**
Housewares	100	183	43	75	112
Plastic dinnerware	100	115	47	154	101
China and other dinnerware	100	136	30	53	117
Flatware	100	156	47	121	105
Glassware	100	222	25	78	115
Silver serving pieces	100	157	73	53	110
Other serving pieces	100	116	26	57	117
Nonelectric cookware	100	326	62	82	109
Tableware, nonelectric kitchenware	100	76	52	66	112
Small appliances	100	73	49	73	111
Small electric kitchen appliances	100	80	46	80	111
Portable heating and cooling equipment	100	50	59	46	113
Miscellaneous household equipment	100	81	41	75	113
Window coverings	100	165	46	96	108
Infants' equipment	100	169	38	235	90
Laundry and cleaning equipment	100	80	59	118	104
Outdoor equipment	100	23	52	52	114
Clocks	100	61	79	102	103
Lamps and lighting fixtures	100	82	46	77	111
Other household decorative items	100	69	41	53	116
Telephones and accessories	100	30	112	105	103
Lawn and garden equipment	100	25	31	29	120
Power tools	100	31	42	95	109
Office furniture for home use	100	84	36	31	119
Hand tools	100	74	11	107	112
Indoor plants and fresh flowers	100	65	35	70	114
Closet and storage items	100	50	20	56	119
Rental of furniture	100	160	277	266	56
Luggage	100	121	71	79	107
Computers and computer hardware, nonbusiness use	100	136	38	84	111
Computer software and accessories, nonbusiness use	100	152	40	69	113
Telephone answering devices	100	100	24	139	106
Calculators	100	173	60	70	110
Business equipment for home use	100	135	95	100	101
Other hardware	100	80	10	159	106
Smoke alarms	100	52	47	96	108
Other household appliances	100	28	46	79	111
Miscellaneous household equipment and parts	100	68	23	40	120

Note: "Asian" and "black" include Hispanics and non-Hispanics who identify themselves as being of the respective race alone. "Hispanic" includes people of any race who identify themselves as Hispanic. "Other" includes people who identify themselves as non-Hispanic and as Alaska Native, American Indian, Asian (who are also included in the "Asian" column), Native Hawaiian or other Pacific Islander, as well as non-Hispanics reporting more than one race. "–" means sample is too small to make a reliable estimate.
Source: Calculations by New Strategist based on the 2004 Consumer Expenditure Survey

Table 8.19 Housing: Household Operations: Total spending by race and Hispanic origin, 2004

(total annual spending on household services, supplies, furnishings, and equipment, by consumer unit race and Hispanic origin groups, 2004; consumer units and dollars in thousands)

	total consumer units	Asian	black	Hispanic	non-Hispanic white and other
Number of consumer units	116,282	3,957	13,773	12,298	90,424
Total spending of all consumer units	$5,046,042,273	$195,707,997	$419,821,562	$462,134,613	$4,174,266,622
Housing, total spending	1,618,468,691	68,923,620	152,094,826	158,445,464	1,311,462,676
HOUSEHOLD SERVICES	**$87,540,578**	**$3,503,924**	**$6,417,254**	**$7,053,272**	**$74,151,297**
Personal services	**34,850,878**	**1,780,729**	**3,315,712**	**4,064,858**	**27,527,778**
Babysitting and child care in own home	4,312,899	175,058	199,158	594,239	3,518,398
Babysitting and child care in someone else's home	3,037,286	47,761	402,585	812,652	1,822,044
Care for elderly, invalids, handicapped, etc.	4,065,219	11,554	183,870	200,826	3,680,257
Day care centers, nurseries, and preschools	22,501,730	1,546,356	2,529,136	2,455,173	17,575,713
Other household services	**52,689,700**	**1,723,194**	**3,101,542**	**2,988,414**	**46,623,519**
Housekeeping services	10,331,656	196,821	326,696	386,280	9,618,401
Gardening, lawn care service	11,056,093	433,925	577,364	509,998	9,968,342
Water-softening service	355,823	1,741	14,875	27,793	312,867
Nonclothing laundry and dry cleaning, sent out	109,305	7,993	4,132	3,197	102,179
Nonclothing laundry and dry cleaning, coin-operated	431,406	17,015	74,787	129,990	229,677
Termite and pest control services	1,400,035	32,250	68,865	81,167	1,250,564
Home security system service fee	1,810,511	72,848	353,828	104,287	1,352,743
Other home services	2,677,974	26,116	93,105	164,670	2,419,746
Termite and pest control products	177,911	5,500	10,192	10,576	157,338
Moving, storage, and freight express	3,943,123	76,489	124,921	216,691	3,606,109
Appliance repair, including at service center	1,689,577	35,415	109,082	89,038	1,491,996
Reupholstering and furniture repair	854,673	17,173	49,032	97,031	708,924
Repairs and rentals of lawn and garden equipment, hand and power tools, etc.	847,696	83,097	28,786	29,392	789,402
Appliance rental	203,494	2,572	91,728	12,913	98,562
Repair of computer systems for nonbusiness use	468,616	13,731	34,570	25,088	408,716
Computer information services	16,216,688	694,018	1,131,314	1,099,195	14,002,156
HOUSEKEEPING SUPPLIES	**69,126,161**	**1,867,110**	**5,157,989**	**6,186,632**	**58,006,996**
Laundry and cleaning supplies	**17,274,854**	**455,095**	**1,706,475**	**2,451,483**	**13,137,703**
Soaps and detergents	9,935,134	295,073	1,079,115	1,550,163	7,318,919
Other laundry cleaning products	7,340,883	160,021	627,222	901,320	5,818,784
Other household products	**33,769,456**	**857,205**	**2,095,424**	**2,581,473**	**29,217,803**
Cleansing and toilet tissue, paper towels, and napkins	9,981,647	313,671	1,046,473	1,290,798	7,661,626
Miscellaneous household products	14,085,239	231,999	750,904	908,084	12,480,320
Lawn and garden supplies	9,702,570	311,535	298,185	382,714	9,075,857
Postage and stationery	**18,081,851**	**554,811**	**1,356,090**	**1,153,675**	**15,651,490**
Stationery, stationery supplies, giftwrap	8,704,871	331,280	570,478	588,090	7,589,286
Postage	8,618,822	185,346	774,180	538,038	7,339,716
Delivery services	758,159	38,185	11,569	27,548	723,392
HOUSEHOLD FURNISHINGS AND EQUIPMENT	**191,411,800**	**6,139,642**	**12,498,309**	**16,025,032**	**163,620,420**
Household textiles	**18,333,020**	**379,555**	**1,473,573**	**1,352,780**	**15,582,768**
Bathroom linens	2,472,155	28,095	279,867	192,464	2,030,019
Bedroom linens	9,967,693	266,069	875,963	738,249	8,390,443
Kitchen and dining room linens	1,144,215	19,310	90,351	70,959	988,334
Curtains and draperies	2,234,940	23,940	140,898	166,884	1,928,744
Slipcovers and decorative pillows	1,060,492	26,591	55,918	106,501	899,719
Sewing materials for household items	1,302,358	10,249	25,205	63,950	1,212,586
Other linens	152,329	5,263	5,234	13,651	133,828
Furniture	**48,486,106**	**2,030,732**	**4,485,453**	**4,320,656**	**39,924,004**
Mattresses and springs	6,228,064	290,563	413,190	590,181	5,228,316
Other bedroom furniture	9,456,052	282,015	1,436,799	1,081,117	7,073,870
Sofas	11,016,557	715,663	975,817	1,217,133	8,857,935
Living room chairs	4,843,145	85,155	391,291	286,666	4,185,727
Living room tables	1,717,485	36,207	138,281	138,844	1,465,773
Kitchen and dining room furniture	4,797,795	304,966	468,007	373,244	3,956,954

	total consumer units	Asian	black	Hispanic	non-Hispanic white and other
Infants' furniture	$981,420	$47,959	$42,145	$116,462	$821,954
Outdoor furniture	1,881,443	25,364	151,778	91,620	1,642,100
Wall units, cabinets, and other furniture	7,564,144	242,841	468,144	425,511	6,691,376
Floor coverings	**6,044,338**	**252,140**	**345,840**	**276,090**	**5,422,727**
Wall-to-wall carpeting	3,253,570	61,492	186,900	158,521	2,908,036
Floor coverings, nonpermanent	2,790,768	190,648	158,940	117,569	2,514,691
Major appliances	**23,714,551**	**548,203**	**1,501,119**	**2,522,689**	**19,706,102**
Dishwashers (built-in), garbage disposals, range hoods	1,667,484	31,696	50,822	106,624	1,510,985
Refrigerators and freezers	5,961,778	207,347	454,647	570,381	4,937,150
Washing machines	3,564,043	92,356	203,840	404,112	2,956,865
Clothes dryers	2,561,692	44,714	108,118	279,534	2,174,697
Cooking stoves, ovens	3,769,862	95,839	323,666	497,946	2,949,631
Microwave ovens	980,257	35,494	90,213	131,097	759,562
Portable dishwasher	141,864	5,144	4,683	16,233	121,168
Window air conditioners	506,990	11,159	46,966	122,119	338,186
Electric floor-cleaning equipment	3,222,174	22,317	160,731	134,048	2,941,493
Sewing machines	417,452	2,176	18,456	28,531	370,738
Miscellaneous household appliances	919,791	–	39,391	231,940	644,723
Small appliances and miscellaneous housewares	**12,170,074**	**662,798**	**640,031**	**957,153**	**10,623,012**
Housewares	9,600,242	598,694	490,870	759,524	8,395,868
Plastic dinnerware	211,633	8,310	11,845	34,434	166,380
China and other dinnerware	1,566,319	72,374	55,918	88,300	1,429,603
Flatware	467,454	24,890	26,031	59,891	382,494
Glassware	2,427,968	183,170	72,859	199,351	2,162,942
Silver serving pieces	34,885	1,860	3,030	1,968	29,840
Other serving pieces	204,656	8,112	6,198	12,421	186,273
Nonelectric cookware	2,104,704	233,344	155,359	182,502	1,789,491
Tableware, nonelectric kitchenware	2,581,460	66,596	159,491	180,535	2,249,749
Small appliances	2,569,832	64,103	149,162	197,629	2,227,143
Small electric kitchen appliances	2,008,190	54,607	109,633	170,204	1,731,620
Portable heating and cooling equipment	561,642	9,497	39,529	27,548	495,524
Miscellaneous household equipment	**82,663,711**	**2,266,253**	**4,052,017**	**6,595,663**	**72,361,806**
Window coverings	2,729,139	152,819	149,024	277,812	2,302,195
Infants' equipment	913,977	52,707	41,319	227,267	642,010
Laundry and cleaning equipment	1,827,953	49,660	128,364	228,620	1,472,103
Outdoor equipment	4,184,989	32,922	258,657	230,465	3,722,756
Clocks	888,394	18,558	83,464	96,170	709,828
Lamps and lighting fixtures	1,907,025	53,499	104,950	155,570	1,648,430
Other household decorative items	18,384,184	433,292	894,694	1,028,974	16,543,975
Telephones and accessories	3,119,846	32,131	415,531	348,033	2,496,607
Lawn and garden equipment	5,673,399	48,988	206,457	172,418	5,294,325
Power tools	3,888,470	40,955	195,026	392,429	3,308,614
Office furniture for home use	1,322,126	37,592	56,332	43,166	1,222,532
Hand tools	710,483	17,886	9,641	80,552	620,309
Indoor plants and fresh flowers	4,828,029	106,127	200,535	357,872	4,287,906
Closet and storage items	2,073,308	35,178	48,343	122,857	1,910,659
Rental of furniture	258,146	14,047	84,842	72,558	113,030
Luggage	770,950	31,775	65,146	64,442	641,106
Computers and computer hardware, nonbusiness use	15,648,069	723,696	709,310	1,389,797	13,548,228
Computer software and accessories, nonbusiness use	2,216,335	114,753	104,124	161,227	1,951,350
Telephone answering devices	72,095	2,453	2,066	10,576	59,680
Calculators	167,446	9,853	11,845	12,421	142,870
Business equipment for home use	109,305	5,025	12,258	11,560	85,903
Other hardware	4,608,256	125,912	56,194	773,544	3,798,712
Smoke alarms	119,770	2,137	6,611	12,175	100,371
Other household appliances	1,457,013	13,889	78,919	121,504	1,256,894
Miscellaneous household equipment and parts	4,788,493	110,282	128,089	203,778	4,481,413

Note: "Asian" and "black" include Hispanics and non-Hispanics who identify themselves as being of the respective race alone. "Hispanic" includes people of any race who identify themselves as Hispanic. "Other" includes people who identify themselves as non-Hispanic and as Alaska Native, American Indian, Asian (who are also included in the "Asian" column), Native Hawaiian or other Pacific Islander, as well as non-Hispanics reporting more than one race. Numbers may not add to total because of rounding and missing subcategories. "–" means sample is too small to make a reliable estimate.
Source: Calculations by New Strategist based on the 2004 Consumer Expenditure Survey

Table 8.20 Housing: Household Operations: Market shares by race and Hispanic origin, 2004

(percentage of total annual spending on household services, supplies, furnishings, and equipment accounted for by consumer unit race and Hispanic origin groups, 2004)

	total consumer units	Asian	black	Hispanic	non-Hispanic white and other
Share of total consumer units	100.0%	3.4%	11.8%	10.6%	77.8%
Share of total before-tax income	100.0	4.2	8.4	8.5	83.3
Share of total spending	100.0	3.9	8.3	9.2	82.7
Share of housing spending	100.0	4.3	9.4	9.8	81.0
HOUSEHOLD SERVICES	100.0	4.0	7.3	8.1	84.7
Personal services	100.0	5.1	9.5	11.7	79.0
Babysitting and child care in own home	100.0	4.1	4.6	13.8	81.6
Babysitting and child care in someone else's home	100.0	1.6	13.3	26.8	60.0
Care for elderly, invalids, handicapped, etc.	100.0	0.3	4.5	4.9	90.5
Day care centers, nurseries, and preschools	100.0	6.9	11.2	10.9	78.1
Other household services	100.0	3.3	5.9	5.7	88.5
Housekeeping services	100.0	1.9	3.2	3.7	93.1
Gardening, lawn care service	100.0	3.9	5.2	4.6	90.2
Water-softening service	100.0	0.5	4.2	7.8	87.9
Nonclothing laundry and dry cleaning, sent out	100.0	7.3	3.8	2.9	93.5
Nonclothing laundry and dry cleaning, coin-operated	100.0	3.9	17.3	30.1	53.2
Termite and pest control services	100.0	2.3	4.9	5.8	89.3
Home security system service fee	100.0	4.0	19.5	5.8	74.7
Other home services	100.0	1.0	3.5	6.1	90.4
Termite and pest control products	100.0	3.1	5.7	5.9	88.4
Moving, storage, and freight express	100.0	1.9	3.2	5.5	91.5
Appliance repair, including at service center	100.0	2.1	6.5	5.3	88.3
Reupholstering and furniture repair	100.0	2.0	5.7	11.4	82.9
Repairs and rentals of lawn and garden equipment, hand and power tools, etc.	100.0	9.8	3.4	3.5	93.1
Appliance rental	100.0	1.3	45.1	6.3	48.4
Repair of computer systems for nonbusiness use	100.0	2.9	7.4	5.4	87.2
Computer information services	100.0	4.3	7.0	6.8	86.3
HOUSEKEEPING SUPPLIES	100.0	2.7	7.5	8.9	83.9
Laundry and cleaning supplies	100.0	2.6	9.9	14.2	76.1
Soaps and detergents	100.0	3.0	10.9	15.6	73.7
Other laundry cleaning products	100.0	2.2	8.5	12.3	79.3
Other household products	100.0	2.5	6.2	7.6	86.5
Cleansing and toilet tissue, paper towels, and napkins	100.0	3.1	10.5	12.9	76.8
Miscellaneous household products	100.0	1.6	5.3	6.4	88.6
Lawn and garden supplies	100.0	3.2	3.1	3.9	93.5
Postage and stationery	100.0	3.1	7.5	6.4	86.6
Stationery, stationery supplies, giftwrap	100.0	3.8	6.6	6.8	87.2
Postage	100.0	2.2	9.0	6.2	85.2
Delivery services	100.0	5.0	1.5	3.6	95.4
HOUSEHOLD FURNISHINGS AND EQUIPMENT	100.0	3.2	6.5	8.4	85.5
Household textiles	100.0	2.1	8.0	7.4	85.0
Bathroom linens	100.0	1.1	11.3	7.8	82.1
Bedroom linens	100.0	2.7	8.8	7.4	84.2
Kitchen and dining room linens	100.0	1.7	7.9	6.2	86.4
Curtains and draperies	100.0	1.1	6.3	7.5	86.3
Slipcovers and decorative pillows	100.0	2.5	5.3	10.0	84.8
Sewing materials for household items	100.0	0.8	1.9	4.9	93.1
Other linens	100.0	3.5	3.4	9.0	87.9
Furniture	100.0	4.2	9.3	8.9	82.3
Mattresses and springs	100.0	4.7	6.6	9.5	83.9
Other bedroom furniture	100.0	3.0	15.2	11.4	74.8
Sofas	100.0	6.5	8.9	11.0	80.4
Living room chairs	100.0	1.8	8.1	5.9	86.4
Living room tables	100.0	2.1	8.1	8.1	85.3
Kitchen and dining room furniture	100.0	6.4	9.8	7.8	82.5

	total consumer units	Asian	black	Hispanic	non-Hispanic white and other
Infants' furniture	100.0%	4.9%	4.3%	11.9%	83.8%
Outdoor furniture	100.0	1.3	8.1	4.9	87.3
Wall units, cabinets, and other furniture	100.0	3.2	6.2	5.6	88.5
Floor coverings	**100.0**	**4.2**	**5.7**	**4.6**	**89.7**
Wall-to-wall carpeting	100.0	1.9	5.7	4.9	89.4
Floor coverings, nonpermanent	100.0	6.8	5.7	4.2	90.1
Major appliances	**100.0**	**2.3**	**6.3**	**10.6**	**83.1**
Dishwashers (built-in), garbage disposals, range hoods	100.0	1.9	3.0	6.4	90.6
Refrigerators and freezers	100.0	3.5	7.6	9.6	82.8
Washing machines	100.0	2.6	5.7	11.3	83.0
Clothes dryers	100.0	1.7	4.2	10.9	84.9
Cooking stoves, ovens	100.0	2.5	8.6	13.2	78.2
Microwave ovens	100.0	3.6	9.2	13.4	77.5
Portable dishwasher	100.0	3.6	3.3	11.4	85.4
Window air conditioners	100.0	2.2	9.3	24.1	66.7
Electric floor-cleaning equipment	100.0	0.7	5.0	4.2	91.3
Sewing machines	100.0	0.5	4.4	6.8	88.8
Miscellaneous household appliances	100.0	–	4.3	25.2	70.1
Small appliances and miscellaneous housewares	**100.0**	**5.4**	**5.3**	**7.9**	**87.3**
Housewares	100.0	6.2	5.1	7.9	87.5
Plastic dinnerware	100.0	3.9	5.6	16.3	78.6
China and other dinnerware	100.0	4.6	3.6	5.6	91.3
Flatware	100.0	5.3	5.6	12.8	81.8
Glassware	100.0	7.5	3.0	8.2	89.1
Silver serving pieces	100.0	5.3	8.7	5.6	85.5
Other serving pieces	100.0	4.0	3.0	6.1	91.0
Nonelectric cookware	100.0	11.1	7.4	8.7	85.0
Tableware, nonelectric kitchenware	100.0	2.6	6.2	7.0	87.2
Small appliances	100.0	2.5	5.8	7.7	86.7
Small electric kitchen appliances	100.0	2.7	5.5	8.5	86.2
Portable heating and cooling equipment	100.0	1.7	7.0	4.9	88.2
Miscellaneous household equipment	**100.0**	**2.7**	**4.9**	**8.0**	**87.5**
Window coverings	100.0	5.6	5.5	10.2	84.4
Infants' equipment	100.0	5.8	4.5	24.9	70.2
Laundry and cleaning equipment	100.0	2.7	7.0	12.5	80.5
Outdoor equipment	100.0	0.8	6.2	5.5	89.0
Clocks	100.0	2.1	9.4	10.8	79.9
Lamps and lighting fixtures	100.0	2.8	5.5	8.2	86.4
Other household decorative items	100.0	2.4	4.9	5.6	90.0
Telephones and accessories	100.0	1.0	13.3	11.2	80.0
Lawn and garden equipment	100.0	0.9	3.6	3.0	93.3
Power tools	100.0	1.1	5.0	10.1	85.1
Office furniture for home use	100.0	2.8	4.3	3.3	92.5
Hand tools	100.0	2.5	1.4	11.3	87.3
Indoor plants and fresh flowers	100.0	2.2	4.2	7.4	88.8
Closet and storage items	100.0	1.7	2.3	5.9	92.2
Rental of furniture	100.0	5.4	32.9	28.1	43.8
Luggage	100.0	4.1	8.5	8.4	83.2
Computers and computer hardware, nonbusiness use	100.0	4.6	4.5	8.9	86.6
Computer software and accessories, nonbusiness use	100.0	5.2	4.7	7.3	88.0
Telephone answering devices	100.0	3.4	2.9	14.7	82.8
Calculators	100.0	5.9	7.1	7.4	85.3
Business equipment for home use	100.0	4.6	11.2	10.6	78.6
Other hardware	100.0	2.7	1.2	16.8	82.4
Smoke alarms	100.0	1.8	5.5	10.2	83.8
Other household appliances	100.0	1.0	5.4	8.3	86.3
Miscellaneous household equipment and parts	100.0	2.3	2.7	4.3	93.6

Note: "Asian" and "black" include Hispanics and non-Hispanics who identify themselves as being of the respective race alone. "Hispanic" includes people of any race who identify themselves as Hispanic. "Other" includes people who identify themselves as non-Hispanic and as Alaska Native, American Indian, Asian (who are also included in the "Asian" column), Native Hawaiian or other Pacific Islander, as well as non-Hispanics reporting more than one race. "–" means sample is too small to make a reliable estimate.
Source: Calculations by New Strategist based on the 2004 Consumer Expenditure Survey

Table 8.21 Housing: Household Operations: Average spending by region, 2004

(average annual spending of consumer units (CU) on household services, supplies, furnishings, and equipment, by region in which consumer unit lives, 2004)

	total consumer units	Northeast	Midwest	South	West
Number of consumer units (in 000s)	116,282	22,051	26,539	41,801	25,891
Average number of persons per CU	2.5	2.4	2.4	2.5	2.6
Average before-tax income of CU	$54,453.00	$61,050.00	$53,567.00	$50,775.00	$55,682.00
Average spending of CU, total	43,394.87	46,114.89	43,370.77	39,173.65	47,921.74
Housing, average spending	**13,918.48**	**15,733.70**	**13,438.35**	**12,250.19**	**15,556.56**
HOUSEHOLD SERVICES	**752.83**	**793.46**	**706.79**	**673.07**	**894.17**
Personal services	**299.71**	**351.93**	**301.10**	**256.55**	**323.48**
Babysitting and child care in own home	37.09	63.69	33.17	24.95	38.03
Babysitting and child care in someone else's home	26.12	15.95	45.13	19.35	26.22
Care for elderly, invalids, handicapped, etc.	34.96	76.94	16.26	17.95	45.82
Day care centers, nurseries, and preschools	193.51	154.25	206.10	193.97	213.31
Other household services	**453.12**	**441.53**	**405.69**	**416.52**	**570.69**
Housekeeping services	88.85	81.67	86.81	77.77	114.95
Gardening, lawn care service	95.08	102.77	79.60	92.04	109.30
Water-softening service	3.06	1.89	6.94	1.12	3.22
Nonclothing laundry and dry cleaning, sent out	0.94	1.42	0.79	0.70	1.08
Nonclothing laundry and dry cleaning, coin-operated	3.71	6.24	2.70	2.49	4.57
Termite and pest control services	12.04	3.65	4.58	18.48	16.46
Home security system service fee	15.57	10.83	12.33	19.61	16.42
Other home services	23.03	33.76	16.06	15.94	32.48
Termite and pest control products	1.53	0.60	0.65	2.18	2.18
Moving, storage, and freight express	33.91	22.92	26.65	24.04	66.65
Appliance repair, including at service center	14.53	17.01	14.69	12.09	16.19
Reupholstering and furniture repair	7.35	3.77	5.14	6.29	14.38
Repairs and rentals of lawn and garden equipment, hand and power tools, etc.	7.29	8.57	7.52	8.22	4.47
Appliance rental	1.75	1.78	1.09	2.51	1.14
Repair of computer systems for nonbusiness use	4.03	3.77	3.18	3.70	5.65
Computer information services	139.46	139.72	135.87	128.39	160.78
HOUSEKEEPING SUPPLIES	**594.47**	**586.10**	**661.12**	**548.97**	**606.28**
Laundry and cleaning supplies	**148.56**	**145.54**	**152.97**	**146.93**	**149.24**
Soaps and detergents	85.44	90.82	81.89	83.53	87.59
Other laundry cleaning products	63.13	54.72	71.07	63.40	61.66
Other household products	**290.41**	**294.40**	**339.62**	**268.35**	**271.48**
Cleansing and toilet tissue, paper towels, and napkins	85.84	88.73	88.65	85.11	81.59
Miscellaneous household products	121.13	133.17	150.44	106.39	104.10
Lawn and garden supplies	83.44	72.51	100.52	76.86	85.79
Postage and stationery	**155.50**	**146.16**	**168.54**	**133.69**	**185.56**
Stationery, stationery supplies, giftwrap	74.86	73.19	84.29	58.09	93.82
Postage	74.12	69.88	81.57	66.64	82.22
Delivery services	6.52	3.10	2.68	8.97	9.52
HOUSEHOLD FURNISHINGS AND EQUIPMENT	**1,646.10**	**1,630.32**	**1,774.93**	**1,432.45**	**1,871.34**
Household textiles	**157.66**	**209.24**	**125.60**	**150.85**	**157.58**
Bathroom linens	21.26	15.10	21.38	21.69	25.75
Bedroom linens	85.72	140.48	53.74	84.07	74.40
Kitchen and dining room linens	9.84	13.11	8.70	10.02	7.88
Curtains and draperies	19.22	25.25	15.74	16.92	21.39
Slipcovers and decorative pillows	9.12	5.00	8.19	11.40	9.93
Sewing materials for household items	11.20	8.64	16.38	5.76	16.83
Other linens	1.31	1.66	1.47	0.97	1.40
Furniture	**416.97**	**381.12**	**438.47**	**356.41**	**523.23**
Mattresses and springs	53.56	51.11	45.73	46.20	75.53
Other bedroom furniture	81.32	63.75	78.84	84.61	93.52
Sofas	94.74	88.31	96.47	77.22	126.73
Living room chairs	41.65	31.49	52.60	34.34	50.87
Living room tables	14.77	13.46	17.04	11.46	18.92
Kitchen and dining room furniture	41.26	58.51	38.48	27.80	51.17

	total consumer units	Northeast	Midwest	South	West
Infants' furniture	$8.44	$9.86	$7.02	$5.65	$13.17
Outdoor furniture	16.18	18.07	16.90	12.33	20.07
Wall units, cabinets, and other furniture	65.05	46.56	85.39	56.81	73.26
Floor coverings	**51.98**	**44.04**	**56.71**	**34.97**	**81.37**
Wall-to-wall carpeting	27.98	23.47	35.45	17.55	41.00
Floor coverings, nonpermanent	24.00	20.57	21.26	17.42	40.37
Major appliances	**203.94**	**216.44**	**234.18**	**160.58**	**231.70**
Dishwashers (built-in), garbage disposals, range hoods	14.34	15.42	18.17	10.64	15.51
Refrigerators and freezers	51.27	52.65	44.89	44.88	66.94
Washing machines	30.65	33.85	29.40	25.63	37.30
Clothes dryers	22.03	23.75	25.57	16.65	25.62
Cooking stoves, ovens	32.42	33.30	30.04	23.97	47.77
Microwave ovens	8.43	8.41	7.10	7.31	11.62
Portable dishwasher	1.22	1.16	2.39	0.77	0.80
Window air conditioners	4.36	5.77	2.62	4.68	4.41
Electric floor-cleaning equipment	27.71	33.79	58.47	17.98	6.15
Sewing machines	3.59	3.23	1.49	4.18	5.11
Miscellaneous household appliances	7.91	5.13	14.01	3.90	10.47
Small appliances and miscellaneous housewares	**104.66**	**94.33**	**97.94**	**99.18**	**129.54**
Housewares	82.56	71.59	74.42	80.24	104.32
Plastic dinnerware	1.82	1.78	2.14	1.45	2.13
China and other dinnerware	13.47	11.69	10.98	13.91	16.89
Flatware	4.02	3.18	3.90	3.36	5.94
Glassware	20.88	14.18	18.12	22.12	27.53
Silver serving pieces	0.30	0.36	0.27	0.30	0.26
Other serving pieces	1.76	1.85	1.63	1.66	2.01
Nonelectric cookware	18.10	16.59	12.61	17.24	26.58
Tableware, nonelectric kitchenware	22.20	21.96	24.77	20.19	22.98
Small appliances	22.10	22.74	23.52	18.94	25.22
Small electric kitchen appliances	17.27	13.23	19.71	15.53	21.02
Portable heating and cooling equipment	4.83	9.51	3.81	3.40	4.20
Miscellaneous household equipment	**710.89**	**685.16**	**822.02**	**630.47**	**747.91**
Window coverings	23.47	34.67	20.08	14.10	32.51
Infants' equipment	7.86	3.48	7.43	7.83	12.14
Laundry and cleaning equipment	15.72	15.33	14.06	14.91	19.11
Outdoor equipment	35.99	20.50	35.28	47.01	32.17
Clocks	7.64	6.89	10.62	5.44	8.78
Lamps and lighting fixtures	16.40	15.32	16.47	18.31	14.16
Other household decorative items	158.10	154.15	210.18	141.20	134.60
Telephones and accessories	26.83	44.22	13.39	25.59	27.85
Lawn and garden equipment	48.79	35.08	75.14	56.78	20.52
Power tools	33.44	36.81	24.33	31.91	42.55
Office furniture for home use	11.37	7.63	8.17	12.00	16.80
Hand tools	6.11	3.09	8.87	5.86	6.24
Indoor plants and fresh flowers	41.52	45.26	51.16	34.77	39.35
Closet and storage items	17.83	15.10	26.60	10.49	23.01
Rental of furniture	2.22	3.15	2.06	1.88	2.14
Luggage	6.63	5.21	7.93	5.32	8.60
Computers and computer hardware, nonbusiness use	134.57	134.24	127.47	106.36	187.65
Computer software and accessories, nonbusiness use	19.06	16.59	17.59	15.68	28.13
Telephone answering devices	0.62	0.83	0.54	0.43	0.86
Calculators	1.44	1.30	1.51	1.34	1.64
Business equipment for home use	0.94	0.28	1.23	0.94	1.20
Other hardware	39.63	23.46	82.65	18.05	43.88
Smoke alarms	1.03	1.44	1.70	0.62	0.64
Other household appliances	12.53	8.97	15.65	12.90	11.74
Miscellaneous household equipment and parts	41.18	52.14	41.93	40.74	31.61

Note: Subcategories may not add to total because some are not shown.
Source: Bureau of Labor Statistics, unpublished tables from the 2004 Consumer Expenditure Survey

Table 8.22 Housing: Household Operations: Indexed spending by region, 2004

(indexed average annual spending of consumer units (CU) on household services, supplies, furnishings, and equipment, by region in which consumer unit lives, 2004; index definition: an index of 100 is the average for all consumer units; an index of 132 means that spending by consumer units in that group is 32 percent above the average for all consumer units; an index of 68 indicates spending that is 32 percent below the average for all consumer units)

	total consumer units	Northeast	Midwest	South	West
Average spending of CU, total	$43,395	$46,115	$43,371	$39,174	$47,922
Average spending of CU, index	100	106	100	90	110
Housing, spending index	100	113	97	88	112
HOUSEHOLD SERVICES	100	105	94	89	119
Personal services	100	117	100	86	108
Babysitting and child care in own home	100	172	89	67	103
Babysitting and child care in someone else's home	100	61	173	74	100
Care for elderly, invalids, handicapped, etc.	100	220	47	51	131
Day care centers, nurseries, and preschools	100	80	107	100	110
Other household services	100	97	90	92	126
Housekeeping services	100	92	98	88	129
Gardening, lawn care service	100	108	84	97	115
Water-softening service	100	62	227	37	105
Nonclothing laundry and dry cleaning, sent out	100	151	84	74	115
Nonclothing laundry and dry cleaning, coin-operated	100	168	73	67	123
Termite and pest control services	100	30	38	153	137
Home security system service fee	100	70	79	126	105
Other home services	100	147	70	69	141
Termite and pest control products	100	39	42	142	142
Moving, storage, and freight express	100	68	79	71	197
Appliance repair, including at service center	100	117	101	83	111
Reupholstering and furniture repair	100	51	70	86	196
Repairs and rentals of lawn and garden equipment, hand and power tools, etc.	100	118	103	113	61
Appliance rental	100	102	62	143	65
Repair of computer systems for nonbusiness use	100	94	79	92	140
Computer information services	100	100	97	92	115
HOUSEKEEPING SUPPLIES	100	99	111	92	102
Laundry and cleaning supplies	100	98	103	99	100
Soaps and detergents	100	106	96	98	103
Other laundry cleaning products	100	87	113	100	98
Other household products	100	101	117	92	93
Cleansing and toilet tissue, paper towels, and napkins	100	103	103	99	95
Miscellaneous household products	100	110	124	88	86
Lawn and garden supplies	100	87	120	92	103
Postage and stationery	100	94	108	86	119
Stationery, stationery supplies, giftwrap	100	98	113	78	125
Postage	100	94	110	90	111
Delivery services	100	48	41	138	146
HOUSEHOLD FURNISHINGS AND EQUIPMENT	100	99	108	87	114
Household textiles	100	133	80	96	100
Bathroom linens	100	71	101	102	121
Bedroom linens	100	164	63	98	87
Kitchen and dining room linens	100	133	88	102	80
Curtains and draperies	100	131	82	88	111
Slipcovers and decorative pillows	100	55	90	125	109
Sewing materials for household items	100	77	146	51	150
Other linens	100	127	112	74	107
Furniture	100	91	105	85	125
Mattresses and springs	100	95	85	86	141
Other bedroom furniture	100	78	97	104	115
Sofas	100	93	102	82	134
Living room chairs	100	76	126	82	122
Living room tables	100	91	115	78	128
Kitchen and dining room furniture	100	142	93	67	124

	total consumer units	Northeast	Midwest	South	West
Infants' furniture	100	117	83	67	156
Outdoor furniture	100	112	104	76	124
Wall units, cabinets, and other furniture	100	72	131	87	113
Floor coverings	**100**	**85**	**109**	**67**	**157**
Wall-to-wall carpeting	100	84	127	63	147
Floor coverings, nonpermanent	100	86	89	73	168
Major appliances	**100**	**106**	**115**	**79**	**114**
Dishwashers (built-in), garbage disposals, range hoods	100	108	127	74	108
Refrigerators and freezers	100	103	88	88	131
Washing machines	100	110	96	84	122
Clothes dryers	100	108	116	76	116
Cooking stoves, ovens	100	103	93	74	147
Microwave ovens	100	100	84	87	138
Portable dishwasher	100	95	196	63	66
Window air conditioners	100	132	60	107	101
Electric floor-cleaning equipment	100	122	211	65	22
Sewing machines	100	90	42	116	142
Miscellaneous household appliances	100	65	177	49	132
Small appliances and miscellaneous housewares	**100**	**90**	**94**	**95**	**124**
Housewares	100	87	90	97	126
Plastic dinnerware	100	98	118	80	117
China and other dinnerware	100	87	82	103	125
Flatware	100	79	97	84	148
Glassware	100	68	87	106	132
Silver serving pieces	100	120	90	100	87
Other serving pieces	100	105	93	94	114
Nonelectric cookware	100	92	70	95	147
Tableware, nonelectric kitchenware	100	99	112	91	104
Small appliances	100	103	106	86	114
Small electric kitchen appliances	100	77	114	90	122
Portable heating and cooling equipment	100	197	79	70	87
Miscellaneous household equipment	**100**	**96**	**116**	**89**	**105**
Window coverings	100	148	86	60	139
Infants' equipment	100	44	95	100	154
Laundry and cleaning equipment	100	98	89	95	122
Outdoor equipment	100	57	98	131	89
Clocks	100	90	139	71	115
Lamps and lighting fixtures	100	93	100	112	86
Other household decorative items	100	98	133	89	85
Telephones and accessories	100	165	50	95	104
Lawn and garden equipment	100	72	154	116	42
Power tools	100	110	73	95	127
Office furniture for home use	100	67	72	106	148
Hand tools	100	51	145	96	102
Indoor plants and fresh flowers	100	109	123	84	95
Closet and storage items	100	85	149	59	129
Rental of furniture	100	142	93	85	96
Luggage	100	79	120	80	130
Computers and computer hardware, nonbusiness use	100	100	95	79	139
Computer software and accessories, nonbusiness use	100	87	92	82	148
Telephone answering devices	100	134	87	69	139
Calculators	100	90	105	93	114
Business equipment for home use	100	30	131	100	128
Other hardware	100	59	209	46	111
Smoke alarms	100	140	165	60	62
Other household appliances	100	72	125	103	94
Miscellaneous household equipment and parts	100	127	102	99	77

Source: Calculations by New Strategist based on the 2004 Consumer Expenditure Survey

Table 8.23 Housing: Household Operations: Total spending by region, 2004

(total annual spending on household services, supplies, furnishings, and equipment, by region in which consumer units live, 2004; consumer units and dollars in thousands)

	total consumer units	Northeast	Midwest	South	West
Number of consumer units	116,282	22,051	26,539	41,801	25,891
Total spending of all consumer units	$5,046,042,273	$1,016,879,439	$1,151,016,865	$1,637,497,744	$1,240,741,770
Housing, total spending	1,618,468,691	346,943,819	356,640,371	512,070,192	402,774,895
HOUSEHOLD SERVICES	**87,540,578**	**17,496,586**	**18,757,500**	**28,134,999**	**23,150,955**
Personal services	**34,850,878**	**7,760,408**	**7,990,893**	**10,724,047**	**8,375,221**
Babysitting and child care in own home	4,312,899	1,404,428	880,299	1,042,935	984,635
Babysitting and child care in someone else's home	3,037,286	351,713	1,197,705	808,849	678,862
Care for elderly, invalids, handicapped, etc.	4,065,219	1,696,604	431,524	750,328	1,186,326
Day care centers, nurseries, and preschools	22,501,730	3,401,367	5,469,688	8,108,140	5,522,809
Other household services	**52,689,700**	**9,736,178**	**10,766,607**	**17,410,953**	**14,775,735**
Housekeeping services	10,331,656	1,800,905	2,303,851	3,250,864	2,976,170
Gardening, lawn care service	11,056,093	2,266,181	2,112,504	3,847,364	2,829,886
Water-softening service	355,823	41,676	184,181	46,817	83,369
Nonclothing laundry and dry cleaning, sent out	109,305	31,312	20,966	29,261	27,962
Nonclothing laundry and dry cleaning, coin-operated	431,406	137,598	71,655	104,084	118,322
Termite and pest control services	1,400,035	80,486	121,549	772,482	426,166
Home security system service fee	1,810,511	238,812	327,226	819,718	425,130
Other home services	2,677,974	744,442	426,216	666,308	840,940
Termite and pest control products	177,911	13,231	17,250	91,126	56,442
Moving, storage, and freight express	3,943,123	505,409	707,264	1,004,896	1,725,635
Appliance repair, including at service center	1,689,577	375,088	389,858	505,374	419,175
Reupholstering and furniture repair	854,673	83,132	136,410	262,928	372,313
Repairs and rentals of lawn and garden equipment, hand and power tools, etc.	847,696	188,977	199,573	343,604	115,733
Appliance rental	203,494	39,251	28,928	104,921	29,516
Repair of computer systems for nonbusiness use	468,616	83,132	84,394	154,664	146,284
Computer information services	16,216,688	3,080,966	3,605,854	5,366,830	4,162,755
HOUSEKEEPING SUPPLIES	**69,126,161**	**12,924,091**	**17,545,464**	**22,947,495**	**15,697,195**
Laundry and cleaning supplies	**17,274,854**	**3,209,303**	**4,059,671**	**6,141,821**	**3,863,973**
Soaps and detergents	9,935,134	2,002,672	2,173,279	3,491,638	2,267,793
Other laundry cleaning products	7,340,883	1,206,631	1,886,127	2,650,183	1,596,439
Other household products	**33,769,456**	**6,491,814**	**9,013,175**	**11,217,298**	**7,028,889**
Cleansing and toilet tissue, paper towels, and napkins	9,981,647	1,956,585	2,352,682	3,557,683	2,112,447
Miscellaneous household products	14,085,239	2,936,532	3,992,527	4,447,208	2,695,253
Lawn and garden supplies	9,702,570	1,598,918	2,667,700	3,212,825	2,221,189
Postage and stationery	**18,081,851**	**3,222,974**	**4,472,883**	**5,588,376**	**4,804,334**
Stationery, stationery supplies, giftwrap	8,704,871	1,613,913	2,236,972	2,428,220	2,429,094
Postage	8,618,822	1,540,924	2,164,786	2,785,619	2,128,758
Delivery services	758,159	68,358	71,125	374,955	246,482
HOUSEHOLD FURNISHINGS AND EQUIPMENT	**191,411,800**	**35,950,186**	**47,104,867**	**59,877,842**	**48,450,864**
Household textiles	**18,333,020**	**4,613,951**	**3,333,298**	**6,305,681**	**4,079,904**
Bathroom linens	2,472,155	332,970	567,404	906,664	666,693
Bedroom linens	9,967,693	3,097,724	1,426,206	3,514,210	1,926,290
Kitchen and dining room linens	1,144,215	289,089	230,889	418,846	204,021
Curtains and draperies	2,234,940	556,788	417,724	707,273	553,808
Slipcovers and decorative pillows	1,060,492	110,255	217,354	476,531	257,098
Sewing materials for household items	1,302,358	190,521	434,709	240,774	435,746
Other linens	152,329	36,605	39,012	40,547	36,247
Furniture	**48,486,106**	**8,404,077**	**11,636,555**	**14,898,294**	**13,546,948**
Mattresses and springs	6,228,064	1,127,027	1,213,628	1,931,206	1,955,547
Other bedroom furniture	9,456,052	1,405,751	2,092,335	3,536,783	2,421,326
Sofas	11,016,557	1,947,324	2,560,217	3,227,873	3,281,166
Living room chairs	4,843,145	694,386	1,395,951	1,435,446	1,317,075
Living room tables	1,717,485	296,806	452,225	479,039	489,858
Kitchen and dining room furniture	4,797,795	1,290,204	1,021,221	1,162,068	1,324,842

	total consumer units	Northeast	Midwest	South	West
Infants' furniture	$981,420	$217,423	$186,304	$236,176	$340,984
Outdoor furniture	1,881,443	398,462	448,509	515,406	519,632
Wall units, cabinets, and other furniture	7,564,144	1,026,695	2,266,165	2,374,715	1,896,775
Floor coverings	**6,044,338**	**971,126**	**1,505,027**	**1,461,781**	**2,106,751**
Wall-to-wall carpeting	3,253,570	517,537	940,808	733,608	1,061,531
Floor coverings, nonpermanent	2,790,768	453,589	564,219	728,173	1,045,220
Major appliances	**23,714,551**	**4,772,718**	**6,214,903**	**6,712,405**	**5,998,945**
Dishwashers (built-in), garbage disposals, range hoods	1,667,484	340,026	482,214	444,763	401,569
Refrigerators and freezers	5,961,778	1,160,985	1,191,336	1,876,029	1,733,144
Washing machines	3,564,043	746,426	780,247	1,071,360	965,734
Clothes dryers	2,561,692	523,711	678,602	695,987	663,327
Cooking stoves, ovens	3,769,862	734,298	797,232	1,001,970	1,236,813
Microwave ovens	980,257	185,449	188,427	305,565	300,853
Portable dishwasher	141,864	25,579	63,428	32,187	20,713
Window air conditioners	506,990	127,234	69,532	195,629	114,179
Electric floor-cleaning equipment	3,222,174	745,103	1,551,735	751,582	159,230
Sewing machines	417,452	71,225	39,543	174,728	132,303
Miscellaneous household appliances	919,791	113,122	371,811	163,024	271,079
Small appliances and miscellaneous housewares	**12,170,074**	**2,080,071**	**2,599,230**	**4,145,823**	**3,353,920**
Housewares	9,600,242	1,578,631	1,975,032	3,354,112	2,700,949
Plastic dinnerware	211,633	39,251	56,793	60,611	55,148
China and other dinnerware	1,566,319	257,776	291,398	581,452	437,299
Flatware	467,454	70,122	103,502	140,451	153,793
Glassware	2,427,968	312,683	480,887	924,638	712,779
Silver serving pieces	34,885	7,938	7,166	12,540	6,732
Other serving pieces	204,656	40,794	43,259	69,390	52,041
Nonelectric cookware	2,104,704	365,826	334,657	720,649	688,183
Tableware, nonelectric kitchenware	2,581,460	484,240	657,371	843,962	594,975
Small appliances	2,569,832	501,440	624,197	791,711	652,971
Small electric kitchen appliances	2,008,190	291,735	523,084	649,170	544,229
Portable heating and cooling equipment	561,642	209,705	101,114	142,123	108,742
Miscellaneous household equipment	82,663,711	15,108,463	21,815,589	26,354,276	19,364,138
Window coverings	**2,729,139**	**764,508**	**532,903**	**589,394**	**841,716**
Infants' equipment	913,977	76,737	197,185	327,302	314,317
Laundry and cleaning equipment	1,827,953	338,042	373,138	623,253	494,777
Outdoor equipment	4,184,989	452,046	936,296	1,965,065	832,913
Clocks	888,394	151,931	281,844	227,397	227,323
Lamps and lighting fixtures	1,907,025	337,821	437,097	765,376	366,617
Other household decorative items	18,384,184	3,399,162	5,577,967	5,902,301	3,484,929
Telephones and accessories	3,119,846	975,095	355,357	1,069,688	721,064
Lawn and garden equipment	5,673,399	773,549	1,994,140	2,373,461	531,283
Power tools	3,888,470	811,697	645,694	1,333,870	1,101,662
Office furniture for home use	1,322,126	168,249	216,824	501,612	434,969
Hand tools	710,483	68,138	235,401	244,954	161,560
Indoor plants and fresh flowers	4,828,029	998,028	1,357,735	1,453,421	1,018,811
Closet and storage items	2,073,308	332,970	705,937	438,492	595,752
Rental of furniture	258,146	69,461	54,670	78,586	55,407
Luggage	770,950	114,886	210,454	222,381	222,663
Computers and computer hardware, nonbusiness use	15,648,069	2,960,126	3,382,926	4,445,954	4,858,446
Computer software and accessories, nonbusiness use	2,216,335	365,826	466,821	655,440	728,314
Telephone answering devices	72,095	18,302	14,331	17,974	22,266
Calculators	167,446	28,666	40,074	56,013	42,461
Business equipment for home use	109,305	6,174	32,643	39,293	31,069
Other hardware	4,608,256	517,316	2,193,448	754,508	1,136,097
Smoke alarms	119,770	31,753	45,116	25,917	16,570
Other household appliances	1,457,013	197,797	415,335	539,233	303,960
Miscellaneous household equipment and parts	4,788,493	1,149,739	1,112,780	1,702,973	818,415

Note: Numbers may not add to total because of rounding and missing subcategories.
Source: Calculations by New Strategist based on the 2004 Consumer Expenditure Survey

Table 8.24 Housing: Household Operations: Market shares by region, 2004

(percentage of total annual spending on household services, supplies, furnishings, and equipment accounted for by consumer units by region, 2004)

	total consumer units	Northeast	Midwest	South	West
Share of total consumer units	**100.0%**	**19.0%**	**22.8%**	**35.9%**	**22.3%**
Share of total before-tax income	**100.0**	**21.3**	**22.5**	**33.5**	**22.8**
Share of total spending	**100.0**	**20.2**	**22.8**	**32.5**	**24.6**
Share of housing spending	**100.0**	**21.4**	**22.0**	**31.6**	**24.9**
HOUSEHOLD SERVICES	**100.0**	**20.0**	**21.4**	**32.1**	**26.4**
Personal services	**100.0**	**22.3**	**22.9**	**30.8**	**24.0**
Babysitting and child care in own home	100.0	32.6	20.4	24.2	22.8
Babysitting and child care in someone else's home	100.0	11.6	39.4	26.6	22.4
Care for elderly, invalids, handicapped, etc.	100.0	41.7	10.6	18.5	29.2
Day care centers, nurseries, and preschools	100.0	15.1	24.3	36.0	24.5
Other household services	**100.0**	**18.5**	**20.4**	**33.0**	**28.0**
Housekeeping services	100.0	17.4	22.3	31.5	28.8
Gardening, lawn care service	100.0	20.5	19.1	34.8	25.6
Water-softening service	100.0	11.7	51.8	13.2	23.4
Nonclothing laundry and dry cleaning, sent out	100.0	28.6	19.2	26.8	25.6
Nonclothing laundry and dry cleaning, coin-operated	100.0	31.9	16.6	24.1	27.4
Termite and pest control services	100.0	5.7	8.7	55.2	30.4
Home security system service fee	100.0	13.2	18.1	45.3	23.5
Other home services	100.0	27.8	15.9	24.9	31.4
Termite and pest control products	100.0	7.4	9.7	51.2	31.7
Moving, storage, and freight express	100.0	12.8	17.9	25.5	43.8
Appliance repair, including at service center	100.0	22.2	23.1	29.9	24.8
Reupholstering and furniture repair	100.0	9.7	16.0	30.8	43.6
Repairs and rentals of lawn and garden equipment, hand and power tools, etc.	100.0	22.3	23.5	40.5	13.7
Appliance rental	100.0	19.3	14.2	51.6	14.5
Repair of computer systems for nonbusiness use	100.0	17.7	18.0	33.0	31.2
Computer information services	100.0	19.0	22.2	33.1	25.7
HOUSEKEEPING SUPPLIES	**100.0**	**18.7**	**25.4**	**33.2**	**22.7**
Laundry and cleaning supplies	**100.0**	**18.6**	**23.5**	**35.6**	**22.4**
Soaps and detergents	100.0	20.2	21.9	35.1	22.8
Other laundry cleaning products	100.0	16.4	25.7	36.1	21.7
Other household products	**100.0**	**19.2**	**26.7**	**33.2**	**20.8**
Cleansing and toilet tissue, paper towels, and napkins	100.0	19.6	23.6	35.6	21.2
Miscellaneous household products	100.0	20.8	28.3	31.6	19.1
Lawn and garden supplies	100.0	16.5	27.5	33.1	22.9
Postage and stationery	**100.0**	**17.8**	**24.7**	**30.9**	**26.6**
Stationery, stationery supplies, giftwrap	100.0	18.5	25.7	27.9	27.9
Postage	100.0	17.9	25.1	32.3	24.7
Delivery services	100.0	9.0	9.4	49.5	32.5
HOUSEHOLD FURNISHINGS AND EQUIPMENT	**100.0**	**18.8**	**24.6**	**31.3**	**25.3**
Household textiles	**100.0**	**25.2**	**18.2**	**34.4**	**22.3**
Bathroom linens	100.0	13.5	23.0	36.7	27.0
Bedroom linens	100.0	31.1	14.3	35.3	19.3
Kitchen and dining room linens	100.0	25.3	20.2	36.6	17.8
Curtains and draperies	100.0	24.9	18.7	31.6	24.8
Slipcovers and decorative pillows	100.0	10.4	20.5	44.9	24.2
Sewing materials for household items	100.0	14.6	33.4	18.5	33.5
Other linens	100.0	24.0	25.6	26.6	23.8
Furniture	**100.0**	**17.3**	**24.0**	**30.7**	**27.9**
Mattresses and springs	100.0	18.1	19.5	31.0	31.4
Other bedroom furniture	100.0	14.9	22.1	37.4	25.6
Sofas	100.0	17.7	23.2	29.3	29.8
Living room chairs	100.0	14.3	28.8	29.6	27.2
Living room tables	100.0	17.3	26.3	27.9	28.5
Kitchen and dining room furniture	100.0	26.9	21.3	24.2	27.6

	total consumer units	Northeast	Midwest	South	West
Infants' furniture	100.0%	22.2%	19.0%	24.1%	34.7%
Outdoor furniture	100.0	21.2	23.8	27.4	27.6
Wall units, cabinets, and other furniture	100.0	13.6	30.0	31.4	25.1
Floor coverings	**100.0**	**16.1**	**24.9**	**24.2**	**34.9**
Wall-to-wall carpeting	100.0	15.9	28.9	22.5	32.6
Floor coverings, nonpermanent	100.0	16.3	20.2	26.1	37.5
Major appliances	**100.0**	**20.1**	**26.2**	**28.3**	**25.3**
Dishwashers (built-in), garbage disposals, range hoods	100.0	20.4	28.9	26.7	24.1
Refrigerators and freezers	100.0	19.5	20.0	31.5	29.1
Washing machines	100.0	20.9	21.9	30.1	27.1
Clothes dryers	100.0	20.4	26.5	27.2	25.9
Cooking stoves, ovens	100.0	19.5	21.1	26.6	32.8
Microwave ovens	100.0	18.9	19.2	31.2	30.7
Portable dishwasher	100.0	18.0	44.7	22.7	14.6
Window air conditioners	100.0	25.1	13.7	38.6	22.5
Electric floor-cleaning equipment	100.0	23.1	48.2	23.3	4.9
Sewing machines	100.0	17.1	9.5	41.9	31.7
Miscellaneous household appliances	100.0	12.3	40.4	17.7	29.5
Small appliances and miscellaneous housewares	**100.0**	**17.1**	**21.4**	**34.1**	**27.6**
Housewares	100.0	16.4	20.6	34.9	28.1
Plastic dinnerware	100.0	18.5	26.8	28.6	26.1
China and other dinnerware	100.0	16.5	18.6	37.1	27.9
Flatware	100.0	15.0	22.1	30.0	32.9
Glassware	100.0	12.9	19.8	38.1	29.4
Silver serving pieces	100.0	22.8	20.5	35.9	19.3
Other serving pieces	100.0	19.9	21.1	33.9	25.4
Nonelectric cookware	100.0	17.4	15.9	34.2	32.7
Tableware, nonelectric kitchenware	100.0	18.8	25.5	32.7	23.0
Small appliances	100.0	19.5	24.3	30.8	25.4
Small electric kitchen appliances	100.0	14.5	26.0	32.3	27.1
Portable heating and cooling equipment	100.0	37.3	18.0	25.3	19.4
Miscellaneous household equipment	**100.0**	**18.3**	**26.4**	**31.9**	**23.4**
Window coverings	100.0	28.0	19.5	21.6	30.8
Infants' equipment	100.0	8.4	21.6	35.8	34.4
Laundry and cleaning equipment	100.0	18.5	20.4	34.1	27.1
Outdoor equipment	100.0	10.8	22.4	47.0	19.9
Clocks	100.0	17.1	31.7	25.6	25.6
Lamps and lighting fixtures	100.0	17.7	22.9	40.1	19.2
Other household decorative items	100.0	18.5	30.3	32.1	19.0
Telephones and accessories	100.0	31.3	11.4	34.3	23.1
Lawn and garden equipment	100.0	13.6	35.1	41.8	9.4
Power tools	100.0	20.9	16.6	34.3	28.3
Office furniture for home use	100.0	12.7	16.4	37.9	32.9
Hand tools	100.0	9.6	33.1	34.5	22.7
Indoor plants and fresh flowers	100.0	20.7	28.1	30.1	21.1
Closet and storage items	100.0	16.1	34.0	21.1	28.7
Rental of furniture	100.0	26.9	21.2	30.4	21.5
Luggage	100.0	14.9	27.3	28.8	28.9
Computers and computer hardware, nonbusiness use	100.0	18.9	21.6	28.4	31.0
Computer software and accessories, nonbusiness use	100.0	16.5	21.1	29.6	32.9
Telephone answering devices	100.0	25.4	19.9	24.9	30.9
Calculators	100.0	17.1	23.9	33.5	25.4
Business equipment for home use	100.0	5.6	29.9	35.9	28.4
Other hardware	100.0	11.2	47.6	16.4	24.7
Smoke alarms	100.0	26.5	37.7	21.6	13.8
Other household appliances	100.0	13.6	28.5	37.0	20.9
Miscellaneous household equipment and parts	100.0	24.0	23.2	35.6	17.1

Note: Numbers may not add to total because of rounding.
Source: Calculations by New Strategist based on the 2004 Consumer Expenditure Survey

Table 8.25 Housing: Household Operations: Average spending by education, 2004

(average annual spending of consumer units (CU) on household services, supplies, furnishings, and equipment, by education of consumer unit reference person, 2004)

	total consumer units	less than high school graduate	high school graduate	some college	associate's degree	college graduate total	bachelor's degree	master's, professional, doctorate
Number of consumer units (in 000s)	116,282	16,829	31,005	25,317	10,678	32,452	20,684	11,768
Average number of persons per CU	2.5	2.7	2.5	2.3	2.6	2.5	2.4	2.5
Average before-tax income of CU	$54,453.00	$29,094.00	$42,334.00	$46,756.00	$58,593.00	$83,825.00	$75,647.00	$98,201.00
Average spending of CU, total	43,394.87	25,421.18	35,438.55	40,877.68	48,177.36	60,712.28	56,728.41	67,801.38
Housing, average spending	13,918.48	8,724.44	11,207.58	12,915.13	14,854.90	19,676.20	18,304.59	22,109.54
HOUSEHOLD SERVICES	752.83	318.16	474.63	656.81	847.39	1,287.90	1,125.41	1,573.48
Personal services	299.71	155.52	200.67	260.59	398.56	467.11	448.78	499.31
Babysitting and child care in own home	37.09	13.19	13.59	17.85	55.18	80.98	69.95	100.37
Babysitting and child care in someone else's home	26.12	20.37	20.20	22.54	45.62	31.14	38.19	18.74
Care for elderly, invalids, handicapped, etc.	34.96	58.02	37.30	50.43	11.22	16.49	19.08	11.94
Day care centers, nurseries, and preschools	193.51	53.84	124.12	146.36	286.35	338.49	321.56	368.26
Other household services	453.12	162.65	273.96	396.22	448.83	820.80	676.62	1,074.17
Housekeeping services	88.85	25.53	36.15	59.47	65.05	202.79	134.62	322.62
Gardening, lawn care service	95.08	36.28	53.91	86.75	93.81	171.82	136.29	234.27
Water-softening service	3.06	1.47	2.50	2.54	5.82	3.92	2.68	6.11
Nonclothing laundry and dry cleaning, sent out	0.94	0.32	0.39	0.84	0.76	1.94	1.60	2.52
Nonclothing laundry and dry cleaning, coin-operated	3.71	7.49	3.08	3.28	2.68	3.03	3.26	2.62
Termite and pest control services	12.04	4.00	6.40	11.07	11.81	22.45	20.99	25.03
Home security system service fee	15.57	3.75	10.13	12.37	12.75	30.34	24.88	39.93
Other home services	23.03	10.75	15.28	13.98	24.88	43.25	35.69	56.54
Termite and pest control products	1.53	0.48	0.83	1.89	1.49	2.49	2.43	2.60
Moving, storage, and freight express	33.91	6.25	15.20	28.07	25.17	73.57	60.26	96.95
Appliance repair, including at service center	14.53	6.13	12.24	14.34	13.05	21.70	19.36	25.83
Reupholstering and furniture repair	7.35	3.83	3.35	5.63	5.74	14.87	10.37	22.78
Repairs and rentals of lawn and garden equipment, hand and power tools, etc.	7.29	6.05	5.97	6.20	6.67	10.26	9.11	12.28
Appliance rental	1.75	3.62	1.56	1.48	2.83	0.80	0.67	1.04
Repair of computer systems for nonbusiness use	4.03	0.86	2.48	4.13	5.24	6.67	6.63	6.74
Computer information services	139.46	45.31	103.88	142.09	170.36	210.06	206.68	215.98
HOUSEKEEPING SUPPLIES	594.47	394.47	507.03	556.69	669.94	785.84	714.89	921.31
Laundry and cleaning supplies	148.56	148.03	142.05	132.67	170.95	159.74	159.40	160.39
Soaps and detergents	85.44	86.22	81.41	79.33	95.61	90.24	92.83	85.29
Other laundry cleaning products	63.13	61.81	60.64	53.34	75.35	69.50	66.57	75.10
Other household products	290.41	163.41	240.58	282.25	338.78	395.04	339.81	500.49
Cleansing and toilet tissue, paper towels, and napkins	85.84	82.88	83.37	84.94	87.78	89.82	90.77	87.99
Miscellaneous household products	121.13	55.46	98.85	112.94	145.64	174.81	142.34	236.81
Lawn and garden supplies	83.44	25.07	58.36	84.38	105.36	130.41	106.70	175.69
Postage and stationery	155.50	83.02	124.40	141.77	160.21	231.07	215.69	260.44
Stationery, stationery supplies, giftwrap	74.86	43.89	56.26	71.34	79.04	110.00	103.28	122.83
Postage	74.12	38.08	65.90	68.94	75.64	103.74	95.00	120.43
Delivery services	6.52	1.05	2.25	1.49	5.53	17.33	17.41	17.18
HOUSEHOLD FURNISHINGS AND EQUIPMENT	1,646.10	684.97	1,211.70	1,620.63	1,777.11	2,536.23	2,276.62	3,004.32
Household textiles	157.66	69.85	137.95	137.03	188.85	227.44	194.07	290.02
Bathroom linens	21.26	9.89	25.99	21.02	18.21	23.54	18.60	32.97
Bedroom linens	85.72	41.35	80.00	65.52	109.33	121.18	101.39	158.97
Kitchen and dining room linens	9.84	5.40	6.51	11.12	11.66	13.88	11.91	17.64
Curtains and draperies	19.22	7.85	11.44	12.72	12.82	39.74	33.33	51.02
Slipcovers and decorative pillows	9.12	1.86	5.01	13.19	21.73	10.17	10.98	8.61
Sewing materials for household items	11.20	2.75	8.08	12.54	13.17	16.86	15.89	18.55
Other linens	1.31	0.75	0.92	0.93	1.94	2.07	1.96	2.27
Furniture	416.97	183.73	288.52	405.52	474.45	650.67	569.23	793.81
Mattresses and springs	53.56	25.10	41.83	51.59	66.76	76.70	68.40	91.29
Other bedroom furniture	81.32	31.67	57.95	71.92	117.87	124.71	129.34	116.58
Sofas	94.74	53.87	67.95	111.95	82.49	132.13	111.50	168.38
Living room chairs	41.65	20.03	28.61	34.96	53.47	66.64	56.39	84.66
Living room tables	14.77	4.30	10.82	12.77	15.22	25.39	24.83	26.38
Kitchen and dining room furniture	41.26	23.14	27.81	33.66	41.35	69.42	51.57	100.81

	total consumer units	less than high school graduate	high school graduate	some college	associate's degree	college graduate total	bachelor's degree	master's, professional, doctorate
Infants' furniture	$8.44	$4.30	$5.48	$6.93	$10.14	$14.01	$14.95	$12.36
Outdoor furniture	16.18	4.98	8.61	12.75	21.95	30.00	23.59	41.27
Wall units, cabinets, and other furniture	65.05	16.34	39.44	69.00	65.20	111.66	88.67	152.07
Floor coverings	**51.98**	**20.48**	**20.71**	**44.91**	**45.07**	**105.99**	**71.30**	**166.98**
Wall-to-wall carpeting	27.98	13.81	12.91	29.32	27.37	48.87	40.10	64.32
Floor coverings, nonpermanent	24.00	6.67	7.80	15.59	17.70	57.12	31.20	102.66
Major appliances	**203.94**	**114.23**	**165.56**	**234.99**	**215.46**	**259.58**	**229.76**	**314.74**
Dishwashers (built-in), garbage disposals, range hoods	14.34	3.44	10.90	15.08	23.24	19.80	18.65	21.82
Refrigerators and freezers	51.27	37.54	44.87	53.79	66.86	57.38	60.86	51.26
Washing machines	30.65	16.20	28.85	36.14	32.47	34.97	31.20	41.61
Clothes dryers	22.03	10.26	22.59	23.18	23.63	26.18	19.95	37.15
Cooking stoves, ovens	32.42	13.07	24.06	36.61	35.85	46.05	42.68	51.97
Microwave ovens	8.43	6.40	6.90	9.56	8.15	10.15	9.72	10.93
Portable dishwasher	1.22	0.64	1.05	1.88	0.86	1.29	0.96	1.88
Window air conditioners	4.36	4.78	3.96	3.39	4.28	5.29	5.67	4.64
Electric floor-cleaning equipment	27.71	5.07	19.48	43.90	11.12	40.78	32.18	57.19
Sewing machines	3.59	0.98	2.83	6.04	6.75	2.72	2.40	3.29
Miscellaneous household appliances	7.91	15.85	0.06	5.41	2.24	14.95	5.49	33.00
Small appliances and miscellaneous housewares	**104.66**	**61.89**	**84.23**	**88.40**	**157.61**	**142.05**	**127.67**	**168.67**
Housewares	82.56	50.21	63.92	66.72	131.61	113.77	103.56	133.07
Plastic dinnerware	1.82	1.67	1.80	1.46	2.41	2.01	1.88	2.23
China and other dinnerware	13.47	5.83	14.02	9.14	20.74	17.73	17.16	18.82
Flatware	4.02	1.28	2.31	3.63	5.24	6.99	5.84	9.00
Glassware	20.88	18.62	16.10	11.56	51.65	24.07	21.51	28.96
Silver serving pieces	0.30	0.20	0.24	0.18	0.28	0.49	0.58	0.31
Other serving pieces	1.76	0.22	1.73	1.43	1.61	2.92	2.93	2.89
Nonelectric cookware	18.10	13.47	13.84	16.62	19.52	25.25	22.62	30.27
Tableware, nonelectric kitchenware	22.20	8.93	13.89	22.70	30.16	34.32	31.03	40.60
Small appliances	22.10	11.68	20.30	21.69	25.99	28.27	24.11	35.60
Small electric kitchen appliances	17.27	9.10	16.29	18.16	20.66	20.64	18.92	23.65
Portable heating and cooling equipment	4.83	2.58	4.01	3.52	5.34	7.64	5.18	11.96
Miscellaneous household equipment	**710.89**	**234.78**	**514.75**	**709.78**	**695.67**	**1,150.50**	**1,084.59**	**1,270.11**
Window coverings	23.47	3.49	11.24	19.74	17.89	50.24	53.72	44.12
Infants' equipment	7.86	7.04	2.21	4.09	17.49	13.55	12.17	16.18
Laundry and cleaning equipment	15.72	10.36	14.36	15.71	21.14	18.15	17.35	19.68
Outdoor equipment	35.99	11.30	24.51	27.27	21.20	70.37	49.29	110.61
Clocks	7.64	1.80	4.67	6.17	8.13	14.40	14.87	13.50
Lamps and lighting fixtures	16.40	4.03	9.11	12.04	10.53	35.12	36.06	33.46
Other household decorative items	158.10	36.46	93.16	131.18	167.64	299.58	320.42	259.80
Telephones and accessories	26.83	26.57	15.71	27.54	29.34	36.53	28.29	52.26
Lawn and garden equipment	48.79	17.31	65.91	55.32	34.89	48.22	51.64	42.21
Power tools	33.44	11.86	31.75	52.48	30.65	33.46	33.84	32.73
Office furniture for home use	11.37	1.40	3.33	12.05	7.10	25.07	13.88	44.74
Hand tools	6.11	3.53	4.21	8.32	9.77	6.33	6.47	6.08
Indoor plants and fresh flowers	41.52	13.86	33.54	33.13	43.41	69.41	65.06	77.05
Closet and storage items	17.83	6.32	7.65	15.19	13.28	36.85	35.62	39.19
Rental of furniture	2.22	4.81	3.78	0.88	0.61	0.96	1.37	0.24
Luggage	6.63	1.52	3.95	5.98	8.45	11.73	12.20	10.91
Computers and computer hardware, nonbusiness use	134.57	42.87	78.20	151.79	143.81	219.50	194.12	264.11
Computer software and accessories, nonbusiness use	19.06	1.98	11.45	19.70	19.42	34.56	32.01	39.06
Telephone answering devices	0.62	0.33	0.44	0.62	0.27	1.07	0.87	1.40
Calculators	1.44	0.67	0.82	1.53	1.64	2.29	1.65	3.42
Business equipment for home use	0.94	0.15	0.82	0.92	1.65	1.25	0.75	2.13
Other hardware	39.63	9.85	44.19	50.45	32.18	44.97	31.26	71.15
Smoke alarms	1.03	0.73	0.91	1.03	1.04	1.28	1.24	1.36
Other household appliances	12.53	2.82	10.96	9.67	9.05	22.42	17.27	31.46
Miscellaneous household equipment and parts	41.18	13.72	37.84	46.96	45.07	53.20	53.17	53.25

Note: Subcategories may not add to total because some are not shown.
Source: Bureau of Labor Statistics, unpublished tables from the 2004 Consumer Expenditure Survey

Table 8.26 Housing: Household Operations: Indexed spending by education, 2004

(indexed average annual spending of consumer units (CU) on household services, supplies, furnishings, and equipment, by education of consumer unit reference person, 2004; index definition: an index of 100 is the average for all consumer units; an index of 132 means that spending by consumer units in that group is 32 percent above the average for all consumer units; an index of 68 indicates spending that is 32 percent below the average for all consumer units)

	total consumer units	less than high school graduate	high school graduate	some college	associate's degree	college graduate total	bachelor's degree	master's, professional, doctorate
Average spending of CU, total	$43,395	$25,421	$35,439	$40,878	$48,177	$60,712	$56,728	$67,801
Average spending of CU, index	100	59	82	94	111	140	131	156
Housing, spending index	100	63	81	93	107	141	132	159
HOUSEHOLD SERVICES	100	42	63	87	113	171	149	209
Personal services	100	52	67	87	133	156	150	167
Babysitting and child care in own home	100	36	37	48	149	218	189	271
Babysitting and child care in someone else's home	100	78	77	86	175	119	146	72
Care for elderly, invalids, handicapped, etc.	100	166	107	144	32	47	55	34
Day care centers, nurseries, and preschools	100	28	64	76	148	175	166	190
Other household services	100	36	60	87	99	181	149	237
Housekeeping services	100	29	41	67	73	228	152	363
Gardening, lawn care service	100	38	57	91	99	181	143	246
Water-softening service	100	48	82	83	190	128	88	200
Nonclothing laundry and dry cleaning, sent out	100	34	41	89	81	206	170	268
Nonclothing laundry and dry cleaning, coin-operated	100	202	83	88	72	82	88	71
Termite and pest control services	100	33	53	92	98	186	174	208
Home security system service fee	100	24	65	79	82	195	160	256
Other home services	100	47	66	61	108	188	155	246
Termite and pest control products	100	31	54	124	97	163	159	170
Moving, storage, and freight express	100	18	45	83	74	217	178	286
Appliance repair, including at service center	100	42	84	99	90	149	133	178
Reupholstering and furniture repair	100	52	46	77	78	202	141	310
Repairs and rentals of lawn and garden equipment, hand and power tools, etc.	100	83	82	85	91	141	125	168
Appliance rental	100	207	89	85	162	46	38	59
Repair of computer systems for nonbusiness use	100	21	62	102	130	166	165	167
Computer information services	100	32	74	102	122	151	148	155
HOUSEKEEPING SUPPLIES	100	66	85	94	113	132	120	155
Laundry and cleaning supplies	100	100	96	89	115	108	107	108
Soaps and detergents	100	101	95	93	112	106	109	100
Other laundry cleaning products	100	98	96	84	119	110	105	119
Other household products	100	56	83	97	117	136	117	172
Cleansing and toilet tissue, paper towels, and napkins	100	97	97	99	102	105	106	103
Miscellaneous household products	100	46	82	93	120	144	118	196
Lawn and garden supplies	100	30	70	101	126	156	128	211
Postage and stationery	100	53	80	91	103	149	139	167
Stationery, stationery supplies, giftwrap	100	59	75	95	106	147	138	164
Postage	100	51	89	93	102	140	128	162
Delivery services	100	16	35	23	85	266	267	263
HOUSEHOLD FURNISHINGS AND EQUIPMENT	100	42	74	98	108	154	138	183
Household textiles	100	44	87	87	120	144	123	184
Bathroom linens	100	47	122	99	86	111	87	155
Bedroom linens	100	48	93	76	128	141	118	185
Kitchen and dining room linens	100	55	66	113	118	141	121	179
Curtains and draperies	100	41	60	66	67	207	173	265
Slipcovers and decorative pillows	100	20	55	145	238	112	120	94
Sewing materials for household items	100	25	72	112	118	151	142	166
Other linens	100	57	70	71	148	158	150	173
Furniture	100	44	69	97	114	156	137	190
Mattresses and springs	100	47	78	96	125	143	128	170
Other bedroom furniture	100	39	71	88	145	153	159	143
Sofas	100	57	72	118	87	139	118	178
Living room chairs	100	48	69	84	128	160	135	203
Living room tables	100	29	73	86	103	172	168	179
Kitchen and dining room furniture	100	56	67	82	100	168	125	244

	total consumer units	less than high school graduate	high school graduate	some college	associate's degree	college graduate total	bachelor's degree	master's, professional, doctorate
Infants' furniture	100	51	65	82	120	166	177	146
Outdoor furniture	100	31	53	79	136	185	146	255
Wall units, cabinets, and other furniture	100	25	61	106	100	172	136	234
Floor coverings	**100**	**39**	**40**	**86**	**87**	**204**	**137**	**321**
Wall-to-wall carpeting	100	49	46	105	98	175	143	230
Floor coverings, nonpermanent	100	28	33	65	74	238	130	428
Major appliances	**100**	**56**	**81**	**115**	**106**	**127**	**113**	**154**
Dishwashers (built-in), garbage disposals, range hoods	100	24	76	105	162	138	130	152
Refrigerators and freezers	100	73	88	105	130	112	119	100
Washing machines	100	53	94	118	106	114	102	136
Clothes dryers	100	47	103	105	107	119	91	169
Cooking stoves, ovens	100	40	74	113	111	142	132	160
Microwave ovens	100	76	82	113	97	120	115	130
Portable dishwasher	100	52	86	154	70	106	79	154
Window air conditioners	100	110	91	78	98	121	130	106
Electric floor-cleaning equipment	100	18	70	158	40	147	116	206
Sewing machines	100	27	79	168	188	76	67	92
Miscellaneous household appliances	100	200	1	68	28	189	69	417
Small appliances and miscellaneous housewares	**100**	**59**	**80**	**84**	**151**	**136**	**122**	**161**
Housewares	100	61	77	81	159	138	125	161
Plastic dinnerware	100	92	99	80	132	110	103	123
China and other dinnerware	100	43	104	68	154	132	127	140
Flatware	100	32	57	90	130	174	145	224
Glassware	100	89	77	55	247	115	103	139
Silver serving pieces	100	67	80	60	93	163	193	103
Other serving pieces	100	13	98	81	91	166	166	164
Nonelectric cookware	100	74	76	92	108	140	125	167
Tableware, nonelectric kitchenware	100	40	63	102	136	155	140	183
Small appliances	100	53	92	98	118	128	109	161
Small electric kitchen appliances	100	53	94	105	120	120	110	137
Portable heating and cooling equipment	100	53	83	73	111	158	107	248
Miscellaneous household equipment	**100**	**33**	**72**	**100**	**98**	**162**	**153**	**179**
Window coverings	100	15	48	84	76	214	229	188
Infants' equipment	100	90	28	52	223	172	155	206
Laundry and cleaning equipment	100	66	91	100	134	115	110	125
Outdoor equipment	100	31	68	76	59	196	137	307
Clocks	100	24	61	81	106	188	195	177
Lamps and lighting fixtures	100	25	56	73	64	214	220	204
Other household decorative items	100	23	59	83	106	189	203	164
Telephones and accessories	100	99	59	103	109	136	105	195
Lawn and garden equipment	100	35	135	113	72	99	106	87
Power tools	100	35	95	157	92	100	101	98
Office furniture for home use	100	12	29	106	62	220	122	393
Hand tools	100	58	69	136	160	104	106	100
Indoor plants and fresh flowers	100	33	81	80	105	167	157	186
Closet and storage items	100	35	43	85	74	207	200	220
Rental of furniture	100	217	170	40	27	43	62	11
Luggage	100	23	60	90	127	177	184	165
Computers and computer hardware, nonbusiness use	100	32	58	113	107	163	144	196
Computer software and accessories, nonbusiness use	100	10	60	103	102	181	168	205
Telephone answering devices	100	53	71	100	44	173	140	226
Calculators	100	47	57	106	114	159	115	238
Business equipment for home use	100	16	87	98	176	133	80	227
Other hardware	100	25	112	127	81	113	79	180
Smoke alarms	100	71	88	100	101	124	120	132
Other household appliances	100	23	87	77	72	179	138	251
Miscellaneous household equipment and parts	100	33	92	114	109	129	129	129

Source: Calculations by New Strategist based on the 2004 Consumer Expenditure Survey

Table 8.27 Housing: Household Operations: Total spending by education, 2004

(total annual spending on household services, supplies, furnishings, and equipment, by consumer unit (CU) educational attainment group, 2004; consumer units and dollars in thousands)

	total consumer units	less than high school graduate	high school graduate	some college	associate's degree	college graduate total	bachelor's degree	master's, professional, doctorate
Number of consumer units	116,282	16,829	31,005	25,317	10,678	32,452	20,684	11,768
Total spending of all CUs	$5,046,042,273	$427,813,038	$1,098,772,243	$1,034,900,225	$514,437,850	$1,970,234,911	$1,173,370,432	$797,886,640
Housing, total spending	1,618,468,691	146,823,601	347,491,018	326,972,346	158,620,622	638,532,042	378,612,140	260,185,067
HOUSEHOLD SERVICES	87,540,578	5,354,315	14,715,903	16,628,459	9,048,430	41,794,931	23,277,980	18,516,713
Personal services	34,850,878	2,617,246	6,221,773	6,597,357	4,255,824	15,158,654	9,282,566	5,875,880
Babysitting and child care in own home	4,312,899	221,975	421,358	451,908	589,212	2,627,963	1,446,846	1,181,154
Babysitting and child care in someone else's home	3,037,286	342,807	626,301	570,645	487,130	1,010,555	789,922	220,532
Care for elderly, invalids, handicapped, etc.	4,065,219	976,419	1,156,487	1,276,736	119,807	535,133	394,651	140,510
Day care centers, nurseries, and preschools	22,501,730	906,073	3,848,341	3,705,396	3,057,645	10,984,677	6,651,147	4,333,684
Other household services	52,689,700	2,737,237	8,494,130	10,031,102	4,792,607	26,636,602	13,995,208	12,640,833
Housekeeping services	10,331,656	429,644	1,120,831	1,505,602	694,604	6,580,941	2,784,480	3,796,592
Gardening, lawn care service	11,056,093	610,556	1,671,480	2,196,250	1,001,703	5,575,903	2,819,022	2,756,889
Water-softening service	355,823	24,739	77,513	64,305	62,146	127,212	55,433	71,902
Nonclothing laundry and dry cleaning, sent out	109,305	5,385	12,092	21,266	8,115	62,957	33,094	29,655
Nonclothing laundry and dry cleaning, coin-operated	431,406	126,049	95,495	83,040	28,617	98,330	67,430	30,832
Termite and pest control services	1,400,035	67,316	198,432	280,259	126,107	728,547	434,157	294,553
Home security system service fee	1,810,511	63,109	314,081	313,171	136,145	984,594	514,618	469,896
Other home services	2,677,974	180,912	473,756	353,932	265,669	1,403,549	738,212	665,363
Termite and pest control products	177,911	8,078	25,734	47,849	15,910	80,805	50,262	30,597
Moving, storage, and freight express	3,943,123	105,181	471,276	710,648	268,765	2,387,494	1,246,418	1,140,908
Appliance repair, including at service center	1,689,577	103,162	379,501	363,046	139,348	704,208	400,442	303,967
Reupholstering and furniture repair	854,673	64,455	103,867	142,535	61,292	482,561	214,493	268,075
Repairs and rentals of lawn and garden equipment, hand and power tools, etc.	847,696	101,815	185,100	156,965	71,222	332,958	188,431	144,511
Appliance rental	203,494	60,921	48,368	37,469	30,219	25,962	13,858	12,239
Repair of computer systems for nonbusiness use	468,616	14,473	76,892	104,559	55,953	216,455	137,135	79,316
Computer information services	16,216,688	762,522	3,220,799	3,597,293	1,819,104	6,816,867	4,274,969	2,541,653
HOUSEKEEPING SUPPLIES	69,126,161	6,638,536	15,720,465	14,093,721	7,153,619	25,502,080	14,786,785	10,841,976
Laundry and cleaning supplies	17,274,854	2,491,197	4,404,260	3,358,806	1,825,404	5,183,882	3,297,030	1,887,470
Soaps and detergents	9,935,134	1,450,996	2,524,117	2,008,398	1,020,924	2,928,468	1,920,096	1,003,693
Other laundry cleaning products	7,340,883	1,040,200	1,880,143	1,350,409	804,587	2,255,414	1,376,934	883,777
Other household products	33,769,456	2,750,027	7,459,183	7,145,723	3,617,493	12,819,838	7,028,630	5,889,766
Cleansing and toilet tissue, paper towels, and napkins	9,981,647	1,394,788	2,584,887	2,150,426	937,315	2,914,839	1,877,487	1,035,466
Miscellaneous household products	14,085,239	933,336	3,064,844	2,859,302	1,555,144	5,672,934	2,944,161	2,786,780
Lawn and garden supplies	9,702,570	421,903	1,809,452	2,136,248	1,125,034	4,232,065	2,206,983	2,067,520
Postage and stationery	18,081,851	1,397,144	3,857,022	3,589,191	1,710,722	7,498,684	4,461,332	3,064,858
Stationery, stationery supplies, giftwrap	8,704,871	738,625	1,744,341	1,806,115	843,989	3,569,720	2,136,244	1,445,463
Postage	8,618,822	640,848	2,043,230	1,745,354	807,684	3,366,570	1,964,980	1,417,220
Delivery services	758,159	17,670	69,761	37,722	59,049	562,393	360,108	202,174
HOUSEHOLD FURNISHINGS, EQUIPMENT	191,411,800	11,527,360	37,568,759	41,029,490	18,975,981	82,305,736	47,089,608	35,354,838
Household textiles	18,333,020	1,175,506	4,277,140	3,469,189	2,016,540	7,380,883	4,014,144	3,412,955
Bathroom linens	2,472,155	166,439	805,820	532,163	194,446	763,920	384,722	387,991
Bedroom linens	9,967,693	695,879	2,480,400	1,658,770	1,167,426	3,932,533	2,097,151	1,870,759
Kitchen and dining room linens	1,144,215	90,877	201,843	281,525	124,505	450,434	246,346	207,588
Curtains and draperies	2,234,940	132,108	354,697	322,032	136,892	1,289,642	689,398	600,403
Slipcovers and decorative pillows	1,060,492	31,302	155,335	333,931	232,033	330,037	227,110	101,322
Sewing materials for household items	1,302,358	46,280	250,520	317,475	140,629	547,141	328,669	218,296
Other linens	152,329	12,622	28,525	23,545	20,715	67,176	40,541	26,713
Furniture	48,486,106	3,091,992	8,945,563	10,266,550	5,066,177	21,115,543	11,773,953	9,341,556
Mattresses and springs	6,228,064	422,408	1,296,939	1,306,104	712,863	2,489,068	1,414,786	1,074,301
Other bedroom furniture	9,456,052	532,974	1,796,740	1,820,799	1,258,616	4,047,089	2,675,269	1,371,913
Sofas	11,016,557	906,578	2,106,790	2,834,238	880,828	4,287,883	2,306,266	1,981,496
Living room chairs	4,843,145	337,085	887,053	885,082	570,953	2,162,601	1,166,371	996,279
Living room tables	1,717,485	72,365	335,474	323,298	162,519	823,956	513,584	310,440
Kitchen and dining room furniture	4,797,795	389,423	862,249	852,170	441,535	2,252,818	1,066,674	1,186,332

	total consumer units	less than high school graduate	high school graduate	some college	associate's degree	college graduate total	bachelor's degree	master's, professional, doctorate
Infants' furniture	$981,420	$72,365	$169,907	$175,447	$108,275	$454,653	$309,226	$145,452
Outdoor furniture	1,881,443	83,808	266,953	322,792	234,382	973,560	487,936	485,665
Wall units, cabinets, and other furniture	7,564,144	274,986	1,222,837	1,746,873	696,206	3,623,590	1,834,050	1,789,560
Floor coverings	**6,044,338**	**344,658**	**642,114**	**1,136,986**	**481,257**	**3,439,587**	**1,474,769**	**1,965,021**
Wall-to-wall carpeting	3,253,570	232,408	400,275	742,294	292,257	1,585,929	829,428	756,918
Floor coverings, nonpermanent	2,790,768	112,249	241,839	394,692	189,001	1,853,658	645,341	1,208,103
Major appliances	**23,714,551**	**1,922,377**	**5,133,188**	**5,949,242**	**2,300,682**	**8,423,890**	**4,752,356**	**3,703,860**
Dishwashers (built-in), garbage disposals, range hoods	1,667,484	57,892	337,955	381,780	248,157	642,550	385,757	256,778
Refrigerators and freezers	5,961,778	631,761	1,391,194	1,361,801	713,931	1,862,096	1,258,828	603,228
Washing machines	3,564,043	272,630	894,494	914,956	346,715	1,134,846	645,341	489,666
Clothes dryers	2,561,692	172,666	700,403	586,848	252,321	849,593	412,646	437,181
Cooking stoves, ovens	3,769,862	219,955	745,980	926,855	382,806	1,494,415	882,793	611,583
Microwave ovens	980,257	107,706	213,935	242,031	87,026	329,388	201,048	128,624
Portable dishwasher	141,864	10,771	32,555	47,596	9,183	41,863	19,857	22,124
Window air conditioners	506,990	80,443	122,780	85,825	45,702	171,671	117,278	54,604
Electric floor-cleaning equipment	3,222,174	85,323	603,977	1,111,416	118,739	1,323,393	665,611	673,012
Sewing machines	417,452	16,492	87,744	152,915	72,077	88,269	49,642	38,717
Miscellaneous household appliances	919,791	266,740	1,860	136,965	23,919	485,157	113,555	388,344
Small appliances and miscellaneous housewares	**12,170,074**	**1,041,547**	**2,611,551**	**2,238,023**	**1,682,960**	**4,609,807**	**2,640,726**	**1,984,909**
Housewares	9,600,242	844,984	1,981,840	1,689,150	1,405,332	3,692,064	2,142,035	1,565,968
Plastic dinnerware	211,633	28,104	55,809	36,963	25,734	65,229	38,886	26,243
China and other dinnerware	1,566,319	98,113	434,690	231,397	221,462	575,374	354,937	221,474
Flatware	467,454	21,541	71,622	91,901	55,953	226,839	120,795	105,912
Glassware	2,427,968	313,356	499,181	292,665	551,519	781,120	444,913	340,801
Silver serving pieces	34,885	3,366	7,441	4,557	2,990	15,901	11,997	3,648
Other serving pieces	204,656	3,702	53,639	36,203	17,192	94,760	60,604	34,010
Nonelectric cookware	2,104,704	226,687	429,109	420,769	208,435	819,413	467,872	356,217
Tableware, nonelectric kitchenware	2,581,460	150,283	430,659	574,696	322,048	1,113,753	641,825	477,781
Small appliances	2,569,832	196,563	629,402	549,126	277,521	917,418	498,691	418,941
Small electric kitchen appliances	2,008,190	153,144	505,071	459,757	220,607	669,809	391,341	278,313
Portable heating and cooling equipment	561,642	43,419	124,330	89,116	57,021	247,933	107,143	140,745
Miscellaneous household equipment	**82,663,711**	**3,951,113**	**15,959,824**	**17,969,500**	**7,428,364**	**37,336,026**	**22,433,660**	**14,946,654**
Window coverings	2,729,139	58,733	348,496	499,758	191,029	1,630,388	1,111,144	519,204
Infants' equipment	913,977	118,476	68,521	103,547	186,758	439,725	251,724	190,406
Laundry and cleaning equipment	1,827,953	174,348	445,232	397,730	225,733	589,004	358,867	231,594
Outdoor equipment	4,184,989	190,168	759,933	690,395	226,374	2,283,647	1,019,514	1,301,658
Clocks	888,394	30,292	144,793	156,206	86,812	467,309	307,571	158,868
Lamps and lighting fixtures	1,907,025	67,821	282,456	304,817	112,439	1,139,714	745,865	393,757
Other household decorative items	18,384,184	613,585	2,888,426	3,321,084	1,790,060	9,721,970	6,627,567	3,057,326
Telephones and accessories	3,119,846	447,147	487,089	697,230	313,293	1,185,472	585,150	614,996
Lawn and garden equipment	5,673,399	291,310	2,043,540	1,400,536	372,555	1,564,835	1,068,122	496,727
Power tools	3,888,470	199,592	984,409	1,328,636	327,281	1,085,844	699,947	385,167
Office furniture for home use	1,322,126	23,561	103,247	305,070	75,814	813,572	287,094	526,500
Hand tools	710,483	59,406	130,531	210,637	104,324	205,421	133,825	71,549
Indoor plants and fresh flowers	4,828,029	233,250	1,039,908	838,752	463,532	2,252,493	1,345,701	906,724
Closet and storage items	2,073,308	106,359	237,188	384,565	141,804	1,195,856	736,764	461,188
Rental of furniture	258,146	80,947	117,199	22,279	6,514	31,154	28,337	2,824
Luggage	770,950	25,580	122,470	151,396	90,229	380,662	252,345	128,389
Computers and computer hardware, nonbusiness use	15,648,069	721,459	2,424,591	3,842,867	1,535,603	7,123,214	4,015,178	3,108,046
Computer software and accessories, nonbusiness use	2,216,335	33,321	355,007	498,745	207,367	1,121,541	662,095	459,658
Telephone answering devices	72,095	5,554	13,642	15,697	2,883	34,724	17,995	16,475
Calculators	167,446	11,275	25,424	38,735	17,512	74,315	34,129	40,247
Business equipment for home use	109,305	2,524	25,424	23,292	17,619	40,565	15,513	25,066
Other hardware	4,608,256	165,766	1,370,111	1,277,243	343,618	1,459,366	646,582	837,293
Smoke alarms	119,770	12,285	28,215	26,077	11,105	41,539	25,648	16,004
Other household appliances	1,457,013	47,458	339,815	244,815	96,636	727,574	357,213	370,221
Miscellaneous household equipment and parts	4,788,493	230,894	1,173,229	1,188,886	481,257	1,726,446	1,099,768	626,646

Note: Numbers may not add to total because of rounding and missing subcategories.
Source: Calculations by New Strategist based on the 2004 Consumer Expenditure Survey

Table 8.28 Housing: Household Operations: Market shares by education, 2004

(percentage of total annual spending on household services, supplies, furnishings, and equipment accounted for by consumer unit educational attainment groups, 2004)

	total consumer units	less than high school graduate	high school graduate	some college	associate's degree	college graduate total	bachelor's degree	master's, professional, doctorate
Share of total consumer units	100.0%	14.5%	26.7%	21.8%	9.2%	27.9%	17.8%	10.1%
Share of total before-tax income	100.0	7.7	20.7	18.7	9.9	43.0	24.7	18.3
Share of total spending	100.0	8.5	21.8	20.5	10.2	39.0	23.3	15.8
Share of housing spending	100.0	9.1	21.5	20.2	9.8	39.5	23.4	16.1
HOUSEHOLD SERVICES	100.0	6.1	16.8	19.0	10.3	47.7	26.6	21.2
Personal services	100.0	7.5	17.9	18.9	12.2	43.5	26.6	16.9
Babysitting and child care in own home	100.0	5.1	9.8	10.5	13.7	60.9	33.5	27.4
Babysitting and child care in someone else's home	100.0	11.3	20.6	18.8	16.0	33.3	26.0	7.3
Care for elderly, invalids, handicapped, etc.	100.0	24.0	28.4	31.4	2.9	13.2	9.7	3.5
Day care centers, nurseries, and preschools	100.0	4.0	17.1	16.5	13.6	48.8	29.6	19.3
Other household services	100.0	5.2	16.1	19.0	9.1	50.6	26.6	24.0
Housekeeping services	100.0	4.2	10.8	14.6	6.7	63.7	27.0	36.7
Gardening, lawn care service	100.0	5.5	15.1	19.9	9.1	50.4	25.5	24.9
Water-softening service	100.0	7.0	21.8	18.1	17.5	35.8	15.6	20.2
Nonclothing laundry and dry cleaning, sent out	100.0	4.9	11.1	19.5	7.4	57.6	30.3	27.1
Nonclothing laundry and dry cleaning, coin-operated	100.0	29.2	22.1	19.2	6.6	22.8	15.6	7.1
Termite and pest control services	100.0	4.8	14.2	20.0	9.0	52.0	31.0	21.0
Home security system service fee	100.0	3.5	17.3	17.3	7.5	54.4	28.4	26.0
Other home services	100.0	6.8	17.7	13.2	9.9	52.4	27.6	24.8
Termite and pest control products	100.0	4.5	14.5	26.9	8.9	45.4	28.3	17.2
Moving, storage, and freight express	100.0	2.7	12.0	18.0	6.8	60.5	31.6	28.9
Appliance repair, including at service center	100.0	6.1	22.5	21.5	8.2	41.7	23.7	18.0
Reupholstering and furniture repair	100.0	7.5	12.2	16.7	7.2	56.5	25.1	31.4
Repairs and rentals of lawn and garden equipment, hand and power tools, etc.	100.0	12.0	21.8	18.5	8.4	39.3	22.2	17.0
Appliance rental	100.0	29.9	23.8	18.4	14.8	12.8	6.8	6.0
Repair of computer systems for nonbusiness use	100.0	3.1	16.4	22.3	11.9	46.2	29.3	16.9
Computer information services	100.0	4.7	19.9	22.2	11.2	42.0	26.4	15.7
HOUSEKEEPING SUPPLIES	100.0	9.6	22.7	20.4	10.3	36.9	21.4	15.7
Laundry and cleaning supplies	100.0	14.4	25.5	19.4	10.6	30.0	19.1	10.9
Soaps and detergents	100.0	14.6	25.4	20.2	10.3	29.5	19.3	10.1
Other laundry cleaning products	100.0	14.2	25.6	18.4	11.0	30.7	18.8	12.0
Other household products	100.0	8.1	22.1	21.2	10.7	38.0	20.8	17.4
Cleansing and toilet tissue, paper towels, and napkins	100.0	14.0	25.9	21.5	9.4	29.2	18.8	10.4
Miscellaneous household products	100.0	6.6	21.8	20.3	11.0	40.3	20.9	19.8
Lawn and garden supplies	100.0	4.3	18.6	22.0	11.6	43.6	22.7	21.3
Postage and stationery	100.0	7.7	21.3	19.8	9.5	41.5	24.7	16.9
Stationery, stationery supplies, giftwrap	100.0	8.5	20.0	20.7	9.7	41.0	24.5	16.6
Postage	100.0	7.4	23.7	20.3	9.4	39.1	22.8	16.4
Delivery services	100.0	2.3	9.2	5.0	7.8	74.2	47.5	26.7
HOUSEHOLD FURNISHINGS AND EQUIPMENT	100.0	6.0	19.6	21.4	9.9	43.0	24.6	18.5
Household textiles	100.0	6.4	23.3	18.9	11.0	40.3	21.9	18.6
Bathroom linens	100.0	6.7	32.6	21.5	7.9	30.9	15.6	15.7
Bedroom linens	100.0	7.0	24.9	16.6	11.7	39.5	21.0	18.8
Kitchen and dining room linens	100.0	7.9	17.6	24.6	10.9	39.4	21.5	18.1
Curtains and draperies	100.0	5.9	15.9	14.4	6.1	57.7	30.8	26.9
Slipcovers and decorative pillows	100.0	3.0	14.6	31.5	21.9	31.1	21.4	9.6
Sewing materials for household items	100.0	3.6	19.2	24.4	10.8	42.0	25.2	16.8
Other linens	100.0	8.3	18.7	15.5	13.6	44.1	26.6	17.5
Furniture	100.0	6.4	18.4	21.2	10.4	43.5	24.3	19.3
Mattresses and springs	100.0	6.8	20.8	21.0	11.4	40.0	22.7	17.2
Other bedroom furniture	100.0	5.6	19.0	19.3	13.3	42.8	28.3	14.5
Sofas	100.0	8.2	19.1	25.7	8.0	38.9	20.9	18.0
Living room chairs	100.0	7.0	18.3	18.3	11.8	44.7	24.1	20.6
Living room tables	100.0	4.2	19.5	18.8	9.5	48.0	29.9	18.1
Kitchen and dining room furniture	100.0	8.1	18.0	17.8	9.2	47.0	22.2	24.7

	total consumer units	less than high school graduate	high school graduate	some college	associate's degree	college graduate total	bachelor's degree	master's, professional, doctorate
Infants' furniture	100.0%	7.4%	17.3%	17.9%	11.0%	46.3%	31.5%	14.8%
Outdoor furniture	100.0	4.5	14.2	17.2	12.5	51.7	25.9	25.8
Wall units, cabinets, and other furniture	100.0	3.6	16.2	23.1	9.2	47.9	24.2	23.7
Floor coverings	**100.0**	**5.7**	**10.6**	**18.8**	**8.0**	**56.9**	**24.4**	**32.5**
Wall-to-wall carpeting	100.0	7.1	12.3	22.8	9.0	48.7	25.5	23.3
Floor coverings, nonpermanent	100.0	4.0	8.7	14.1	6.8	66.4	23.1	43.3
Major appliances	**100.0**	**8.1**	**21.6**	**25.1**	**9.7**	**35.5**	**20.0**	**15.6**
Dishwashers (built-in), garbage disposals, range hoods	100.0	3.5	20.3	22.9	14.9	38.5	23.1	15.4
Refrigerators and freezers	100.0	10.6	23.3	22.8	12.0	31.2	21.1	10.1
Washing machines	100.0	7.6	25.1	25.7	9.7	31.8	18.1	13.7
Clothes dryers	100.0	6.7	27.3	22.9	9.8	33.2	16.1	17.1
Cooking stoves, ovens	100.0	5.8	19.8	24.6	10.2	39.6	23.4	16.2
Microwave ovens	100.0	11.0	21.8	24.7	8.9	33.6	20.5	13.1
Portable dishwasher	100.0	7.6	22.9	33.6	6.5	29.5	14.0	15.6
Window air conditioners	100.0	15.9	24.2	16.9	9.0	33.9	23.1	10.8
Electric floor-cleaning equipment	100.0	2.6	18.7	34.5	3.7	41.1	20.7	20.9
Sewing machines	100.0	4.0	21.0	36.6	17.3	21.1	11.9	9.3
Miscellaneous household appliances	100.0	29.0	0.2	14.9	2.6	52.7	12.3	42.2
Small appliances and miscellaneous housewares	**100.0**	**8.6**	**21.5**	**18.4**	**13.8**	**37.9**	**21.7**	**16.3**
Housewares	100.0	8.8	20.6	17.6	14.6	38.5	22.3	16.3
Plastic dinnerware	100.0	13.3	26.4	17.5	12.2	30.8	18.4	12.4
China and other dinnerware	100.0	6.3	27.8	14.8	14.1	36.7	22.7	14.1
Flatware	100.0	4.6	15.3	19.7	12.0	48.5	25.8	22.7
Glassware	100.0	12.9	20.6	12.1	22.7	32.2	18.3	14.0
Silver serving pieces	100.0	9.6	21.3	13.1	8.6	45.6	34.4	10.5
Other serving pieces	100.0	1.8	26.2	17.7	8.4	46.3	29.6	16.6
Nonelectric cookware	100.0	10.8	20.4	20.0	9.9	38.9	22.2	16.9
Tableware, nonelectric kitchenware	100.0	5.8	16.7	22.3	12.5	43.1	24.9	18.5
Small appliances	100.0	7.6	24.5	21.4	10.8	35.7	19.4	16.3
Small electric kitchen appliances	100.0	7.6	25.2	22.9	11.0	33.4	19.5	13.9
Portable heating and cooling equipment	100.0	7.7	22.1	15.9	10.2	44.1	19.1	25.1
Miscellaneous household equipment	**100.0**	**4.8**	**19.3**	**21.7**	**9.0**	**45.2**	**27.1**	**18.1**
Window coverings	100.0	2.2	12.8	18.3	7.0	59.7	40.7	19.0
Infants' equipment	100.0	13.0	7.5	11.3	20.4	48.1	27.5	20.8
Laundry and cleaning equipment	100.0	9.5	24.4	21.8	12.3	32.2	19.6	12.7
Outdoor equipment	100.0	4.5	18.2	16.5	5.4	54.6	24.4	31.1
Clocks	100.0	3.4	16.3	17.6	9.8	52.6	34.6	17.9
Lamps and lighting fixtures	100.0	3.6	14.8	16.0	5.9	59.8	39.1	20.6
Other household decorative items	100.0	3.3	15.7	18.1	9.7	52.9	36.1	16.6
Telephones and accessories	100.0	14.3	15.6	22.3	10.0	38.0	18.8	19.7
Lawn and garden equipment	100.0	5.1	36.0	24.7	6.6	27.6	18.8	8.8
Power tools	100.0	5.1	25.3	34.2	8.4	27.9	18.0	9.9
Office furniture for home use	100.0	1.8	7.8	23.1	5.7	61.5	21.7	39.8
Hand tools	100.0	8.4	18.4	29.6	14.7	28.9	18.8	10.1
Indoor plants and fresh flowers	100.0	4.8	21.5	17.4	9.6	46.7	27.9	18.8
Closet and storage items	100.0	5.1	11.4	18.5	6.8	57.7	35.5	22.2
Rental of furniture	100.0	31.4	45.4	8.6	2.5	12.1	11.0	1.1
Luggage	100.0	3.3	15.9	19.6	11.7	49.4	32.7	16.7
Computers and computer hardware, nonbusiness use	100.0	4.6	15.5	24.6	9.8	45.5	25.7	19.9
Computer software and accessories, nonbusiness use	100.0	1.5	16.0	22.5	9.4	50.6	29.9	20.7
Telephone answering devices	100.0	7.7	18.9	21.8	4.0	48.2	25.0	22.9
Calculators	100.0	6.7	15.2	23.1	10.5	44.4	20.4	24.0
Business equipment for home use	100.0	2.3	23.3	21.3	16.1	37.1	14.2	22.9
Other hardware	100.0	3.6	29.7	27.7	7.5	31.7	14.0	18.2
Smoke alarms	100.0	10.3	23.6	21.8	9.3	34.7	21.4	13.4
Other household appliances	100.0	3.3	23.3	16.8	6.6	49.9	24.5	25.4
Miscellaneous household equipment and parts	100.0	4.8	24.5	24.8	10.1	36.1	23.0	13.1

Note: Numbers may not add to total because of rounding.
Source: Calculations by New Strategist based on the 2004 Consumer Expenditure Survey

Chapter 9. Spending on Housing: Shelter and Utilities, 2004

Housing is by far Americans' biggest expense. In 2004, housing costs—including shelter, utilities, and household operations—absorbed 32.1 percent of average household expenditures. That figure was slightly below the 32.4 percent in 2000 as lower mortgage interest rates reduced some housing costs. Spending on shelter rose 2 percent between 2000 and 2004, after adjusting for inflation. Spending on owned homes climbed 5 percent, while spending on rented homes fell 1 percent. Spending on "other lodging," such as hotels and motels, declined by 10 percent as the lackluster economy cut travel spending. Spending on utilities and fuels increased 7 percent because of rising energy prices.

Overall housing costs are highest for householders aged 35 to 44, at $16,794 in 2004. This age group spends much more than any other on mortgage interest—an average of $4,419 in 2004. Second in spending on mortgage interest are householders aged 45 to 54, devoting $3,784 to this item in 2004. Spending on maintenance and repair services for owned homes is greatest among householders aged 55 to 64. Householders aged 25 to 34 spend the most on rent.

Households with incomes of $100,000 or more spent $28,140 on housing in 2004, more than twice the $13,918 spent by the average household. The affluent devote more than $7,172 to mortgage interest alone. The most affluent households account for a large share of the market in a number of shelter categories: 40 percent of the market for lodging on trips, 51 percent of the market for owned vacation homes, and 50 percent of the market for housing while attending school.

Among household types, married couples with children under age 6 spend the most on housing, averaging $21,045 in 2004. Behind this figure is the high cost of housing for recent homebuyers—many married couples with young children are new homeowners. This household type spends more than twice as much as the average household on mortgage interest. Married couples without children at home (most of them empty-nesters) spend 75 percent more than average on owned vacation homes and 68 percent more than average for lodging on trips.

Asian households spend 25 percent more than the average household on housing, while the spending of black and Hispanic households is below average. Asians spend 67 percent more than average on mortgage interest, in part because many Asians live in California where housing costs are high. Blacks spend 40 percent more than the average household on rent, while Hispanics spend 60 percent more. Blacks spend 16 percent more than average on residential telephone service, while Hispanics spend more than three times the average on phone cards.

Households in the West spend the most on housing, $15,557 in 2004, because of the high cost of housing in California. Housing costs are lowest in the South, at $12,250. Northeastern households spend 53 percent more than average on property taxes. Western households spend 26 percent more than the average household on mortgage interest and 33 percent more than average for lodging on trips. Households in the South spend 21 percent more than average on electricity.

Not surprisingly, college graduates (who dominate the nation's affluent households) spend the most on housing, an average of $19,676 in 2004. They spend far more than the average household on almost every shelter category. They spend 62 percent more than average on mortgage interest, more than twice the average on lodging while on trips, and 84 percent more on owned vacation homes.

Table 9.1 Housing: Shelter and Utilities: Average spending by age, 2004

(average annual spending of consumer units (CU) on shelter and utilities, by age of consumer unit reference person, 2004)

	total consumer units	under 25	25 to 34	35 to 44	45 to 54	55 to 64	65 to 74	75+
Number of consumer units (in 000s)	116,282	8,817	19,439	24,070	23,712	17,479	11,230	11,536
Average number of persons per CU	2.5	1.9	2.9	3.2	2.7	2.1	1.9	1.5
Average before-tax income of CU	$54,453.00	$22,840.00	$52,484.00	$65,515.00	$70,434.00	$61,031.00	$42,137.00	$28,028.00
Average spending of CU, total	43,394.87	24,534.56	42,700.54	50,401.62	52,764.36	47,298.58	36,511.98	25,763.32
Housing, average spending	13,918.48	7,648.84	14,378.71	16,793.61	16,163.91	14,339.42	11,151.62	9,381.21
SHELTER	7,998.43	4,900.53	8,729.29	9,855.85	9,313.46	7,882.98	5,784.39	4,886.25
Owned dwellings*	5,324.49	1,009.48	4,700.01	7,025.32	6,967.84	5,970.31	4,134.07	2,928.45
Mortgage interest and charges	2,936.18	614.58	3,189.59	4,574.95	4,009.69	2,812.61	1,317.05	421.06
Mortgage interest	2,785.37	606.14	3,066.26	4,419.20	3,784.00	2,583.01	1,188.40	377.16
Interest paid, home equity loan	57.73	1.38	53.76	58.14	89.16	74.22	57.03	17.72
Interest paid, home equity line of credit	92.89	7.07	69.57	97.61	136.53	154.79	70.59	26.19
Property taxes	1,391.17	235.78	908.96	1,562.17	1,746.88	1,759.50	1,533.59	1,302.20
Maintenance, repairs, insurance, other expenses	997.14	159.11	601.47	888.20	1,211.27	1,398.20	1,283.43	1,205.19
Homeowner's insurance	314.75	50.41	202.17	321.63	374.17	408.15	398.63	346.81
Ground rent	40.10	12.24	32.09	38.44	33.92	49.55	56.47	60.76
Maintenance and repair services	530.63	66.27	276.95	417.74	660.47	804.98	729.14	672.80
Painting and papering	59.71	8.80	34.82	50.01	69.51	96.32	87.54	58.12
Plumbing and water heating	49.48	8.58	15.26	47.52	60.81	62.07	77.37	72.93
Heat, air conditioning, electrical work	89.48	19.89	59.76	63.98	117.88	124.02	112.51	112.79
Roofing and gutters	96.28	8.22	49.88	88.21	104.12	114.64	142.34	169.83
Other repair and maintenance services	177.49	1.54	93.43	120.01	224.37	309.28	246.87	209.96
Repair, replacement of hard-surface flooring	52.71	18.96	21.45	43.70	78.69	87.98	54.07	41.80
Repair of built-in appliances	5.49	0.27	2.35	4.29	5.09	10.67	8.43	7.38
Maintenance and repair materials	73.33	23.58	69.16	81.60	109.28	87.44	61.32	17.51
Paints, wallpaper, and supplies	15.18	2.82	21.77	15.98	20.92	13.83	11.78	5.43
Tools, equipment for painting, wallpapering	1.63	0.30	2.34	1.72	2.25	1.49	1.26	0.58
Plumbing supplies and equipment	5.79	0.72	3.25	8.92	8.42	4.43	5.56	4.24
Electrical supplies, heating and cooling equipment	3.23	0.45	2.88	4.17	4.62	4.78	1.64	0.28
Hard-surface flooring, repair and replacement	9.34	2.28	6.86	13.49	15.14	7.30	10.38	0.41
Roofing and gutters	6.42	11.67	8.18	6.30	8.41	5.35	2.78	0.77
Plaster, paneling, siding, windows, doors, screens, awnings	13.02	1.00	9.87	12.85	17.00	26.39	11.26	1.17
Patio, walk, fence, driveway, masonry, brick, and stucco materials	1.57	0.04	0.75	1.39	3.14	2.79	0.72	0.24
Miscellaneous supplies and equipment	17.16	4.29	13.28	16.78	29.39	21.10	15.93	4.39
Property management and security	34.91	6.05	18.60	26.66	31.68	43.84	34.51	95.16
Property management	28.55	4.35	16.26	21.82	28.59	36.03	25.10	73.75
Management and upkeep services for security	6.36	1.70	2.34	4.84	3.09	7.81	9.41	21.41
Parking	3.43	0.56	2.51	2.13	1.75	4.24	3.36	12.15
Rented dwellings	2,201.09	3,646.77	3,802.04	2,449.74	1,635.51	1,169.18	1,123.08	1,654.95
Rent	2,125.93	3,604.42	3,706.94	2,382.59	1,591.87	1,093.04	1,053.99	1,502.45
Rent as pay	36.08	32.63	72.19	34.98	22.89	25.33	12.14	46.90
Maintenance, insurance, and other expenses	39.07	9.72	22.90	32.18	20.75	50.82	56.95	105.59
Tenant's insurance	7.06	6.07	11.53	6.31	6.01	5.23	5.76	8.06
Maintenance and repair services	26.94	1.40	4.34	20.01	7.61	40.49	50.85	94.90
Maintenance and repair materials	5.07	2.25	7.03	5.85	7.13	5.10	0.34	2.63
Other lodging	472.85	244.28	227.24	380.78	710.11	743.48	527.25	302.84
Owned vacation homes	137.22	2.83	28.24	89.30	190.48	272.75	211.95	136.01
Mortgage interest and charges	54.04	1.66	18.41	47.69	83.20	97.74	55.36	39.93
Property taxes	57.51	1.17	6.88	28.48	79.34	131.40	91.32	56.71
Maintenance, insurance, and other expenses	25.67	–	2.95	13.13	27.94	43.61	65.27	39.37
Housing while attending school	57.73	159.25	8.92	10.85	150.86	70.68	5.56	–
Lodging on trips	277.89	82.21	190.09	280.62	368.77	400.05	309.74	166.84

	total consumer units	under 25	25 to 34	35 to 44	45 to 54	55 to 64	65 to 74	75+
UTILITIES, FUELS, PUBLIC SERVICES	**$2,926.65**	**$1,413.04**	**$2,687.02**	**$3,308.62**	**$3,412.89**	**$3,222.25**	**$2,881.16**	**$2,287.22**
Natural gas	**424.02**	**135.05**	**365.55**	**473.93**	**472.66**	**477.01**	**478.05**	**406.38**
Electricity	**1,064.41**	**506.55**	**957.37**	**1,210.96**	**1,231.49**	**1,176.74**	**1,071.59**	**844.80**
Fuel oil and other fuels	**120.53**	**28.13**	**61.18**	**103.83**	**149.38**	**161.15**	**163.34**	**163.53**
Fuel oil	64.19	14.27	31.04	53.90	76.85	86.13	90.95	94.42
Bottled and tank gas	45.20	11.53	26.38	40.32	56.26	58.29	57.58	58.18
Wood and other fuels	10.61	2.33	3.75	8.91	15.00	16.38	14.81	10.24
Telephone services	**990.22**	**642.39**	**1,027.90**	**1,144.76**	**1,178.11**	**1,039.95**	**815.43**	**578.70**
Residential telephone and pay phones	592.31	245.25	536.85	664.51	681.74	673.33	596.40	489.82
Cellular phone service	378.39	371.32	464.67	451.23	479.39	353.38	207.65	82.91
Pager service	1.01	0.44	1.56	0.98	1.09	0.97	0.65	0.78
Phone cards	18.51	25.38	24.82	28.03	15.89	12.28	10.73	5.19
Water and other public services	**327.47**	**100.92**	**275.02**	**375.15**	**381.26**	**367.39**	**352.76**	**293.83**
Water and sewerage maintenance	242.54	76.94	207.40	281.46	281.85	265.79	259.16	214.90
Trash and garbage collection	82.77	23.98	66.48	91.41	97.19	97.95	89.96	77.48
Septic tank cleaning	2.16	–	1.14	2.27	2.22	3.66	3.64	1.45

* See Appendix B for information about mortgage principal reduction.
Note: Subcategories may not add to total because some are not shown. "–" means sample is too small to make a reliable estimate.
Source: Bureau of Labor Statistics, unpublished tables from the 2004 Consumer Expenditure Survey

Table 9.2 Housing: Shelter and Utilities: Indexed spending by age, 2004

(indexed average annual spending of consumer units (CU) on shelter and utilities, by age of consumer unit reference person, 2004; index definition: an index of 100 is the average for all consumer units; an index of 132 means that spending by consumer units in that group is 32 percent above the average for all consumer units; an index of 68 indicates spending that is 32 percent below the average for all consumer units)

	total consumer units	under 25	25 to 34	35 to 44	45 to 54	55 to 64	65 to 74	75+
Average spending of CU, total	$43,395	$24,535	$42,701	$50,402	$52,764	$47,299	$36,512	$25,763
Average spending of CU, index	100	57	98	116	122	109	84	59
Housing, spending index	100	55	103	121	116	103	80	67
SHELTER	100	61	109	123	116	99	72	61
Owned dwellings*	100	19	88	132	131	112	78	55
Mortgage interest and charges	100	21	109	156	137	96	45	14
Mortgage interest	100	22	110	159	136	93	43	14
Interest paid, home equity loan	100	2	93	101	154	129	99	31
Interest paid, home equity line of credit	100	8	75	105	147	167	76	28
Property taxes	100	17	65	112	126	126	110	94
Maintenance, repairs, insurance, other expenses	100	16	60	89	121	140	129	121
Homeowner's insurance	100	16	64	102	119	130	127	110
Ground rent	100	31	80	96	85	124	141	152
Maintenance and repair services	100	12	52	79	124	152	137	127
Painting and papering	100	15	58	84	116	161	147	97
Plumbing and water heating	100	17	31	96	123	125	156	147
Heat, air conditioning, electrical work	100	22	67	72	132	139	126	126
Roofing and gutters	100	9	52	92	108	119	148	176
Other repair and maintenance services	100	1	53	68	126	174	139	118
Repair, replacement of hard-surface flooring	100	36	41	83	149	167	103	79
Repair of built-in appliances	100	5	43	78	93	194	154	134
Maintenance and repair materials	100	32	94	111	149	119	84	24
Paints, wallpaper, and supplies	100	19	143	105	138	91	78	36
Tools, equipment for painting, wallpapering	100	18	144	106	138	91	77	36
Plumbing supplies and equipment	100	12	56	154	145	77	96	73
Electrical supplies, heating and cooling equipment	100	14	89	129	143	148	51	9
Hard-surface flooring, repair and replacement	100	24	73	144	162	78	111	4
Roofing and gutters	100	182	127	98	131	83	43	12
Plaster, paneling, siding, windows, doors, screens, awnings	100	8	76	99	131	203	86	9
Patio, walk, fence, driveway, masonry, brick, and stucco materials	100	3	48	89	200	178	46	15
Miscellaneous supplies and equipment	100	25	77	98	171	123	93	26
Property management and security	100	17	53	76	91	126	99	273
Property management	100	15	57	76	100	126	88	258
Management and upkeep services for security	100	27	37	76	49	123	148	337
Parking	100	16	73	62	51	124	98	354
Rented dwellings	100	166	173	111	74	53	51	75
Rent	100	170	174	112	75	51	50	71
Rent as pay	100	90	200	97	63	70	34	130
Maintenance, insurance, and other expenses	100	25	59	82	53	130	146	270
Tenant's insurance	100	86	163	89	85	74	82	114
Maintenance and repair services	100	5	16	74	28	150	189	352
Maintenance and repair materials	100	44	139	115	141	101	7	52
Other lodging	100	52	48	81	150	157	112	64
Owned vacation homes	100	2	21	65	139	199	154	99
Mortgage interest and charges	100	3	34	88	154	181	102	74
Property taxes	100	2	12	50	138	228	159	99
Maintenance, insurance, and other expenses	100	–	11	51	109	170	254	153
Housing while attending school	100	276	15	19	261	122	10	–
Lodging on trips	100	30	68	101	133	144	111	60

	total consumer units	under 25	25 to 34	35 to 44	45 to 54	55 to 64	65 to 74	75+
UTILITIES, FUELS, AND PUBLIC SERVICES	100	48	92	113	117	110	98	78
Natural gas	100	32	86	112	111	112	113	96
Electricity	100	48	90	114	116	111	101	79
Fuel oil and other fuels	100	23	51	86	124	134	136	136
Fuel oil	100	22	48	84	120	134	142	147
Bottled and tank gas	100	26	58	89	124	129	127	129
Wood and other fuels	100	22	35	84	141	154	140	97
Telephone services	100	65	104	116	119	105	82	58
Residential telephone and pay phones	100	41	91	112	115	114	101	83
Cellular phone service	100	98	123	119	127	93	55	22
Pager service	100	44	154	97	108	96	64	77
Phone cards	100	137	134	151	86	66	58	28
Water and other public services	100	31	84	115	116	112	108	90
Water and sewerage maintenance	100	32	86	116	116	110	107	89
Trash and garbage collection	100	29	80	110	117	118	109	94
Septic tank cleaning	100	–	53	105	103	169	169	67

* See Appendix B for information about mortgage principal reduction.
Note: "–" means sample is too small to make a reliable estimate.
Source: Calculations by New Strategist based on the 2004 Consumer Expenditure Survey

Table 9.3 Housing: Shelter and Utilities: Total spending by age, 2004

(total annual spending on shelter and utilities, by consumer unit (CU) age groups, 2004; consumer units and dollars in thousands)

	total consumer units	under 25	25 to 34	35 to 44	45 to 54	55 to 64	65 to 74	75+
Number of consumer units	116,282	8,817	19,439	24,070	23,712	17,479	11,230	11,536
Total spending of all CUs	$5,046,042,273	$216,321,216	$830,055,797	$1,213,166,993	$1,251,148,504	$826,731,880	$410,029,535	$297,205,660
Housing, total spending	1,618,468,691	67,439,822	279,507,744	404,222,193	383,278,634	250,638,722	125,232,693	108,221,639
SHELTER	930,073,437	43,207,973	169,688,668	237,230,310	220,840,764	137,786,607	64,958,700	56,367,780
Owned dwellings*	619,142,346	8,900,585	91,363,494	169,099,452	165,221,422	104,355,048	46,425,606	33,782,599
Mortgage interest and charges	341,424,883	5,418,752	62,002,440	110,119,047	95,077,769	49,161,610	14,790,472	4,857,348
Mortgage interest	323,888,394	5,344,336	59,605,028	106,370,144	89,726,208	45,148,432	13,345,732	4,350,918
Interest paid, home equity loan	6,712,960	12,167	1,045,041	1,399,430	2,114,162	1,297,291	640,447	204,418
Interest paid, home equity line of credit	10,801,435	62,336	1,352,371	2,349,473	3,237,399	2,705,574	792,726	302,128
Property taxes	161,768,030	2,078,872	17,669,273	37,601,432	41,422,019	30,754,301	17,222,216	15,022,179
Maintenance, repairs, insurance, other expenses	115,949,433	1,402,873	11,691,975	21,378,974	28,721,634	24,439,138	14,412,919	13,903,072
Homeowner's insurance	36,599,760	444,465	3,929,983	7,741,634	8,872,319	7,134,054	4,476,615	4,000,800
Ground rent	4,662,908	107,920	623,798	925,251	804,311	866,084	634,158	700,927
Maintenance and repair services	61,702,718	584,303	5,383,631	10,055,002	15,661,065	14,070,245	8,188,242	7,761,421
Painting and papering	6,943,198	77,590	676,866	1,203,741	1,648,221	1,683,577	983,074	670,472
Plumbing and water heating	5,753,633	75,650	296,639	1,143,806	1,441,927	1,084,922	868,865	841,320
Heat, air conditioning, electrical work	10,404,913	175,370	1,161,675	1,539,999	2,795,171	2,167,746	1,263,487	1,301,145
Roofing and gutters	11,195,631	72,476	969,617	2,123,215	2,468,893	2,003,793	1,598,478	1,959,159
Other repair and maintenance services	20,638,892	13,578	1,816,186	2,888,641	5,320,261	5,405,905	2,772,350	2,422,099
Repair, replacement of hard-surface flooring	6,129,224	167,170	416,967	1,051,859	1,865,897	1,537,802	607,206	482,205
Repair of built-in appliances	638,388	2,381	45,682	103,260	120,694	186,501	94,669	85,136
Maintenance and repair materials	8,526,959	207,905	1,344,401	1,964,112	2,591,247	1,528,364	688,624	201,995
Paints, wallpaper, and supplies	1,765,161	24,864	423,187	384,639	496,055	241,735	132,289	62,640
Tools, equipment for painting, wallpapering	189,540	2,645	45,487	41,400	53,352	26,044	14,150	6,691
Plumbing supplies and equipment	673,273	6,348	63,177	214,704	199,655	77,432	62,439	48,913
Electrical supplies, heating and cooling equipment	375,591	3,968	55,984	100,372	109,549	83,550	18,417	3,230
Hard-surface flooring, repair and replacement	1,086,074	20,103	133,352	324,704	359,000	127,597	116,567	4,730
Roofing and gutters	746,530	102,894	159,011	151,641	199,418	93,513	31,219	8,883
Plaster, paneling, siding, windows, doors, screens, awnings	1,513,992	8,817	191,863	309,300	403,104	461,271	126,450	13,497
Patio, walk, fence, driveway, masonry, brick, and stucco materials	182,563	353	14,579	33,457	74,456	48,766	8,086	2,769
Miscellaneous supplies and equipment	1,995,399	37,825	258,150	403,895	696,896	368,807	178,894	50,643
Property management and security	4,059,405	53,343	361,565	641,706	751,196	766,279	387,547	1,097,766
Property management	3,319,851	38,354	316,078	525,207	677,926	629,768	281,873	850,780
Management and upkeep services for security	739,554	14,989	45,487	116,499	73,270	136,511	105,674	246,986
Parking	398,847	4,938	48,792	51,269	41,496	74,111	37,733	140,162
Rented dwellings	255,947,147	32,153,571	73,907,856	58,965,242	38,781,213	20,436,097	12,612,188	19,091,503
Rent	247,207,392	31,780,171	72,059,207	57,348,941	37,746,421	19,105,246	11,836,308	17,332,263
Rent as pay	4,195,455	287,699	1,403,301	841,969	542,768	442,743	136,332	541,038
Maintenance, insurance, and other expenses	4,543,138	85,701	445,153	774,573	492,024	888,283	639,549	1,218,086
Tenant's insurance	820,951	53,519	224,132	151,882	142,509	91,415	64,685	92,980
Maintenance and repair services	3,132,637	12,344	84,365	481,641	180,448	707,725	571,046	1,094,766
Maintenance and repair materials	589,550	19,838	136,656	140,810	169,067	89,143	3,818	30,340
Other lodging	54,983,944	2,153,817	4,417,318	9,165,375	16,838,128	12,995,287	5,921,018	3,493,562
Owned vacation homes	15,956,216	24,952	548,957	2,149,451	4,516,662	4,767,397	2,380,199	1,569,011
Mortgage interest and charges	6,283,879	14,636	357,872	1,147,898	1,972,838	1,708,397	621,693	460,632
Property taxes	6,687,378	10,316	133,740	685,514	1,881,310	2,296,741	1,025,524	654,207
Maintenance, insurance, and other expenses	2,984,959	–	57,345	316,039	662,513	762,259	732,982	454,172
Housing while attending school	6,712,960	1,404,107	173,396	261,160	3,577,192	1,235,416	62,439	–
Lodging on trips	32,313,605	724,846	3,695,160	6,754,523	8,744,274	6,992,474	3,478,380	1,924,666

	total consumer units	under 25	25 to 34	35 to 44	45 to 54	55 to 64	65 to 74	75+
UTILITIES, FUELS, PUBLIC SERVICES	$340,316,715	$12,458,774	$52,232,982	$79,638,483	$80,926,448	$56,321,708	$32,355,427	$26,385,370
Natural gas	49,305,894	1,190,736	7,105,926	11,407,495	11,207,714	8,337,658	5,368,502	4,688,000
Electricity	123,771,724	4,466,251	18,610,315	29,147,807	29,201,091	20,568,238	12,033,956	9,745,613
Fuel oil and other fuels	14,015,469	248,022	1,189,278	2,499,188	3,542,099	2,816,741	1,834,308	1,886,482
Fuel oil	7,464,142	125,819	603,387	1,297,373	1,822,267	1,505,466	1,021,369	1,089,229
Bottled and tank gas	5,255,946	101,660	512,801	970,502	1,334,037	1,018,851	646,623	671,164
Wood and other fuels	1,233,752	20,544	72,896	214,464	355,680	286,306	166,316	118,129
Telephone services	115,144,762	5,663,953	19,981,348	27,554,373	27,935,344	18,177,286	9,157,279	6,675,883
Residential telephone and pay phones	68,874,991	2,162,369	10,435,827	15,994,756	16,165,419	11,769,135	6,697,572	5,650,564
Cellular phone service	43,999,946	3,273,928	9,032,720	10,861,106	11,367,296	6,176,729	2,331,910	956,450
Pager service	117,445	3,879	30,325	23,589	25,846	16,955	7,300	8,998
Phone cards	2,152,380	223,775	482,476	674,682	376,784	214,642	120,498	59,872
Water and other public services	38,078,867	889,812	5,346,114	9,029,861	9,040,437	6,421,610	3,961,495	3,389,623
Water and sewerage maintenance	28,203,036	678,380	4,031,649	6,774,742	6,683,227	4,645,743	2,910,367	2,479,086
Trash and garbage collection	9,624,661	211,432	1,292,305	2,200,239	2,304,569	1,712,068	1,010,251	893,809
Septic tank cleaning	251,169	–	22,160	54,639	52,641	63,973	40,877	16,727

See Appendix B for information about mortgage principal reduction.
Note: Numbers may not add to total because of rounding and missing subcategories. "–" means sample is too small to make a reliable estimate.
Source: Calculations by New Strategist based on the 2004 Consumer Expenditure Survey

Table 9.4 Housing: Shelter and Utilities: Market shares by age, 2004

(percentage of total annual spending on shelter and utilities accounted for by consumer unit age groups, 2004)

	total consumer units	under 25	25 to 34	35 to 44	45 to 54	55 to 64	65 to 74	75+
Share of total consumer units	100.0%	7.6%	16.7%	20.7%	20.4%	15.0%	9.7%	9.9%
Share of total before-tax income	100.0	3.2	16.1	24.9	26.4	16.8	7.5	5.1
Share of total spending	100.0	4.3	16.4	24.0	24.8	16.4	8.1	5.9
Share of housing spending	100.0	4.2	17.3	25.0	23.7	15.5	7.7	6.7
SHELTER	100.0	4.6	18.2	25.5	23.7	14.8	7.0	6.1
Owned dwellings*	100.0	1.4	14.8	27.3	26.7	16.9	7.5	5.5
Mortgage interest and charges	100.0	1.6	18.2	32.3	27.8	14.4	4.3	1.4
Mortgage interest	100.0	1.7	18.4	32.8	27.7	13.9	4.1	1.3
Interest paid, home equity loan	100.0	0.2	15.6	20.8	31.5	19.3	9.5	3.0
Interest paid, home equity line of credit	100.0	0.6	12.5	21.8	30.0	25.0	7.3	2.8
Property taxes	100.0	1.3	10.9	23.2	25.6	19.0	10.6	9.3
Maintenance, repairs, insurance, other expenses	100.0	1.2	10.1	18.4	24.8	21.1	12.4	12.0
Homeowner's insurance	100.0	1.2	10.7	21.2	24.2	19.5	12.2	10.9
Ground rent	100.0	2.3	13.4	19.8	17.2	18.6	13.6	15.0
Maintenance and repair services	100.0	0.9	8.7	16.3	25.4	22.8	13.3	12.6
Painting and papering	100.0	1.1	9.7	17.3	23.7	24.2	14.2	9.7
Plumbing and water heating	100.0	1.3	5.2	19.9	25.1	18.9	15.1	14.6
Heat, air conditioning, electrical work	100.0	1.7	11.2	14.8	26.9	20.8	12.1	12.5
Roofing and gutters	100.0	0.6	8.7	19.0	22.1	17.9	14.3	17.5
Other repair and maintenance services	100.0	0.1	8.8	14.0	25.8	26.2	13.4	11.7
Repair, replacement of hard-surface flooring	100.0	2.7	6.8	17.2	30.4	25.1	9.9	7.9
Repair of built-in appliances	100.0	0.4	7.2	16.2	18.9	29.2	14.8	13.3
Maintenance and repair materials	100.0	2.4	15.8	23.0	30.4	17.9	8.1	2.4
Paints, wallpaper, and supplies	100.0	1.4	24.0	21.8	28.1	13.7	7.5	3.5
Tools, equipment for painting, wallpapering	100.0	1.4	24.0	21.8	28.1	13.7	7.5	3.5
Plumbing supplies and equipment	100.0	0.9	9.4	31.9	29.7	11.5	9.3	7.3
Electrical supplies, heating and cooling equipment	100.0	1.1	14.9	26.7	29.2	22.2	4.9	0.9
Hard-surface flooring, repair and replacement	100.0	1.9	12.3	29.9	33.1	11.7	10.7	0.4
Roofing and gutters	100.0	13.8	21.3	20.3	26.7	12.5	4.2	1.2
Plaster, paneling, siding, windows, doors, screens, awnings	100.0	0.6	12.7	20.4	26.6	30.5	8.4	0.9
Patio, walk, fence, driveway, masonry, brick, and stucco materials	100.0	0.2	8.0	18.3	40.8	26.7	4.4	1.5
Miscellaneous supplies and equipment	100.0	1.9	12.9	20.2	34.9	18.5	9.0	2.5
Property management and security	100.0	1.3	8.9	15.8	18.5	18.9	9.5	27.0
Property management	100.0	1.2	9.5	15.8	20.4	19.0	8.5	25.6
Management and upkeep services for security	100.0	2.0	6.2	15.8	9.9	18.5	14.3	33.4
Parking	100.0	1.2	12.2	12.9	10.4	18.6	9.5	35.1
Rented dwellings	100.0	12.6	28.9	23.0	15.2	8.0	4.9	7.5
Rent	100.0	12.9	29.1	23.2	15.3	7.7	4.8	7.0
Rent as pay	100.0	6.9	33.4	20.1	12.9	10.6	3.2	12.9
Maintenance, insurance, and other expenses	100.0	1.9	9.8	17.0	10.8	19.6	14.1	26.8
Tenant's insurance	100.0	6.5	27.3	18.5	17.4	11.1	7.9	11.3
Maintenance and repair services	100.0	0.4	2.7	15.4	5.8	22.6	18.2	34.9
Maintenance and repair materials	100.0	3.4	23.2	23.9	28.7	15.1	0.6	5.1
Other lodging	100.0	3.9	8.0	16.7	30.6	23.6	10.8	6.4
Owned vacation homes	100.0	0.2	3.4	13.5	28.3	29.9	14.9	9.8
Mortgage interest and charges	100.0	0.2	5.7	18.3	31.4	27.2	9.9	7.3
Property taxes	100.0	0.2	2.0	10.3	28.1	34.3	15.3	9.8
Maintenance, insurance, and other expenses	100.0	–	1.9	10.6	22.2	25.5	24.6	15.2
Housing while attending school	100.0	20.9	2.6	3.9	53.3	18.4	0.9	–
Lodging on trips	100.0	2.2	11.4	20.9	27.1	21.6	10.8	6.0

	total consumer units	under 25	25 to 34	35 to 44	45 to 54	55 to 64	65 to 74	75+
UTILITIES, FUELS, AND PUBLIC SERVICES	100.0%	3.7%	15.3%	23.4%	23.8%	16.5%	9.5%	7.8%
Natural gas	100.0	2.4	14.4	23.1	22.7	16.9	10.9	9.5
Electricity	100.0	3.6	15.0	23.5	23.6	16.6	9.7	7.9
Fuel oil and other fuels	100.0	1.8	8.5	17.8	25.3	20.1	13.1	13.5
Fuel oil	100.0	1.7	8.1	17.4	24.4	20.2	13.7	14.6
Bottled and tank gas	100.0	1.9	9.8	18.5	25.4	19.4	12.3	12.8
Wood and other fuels	100.0	1.7	5.9	17.4	28.8	23.2	13.5	9.6
Telephone services	100.0	4.9	17.4	23.9	24.3	15.8	8.0	5.8
Residential telephone and pay phones	100.0	3.1	15.2	23.2	23.5	17.1	9.7	8.2
Cellular phone service	100.0	7.4	20.5	24.7	25.8	14.0	5.3	2.2
Pager service	100.0	3.3	25.8	20.1	22.0	14.4	6.2	7.7
Phone cards	100.0	10.4	22.4	31.3	17.5	10.0	5.6	2.8
Water and other public services	100.0	2.3	14.0	23.7	23.7	16.9	10.4	8.9
Water and sewerage maintenance	100.0	2.4	14.3	24.0	23.7	16.5	10.3	8.8
Trash and garbage collection	100.0	2.2	13.4	22.9	23.9	17.8	10.5	9.3
Septic tank cleaning	100.0	–	8.8	21.8	21.0	25.5	16.3	6.7

See Appendix B for information about mortgage principal reduction.

Note: Numbers may not add to total because of rounding. "–" means sample is too small to make a reliable estimate.

Source: Calculations by New Strategist based on the 2004 Consumer Expenditure Survey

Table 9.5 Housing: Shelter and Utilities: Average spending by income, 2004

(average annual spending on shelter and utilities, by before-tax income of consumer units (CU), 2004)

	total consumer units	under $20,000	$20,000– $39,999	$40,000– $49,999	$50,000– $69,999	$70,000– $79,999	$80,000– $99,999	$100,000 or more
Number of consumer units (in 000s)	116,282	28,898	27,297	11,374	18,069	6,461	9,246	14,937
Average number of persons per CU	2.5	1.8	2.3	2.6	2.8	3.0	3.1	3.2
Average before-tax income of CU	$54,453.00	$10,923.47	$29,561.76	$44,645.00	$59,259.00	$74,437.00	$88,811.00	$155,901.00
Average spending of CU, total	43,394.87	18,865.37	30,400.94	38,204.07	47,750.13	55,012.03	65,446.39	93,525.67
Housing, average spending	13,918.48	7,098.03	10,362.24	12,383.34	14,698.87	17,421.88	20,397.04	28,139.97
SHELTER	**7,998.43**	**4,134.89**	**5,938.23**	**7,073.90**	**8,421.43**	**10,212.97**	**11,761.49**	**16,143.23**
Owned dwellings*	**5,324.49**	**1,524.86**	**2,924.78**	**4,362.61**	**5,916.88**	**8,051.24**	**9,603.76**	**13,248.55**
Mortgage interest and charges	2,936.18	542.99	1,384.20	2,431.11	3,459.01	4,871.16	5,681.12	7,618.51
Mortgage interest	2,785.37	512.06	1,312.44	2,332.37	3,289.39	4,647.85	5,422.69	7,172.40
Interest paid, home equity loan	57.73	13.27	31.59	50.25	74.25	93.79	92.46	140.14
Interest paid, home equity line of credit	92.89	17.67	40.17	47.47	94.79	129.52	165.97	305.97
Property taxes	1,391.17	536.10	829.11	1,098.34	1,466.45	1,883.84	2,252.54	3,458.26
Maintenance, repairs, insurance, other expenses	997.14	445.76	711.46	833.16	991.42	1,296.23	1,670.10	2,171.78
Homeowner's insurance	314.75	141.02	241.47	289.47	360.45	411.11	492.69	596.91
Ground rent	40.10	55.00	65.66	39.54	21.94	14.40	28.13	5.45
Maintenance and repair services	530.63	216.45	321.88	392.03	464.41	721.43	961.24	1,356.56
Painting and papering	59.71	14.19	19.36	31.54	67.36	67.83	83.06	215.75
Plumbing and water heating	49.48	23.51	36.22	32.05	56.87	52.99	90.45	101.40
Heat, air conditioning, electrical work	89.48	45.38	58.60	72.95	75.43	156.67	122.63	211.19
Roofing and gutters	96.28	40.64	92.34	83.68	75.39	99.06	116.47	232.27
Other repair and maintenance services	177.49	76.84	87.99	124.26	125.13	267.32	410.26	456.71
Repair, replacement of hard-surface flooring	52.71	13.47	24.73	44.84	58.42	70.12	128.39	124.45
Repair of built-in appliances	5.49	2.41	2.63	2.71	5.80	7.45	9.99	14.78
Maintenance and repair materials	73.33	16.11	47.25	73.70	110.38	104.44	129.07	138.63
Paints, wallpaper, and supplies	15.18	3.35	7.10	19.07	18.89	21.05	32.59	32.08
Tools, equipment for painting, wallpapering	1.63	0.36	0.76	2.05	2.03	2.26	3.50	3.45
Plumbing supplies and equipment	5.79	1.70	5.00	6.23	10.21	9.23	9.32	5.75
Electrical supplies, heating and cooling equipment	3.23	0.34	1.06	3.92	4.50	4.50	4.83	9.27
Hard-surface flooring, repair and replacement	9.34	4.81	6.84	7.42	12.26	15.19	16.85	14.88
Roofing and gutters	6.42	1.45	9.06	2.40	9.36	3.37	7.78	11.64
Plaster, paneling, siding, windows, doors, screens, awnings	13.02	1.82	4.72	10.87	25.68	25.43	25.95	22.84
Patio, walk, fence, driveway, masonry, brick, and stucco materials	1.57	0.06	1.11	2.04	3.20	2.66	1.64	2.49
Miscellaneous supplies and equipment	17.16	3.28	11.61	19.69	24.24	20.74	26.62	36.24
Property management and security	34.91	14.75	32.45	35.50	30.68	41.55	53.63	68.60
Property management	28.55	12.27	26.43	28.27	26.07	35.32	43.04	55.24
Management and upkeep services for security	6.36	2.49	6.03	7.23	4.60	6.23	10.59	13.36
Parking	3.43	2.43	2.77	2.93	3.57	3.30	5.35	5.63
Rented dwellings	**2,201.09**	**2,472.42**	**2,825.62**	**2,456.52**	**2,085.43**	**1,637.71**	**1,324.70**	**1,266.41**
Rent	2,125.93	2,320.86	2,777.63	2,405.47	2,042.47	1,550.97	1,303.07	1,204.02
Rent as pay	36.08	91.54	23.57	25.68	16.55	19.99	0.12	12.45
Maintenance, insurance, and other expenses	39.07	60.03	24.43	25.37	26.40	66.75	21.50	49.95
Tenant's insurance	7.06	6.01	7.57	7.80	8.66	8.60	7.64	4.66
Maintenance and repair services	26.94	49.87	12.23	12.12	10.84	55.31	11.61	37.42
Maintenance and repair materials	5.07	4.15	4.63	5.45	6.90	2.83	2.25	7.87
Other lodging	**472.85**	**137.61**	**187.83**	**254.78**	**419.11**	**524.03**	**833.04**	**1,628.27**
Owned vacation homes	137.22	22.82	52.28	63.65	93.41	147.44	263.38	540.29
Mortgage interest and charges	54.04	10.10	8.02	21.91	31.95	60.34	120.85	235.15
Property taxes	57.51	9.21	30.64	29.37	41.97	57.11	95.18	217.10
Maintenance, insurance, and other expenses	25.67	6.03	13.61	12.37	19.49	30.00	47.35	88.04
Housing while attending school	57.73	53.73	5.61	6.93	26.67	46.72	86.49	223.95
Lodging on trips	277.89	61.06	129.94	184.20	299.03	329.87	483.17	864.03

	total consumer units	under $20,000	$20,000– $39,999	$40,000– $49,999	$50,000– $69,999	$70,000– $79,999	$80,000– $99,999	$100,000 or more
UTILITIES, FUELS, AND PUBLIC SERVICES	**$2,926.65**	**$1,810.87**	**$2,531.00**	**$2,935.41**	**$3,270.31**	**$3,551.79**	**$3,903.01**	**$4,511.22**
Natural gas	**424.02**	**250.10**	**370.00**	**433.92**	**450.33**	**539.82**	**534.60**	**701.29**
Electricity	**1,064.41**	**712.66**	**941.02**	**1,070.20**	**1,155.95**	**1,231.80**	**1,392.54**	**1,579.81**
Fuel oil and other fuels	**120.53**	**84.36**	**106.47**	**106.50**	**129.87**	**129.32**	**155.84**	**189.94**
Fuel oil	64.19	41.05	58.09	48.62	59.21	76.95	84.33	120.05
Bottled and tank gas	45.20	31.97	36.64	46.31	57.57	46.35	62.74	59.26
Wood and other fuels	10.61	10.49	10.95	11.56	12.88	6.01	8.77	9.91
Telephone services	**990.22**	**588.34**	**841.28**	**984.23**	**1,147.71**	**1,251.75**	**1,369.83**	**1,505.83**
Residential telephone and pay phones	592.31	411.43	541.84	613.05	654.90	693.55	729.83	814.07
Cellular phone service	378.39	160.32	278.60	350.25	468.69	545.87	616.27	675.13
Pager service	1.01	0.32	1.14	0.98	1.47	0.30	1.97	1.27
Phone cards	18.51	16.28	19.71	19.95	22.65	12.04	21.76	15.37
Water and other public services	**327.47**	**175.40**	**272.22**	**340.57**	**386.45**	**399.10**	**450.19**	**534.34**
Water and sewerage maintenance	242.54	132.06	201.69	252.88	285.65	288.57	334.86	393.86
Trash and garbage collection	82.77	42.88	69.23	86.56	97.46	108.54	110.59	135.64
Septic tank cleaning	2.16	0.55	1.30	1.12	3.34	1.98	4.74	4.84

* See Appendix B for information about mortgage principal reduction.

Note: Subcategories may not add to total because some are not shown.

Source: Bureau of Labor Statistics, unpublished tables from the 2004 Consumer Expenditure Survey; calculations by New Strategist

Table 9.6 Housing: Shelter and Utilities: Indexed spending by income, 2004

(indexed average annual spending of consumer units (CU) on shelter and utilities, by before-tax income of consumer unit, 2004; index definition: an index of 100 is the average for all consumer units; an index of 132 means that spending by consumer units in that group is 32 percent above the average for all consumer units; an index of 68 indicates spending that is 32 percent below the average for all consumer units)

	total consumer units	under $20,000	$20,000–$39,999	$40,000–$49,999	$50,000–$69,999	$70,000–$79,999	$80,000–$99,999	$100,000 or more
Average spending of CU, total	$43,395	$18,865	$30,401	$38,204	$47,750	$55,012	$65,446	$93,526
Average spending of CU, index	100	43	70	88	110	127	151	216
Housing, spending index	**100**	**51**	**74**	**89**	**106**	**125**	**147**	**202**
SHELTER	**100**	**52**	**74**	**88**	**105**	**128**	**147**	**202**
Owned dwellings*	**100**	**29**	**55**	**82**	**111**	**151**	**180**	**249**
Mortgage interest and charges	100	18	47	83	118	166	193	259
Mortgage interest	100	18	47	84	118	167	195	258
Interest paid, home equity loan	100	23	55	87	129	162	160	243
Interest paid, home equity line of credit	100	19	43	51	102	139	179	329
Property taxes	100	39	60	79	105	135	162	249
Maintenance, repairs, insurance, other expenses	100	45	71	84	99	130	167	218
Homeowner's insurance	100	45	77	92	115	131	157	190
Ground rent	100	137	164	99	55	36	70	14
Maintenance and repair services	100	41	61	74	88	136	181	256
Painting and papering	100	24	32	53	113	114	139	361
Plumbing and water heating	100	48	73	65	115	107	183	205
Heat, air conditioning, electrical work	100	51	65	82	84	175	137	236
Roofing and gutters	100	42	96	87	78	103	121	241
Other repair and maintenance services	100	43	50	70	70	151	231	257
Repair, replacement of hard-surface flooring	100	26	47	85	111	133	244	236
Repair of built-in appliances	100	44	48	49	106	136	182	269
Maintenance and repair materials	100	22	64	101	151	142	176	189
Paints, wallpaper, and supplies	100	22	47	126	124	139	215	211
Tools, equipment for painting, wallpapering	100	22	47	126	125	139	215	212
Plumbing supplies and equipment	100	29	86	108	176	159	161	99
Electrical supplies, heating and cooling equipment	100	11	33	121	139	139	150	287
Hard-surface flooring, repair and replacement	100	51	73	79	131	163	180	159
Roofing and gutters	100	23	141	37	146	52	121	181
Plaster, paneling, siding, windows, doors, screens, awnings	100	14	36	83	197	195	199	175
Patio, walk, fence, driveway, masonry, brick, and stucco materials	100	4	71	130	204	169	104	159
Miscellaneous supplies and equipment	100	19	68	115	141	121	155	211
Property management and security	100	42	93	102	88	119	154	197
Property management	100	43	93	99	91	124	151	193
Management and upkeep services for security	100	39	95	114	72	98	167	210
Parking	100	71	81	85	104	96	156	164
Rented dwellings	**100**	**112**	**128**	**112**	**95**	**74**	**60**	**58**
Rent	100	109	131	113	96	73	61	57
Rent as pay	100	254	65	71	46	55	0	35
Maintenance, insurance, and other expenses	100	154	63	65	68	171	55	128
Tenant's insurance	100	85	107	110	123	122	108	66
Maintenance and repair services	100	185	45	45	40	205	43	139
Maintenance and repair materials	100	82	91	107	136	56	44	155
Other lodging	**100**	**29**	**40**	**54**	**89**	**111**	**176**	**344**
Owned vacation homes	100	17	38	46	68	107	192	394
Mortgage interest and charges	100	19	15	41	59	112	224	435
Property taxes	100	16	53	51	73	99	166	377
Maintenance, insurance, and other expenses	100	23	53	48	76	117	184	343
Housing while attending school	100	93	10	12	46	81	150	388
Lodging on trips	100	22	47	66	108	119	174	311

	total consumer units	under $20,000	$20,000– $39,999	$40,000– $49,999	$50,000– $69,999	$70,000– $79,999	$80,000– $99,999	$100,000 or more
UTILITIES, FUELS, AND PUBLIC SERVICES	**100**	**62**	**86**	**100**	**112**	**121**	**133**	**154**
Natural gas	**100**	**59**	**87**	**102**	**106**	**127**	**126**	**165**
Electricity	**100**	**67**	**88**	**101**	**109**	**116**	**131**	**148**
Fuel oil and other fuels	**100**	**70**	**88**	**88**	**108**	**107**	**129**	**158**
Fuel oil	100	64	90	76	92	120	131	187
Bottled and tank gas	100	71	81	102	127	103	139	131
Wood and other fuels	100	99	103	109	121	57	83	93
Telephone services	**100**	**59**	**85**	**99**	**116**	**126**	**138**	**152**
Residential telephone and pay phones	100	69	91	104	111	117	123	137
Cellular phone service	100	42	74	93	124	144	163	178
Pager service	100	32	113	97	146	30	195	126
Phone cards	100	88	106	108	122	65	118	83
Water and other public services	**100**	**54**	**83**	**104**	**118**	**122**	**137**	**163**
Water and sewerage maintenance	100	54	83	104	118	119	138	162
Trash and garbage collection	100	52	84	105	118	131	134	164
Septic tank cleaning	100	26	60	52	155	92	219	224

* See Appendix B for information about mortgage principal reduction.
Source: Calculations by New Strategist based on the 2004 Consumer Expenditure Survey

Table 9.7 Housing: Shelter and Utilities: Total spending by income, 2004

(total annual spending on shelter and utilities, by before-tax income group of consumer units (CU), 2004; consumer units and dollars in thousands)

	total consumer units	under $20,000	$20,000–$39,999	$40,000–$49,999	$50,000–$69,999	$70,000–$79,999	$80,000–$99,999	$100,000 or more
Number of consumer units	116,282	28,898	27,297	11,374	18,069	6,461	9,246	14,937
Total spending of all CUs	$5,046,042,273	$545,171,431	$829,854,379	$434,533,092	$862,797,099	$355,432,726	$605,117,322	$1,396,992,933
Housing, total spending	1,618,468,691	205,118,748	282,858,140	140,848,109	265,593,882	112,562,767	188,591,032	420,326,732
SHELTER	930,073,437	119,490,120	162,095,858	80,458,539	152,166,819	65,985,999	108,746,737	241,131,427
Owned dwellings*	619,142,346	44,065,540	79,837,659	49,620,326	106,912,105	52,019,062	88,796,365	197,893,591
Mortgage interest and charges	341,424,883	15,691,435	37,784,516	27,651,445	62,500,852	31,472,565	52,527,636	113,797,684
Mortgage interest	323,888,394	14,797,544	35,825,618	26,528,376	59,435,988	30,029,759	50,138,192	107,134,139
Interest paid, home equity loan	6,712,960	383,384	862,255	571,544	1,341,623	605,977	854,885	2,093,271
Interest paid, home equity line of credit	10,801,435	510,507	1,096,643	539,924	1,712,761	836,829	1,534,559	4,570,274
Property taxes	161,768,030	15,492,346	22,632,184	12,492,519	26,497,285	12,171,490	20,826,985	51,656,030
Maintenance, repairs, insurance, other expenses	115,949,433	12,881,669	19,420,817	9,476,362	17,913,968	8,374,942	15,441,745	32,439,878
Homeowner's insurance	36,599,760	4,075,234	6,591,355	3,292,432	6,512,971	2,656,182	4,555,412	8,916,045
Ground rent	4,662,908	1,589,516	1,792,333	449,728	396,434	93,038	260,090	81,407
Maintenance and repair services	61,702,718	6,254,978	8,786,326	4,458,949	8,391,424	4,661,159	8,887,625	20,262,937
Painting and papering	6,943,198	410,155	528,419	358,736	1,217,128	438,250	767,973	3,222,658
Plumbing and water heating	5,753,633	679,278	988,602	364,537	1,027,584	342,368	836,301	1,514,612
Heat, air conditioning, electrical work	10,404,913	1,311,532	1,599,520	829,733	1,362,945	1,012,245	1,133,837	3,154,545
Roofing and gutters	11,195,631	1,174,481	2,520,717	951,776	1,362,222	640,027	1,076,882	3,469,417
Other repair and maintenance services	20,638,892	2,220,634	2,401,747	1,413,333	2,260,974	1,727,155	3,793,264	6,821,877
Repair, replacement of hard-surface flooring	6,129,224	389,275	675,099	510,010	1,055,591	453,045	1,187,094	1,858,910
Repair of built-in appliances	638,388	69,589	71,818	30,824	104,800	48,134	92,368	220,769
Maintenance and repair materials	8,526,959	465,428	1,289,763	838,264	1,994,456	674,787	1,193,381	2,070,716
Paints, wallpaper, and supplies	1,765,161	96,799	193,751	216,902	341,323	136,004	301,327	479,179
Tools, equipment for painting, wallpapering	189,540	10,354	20,756	23,317	36,680	14,602	32,361	51,533
Plumbing supplies and equipment	673,273	49,050	136,573	70,860	184,484	59,635	86,173	85,888
Electrical supplies, heating and cooling equipment	375,591	9,858	28,806	44,586	81,311	29,075	44,658	138,466
Hard-surface flooring, repair and replacement	1,086,074	138,910	186,744	84,395	221,526	98,143	155,795	222,263
Roofing and gutters	746,530	41,790	247,217	27,298	169,126	21,774	71,934	173,867
Plaster, paneling, siding, windows, doors, screens, awnings	1,513,992	52,486	128,810	123,635	464,012	164,303	239,934	341,161
Patio, walk, fence, driveway, masonry, brick, and stucco materials	182,563	1,800	30,271	23,203	57,821	17,186	15,163	37,193
Miscellaneous supplies and equipment	1,995,399	94,849	316,825	223,954	437,993	134,001	246,129	541,317
Property management and security	4,059,405	426,364	885,831	403,777	554,357	268,455	495,863	1,024,678
Property management	3,319,851	354,538	721,360	321,543	471,059	228,203	397,948	825,120
Management and upkeep services for security	739,554	71,826	164,471	82,234	83,117	40,252	97,915	199,558
Parking	398,847	70,141	75,481	33,326	64,506	21,321	49,466	84,095
Rented dwellings	255,947,147	71,447,942	77,130,969	27,940,458	37,681,635	10,581,244	12,248,176	18,916,366
Rent	247,207,392	67,068,111	75,820,866	27,359,816	36,905,390	10,020,817	12,048,185	17,984,447
Rent as pay	4,195,455	2,645,195	643,319	292,084	299,042	129,155	1,110	185,966
Maintenance, insurance, and other expenses	4,543,138	1,734,735	666,783	288,558	477,022	431,272	198,789	746,103
Tenant's insurance	820,951	173,757	206,560	88,717	156,478	55,565	70,639	69,606
Maintenance and repair services	3,132,637	1,441,012	333,969	137,853	195,868	357,358	107,346	558,943
Maintenance and repair materials	589,550	119,922	126,396	61,988	124,676	18,285	20,804	117,554
Other lodging	54,983,944	3,976,711	5,127,230	2,897,868	7,572,899	3,385,758	7,702,288	24,321,469
Owned vacation homes	15,956,216	659,315	1,427,095	723,955	1,687,825	952,610	2,435,211	8,070,312
Mortgage interest and charges	6,283,879	291,870	218,968	249,204	577,305	389,857	1,117,379	3,512,436
Property taxes	6,687,378	266,232	836,479	334,054	758,356	368,988	880,034	3,242,823
Maintenance, insurance, and other expenses	2,984,959	174,152	371,648	140,696	352,165	193,830	437,798	1,315,053
Housing while attending school	6,712,960	1,552,822	153,103	78,822	481,900	301,858	799,687	3,345,141
Lodging on trips	32,313,605	1,764,573	3,546,902	2,095,091	5,403,173	2,131,290	4,467,390	12,906,016

	total consumer units	under $20,000	$20,000– $39,999	$40,000– $49,999	$50,000– $69,999	$70,000– $79,999	$80,000– $99,999	$100,000 or more
UTILITIES, FUELS, PUBLIC SERVICES	**$340,316,715**	**$52,330,398**	**$69,088,593**	**$33,387,353**	**$59,091,231**	**$22,948,115**	**$36,087,230**	**$67,384,093**
Natural gas	**49,305,894**	**7,227,271**	**10,099,870**	**4,935,406**	**8,137,013**	**3,487,777**	**4,942,912**	**10,475,169**
Electricity	**123,771,724**	**20,594,430**	**25,687,019**	**12,172,455**	**20,886,861**	**7,958,660**	**12,875,425**	**23,597,622**
Fuel oil and other fuels	**14,015,469**	**2,437,954**	**2,906,441**	**1,211,331**	**2,346,621**	**835,537**	**1,440,897**	**2,837,134**
Fuel oil	7,464,142	1,186,149	1,585,682	553,004	1,069,865	497,174	779,715	1,793,187
Bottled and tank gas	5,255,946	923,933	1,000,157	526,730	1,040,232	299,467	580,094	885,167
Wood and other fuels	1,233,752	303,055	298,934	131,483	232,729	38,831	81,087	148,026
Telephone services	**115,144,762**	**17,001,973**	**22,964,353**	**11,194,632**	**20,737,972**	**8,087,557**	**12,665,448**	**22,492,583**
Residential telephone and pay phones	68,874,991	11,889,386	14,790,672	6,972,831	11,833,388	4,481,027	6,748,008	12,159,764
Cellular phone service	43,999,946	4,633,058	7,604,976	3,983,744	8,468,760	3,526,866	5,698,032	10,084,417
Pager service	117,445	9,206	31,046	11,147	26,561	1,938	18,215	18,970
Phone cards	2,152,380	470,367	537,932	226,911	409,263	77,790	201,193	229,582
Water and other public services	**38,078,867**	**5,068,842**	**7,430,778**	**3,873,643**	**6,982,765**	**2,578,585**	**4,162,457**	**7,981,437**
Water and sewerage maintenance	28,203,036	3,816,191	5,505,574	2,876,257	5,161,410	1,864,451	3,096,116	5,883,087
Trash and garbage collection	9,624,661	1,239,280	1,889,839	984,533	1,761,005	701,277	1,022,515	2,026,055
Septic tank cleaning	251,169	15,989	35,365	12,739	60,350	12,793	43,826	72,295

* See Appendix B for information about mortgage principal reduction.
Note: Numbers may not add to total because of rounding and missing subcategories.
Source: Calculations by New Strategist based on the 2004 Consumer Expenditure Survey

Table 9.8 Housing: Shelter and Utilities: Market shares by income, 2004

(percentage of total annual spending on shelter and utilities accounted for by before-tax income group of consumer units, 2004)

	total consumer units	under $20,000	$20,000–$39,999	$40,000–$49,999	$50,000–$69,999	$70,000–$79,999	$80,000–$99,999	$100,000 or more
Share of total consumer units	100.0%	24.9%	23.5%	9.8%	15.5%	5.6%	8.0%	12.8%
Share of total before-tax income	100.0	5.0	12.7	8.0	16.9	7.6	13.0	36.8
Share of total spending	100.0	10.8	16.4	8.6	17.1	7.0	12.0	27.7
Share of housing spending	100.0	12.7	17.5	8.7	16.4	7.0	11.7	26.0
SHELTER	**100.0**	**12.8**	**17.4**	**8.7**	**16.4**	**7.1**	**11.7**	**25.9**
Owned dwellings*	100.0	7.1	12.9	8.0	17.3	8.4	14.3	32.0
Mortgage interest and charges	100.0	4.6	11.1	8.1	18.3	9.2	15.4	33.3
Mortgage interest	100.0	4.6	11.1	8.2	18.4	9.3	15.5	33.1
Interest paid, home equity loan	100.0	5.7	12.8	8.5	20.0	9.0	12.7	31.2
Interest paid, home equity line of credit	100.0	4.7	10.2	5.0	15.9	7.7	14.2	42.3
Property taxes	100.0	9.6	14.0	7.7	16.4	7.5	12.9	31.9
Maintenance, repairs, insurance, other expenses	100.0	11.1	16.7	8.2	15.4	7.2	13.3	28.0
Homeowner's insurance	100.0	11.1	18.0	9.0	17.8	7.3	12.4	24.4
Ground rent	100.0	34.1	38.4	9.6	8.5	2.0	5.6	1.7
Maintenance and repair services	100.0	10.1	14.2	7.2	13.6	7.6	14.4	32.8
Painting and papering	100.0	5.9	7.6	5.2	17.5	6.3	11.1	46.4
Plumbing and water heating	100.0	11.8	17.2	6.3	17.9	6.0	14.5	26.3
Heat, air conditioning, electrical work	100.0	12.6	15.4	8.0	13.1	9.7	10.9	30.3
Roofing and gutters	100.0	10.5	22.5	8.5	12.2	5.7	9.6	31.0
Other repair and maintenance services	100.0	10.8	11.6	6.8	11.0	8.4	18.4	33.1
Repair, replacement of hard-surface flooring	100.0	6.4	11.0	8.3	17.2	7.4	19.4	30.3
Repair of built-in appliances	100.0	10.9	11.2	4.8	16.4	7.5	14.5	34.6
Maintenance and repair materials	100.0	5.5	15.1	9.8	23.4	7.9	14.0	24.3
Paints, wallpaper, and supplies	100.0	5.5	11.0	12.3	19.3	7.7	17.1	27.1
Tools, equipment for painting, wallpapering	100.0	5.5	11.0	12.3	19.4	7.7	17.1	27.2
Plumbing supplies and equipment	100.0	7.3	20.3	10.5	27.4	8.9	12.8	12.8
Electrical supplies, heating and cooling equipment	100.0	2.6	7.7	11.9	21.6	7.7	11.9	36.9
Hard-surface flooring, repair and replacement	100.0	12.8	17.2	7.8	20.4	9.0	14.3	20.5
Roofing and gutters	100.0	5.6	33.1	3.7	22.7	2.9	9.6	23.3
Plaster, paneling, siding, windows, doors, screens, awnings	100.0	3.5	8.5	8.2	30.6	10.9	15.8	22.5
Patio, walk, fence, driveway, masonry, brick, and stucco materials	100.0	1.0	16.6	12.7	31.7	9.4	8.3	20.4
Miscellaneous supplies and equipment	100.0	4.8	15.9	11.2	22.0	6.7	12.3	27.1
Property management and security	100.0	10.5	21.8	9.9	13.7	6.6	12.2	25.2
Property management	100.0	10.7	21.7	9.7	14.2	6.9	12.0	24.9
Management and upkeep services for security	100.0	9.7	22.2	11.1	11.2	5.4	13.2	27.0
Parking	100.0	17.6	18.9	8.4	16.2	5.3	12.4	21.1
Rented dwellings	**100.0**	**27.9**	**30.1**	**10.9**	**14.7**	**4.1**	**4.8**	**7.4**
Rent	100.0	27.1	30.7	11.1	14.9	4.1	4.9	7.3
Rent as pay	100.0	63.0	15.3	7.0	7.1	3.1	0.0	4.4
Maintenance, insurance, and other expenses	100.0	38.2	14.7	6.4	10.5	9.5	4.4	16.4
Tenant's insurance	100.0	21.2	25.2	10.8	19.1	6.8	8.6	8.5
Maintenance and repair services	100.0	46.0	10.7	4.4	6.3	11.4	3.4	17.8
Maintenance and repair materials	100.0	20.3	21.4	10.5	21.1	3.1	3.5	19.9
Other lodging	**100.0**	**7.2**	**9.3**	**5.3**	**13.8**	**6.2**	**14.0**	**44.2**
Owned vacation homes	100.0	4.1	8.9	4.5	10.6	6.0	15.3	50.6
Mortgage interest and charges	100.0	4.6	3.5	4.0	9.2	6.2	17.8	55.9
Property taxes	100.0	4.0	12.5	5.0	11.3	5.5	13.2	48.5
Maintenance, insurance, and other expenses	100.0	5.8	12.5	4.7	11.8	6.5	14.7	44.1
Housing while attending school	100.0	23.1	2.3	1.2	7.2	4.5	11.9	49.8
Lodging on trips	100.0	5.5	11.0	6.5	16.7	6.6	13.8	39.9

	total consumer units	under $20,000	$20,000– $39,999	$40,000– $49,999	$50,000– $69,999	$70,000– $79,999	$80,000– $99,999	$100,000 or more
UTILITIES, FUELS, AND PUBLIC SERVICES	**100.0%**	**15.4%**	**20.3%**	**9.8%**	**17.4%**	**6.7%**	**10.6%**	**19.8%**
Natural gas	**100.0**	**14.7**	**20.5**	**10.0**	**16.5**	**7.1**	**10.0**	**21.2**
Electricity	**100.0**	**16.6**	**20.8**	**9.8**	**16.9**	**6.4**	**10.4**	**19.1**
Fuel oil and other fuels	**100.0**	**17.4**	**20.7**	**8.6**	**16.7**	**6.0**	**10.3**	**20.2**
Fuel oil	100.0	15.9	21.2	7.4	14.3	6.7	10.4	24.0
Bottled and tank gas	100.0	17.6	19.0	10.0	19.8	5.7	11.0	16.8
Wood and other fuels	100.0	24.6	24.2	10.7	18.9	3.1	6.6	12.0
Telephone services	**100.0**	**14.8**	**19.9**	**9.7**	**18.0**	**7.0**	**11.0**	**19.5**
Residential telephone and pay phones	100.0	17.3	21.5	10.1	17.2	6.5	9.8	17.7
Cellular phone service	100.0	10.5	17.3	9.1	19.2	8.0	13.0	22.9
Pager service	100.0	7.8	26.4	9.5	22.6	1.7	15.5	16.2
Phone cards	100.0	21.9	25.0	10.5	19.0	3.6	9.3	10.7
Water and other public services	**100.0**	**13.3**	**19.5**	**10.2**	**18.3**	**6.8**	**10.9**	**21.0**
Water and sewerage maintenance	100.0	13.5	19.5	10.2	18.3	6.6	11.0	20.9
Trash and garbage collection	100.0	12.9	19.6	10.2	18.3	7.3	10.6	21.1
Septic tank cleaning	100.0	6.4	14.1	5.1	24.0	5.1	17.4	28.8

* See Appendix B for information about mortgage principal reduction.
Note: Numbers may not add to total because of rounding.
Source: Calculations by New Strategist based on the 2004 Consumer Expenditure Survey

Table 9.9 Housing: Shelter and Utilities: Average spending by high-income consumer units, 2004

(average annual spending on shelter and utilities, by before-tax income of high-income consumer units (CU), 2004)

	total consumer units	$100,000 or more	$100,000–$119,999	$120,000–$149,999	$150,000 or more
Number of consumer units (in 000s)	116,282	14,937	5,625	4,245	5,067
Average number of persons per CU	2.5	3.2	3.1	3.3	3.2
Average before-tax income of CU	$54,453.00	$155,901.00	$108,751.00	$132,292.00	$228,021.00
Average spending of CU, total	43,394.87	93,525.67	75,213.14	87,298.57	119,448.79
Housing, average spending	**13,918.48**	**28,139.97**	**22,273.31**	**26,339.36**	**36,246.25**
SHELTER	**7,998.43**	**16,143.23**	**12,871.08**	**14,868.77**	**20,843.27**
Owned dwellings*	**5,324.49**	**13,248.55**	**10,421.42**	**12,526.80**	**16,991.53**
Mortgage interest and charges	2,936.18	7,618.51	6,138.55	7,306.39	9,522.86
Mortgage interest	2,785.37	7,172.40	5,808.99	6,861.47	8,946.36
Interest paid, home equity loan	57.73	140.14	118.85	131.12	171.33
Interest paid, home equity line of credit	92.89	305.97	210.71	313.79	405.17
Property taxes	1,391.17	3,458.26	2,570.42	3,172.62	4,683.14
Maintenance, repairs, insurance, other expenses	997.14	2,171.78	1,712.45	2,047.79	2,785.54
Homeowner's insurance	314.75	596.91	480.88	555.57	760.35
Ground rent	40.10	5.45	0.02	16.29	2.40
Maintenance and repair services	530.63	1,356.56	1,061.22	1,294.53	1,736.37
Painting and papering	59.71	215.75	99.66	206.75	352.17
Plumbing and water heating	49.48	101.40	92.02	81.38	128.59
Heat, air conditioning, electrical work	89.48	211.19	133.03	213.02	296.42
Roofing and gutters	96.28	232.27	252.33	189.17	246.10
Other repair and maintenance services	177.49	456.71	359.12	453.08	568.08
Repair, replacement of hard-surface flooring	52.71	124.45	115.92	136.60	123.75
Repair of built-in appliances	5.49	14.78	9.13	14.52	21.27
Maintenance and repair materials	73.33	138.63	109.92	135.01	173.54
Paints, wallpaper, and supplies	15.18	32.08	25.99	33.82	37.37
Tools, equipment for painting, wallpapering	1.63	3.45	2.79	3.63	4.01
Plumbing supplies and equipment	5.79	5.75	5.86	5.55	5.80
Electrical supplies, heating and cooling equipment	3.23	9.27	7.01	11.76	9.68
Hard-surface flooring, repair and replacement	9.34	14.88	10.77	14.94	19.40
Roofing and gutters	6.42	11.64	14.52	5.08	13.94
Plaster, paneling, siding, windows, doors, screens, awnings	13.02	22.84	13.61	29.64	27.38
Patio, walk, fence, driveway, masonry, brick, and stucco materials	1.57	2.49	1.40	3.73	2.67
Miscellaneous supplies and equipment	17.16	36.24	27.97	26.86	53.28
Property management and security	34.91	68.60	51.55	42.86	109.08
Property management	28.55	55.24	39.56	37.41	87.58
Management and upkeep services for security	6.36	13.36	11.99	5.45	21.50
Parking	3.43	5.63	8.87	3.53	3.81
Rented dwellings	**2,201.09**	**1,266.41**	**1,496.12**	**1,018.86**	**1,218.81**
Rent	2,125.93	1,204.02	1,439.08	969.82	1,139.28
Rent as pay	36.08	12.45	3.99	17.37	17.71
Maintenance, insurance, and other expenses	39.07	49.95	53.05	31.66	61.82
Tenant's insurance	7.06	4.66	6.11	4.32	3.33
Maintenance and repair services	26.94	37.42	38.35	12.99	56.84
Maintenance and repair materials	5.07	7.87	8.59	14.35	1.65
Other lodging	**472.85**	**1,628.27**	**953.53**	**1,323.11**	**2,632.92**
Owned vacation homes	137.22	540.29	301.04	373.58	945.53
Mortgage interest and charges	54.04	235.15	155.16	160.42	386.54
Property taxes	57.51	217.10	116.30	128.69	403.07
Maintenance, insurance, and other expenses	25.67	88.04	29.58	84.47	155.92
Housing while attending school	57.73	223.95	69.17	199.19	416.52
Lodging on trips	277.89	864.03	583.32	750.35	1,270.87

	total consumer units	$100,000 or more	$100,000– $119,999	$120,000– $149,999	$150,000 or more
UTILITIES, FUELS, AND PUBLIC SERVICES	**$2,926.65**	**$4,511.22**	**$3,976.74**	**$4,446.16**	**$5,159.03**
Natural gas	**424.02**	**701.29**	**586.58**	**728.98**	**805.42**
Electricity	**1,064.41**	**1,579.81**	**1,343.48**	**1,541.17**	**1,874.53**
Fuel oil and other fuels	**120.53**	**189.94**	**167.17**	**152.75**	**246.37**
Fuel oil	64.19	120.05	102.45	79.77	173.34
Bottled and tank gas	45.20	59.26	54.28	62.30	62.23
Wood and other fuels	10.61	9.91	10.45	8.12	10.80
Telephone services	**990.22**	**1,505.83**	**1,404.39**	**1,493.51**	**1,628.77**
Residential telephone and pay phones	592.31	814.07	729.10	797.57	922.21
Cellular phone service	378.39	675.13	656.23	680.12	691.93
Pager service	1.01	1.27	2.34	–	1.15
Phone cards	18.51	15.37	16.72	15.82	13.49
Water and other public services	**327.47**	**534.34**	**475.11**	**529.75**	**603.94**
Water and sewerage maintenance	242.54	393.86	348.09	390.90	447.15
Trash and garbage collection	82.77	135.64	123.29	133.57	151.08
Septic tank cleaning	2.16	4.84	3.73	5.28	5.71

* See Appendix B for information about mortgage principal reduction.
Note: Subcategories may not add to total because some are not shown. "–" means sample is too small to make a reliable estimate.
Source: Bureau of Labor Statistics, unpublished tables from the 2004 Consumer Expenditure Survey; calculations by New Strategist

Table 9.10 Housing: Shelter and Utilities: Indexed spending by high-income consumer units, 2004

(indexed average annual spending of high-income consumer units (CU) on shelter and utilities, by before-tax income of consumer unit, 2004; index definition: an index of 100 is the average for all consumer units; an index of 132 means that spending by consumer units in that group is 32 percent above the average for all consumer units; an index of 68 indicates spending that is 32 percent below the average for all consumer units)

	total consumer units	$100,000 or more	$100,000– $119,999	$120,000– $149,999	$150,000 or more
Average spending of CU, total	$43,395	$93,526	$75,213	$87,299	$119,449
Average spending of CU, index	100	216	173	201	275
Housing, spending index	**100**	**202**	**160**	**189**	**260**
SHELTER	**100**	**202**	**161**	**186**	**261**
Owned dwellings*	**100**	**249**	**196**	**235**	**319**
Mortgage interest and charges	100	259	209	249	324
Mortgage interest	100	258	209	246	321
Interest paid, home equity loan	100	243	206	227	297
Interest paid, home equity line of credit	100	329	227	338	436
Property taxes	100	249	185	228	337
Maintenance, repairs, insurance, other expenses	100	218	172	205	279
Homeowner's insurance	100	190	153	177	242
Ground rent	100	14	0	41	6
Maintenance and repair services	100	256	200	244	327
Painting and papering	100	361	167	346	590
Plumbing and water heating	100	205	186	164	260
Heat, air conditioning, electrical work	100	236	149	238	331
Roofing and gutters	100	241	262	196	256
Other repair and maintenance services	100	257	202	255	320
Repair, replacement of hard-surface flooring	100	236	220	259	235
Repair of built-in appliances	100	269	166	264	387
Maintenance and repair materials	100	189	150	184	237
Paints, wallpaper, and supplies	100	211	171	223	246
Tools, equipment for painting, wallpapering	100	212	171	223	246
Plumbing supplies and equipment	100	99	101	96	100
Electrical supplies, heating and cooling equipment	100	287	217	364	300
Hard-surface flooring, repair and replacement	100	159	115	160	208
Roofing and gutters	100	181	226	79	217
Plaster, paneling, siding, windows, doors, screens, awnings	100	175	105	228	210
Patio, walk, fence, driveway, masonry, brick, and stucco materials	100	159	89	238	170
Miscellaneous supplies and equipment	100	211	163	157	310
Property management and security	100	197	148	123	312
Property management	100	193	139	131	307
Management and upkeep services for security	100	210	189	86	338
Parking	100	164	259	103	111
Rented dwellings	**100**	**58**	**68**	**46**	**55**
Rent	100	57	68	46	54
Rent as pay	100	35	11	48	49
Maintenance, insurance, and other expenses	100	128	136	81	158
Tenant's insurance	100	66	87	61	47
Maintenance and repair services	100	139	142	48	211
Maintenance and repair materials	100	155	169	283	33
Other lodging	**100**	**344**	**202**	**280**	**557**
Owned vacation homes	100	394	219	272	689
Mortgage interest and charges	100	435	287	297	715
Property taxes	100	377	202	224	701
Maintenance, insurance, and other expenses	100	343	115	329	607
Housing while attending school	100	388	120	345	721
Lodging on trips	100	311	210	270	457

	total consumer units	$100,000 or more	$100,000– $119,999	$120,000– $149,999	$150,000 or more
UTILITIES, FUELS, AND PUBLIC SERVICES	100	154	136	152	176
Natural gas	100	165	138	172	190
Electricity	100	148	126	145	176
Fuel oil and other fuels	100	158	139	127	204
Fuel oil	100	187	160	124	270
Bottled and tank gas	100	131	120	138	138
Wood and other fuels	100	93	98	77	102
Telephone services	100	152	142	151	164
Residential telephone and pay phones	100	137	123	135	156
Cellular phone service	100	178	173	180	183
Pager service	100	126	232	–	114
Phone cards	100	83	90	85	73
Water and other public services	100	163	145	162	184
Water and sewerage maintenance	100	162	144	161	184
Trash and garbage collection	100	164	149	161	183
Septic tank cleaning	100	224	173	244	264

* See Appendix B for information about mortgage principal reduction.
Note: "–" means sample is too small to make a reliable estimate.
Source: Calculations by New Strategist based on the 2004 Consumer Expenditure Survey

Table 9.11 Housing: Shelter and Utilities: Total spending by high-income consumer units, 2004

(total annual spending on shelter and utilities, by before-tax income group of high-income consumer units (CU), 2004; consumer units and dollars in thousands)

	total consumer units	$100,000 or more	$100,000– $119,999	$120,000– $149,999	$150,000 or more
Number of consumer units	116,282	14,937	5,625	4,245	5,067
Total spending of all CUs	$5,046,042,273	$1,396,992,933	$423,073,913	$370,582,430	$605,247,019
Housing, total spending	1,618,468,691	420,326,732	125,287,369	111,810,583	183,659,749
SHELTER	930,073,437	241,131,427	72,399,825	63,117,929	105,612,849
Owned dwellings*	619,142,346	197,893,591	58,620,488	53,176,266	86,096,083
Mortgage interest and charges	341,424,883	113,797,684	34,529,344	31,015,626	48,252,332
Mortgage interest	323,888,394	107,134,139	32,675,569	29,126,940	45,331,206
Interest paid, home equity loan	6,712,960	2,093,271	668,531	556,604	868,129
Interest paid, home equity line of credit	10,801,435	4,570,274	1,185,244	1,332,039	2,052,996
Property taxes	161,768,030	51,656,030	14,458,613	13,467,772	23,729,470
Maintenance, repairs, insurance, other expenses	115,949,433	32,439,878	9,632,531	8,692,869	14,114,331
Homeowner's insurance	36,599,760	8,916,045	2,704,950	2,358,395	3,852,693
Ground rent	4,662,908	81,407	113	69,151	12,161
Maintenance and repair services	61,702,718	20,262,937	5,969,363	5,495,280	8,798,187
Painting and papering	6,943,198	3,222,658	560,588	877,654	1,784,445
Plumbing and water heating	5,753,633	1,514,612	517,613	345,458	651,566
Heat, air conditioning, electrical work	10,404,913	3,154,545	748,294	904,270	1,501,960
Roofing and gutters	11,195,631	3,469,417	1,419,356	803,027	1,246,989
Other repair and maintenance services	20,638,892	6,821,877	2,020,050	1,923,325	2,878,461
Repair, replacement of hard-surface flooring	6,129,224	1,858,910	652,050	579,867	627,041
Repair of built-in appliances	638,388	220,769	51,356	61,637	107,775
Maintenance and repair materials	8,526,959	2,070,716	618,300	573,117	879,327
Paints, wallpaper, and supplies	1,765,161	479,179	146,194	143,566	189,354
Tools, equipment for painting, wallpapering	189,540	51,533	15,694	15,409	20,319
Plumbing supplies and equipment	673,273	85,888	32,963	23,560	29,389
Electrical supplies, heating and cooling equipment	375,591	138,466	39,431	49,921	49,049
Hard-surface flooring, repair and replacement	1,086,074	222,263	60,581	63,420	98,300
Roofing and gutters	746,530	173,867	81,675	21,565	70,634
Plaster, paneling, siding, windows, doors, screens, awnings	1,513,992	341,161	76,556	125,822	138,734
Patio, walk, fence, driveway, masonry, brick, and stucco materials	182,563	37,193	7,875	15,834	13,529
Miscellaneous supplies and equipment	1,995,399	541,317	157,331	114,021	269,970
Property management and security	4,059,405	1,024,678	289,969	181,941	552,708
Property management	3,319,851	825,120	222,525	158,805	443,768
Management and upkeep services for security	739,554	199,558	67,444	23,135	108,941
Parking	398,847	84,095	49,894	14,985	19,305
Rented dwellings	255,947,147	18,916,366	8,415,675	4,325,061	6,175,710
Rent	247,207,392	17,984,447	8,094,825	4,116,886	5,772,732
Rent as pay	4,195,455	185,966	22,444	73,736	89,737
Maintenance, insurance, and other expenses	4,543,138	746,103	298,406	134,397	313,242
Tenant's insurance	820,951	69,606	34,369	18,338	16,873
Maintenance and repair services	3,132,637	558,943	215,719	55,143	288,008
Maintenance and repair materials	589,550	117,554	48,319	60,916	8,361
Other lodging	54,983,944	24,321,469	5,363,606	5,616,602	13,341,006
Owned vacation homes	15,956,216	8,070,312	1,693,350	1,585,847	4,791,001
Mortgage interest and charges	6,283,879	3,512,436	872,775	680,983	1,958,598
Property taxes	6,687,378	3,242,823	654,188	546,289	2,042,356
Maintenance, insurance, and other expenses	2,984,959	1,315,053	166,388	358,575	790,047
Housing while attending school	6,712,960	3,345,141	389,081	845,562	2,110,507
Lodging on trips	32,313,605	12,906,016	3,281,175	3,185,236	6,439,498

	total consumer units	$100,000 or more	$100,000– $119,999	$120,000– $149,999	$150,000 or more
UTILITIES, FUELS, AND PUBLIC SERVICES	**$340,316,715**	**$67,384,093**	**$22,369,163**	**$18,873,949**	**$26,140,805**
Natural gas	**49,305,894**	**10,475,169**	**3,299,513**	**3,094,520**	**4,081,063**
Electricity	**123,771,724**	**23,597,622**	**7,557,075**	**6,542,267**	**9,498,244**
Fuel oil and other fuels	**14,015,469**	**2,837,134**	**940,331**	**648,424**	**1,248,357**
Fuel oil	7,464,142	1,793,187	576,281	338,624	878,314
Bottled and tank gas	5,255,946	885,167	305,325	264,464	315,319
Wood and other fuels	1,233,752	148,026	58,781	34,469	54,724
Telephone services	**115,144,762**	**22,492,583**	**7,899,694**	**6,339,950**	**8,252,978**
Residential telephone and pay phones	68,874,991	12,159,764	4,101,188	3,385,685	4,672,838
Cellular phone service	43,999,946	10,084,417	3,691,294	2,887,109	3,506,009
Pager service	117,445	18,970	13,163	–	5,827
Phone cards	2,152,380	229,582	94,050	67,156	68,354
Water and other public services	**38,078,867**	**7,981,437**	**2,672,494**	**2,248,789**	**3,060,164**
Water and sewerage maintenance	28,203,036	5,883,087	1,958,006	1,659,371	2,265,709
Trash and garbage collection	9,624,661	2,026,055	693,506	567,005	765,522
Septic tank cleaning	251,169	72,295	20,981	22,414	28,933

* See Appendix B for information about mortgage principal reduction.
Note: Numbers may not add to total because of rounding and missing subcategories. "–" means sample is too small to make a reliable estimate.
Source: Calculations by New Strategist based on the 2004 Consumer Expenditure Survey

Table 9.12 Housing: Shelter and Utilities: Market shares by high-income consumer units, 2004

(percentage of total annual spending on shelter and utilities accounted for by before-tax income group of high-income consumer units, 2004)

	total consumer units	$100,000 or more	$100,000–$119,999	$120,000–$149,999	$150,000 or more
Share of total consumer units	100.0%	12.8%	4.8%	3.7%	4.4%
Share of total before-tax income	100.0	36.8	9.7	8.9	18.2
Share of total spending	100.0	27.7	8.4	7.3	12.0
Share of housing spending	100.0	26.0	7.7	6.9	11.3
SHELTER	100.0	25.9	7.8	6.8	11.4
Owned dwellings*	100.0	32.0	9.5	8.6	13.9
Mortgage interest and charges	100.0	33.3	10.1	9.1	14.1
Mortgage interest	100.0	33.1	10.1	9.0	14.0
Interest paid, home equity loan	100.0	31.2	10.0	8.3	12.9
Interest paid, home equity line of credit	100.0	42.3	11.0	12.3	19.0
Property taxes	100.0	31.9	8.9	8.3	14.7
Maintenance, repairs, insurance, other expenses	100.0	28.0	8.3	7.5	12.2
Homeowner's insurance	100.0	24.4	7.4	6.4	10.5
Ground rent	100.0	1.7	0.0	1.5	0.3
Maintenance and repair services	100.0	32.8	9.7	8.9	14.3
Painting and papering	100.0	46.4	8.1	12.6	25.7
Plumbing and water heating	100.0	26.3	9.0	6.0	11.3
Heat, air conditioning, electrical work	100.0	30.3	7.2	8.7	14.4
Roofing and gutters	100.0	31.0	12.7	7.2	11.1
Other repair and maintenance services	100.0	33.1	9.8	9.3	13.9
Repair, replacement of hard-surface flooring	100.0	30.3	10.6	9.5	10.2
Repair of built-in appliances	100.0	34.6	8.0	9.7	16.9
Maintenance and repair materials	100.0	24.3	7.3	6.7	10.3
Paints, wallpaper, and supplies	100.0	27.1	8.3	8.1	10.7
Tools, equipment for painting, wallpapering	100.0	27.2	8.3	8.1	10.7
Plumbing supplies and equipment	100.0	12.8	4.9	3.5	4.4
Electrical supplies, heating and cooling equipment	100.0	36.9	10.5	13.3	13.1
Hard-surface flooring, repair and replacement	100.0	20.5	5.6	5.8	9.1
Roofing and gutters	100.0	23.3	10.9	2.9	9.5
Plaster, paneling, siding, windows, doors, screens, awnings	100.0	22.5	5.1	8.3	9.2
Patio, walk, fence, driveway, masonry, brick, and stucco materials	100.0	20.4	4.3	8.7	7.4
Miscellaneous supplies and equipment	100.0	27.1	7.9	5.7	13.5
Property management and security	100.0	25.2	7.1	4.5	13.6
Property management	100.0	24.9	6.7	4.8	13.4
Management and upkeep services for security	100.0	27.0	9.1	3.1	14.7
Parking	100.0	21.1	12.5	3.8	4.8
Rented dwellings	100.0	7.4	3.3	1.7	2.4
Rent	100.0	7.3	3.3	1.7	2.3
Rent as pay	100.0	4.4	0.5	1.8	2.1
Maintenance, insurance, and other expenses	100.0	16.4	6.6	3.0	6.9
Tenant's insurance	100.0	8.5	4.2	2.2	2.1
Maintenance and repair services	100.0	17.8	6.9	1.8	9.2
Maintenance and repair materials	100.0	19.9	8.2	10.3	1.4
Other lodging	100.0	44.2	9.8	10.2	24.3
Owned vacation homes	100.0	50.6	10.6	9.9	30.0
Mortgage interest and charges	100.0	55.9	13.9	10.8	31.2
Property taxes	100.0	48.5	9.8	8.2	30.5
Maintenance, insurance, and other expenses	100.0	44.1	5.6	12.0	26.5
Housing while attending school	100.0	49.8	5.8	12.6	31.4
Lodging on trips	100.0	39.9	10.2	9.9	19.9

	total consumer units	$100,000 or more	$100,000– $119,999	$120,000– $149,999	$150,000 or more
UTILITIES, FUELS, AND PUBLIC SERVICES	**100.0%**	**19.8%**	**6.6%**	**5.5%**	**7.7%**
Natural gas	**100.0**	**21.2**	**6.7**	**6.3**	**8.3**
Electricity	**100.0**	**19.1**	**6.1**	**5.3**	**7.7**
Fuel oil and other fuels	**100.0**	**20.2**	**6.7**	**4.6**	**8.9**
Fuel oil	100.0	24.0	7.7	4.5	11.8
Bottled and tank gas	100.0	16.8	5.8	5.0	6.0
Wood and other fuels	100.0	12.0	4.8	2.8	4.4
Telephone services	**100.0**	**19.5**	**6.9**	**5.5**	**7.2**
Residential telephone and pay phones	100.0	17.7	6.0	4.9	6.8
Cellular phone service	100.0	22.9	8.4	6.6	8.0
Pager service	100.0	16.2	11.2	–	5.0
Phone cards	100.0	10.7	4.4	3.1	3.2
Water and other public services	**100.0**	**21.0**	**7.0**	**5.9**	**8.0**
Water and sewerage maintenance	100.0	20.9	6.9	5.9	8.0
Trash and garbage collection	100.0	21.1	7.2	5.9	8.0
Septic tank cleaning	100.0	28.8	8.4	8.9	11.5

* See Appendix B for information about mortgage principal reduction.

Note: Numbers may not add to total because of rounding. "–" means sample is too small to make a reliable estimate.

Source: Calculations by New Strategist based on the 2004 Consumer Expenditure Survey

Table 9.13 Housing: Shelter and Utilities: Average spending by household type, 2004

(average annual spending of consumer units (CU) on shelter and utilities, by type of consumer unit, 2004)

	total married couples	married couples, no children	married couples with children				single parent, at least one child <18	single person
			total	oldest child under 6	oldest child 6 to 17	oldest child 18 or older		
Number of consumer units (in 000s)	59,797	25,585	29,279	5,604	15,376	8,300	6,892	33,686
Average number of persons per CU	3.2	2.0	3.9	3.5	4.1	3.9	2.9	1.0
Average before-tax income of CU	$73,001.00	$64,434.00	$79,764.00	$75,293.00	$78,508.00	$85,109.00	$31,055.00	$28,143.00
Average spending of CU, total	55,606.57	49,690.43	60,660.88	55,981.04	60,577.88	64,161.69	32,824.46	25,423.35
Housing, average spending	17,004.54	14,706.43	18,912.20	21,045.02	18,900.14	17,502.90	12,029.78	9,244.07
SHELTER	**9,427.20**	**8,030.78**	**10,657.95**	**11,944.05**	**10,838.46**	**9,455.22**	**7,043.09**	**5,840.90**
Owned dwellings*	**7,291.33**	**5,946.97**	**8,472.50**	**9,253.82**	**8,643.74**	**7,627.76**	**3,314.06**	**2,916.43**
Mortgage interest and charges	4,152.18	2,793.44	5,315.02	6,243.25	5,432.70	4,470.28	2,037.29	1,360.14
Mortgage interest	3,936.22	2,619.41	5,071.42	5,991.98	5,216.89	4,180.38	1,947.15	1,297.31
Interest paid, home equity loan	80.40	61.98	91.61	87.40	86.95	103.08	31.71	23.64
Interest paid, home equity line of credit	135.36	111.98	151.63	163.87	128.17	186.83	58.43	38.90
Property taxes	1,884.56	1,813.88	1,957.66	1,906.62	1,960.57	1,986.72	729.17	831.68
Maintenance, repairs, insurance, other expenses	1,254.59	1,339.66	1,199.83	1,103.95	1,250.47	1,170.76	547.59	724.61
Homeowner's insurance	416.56	439.20	404.42	317.56	411.41	450.11	154.46	206.62
Ground rent	36.44	42.57	25.92	14.56	32.26	21.86	44.59	48.95
Maintenance and repair services	665.25	718.81	630.13	631.14	683.25	531.04	310.52	383.11
Painting and papering	76.97	83.59	70.04	99.42	67.00	55.83	48.62	38.47
Plumbing and water heating	58.87	65.58	56.32	51.92	45.69	78.97	27.76	40.06
Heat, air conditioning, electrical work	105.98	102.39	109.74	149.29	109.87	82.80	48.21	73.45
Roofing and gutters	114.13	108.85	118.97	151.74	119.35	96.12	45.06	72.32
Other repair and maintenance services	227.73	272.40	192.04	145.39	236.55	141.10	103.39	127.59
Repair, replacement of hard-surface flooring	73.53	75.29	76.58	29.03	97.58	69.78	34.52	28.45
Repair of built-in appliances	8.04	10.71	6.45	4.35	7.21	6.44	2.96	2.78
Maintenance and repair materials	99.16	80.23	117.49	107.60	106.23	145.02	26.25	33.99
Paints, wallpaper, and supplies	19.18	15.66	22.35	20.05	22.64	23.35	9.24	7.28
Tools, equipment for painting, wallpapering	2.06	1.68	2.40	2.15	2.43	2.51	0.99	0.78
Plumbing supplies and equipment	7.19	6.33	8.81	7.56	8.71	9.84	2.75	4.16
Electrical supplies, heating and cooling equipment	4.31	4.17	4.81	7.32	2.24	7.89	1.19	2.16
Hard-surface flooring, repair and replacement	12.47	7.25	18.46	28.07	11.92	24.08	1.99	4.98
Roofing and gutters	6.72	5.59	7.93	14.72	7.24	4.61	2.31	1.59
Plaster, paneling, siding, windows, doors, screens, awnings	18.68	13.43	23.13	5.17	26.71	28.63	1.45	6.26
Patio, walk, fence, driveway, masonry, brick, and stucco materials	2.05	1.54	2.68	1.20	1.55	5.78	0.16	0.45
Miscellaneous supplies and equipment	26.49	24.58	26.92	21.34	22.78	38.34	6.17	6.33
Property management and security	34.00	53.44	20.25	30.36	16.01	21.28	10.81	46.63
Property management	26.79	41.49	16.39	24.72	12.92	17.20	8.89	39.30
Management and upkeep services for security	7.21	11.94	3.86	5.64	3.09	4.09	1.92	7.32
Parking	3.17	5.40	1.62	2.73	1.31	1.44	0.96	5.32
Rented dwellings	**1,463.06**	**1,307.50**	**1,557.78**	**2,333.63**	**1,544.70**	**1,058.19**	**3,509.91**	**2,659.25**
Rent	1,424.08	1,251.41	1,531.07	2,286.36	1,522.86	1,036.34	3,316.11	2,545.21
Rent as pay	8.89	9.95	9.46	18.17	11.39	–	164.86	51.26
Maintenance, insurance, and other expenses	30.09	46.14	17.25	29.10	10.45	21.85	28.94	62.78
Tenant's insurance	5.74	7.43	4.97	7.14	3.87	5.56	6.44	9.13
Maintenance and repair services	20.38	32.57	9.76	19.95	3.77	14.00	16.72	49.87
Maintenance and repair materials	3.96	6.13	2.52	2.02	2.82	2.29	5.78	3.78
Other lodging	**672.80**	**776.31**	**627.66**	**356.60**	**650.02**	**769.27**	**219.12**	**265.22**
Owned vacation homes	193.20	239.63	162.13	104.44	163.99	197.64	68.86	77.37
Mortgage interest and charges	76.78	86.55	72.81	61.85	61.91	100.41	16.82	29.28
Property taxes	80.22	94.93	69.01	29.56	84.58	66.78	43.66	34.03
Maintenance, insurance, and other expenses	36.19	58.15	20.31	13.03	17.50	30.45	8.38	14.07
Housing while attending school	75.44	70.02	87.19	5.76	71.04	172.07	8.93	61.14
Lodging on trips	404.16	466.66	378.34	246.39	414.98	399.56	141.34	126.70

	total married couples	married couples, no children	married couples with children				single parent, at least one child <18	single person
			total	oldest child under 6	oldest child 6 to 17	oldest child 18 or older		
UTILITIES, FUELS, AND PUBLIC SERVICES	**$3,571.88**	**$3,176.15**	**$3,838.58**	**$3,325.38**	**$3,809.18**	**$4,239.53**	**$2,754.55**	**$1,829.83**
Natural gas	**511.59**	**448.40**	**561.07**	**545.63**	**548.98**	**593.88**	**380.47**	**274.01**
Electricity	**1,302.40**	**1,173.39**	**1,380.69**	**1,114.38**	**1,419.06**	**1,489.43**	**1,064.71**	**648.85**
Fuel oil and other fuels	**156.41**	**163.01**	**149.43**	**110.26**	**148.74**	**177.18**	**67.16**	**84.48**
Fuel oil	80.25	80.34	81.41	62.08	75.76	104.91	36.32	49.64
Bottled and tank gas	61.75	67.08	54.22	41.03	60.79	50.93	24.81	27.84
Wood and other fuels	13.55	15.42	12.20	4.52	11.67	18.37	6.04	6.79
Telephone services	**1,179.26**	**1,013.25**	**1,300.48**	**1,165.82**	**1,248.65**	**1,487.40**	**978.81**	**634.45**
Residential telephone and pay phones	697.22	637.39	732.44	655.64	721.23	805.04	587.72	405.04
Cellular phone service	461.63	361.27	546.01	484.38	506.46	660.88	367.57	217.16
Pager service	1.39	1.56	1.05	0.89	0.81	1.59	0.28	0.69
Phone cards	19.01	13.03	20.98	24.91	20.14	19.89	23.24	11.56
Water and other public services	**422.23**	**378.10**	**446.90**	**389.29**	**443.75**	**491.64**	**263.41**	**188.03**
Water and sewerage maintenance	312.84	273.67	335.73	285.50	333.16	374.40	202.76	134.99
Trash and garbage collection	105.81	100.57	107.67	98.21	108.16	113.16	60.53	52.51
Septic tank cleaning	3.58	3.87	3.50	5.58	2.43	4.08	0.12	0.54

* See Appendix B for information about mortgage principal reduction.

Note: Average spending figures for total consumer units can be found on Average Spending by Age and Average Spending by Region tables. Subcategories may not add to total because some are not shown. "–" means sample is too small to make a reliable estimate.

Source: Bureau of Labor Statistics, unpublished tables from the 2004 Consumer Expenditure Survey

Table 9.14 Housing: Shelter and Utilities: Indexed spending by household type, 2004

(indexed average annual spending of consumer units (CU) on shelter and utilities, by type of consumer unit, 2004; index definition: an index of 100 is the average for all consumer units; an index of 132 means that spending by consumer units in that group is 32 percent above the average for all consumer units; an index of 68 indicates spending that is 32 percent below the average for all consumer units)

	total married couples	married couples, no children	married couples with children total	married couples with children oldest child under 6	married couples with children oldest child 6 to 17	married couples with children oldest child 18 or older	single parent, at least one child <18	single person
Average spending of CU, total	$55,607	$49,690	$60,661	$55,981	$60,578	$64,162	$32,824	$25,423
Average spending of CU, index	128	115	140	129	140	148	76	59
Housing, spending index	**122**	**106**	**136**	**151**	**136**	**126**	**86**	**66**
SHELTER	**118**	**100**	**133**	**149**	**136**	**118**	**88**	**73**
Owned dwellings*	**137**	**112**	**159**	**174**	**162**	**143**	**62**	**55**
Mortgage interest and charges	141	95	181	213	185	152	69	46
Mortgage interest	141	94	182	215	187	150	70	47
Interest paid, home equity loan	139	107	159	151	151	179	55	41
Interest paid, home equity line of credit	146	121	163	176	138	201	63	42
Property taxes	135	130	141	137	141	143	52	60
Maintenance, repairs, insurance, other expenses	126	134	120	111	125	117	55	73
Homeowner's insurance	132	140	128	101	131	143	49	66
Ground rent	91	106	65	36	80	55	111	122
Maintenance and repair services	125	135	119	119	129	100	59	72
Painting and papering	129	140	117	167	112	94	81	64
Plumbing and water heating	119	133	114	105	92	160	56	81
Heat, air conditioning, electrical work	118	114	123	167	123	93	54	82
Roofing and gutters	119	113	124	158	124	100	47	75
Other repair and maintenance services	128	153	108	82	133	79	58	72
Repair, replacement of hard-surface flooring	139	143	145	55	185	132	65	54
Repair of built-in appliances	146	195	117	79	131	117	54	51
Maintenance and repair materials	135	109	160	147	145	198	36	46
Paints, wallpaper, and supplies	126	103	147	132	149	154	61	48
Tools, equipment for painting, wallpapering	126	103	147	132	149	154	61	48
Plumbing supplies and equipment	124	109	152	131	150	170	47	72
Electrical supplies, heating and cooling equipment	133	129	149	227	69	244	37	67
Hard-surface flooring, repair and replacement	134	78	198	301	128	258	21	53
Roofing and gutters	105	87	124	229	113	72	36	25
Plaster, paneling, siding, windows, doors, screens, awnings	143	103	178	40	205	220	11	48
Patio, walk, fence, driveway, masonry, brick, and stucco materials	131	98	171	76	99	368	10	29
Miscellaneous supplies and equipment	154	143	157	124	133	223	36	37
Property management and security	97	153	58	87	46	61	31	134
Property management	94	145	57	87	45	60	31	138
Management and upkeep services for security	113	188	61	89	49	64	30	115
Parking	92	157	47	80	38	42	28	155
Rented dwellings	**66**	**59**	**71**	**106**	**70**	**48**	**159**	**121**
Rent	67	59	72	108	72	49	156	120
Rent as pay	25	28	26	50	32	–	457	142
Maintenance, insurance, and other expenses	77	118	44	74	27	56	74	161
Tenant's insurance	81	105	70	101	55	79	91	129
Maintenance and repair services	76	121	36	74	14	52	62	185
Maintenance and repair materials	78	121	50	40	56	45	114	75
Other lodging	**142**	**164**	**133**	**75**	**137**	**163**	**46**	**56**
Owned vacation homes	141	175	118	76	120	144	50	56
Mortgage interest and charges	142	160	135	114	115	186	31	54
Property taxes	139	165	120	51	147	116	76	59
Maintenance, insurance, and other expenses	141	227	79	51	68	119	33	55
Housing while attending school	131	121	151	10	123	298	15	106
Lodging on trips	145	168	136	89	149	144	51	46

	total married couples	married couples, no children	married couples with children				single parent, at least one child <18	single person
			total	oldest child under 6	oldest child 6 to 17	oldest child 18 or older		
UTILITIES, FUELS, AND PUBLIC SERVICES	**122**	**109**	**131**	**114**	**130**	**145**	**94**	**63**
Natural gas	**121**	**106**	**132**	**129**	**129**	**140**	**90**	**65**
Electricity	**122**	**110**	**130**	**105**	**133**	**140**	**100**	**61**
Fuel oil and other fuels	**130**	**135**	**124**	**91**	**123**	**147**	**56**	**70**
Fuel oil	125	125	127	97	118	163	57	77
Bottled and tank gas	137	148	120	91	134	113	55	62
Wood and other fuels	128	145	115	43	110	173	57	64
Telephone services	**119**	**102**	**131**	**118**	**126**	**150**	**99**	**64**
Residential telephone and pay phones	118	108	124	111	122	136	99	68
Cellular phone service	122	95	144	128	134	175	97	57
Pager service	138	154	104	88	80	157	28	68
Phone cards	103	70	113	135	109	107	126	62
Water and other public services	**129**	**115**	**136**	**119**	**136**	**150**	**80**	**57**
Water and sewerage maintenance	129	113	138	118	137	154	84	56
Trash and garbage collection	128	122	130	119	131	137	73	63
Septic tank cleaning	166	179	162	258	113	189	6	25

* See Appendix B for information about mortgage principal reduction.

Note: Spending index for total consumer units is 100. "–" means sample is too small to make a reliable estimate.

Source: Calculations by New Strategist based on the 2004 Consumer Expenditure Survey

Table 9.15 Housing: Shelter and Utilities: Total spending by household type, 2004

(total annual spending on shelter and utilities, by consumer unit (CU) type, 2004; consumer units and dollars in thousands)

	total married couples	married couples, no children	married couples with children				single parent, at least one child <18	single person
			total	oldest child under 6	oldest child 6 to 17	oldest child 18 or older		
Number of consumer units	59,797	25,585	29,279	5,604	15,376	8,300	6,892	33,686
Total spending of all CUs	$3,325,106,066	$1,271,329,652	$1,776,089,906	$313,717,748	$931,445,483	$532,542,027	$226,226,178	$856,410,968
Housing, total spending	1,016,820,478	376,264,012	553,730,304	117,936,292	290,608,553	145,274,070	82,909,244	311,395,742
SHELTER	563,718,278	205,467,506	312,054,118	66,934,456	166,652,161	78,478,326	48,540,976	196,756,557
Owned dwellings*	435,999,660	152,153,227	248,066,328	51,858,407	132,906,146	63,310,408	22,840,502	98,242,861
Mortgage interest and charges	248,287,907	71,470,162	155,618,471	34,987,173	83,533,195	37,103,324	14,041,003	45,817,676
Mortgage interest	235,374,147	67,017,605	148,496,106	33,579,056	80,214,901	34,697,154	13,419,758	43,701,185
Interest paid, home equity loan	4,807,679	1,585,758	2,682,249	489,790	1,336,943	855,564	218,545	796,337
Interest paid, home equity line of credit	8,094,122	2,865,008	4,439,575	918,327	1,970,742	1,550,689	402,700	1,310,385
Property taxes	112,691,034	46,408,120	57,318,327	10,684,698	30,145,724	16,489,776	5,025,440	28,015,972
Maintenance, repairs, insurance, other expenses	75,020,718	34,275,201	35,129,823	6,186,536	19,227,227	9,717,308	3,773,990	24,409,212
Homeowner's insurance	24,909,038	11,236,932	11,841,013	1,779,606	6,325,840	3,735,913	1,064,538	6,960,201
Ground rent	2,179,003	1,089,153	758,912	81,594	496,030	181,438	307,314	1,648,930
Maintenance and repair services	39,779,954	18,390,754	18,449,576	3,536,909	10,505,652	4,407,632	2,140,104	12,905,443
Painting and papering	4,602,575	2,138,650	2,050,701	557,150	1,030,192	463,389	335,089	1,295,900
Plumbing and water heating	3,520,249	1,677,864	1,648,993	290,960	702,529	655,451	191,322	1,349,461
Heat, air conditioning, electrical work	6,337,286	2,619,648	3,213,077	836,621	1,689,361	687,240	332,263	2,474,237
Roofing and gutters	6,824,632	2,784,927	3,483,323	850,351	1,835,126	797,796	310,554	2,436,172
Other repair and maintenance services	13,617,571	6,969,354	5,622,739	814,766	3,637,193	1,171,130	712,564	4,297,997
Repair, replacement of hard-surface flooring	4,396,873	1,926,295	2,242,186	162,684	1,500,390	579,174	237,912	958,367
Repair of built-in appliances	480,768	274,015	188,850	24,377	110,861	53,452	20,400	93,647
Maintenance and repair materials	5,929,471	2,052,685	3,439,990	602,990	1,633,392	1,203,666	180,915	1,144,987
Paints, wallpaper, and supplies	1,146,906	400,661	654,386	112,360	348,113	193,805	63,682	245,234
Tools, equipment for painting, wallpapering	123,182	42,983	70,270	12,049	37,364	20,833	6,823	26,275
Plumbing supplies and equipment	429,940	161,953	257,948	42,366	133,925	81,672	18,953	140,134
Electrical supplies, heating and cooling equipment	257,725	106,689	140,832	41,021	34,442	65,487	8,201	72,762
Hard-surface flooring, repair and replacement	745,669	185,491	540,490	157,304	183,282	199,864	13,715	167,756
Roofing and gutters	401,836	143,020	232,182	82,491	111,322	38,263	15,921	53,561
Plaster, paneling, siding, windows, doors, screens, awnings	1,117,008	343,607	677,223	28,973	410,693	237,629	9,993	210,874
Patio, walk, fence, driveway, masonry, brick, and stucco materials	122,584	39,401	78,468	6,725	23,833	47,974	1,103	15,159
Miscellaneous supplies and equipment	1,584,023	628,879	788,191	119,589	350,265	318,222	42,524	213,232
Property management and security	2,033,098	1,367,262	592,900	170,137	246,170	176,624	74,503	1,570,778
Property management	1,601,962	1,061,522	479,883	138,531	198,658	142,760	61,270	1,323,860
Management and upkeep services for security	431,136	305,485	113,017	31,607	47,512	33,947	13,233	246,582
Parking	189,556	138,159	47,432	15,299	20,143	11,952	6,616	179,210
Rented dwellings	87,486,599	33,452,388	45,610,241	13,077,663	23,751,307	8,782,977	24,190,300	89,579,496
Rent	85,155,712	32,017,325	44,828,199	12,812,761	23,415,495	8,601,622	22,854,630	85,737,944
Rent as pay	531,595	254,571	276,979	101,825	175,133	—	1,136,215	1,726,744
Maintenance, insurance, and other expenses	1,799,292	1,180,492	505,063	163,076	160,679	181,355	199,454	2,114,807
Tenant's insurance	343,235	190,097	145,517	40,013	59,505	46,148	44,384	307,553
Maintenance and repair services	1,218,663	833,303	285,763	111,800	57,968	116,200	115,234	1,679,921
Maintenance and repair materials	236,796	156,836	73,783	11,320	43,360	19,007	39,836	127,333
Other lodging	40,231,422	19,861,891	18,377,257	1,998,386	9,994,708	6,384,941	1,510,175	8,934,201
Owned vacation homes	11,552,780	6,130,934	4,747,004	585,282	2,521,510	1,640,412	474,583	2,606,286
Mortgage interest and charges	4,591,214	2,214,382	2,131,804	346,607	951,928	833,403	115,923	986,326
Property taxes	4,796,915	2,428,784	2,020,544	165,654	1,300,502	554,274	300,905	1,146,335
Maintenance, insurance, and other expenses	2,164,053	1,487,768	594,656	73,020	269,080	252,735	57,755	473,962
Housing while attending school	4,511,086	1,791,462	2,552,836	32,279	1,092,311	1,428,181	61,546	2,059,562
Lodging on trips	24,167,556	11,939,496	11,077,417	1,380,770	6,380,732	3,316,348	974,115	4,268,016

	total married couples	married couples, no children	married couples with children				single parent, at least one child <18	single person
			total	oldest child under 6	oldest child 6 to 17	oldest child 18 or older		
UTILITIES, FUELS, PUBLIC SERVICES	$213,587,708	$81,261,798	$112,389,784	$18,635,430	$58,569,952	$35,188,099	$18,984,359	$61,639,653
Natural gas	30,591,547	11,472,314	16,427,569	3,057,711	8,441,116	4,929,204	2,622,199	9,230,301
Electricity	77,879,613	30,021,183	40,425,223	6,244,986	21,819,467	12,362,269	7,337,981	21,857,161
Fuel oil and other fuels	9,352,849	4,170,611	4,375,161	617,897	2,287,026	1,470,594	462,867	2,845,793
Fuel oil	4,798,709	2,055,499	2,383,603	347,896	1,164,886	870,753	250,317	1,672,173
Bottled and tank gas	3,692,465	1,716,242	1,587,507	229,932	934,707	422,719	170,991	937,818
Wood and other fuels	810,249	394,521	357,204	25,330	179,438	152,471	41,628	228,728
Telephone services	70,516,210	25,924,001	38,076,754	6,533,255	19,199,242	12,345,420	6,745,959	21,372,083
Residential telephone and pay phones	41,691,664	16,307,623	21,445,111	3,674,207	11,089,632	6,681,832	4,050,566	13,644,177
Cellular phone service	27,604,089	9,243,093	15,986,627	2,714,466	7,787,329	5,485,304	2,533,292	7,315,252
Pager service	83,118	39,913	30,743	4,988	12,455	13,197	1,930	23,243
Phone cards	1,136,741	333,373	614,273	139,596	309,673	165,087	160,170	389,410
Water and other public services	25,248,087	9,673,689	13,084,785	2,181,581	6,823,100	4,080,612	1,815,422	6,333,979
Water and sewerage maintenance	18,706,893	7,001,847	9,829,839	1,599,942	5,122,668	3,107,520	1,397,422	4,547,273
Trash and garbage collection	6,327,121	2,573,083	3,152,470	550,369	1,663,068	939,228	417,173	1,768,852
Septic tank cleaning	214,073	99,014	102,477	31,270	37,364	33,864	827	18,190

* See Appendix B for information about mortgage principal reduction.
Note: Total spending figures for total consumer units can be found on Total Spending by Age and Total Spending by Region tables. Spending by type of consumer unit will not add to total because not all types of consumer units are shown. Numbers may not add to category total because of rounding and missing subcategories. "–" means sample is too small to make a reliable estimate.
Source: Calculations by New Strategist based on the 2004 Consumer Expenditure Survey

Table 9.16 Housing: Shelter and Utilities: Market shares by household type, 2004

(percentage of total annual spending on shelter and utilities accounted for by types of consumer units, 2004)

	total married couples	married couples, no children	married couples with children				single parent, at least one child <18	single person
			total	oldest child under 6	oldest child 6 to 17	oldest child 18 or older		
Share of total consumer units	51.4%	22.0%	25.2%	4.8%	13.2%	7.1%	5.9%	29.0%
Share of total before-tax income	68.9	26.0	36.9	6.7	19.1	11.2	3.4	15.0
Share of total spending	65.9	25.2	35.2	6.2	18.5	10.6	4.5	17.0
Share of housing spending	62.8	23.2	34.2	7.3	18.0	9.0	5.1	19.2
SHELTER	**60.6**	**22.1**	**33.6**	**7.2**	**17.9**	**8.4**	**5.2**	**21.2**
Owned dwellings*	**70.4**	**24.6**	**40.1**	**8.4**	**21.5**	**10.2**	**3.7**	**15.9**
Mortgage interest and charges	72.7	20.9	45.6	10.2	24.5	10.9	4.1	13.4
Mortgage interest	72.7	20.7	45.8	10.4	24.8	10.7	4.1	13.5
Interest paid, home equity loan	71.6	23.6	40.0	7.3	19.9	12.7	3.3	11.9
Interest paid, home equity line of credit	74.9	26.5	41.1	8.5	18.2	14.4	3.7	12.1
Property taxes	69.7	28.7	35.4	6.6	18.6	10.2	3.1	17.3
Maintenance, repairs, insurance, other expenses	64.7	29.6	30.3	5.3	16.6	8.4	3.3	21.1
Homeowner's insurance	68.1	30.7	32.4	4.9	17.3	10.2	2.9	19.0
Ground rent	46.7	23.4	16.3	1.7	10.6	3.9	6.6	35.4
Maintenance and repair services	64.5	29.8	29.9	5.7	17.0	7.1	3.5	20.9
Painting and papering	66.3	30.8	29.5	8.0	14.8	6.7	4.8	18.7
Plumbing and water heating	61.2	29.2	28.7	5.1	12.2	11.4	3.3	23.5
Heat, air conditioning, electrical work	60.9	25.2	30.9	8.0	16.2	6.6	3.2	23.8
Roofing and gutters	61.0	24.9	31.1	7.6	16.4	7.1	2.8	21.8
Other repair and maintenance services	66.0	33.8	27.2	3.9	17.6	5.7	3.5	20.8
Repair, replacement of hard-surface flooring	71.7	31.4	36.6	2.7	24.5	9.4	3.9	15.6
Repair of built-in appliances	75.3	42.9	29.6	3.8	17.4	8.4	3.2	14.7
Maintenance and repair materials	69.5	24.1	40.3	7.1	19.2	14.1	2.1	13.4
Paints, wallpaper, and supplies	65.0	22.7	37.1	6.4	19.7	11.0	3.6	13.9
Tools, equipment for painting, wallpapering	65.0	22.7	37.1	6.4	19.7	11.0	3.6	13.9
Plumbing supplies and equipment	63.9	24.1	38.3	6.3	19.9	12.1	2.8	20.8
Electrical supplies, heating and cooling equipment	68.6	28.4	37.5	10.9	9.2	17.4	2.2	19.4
Hard-surface flooring, repair and replacement	68.7	17.1	49.8	14.5	16.9	18.4	1.3	15.4
Roofing and gutters	53.8	19.2	31.1	11.0	14.9	5.1	2.1	7.2
Plaster, paneling, siding, windows, doors, screens, awnings	73.8	22.7	44.7	1.9	27.1	15.7	0.7	13.9
Patio, walk, fence, driveway, masonry, brick, and stucco materials	67.1	21.6	43.0	3.7	13.1	26.3	0.6	8.3
Miscellaneous supplies and equipment	79.4	31.5	39.5	6.0	17.6	15.9	2.1	10.7
Property management and security	50.1	33.7	14.6	4.2	6.1	4.4	1.8	38.7
Property management	48.3	32.0	14.5	4.2	6.0	4.3	1.8	39.9
Management and upkeep services for security	58.3	41.3	15.3	4.3	6.4	4.6	1.8	33.3
Parking	47.5	34.6	11.9	3.8	5.1	3.0	1.7	44.9
Rented dwellings	**34.2**	**13.1**	**17.8**	**5.1**	**9.3**	**3.4**	**9.5**	**35.0**
Rent	34.4	13.0	18.1	5.2	9.5	3.5	9.2	34.7
Rent as pay	12.7	6.1	6.6	2.4	4.2	–	27.1	41.2
Maintenance, insurance, and other expenses	39.6	26.0	11.1	3.6	3.5	4.0	4.4	46.5
Tenant's insurance	41.8	23.2	17.7	4.9	7.2	5.6	5.4	37.5
Maintenance and repair services	38.9	26.6	9.1	3.6	1.9	3.7	3.7	53.6
Maintenance and repair materials	40.2	26.6	12.5	1.9	7.4	3.2	6.8	21.6
Other lodging	**73.2**	**36.1**	**33.4**	**3.6**	**18.2**	**11.6**	**2.7**	**16.2**
Owned vacation homes	72.4	38.4	29.8	3.7	15.8	10.3	3.0	16.3
Mortgage interest and charges	73.1	35.2	33.9	5.5	15.1	13.3	1.8	15.7
Property taxes	71.7	36.3	30.2	2.5	19.4	8.3	4.5	17.1
Maintenance, insurance, and other expenses	72.5	49.8	19.9	2.4	9.0	8.5	1.9	15.9
Housing while attending school	67.2	26.7	38.0	0.5	16.3	21.3	0.9	30.7
Lodging on trips	74.8	36.9	34.3	4.3	19.7	10.3	3.0	13.2

	total married couples	married couples, no children	married couples with children				single parent, at least one child <18	single person
			total	oldest child under 6	oldest child 6 to 17	oldest child 18 or older		
UTILITIES, FUELS, AND PUBLIC SERVICES	**62.8%**	**23.9%**	**33.0%**	**5.5%**	**17.2%**	**10.3%**	**5.6%**	**18.1%**
Natural gas	**62.0**	**23.3**	**33.3**	**6.2**	**17.1**	**10.0**	**5.3**	**18.7**
Electricity	**62.9**	**24.3**	**32.7**	**5.0**	**17.6**	**10.0**	**5.9**	**17.7**
Fuel oil and other fuels	**66.7**	**29.8**	**31.2**	**4.4**	**16.3**	**10.5**	**3.3**	**20.3**
Fuel oil	64.3	27.5	31.9	4.7	15.6	11.7	3.4	22.4
Bottled and tank gas	70.3	32.7	30.2	4.4	17.8	8.0	3.3	17.8
Wood and other fuels	65.7	32.0	29.0	2.1	14.5	12.4	3.4	18.5
Telephone services	**61.2**	**22.5**	**33.1**	**5.7**	**16.7**	**10.7**	**5.9**	**18.6**
Residential telephone and pay phones	60.5	23.7	31.1	5.3	16.1	9.7	5.9	19.8
Cellular phone service	62.7	21.0	36.3	6.2	17.7	12.5	5.8	16.6
Pager service	70.8	34.0	26.2	4.2	10.6	11.2	1.6	19.8
Phone cards	52.8	15.5	28.5	6.5	14.4	7.7	7.4	18.1
Water and other public services	**66.3**	**25.4**	**34.4**	**5.7**	**17.9**	**10.7**	**4.8**	**16.6**
Water and sewerage maintenance	66.3	24.8	34.9	5.7	18.2	11.0	5.0	16.1
Trash and garbage collection	65.7	26.7	32.8	5.7	17.3	9.8	4.3	18.4
Septic tank cleaning	85.2	39.4	40.8	12.4	14.9	13.5	0.3	7.2

* See Appendix B for information about mortgage principal reduction.
Note: Market share for total consumer units is 100.0%. Market shares by type of consumer unit will not add to total because not all types of consumer units are shown. "–" means sample is too small to make a reliable estimate.
Source: Calculations by New Strategist based on the 2004 Consumer Expenditure Survey

Table 9.17 Housing: Shelter and Utilities: Average spending by race and Hispanic origin, 2004

(average annual spending of consumer units (CU) on shelter and utilities, by race and Hispanic origin of consumer unit reference person, 2004)

	total consumer units	Asian	black	Hispanic	non-Hispanic white and other
Number of consumer units (in 000s)	116,282	3,957	13,773	12,298	90,424
Average number of persons per CU	2.5	2.8	2.6	3.3	2.3
Average before-tax income of CU	$54,453.00	$67,705.00	$38,503.00	$43,693.00	$58,314.00
Average spending of CU, total	43,394.87	49,458.68	30,481.49	37,578.03	46,163.26
Housing, average spending	**13,918.48**	**17,418.15**	**11,042.97**	**12,883.84**	**14,503.48**
SHELTER	**7,998.43**	**11,728.43**	**6,410.60**	**7,833.35**	**8,266.19**
Owned dwellings*	**5,324.49**	**7,733.71**	**3,164.96**	**4,106.53**	**5,817.01**
Mortgage interest and charges	2,936.18	4,810.03	1,936.45	2,588.59	3,134.46
Mortgage interest	2,785.37	4,642.19	1,873.07	2,498.70	2,962.41
Interest paid, home equity loan	57.73	76.94	35.22	42.88	63.04
Interest paid, home equity line of credit	92.89	90.90	28.17	47.00	108.77
Property taxes	1,391.17	1,899.82	742.67	866.41	1,559.86
Maintenance, repairs, insurance, other expenses	997.14	1,023.86	485.83	651.53	1,122.68
Homeowner's insurance	314.75	319.30	193.46	215.19	346.64
Ground rent	40.10	36.88	14.02	47.25	43.00
Maintenance and repair services	530.63	567.41	229.32	305.93	608.20
Painting and papering	59.71	67.01	15.42	33.72	69.95
Plumbing and water heating	49.48	65.89	26.94	29.02	55.87
Heat, air conditioning, electrical work	89.48	100.07	38.15	41.95	103.55
Roofing and gutters	96.28	78.92	51.48	52.49	108.83
Other repair and maintenance services	177.49	121.49	59.84	105.61	204.77
Repair, replacement of hard-surface flooring	52.71	131.23	36.14	41.18	58.60
Repair of built-in appliances	5.49	2.81	1.37	1.97	6.64
Maintenance and repair materials	73.33	39.87	29.71	58.25	81.87
Paints, wallpaper, and supplies	15.18	12.93	8.41	16.56	16.01
Tools, equipment for painting, wallpapering	1.63	1.39	0.90	1.78	1.72
Plumbing supplies and equipment	5.79	1.51	2.33	2.06	6.80
Electrical supplies, heating and cooling equipment	3.23	0.10	1.29	0.78	3.85
Hard-surface flooring, repair and replacement	9.34	11.81	2.84	6.50	10.69
Roofing and gutters	6.42	0.92	0.86	13.07	6.35
Plaster, paneling, siding, windows, doors, screens, awnings	13.02	1.48	7.04	4.31	15.09
Patio, walk, fence, driveway, masonry, brick, and stucco materials	1.57	–	0.88	1.58	1.67
Miscellaneous supplies and equipment	17.16	9.72	5.15	11.62	19.70
Property management and security	34.91	53.86	18.61	22.67	38.97
Property management	28.55	44.31	17.63	19.67	31.35
Management and upkeep services for security	6.36	9.55	0.98	3.01	7.62
Parking	3.43	6.54	0.70	2.24	3.99
Rented dwellings	**2,201.09**	**3,537.04**	**3,096.80**	**3,500.94**	**1,894.26**
Rent	2,125.93	3,499.64	2,967.43	3,409.82	1,829.26
Rent as pay	36.08	25.77	111.08	70.34	20.31
Maintenance, insurance, and other expenses	39.07	11.63	18.29	20.79	44.69
Tenant's insurance	7.06	1.53	6.39	3.55	7.63
Maintenance and repair services	26.94	4.98	7.57	11.21	31.96
Maintenance and repair materials	5.07	5.11	4.34	6.02	5.10
Other lodging	**472.85**	**457.68**	**148.84**	**225.88**	**554.92**
Owned vacation homes	137.22	38.80	28.96	63.63	163.40
Mortgage interest and charges	54.04	21.71	10.21	31.72	63.63
Property taxes	57.51	12.08	15.28	22.59	68.55
Maintenance, insurance, and other expenses	25.67	5.01	3.46	9.33	31.22
Housing while attending school	57.73	149.72	22.20	22.83	67.76
Lodging on trips	277.89	269.16	97.68	139.42	323.77

	total consumer units	Asian	black	Hispanic	non-Hispanic white and other
UTILITIES, FUELS, AND PUBLIC SERVICES	**$2,926.65**	**$2,780.78**	**$2,884.50**	**$2,670.84**	**$2,966.28**
Natural gas	**424.02**	**441.53**	**452.03**	**337.42**	**431.56**
Electricity	**1,064.41**	**876.14**	**1,088.26**	**909.35**	**1,080.83**
Fuel oil and other fuels	**120.53**	**40.29**	**52.07**	**73.08**	**137.53**
Fuel oil	64.19	28.16	31.19	35.05	73.42
Bottled and tank gas	45.20	11.43	16.10	29.84	51.62
Wood and other fuels	10.61	0.70	4.78	8.19	11.82
Telephone services	**990.22**	**1,078.14**	**1,025.02**	**1,030.59**	**979.34**
Residential telephone and pay phones	592.31	552.53	688.72	584.51	578.55
Cellular phone service	378.39	468.23	316.03	389.44	386.43
Pager service	1.01	2.19	0.85	0.93	1.04
Phone cards	18.51	55.18	19.43	55.71	13.32
Water and other public services	**327.47**	**344.68**	**267.12**	**320.41**	**337.01**
Water and sewerage maintenance	242.54	265.26	216.46	243.58	245.93
Trash and garbage collection	82.77	78.64	49.94	75.83	88.56
Septic tank cleaning	2.16	0.77	0.72	1.00	2.53

* See Appendix B for information about mortgage principal reduction.
Note: "Asian" and "black" include Hispanics and non-Hispanics who identify themselves as being of the respective race alone. "Hispanic" includes people of any race who identify themselves as Hispanic. "Other" includes people who identify themselves as non-Hispanic and as Alaska Native, American Indian, Asian (who are also included in the "Asian" column), Native Hawaiian or other Pacific Islander, as well as non-Hispanics reporting more than one race. Subcategories may not add to total because some are not shown. "–" means sample is too small to make a reliable estimate.
Source: Bureau of Labor Statistics, unpublished tables from the 2004 Consumer Expenditure Survey

Table 9.18 Housing: Shelter and Utilities: Indexed spending by race and Hispanic origin, 2004

(indexed average annual spending of consumer units (CU) on shelter and utilities, by race and Hispanic origin of consumer unit reference person, 2004; index definition: an index of 100 is the average for all consumer units; an index of 132 means that spending by consumer units in that group is 32 percent above the average for all consumer units; an index of 68 indicates spending that is 32 percent below the average for all consumer units)

	total consumer units	Asian	black	Hispanic	non-Hispanic white and other
Average spending of CU, total	$43,395	$49,459	$30,481	$37,578	$46,163
Average spending of CU, index	100	114	70	87	106
Housing, spending index	100	125	79	93	104
SHELTER	100	147	80	98	103
Owned dwellings*	100	145	59	77	109
Mortgage interest and charges	100	164	66	88	107
Mortgage interest	100	167	67	90	106
Interest paid, home equity loan	100	133	61	74	109
Interest paid, home equity line of credit	100	98	30	51	117
Property taxes	100	137	53	62	112
Maintenance, repairs, insurance, other expenses	100	103	49	65	113
Homeowner's insurance	100	101	61	68	110
Ground rent	100	92	35	118	107
Maintenance and repair services	100	107	43	58	115
Painting and papering	100	112	26	56	117
Plumbing and water heating	100	133	54	59	113
Heat, air conditioning, electrical work	100	112	43	47	116
Roofing and gutters	100	82	53	55	113
Other repair and maintenance services	100	68	34	60	115
Repair, replacement of hard-surface flooring	100	249	69	78	111
Repair of built-in appliances	100	51	25	36	121
Maintenance and repair materials	100	54	41	79	112
Paints, wallpaper, and supplies	100	85	55	109	105
Tools, equipment for painting, wallpapering	100	85	55	109	106
Plumbing supplies and equipment	100	26	40	36	117
Electrical supplies, heating and cooling equipment	100	3	40	24	119
Hard-surface flooring, repair and replacement	100	126	30	70	114
Roofing and gutters	100	14	13	204	99
Plaster, paneling, siding, windows, doors, screens, awnings	100	11	54	33	116
Patio, walk, fence, driveway, masonry, brick, and stucco materials	100	–	56	101	106
Miscellaneous supplies and equipment	100	57	30	68	115
Property management and security	100	154	53	65	112
Property management	100	155	62	69	110
Management and upkeep services for security	100	150	15	47	120
Parking	100	191	20	65	116
Rented dwellings	100	161	141	159	86
Rent	100	165	140	160	86
Rent as pay	100	71	308	195	56
Maintenance, insurance, and other expenses	100	30	47	53	114
Tenant's insurance	100	22	91	50	108
Maintenance and repair services	100	18	28	42	119
Maintenance and repair materials	100	101	86	119	101
Other lodging	100	97	31	48	117
Owned vacation homes	100	28	21	46	119
Mortgage interest and charges	100	40	19	59	118
Property taxes	100	21	27	39	119
Maintenance, insurance, and other expenses	100	20	13	36	122
Housing while attending school	100	259	38	40	117
Lodging on trips	100	97	35	50	117

	total consumer units	Asian	black	Hispanic	non-Hispanic white and other
UTILITIES, FUELS, AND PUBLIC SERVICES	**100**	**95**	**99**	**91**	**101**
Natural gas	**100**	**104**	**107**	**80**	**102**
Electricity	**100**	**82**	**102**	**85**	**102**
Fuel oil and other fuels	**100**	**33**	**43**	**61**	**114**
Fuel oil	100	44	49	55	114
Bottled and tank gas	100	25	36	66	114
Wood and other fuels	100	7	45	77	111
Telephone services	**100**	**109**	**104**	**104**	**99**
Residential telephone and pay phones	100	93	116	99	98
Cellular phone service	100	124	84	103	102
Pager service	100	217	84	92	103
Phone cards	100	298	105	301	72
Water and other public services	**100**	**105**	**82**	**98**	**103**
Water and sewerage maintenance	100	109	89	100	101
Trash and garbage collection	100	95	60	92	107
Septic tank cleaning	100	36	33	46	117

* See Appendix B for information about mortgage principal reduction.
Note: "Asian" and "black" include Hispanics and non-Hispanics who identify themselves as being of the respective race alone. "Hispanic" includes people of any race who identify themselves as Hispanic. "Other" includes people who identify themselves as non-Hispanic and as Alaska Native, American Indian, Asian (who are also included in the "Asian" column), Native Hawaiian or other Pacific Islander, as well as non-Hispanics reporting more than one race. "–" means sample is too small to make a reliable estimate.
Source: Calculations by New Strategist based on the 2004 Consumer Expenditure Survey

Table 9.19 Housing: Shelter and Utilities: Total spending by race and Hispanic origin, 2004

(total annual spending on shelter and utilities, by consumer unit race and Hispanic origin groups, 2004; consumer units and dollars in thousands)

	total consumer units	Asian	black	Hispanic	non-Hispanic white and other
Number of consumer units	116,282	3,957	13,773	12,298	90,424
Total spending of all consumer units	$5,046,042,273	$195,707,997	$419,821,562	$462,134,613	$4,174,266,622
Housing, total spending	1,618,468,691	68,923,620	152,094,826	158,445,464	1,311,462,676
SHELTER	**930,073,437**	**46,409,398**	**88,293,194**	**96,334,538**	**747,461,965**
Owned dwellings*	**619,142,346**	**30,602,290**	**43,590,994**	**50,502,106**	**525,997,312**
Mortgage interest and charges	341,424,883	19,033,289	26,670,726	31,834,480	283,430,411
Mortgage interest	323,888,394	18,369,146	25,797,793	30,729,013	267,872,962
Interest paid, home equity loan	6,712,960	304,452	485,085	527,338	5,700,329
Interest paid, home equity line of credit	10,801,435	359,691	387,985	578,006	9,835,418
Property taxes	161,768,030	7,517,588	10,228,794	10,655,110	141,048,781
Maintenance, repairs, insurance, other expenses	115,949,433	4,051,414	6,691,337	8,012,516	101,517,216
Homeowner's insurance	36,599,760	1,263,470	2,664,525	2,646,407	31,344,575
Ground rent	4,662,908	145,934	193,097	581,081	3,888,232
Maintenance and repair services	61,702,718	2,245,241	3,158,424	3,762,327	54,995,877
Painting and papering	6,943,198	265,159	212,380	414,689	6,325,159
Plumbing and water heating	5,753,633	260,727	371,045	356,888	5,051,989
Heat, air conditioning, electrical work	10,404,913	395,977	525,440	515,901	9,363,405
Roofing and gutters	11,195,631	312,286	709,034	645,522	9,840,844
Other repair and maintenance services	20,638,892	480,736	824,176	1,298,792	18,516,122
Repair, replacement of hard-surface flooring	6,129,224	519,277	497,756	506,432	5,298,846
Repair of built-in appliances	638,388	11,119	18,869	24,227	600,415
Maintenance and repair materials	8,526,959	157,766	409,196	716,359	7,403,013
Paints, wallpaper, and supplies	1,765,161	51,164	115,831	203,655	1,447,688
Tools, equipment for painting, wallpapering	189,540	5,500	12,396	21,890	155,529
Plumbing supplies and equipment	673,273	5,975	32,091	25,334	614,883
Electrical supplies, heating and cooling equipment	375,591	396	17,767	9,592	348,132
Hard-surface flooring, repair and replacement	1,086,074	46,732	39,115	79,937	966,633
Roofing and gutters	746,530	3,640	11,845	160,735	574,192
Plaster, paneling, siding, windows, doors, screens, awnings	1,513,992	5,856	96,962	53,004	1,364,498
Patio, walk, fence, driveway, masonry, brick, and stucco materials	182,563	–	12,120	19,431	151,008
Miscellaneous supplies and equipment	1,995,399	38,462	70,931	142,903	1,781,353
Property management and security	4,059,405	213,124	256,316	278,796	3,523,823
Property management	3,319,851	175,335	242,818	241,902	2,834,792
Management and upkeep services for security	739,554	37,789	13,498	37,017	689,031
Parking	398,847	25,879	9,641	27,548	360,792
Rented dwellings	**255,947,147**	**13,996,067**	**42,652,226**	**43,054,560**	**171,286,566**
Rent	247,207,392	13,848,075	40,870,413	41,933,966	165,409,006
Rent as pay	4,195,455	101,972	1,529,905	865,041	1,836,511
Maintenance, insurance, and other expenses	4,543,138	46,020	251,908	255,675	4,041,049
Tenant's insurance	820,951	6,054	88,009	43,658	689,935
Maintenance and repair services	3,132,637	19,706	104,262	137,861	2,889,951
Maintenance and repair materials	589,550	20,220	59,775	74,034	461,162
Other lodging	**54,983,944**	**1,811,040**	**2,049,973**	**2,777,872**	**50,178,086**
Owned vacation homes	15,956,216	153,532	398,866	782,522	14,775,282
Mortgage interest and charges	6,283,879	85,906	140,622	390,093	5,753,679
Property taxes	6,687,378	47,801	210,451	277,812	6,198,565
Maintenance, insurance, and other expenses	2,984,959	19,825	47,655	114,740	2,823,037
Housing while attending school	6,712,960	592,442	305,761	280,763	6,127,130
Lodging on trips	32,313,605	1,065,066	1,345,347	1,714,587	29,276,578

	total consumer units	Asian	black	Hispanic	non-Hispanic white and other
UTILITIES, FUELS, AND PUBLIC SERVICES	$340,316,715	$11,003,546	$39,728,219	$32,845,990	$268,222,903
Natural gas	49,305,894	1,747,134	6,225,809	4,149,591	39,023,381
Electricity	123,771,724	3,466,886	14,988,605	11,183,186	97,732,972
Fuel oil and other fuels	14,015,469	159,428	717,160	898,738	12,436,013
Fuel oil	7,464,142	111,429	429,580	431,045	6,638,930
Bottled and tank gas	5,255,946	45,229	221,745	366,972	4,667,687
Wood and other fuels	1,233,752	2,770	65,835	100,721	1,068,812
Telephone services	115,144,762	4,266,200	14,117,600	12,674,196	88,555,840
Residential telephone and pay phones	68,874,991	2,186,361	9,485,741	7,188,304	52,314,805
Cellular phone service	43,999,946	1,852,786	4,352,681	4,789,333	34,942,546
Pager service	117,445	8,666	11,707	11,437	94,041
Phone cards	2,152,380	218,347	267,609	685,122	1,204,448
Water and other public services	38,078,867	1,363,899	3,679,044	3,940,402	30,473,792
Water and sewerage maintenance	28,203,036	1,049,634	2,981,304	2,995,547	22,237,974
Trash and garbage collection	9,624,661	311,178	687,824	932,557	8,007,949
Septic tank cleaning	251,169	3,047	9,917	12,298	228,773

* See Appendix B for information about mortgage principal reduction.

Note: "Asian" and "black" include Hispanics and non-Hispanics who identify themselves as being of the respective race alone. "Hispanic" includes people of any race who identify themselves as Hispanic. "Other" includes people who identify themselves as non-Hispanic and as Alaska Native, American Indian, Asian (who are also included in the "Asian" column), Native Hawaiian or other Pacific Islander, as well as non-Hispanics reporting more than one race. "–" means sample is too small to make a reliable estimate.

Source: Calculations by New Strategist based on the 2004 Consumer Expenditure Survey

Table 9.20 Housing: Shelter and Utilities: Market shares by race and Hispanic origin, 2004

(percentage of total annual spending on shelter and utilities accounted for by consumer unit race and Hispanic origin groups, 2004)

	total consumer units	Asian	black	Hispanic	non-Hispanic white and other
Share of total consumer units	100.0%	3.4%	11.8%	10.6%	77.8%
Share of total before-tax income	100.0	4.2	8.4	8.5	83.3
Share of total spending	100.0	3.9	8.3	9.2	82.7
Share of housing spending	100.0	4.3	9.4	9.8	81.0
SHELTER	**100.0**	**5.0**	**9.5**	**10.4**	**80.4**
Owned dwellings*	**100.0**	**4.9**	**7.0**	**8.2**	**85.0**
Mortgage interest and charges	100.0	5.6	7.8	9.3	83.0
Mortgage interest	100.0	5.7	8.0	9.5	82.7
Interest paid, home equity loan	100.0	4.5	7.2	7.9	84.9
Interest paid, home equity line of credit	100.0	3.3	3.6	5.4	91.1
Property taxes	100.0	4.6	6.3	6.6	87.2
Maintenance, repairs, insurance, other expenses	100.0	3.5	5.8	6.9	87.6
Homeowner's insurance	100.0	3.5	7.3	7.2	85.6
Ground rent	100.0	3.1	4.1	12.5	83.4
Maintenance and repair services	100.0	3.6	5.1	6.1	89.1
Painting and papering	100.0	3.8	3.1	6.0	91.1
Plumbing and water heating	100.0	4.5	6.4	6.2	87.8
Heat, air conditioning, electrical work	100.0	3.8	5.0	5.0	90.0
Roofing and gutters	100.0	2.8	6.3	5.8	87.9
Other repair and maintenance services	100.0	2.3	4.0	6.3	89.7
Repair, replacement of hard-surface flooring	100.0	8.5	8.1	8.3	86.5
Repair of built-in appliances	100.0	1.7	3.0	3.8	94.1
Maintenance and repair materials	100.0	1.9	4.8	8.4	86.8
Paints, wallpaper, and supplies	100.0	2.9	6.6	11.5	82.0
Tools, equipment for painting, wallpapering	100.0	2.9	6.5	11.5	82.1
Plumbing supplies and equipment	100.0	0.9	4.8	3.8	91.3
Electrical supplies, heating and cooling equipment	100.0	0.1	4.7	2.6	92.7
Hard-surface flooring, repair and replacement	100.0	4.3	3.6	7.4	89.0
Roofing and gutters	100.0	0.5	1.6	21.5	76.9
Plaster, paneling, siding, windows, doors, screens, awnings	100.0	0.4	6.4	3.5	90.1
Patio, walk, fence, driveway, masonry, brick, and stucco materials	100.0	–	6.6	10.6	82.7
Miscellaneous supplies and equipment	100.0	1.9	3.6	7.2	89.3
Property management and security	100.0	5.3	6.3	6.9	86.8
Property management	100.0	5.3	7.3	7.3	85.4
Management and upkeep services for security	100.0	5.1	1.8	5.0	93.2
Parking	100.0	6.5	2.4	6.9	90.5
Rented dwellings	**100.0**	**5.5**	**16.7**	**16.8**	**66.9**
Rent	100.0	5.6	16.5	17.0	66.9
Rent as pay	100.0	2.4	36.5	20.6	43.8
Maintenance, insurance, and other expenses	100.0	1.0	5.5	5.6	88.9
Tenant's insurance	100.0	0.7	10.7	5.3	84.0
Maintenance and repair services	100.0	0.6	3.3	4.4	92.3
Maintenance and repair materials	100.0	3.4	10.1	12.6	78.2
Other lodging	**100.0**	**3.3**	**3.7**	**5.1**	**91.3**
Owned vacation homes	100.0	1.0	2.5	4.9	92.6
Mortgage interest and charges	100.0	1.4	2.2	6.2	91.6
Property taxes	100.0	0.7	3.1	4.2	92.7
Maintenance, insurance, and other expenses	100.0	0.7	1.6	3.8	94.6
Housing while attending school	100.0	8.8	4.6	4.2	91.3
Lodging on trips	100.0	3.3	4.2	5.3	90.6

	total consumer units	Asian	black	Hispanic	non-Hispanic white and other
UTILITIES, FUELS, AND PUBLIC SERVICES	**100.0%**	**3.2%**	**11.7%**	**9.7%**	**78.8%**
Natural gas	**100.0**	**3.5**	**12.6**	**8.4**	**79.1**
Electricity	**100.0**	**2.8**	**12.1**	**9.0**	**79.0**
Fuel oil and other fuels	**100.0**	**1.1**	**5.1**	**6.4**	**88.7**
Fuel oil	100.0	1.5	5.8	5.8	88.9
Bottled and tank gas	100.0	0.9	4.2	7.0	88.8
Wood and other fuels	100.0	0.2	5.3	8.2	86.6
Telephone services	**100.0**	**3.7**	**12.3**	**11.0**	**76.9**
Residential telephone and pay phones	100.0	3.2	13.8	10.4	76.0
Cellular phone service	100.0	4.2	9.9	10.9	79.4
Pager service	100.0	7.4	10.0	9.7	80.1
Phone cards	100.0	10.1	12.4	31.8	56.0
Water and other public services	**100.0**	**3.6**	**9.7**	**10.3**	**80.0**
Water and sewerage maintenance	100.0	3.7	10.6	10.6	78.8
Trash and garbage collection	100.0	3.2	7.1	9.7	83.2
Septic tank cleaning	100.0	1.2	3.9	4.9	91.1

* See Appendix B for information about mortgage principal reduction.
Note: "Asian" and "black" include Hispanics and non-Hispanics who identify themselves as being of the respective race alone. "Hispanic" includes people of any race who identify themselves as Hispanic. "Other" includes people who identify themselves as non-Hispanic and as Alaska Native, American Indian, Asian (who are also included in the "Asian" column), Native Hawaiian or other Pacific Islander, as well as non-Hispanics reporting more than one race. "–" means sample is too small to make a reliable estimate.
Source: Calculations by New Strategist based on the 2004 Consumer Expenditure Survey

Table 9.21 Housing: Shelter and Utilities: Average spending by region, 2004

(average annual spending of consumer units (CU) on shelter and utilities, by region in which consumer unit lives, 2004)

	total consumer units	Northeast	Midwest	South	West
Number of consumer units (in 000s)	116,282	22,051	26,539	41,801	25,891
Average number of persons per CU	2.5	2.4	2.4	2.5	2.6
Average before-tax income of CU	$54,453.00	$61,050.00	$53,567.00	$50,775.00	$55,682.00
Average spending of CU, total	43,394.87	46,114.89	43,370.77	39,173.65	47,921.74
Housing, average spending	13,918.48	15,733.70	13,438.35	12,250.19	15,556.56
SHELTER	7,998.43	9,625.51	7,338.56	6,620.81	9,513.25
Owned dwellings*	5,324.49	6,387.19	5,259.90	4,456.42	5,887.13
Mortgage interest and charges	2,936.18	3,056.84	2,749.70	2,531.46	3,678.01
Mortgage interest	2,785.37	2,847.31	2,572.48	2,432.45	3,520.63
Interest paid, home equity loan	57.73	91.92	51.58	47.50	51.43
Interest paid, home equity line of credit	92.89	117.08	125.64	51.25	105.95
Property taxes	1,391.17	2,130.80	1,530.01	1,046.42	1,175.55
Maintenance, repairs, insurance, other expenses	997.14	1,199.56	980.20	878.54	1,033.57
Homeowner's insurance	314.75	255.33	348.70	341.96	286.61
Ground rent	40.10	28.30	29.73	31.11	75.27
Maintenance and repair services	530.63	762.75	489.15	420.35	553.52
Painting and papering	59.71	65.79	55.92	46.77	79.31
Plumbing and water heating	49.48	51.83	50.86	43.53	55.66
Heat, air conditioning, electrical work	89.48	144.20	76.68	70.20	87.11
Roofing and gutters	96.28	167.27	85.88	78.12	75.80
Other repair and maintenance services	177.49	287.08	156.07	125.63	189.86
Repair, replacement of hard-surface flooring	52.71	38.73	60.00	50.91	60.04
Repair of built-in appliances	5.49	7.84	3.73	5.21	5.74
Maintenance and repair materials	73.33	95.32	78.53	55.71	77.71
Paints, wallpaper, and supplies	15.18	17.27	19.48	11.77	14.50
Tools, equipment for painting, wallpapering	1.63	1.86	2.09	1.26	1.56
Plumbing supplies and equipment	5.79	7.29	6.13	4.77	5.79
Electrical supplies, heating and cooling equipment	3.23	4.26	3.81	2.22	3.38
Hard-surface flooring, repair and replacement	9.34	4.64	11.29	10.38	9.66
Roofing and gutters	6.42	3.73	3.49	6.95	10.86
Plaster, paneling, siding, windows, doors, screens, awnings	13.02	20.81	14.71	6.22	15.64
Patio, walk, fence, driveway, masonry, brick, and stucco materials	1.57	1.84	2.35	1.13	1.23
Miscellaneous supplies and equipment	17.16	33.62	15.19	11.01	15.09
Property management and security	34.91	54.77	30.52	25.65	37.44
Property management	28.55	50.21	25.79	18.08	29.83
Management and upkeep services for security	6.36	4.57	4.73	7.56	7.61
Parking	3.43	3.08	3.57	3.77	3.02
Rented dwellings	2,201.09	2,673.59	1,555.85	1,825.51	3,066.44
Rent	2,125.93	2,582.01	1,502.59	1,767.68	2,954.87
Rent as pay	36.08	47.45	23.93	28.99	50.31
Maintenance, insurance, and other expenses	39.07	44.13	29.33	28.85	61.26
Tenant's insurance	7.06	6.06	9.11	6.22	7.19
Maintenance and repair services	26.94	30.96	17.52	17.64	48.18
Maintenance and repair materials	5.07	7.12	2.70	4.98	5.90
Other lodging	472.85	564.74	522.81	338.88	559.68
Owned vacation homes	137.22	181.84	189.02	104.31	99.27
Mortgage interest and charges	54.04	68.38	61.64	44.79	48.98
Property taxes	57.51	85.71	84.00	39.99	34.61
Maintenance, insurance, and other expenses	25.67	27.74	43.39	19.52	15.68
Housing while attending school	57.73	81.85	47.00	30.94	91.46
Lodging on trips	277.89	301.05	286.78	203.64	368.95

	total consumer units	Northeast	Midwest	South	West
UTILITIES, FUELS, AND PUBLIC SERVICES	$2,926.65	$3,098.30	$2,956.95	$2,974.88	$2,671.52
Natural gas	424.02	563.62	630.90	255.49	365.13
Electricity	1,064.41	985.33	958.04	1,288.01	879.82
Fuel oil and other fuels	120.53	321.52	105.24	68.95	48.33
Fuel oil	64.19	264.81	18.89	22.80	6.62
Bottled and tank gas	45.20	33.26	82.10	36.89	30.94
Wood and other fuels	10.61	20.67	4.25	9.26	10.77
Telephone services	990.22	987.91	945.81	1,031.34	971.31
Residential telephone and pay phones	592.31	637.95	551.69	634.77	526.52
Cellular phone service	378.39	331.07	378.26	378.50	418.63
Pager service	1.01	1.17	1.11	0.70	1.26
Phone cards	18.51	17.73	14.74	17.37	24.90
Water and other public services	327.47	239.91	316.97	331.09	406.94
Water and sewerage maintenance	242.54	185.67	228.56	254.09	286.66
Trash and garbage collection	82.77	49.46	86.20	75.95	118.63
Septic tank cleaning	2.16	4.78	2.22	1.05	1.65

* See Appendix B for information about mortgage principal reduction.
Note: Subcategories may not add to total because some are not shown.
Source: Bureau of Labor Statistics, unpublished tables from the 2004 Consumer Expenditure Survey

Table 9.22 Housing: Shelter and Utilities: Indexed spending by region, 2004

(indexed average annual spending of consumer units (CU) on shelter and utilities, by region in which consumer unit lives, 2004; index definition: an index of 100 is the average for all consumer units; an index of 132 means that spending by consumer units in that group is 32 percent above the average for all consumer units; an index of 68 indicates spending that is 32 percent below the average for all consumer units)

	total consumer units	Northeast	Midwest	South	West
Average spending of CU, total	$43,395	$46,115	$43,371	$39,174	$47,922
Average spending of CU, index	100	106	100	90	110
Housing, spending index	100	113	97	88	112
SHELTER	100	120	92	83	119
Owned dwellings*	100	120	99	84	111
Mortgage interest and charges	100	104	94	86	125
Mortgage interest	100	102	92	87	126
Interest paid, home equity loan	100	159	89	82	89
Interest paid, home equity line of credit	100	126	135	55	114
Property taxes	100	153	110	75	85
Maintenance, repairs, insurance, other expenses	100	120	98	88	104
Homeowner's insurance	100	81	111	109	91
Ground rent	100	71	74	78	188
Maintenance and repair services	100	144	92	79	104
Painting and papering	100	110	94	78	133
Plumbing and water heating	100	105	103	88	112
Heat, air conditioning, electrical work	100	161	86	78	97
Roofing and gutters	100	174	89	81	79
Other repair and maintenance services	100	162	88	71	107
Repair, replacement of hard-surface flooring	100	73	114	97	114
Repair of built-in appliances	100	143	68	95	105
Maintenance and repair materials	100	130	107	76	106
Paints, wallpaper, and supplies	100	114	128	78	96
Tools, equipment for painting, wallpapering	100	114	128	77	96
Plumbing supplies and equipment	100	126	106	82	100
Electrical supplies, heating and cooling equipment	100	132	118	69	105
Hard-surface flooring, repair and replacement	100	50	121	111	103
Roofing and gutters	100	58	54	108	169
Plaster, paneling, siding, windows, doors, screens, awnings	100	160	113	48	120
Patio, walk, fence, driveway, masonry, brick, and stucco materials	100	117	150	72	78
Miscellaneous supplies and equipment	100	196	89	64	88
Property management and security	100	157	87	73	107
Property management	100	176	90	63	104
Management and upkeep services for security	100	72	74	119	120
Parking	100	90	104	110	88
Rented dwellings	100	121	71	83	139
Rent	100	121	71	83	139
Rent as pay	100	132	66	80	139
Maintenance, insurance, and other expenses	100	113	75	74	157
Tenant's insurance	100	86	129	88	102
Maintenance and repair services	100	115	65	65	179
Maintenance and repair materials	100	140	53	98	116
Other lodging	100	119	111	72	118
Owned vacation homes	100	133	138	76	72
Mortgage interest and charges	100	127	114	83	91
Property taxes	100	149	146	70	60
Maintenance, insurance, and other expenses	100	108	169	76	61
Housing while attending school	100	142	81	54	158
Lodging on trips	100	108	103	73	133

	total consumer units	Northeast	Midwest	South	West
UTILITIES, FUELS, AND PUBLIC SERVICES	**100**	**106**	**101**	**102**	**91**
Natural gas	**100**	**133**	**149**	**60**	**86**
Electricity	**100**	**93**	**90**	**121**	**83**
Fuel oil and other fuels	**100**	**267**	**87**	**57**	**40**
Fuel oil	100	413	29	36	10
Bottled and tank gas	100	74	182	82	68
Wood and other fuels	100	195	40	87	102
Telephone services	**100**	**100**	**96**	**104**	**98**
Residential telephone and pay phones	100	108	93	107	89
Cellular phone service	100	87	100	100	111
Pager service	100	116	110	69	125
Phone cards	100	96	80	94	135
Water and other public services	**100**	**73**	**97**	**101**	**124**
Water and sewerage maintenance	100	77	94	105	118
Trash and garbage collection	100	60	104	92	143
Septic tank cleaning	100	221	103	49	76

* See Appendix B for information about mortgage principal reduction.
Source: Calculations by New Strategist based on the 2004 Consumer Expenditure Survey

Table 9.23 Housing: Shelter and Utilities: Total spending by region, 2004

(total annual spending on shelter and utilities, by region in which consumer units live, 2004; consumer units and dollars in thousands)

	total consumer units	Northeast	Midwest	South	West
Number of consumer units	116,282	22,051	26,539	41,801	25,891
Total spending of all consumer units	$5,046,042,273	$1,016,879,439	$1,151,016,865	$1,637,497,744	$1,240,741,770
Housing, total spending	1,618,468,691	346,943,819	356,640,371	512,070,192	402,774,895
SHELTER	930,073,437	212,252,121	194,758,044	276,756,479	246,307,556
Owned dwellings*	619,142,346	140,843,927	139,592,486	186,282,812	152,423,683
Mortgage interest and charges	341,424,883	67,406,379	72,974,288	105,817,559	95,227,357
Mortgage interest	323,888,394	62,786,033	68,271,047	101,678,842	91,152,631
Interest paid, home equity loan	6,712,960	2,026,928	1,368,882	1,985,548	1,331,574
Interest paid, home equity line of credit	10,801,435	2,581,731	3,334,360	2,142,301	2,743,151
Property taxes	161,768,030	46,986,271	40,604,935	43,741,402	30,436,165
Maintenance, repairs, insurance, other expenses	115,949,433	26,451,498	26,013,528	36,723,851	26,760,161
Homeowner's insurance	36,599,760	5,630,282	9,254,149	14,294,270	7,420,620
Ground rent	4,662,908	624,043	789,004	1,300,429	1,948,816
Maintenance and repair services	61,702,718	16,819,400	12,981,552	17,571,050	14,331,186
Painting and papering	6,943,198	1,450,735	1,484,061	1,955,033	2,053,415
Plumbing and water heating	5,753,633	1,142,903	1,349,774	1,819,598	1,441,093
Heat, air conditioning, electrical work	10,404,913	3,179,754	2,035,011	2,934,430	2,255,365
Roofing and gutters	11,195,631	3,688,471	2,279,169	3,265,494	1,962,538
Other repair and maintenance services	20,638,892	6,330,401	4,141,942	5,251,460	4,915,665
Repair, replacement of hard-surface flooring	6,129,224	854,035	1,592,340	2,128,089	1,554,496
Repair of built-in appliances	638,388	172,880	98,990	217,783	148,614
Maintenance and repair materials	8,526,959	2,101,901	2,084,108	2,328,734	2,011,990
Paints, wallpaper, and supplies	1,765,161	380,821	516,980	491,998	375,420
Tools, equipment for painting, wallpapering	189,540	41,015	55,467	52,669	40,390
Plumbing supplies and equipment	673,273	160,752	162,684	199,391	149,909
Electrical supplies, heating and cooling equipment	375,591	93,937	101,114	92,798	87,512
Hard-surface flooring, repair and replacement	1,086,074	102,317	299,625	433,894	250,107
Roofing and gutters	746,530	82,250	92,621	290,517	281,176
Plaster, paneling, siding, windows, doors, screens, awnings	1,513,992	458,881	390,389	260,002	404,935
Patio, walk, fence, driveway, masonry, brick, and stucco materials	182,563	40,574	62,367	47,235	31,846
Miscellaneous supplies and equipment	1,995,399	741,355	403,127	460,229	390,695
Property management and security	4,059,405	1,207,733	809,970	1,072,196	969,359
Property management	3,319,851	1,107,181	684,441	755,762	772,329
Management and upkeep services for security	739,554	100,773	125,529	316,016	197,031
Parking	398,847	67,917	94,744	157,590	78,191
Rented dwellings	255,947,147	58,955,333	41,290,703	76,308,144	79,393,198
Rent	247,207,392	56,935,903	39,877,236	73,890,792	76,504,539
Rent as pay	4,195,455	1,046,320	635,078	1,211,811	1,302,576
Maintenance, insurance, and other expenses	4,543,138	973,111	778,389	1,205,959	1,586,083
Tenant's insurance	820,951	133,629	241,770	260,002	186,156
Maintenance and repair services	3,132,637	682,699	464,963	737,370	1,247,428
Maintenance and repair materials	589,550	157,003	71,655	208,169	152,757
Other lodging	54,983,944	12,453,082	13,874,855	14,165,523	14,490,675
Owned vacation homes	15,956,216	4,009,754	5,016,402	4,360,262	2,570,200
Mortgage interest and charges	6,283,879	1,507,847	1,635,864	1,872,267	1,268,141
Property taxes	6,687,378	1,889,991	2,229,276	1,671,622	896,088
Maintenance, insurance, and other expenses	2,984,959	611,695	1,151,527	815,956	405,971
Housing while attending school	6,712,960	1,804,874	1,247,333	1,293,323	2,367,991
Lodging on trips	32,313,605	6,638,454	7,610,854	8,512,356	9,552,484

	total consumer units	Northeast	Midwest	South	West
UTILITIES, FUELS, AND PUBLIC SERVICES	$340,316,715	$68,320,613	$78,474,496	$124,352,959	$69,168,324
Natural gas	49,305,894	12,428,385	16,743,455	10,679,737	9,453,581
Electricity	123,771,724	21,727,512	25,425,424	53,840,106	22,779,420
Fuel oil and other fuels	14,015,469	7,089,838	2,792,964	2,882,179	1,251,312
Fuel oil	7,464,142	5,839,325	501,322	953,063	171,398
Bottled and tank gas	5,255,946	733,416	2,178,852	1,542,039	801,068
Wood and other fuels	1,233,752	455,794	112,791	387,077	278,846
Telephone services	115,144,762	21,784,403	25,100,852	43,111,043	25,148,187
Residential telephone and pay phones	68,874,991	14,067,435	14,641,301	26,534,021	13,632,129
Cellular phone service	43,999,946	7,300,425	10,038,642	15,821,679	10,838,749
Pager service	117,445	25,800	29,458	29,261	32,623
Phone cards	2,152,380	390,964	391,185	726,083	644,686
Water and other public services	38,078,867	5,290,255	8,412,067	13,839,893	10,536,084
Water and sewerage maintenance	28,203,036	4,094,209	6,065,754	10,621,216	7,421,914
Trash and garbage collection	9,624,661	1,090,642	2,287,662	3,174,786	3,071,449
Septic tank cleaning	251,169	105,404	58,917	43,891	42,720

* See Appendix B for information about mortgage principal reduction.
Note: Numbers may not add to total because of rounding and missing subcategories.
Source: Calculations by New Strategist based on the 2004 Consumer Expenditure Survey

Table 9.24 Housing: Shelter and Utilities: Market shares by region, 2004

(percentage of total annual spending on shelter and utilities accounted for by consumer units by region, 2004)

	total consumer units	Northeast	Midwest	South	West
Share of total consumer units	100.0%	19.0%	22.8%	35.9%	22.3%
Share of total before-tax income	100.0	21.3	22.5	33.5	22.8
Share of total spending	100.0	20.2	22.8	32.5	24.6
Share of housing spending	100.0	21.4	22.0	31.6	24.9
SHELTER	100.0	22.8	20.9	29.8	26.5
Owned dwellings*	100.0	22.7	22.5	30.1	24.6
Mortgage interest and charges	100.0	19.7	21.4	31.0	27.9
Mortgage interest	100.0	19.4	21.1	31.4	28.1
Interest paid, home equity loan	100.0	30.2	20.4	29.6	19.8
Interest paid, home equity line of credit	100.0	23.9	30.9	19.8	25.4
Property taxes	100.0	29.0	25.1	27.0	18.8
Maintenance, repairs, insurance, other expenses	100.0	22.8	22.4	31.7	23.1
Homeowner's insurance	100.0	15.4	25.3	39.1	20.3
Ground rent	100.0	13.4	16.9	27.9	41.8
Maintenance and repair services	100.0	27.3	21.0	28.5	23.2
Painting and papering	100.0	20.9	21.4	28.2	29.6
Plumbing and water heating	100.0	19.9	23.5	31.6	25.0
Heat, air conditioning, electrical work	100.0	30.6	19.6	28.2	21.7
Roofing and gutters	100.0	32.9	20.4	29.2	17.5
Other repair and maintenance services	100.0	30.7	20.1	25.4	23.8
Repair, replacement of hard-surface flooring	100.0	13.9	26.0	34.7	25.4
Repair of built-in appliances	100.0	27.1	15.5	34.1	23.3
Maintenance and repair materials	100.0	24.7	24.4	27.3	23.6
Paints, wallpaper, and supplies	100.0	21.6	29.3	27.9	21.3
Tools, equipment for painting, wallpapering	100.0	21.6	29.3	27.8	21.3
Plumbing supplies and equipment	100.0	23.9	24.2	29.6	22.3
Electrical supplies, heating and cooling equipment	100.0	25.0	26.9	24.7	23.3
Hard-surface flooring, repair and replacement	100.0	9.4	27.6	40.0	23.0
Roofing and gutters	100.0	11.0	12.4	38.9	37.7
Plaster, paneling, siding, windows, doors, screens, awnings	100.0	30.3	25.8	17.2	26.7
Patio, walk, fence, driveway, masonry, brick, and stucco materials	100.0	22.2	34.2	25.9	17.4
Miscellaneous supplies and equipment	100.0	37.2	20.2	23.1	19.6
Property management and security	100.0	29.8	20.0	26.4	23.9
Property management	100.0	33.4	20.6	22.8	23.3
Management and upkeep services for security	100.0	13.6	17.0	42.7	26.6
Parking	100.0	17.0	23.8	39.5	19.6
Rented dwellings	100.0	23.0	16.1	29.8	31.0
Rent	100.0	23.0	16.1	29.9	30.9
Rent as pay	100.0	24.9	15.1	28.9	31.0
Maintenance, insurance, and other expenses	100.0	21.4	17.1	26.5	34.9
Tenant's insurance	100.0	16.3	29.5	31.7	22.7
Maintenance and repair services	100.0	21.8	14.8	23.5	39.8
Maintenance and repair materials	100.0	26.6	12.2	35.3	25.9
Other lodging	100.0	22.6	25.2	25.8	26.4
Owned vacation homes	100.0	25.1	31.4	27.3	16.1
Mortgage interest and charges	100.0	24.0	26.0	29.8	20.2
Property taxes	100.0	28.3	33.3	25.0	13.4
Maintenance, insurance, and other expenses	100.0	20.5	38.6	27.3	13.6
Housing while attending school	100.0	26.9	18.6	19.3	35.3
Lodging on trips	100.0	20.5	23.6	26.3	29.6

	total consumer units	Northeast	Midwest	South	West
UTILITIES, FUELS, AND PUBLIC SERVICES	**100.0%**	**20.1%**	**23.1%**	**36.5%**	**20.3%**
Natural gas	**100.0**	**25.2**	**34.0**	**21.7**	**19.2**
Electricity	**100.0**	**17.6**	**20.5**	**43.5**	**18.4**
Fuel oil and other fuels	**100.0**	**50.6**	**19.9**	**20.6**	**8.9**
Fuel oil	100.0	78.2	6.7	12.8	2.3
Bottled and tank gas	100.0	14.0	41.5	29.3	15.2
Wood and other fuels	100.0	36.9	9.1	31.4	22.6
Telephone services	**100.0**	**18.9**	**21.8**	**37.4**	**21.8**
Residential telephone and pay phones	100.0	20.4	21.3	38.5	19.8
Cellular phone service	100.0	16.6	22.8	36.0	24.6
Pager service	100.0	22.0	·25.1	24.9	27.8
Phone cards	100.0	18.2	18.2	33.7	30.0
Water and other public services	**100.0**	**13.9**	**22.1**	**36.3**	**27.7**
Water and sewerage maintenance	100.0	14.5	21.5	37.7	26.3
Trash and garbage collection	100.0	11.3	23.8	33.0	31.9
Septic tank cleaning	100.0	42.0	23.5	17.5	17.0

* See Appendix B for information about mortgage principal reduction.
Note: Numbers may not add to total because of rounding.
Source: Calculations by New Strategist based on the 2004 Consumer Expenditure Survey

Table 9.25 Housing: Shelter and Utilities: Average spending by education, 2004

(average annual spending of consumer units (CU) on shelter and utilities, by education of consumer unit reference person, 2004)

	total consumer units	less than high school graduate	high school graduate	some college	associate's degree	college graduate		
						total	bachelor's degree	master's, professional, doctorate
Number of consumer units (in 000s)	116,282	16,829	31,005	25,317	10,678	32,452	20,684	11,768
Average number of persons per CU	2.5	2.7	2.5	2.3	2.6	2.5	2.4	2.5
Average before-tax income of CU	$54,453.00	$29,094.00	$42,334.00	$46,756.00	$58,593.00	$83,825.00	$75,647.00	$98,201.00
Average spending of CU, total	43,394.87	25,421.18	35,438.55	40,877.68	48,177.36	60,712.28	56,728.41	67,801.38
Housing, average spending	13,918.48	8,724.44	11,207.58	12,915.13	14,854.90	19,676.20	18,304.59	22,109.54
SHELTER	**7,998.43**	**4,912.79**	**6,176.93**	**7,363.73**	**8,388.68**	**11,705.69**	**10,955.61**	**13,024.08**
Owned dwellings*	5,324.49	2,411.61	3,869.02	4,622.71	6,062.37	8,530.39	7,689.34	10,008.69
Mortgage interest and charges	2,936.18	1,245.20	2,043.99	2,562.70	3,523.49	4,763.66	4,403.77	5,396.23
Mortgage interest	2,785.37	1,201.41	1,931.43	2,431.85	3,340.15	4,515.93	4,180.78	5,105.04
Interest paid, home equity loan	57.73	27.56	49.10	45.19	71.88	86.74	90.02	80.98
Interest paid, home equity line of credit	92.89	15.66	63.47	85.66	110.29	160.98	132.97	210.21
Property taxes	1,391.17	689.34	1,058.00	1,155.03	1,445.36	2,239.85	1,947.48	2,753.75
Maintenance, repairs, insurance, other expenses	997.14	477.07	767.02	904.98	1,093.51	1,526.88	1,338.09	1,858.71
Homeowner's insurance	314.75	183.46	283.19	288.62	366.45	416.35	374.67	489.62
Ground rent	40.10	74.18	50.46	35.51	44.10	14.78	12.54	18.71
Maintenance and repair services	530.63	182.52	348.47	477.60	533.99	925.47	795.31	1,154.26
Painting and papering	59.71	13.17	32.39	40.92	37.12	132.04	97.64	192.51
Plumbing and water heating	49.48	13.91	39.43	39.36	65.68	80.08	60.39	114.67
Heat, air conditioning, electrical work	89.48	26.62	69.28	79.76	121.51	138.41	126.64	159.11
Roofing and gutters	96.28	63.06	81.36	95.55	82.44	132.89	122.82	150.59
Other repair and maintenance services	177.49	49.97	96.46	159.30	171.33	337.26	293.37	414.40
Repair, replacement of hard-surface flooring	52.71	15.18	24.99	57.90	51.69	94.93	86.78	109.26
Repair of built-in appliances	5.49	0.60	4.55	4.81	4.21	9.87	7.68	13.71
Maintenance and repair materials	73.33	32.44	61.30	62.78	122.23	98.17	97.39	99.52
Paints, wallpaper, and supplies	15.18	7.19	10.52	10.73	27.58	23.17	24.21	21.35
Tools, equipment for painting, wallpapering	1.63	0.77	1.13	1.15	2.96	2.49	2.60	2.29
Plumbing supplies and equipment	5.79	3.25	4.24	5.26	13.82	6.34	4.05	10.36
Electrical supplies, heating and cooling equipment	3.23	0.38	2.63	3.20	4.35	4.93	4.92	4.93
Hard-surface flooring, repair and replacement	9.34	6.05	3.38	8.37	15.24	15.55	17.91	11.40
Roofing and gutters	6.42	2.31	6.97	6.35	4.55	8.70	9.61	7.10
Plaster, paneling, siding, windows, doors, screens, awnings	13.02	6.50	8.69	14.32	23.54	16.07	15.34	17.34
Patio, walk, fence, driveway, masonry, brick, and stucco materials	1.57	0.49	1.68	2.14	1.14	1.72	2.06	1.11
Miscellaneous supplies and equipment	17.16	5.50	22.05	11.26	29.04	19.21	16.69	23.65
Property management and security	34.91	4.09	21.72	37.09	23.19	65.64	51.55	90.42
Property management	28.55	3.20	18.73	30.26	18.59	53.02	38.69	78.21
Management and upkeep services for security	6.36	0.89	2.99	6.83	4.60	12.62	12.86	12.22
Parking	3.43	0.38	1.89	3.38	3.56	6.47	6.64	6.17
Rented dwellings	**2,201.09**	**2,425.04**	**2,066.27**	**2,302.81**	**1,862.73**	**2,245.73**	**2,461.94**	**1,865.70**
Rent	2,125.93	2,328.49	1,997.34	2,249.35	1,803.86	2,153.45	2,371.27	1,770.59
Rent as pay	36.08	84.17	37.58	31.91	26.19	16.23	13.51	21.01
Maintenance, insurance, and other expenses	39.07	12.38	31.35	21.55	32.68	76.06	77.17	74.10
Tenant's insurance	7.06	3.33	5.31	7.40	9.25	9.69	9.60	9.85
Maintenance and repair services	26.94	3.90	21.74	6.06	15.61	63.87	65.05	61.80
Maintenance and repair materials	5.07	5.15	4.31	8.09	7.82	2.49	2.51	2.46
Other lodging	**472.85**	**76.13**	**241.64**	**438.21**	**463.59**	**929.57**	**804.33**	**1,149.70**
Owned vacation homes	137.22	27.19	79.21	144.42	109.99	253.05	226.12	300.39
Mortgage interest and charges	54.04	4.58	28.21	50.51	36.48	112.91	110.37	117.36
Property taxes	57.51	17.54	30.31	66.58	48.33	100.16	85.89	125.24
Maintenance, insurance, and other expenses	25.67	5.07	20.68	27.33	25.18	39.99	29.86	57.78
Housing while attending school	57.73	5.84	11.57	75.56	72.46	110.00	88.52	147.75
Lodging on trips	277.89	43.11	150.86	218.22	281.15	566.51	489.68	701.56

	total consumer units	less than high school graduate	high school graduate	some college	associate's degree	college graduate		
						total	bachelor's degree	master's, professional, doctorate
UTILITIES, FUELS, AND PUBLIC SERVICES	$2,926.65	$2,414.05	$2,837.29	$2,717.27	$3,171.78	$3,360.53	$3,232.06	$3,586.35
Natural gas	424.02	334.69	414.89	367.28	436.13	519.33	482.46	584.15
Electricity	1,064.41	937.12	1,070.26	1,004.55	1,129.99	1,149.96	1,111.12	1,218.21
Fuel oil and other fuels	120.53	102.94	134.00	104.87	134.84	124.31	112.87	144.41
Fuel oil	64.19	43.34	67.84	56.56	69.31	75.80	64.66	95.38
Bottled and tank gas	45.20	49.04	52.10	37.29	57.51	38.73	37.62	40.68
Wood and other fuels	10.61	10.09	12.81	10.59	8.01	9.66	10.41	8.35
Telephone services	990.22	777.81	920.61	937.39	1,111.90	1,168.05	1,148.68	1,202.08
Residential telephone and pay phones	592.31	543.67	583.50	537.84	607.78	663.35	641.83	701.16
Cellular phone service	378.39	199.12	321.31	382.41	486.51	487.18	491.78	479.10
Pager service	1.01	1.23	0.45	1.28	1.90	0.92	0.70	1.30
Phone cards	18.51	33.79	15.35	15.86	15.72	16.60	14.37	20.52
Water and other public services	327.47	261.49	297.52	303.17	358.91	398.89	376.93	437.50
Water and sewerage maintenance	242.54	200.64	223.25	221.73	257.76	293.92	277.21	323.30
Trash and garbage collection	82.77	59.79	72.64	79.49	97.49	102.07	97.36	110.35
Septic tank cleaning	2.16	1.06	1.63	1.95	3.66	2.90	2.36	3.85

* See Appendix B for information about mortgage principal reduction.
Note: Subcategories may not add to total because some are not shown.
Source: Bureau of Labor Statistics, unpublished tables from the 2004 Consumer Expenditure Survey

Table 9.26 Housing: Shelter and Utilities: Indexed spending by education, 2004

(indexed average annual spending of consumer units (CU) on shelter and utilities, by education of consumer unit reference person, 2004; index definition: an index of 100 is the average for all consumer units; an index of 132 means that spending by consumer units in that group is 32 percent above the average for all consumer units; an index of 68 indicates spending that is 32 percent below the average for all consumer units)

	total consumer units	less than high school graduate	high school graduate	some college	associate's degree	college graduate total	bachelor's degree	master's, professional, doctorate
Average spending of CU, total	$43,395	$25,421	$35,439	$40,878	$48,177	$60,712	$56,728	$67,801
Average spending of CU, index	100	59	82	94	111	140	131	156
Housing, spending index	100	63	81	93	107	141	132	159
SHELTER	100	61	77	92	105	146	137	163
Owned dwellings*	100	45	73	87	114	160	144	188
Mortgage interest and charges	100	42	70	87	120	162	150	184
Mortgage interest	100	43	69	87	120	162	150	183
Interest paid, home equity loan	100	48	85	78	125	150	156	140
Interest paid, home equity line of credit	100	17	68	92	119	173	143	226
Property taxes	100	50	76	83	104	161	140	198
Maintenance, repairs, insurance, other expenses	100	48	77	91	110	153	134	186
Homeowner's insurance	100	58	90	92	116	132	119	156
Ground rent	100	185	126	89	110	37	31	47
Maintenance and repair services	100	34	66	90	101	174	150	218
Painting and papering	100	22	54	69	62	221	164	322
Plumbing and water heating	100	28	80	80	133	162	122	232
Heat, air conditioning, electrical work	100	30	77	89	136	155	142	178
Roofing and gutters	100	65	85	99	86	138	128	156
Other repair and maintenance services	100	28	54	90	97	190	165	233
Repair, replacement of hard-surface flooring	100	29	47	110	98	180	165	207
Repair of built-in appliances	100	11	83	88	77	180	140	250
Maintenance and repair materials	100	44	84	86	167	134	133	136
Paints, wallpaper, and supplies	100	47	69	71	182	153	159	141
Tools, equipment for painting, wallpapering	100	47	69	71	182	153	160	140
Plumbing supplies and equipment	100	56	73	91	239	109	70	179
Electrical supplies, heating and cooling equipment	100	12	81	99	135	153	152	153
Hard-surface flooring, repair and replacement	100	65	36	90	163	166	192	122
Roofing and gutters	100	36	109	99	71	136	150	111
Plaster, paneling, siding, windows, doors, screens, awnings	100	50	67	110	181	123	118	133
Patio, walk, fence, driveway, masonry, brick, and stucco materials	100	31	107	136	73	110	131	71
Miscellaneous supplies and equipment	100	32	128	66	169	112	97	138
Property management and security	100	12	62	106	66	188	148	259
Property management	100	11	66	106	65	186	136	274
Management and upkeep services for security	100	14	47	107	72	198	202	192
Parking	100	11	55	99	104	189	194	180
Rented dwellings	100	110	94	105	85	102	112	85
Rent	100	110	94	106	85	101	112	83
Rent as pay	100	233	104	88	73	45	37	58
Maintenance, insurance, and other expenses	100	32	80	55	84	195	198	190
Tenant's insurance	100	47	75	105	131	137	136	140
Maintenance and repair services	100	14	81	22	58	237	241	229
Maintenance and repair materials	100	102	85	160	154	49	50	49
Other lodging	100	16	51	93	98	197	170	243
Owned vacation homes	100	20	58	105	80	184	165	219
Mortgage interest and charges	100	8	52	93	68	209	204	217
Property taxes	100	30	53	116	84	174	149	218
Maintenance, insurance, and other expenses	100	20	81	106	98	156	116	225
Housing while attending school	100	10	20	131	126	191	153	256
Lodging on trips	100	16	54	79	101	204	176	252

	total consumer units	less than high school graduate	high school graduate	some college	associate's degree	college graduate total	bachelor's degree	master's, professional, doctorate
UTILITIES, FUELS, AND PUBLIC SERVICES	**100**	**82**	**97**	**93**	**108**	**115**	**110**	**123**
Natural gas	**100**	**79**	**98**	**87**	**103**	**122**	**114**	**138**
Electricity	**100**	**88**	**101**	**94**	**106**	**108**	**104**	**114**
Fuel oil and other fuels	**100**	**85**	**111**	**87**	**112**	**103**	**94**	**120**
Fuel oil	100	68	106	88	108	118	101	149
Bottled and tank gas	100	108	115	83	127	86	83	90
Wood and other fuels	100	95	121	100	75	91	98	79
Telephone services	**100**	**79**	**93**	**95**	**112**	**118**	**116**	**121**
Residential telephone and pay phones	100	92	99	91	103	112	108	118
Cellular phone service	100	53	85	101	129	129	130	127
Pager service	100	122	45	127	188	91	69	129
Phone cards	100	183	83	86	85	90	78	111
Water and other public services	**100**	**80**	**91**	**93**	**110**	**122**	**115**	**134**
Water and sewerage maintenance	100	83	92	91	106	121	114	133
Trash and garbage collection	100	72	88	96	118	123	118	133
Septic tank cleaning	100	49	75	90	169	134	109	178

See Appendix B for information about mortgage principal reduction.
Source: Calculations by New Strategist based on the 2004 Consumer Expenditure Survey

Table 9.27 Housing: Shelter and Utilities: Total spending by education, 2004

(total annual spending on shelter and utilities, by consumer unit (CU) educational attainment group, 2004; consumer units and dollars in thousands)

	total consumer units	less than high school graduate	high school graduate	some college	associate's degree	college graduate total	college graduate bachelor's degree	college graduate master's, professional, doctorate
Number of consumer units	116,282	16,829	31,005	25,317	10,678	32,452	20,684	11,768
Total spending of all CUs	$5,046,042,273	$427,813,038	$1,098,772,243	$1,034,900,225	$514,437,850	$1,970,234,911	$1,173,370,432	$797,886,640
Housing, total spending	1,618,468,691	146,823,601	347,491,018	326,972,346	158,620,622	638,532,042	378,612,140	260,185,067
SHELTER	930,073,437	82,677,343	191,515,715	186,427,552	89,574,325	379,873,052	226,605,837	153,267,373
Owned dwellings*	619,142,346	40,584,985	119,958,965	117,033,149	64,733,987	276,828,216	159,046,309	117,782,264
Mortgage interest and charges	341,424,883	20,955,471	63,373,910	64,879,876	37,623,826	154,590,294	91,087,579	63,502,835
Mortgage interest	323,888,394	20,218,529	59,883,987	61,567,146	35,666,122	146,550,960	86,475,254	60,076,111
Interest paid, home equity loan	6,712,960	463,807	1,522,346	1,144,075	767,535	2,814,886	1,861,974	952,973
Interest paid, home equity line of credit	10,801,435	263,542	1,967,887	2,168,654	1,177,677	5,224,123	2,750,351	2,473,751
Property taxes	161,768,030	11,600,903	32,803,290	29,241,895	15,433,554	72,687,612	40,281,676	32,406,130
Maintenance, repairs, insurance, other expenses	115,949,433	8,028,611	23,781,455	22,911,379	11,676,500	49,550,310	27,677,054	21,873,299
Homeowner's insurance	36,599,760	3,087,448	8,780,306	7,306,993	3,912,953	13,511,390	7,749,674	5,761,848
Ground rent	4,662,908	1,248,375	1,564,512	899,007	470,900	479,641	259,377	220,179
Maintenance and repair services	61,702,718	3,071,629	10,804,312	12,091,399	5,701,945	30,033,352	16,450,192	13,583,332
Painting and papering	6,943,198	221,638	1,004,252	1,035,972	396,367	4,284,962	2,019,586	2,265,458
Plumbing and water heating	5,753,633	234,091	1,222,527	996,477	701,331	2,598,756	1,249,107	1,349,437
Heat, air conditioning, electrical work	10,404,913	447,988	2,148,026	2,019,284	1,297,484	4,491,681	2,619,422	1,872,406
Roofing and gutters	11,195,631	1,061,237	2,522,567	2,419,039	880,294	4,312,546	2,540,409	1,772,143
Other repair and maintenance services	20,638,892	840,945	2,990,742	4,032,998	1,829,462	10,944,762	6,068,065	4,876,659
Repair, replacement of hard-surface flooring	6,129,224	255,464	774,815	1,465,854	551,946	3,080,668	1,794,958	1,285,772
Repair of built-in appliances	638,388	10,097	141,073	121,775	44,954	320,301	158,853	161,339
Maintenance and repair materials	8,526,959	545,933	1,900,607	1,589,401	1,305,172	3,185,813	2,014,415	1,171,151
Paints, wallpaper, and supplies	1,765,161	121,001	326,173	271,651	294,499	751,913	500,760	251,247
Tools, equipment for painting, wallpapering	189,540	12,958	35,036	29,115	31,607	80,805	53,778	26,949
Plumbing supplies and equipment	673,273	54,694	131,461	133,167	147,570	205,746	83,770	121,916
Electrical supplies, heating and cooling equipment	375,591	6,395	81,543	81,014	46,449	159,988	101,765	58,016
Hard-surface flooring, repair and replacement	1,086,074	101,815	104,797	211,903	162,733	504,629	370,450	134,155
Roofing and gutters	746,530	38,875	216,105	160,763	48,585	282,332	198,773	83,553
Plaster, paneling, siding, windows, doors, screens, awnings	1,513,992	109,389	269,433	362,539	251,360	521,504	317,293	204,057
Patio, walk, fence, driveway, masonry, brick, and stucco materials	182,563	8,246	52,088	54,178	12,173	55,817	42,609	13,062
Miscellaneous supplies and equipment	1,995,399	92,560	683,660	285,069	310,089	623,403	345,216	278,313
Property management and security	4,059,405	68,831	673,429	939,008	247,623	2,130,149	1,066,260	1,064,063
Property management	3,319,851	53,853	580,724	766,092	198,504	1,720,605	800,264	920,375
Management and upkeep services for security	739,554	14,978	92,705	172,915	49,119	409,544	265,996	143,805
Parking	398,847	6,395	58,599	85,571	38,014	209,964	137,342	72,609
Rented dwellings	255,947,147	40,810,998	64,064,701	58,300,241	19,890,231	72,878,430	50,922,767	21,955,558
Rent	247,207,392	39,186,158	61,927,527	56,946,794	19,261,617	69,883,759	49,047,349	20,836,303
Rent as pay	4,195,455	1,416,497	1,165,168	807,865	279,657	526,696	279,441	247,246
Maintenance, insurance, and other expenses	4,543,138	208,343	972,007	545,581	348,957	2,468,299	1,596,184	872,009
Tenant's insurance	820,951	56,041	164,637	187,346	98,772	314,460	198,566	115,915
Maintenance and repair services	3,132,637	65,633	674,049	153,421	166,684	2,072,709	1,345,494	727,262
Maintenance and repair materials	589,550	86,669	133,632	204,815	83,502	80,805	51,917	28,949
Other lodging	54,983,944	1,281,192	7,492,048	11,094,163	4,950,214	30,166,406	16,636,762	13,529,670
Owned vacation homes	15,956,216	457,581	2,455,906	3,656,281	1,174,473	8,211,979	4,677,066	3,534,990
Mortgage interest and charges	6,283,879	77,077	874,651	1,278,762	389,533	3,664,155	2,282,893	1,381,092
Property taxes	6,687,378	295,181	939,762	1,685,606	516,068	3,250,392	1,776,549	1,473,824
Maintenance, insurance, and other expenses	2,984,959	85,323	641,183	691,914	268,872	1,297,755	617,624	679,955
Housing while attending school	6,712,960	98,281	358,728	1,912,953	773,728	3,569,720	1,830,948	1,738,722
Lodging on trips	32,313,605	725,498	4,677,414	5,524,676	3,002,120	18,384,383	10,128,541	8,255,958

	total consumer units	less than high school graduate	high school graduate	some college	associate's degree	college graduate total	bachelor's degree	master's, professional, doctorate
UTILITIES, FUELS, PUBLIC SERVICES	$340,316,715	$40,626,047	$87,970,176	$68,793,125	$33,868,267	$109,055,920	$66,851,929	$42,204,167
Natural gas	49,305,894	5,632,498	12,863,664	9,298,428	4,656,996	16,853,297	9,979,203	6,874,277
Electricity	123,771,724	15,770,792	33,183,411	25,432,192	12,066,033	37,318,502	22,982,406	14,335,895
Fuel oil and other fuels	14,015,469	1,732,377	4,154,670	2,654,994	1,439,822	4,034,108	2,334,603	1,699,417
Fuel oil	7,464,142	729,369	2,103,379	1,431,930	740,092	2,459,862	1,337,427	1,122,432
Bottled and tank gas	5,255,946	825,294	1,615,361	944,071	614,092	1,256,866	778,132	478,722
Wood and other fuels	1,233,752	169,805	397,174	268,107	85,531	313,486	215,320	98,263
Telephone services	115,144,762	13,089,764	28,543,513	23,731,903	11,872,868	37,905,559	23,759,297	14,146,077
Residential telephone and pay phones	68,874,991	9,149,422	18,091,418	13,616,495	6,489,875	21,527,034	13,275,612	8,251,251
Cellular phone service	43,999,946	3,350,990	9,962,217	9,681,474	5,194,954	15,809,965	10,171,978	5,638,049
Pager service	117,445	20,700	13,952	32,406	20,288	29,856	14,479	15,298
Phone cards	2,152,380	568,652	475,927	401,528	167,858	538,703	297,229	241,479
Water and other public services	38,078,867	4,400,615	9,224,608	7,675,355	3,832,441	12,944,778	7,796,420	5,148,500
Water and sewerage maintenance	28,203,036	3,376,571	6,921,866	5,613,538	2,752,361	9,538,292	5,733,812	3,804,594
Trash and garbage collection	9,624,661	1,006,206	2,252,203	2,012,448	1,040,998	3,312,376	2,013,794	1,298,599
Septic tank cleaning	251,169	17,839	50,538	49,368	39,081	94,111	48,814	45,307

* See Appendix B for information about mortgage principal reduction.
Note: Numbers may not add to total because of rounding and missing subcategories.
Source: Calculations by New Strategist based on the 2004 Consumer Expenditure Survey

Table 9.28 Housing: Shelter and Utilities: Market shares by education, 2004

(percentage of total annual spending on shelter and utilities accounted for by consumer unit educational attainment groups, 2004)

	total consumer units	less than high school graduate	high school graduate	some college	associate's degree	college graduate total	bachelor's degree	master's, professional, doctorate
Share of total consumer units	100.0%	14.5%	26.7%	21.8%	9.2%	27.9%	17.8%	10.1%
Share of total before-tax income	100.0	7.7	20.7	18.7	9.9	43.0	24.7	18.3
Share of total spending	100.0	8.5	21.8	20.5	10.2	39.0	23.3	15.8
Share of housing spending	100.0	9.1	21.5	20.2	9.8	39.5	23.4	16.1
SHELTER	100.0	8.9	20.6	20.0	9.6	40.8	24.4	16.5
Owned dwellings*	100.0	6.6	19.4	18.9	10.5	44.7	25.7	19.0
Mortgage interest and charges	100.0	6.1	18.6	19.0	11.0	45.3	26.7	18.6
Mortgage interest	100.0	6.2	18.5	19.0	11.0	45.2	26.7	18.5
Interest paid, home equity loan	100.0	6.9	22.7	17.0	11.4	41.9	27.7	14.2
Interest paid, home equity line of credit	100.0	2.4	18.2	20.1	10.9	48.4	25.5	22.9
Property taxes	100.0	7.2	20.3	18.1	9.5	44.9	24.9	20.0
Maintenance, repairs, insurance, other expenses	100.0	6.9	20.5	19.8	10.1	42.7	23.9	18.9
Homeowner's insurance	100.0	8.4	24.0	20.0	10.7	36.9	21.2	15.7
Ground rent	100.0	26.8	33.6	19.3	10.1	10.3	5.6	4.7
Maintenance and repair services	100.0	5.0	17.5	19.6	9.2	48.7	26.7	22.0
Painting and papering	100.0	3.2	14.5	14.9	5.7	61.7	29.1	32.6
Plumbing and water heating	100.0	4.1	21.2	17.3	12.2	45.2	21.7	23.5
Heat, air conditioning, electrical work	100.0	4.3	20.6	19.4	12.5	43.2	25.2	18.0
Roofing and gutters	100.0	9.5	22.5	21.6	7.9	38.5	22.7	15.8
Other repair and maintenance services	100.0	4.1	14.5	19.5	8.9	53.0	29.4	23.6
Repair, replacement of hard-surface flooring	100.0	4.2	12.6	23.9	9.0	50.3	29.3	21.0
Repair of built-in appliances	100.0	1.6	22.1	19.1	7.0	50.2	24.9	25.3
Maintenance and repair materials	100.0	6.4	22.3	18.6	15.3	37.4	23.6	13.7
Paints, wallpaper, and supplies	100.0	6.9	18.5	15.4	16.7	42.6	28.4	14.2
Tools, equipment for painting, wallpapering	100.0	6.8	18.5	15.4	16.7	42.6	28.4	14.2
Plumbing supplies and equipment	100.0	8.1	19.5	19.8	21.9	30.6	12.4	18.1
Electrical supplies, heating and cooling equipment	100.0	1.7	21.7	21.6	12.4	42.6	27.1	15.4
Hard-surface flooring, repair and replacement	100.0	9.4	9.6	19.5	15.0	46.5	34.1	12.4
Roofing and gutters	100.0	5.2	28.9	21.5	6.5	37.8	26.6	11.2
Plaster, paneling, siding, windows, doors, screens, awnings	100.0	7.2	17.8	23.9	16.6	34.4	21.0	13.5
Patio, walk, fence, driveway, masonry, brick, and stucco materials	100.0	4.5	28.5	29.7	6.7	30.6	23.3	7.2
Miscellaneous supplies and equipment	100.0	4.6	34.3	14.3	15.5	31.2	17.3	13.9
Property management and security	100.0	1.7	16.6	23.1	6.1	52.5	26.3	26.2
Property management	100.0	1.6	17.5	23.1	6.0	51.8	24.1	27.7
Management and upkeep services for security	100.0	2.0	12.5	23.4	6.6	55.4	36.0	19.4
Parking	100.0	1.6	14.7	21.5	9.5	52.6	34.4	18.2
Rented dwellings	100.0	15.9	25.0	22.8	7.8	28.5	19.9	8.6
Rent	100.0	15.9	25.1	23.0	7.8	28.3	19.8	8.4
Rent as pay	100.0	33.8	27.8	19.3	6.7	12.6	6.7	5.9
Maintenance, insurance, and other expenses	100.0	4.6	21.4	12.0	7.7	54.3	35.1	19.2
Tenant's insurance	100.0	6.8	20.1	22.8	12.0	38.3	24.2	14.1
Maintenance and repair services	100.0	2.1	21.5	4.9	5.3	66.2	43.0	23.2
Maintenance and repair materials	100.0	14.7	22.7	34.7	14.2	13.7	8.8	4.9
Other lodging	100.0	2.3	13.6	20.2	9.0	54.9	30.3	24.6
Owned vacation homes	100.0	2.9	15.4	22.9	7.4	51.5	29.3	22.2
Mortgage interest and charges	100.0	1.2	13.9	20.3	6.2	58.3	36.3	22.0
Property taxes	100.0	4.4	14.1	25.2	7.7	48.6	26.6	22.0
Maintenance, insurance, and other expenses	100.0	2.9	21.5	23.2	9.0	43.5	20.7	22.8
Housing while attending school	100.0	1.5	5.3	28.5	11.5	53.2	27.3	25.9
Lodging on trips	100.0	2.2	14.5	17.1	9.3	56.9	31.3	25.5

	total consumer units	less than high school graduate	high school graduate	some college	associate's degree	college graduate total	bachelor's degree	master's, professional, doctorate
UTILITIES, FUELS, AND PUBLIC SERVICES	100.0%	11.9%	25.8%	20.2%	10.0%	32.0%	19.6%	12.4%
Natural gas	100.0	11.4	26.1	18.9	9.4	34.2	20.2	13.9
Electricity	100.0	12.7	26.8	20.5	9.7	30.2	18.6	11.6
Fuel oil and other fuels	100.0	12.4	29.6	18.9	10.3	28.8	16.7	12.1
Fuel oil	100.0	9.8	28.2	19.2	9.9	33.0	17.9	15.0
Bottled and tank gas	100.0	15.7	30.7	18.0	11.7	23.9	14.8	9.1
Wood and other fuels	100.0	13.8	32.2	21.7	6.9	25.4	17.5	8.0
Telephone services	100.0	11.4	24.8	20.6	10.3	32.9	20.6	12.3
Residential telephone and pay phones	100.0	13.3	26.3	19.8	9.4	31.3	19.3	12.0
Cellular phone service	100.0	7.6	22.6	22.0	11.8	35.9	23.1	12.8
Pager service	100.0	17.6	11.9	27.6	17.3	25.4	12.3	13.0
Phone cards	100.0	26.4	22.1	18.7	7.8	25.0	13.8	11.2
Water and other public services	100.0	11.6	24.2	20.2	10.1	34.0	20.5	13.5
Water and sewerage maintenance	100.0	12.0	24.5	19.9	9.8	33.8	20.3	13.5
Trash and garbage collection	100.0	10.5	23.4	20.9	10.8	34.4	20.9	13.5
Septic tank cleaning	100.0	7.1	20.1	19.7	15.6	37.5	19.4	18.0

* See Appendix B for information about mortgage principal reduction.
Note: Numbers may not add to total because of rounding.
Source: Calculations by New Strategist based on the 2004 Consumer Expenditure Survey

Chapter 10. Spending on Personal Care, Reading, Education, and Tobacco, 2004

The average household spent 6 percent less on personal care products and services in 2004 than in 2000, after adjusting for inflation. Spending on reading material also fell during those years—down a substantial 19 percent as the Internet cut household spending on magazines and newspapers. Not surprisingly, spending on education rose 16 percent as college tuition soared. The average household spent 18 percent less on tobacco in 2004 than in 2000 as smoking declined in popularity.

Spending on personal care products and services is highest among householders aged 45 to 54, at $690 in 2004. The biggest spenders on reading material are householders aged 55 to 64. This age group spends 38 percent more than the average household on books. Householders aged 65 or older are the biggest spenders on newspaper subscriptions. Education spending is greatest for the youngest householders, who are most likely to be paying their way through college. Householders aged 45 to 54 (the parents of college students) are the second-biggest spenders on education.

Households with incomes of $100,000 or more spend twice as much as the average household on personal care products and services. This high-income group also spends more than twice the average on reading material and more than three times the average on education. Households with incomes of $100,000 or more spend 13 percent less than average on tobacco. Households with incomes below $50,000 account for the 56 percent majority of spending on tobacco.

Not surprisingly, spending on education is highest among married couples with children aged 18 or older at home because many have children in college. Couples with school-aged or older children at home spend the most on personal care products and services because they have the largest households. Married couples without children at home spend the most on reading material—particularly newspaper and magazine subscriptions. Tobacco spending is highest for couples with adult children at home.

Asian, black, and Hispanic householders spend about an average amount on personal care products and services, but on a number of individual personal care items their spending is well above average. Blacks spend more than four times the average on wigs and hairpieces, for example. Asian households spend more than double the average on college tuition.

Households in the Northeast spend 22 percent more than average on newspaper subscriptions, while households in the South spend 25 percent less than average on this item. Households in the West spend the most on books—37 percent more than average. Spending on cigarettes is greatest in the Midwest—20 percent above average. Household spending on education is 27 percent above average in the Northeast and 30 percent below average in the South.

College graduates spend more than other householders on personal care products and services, reading material, and education. They spend twice the average on college tuition and more than twice the average on books. Householders with no more than a high school diploma spend the most on tobacco, 32 percent more than the average household.

Table 10.1 Personal Care, Reading, Education, Tobacco: Average spending by age, 2004

(average annual spending of consumer units (CU) on personal care, reading, education, and tobacco products, by age of consumer unit reference person, 2004)

	total consumer units	under 25	25 to 34	35 to 44	45 to 54	55 to 64	65 to 74	75+
Number of consumer units (in 000s)	116,282	8,817	19,439	24,070	23,712	17,479	11,230	11,536
Average number of persons per CU	2.5	1.9	2.9	3.2	2.7	2.1	1.9	1.5
Average before-tax income of CU	$54,453.00	$22,840.00	$52,484.00	$65,515.00	$70,434.00	$61,031.00	$42,137.00	$28,028.00
Average spending of CU, total	43,394.87	24,534.56	42,700.54	50,401.62	52,764.36	47,298.58	36,511.98	25,763.32
PERSONAL CARE PRODUCTS AND SERVICES	**581.09**	**334.39**	**552.25**	**659.93**	**689.57**	**627.53**	**514.26**	**420.80**
Personal care products	**317.00**	**203.07**	**314.12**	**380.60**	**395.28**	**324.08**	**239.02**	**175.84**
Hair care products	63.90	47.14	66.32	75.85	85.94	62.12	43.82	22.97
Hair accessories	6.37	4.80	8.31	8.12	7.57	5.57	3.09	2.37
Wigs and hairpieces	1.90	3.43	1.72	0.95	2.38	2.72	2.26	0.48
Oral hygiene products	34.63	21.72	32.74	37.60	41.33	35.55	35.37	25.42
Shaving products	18.71	13.14	19.67	22.79	24.22	20.11	7.80	9.79
Cosmetics, perfume, and bath products	147.41	82.47	141.94	182.03	178.71	159.63	115.28	80.40
Deodorants, feminine hygiene, miscellaneous products	34.33	25.04	35.04	41.17	43.79	28.22	23.23	26.23
Electric personal care appliances	9.74	5.33	8.38	12.09	11.34	10.16	8.16	8.18
Personal care services	**264.09**	**131.32**	**238.14**	**279.33**	**294.30**	**303.45**	**275.24**	**244.96**
READING	**130.41**	**50.75**	**93.51**	**122.61**	**148.60**	**177.07**	**157.68**	**135.25**
Newspaper subscriptions	41.76	3.70	13.94	28.50	46.06	59.95	69.43	82.06
Newspaper, nonsubscription	9.44	4.95	7.97	9.86	10.92	11.59	11.05	6.65
Magazine subscriptions	14.88	6.18	9.69	12.68	16.60	20.33	20.68	17.42
Magazines, nonsubscription	8.36	8.51	10.13	9.77	8.95	8.85	4.95	3.65
Books purchased through book clubs	5.50	1.06	4.31	5.81	6.52	7.57	6.84	3.75
Books not purchased through book clubs	49.69	26.31	46.75	55.81	59.45	65.43	44.66	20.73
EDUCATION	**905.41**	**1,820.54**	**726.48**	**785.92**	**1,567.35**	**729.88**	**352.33**	**197.77**
College tuition	541.35	1,416.89	471.78	253.40	993.00	489.60	147.31	123.82
Elementary and high school tuition	142.80	14.36	50.78	284.63	246.18	62.39	130.52	21.41
Other school tuition	27.13	29.17	22.36	26.12	56.36	21.70	3.07	7.26
Other school expenses including rentals	48.84	37.47	58.27	46.29	77.81	50.95	16.19	16.03
Books, supplies for college	58.86	270.11	49.98	31.67	80.34	36.76	8.94	7.06
Books, supplies for elementary, high school	13.56	2.94	12.13	27.59	19.61	7.88	2.70	1.52
Books, supplies for day care, nursery school	2.32	1.84	2.92	3.92	1.90	2.73	0.49	0.36
Miscellaneous school expenses and supplies	70.55	47.77	58.26	112.29	92.16	57.88	43.10	20.31
TOBACCO PRODUCTS, SMOKING SUPPLIES	**288.13**	**235.67**	**283.38**	**349.66**	**375.34**	**300.53**	**197.24**	**98.29**
Cigarettes	264.05	213.84	262.87	325.76	339.13	272.87	183.08	86.75
Other tobacco products	22.07	17.38	19.19	21.49	35.08	25.24	12.83	9.13
Smoking accessories	2.02	4.46	1.32	2.42	1.13	2.41	1.33	2.41

Note: Subcategories may not add to total because some are not shown.
Source: Bureau of Labor Statistics, unpublished tables from the 2004 Consumer Expenditure Survey

Table 10.2 Personal Care, Reading, Education, Tobacco: Indexed spending by age, 2004

(indexed average annual spending of consumer units (CU) on personal care, reading, education, and tobacco products, by age of consumer unit reference person, 2004; index definition: an index of 100 is the average for all consumer units; an index of 132 means that spending by consumer units in that group is 32 percent above the average for all consumer units; an index of 68 indicates spending that is 32 percent below the average for all consumer units)

	total consumer units	under 25	25 to 34	35 to 44	45 to 54	55 to 64	65 to 74	75+
Average spending of CU, total	$43,395	$24,535	$42,701	$50,402	$52,764	$47,299	$36,512	$25,763
Average spending of CU, index	100	57	98	116	122	109	84	59
PERSONAL CARE PRODUCTS AND SERVICES	**100**	**58**	**95**	**114**	**119**	**108**	**88**	**72**
Personal care products	**100**	**64**	**99**	**120**	**125**	**102**	**75**	**55**
Hair care products	100	74	104	119	134	97	69	36
Hair accessories	100	75	130	127	119	87	49	37
Wigs and hairpieces	100	181	91	50	125	143	119	25
Oral hygiene products	100	63	95	109	119	103	102	73
Shaving products	100	70	105	122	129	107	42	52
Cosmetics, perfume, and bath products	100	56	96	123	121	108	78	55
Deodorants, feminine hygiene, miscellaneous products	100	73	102	120	128	82	68	76
Electric personal care appliances	100	55	86	124	116	104	84	84
Personal care services	**100**	**50**	**90**	**106**	**111**	**115**	**104**	**93**
READING	**100**	**39**	**72**	**94**	**114**	**136**	**121**	**104**
Newspaper subscriptions	100	9	33	68	110	144	166	197
Newspaper, nonsubscription	100	52	84	104	116	123	117	70
Magazine subscriptions	100	42	65	85	112	137	139	117
Magazines, nonsubscription	100	102	121	117	107	106	59	44
Books purchased through book clubs	100	19	78	106	119	138	124	68
Books not purchased through book clubs	100	53	94	112	120	132	90	42
EDUCATION	**100**	**201**	**80**	**87**	**173**	**81**	**39**	**22**
College tuition	100	262	87	47	183	90	27	23
Elementary and high school tuition	100	10	36	199	172	44	91	15
Other school tuition	100	108	82	96	208	80	11	27
Other school expenses including rentals	100	77	119	95	159	104	33	33
Books, supplies for college	100	459	85	54	136	62	15	12
Books, supplies for elementary, high school	100	22	89	203	145	58	20	11
Books, supplies for day care, nursery school	100	79	126	169	82	118	21	16
Miscellaneous school expenses and supplies	100	68	83	159	131	82	61	29
TOBACCO PRODUCTS AND SMOKING SUPPLIES	**100**	**82**	**98**	**121**	**130**	**104**	**68**	**34**
Cigarettes	100	81	100	123	128	103	69	33
Other tobacco products	100	79	87	97	159	114	58	41
Smoking accessories	100	221	65	120	56	119	66	119

Source: Calculations by New Strategist based on the 2004 Consumer Expenditure Survey

Table 10.3 Personal Care, Reading, Education, and Tobacco: Total spending by age, 2004

(total annual spending on personal care, reading, education, and tobacco products, by consumer unit (CU) age groups, 2004; consumer units and dollars in thousands)

	total consumer units	under 25	25 to 34	35 to 44	45 to 54	55 to 64	65 to 74	75+
Number of consumer units	116,282	8,817	19,439	24,070	23,712	17,479	11,230	11,536
Total spending of all CUs	$5,046,042,273	$216,321,216	$830,055,797	$1,213,166,993	$1,251,148,504	$826,731,880	$410,029,535	$297,205,660
PERSONAL CARE PRODUCTS, SERVICES	**67,570,307**	**2,948,317**	**10,735,188**	**15,884,515**	**16,351,084**	**10,968,597**	**5,775,140**	**4,854,349**
Personal care products	**36,861,394**	**1,790,468**	**6,106,179**	**9,161,042**	**9,372,879**	**5,664,594**	**2,684,195**	**2,028,490**
Hair care products	7,430,420	415,633	1,289,194	1,825,710	2,037,809	1,085,795	492,099	264,982
Hair accessories	740,716	42,322	161,538	195,448	179,500	97,358	34,701	27,340
Wigs and hairpieces	220,936	30,242	33,435	22,867	56,435	47,543	25,380	5,537
Oral hygiene products	4,026,846	191,505	636,433	905,032	980,017	621,378	397,205	293,245
Shaving products	2,175,636	115,855	382,365	548,555	574,305	351,503	87,594	112,937
Cosmetics, perfume, and bath products	17,141,130	727,138	2,759,172	4,381,462	4,237,572	2,790,173	1,294,594	927,494
Deodorants, feminine hygiene, misc. products	3,991,961	220,778	681,143	990,962	1,038,348	493,257	260,873	302,589
Electric personal care appliances	1,132,587	46,995	162,899	291,006	268,894	177,587	91,637	94,364
Personal care services	**30,708,913**	**1,157,848**	**4,629,203**	**6,723,473**	**6,978,442**	**5,304,003**	**3,090,945**	**2,825,859**
READING	**15,164,336**	**447,463**	**1,817,741**	**2,951,223**	**3,523,603**	**3,095,007**	**1,770,746**	**1,560,244**
Newspaper subscriptions	4,855,936	32,623	270,980	685,995	1,092,175	1,047,866	779,699	946,644
Newspaper, nonsubscription	1,097,702	43,644	154,929	237,330	258,935	202,582	124,092	76,714
Magazine subscriptions	1,730,276	54,489	188,364	305,208	393,619	355,348	232,236	200,957
Magazines, nonsubscription	972,118	75,033	196,917	235,164	212,222	154,689	55,589	42,106
Books purchased through book clubs	639,551	9,346	83,782	139,847	154,602	132,316	76,813	43,260
Books not purchased through book clubs	5,778,053	231,975	908,773	1,343,347	1,409,678	1,143,651	501,532	239,141
EDUCATION	**105,282,886**	**16,051,701**	**14,122,045**	**18,917,094**	**37,165,003**	**12,757,573**	**3,956,666**	**2,281,475**
College tuition	62,949,261	12,492,719	9,170,931	6,099,338	23,546,016	8,557,718	1,654,291	1,428,388
Elementary and high school tuition	16,605,070	126,612	987,112	6,851,044	5,837,420	1,090,515	1,465,740	246,986
Other school tuition	3,154,731	257,192	434,656	628,708	1,336,408	379,294	34,476	83,751
Other school expenses including rentals	5,679,213	330,373	1,132,711	1,114,200	1,845,031	890,555	181,814	184,922
Books, supplies for college	6,844,359	2,381,560	971,561	762,297	1,905,022	642,528	100,396	81,444
Books, supplies for elementary, high school	1,576,784	25,922	235,795	664,091	464,992	137,735	30,321	17,535
Books, supplies for day care, nursery school	269,774	16,223	56,762	94,354	45,053	47,718	5,503	4,153
Miscellaneous school expenses and supplies	8,203,695	421,188	1,132,516	2,702,820	2,185,298	1,011,685	484,013	234,296
TOBACCO PRODUCTS, SMOKING SUPPLIES	**33,504,333**	**2,077,902**	**5,508,624**	**8,416,316**	**8,900,062**	**5,252,964**	**2,215,005**	**1,133,873**
Cigarettes	30,704,262	1,885,427	5,109,930	7,841,043	8,041,451	4,769,495	2,055,988	1,000,748
Other tobacco products	2,566,344	153,239	373,034	517,264	831,817	441,170	144,081	105,324
Smoking accessories	234,890	39,324	25,659	58,249	26,795	42,124	14,936	27,802

Note: Numbers may not add to total because of rounding and missing subcategories.
Source: Calculations by New Strategist based on the 2004 Consumer Expenditure Survey

Table 10.4 Personal Care, Reading, Education, and Tobacco: Market shares by age, 2004

(percentage of total annual spending on personal care, reading, education, and tobacco products accounted for by consumer unit age groups, 2004)

	total consumer units	under 25	25 to 34	35 to 44	45 to 54	55 to 64	65 to 74	75+
Share of total consumer units	100.0%	7.6%	16.7%	20.7%	20.4%	15.0%	9.7%	9.9%
Share of total before-tax income	100.0	3.2	16.1	24.9	26.4	16.8	7.5	5.1
Share of total spending	100.0	4.3	16.4	24.0	24.8	16.4	8.1	5.9
PERSONAL CARE PRODUCTS AND SERVICES	100.0	4.4	15.9	23.5	24.2	16.2	8.5	7.2
Personal care products	100.0	4.9	16.6	24.9	25.4	15.4	7.3	5.5
Hair care products	100.0	5.6	17.4	24.6	27.4	14.6	6.6	3.6
Hair accessories	100.0	5.7	21.8	26.4	24.2	13.1	4.7	3.7
Wigs and hairpieces	100.0	13.7	15.1	10.3	25.5	21.5	11.5	2.5
Oral hygiene products	100.0	4.8	15.8	22.5	24.3	15.4	9.9	7.3
Shaving products	100.0	5.3	17.6	25.2	26.4	16.2	4.0	5.2
Cosmetics, perfume, and bath products	100.0	4.2	16.1	25.6	24.7	16.3	7.6	5.4
Deodorants, feminine hygiene, miscellaneous products	100.0	5.5	17.1	24.8	26.0	12.4	6.5	7.6
Electric personal care appliances	100.0	4.1	14.4	25.7	23.7	15.7	8.1	8.3
Personal care services	100.0	3.8	15.1	21.9	22.7	17.3	10.1	9.2
READING	100.0	3.0	12.0	19.5	23.2	20.4	11.7	10.3
Newspaper subscriptions	100.0	0.7	5.6	14.1	22.5	21.6	16.1	19.5
Newspaper, nonsubscription	100.0	4.0	14.1	21.6	23.6	18.5	11.3	7.0
Magazine subscriptions	100.0	3.1	10.9	17.6	22.7	20.5	13.4	11.6
Magazines, nonsubscription	100.0	7.7	20.3	24.2	21.8	15.9	5.7	4.3
Books purchased through book clubs	100.0	1.5	13.1	21.9	24.2	20.7	12.0	6.8
Books not purchased through book clubs	100.0	4.0	15.7	23.2	24.4	19.8	8.7	4.1
EDUCATION	100.0	15.2	13.4	18.0	35.3	12.1	3.8	2.2
College tuition	100.0	19.8	14.6	9.7	37.4	13.6	2.6	2.3
Elementary and high school tuition	100.0	0.8	5.9	41.3	35.2	6.6	8.8	1.5
Other school tuition	100.0	8.2	13.8	19.9	42.4	12.0	1.1	2.7
Other school expenses including rentals	100.0	5.8	19.9	19.6	32.5	15.7	3.2	3.3
Books, supplies for college	100.0	34.8	14.2	11.1	27.8	9.4	1.5	1.2
Books, supplies for elementary, high school	100.0	1.6	15.0	42.1	29.5	8.7	1.9	1.1
Books, supplies for day care, nursery school	100.0	6.0	21.0	35.0	16.7	17.7	2.0	1.5
Miscellaneous school expenses and supplies	100.0	5.1	13.8	32.9	26.6	12.3	5.9	2.9
TOBACCO PRODUCTS AND SMOKING SUPPLIES	100.0	6.2	16.4	25.1	26.6	15.7	6.6	3.4
Cigarettes	100.0	6.1	16.6	25.5	26.2	15.5	6.7	3.3
Other tobacco products	100.0	6.0	14.5	20.2	32.4	17.2	5.6	4.1
Smoking accessories	100.0	16.7	10.9	24.8	11.4	17.9	6.4	11.8

Note: Numbers may not add to total because of rounding.
Source: Calculations by New Strategist based on the 2004 Consumer Expenditure Survey

Table 10.5 Personal Care, Reading, Education, and Tobacco: Average spending by income, 2004

(average annual spending on personal care, reading, education, and tobacco products, by before-tax income of consumer units (CU), 2004)

	total consumer units	under $20,000	$20,000– $39,999	$40,000– $49,999	$50,000– $69,999	$70,000– $79,999	$80,000– $99,999	$100,000 or more
Number of consumer units (in 000s)	116,282	28,898	27,297	11,374	18,069	6,461	9,246	14,937
Average number of persons per CU	2.5	1.8	2.3	2.6	2.8	3.0	3.1	3.2
Average before-tax income of CU	$54,453.00	$10,923.47	$29,561.76	$44,645.00	$59,259.00	$74,437.00	$88,811.00	$155,901.00
Average spending of CU, total	43,394.87	18,865.37	30,400.94	38,204.07	47,750.13	55,012.03	65,446.39	93,525.67
PERSONAL CARE PRODUCTS AND SERVICES	**581.09**	**276.97**	**429.57**	**550.47**	**600.28**	**658.12**	**852.42**	**1,207.19**
Personal care products	**317.00**	**160.54**	**245.86**	**318.14**	**319.38**	**313.91**	**436.99**	**634.98**
Hair care products	63.90	31.62	52.63	61.33	71.61	71.59	66.70	127.34
Hair accessories	6.37	4.49	5.35	6.02	5.74	5.79	7.61	11.76
Wigs and hairpieces	1.90	1.54	2.67	1.09	2.01	2.79	1.83	1.36
Oral hygiene products	34.63	21.05	27.44	34.76	33.51	35.86	48.31	62.93
Shaving products	18.71	7.74	13.69	18.55	17.49	21.93	24.33	43.09
Cosmetics, perfume, and bath products	147.41	68.16	112.09	152.31	144.60	125.24	217.39	311.37
Deodorants, feminine hygiene, miscellaneous products	34.33	24.89	24.92	33.47	32.68	36.74	47.04	60.95
Electric personal care appliances	9.74	2.35	7.07	10.61	11.74	13.97	23.79	16.18
Personal care services	**264.09**	**116.42**	**183.70**	**232.33**	**280.91**	**344.20**	**415.43**	**572.21**
READING	**130.41**	**60.31**	**88.61**	**118.49**	**137.24**	**159.13**	**196.58**	**289.77**
Newspaper subscriptions	41.76	23.83	30.38	37.35	43.10	49.55	56.62	86.41
Newspaper, nonsubscription	9.44	5.70	9.66	11.22	9.65	13.64	12.76	10.82
Magazine subscriptions	14.88	5.84	10.22	16.67	15.27	18.53	23.77	31.98
Magazines, nonsubscription	8.36	3.96	6.15	8.66	8.60	9.89	12.86	16.92
Books purchased through book clubs	5.50	2.59	2.91	5.89	7.70	5.68	6.82	12.03
Books not purchased through book clubs	49.69	17.32	29.11	38.65	52.09	61.85	83.37	129.31
EDUCATION	**905.41**	**581.68**	**316.11**	**417.00**	**706.47**	**940.01**	**1,539.94**	**2,805.69**
College tuition	541.35	436.01	184.73	237.15	415.01	445.14	948.44	1,570.96
Elementary and high school tuition	142.80	9.66	18.02	53.55	72.99	196.40	287.87	667.85
Other school tuition	27.13	7.57	12.47	5.85	15.20	62.63	19.60	111.68
Other school expenses including rentals	48.84	13.32	23.56	27.91	42.46	58.70	79.04	164.48
Books, supplies for college	58.86	81.58	29.26	25.17	51.54	60.90	70.90	95.19
Books, supplies for elementary, high school	13.56	4.33	9.35	14.24	14.56	14.62	21.02	32.29
Books, supplies for day care, nursery school	2.32	1.27	1.94	1.51	3.89	4.49	2.49	2.71
Miscellaneous school expenses and supplies	70.55	27.94	36.77	51.63	90.82	97.12	110.59	160.52
TOBACCO PRODUCTS, SMOKING SUPPLIES	**288.13**	**227.06**	**305.12**	**329.09**	**339.47**	**336.61**	**303.34**	**251.72**
Cigarettes	264.05	212.73	287.87	303.24	304.03	294.32	269.54	225.07
Other tobacco products	22.07	12.72	15.96	24.42	31.63	39.87	30.76	24.86
Smoking accessories	2.02	1.61	1.28	1.42	3.81	2.42	3.04	1.78

Note: Subcategories may not add to total because some are not shown.
Source: Bureau of Labor Statistics, unpublished tables from the 2004 Consumer Expenditure Survey; calculations by New Strategist

Table 10.6 Personal Care, Reading, Education, and Tobacco: Indexed spending by income, 2004

(indexed average annual spending of consumer units (CU) on personal care, reading, education, and tobacco products, by before-tax income of consumer unit, 2004; index definition: an index of 100 is the average for all consumer units; an index of 132 means that spending by consumer units in that group is 32 percent above the average for all consumer units; an index of 68 indicates spending that is 32 percent below the average for all consumer units)

	total consumer units	under $20,000	$20,000–$39,999	$40,000–$49,999	$50,000–$69,999	$70,000–$79,999	$80,000–$99,999	$100,000 or more
Average spending of CU, total	$43,395	$18,865	$30,401	$38,204	$47,750	$55,012	$65,446	$93,526
Average spending of CU, index	100	43	70	88	110	127	151	216
PERSONAL CARE PRODUCTS AND SERVICES	100	48	74	95	103	113	147	208
Personal care products	100	51	78	100	101	99	138	200
Hair care products	100	49	82	96	112	112	104	199
Hair accessories	100	70	84	95	90	91	119	185
Wigs and hairpieces	100	81	141	57	106	147	96	72
Oral hygiene products	100	61	79	100	97	104	140	182
Shaving products	100	41	73	99	93	117	130	230
Cosmetics, perfume, and bath products	100	46	76	103	98	85	147	211
Deodorants, feminine hygiene, miscellaneous products	100	73	73	97	95	107	137	178
Electric personal care appliances	100	24	73	109	121	143	244	166
Personal care services	100	44	70	88	106	130	157	217
READING	100	46	68	91	105	122	151	222
Newspaper subscriptions	100	57	73	89	103	119	136	207
Newspaper, nonsubscription	100	60	102	119	102	144	135	115
Magazine subscriptions	100	39	69	112	103	125	160	215
Magazines, nonsubscription	100	47	74	104	103	118	154	202
Books purchased through book clubs	100	47	53	107	140	103	124	219
Books not purchased through book clubs	100	35	59	78	105	124	168	260
EDUCATION	100	64	35	46	78	104	170	310
College tuition	100	81	34	44	77	82	175	290
Elementary and high school tuition	100	7	13	38	51	138	202	468
Other school tuition	100	28	46	22	56	231	72	412
Other school expenses including rentals	100	27	48	57	87	120	162	337
Books, supplies for college	100	139	50	43	88	103	120	162
Books, supplies for elementary, high school	100	32	69	105	107	108	155	238
Books, supplies for day care, nursery school	100	55	84	65	168	194	107	117
Miscellaneous school expenses and supplies	100	40	52	73	129	138	157	228
TOBACCO PRODUCTS AND SMOKING SUPPLIES	100	79	106	114	118	117	105	87
Cigarettes	100	81	109	115	115	111	102	85
Other tobacco products	100	58	72	111	143	181	139	113
Smoking accessories	100	80	63	70	189	120	150	88

Source: Calculations by New Strategist based on the 2004 Consumer Expenditure Survey

Table 10.7 Personal Care, Reading, Education, and Tobacco: Total spending by income, 2004

(total annual spending on personal care, reading, education, and tobacco products, by before-tax income group of consumer units (CU), 2004; consumer units and dollars in thousands)

	total consumer units	under $20,000	$20,000–$39,999	$40,000–$49,999	$50,000–$69,999	$70,000–$79,999	$80,000–$99,999	$100,000 or more
Number of consumer units	116,282	28,898	27,297	11,374	18,069	6,461	9,246	14,937
Total spending of all CUs	$5,046,042,273	$545,171,431	$829,854,379	$434,533,092	$862,797,099	$355,432,726	$605,117,322	$1,396,992,933
PERSONAL CARE PRODUCTS, SERVICES	**67,570,307**	**8,003,885**	**11,725,837**	**6,261,046**	**10,846,459**	**4,252,113**	**7,881,475**	**18,031,797**
Personal care products	**36,861,394**	**4,639,374**	**6,711,191**	**3,618,524**	**5,770,877**	**2,028,173**	**4,040,410**	**9,484,696**
Hair care products	7,430,420	913,786	1,436,641	697,567	1,293,921	462,543	616,708	1,902,078
Hair accessories	740,716	129,758	146,118	68,471	103,716	37,409	70,362	175,659
Wigs and hairpieces	220,936	44,582	72,972	12,398	36,319	18,026	16,920	20,314
Oral hygiene products	4,026,846	608,339	748,910	395,360	605,492	231,691	446,674	939,985
Shaving products	2,175,636	223,804	373,657	210,988	316,027	141,690	224,955	643,635
Cosmetics, perfume, and bath products	17,141,130	1,969,667	3,059,817	1,732,374	2,612,777	809,176	2,009,988	4,650,934
Deodorants, feminine hygiene, misc. products	3,991,961	719,347	680,108	380,688	590,495	237,377	434,932	910,410
Electric personal care appliances	1,132,587	68,047	193,099	120,678	212,130	90,260	219,962	241,681
Personal care services	**30,708,913**	**3,364,440**	**5,014,504**	**2,642,521**	**5,075,763**	**2,223,876**	**3,841,066**	**8,547,101**
READING	**15,164,336**	**1,742,829**	**2,418,883**	**1,347,705**	**2,479,790**	**1,028,139**	**1,817,579**	**4,328,294**
Newspaper subscriptions	4,855,936	688,768	829,262	424,819	778,774	320,143	523,509	1,290,706
Newspaper, nonsubscription	1,097,702	164,848	263,648	127,616	174,366	88,128	117,979	161,618
Magazine subscriptions	1,730,276	168,689	278,925	189,605	275,914	119,722	219,777	477,685
Magazines, nonsubscription	972,118	114,432	167,905	98,499	155,393	63,899	118,904	252,734
Books purchased through book clubs	639,551	74,884	79,358	66,993	139,131	36,698	63,058	179,692
Books not purchased through book clubs	5,778,053	500,480	794,667	439,605	941,214	399,613	770,839	1,931,503
EDUCATION	**105,282,886**	**16,809,381**	**8,628,871**	**4,742,958**	**12,765,206**	**6,073,405**	**14,238,285**	**41,908,592**
College tuition	62,949,261	12,599,876	5,042,473	2,697,344	7,498,816	2,876,050	8,769,276	23,465,430
Elementary and high school tuition	16,605,070	279,086	491,975	609,078	1,318,856	1,268,940	2,661,646	9,975,675
Other school tuition	3,154,731	218,657	340,462	66,538	274,649	404,652	181,222	1,668,164
Other school expenses including rentals	5,679,213	384,893	643,235	317,448	767,210	379,261	730,804	2,456,838
Books, supplies for college	6,844,359	2,357,555	798,636	286,284	931,276	393,475	655,541	1,421,853
Books, supplies for elementary, high school	1,576,784	125,061	255,319	161,966	263,085	94,460	194,351	482,316
Books, supplies for day care, nursery school	269,774	36,576	53,076	17,175	70,288	29,010	23,023	40,479
Miscellaneous school expenses and supplies	8,203,695	807,532	1,003,847	587,240	1,641,027	627,492	1,022,515	2,397,687
TOBACCO PRODUCTS, SMOKING SUPPLIES	**33,504,333**	**6,561,628**	**8,328,756**	**3,743,070**	**6,133,883**	**2,174,837**	**2,804,682**	**3,759,942**
Cigarettes	30,704,262	6,147,616	7,857,954	3,449,052	5,493,518	1,901,602	2,492,167	3,361,871
Other tobacco products	2,566,344	367,507	435,705	277,753	571,522	257,600	284,407	371,334
Smoking accessories	234,890	46,488	34,965	16,151	68,843	15,636	28,108	26,588

Note: Numbers may not add to total because of rounding and missing subcategories.
Source: Calculations by New Strategist based on the 2004 Consumer Expenditure Survey

Table 10.8 Personal Care, Reading, Education, and Tobacco: Market shares by income, 2004

(percentage of total annual spending on personal care, reading, education, and tobacco products accounted for by before-tax income group of consumer units, 2004)

	total consumer units	under $20,000	$20,000–$39,999	$40,000–$49,999	$50,000–$69,999	$70,000–$79,999	$80,000–$99,999	$100,000 or more
Share of total consumer units	100.0%	24.9%	23.5%	9.8%	15.5%	5.6%	8.0%	12.8%
Share of total before-tax income	100.0	5.0	12.7	8.0	16.9	7.6	13.0	36.8
Share of total spending	100.0	10.8	16.4	8.6	17.1	7.0	12.0	27.7
PERSONAL CARE PRODUCTS AND SERVICES	**100.0**	**11.8**	**17.4**	**9.3**	**16.1**	**6.3**	**11.7**	**26.7**
Personal care products	**100.0**	**12.6**	**18.2**	**9.8**	**15.7**	**5.5**	**11.0**	**25.7**
Hair care products	100.0	12.3	19.3	9.4	17.4	6.2	8.3	25.6
Hair accessories	100.0	17.5	19.7	9.2	14.0	5.1	9.5	23.7
Wigs and hairpieces	100.0	20.2	33.0	5.6	16.4	8.2	7.7	9.2
Oral hygiene products	100.0	15.1	18.6	9.8	15.0	5.8	11.1	23.3
Shaving products	100.0	10.3	17.2	9.7	14.5	6.5	10.3	29.6
Cosmetics, perfume, and bath products	100.0	11.5	17.9	10.1	15.2	4.7	11.7	27.1
Deodorants, feminine hygiene, miscellaneous products	100.0	18.0	17.0	9.5	14.8	5.9	10.9	22.8
Electric personal care appliances	100.0	6.0	17.0	10.7	18.7	8.0	19.4	21.3
Personal care services	**100.0**	**11.0**	**16.3**	**8.6**	**16.5**	**7.2**	**12.5**	**27.8**
READING	**100.0**	**11.5**	**16.0**	**8.9**	**16.4**	**6.8**	**12.0**	**28.5**
Newspaper subscriptions	100.0	14.2	17.1	8.7	16.0	6.6	10.8	26.6
Newspaper, nonsubscription	100.0	15.0	24.0	11.6	15.9	8.0	10.7	14.7
Magazine subscriptions	100.0	9.7	16.1	11.0	15.9	6.9	12.7	27.6
Magazines, nonsubscription	100.0	11.8	17.3	10.1	16.0	6.6	12.2	26.0
Books purchased through book clubs	100.0	11.7	12.4	10.5	21.8	5.7	9.9	28.1
Books not purchased through book clubs	100.0	8.7	13.8	7.6	16.3	6.9	13.3	33.4
EDUCATION	**100.0**	**16.0**	**8.2**	**4.5**	**12.1**	**5.8**	**13.5**	**39.8**
College tuition	100.0	20.0	8.0	4.3	11.9	4.6	13.9	37.3
Elementary and high school tuition	100.0	1.7	3.0	3.7	7.9	7.6	16.0	60.1
Other school tuition	100.0	6.9	10.8	2.1	8.7	12.8	5.7	52.9
Other school expenses including rentals	100.0	6.8	11.3	5.6	13.5	6.7	12.9	43.3
Books, supplies for college	100.0	34.4	11.7	4.2	13.6	5.7	9.6	20.8
Books, supplies for elementary, high school	100.0	7.9	16.2	10.3	16.7	6.0	12.3	30.6
Books, supplies for day care, nursery school	100.0	13.6	19.7	6.4	26.1	10.8	8.5	15.0
Miscellaneous school expenses and supplies	100.0	9.8	12.2	7.2	20.0	7.6	12.5	29.2
TOBACCO PRODUCTS, SMOKING SUPPLIES	**100.0**	**19.6**	**24.9**	**11.2**	**18.3**	**6.5**	**8.4**	**11.2**
Cigarettes	100.0	20.0	25.6	11.2	17.9	6.2	8.1	10.9
Other tobacco products	100.0	14.3	17.0	10.8	22.3	10.0	11.1	14.5
Smoking accessories	100.0	19.8	14.9	6.9	29.3	6.7	12.0	11.3

Note: Numbers may not add to total because of rounding.
Source: Calculations by New Strategist based on the 2004 Consumer Expenditure Survey

Table 10.9 Personal Care, Reading, Education, and Tobacco: Average spending by high-income consumer units, 2004

(average annual spending on personal care, reading, education, and tobacco products, by before-tax income of high-income consumer units (CU), 2004)

	total consumer units	$100,000 or more	$100,000–$119,999	$120,000–$149,999	$150,000 or more
Number of consumer units (in 000s)	116,282	14,937	5,625	4,245	5,067
Average number of persons per CU	2.5	3.2	3.1	3.3	3.2
Average before-tax income of CU	$54,453.00	$155,901.00	$108,751.00	$132,292.00	$228,021.00
Average spending of CU, total	43,394.87	93,525.67	75,213.14	87,298.57	119,448.79
PERSONAL CARE PRODUCTS AND SERVICES	**581.09**	**1,207.19**	**1,030.13**	**1,190.55**	**1,427.06**
Personal care products	**317.00**	**634.98**	**562.24**	**630.56**	**728.80**
Hair care products	63.90	127.34	108.88	120.21	157.23
Hair accessories	6.37	11.76	13.07	10.67	11.27
Wigs and hairpieces	1.90	1.36	1.76	0.71	1.44
Oral hygiene products	34.63	62.93	50.68	61.73	79.19
Shaving products	18.71	43.09	39.30	39.78	51.08
Cosmetics, perfume, and bath products	147.41	311.37	280.03	320.74	340.43
Deodorants, feminine hygiene, miscellaneous products	34.33	60.95	55.96	56.21	71.89
Electric personal care appliances	9.74	16.18	12.57	20.50	16.26
Personal care services	**264.09**	**572.21**	**467.88**	**560.00**	**698.26**
READING	**130.41**	**289.77**	**227.43**	**297.77**	**352.86**
Newspaper subscriptions	41.76	86.41	70.68	90.77	100.21
Newspaper, nonsubscription	9.44	10.82	12.65	8.83	10.46
Magazine subscriptions	14.88	31.98	24.51	32.71	39.66
Magazines, nonsubscription	8.36	16.92	15.73	14.57	20.23
Books purchased through book clubs	5.50	12.03	8.34	11.67	16.42
Books not purchased through book clubs	49.69	129.31	95.45	138.67	159.05
EDUCATION	**905.41**	**2,805.69**	**1,865.40**	**2,166.39**	**4,381.58**
College tuition	541.35	1,570.96	937.60	1,391.73	2,424.19
Elementary and high school tuition	142.80	667.85	357.64	257.23	1,356.22
Other school tuition	27.13	111.68	149.46	77.91	98.04
Other school expenses including rentals	48.84	164.48	116.38	151.30	228.92
Books, supplies for college	58.86	95.19	70.27	104.29	115.24
Books, supplies for elementary, high school	13.56	32.29	35.37	24.15	35.67
Books, supplies for day care, nursery school	2.32	2.71	2.46	3.78	2.10
Miscellaneous school expenses and supplies	70.55	160.52	196.22	155.99	121.21
TOBACCO PRODUCTS AND SMOKING SUPPLIES	**288.13**	**251.72**	**278.98**	**290.13**	**189.17**
Cigarettes	264.05	225.07	255.04	261.88	160.98
Other tobacco products	22.07	24.86	21.33	26.46	27.44
Smoking accessories	2.02	1.78	2.61	1.79	0.75

Note: Subcategories may not add to total because some are not shown.
Source: Bureau of Labor Statistics, unpublished tables from the 2004 Consumer Expenditure Survey; calculations by New Strategist

Table 10.10 Personal Care, Reading, Education, and Tobacco: Indexed spending by high-income consumer units, 2004

(indexed average annual spending of high-income consumer units (CU) on personal care, reading, education, and tobacco products, by before-tax income of consumer unit, 2004; index definition: an index of 100 is the average for all consumer units; an index of 132 means that spending by consumer units in that group is 32 percent above the average for all consumer units; an index of 68 indicates spending that is 32 percent below the average for all consumer units)

	total consumer units	$100,000 or more	$100,000–$119,999	$120,000–$149,999	$150,000 or more
Average spending of CU, total	$43,395	$93,526	$75,213	$87,299	$119,449
Average spending of CU, index	100	216	173	201	275
PERSONAL CARE PRODUCTS AND SERVICES	**100**	**208**	**177**	**205**	**246**
Personal care products	**100**	**200**	**177**	**199**	**230**
Hair care products	100	199	170	188	246
Hair accessories	100	185	205	168	177
Wigs and hairpieces	100	72	93	37	76
Oral hygiene products	100	182	146	178	229
Shaving products	100	230	210	213	273
Cosmetics, perfume, and bath products	100	211	190	218	231
Deodorants, feminine hygiene, miscellaneous products	100	178	163	164	209
Electric personal care appliances	100	166	129	210	167
Personal care services	**100**	**217**	**177**	**212**	**264**
READING	**100**	**222**	**174**	**228**	**271**
Newspaper subscriptions	100	207	169	217	240
Newspaper, nonsubscription	100	115	134	94	111
Magazine subscriptions	100	215	165	220	267
Magazines, nonsubscription	100	202	188	174	242
Books purchased through book clubs	100	219	152	212	299
Books not purchased through book clubs	100	260	192	279	320
EDUCATION	**100**	**310**	**206**	**239**	**484**
College tuition	100	290	173	257	448
Elementary and high school tuition	100	468	250	180	950
Other school tuition	100	412	551	287	361
Other school expenses including rentals	100	337	238	310	469
Books, supplies for college	100	162	119	177	196
Books, supplies for elementary, high school	100	238	261	178	263
Books, supplies for day care, nursery school	100	117	106	163	91
Miscellaneous school expenses and supplies	100	228	278	221	172
TOBACCO PRODUCTS AND SMOKING SUPPLIES	**100**	**87**	**97**	**101**	**66**
Cigarettes	100	85	97	99	61
Other tobacco products	100	113	97	120	124
Smoking accessories	100	88	129	89	37

Source: Calculations by New Strategist based on the 2004 Consumer Expenditure Survey

Table 10.11 Personal Care, Reading, Education, and Tobacco: Total spending by high-income consumer units, 2004

(total annual spending on personal care, reading, education, and tobacco products, by before-tax income group of high-income consumer units (CU), 2004; consumer units and dollars in thousands)

	total consumer units	$100,000 or more	$100,000–$119,999	$120,000–$149,999	$150,000 or more
Number of consumer units	116,282	14,937	5,625	4,245	5,067
Total spending of all CUs	$5,046,042,273	$1,396,992,933	$423,073,913	$370,582,430	$605,247,019
PERSONAL CARE PRODUCTS AND SERVICES	67,570,307	18,031,797	5,794,481	5,053,885	7,230,913
Personal care products	36,861,394	9,484,696	3,162,600	2,676,727	3,692,830
Hair care products	7,430,420	1,902,078	612,450	510,291	796,684
Hair accessories	740,716	175,659	73,519	45,294	57,105
Wigs and hairpieces	220,936	20,314	9,900	3,014	7,296
Oral hygiene products	4,026,846	939,985	285,075	262,044	401,256
Shaving products	2,175,636	643,635	221,063	168,866	258,822
Cosmetics, perfume, and bath products	17,141,130	4,650,934	1,575,169	1,361,541	1,724,959
Deodorants, feminine hygiene, miscellaneous products	3,991,961	910,410	314,775	238,611	364,267
Electric personal care appliances	1,132,587	241,681	70,706	87,023	82,389
Personal care services	30,708,913	8,547,101	2,631,825	2,377,200	3,538,083
READING	15,164,336	4,328,294	1,279,294	1,264,034	1,787,942
Newspaper subscriptions	4,855,936	1,290,706	397,575	385,319	507,764
Newspaper, nonsubscription	1,097,702	161,618	71,156	37,483	53,001
Magazine subscriptions	1,730,276	477,685	137,869	138,854	200,957
Magazines, nonsubscription	972,118	252,734	88,481	61,850	102,505
Books purchased through book clubs	639,551	179,692	46,913	49,539	83,200
Books not purchased through book clubs	5,778,053	1,931,503	536,906	588,654	805,906
EDUCATION	105,282,886	41,908,592	10,492,875	9,196,326	22,201,466
College tuition	62,949,261	23,465,430	5,274,000	5,907,894	12,283,371
Elementary and high school tuition	16,605,070	9,975,675	2,011,725	1,091,941	6,871,967
Other school tuition	3,154,731	1,668,164	840,713	330,728	496,769
Other school expenses including rentals	5,679,213	2,456,838	654,638	642,269	1,159,938
Books, supplies for college	6,844,359	1,421,853	395,269	442,711	583,921
Books, supplies for elementary, high school	1,576,784	482,316	198,956	102,517	180,740
Books, supplies for day care, nursery school	269,774	40,479	13,838	16,046	10,641
Miscellaneous school expenses and supplies	8,203,695	2,397,687	1,103,738	662,178	614,171
TOBACCO PRODUCTS AND SMOKING SUPPLIES	33,504,333	3,759,942	1,569,263	1,231,602	958,524
Cigarettes	30,704,262	3,361,871	1,434,600	1,111,681	815,686
Other tobacco products	2,566,344	371,334	119,981	112,323	139,038
Smoking accessories	234,890	26,588	14,681	7,599	3,800

Note: Numbers may not add to total because of rounding and missing subcategories.
Source: Calculations by New Strategist based on the 2004 Consumer Expenditure Survey

Table 10.12 Personal Care, Reading, Education, and Tobacco: Market shares by high-income consumer units, 2004

(percentage of total annual spending on personal care, reading, education, and tobacco products accounted for by before-tax income group of high-income consumer units, 2004)

	total consumer units	$100,000 or more	$100,000–$119,999	$120,000–$149,999	$150,000 or more
Share of total consumer units	100.0%	12.8%	4.8%	3.7%	4.4%
Share of total before-tax income	100.0	36.8	9.7	8.9	18.2
Share of total spending	100.0	27.7	8.4	7.3	12.0
PERSONAL CARE PRODUCTS AND SERVICES	100.0	26.7	8.6	7.5	10.7
Personal care products	100.0	25.7	8.6	7.3	10.0
Hair care products	100.0	25.6	8.2	6.9	10.7
Hair accessories	100.0	23.7	9.9	6.1	7.7
Wigs and hairpieces	100.0	9.2	4.5	1.4	3.3
Oral hygiene products	100.0	23.3	7.1	6.5	10.0
Shaving products	100.0	29.6	10.2	7.8	11.9
Cosmetics, perfume, and bath products	100.0	27.1	9.2	7.9	10.1
Deodorants, feminine hygiene, miscellaneous products	100.0	22.8	7.9	6.0	9.1
Electric personal care appliances	100.0	21.3	6.2	7.7	7.3
Personal care services	100.0	27.8	8.6	7.7	11.5
READING	100.0	28.5	8.4	8.3	11.8
Newspaper subscriptions	100.0	26.6	8.2	7.9	10.5
Newspaper, nonsubscription	100.0	14.7	6.5	3.4	4.8
Magazine subscriptions	100.0	27.6	8.0	8.0	11.6
Magazines, nonsubscription	100.0	26.0	9.1	6.4	10.5
Books purchased through book clubs	100.0	28.1	7.3	7.7	13.0
Books not purchased through book clubs	100.0	33.4	9.3	10.2	13.9
EDUCATION	100.0	39.8	10.0	8.7	21.1
College tuition	100.0	37.3	8.4	9.4	19.5
Elementary and high school tuition	100.0	60.1	12.1	6.6	41.4
Other school tuition	100.0	52.9	26.6	10.5	15.7
Other school expenses including rentals	100.0	43.3	11.5	11.3	20.4
Books, supplies for college	100.0	20.8	5.8	6.5	8.5
Books, supplies for elementary, high school	100.0	30.6	12.6	6.5	11.5
Books, supplies for day care, nursery school	100.0	15.0	5.1	5.9	3.9
Miscellaneous school expenses and supplies	100.0	29.2	13.5	8.1	7.5
TOBACCO PRODUCTS AND SMOKING SUPPLIES	100.0	11.2	4.7	3.7	2.9
Cigarettes	100.0	10.9	4.7	3.6	2.7
Other tobacco products	100.0	14.5	4.7	4.4	5.4
Smoking accessories	100.0	11.3	6.3	3.2	1.6

Note: Numbers may not add to total because of rounding.
Source: Calculations by New Strategist based on the 2004 Consumer Expenditure Survey

Table 10.13 Personal Care, Reading, Education, and Tobacco: Average spending by household type, 2004

(average annual spending of consumer units (CU) on personal care, reading, education, and tobacco products, by type of consumer unit, 2004)

	total married couples	married couples, no children	married couples with children				single parent, at least one child <18	single person
			total	oldest child under 6	oldest child 6 to 17	oldest child 18 or older		
Number of consumer units (in 000s)	59,797	25,585	29,279	5,604	15,376	8,300	6,892	33,686
Average number of persons per CU	3.2	2.0	3.9	3.5	4.1	3.9	2.9	1.0
Average before-tax income of CU	$73,001.00	$64,434.00	$79,764.00	$75,293.00	$78,508.00	$85,109.00	$31,055.00	$28,143.00
Average spending of CU, total	55,606.57	49,690.43	60,660.88	55,981.04	60,577.88	64,161.69	32,824.46	25,423.35
PERSONAL CARE PRODUCTS AND SERVICES	710.54	655.95	747.95	603.93	731.85	891.37	517.30	355.46
Personal care products	383.76	324.73	420.92	321.28	404.93	534.15	298.64	187.33
Hair care products	78.03	60.50	90.66	73.66	97.37	90.30	62.89	34.78
Hair accessories	6.98	5.41	7.98	8.32	7.79	8.08	10.35	4.04
Wigs and hairpieces	1.93	2.09	1.83	1.11	1.65	2.65	3.01	1.35
Oral hygiene products	43.14	41.35	44.79	44.52	42.88	48.99	30.56	19.98
Shaving products	21.40	18.13	23.91	13.07	24.38	31.63	14.50	14.09
Cosmetics, perfume, and bath products	177.86	148.65	195.56	140.71	172.14	288.44	127.20	88.69
Deodorants, feminine hygiene, miscellaneous products	41.14	34.20	44.81	35.97	47.57	46.15	40.52	19.26
Electric personal care appliances	13.28	14.40	11.39	3.91	11.14	17.91	9.61	5.14
Personal care services	326.79	331.22	327.03	282.66	326.92	357.22	218.66	168.12
READING	165.69	186.06	153.02	139.38	157.63	153.69	68.13	97.45
Newspaper subscriptions	55.99	72.20	43.84	33.08	42.10	54.34	12.62	30.11
Newspaper, nonsubscription	9.98	9.50	10.37	9.28	10.02	11.74	8.50	8.78
Magazine subscriptions	19.17	24.93	15.08	16.37	15.69	13.08	5.95	10.28
Magazines, nonsubscription	9.97	9.21	10.70	11.96	10.32	10.55	7.56	6.01
Books purchased through book clubs	7.62	8.49	6.99	10.47	7.02	4.59	3.32	3.28
Books not purchased through book clubs	62.51	61.32	65.58	58.22	71.63	59.34	30.07	37.13
EDUCATION	1,154.49	828.48	1,485.37	413.62	1,439.11	2,294.49	699.57	629.29
College tuition	646.22	618.70	700.96	197.03	423.06	1,555.99	275.98	454.73
Elementary and high school tuition	232.30	40.72	412.85	55.01	646.35	221.91	204.09	23.43
Other school tuition	40.94	25.37	55.41	33.33	27.82	121.43	8.20	13.63
Other school expenses including rentals	67.25	42.27	91.70	57.20	87.94	121.97	43.00	23.19
Books, supplies for college	54.57	41.55	65.18	13.31	36.46	153.40	36.27	69.16
Books, supplies for elementary, high school	19.63	2.03	34.86	2.83	53.75	21.50	37.28	1.19
Books, supplies for day care, nursery school	3.28	2.11	4.61	5.55	4.69	3.82	2.08	1.23
Miscellaneous school expenses and supplies	90.31	55.74	119.80	49.37	159.03	94.48	92.67	42.74
TOBACCO PRODUCTS, SMOKING SUPPLIES	300.73	248.91	324.40	210.66	318.01	412.90	277.31	166.99
Cigarettes	271.10	222.19	293.32	185.44	287.88	376.24	265.90	148.90
Other tobacco products	27.66	25.47	29.13	20.88	28.90	35.14	10.36	16.14
Smoking accessories	1.97	1.25	1.95	4.33	1.23	1.52	1.06	1.95

Note: Average spending figures for total consumer units can be found on Average Spending by Age and Average Spending by Region tables. Subcategories may not add to total because some are not shown.
Source: Bureau of Labor Statistics, unpublished tables from the 2004 Consumer Expenditure Survey

Table 10.14 Personal Care, Reading, Education, and Tobacco: Indexed spending by household type, 2004

(indexed average annual spending of consumer units (CU) on personal care, reading, education, and tobacco products, by type of consumer unit, 2004; index definition: an index of 100 is the average for all consumer units; an index of 132 means that spending by consumer units in that group is 32 percent above the average for all consumer units; an index of 68 indicates spending that is 32 percent below the average for all consumer units)

| | total married couples | married couples, no children | married couples with children | | | | single parent, at least one child <18 | single person |
			total	oldest child under 6	oldest child 6 to 17	oldest child 18 or older		
Average spending of CU, total	$55,607	$49,690	$60,661	$55,981	$60,578	$64,162	$32,824	$25,423
Average spending of CU, index	128	115	140	129	140	148	76	59
PERSONAL CARE PRODUCTS AND SERVICES	**122**	**113**	**129**	**104**	**126**	**153**	**89**	**61**
Personal care products	**121**	**102**	**133**	**101**	**128**	**169**	**94**	**59**
Hair care products	122	95	142	115	152	141	98	54
Hair accessories	110	85	125	131	122	127	162	63
Wigs and hairpieces	102	110	96	58	87	139	158	71
Oral hygiene products	125	119	129	129	124	141	88	58
Shaving products	114	97	128	70	130	169	77	75
Cosmetics, perfume, and bath products	121	101	133	95	117	196	86	60
Deodorants, feminine hygiene, miscellaneous products	120	100	131	105	139	134	118	56
Electric personal care appliances	136	148	117	40	114	184	99	53
Personal care services	**124**	**125**	**124**	**107**	**124**	**135**	**83**	**64**
READING	**127**	**143**	**117**	**107**	**121**	**118**	**52**	**75**
Newspaper subscriptions	134	173	105	79	101	130	30	72
Newspaper, nonsubscription	106	101	110	98	106	124	90	93
Magazine subscriptions	129	168	101	110	105	88	40	69
Magazines, nonsubscription	119	110	128	143	123	126	90	72
Books purchased through book clubs	139	154	127	190	128	83	60	60
Books not purchased through book clubs	126	123	132	117	144	119	61	75
EDUCATION	**128**	**92**	**164**	**46**	**159**	**253**	**77**	**70**
College tuition	119	114	129	36	78	287	51	84
Elementary and high school tuition	163	29	289	39	453	155	143	16
Other school tuition	151	94	204	123	103	448	30	50
Other school expenses including rentals	138	87	188	117	180	250	88	47
Books, supplies for college	93	71	111	23	62	261	62	117
Books, supplies for elementary, high school	145	15	257	21	396	159	275	9
Books, supplies for day care, nursery school	141	91	199	239	202	165	90	53
Miscellaneous school expenses and supplies	128	79	170	70	225	134	131	61
TOBACCO PRODUCTS AND SMOKING SUPPLIES	**104**	**86**	**113**	**73**	**110**	**143**	**96**	**58**
Cigarettes	103	84	111	70	109	142	101	56
Other tobacco products	125	115	132	95	131	159	47	73
Smoking accessories	98	62	97	214	61	75	52	97

Note: Spending index for total consumer units is 100. "–" means sample is too small to make a reliable estimate.
Source: Calculations by New Strategist based on the 2004 Consumer Expenditure Survey

Table 10.15 Personal Care, Reading, Education, and Tobacco: Total spending by household type, 2004

(total annual spending on personal care, reading, education, and tobacco products, by consumer unit (CU) type, 2004; consumer units and dollars in thousands)

	total married couples	married couples, no children	married couples with children total	oldest child under 6	oldest child 6 to 17	oldest child 18 or older	single parent, at least one child <18	single person
Number of consumer units	59,797	25,585	29,279	5,604	15,376	8,300	6,892	33,686
Total spending of all CUs	$3,325,106,066	$1,271,329,652	$1,776,089,906	$313,717,748	$931,445,483	$532,542,027	$226,226,178	$856,410,968
PERSONAL CARE PRODUCTS, SERVICES	**42,488,160**	**16,782,481**	**21,899,228**	**3,384,424**	**11,252,926**	**7,398,371**	**3,565,232**	**11,974,026**
Personal care products	**22,947,697**	**8,308,217**	**12,324,117**	**1,800,453**	**6,226,204**	**4,433,445**	**2,058,227**	**6,310,398**
Hair care products	4,665,960	1,547,893	2,654,434	412,791	1,497,161	749,490	433,438	1,171,599
Hair accessories	417,383	138,415	233,646	46,625	119,779	67,064	71,332	136,091
Wigs and hairpieces	115,408	53,473	53,581	6,220	25,370	21,995	20,745	45,476
Oral hygiene products	2,579,643	1,057,940	1,311,406	249,490	659,323	406,617	210,620	673,046
Shaving products	1,279,656	463,856	700,061	73,244	374,867	262,529	99,934	474,636
Cosmetics, perfume, and bath products	10,635,494	3,803,210	5,725,801	788,539	2,646,825	2,394,052	876,662	2,987,611
Deodorants, feminine hygiene, miscellaneous products	2,460,049	875,007	1,311,992	201,576	731,436	383,045	279,264	648,792
Electric personal care appliances	794,104	368,424	333,488	21,912	171,289	148,653	66,232	173,146
Personal care services	**19,541,062**	**8,474,264**	**9,575,111**	**1,584,027**	**5,026,722**	**2,964,926**	**1,507,005**	**5,663,290**
READING	**9,907,765**	**4,760,345**	**4,480,273**	**781,086**	**2,423,719**	**1,275,627**	**469,552**	**3,282,701**
Newspaper subscriptions	3,348,034	1,847,237	1,283,591	185,380	647,330	451,022	86,977	1,014,285
Newspaper, nonsubscription	596,774	243,058	303,623	52,005	154,068	97,442	58,582	295,763
Magazine subscriptions	1,146,308	637,834	441,527	91,737	241,249	108,564	41,007	346,292
Magazines, nonsubscription	596,176	235,638	313,285	67,024	158,680	87,565	52,104	202,453
Books purchased through book clubs	455,653	217,217	204,660	58,674	107,940	38,097	22,881	110,490
Books not purchased through book clubs	3,737,910	1,568,872	1,920,117	326,265	1,101,383	492,522	207,242	1,250,761
EDUCATION	**69,035,039**	**21,196,661**	**43,490,148**	**2,317,926**	**22,127,755**	**19,044,267**	**4,821,436**	**21,198,263**
College tuition	38,642,017	15,829,440	20,523,408	1,104,156	6,504,971	12,914,717	1,902,054	15,318,035
Elementary and high school tuition	13,890,843	1,041,821	12,087,835	308,276	9,938,278	1,841,853	1,406,588	789,263
Other school tuition	2,448,089	649,091	1,622,349	186,781	427,760	1,007,869	56,514	459,140
Other school expenses including rentals	4,021,348	1,081,478	2,684,884	320,549	1,352,165	1,012,351	296,356	781,178
Books, supplies for college	3,263,122	1,063,057	1,908,405	74,589	560,609	1,273,220	249,973	2,329,724
Books, supplies for elementary, high school	1,173,815	51,938	1,020,666	15,859	826,460	178,450	256,934	40,086
Books, supplies for day care, nursery school	196,134	53,984	134,976	31,102	72,113	31,706	14,335	41,434
Miscellaneous school expenses and supplies	5,400,267	1,426,108	3,507,624	276,669	2,445,245	784,184	638,682	1,439,740
TOBACCO PRODUCTS, SMOKING SUPPLIES	**17,982,752**	**6,368,362**	**9,498,108**	**1,180,539**	**4,889,722**	**3,427,070**	**1,911,221**	**5,625,225**
Cigarettes	16,210,967	5,684,731	8,588,116	1,039,206	4,426,443	3,122,792	1,832,583	5,015,845
Other tobacco products	1,653,985	651,650	852,897	117,012	444,366	291,662	71,401	543,692
Smoking accessories	117,800	31,981	57,094	24,265	18,912	12,616	7,306	65,688

Note: Total spending figures for total consumer units can be found on Total Spending by Age and Total Spending by Region tables. Spending by type of consumer unit will not add to total because not all types of consumer units are shown. Numbers may not add to category total because of rounding and missing subcategories. "–" means sample is too small to make a reliable estimate.
Source: Calculations by New Strategist based on the 2004 Consumer Expenditure Survey

Table 10.16 Personal Care, Reading, Education, and Tobacco: Market shares by household type, 2004

(percentage of total annual spending on personal care, reading, education, and tobacco products accounted for by types of consumer units, 2004)

	total married couples	married couples, no children	married couples with children				single parent, at least one child <18	single person
			total	oldest child under 6	oldest child 6 to 17	oldest child 18 or older		
Share of total consumer units	**51.4%**	**22.0%**	**25.2%**	**4.8%**	**13.2%**	**7.1%**	**5.9%**	**29.0%**
Share of total before-tax income	**68.9**	**26.0**	**36.9**	**6.7**	**19.1**	**11.2**	**3.4**	**15.0**
Share of total spending	**65.9**	**25.2**	**35.2**	**6.2**	**18.5**	**10.6**	**4.5**	**17.0**
PERSONAL CARE PRODUCTS AND SERVICES	**62.9**	**24.8**	**32.4**	**5.0**	**16.7**	**10.9**	**5.3**	**17.7**
Personal care products	**62.3**	**22.5**	**33.4**	**4.9**	**16.9**	**12.0**	**5.6**	**17.1**
Hair care products	62.8	20.8	35.7	5.6	20.1	10.1	5.8	15.8
Hair accessories	56.3	18.7	31.5	6.3	16.2	9.1	9.6	18.4
Wigs and hairpieces	52.2	24.2	24.3	2.8	11.5	10.0	9.4	20.6
Oral hygiene products	64.1	26.3	32.6	6.2	16.4	10.1	5.2	16.7
Shaving products	58.8	21.3	32.2	3.4	17.2	12.1	4.6	21.8
Cosmetics, perfume, and bath products	62.0	22.2	33.4	4.6	15.4	14.0	5.1	17.4
Deodorants, feminine hygiene, miscellaneous products	61.6	21.9	32.9	5.0	18.3	9.6	7.0	16.3
Electric personal care appliances	70.1	32.5	29.4	1.9	15.1	13.1	5.8	15.3
Personal care services	**63.6**	**27.6**	**31.2**	**5.2**	**16.4**	**9.7**	**4.9**	**18.4**
READING	**65.3**	**31.4**	**29.5**	**5.2**	**16.0**	**8.4**	**3.1**	**21.6**
Newspaper subscriptions	68.9	38.0	26.4	3.8	13.3	9.3	1.8	20.9
Newspaper, nonsubscription	54.4	22.1	27.7	4.7	14.0	8.9	5.3	26.9
Magazine subscriptions	66.3	36.9	25.5	5.3	13.9	6.3	2.4	20.0
Magazines, nonsubscription	61.3	24.2	32.2	6.9	16.3	9.0	5.4	20.8
Books purchased through book clubs	71.2	34.0	32.0	9.2	16.9	6.0	3.6	17.3
Books not purchased through book clubs	64.7	27.2	33.2	5.6	19.1	8.5	3.6	21.6
EDUCATION	**65.6**	**20.1**	**41.3**	**2.2**	**21.0**	**18.1**	**4.6**	**20.1**
College tuition	61.4	25.1	32.6	1.8	10.3	20.5	3.0	24.3
Elementary and high school tuition	83.7	6.3	72.8	1.9	59.9	11.1	8.5	4.8
Other school tuition	77.6	20.6	51.4	5.9	13.6	31.9	1.8	14.6
Other school expenses including rentals	70.8	19.0	47.3	5.6	23.8	17.8	5.2	13.8
Books, supplies for college	47.7	15.5	27.9	1.1	8.2	18.6	3.7	34.0
Books, supplies for elementary, high school	74.4	3.3	64.7	1.0	52.4	11.3	16.3	2.5
Books, supplies for day care, nursery school	72.7	20.0	50.0	11.5	26.7	11.8	5.3	15.4
Miscellaneous school expenses and supplies	65.8	17.4	42.8	3.4	29.8	9.6	7.8	17.5
TOBACCO PRODUCTS AND SMOKING SUPPLIES	**53.7**	**19.0**	**28.3**	**3.5**	**14.6**	**10.2**	**5.7**	**16.8**
Cigarettes	52.8	18.5	28.0	3.4	14.4	10.2	6.0	16.3
Other tobacco products	64.4	25.4	33.2	4.6	17.3	11.4	2.8	21.2
Smoking accessories	50.2	13.6	24.3	10.3	8.1	5.4	3.1	28.0

Note: Market share for total consumer units is 100.0%. Market shares by type of consumer unit will not add to total because not all types of consumer units are shown. "–" means sample is too small to make a reliable estimate.
Source: Calculations by New Strategist based on the 2004 Consumer Expenditure Survey

Table 10.17 Personal Care, Reading, Education, and Tobacco: Average spending by race and Hispanic origin, 2004

(average annual spending of consumer units (CU) on personal care, reading, education, and tobacco products, by race and Hispanic origin of consumer unit reference person, 2004)

	total consumer units	Asian	black	Hispanic	non-Hispanic white and other
Number of consumer units (in 000s)	116,282	3,957	13,773	12,298	90,424
Average number of persons per CU	2.5	2.8	2.6	3.3	2.3
Average before-tax income of CU	$54,453.00	$67,705.00	$38,503.00	$43,693.00	$58,314.00
Average spending of CU, total	43,394.87	49,458.68	30,481.49	37,578.03	46,163.26
PERSONAL CARE PRODUCTS AND SERVICES	581.09	506.43	503.24	519.43	601.76
Personal care products	317.00	303.27	249.01	321.21	327.26
Hair care products	63.90	61.97	44.17	72.65	66.02
Hair accessories	6.37	4.53	8.39	5.99	6.11
Wigs and hairpieces	1.90	0.04	7.76	1.84	1.03
Oral hygiene products	34.63	37.49	28.88	35.36	35.40
Shaving products	18.71	11.50	11.76	11.18	20.82
Cosmetics, perfume, and bath products	147.41	165.42	111.90	155.91	151.62
Deodorants, feminine hygiene, miscellaneous products	34.33	20.71	31.03	31.43	35.35
Electric personal care appliances	9.74	1.62	5.11	6.85	10.91
Personal care services	264.09	203.16	254.23	198.22	274.49
READING	130.41	112.48	53.33	53.17	152.45
Newspaper subscriptions	41.76	30.50	16.18	12.16	49.59
Newspaper, nonsubscription	9.44	4.18	8.31	5.86	10.10
Magazine subscriptions	14.88	10.77	3.96	5.32	17.83
Magazines, nonsubscription	8.36	5.98	5.34	4.03	9.41
Books purchased through book clubs	5.50	2.14	1.60	4.03	6.29
Books not purchased through book clubs	49.69	58.91	17.91	18.90	58.61
EDUCATION	905.41	2,086.77	573.45	438.12	1,018.77
College tuition	541.35	1,452.99	307.62	208.06	621.52
Elementary and high school tuition	142.80	291.55	61.11	106.89	160.38
Other school tuition	27.13	27.47	9.07	12.59	31.79
Other school expenses including rentals	48.84	78.42	27.37	24.02	55.38
Books, supplies for college	58.86	126.62	39.25	35.10	65.11
Books, supplies for elementary, high school	13.56	18.91	9.37	14.00	14.16
Books, supplies for day care, nursery school	2.32	2.26	1.75	1.56	2.50
Miscellaneous school expenses and supplies	70.55	88.54	117.91	35.89	67.94
TOBACCO PRODUCTS AND SMOKING SUPPLIES	288.13	102.87	200.46	154.98	319.31
Cigarettes	264.05	101.94	188.62	144.79	291.53
Other tobacco products	22.07	0.28	10.83	7.20	25.75
Smoking accessories	2.02	0.66	1.00	2.98	2.04

Note: "Asian" and "black" include Hispanics and non-Hispanics who identify themselves as being of the respective race alone. "Hispanic" includes people of any race who identify themselves as Hispanic. "Other" includes people who identify themselves as non-Hispanic and as Alaska Native, American Indian, Asian (who are also included in the "Asian" column), Native Hawaiian or other Pacific Islander, as well as non-Hispanics reporting more than one race. Subcategories may not add to total because some are not shown.
Source: Bureau of Labor Statistics, unpublished tables from the 2004 Consumer Expenditure Survey

Table 10.18 Personal Care, Reading, Education, and Tobacco: Indexed spending by race and Hispanic origin, 2004

(indexed average annual spending of consumer units (CU) on personal care, reading, education, and tobacco products, by race and Hispanic origin of consumer unit reference person, 2004; index definition: an index of 100 is the average for all consumer units; an index of 132 means that spending by consumer units in that group is 32 percent above the average for all consumer units; an index of 68 indicates spending that is 32 percent below the average for all consumer units)

	total consumer units	Asian	black	Hispanic	non-Hispanic white and other
Average spending of CU, total	$43,395	$49,459	$30,481	$37,578	$46,163
Average spending of CU, index	100	114	70	87	106
PERSONAL CARE PRODUCTS AND SERVICES	**100**	**87**	**87**	**89**	**104**
Personal care products	**100**	**96**	**79**	**101**	**103**
Hair care products	100	97	69	114	103
Hair accessories	100	71	132	94	96
Wigs and hairpieces	100	2	408	97	54
Oral hygiene products	100	108	83	102	102
Shaving products	100	61	63	60	111
Cosmetics, perfume, and bath products	100	112	76	106	103
Deodorants, feminine hygiene, miscellaneous products	100	60	90	92	103
Electric personal care appliances	100	17	52	70	112
Personal care services	**100**	**77**	**96**	**75**	**104**
READING	**100**	**86**	**41**	**41**	**117**
Newspaper subscriptions	100	73	39	29	119
Newspaper, nonsubscription	100	44	88	62	107
Magazine subscriptions	100	72	27	36	120
Magazines, nonsubscription	100	72	64	48	113
Books purchased through book clubs	100	39	29	73	114
Books not purchased through book clubs	100	119	36	38	118
EDUCATION	**100**	**230**	**63**	**48**	**113**
College tuition	100	268	57	38	115
Elementary and high school tuition	100	204	43	75	112
Other school tuition	100	101	33	46	117
Other school expenses including rentals	100	161	56	49	113
Books, supplies for college	100	215	67	60	111
Books, supplies for elementary, high school	100	139	69	103	104
Books, supplies for day care, nursery school	100	97	75	67	108
Miscellaneous school expenses and supplies	100	125	167	51	96
TOBACCO PRODUCTS AND SMOKING SUPPLIES	**100**	**36**	**70**	**54**	**111**
Cigarettes	100	39	71	55	110
Other tobacco products	100	1	49	33	117
Smoking accessories	100	33	50	148	101

Note: "Asian" and "black" include Hispanics and non-Hispanics who identify themselves as being of the respective race alone. "Hispanic" includes people of any race who identify themselves as Hispanic. "Other" includes people who identify themselves as non-Hispanic and as Alaska Native, American Indian, Asian (who are also included in the "Asian" column), Native Hawaiian or other Pacific Islander, as well as non-Hispanics reporting more than one race.
Source: Calculations by New Strategist based on the 2004 Consumer Expenditure Survey

Table 10.19 Personal Care, Reading, Education, and Tobacco: Total spending by race and Hispanic origin, 2004

(total annual spending on personal care, reading, education, and tobacco products, by consumer unit race and Hispanic origin groups, 2004; consumer units and dollars in thousands)

	total consumer units	Asian	black	Hispanic	non-Hispanic white and other
Number of consumer units	116,282	3,957	13,773	12,298	90,424
Total spending of all consumer units	$5,046,042,273	$195,707,997	$419,821,562	$462,134,613	$4,174,266,622
PERSONAL CARE PRODUCTS AND SERVICES	**67,570,307**	**2,003,944**	**6,931,125**	**6,387,950**	**54,413,546**
Personal care products	**36,861,394**	**1,200,039**	**3,429,615**	**3,950,241**	**29,592,158**
Hair care products	7,430,420	245,215	608,353	893,450	5,969,792
Hair accessories	740,716	17,925	115,555	73,665	552,491
Wigs and hairpieces	220,936	158	106,878	22,628	93,137
Oral hygiene products	4,026,846	148,348	397,764	434,857	3,201,010
Shaving products	2,175,636	45,506	161,970	137,492	1,882,628
Cosmetics, perfume, and bath products	17,141,130	654,567	1,541,199	1,917,381	13,710,087
Deodorants, feminine hygiene, miscellaneous products	3,991,961	81,949	427,376	386,526	3,196,488
Electric personal care appliances	1,132,587	6,410	70,380	84,241	986,526
Personal care services	**30,708,913**	**803,904**	**3,501,510**	**2,437,710**	**24,820,484**
READING	**15,164,336**	**445,083**	**734,514**	**653,885**	**13,785,139**
Newspaper subscriptions	4,855,936	120,689	222,847	149,544	4,484,126
Newspaper, nonsubscription	1,097,702	16,540	114,454	72,066	913,282
Magazine subscriptions	1,730,276	42,617	54,541	65,425	1,612,260
Magazines, nonsubscription	972,118	23,663	73,548	49,561	850,890
Books purchased through book clubs	639,551	8,468	22,037	49,561	568,767
Books not purchased through book clubs	5,778,053	233,107	246,674	232,432	5,299,751
EDUCATION	**105,282,886**	**8,257,349**	**7,898,127**	**5,388,000**	**92,121,258**
College tuition	62,949,261	5,749,481	4,236,850	2,558,722	56,200,324
Elementary and high school tuition	16,605,070	1,153,663	841,668	1,314,533	14,502,201
Other school tuition	3,154,731	108,699	124,921	154,832	2,874,579
Other school expenses including rentals	5,679,213	310,308	376,967	295,398	5,007,681
Books, supplies for college	6,844,359	501,035	540,590	431,660	5,887,507
Books, supplies for elementary, high school	1,576,784	74,827	129,053	172,172	1,280,404
Books, supplies for day care, nursery school	269,774	8,943	24,103	19,185	226,060
Miscellaneous school expenses and supplies	8,203,695	350,353	1,623,974	441,375	6,143,407
TOBACCO PRODUCTS AND SMOKING SUPPLIES	**33,504,333**	**407,057**	**2,760,936**	**1,905,944**	**28,873,287**
Cigarettes	30,704,262	403,377	2,597,863	1,780,627	26,361,309
Other tobacco products	2,566,344	1,108	149,162	88,546	2,328,418
Smoking accessories	234,890	2,612	13,773	36,648	184,465

Note: "Asian" and "black" include Hispanics and non-Hispanics who identify themselves as being of the respective race alone. "Hispanic" includes people of any race who identify themselves as Hispanic. "Other" includes people who identify themselves as non-Hispanic and as Alaska Native, American Indian, Asian (who are also included in the "Asian" column), Native Hawaiian or other Pacific Islander, as well as non-Hispanics reporting more than one race. Numbers may not add to total because of rounding and missing subcategories.
Source: Calculations by New Strategist based on the 2004 Consumer Expenditure Survey

Table 10.20 Personal Care, Reading, Education, and Tobacco: Market shares by race and Hispanic origin, 2004

(percentage of total annual spending on personal care, reading, education, and tobacco products accounted for by consumer unit race and Hispanic origin groups, 2004)

	total consumer units	Asian	black	Hispanic	non-Hispanic white and other
Share of total consumer units	**100.0%**	**3.4%**	**11.8%**	**10.6%**	**77.8%**
Share of total before-tax income	**100.0**	**4.2**	**8.4**	**8.5**	**83.3**
Share of total spending	**100.0**	**3.9**	**8.3**	**9.2**	**82.7**
PERSONAL CARE PRODUCTS AND SERVICES	**100.0**	**3.0**	**10.3**	**9.5**	**80.5**
Personal care products	**100.0**	**3.3**	**9.3**	**10.7**	**80.3**
Hair care products	100.0	3.3	8.2	12.0	80.3
Hair accessories	100.0	2.4	15.6	9.9	74.6
Wigs and hairpieces	100.0	0.1	48.4	10.2	42.2
Oral hygiene products	100.0	3.7	9.9	10.8	79.5
Shaving products	100.0	2.1	7.4	6.3	86.5
Cosmetics, perfume, and bath products	100.0	3.8	9.0	11.2	80.0
Deodorants, feminine hygiene, miscellaneous products	100.0	2.1	10.7	9.7	80.1
Electric personal care appliances	100.0	0.6	6.2	7.4	87.1
Personal care services	**100.0**	**2.6**	**11.4**	**7.9**	**80.8**
READING	**100.0**	**2.9**	**4.8**	**4.3**	**90.9**
Newspaper subscriptions	100.0	2.5	4.6	3.1	92.3
Newspaper, nonsubscription	100.0	1.5	10.4	6.6	83.2
Magazine subscriptions	100.0	2.5	3.2	3.8	93.2
Magazines, nonsubscription	100.0	2.4	7.6	5.1	87.5
Books purchased through book clubs	100.0	1.3	3.4	7.7	88.9
Books not purchased through book clubs	100.0	4.0	4.3	4.0	91.7
EDUCATION	**100.0**	**7.8**	**7.5**	**5.1**	**87.5**
College tuition	100.0	9.1	6.7	4.1	89.3
Elementary and high school tuition	100.0	6.9	5.1	7.9	87.3
Other school tuition	100.0	3.4	4.0	4.9	91.1
Other school expenses including rentals	100.0	5.5	6.6	5.2	88.2
Books, supplies for college	100.0	7.3	7.9	6.3	86.0
Books, supplies for elementary, high school	100.0	4.7	8.2	10.9	81.2
Books, supplies for day care, nursery school	100.0	3.3	8.9	7.1	83.8
Miscellaneous school expenses and supplies	100.0	4.3	19.8	5.4	74.9
TOBACCO PRODUCTS AND SMOKING SUPPLIES	**100.0**	**1.2**	**8.2**	**5.7**	**86.2**
Cigarettes	100.0	1.3	8.5	5.8	85.9
Other tobacco products	100.0	0.0	5.8	3.5	90.7
Smoking accessories	100.0	1.1	5.9	15.6	78.5

Note: "Asian" and "black" include Hispanics and non-Hispanics who identify themselves as being of the respective race alone. "Hispanic" includes people of any race who identify themselves as Hispanic. "Other" includes people who identify themselves as non-Hispanic and as Alaska Native, American Indian, Asian (who are also included in the "Asian" column), Native Hawaiian or other Pacific Islander, as well as non-Hispanics reporting more than one race. Numbers may not add to total because of rounding.
Source: Calculations by New Strategist based on the 2004 Consumer Expenditure Survey

Table 10.21 Personal Care, Reading, Education, and Tobacco: Average spending by region, 2004

(average annual spending of consumer units (CU) on personal care, reading, education, and tobacco products, by region in which consumer unit lives, 2004)

	total consumer units	Northeast	Midwest	South	West
Number of consumer units (in 000s)	116,282	22,051	26,539	41,801	25,891
Average number of persons per CU	2.5	2.4	2.4	2.5	2.6
Average before-tax income of CU	$54,453.00	$61,050.00	$53,567.00	$50,775.00	$55,682.00
Average spending of CU, total	43,394.87	46,114.89	43,370.77	39,173.65	47,921.74
PERSONAL CARE PRODUCTS AND SERVICES	**581.09**	**631.50**	**562.92**	**542.25**	**619.86**
Personal care products	**317.00**	**338.65**	**295.63**	**303.55**	**342.54**
Hair care products	63.90	72.68	65.29	55.22	69.01
Hair accessories	6.37	5.52	6.40	6.08	7.57
Wigs and hairpieces	1.90	1.54	1.20	2.12	2.59
Oral hygiene products	34.63	38.05	30.13	33.39	38.39
Shaving products	18.71	23.02	18.95	16.26	18.73
Cosmetics, perfume, and bath products	147.41	151.53	130.92	148.10	159.96
Deodorants, feminine hygiene, miscellaneous products	34.33	35.82	35.09	33.48	33.61
Electric personal care appliances	9.74	10.48	7.64	8.90	12.68
Personal care services	**264.09**	**292.85**	**267.29**	**238.70**	**277.33**
READING	**130.41**	**144.78**	**150.39**	**97.73**	**150.48**
Newspaper subscriptions	41.76	50.94	51.34	31.13	41.28
Newspaper, nonsubscription	9.44	17.01	10.33	7.11	5.86
Magazine subscriptions	14.88	16.67	16.56	11.13	17.69
Magazines, nonsubscription	8.36	8.25	9.87	6.97	9.14
Books purchased through book clubs	5.50	4.22	7.22	4.38	6.65
Books not purchased through book clubs	49.69	47.43	53.90	36.88	67.98
EDUCATION	**905.41**	**1,152.32**	**928.20**	**631.02**	**1,115.23**
College tuition	541.35	742.42	589.97	307.90	697.17
Elementary and high school tuition	142.80	175.95	137.37	133.55	135.07
Other school tuition	27.13	47.67	16.58	18.93	33.68
Other school expenses including rentals	48.84	56.87	55.92	37.27	53.45
Books, supplies for college	58.86	54.55	60.53	40.16	91.02
Books, supplies for elementary, high school	13.56	11.17	14.32	15.22	12.12
Books, supplies for day care, nursery school	2.32	2.26	1.73	2.18	3.19
Miscellaneous school expenses and supplies	70.55	61.42	51.77	75.81	89.53
TOBACCO PRODUCTS AND SMOKING SUPPLIES	**288.13**	**296.16**	**339.97**	**291.04**	**223.48**
Cigarettes	264.05	276.33	317.79	261.77	202.18
Other tobacco products	22.07	18.36	20.85	26.87	18.71
Smoking accessories	2.02	1.47	1.33	2.40	2.59

Note: Subcategories may not add to total because some are not shown.
Source: Bureau of Labor Statistics, unpublished tables from the 2004 Consumer Expenditure Survey

Table 10.22 Personal Care, Reading, Education, and Tobacco: Indexed spending by region, 2004

(indexed average annual spending of consumer units (CU) on personal care, reading, education, and tobacco products, by region in which consumer unit lives, 2004; index definition: an index of 100 is the average for all consumer units; an index of 132 means that spending by consumer units in that group is 32 percent above the average for all consumer units; an index of 68 indicates spending that is 32 percent below the average for all consumer units)

	total consumer units	Northeast	Midwest	South	West
Average spending of CU, total	$43,395	$46,115	$43,371	$39,174	$47,922
Average spending of CU, index	100	106	100	90	110
PERSONAL CARE PRODUCTS AND SERVICES	100	109	97	93	107
Personal care products	100	107	93	96	108
Hair care products	100	114	102	86	108
Hair accessories	100	87	100	95	119
Wigs and hairpieces	100	81	63	112	136
Oral hygiene products	100	110	87	96	111
Shaving products	100	123	101	87	100
Cosmetics, perfume, and bath products	100	103	89	100	109
Deodorants, feminine hygiene, miscellaneous products	100	104	102	98	98
Electric personal care appliances	100	108	78	91	130
Personal care services	100	111	101	90	105
READING	100	111	115	75	115
Newspaper subscriptions	100	122	123	75	99
Newspaper, nonsubscription	100	180	109	75	62
Magazine subscriptions	100	112	111	75	119
Magazines, nonsubscription	100	99	118	83	109
Books purchased through book clubs	100	77	131	80	121
Books not purchased through book clubs	100	95	108	74	137
EDUCATION	100	127	103	70	123
College tuition	100	137	109	57	129
Elementary and high school tuition	100	123	96	94	95
Other school tuition	100	176	61	70	124
Other school expenses including rentals	100	116	114	76	109
Books, supplies for college	100	93	103	68	155
Books, supplies for elementary, high school	100	82	106	112	89
Books, supplies for day care, nursery school	100	97	75	94	138
Miscellaneous school expenses and supplies	100	87	73	107	127
TOBACCO PRODUCTS AND SMOKING SUPPLIES	100	103	118	101	78
Cigarettes	100	105	120	99	77
Other tobacco products	100	83	94	122	85
Smoking accessories	100	73	66	119	128

Source: Calculations by New Strategist based on the 2004 Consumer Expenditure Survey

Table 10.23 Personal Care, Reading, Education, and Tobacco: Total spending by region, 2004

(total annual spending on personal care, reading, education, and tobacco products, by region in which consumer units live, 2004; consumer units and dollars in thousands)

	total consumer units	Northeast	Midwest	South	West
Number of consumer units	**116,282**	**22,051**	**26,539**	**41,801**	**25,891**
Total spending of all consumer units	**$5,046,042,273**	**$1,016,879,439**	**$1,151,016,865**	**$1,637,497,744**	**$1,240,741,770**
PERSONAL CARE PRODUCTS AND SERVICES	**67,570,307**	**13,925,207**	**14,939,334**	**22,666,592**	**16,048,795**
Personal care products	**36,861,394**	**7,467,571**	**7,845,725**	**12,688,694**	**8,868,703**
Hair care products	7,430,420	1,602,667	1,732,731	2,308,251	1,786,738
Hair accessories	740,716	121,722	169,850	254,150	195,995
Wigs and hairpieces	220,936	33,959	31,847	88,618	67,058
Oral hygiene products	4,026,846	839,041	799,620	1,395,735	993,955
Shaving products	2,175,636	507,614	502,914	679,684	484,938
Cosmetics, perfume, and bath products	17,141,130	3,341,388	3,474,486	6,190,728	4,141,524
Deodorants, feminine hygiene, miscellaneous products	3,991,961	789,867	931,254	1,399,497	870,197
Electric personal care appliances	1,132,587	231,094	202,758	372,029	328,298
Personal care services	**30,708,913**	**6,457,635**	**7,093,609**	**9,977,899**	**7,180,351**
READING	**15,164,336**	**3,192,544**	**3,991,200**	**4,085,212**	**3,896,078**
Newspaper subscriptions	4,855,936	1,123,278	1,362,512	1,301,265	1,068,780
Newspaper, nonsubscription	1,097,702	375,088	274,148	297,205	151,721
Magazine subscriptions	1,730,276	367,590	439,486	465,245	458,012
Magazines, nonsubscription	972,118	181,921	261,940	291,353	236,644
Books purchased through book clubs	639,551	93,055	191,612	183,088	172,175
Books not purchased through book clubs	5,778,053	1,045,879	1,430,452	1,541,621	1,760,070
EDUCATION	**105,282,886**	**25,409,808**	**24,633,500**	**26,377,267**	**28,874,420**
College tuition	62,949,261	16,371,103	15,657,214	12,870,528	18,050,428
Elementary and high school tuition	16,605,070	3,879,873	3,645,662	5,582,524	3,497,097
Other school tuition	3,154,731	1,051,171	440,017	791,293	872,009
Other school expenses including rentals	5,679,213	1,254,040	1,484,061	1,557,923	1,383,874
Books, supplies for college	6,844,359	1,202,882	1,606,406	1,678,728	2,356,599
Books, supplies for elementary, high school	1,576,784	246,310	380,038	636,211	313,799
Books, supplies for day care, nursery school	269,774	49,835	45,912	91,126	82,592
Miscellaneous school expenses and supplies	8,203,695	1,354,372	1,373,924	3,168,934	2,318,021
TOBACCO PRODUCTS AND SMOKING SUPPLIES	**33,504,333**	**6,530,624**	**9,022,464**	**12,165,763**	**5,786,121**
Cigarettes	30,704,262	6,093,353	8,433,829	10,942,248	5,234,642
Other tobacco products	2,566,344	404,856	553,338	1,123,193	484,421
Smoking accessories	234,890	32,415	35,297	100,322	67,058

Note: Numbers may not add to total because of rounding and missing subcategories.
Source: Calculations by New Strategist based on the 2004 Consumer Expenditure Survey

Table 10.24 Personal Care, Reading, Education, and Tobacco: Market shares by region, 2004

(percentage of total annual spending on personal care, reading, education, and tobacco products accounted for by consumer units by region, 2004)

	total consumer units	Northeast	Midwest	South	West
Share of total consumer units	**100.0%**	**19.0%**	**22.8%**	**35.9%**	**22.3%**
Share of total before-tax income	**100.0**	**21.3**	**22.5**	**33.5**	**22.8**
Share of total spending	**100.0**	**20.2**	**22.8**	**32.5**	**24.6**
PERSONAL CARE PRODUCTS AND SERVICES	**100.0**	**20.6**	**22.1**	**33.5**	**23.8**
Personal care products	**100.0**	**20.3**	**21.3**	**34.4**	**24.1**
Hair care products	100.0	21.6	23.3	31.1	24.0
Hair accessories	100.0	16.4	22.9	34.3	26.5
Wigs and hairpieces	100.0	15.4	14.4	40.1	30.4
Oral hygiene products	100.0	20.8	19.9	34.7	24.7
Shaving products	100.0	23.3	23.1	31.2	22.3
Cosmetics, perfume, and bath products	100.0	19.5	20.3	36.1	24.2
Deodorants, feminine hygiene, miscellaneous products	100.0	19.8	23.3	35.1	21.8
Electric personal care appliances	100.0	20.4	17.9	32.8	29.0
Personal care services	**100.0**	**21.0**	**23.1**	**32.5**	**23.4**
READING	**100.0**	**21.1**	**26.3**	**26.9**	**25.7**
Newspaper subscriptions	100.0	23.1	28.1	26.8	22.0
Newspaper, nonsubscription	100.0	34.2	25.0	27.1	13.8
Magazine subscriptions	100.0	21.2	25.4	26.9	26.5
Magazines, nonsubscription	100.0	18.7	26.9	30.0	24.3
Books purchased through book clubs	100.0	14.6	30.0	28.6	26.9
Books not purchased through book clubs	100.0	18.1	24.8	26.7	30.5
EDUCATION	**100.0**	**24.1**	**23.4**	**25.1**	**27.4**
College tuition	100.0	26.0	24.9	20.4	28.7
Elementary and high school tuition	100.0	23.4	22.0	33.6	21.1
Other school tuition	100.0	33.3	13.9	25.1	27.6
Other school expenses including rentals	100.0	22.1	26.1	27.4	24.4
Books, supplies for college	100.0	17.6	23.5	24.5	34.4
Books, supplies for elementary, high school	100.0	15.6	24.1	40.3	19.9
Books, supplies for day care, nursery school	100.0	18.5	17.0	33.8	30.6
Miscellaneous school expenses and supplies	100.0	16.5	16.7	38.6	28.3
TOBACCO PRODUCTS AND SMOKING SUPPLIES	**100.0**	**19.5**	**26.9**	**36.3**	**17.3**
Cigarettes	100.0	19.8	27.5	35.6	17.0
Other tobacco products	100.0	15.8	21.6	43.8	18.9
Smoking accessories	100.0	13.8	15.0	42.7	28.5

Note: Numbers may not add to total because of rounding.
Source: Calculations by New Strategist based on the 2004 Consumer Expenditure Survey

Table 10.25 Personal Care, Reading, Education, and Tobacco: Average spending by education, 2004

(average annual spending of consumer units (CU) on personal care, reading, education, and tobacco products, by education of consumer unit reference person, 2004)

	total consumer units	less than high school graduate	high school graduate	some college	associate's degree	college graduate total	bachelor's degree	master's, professional, doctorate
Number of consumer units (in 000s)	116,282	16,829	31,005	25,317	10,678	32,452	20,684	11,768
Average number of persons per CU	2.5	2.7	2.5	2.3	2.6	2.5	2.4	2.5
Average before-tax income of CU	$54,453.00	$29,094.00	$42,334.00	$46,756.00	$58,593.00	$83,825.00	$75,647.00	$98,201.00
Average spending of CU, total	43,394.87	25,421.18	35,438.55	40,877.68	48,177.36	60,712.28	56,728.41	67,801.38
PERSONAL CARE PRODUCTS AND SERVICES	**581.09**	**361.49**	**480.66**	**554.10**	**684.35**	**779.40**	**753.74**	**825.27**
Personal care products	**317.00**	**231.17**	**274.50**	**304.30**	**394.92**	**387.76**	**382.79**	**397.28**
Hair care products	63.90	47.49	54.18	69.96	77.54	73.36	76.10	68.12
Hair accessories	6.37	5.46	6.02	5.69	9.19	6.82	6.53	7.38
Wigs and hairpieces	1.90	2.67	1.41	2.85	2.27	1.13	1.29	0.83
Oral hygiene products	34.63	24.92	31.89	30.83	44.65	41.94	40.00	45.64
Shaving products	18.71	11.25	14.96	15.66	19.81	28.01	25.27	33.24
Cosmetics, perfume, and bath products	147.41	104.97	126.33	136.56	192.07	183.92	185.92	180.09
Deodorants, feminine hygiene, miscellaneous products	34.33	28.18	31.45	30.64	41.27	40.80	37.63	46.86
Electric personal care appliances	9.74	6.23	8.27	12.11	8.12	11.79	10.04	15.13
Personal care services	**264.09**	**130.32**	**206.16**	**249.80**	**289.42**	**391.64**	**370.96**	**427.98**
READING	**130.41**	**44.62**	**85.33**	**116.30**	**130.43**	**228.97**	**193.02**	**292.29**
Newspaper subscriptions	41.76	21.23	35.40	37.26	41.16	62.18	53.56	77.32
Newspaper, nonsubscription	9.44	6.05	10.04	9.72	10.74	10.00	9.95	10.08
Magazine subscriptions	14.88	3.81	8.86	14.10	14.93	26.96	24.43	31.40
Magazines, nonsubscription	8.36	2.54	6.16	8.96	9.54	12.61	12.40	12.99
Books purchased through book clubs	5.50	1.26	4.16	5.05	4.97	9.51	7.52	12.99
Books not purchased through book clubs	49.69	7.63	20.55	40.92	48.81	106.47	84.91	144.37
EDUCATION	**905.41**	**133.01**	**364.24**	**980.94**	**808.46**	**1,797.44**	**1,496.85**	**2,326.02**
College tuition	541.35	64.62	195.95	636.93	435.82	1,078.74	937.02	1,327.85
Elementary and high school tuition	142.80	18.28	58.34	78.11	102.50	351.81	261.70	510.20
Other school tuition	27.13	1.30	7.80	25.12	30.55	59.43	34.43	103.37
Other school expenses including rentals	48.84	7.63	16.05	40.88	45.28	108.94	71.97	173.92
Books, supplies for college	58.86	6.18	25.54	116.34	57.11	73.76	72.11	76.66
Books, supplies for elementary, high school	13.56	8.93	9.62	11.94	13.99	20.84	17.75	26.28
Books, supplies for day care, nursery school	2.32	0.88	1.75	1.82	3.01	3.77	3.22	4.73
Miscellaneous school expenses and supplies	70.55	25.19	49.21	69.81	120.21	100.15	98.65	103.01
TOBACCO PRODUCTS, SMOKING SUPPLIES	**288.13**	**346.85**	**379.74**	**308.40**	**311.93**	**146.56**	**165.69**	**113.16**
Cigarettes	264.05	325.11	351.68	284.67	283.46	126.18	148.62	86.72
Other tobacco products	22.07	19.88	26.45	22.05	24.48	18.23	16.33	21.56
Smoking accessories	2.02	1.85	1.60	1.69	3.99	2.16	0.74	4.87

Note: Subcategories may not add to total because some are not shown.
Source: Bureau of Labor Statistics, unpublished tables from the 2004 Consumer Expenditure Survey

Table 10.26 Personal Care, Reading, Education, and Tobacco: Indexed spending by education, 2004

(indexed average annual spending of consumer units (CU) on personal care, reading, education, and tobacco products, by education of consumer unit reference person, 2004; index definition: an index of 100 is the average for all consumer units; an index of 132 means that spending by consumer units in that group is 32 percent above the average for all consumer units; an index of 68 indicates spending that is 32 percent below the average for all consumer units)

	total consumer units	less than high school graduate	high school graduate	some college	associate's degree	college graduate		
						total	bachelor's degree	master's, professional, doctorate
Average spending of CU, total	$43,395	$25,421	$35,439	$40,878	$48,177	$60,712	$56,728	$67,801
Average spending of CU, index	100	59	82	94	111	140	131	156
PERSONAL CARE PRODUCTS AND SERVICES	**100**	**62**	**83**	**95**	**118**	**134**	**130**	**142**
Personal care products	**100**	**73**	**87**	**96**	**125**	**122**	**121**	**125**
Hair care products	100	74	85	109	121	115	119	107
Hair accessories	100	86	95	89	144	107	103	116
Wigs and hairpieces	100	141	74	150	119	59	68	44
Oral hygiene products	100	72	92	89	129	121	116	132
Shaving products	100	60	80	84	106	150	135	178
Cosmetics, perfume, and bath products	100	71	86	93	130	125	126	122
Deodorants, feminine hygiene, miscellaneous products	100	82	92	89	120	119	110	136
Electric personal care appliances	100	64	85	124	83	121	103	155
Personal care services	**100**	**49**	**78**	**95**	**110**	**148**	**140**	**162**
READING	**100**	**34**	**65**	**89**	**100**	**176**	**148**	**224**
Newspaper subscriptions	100	51	85	89	99	149	128	185
Newspaper, nonsubscription	100	64	106	103	114	106	105	107
Magazine subscriptions	100	26	60	95	100	181	164	211
Magazines, nonsubscription	100	30	74	107	114	151	148	155
Books purchased through book clubs	100	23	76	92	90	173	137	236
Books not purchased through book clubs	100	15	41	82	98	214	171	291
EDUCATION	**100**	**15**	**40**	**108**	**89**	**199**	**165**	**257**
College tuition	100	12	36	118	81	199	173	245
Elementary and high school tuition	100	13	41	55	72	246	183	357
Other school tuition	100	5	29	93	113	219	127	381
Other school expenses including rentals	100	16	33	84	93	223	147	356
Books, supplies for college	100	10	43	198	97	125	123	130
Books, supplies for elementary, high school	100	66	71	88	103	154	131	194
Books, supplies for day care, nursery school	100	38	75	78	130	163	139	204
Miscellaneous school expenses and supplies	100	36	70	99	170	142	140	146
TOBACCO PRODUCTS AND SMOKING SUPPLIES	**100**	**120**	**132**	**107**	**108**	**51**	**58**	**39**
Cigarettes	100	123	133	108	107	48	56	33
Other tobacco products	100	90	120	100	111	83	74	98
Smoking accessories	100	92	79	84	198	107	37	241

Source: Calculations by New Strategist based on the 2004 Consumer Expenditure Survey

Table 10.27 Personal Care, Reading, Education, and Tobacco: Total spending by education, 2004

(total annual spending on personal care, reading, education, and tobacco products, by consumer unit (CU) educational attainment group, 2004; consumer units and dollars in thousands)

	total consumer units	less than high school graduate	high school graduate	some college	associate's degree	college graduate total	bachelor's degree	master's, professional, doctorate
Number of consumer units	116,282	16,829	31,005	25,317	10,678	32,452	20,684	11,768
Total spending of all CUs	$5,046,042,273	$427,813,038	$1,098,772,243	$1,034,900,225	$514,437,850	$1,970,234,911	$1,173,370,432	$797,886,640
PERSONAL CARE PRODUCTS, SERVICES	**67,570,307**	**6,083,515**	**14,902,863**	**14,028,150**	**7,307,489**	**25,293,089**	**15,590,358**	**9,711,777**
Personal care products	**36,861,394**	**3,890,360**	**8,510,873**	**7,703,963**	**4,216,956**	**12,583,588**	**7,917,628**	**4,675,191**
Hair care products	7,430,420	799,209	1,679,851	1,771,177	827,972	2,380,679	1,574,052	801,636
Hair accessories	740,716	91,886	186,650	144,054	98,131	221,323	135,067	86,848
Wigs and hairpieces	220,936	44,933	43,717	72,153	24,239	36,671	26,682	9,767
Oral hygiene products	4,026,846	419,379	988,749	780,523	476,773	1,361,037	827,360	537,092
Shaving products	2,175,636	189,326	463,835	396,464	211,531	908,981	522,685	391,168
Cosmetics, perfume, and bath products	17,141,130	1,766,540	3,916,862	3,457,290	2,050,923	5,968,572	3,845,569	2,119,299
Deodorants, feminine hygiene, misc. products	3,991,961	474,241	975,107	775,713	440,681	1,324,042	778,339	551,448
Electric personal care appliances	1,132,587	104,845	256,411	306,589	86,705	382,609	207,667	178,050
Personal care services	**30,708,913**	**2,193,155**	**6,391,991**	**6,324,187**	**3,090,427**	**12,709,501**	**7,672,937**	**5,036,469**
READING	**15,164,336**	**750,910**	**2,645,657**	**2,944,367**	**1,392,732**	**7,430,534**	**3,992,426**	**3,439,669**
Newspaper subscriptions	4,855,936	357,280	1,097,577	943,311	439,506	2,017,865	1,107,835	909,902
Newspaper, nonsubscription	1,097,702	101,815	311,290	246,081	114,682	324,520	205,806	118,621
Magazine subscriptions	1,730,276	64,118	274,704	356,970	159,423	874,906	505,310	369,515
Magazines, nonsubscription	972,118	42,746	190,991	226,840	101,868	409,220	256,482	152,866
Books purchased through book clubs	639,551	21,205	128,981	127,851	53,070	308,619	155,544	152,866
Books not purchased through book clubs	5,778,053	128,405	637,153	1,035,972	521,193	3,455,164	1,756,278	1,698,946
EDUCATION	**105,282,886**	**2,238,425**	**11,293,261**	**24,834,458**	**8,632,736**	**58,330,523**	**30,960,845**	**27,372,603**
College tuition	62,949,261	1,087,490	6,075,430	16,125,157	4,653,686	35,007,270	19,381,322	15,626,139
Elementary and high school tuition	16,605,070	307,634	1,808,832	1,977,511	1,094,495	11,416,938	5,413,003	6,004,034
Other school tuition	3,154,731	21,878	241,839	635,963	326,213	1,928,622	712,150	1,216,458
Other school expenses including rentals	5,679,213	128,405	497,630	1,034,959	483,500	3,535,321	1,488,627	2,046,691
Books, supplies for college	6,844,359	104,003	791,868	2,945,380	609,821	2,393,660	1,491,523	902,135
Books, supplies for elementary, high school	1,576,784	150,283	298,268	302,285	149,385	676,300	367,141	309,263
Books, supplies for day care, nursery school	269,774	14,810	54,259	46,077	32,141	122,344	66,602	55,663
Miscellaneous school expenses and supplies	8,203,695	423,923	1,525,756	1,767,380	1,283,602	3,250,068	2,040,477	1,212,222
TOBACCO PRODUCTS, SMOKING SUPPLIES	**33,504,333**	**5,837,139**	**11,773,839**	**7,807,763**	**3,330,789**	**4,756,165**	**3,427,132**	**1,331,667**
Cigarettes	30,704,262	5,471,276	10,903,838	7,206,990	3,026,786	4,094,793	3,074,056	1,020,521
Other tobacco products	2,566,344	334,561	820,082	558,240	261,397	591,600	337,770	253,718
Smoking accessories	234,890	31,134	49,608	42,786	42,605	70,096	15,306	57,310

Note: Numbers may not add to total because of rounding and missing subcategories.
Source: Calculations by New Strategist based on the 2004 Consumer Expenditure Survey

Table 10.28 Personal Care, Reading, Education, and Tobacco: Market shares by education, 2004

(percentage of total annual spending on personal care, reading, education, and tobacco products accounted for by consumer unit educational attainment groups, 2004)

	total consumer units	less than high school graduate	high school graduate	some college	associate's degree	college graduate total	bachelor's degree	master's, professional, doctorate
Share of total consumer units	**100.0%**	**14.5%**	**26.7%**	**21.8%**	**9.2%**	**27.9%**	**17.8%**	**10.1%**
Share of total before-tax income	**100.0**	**7.7**	**20.7**	**18.7**	**9.9**	**43.0**	**24.7**	**18.3**
Share of total spending	**100.0**	**8.5**	**21.8**	**20.5**	**10.2**	**39.0**	**23.3**	**15.8**
PERSONAL CARE PRODUCTS AND SERVICES	**100.0**	**9.0**	**22.1**	**20.8**	**10.8**	**37.4**	**23.1**	**14.4**
Personal care products	**100.0**	**10.6**	**23.1**	**20.9**	**11.4**	**34.1**	**21.5**	**12.7**
Hair care products	100.0	10.8	22.6	23.8	11.1	32.0	21.2	10.8
Hair accessories	100.0	12.4	25.2	19.4	13.2	29.9	18.2	11.7
Wigs and hairpieces	100.0	20.3	19.8	32.7	11.0	16.6	12.1	4.4
Oral hygiene products	100.0	10.4	24.6	19.4	11.8	33.8	20.5	13.3
Shaving products	100.0	8.7	21.3	18.2	9.7	41.8	24.0	18.0
Cosmetics, perfume, and bath products	100.0	10.3	22.9	20.2	12.0	34.8	22.4	12.4
Deodorants, feminine hygiene, miscellaneous products	100.0	11.9	24.4	19.4	11.0	33.2	19.5	13.8
Electric personal care appliances	100.0	9.3	22.6	27.1	7.7	33.8	18.3	15.7
Personal care services	**100.0**	**7.1**	**20.8**	**20.6**	**10.1**	**41.4**	**25.0**	**16.4**
READING	**100.0**	**5.0**	**17.4**	**19.4**	**9.2**	**49.0**	**26.3**	**22.7**
Newspaper subscriptions	100.0	7.4	22.6	19.4	9.1	41.6	22.8	18.7
Newspaper, nonsubscription	100.0	9.3	28.4	22.4	10.4	29.6	18.7	10.8
Magazine subscriptions	100.0	3.7	15.9	20.6	9.2	50.6	29.2	21.4
Magazines, nonsubscription	100.0	4.4	19.6	23.3	10.5	42.1	26.4	15.7
Books purchased through book clubs	100.0	3.3	20.2	20.0	8.3	48.3	24.3	23.9
Books not purchased through book clubs	100.0	2.2	11.0	17.9	9.0	59.8	30.4	29.4
EDUCATION	**100.0**	**2.1**	**10.7**	**23.6**	**8.2**	**55.4**	**29.4**	**26.0**
College tuition	100.0	1.7	9.7	25.6	7.4	55.6	30.8	24.8
Elementary and high school tuition	100.0	1.9	10.9	11.9	6.6	68.8	32.6	36.2
Other school tuition	100.0	0.7	7.7	20.2	10.3	61.1	22.6	38.6
Other school expenses including rentals	100.0	2.3	8.8	18.2	8.5	62.3	26.2	36.0
Books, supplies for college	100.0	1.5	11.6	43.0	8.9	35.0	21.8	13.2
Books, supplies for elementary, high school	100.0	9.5	18.9	19.2	9.5	42.9	23.3	19.6
Books, supplies for day care, nursery school	100.0	5.5	20.1	17.1	11.9	45.4	24.7	20.6
Miscellaneous school expenses and supplies	100.0	5.2	18.6	21.5	15.6	39.6	24.9	14.8
TOBACCO PRODUCTS, SMOKING SUPPLIES	**100.0**	**17.4**	**35.1**	**23.3**	**9.9**	**14.2**	**10.2**	**4.0**
Cigarettes	100.0	17.8	35.5	23.5	9.9	13.3	10.0	3.3
Other tobacco products	100.0	13.0	32.0	21.8	10.2	23.1	13.2	9.9
Smoking accessories	100.0	13.3	21.1	18.2	18.1	29.8	6.5	24.4

Note: Numbers may not add to total because of rounding.
Source: Calculations by New Strategist based on the 2004 Consumer Expenditure Survey

Chapter 11. Spending on Transportation, 2004

Transportation is the second-largest household expenditure category, and the average of $7,801 devoted to transportation in 2004 consumed 18 percent of the average household budget. Spending trends have been mixed in the transportation category during the past four years. Households devoted much less to new cars (down 33 percent) and much more to new trucks (up 43 percent) between 2000 and 2004. Spending on vehicle maintenance and repairs declined 5 percent as warranties on new cars and trucks reduced repair bills. Gasoline and motor oil spending by the average household rose 13 percent between 2000 and 2004—a trend that has now most certainly accelerated with the recent petroleum price rise. Spending on public transportation fell 6 percent between 2000 and 2004.

Householders aged 45 to 54 spend the most on transportation, an average of $9,343 in 2004—or 20 percent more than the average household. These are also the most affluent households, which accounts for their above-average spending. Householders aged 55 to 64 spend the most on new cars, however. Spending on public transportation also peaks in the 55-to-64 age group. Householders aged 55 to 64 spend 31 percent more than the average household on airline fares and 43 percent more on intercity train fares. Householders aged 65 to 74 spend 70 percent more than average on ship fares.

Households with incomes of $100,000 or more spend twice the average on transportation. They spend more than twice the average on new cars and trucks, more than three times the average on airline fares and auto rentals on trips, and nearly four times the average on ship fares. Households with incomes below $70,000 control 60 percent of spending on used cars and trucks.

Married couples with children aged 18 or older at home spend the most on transportation because they are more likely to have two or more vehicles. In 2004 this household type spent more than twice the average on new trucks and 79 percent more than the average on used cars and trucks. Married couples without children at home (most of them empty- nesters) spend 47 percent more than the average household on airline fares and more than twice the average on ship fares.

Blacks and Hispanics spend less than the average household on transportation, but on some categories their spending is well above average. Hispanics spend 46 percent above average on used trucks. Blacks spend 94 percent more than average on mass transit, while Hispanics spend 44 percent more. Asians spend more than twice the average on airline fares. They also spend more than twice the average on mass transit fares.

Households in the West spend the most on transportation, $8,966 in 2004. Households in the South spend the most on used trucks, however, 9 percent more than the average household. Households in the Northeast spend three times more than the average household on mass transit.

Because they dominate affluent households, college graduates spend 25 percent more than average on transportation—$9,766 in 2004. Households headed by people with associate's degrees spend even more—$9,872, including 74 percent more than average on new trucks. College graduates spend more than twice the average on public transportation, including airline and ship fares, controlling 59 percent of the market for airline fares and 62 percent of the market for ship fares.

Table 11.1 Transportation: Average spending by age, 2004

(average annual spending of consumer units (CU) on transportation, by age of consumer unit reference person, 2004)

	total consumer units	under 25	25 to 34	35 to 44	45 to 54	55 to 64	65 to 74	75+
Number of consumer units (in 000s)	116,282	8,817	19,439	24,070	23,712	17,479	11,230	11,536
Average number of persons per CU	2.5	1.9	2.9	3.2	2.7	2.1	1.9	1.5
Average before-tax income of CU	$54,453.00	$22,840.00	$52,484.00	$65,515.00	$70,434.00	$61,031.00	$42,137.00	$28,028.00
Average spending of CU, total	43,394.87	24,534.56	42,700.54	50,401.62	52,764.36	47,298.58	36,511.98	25,763.32
Transportation, average spending	**7,801.38**	**4,704.39**	**8,485.38**	**9,182.80**	**9,343.11**	**8,420.61**	**6,506.10**	**3,286.46**
VEHICLE PURCHASES	**3,397.07**	**2,034.84**	**4,032.96**	**4,189.78**	**3,790.40**	**3,616.25**	**2,821.66**	**1,132.27**
Cars and trucks, new	**1,748.38**	**542.06**	**1,900.72**	**2,204.39**	**1,826.89**	**2,311.41**	**1,561.02**	**630.11**
New cars	672.87	199.79	792.28	701.75	608.83	923.30	738.98	460.82
New trucks	1,075.51	342.28	1,108.43	1,502.65	1,218.07	1,388.11	822.05	169.29
Cars and trucks, used	**1,582.25**	**1,430.03**	**2,086.41**	**1,906.61**	**1,825.79**	**1,246.73**	**1,251.40**	**502.05**
Used cars	760.60	815.59	871.87	810.91	915.20	657.02	692.81	331.27
Used trucks	821.64	614.44	1,214.54	1,095.70	910.58	589.71	558.58	170.78
Other vehicles	**66.45**	**62.74**	**45.83**	**78.78**	**137.72**	**58.11**	**9.24**	**0.11**
GASOLINE AND MOTOR OIL	**1,597.56**	**1,129.60**	**1,678.82**	**1,876.80**	**1,980.02**	**1,666.37**	**1,258.73**	**675.14**
Gasoline	1,466.54	1,048.00	1,553.98	1,737.48	1,813.24	1,514.05	1,125.15	621.42
Diesel fuel	20.50	6.43	15.73	25.48	36.39	16.01	16.90	6.56
Gasoline on trips	100.35	65.88	98.65	102.85	116.56	125.89	108.63	44.29
Motor oil	9.01	8.62	9.46	9.95	12.65	8.17	6.96	2.42
Motor oil on trips	1.01	0.67	1.00	1.04	1.18	1.27	1.10	0.45
OTHER VEHICLE EXPENSES	**2,365.41**	**1,325.70**	**2,407.41**	**2,681.18**	**3,061.08**	**2,531.66**	**1,901.61**	**1,199.53**
Vehicle finance charges	**323.41**	**147.21**	**408.32**	**434.16**	**397.87**	**336.43**	**182.48**	**48.36**
Automobile finance charges	133.28	79.40	157.75	155.00	170.65	152.76	87.77	25.84
Truck finance charges	166.90	65.72	233.04	243.34	203.30	145.73	75.25	19.73
Motorcycle and plane finance charges	3.27	0.82	4.58	4.40	3.98	4.77	–	0.04
Other vehicle finance charges	19.97	1.27	12.95	31.41	19.94	33.16	19.46	2.75
Maintenance and repairs	**651.66**	**399.69**	**602.37**	**687.35**	**837.92**	**741.59**	**585.46**	**398.19**
Coolant, additives, brake and transmission fluids	2.93	2.99	3.06	3.12	4.00	2.75	2.54	0.77
Tires—purchased, replaced, installed	94.09	50.02	94.53	103.91	124.63	107.90	75.03	41.38
Parts, equipment, and accessories	43.03	36.79	48.72	49.59	49.64	42.97	38.87	15.11
Vehicle audio equipment, excluding labor	8.28	35.01	7.53	14.56	2.79	4.42	–	
Vehicle products	4.31	4.96	6.41	3.77	4.74	3.87	3.00	2.32
Miscellaneous auto repair, servicing	50.26	7.50	57.45	54.32	47.15	55.02	44.17	68.96
Body work and painting	36.50	31.18	30.50	29.32	53.73	51.15	27.55	16.78
Clutch and transmission repair	39.27	27.70	36.77	38.34	59.52	35.16	43.20	15.06
Drive shaft and rear-end repair	6.21	2.71	3.82	5.50	8.78	11.52	3.76	3.41
Brake work	44.56	21.40	43.36	45.41	51.42	54.69	43.45	34.14
Repair to steering or front-end	15.19	11.09	10.38	15.75	23.97	19.73	8.74	6.60
Repair to engine cooling system	17.95	12.69	16.49	19.06	20.19	24.48	13.12	12.32
Motor tune-up	41.77	14.49	37.71	48.31	51.24	49.78	42.66	23.38
Lube, oil change, and oil filters	56.23	33.44	53.01	58.87	66.95	67.48	57.88	32.90
Front-end alignment, wheel balance, rotation	9.13	3.62	13.33	8.19	9.20	10.21	10.34	5.20
Shock absorber replacement	2.76	0.48	3.69	1.71	3.93	3.85	2.44	1.40
Gas tank repair, replacement	3.32	1.10	1.86	5.08	3.91	3.44	5.11	0.53
Tire repair and other repair work	49.93	23.12	37.33	50.41	71.05	61.05	46.77	33.51
Vehicle air conditioning repair	14.23	5.69	8.07	14.71	19.22	20.54	15.11	9.48
Exhaust system repair	10.19	6.43	8.65	13.27	10.88	11.96	9.51	5.79
Electrical system repair	22.54	14.10	17.26	21.68	32.57	25.16	21.96	15.68
Motor repair, replacement	69.92	53.18	55.40	71.58	113.01	59.36	52.22	48.42
Auto repair service policy	9.05	–	7.05	10.90	5.40	15.09	18.03	5.06
Vehicle insurance	**964.37**	**535.32**	**943.79**	**1,068.20**	**1,272.71**	**972.77**	**824.71**	**599.80**

	total consumer units	under 25	25 to 34	35 to 44	45 to 54	55 to 64	65 to 74	75+
Vehicle rental, leases, licenses, other charges	**$425.96**	**$243.47**	**$452.93**	**$491.47**	**$552.58**	**$480.88**	**$308.96**	**$153.19**
Leased and rented vehicles	254.85	134.83	282.00	301.54	351.47	284.02	151.69	60.97
Rented vehicles	38.27	14.63	34.72	42.69	45.08	53.53	38.84	15.39
Auto rental	5.64	5.79	8.28	4.21	6.67	4.17	8.89	1.01
Auto rental on trips	21.18	6.90	13.79	24.75	29.47	29.42	17.01	11.65
Truck rental	4.72	0.37	4.38	7.32	4.63	5.53	5.63	1.22
Truck rental on trips	4.54	0.81	4.68	6.31	3.18	8.63	3.46	1.12
Leased vehicles	216.58	120.20	247.27	258.86	306.40	230.49	112.85	45.58
Car lease payments	104.73	78.69	114.76	116.75	143.33	113.56	64.72	28.87
Truck lease payments	96.04	23.89	112.16	124.50	141.04	104.45	37.59	16.27
Vehicle registration, state	80.92	36.88	89.59	90.26	90.04	91.22	76.09	50.83
Vehicle registration, local	6.90	2.94	7.31	6.15	9.48	7.28	8.81	3.02
Driver's license	7.16	5.88	7.38	8.18	8.29	7.14	6.42	4.07
Vehicle inspection	9.29	3.88	8.45	10.71	10.77	10.04	9.96	7.09
Parking fees	29.41	30.16	25.54	36.07	36.66	32.47	25.31	5.94
Parking fees in home city, excluding residence	23.87	27.93	20.06	29.84	30.59	24.38	19.23	4.70
Parking fees on trips	5.54	2.23	5.48	6.23	6.07	8.09	6.08	1.24
Tolls	14.60	14.52	16.69	18.22	16.55	18.70	4.21	2.96
Tolls on trips	4.63	1.79	4.42	4.53	5.64	7.21	4.20	1.75
Towing charges	5.08	10.92	5.15	6.26	5.43	2.83	4.11	1.72
Automobile service clubs	13.12	1.69	6.41	9.54	18.23	19.96	18.17	14.83
PUBLIC TRANSPORTATION	**441.33**	**214.25**	**366.19**	**435.04**	**511.61**	**606.32**	**524.10**	**279.52**
Airline fares	275.94	119.55	232.92	278.57	337.87	361.10	331.37	152.23
Intercity bus fares	9.35	7.57	6.41	7.08	8.78	13.10	16.34	9.08
Intracity mass transit fares	46.32	32.31	54.28	67.09	51.57	44.47	21.22	16.71
Local transportation on trips	10.00	3.38	7.95	8.15	10.94	16.21	13.02	8.04
Taxi fares and limousine service on trips	5.87	1.99	4.67	4.79	6.43	9.52	7.65	4.72
Taxi fares and limousine service	23.18	28.68	19.80	18.22	13.66	57.32	19.33	6.53
Intercity train fares	17.84	7.25	15.18	16.52	17.89	25.43	26.24	13.38
Ship fares	52.10	12.66	24.45	33.81	62.83	78.91	88.51	68.84
School bus	0.74	0.85	0.53	0.83	1.65	0.28	0.41	–

Note: Subcategories may not add to total because some are not shown. "–" means sample is too small to make a reliable estimate.
Source: Bureau of Labor Statistics, unpublished tables from the 2004 Consumer Expenditure Survey

Table 11.2 Transportation: Indexed spending by age, 2004

(indexed average annual spending of consumer units (CU) on transportation, by age of consumer unit reference person, 2004; index definition: an index of 100 is the average for all consumer units; an index of 132 means that spending by consumer units in that group is 32 percent above the average for all consumer units; an index of 68 indicates spending that is 32 percent below the average for all consumer units)

	total consumer units	under 25	25 to 34	35 to 44	45 to 54	55 to 64	65 to 74	75+
Average spending of CU, total	$43,395	$24,535	$42,701	$50,402	$52,764	$47,299	$36,512	$25,763
Average spending of CU, index	100	57	98	116	122	109	84	59
Transportation, spending index	**100**	**60**	**109**	**118**	**120**	**108**	**83**	**42**
VEHICLE PURCHASES	**100**	**60**	**119**	**123**	**112**	**106**	**83**	**33**
Cars and trucks, new	**100**	**31**	**109**	**126**	**104**	**132**	**89**	**36**
New cars	100	30	118	104	90	137	110	68
New trucks	100	32	103	140	113	129	76	16
Cars and trucks, used	**100**	**90**	**132**	**120**	**115**	**79**	**79**	**32**
Used cars	100	107	115	107	120	86	91	44
Used trucks	100	75	148	133	111	72	68	21
Other vehicles	**100**	**94**	**69**	**119**	**207**	**87**	**14**	**0**
GASOLINE AND MOTOR OIL	**100**	**71**	**105**	**117**	**124**	**104**	**79**	**42**
Gasoline	100	71	106	118	124	103	77	42
Diesel fuel	100	31	77	124	178	78	82	32
Gasoline on trips	100	66	98	102	116	125	108	44
Motor oil	100	96	105	110	140	91	77	27
Motor oil on trips	100	66	99	103	117	126	109	45
OTHER VEHICLE EXPENSES	**100**	**56**	**102**	**113**	**129**	**107**	**80**	**51**
Vehicle finance charges	**100**	**46**	**126**	**134**	**123**	**104**	**56**	**15**
Automobile finance charges	100	60	118	116	128	115	66	19
Truck finance charges	100	39	140	146	122	87	45	12
Motorcycle and plane finance charges	100	25	140	135	122	146	–	1
Other vehicle finance charges	100	6	65	157	100	166	97	14
Maintenance and repairs	**100**	**61**	**92**	**105**	**129**	**114**	**90**	**61**
Coolant, additives, brake and transmission fluids	100	102	104	106	137	94	87	26
Tires—purchased, replaced, installed	100	53	100	110	132	115	80	44
Parts, equipment, and accessories	100	85	113	115	115	100	90	35
Vehicle audio equipment, excluding labor	100	423	91	176	34	53	–	–
Vehicle products	100	115	149	87	110	90	70	54
Miscellaneous auto repair, servicing	100	15	114	108	94	109	88	137
Body work and painting	100	85	84	80	147	140	75	46
Clutch and transmission repair	100	71	94	98	152	90	110	38
Drive shaft and rear-end repair	100	44	62	89	141	186	61	55
Brake work	100	48	97	102	115	123	98	77
Repair to steering or front-end	100	73	68	104	158	130	58	43
Repair to engine cooling system	100	71	92	106	112	136	73	69
Motor tune-up	100	35	90	116	123	119	102	56
Lube, oil change, and oil filters	100	59	94	105	119	120	103	59
Front-end alignment, wheel balance, rotation	100	40	146	90	101	112	113	57
Shock absorber replacement	100	17	134	62	142	139	88	51
Gas tank repair, replacement	100	33	56	153	118	104	154	16
Tire repair and other repair work	100	46	75	101	142	122	94	67
Vehicle air conditioning repair	100	40	57	103	135	144	106	67
Exhaust system repair	100	63	85	130	107	117	93	57
Electrical system repair	100	63	77	96	144	112	97	70
Motor repair, replacement	100	76	79	102	162	85	75	69
Auto repair service policy	100	–	78	120	60	167	199	56
Vehicle insurance	**100**	**56**	**98**	**111**	**132**	**101**	**86**	**62**

	total consumer units	under 25	25 to 34	35 to 44	45 to 54	55 to 64	65 to 74	75+
Vehicle rental, leases, licenses, other charges	**100**	**57**	**106**	**115**	**130**	**113**	**73**	**36**
Leased and rented vehicles	100	53	111	118	138	111	60	24
Rented vehicles	100	38	91	112	118	140	101	40
Auto rental	100	103	147	75	118	74	158	18
Auto rental on trips	100	33	65	117	139	139	80	55
Truck rental	100	8	93	155	98	117	119	26
Truck rental on trips	100	18	103	139	70	190	76	25
Leased vehicles	100	55	114	120	141	106	52	21
Car lease payments	100	75	110	111	137	108	62	28
Truck lease payments	100	25	117	130	147	109	39	17
Vehicle registration, state	100	46	111	112	111	113	94	63
Vehicle registration, local	100	43	106	89	137	106	128	44
Driver's license	100	82	103	114	116	100	90	57
Vehicle inspection	100	42	91	115	116	108	107	76
Parking fees	100	103	87	123	125	110	86	20
Parking fees in home city, excluding residence	100	117	84	125	128	102	81	20
Parking fees on trips	100	40	99	112	110	146	110	22
Tolls	100	99	114	125	113	128	29	20
Tolls on trips	100	39	95	98	122	156	91	38
Towing charges	100	215	101	123	107	56	81	34
Automobile service clubs	100	13	49	73	139	152	138	113
PUBLIC TRANSPORTATION	**100**	**49**	**83**	**99**	**116**	**137**	**119**	**63**
Airline fares	100	43	84	101	122	131	120	55
Intercity bus fares	100	81	69	76	94	140	175	97
Intracity mass transit fares	100	70	117	145	111	96	46	36
Local transportation on trips	100	34	80	82	109	162	130	80
Taxi fares and limousine service on trips	100	34	80	82	110	162	130	80
Taxi fares and limousine service	100	124	85	79	59	247	83	28
Intercity train fares	100	41	85	93	100	143	147	75
Ship fares	100	24	47	65	121	151	170	132
School bus	100	115	72	112	223	38	55	–

Note: "–" means sample is too small to make a reliable estimate.
Source: Calculations by New Strategist based on the 2004 Consumer Expenditure Survey

Table 11.3 Transportation: Total spending by age, 2004

(total annual spending on transportation, by consumer unit (CU) age groups, 2004; consumer units and dollars in thousands)

	total consumer units	under 25	25 to 34	35 to 44	45 to 54	55 to 64	65 to 74	75+
Number of consumer units	116,282	8,817	19,439	24,070	23,712	17,479	11,230	11,536
Total spending of all CUs	$5,046,042,273	$216,321,216	$830,055,797	$1,213,166,993	$1,251,148,504	$826,731,880	$410,029,535	$297,205,660
Transportation, total spending	907,160,069	41,478,607	164,947,302	221,029,996	221,543,824	147,183,842	73,063,503	37,912,603
VEHICLE PURCHASES	395,018,094	17,941,184	78,396,709	100,848,005	89,877,965	63,208,434	31,687,242	13,061,867
Cars and trucks, new	203,305,123	4,779,343	36,948,096	53,059,667	43,319,216	40,401,135	17,530,255	7,268,949
New cars	78,242,669	1,761,548	15,401,131	16,891,123	14,436,577	16,138,361	8,298,745	5,316,020
New trucks	125,062,454	3,017,883	21,546,771	36,168,786	28,882,876	24,262,775	9,231,622	1,952,929
Cars and trucks, used	183,987,195	12,608,575	40,557,724	45,892,103	43,293,132	21,791,594	14,053,222	5,791,649
Used cars	88,444,089	7,191,057	16,948,281	19,518,604	21,701,222	11,484,053	7,780,256	3,821,531
Used trucks	95,541,942	5,417,517	23,609,443	26,373,499	21,591,673	10,307,541	6,272,853	1,970,118
Other vehicles	7,726,939	553,179	890,889	1,896,235	3,265,617	1,015,705	103,765	1,269
GASOLINE AND MOTOR OIL	185,767,472	9,959,683	32,634,582	45,174,576	46,950,234	29,126,481	14,135,538	7,788,415
Gasoline	170,532,204	9,240,216	30,207,817	41,821,144	42,995,547	26,464,080	12,635,435	7,168,701
Diesel fuel	2,383,781	56,693	305,775	613,304	862,880	279,839	189,787	75,676
Gasoline on trips	11,668,899	580,864	1,917,657	2,475,600	2,763,871	2,200,431	1,219,915	510,929
Motor oil	1,047,701	76,003	183,893	239,497	299,957	142,803	78,161	27,917
Motor oil on trips	117,445	5,907	19,439	25,033	27,980	22,198	12,353	5,191
OTHER VEHICLE EXPENSES	275,054,606	11,688,697	46,797,643	64,536,003	72,584,329	44,250,885	21,355,080	13,837,778
Vehicle finance charges	37,606,762	1,297,951	7,937,332	10,450,231	9,434,293	5,880,460	2,049,250	557,881
Automobile finance charges	15,498,065	700,070	3,066,502	3,730,850	4,046,453	2,670,092	985,657	298,090
Truck finance charges	19,407,466	579,453	4,530,065	5,857,194	4,820,650	2,547,215	845,058	227,605
Motorcycle and plane finance charges	380,242	7,230	89,031	105,908	94,374	83,375	–	461
Other vehicle finance charges	2,322,152	11,198	251,735	756,039	472,817	579,604	218,536	31,724
Maintenance and repairs	75,776,328	3,524,067	11,709,470	16,544,515	19,868,759	12,962,252	6,574,716	4,593,520
Coolant, additives, brake and transmission fluids	340,706	26,363	59,483	75,098	94,848	48,067	28,524	8,883
Tires—purchased, replaced, installed	10,940,973	441,026	1,837,569	2,501,114	2,955,227	1,885,984	842,587	477,360
Parts, equipment, and accessories	5,003,614	324,377	947,068	1,193,631	1,177,064	751,073	436,510	174,309
Vehicle audio equipment, excluding labor	962,815	308,683	146,376	350,459	66,156	77,257	–	–
Vehicle products	501,175	43,732	124,604	90,744	112,395	67,644	33,690	26,764
Miscellaneous auto repair, servicing	5,844,333	66,128	1,116,771	1,307,482	1,118,021	961,695	496,029	795,523
Body work and painting	4,244,293	274,914	592,890	705,732	1,274,046	894,051	309,387	193,574
Clutch and transmission repair	4,566,394	244,231	714,772	922,844	1,411,338	614,562	485,136	173,732
Drive shaft and rear-end repair	722,111	23,894	74,257	132,385	208,191	201,358	42,225	39,338
Brake work	5,181,526	188,684	842,875	1,093,019	1,219,271	955,927	487,944	393,839
Repair to steering or front-end	1,766,324	97,781	201,777	379,103	568,377	344,861	98,150	76,138
Repair to engine cooling system	2,087,262	111,888	320,549	458,774	478,745	427,886	147,338	142,124
Motor tune-up	4,857,099	127,758	733,045	1,162,822	1,215,003	870,105	479,072	269,712
Lube, oil change, and oil filters	6,538,537	294,840	1,030,461	1,417,001	1,587,518	1,179,483	649,992	379,534
Front-end alignment, wheel balance, rotation	1,061,655	31,918	259,122	197,133	218,150	178,461	116,118	59,987
Shock absorber replacement	320,938	4,232	71,730	41,160	93,188	67,294	27,401	16,150
Gas tank repair, replacement	386,056	9,699	36,157	122,276	92,714	60,128	57,385	6,114
Tire repair and other repair work	5,805,960	203,849	725,658	1,213,369	1,684,738	1,067,093	525,227	386,571
Vehicle air conditioning repair	1,654,693	50,169	156,873	354,070	455,745	359,019	169,685	109,361
Exhaust system repair	1,184,914	56,693	168,147	319,409	257,987	209,049	106,797	66,793
Electrical system repair	2,620,996	124,320	335,517	521,838	772,300	439,772	246,611	180,884
Motor repair, replacement	8,130,437	468,888	1,076,921	1,722,931	2,679,693	1,037,553	586,431	558,573
Auto repair service policy	1,052,352	–	137,045	262,363	128,045	263,758	202,477	58,372
Vehicle insurance	112,138,872	4,719,916	18,346,334	25,711,574	30,178,500	17,003,047	9,261,493	6,919,293

	total consumer units	under 25	25 to 34	35 to 44	45 to 54	55 to 64	65 to 74	75+
Vehicle rental, leases, licenses, other charges	**$49,531,481**	**$2,146,675**	**$8,804,506**	**$11,829,683**	**$13,102,777**	**$8,405,302**	**$3,469,621**	**$1,767,200**
Leased and rented vehicles	29,634,468	1,188,796	5,481,798	7,258,068	8,334,057	4,964,386	1,703,479	703,350
Rented vehicles	4,450,112	128,993	674,922	1,027,548	1,068,937	935,651	436,173	177,539
Auto rental	655,830	51,050	160,955	101,335	158,159	72,887	99,835	11,651
Auto rental on trips	2,462,853	60,837	268,064	595,733	698,793	514,232	191,022	134,394
Truck rental	548,851	3,262	85,143	176,192	109,787	96,659	63,225	14,074
Truck rental on trips	527,920	7,142	90,975	151,882	75,404	150,844	38,856	12,920
Leased vehicles	25,184,356	1,059,803	4,806,682	6,230,760	7,265,357	4,028,735	1,267,306	525,811
Car lease payments	12,178,214	693,810	2,230,820	2,810,173	3,398,641	1,984,915	726,806	333,044
Truck lease payments	11,167,723	210,638	2,180,278	2,996,715	3,344,340	1,825,682	422,136	187,691
Vehicle registration, state	9,409,539	325,171	1,741,540	2,172,558	2,135,028	1,594,434	854,491	586,375
Vehicle registration, local	802,346	25,922	142,099	148,031	224,790	127,247	98,936	34,839
Driver's license	832,579	51,844	143,460	196,893	196,572	124,800	72,097	46,952
Vehicle inspection	1,080,260	34,210	164,260	257,790	255,378	175,489	111,851	81,790
Parking fees	3,419,854	265,921	496,472	868,205	869,282	567,543	284,231	68,524
Parking fees in home city, excluding residence	2,775,651	246,259	389,946	718,249	725,350	426,138	215,953	54,219
Parking fees on trips	644,202	19,662	106,526	149,956	143,932	141,405	68,278	14,305
Tolls	1,697,717	128,023	324,437	438,555	392,434	326,857	47,278	34,147
Tolls on trips	538,386	15,782	85,920	109,037	133,736	126,024	47,166	20,188
Towing charges	590,713	96,282	100,111	150,678	128,756	49,466	46,155	19,842
Automobile service clubs	1,525,620	14,901	124,604	229,628	432,270	348,881	204,049	171,079
PUBLIC TRANSPORTATION	**51,318,735**	**1,889,042**	**7,118,367**	**10,471,413**	**12,131,296**	**10,597,867**	**5,885,643**	**3,224,543**
Airline fares	32,086,855	1,054,072	4,527,732	6,705,180	8,011,573	6,311,667	3,721,285	1,756,125
Intercity bus fares	1,087,237	66,745	124,604	170,416	208,191	228,975	183,498	104,747
Intracity mass transit fares	5,386,182	284,877	1,055,149	1,614,856	1,222,828	777,291	238,301	192,767
Local transportation on trips	1,162,820	29,801	154,540	196,171	259,409	283,335	146,215	92,749
Taxi fares and limousine service on trips	682,575	17,546	90,780	115,295	152,468	166,400	85,910	54,450
Taxi fares and limousine service	2,695,417	252,872	384,892	438,555	323,906	1,001,896	217,076	75,330
Intercity train fares	2,074,471	63,923	295,084	397,636	424,208	444,491	294,675	154,352
Ship fares	6,058,292	111,623	475,284	813,807	1,489,825	1,379,268	993,967	794,138
School bus	86,049	7,494	10,303	19,978	39,125	4,894	4,604	–

Note: Numbers may not add to total because of rounding and missing subcategories. "–" means sample is too small to make a reliable estimate.
Source: Calculations by New Strategist based on the 2004 Consumer Expenditure Survey

Table 11.4 Transportation: Market shares by age, 2004

(percentage of total annual spending on transportation accounted for by consumer unit age groups, 2004)

	total consumer units	under 25	25 to 34	35 to 44	45 to 54	55 to 64	65 to 74	75+
Share of total consumer units	100.0%	7.6%	16.7%	20.7%	20.4%	15.0%	9.7%	9.9%
Share of total before-tax income	100.0	3.2	16.1	24.9	26.4	16.8	7.5	5.1
Share of total spending	100.0	4.3	16.4	24.0	24.8	16.4	8.1	5.9
Share of transportation spending	100.0	4.6	18.2	24.4	24.4	16.2	8.1	4.2
VEHICLE PURCHASES	100.0	4.5	19.8	25.5	22.8	16.0	8.0	3.3
Cars and trucks, new	100.0	2.4	18.2	26.1	21.3	19.9	8.6	3.6
New cars	100.0	2.3	19.7	21.6	18.5	20.6	10.6	6.8
New trucks	100.0	2.4	17.2	28.9	23.1	19.4	7.4	1.6
Cars and trucks, used	100.0	6.9	22.0	24.9	23.5	11.8	7.6	3.1
Used cars	100.0	8.1	19.2	22.1	24.5	13.0	8.8	4.3
Used trucks	100.0	5.7	24.7	27.6	22.6	10.8	6.6	2.1
Other vehicles	100.0	7.2	11.5	24.5	42.3	13.1	1.3	0.0
GASOLINE AND MOTOR OIL	100.0	5.4	17.6	24.3	25.3	15.7	7.6	4.2
Gasoline	100.0	5.4	17.7	24.5	25.2	15.5	7.4	4.2
Diesel fuel	100.0	2.4	12.8	25.7	36.2	11.7	8.0	3.2
Gasoline on trips	100.0	5.0	16.4	21.2	23.7	18.9	10.5	4.4
Motor oil	100.0	7.3	17.6	22.9	28.6	13.6	7.5	2.7
Motor oil on trips	100.0	5.0	16.6	21.3	23.8	18.9	10.5	4.4
OTHER VEHICLE EXPENSES	100.0	4.2	17.0	23.5	26.4	16.1	7.8	5.0
Vehicle finance charges	100.0	3.5	21.1	27.8	25.1	15.6	5.4	1.5
Automobile finance charges	100.0	4.5	19.8	24.1	26.1	17.2	6.4	1.9
Truck finance charges	100.0	3.0	23.3	30.2	24.8	13.1	4.4	1.2
Motorcycle and plane finance charges	100.0	1.9	23.4	27.9	24.8	21.9	–	0.1
Other vehicle finance charges	100.0	0.5	10.8	32.6	20.4	25.0	9.4	1.4
Maintenance and repairs	100.0	4.7	15.5	21.8	26.2	17.1	8.7	6.1
Coolant, additives, brake and transmission fluids	100.0	7.7	17.5	22.0	27.8	14.1	8.4	2.6
Tires—purchased, replaced, installed	100.0	4.0	16.8	22.9	27.0	17.2	7.7	4.4
Parts, equipment, and accessories	100.0	6.5	18.9	23.9	23.5	15.0	8.7	3.5
Vehicle audio equipment, excluding labor	100.0	32.1	15.2	36.4	6.9	8.0	–	–
Vehicle products	100.0	8.7	24.9	18.1	22.4	13.5	6.7	5.3
Miscellaneous auto repair, servicing	100.0	1.1	19.1	22.4	19.1	16.5	8.5	13.6
Body work and painting	100.0	6.5	14.0	16.6	30.0	21.1	7.3	4.6
Clutch and transmission repair	100.0	5.3	15.7	20.2	30.9	13.5	10.6	3.8
Drive shaft and rear-end repair	100.0	3.3	10.3	18.3	28.8	27.9	5.8	5.4
Brake work	100.0	3.6	16.3	21.1	23.5	18.4	9.4	7.6
Repair to steering or front-end	100.0	5.5	11.4	21.5	32.2	19.5	5.6	4.3
Repair to engine cooling system	100.0	5.4	15.4	22.0	22.9	20.5	7.1	6.8
Motor tune-up	100.0	2.6	15.1	23.9	25.0	17.9	9.9	5.6
Lube, oil change, and oil filters	100.0	4.5	15.8	21.7	24.3	18.0	9.9	5.8
Front-end alignment, wheel balance, rotation	100.0	3.0	24.4	18.6	20.5	16.8	10.9	5.7
Shock absorber replacement	100.0	1.3	22.4	12.8	29.0	21.0	8.5	5.0
Gas tank repair, replacement	100.0	2.5	9.4	31.7	24.0	15.6	14.9	1.6
Tire repair and other repair work	100.0	3.5	12.5	20.9	29.0	18.4	9.0	6.7
Vehicle air conditioning repair	100.0	3.0	9.5	21.4	27.5	21.7	10.3	6.6
Exhaust system repair	100.0	4.8	14.2	27.0	21.8	17.6	9.0	5.6
Electrical system repair	100.0	4.7	12.8	19.9	29.5	16.8	9.4	6.9
Motor repair, replacement	100.0	5.8	13.2	21.2	33.0	12.8	7.2	6.9
Auto repair service policy	100.0	–	13.0	24.9	12.2	25.1	19.2	5.5
Vehicle insurance	100.0	4.2	16.4	22.9	26.9	15.2	8.3	6.2

	total consumer units	under 25	25 to 34	35 to 44	45 to 54	55 to 64	65 to 74	75+
Vehicle rental, leases, licenses, other charges	**100.0%**	**4.3%**	**17.8%**	**23.9%**	**26.5%**	**17.0%**	**7.0%**	**3.6%**
Leased and rented vehicles	100.0	4.0	18.5	24.5	28.1	16.8	5.7	2.4
Rented vehicles	100.0	2.9	15.2	23.1	24.0	21.0	9.8	4.0
Auto rental	100.0	7.8	24.5	15.5	24.1	11.1	15.2	1.8
Auto rental on trips	100.0	2.5	10.9	24.2	28.4	20.9	7.8	5.5
Truck rental	100.0	0.6	15.5	32.1	20.0	17.6	11.5	2.6
Truck rental on trips	100.0	1.4	17.2	28.8	14.3	28.6	7.4	2.4
Leased vehicles	100.0	4.2	19.1	24.7	28.8	16.0	5.0	2.1
Car lease payments	100.0	5.7	18.3	23.1	27.9	16.3	6.0	2.7
Truck lease payments	100.0	1.9	19.5	26.8	29.9	16.3	3.8	1.7
Vehicle registration, state	100.0	3.5	18.5	23.1	22.7	16.9	9.1	6.2
Vehicle registration, local	100.0	3.2	17.7	18.4	28.0	15.9	12.3	4.3
Driver's license	100.0	6.2	17.2	23.6	23.6	15.0	8.7	5.6
Vehicle inspection	100.0	3.2	15.2	23.9	23.6	16.2	10.4	7.6
Parking fees	100.0	7.8	14.5	25.4	25.4	16.6	8.3	2.0
Parking fees in home city, excluding residence	100.0	8.9	14.0	25.9	26.1	15.4	7.8	2.0
Parking fees on trips	100.0	3.1	16.5	23.3	22.3	22.0	10.6	2.2
Tolls	100.0	7.5	19.1	25.8	23.1	19.3	2.8	2.0
Tolls on trips	100.0	2.9	16.0	20.3	24.8	23.4	8.8	3.7
Towing charges	100.0	16.3	16.9	25.5	21.8	8.4	7.8	3.4
Automobile service clubs	100.0	1.0	8.2	15.1	28.3	22.9	13.4	11.2
PUBLIC TRANSPORTATION	**100.0**	**3.7**	**13.9**	**20.4**	**23.6**	**20.7**	**11.5**	**6.3**
Airline fares	100.0	3.3	14.1	20.9	25.0	19.7	11.6	5.5
Intercity bus fares	100.0	6.1	11.5	15.7	19.1	21.1	16.9	9.6
Intracity mass transit fares	100.0	5.3	19.6	30.0	22.7	14.4	4.4	3.6
Local transportation on trips	100.0	2.6	13.3	16.9	22.3	24.4	12.6	8.0
Taxi fares and limousine service on trips	100.0	2.6	13.3	16.9	22.3	24.4	12.6	8.0
Taxi fares and limousine service	100.0	9.4	14.3	16.3	12.0	37.2	8.1	2.8
Intercity train fares	100.0	3.1	14.2	19.2	20.4	21.4	14.2	7.4
Ship fares	100.0	1.8	7.8	13.4	24.6	22.8	16.4	13.1
School bus	100.0	8.7	12.0	23.2	45.5	5.7	5.4	–

Note: Numbers may not add to total because of rounding. "–" means sample is too small to make a reliable estimate.
Source: Calculations by New Strategist based on the 2004 Consumer Expenditure Survey

Table 11.5 Transportation: Average spending by income, 2004

(average annual spending on transportation, by before-tax income of consumer units (CU), 2004)

	total consumer units	under $20,000	$20,000–$39,999	$40,000–$49,999	$50,000–$69,999	$70,000–$79,999	$80,000–$99,999	$100,000 or more
Number of consumer units (in 000s)	116,282	28,898	27,297	11,374	18,069	6,461	9,246	14,937
Average number of persons per CU	2.5	1.8	2.3	2.6	2.8	3.0	3.1	3.2
Average before-tax income of CU	$54,453.00	$10,923.47	$29,561.76	$44,645.00	$59,259.00	$74,437.00	$88,811.00	$155,901.00
Average spending of CU, total	43,394.87	18,865.37	30,400.94	38,204.07	47,750.13	55,012.03	65,446.39	93,525.67
Transportation, average spending	**7,801.38**	**2,862.72**	**5,678.25**	**7,030.76**	**9,699.90**	**9,964.51**	**12,446.15**	**15,706.86**
VEHICLE PURCHASES	**3,397.07**	**1,036.93**	**2,419.18**	**2,867.48**	**4,538.51**	**4,218.13**	**5,516.38**	**7,105.82**
Cars and trucks, new	**1,748.38**	**403.26**	**1,068.84**	**1,336.59**	**2,254.49**	**2,139.49**	**3,165.86**	**4,247.37**
New cars	672.87	173.41	469.42	514.12	1,035.77	638.12	815.48	1,619.61
New trucks	1,075.51	229.84	599.42	822.47	1,218.72	1,501.37	2,350.39	2,627.76
Cars and trucks, used	**1,582.25**	**627.95**	**1,339.33**	**1,449.49**	**2,123.19**	**1,974.46**	**2,231.48**	**2,747.64**
Used cars	760.60	370.18	654.08	573.20	934.15	952.40	947.95	1,444.47
Used trucks	821.64	257.78	685.26	876.29	1,189.04	1,022.06	1,283.53	1,303.17
Other vehicles	**66.45**	**7.63**	**11.01**	**81.39**	**160.83**	**104.19**	**119.03**	**110.81**
GASOLINE AND MOTOR OIL	**1,597.56**	**778.64**	**1,306.40**	**1,620.97**	**1,953.34**	**2,130.64**	**2,366.46**	**2,559.30**
Gasoline	1,466.54	726.88	1,212.26	1,510.75	1,781.68	1,971.48	2,134.65	2,315.38
Diesel fuel	20.50	4.99	9.55	15.55	35.55	22.09	49.64	37.35
Gasoline on trips	100.35	41.14	75.24	83.29	122.79	123.97	169.89	193.41
Motor oil	9.01	5.22	8.59	10.54	11.60	10.62	10.57	11.20
Motor oil on trips	1.01	0.42	0.76	0.84	1.24	1.25	1.72	1.95
OTHER VEHICLE EXPENSES	**2,365.41**	**908.74**	**1,725.63**	**2,259.30**	**2,795.44**	**3,184.07**	**3,811.71**	**4,658.61**
Vehicle finance charges	**323.41**	**70.96**	**210.61**	**357.90**	**445.38**	**558.79**	**563.92**	**593.47**
Automobile finance charges	133.28	37.12	102.07	144.62	183.42	200.60	211.64	229.42
Truck finance charges	166.90	31.33	100.26	185.72	238.20	300.12	305.01	307.24
Motorcycle and plane finance charges	3.27	0.21	1.13	2.62	4.45	5.80	8.91	7.60
Other vehicle finance charges	19.97	3.34	7.15	24.94	19.30	52.27	38.37	49.21
Maintenance and repairs	**651.66**	**313.57**	**483.07**	**570.91**	**754.72**	**830.13**	**1,048.47**	**1,224.54**
Coolant, additives, brake and transmission fluids	2.93	2.21	2.90	3.97	3.27	3.22	2.99	3.05
Tires—purchased, replaced, installed	94.09	38.74	73.63	104.29	106.67	121.62	147.32	170.71
Parts, equipment, and accessories	43.03	24.86	35.69	39.73	53.23	74.93	51.80	62.55
Vehicle audio equipment, excluding labor	8.28	38.50	3.70	–	16.35	0.96	23.54	2.56
Vehicle products	4.31	2.55	3.69	3.54	4.63	4.69	7.60	6.54
Miscellaneous auto repair, servicing	50.26	49.94	35.07	23.52	50.38	50.02	44.50	99.01
Body work and painting	36.50	14.87	22.95	20.53	35.56	37.30	59.98	101.52
Clutch and transmission repair	39.27	15.56	30.80	38.10	53.14	42.11	77.16	60.05
Drive shaft and rear-end repair	6.21	2.21	2.12	5.08	5.47	12.11	16.93	15.01
Brake work	44.56	16.15	33.13	40.86	51.39	59.56	86.73	82.37
Repair to steering or front-end	15.19	6.41	9.45	13.79	18.70	32.07	22.98	27.36
Repair to engine cooling system	17.95	9.53	14.44	19.12	22.56	34.70	21.81	24.56
Motor tune-up	41.77	14.82	31.20	30.44	50.14	52.29	70.75	89.27
Lube, oil change, and oil filters	56.23	25.53	43.19	55.96	68.98	73.96	91.03	95.06
Front-end alignment, wheel balance, rotation	9.13	3.32	7.36	9.35	14.27	14.05	13.18	12.56
Shock absorber replacement	2.76	0.83	2.31	3.20	2.19	2.22	7.82	4.77
Gas tank repair, replacement	3.32	–	2.39	2.20	4.18	5.17	4.50	5.56
Tire repair and other repair work	49.93	23.08	33.15	41.72	58.31	67.82	81.80	101.20
Vehicle air conditioning repair	14.23	4.46	11.08	14.10	13.23	25.02	23.21	29.97
Exhaust system repair	10.19	5.64	8.68	9.25	14.94	9.68	14.43	14.31
Electrical system repair	22.54	9.78	17.61	21.54	27.22	34.47	36.89	37.32
Motor repair, replacement	69.92	29.41	52.00	62.51	69.42	65.23	120.12	158.27
Auto repair service policy	9.05	1.24	6.51	8.11	10.53	6.93	21.40	20.96
Vehicle insurance	**964.37**	**410.26**	**789.07**	**1,032.15**	**1,145.81**	**1,245.33**	**1,431.07**	**1,675.27**

	total consumer units	under $20,000	$20,000– $39,999	$40,000– $49,999	$50,000– $69,999	$70,000– $79,999	$80,000– $99,999	$100,000 or more
Vehicle rental, leases, licenses, other charges	**$425.96**	**$113.93**	**$242.87**	**$298.35**	**$449.52**	**$549.82**	**$768.24**	**$1,165.33**
Leased and rented vehicles	254.85	41.22	115.99	158.11	259.28	342.32	503.05	798.71
Rented vehicles	38.27	10.44	18.37	20.90	38.69	40.77	73.28	118.40
Auto rental	5.64	2.02	3.00	2.47	6.95	5.08	11.94	14.62
Auto rental on trips	21.18	3.88	9.40	10.67	24.25	26.14	38.87	67.38
Truck rental	4.72	1.58	3.09	5.30	3.99	3.21	11.33	11.62
Truck rental on trips	4.54	0.91	2.48	2.45	3.50	6.29	9.77	14.20
Leased vehicles	216.58	30.77	97.62	137.22	220.59	301.55	429.77	680.31
Car lease payments	104.73	21.76	52.89	64.86	105.02	131.20	181.94	330.75
Truck lease payments	96.04	8.36	40.63	68.14	100.59	152.24	224.25	278.97
Vehicle registration, state	80.92	31.52	69.93	75.38	95.77	96.77	136.58	141.51
Vehicle registration, local	6.90	3.07	7.01	4.74	8.74	7.46	7.66	12.79
Driver's license	7.16	4.38	6.09	7.00	8.34	8.34	8.77	11.69
Vehicle inspection	9.29	4.99	6.95	8.80	11.16	11.68	11.97	17.34
Parking fees	29.41	11.42	11.83	17.28	30.44	30.04	46.63	93.43
Parking fees in home city, excluding residence	23.87	9.93	8.97	14.02	23.65	23.04	37.65	77.69
Parking fees on trips	5.54	1.49	2.86	3.26	6.79	6.99	8.98	15.74
Tolls	14.60	5.77	7.34	10.66	12.23	22.96	23.35	39.66
Tolls on trips	4.63	1.99	2.67	2.70	5.55	6.77	7.03	11.22
Towing charges	5.08	4.03	4.74	4.41	5.38	5.33	4.53	8.16
Automobile service clubs	13.12	5.53	10.32	9.27	12.63	18.14	18.67	30.83
PUBLIC TRANSPORTATION	**441.33**	**138.41**	**227.05**	**283.00**	**412.62**	**431.67**	**751.60**	**1,383.13**
Airline fares	275.94	75.69	135.41	188.26	265.93	288.36	484.54	864.59
Intercity bus fares	9.35	5.91	7.80	6.71	9.72	7.89	13.61	18.39
Intracity mass transit fares	46.32	35.20	31.88	33.88	35.46	39.91	72.62	103.29
Local transportation on trips	10.00	2.07	5.49	6.16	8.69	11.27	17.25	33.02
Taxi fares and limousine service on trips	5.87	1.22	3.22	3.62	5.10	6.62	10.13	19.39
Taxi fares and limousine service	23.18	8.83	14.09	12.39	23.41	19.12	35.46	66.40
Intercity train fares	17.84	4.61	12.57	9.37	22.94	26.59	30.77	41.54
Ship fares	52.10	4.89	16.18	21.94	41.37	30.78	85.67	233.44
School bus	0.74	–	0.79	0.67	–	1.13	1.55	3.07

Note: Subcategories may not add to total because some are not shown. "–" means sample is too small to make a reliable estimate.
Source: Bureau of Labor Statistics, unpublished tables from the 2004 Consumer Expenditure Survey; calculations by New Strategist

Table 11.6 Transportation: Indexed spending by income, 2004

(indexed average annual spending of consumer units (CU) on transportation, by before-tax income of consumer unit, 2004; index definition: an index of 100 is the average for all consumer units; an index of 132 means that spending by consumer units in that group is 32 percent above the average for all consumer units; an index of 68 indicates spending that is 32 percent below the average for all consumer units)

	total consumer units	under $20,000	$20,000–$39,999	$40,000–$49,999	$50,000–$69,999	$70,000–$79,999	$80,000–$99,999	$100,000 or more
Average spending of CU, total	$43,395	$18,865	$30,401	$38,204	$47,750	$55,012	$65,446	$93,526
Average spending of CU, index	100	43	70	88	110	127	151	216
Transportation, spending index	100	37	73	90	124	128	160	201
VEHICLE PURCHASES	100	31	71	84	134	124	162	209
Cars and trucks, new	100	23	61	76	129	122	181	243
New cars	100	26	70	76	154	95	121	241
New trucks	100	21	56	76	113	140	219	244
Cars and trucks, used	100	40	85	92	134	125	141	174
Used cars	100	49	86	75	123	125	125	190
Used trucks	100	31	83	107	145	124	156	159
Other vehicles	100	11	17	122	242	157	179	167
GASOLINE AND MOTOR OIL	100	49	82	101	122	133	148	160
Gasoline	100	50	83	103	121	134	146	158
Diesel fuel	100	24	47	76	173	108	242	182
Gasoline on trips	100	41	75	83	122	124	169	193
Motor oil	100	58	95	117	129	118	117	124
Motor oil on trips	100	41	75	83	123	124	170	193
OTHER VEHICLE EXPENSES	100	38	73	96	118	135	161	197
Vehicle finance charges	100	22	65	111	138	173	174	184
Automobile finance charges	100	28	77	109	138	151	159	172
Truck finance charges	100	19	60	111	143	180	183	184
Motorcycle and plane finance charges	100	6	34	80	136	177	272	232
Other vehicle finance charges	100	17	36	125	97	262	192	246
Maintenance and repairs	100	48	74	88	116	127	161	188
Coolant, additives, brake and transmission fluids	100	75	99	135	112	110	102	104
Tires—purchased, replaced, installed	100	41	78	111	113	129	157	181
Parts, equipment, and accessories	100	58	83	92	124	174	120	145
Vehicle audio equipment, excluding labor	100	465	45	–	197	12	284	31
Vehicle products	100	59	86	82	107	109	176	152
Miscellaneous auto repair, servicing	100	99	70	47	100	100	89	197
Body work and painting	100	41	63	56	97	102	164	278
Clutch and transmission repair	100	40	78	97	135	107	196	153
Drive shaft and rear-end repair	100	36	34	82	88	195	273	242
Brake work	100	36	74	92	115	134	195	185
Repair to steering or front-end	100	42	62	91	123	211	151	180
Repair to engine cooling system	100	53	80	107	126	193	122	137
Motor tune-up	100	35	75	73	120	125	169	214
Lube, oil change, and oil filters	100	45	77	100	123	132	162	169
Front-end alignment, wheel balance, rotation	100	36	81	102	156	154	144	138
Shock absorber replacement	100	30	84	116	79	80	283	173
Gas tank repair, replacement	100	–	72	66	126	156	136	167
Tire repair and other repair work	100	46	66	84	117	136	164	203
Vehicle air conditioning repair	100	31	78	99	93	176	163	211
Exhaust system repair	100	55	85	91	147	95	142	140
Electrical system repair	100	43	78	96	121	153	164	166
Motor repair, replacement	100	42	74	89	99	93	172	226
Auto repair service policy	100	14	72	90	116	77	236	232
Vehicle insurance	100	43	82	107	119	129	148	174

	total consumer units	under $20,000	$20,000– $39,999	$40,000– $49,999	$50,000– $69,999	$70,000– $79,999	$80,000– $99,999	$100,000 or more
Vehicle rental, leases, licenses, other charges	**100**	**27**	**57**	**70**	**106**	**129**	**180**	**274**
Leased and rented vehicles	100	16	46	62	102	134	197	313
Rented vehicles	100	27	48	55	101	107	191	309
Auto rental	100	36	53	44	123	90	212	259
Auto rental on trips	100	18	44	50	114	123	184	318
Truck rental	100	33	65	112	85	68	240	246
Truck rental on trips	100	20	55	54	77	139	215	313
Leased vehicles	100	14	45	63	102	139	198	314
Car lease payments	100	21	51	62	100	125	174	316
Truck lease payments	100	9	42	71	105	159	233	290
Vehicle registration, state	100	39	86	93	118	120	169	175
Vehicle registration, local	100	45	102	69	127	108	111	185
Driver's license	100	61	85	98	116	116	122	163
Vehicle inspection	100	54	75	95	120	126	129	187
Parking fees	100	39	40	59	104	102	159	318
Parking fees in home city, excluding residence	100	42	38	59	99	97	158	325
Parking fees on trips	100	27	52	59	123	126	162	284
Tolls	100	40	50	73	84	157	160	272
Tolls on trips	100	43	58	58	120	146	152	242
Towing charges	100	79	93	87	106	105	89	161
Automobile service clubs	100	42	79	71	96	138	142	235
PUBLIC TRANSPORTATION	**100**	**31**	**51**	**64**	**93**	**98**	**170**	**313**
Airline fares	100	27	49	68	96	105	176	313
Intercity bus fares	100	63	83	72	104	84	146	197
Intracity mass transit fares	100	76	69	73	77	86	157	223
Local transportation on trips	100	21	55	62	87	113	173	330
Taxi fares and limousine service on trips	100	21	55	62	87	113	173	330
Taxi fares and limousine service	100	38	61	53	101	82	153	286
Intercity train fares	100	26	70	53	129	149	172	233
Ship fares	100	9	31	42	79	59	164	448
School bus	100	–	107	91	–	153	209	415

Note: "–" means sample is too small to make a reliable estimate.
Source: Calculations by New Strategist based on the 2004 Consumer Expenditure Survey

Table 11.7 Transportation: Total spending by income, 2004

(total annual spending on transportation, by before-tax income group of consumer units (CU), 2004; consumer units and dollars in thousands)

	total consumer units	under $20,000	$20,000–$39,999	$40,000–$49,999	$50,000–$69,999	$70,000–$79,999	$80,000–$99,999	$100,000 or more
Number of consumer units	116,282	28,898	27,297	11,374	18,069	6,461	9,246	14,937
Total spending of all CUs	$5,046,042,273	$545,171,431	$829,854,379	$434,533,092	$862,797,099	$355,432,726	$605,117,322	$1,396,992,933
Transportation, total spending	907,160,069	82,726,903	154,999,209	79,967,864	175,267,493	64,380,699	115,077,103	234,613,368
VEHICLE PURCHASES	395,018,094	29,965,269	66,036,373	32,614,718	82,006,337	27,253,338	51,004,449	106,139,633
Cars and trucks, new	203,305,123	11,653,273	29,176,095	15,202,375	40,736,380	13,823,245	29,271,542	63,442,966
New cars	78,242,669	5,011,346	12,813,726	5,847,601	18,715,328	4,122,893	7,539,928	24,192,115
New trucks	125,062,454	6,641,837	16,362,379	9,354,774	22,021,052	9,700,352	21,731,706	39,250,851
Cars and trucks, used	183,987,195	18,146,631	36,559,672	16,486,499	38,363,920	12,756,986	20,632,264	41,041,499
Used cars	88,444,089	10,697,369	17,854,329	6,519,577	16,879,156	6,153,456	8,764,746	21,576,048
Used trucks	95,541,942	7,449,262	18,705,485	9,966,922	21,484,764	6,603,530	11,867,518	19,465,450
Other vehicles	7,726,939	220,479	300,595	925,730	2,906,037	673,172	1,100,551	1,655,169
GASOLINE AND MOTOR OIL	185,767,472	22,501,034	35,660,724	18,436,913	35,294,900	13,766,065	21,880,289	38,228,264
Gasoline	170,532,204	21,005,357	33,090,945	17,183,271	32,193,176	12,737,732	19,736,974	34,584,831
Diesel fuel	2,383,781	144,200	260,757	176,866	642,353	142,723	458,971	557,897
Gasoline on trips	11,668,899	1,188,743	2,053,699	947,340	2,218,693	800,970	1,570,803	2,888,965
Motor oil	1,047,701	150,717	234,389	119,882	209,600	68,616	97,730	167,294
Motor oil on trips	117,445	12,063	20,793	9,554	22,406	8,076	15,903	29,127
OTHER VEHICLE EXPENSES	275,054,606	26,260,695	47,104,405	25,697,278	50,510,805	20,572,276	35,243,071	69,585,658
Vehicle finance charges	37,606,762	2,050,709	5,748,977	4,070,755	8,047,571	3,610,342	5,214,004	8,864,661
Automobile finance charges	15,498,065	1,072,718	2,786,252	1,644,908	3,314,216	1,296,077	1,956,823	3,426,847
Truck finance charges	19,407,466	905,417	2,736,912	2,112,379	4,304,036	1,939,075	2,820,122	4,589,244
Motorcycle and plane finance charges	380,242	5,958	30,741	29,800	80,407	37,474	82,382	113,521
Other vehicle finance charges	2,322,152	96,516	195,072	283,668	348,732	337,716	354,769	735,050
Maintenance and repairs	75,776,328	9,061,611	13,186,332	6,493,530	13,637,036	5,363,470	9,694,154	18,290,954
Coolant, additives, brake and transmission fluids	340,706	63,875	79,103	45,155	59,086	20,804	27,646	45,558
Tires— purchased, replaced, installed	10,940,973	1,119,371	2,009,855	1,186,194	1,927,420	785,787	1,362,121	2,549,895
Parts, equipment, and accessories	5,003,614	718,497	974,178	451,889	961,813	484,123	478,943	934,309
Vehicle audio equipment, excluding labor	962,815	1,112,573	100,954	—	295,428	6,203	217,651	38,239
Vehicle products	501,175	73,626	100,619	40,264	83,659	30,302	70,270	97,688
Miscellaneous auto repair, servicing	5,844,333	1,443,173	957,202	267,516	910,316	323,179	411,447	1,478,912
Body work and painting	4,244,293	429,777	626,552	233,508	642,534	240,995	554,575	1,516,404
Clutch and transmission repair	4,566,394	449,764	840,831	433,349	960,187	272,073	713,421	896,967
Drive shaft and rear-end repair	722,111	63,906	57,970	57,780	98,837	78,243	156,535	224,204
Brake work	5,181,526	466,719	904,472	464,742	928,566	384,817	801,906	1,230,361
Repair to steering or front-end	1,766,324	185,105	258,030	156,847	337,890	207,204	212,473	408,676
Repair to engine cooling system	2,087,262	275,522	394,203	217,471	407,637	224,197	201,655	366,853
Motor tune-up	4,857,099	428,356	851,539	346,225	905,980	337,846	654,155	1,333,426
Lube, oil change, and oil filters	6,538,537	737,655	1,179,058	636,489	1,246,400	477,856	841,663	1,419,911
Front-end alignment, wheel balance, rotation	1,061,655	95,966	200,780	106,347	257,845	90,777	121,862	187,609
Shock absorber replacement	320,938	23,998	63,072	36,397	39,571	14,343	72,304	71,249
Gas tank repair, replacement	386,056	—	65,245	25,023	75,528	33,403	41,607	83,050
Tire repair and other repair work	5,805,960	667,061	904,924	474,523	1,053,603	438,185	756,323	1,511,624
Vehicle air conditioning repair	1,654,693	129,029	302,585	160,373	239,053	161,654	214,600	447,662
Exhaust system repair	1,184,914	163,043	236,982	105,210	269,951	62,542	133,420	213,748
Electrical system repair	2,620,996	282,494	480,588	244,996	491,838	222,711	341,085	557,449
Motor repair, replacement	8,130,437	849,855	1,419,570	710,989	1,254,350	421,451	1,110,630	2,364,079
Auto repair service policy	1,052,352	35,911	177,747	92,243	190,267	44,775	197,864	313,080
Vehicle insurance	112,138,872	11,855,799	21,539,242	11,739,674	20,703,641	8,046,077	13,231,673	25,023,508

	total consumer units	under $20,000	$20,000– $39,999	$40,000– $49,999	$50,000– $69,999	$70,000– $79,999	$80,000– $99,999	$100,000 or more
Vehicle rental, leases, licenses, other charges	**$49,531,481**	**$3,292,413**	**$6,629,712**	**$3,393,433**	**$8,122,377**	**$3,552,387**	**$7,103,147**	**$17,406,534**
Leased and rented vehicles	29,634,468	1,191,078	3,166,291	1,798,343	4,684,930	2,211,730	4,651,200	11,930,331
Rented vehicles	4,450,112	301,738	501,566	237,717	699,090	263,415	677,547	1,768,541
Auto rental	655,830	58,509	81,931	28,094	125,580	32,822	110,397	218,379
Auto rental on trips	2,462,853	112,022	256,536	121,361	438,173	168,891	359,392	1,006,455
Truck rental	548,851	45,650	84,228	60,282	72,095	20,740	104,757	173,568
Truck rental on trips	527,920	26,292	67,616	27,866	63,242	40,640	90,333	212,105
Leased vehicles	25,184,356	889,258	2,664,725	1,560,740	3,985,841	1,948,315	3,973,653	10,161,790
Car lease payments	12,178,214	628,783	1,443,715	737,718	1,897,606	847,683	1,682,217	4,940,413
Truck lease payments	11,167,723	241,608	1,109,167	775,024	1,817,561	983,623	2,073,416	4,166,975
Vehicle registration, state	9,409,539	910,750	1,908,863	857,372	1,730,468	625,231	1,262,819	2,113,735
Vehicle registration, local	802,346	88,840	191,278	53,913	157,923	48,199	70,824	191,044
Driver's license	832,579	126,648	166,230	79,618	150,695	53,885	81,087	174,614
Vehicle inspection	1,080,260	144,314	189,663	100,091	201,650	75,464	110,675	259,008
Parking fees	3,419,854	329,949	322,968	196,543	550,020	194,088	431,141	1,395,564
Parking fees in home city, excluding residence	2,775,651	286,942	244,967	159,463	427,332	148,861	348,112	1,160,456
Parking fees on trips	644,202	43,007	78,001	37,079	122,689	45,162	83,029	235,108
Tolls	1,697,717	166,884	200,443	121,247	220,984	148,345	215,894	592,401
Tolls on trips	538,386	57,545	72,910	30,710	100,283	43,741	64,999	167,593
Towing charges	590,713	116,433	129,315	50,159	97,211	34,437	41,884	121,886
Automobile service clubs	1,525,620	159,929	281,633	105,437	228,211	117,203	172,623	460,508
PUBLIC TRANSPORTATION	**51,318,735**	**3,999,906**	**6,197,839**	**3,218,842**	**7,455,631**	**2,789,020**	**6,949,294**	**20,659,813**
Airline fares	32,086,855	2,187,156	3,696,231	2,141,269	4,805,089	1,863,094	4,480,057	12,914,381
Intercity bus fares	1,087,237	170,704	212,964	76,320	175,631	50,977	125,838	274,691
Intracity mass transit fares	5,386,182	1,017,232	870,331	385,351	640,727	257,859	671,445	1,542,843
Local transportation on trips	1,162,820	59,903	149,753	70,064	157,020	72,815	159,494	493,220
Taxi fares and limousine service on trips	682,575	35,199	87,956	41,174	92,152	42,772	93,662	289,628
Taxi fares and limousine service	2,695,417	255,265	384,593	140,924	422,995	123,534	327,863	991,817
Intercity train fares	2,074,471	133,105	343,192	106,574	414,503	171,798	284,499	620,483
Ship fares	6,058,292	141,296	441,622	249,546	747,515	198,870	792,105	3,486,893
School bus	86,049	–	21,565	7,621	–	7,301	14,331	45,857

Note: Numbers may not add to total because of rounding and missing subcategories. "–" means sample is too small to make a reliable estimate.
Source: Calculations by New Strategist based on the 2004 Consumer Expenditure Survey

Table 11.8 Transportation: Market shares by income, 2004

(percentage of total annual spending on transportation accounted for by before-tax income group of consumer units, 2004)

	total consumer units	under $20,000	$20,000–$39,999	$40,000–$49,999	$50,000–$69,999	$70,000–$79,999	$80,000–$99,999	$100,000 or more
Share of total consumer units	100.0%	24.9%	23.5%	9.8%	15.5%	5.6%	8.0%	12.8%
Share of total before-tax income	100.0	5.0	12.7	8.0	16.9	7.6	13.0	36.8
Share of total spending	100.0	10.8	16.4	8.6	17.1	7.0	12.0	27.7
Share of transportation spending	100.0	9.1	17.1	8.8	19.3	7.1	12.7	25.9
VEHICLE PURCHASES	**100.0**	**7.6**	**16.7**	**8.3**	**20.8**	**6.9**	**12.9**	**26.9**
Cars and trucks, new	**100.0**	**5.7**	**14.4**	**7.5**	**20.0**	**6.8**	**14.4**	**31.2**
New cars	100.0	6.4	16.4	7.5	23.9	5.3	9.6	30.9
New trucks	100.0	5.3	13.1	7.5	17.6	7.8	17.4	31.4
Cars and trucks, used	**100.0**	**9.9**	**19.9**	**9.0**	**20.9**	**6.9**	**11.2**	**22.3**
Used cars	100.0	12.1	20.2	7.4	19.1	7.0	9.9	24.4
Used trucks	100.0	7.8	19.6	10.4	22.5	6.9	12.4	20.4
Other vehicles	**100.0**	**2.9**	**3.9**	**12.0**	**37.6**	**8.7**	**14.2**	**21.4**
GASOLINE AND MOTOR OIL	**100.0**	**12.1**	**19.2**	**9.9**	**19.0**	**7.4**	**11.8**	**20.6**
Gasoline	100.0	12.3	19.4	10.1	18.9	7.5	11.6	20.3
Diesel fuel	100.0	6.0	10.9	7.4	26.9	6.0	19.3	23.4
Gasoline on trips	100.0	10.2	17.6	8.1	19.0	6.9	13.5	24.8
Motor oil	100.0	14.4	22.4	11.4	20.0	6.5	9.3	16.0
Motor oil on trips	100.0	10.3	17.7	8.1	19.1	6.9	13.5	24.8
OTHER VEHICLE EXPENSES	**100.0**	**9.5**	**17.1**	**9.3**	**18.4**	**7.5**	**12.8**	**25.3**
Vehicle finance charges	**100.0**	**5.5**	**15.3**	**10.8**	**21.4**	**9.6**	**13.9**	**23.6**
Automobile finance charges	100.0	6.9	18.0	10.6	21.4	8.4	12.6	22.1
Truck finance charges	100.0	4.7	14.1	10.9	22.2	10.0	14.5	23.6
Motorcycle and plane finance charges	100.0	1.6	8.1	7.8	21.1	9.9	21.7	29.9
Other vehicle finance charges	100.0	4.2	8.4	12.2	15.0	14.5	15.3	31.7
Maintenance and repairs	**100.0**	**12.0**	**17.4**	**8.6**	**18.0**	**7.1**	**12.8**	**24.1**
Coolant, additives, brake and transmission fluids	100.0	18.7	23.2	13.3	17.3	6.1	8.1	13.4
Tires—purchased, replaced, installed	100.0	10.2	18.4	10.8	17.6	7.2	12.4	23.3
Parts, equipment, and accessories	100.0	14.4	19.5	9.0	19.2	9.7	9.6	18.7
Vehicle audio equipment, excluding labor	100.0	115.6	10.5	–	30.7	0.6	22.6	4.0
Vehicle products	100.0	14.7	20.1	8.0	16.7	6.0	14.0	19.5
Miscellaneous auto repair, servicing	100.0	24.7	16.4	4.6	15.6	5.5	7.0	25.3
Body work and painting	100.0	10.1	14.8	5.5	15.1	5.7	13.1	35.7
Clutch and transmission repair	100.0	9.8	18.4	9.5	21.0	6.0	15.6	19.6
Drive shaft and rear-end repair	100.0	8.8	8.0	8.0	13.7	10.8	21.7	31.0
Brake work	100.0	9.0	17.5	9.0	17.9	7.4	15.5	23.7
Repair to steering or front-end	100.0	10.5	14.6	8.9	19.1	11.7	12.0	23.1
Repair to engine cooling system	100.0	13.2	18.9	10.4	19.5	10.7	9.7	17.6
Motor tune-up	100.0	8.8	17.5	7.1	18.7	7.0	13.5	27.5
Lube, oil change, and oil filters	100.0	11.3	18.0	9.7	19.1	7.3	12.9	21.7
Front-end alignment, wheel balance, rotation	100.0	9.0	18.9	10.0	24.3	8.6	11.5	17.7
Shock absorber replacement	100.0	7.5	19.7	11.3	12.3	4.5	22.5	22.2
Gas tank repair, replacement	100.0	–	16.9	6.5	19.6	8.7	10.8	21.5
Tire repair and other repair work	100.0	11.5	15.6	8.2	18.1	7.5	13.0	26.0
Vehicle air conditioning repair	100.0	7.8	18.3	9.7	14.4	9.8	13.0	27.1
Exhaust system repair	100.0	13.8	20.0	8.9	22.8	5.3	11.3	18.0
Electrical system repair	100.0	10.8	18.3	9.3	18.8	8.5	13.0	21.3
Motor repair, replacement	100.0	10.5	17.5	8.7	15.4	5.2	13.7	29.1
Auto repair service policy	100.0	3.4	16.9	8.8	18.1	4.3	18.8	29.8
Vehicle insurance	**100.0**	**10.6**	**19.2**	**10.5**	**18.5**	**7.2**	**11.8**	**22.3**

	total consumer units	under $20,000	$20,000– $39,999	$40,000– $49,999	$50,000– $69,999	$70,000– $79,999	$80,000– $99,999	$100,000 or more
Vehicle rental, leases, licenses, other charges	**100.0%**	**6.6%**	**13.4%**	**6.9%**	**16.4%**	**7.2%**	**14.3%**	**35.1%**
Leased and rented vehicles	100.0	4.0	10.7	6.1	15.8	7.5	15.7	40.3
Rented vehicles	100.0	6.8	11.3	5.3	15.7	5.9	15.2	39.7
Auto rental	100.0	8.9	12.5	4.3	19.1	5.0	16.8	33.3
Auto rental on trips	100.0	4.5	10.4	4.9	17.8	6.9	14.6	40.9
Truck rental	100.0	8.3	15.3	11.0	13.1	3.8	19.1	31.6
Truck rental on trips	100.0	5.0	12.8	5.3	12.0	7.7	17.1	40.2
Leased vehicles	100.0	3.5	10.6	6.2	15.8	7.7	15.8	40.3
Car lease payments	100.0	5.2	11.9	6.1	15.6	7.0	13.8	40.6
Truck lease payments	100.0	2.2	9.9	6.9	16.3	8.8	18.6	37.3
Vehicle registration, state	100.0	9.7	20.3	9.1	18.4	6.6	13.4	22.5
Vehicle registration, local	100.0	11.1	23.8	6.7	19.7	6.0	8.8	23.8
Driver's license	100.0	15.2	20.0	9.6	18.1	6.5	9.7	21.0
Vehicle inspection	100.0	13.4	17.6	9.3	18.7	7.0	10.2	24.0
Parking fees	100.0	9.6	9.4	5.7	16.1	5.7	12.6	40.8
Parking fees in home city, excluding residence	100.0	10.3	8.8	5.7	15.4	5.4	12.5	41.8
Parking fees on trips	100.0	6.7	12.1	5.8	19.0	7.0	12.9	36.5
Tolls	100.0	9.8	11.8	7.1	13.0	8.7	12.7	34.9
Tolls on trips	100.0	10.7	13.5	5.7	18.6	8.1	12.1	31.1
Towing charges	100.0	19.7	21.9	8.5	16.5	5.8	7.1	20.6
Automobile service clubs	100.0	10.5	18.5	6.9	15.0	7.7	11.3	30.2
PUBLIC TRANSPORTATION	**100.0**	**7.8**	**12.1**	**6.3**	**14.5**	**5.4**	**13.5**	**40.3**
Airline fares	100.0	6.8	11.5	6.7	15.0	5.8	14.0	40.2
Intercity bus fares	100.0	15.7	19.6	7.0	16.2	4.7	11.6	25.3
Intracity mass transit fares	100.0	18.9	16.2	7.2	11.9	4.8	12.5	28.6
Local transportation on trips	100.0	5.2	12.9	6.0	13.5	6.3	13.7	42.4
Taxi fares and limousine service on trips	100.0	5.2	12.9	6.0	13.5	6.3	13.7	42.4
Taxi fares and limousine service	100.0	9.5	14.3	5.2	15.7	4.6	12.2	36.8
Intercity train fares	100.0	6.4	16.5	5.1	20.0	8.3	13.7	29.9
Ship fares	100.0	2.3	7.3	4.1	12.3	3.3	13.1	57.6
School bus	100.0	–	25.1	8.9	–	8.5	16.7	53.3

Note: Numbers may not add to total because of rounding. "–" means sample is too small to make a reliable estimate.
Source: Calculations by New Strategist based on the 2004 Consumer Expenditure Survey

Table 11.9 Transportation: Average spending by high-income consumer units, 2004

(average annual spending on transportation, by before-tax income of high-income consumer units (CU), 2004)

	total consumer units	$100,000 or more	$100,000– $119,999	$120,000– $149,999	$150,000 or more
Number of consumer units (in 000s)	116,282	14,937	5,625	4,245	5,067
Average number of persons per CU	2.5	3.2	3.1	3.3	3.2
Average before-tax income of CU	$54,453.00	$155,901.00	$108,751.00	$132,292.00	$228,021.00
Average spending of CU, total	43,394.87	93,525.67	75,213.14	87,298.57	119,448.79
Transportation, average spending	7,801.38	15,706.86	13,520.44	15,515.36	18,307.86
VEHICLE PURCHASES	**3,397.07**	**7,105.82**	**6,012.79**	**7,028.16**	**8,384.21**
Cars and trucks, new	**1,748.38**	**4,247.37**	**3,210.38**	**4,583.55**	**5,116.86**
New cars	672.87	1,619.61	1,101.01	1,730.76	2,102.17
New trucks	1,075.51	2,627.76	2,109.36	2,852.79	3,014.69
Cars and trucks, used	**1,582.25**	**2,747.64**	**2,723.11**	**2,292.03**	**3,156.56**
Used cars	760.60	1,444.47	1,388.85	1,242.32	1,675.56
Used trucks	821.64	1,303.17	1,334.26	1,049.71	1,481.01
Other vehicles	**66.45**	**110.81**	**79.31**	**152.57**	**110.78**
GASOLINE AND MOTOR OIL	**1,597.56**	**2,559.30**	**2,451.62**	**2,686.06**	**2,572.65**
Gasoline	1,466.54	2,315.38	2,209.55	2,440.13	2,328.34
Diesel fuel	20.50	37.35	43.24	30.78	36.34
Gasoline on trips	100.35	193.41	185.18	200.28	196.80
Motor oil	9.01	11.20	11.79	12.85	9.18
Motor oil on trips	1.01	1.95	1.87	2.02	1.99
OTHER VEHICLE EXPENSES	**2,365.41**	**4,658.61**	**4,161.78**	**4,581.95**	**5,277.77**
Vehicle finance charges	**323.41**	**593.47**	**574.89**	**655.28**	**562.32**
Automobile finance charges	133.28	229.42	222.43	247.54	221.98
Truck finance charges	166.90	307.24	309.76	338.77	278.04
Motorcycle and plane finance charges	3.27	7.60	5.37	11.98	6.42
Other vehicle finance charges	19.97	49.21	37.34	56.98	55.88
Maintenance and repairs	**651.66**	**1,224.54**	**1,083.12**	**1,226.86**	**1,383.20**
Coolant, additives, brake and transmission fluids	2.93	3.05	3.62	3.50	2.05
Tires—purchased, replaced, installed	94.09	170.71	156.32	173.43	184.42
Parts, equipment, and accessories	43.03	62.55	65.19	81.89	43.43
Vehicle audio equipment, excluding labor	8.28	2.56	0.95	5.75	1.30
Vehicle products	4.31	6.54	5.08	10.62	4.21
Miscellaneous auto repair, servicing	50.26	99.01	124.53	53.43	113.68
Body work and painting	36.50	101.52	85.59	94.35	125.22
Clutch and transmission repair	39.27	60.05	46.41	60.43	74.87
Drive shaft and rear-end repair	6.21	15.01	16.96	11.41	15.87
Brake work	44.56	82.37	72.27	84.75	91.58
Repair to steering or front-end	15.19	27.36	18.09	22.98	41.33
Repair to engine cooling system	17.95	24.56	22.70	23.18	27.76
Motor tune-up	41.77	89.27	75.33	88.57	105.33
Lube, oil change, and oil filters	56.23	95.06	85.34	98.73	102.77
Front-end alignment, wheel balance, rotation	9.13	12.56	9.97	14.19	14.08
Shock absorber replacement	2.76	4.77	3.14	5.30	6.15
Gas tank repair, replacement	3.32	5.56	3.53	8.75	4.82
Tire repair and other repair work	49.93	101.20	84.32	113.13	109.95
Vehicle air conditioning repair	14.23	29.97	23.62	35.45	32.44
Exhaust system repair	10.19	14.31	11.31	12.56	19.12
Electrical system repair	22.54	37.32	25.58	50.01	39.72
Motor repair, replacement	69.92	158.27	118.25	141.60	216.65
Auto repair service policy	9.05	20.96	25.04	32.86	6.45
Vehicle insurance	**964.37**	**1,675.27**	**1,583.52**	**1,743.84**	**1,719.66**

	total consumer units	$100,000 or more	$100,000– $119,999	$120,000– $149,999	$150,000 or more
Vehicle rental, leases, licenses, other charges	**$425.96**	**$1,165.33**	**$920.24**	**$955.98**	**$1,612.59**
Leased and rented vehicles	254.85	798.71	602.75	600.25	1,182.51
Rented vehicles	38.27	118.40	79.06	85.11	189.97
Auto rental	5.64	14.62	7.12	9.28	27.42
Auto rental on trips	21.18	67.38	51.01	53.61	97.09
Truck rental	4.72	11.62	11.15	6.68	16.27
Truck rental on trips	4.54	14.20	3.40	11.96	28.06
Leased vehicles	216.58	680.31	523.70	515.14	992.54
Car lease payments	104.73	330.75	232.92	259.93	498.68
Truck lease payments	96.04	278.97	227.21	205.29	398.14
Vehicle registration, state	80.92	141.51	120.45	146.68	160.56
Vehicle registration, local	6.90	12.79	14.94	14.06	9.33
Driver's license	7.16	11.69	13.37	10.65	10.69
Vehicle inspection	9.29	17.34	16.49	17.61	18.05
Parking fees	29.41	93.43	60.53	85.45	136.63
Parking fees in home city, excluding residence	23.87	77.69	48.57	71.15	115.50
Parking fees on trips	5.54	15.74	11.95	14.30	21.14
Tolls	14.60	39.66	38.60	41.56	39.04
Tolls on trips	4.63	11.22	12.64	8.27	12.10
Towing charges	5.08	8.16	9.38	7.92	7.01
Automobile service clubs	13.12	30.83	31.09	23.53	36.66
PUBLIC TRANSPORTATION	**441.33**	**1,383.13**	**894.25**	**1,219.19**	**2,073.23**
Airline fares	275.94	864.59	569.29	789.04	1,255.68
Intercity bus fares	9.35	18.39	11.87	13.44	29.77
Intracity mass transit fares	46.32	103.29	82.49	91.34	136.40
Local transportation on trips	10.00	33.02	20.52	25.90	52.87
Taxi fares and limousine service on trips	5.87	19.39	12.05	15.21	31.05
Taxi fares and limousine service	23.18	66.40	40.90	25.83	138.73
Intercity train fares	17.84	41.54	25.60	39.22	61.17
Ship fares	52.10	233.44	129.84	218.16	361.25
School bus	0.74	3.07	1.68	1.06	6.30

Note: Subcategories may not add to total because some are not shown.
Source: Bureau of Labor Statistics, unpublished tables from the 2004 Consumer Expenditure Survey; calculations by New Strategist

Table 11.10 Transportation: Indexed spending by high-income consumer units, 2004

(indexed average annual spending of high-income consumer units (CU) on transportation, by before-tax income of consumer unit, 2004; index definition: an index of 100 is the average for all consumer units; an index of 132 means that spending by consumer units in that group is 32 percent above the average for all consumer units; an index of 68 indicates spending that is 32 percent below the average for all consumer units)

	total consumer units	$100,000 or more	$100,000– $119,999	$120,000– $149,999	$150,000 or more
Average spending of CU, total	$43,395	$93,526	$75,213	$87,299	$119,449
Average spending of CU, index	100	216	173	201	275
Transportation, spending index	100	201	173	199	235
VEHICLE PURCHASES	100	209	177	207	247
Cars and trucks, new	100	243	184	262	293
New cars	100	241	164	257	312
New trucks	100	244	196	265	280
Cars and trucks, used	100	174	172	145	199
Used cars	100	190	183	163	220
Used trucks	100	159	162	128	180
Other vehicles	100	167	119	230	167
GASOLINE AND MOTOR OIL	100	160	153	168	161
Gasoline	100	158	151	166	159
Diesel fuel	100	182	211	150	177
Gasoline on trips	100	193	185	200	196
Motor oil	100	124	131	143	102
Motor oil on trips	100	193	185	200	197
OTHER VEHICLE EXPENSES	100	197	176	194	223
Vehicle finance charges	100	184	178	203	174
Automobile finance charges	100	172	167	186	167
Truck finance charges	100	184	186	203	167
Motorcycle and plane finance charges	100	232	164	366	196
Other vehicle finance charges	100	246	187	285	280
Maintenance and repairs	100	188	166	188	212
Coolant, additives, brake and transmission fluids	100	104	124	119	70
Tires—purchased, replaced, installed	100	181	166	184	196
Parts, equipment, and accessories	100	145	151	190	101
Vehicle audio equipment, excluding labor	100	31	11	69	16
Vehicle products	100	152	118	246	98
Miscellaneous auto repair, servicing	100	197	248	106	226
Body work and painting	100	278	234	258	343
Clutch and transmission repair	100	153	118	154	191
Drive shaft and rear-end repair	100	242	273	184	256
Brake work	100	185	162	190	206
Repair to steering or front-end	100	180	119	151	272
Repair to engine cooling system	100	137	126	129	155
Motor tune-up	100	214	180	212	252
Lube, oil change, and oil filters	100	169	152	176	183
Front-end alignment, wheel balance, rotation	100	138	109	155	154
Shock absorber replacement	100	173	114	192	223
Gas tank repair, replacement	100	167	106	264	145
Tire repair and other repair work	100	203	169	227	220
Vehicle air conditioning repair	100	211	166	249	228
Exhaust system repair	100	140	111	123	188
Electrical system repair	100	166	113	222	176
Motor repair, replacement	100	226	169	203	310
Auto repair service policy	100	232	277	363	71
Vehicle insurance	100	174	164	181	178

	total consumer units	$100,000 or more	$100,000– $119,999	$120,000– $149,999	$150,000 or more
Vehicle rental, leases, licenses, other charges	**100**	**274**	**216**	**224**	**379**
Leased and rented vehicles	100	313	237	236	464
Rented vehicles	100	309	207	222	496
Auto rental	100	259	126	165	486
Auto rental on trips	100	318	241	253	458
Truck rental	100	246	236	142	345
Truck rental on trips	100	313	75	263	618
Leased vehicles	100	314	242	238	458
Car lease payments	100	316	222	248	476
Truck lease payments	100	290	237	214	415
Vehicle registration, state	100	175	149	181	198
Vehicle registration, local	100	185	217	204	135
Driver's license	100	163	187	149	149
Vehicle inspection	100	187	178	190	194
Parking fees	100	318	206	291	465
Parking fees in home city, excluding residence	100	325	203	298	484
Parking fees on trips	100	284	216	258	382
Tolls	100	272	264	285	267
Tolls on trips	100	242	273	179	261
Towing charges	100	161	185	156	138
Automobile service clubs	100	235	237	179	279
PUBLIC TRANSPORTATION	**100**	**313**	**203**	**276**	**470**
Airline fares	100	313	206	286	455
Intercity bus fares	100	197	127	144	318
Intracity mass transit fares	100	223	178	197	294
Local transportation on trips	100	330	205	259	529
Taxi fares and limousine service on trips	100	330	205	259	529
Taxi fares and limousine service	100	286	176	111	598
Intercity train fares	100	233	143	220	343
Ship fares	100	448	249	419	693
School bus	100	415	227	143	851

Source: Calculations by New Strategist based on the 2004 Consumer Expenditure Survey

Table 11.11 Transportation: Total spending by high-income consumer units, 2004

(total annual spending on transportation, by before-tax income group of high-income consumer units (CU), 2004; consumer units and dollars in thousands)

	total consumer units	$100,000 or more	$100,000–$119,999	$120,000–$149,999	$150,000 or more
Number of consumer units	116,282	14,937	5,625	4,245	5,067
Total spending of all CUs	$5,046,042,273	$1,396,992,933	$423,073,913	$370,582,430	$605,247,019
Transportation, total spending	907,160,069	234,613,368	76,052,475	65,862,703	92,765,927
VEHICLE PURCHASES	395,018,094	106,139,633	33,821,944	29,834,539	42,482,792
Cars and trucks, new	203,305,123	63,442,966	18,058,388	19,457,170	25,927,130
New cars	78,242,669	24,192,115	6,193,181	7,347,076	10,651,695
New trucks	125,062,454	39,250,851	11,865,150	12,110,094	15,275,434
Cars and trucks, used	183,987,195	41,041,499	15,317,494	9,729,667	15,994,290
Used cars	88,444,089	21,576,048	7,812,281	5,273,648	8,490,063
Used trucks	95,541,942	19,465,450	7,505,213	4,456,019	7,504,278
Other vehicles	7,726,939	1,655,169	446,119	647,660	561,322
GASOLINE AND MOTOR OIL	185,767,472	38,228,264	13,790,363	11,402,325	13,035,618
Gasoline	170,532,204	34,584,831	12,428,719	10,358,352	11,797,699
Diesel fuel	2,383,781	557,897	243,225	130,661	184,135
Gasoline on trips	11,668,899	2,888,965	1,041,638	850,189	997,186
Motor oil	1,047,701	167,294	66,319	54,548	46,515
Motor oil on trips	117,445	29,127	10,519	8,575	10,083
OTHER VEHICLE EXPENSES	275,054,606	69,585,658	23,410,013	19,450,378	26,742,461
Vehicle finance charges	37,606,762	8,864,661	3,233,756	2,781,664	2,849,275
Automobile finance charges	15,498,065	3,426,847	1,251,169	1,050,807	1,124,773
Truck finance charges	19,407,466	4,589,244	1,742,400	1,438,079	1,408,829
Motorcycle and plane finance charges	380,242	113,521	30,206	50,855	32,530
Other vehicle finance charges	2,322,152	735,050	210,038	241,880	283,144
Maintenance and repairs	75,776,328	18,290,954	6,092,550	5,208,021	7,008,674
Coolant, additives, brake and transmission fluids	340,706	45,558	20,363	14,858	10,387
Tires—purchased, replaced, installed	10,940,973	2,549,895	879,300	736,210	934,456
Parts, equipment, and accessories	5,003,614	934,309	366,694	347,623	220,060
Vehicle audio equipment, excluding labor	962,815	38,239	5,344	24,409	6,587
Vehicle products	501,175	97,688	28,575	45,082	21,332
Miscellaneous auto repair, servicing	5,844,333	1,478,912	700,481	226,810	576,017
Body work and painting	4,244,293	1,516,404	481,444	400,516	634,490
Clutch and transmission repair	4,566,394	896,967	261,056	256,525	379,366
Drive shaft and rear-end repair	722,111	224,204	95,400	48,435	80,413
Brake work	5,181,526	1,230,361	406,519	359,764	464,036
Repair to steering or front-end	1,766,324	408,676	101,756	97,550	209,419
Repair to engine cooling system	2,087,262	366,853	127,688	98,399	140,660
Motor tune-up	4,857,099	1,333,426	423,731	375,980	533,707
Lube, oil change, and oil filters	6,538,537	1,419,911	480,038	419,109	520,736
Front-end alignment, wheel balance, rotation	1,061,655	187,609	56,081	60,237	71,343
Shock absorber replacement	320,938	71,249	17,663	22,499	31,162
Gas tank repair, replacement	386,056	83,050	19,856	37,144	24,423
Tire repair and other repair work	5,805,960	1,511,624	474,300	480,237	557,117
Vehicle air conditioning repair	1,654,693	447,662	132,863	150,485	164,373
Exhaust system repair	1,184,914	213,748	63,619	53,317	96,881
Electrical system repair	2,620,996	557,449	143,888	212,292	201,261
Motor repair, replacement	8,130,437	2,364,079	665,156	601,092	1,097,766
Auto repair service policy	1,052,352	313,080	140,850	139,491	32,682
Vehicle insurance	112,138,872	25,023,508	8,907,300	7,402,601	8,713,517

	total consumer units	$100,000 or more	$100,000– $119,999	$120,000– $149,999	$150,000 or more
Vehicle rental, leases, licenses, other charges	**$49,531,481**	**$17,406,534**	**$5,176,350**	**$4,058,135**	**$8,170,994**
Leased and rented vehicles	29,634,468	11,930,331	3,390,469	2,548,061	5,991,778
Rented vehicles	4,450,112	1,768,541	444,713	361,292	962,578
Auto rental	655,830	218,379	40,050	39,394	138,937
Auto rental on trips	2,462,853	1,006,455	286,931	227,574	491,955
Truck rental	548,851	173,568	62,719	28,357	82,440
Truck rental on trips	527,920	212,105	19,125	50,770	142,180
Leased vehicles	25,184,356	10,161,790	2,945,813	2,186,769	5,029,200
Car lease payments	12,178,214	4,940,413	1,310,175	1,103,403	2,526,812
Truck lease payments	11,167,723	4,166,975	1,278,056	871,456	2,017,375
Vehicle registration, state	9,409,539	2,113,735	677,531	622,657	813,558
Vehicle registration, local	802,346	191,044	84,038	59,685	47,275
Driver's license	832,579	174,614	75,206	45,209	54,166
Vehicle inspection	1,080,260	259,008	92,756	74,754	91,459
Parking fees	3,419,854	1,395,564	340,481	362,735	692,304
Parking fees in home city, excluding residence	2,775,651	1,160,456	273,206	302,032	585,239
Parking fees on trips	644,202	235,108	67,219	60,704	107,116
Tolls	1,697,717	592,401	217,125	176,422	197,816
Tolls on trips	538,386	167,593	71,100	35,106	61,311
Towing charges	590,713	121,886	52,763	33,620	35,520
Automobile service clubs	1,525,620	460,508	174,881	99,885	185,756
PUBLIC TRANSPORTATION	**51,318,735**	**20,659,813**	**5,030,156**	**5,175,462**	**10,505,056**
Airline fares	32,086,855	12,914,381	3,202,256	3,349,475	6,362,531
Intercity bus fares	1,087,237	274,691	66,769	57,053	150,845
Intracity mass transit fares	5,386,182	1,542,843	464,006	387,738	691,139
Local transportation on trips	1,162,820	493,220	115,425	109,946	267,892
Taxi fares and limousine service on trips	682,575	289,628	67,781	64,566	157,330
Taxi fares and limousine service	2,695,417	991,817	230,063	109,648	702,945
Intercity train fares	2,074,471	620,483	144,000	166,489	309,948
Ship fares	6,058,292	3,486,893	730,350	926,089	1,830,454
School bus	86,049	45,857	9,450	4,500	31,922

Note: Numbers may not add to total because of rounding and missing subcategories.
Source: Calculations by New Strategist based on the 2004 Consumer Expenditure Survey

Table 11.12 Transportation: Market shares by high-income consumer units, 2004

(percentage of total annual spending on transportation accounted for by before-tax income group of high-income consumer units, 2004)

	total consumer units	$100,000 or more	$100,000– $119,999	$120,000– $149,999	$150,000 or more
Share of total consumer units	100.0%	12.8%	4.8%	3.7%	4.4%
Share of total before-tax income	100.0	36.8	9.7	8.9	18.2
Share of total spending	100.0	27.7	8.4	7.3	12.0
Share of transportation spending	100.0	25.9	8.4	7.3	10.2
VEHICLE PURCHASES	100.0	26.9	8.6	7.6	10.8
Cars and trucks, new	100.0	31.2	8.9	9.6	12.8
New cars	100.0	30.9	7.9	9.4	13.6
New trucks	100.0	31.4	9.5	9.7	12.2
Cars and trucks, used	100.0	22.3	8.3	5.3	8.7
Used cars	100.0	24.4	8.8	6.0	9.6
Used trucks	100.0	20.4	7.9	4.7	7.9
Other vehicles	100.0	21.4	5.8	8.4	7.3
GASOLINE AND MOTOR OIL	100.0	20.6	7.4	6.1	7.0
Gasoline	100.0	20.3	7.3	6.1	6.9
Diesel fuel	100.0	23.4	10.2	5.5	7.7
Gasoline on trips	100.0	24.8	8.9	7.3	8.5
Motor oil	100.0	16.0	6.3	5.2	4.4
Motor oil on trips	100.0	24.8	9.0	7.3	8.6
OTHER VEHICLE EXPENSES	100.0	25.3	8.5	7.1	9.7
Vehicle finance charges	100.0	23.6	8.6	7.4	7.6
Automobile finance charges	100.0	22.1	8.1	6.8	7.3
Truck finance charges	100.0	23.6	9.0	7.4	7.3
Motorcycle and plane finance charges	100.0	29.9	7.9	13.4	8.6
Other vehicle finance charges	100.0	31.7	9.0	10.4	12.2
Maintenance and repairs	100.0	24.1	8.0	6.9	9.2
Coolant, additives, brake and transmission fluids	100.0	13.4	6.0	4.4	3.0
Tires– purchased, replaced, installed	100.0	23.3	8.0	6.7	8.5
Parts, equipment, and accessories	100.0	18.7	7.3	6.9	4.4
Vehicle audio equipment, excluding labor	100.0	4.0	0.6	2.5	0.7
Vehicle products	100.0	19.5	5.7	9.0	4.3
Miscellaneous auto repair, servicing	100.0	25.3	12.0	3.9	9.9
Body work and painting	100.0	35.7	11.3	9.4	14.9
Clutch and transmission repair	100.0	19.6	5.7	5.6	8.3
Drive shaft and rear-end repair	100.0	31.0	13.2	6.7	11.1
Brake work	100.0	23.7	7.8	6.9	9.0
Repair to steering or front-end	100.0	23.1	5.8	5.5	11.9
Repair to engine cooling system	100.0	17.6	6.1	4.7	6.7
Motor tune-up	100.0	27.5	8.7	7.7	11.0
Lube, oil change, and oil filters	100.0	21.7	7.3	6.4	8.0
Front-end alignment, wheel balance, rotation	100.0	17.7	5.3	5.7	6.7
Shock absorber replacement	100.0	22.2	5.5	7.0	9.7
Gas tank repair, replacement	100.0	21.5	5.1	9.6	6.3
Tire repair and other repair work	100.0	26.0	8.2	8.3	9.6
Vehicle air conditioning repair	100.0	27.1	8.0	9.1	9.9
Exhaust system repair	100.0	18.0	5.4	4.5	8.2
Electrical system repair	100.0	21.3	5.5	8.1	7.7
Motor repair, replacement	100.0	29.1	8.2	7.4	13.5
Auto repair service policy	100.0	29.8	13.4	13.3	3.1
Vehicle insurance	100.0	22.3	7.9	6.6	7.8

	total consumer units	$100,000 or more	$100,000– $119,999	$120,000– $149,999	$150,000 or more
Vehicle rental, leases, licenses, other charges	**100.0%**	**35.1%**	**10.5%**	**8.2%**	**16.5%**
Leased and rented vehicles	100.0	40.3	11.4	8.6	20.2
Rented vehicles	100.0	39.7	10.0	8.1	21.6
Auto rental	100.0	33.3	6.1	6.0	21.2
Auto rental on trips	100.0	40.9	11.7	9.2	20.0
Truck rental	100.0	31.6	11.4	5.2	15.0
Truck rental on trips	100.0	40.2	3.6	9.6	26.9
Leased vehicles	100.0	40.3	11.7	8.7	20.0
Car lease payments	100.0	40.6	10.8	9.1	20.7
Truck lease payments	100.0	37.3	11.4	7.8	18.1
Vehicle registration, state	100.0	22.5	7.2	6.6	8.6
Vehicle registration, local	100.0	23.8	10.5	7.4	5.9
Driver's license	100.0	21.0	9.0	5.4	6.5
Vehicle inspection	100.0	24.0	8.6	6.9	8.5
Parking fees	100.0	40.8	10.0	10.6	20.2
Parking fees in home city, excluding residence	100.0	41.8	9.8	10.9	21.1
Parking fees on trips	100.0	36.5	10.4	9.4	16.6
Tolls	100.0	34.9	12.8	10.4	11.7
Tolls on trips	100.0	31.1	13.2	6.5	11.4
Towing charges	100.0	20.6	8.9	5.7	6.0
Automobile service clubs	100.0	30.2	11.5	6.5	12.2
PUBLIC TRANSPORTATION	**100.0**	**40.3**	**9.8**	**10.1**	**20.5**
Airline fares	100.0	40.2	10.0	10.4	19.8
Intercity bus fares	100.0	25.3	6.1	5.2	13.9
Intracity mass transit fares	100.0	28.6	8.6	7.2	12.8
Local transportation on trips	100.0	42.4	9.9	9.5	23.0
Taxi fares and limousine service on trips	100.0	42.4	9.9	9.5	23.0
Taxi fares and limousine service	100.0	36.8	8.5	4.1	26.1
Intercity train fares	100.0	29.9	6.9	8.0	14.9
Ship fares	100.0	57.6	12.1	15.3	30.2
School bus	100.0	53.3	11.0	5.2	37.1

Note: Numbers may not add to total because of rounding.
Source: Calculations by New Strategist based on the 2004 Consumer Expenditure Survey

Table 11.13 Transportation: Average spending by household type, 2004

(average annual spending of consumer units (CU) on transportation, by type of consumer unit, 2004)

	total married couples	married couples, no children	married couples with children				single parent, at least one child <18	single person
			total	oldest child under 6	oldest child 6 to 17	oldest child 18 or older		
Number of consumer units (in 000s)	59,797	25,585	29,279	5,604	15,376	8,300	6,892	33,686
Average number of persons per CU	3.2	2.0	3.9	3.5	4.1	3.9	2.9	1.0
Average before-tax income of CU	$73,001.00	$64,434.00	$79,764.00	$75,293.00	$78,508.00	$85,109.00	$31,055.00	$28,143.00
Average spending of CU, total	55,606.57	49,690.43	60,660.88	55,981.04	60,577.88	64,161.69	32,824.46	25,423.35
Transportation, average spending	**10,485.78**	**8,975.18**	**11,883.71**	**10,598.75**	**11,376.57**	**13,693.78**	**5,446.03**	**3,940.64**
VEHICLE PURCHASES	**4,723.70**	**3,806.39**	**5,579.46**	**5,141.78**	**5,369.75**	**6,263.45**	**2,304.25**	**1,599.77**
Cars and trucks, new	**2,609.20**	**2,295.31**	**2,968.56**	**2,943.98**	**2,769.36**	**3,354.16**	**797.66**	**795.65**
New cars	918.42	993.21	873.93	804.94	788.79	1,078.23	172.35	392.30
New trucks	1,690.79	1,302.10	2,094.63	2,139.04	1,980.57	2,275.94	625.31	403.36
Cars and trucks, used	**2,020.71**	**1,369.47**	**2,545.83**	**2,169.08**	**2,525.82**	**2,837.25**	**1,462.78**	**776.30**
Used cars	906.86	704.86	1,036.66	952.72	886.83	1,370.92	891.29	443.13
Used trucks	1,113.85	664.62	1,509.16	1,216.36	1,639.00	1,466.34	571.48	333.17
Other vehicles	**93.78**	**141.60**	**65.07**	**28.72**	**74.57**	**72.03**	**43.81**	**27.82**
GASOLINE AND MOTOR OIL	**2,086.77**	**1,751.83**	**2,361.73**	**1,990.51**	**2,276.54**	**2,770.18**	**1,216.37**	**805.92**
Gasoline	1,903.15	1,561.28	2,181.06	1,854.97	2,096.71	2,557.49	1,148.02	741.30
Diesel fuel	32.82	31.19	34.58	14.49	37.49	42.76	2.02	7.95
Gasoline on trips	137.08	147.54	131.13	109.11	127.85	152.06	59.93	52.30
Motor oil	12.06	9.69	13.63	10.84	13.19	16.33	5.80	3.84
Motor oil on trips	1.38	1.49	1.32	1.10	1.29	1.54	0.61	0.53
OTHER VEHICLE EXPENSES	**3,079.92**	**2,752.91**	**3,381.26**	**3,014.96**	**3,188.42**	**3,985.80**	**1,715.94**	**1,280.84**
Vehicle finance charges	**451.11**	**372.03**	**518.91**	**484.24**	**516.04**	**547.64**	**210.81**	**126.54**
Automobile finance charges	166.49	145.89	178.84	168.23	156.49	227.40	101.73	71.99
Truck finance charges	244.96	173.30	308.60	304.67	326.03	278.98	103.24	51.81
Motorcycle and plane finance charges	4.57	5.08	3.87	1.77	3.88	5.27	1.30	1.13
Other vehicle finance charges	35.10	47.76	27.59	9.57	29.63	35.99	4.54	1.60
Maintenance and repairs	**830.13**	**771.18**	**880.72**	**722.33**	**880.75**	**986.94**	**477.45**	**403.76**
Coolant, additives, brake and transmission fluids	3.53	2.55	3.99	3.12	3.76	4.98	2.86	1.63
Tires—purchased, replaced, installed	124.50	110.52	134.14	110.47	143.39	133.00	61.51	54.68
Parts, equipment, and accessories	55.57	45.28	64.25	70.88	56.05	74.95	34.95	25.08
Vehicle audio equipment, excluding labor	6.37	5.86	7.84	3.60	7.91	11.10	15.98	13.72
Vehicle products	5.21	6.19	3.94	5.89	3.51	3.27	4.92	1.14
Miscellaneous auto repair, servicing	60.89	51.75	73.66	46.65	93.64	53.64	21.77	40.57
Body work and painting	48.76	47.22	52.09	36.23	44.46	76.92	18.76	21.14
Clutch and transmission repair	49.97	46.84	46.15	29.36	53.00	44.80	46.50	20.89
Drive shaft and rear-end repair	8.93	6.90	11.02	7.52	13.04	9.64	4.12	3.77
Brake work	58.51	55.66	58.56	63.16	58.40	55.77	34.46	24.17
Repair to steering or front-end	20.72	20.09	20.94	13.71	19.69	28.13	6.93	8.68
Repair to engine cooling system	21.44	24.02	19.23	13.11	20.37	21.24	16.66	11.76
Motor tune-up	51.26	47.95	53.48	40.01	58.47	53.32	25.80	30.44
Lube, oil change, and oil filters	72.10	68.88	75.87	67.72	72.18	88.23	41.27	35.06
Front-end alignment, wheel balance, rotation	10.42	11.59	9.05	6.98	9.91	8.83	7.97	7.92
Shock absorber replacement	3.73	4.97	3.10	1.19	3.50	3.64	4.18	1.01
Gas tank repair, replacement	3.90	4.44	3.32	2.30	2.97	4.88	1.89	2.88
Tire repair and other repair work	62.58	51.18	73.29	58.39	69.43	90.51	31.79	34.21
Vehicle air conditioning repair	18.99	23.67	15.40	5.42	15.24	22.44	10.35	7.12
Exhaust system repair	11.52	10.03	11.73	11.98	10.49	13.86	10.16	6.89
Electrical system repair	29.46	27.92	29.44	13.84	32.35	34.57	15.42	13.58
Motor repair, replacement	91.53	90.67	96.15	90.71	81.10	127.68	52.89	32.66
Auto repair service policy	10.20	7.00	14.08	20.08	7.85	21.57	6.29	4.77
Vehicle insurance	**1,225.76**	**1,075.40**	**1,356.33**	**1,105.01**	**1,198.89**	**1,817.67**	**725.48**	**537.18**

	total married couples	married couples, no children	married couples with children				single parent, at least one child <18	single person
			total	oldest child under 6	oldest child 6 to 17	oldest child 18 or older		
Vehicle rental, leases, licenses, other charges	**$572.91**	**$534.31**	**$625.30**	**$703.38**	**$592.74**	**$633.55**	**$302.20**	**$213.36**
Leased and rented vehicles	350.69	313.56	397.25	493.98	368.30	385.56	192.13	115.34
Rented vehicles	52.32	64.52	45.45	33.09	46.71	51.47	22.32	20.58
Auto rental	5.30	7.24	4.28	2.82	5.13	3.71	9.52	3.80
Auto rental on trips	30.85	37.97	26.58	20.38	29.74	24.92	5.68	10.40
Truck rental	7.01	8.26	6.76	6.65	5.59	9.00	3.93	1.46
Truck rental on trips	6.42	5.41	7.49	3.25	5.97	13.16	3.19	2.64
Leased vehicles	298.37	249.04	351.80	460.89	321.59	334.09	169.81	94.76
Car lease payments	134.22	123.75	147.48	169.51	121.31	181.10	91.15	47.72
Truck lease payments	138.60	93.68	179.99	239.89	180.62	138.39	64.58	45.35
Vehicle registration, state	109.86	106.81	115.78	112.71	112.46	123.99	55.00	41.90
Vehicle registration, local	8.69	9.63	7.70	9.10	7.78	6.62	5.51	5.10
Driver's license	9.02	7.85	9.89	8.36	9.59	11.49	5.15	4.18
Vehicle inspection	12.06	11.17	12.71	11.21	12.14	14.79	4.81	5.50
Parking fees	36.25	35.51	37.85	28.13	43.89	33.20	21.03	20.66
Parking fees in home city, excluding residence	28.55	26.09	30.97	21.55	36.71	26.68	17.40	17.94
Parking fees on trips	7.70	9.42	6.88	6.58	7.18	6.53	3.63	2.73
Tolls	17.60	17.89	17.96	19.12	14.60	24.04	6.18	5.49
Tolls on trips	6.21	7.16	5.58	5.18	5.37	6.24	2.16	2.46
Towing charges	5.53	3.47	6.96	5.40	5.13	11.41	5.34	3.42
Automobile service clubs	17.00	21.26	13.63	10.18	13.50	16.21	4.88	9.31
PUBLIC TRANSPORTATION	**595.39**	**664.06**	**561.26**	**451.49**	**541.86**	**674.35**	**209.47**	**254.10**
Airline fares	382.60	405.88	376.73	288.87	383.26	423.96	109.16	158.75
Intercity bus fares	11.91	15.04	10.02	3.76	10.40	13.55	4.92	6.40
Intracity mass transit fares	45.36	28.04	56.63	61.75	48.11	68.97	59.23	32.22
Local transportation on trips	13.07	17.48	10.49	7.81	10.60	12.11	2.76	6.67
Taxi fares and limousine service on trips	7.68	10.26	6.16	4.59	6.22	7.11	1.62	3.92
Taxi fares and limousine service	26.85	19.70	32.51	38.51	16.29	61.52	9.20	19.29
Intercity train fares	22.17	29.09	18.59	11.85	21.56	17.63	5.75	14.43
Ship fares	84.63	138.35	48.00	34.36	42.33	67.72	15.44	12.42
School bus	1.13	0.21	2.13	–	3.09	1.78	1.39	–

Note: Average spending figures for total consumer units can be found on Average Spending by Age and Average Spending by Region tables. Subcategories may not add to total because some are not shown. "–" means sample is too small to make a reliable estimate.
Source: Bureau of Labor Statistics, unpublished tables from the 2004 Consumer Expenditure Survey

Table 11.14 Transportation: Indexed spending by household type, 2004

(indexed average annual spending of consumer units (CU) on transportation, by type of consumer unit, 2004; index definition: an index of 100 is the average for all consumer units; an index of 132 means that spending by consumer units in that group is 32 percent above the average for all consumer units; an index of 68 indicates spending that is 32 percent below the average for all consumer units)

	total married couples	married couples, no children	married couples with children				single parent, at least one child <18	single person
			total	oldest child under 6	oldest child 6 to 17	oldest child 18 or older		
Average spending of CU, total	$55,607	$49,690	$60,661	$55,981	$60,578	$64,162	$32,824	$25,423
Average spending of CU, index	128	115	140	129	140	148	76	59
Transportation, spending index	134	115	152	136	146	176	70	51
VEHICLE PURCHASES	**139**	**112**	**164**	**151**	**158**	**184**	**68**	**47**
Cars and trucks, new	**149**	**131**	**170**	**168**	**158**	**192**	**46**	**46**
New cars	136	148	130	120	117	160	26	58
New trucks	157	121	195	199	184	212	58	38
Cars and trucks, used	**128**	**87**	**161**	**137**	**160**	**179**	**92**	**49**
Used cars	119	93	136	125	117	180	117	58
Used trucks	136	81	184	148	199	178	70	41
Other vehicles	**141**	**213**	**98**	**43**	**112**	**108**	**66**	**42**
GASOLINE AND MOTOR OIL	**131**	**110**	**148**	**125**	**143**	**173**	**76**	**50**
Gasoline	130	106	149	126	143	174	78	51
Diesel fuel	160	152	169	71	183	209	10	39
Gasoline on trips	137	147	131	109	127	152	60	52
Motor oil	134	108	151	120	146	181	64	43
Motor oil on trips	137	148	131	109	128	152	60	52
OTHER VEHICLE EXPENSES	**130**	**116**	**143**	**127**	**135**	**169**	**73**	**54**
Vehicle finance charges	**139**	**115**	**160**	**150**	**160**	**169**	**65**	**39**
Automobile finance charges	125	109	134	126	117	171	76	54
Truck finance charges	147	104	185	183	195	167	62	31
Motorcycle and plane finance charges	140	155	118	54	119	161	40	35
Other vehicle finance charges	176	239	138	48	148	180	23	8
Maintenance and repairs	**127**	**118**	**135**	**111**	**135**	**151**	**73**	**62**
Coolant, additives, brake and transmission fluids	120	87	136	106	128	170	98	56
Tires—purchased, replaced, installed	132	117	143	117	152	141	65	58
Parts, equipment, and accessories	129	105	149	165	130	174	81	58
Vehicle audio equipment, excluding labor	77	71	95	43	96	134	193	166
Vehicle products	121	144	91	137	81	76	114	26
Miscellaneous auto repair, servicing	121	103	147	93	186	107	43	81
Body work and painting	134	129	143	99	122	211	51	58
Clutch and transmission repair	127	119	118	75	135	114	118	53
Drive shaft and rear-end repair	144	111	177	121	210	155	66	61
Brake work	131	125	131	142	131	125	77	54
Repair to steering or front-end	136	132	138	90	130	185	46	57
Repair to engine cooling system	119	134	107	73	113	118	93	66
Motor tune-up	123	115	128	96	140	128	62	73
Lube, oil change, and oil filters	128	122	135	120	128	157	73	62
Front-end alignment, wheel balance, rotation	114	127	99	76	109	97	87	87
Shock absorber replacement	135	180	112	43	127	132	151	37
Gas tank repair, replacement	117	134	100	69	89	147	57	87
Tire repair and other repair work	125	103	147	117	139	181	64	69
Vehicle air conditioning repair	133	166	108	38	107	158	73	50
Exhaust system repair	113	98	115	118	103	136	100	68
Electrical system repair	131	124	131	61	144	153	68	60
Motor repair, replacement	131	130	138	130	116	183	76	47
Auto repair service policy	113	77	156	222	87	238	70	53
Vehicle insurance	**127**	**112**	**141**	**115**	**124**	**188**	**75**	**56**

	total married couples	married couples, no children	married couples with children				single parent, at least one child <18	single person
			total	oldest child under 6	oldest child 6 to 17	oldest child 18 or older		
Vehicle rental, leases, licenses, other charges	**134**	**125**	**147**	**165**	**139**	**149**	**71**	**50**
Leased and rented vehicles	138	123	156	194	145	151	75	45
Rented vehicles	137	169	119	86	122	134	58	54
Auto rental	94	128	76	50	91	66	169	67
Auto rental on trips	146	179	125	96	140	118	27	49
Truck rental	149	175	143	141	118	191	83	31
Truck rental on trips	141	119	165	72	131	290	70	58
Leased vehicles	138	115	162	213	148	154	78	44
Car lease payments	128	118	141	162	116	173	87	46
Truck lease payments	144	98	187	250	188	144	67	47
Vehicle registration, state	136	132	143	139	139	153	68	52
Vehicle registration, local	126	140	112	132	113	96	80	74
Driver's license	126	110	138	117	134	160	72	58
Vehicle inspection	130	120	137	121	131	159	52	59
Parking fees	123	121	129	96	149	113	72	70
Parking fees in home city, excluding residence	120	109	130	90	154	112	73	75
Parking fees on trips	139	170	124	119	130	118	66	49
Tolls	121	123	123	131	100	165	42	38
Tolls on trips	134	155	121	112	116	135	47	53
Towing charges	109	68	137	106	101	225	105	67
Automobile service clubs	130	162	104	78	103	124	37	71
PUBLIC TRANSPORTATION	**135**	**150**	**127**	**102**	**123**	**153**	**47**	**58**
Airline fares	139	147	137	105	139	154	40	58
Intercity bus fares	127	161	107	40	111	145	53	68
Intracity mass transit fares	98	61	122	133	104	149	128	70
Local transportation on trips	131	175	105	78	106	121	28	67
Taxi fares and limousine service on trips	131	175	105	78	106	121	28	67
Taxi fares and limousine service	116	85	140	166	70	265	40	83
Intercity train fares	124	163	104	66	121	99	32	81
Ship fares	162	266	92	66	81	130	30	24
School bus	153	28	288	–	418	241	188	–

Note: Spending index for total consumer units is 100. "–" means sample is too small to make a reliable estimate.
Source: Calculations by New Strategist based on the 2004 Consumer Expenditure Survey

Table 11.15 Transportation: Total spending by household type, 2004

(total annual spending on transportation, by consumer unit (CU) type, 2004; consumer units and dollars in thousands)

	total married couples	married couples, no children	married couples with children				single parent, at least one child <18	single person
			total	oldest child under 6	oldest child 6 to 17	oldest child 18 or older		
Number of consumer units	59,797	25,585	29,279	5,604	15,376	8,300	6,892	33,686
Total spending of all CUs	$3,325,106,066	$1,271,329,652	$1,776,089,906	$313,717,748	$931,445,483	$532,542,027	$226,226,178	$856,410,968
Transportation, total spending	627,018,187	229,629,980	347,943,145	59,395,395	174,926,140	113,658,374	37,534,039	132,744,399
VEHICLE PURCHASES	282,463,089	97,386,488	163,361,009	28,814,535	82,565,276	51,986,635	15,880,891	53,889,852
Cars and trucks, new	156,022,332	58,725,506	86,916,468	16,498,064	42,581,679	27,839,528	5,497,473	26,802,266
New cars	54,918,761	25,411,278	25,587,796	4,510,884	12,128,435	8,949,309	1,187,836	13,215,018
New trucks	101,104,170	33,314,229	61,328,672	11,987,180	30,453,244	18,890,302	4,309,637	13,587,585
Cars and trucks, used	120,832,396	35,037,890	74,539,357	12,155,524	38,837,008	23,549,175	10,081,480	26,150,442
Used cars	54,227,507	18,033,843	30,352,368	5,339,043	13,635,898	11,378,636	6,142,771	14,927,277
Used trucks	66,604,888	17,004,303	44,186,696	6,816,481	25,201,264	12,170,622	3,938,640	11,223,165
Other vehicles	5,607,763	3,622,836	1,905,185	160,947	1,146,588	597,849	301,939	937,145
GASOLINE AND MOTOR OIL	124,782,586	44,820,571	69,149,093	11,154,818	35,004,079	22,992,494	8,383,222	27,148,221
Gasoline	113,802,661	39,945,349	63,859,256	10,395,252	32,239,013	21,227,167	7,912,154	24,971,432
Diesel fuel	1,962,538	797,996	1,012,468	81,202	576,446	354,908	13,922	267,804
Gasoline on trips	8,196,973	3,774,811	3,839,355	611,452	1,965,822	1,262,098	413,038	1,761,778
Motor oil	721,152	247,919	399,073	60,747	202,809	135,539	39,974	129,354
Motor oil on trips	82,520	38,122	38,648	6,164	19,835	12,782	4,204	17,854
OTHER VEHICLE EXPENSES	184,169,976	70,433,202	98,999,912	16,895,836	49,025,146	33,082,140	11,826,258	43,146,376
Vehicle finance charges	26,975,025	9,518,388	15,193,166	2,713,681	7,934,631	4,545,412	1,452,903	4,262,626
Automobile finance charges	9,955,603	3,732,596	5,236,256	942,761	2,406,190	1,887,420	701,123	2,425,055
Truck finance charges	14,647,873	4,433,881	9,035,499	1,707,371	5,013,037	2,315,534	711,530	1,745,272
Motorcycle and plane finance charges	273,272	129,972	113,310	9,919	59,659	43,741	8,960	38,065
Other vehicle finance charges	2,098,875	1,221,940	807,808	53,630	455,591	298,717	31,290	53,898
Maintenance and repairs	49,639,284	19,730,640	25,786,601	4,047,937	13,542,412	8,191,602	3,290,585	13,601,059
Coolant, additives, brake and transmission fluids	211,083	65,242	116,823	17,484	57,814	41,334	19,711	54,908
Tires—purchased, replaced, installed	7,444,727	2,827,654	3,927,485	619,074	2,204,765	1,103,900	423,927	1,841,950
Parts, equipment, and accessories	3,322,919	1,158,489	1,881,176	397,212	861,825	622,085	240,875	844,845
Vehicle audio equipment, excluding labor	380,907	149,928	229,547	20,174	121,624	92,130	110,134	462,172
Vehicle products	311,542	158,371	115,359	33,008	53,970	27,141	33,909	38,402
Miscellaneous auto repair, servicing	3,641,039	1,324,024	2,156,691	261,427	1,439,809	445,212	150,039	1,366,641
Body work and painting	2,915,702	1,208,124	1,525,143	203,033	683,617	638,436	129,294	712,122
Clutch and transmission repair	2,988,056	1,198,401	1,351,226	164,533	814,928	371,840	320,478	703,701
Drive shaft and rear-end repair	533,987	176,537	322,655	42,142	200,503	80,012	28,395	126,996
Brake work	3,498,722	1,424,061	1,714,578	353,949	897,958	462,891	237,498	814,191
Repair to steering or front-end	1,238,994	514,003	613,102	76,831	302,753	233,479	47,762	292,394
Repair to engine cooling system	1,282,048	614,552	563,035	73,468	313,209	176,292	114,821	396,147
Motor tune-up	3,065,194	1,226,801	1,565,841	224,216	899,035	442,556	177,814	1,025,402
Lube, oil change, and oil filters	4,311,364	1,762,295	2,221,398	379,503	1,109,840	732,309	284,433	1,181,031
Front-end alignment, wheel balance, rotation	623,085	296,530	264,975	39,116	152,376	73,289	54,929	266,793
Shock absorber replacement	223,043	127,157	90,765	6,669	53,816	30,212	28,809	34,023
Gas tank repair, replacement	233,208	113,597	97,206	12,889	45,667	40,504	13,026	97,016
Tire repair and other repair work	3,742,096	1,309,440	2,145,858	327,218	1,067,556	751,233	219,097	1,152,398
Vehicle air conditioning repair	1,135,545	605,597	450,897	30,374	234,330	186,252	71,332	239,844
Exhaust system repair	688,861	256,618	343,443	67,136	161,294	115,038	70,023	232,097
Electrical system repair	1,761,620	714,333	861,974	77,559	497,414	286,931	106,275	457,456
Motor repair, replacement	5,473,219	2,319,792	2,815,176	508,339	1,246,994	1,059,744	364,518	1,100,185
Auto repair service policy	609,929	179,095	412,248	112,528	120,702	179,031	43,351	160,682
Vehicle insurance	73,296,771	27,514,109	39,711,986	6,192,476	18,434,133	15,086,661	5,000,008	18,095,445

	total married couples	married couples, no children	married couples with children				single parent, at least one child <18	single person
			total	oldest child under 6	oldest child 6 to 17	oldest child 18 or older		
Vehicle rental, leases, licenses, other charges	**$34,258,299**	**$13,670,321**	**$18,308,159**	**$3,941,742**	**$9,113,970**	**$5,258,465**	**$2,082,762**	**$7,187,245**
Leased and rented vehicles	20,970,210	8,022,433	11,631,083	2,768,264	5,662,981	3,200,148	1,324,160	3,885,343
Rented vehicles	3,128,579	1,650,744	1,330,731	185,436	718,213	427,201	153,829	693,258
Auto rental	316,924	185,235	125,314	15,803	78,879	30,793	65,612	128,007
Auto rental on trips	1,844,737	971,462	778,236	114,210	457,282	206,836	39,147	350,334
Truck rental	419,177	211,332	197,926	37,267	85,952	74,700	27,086	49,182
Truck rental on trips	383,897	138,415	219,300	18,213	91,795	109,228	21,985	88,931
Leased vehicles	17,841,631	6,371,688	10,300,352	2,582,828	4,944,768	2,772,947	1,170,331	3,192,085
Car lease payments	8,025,953	3,166,144	4,318,067	949,934	1,865,263	1,503,130	628,206	1,607,496
Truck lease payments	8,287,864	2,396,803	5,269,927	1,344,344	2,777,213	1,148,637	445,085	1,527,660
Vehicle registration, state	6,569,298	2,732,734	3,389,923	631,627	1,729,185	1,029,117	379,060	1,411,443
Vehicle registration, local	519,636	246,384	225,448	50,996	119,625	54,946	37,975	171,799
Driver's license	539,369	200,842	289,569	46,849	147,456	95,367	35,494	140,807
Vehicle inspection	721,152	285,784	372,136	62,821	186,665	122,757	33,151	185,273
Parking fees	2,167,641	908,523	1,108,210	157,641	674,853	275,560	144,939	695,953
Parking fees in home city, excluding residence	1,707,204	667,513	906,771	120,766	564,453	221,444	119,921	604,327
Parking fees on trips	460,437	241,011	201,440	36,874	110,400	54,199	25,018	91,963
Tolls	1,052,427	457,716	525,851	107,148	224,490	199,532	42,593	184,936
Tolls on trips	371,339	183,189	163,377	29,029	82,569	51,792	14,887	82,868
Towing charges	330,677	88,780	203,782	30,262	78,879	94,703	36,803	115,206
Automobile service clubs	1,016,549	543,937	399,073	57,049	207,576	134,543	33,633	313,617
PUBLIC TRANSPORTATION	**35,602,536**	**16,989,975**	**16,433,132**	**2,530,150**	**8,331,639**	**5,597,105**	**1,443,667**	**8,559,613**
Airline fares	22,878,332	10,384,440	11,030,278	1,618,827	5,893,006	3,518,868	752,331	5,347,653
Intercity bus fares	712,182	384,798	293,376	21,071	159,910	112,465	33,909	215,590
Intracity mass transit fares	2,712,392	717,403	1,658,070	346,047	739,739	572,451	408,213	1,085,363
Local transportation on trips	781,547	447,226	307,137	43,767	162,986	100,513	19,022	224,686
Taxi fares and limousine service on trips	459,241	262,502	180,359	25,722	95,639	59,013	11,165	132,049
Taxi fares and limousine service	1,605,549	504,025	951,860	215,810	250,475	510,616	63,406	649,803
Intercity train fares	1,325,699	744,268	544,297	66,407	331,507	146,329	39,629	486,089
Ship fares	5,060,620	3,539,685	1,405,392	192,553	650,866	562,076	106,412	418,380
School bus	67,571	5,373	62,364	–	47,512	14,774	9,580	–

Note: Total spending figures for total consumer units can be found on Total Spending by Age and Total Spending by Region tables. Spending by type of consumer unit will not add to total because not all types of consumer units are shown. Numbers may not add to category total because of rounding and missing subcategories. "–" means sample is too small to make a reliable estimate.
Source: Calculations by New Strategist based on the 2004 Consumer Expenditure Survey

Table 11.16 Transportation: Market shares by household type, 2004

(percentage of total annual spending on transportation accounted for by types of consumer units, 2004)

	total married couples	married couples, no children	married couples with children			single parent, at least one child <18	single person
			total	oldest child under 6	oldest child 6 to 17	oldest child 18 or older		
Share of total consumer units	51.4%	22.0%	25.2%	4.8%	13.2%	7.1%	5.9%	29.0%
Share of total before-tax income	68.9	26.0	36.9	6.7	19.1	11.2	3.4	15.0
Share of total spending	65.9	25.2	35.2	6.2	18.5	10.6	4.5	17.0
Share of transportation spending	69.1	25.3	38.4	6.5	19.3	12.5	4.1	14.6
VEHICLE PURCHASES	**71.5**	**24.7**	**41.4**	**7.3**	**20.9**	**13.2**	**4.0**	**13.6**
Cars and trucks, new	**76.7**	**28.9**	**42.8**	**8.1**	**20.9**	**13.7**	**2.7**	**13.2**
New cars	70.2	32.5	32.7	5.8	15.5	11.4	1.5	16.9
New trucks	80.8	26.6	49.0	9.6	24.4	15.1	3.4	10.9
Cars and trucks, used	**65.7**	**19.0**	**40.5**	**6.6**	**21.1**	**12.8**	**5.5**	**14.2**
Used cars	61.3	20.4	34.3	6.0	15.4	12.9	6.9	16.9
Used trucks	69.7	17.8	46.2	7.1	26.4	12.7	4.1	11.7
Other vehicles	**72.6**	**46.9**	**24.7**	**2.1**	**14.8**	**7.7**	**3.9**	**12.1**
GASOLINE AND MOTOR OIL	**67.2**	**24.1**	**37.2**	**6.0**	**18.8**	**12.4**	**4.5**	**14.6**
Gasoline	66.7	23.4	37.4	6.1	18.9	12.4	4.6	14.6
Diesel fuel	82.3	33.5	42.5	3.4	24.2	14.9	0.6	11.2
Gasoline on trips	70.2	32.3	32.9	5.2	16.8	10.8	3.5	15.1
Motor oil	68.8	23.7	38.1	5.8	19.4	12.9	3.8	12.3
Motor oil on trips	70.3	32.5	32.9	5.2	16.9	10.9	3.6	15.2
OTHER VEHICLE EXPENSES	**67.0**	**25.6**	**36.0**	**6.1**	**17.8**	**12.0**	**4.3**	**15.7**
Vehicle finance charges	**71.7**	**25.3**	**40.4**	**7.2**	**21.1**	**12.1**	**3.9**	**11.3**
Automobile finance charges	64.2	24.1	33.8	6.1	15.5	12.2	4.5	15.6
Truck finance charges	75.5	22.8	46.6	8.8	25.8	11.9	3.7	9.0
Motorcycle and plane finance charges	71.9	34.2	29.8	2.6	15.7	11.5	2.4	10.0
Other vehicle finance charges	90.4	52.6	34.8	2.3	19.6	12.9	1.3	2.3
Maintenance and repairs	**65.5**	**26.0**	**34.0**	**5.3**	**17.9**	**10.8**	**4.3**	**17.9**
Coolant, additives, brake and transmission fluids	62.0	19.1	34.3	5.1	17.0	12.1	5.8	16.1
Tires—purchased, replaced, installed	68.0	25.8	35.9	5.7	20.2	10.1	3.9	16.8
Parts, equipment, and accessories	66.4	23.2	37.6	7.9	17.2	12.4	4.8	16.9
Vehicle audio equipment, excluding labor	39.6	15.6	23.8	2.1	12.6	9.6	11.4	48.0
Vehicle products	62.2	31.6	23.0	6.6	10.8	5.4	6.8	7.7
Miscellaneous auto repair, servicing	62.3	22.7	36.9	4.5	24.6	7.6	2.6	23.4
Body work and painting	68.7	28.5	35.9	4.8	16.1	15.0	3.0	16.8
Clutch and transmission repair	65.4	26.2	29.6	3.6	17.8	8.1	7.0	15.4
Drive shaft and rear-end repair	73.9	24.4	44.7	5.8	27.8	11.1	3.9	17.6
Brake work	67.5	27.5	33.1	6.8	17.3	8.9	4.6	15.7
Repair to steering or front-end	70.1	29.1	34.7	4.3	17.1	13.2	2.7	16.6
Repair to engine cooling system	61.4	29.4	27.0	3.5	15.0	8.4	5.5	19.0
Motor tune-up	63.1	25.3	32.2	4.6	18.5	9.1	3.7	21.1
Lube, oil change, and oil filters	65.9	27.0	34.0	5.8	17.0	11.2	4.4	18.1
Front-end alignment, wheel balance, rotation	58.7	27.9	25.0	3.7	14.4	6.9	5.2	25.1
Shock absorber replacement	69.5	39.6	28.3	2.1	16.8	9.4	9.0	10.6
Gas tank repair, replacement	60.4	29.4	25.2	3.3	11.8	10.5	3.4	25.1
Tire repair and other repair work	64.5	22.6	37.0	5.6	18.4	12.9	3.8	19.8
Vehicle air conditioning repair	68.6	36.6	27.2	1.8	14.2	11.3	4.3	14.5
Exhaust system repair	58.1	21.7	29.0	5.7	13.6	9.7	5.9	19.6
Electrical system repair	67.2	27.3	32.9	3.0	19.0	10.9	4.1	17.5
Motor repair, replacement	67.3	28.5	34.6	6.3	15.3	13.0	4.5	13.5
Auto repair service policy	58.0	17.0	39.2	10.7	11.5	17.0	4.1	15.3
Vehicle insurance	**65.4**	**24.5**	**35.4**	**5.5**	**16.4**	**13.5**	**4.5**	**16.1**

	total married couples	married couples, no children	married couples with children				single parent, at least one child <18	single person
			total	oldest child under 6	oldest child 6 to 17	oldest child 18 or older		
Vehicle rental, leases, licenses, other charges	**69.2%**	**27.6%**	**37.0%**	**8.0%**	**18.4%**	**10.6%**	**4.2%**	**14.5%**
Leased and rented vehicles	70.8	27.1	39.2	9.3	19.1	10.8	4.5	13.1
Rented vehicles	70.3	37.1	29.9	4.2	16.1	9.6	3.5	15.6
Auto rental	48.3	28.2	19.1	2.4	12.0	4.7	10.0	19.5
Auto rental on trips	74.9	39.4	31.6	4.6	18.6	8.4	1.6	14.2
Truck rental	76.4	38.5	36.1	6.8	15.7	13.6	4.9	9.0
Truck rental on trips	72.7	26.2	41.5	3.4	17.4	20.7	4.2	16.8
Leased vehicles	70.8	25.3	40.9	10.3	19.6	11.0	4.6	12.7
Car lease payments	65.9	26.0	35.5	7.8	15.3	12.3	5.2	13.2
Truck lease payments	74.2	21.5	47.2	12.0	24.9	10.3	4.0	13.7
Vehicle registration, state	69.8	29.0	36.0	6.7	18.4	10.9	4.0	15.0
Vehicle registration, local	64.8	30.7	28.1	6.4	14.9	6.8	4.7	21.4
Driver's license	64.8	24.1	34.8	5.6	17.7	11.5	4.3	16.9
Vehicle inspection	66.8	26.5	34.4	5.8	17.3	11.4	3.1	17.2
Parking fees	63.4	26.6	32.4	4.6	19.7	8.1	4.2	20.4
Parking fees in home city, excluding residence	61.5	24.0	32.7	4.4	20.3	8.0	4.3	21.8
Parking fees on trips	71.5	37.4	31.3	5.7	17.1	8.4	3.9	14.3
Tolls	62.0	27.0	31.0	6.3	13.2	11.8	2.5	10.9
Tolls on trips	69.0	34.0	30.3	5.4	15.3	9.6	2.8	15.4
Towing charges	56.0	15.0	34.5	5.1	13.4	16.0	6.2	19.5
Automobile service clubs	66.6	35.7	26.2	3.7	13.6	8.8	2.2	20.6
PUBLIC TRANSPORTATION	**69.4**	**33.1**	**32.0**	**4.9**	**16.2**	**10.9**	**2.8**	**16.7**
Airline fares	71.3	32.4	34.4	5.0	18.4	11.0	2.3	16.7
Intercity bus fares	65.5	35.4	27.0	1.9	14.7	10.3	3.1	19.8
Intracity mass transit fares	50.4	13.3	30.8	6.4	13.7	10.6	7.6	20.2
Local transportation on trips	67.2	38.5	26.4	3.8	14.0	8.6	1.6	19.3
Taxi fares and limousine service on trips	67.3	38.5	26.4	3.8	14.0	8.6	1.6	19.3
Taxi fares and limousine service	59.6	18.7	35.3	8.0	9.3	18.9	2.4	24.1
Intercity train fares	63.9	35.9	26.2	3.2	16.0	7.1	1.9	23.4
Ship fares	83.5	58.4	23.2	3.2	10.7	9.3	1.8	6.9
School bus	78.5	6.2	72.5	–	55.2	17.2	11.1	–

Note: Market share for total consumer units is 100.0%. Market shares by type of consumer unit will not add to total because not all types of consumer units are shown. "–" means sample is too small to make a reliable estimate.
Source: Calculations by New Strategist based on the 2004 Consumer Expenditure Survey

Table 11.17 Transportation: Average spending by race and Hispanic origin, 2004

(average annual spending by consumer units (CU) on transportation, by race and Hispanic origin of consumer unit reference person, 2004)

	total consumer units	Asian	black	Hispanic	non-Hispanic white and other
Number of consumer units (in 000s)	116,282	3,957	13,773	12,298	90,424
Average number of persons per CU	2.5	2.8	2.6	3.3	2.3
Average before-tax income of CU	$54,453.00	$67,705.00	$38,503.00	$43,693.00	$58,314.00
Average spending of CU, total	43,394.87	49,458.68	30,481.49	37,578.03	46,163.26
Transportation, average spending	7,801.38	8,556.48	4,976.36	7,497.29	8,272.66
VEHICLE PURCHASES	3,397.07	3,676.02	1,759.06	3,444.85	3,638.97
Cars and trucks, new	1,748.38	2,307.14	786.13	1,603.91	1,917.39
New cars	672.87	934.05	338.38	736.37	713.59
New trucks	1,075.51	1,373.09	447.75	867.54	1,203.80
Cars and trucks, used	1,582.25	1,353.78	960.24	1,832.83	1,639.17
Used cars	760.60	1,182.39	618.95	635.74	797.36
Used trucks	821.64	171.39	341.28	1,197.09	841.81
Other vehicles	66.45	15.10	12.69	8.12	82.41
GASOLINE AND MOTOR OIL	1,597.56	1,637.25	1,230.96	1,649.73	1,645.67
Gasoline	1,466.54	1,532.70	1,182.93	1,549.55	1,497.94
Diesel fuel	20.50	13.89	2.62	8.84	24.76
Gasoline on trips	100.35	84.18	39.75	79.11	112.39
Motor oil	9.01	5.62	5.26	11.43	9.26
Motor oil on trips	1.01	0.85	0.40	0.80	1.14
OTHER VEHICLE EXPENSES	2,365.41	2,329.90	1,696.15	2,048.14	2,511.05
Vehicle finance charges	323.41	259.91	240.47	284.55	340.97
Automobile finance charges	133.28	139.72	140.43	108.02	135.54
Truck finance charges	166.90	119.67	99.01	171.53	176.39
Motorcycle and plane finance charges	3.27	–	0.87	1.61	3.85
Other vehicle finance charges	19.97	0.52	0.16	3.39	25.19
Maintenance and repairs	651.66	701.46	427.42	573.99	697.15
Coolant, additives, brake and transmission fluids	2.93	2.52	2.47	4.01	2.86
Tires—purchased, replaced, installed	94.09	80.94	58.08	89.12	100.12
Parts, equipment, and accessories	43.03	27.13	18.78	48.99	45.87
Vehicle audio equipment, excluding labor	8.28	–	12.97	0.71	8.70
Vehicle products	4.31	1.85	3.48	2.06	4.75
Miscellaneous auto repair, servicing	50.26	70.15	33.79	20.04	56.99
Body work and painting	36.50	49.03	24.76	38.38	38.31
Clutch and transmission repair	39.27	29.47	18.46	36.81	42.79
Drive shaft and rear-end repair	6.21	2.75	4.32	3.54	6.91
Brake work	44.56	49.54	31.27	35.17	48.03
Repair to steering or front-end	15.19	15.12	8.40	12.96	16.57
Repair to engine cooling system	17.95	16.76	13.47	16.56	18.86
Motor tune-up	41.77	58.03	32.12	32.77	44.46
Lube, oil change, and oil filters	56.23	64.81	36.23	46.90	60.51
Front-end alignment, wheel balance, rotation	9.13	8.72	6.55	6.87	9.84
Shock absorber replacement	2.76	3.07	1.27	2.38	3.05
Gas tank repair, replacement	3.32	5.64	2.03	3.88	3.44
Tire repair and other repair work	49.93	47.35	35.40	41.27	53.31
Vehicle air conditioning repair	14.23	14.76	11.40	13.28	14.82
Exhaust system repair	10.19	8.93	5.80	7.02	11.27
Electrical system repair	22.54	22.35	12.01	19.49	24.68
Motor repair, replacement	69.92	103.73	43.90	88.12	71.46
Auto repair service policy	9.05	18.81	10.47	3.65	9.54
Vehicle insurance	964.37	954.35	745.07	864.54	1,011.56

	total consumer units	Asian	black	Hispanic	non-Hispanic white and other
Vehicle rental, leases, licenses, other charges	**$425.96**	**$414.18**	**$283.18**	**$325.07**	**$461.37**
Leased and rented vehicles	254.85	214.16	200.57	171.57	274.23
Rented vehicles	38.27	51.05	27.48	26.35	41.44
Auto rental	5.64	2.53	8.06	5.19	5.32
Auto rental on trips	21.18	41.95	7.95	11.88	24.41
Truck rental	4.72	4.01	8.73	1.17	4.58
Truck rental on trips	4.54	2.57	2.74	0.20	5.39
Leased vehicles	216.58	163.11	173.09	145.21	232.79
Car lease payments	104.73	57.98	87.95	40.99	115.70
Truck lease payments	96.04	100.50	78.14	88.03	100.02
Vehicle registration, state	80.92	75.23	32.13	75.46	88.97
Vehicle registration, local	6.90	4.15	5.95	4.47	7.38
Driver's license	7.16	6.40	4.13	5.51	7.84
Vehicle inspection	9.29	11.68	4.58	9.56	9.97
Parking fees	29.41	52.85	15.46	18.07	33.20
Parking fees in home city, excluding residence	23.87	44.99	13.57	14.66	26.83
Parking fees on trips	5.54	7.85	1.89	3.41	6.37
Tolls	14.60	26.28	5.30	21.94	14.99
Tolls on trips	4.63	5.92	3.05	3.24	5.08
Towing charges	5.08	5.04	6.36	7.03	4.81
Automobile service clubs	13.12	12.47	5.66	8.22	14.90
PUBLIC TRANSPORTATION	**441.33**	**913.32**	**290.20**	**354.56**	**476.97**
Airline fares	275.94	630.07	127.03	223.94	305.78
Intercity bus fares	9.35	13.87	7.62	8.14	9.76
Intracity mass transit fares	46.32	128.92	89.68	66.67	37.07
Local transportation on trips	10.00	18.57	3.95	4.23	11.68
Taxi fares and limousine service on trips	5.87	10.91	2.32	2.49	6.86
Taxi fares and limousine service	23.18	8.11	24.51	26.54	23.36
Intercity train fares	17.84	26.54	10.13	5.45	20.65
Ship fares	52.10	75.10	23.69	15.51	61.27
School bus	0.74	1.23	1.27	1.59	0.54

Note: "Asian" and "black" include Hispanics and non-Hispanics who identify themselves as being of the respective race alone. "Hispanic" includes people of any race who identify themselves as Hispanic. "Other" includes people who identify themselves as non-Hispanic and as Alaska Native, American Indian, Asian (who are also included in the "Asian" column), Native Hawaiian or other Pacific Islander, as well as non-Hispanics reporting more than one race. Subcategories may not add to total because some are not shown. "–" means sample is too small to make a reliable estimate.
Source: Bureau of Labor Statistics, unpublished tables from the 2004 Consumer Expenditure Survey

Table 11.18 Transportation: Indexed spending by race and Hispanic origin, 2004

(indexed average annual spending of consumer units (CU) on transportation, by race and Hispanic origin of consumer unit reference person, 2004; index definition: an index of 100 is the average for all consumer units; an index of 132 means that spending by consumer units in that group is 32 percent above the average for all consumer units; an index of 68 indicates spending that is 32 percent below the average for all consumer units)

	total consumer units	Asian	black	Hispanic	non-Hispanic white and other
Average spending of CU, total	$43,395	$49,459	$30,481	$37,578	$46,163
Average spending of CU, index	100	114	70	87	106
Transportation, spending index	100	110	64	96	106
VEHICLE PURCHASES	100	108	52	101	107
Cars and trucks, new	100	132	45	92	110
New cars	100	139	50	109	106
New trucks	100	128	42	81	112
Cars and trucks, used	100	86	61	116	104
Used cars	100	155	81	84	105
Used trucks	100	21	42	146	102
Other vehicles	100	23	19	12	124
GASOLINE AND MOTOR OIL	100	102	77	103	103
Gasoline	100	105	81	106	102
Diesel fuel	100	68	13	43	121
Gasoline on trips	100	84	40	79	112
Motor oil	100	62	58	127	103
Motor oil on trips	100	84	40	79	113
OTHER VEHICLE EXPENSES	100	98	72	87	106
Vehicle finance charges	100	80	74	88	105
Automobile finance charges	100	105	105	81	102
Truck finance charges	100	72	59	103	106
Motorcycle and plane finance charges	100	–	27	49	118
Other vehicle finance charges	100	3	1	17	126
Maintenance and repairs	100	108	66	88	107
Coolant, additives, brake and transmission fluids	100	86	84	137	98
Tires—purchased, replaced, installed	100	86	62	95	106
Parts, equipment, and accessories	100	63	44	114	107
Vehicle audio equipment, excluding labor	100	–	157	9	105
Vehicle products	100	43	81	48	110
Miscellaneous auto repair, servicing	100	140	67	40	113
Body work and painting	100	134	68	105	105
Clutch and transmission repair	100	75	47	94	109
Drive shaft and rear-end repair	100	44	70	57	111
Brake work	100	111	70	79	108
Repair to steering or front-end	100	100	55	85	109
Repair to engine cooling system	100	93	75	92	105
Motor tune-up	100	139	77	78	106
Lube, oil change, and oil filters	100	115	64	83	108
Front-end alignment, wheel balance, rotation	100	96	72	75	108
Shock absorber replacement	100	111	46	86	111
Gas tank repair, replacement	100	170	61	117	104
Tire repair and other repair work	100	95	71	83	107
Vehicle air conditioning repair	100	104	80	93	104
Exhaust system repair	100	88	57	69	111
Electrical system repair	100	99	53	86	109
Motor repair, replacement	100	148	63	126	102
Auto repair service policy	100	208	116	40	105
Vehicle insurance	100	99	77	90	105

	total consumer units	Asian	black	Hispanic	non-Hispanic white and other
Vehicle rental, leases, licenses, other charges	**100**	**97**	**66**	**76**	**108**
Leased and rented vehicles	100	84	79	67	108
Rented vehicles	100	133	72	69	108
Auto rental	100	45	143	92	94
Auto rental on trips	100	198	38	56	115
Truck rental	100	85	185	25	97
Truck rental on trips	100	57	60	4	119
Leased vehicles	100	75	80	67	107
Car lease payments	100	55	84	39	110
Truck lease payments	100	105	81	92	104
Vehicle registration, state	100	93	40	93	110
Vehicle registration, local	100	60	86	65	107
Driver's license	100	89	58	77	109
Vehicle inspection	100	126	49	103	107
Parking fees	100	180	53	61	113
Parking fees in home city, excluding residence	100	188	57	61	112
Parking fees on trips	100	142	34	62	115
Tolls	100	180	36	150	103
Tolls on trips	100	128	66	70	110
Towing charges	100	99	125	138	95
Automobile service clubs	100	95	43	63	114
PUBLIC TRANSPORTATION	**100**	**207**	**66**	**80**	**108**
Airline fares	100	228	46	81	111
Intercity bus fares	100	148	81	87	104
Intracity mass transit fares	100	278	194	144	80
Local transportation on trips	100	186	40	42	117
Taxi fares and limousine service on trips	100	186	40	42	117
Taxi fares and limousine service	100	35	106	114	101
Intercity train fares	100	149	57	31	116
Ship fares	100	144	45	30	118
School bus	100	166	172	215	73

Note: "Asian" and "black" include Hispanics and non-Hispanics who identify themselves as being of the respective race alone. "Hispanic" includes people of any race who identify themselves as Hispanic. "Other" includes people who identify themselves as non-Hispanic and as Alaska Native, American Indian, Asian (who are also included in the "Asian" column), Native Hawaiian or other Pacific Islander, as well as non-Hispanics reporting more than one race. "–" means sample is too small to make a reliable estimate.
Source: Calculations by New Strategist based on the 2004 Consumer Expenditure Survey

Table 11.19 Transportation: Total spending by race and Hispanic origin, 2004

(total annual spending on transportation, by consumer unit race and Hispanic origin groups, 2004; consumer units and dollars in thousands)

	total consumer units	Asian	black	Hispanic	non-Hispanic white and other
Number of consumer units	116,282	3,957	13,773	12,298	90,424
Total spending of all consumer units	$5,046,042,273	$195,707,997	$419,821,562	$462,134,613	$4,174,266,622
Transportation, total spending	907,160,069	33,857,991	68,539,406	92,201,672	748,047,008
VEHICLE PURCHASES	395,018,094	14,546,011	24,227,533	42,364,765	329,050,223
Cars and trucks, new	203,305,123	9,129,353	10,827,368	19,724,885	173,378,073
New cars	78,242,669	3,696,036	4,660,508	9,055,878	64,525,662
New trucks	125,062,454	5,433,317	6,166,861	10,669,007	108,852,411
Cars and trucks, used	183,987,195	5,356,907	13,225,386	22,540,143	148,220,308
Used cars	88,444,089	4,678,717	8,524,798	7,818,331	72,100,481
Used trucks	95,541,942	678,190	4,700,449	14,721,813	76,119,827
Other vehicles	7,726,939	59,751	174,779	99,860	7,451,842
GASOLINE AND MOTOR OIL	185,767,472	6,478,598	16,954,012	20,288,380	148,808,064
Gasoline	170,532,204	6,064,894	16,292,495	19,056,366	135,449,727
Diesel fuel	2,383,781	54,963	36,085	108,714	2,238,898
Gasoline on trips	11,668,899	333,100	547,477	972,895	10,162,753
Motor oil	1,047,701	22,238	72,446	140,566	837,326
Motor oil on trips	117,445	3,363	5,509	9,838	103,083
OTHER VEHICLE EXPENSES	275,054,606	9,219,414	23,361,074	25,188,026	227,059,185
Vehicle finance charges	37,606,762	1,028,464	3,311,993	3,499,396	30,831,871
Automobile finance charges	15,498,065	552,872	1,934,142	1,328,430	12,256,069
Truck finance charges	19,407,466	473,534	1,363,665	2,109,476	15,949,889
Motorcycle and plane finance charges	380,242	–	11,983	19,800	348,132
Other vehicle finance charges	2,322,152	2,058	2,204	41,690	2,277,781
Maintenance and repairs	75,776,328	2,775,677	5,886,856	7,058,929	63,039,092
Coolant, additives, brake and transmission fluids	340,706	9,972	34,019	49,315	258,613
Tires—purchased, replaced, installed	10,940,973	320,280	799,936	1,095,998	9,053,251
Parts, equipment, and accessories	5,003,614	107,353	258,657	602,479	4,147,749
Vehicle audio equipment, excluding labor	962,815	–	178,636	8,732	786,689
Vehicle products	501,175	7,320	47,930	25,334	429,514
Miscellaneous auto repair, servicing	5,844,333	277,584	465,390	246,452	5,153,264
Body work and painting	4,244,293	194,012	341,019	471,997	3,464,143
Clutch and transmission repair	4,566,394	116,613	254,250	452,689	3,869,243
Drive shaft and rear-end repair	722,111	10,882	59,499	43,535	624,830
Brake work	5,181,526	196,030	430,682	432,521	4,343,065
Repair to steering or front-end	1,766,324	59,830	115,693	159,382	1,498,326
Repair to engine cooling system	2,087,262	66,319	185,522	203,655	1,705,397
Motor tune-up	4,857,099	229,625	442,389	403,005	4,020,251
Lube, oil change, and oil filters	6,538,537	256,453	498,996	576,776	5,471,556
Front-end alignment, wheel balance, rotation	1,061,655	34,505	90,213	84,487	889,772
Shock absorber replacement	320,938	12,148	17,492	29,269	275,793
Gas tank repair, replacement	386,056	22,317	27,959	47,716	311,059
Tire repair and other repair work	5,805,960	187,364	487,564	507,538	4,820,503
Vehicle air conditioning repair	1,654,693	58,405	157,012	163,317	1,340,084
Exhaust system repair	1,184,914	35,336	79,883	86,332	1,019,078
Electrical system repair	2,620,996	88,439	165,414	239,688	2,231,664
Motor repair, replacement	8,130,437	410,460	604,635	1,083,700	6,461,699
Auto repair service policy	1,052,352	74,431	144,203	44,888	862,645
Vehicle insurance	112,138,872	3,776,363	10,261,849	10,632,113	91,469,301

	total consumer units	Asian	black	Hispanic	non-Hispanic white and other
Vehicle rental, leases, licenses, other charges	**$49,531,481**	**$1,638,910**	**$3,900,238**	**$3,997,711**	**$41,718,921**
Leased and rented vehicles	29,634,468	847,431	2,762,451	2,109,968	24,796,974
Rented vehicles	4,450,112	202,005	378,482	324,052	3,747,171
Auto rental	655,830	10,011	111,010	63,827	481,056
Auto rental on trips	2,462,853	165,996	109,495	146,100	2,207,250
Truck rental	548,851	15,868	120,238	14,389	414,142
Truck rental on trips	527,920	10,169	37,738	2,460	487,385
Leased vehicles	25,184,356	645,426	2,383,969	1,785,793	21,049,803
Car lease payments	12,178,214	229,427	1,211,335	504,095	10,462,057
Truck lease payments	11,167,723	397,679	1,076,222	1,082,593	9,044,208
Vehicle registration, state	9,409,539	297,685	442,526	928,007	8,045,023
Vehicle registration, local	802,346	16,422	81,949	54,972	667,329
Driver's license	832,579	25,325	56,882	67,762	708,924
Vehicle inspection	1,080,260	46,218	63,080	117,569	901,527
Parking fees	3,419,854	209,127	212,931	222,225	3,002,077
Parking fees in home city, excluding residence	2,775,651	178,025	186,900	180,289	2,426,076
Parking fees on trips	644,202	31,062	26,031	41,936	576,001
Tolls	1,697,717	103,990	72,997	269,818	1,355,456
Tolls on trips	538,386	23,425	42,008	39,846	459,354
Towing charges	590,713	19,943	87,596	86,455	434,939
Automobile service clubs	1,525,620	49,344	77,955	101,090	1,347,318
PUBLIC TRANSPORTATION	**51,318,735**	**3,614,007**	**3,996,925**	**4,360,379**	**43,129,535**
Airline fares	32,086,855	2,493,187	1,749,584	2,754,014	27,649,851
Intercity bus fares	1,087,237	54,884	104,950	100,106	882,538
Intracity mass transit fares	5,386,182	510,136	1,235,163	819,908	3,352,018
Local transportation on trips	1,162,820	73,481	54,403	52,021	1,056,152
Taxi fares and limousine service on trips	682,575	43,171	31,953	30,622	620,309
Taxi fares and limousine service	2,695,417	32,091	337,576	326,389	2,112,305
Intercity train fares	2,074,471	105,019	139,520	67,024	1,867,256
Ship fares	6,058,292	297,171	326,282	190,742	5,540,278
School bus	86,049	4,867	17,492	19,554	48,829

Note: "Asian" and "black" include Hispanics and non-Hispanics who identify themselves as being of the respective race alone. "Hispanic" includes people of any race who identify themselves as Hispanic. "Other" includes people who identify themselves as non-Hispanic and as Alaska Native, American Indian, Asian (who are also included in the "Asian" column), Native Hawaiian or other Pacific Islander, as well as non-Hispanics reporting more than one race. Numbers may not add to total because of rounding and missing subcategories. "–" means sample is too small to make a reliable estimate.
Source: Calculations by New Strategist based on the 2004 Consumer Expenditure Survey

Table 11.20 Transportation: Market shares by race and Hispanic origin, 2004

(percentage of total annual spending on transportation accounted for by consumer unit race and Hispanic origin groups, 2004)

	total consumer units	Asian	black	Hispanic	non-Hispanic white and other
Share of total consumer units	100.0%	3.4%	11.8%	10.6%	77.8%
Share of total before-tax income	100.0	4.2	8.4	8.5	83.3
Share of total spending	100.0	3.9	8.3	9.2	82.7
Share of transportation spending	100.0	3.7	7.6	10.2	82.5
VEHICLE PURCHASES	100.0	3.7	6.1	10.7	83.3
Cars and trucks, new	100.0	4.5	5.3	9.7	85.3
New cars	100.0	4.7	6.0	11.6	82.5
New trucks	100.0	4.3	4.9	8.5	87.0
Cars and trucks, used	100.0	2.9	7.2	12.3	80.6
Used cars	100.0	5.3	9.6	8.8	81.5
Used trucks	100.0	0.7	4.9	15.4	79.7
Other vehicles	100.0	0.8	2.3	1.3	96.4
GASOLINE AND MOTOR OIL	100.0	3.5	9.1	10.9	80.1
Gasoline	100.0	3.6	9.6	11.2	79.4
Diesel fuel	100.0	2.3	1.5	4.6	93.9
Gasoline on trips	100.0	2.9	4.7	8.3	87.1
Motor oil	100.0	2.1	6.9	13.4	79.9
Motor oil on trips	100.0	2.9	4.7	8.4	87.8
OTHER VEHICLE EXPENSES	100.0	3.4	8.5	9.2	82.6
Vehicle finance charges	100.0	2.7	8.8	9.3	82.0
Automobile finance charges	100.0	3.6	12.5	8.6	79.1
Truck finance charges	100.0	2.4	7.0	10.9	82.2
Motorcycle and plane finance charges	100.0	–	3.2	5.2	91.6
Other vehicle finance charges	100.0	0.1	0.1	1.8	98.1
Maintenance and repairs	100.0	3.7	7.8	9.3	83.2
Coolant, additives, brake and transmission fluids	100.0	2.9	10.0	14.5	75.9
Tires—purchased, replaced, installed	100.0	2.9	7.3	10.0	82.7
Parts, equipment, and accessories	100.0	2.1	5.2	12.0	82.9
Vehicle audio equipment, excluding labor	100.0	–	18.6	0.9	81.7
Vehicle products	100.0	1.5	9.6	5.1	85.7
Miscellaneous auto repair, servicing	100.0	4.7	8.0	4.2	88.2
Body work and painting	100.0	4.6	8.0	11.1	81.6
Clutch and transmission repair	100.0	2.6	5.6	9.9	84.7
Drive shaft and rear-end repair	100.0	1.5	8.2	6.0	86.5
Brake work	100.0	3.8	8.3	8.3	83.8
Repair to steering or front-end	100.0	3.4	6.5	9.0	84.8
Repair to engine cooling system	100.0	3.2	8.9	9.8	81.7
Motor tune-up	100.0	4.7	9.1	8.3	82.8
Lube, oil change, and oil filters	100.0	3.9	7.6	8.8	83.7
Front-end alignment, wheel balance, rotation	100.0	3.3	8.5	8.0	83.8
Shock absorber replacement	100.0	3.8	5.5	9.1	85.9
Gas tank repair, replacement	100.0	5.8	7.2	12.4	80.6
Tire repair and other repair work	100.0	3.2	8.4	8.7	83.0
Vehicle air conditioning repair	100.0	3.5	9.5	9.9	81.0
Exhaust system repair	100.0	3.0	6.7	7.3	86.0
Electrical system repair	100.0	3.4	6.3	9.1	85.1
Motor repair, replacement	100.0	5.0	7.4	13.3	79.5
Auto repair service policy	100.0	7.1	13.7	4.3	82.0
Vehicle insurance	100.0	3.4	9.2	9.5	81.6

	total consumer units	Asian	black	Hispanic	non-Hispanic white and other
Vehicle rental, leases, licenses, other charges	**100.0%**	**3.3%**	**7.9%**	**8.1%**	**84.2%**
Leased and rented vehicles	100.0	2.9	9.3	7.1	83.7
Rented vehicles	100.0	4.5	8.5	7.3	84.2
Auto rental	100.0	1.5	16.9	9.7	73.4
Auto rental on trips	100.0	6.7	4.4	5.9	89.6
Truck rental	100.0	2.9	21.9	2.6	75.5
Truck rental on trips	100.0	1.9	7.1	0.5	92.3
Leased vehicles	100.0	2.6	9.5	7.1	83.6
Car lease payments	100.0	1.9	9.9	4.1	85.9
Truck lease payments	100.0	3.6	9.6	9.7	81.0
Vehicle registration, state	100.0	3.2	4.7	9.9	85.5
Vehicle registration, local	100.0	2.0	10.2	6.9	83.2
Driver's license	100.0	3.0	6.8	8.1	85.1
Vehicle inspection	100.0	4.3	5.8	10.9	83.5
Parking fees	100.0	6.1	6.2	6.5	87.8
Parking fees in home city, excluding residence	100.0	6.4	6.7	6.5	87.4
Parking fees on trips	100.0	4.8	4.0	6.5	89.4
Tolls	100.0	6.1	4.3	15.9	79.8
Tolls on trips	100.0	4.4	7.8	7.4	85.3
Towing charges	100.0	3.4	14.8	14.6	73.6
Automobile service clubs	100.0	3.2	5.1	6.6	88.3
PUBLIC TRANSPORTATION	**100.0**	**7.0**	**7.8**	**8.5**	**84.0**
Airline fares	100.0	7.8	5.5	8.6	86.2
Intercity bus fares	100.0	5.0	9.7	9.2	81.2
Intracity mass transit fares	100.0	9.5	22.9	15.2	62.2
Local transportation on trips	100.0	6.3	4.7	4.5	90.8
Taxi fares and limousine service on trips	100.0	6.3	4.7	4.5	90.9
Taxi fares and limousine service	100.0	1.2	12.5	12.1	78.4
Intercity train fares	100.0	5.1	6.7	3.2	90.0
Ship fares	100.0	4.9	5.4	3.1	91.4
School bus	100.0	5.7	20.3	22.7	56.7

Note: "Asian" and "black" include Hispanics and non-Hispanics who identify themselves as being of the respective race alone. "Hispanic" includes people of any race who identify themselves as Hispanic. "Other" includes people who identify themselves as non-Hispanic and as Alaska Native, American Indian, Asian (who are also included in the "Asian" column), Native Hawaiian or other Pacific Islander, as well as non-Hispanics reporting more than one race. "–" means sample is too small to make a reliable estimate.
Source: Calculations by New Strategist based on the 2004 Consumer Expenditure Survey

Table 11.21 Transportation: Average spending by region, 2004

(average annual spending of consumer units (CU) on transportation, by region in which consumer unit lives, 2004)

	total consumer units	Northeast	Midwest	South	West
Number of consumer units (in 000s)	116,282	22,051	26,539	41,801	25,891
Average number of persons per CU	2.5	2.4	2.4	2.5	2.6
Average before-tax income of CU	$54,453.00	$61,050.00	$53,567.00	$50,775.00	$55,682.00
Average spending of CU, total	43,394.87	46,114.89	43,370.77	39,173.65	47,921.74
Transportation, average spending	**7,801.38**	**7,621.85**	**7,709.79**	**7,232.79**	**8,965.53**
VEHICLE PURCHASES	**3,397.07**	**3,195.56**	**3,314.52**	**3,195.14**	**3,979.34**
Cars and trucks, new	**1,748.38**	**1,589.79**	**1,609.89**	**1,626.94**	**2,221.47**
New cars	672.87	656.35	515.94	626.47	922.72
New trucks	1,075.51	933.45	1,093.95	1,000.47	1,298.75
Cars and trucks, used	**1,582.25**	**1,511.89**	**1,621.23**	**1,520.10**	**1,702.55**
Used cars	760.60	871.33	767.36	627.63	874.07
Used trucks	821.64	640.56	853.87	892.48	828.47
Other vehicles	**66.45**	**93.88**	**83.40**	**48.10**	**55.32**
GASOLINE AND MOTOR OIL	**1,597.56**	**1,385.91**	**1,619.57**	**1,597.72**	**1,755.00**
Gasoline	1,466.54	1,304.04	1,476.52	1,479.64	1,573.54
Diesel fuel	20.50	10.41	16.40	19.66	34.65
Gasoline on trips	100.35	65.81	114.01	88.51	134.90
Motor oil	9.01	4.98	10.87	9.02	10.55
Motor oil on trips	1.01	0.66	1.15	0.89	1.36
OTHER VEHICLE EXPENSES	**2,365.41**	**2,396.38**	**2,412.88**	**2,160.00**	**2,621.74**
Vehicle finance charges	**323.41**	**256.23**	**331.38**	**357.27**	**317.82**
Automobile finance charges	133.28	110.02	129.87	147.39	133.78
Truck finance charges	166.90	127.35	174.71	187.46	159.38
Motorcycle and plane finance charges	3.27	2.79	3.41	3.97	2.40
Other vehicle finance charges	19.97	16.06	23.38	18.44	22.26
Maintenance and repairs	**651.66**	**590.35**	**653.79**	**577.75**	**820.93**
Coolant, additives, brake and transmission fluids	2.93	2.04	3.60	2.92	3.04
Tires—purchased, replaced, installed	94.09	75.30	96.34	86.78	119.58
Parts, equipment, and accessories	43.03	23.86	40.99	39.39	67.34
Vehicle audio equipment, excluding labor	8.28	5.42	8.49	12.61	3.47
Vehicle products	4.31	4.42	5.13	4.54	2.99
Miscellaneous auto repair, servicing	50.26	37.97	54.38	59.35	41.76
Body work and painting	36.50	36.21	29.37	33.00	49.71
Clutch and transmission repair	39.27	28.71	41.57	38.39	47.32
Drive shaft and rear-end repair	6.21	4.23	6.41	4.68	10.14
Brake work	44.56	50.73	47.30	35.61	50.96
Repair to steering or front-end	15.19	20.23	13.83	10.31	20.17
Repair to engine cooling system	17.95	16.92	18.12	14.15	24.79
Motor tune-up	41.77	41.05	34.56	30.15	68.53
Lube, oil change, and oil filters	56.23	48.53	64.01	49.74	65.29
Front-end alignment, wheel balance, rotation	9.13	8.39	10.13	6.15	13.53
Shock absorber replacement	2.76	2.67	2.79	1.09	5.50
Gas tank repair, replacement	3.32	2.94	2.76	2.52	5.53
Tire repair and other repair work	49.93	49.55	49.56	41.52	64.22
Vehicle air conditioning repair	14.23	11.11	14.38	13.99	17.14
Exhaust system repair	10.19	16.06	10.92	6.25	10.80
Electrical system repair	22.54	18.50	25.12	18.14	30.45
Motor repair, replacement	69.92	80.73	63.00	58.28	86.62
Auto repair service policy	9.05	4.77	11.04	8.17	12.06
Vehicle insurance	**964.37**	**990.94**	**923.56**	**943.97**	**1,016.54**

	total consumer units	Northeast	Midwest	South	West
Vehicle rental, leases, licenses, other charges	**$425.96**	**$558.87**	**$504.16**	**$281.01**	**$466.45**
Leased and rented vehicles	254.85	370.98	311.77	156.33	256.64
Rented vehicles	38.27	37.69	34.13	29.54	57.08
Auto rental	5.64	9.59	3.14	4.93	5.99
Auto rental on trips	21.18	20.86	20.77	12.94	35.18
Truck rental	4.72	5.10	3.19	5.07	5.38
Truck rental on trips	4.54	2.12	3.89	3.83	8.41
Leased vehicles	216.58	333.29	277.64	126.79	199.56
Car lease payments	104.73	174.82	116.20	61.00	103.88
Truck lease payments	96.04	132.38	140.60	56.73	82.86
Vehicle registration, state	80.92	39.63	112.52	56.56	123.02
Vehicle registration, local	6.90	3.09	5.66	12.54	2.30
Driver's license	7.16	10.39	6.65	5.63	7.41
Vehicle inspection	9.29	18.75	2.89	7.29	11.04
Parking fees	29.41	44.94	33.27	18.42	29.98
Parking fees in home city, excluding residence	23.87	38.04	27.82	13.85	23.95
Parking fees on trips	5.54	6.90	5.45	4.56	6.04
Tolls	14.60	38.91	9.96	8.82	7.83
Tolls on trips	4.63	9.03	3.96	3.70	3.05
Towing charges	5.08	5.40	4.31	4.24	6.97
Automobile service clubs	13.12	17.76	13.16	7.49	18.21
PUBLIC TRANSPORTATION	**441.33**	**643.99**	**362.82**	**279.93**	**609.46**
Airline fares	275.94	296.45	239.17	193.79	428.81
Intercity bus fares	9.35	10.79	6.78	7.39	13.91
Intracity mass transit fares	46.32	145.43	23.72	14.33	36.71
Local transportation on trips	10.00	14.41	9.68	5.85	13.26
Taxi fares and limousine service on trips	5.87	8.46	5.69	3.43	7.79
Taxi fares and limousine service	23.18	76.18	16.64	5.42	13.08
Intercity train fares	17.84	25.25	13.16	12.31	25.24
Ship fares	52.10	65.84	47.16	36.87	70.03
School bus	0.74	1.17	0.81	0.54	0.63

Note: Subcategories may not add to total because some are not shown.
Source: Bureau of Labor Statistics, unpublished tables from the 2004 Consumer Expenditure Survey

Table 11.22 Transportation: Indexed spending by region, 2004

(indexed average annual spending of consumer units (CU) on transportation, by region in which consumer unit lives, 2004; index definition: an index of 100 is the average for all consumer units; an index of 132 means that spending by consumer units in that group is 32 percent above the average for all consumer units; an index of 68 indicates spending that is 32 percent below the average for all consumer units)

	total consumer units	Northeast	Midwest	South	West
Average spending of CU, total	$43,395	$46,115	$43,371	$39,174	$47,922
Average spending of CU, index	100	106	100	90	110
Transportation, spending index	100	98	99	93	115
VEHICLE PURCHASES	100	94	98	94	117
Cars and trucks, new	100	91	92	93	127
New cars	100	98	77	93	137
New trucks	100	87	102	93	121
Cars and trucks, used	100	96	102	96	108
Used cars	100	115	101	83	115
Used trucks	100	78	104	109	101
Other vehicles	100	141	126	72	83
GASOLINE AND MOTOR OIL	100	87	101	100	110
Gasoline	100	89	101	101	107
Diesel fuel	100	51	80	96	169
Gasoline on trips	100	66	114	88	134
Motor oil	100	55	121	100	117
Motor oil on trips	100	65	114	88	135
OTHER VEHICLE EXPENSES	100	101	102	91	111
Vehicle finance charges	100	79	102	110	98
Automobile finance charges	100	83	97	111	100
Truck finance charges	100	76	105	112	95
Motorcycle and plane finance charges	100	85	104	121	73
Other vehicle finance charges	100	80	117	92	111
Maintenance and repairs	100	91	100	89	126
Coolant, additives, brake and transmission fluids	100	70	123	100	104
Tires—purchased, replaced, installed	100	80	102	92	127
Parts, equipment, and accessories	100	55	95	92	156
Vehicle audio equipment, excluding labor	100	65	103	152	42
Vehicle products	100	103	119	105	69
Miscellaneous auto repair, servicing	100	76	108	118	83
Body work and painting	100	99	80	90	136
Clutch and transmission repair	100	73	106	98	120
Drive shaft and rear-end repair	100	68	103	75	163
Brake work	100	114	106	80	114
Repair to steering or front-end	100	133	91	68	133
Repair to engine cooling system	100	94	101	79	138
Motor tune-up	100	98	83	72	164
Lube, oil change, and oil filters	100	86	114	88	116
Front-end alignment, wheel balance, rotation	100	92	111	67	148
Shock absorber replacement	100	97	101	39	199
Gas tank repair, replacement	100	89	83	76	167
Tire repair and other repair work	100	99	99	83	129
Vehicle air conditioning repair	100	78	101	98	120
Exhaust system repair	100	158	107	61	106
Electrical system repair	100	82	111	80	135
Motor repair, replacement	100	115	90	83	124
Auto repair service policy	100	53	122	90	133
Vehicle insurance	100	103	96	98	105

	total consumer units	Northeast	Midwest	South	West
Vehicle rental, leases, licenses, other charges	**100**	**131**	**118**	**66**	**110**
Leased and rented vehicles	100	146	122	61	101
Rented vehicles	100	98	89	77	149
Auto rental	100	170	56	87	106
Auto rental on trips	100	98	98	61	166
Truck rental	100	108	68	107	114
Truck rental on trips	100	47	86	84	185
Leased vehicles	100	154	128	59	92
Car lease payments	100	167	111	58	99
Truck lease payments	100	138	146	59	86
Vehicle registration, state	100	49	139	70	152
Vehicle registration, local	100	45	82	182	33
Driver's license	100	145	93	79	103
Vehicle inspection	100	202	31	78	119
Parking fees	100	153	113	63	102
Parking fees in home city, excluding residence	100	159	117	58	100
Parking fees on trips	100	125	98	82	109
Tolls	100	267	68	60	54
Tolls on trips	100	195	86	80	66
Towing charges	100	106	85	83	137
Automobile service clubs	100	135	100	57	139
PUBLIC TRANSPORTATION	**100**	**146**	**82**	**63**	**138**
Airline fares	100	107	87	70	155
Intercity bus fares	100	115	73	79	149
Intracity mass transit fares	100	314	51	31	79
Local transportation on trips	100	144	97	59	133
Taxi fares and limousine service on trips	100	144	97	58	133
Taxi fares and limousine service	100	329	72	23	56
Intercity train fares	100	142	74	69	141
Ship fares	100	126	91	71	134
School bus	100	158	109	73	85

Source: Calculations by New Strategist based on the 2004 Consumer Expenditure Survey

Table 11.23 Transportation: Total spending by region, 2004

(total annual spending on transportation, by region in which consumer units live, 2004; consumer units and dollars in thousands)

	total consumer units	Northeast	Midwest	South	West
Number of consumer units	116,282	22,051	26,539	41,801	25,891
Total spending of all consumer units	$5,046,042,273	$1,016,879,439	$1,151,016,865	$1,637,497,744	$1,240,741,770
Transportation, total spending	907,160,069	168,069,414	204,610,117	302,337,855	232,126,537
VEHICLE PURCHASES	395,018,094	70,465,294	87,964,046	133,560,047	103,029,092
Cars and trucks, new	203,305,123	35,056,459	42,724,871	68,007,719	57,516,080
New cars	78,242,669	14,473,174	13,692,532	26,187,072	23,890,144
New trucks	125,062,454	20,583,506	29,032,339	41,820,646	33,625,936
Cars and trucks, used	183,987,195	33,338,686	43,025,823	63,541,700	44,080,722
Used cars	88,444,089	19,213,698	20,364,967	26,235,562	22,630,546
Used trucks	95,541,942	14,124,989	22,660,856	37,306,556	21,449,917
Other vehicles	7,726,939	2,070,148	2,213,353	2,010,628	1,432,290
GASOLINE AND MOTOR OIL	185,767,472	30,560,701	42,981,768	66,786,294	45,438,705
Gasoline	170,532,204	28,755,386	39,185,364	61,850,432	40,740,524
Diesel fuel	2,383,781	229,551	435,240	821,808	897,123
Gasoline on trips	11,668,899	1,451,176	3,025,711	3,699,807	3,492,696
Motor oil	1,047,701	109,814	288,479	377,045	273,150
Motor oil on trips	117,445	14,554	30,520	37,203	35,212
OTHER VEHICLE EXPENSES	275,054,606	52,842,575	64,035,422	90,290,160	67,879,470
Vehicle finance charges	37,606,762	5,650,128	8,794,494	14,934,243	8,228,678
Automobile finance charges	15,498,065	2,426,051	3,446,620	6,161,049	3,463,698
Truck finance charges	19,407,466	2,808,195	4,636,629	7,836,015	4,126,508
Motorcycle and plane finance charges	380,242	61,522	90,498	165,950	62,138
Other vehicle finance charges	2,322,152	354,139	620,482	770,810	576,334
Maintenance and repairs	75,776,328	13,017,808	17,350,933	24,150,528	21,254,699
Coolant, additives, brake and transmission fluids	340,706	44,984	95,540	122,059	78,709
Tires—purchased, replaced, installed	10,940,973	1,660,440	2,556,767	3,627,491	3,096,046
Parts, equipment, and accessories	5,003,614	526,137	1,087,834	1,646,541	1,743,500
Vehicle audio equipment, excluding labor	962,815	119,516	225,316	527,111	89,842
Vehicle products	501,175	97,465	136,145	189,777	77,414
Miscellaneous auto repair, servicing	5,844,333	837,276	1,443,191	2,480,889	1,081,208
Body work and painting	4,244,293	798,467	779,450	1,379,433	1,287,042
Clutch and transmission repair	4,566,394	633,084	1,103,226	1,604,740	1,225,162
Drive shaft and rear-end repair	722,111	93,276	170,115	195,629	262,535
Brake work	5,181,526	1,118,647	1,255,295	1,488,534	1,319,405
Repair to steering or front-end	1,766,324	446,092	367,034	430,968	522,221
Repair to engine cooling system	2,087,262	373,103	480,887	591,484	641,838
Motor tune-up	4,857,099	905,194	917,188	1,260,300	1,774,310
Lube, oil change, and oil filters	6,538,537	1,070,135	1,698,761	2,079,182	1,690,423
Front-end alignment, wheel balance, rotation	1,061,655	185,008	268,840	257,076	350,305
Shock absorber replacement	320,938	58,876	74,044	45,563	142,401
Gas tank repair, replacement	386,056	64,830	73,248	105,339	143,177
Tire repair and other repair work	5,805,960	1,092,627	1,315,273	1,735,578	1,662,720
Vehicle air conditioning repair	1,654,693	244,987	381,631	584,796	443,772
Exhaust system repair	1,184,914	354,139	289,806	261,256	279,623
Electrical system repair	2,620,996	407,944	666,660	758,270	788,381
Motor repair, replacement	8,130,437	1,780,177	1,671,957	2,436,162	2,242,678
Auto repair service policy	1,052,352	105,183	292,991	341,514	312,245
Vehicle insurance	112,138,872	21,851,218	24,510,359	39,458,890	26,319,237

	total consumer units	Northeast	Midwest	South	West
Vehicle rental, leases, licenses, other charges	**$49,531,481**	**$12,323,642**	**$13,379,902**	**$11,746,499**	**$12,076,857**
Leased and rented vehicles	29,634,468	8,180,480	8,274,064	6,534,750	6,644,666
Rented vehicles	4,450,112	831,102	905,776	1,234,802	1,477,858
Auto rental	655,830	211,469	83,332	206,079	155,087
Auto rental on trips	2,462,853	459,984	551,215	540,905	910,845
Truck rental	548,851	112,460	84,659	211,931	139,294
Truck rental on trips	527,920	46,748	103,237	160,098	217,743
Leased vehicles	25,184,356	7,349,378	7,368,288	5,299,949	5,166,808
Car lease payments	12,178,214	3,854,956	3,083,832	2,549,861	2,689,557
Truck lease payments	11,167,723	2,919,111	3,731,383	2,371,371	2,145,328
Vehicle registration, state	9,409,539	873,881	2,986,168	2,364,265	3,185,111
Vehicle registration, local	802,346	68,138	150,211	524,185	59,549
Driver's license	832,579	229,110	176,484	235,340	191,852
Vehicle inspection	1,080,260	413,456	76,698	304,729	285,837
Parking fees	3,419,854	990,972	882,953	769,974	776,212
Parking fees in home city, excluding residence	2,775,651	838,820	738,315	578,944	620,089
Parking fees on trips	644,202	152,152	144,638	190,613	156,382
Tolls	1,697,717	858,004	264,328	368,685	202,727
Tolls on trips	538,386	199,121	105,094	154,664	78,968
Towing charges	590,713	119,075	114,383	177,236	180,460
Automobile service clubs	1,525,620	391,626	349,253	313,089	471,475
PUBLIC TRANSPORTATION	**51,318,735**	**14,200,623**	**9,628,880**	**11,701,354**	**15,779,529**
Airline fares	32,086,855	6,537,019	6,347,333	8,100,616	11,102,320
Intercity bus fares	1,087,237	237,930	179,934	308,909	360,144
Intracity mass transit fares	5,386,182	3,206,877	629,505	599,008	950,459
Local transportation on trips	1,162,820	317,755	256,898	244,536	343,315
Taxi fares and limousine service on trips	682,575	186,551	151,007	143,377	201,691
Taxi fares and limousine service	2,695,417	1,679,845	441,609	226,561	338,654
Intercity train fares	2,074,471	556,788	349,253	514,570	653,489
Ship fares	6,058,292	1,451,838	1,251,579	1,541,203	1,813,147
School bus	86,049	25,800	21,497	22,573	16,311

Note: Numbers may not add to total because of rounding and missing subcategories.
Source: Calculations by New Strategist based on the 2004 Consumer Expenditure Survey

Table 11.24 Transportation: Market shares by region, 2004

(percentage of total annual spending on transportation accounted for by consumer units by region, 2004)

	total consumer units	Northeast	Midwest	South	West
Share of total consumer units	100.0%	19.0%	22.8%	35.9%	22.3%
Share of total before-tax income	100.0	21.3	22.5	33.5	22.8
Share of total spending	100.0	20.2	22.8	32.5	24.6
Share of transportation spending	100.0	18.5	22.6	33.3	25.6
VEHICLE PURCHASES	100.0	17.8	22.3	33.8	26.1
Cars and trucks, new	100.0	17.2	21.0	33.5	28.3
New cars	100.0	18.5	17.5	33.5	30.5
New trucks	100.0	16.5	23.2	33.4	26.9
Cars and trucks, used	100.0	18.1	23.4	34.5	24.0
Used cars	100.0	21.7	23.0	29.7	25.6
Used trucks	100.0	14.8	23.7	39.0	22.5
Other vehicles	100.0	26.8	28.6	26.0	18.5
GASOLINE AND MOTOR OIL	100.0	16.5	23.1	36.0	24.5
Gasoline	100.0	16.9	23.0	36.3	23.9
Diesel fuel	100.0	9.6	18.3	34.5	37.6
Gasoline on trips	100.0	12.4	25.9	31.7	29.9
Motor oil	100.0	10.5	27.5	36.0	26.1
Motor oil on trips	100.0	12.4	26.0	31.7	30.0
OTHER VEHICLE EXPENSES	100.0	19.2	23.3	32.8	24.7
Vehicle finance charges	100.0	15.0	23.4	39.7	21.9
Automobile finance charges	100.0	15.7	22.2	39.8	22.3
Truck finance charges	100.0	14.5	23.9	40.4	21.3
Motorcycle and plane finance charges	100.0	16.2	23.8	43.6	16.3
Other vehicle finance charges	100.0	15.3	26.7	33.2	24.8
Maintenance and repairs	100.0	17.2	22.9	31.9	28.0
Coolant, additives, brake and transmission fluids	100.0	13.2	28.0	35.8	23.1
Tires—purchased, replaced, installed	100.0	15.2	23.4	33.2	28.3
Parts, equipment, and accessories	100.0	10.5	21.7	32.9	34.8
Vehicle audio equipment, excluding labor	100.0	12.4	23.4	54.7	9.3
Vehicle products	100.0	19.4	27.2	37.9	15.4
Miscellaneous auto repair, servicing	100.0	14.3	24.7	42.4	18.5
Body work and painting	100.0	18.8	18.4	32.5	30.3
Clutch and transmission repair	100.0	13.9	24.2	35.1	26.8
Drive shaft and rear-end repair	100.0	12.9	23.6	27.1	36.4
Brake work	100.0	21.6	24.2	28.7	25.5
Repair to steering or front-end	100.0	25.3	20.8	24.4	29.6
Repair to engine cooling system	100.0	17.9	23.0	28.3	30.8
Motor tune-up	100.0	18.6	18.9	25.9	36.5
Lube, oil change, and oil filters	100.0	16.4	26.0	31.8	25.9
Front-end alignment, wheel balance, rotation	100.0	17.4	25.3	24.2	33.0
Shock absorber replacement	100.0	18.3	23.1	14.2	44.4
Gas tank repair, replacement	100.0	16.8	19.0	27.3	37.1
Tire repair and other repair work	100.0	18.8	22.7	29.9	28.6
Vehicle air conditioning repair	100.0	14.8	23.1	35.3	26.8
Exhaust system repair	100.0	29.9	24.5	22.0	23.6
Electrical system repair	100.0	15.6	25.4	28.9	30.1
Motor repair, replacement	100.0	21.9	20.6	30.0	27.6
Auto repair service policy	100.0	10.0	27.8	32.5	29.7
Vehicle insurance	100.0	19.5	21.9	35.2	23.5

	total consumer units	Northeast	Midwest	South	West
Vehicle rental, leases, licenses, other charges	**100.0%**	**24.9%**	**27.0%**	**23.7%**	**24.4%**
Leased and rented vehicles	100.0	27.6	27.9	22.1	22.4
Rented vehicles	100.0	18.7	20.4	27.7	33.2
Auto rental	100.0	32.2	12.7	31.4	23.6
Auto rental on trips	100.0	18.7	22.4	22.0	37.0
Truck rental	100.0	20.5	15.4	38.6	25.4
Truck rental on trips	100.0	8.9	19.6	30.3	41.2
Leased vehicles	100.0	29.2	29.3	21.0	20.5
Car lease payments	100.0	31.7	25.3	20.9	22.1
Truck lease payments	100.0	26.1	33.4	21.2	19.2
Vehicle registration, state	100.0	9.3	31.7	25.1	33.8
Vehicle registration, local	100.0	8.5	18.7	65.3	7.4
Driver's license	100.0	27.5	21.2	28.3	23.0
Vehicle inspection	100.0	38.3	7.1	28.2	26.5
Parking fees	100.0	29.0	25.8	22.5	22.7
Parking fees in home city, excluding residence	100.0	30.2	26.6	20.9	22.3
Parking fees on trips	100.0	23.6	22.5	29.6	24.3
Tolls	100.0	50.5	15.6	21.7	11.9
Tolls on trips	100.0	37.0	19.5	28.7	14.7
Towing charges	100.0	20.2	19.4	30.0	30.5
Automobile service clubs	100.0	25.7	22.9	20.5	30.9
PUBLIC TRANSPORTATION	**100.0**	**27.7**	**18.8**	**22.8**	**30.7**
Airline fares	100.0	20.4	19.8	25.2	34.6
Intercity bus fares	100.0	21.9	16.5	28.4	33.1
Intracity mass transit fares	100.0	59.5	11.7	11.1	17.6
Local transportation on trips	100.0	27.3	22.1	21.0	29.5
Taxi fares and limousine service on trips	100.0	27.3	22.1	21.0	29.5
Taxi fares and limousine service	100.0	62.3	16.4	8.4	12.6
Intercity train fares	100.0	26.8	16.8	24.8	31.5
Ship fares	100.0	24.0	20.7	25.4	29.9
School bus	100.0	30.0	25.0	26.2	19.0

Note: Numbers may not add to total because of rounding.
Source: Calculations by New Strategist based on the 2004 Consumer Expenditure Survey

Table 11.25 Transportation: Average spending by education, 2004

(average annual spending of consumer units (CU) on transportation, by education of consumer unit reference person, 2004)

	total consumer units	less than high school graduate	high school graduate	some college	associate's degree	college graduate total	bachelor's degree	master's, professional, doctorate
Number of consumer units (in 000s)	116,282	16,829	31,005	25,317	10,678	32,452	20,684	11,768
Average number of per sons per CU	2.5	2.7	2.5	2.3	2.6	2.5	2.4	2.5
Average before-tax income of CU	$54,453.00	$29,094.00	$42,334.00	$46,756.00	$58,593.00	$83,825.00	$75,647.00	$98,201.00
Average spending of CU, total	43,394.87	25,421.18	35,438.55	40,877.68	48,177.36	60,712.28	56,728.41	67,801.38
Transportation, average spending	**7,801.38**	**4,472.34**	**6,819.04**	**7,829.44**	**9,872.12**	**9,766.03**	**9,719.97**	**9,847.56**
VEHICLE PURCHASES	**3,397.07**	**1,921.91**	**3,046.01**	**3,590.03**	**4,775.84**	**3,893.29**	**4,071.65**	**3,579.80**
Cars and trucks, new	**1,748.38**	**668.45**	**1,445.39**	**1,924.98**	**2,695.94**	**2,148.35**	**2,280.50**	**1,916.07**
New cars	672.87	411.29	535.08	796.62	824.13	793.87	793.49	794.52
New trucks	1,075.51	257.16	910.31	1,128.36	1,871.81	1,354.48	1,487.00	1,121.55
Cars and trucks, used	**1,582.25**	**1,232.14**	**1,540.59**	**1,588.78**	**1,932.72**	**1,683.20**	**1,738.71**	**1,585.64**
Used cars	760.60	518.39	704.95	851.03	572.51	930.73	936.44	920.70
Used trucks	821.64	713.75	835.63	737.75	1,360.21	752.47	802.26	664.94
Other vehicles	**66.45**	**21.32**	**60.03**	**76.28**	**147.17**	**61.74**	**52.44**	**78.09**
GASOLINE AND MOTOR OIL	**1,597.56**	**1,142.34**	**1,537.14**	**1,574.41**	**1,852.28**	**1,825.59**	**1,816.96**	**1,840.76**
Gasoline	1,466.54	1,081.75	1,426.34	1,436.89	1,684.23	1,655.99	1,651.40	1,664.06
Diesel fuel	20.50	10.88	26.43	19.67	36.73	15.13	18.27	9.61
Gasoline on trips	100.35	39.87	73.25	107.93	117.75	145.97	137.71	160.50
Motor oil	9.01	9.44	9.86	8.82	12.39	7.03	8.20	4.96
Motor oil on trips	1.01	0.40	0.74	1.09	1.19	1.47	1.39	1.62
OTHER VEHICLE EXPENSES	**2,365.41**	**1,258.88**	**2,026.61**	**2,323.66**	**2,850.58**	**3,139.51**	**3,051.75**	**3,293.26**
Vehicle finance charges	**323.41**	**168.05**	**314.94**	**327.69**	**416.49**	**378.11**	**393.62**	**350.86**
Automobile finance charges	133.28	71.37	118.89	138.44	177.70	160.48	161.14	159.31
Truck finance charges	166.90	92.95	174.43	163.40	209.55	186.74	196.14	170.24
Motorcycle and plane finance charges	3.27	0.75	2.77	4.57	5.12	3.43	4.17	2.14
Other vehicle finance charges	19.97	2.97	18.85	21.28	24.11	27.46	32.18	19.16
Maintenance and repairs	**651.66**	**332.35**	**496.66**	**696.27**	**787.24**	**889.10**	**835.00**	**983.36**
Coolant, additives, brake and transmission fluids	2.93	3.32	3.16	3.28	3.55	2.05	2.08	1.99
Tires—purchased, replaced, installed	94.09	53.89	75.71	95.01	111.18	126.14	119.17	138.40
Parts, equipment, and accessories	43.03	30.55	46.64	43.70	54.68	41.71	42.32	40.63
Vehicle audio equipment, excluding labor	8.28	3.37	7.11	18.10	–	7.45	3.82	14.38
Vehicle products	4.31	2.10	3.78	6.17	5.37	4.33	4.09	4.78
Miscellaneous auto repair, servicing	50.26	18.64	29.16	76.25	68.11	63.18	72.54	45.32
Body work and painting	36.50	13.98	20.18	40.42	47.36	57.14	46.91	75.14
Clutch and transmission repair	39.27	20.81	30.93	42.59	42.69	53.10	51.75	55.48
Drive shaft and rear-end repair	6.21	1.37	2.20	7.92	11.26	9.54	9.18	10.19
Brake work	44.56	21.26	31.83	49.85	50.12	62.85	60.59	66.81
Repair to steering or front-end	15.19	8.00	12.13	14.67	17.92	21.35	22.59	19.18
Repair to engine cooling system	17.95	8.94	14.17	17.02	22.87	25.34	25.06	25.83
Motor tune-up	41.77	15.23	30.34	43.45	45.56	63.90	51.75	85.27
Lube, oil change, and oil filters	56.23	27.63	47.58	56.36	64.75	76.43	73.80	81.05
Front-end alignment, wheel balance, rotation	9.13	4.80	8.96	7.30	9.30	12.89	12.78	13.10
Shock absorber replacement	2.76	1.33	2.21	2.12	2.12	4.74	4.45	5.26
Gas tank repair, replacement	3.32	2.43	2.01	4.31	2.00	4.75	4.73	4.77
Tire repair and other repair work	49.93	22.16	35.43	51.23	45.54	78.62	76.46	82.40
Vehicle air conditioning repair	14.23	6.25	8.01	15.79	18.63	21.66	17.28	29.35
Exhaust system repair	10.19	7.27	8.81	8.71	13.09	13.22	10.46	18.09
Electrical system repair	22.54	13.38	15.48	23.73	33.90	29.38	26.57	34.32
Motor repair, replacement	69.92	45.47	53.32	59.24	107.67	94.39	82.60	115.11
Auto repair service policy	9.05	0.17	7.52	9.05	9.56	14.93	14.02	16.54
Vehicle insurance	**964.37**	**603.99**	**926.61**	**923.50**	**1,126.75**	**1,165.81**	**1,142.58**	**1,206.64**

	total consumer units	less than high school graduate	high school graduate	some college	associate's degree	college graduate total	college graduate bachelor's degree	college graduate master's, professional, doctorate
Vehicle rental, leases, licenses, other charges	**$425.96**	**$154.50**	**$288.40**	**$376.20**	**$520.11**	**$706.49**	**$680.56**	**$752.41**
Leased and rented vehicles	254.85	69.63	161.46	204.43	311.23	460.89	459.69	463.01
Rented vehicles	38.27	13.03	19.52	25.86	42.23	77.64	69.08	92.68
Auto rental	5.64	5.68	2.50	3.62	10.08	8.74	7.83	10.35
Auto rental on trips	21.18	2.43	8.87	16.40	19.97	46.79	39.65	59.34
Truck rental	4.72	4.44	2.75	2.28	5.18	8.48	9.38	6.89
Truck rental on trips	4.54	0.48	2.26	3.29	2.06	10.62	8.38	14.56
Leased vehicles	216.58	56.59	141.95	178.58	269.00	383.25	390.60	370.32
Car lease payments	104.73	22.36	61.38	91.02	116.71	195.61	198.74	190.10
Truck lease payments	96.04	32.72	71.48	69.86	143.31	157.20	159.86	152.51
Vehicle registration, state	80.92	45.69	69.74	83.13	106.99	99.56	96.04	105.77
Vehicle registration, local	6.90	5.22	4.84	6.88	10.53	8.55	8.44	8.74
Driver's license	7.16	4.57	6.80	6.86	8.18	8.75	8.87	8.54
Vehicle inspection	9.29	6.16	9.23	8.34	9.54	11.64	10.72	13.28
Parking fees	29.41	6.19	13.14	25.72	27.49	60.52	45.22	87.42
Parking fees in home city, excluding residence	23.87	4.72	10.10	21.09	21.25	50.01	35.77	75.03
Parking fees on trips	5.54	1.47	3.04	4.63	6.24	10.51	9.44	12.38
Tolls	14.60	8.12	6.82	19.05	17.24	21.54	19.25	25.90
Tolls on trips	4.63	1.91	2.47	3.94	5.04	8.50	8.61	8.30
Towing charges	5.08	3.01	4.04	5.63	7.40	5.97	5.83	6.21
Automobile service clubs	13.12	4.00	9.85	12.23	16.46	20.56	17.90	25.25
PUBLIC TRANSPORTATION	**441.33**	**149.21**	**209.28**	**341.34**	**393.42**	**907.64**	**779.60**	**1,133.73**
Airline fares	275.94	76.53	123.79	212.99	259.68	579.19	477.64	757.69
Intercity bus fares	9.35	5.07	5.70	9.82	9.51	14.64	12.85	17.78
Intracity mass transit fares	46.32	49.05	31.78	33.94	25.53	75.28	66.26	91.15
Local transportation on trips	10.00	1.59	5.02	8.76	8.33	20.62	17.24	26.56
Taxi fares and limousine service on trips	5.87	0.93	2.95	5.14	4.89	12.11	10.13	15.60
Taxi fares and limousine service	23.18	6.66	7.00	17.80	8.92	55.43	48.49	68.68
Intercity train fares	17.84	3.86	9.11	17.77	16.63	33.87	29.95	40.78
Ship fares	52.10	4.84	23.38	34.55	59.86	115.17	116.21	113.33
School bus	0.74	0.67	0.55	0.57	0.07	1.32	0.84	2.17

Note: Subcategories may not add to total because some are not shown. "–" means sample is too small to make a reliable estimate.
Source: Bureau of Labor Statistics, unpublished tables from the 2004 Consumer Expenditure Survey

Table 11.26 Transportation: Indexed spending by education, 2004

(indexed average annual spending of consumer units (CU) on transportation, by education of consumer unit reference person, 2004; index definition: an index of 100 is the average for all consumer units; an index of 132 means that spending by consumer units in that group is 32 percent above the average for all consumer units; an index of 68 indicates spending that is 32 percent below the average for all consumer units)

	total consumer units	less than high school graduate	high school graduate	some college	associate's degree	college graduate total	bachelor's degree	master's, professional, doctorate
Average spending of CU, total	$43,395	$25,421	$35,439	$40,878	$48,177	$60,712	$56,728	$67,801
Average spending of CU, index	100	59	82	94	111	140	131	156
Transportation, spending index	100	57	87	100	127	125	125	126
VEHICLE PURCHASES	100	57	90	106	141	115	120	105
Cars and trucks, new	100	38	83	110	154	123	130	110
New cars	100	61	80	118	122	118	118	118
New trucks	100	24	85	105	174	126	138	104
Cars and trucks, used	100	78	97	100	122	106	110	100
Used cars	100	68	93	112	75	122	123	121
Used trucks	100	87	102	90	166	92	98	81
Other vehicles	100	32	90	115	221	93	79	118
GASOLINE AND MOTOR OIL	100	72	96	99	116	114	114	115
Gasoline	100	74	97	98	115	113	113	113
Diesel fuel	100	53	129	96	179	74	89	47
Gasoline on trips	100	40	73	108	117	145	137	160
Motor oil	100	105	109	98	138	78	91	55
Motor oil on trips	100	40	73	108	118	146	138	160
OTHER VEHICLE EXPENSES	100	53	86	98	121	133	129	139
Vehicle finance charges	100	52	97	101	129	117	122	108
Automobile finance charges	100	54	89	104	133	120	121	120
Truck finance charges	100	56	105	98	126	112	118	102
Motorcycle and plane finance charges	100	23	85	140	157	105	128	65
Other vehicle finance charges	100	15	94	107	121	138	161	96
Maintenance and repairs	100	51	76	107	121	136	128	151
Coolant, additives, brake and transmission fluids	100	113	108	112	121	70	71	68
Tires—purchased, replaced, installed	100	57	80	101	118	134	127	147
Parts, equipment, and accessories	100	71	108	102	127	97	98	94
Vehicle audio equipment, excluding labor	100	41	86	219	–	90	46	174
Vehicle products	100	49	88	143	125	100	95	111
Miscellaneous auto repair, servicing	100	37	58	152	136	126	144	90
Body work and painting	100	38	55	111	130	157	129	206
Clutch and transmission repair	100	53	79	108	109	135	132	141
Drive shaft and rear-end repair	100	22	35	128	181	154	148	164
Brake work	100	48	71	112	112	141	136	150
Repair to steering or front-end	100	53	80	97	118	141	149	126
Repair to engine cooling system	100	50	79	95	127	141	140	144
Motor tune-up	100	36	73	104	109	153	124	204
Lube, oil change, and oil filters	100	49	85	100	115	136	131	144
Front-end alignment, wheel balance, rotation	100	53	98	80	102	141	140	143
Shock absorber replacement	100	48	80	77	77	172	161	191
Gas tank repair, replacement	100	73	61	130	60	143	142	144
Tire repair and other repair work	100	44	71	103	91	157	153	165
Vehicle air conditioning repair	100	44	56	111	131	152	121	206
Exhaust system repair	100	71	86	85	128	130	103	178
Electrical system repair	100	59	69	105	150	130	118	152
Motor repair, replacement	100	65	76	85	154	135	118	165
Auto repair service policy	100	2	83	100	106	165	155	183
Vehicle insurance	100	63	96	96	117	121	118	125

	total consumer units	less than high school graduate	high school graduate	some college	associate's degree	college graduate total	college graduate bachelor's degree	college graduate master's, professional, doctorate
Vehicle rental, leases, licenses, other charges	**100**	**36**	**68**	**88**	**122**	**166**	**160**	**177**
Leased and rented vehicles	100	27	63	80	122	181	180	182
Rented vehicles	100	34	51	68	110	203	181	242
Auto rental	100	101	44	64	179	155	139	184
Auto rental on trips	100	11	42	77	94	221	187	280
Truck rental	100	94	58	48	110	180	199	146
Truck rental on trips	100	11	50	72	45	234	185	321
Leased vehicles	100	26	66	82	124	177	180	171
Car lease payments	100	21	59	87	111	187	190	182
Truck lease payments	100	34	74	73	149	164	166	159
Vehicle registration, state	100	56	86	103	132	123	119	131
Vehicle registration, local	100	76	70	100	153	124	122	127
Driver's license	100	64	95	96	114	122	124	119
Vehicle inspection	100	66	99	90	103	125	115	143
Parking fees	100	21	45	87	93	206	154	297
Parking fees in home city, excluding residence	100	20	42	88	89	210	150	314
Parking fees on trips	100	27	55	84	113	190	170	223
Tolls	100	56	47	130	118	148	132	177
Tolls on trips	100	41	53	85	109	184	186	179
Towing charges	100	59	80	111	146	118	115	122
Automobile service clubs	100	30	75	93	125	157	136	192
PUBLIC TRANSPORTATION	**100**	**34**	**47**	**77**	**89**	**206**	**177**	**257**
Airline fares	100	28	45	77	94	210	173	275
Intercity bus fares	100	54	61	105	102	157	137	190
Intracity mass transit fares	100	106	69	73	55	163	143	197
Local transportation on trips	100	16	50	88	83	206	172	266
Taxi fares and limousine service on trips	100	16	50	88	83	206	173	266
Taxi fares and limousine service	100	29	30	77	38	239	209	296
Intercity train fares	100	22	51	100	93	190	168	229
Ship fares	100	9	45	66	115	221	223	218
School bus	100	91	74	77	9	178	114	293

Note: "–" means sample is too small to make a reliable estimate.
Source: Calculations by New Strategist based on the 2004 Consumer Expenditure Survey

Table 11.27 Transportation: Total spending by education, 2004

(total annual spending on transportation, by consumer unit (CU) educational attainment group, 2004; consumer units and dollars in thousands)

	total consumer units	less than high school graduate	high school graduate	some college	associate's degree	college graduate total	college graduate bachelor's degree	college graduate master's, professional, doctorate
Number of consumer units	116,282	16,829	31,005	25,317	10,678	32,452	20,684	11,768
Total spending of all CUs	$5,046,042,273	$427,813,038	$1,098,772,243	$1,034,900,225	$514,437,850	$1,970,234,911	$1,173,370,432	$797,886,640
Transportation, total spending	907,160,069	75,265,010	211,424,335	198,217,932	105,414,497	316,927,206	201,047,859	115,886,086
VEHICLE PURCHASES	395,018,094	32,343,823	94,441,540	90,888,790	50,996,420	126,345,047	84,218,009	42,127,086
Cars and trucks, new	203,305,123	11,249,345	44,814,317	48,734,719	28,787,247	69,718,254	47,169,862	22,548,312
New cars	78,242,669	6,921,599	16,590,155	20,168,029	8,800,060	25,762,669	16,412,547	9,349,911
New trucks	125,062,454	4,327,746	28,224,162	28,566,690	19,987,187	43,955,585	30,757,108	13,198,400
Cars and trucks, used	183,987,195	20,735,684	47,765,993	40,223,143	20,637,584	54,623,206	35,963,478	18,659,812
Used cars	88,444,089	8,723,985	21,856,975	21,545,527	6,113,262	30,204,050	19,369,325	10,834,798
Used trucks	95,541,942	12,011,699	25,908,708	18,677,617	14,524,322	24,419,156	16,593,946	7,825,014
Other vehicles	7,726,939	358,794	1,861,230	1,931,181	1,571,481	2,003,586	1,084,669	918,963
GASOLINE AND MOTOR OIL	185,767,472	19,224,440	47,659,026	39,859,338	19,778,646	59,244,047	37,582,001	21,662,064
Gasoline	170,532,204	18,204,771	44,223,672	36,377,744	17,984,208	53,740,187	34,157,558	19,582,658
Diesel fuel	2,383,781	183,100	819,462	497,985	392,203	490,999	377,897	113,090
Gasoline on trips	11,668,899	670,972	2,271,116	2,732,464	1,257,335	4,737,018	2,848,394	1,888,764
Motor oil	1,047,701	158,866	305,709	223,296	132,300	228,138	169,609	58,369
Motor oil on trips	117,445	6,732	22,944	27,596	12,707	47,704	28,751	19,064
OTHER VEHICLE EXPENSES	275,054,606	21,185,692	62,835,043	58,828,100	30,438,493	101,883,379	63,122,397	38,755,084
Vehicle finance charges	37,606,762	2,828,113	9,764,715	8,296,128	4,447,280	12,270,426	8,141,636	4,128,920
Automobile finance charges	15,498,065	1,201,086	3,686,184	3,504,885	1,897,481	5,207,897	3,333,020	1,874,760
Truck finance charges	19,407,466	1,564,256	5,408,202	4,136,798	2,237,575	6,060,086	4,056,960	2,003,384
Motorcycle and plane finance charges	380,242	12,622	85,884	115,699	54,671	111,310	86,252	25,184
Other vehicle finance charges	2,322,152	49,982	584,444	538,746	257,447	891,132	665,611	225,475
Maintenance and repairs	75,776,328	5,593,118	15,398,943	17,627,468	8,406,149	28,853,073	17,271,140	11,572,180
Coolant, additives, brake and transmission fluids	340,706	55,872	97,976	83,040	37,907	66,527	43,023	23,418
Tires—purchased, replaced, installed	10,940,973	906,915	2,347,389	2,405,368	1,187,180	4,093,495	2,464,912	1,628,691
Parts, equipment, and accessories	5,003,614	514,126	1,446,073	1,106,353	583,873	1,353,573	875,347	478,134
Vehicle audio equipment, excluding labor	962,815	56,714	220,446	458,238	–	241,767	79,013	169,224
Vehicle products	501,175	35,341	117,199	156,206	57,341	140,517	84,598	56,251
Miscellaneous auto repair, servicing	5,844,333	313,693	904,106	1,930,421	727,279	2,050,317	1,500,417	533,326
Body work and painting	4,244,293	235,269	625,681	1,023,313	505,710	1,854,307	970,286	884,248
Clutch and transmission repair	4,566,394	350,211	958,985	1,078,251	455,844	1,723,201	1,070,397	652,889
Drive shaft and rear-end repair	722,111	23,056	68,211	200,511	120,234	309,592	189,879	119,916
Brake work	5,181,526	357,785	986,889	1,262,052	535,181	2,039,608	1,253,244	786,220
Repair to steering or front-end	1,766,324	134,632	376,091	371,400	191,350	692,850	467,252	225,710
Repair to engine cooling system	2,087,262	150,451	439,341	430,895	244,206	822,334	518,341	303,967
Motor tune-up	4,857,099	256,306	940,692	1,100,024	486,490	2,073,683	1,070,397	1,003,457
Lube, oil change, and oil filters	6,538,537	464,985	1,475,218	1,426,866	691,401	2,480,306	1,526,479	953,796
Front-end alignment, wheel balance, rotation	1,061,655	80,779	277,805	184,814	99,305	418,306	264,342	154,161
Shock absorber replacement	320,938	22,383	68,521	53,672	22,637	153,822	92,044	61,900
Gas tank repair, replacement	386,056	40,894	62,320	109,116	21,356	154,147	97,835	56,133
Tire repair and other repair work	5,805,960	372,931	1,098,507	1,296,990	486,276	2,551,376	1,581,499	969,683
Vehicle air conditioning repair	1,654,693	105,181	248,350	399,755	198,931	702,910	357,420	345,391
Exhaust system repair	1,184,914	122,347	273,154	220,511	139,775	429,015	216,355	212,883
Electrical system repair	2,620,996	225,172	479,957	600,772	361,984	953,440	549,574	403,878
Motor repair, replacement	8,130,437	765,215	1,653,187	1,499,779	1,149,700	3,063,144	1,708,498	1,354,614
Auto repair service policy	1,052,352	2,861	233,158	229,119	102,082	484,508	289,990	194,643
Vehicle insurance	112,138,872	10,164,548	28,729,543	23,380,250	12,031,437	37,832,866	23,633,125	14,199,740

	total consumer units	less than high school graduate	high school graduate	some college	associate's degree	college graduate		master's, professional, doctorate
						total	bachelor's degree	
Vehicle rental, leases, licenses, other charges	**$49,531,481**	**$2,600,081**	**$8,941,842**	**$9,524,255**	**$5,553,735**	**$22,927,013**	**$14,076,703**	**$8,854,361**
Leased and rented vehicles	29,634,468	1,171,803	5,006,067	5,175,554	3,323,314	14,956,802	9,508,228	5,448,702
Rented vehicles	4,450,112	219,282	605,218	654,698	450,932	2,519,573	1,428,851	1,090,658
Auto rental	655,830	95,589	77,513	91,648	107,634	283,630	161,956	121,799
Auto rental on trips	2,462,853	40,894	275,014	415,199	213,240	1,518,429	820,121	698,313
Truck rental	548,851	74,721	85,264	57,723	55,312	275,193	194,016	81,082
Truck rental on trips	527,920	8,078	70,071	83,293	21,997	344,640	173,332	171,342
Leased vehicles	25,184,356	952,353	4,401,160	4,521,110	2,872,382	12,437,229	8,079,170	4,357,926
Car lease payments	12,178,214	376,296	1,903,087	2,304,353	1,246,229	6,347,936	4,110,738	2,237,097
Truck lease payments	11,167,723	550,645	2,216,237	1,768,646	1,530,264	5,101,454	3,306,544	1,794,738
Vehicle registration, state	9,409,539	768,917	2,162,289	2,104,602	1,142,439	3,230,921	1,986,491	1,244,701
Vehicle registration, local	802,346	87,847	150,064	174,181	112,439	277,465	174,573	102,852
Driver's license	832,579	76,909	210,834	173,675	87,346	283,955	183,467	100,499
Vehicle inspection	1,080,260	103,667	286,176	211,144	101,868	377,741	221,732	156,279
Parking fees	3,419,854	104,172	407,406	651,153	293,538	1,963,995	935,330	1,028,759
Parking fees in home city, excluding residence	2,775,651	79,433	313,151	533,936	226,908	1,622,925	739,867	882,953
Parking fees on trips	644,202	24,739	94,255	117,218	66,631	341,071	195,257	145,688
Tolls	1,697,717	136,651	211,454	482,289	184,089	699,016	398,167	304,791
Tolls on trips	538,386	32,143	76,582	99,749	53,817	275,842	178,089	97,674
Towing charges	590,713	50,655	125,260	142,535	79,017	193,738	120,588	73,079
Automobile service clubs	1,525,620	67,316	305,399	309,627	175,760	667,213	370,244	297,142
PUBLIC TRANSPORTATION	**51,318,735**	**2,511,055**	**6,488,726**	**8,641,705**	**4,200,939**	**29,454,733**	**16,125,246**	**13,341,735**
Airline fares	32,086,855	1,287,923	3,838,109	5,392,268	2,772,863	18,795,874	9,879,506	8,916,496
Intercity bus fares	1,087,237	85,323	176,729	248,613	101,548	475,097	265,789	209,235
Intracity mass transit fares	5,386,182	825,462	985,339	859,259	272,609	2,442,987	1,370,522	1,072,653
Local transportation on trips	1,162,820	26,758	155,645	221,777	88,948	669,160	356,592	312,558
Taxi fares and limousine service on trips	682,575	15,651	91,465	130,129	52,215	392,994	209,529	183,581
Taxi fares and limousine service	2,695,417	112,081	217,035	450,643	95,248	1,798,814	1,002,967	808,226
Intercity train fares	2,074,471	64,960	282,456	449,883	177,575	1,099,149	619,486	479,899
Ship fares	6,058,292	81,452	724,897	874,702	639,185	3,737,497	2,403,688	1,333,667
School bus	86,049	11,275	17,053	14,431	747	42,837	17,375	25,537

Note: Numbers may not add to total because of rounding and missing subcategories. "–" means sample is too small to make a reliable estimate.
Source: Calculations by New Strategist based on the 2004 Consumer Expenditure Survey

Table 11.28 Transportation: Market shares by education, 2004

(percentage of total annual spending on transportation accounted for by consumer unit educational attainment groups, 2004)

	total consumer units	less than high school graduate	high school graduate	some college	associate's degree	college graduate total	bachelor's degree	master's, professional, doctorate
Share of total consumer units	100.0%	14.5%	26.7%	21.8%	9.2%	27.9%	17.8%	10.1%
Share of total before-tax income	100.0	7.7	20.7	18.7	9.9	43.0	24.7	18.3
Share of total spending	100.0	8.5	21.8	20.5	10.2	39.0	23.3	15.8
Share of transportation spending	100.0	8.3	23.3	21.9	11.6	34.9	22.2	12.8
VEHICLE PURCHASES	100.0	8.2	23.9	23.0	12.9	32.0	21.3	10.7
Cars and trucks, new	100.0	5.5	22.0	24.0	14.2	34.3	23.2	11.1
New cars	100.0	8.8	21.2	25.8	11.2	32.9	21.0	11.9
New trucks	100.0	3.5	22.6	22.8	16.0	35.1	24.6	10.6
Cars and trucks, used	100.0	11.3	26.0	21.9	11.2	29.7	19.5	10.1
Used cars	100.0	9.9	24.7	24.4	6.9	34.2	21.9	12.3
Used trucks	100.0	12.6	27.1	19.5	15.2	25.6	17.4	8.2
Other vehicles	100.0	4.6	24.1	25.0	20.3	25.9	14.0	11.9
GASOLINE AND MOTOR OIL	100.0	10.3	25.7	21.5	10.6	31.9	20.2	11.7
Gasoline	100.0	10.7	25.9	21.3	10.5	31.5	20.0	11.5
Diesel fuel	100.0	7.7	34.4	20.9	16.5	20.6	15.9	4.7
Gasoline on trips	100.0	5.8	19.5	23.4	10.8	40.6	24.4	16.2
Motor oil	100.0	15.2	29.2	21.3	12.6	21.8	16.2	5.6
Motor oil on trips	100.0	5.7	19.5	23.5	10.8	40.6	24.5	16.2
OTHER VEHICLE EXPENSES	100.0	7.7	22.8	21.4	11.1	37.0	22.9	14.1
Vehicle finance charges	100.0	7.5	26.0	22.1	11.8	32.6	21.6	11.0
Automobile finance charges	100.0	7.7	23.8	22.6	12.2	33.6	21.5	12.1
Truck finance charges	100.0	8.1	27.9	21.3	11.5	31.2	20.9	10.3
Motorcycle and plane finance charges	100.0	3.3	22.6	30.4	14.4	29.3	22.7	6.6
Other vehicle finance charges	100.0	2.2	25.2	23.2	11.1	38.4	28.7	9.7
Maintenance and repairs	100.0	7.4	20.3	23.3	11.1	38.1	22.8	15.3
Coolant, additives, brake and transmission fluids	100.0	16.4	28.8	24.4	11.1	19.5	12.6	6.9
Tires—purchased, replaced, installed	100.0	8.3	21.5	22.0	10.9	37.4	22.5	14.9
Parts, equipment, and accessories	100.0	10.3	28.9	22.1	11.7	27.1	17.5	9.6
Vehicle audio equipment, excluding labor	100.0	5.9	22.9	47.6	–	25.1	8.2	17.6
Vehicle products	100.0	7.1	23.4	31.2	11.4	28.0	16.9	11.2
Miscellaneous auto repair, servicing	100.0	5.4	15.5	33.0	12.4	35.1	25.7	9.1
Body work and painting	100.0	5.5	14.7	24.1	11.9	43.7	22.9	20.8
Clutch and transmission repair	100.0	7.7	21.0	23.6	10.0	37.7	23.4	14.3
Drive shaft and rear-end repair	100.0	3.2	9.4	27.8	16.7	42.9	26.3	16.6
Brake work	100.0	6.9	19.0	24.4	10.3	39.4	24.2	15.2
Repair to steering or front-end	100.0	7.6	21.3	21.0	10.8	39.2	26.5	12.8
Repair to engine cooling system	100.0	7.2	21.0	20.6	11.7	39.4	24.8	14.6
Motor tune-up	100.0	5.3	19.4	22.6	10.0	42.7	22.0	20.7
Lube, oil change, and oil filters	100.0	7.1	22.6	21.8	10.6	37.9	23.3	14.6
Front-end alignment, wheel balance, rotation	100.0	7.6	26.2	17.4	9.4	39.4	24.9	14.5
Shock absorber replacement	100.0	7.0	21.4	16.7	7.1	47.9	28.7	19.3
Gas tank repair, replacement	100.0	10.6	16.1	28.3	5.5	39.9	25.3	14.5
Tire repair and other repair work	100.0	6.4	18.9	22.3	8.4	43.9	27.2	16.7
Vehicle air conditioning repair	100.0	6.4	15.0	24.2	12.0	42.5	21.6	20.9
Exhaust system repair	100.0	10.3	23.1	18.6	11.8	36.2	18.3	18.0
Electrical system repair	100.0	8.6	18.3	22.9	13.8	36.4	21.0	15.4
Motor repair, replacement	100.0	9.4	20.3	18.4	14.1	37.7	21.0	16.7
Auto repair service policy	100.0	0.3	22.2	21.8	9.7	46.0	27.6	18.5
Vehicle insurance	100.0	9.1	25.6	20.8	10.7	33.7	21.1	12.7

	total consumer units	less than high school graduate	high school graduate	some college	associate's degree	college graduate		
						total	bachelor's degree	master's, professional, doctorate
Vehicle rental, leases, licenses, other charges	**100.0%**	**5.2%**	**18.1%**	**19.2%**	**11.2%**	**46.3%**	**28.4%**	**17.9%**
Leased and rented vehicles	100.0	4.0	16.9	17.5	11.2	50.5	32.1	18.4
Rented vehicles	100.0	4.9	13.6	14.7	10.1	56.6	32.1	24.5
Auto rental	100.0	14.6	11.8	14.0	16.4	43.2	24.7	18.6
Auto rental on trips	100.0	1.7	11.2	16.9	8.7	61.7	33.3	28.4
Truck rental	100.0	13.6	15.5	10.5	10.1	50.1	35.3	14.8
Truck rental on trips	100.0	1.5	13.3	15.8	4.2	65.3	32.8	32.5
Leased vehicles	100.0	3.8	17.5	18.0	11.4	49.4	32.1	17.3
Car lease payments	100.0	3.1	15.6	18.9	10.2	52.1	33.8	18.4
Truck lease payments	100.0	4.9	19.8	15.8	13.7	45.7	29.6	16.1
Vehicle registration, state	100.0	8.2	23.0	22.4	12.1	34.3	21.1	13.2
Vehicle registration, local	100.0	10.9	18.7	21.7	14.0	34.6	21.8	12.8
Driver's license	100.0	9.2	25.3	20.9	10.5	34.1	22.0	12.1
Vehicle inspection	100.0	9.6	26.5	19.5	9.4	35.0	20.5	14.5
Parking fees	100.0	3.0	11.9	19.0	8.6	57.4	27.4	30.1
Parking fees in home city, excluding residence	100.0	2.9	11.3	19.2	8.2	58.5	26.7	31.8
Parking fees on trips	100.0	3.8	14.6	18.2	10.3	52.9	30.3	22.6
Tolls	100.0	8.0	12.5	28.4	10.8	41.2	23.5	18.0
Tolls on trips	100.0	6.0	14.2	18.5	10.0	51.2	33.1	18.1
Towing charges	100.0	8.6	21.2	24.1	13.4	32.8	20.4	12.4
Automobile service clubs	100.0	4.4	20.0	20.3	11.5	43.7	24.3	19.5
PUBLIC TRANSPORTATION	**100.0**	**4.9**	**12.6**	**16.8**	**8.2**	**57.4**	**31.4**	**26.0**
Airline fares	100.0	4.0	12.0	16.8	8.6	58.6	30.8	27.8
Intercity bus fares	100.0	7.8	16.3	22.9	9.3	43.7	24.4	19.2
Intracity mass transit fares	100.0	15.3	18.3	16.0	5.1	45.4	25.4	19.9
Local transportation on trips	100.0	2.3	13.4	19.1	7.6	57.5	30.7	26.9
Taxi fares and limousine service on trips	100.0	2.3	13.4	19.1	7.6	57.6	30.7	26.9
Taxi fares and limousine service	100.0	4.2	8.1	16.7	3.5	66.7	37.2	30.0
Intercity train fares	100.0	3.1	13.6	21.7	8.6	53.0	29.9	23.1
Ship fares	100.0	1.3	12.0	14.4	10.6	61.7	39.7	22.0
School bus	100.0	13.1	19.8	16.8	0.9	49.8	20.2	29.7

Note: Numbers may not add to total because of rounding. "–" means sample is too small to make a reliable estimate.
Source: Calculations by New Strategist based on the 2004 Consumer Expenditure Survey

Appendix A: About the Consumer Expenditure Survey

History

The Consumer Expenditure Survey (CEX) is an ongoing study of the day-to-day spending of American households. In taking the survey, government interviewers collect spending data on products and services as well as the amount and sources of household income, changes in savings and debt, and demographic and economic characteristics of household members. The Bureau of the Census collects the data for the CEX under contract with the Bureau of Labor Statistics (BLS), which is responsible for analysis and release of the survey data.

Since the late 19th century, the federal government has conducted expenditure surveys about every ten years. Although the results have been used for a variety of purposes, their primary application is to track consumer prices. In 1980 the CEX became a continuous survey with annual release of data (with a lag time of about two years between data collection and release). The survey is used to update prices for the market basket of products and services used in calculating the Consumer Price Index.

Description of the Consumer Expenditure Survey

The CEX comprises two surveys: an interview survey and a diary survey. In the interview portion of the survey, respondents are asked each quarter for five consecutive quarters to report their expenditures for the previous three months. The purchase of big-ticket items, such as houses, cars, and major appliances, or recurring expenses, such as insurance premiums, utility payments, and rent, are recorded by the interview survey. About 95 percent of all expenditures are covered by the interview component.

Expenditures on low-cost, frequently purchased items are recorded during a two-week period by the diary survey. These detailed records include expenses for food and beverages purchased in grocery stores and at restaurants, as well as other items such as tobacco, housekeeping supplies, nonprescription drugs, and personal care products and services. The diary survey is intended to capture expenditures respondents are likely to forget or recall incorrectly over longer periods of time.

The average spending figures shown in this book are the integrated data from both the diary and the interview components of the survey. Integrated data provide a more complete accounting of consumer expenditures than either component of the survey is designed to do alone.

Data collection and processing

Two separate, nationally representative samples are used for the interview and diary surveys. For the interview survey, about 7,500 consumer units are interviewed on a rotating panel basis each quarter for five consecutive quarters. Another 7,500 consumer units keep weekly diaries of spending for two consecutive weeks. Data collection is carried out in 105 areas of the country.

The BLS reviews, audits, and cleans the data, and then weights them to reflect the number and characteristics of all U.S. consumer units. Like any sample survey, the CEX is subject to two major types of error. Nonsampling error occurs when respondents misinterpret questions or interviewers are inconsistent in the way they ask questions or record answers. Respondents may forget items, recall expenses incorrectly, or deliberately give wrong answers. A respondent may remember how much he or she spent at the grocery store but forget the items picked up at a local convenience store. Most surveys of alcohol consumption or spending on alcohol suffer from this type of underreporting, for example. Nonsampling error can also be caused by mistakes during the various stages of data processing and refinement.

Sampling error occurs when a sample does not accurately represent the population it is supposed to represent. This kind of error is present in every sample-based survey and is minimized by using a proper sampling procedure. Standard error tables documenting the extent of sampling error in the CEX are available from the BLS at http://www.bls.gov/cex/csxstnderror.htm.

Although the CEX is the best source of information about the spending behavior of American households, it should be treated with caution because of the above problems. Comparisons with consumption data from other sources show that CEX data tend to underestimate expenditures except for rent, fuel, telephone service, furniture, transportation, and personal care services. Despite these problems, the data reveal important spending patterns by demographic segment that can be used to better understand consumer behavior.

The definition of consumer unit

The CEX uses consumer unit as its sampling unit instead of household, which is the sampling unit used by the Census Bureau. The term "household" is used interchangeably with the term "consumer unit" in this book for convenience, although they are not exactly the same. Some households contain more than one consumer unit.

The BLS defines consumer unit as either (1) members of a household who are related by blood, marriage, adoption, or other legal arrangements; (2) a person living alone or sharing a household with others or living as a roomer in a private home or lodging house or in permanent living quarters in a hotel or motel, but who is financially independent; or (3) two or more persons living together who pool their income to make joint expenditure decisions. The BLS defines financial independence in terms of "the three major expense categories: housing, food, and other living expenses. To be considered financially independent, at least two of the three major expense categories have to be provided by the respondent."

The Census Bureau uses household as its sampling unit in the decennial census and in the monthly Current Population Survey. The Census Bureau's household "consists of all persons who occupy a housing unit. A house, an apartment or other groups of rooms, or a single room is regarded as a housing unit when it is occupied or intended for occupancy as separate living quarters; that is, when the occupants do not live and eat with any other persons in the structure and there is direct access from the outside or through a common hall." The definition goes on to specify that "a household includes the related family members and all the unrelated persons, if any, such as lodgers, foster children, wards, or employees who share the housing unit. A person living alone in a housing unit or a group of unrelated persons sharing a housing unit as partners is also counted as a household. The count of households excludes group quarters."

Because there can be more than one consumer unit in a household, consumer units outnumber households by several million. Most of the excess consumer units are headed by young adults, under age 25.

For more information

If you want to know more about the CEX, contact the CEX specialists at the BLS at (202) 691-6900 or visit the CEX home page at http://www.bls.gov/cex/. The web site includes news releases, technical documentation, and current and historical CEX data. The detailed average spending data shown in chapters 2 through 11 of *Household Spending* are available only by special request from the BLS.

Appendix B: Mortgage Principal and Capital Improvements, 2004

The spending statistics reported by the Consumer Expenditure Survey do not include spending on mortgage principal reduction or capital improvements. Because the survey treats home equity as an asset, principal reduction and capital improvements are regarded as asset accumulation rather than expenditures. The following table shows the average amount spent by households in 2004 for mortgage principal reduction and capital improvements. Adding these figures to expenditures for the category "owned dwellings" gives a more complete picture of the average amount households devote to housing.

(average annual reduction in mortgage principal and change in capital improvement for owned homes, by age of consumer unit reference person, average before-tax income of consumer unit, type of consumer unit, race and Hispanic origin of consumer unit reference person, region in which consumer unit lives, and educational attainment of consumer unit reference person, 2004)

	total consumer units	under 25	25 to 34	35 to 44	45 to 54	55 to 64	65 to 74	75+
AGE OF REFERENCE PERSON								
Reduction of mortgage principal	−$1,306.43	−$164.66	−$1,136.98	−$1,884.52	−$1,933.51	−$1,513.77	−$716.71	−$229.39
Change in capital improvements	734.73	42.70	392.42	988.13	958.98	959.13	655.18	588.23

	total consumer units	under $20,000	$20,000– $39,999	$40,000– $49,999	$50,000– $69,999	$70,000– $79,999	$80,000– $99,999	$100,000 or more
BEFORE-TAX INCOME OF CONSUMER UNIT								
Reduction of mortgage principal	−$1,306.43	−$269.16	−$581.68	−$956.74	−$1,398.49	−$2,340.69	−$2,449.66	−$3,637.55
Change in capital improvements	896.85	147.16	470.34	529.96	851.68	1,074.34	1,447.76	3,042.92

	total consumer units	total married couples	married couples, no children	married couples with children total	oldest child under 6	oldest child 6 to 17	oldest child 18 or older	with child under 18	single person
TYPE OF CONSUMER UNIT									
Reduction of mortgage principal	−$1,306.43	−$1,866.69	−$1,323.90	−$2,364.17	−$2,600.95	−$2,354.83	−$2,221.59	−$722.19	−$582.48
Change in capital improvements	896.85	1,212.20	908.19	1,503.75	2,662.50	1,373.33	963.02	253.66	399.28

	total consumer units	Asian	black	Hispanic	non-Hispanic white and other
RACE/HISPANIC ORIGIN OF REFERENCE PERSON					
Reduction of mortgage principal	−$1,306.43	−$2,258.98	−$758.87	−$974.38	−$1,434.69
Change in capital improvements	896.85	689.14	326.51	669.26	1,013.71

	total consumer units	Northeast	Midwest	South	West
REGION					
Reduction of mortgage principal	−$1,306.43	−$1,333.98	−$1,468.02	−$1,079.11	−$1,484.34
Change in capital improvements	896.85	1,094.55	843.13	609.82	1,246.94

	total consumer units	less than high school graduate	high school graduate	some college	associate's degree	college graduate total	bachelor's degree	graduate degree
EDUCATIONAL ATTAINMENT OF REFERENCE PERSON								
Reduction of mortgage principal	−$1,306.43	−$511.62	−$857.31	−$1,031.49	−$1,650.42	−$2,249.02	−$2,069.54	−$2,564.50
Change in capital improvements	896.85	275.92	619.87	730.65	623.2	1,703.19	1,286.15	2,436.23

Note: "Asian" and "black" include Hispanics and non-Hispanics who identify themselves as being of the respective race alone. "Hispanic" includes people of any race who identify themselves as Hispanic. "Other" includes people who identify themselves as non-Hispanic and as Alaska Native, American Indian, Asian (who are also included in the "Asian" column), Native Hawaiian or other Pacific Islander, as well as non-Hispanics reporting more than one race. Subcategories may not add to total because some are not shown.
Source: Bureau of Labor Statistics, 2004 Consumer Expenditure Survey

Appendix C: Percent Reporting Expenditure and Amount Spent, Average Quarter 2004

(percent of consumer units reporting expenditure and amount spent by purchasers during an average quarter, 2004)

	percent reporting expenditure during quarter	average amount spent by purchasers per quarter
FOOD	**99.54%**	**$1,398.14**
Food at home	**98.95**	**1,026.31**
Grocery stores	98.55	958.26
Convenience stores	24.17	252.20
Groceries purchased on trips	10.47	97.56
Food away from home	**80.23**	**468.87**
Meals at restaurants and carryouts	77.96	356.96
Board (including at school)	1.02	683.58
Catered affairs	1.01	1,449.50
Restaurant food on trips	25.07	230.90
School lunches	9.77	162.21
Meals as pay	1.81	337.71
ALCOHOLIC BEVERAGES	**38.55**	**206.89**
At home	**30.97**	**137.10**
Beer and wine	29.97	120.15
Other alcoholic beverages	8.11	79.59
Away from home	**25.63**	**145.51**
Alcoholic beverages at restaurants, taverns	19.79	139.98
Alcoholic beverages purchased on trips	12.10	79.28
HOUSING	**99.49**	**3,247.42**
Shelter	**97.63**	**2,048.15**
• Owned dwellings	**67.79**	**1,963.60**
Mortgage interest and charges	43.43	1,690.18
Mortgage interest	40.51	1,718.94
Interest paid, home equity loan	2.83	509.98
Interest paid, home equity line of credit	4.68	496.21
Property taxes	66.36	524.10
Maintenance, repairs, insurance, other expenses	37.33	667.79
Homeowner's insurance	26.26	299.65
Ground rent	1.30	771.15
Maintenance and repair services	12.18	1,089.14
Painting and papering	1.12	1,332.81
Plumbing and water heating	3.86	320.47
Heat, air conditioning, electrical work	4.24	527.59
Roofing and gutters	1.23	1,956.91
Other repair and maintenance services	3.55	1,249.93
Repair/replacement of hard-surface flooring	0.62	2,125.40
Repair of built-in appliances	0.91	150.82
Maintenance and repair materials	5.89	311.25
Paints, wallpaper, and supplies	2.55	148.82
Tools/equipment for painting, wallpapering	2.55	15.98
Plumbing supplies and equipment	0.87	166.38
Electrical supplies, heating/cooling equipment	0.44	183.52
Hard-surface flooring, repair and replacement	0.39	598.72
Roofing and gutters	0.36	445.83
Plaster, paneling, siding, windows, doors, screens, awnings	0.80	406.88
Patio, walk, fence, driveway, masonry, brick, and stucco work	0.44	89.20
Miscellaneous supplies and equipment	1.75	245.14
Insulation, other maintenance/repair	1.75	245.14

	percent reporting expenditure during quarter	average amount spent by purchasers per quarter
Property management and security	4.65%	$187.69
Property management	4.33	164.84
Management and upkeep services for security	1.43	111.19
Parking	1.17	73.29
• Rented dwellings	**30.58**	**1,799.45**
Rent	30.16	1,762.21
Rent as pay	0.80	1,127.50
Maintenance, insurance, and other expenses	2.97	328.87
Tenant's insurance	2.03	86.95
Maintenance and repair services	0.42	1,603.57
Maintenance and repair materials	0.65	195.00
• Other lodging	**18.91**	**625.13**
Owned vacation homes	3.68	932.20
Mortgage interest and charges	1.06	1,274.53
Property taxes	3.51	409.62
Maintenance, insurance, and other expenses	1.14	562.94
Housing while attending school	0.96	1,503.39
Lodging on trips	15.67	443.35
Utilities, fuels, public services	**97.35**	**751.58**
Natural gas	50.35	210.54
Electricity	91.16	291.91
Fuel oil and other fuels	10.24	294.26
Fuel oil	3.79	423.42
Bottled gas	5.56	203.24
Wood and other fuels	1.55	171.13
Telephone services	94.50	261.96
Residential phone service and pay phones	87.43	169.37
Cellular phone service	45.95	205.87
Pager service	0.32	78.91
Phone cards	9.08	50.96
Water and other public services	60.35	135.65
Water and sewerage maintenance	53.94	112.41
Trash and garbage collection	36.39	56.86
Septic tank cleaning	0.27	200.00
Household services	**60.29**	**311.95**
Personal services	7.99	937.77
Babysitting and child care in own home	1.89	490.61
Babysitting and child care in someone else's home	1.16	562.93
Care for elderly, invalids, handicapped, etc.	0.39	2,241.03
Adult day care centers	0.06	3,345.83
Day care centers, nurseries and preschools	5.47	884.41
Other household services	57.88	195.48
Housekeeping services	5.96	372.69
Gardening, lawn care service	13.71	173.38
Water softening service	1.19	64.29
Nonclothing laundry and dry cleaning, sent out	0.59	39.83
Nonclothing laundry and dry cleaning, coin-operated	4.25	21.82
Termite/pest control services	2.70	111.48
Home security system service fee	3.72	104.64
Other home services	2.40	239.90
Termite/pest control products	1.61	23.76
Moving, storage, and freight express	1.76	481.68
Appliance repair, including at service center	2.45	148.27
Reupholstering and furniture repair	0.55	334.09
Repairs/rentals of lawn/garden equipment, hand/power tools, etc.	1.16	157.11
Appliance rental	0.31	141.13
Rental of office equipment for nonbusiness use	0.06	183.33
Repair of computer systems for nonbusiness use	0.60	167.92
Computer information services	45.09	77.32

	percent reporting expenditure during quarter	average amount spent by purchasers per quarter
Household furnishings and equipment	**50.89%**	**$612.13**
Household textiles	19.46	117.66
Bathroom linens	6.51	44.12
Bedroom linens	10.47	100.48
Kitchen and dining room linens	2.34	28.95
Curtains and draperies	2.41	199.38
Slipcovers and decorative pillows	1.38	64.86
Sewing materials for household items	3.83	73.11
Other linens	0.78	41.99
Furniture	11.04	944.23
Mattress and springs	1.82	735.71
Other bedroom furniture	2.35	865.11
Sofas	2.28	1,038.82
Living room chairs	2.15	484.30
Living room tables	1.57	235.19
Kitchen and dining room furniture	1.54	669.81
Infants' furniture	0.88	239.77
Outdoor furniture	1.49	271.48
Wall units, cabinets, and other furniture	3.32	489.83
Floor coverings	3.45	376.67
Wall-to-wall carpeting, replacement (owner)	0.40	1,611.25
Floor coverings, nonpermanent	3.05	196.72
Major appliances	8.51	541.54
Dishwashers (built-in), garbage disposals, range hoods (owner)	0.77	453.90
Refrigerators and freezers (renter)	0.32	431.25
Refrigerators and freezers (owner)	1.45	788.79
Washing machines (renter)	0.36	328.47
Washing machines (owner)	1.21	535.54
Clothes dryers (renter)	0.29	276.72
Clothes dryers (owner)	1.02	461.27
Cooking stoves, ovens (renter)	0.17	433.82
Cooking stoves, ovens (owner)	0.94	783.78
Microwave ovens (renter)	0.54	74.07
Microwave ovens (owner)	1.04	164.18
Window air conditioners (renter)	0.16	134.38
Window air conditioners (owner)	0.33	265.15
Electric floor-cleaning equipment	2.30	174.24
Sewing machines	0.33	271.97
Small appliances and miscellaneous housewares	15.53	83.23
Housewares	9.63	76.84
Plastic dinnerware	1.82	25.00
China and other dinnerware	2.61	76.05
Flatware	1.53	65.69
Glassware	2.38	34.98
Silver serving pieces	0.14	92.86
Other serving pieces	0.93	47.31
Nonelectric cookware	3.63	70.32
Small appliances	7.78	71.02
Small electric kitchen appliances	6.69	64.54
Portable heating and cooling equipment	1.41	85.64
Miscellaneous household equipment	34.31	327.51
Window coverings	1.88	312.10
Infants' equipment	0.62	111.69
Outdoor equipment	1.04	224.28
Clocks	1.81	49.03
Lamps and lighting fixtures	3.57	114.85
Other household decorative items	8.53	207.30
Telephones and accessories	4.39	81.38
Lawn and garden equipment	2.63	463.78
Power tools	2.23	203.25

	percent reporting expenditure during quarter	average amount spent by purchasers per quarter
Small miscellaneous furnishings	1.03%	$275.97
Hand tools	2.09	73.09
Indoor plants and fresh flowers	12.84	80.84
Closet and storage items	1.75	57.00
Rental of furniture	0.21	264.29
Luggage	1.54	107.63
Computers and computer hardware, nonbusiness use	4.65	723.49
Computer software and accessories, nonbusiness use	4.15	114.82
Telephone answering devices	0.38	40.79
Calculators	0.90	40.00
Business equipment for home use	0.27	87.04
Smoke alarms (owner)	0.58	39.22
Smoke alarms (renter)	0.12	25.00
Other household appliances (owner)	1.09	260.78
Other household appliances (renter)	0.32	90.63
APPAREL AND SERVICES	**74.40**	**406.77**
Men's and boys'	**36.69**	**203.15**
• Men's apparel	**30.38**	**183.12**
Suits	1.93	310.75
Sportcoats and tailored jackets	1.56	134.29
Coats and jackets	4.98	111.45
Underwear	7.03	27.95
Hosiery	6.45	17.17
Nightwear	1.55	33.87
Accessories	5.22	39.13
Sweaters and vests	3.10	79.35
Active sportswear	4.10	63.05
Shirts	16.33	74.54
Pants	17.10	85.42
Shorts and shorts sets	4.90	53.72
Uniforms	0.99	100.76
Costumes	0.83	107.53
• Boys' (aged 2 to 15) apparel	**11.26**	**167.87**
Coats and jackets	2.39	62.66
Sweaters	1.04	71.63
Shirts	6.31	59.67
Underwear	3.03	29.37
Nightwear	1.24	30.44
Hosiery	2.84	15.58
Accessories	1.41	23.76
Suits, sportcoats, and vests	0.64	101.17
Pants	6.65	84.17
Shorts and shorts sets	3.31	58.69
Uniforms	0.95	100.53
Active sportswear	1.91	56.15
Costumes	1.40	45.54
Women's and girls'	**46.07**	**256.90**
• Women's apparel	**40.62**	**232.78**
Coats and jackets	7.74	104.81
Dresses	8.51	137.98
Sportcoats and tailored jackets	2.26	96.90
Sweaters and vests	9.57	79.70
Shirts, blouses, and tops	21.19	71.06
Skirts	5.52	51.22
Pants	21.13	85.40
Shorts and shorts sets	5.78	52.47
Active sportswear	5.71	64.80
Nightwear	5.67	43.12
Undergarments	10.88	46.48

	percent reporting expenditure during quarter	average amount spent by purchasers per quarter
Hosiery	9.72%	$18.21
Suits	3.32	177.48
Accessories	8.15	52.70
Uniforms	1.66	89.91
Costumes	1.19	106.93
• Girls' (aged 2 to 15) apparel	**12.64**	**188.25**
Coats and jackets	2.83	66.17
Dresses and suits	2.86	69.14
Shirts, blouses, and sweaters	7.13	77.91
Skirts and pants	7.10	85.63
Shorts and shorts sets	3.35	62.69
Active sportswear	2.60	59.33
Underwear and nightwear	4.26	36.85
Hosiery	2.79	15.77
Accessories	2.34	28.95
Uniforms	0.82	117.07
Costumes	1.78	57.58
Children's (under age two) apparel	**13.32**	**120.16**
Coats, jackets, and snowsuits	1.20	51.67
Outerwear including dresses	7.26	71.35
Underwear	7.39	104.70
Nightwear and loungewear	2.68	32.56
Accessories	3.55	45.00
Footwear	**31.57**	**100.86**
Men's	11.44	87.65
Boys'	5.61	66.35
Women's	17.95	80.84
Girls'	6.05	59.17
Other apparel products and services	**39.90**	**155.14**
Material for making clothes	1.31	59.54
Sewing patterns and notions	1.79	19.97
Watches	4.23	127.13
Jewelry	8.08	351.86
Shoe repair and other shoe services	0.83	33.73
Coin-operated apparel laundry and dry cleaning	13.89	62.74
Apparel alteration, repair, and tailoring services	2.88	44.44
Clothing rental	0.42	135.71
Watch and jewelry repair	1.90	50.26
Professional laundry, dry cleaning	18.39	81.81
Clothing storage	0.10	117.50
TRANSPORTATION	**94.36**	**2,047.93**
Vehicle purchases	**6.06**	**14,014.32**
Cars and trucks, new	1.70	25,711.47
New cars	0.77	21,846.43
New trucks	0.94	28,603.99
Cars and trucks, used	4.21	9,395.78
Used cars	2.35	8,091.49
Used trucks	1.94	10,588.14
Other vehicles	0.25	6,645.00
New motorcycles	0.13	9,042.31
Used motorcycles	0.12	3,918.75
Gasoline and motor oil	**90.26**	**442.45**
Gasoline	89.66	408.92
Diesel fuel	1.58	324.37
Gasoline on trips	22.10	113.52
Motor oil	10.19	22.11
Motor oil on trips	22.10	1.14

	percent reporting expenditure during quarter	average amount spent by purchasers per quarter
Other vehicle expenses	**80.14%**	**$718.88**
Vehicle finance charges	33.58	240.78
Automobile finance charges	18.32	181.88
Truck finance charges	18.37	227.14
Motorcycle and plane finance charges	0.71	115.14
Other vehicle finance charges	1.37	364.42
Maintenance and repairs	50.85	297.59
Coolant, additives, brake, transmission fluids	5.70	12.85
Tires	8.36	281.37
Parts, equipment, and accessories	10.31	104.34
Vehicle audio equipment	0.12	208.33
Body work and painting	1.71	533.63
Clutch, transmission repair	1.62	606.02
Drive shaft and rear-end repair	0.36	431.25
Brake work	4.53	245.92
Repair to steering or front-end	1.05	361.67
Repair to engine cooling system	1.83	245.22
Motor tune-up	4.65	224.57
Lube, oil change, and oil filters	32.74	42.94
Front-end alignment, wheel balance, rotation	2.08	109.74
Shock absorber replacement	0.29	237.93
Repair tires and other repair work	8.00	156.03
Exhaust system repair	1.17	217.74
Electrical system repair	2.51	224.50
Motor repair, replacement	2.73	640.29
Auto repair service policy	0.35	646.43
Vehicle accessories, including labor	0.67	477.99
Vehicle audio equipment, including labor	0.50	299.00
Vehicle air conditioning repair	1.31	271.56
Vehicle insurance	52.95	455.32
Vehicle rental, leases, licenses, other charges	38.63	266.22
Leased and rented vehicles	6.52	977.19
Rented vehicles	3.09	309.63
Auto rental	0.55	256.36
Auto rental on trips	1.95	271.54
Truck rental	0.35	337.14
Truck rental on trips	0.32	354.69
Leased vehicles	3.69	1,467.34
Car lease payments	2.19	1,195.55
Truck lease payments	1.80	1,333.89
Vehicle registration, state	16.22	124.72
Vehicle registration, local	2.01	85.82
Driver's license	5.86	30.55
Vehicle inspection	5.89	39.43
Parking fees	11.85	62.05
Parking fees in home city, excluding residence	9.02	66.16
Parking fees on trips	3.71	37.33
Tolls on trips	7.28	15.90
Towing charges	1.14	111.40
Automobile service clubs	3.93	83.46
Public transportation	**18.19**	**592.03**
Airline fares	10.35	666.52
Intercity bus fares	4.14	56.46
Intracity mass transit fares	6.65	174.14
Local transportation on trips	5.41	46.21
Taxi fares and limousine service on trips	5.41	27.13
Taxi fares and limousine service	2.97	106.14
Intercity train fares	3.84	116.15
Ship fares	2.74	475.36
School bus	0.08	231.25

	percent reporting expenditure during quarter	average amount spent by purchasers per quarter
HEALTH CARE	**78.68%**	**$766.33**
Health insurance	**64.74**	**514.25**
Commercial health insurance	14.50	469.86
Traditional fee-for-service health plan (not BCBS)	4.23	425.24
Preferred-provider health plan (not BCBS)	10.41	481.68
Blue Cross, Blue Shield	20.92	485.05
Traditional fee-for-service health plan	3.39	511.21
Preferred-provider health plan	8.58	494.11
Health maintenance organization	6.60	430.34
Commercial Medicare supplement	2.43	481.89
Other BCBS health insurance	0.74	220.95
Health maintenance plans (HMOs)	15.69	433.57
Medicare payments	23.35	263.60
Commercial Medicare supplements/other health insurance	11.26	299.71
Commercial Medicare supplement (not BCBS)	4.87	476.90
Other health insurance (not BCBS)	6.78	155.24
Medical services	**40.59**	**399.34**
Physician's services	26.45	138.54
Dental services	14.18	424.19
Eye care services	7.27	133.73
Service by professionals other than physician	5.96	165.86
Lab tests, X-rays	4.54	147.30
Hospital room	1.64	609.91
Hospital services other than room	2.65	483.02
Care in convalescent or nursing home	0.26	3,974.04
Other medical services	2.44	240.37
Prescription drugs	**43.46**	**201.00**
Medical supplies	**8.46**	**243.23**
Eyeglasses and contact lenses	6.76	175.89
Hearing aids	1.02	372.79
Medical equipment for general use	1.20	140.63
Supportive/convalescent medical equipment	1.03	173.79
Rental of medical equipment	0.51	92.16
Rental of supportive, convalescent medical equipment	0.58	161.21
ENTERTAINMENT	**89.31**	**585.28**
Fees and admissions	**47.60**	**277.28**
Recreation expenses on trips	9.33	72.45
Social, recreation, civic club membership	10.85	226.24
Fees for participant sports	10.75	172.05
Participant sports on trips	4.32	154.63
Movie, theater, opera, ballet	31.22	74.04
Movie, other admissions on trips	9.78	122.78
Admission to sports events	6.65	135.53
Admission to sports events on trips	9.78	40.93
Fees for recreational lessons	6.84	301.24
Other entertainment services on trips	9.33	72.45
Television, radios, and sound equipment	**82.58**	**235.27**
Television	76.77	212.52
Community antenna or cable TV	71.16	165.48
Color TV, console	0.95	1,380.53
Color TV, portable, table model	2.58	385.66
VCRs and video disc players	3.53	170.33
Video cassettes, tapes, and discs	17.51	60.87
Video game hardware and software	4.36	105.16
Repair of TV, radio, and sound equipment	0.54	139.81
Rental of televisions	0.09	225.00

	percent reporting expenditure during quarter	average amount spent by purchasers per quarter
Radios and sound equipment	36.95%	$84.27
Radios	1.11	87.39
Tape recorders and players	0.31	95.97
Sound components and component systems	1.40	251.43
Compact disc, tape, record, video mail order clubs	1.74	59.63
Records, CDs, audio tapes, needles	17.32	50.89
Rental of VCR, radio, sound equipment	0.05	55.00
Musical instruments and accessories	1.35	371.48
Rental and repair of musical instruments	0.32	178.13
Rental of video cassettes, tapes, discs, films	25.17	35.37
Sound equipment accessories	1.03	173.30
Satellite dishes	0.14	137.50
Pets, toys, and playground equipment	**37.01**	**203.94**
Pets	27.71	174.03
Pet purchase, supplies, and medicines	22.46	99.55
Pet services	4.96	126.36
Veterinary services	8.36	234.39
Toys, games, hobbies, and tricycles	14.34	172.96
Playground equipment	0.31	268.55
Other entertainment supplies, equipment, services	**28.96**	**417.67**
Unmotored recreational vehicles	0.18	7,693.06
Boat without motor and boat trailers	0.11	3,993.18
Trailer and other attachable campers	0.08	11,818.75
Motorized recreational vehicles	0.31	18,516.13
Rental of recreational vehicles	0.54	287.50
Outboard motors	0.06	541.67
Docking and landing fees	0.40	351.25
Sports, recreation, exercise equipment	11.02	242.97
Athletic gear, game tables, exercise equipment	5.80	193.45
Bicycles	1.51	187.75
Camping equipment	1.04	137.26
Hunting and fishing equipment	2.23	246.19
Winter sports equipment	0.37	281.76
Water sports equipment	0.56	207.59
Other sports equipment	1.24	239.72
Rental and repair of miscellaneous sports equipment	0.36	172.92
Photographic equipment and supplies	22.16	88.70
Film	13.74	22.16
Film processing	15.31	33.16
Repair and rental of photographic equipment	0.13	190.38
Photographic equipment	2.31	312.99
Photographer fees	2.60	156.06
PERSONAL CARE PRODUCTS AND SERVICES	**64.81**	**105.01**
Wigs and hairpieces	0.70	67.86
Electric personal care appliances	3.49	44.56
Personal care services	63.84	103.42
READING	**48.40**	**67.18**
Newspaper subscriptions	21.92	47.63
Newspapers, nonsubscriptions	13.59	17.37
Magazine subscriptions	8.36	44.50
Magazines, nonsubscriptions	10.20	20.49
Books purchased through book clubs	2.16	63.66
Books not purchased through book clubs	19.67	63.15
EDUCATION	**15.43**	**1,352.66**
College tuition	5.34	2,534.41
Elementary/high school tuition	1.88	1,898.94
Other schools tuition	0.71	955.28
Other school expenses including rentals	4.05	301.48

	percent reporting expenditure during quarter	average amount spent by purchasers per quarter
Books, supplies for college	4.64%	$317.13
Books, supplies for elementary, high school	3.76	90.16
Books, supplies for day care, nursery school	0.56	103.57
TOBACCO PRODUCTS AND SMOKING SUPPLIES	**22.50**	**317.90**
Cigarettes	20.05	329.24
Other tobacco products	3.35	164.70
FINANCIAL PRODUCTS AND SERVICES		
Miscellaneous financial products and services	**40.87**	**387.52**
Lottery and gambling losses	12.71	101.14
Legal fees	2.34	1,362.18
Funeral expenses	1.32	1,245.83
Safe deposit box rental	2.25	35.78
Checking accounts, other bank service charges	13.16	35.52
Cemetery lots, vaults, and maintenance fees	0.65	518.46
Accounting fees	4.88	262.40
Finance charges, except mortgage and vehicles	6.49	609.32
Occupational expenses	6.50	165.77
Expenses for other properties	5.31	431.40
Credit card memberships	1.03	58.50
Shopping club membership fees	3.00	47.67
Cash contributions	**48.31**	**728.65**
Support for college students	1.92	1,074.09
Alimony expenditures	0.36	3,284.03
Child support expenditures	3.07	1,344.46
Gifts to nonhousehold members of stocks, bonds and mutual funds	0.32	1,950.78
Cash contributions to charities	16.51	238.51
Cash contributions to religious organizations	30.80	458.69
Cash contributions to educational organizations	2.09	550.96
Cash contributions to political organizations	2.34	177.14
Other cash gifts	13.19	574.17
Personal insurance and pensions	**85.27**	**1,414.10**
Life and other personal insurance	34.96	279.13
Life, endowment, annuity, other personal insurance	34.22	276.29
Other nonhealth insurance	1.92	158.33
Pensions and Social Security	**80.58**	**1,375.29**
Deductions for government retirement	2.93	669.37
Deductions for railroad retirement	0.06	1,112.50
Deductions for private pensions	10.97	1,181.84
Nonpayroll deposit to retirement plans	7.60	1,317.57
Deductions for Social Security	80.38	1,067.62
PERSONAL TAXES	**55.64**	**973.15**
Federal income taxes	50.23	756.00
State and local income taxes	35.69	330.71
Other taxes	15.59	280.28
GIFTS	**30.32**	**648.08**
Food	**1.03**	**898.79**
Housing	**11.51**	**320.63**
Household textiles	2.50	74.70
Appliances and miscellaneous housewares	2.16	145.49
Major appliances	0.41	354.88
Small appliances and miscellaneous housewares	1.84	91.71
Miscellaneous household equipment	5.54	128.20
Other housing	3.62	684.88

	percent reporting expenditure during quarter	average amount spent by purchasers per quarter
Apparel and services	**17.78%**	**$226.17**
Males aged two or older	4.89	202.30
Females aged two or older	6.51	227.30
Children under age two	8.60	82.33
Other apparel products and services	5.07	166.52
Jewelry and watches	2.20	273.07
All other apparel products and services	3.14	77.55
Transportation	**1.32**	**873.11**
Health care	**1.40**	**744.64**
Entertainment	**7.81**	**196.90**
Toys, games, hobbies, and tricycles	4.68	147.70
Other entertainment	3.99	212.16
Education	**2.11**	**2,816.47**
All other gifts	**4.19**	**319.09**

Source: Calculations by New Strategist based on the 2004 Consumer Expenditure Survey

Appendix D: Spending by Product and Service Ranked by Amount Spent, 2004

(average annual spending of consumer units on products and services, ranked by amount spent, 2004)

Deductions for Social Security	$3,432.61
Vehicle purchases (net outlay)	3,397.07
Groceries (also shown by individual category)	3,346.82
Mortgage interest	2,785.37
Restaurants (also shown by meal category)	2,259.72
Rent	2,125.93
Gasoline and motor oil	1,597.56
Federal income taxes	1,518.95
Property taxes	1,391.17
Health insurance	1,331.71
Electricity	1,064.41
Vehicle insurance	964.37
Restaurant dinners	795.59
Restaurant lunches	725.07
Vehicle maintenance and repairs	651.66
Women's clothes	631.01
Residential phone service	592.31
Cash contributions to church, religious organizations	565.11
College tuition	541.35
Maintenance and repair services, owned homes	530.63
Deductions for private pensions	518.59
Cable TV or community antenna	471.01
Alcoholic beverages (beer and wine also shown separately)	459.27
Natural gas	424.02
Nonpayroll deposit to retirement plans	400.54
State and local income taxes	397.82
Life and other personal insurance	390.34
Cellular phone service	378.39
Prescription drugs	349.41
Vehicle finance charges	323.41
Men's clothes	317.28
Homeowner's insurance	314.75
Cash gifts to nonhousehold members	302.93
Restaurant snacks	297.45
Lodging on trips	277.89
Airline fares	275.94
Beef	265.34
Personal care services	264.09
Cigarettes	264.05
Water and sewerage maintenance	242.54
Dental services	240.60
Motorized recreational vehicles	229.60
Leased vehicles	216.58
Restaurant breakfasts	210.06
Beer	207.63
Day care centers, nurseries, and preschools	193.51
Fresh fruits	186.74
Fresh vegetables	182.94
Pork	181.14
Child support	165.10
Finance charges other than mortgage and vehicle	158.18
Decorative items for the home	158.10
Cash contributions to charities	157.51

Poultry	$155.61
Women's footwear	153.81
Interest paid, home equity loan/line of credit	150.62
Laundry and cleaning supplies	148.56
Cosmetics, perfume, bath preparations	147.41
Physician's services	146.58
Taxes except federal, state, local, personal property, and property	146.39
Elementary and high school tuition	142.80
Carbonated drinks	141.89
Movie, theater, opera, ballet tickets	140.49
Computer information services (Internet)	139.46
Owned vacation homes	137.22
Computers and computer hardware, nonbusiness use	134.57
Fresh milk	128.94
Fish and seafood	127.80
Legal fees	127.50
School expenses (except tuition, books, supplies)	119.39
Wine	116.84
Jewelry	113.72
Cheese	113.67
Men's footwear	110.67
Pet food	110.31
Girls' (2 to 15) clothes	107.60
Prepared food except frozen, salads, and desserts	102.74
Fees for participant sports	100.70
Toys, games, arts and crafts, and tricycles	99.21
Social, recreation, civic club membership	98.19
Gardening, lawn care service	95.08
Sofas	94.74
Televisions	92.75
Expenses for other properties	91.63
Boys' (2 to 15) clothes	88.88
Housekeeping services	88.85
Ready-to-eat and cooked cereals	86.69
Potato chips and other snacks	86.06
Cleansing and toilet tissue, paper towels, and napkins	85.84
Bedroom linens	85.72
Lawn and garden supplies	83.44
Candy and chewing gum	83.13
Trash and garbage collection	82.77
Support for college students	82.49
Fees for recreational lessons	82.42
Bedroom furniture except mattress and springs	81.32
Vehicle registration, state	80.92
Nonprescription drugs	80.31
Infants' (under age 2) clothes	78.51
Deductions for government retirement	78.45
Veterinary services	78.38
Frozen prepared foods, except meals	78.11
Stationery, stationery supplies, giftwrap	74.86
Postage	74.12
Home maintenance and repair materials, owned homes	73.33
Lunch meats (cold cuts)	72.99
Nonalcoholic beverages (except carbonated, coffee, fruit-flavored drinks, and tea) and ice	70.10
Lottery and gambling losses	66.54
Funeral expenses	65.78
Wall units, cabinets, and other occasional furniture	65.05
Fuel oil	64.19
Hair care products	63.90
School lunches	63.39
Babysitting and child care	63.21
Ice cream products	60.22

Professional laundry and dry cleaning	$60.18
School books, supplies, equipment for college	58.86
Catered affairs	58.56
Pet purchase, supplies, medicine	57.85
Housing while attending school	57.73
Unmotored recreational vehicles	55.39
Books, except for school	55.19
Canned and bottled fruit juice	55.05
Mattress and springs	53.56
Athletic gear, game tables, and exercise equipment	53.07
Bread, other than white	52.59
Ship fares	52.10
Admission to sporting events	52.06
Refrigerators, freezers	51.27
Accounting fees	51.22
Hospital services other than room	51.20
Nonprescription vitamins	50.57
Lawn and garden equipment	48.79
Eyeglasses and contact lenses	47.56
Alimony	47.29
Cookies	46.57
Intracity mass transit fares	46.32
Cash contributions to educational institutions	46.06
Bottled gas	45.20
Occupational expenses	43.10
Video cassettes, tapes, and discs	42.63
Biscuits and rolls	42.11
Eggs	41.84
Newspaper subscriptions	41.76
Living room chairs	41.65
Indoor plants, fresh flowers	41.52
Care in convalescent or nursing home	41.33
Kitchen, dining room furniture	41.26
Sauces and gravies	40.94
Groceries on trips	40.86
Ground rent	40.10
Hospital room	40.01
Medical services by professionals other than physician	39.54
Coffee	39.12
Cakes and cupcakes	39.04
Eyecare services	38.89
Alcoholic beverages purchased on trips	38.37
Rented vehicles	38.27
Canned and packaged soups	36.50
Rent as pay	36.08
Outdoor equipment	35.99
Boys' footwear	35.92
Rental of video cassettes, tapes, films, and discs	35.61
CDs, audio tapes, records	35.26
White bread	35.04
Care for elderly, invalids, handicapped	34.96
Coin-operated apparel laundry and dry cleaning	34.86
Oral hygiene products	34.63
Canned vegetables	34.49
Deodorants, feminine hygiene, miscellaneous personal care	34.33
Moving, storage, freight express	33.91
Power tools	33.44
Photographic equipment and supplies (except film)	33.16
Film and film processing	32.49
Cooking stoves, ovens	32.42
Hunting and fishing equipment	31.82
Frozen meals	31.79
Topicals and dressings	31.53
Personal property taxes	31.17

Nuts	$31.01
Washing machines	30.65
Baby food	30.08
Parking fees	29.41
Taxi fares and limousine services	29.05
Fats and oils	28.56
Property management, owned home	28.55
Frozen vegetables	28.50
Girls' footwear	28.34
Wall-to-wall carpeting	27.98
Food or board at school	27.89
Electric floor-cleaning equipment	27.71
Salad dressings	27.44
School tuition (except college, elementary, high school)	27.13
Maintenance and repair services, rented home	26.94
Telephones and accessories	26.83
Lab tests, X-rays	26.75
Pasta, cornmeal and other cereal products	26.55
Frozen and refrigerated bakery products	26.32
Prepared salads	25.43
Pet services	25.07
Gifts of stocks, bonds, and mutual funds to nonhousehold members	24.97
Crackers	24.60
Meals as pay	24.45
VCRs and video disc players	24.05
Floor coverings, nonpermanent	24.00
Sweetrolls, coffee cakes, doughnuts	23.59
Window coverings	23.47
Sound equipment	23.39
Frankfurters	22.52
Salt, spices, other seasonings	22.22
Tableware, nonelectric kitchenware	22.20
Fresh fruit juice	22.07
Tobacco products except cigarettes	22.07
Jams, preserves, other sweets	22.04
Clothes dryers	22.03
Butter	21.81
Watches	21.51
Bathroom linens	21.26
Glassware	20.88
Musical instruments and accessories	20.06
Baking needs	19.97
Noncarbonated fruit-flavored drinks	19.79
Tolls	19.23
Curtains and draperies	19.22
Computer software and accessories for nonbusiness use	19.06
Shaving needs	18.71
Checking accounts, other bank service charges	18.70
Phone cards	18.51
Rice	18.46
Video game hardware and software	18.34
Nonelectric cookware	18.10
Intercity train fares	17.84
Closet and storage items	17.83
Tea	17.63
Small electric kitchen appliances	17.27
Cash contributions to political organizations	16.58
Lamps and lighting fixtures	16.40
Photographer fees	16.23
Canned fruits	16.19
Outdoor furniture	16.18
Sugar	16.10
Laundry and cleaning equipment	15.72
Home security system service fee	15.57

Cream	$15.39
Hearing aids	15.21
Magazine subscriptions	14.88
Living room tables	14.77
Appliance repair, including at service center	14.53
Dishwashers (built-in), garbage disposals, range hoods	14.34
Pies, tarts, turnovers	13.99
Prepared flour mixes	13.78
School books, supplies, equipment for elementary, high school	13.56
Camping equipment	13.48
Cemetery lots, vaults, maintenance fees	13.48
China and other dinnerware	13.47
Automobile service clubs	13.12
Material for making clothes	13.05
Peanut butter	12.52
Lamb, organ meats	12.48
Services for termite/pest control	12.04
Office furniture for home use	11.37
Bicycles	11.34
Sewing materials for household items (except clothes)	11.20
Prepared desserts	10.91
Nondairy cream and imitation milk	10.80
Wood	10.61
Olives, pickles, relishes	10.52
Local transportation on trips	10.00
Kitchen and dining room linens	9.84
Electric personal care appliances	9.74
Tape recorders and players	9.71
Dried vegetables	9.58
Margarine	9.57
Newspapers, nonsubscriptions	9.44
Intercity bus fares	9.35
Vehicle inspection	9.29
Slipcovers, decorative pillows	9.12
Vegetable juice	9.06
Infants' furniture	8.44
Microwave ovens	8.43
Magazines, nonsubscriptions	8.36
Flour	8.32
Adult day care centers	8.03
Infants' equipment	7.86
Sewing patterns and notions	7.82
Clocks	7.64
Reupholstering, furniture repair	7.35
Repairs/rentals of household equipment	7.29
Driver's license	7.16
Supportive and convalescent medical equipment	7.16
Tenant's insurance	7.06
Vehicle registration, local	6.90
Artificial sweeteners	6.85
Medical equipment for general use	6.75
Luggage	6.63
Delivery services	6.52
Frozen fruit juice	6.44
Hair accessories	6.37
Management and upkeep for security, owned home	6.36
Dried fruit	6.35
Hand tools	6.11
Shopping club membership fees	5.72
Docking and landing fees	5.62
Alteration, repair and tailoring of apparel and accessories	5.12
Towing charges	5.08
Maintenance and repair materials, rented home	5.07
Portable heating and cooling equipment	4.83

Water sports equipment	$4.65
Window air conditioners	4.36
Winter sports equipment	4.17
Compact disc, tape, record, and video mail order clubs	4.15
Repair of computer systems for nonbusiness use	4.03
Flatware	4.02
Watch and jewelry repair	3.82
Fireworks	3.75
Rental of supportive, convalescent medical equipment	3.74
Coin-operated household laundry and dry cleaning (nonclothing)	3.71
Radios	3.67
Sewing machines	3.59
Frozen fruits	3.53
Parking at owned home	3.43
Playground equipment	3.33
Bread and cracker products	3.25
Safe deposit box rental	3.22
Water softening service	3.06
Repair of TV, radio, and sound equipment	3.02
Deductions for railroad retirement	2.67
Rental and repair of sports equipment	2.49
Credit card memberships	2.41
School books, supplies, equipment for day care, nursery, other	2.32
Clothing rental	2.28
Rental and repair of musical instruments	2.28
Rental of furniture	2.22
Septic tank cleaning	2.16
Visual goods	2.10
Smoking accessories	2.02
Wigs and hairpieces	1.90
Rental of medical equipment	1.88
Plastic dinnerware	1.82
Appliance rental	1.75
Termite/pest control products	1.53
Pinball, electronic video games	1.51
Calculators	1.44
Portable dishwasher	1.22
Shoe repair and other shoe service	1.12
Smoke alarms	1.03
Pager service	1.01
Repair and rental of photographic equipment	0.99
Professional laundry and dry cleaning, sent out (nonclothing)	0.94
Business equipment for home use	0.94
Rental of televisions	0.81
Satellite dishes	0.77
School bus	0.74
Telephone answering devices	0.62
Repair of miscellaneous household equipment and furnishings	0.54
Clothing storage	0.47
Silver serving pieces	0.30
Rental of VCR, radio, and sound equipment	0.11

Source: Calculations by New Strategist based on the 2004 Consumer Expenditure Survey

Glossary

alcoholic beverages Includes beer and ale, wine, whiskey, gin, vodka, rum, and other alcoholic beverages.

annual spending The annual amount spent per household. The Bureau of Labor Statistics calculates the annual average for all households in a segment, not just for those purchasing an item. The averages are calculated by integrating the results of the diary (weekly) and interview (quarterly) portions of the Consumer Expenditure Survey. For items purchased by most households—such as bread—average annual spending figures are a fairly accurate account of actual spending. For products and services purchased by few households during a year's time—such as cars—the average annual amount spent is much less than what purchasers spend. For more about the methodology of the Consumer Expenditure Survey, see Appendix A.

apparel, accessories, and related services Includes the following:

• *men's and boys' apparel* Includes coats, jackets, sweaters, vests, sport coats, tailored jackets, slacks, shorts and short sets, sportswear, shirts, underwear, nightwear, hosiery, uniforms, and other accessories.

• *women's and girls' apparel* Includes coats, jackets, furs, sport coats, tailored jackets, sweaters, vests, blouses, shirts, dresses, dungarees, culottes, slacks, shorts, sportswear, underwear, nightwear, uniforms, hosiery, and other accessories.

• *infants' apparel* Includes coats, jackets, snowsuits, underwear, diapers, dresses, crawlers, sleeping garments, hosiery, footwear, and other accessories for children.

• *footwear* Includes articles such as shoes, slippers, boots, and other similar items. It excludes footwear for babies and footwear used for sports such as bowling or golf shoes.

• *other apparel products and services* Includes material for making clothes, shoe repair, alterations and sewing patterns and notions, clothing rental, clothing storage, dry cleaning, sent-out laundry, watches, jewelry, and repairs to watches and jewelry.

cash contributions Includes cash contributed to persons or organizations outside the consumer unit including alimony and child support payments, care of students away from home, and contributions to religious, educational, charitable, or political organizations.

consumer unit Defined as follows:

• All members of a household who are related by blood, marriage, adoption, or other legal arrangements.

• A person living alone or sharing a household with others or living as a roomer in a private home or lodging house or in permanent living quarters in a hotel or motel, but who is financially independent.

• Two persons or more living together who pool their income to make joint expenditure decisions. Financial independence is determined by the three major expense categories: housing, food, and other living expenses. To be considered financially

independent, at least two of the three major expense categories have to be provided by the respondent. For convenience, called households in the text of this report.

education Includes tuition, fees, books, supplies, and equipment for public and private nursery schools, elementary and high schools, colleges and universities, and other schools.

entertainment Includes the following:

• *fees and admissions* Includes fees for participant sports; admissions to sporting events, movies, concerts, plays; health, swimming, tennis, and country club memberships, and other social recreational and fraternal organizations; recreational lessons or instructions; and recreational expenses on trips.

• *television, radio, and sound equipment* Includes television sets, video recorders, video cassettes, tapes, discs, disc players, video game hardware, video game cartridges, cable TV, radios, phonographs, tape recorders and players, sound components, records and tapes, musical instruments, and rental and repair of TV and sound equipment.

• *pets, toys, hobbies, and playground equipment* Includes pet food, pet services, veterinary expenses, toys, games, hobbies, and playground equipment.

• *other entertainment equipment and services* Includes indoor exercise equipment, athletic shoes, bicycles, trailers, campers, camping equipment, rental of cameras and trailers, hunting and fishing equipment, sports equipment, winter sports equipment, water sports equipment, boats, boat motors and boat trailers, rental of boats, landing and docking fees, rental and repair of sports equipment, photographic equipment, film and film processing, photographer fees, repair and rental of photo equipment, fireworks, pinball and electronic video games.

expenditure The transaction cost including excise and sales taxes of goods and services acquired during the survey period. The full cost of each purchase is recorded even though full payment may not have been made at the date of purchase. Expenditure estimates include gifts. Excluded from expenditures are purchases or portions of purchases directly assignable to business purposes and periodic credit or installment payments on goods and services already acquired.

federal income tax Includes federal income tax withheld in the survey year to pay for income earned in survey year plus additional tax paid in survey year to cover any underpayment or underwithholding of tax in the year prior to the survey.

financial products and services Includes union dues, professional dues and fees, other occupational expenses, funerals, cemetery lots, and unclassified fees and personal services.

food Includes the following:

• *food at home* Refers to the total expenditures for food at grocery stores or other food stores during the interview period. It is calculated by multiplying the number of visits to a grocery or other food store by the average amount spent per visit. It excludes the purchase of nonfood items.

• *food away from home* Includes all meals (breakfast, lunch, brunch, and dinner) at restaurants, carryouts, and vending machines, including tips, plus meals as pay, special catered affairs such as weddings, bar mitzvahs, and confirmations, and meals away from home on trips.

gifts for nonhousehold members Includes gift expenditures for people outside of the consumer unit. The amount spent on gifts is also included in individual product and service categories.

health care Includes the following:

• *health insurance* Includes health maintenance plans (HMOs), Blue Cross/Blue Shield, commercial health insurance, Medicare, Medicare supplemental insurance, and other health insurance.

• *medical services* Includes hospital room and services, physicians' services, services of a practitioner other than a physician, eye and dental care, lab tests, X-rays, nursing, therapy services, care in convalescent or nursing home, and other medical care.

• *drugs* Includes prescription and nonprescription drugs, internal and respiratory over-the-counter drugs.

• *medical supplies* Includes eyeglasses and contact lenses, topicals and dressings, antiseptics, bandages, cotton, first aid kits, contraceptives; medical equipment for general use such as syringes, ice bags, thermometers, vaporizers, heating pads; supportive or convalescent medical equipment such as hearing aids, braces, canes, crutches, and walkers.

household According to the Census Bureau, all the people who occupy a household. A group of unrelated people who share a housing unit as roommates or unmarried partners is also counted as a household. Households do not include group quarters such as college dormitories, prisons, or nursing homes. A household may contain more than one consumer unit. The terms "household" and "consumer unit" are used interchangeably in this report.

household furnishings and equipment Includes the following:

• *household textiles* Includes bathroom, kitchen, dining room, and other linens, curtains and drapes, slipcovers and decorative pillows, and sewing materials.

• *furniture* Includes living room, dining room, kitchen, bedroom, nursery, porch, lawn, and other outdoor furniture.

• *carpet, rugs, and other floor coverings* Includes installation and replacement of wall-to-wall carpets, room-size rugs, and other soft floor coverings.

• *major appliances* Includes refrigerators, freezers, dishwashers, stoves, ovens, garbage disposals, vacuum cleaners, microwaves, air-conditioners, sewing machines, washing machines and dryers, and floor-cleaning equipment.

• *small appliances and miscellaneous housewares* Includes small electrical kitchen appliances, portable heating and cooling equipment, china and other dinnerware, flatware, glassware, silver and other serving pieces, nonelectric cookware, and plastic dinnerware. Excludes personal care appliances.

• *miscellaneous household equipment* Includes typewriters, luggage, lamps and other light fixtures, window coverings, clocks, lawn mowers and gardening equipment, other hand and power tools, telephone answering devices, telephone accessories, computers and computer hardware for home use, calculators, office equipment for home use, floral arrangements and house plants, rental of furniture, closet and storage items, household decorative items, infants' equipment, outdoor equipment, smoke alarms, other household appliances, and small miscellaneous furnishing.

household services Includes the following:

• *personal services* Includes baby sitting, day care, and care of elderly and handicapped persons.

• *other household services* Includes housekeeping services, gardening and lawn care services, coin-operated laundry and dry-cleaning of household textiles, termite and pest control products, moving, storage, and freight expenses, repair of household appliances and other household equipment, reupholstering and furniture repair, rental and repair of lawn and gardening tools, and rental of other household equipment.

housekeeping supplies Includes soaps, detergents, other laundry cleaning products, cleansing and toilet tissue, paper towels, napkins, and miscellaneous household products; lawn and garden supplies, postage, stationery, stationery supplies, and gift wrap.

income before taxes The total money earnings and selected money receipts accruing to a consumer unit during the 12 months prior to the interview date. Income includes the following components:

• *wages and salaries* Includes total money earnings for all members of the consumer unit aged 14 or older from all jobs, including civilian wages and salaries, Armed Forces pay and allowances, piece-rate payments, commissions, tips, National Guard or Reserve pay (received for training periods), and cash bonuses before deductions for taxes, pensions, union dues, etc.

• *self-employment income* Includes net business and farm income, which consists of net income (gross receipts minus operating expenses) from a profession or unincorporated business or from the operation of a farm by an owner, tenant, or sharecropper. If the business or farm is a partnership, only an appropriate share of net income is recorded. Losses are also recorded.

• *Social Security, private and government retirement* Includes payments by the federal government made under retirement, survivor, and disability insurance programs to retired persons, dependents of deceased insured workers, or to disabled workers; and private pensions or retirement benefits received by retired persons or their survivors, either directly or through an insurance company.

• *interest, dividends, rental income, and other property income* Includes interest income on savings or bonds; payments made by a corporation to its stockholders, periodic receipts from estates or trust funds; net income or loss from the rental of property, real estate, or farms, and net income or loss from roomers or boarders.

• *unemployment and workers' compensation and veterans' benefits* Includes income from unemployment compensation and workers' compensation, and veterans' payments including educational benefits, but excluding military retirement.

• *public assistance, supplemental security income, and food stamps* Includes public assistance or welfare, including money received from job training grants; supplemental security income paid by federal, state, and local welfare agencies to low-income persons who are aged 65 or older, blind, or disabled; and the value of food stamps obtained.

• *regular contributions for support* Includes alimony and child support as well as any regular contributions from persons outside the consumer unit.

• *other income* Includes money income from care of foster children, cash scholarships, fellowships, or stipends not based on working; and meals and rent as pay.

indexed spending The indexed spending figures compare the spending of each demographic segment with that of the average household. To compute an index, the amount spent on an item by a demographic segment is divided by the amount spent on the item by the average household. That figure is then multiplied by 100. An index of 100 is the average for all households. An index of 132 means average spending by households in a segment is 32 percent above average (100 plus 32). An index of 75 means average spending by households in a segment is 25 percent below average (100 minus 25). Indexed spending figures identify the consumer units that spend the most on a product or service.

life and other personal insurance Includes premiums from whole life and term insurance; endowments; income and other life insurance; mortgage guarantee insurance; mortgage life insurance; premiums for personal life liability, accident and disability; and other nonhealth insurance not for homes and vehicles.

market share The market share is the percentage of total household spending on an item that is accounted for by a demographic segment. Market shares are calculated by dividing a demographic segment's total spending on an item by the total spending of all households on the item. Total spending on an item for all households is calculated by multiplying average spending by the total number of households. Total spending

on an item for each demographic segment is calculated by multiplying the segment's average spending by the number of households in the segment. Market shares reveal the demographic segments that account for the largest share of spending on a product or service.

pensions and Social Security Includes all Social Security contributions paid by employees; employees' contributions to railroad retirement, government retirement, and private pensions programs; retirement programs for the self-employed.

personal care Includes products for the hair, oral hygiene products, shaving needs, cosmetics and bath products, suntan lotions and hand creams, electric personal care appliances, incontinence products, other personal care products, personal care services such as hair care services (haircuts, bleaching, tinting, coloring, conditioning treatments, permanents, press, and curls), styling and other services for wigs and hairpieces, body massages or slenderizing treatments, facials, manicures, pedicures, shaves, and electrolysis.

quarterly spending Quarterly spending data are collected in the interview portion of the Consumer Expenditure Survey. The quarterly spending tables show the percentage of households purchasing an item during an average quarter, and the amount spent during the quarter on the item by purchasers. Not all items are included in the interview portion of the Consumer Expenditure Survey. For more about the methodology of the Consumer Expenditure Survey, see Appendix A.

reading Includes subscriptions for newspapers, magazines, and books through book clubs; purchase of single-copy newspapers and magazines, books, and encyclopedias and other reference books.

reference person The first member mentioned by the respondent when asked to "Start with the name of the person or one of the persons who owns or rents the home." It is with respect to this person that the relationship of other consumer unit members is determined. Also called the householder or head of household.

shelter Includes the following:

• *owned dwellings* Includes interest on mortgages, property taxes and insurance, refinancing and prepayment charges, ground rent, expenses for property management/security, homeowners' insurance, fire insurance and extended coverage, landscaping expenses for repairs and maintenance contracted out (including periodic maintenance and service contracts), and expenses of materials for owner-performed repairs and maintenance for dwellings used or maintained by the consumer unit, but not dwellings maintained for business or rent.

• *rented dwellings* Includes rent paid for dwellings, rent received as pay, parking fees, maintenance, and other expenses.

• *other lodging* Includes all expenses for vacation homes, school, college, hotels, motels, cottages, trailer camps, and other lodging while out of town.

• *utilities, fuels, and public services* Includes natural gas, electricity, fuel oil, coal, bottled gas, wood, and other fuels; telephone services; water, garbage and trash collection, sewerage maintenance, septic tank cleaning, and other public services.

state and local income taxes Includes state and local income taxes withheld in the survey year to pay for income earned in survey year plus additional taxes paid in the survey year to cover any underpayment or underwithholding of taxes in the year prior to the survey.

tobacco and smoking supplies Includes cigarettes, cigars, snuff, loose smoking tobacco, chewing tobacco, and smoking accessories such as cigarette or cigar holders, pipes, flints, lighters, pipe cleaners, and other smoking products and accessories.

transportation Includes the following:

• *vehicle purchases (net outlay)* Includes the net outlay (purchase price minus trade-in value) on new and used domestic and imported cars and trucks and other vehicles, including motorcycles and private planes.

• *gasoline and motor oil* Includes gasoline, diesel fuel, and motor oil.

• *other vehicle expenses* Includes vehicle finance charges, maintenance and repairs, vehicle insurance, and vehicle rental licenses and other charges.

• *vehicle finance charges* Includes the dollar amount of interest paid for a loan contracted for the purchase of vehicles described above.

• *maintenance and repairs* Includes tires, batteries, tubes, lubrication, filters, coolant, additives, brake and transmission fluids, oil change, brake adjustment and repair, front-end alignment, wheel balancing, steering repair, shock absorber replacement, clutch and transmission repair, electrical system repair, repair to cooling system, drive train repair, drive shaft and rear-end repair, tire repair, other maintenance and services, and auto repair policies.

• *vehicle insurance* Includes the premium paid for insuring cars, trucks, and other vehicles.

• *vehicle rental, licenses, and other charges* Includes leased and rented cars, trucks, motorcycles, and aircraft, inspection fees, state and local registration, driver's license fees, parking fees, towing charges, and tolls on trips.

• *public transportation* Includes fares for mass transit, buses, trains, airlines, taxis, private school buses, and fares paid on trips for trains, boats, taxis, buses, and trains.

Index

accounting fees, 161–189
admissions
    to entertainment events, 7–44, 103–159
    to movies, theater, opera, ballet, 103–159
    to sporting events, 103–159
air conditioners, window units, 365–421
    maintenance and repair of, 423–479
airline fares, 511–567
    gifts of, 305–333
alarms, smoke, 365–421
alcoholic beverages, 7–44, 191–303. *See also* Beer; Wine; *and* Whiskey.
    at catered affairs, 191–303
    at home, 191–303
    from fast-food restaurants, 191–303
    from full-service restaurants, 191–303
    gifts of, 7–44, 305–333
    purchased on trips, 191–303
alimony, 161–189
apparel
    boys', 7–44, 45–101
    gifts of, 7–44, 305–333
    girls', 7–44, 45–101
    infants', 7–44, 45–101
    men's, 7–44, 45–101
    repair, 45–101
    shoes, 7–44, 45–101
    shoes, gifts of, 305–333
    women's, 7–44, 45–101
apples, 191–303
appliances
    gifts of, 7–44, 305–333
    kitchen, 365–421
    major, 7–44, 365–421
    personal care, 365–421
    repair, 365–421
    small, 7–44, 365–421
artificial sweeteners, 191–303
athletic gear, 103–159
    gifts of, 305–333
audio tapes, 103–159
auto rental, 511–567
    on trips, 511–567
automobile service clubs, 511–567
automobiles. *See* Cars *and* Trucks.

baby food, 191–303
babysitting. *See also* Day care centers, nursery schools, and preschools.
    other home, 481–509
    own home, 481–509
bacon, 191–303
bakery products, 7–44, 191–303
    frozen and refrigerated, 191–303
baking needs, 191–303
ballet tickets, 103–159
bananas, 191–303
bank service charges, 161–189
bath products, 481–509
    gifts of, 305–333
bathroom linens, 365–421
    gifts of, 305–333
bedroom furniture, 365–421
    gifts of, 305–333

bedroom linens, 365–421
    gifts of, 305–333
beds. *See* Mattresses and springs.
beef, 7–44, 191–303
beer and ale, 191–303
    gifts of, 305–333
bicycles, 103–159
biscuits and rolls, 191–303
blouses and tops, 45–101
Blue Cross, Blue Shield. *See* Health insurance.
board, including at school, 191–303
    gifts of, 305–333
boats, 103–159
bologna, 191–303
books, 481–509
    and supplies for college, 481–509
    and supplies for college, gifts of, 305–333
    and supplies for daycare and nursery school, 481–509
    and supplies for elementary and high school, 481–509
    purchased through book clubs, 481–509
boys' apparel, 7–44, 45–101
    gifts of, 7–44, 305–333
bread, 191–303
bread and cracker products, 191–303
breakfast and brunch, at restaurants, 191–303
bus fares, intercity, 511–567
business equipment and office furniture for home use, 365–421
butter, 191–303

cabinets, 365–421
cable TV and community antenna, 103–159
    gifts of, 305–333
cafeterias, meals from, 191–303
cakes, 191–303
    gifts of, 305–333
calculators, 365–421
campers, motorized, 103–159
camping equipment, 103–159
candy, 191–303
    gifts of, 305–333
carbonated drinks, 191–303
carpeting, wall-to-wall, 365–421
cars
    gifts of, 305–333
    lease payments, 511–567
    new, 7–44, 511–567
    rental, 511–567
    used, 7–44, 511–567
catered affairs, 191–303
    gifts of, 305–333
CD, tape, record, video mail order clubs, 103–159
CDs, 103–159
cellular phone service, 423–479
cemetery lots, vaults, maintenance fees, 161–189
cereal, 7–44, 191–303
chairs, living room, 365–421
charitable contributions, 161–189
checking accounts, 161–189
cheese, 191–303
chewing gum, 191–303
    gifts of, 305–333
chicken. *See* Poultry.
child care. *See* Babysitting; *and* Day care centers, nursery schools, and preschools.